CANADA

W9-AUD-885

Lake Superior

MINNESOTA
Duluth

St. Paul
apolis

Mississippi River

WISCONSIN

Green Bay

MICHIGAN

Lake Huron

Lake Michigan

Grand Rapids

Madison ★

Milwaukee

Lansing

Rockford

Detroit

Lake Erie

IOWA

Cedar Rapids

Moines ★

Davenport

Peoria

Chicago

Gary

Fort Wayne

Toledo

Cleveland

Akron

CENTRAL

OHIO

Wheeling

Columbus ★

Lake Ontario

Rochester

Syracuse

Buffalo

NEW YORK

Albany ★

VT
Burlington

Montpelier ★

ADIRONDACK MTS.

St. Lawrence River

Augusta ★

MAINE

Lewiston

Portland

NH
Concord ★

Manchester

Boston ★

Cape Cod

MA

Worcester

CT

Hartford ★

RI

Providence ★

Bridgeport

PENNSYLVANIA

ALLEGHENY MTS.

Pittsburgh

Harrisburg ★

Philadelphia

NEW JERSEY

Jersey City

Newark

Trenton ★

New York City

LONG ISLAND

Wilmington

DELAWARE

Dover ★

ILLINOIS

INDIANA

Springfield ★

Indianapolis ★

Cincinnati

WEST VIRGINIA

Huntington

Charleston ★

Baltimore

WASHINGTON, D.C. ✪

Annapolis ★

MARYLAND

DELMARVA PENINSULA

PLAINS

Kansas City

Jefferson City ★

St. Louis

Louisville

Frankfort ★

Lexington

KENTUCKY

Ohio River

VIRGINIA

Richmond ★

Newport News

Norfolk

Chesapeake Bay

35° North Latitude

70° West Longitude

MISSOURI

Springfield

OZARK PLATEAU

Nashville ★

Knoxville

TENNESSEE

Tennessee River

APPALACHIAN MOUNTAINS

BLUE RIDGE MTS.

Mt. Mitchell ▲ 6,684 ft. (2,030 m)

PIEDMONT

Winston-Salem

Greensboro

Raleigh ★

NORTH CAROLINA

Charlotte

Greenville

Cape Hatteras

ARKANSAS

Fort Smith

Little Rock ★

Pine Bluff

Memphis

Huntsville

Birmingham

PIEDMONT

Atlanta ★

SOUTH CAROLINA

Columbia ★

COASTAL PLAIN

Charleston

Cape Fear

0   200 Miles
0   200 Kilometers

MISSISSIPPI

ALABAMA

GEORGIA

Macon

Columbus

Savannah

The United States: Physical-Political

Jackson ★

Meridian

Montgomery ★

Alabama River

LOUISIANA

Shreveport

Baton Rouge ★

PLAIN

Biloxi

Mobile

Tallahassee ★

FLORIDA

Jacksonville

Cape Canaveral

Land Elevation

Feet		Meters
10,000		3,000
7,000		2,000
3,000		1,000
700		200
(Sea Level) 0		0 (Sea Level)
Below Sea Level		Below Sea Level

COASTAL

New Orleans

Mississippi Delta

Gulf of Mexico

FLORIDA PENINSULA

St. Petersburg

Tampa

Lake Okeechobee

Fort Lauderdale

Miami

——— International boundaries

——— State boundaries

✪ National capital

★ State capital

Florida Keys

Straits of Florida

ATLANTIC OCEAN

20°N

PUERTO RICO (U.S.)

San Juan

0   100 Miles
0   100 Kilometers

CUBA

ATLANTIC OCEAN

Bay of

Vivian A. Miller
Nicholas Miller
P.O. Box 518
Lansing, IL 60438

THE AMERICAN PEOPLE

THE *AMERICAN PEOPLE*

Creating a Nation and a Society

Fourth Edition

GENERAL EDITORS

Gary B. Nash
University of California, Los Angeles

Julie Roy Jeffrey
Goucher College

John R. Howe
University of Minnesota

Peter J. Frederick
Wabash College

Allen F. Davis
Temple University

Allan M. Winkler
Miami University

 LONGMAN

An imprint of Addison Wesley Longman, Inc.

New York • Menlo Park, California • Reading, Massachusetts • Harlow, England
Don Mills, Ontario • Sydney • Mexico City • Madrid • Amsterdam

Acquisitions Editor: Bruce Borland
Developmental Editor: Betty Slack
Coordination, Design, Art, and Page Makeup: Thompson Steele Production Services
Executive Editor: Pamela Gordon
Marketing Manager: Sue Westmoreland
Supplements Editor: Jessica Bayne
Cover Designer: Kay Petronio
Cover Illustration: PhotoDisk, Inc.
Photo Researcher: Corrine Johns
Full-Service Production Manager: Eric Jorgensen
Manufacturing Manager: Hilda Koparanian
Printer and Binder: RR Donnelley & Sons Company
Cover Printer: The Lehigh Press Inc.

For permission to use copyrighted material, grateful acknowledgment is made to the following copyright holders:

p. 354 "Land Sales Chart (1800-1860)" from *America Moves West,* Fifth Edition by Robert E. Riegel and Robert G. Athearn, copyright © 1971 by Holt, Rinehart and Winston, Inc., reprinted by permission of the publisher.

p. 384 William J. Faulkner, *The Days When the Animals Talked.* Copyright © 1977 by William J. Faulkner. Used by permission of Marie Brown Associates.

p. 639 Zunz, *The Changing Face of Inequality* (1982), p. 234.

p. 891 From "The Good War" by Studs Terkel. Copyright © 1984 by Studs Terkel. Reprinted by permission of Pantheon Books, a division of Random House, Inc.

p. 925 Words and music by Malvina Reynolds. © 1962 Schroeder Music Co. (ASCAP). Used by permission. All rights reserved.

p. 976–977 George H. Gallop, *The Gallop Poll: Public Opinion, 1935-1971,* vol. 2 (New York: Random House, 1972). © American Institute of Public Opinion.

p. 1044 "I Am Woman", words by Helen Reddy, music by Ray Burton. Copyright © 1971 by Irving Music, Inc. and Buggerlugs Music Co. (BMI). All rights reserved. Reprinted by permission.

p. 1050 Passages from *I Am Joaquim* by Rodolfo "Corky" Gonzalez. New York: Bantam Books, 1972. Copyright by Rodolfo Gonzalez.

p. 1059 Excerpt from "The Times They Are A-Changin'" by Bob Dylan. Copyright © 1963, 1964 by Warner Brothers Music. Copyright renewed 1991 by Special Rider Music. All rights reserved. International copyright secured. Reprinted by permission.

Library of Congress Cataloging-in-Publication Data
The American people : creating a nation and a society / general editors, Gary B. Nash ... [et al.]. — 4th ed.
　　p.　　cm.
　　Includes bibliographical references and index.
　　ISBN 0–673–98575-X
　　1. United States—History. I. Nash, Gary B.
E178.1
973—dc21　　　96–52439

ISBN 0-673-98575-X (College Edition)
ISBN 0-321-04490-8 (School Edition)

4 5 6 7 8 9 10 11 - DOW - 03 02 01 00 99

Brief Contents

Detailed Contents

PART I

A Colonizing People, 1492–1776   2

P A R T   I I

A Revolutionary People, 1775-1828

PART III

An Expanding People, 1820–1877   318

PART V

A Modernizing People, 1900–1945   *722*

PART VI

A Resilient People, 1945–1997   910

Recovering the Past

The American People Gather

Diagraphics

aps

Figures

ables

Preface

The Yoruba people of West Africa have an old saying, "However far the stream flows, it never forgets its source." Why, we wonder, do such ancient societies as the Yoruba find history so important, whereas today's American students question its relevance? This book aims to end such skepticism about the usefulness of history.

As we near the end of the twentieth century, in an ethnically and racially diverse society caught up in an interdependent global society, history is of central importance in preparing us to exercise our rights and responsibilities as free people. History cannot make good citizens, but without history we cannot understand the choices before us and think wisely about them. Lacking a collective memory of the past, we lapse into a kind of amnesia, unaware of the human condition and the long struggles of men and women everywhere to deal with the problems of their day and to create a better society. Unfurnished with historical knowledge, we deprive ourselves of knowing about the huge range of approaches people have taken to political, economic, and social life; to solving problems; and to conquering the obstacles in their way.

History has a deeper, even more fundamental importance: the cultivation of the private person whose self-knowledge and self-respect provides the foundation for a life of dignity and fulfillment. Historical memory is the key to self-identity; to seeing one's place in the long stream of time, in the story of humankind. "It is true that history cannot satisfy our appetite when we are hungry, nor keep us warm when the cold wind blows," says the New York Chinatown History Project. "But it is also true that if younger generations do not understand the hardships and triumphs of their elders, then we will be a people without a past. As such, we will be like water without a source, a tree without roots."

When we study our own history, that of the American people, we see a rich and extraordinarily complex human story. This country, whose written history began with a convergence of Native Americans, Europeans, and Africans, has always been a nation of diverse peoples—a magnificent mosaic of cultures, religions, and skin shades. This book explores how American society assumed its present shape and developed its present forms of government; how as a nation we have conducted our foreign affairs and managed our economy; how as individuals and in groups we have lived, worked, loved, married, raised families, voted, argued, protested, and struggled to fulfill our dreams and the noble ideals of the American experiment.

Several ways of making the past understandable distinguish this book from most textbooks written in the last twenty years. The coverage of public events like presidential elections, diplomatic treaties, and economic legislation is integrated with the private human stories that pervade them. Within a chronological framework, we have woven together our history as a nation, as a people, and as a society. When, for example, national political events are discussed, we analyze their impact on social and economic life at the state and local level. Wars are described not only as they unfolded on the battlefield and in the salons of diplomats, but also on the home front, where they are history's greatest motor of social change. The interaction of ordinary Americans with extraordinary events runs as a theme throughout this book.

Above all, we have tried to show the "humanness" of our history as it is revealed in people's everyday lives. The authors have often used the words of ordinary Americans to capture the authentic human voices of those who participated in and responded to epic events such as war, slavery, industrialization, and reform movements.

Goals and Themes of the Book

Our primary goal is to provide students with a rich, balanced, and thought-provoking treatment of the American past. By this, we mean a history that treats the lives and experiences of Americans of all national origins and cultural backgrounds, at all levels of society, and in all regions of the country. It also means a history that seeks connections between the many factors—political, economic, technological, social, religious, intellectual, and biological—that have molded and remolded American society over four centuries. And, finally, it means a history that encourages students to think about how we have all inherited a complex past filled with both notable achievements and thorny problems. The only history befitting a democratic nation is one that inspires students to initiate a frank and searching dialogue with their past.

To speak of a dialogue about the past presumes that history is interpretive. Students should understand that historians are continually reinterpreting the past. New interpretations are often based on the discovery of new evidence, but more often new interpretations emerge because historians reevaluate old evidence in the light of new ideas that spring from the times in which they write and from their personal views of the world.

Through this book, we also hope to promote class discussions, which can be organized around six questions that we see as basic to the American historical experience:

1. How has this nation been peopled, from the first inhabitants to the many groups that arrived in slavery or servitude during the colonial period down to the voluntary immigrants of today? How have these waves of newcomers contributed to the American cultural mosaic? To what extent have different immigrant groups preserved elements of their ethnic, racial, and religious heritages? How have the tensions between cultural assimilation and cultural preservation been played out, in the past and today?

2. To what extent have Americans developed a stable, democratic political system flexible enough to address the wholesale changes occurring in the last two centuries and to what degree has this political system been consistent with the principles of our nation's founding?

3. How have economic and technological changes affected daily life, work, family organization, leisure, sexual behavior, the division of wealth, and community relations in the United States?

4. Has American religion served more to promote or retard social reform in our history? Whatever their varied sources, how have the recurring reform movements in our history dealt with economic, political, and social problems in attempting to square the ideals of American life with the reality?

5. What has been the role of our nation in the world? To what extent has the United States served as a model for other peoples, as an interventionist savior of other nations around the globe, and as an interfering expansionist in the affairs of other nations?

6. How have American beliefs and values changed over more than four hundred years of history, and how have they varied between different groups—women and men; Americans of many colors and cultures; people of different regions, religions, sexual orientations, ages, and classes?

In writing a history that revolves around these themes, we have tried to convey two dynamics that operate in all societies. First, we observe people continuously adjusting to new developments, such as industrialization and urbanization, over which they seemingly have little control; yet we realize that people are not paralyzed by history but are the fundamental creators of it. They retain the ability, individually and collectively, to shape the world in which they live and thus in considerable degree to control their own lives.

Second, we emphasize the connections that always exist among social, political, economic, and cultural events. Just as our individual lives are never neatly parceled into separate spheres of activity, the life of a society is made up of a complicated and often messy mixture of forces, events, and accidental occurrences. In this text, political and economic, technological and cultural factors are intertwined like strands in a rope.

Structure of the Book

Part Organization

The chapters of this book are grouped into six parts that relate to major periods in American history. Each part begins with a *Comparative Chronology* summarizing the political and diplomatic, social and economic, and cultural and technological events of the period.

Chapter Structure

Every chapter begins with a *personal story* recalling the experience of an ordinary or lesser-known American. Chapter 1, for example, is introduced with the tragic account of Opechancanough, a Powhatan tribesman whose entire life of nearly ninety years was consumed by a struggle against the land, hunger, and alien values brought by Spanish and English newcomers. This brief anecdote introduces the overarching themes and major concepts of the chapter, in this case the meeting of three societies—Native American, European, and African—in the North American wilderness, each with different cultural values, life-styles, and aspirations. In addition, the personal story launches the chapter by engaging the student with a human account, suggesting that history was shaped by ordinary as well as extraordinary people. Following the personal story and easily identifiable by its visual separation from the anecdote and the body of the chapter, a *brief chapter overview* links the biographical sketch to the text. Students should read these crucial transition paragraphs carefully for two reasons: first, to identify the three or four major themes of the chapter; and second, to understand the organizational structure of the chapter.

We aim to facilitate the learning process for students in other ways as well. Every chapter ends with pedagogical features to reinforce and expand the presentation. A *Conclusion* briefly summarizes the main concepts and developments elaborated in the chapter and serves as a bridge to the following chapter. A list of *Recommended Readings* provides supplementary sources for further study or research; novels contemporary to the period are often included. Finally, a *Timeline* reviews the major events and developments covered in the chapter. Each map, figure, and table has been chosen to relate clearly to the narrative.

Special Features

A distinctive feature of this book is the two-page *Recovering the Past* presented in each chapter. These RTPs, as the authors affectionately call them, introduce students to the fascinating variety of evidence—ranging from sermons, folk tales, and diaries to tombstones, advertising, and popular music—that historians have learned to employ in reconstructing the past. Each RTP gives basic information about the source and its use by historians and then raises questions for students to consider as they study the example reproduced for their inspection.

In addition to the "Recovering the Past" sections, we have provided other elements that will facilitate learning for students.

- *The American People Gather* is a new element that helps students see how the temper and character of American society has changed over nearly 400 years in the way people from every rank mingle with their fellow Americans in their leisure time. Choosing particularly important scenes where people gathered, from taverns to rock music festivals, we show how Americans reflect the changing values, tastes, and priorities of their era.

- In a series of *Diagraphics*, another new feature, we bring together, in visually engaging ways, economic data that portrays how political, social, and technological changes are closely intertwined at particular moments in American history. One diagraphic, for example, suggests the broad impact of new methods of steel production during the nineteenth century on the ways in which Americans worked, travelled, constructed their buildings, and waged war.

- The program of *color illustrations*—paintings, cartoons, photographs, maps, and figures—amplifies important themes while presenting visual evidence for student reflection and analysis. Captions on all photographs, maps, and figures are designed to help students understand and interpret the information presented. Summary tables, which we refer to as "talking boxes," recap points discussed in the narrative, pulling the material together in a format designed for ease of student study. Examples of such "talking boxes" include "Significant Factors Promoting Economic Growth, 1820–1860" in Chapter 10 and "Conflicting Aims During the Cold War" in Chapter 27.

The Fourth Edition

The fourth edition of *The American People* has benefited from both the helpful comments of scholars and the experience of teachers and students who used previous editions of the book. Some of the modifications are small, but others, like the reorganization of the chapters on the period following World War II and the contemporary period, are substantial. Strengthening the thematic unity of the book has been one of our major goals in this revision. In particular, we have made a special effort to address the role of religion in the unfolding of the American story and to provide a more thorough coverage of the American West.

Major Changes in Fourth Edition

- *Chapter 1:* added material on environmental devastation wrought by earliest American inhabitants, including discussion of the depletion of megafauna, deforestation, and salinization; new diagraphic feature on The Columbian Exchange
- *Chapter 2:* new section on New Spain's Northern Frontier; discussion of Pope's revolt and the decline of Florida's missions
- *Chapter 3:* added new diagraphic feature on the African Slave Trade
- *Chapter 4:* added material on French settlement and the French inland empire; discussion of the relationships between Native Americans and French fur traders, the development of mixed race communities, and French settlement in the heartland from the Mississippi Valley to the Gulf of Mexico; new feature on The American People Gather . . . at Colonial Taverns
- *Chapter 6:* added material on Indian allies of the Americans in Revolutionary War
- *Chapter 8:* added material on shifting political alignments among workers and artisans at the end of the 18th century
- *Chapter 9* is reorganized; new section on A Nation of Regions includes discussion of the effects on the environment of the expanding population and increased agricultural activity,

and a new subsection on The Urban Northeast; expanded introduction to the section on Indian-White Relations in the Early Republic; a new section on The Evangelical Impulse, which discusses religious revivalism in the early Republic; added discussion of black churches and African American religious congregations as cornerstone of black community life; a new section on A New Style of Politics, which discusses the beginning of party politics and mass democratic politics; new feature on The American People Gather . . . at Agriculture Fairs; diagraphic feature on The Movement of White and Black Population into Trans-Appalachia

- *Chapter 11* has expanded discussion of African American churches, independent urban black churches, and African American Catholics
- *Chapter 12* is reorganized; the first section of chapter now deals with religious revival (the Second Great Awakening) and reform philosophy (Transcendentalism); discussion of Jackson's presidency reorganized and now includes a separate section on Jackson's Indian Policy; new section on The Dilemmas of Reform; new feature on The American People Gather . . . at Minstrel Shows
- *Chapter 13:* new material on religious idealism as a motive for westward migration
- *Chapter 14:* added material on growth of Catholic Church in the United States
- *Chapter 17* has been retitled The Realities of Rural America to reflect better chapter's content; new feature on The American People Gather . . . at Buffalo Bill's Wild West Show
- *Chapter 21:* added discussion of the links between progressive social justice and Protestant social gospel movements; new material on The Men and Religion Forward Movement; new feature on The American People Gather . . . at Amusement Parks
- *Chapter 23:* expanded discussion of religion during the 1920s including two sections, one on Religious Intolerance and the other on Religious Fundamentalism; diagraphic feature on The Impact of the Automobile
- *Chapter 24:* new section on The New Deal and the West

■ *Chapter 25:* added material on the impact of war industry on the West

Chapters 26-30 have been reorganized

■ *Chapter 26:* begins with a demographic profile of the United States and deals with postwar growth and social change, covering the period from 1945 to 1970; added material on African American families and communities

■ *Chapter 27:* covers the Cold War from its beginning through Vietnam; covers foreign policy in general through the 1960s including the Bay of Pigs and the Cuban missile crisis; new section on The Continuing Cold War

■ *Chapter 28* has been retitled High Water and Ebb Tide of the Liberal State to reflect more accurately the chapter's content; new opening anecdote; chapter covers domestic politics from 1945 to 1980, including discussion of the origins of the welfare state under presidents Truman and Eisenhower

■ *Chapter 29:* provides post-World War II background to reform movements and covers reform movements to 1980

■ *Chapter 30:* carries the story from 1980 to the present, including discussion of the 1996 election; covers the economy, the political shift to the right, the end to social reform and the end of the Cold War

Our aim has been to write a balanced and vivid history of the development of the American nation and its society. We have also tried to provide the support materials necessary to make teaching and learning enjoyable and rewarding. The reader will be the judge of our success. The authors welcome your comments.

GARY B. NASH
JULIE ROY JEFFREY

Supplements

For Qualified College Adopters

Teaching the American People. Julie Roy Jeffrey and Peter J. Frederick with Neal Brooks and Elizabeth Nix of Essex Community College. This guide was written based on ideas generated in "active learning" workshops and is tied closely to the text. In addition to suggestions on how to generate lively class discussion and involve students in active learning, this supplement also offers a file of exam questions and lists of resources, including films, slides, photo collections, records and audiocassettes.

Comprehensive American History Transparency Set. This vast collection of American history map transparencies includes over two hundred map transparencies ranging from the first Native Americans to the end of the Cold War, covering wars, social trends, elections, immigration and demographics. Also included are a reproducible set of student map exercises, teaching tips, and correlation charts.

American Impressions: A CD-ROM for U.S. History. This unique CD-ROM for the U.S. History course is organized in a topical and thematic framework which allows in depth coverage with a media-centered focus. Hundreds of photos, maps, works of art, graphics, and historical film clips are organized into narrated vignettes and interactive activities to create a tool for both professors and students. Topics include "The Encounter Period," "Revolution to Republic," "A Century of Labor and Reform," and "The Struggle for Equality." A guide for instructors provides teaching tips and suggestions for using advanced media in the classroom. The CD-ROM is available in both Macintosh and Windows formats.

Visual Archives of American History, 2/e. This two-sided video laserdisc explores history from the meeting of three cultures to the present. It is an encyclopedic chronology of U.S. history offering hundreds of photographs and illustrations, a variety of source and reference maps—several of which are animated—plus fifty minutes of video. For ease in planning lectures, a manual listing barcodes for scanning and frame numbers for all the material is available.

Discovering American History Through Maps and Views. Created by Gerald Danzer of the University of Illinois at Chicago, the recipient of the AHA's 1990 James Harvey Robinson Prize for his work in the development of map transparencies—this set of 140 four-color acetates is a unique instructional tool. It contains an introduction on teaching history through maps and a detailed commentary on each transparency. The collection includes cartographic and pictorial maps, views and photos, urban plans, building diagrams, and works of art.

A Guide to Teaching American History Through Film. Written by Randy Roberts of Purdue University, this guide provides instructors with a creative and practical tool for stimulating classroom discussion. The sections include "American Films: A Historian's Perspective," a list of films, practical suggestions and bibliography. The film listing is presented in narrative form, developing connections between each film and the topics being discussed.

Video Lecture Launchers. Prepared by Mark Newman, University of Illinois at Chicago, these video lecture launchers (each 2 to 5 minutes in duration) cover key issues in American history from 1877 to the present. The launchers are accompanied by an Instructor's Manual.

Transparencies. A set of 40 map transparencies drawn from the text.

"This Is America" *Immigration Video.* Produced by the American Museum of Immigration, this video tells the story of American immigrants, relating their personal stories and accomplishments. By showing how the richness of our culture is due to the contributions of millions of immigrant Americans, the videos make the point that America's strength lies in the ethnically and culturally diverse backgrounds of its citizens.

Telecourse Packages. The American Adventure: Beginnings to 1877 and *American in Perspective: U.S. History Since 1877*—produced and distributed by the LeCroy Center for Educational Telecommunications, Dallas Country Community College District—are designed as a component of a comprehensive earning package consisting of the 26-lesson telecourse program, *The American People,* and a telecourse study guide. *Telecourse Guide for the American Adventure* and *Telecourse Study Guides for America in Perspective* contain numerous study aids, self-tests, enrichment ideas, suggested readings, all keyed to specific pages in *The American People.* The study guide can be ordered through your Longman representative.

Test Bank. This test bank, prepared by Charles Cook, Houston Comunity College, J. H. Smallwood, North Texas State University, and Elizabeth Neumeyer, Kellogg Community College, contains more than 3500 objective, conceptual, and essay questions. All questions are keyed to specific pages in the text.

Test Gen Computerized Testing System. This flexible, easy-to-master computer test bank includes all the test items in the printed test bank. The software allows you to edit existing questions and add your own items. Tests can be printed in several different formats and can include figures such as graphs and tables. Available for Windows and Macintosh computers.

QuizMaster. This new program enables you to design Test Gen generated tests that your students can take on a computer rather than in printed form. QuizMaster can be obtained free through your sales representative.

Grades. A grade-keeping and classroom management software program that maintains data for up to 200 students.

For Students

Study Guides and Practice Tests. This two-volume study guide, created by Julie Roy Jeffrey and Peter J. Frederick, with Neal Brooks and Elizabeth Nix of Essex Community College includes chapter outlines, significant themes and highlights, a glossary, learning enrichment ideas, sample test questions, exercises for identification and interpretation and geography exercises based on maps in the text.

Longman American History Atlas. This full color historical atlas includes more than 100 maps, all designed especially for this volume. This valuable reference tool is available shrinkwrapped with *The American People* at low cost.

America Through the Eyes of Its People: Primary Sources in American History, Second Edition. This one-volume collection of primary documents portrays the rich and varied tapestry of American life. It contains documents by women, Native Americans, African-Americans, Hispanics, and others who helped to shape the course of U.S. history along with student study questions and contextual headnotes.

Retracing the Past, Third Edition. This two-volume set of readers is edited by Ronald Schultz of the University of Wyoming and Gary B. Nash. These secondary source readings cover economic, political and social history with special emphasis on women, racial and ethnic groups and working-class people.

Leaarning to Think Critically: Films and Myths About American History. Randy Roberts and Robert May of Purdue University use well-known films such as *Gone with the Wind* and *Casablanca* to explore some common myths about America and its past. This short handbook subjects some popular beliefs to historical scrutiny in order to help students develop a method of inquiry for approaching the subject of history in general.

Mapping America: A Guide to Historical Geography. This workbook by Ken Weatherbie of Del Mar College was revised specifically for this new edition. Each volume contains 18 exercises corresponding to the map program in the text each concluding with interpretive questions about the role of geography in American history. This free item is designed to be packaged with *The American People*.

Mapping American History: Student Activities. Written by Gerald Danzer of the University of Illinois at Chicago, this free map workbook for students features exercises designed to teach students to interpret and analyze cartographic materials as historical documents. This free item is designed to be packaged with *The American People*.

TimeLink Computer Atlas of American History. This atlas, compiled by William Hamblin of Brigham Young University, is an introductory software tutorial and textbook companion. This Macintosh program presents the historical geography of the continental United States from colonial times to the settling of the West and the admission of the last continental state in 1912. The program covers territories in different time periods, provides quizzes, and includes a special Civil War module.

Acknowledgments

The authors wish to thank the following reviewers who gave generously of their time and expertise and whose thoughtful and constructive work have contributed greatly to this edition:

John Alexander, University of Cincinnati
Terry Alford, Northern Virginia Community College
Jackie R. Booker, Western Connecticut State University
Neal Brooks, Essex Community College
Dickson D. Bruce, Jr., University of California, Irvine
Jane Censer, George Mason University
David Culbert, Louisiana State University
Mark T. Dalhouse, Northeast Missouri State University
Dennis B. Downey, Millersville University
Robert Farrar, Spokane Falls Community College
Brian Gordon, St. Louis Community College
Carol Gruber, William Paterson College
Link Hullar, Kingwood College
Robert J. Kolesar, John Carroll University
Patricia M. Lisella, Iona College
Paul K. Longmore, San Francisco State University
Rita Loos, Framingham State College
Suzanne Marshall, Jacksonville State University
Art McCoole, Cuyamaca College
Otis L. Miller, Belleville Area College
William G. Morris, Midland College
Carla Pestana, Ohio State University
Jud Sage, Northern Virginia Community College
Phil Schaeffer, Olympic College
Nancy Shoemaker, University of Wisconsin, Eau Claire
Bradley Skelcher, Delaware State University
Jo Snider, Southwest Texas State University
Katherine Scott Sturdevant, Pikes Peak Community College
Stephen Strausberg, University of Arkansas
Nan M. Sumner-Mack, Hawaii Community College
Cynthia Taylor, Santa Rosa Junior College
Paul B. Weinstein, University of Akron—Wayne College
Joan Welker, Prince George's Community College
Kenneth H. Williams, Alcorn State University
Mitch Yamasaki, Chaminade University
Charles Zappia, San Diego Mesa College

Over the years, as previous editions of this text were being developed, many of our colleagues read and criticized the various drafts of the manuscript. For their thoughtful evaluations and constructive suggestions, the authors wish to express their gratitude to the following reviewers:

Richard H. Abbott, Eastern Michigan University
Kenneth G. Alfers, Mountain View College
Gregg Andrews, Southwest Texas State University
Robert Asher, University of Connecticut, Storrs
Harry Baker, University of Arkansas at Little Rock
Michael Batinski, Southern Illinois University
Gary Bell, Sam Houston State University
Virginia Bellows, Tulsa Junior College
Spencer Bennett, Siena Heights College
James Bradford, Texas A&M University
Jeffrey P. Brown, New Mexico State University
David Brundage, University of California, Santa Cruz
Colin Calloway, University of Wyoming
D'Ann Campbell, Indiana University
Vincent A. Clark, Johnson County Community College
Neil Clough, North Seattle Community College
Matthew Ware Coulter, Collin County Community College
David Culbert, Louisiana State University
Bruce Dierenfield, Canisius College
John Dittmer, DePauw University
Gordon Dodds, Portland State University
Richard Donley, Eastern Washington University
Robert Downtain, Tarrant County Community College
Bernard Friedman, Indiana University–Purdue University at Indianapolis
Bruce Glasrud, California State University, Hayward
Richard Griswold del Castillo, San Diego State University
Colonel Williams L. Harris, The Citadel Military College
Robert Haws, University of Mississippi
Jerrold Hirsch, Northeast Missouri State University
Frederick Hoxie, D'Arcy McNickle Center for the History of the American Indian
John S. Hughes, University of Texas
Donald M. Jacobs, Northeastern University
Delores Janiewski, University of Idaho
David Johnson, Portland State University
Richard Kern, University of Findlay
Monte Lewis, Cisco Junior College
William Link, University of North Carolina, Greensboro

Ronald Lora, University of Toledo
George M. Lubick, Northern Arizona University
John C. Massman, St. Cloud State University
Vern Mattson, University of Nevada at Las Vegas
John McCormick, Delaware County Community College
Sylvia McGrath, Stephen F. Austin University
James E. McMillan, Denison University
Walter Miszczenko, Boise State University
Norma Mitchell, Troy State University
Gerald F. Moran, University of Michigan, Dearborn
Marian Morton, John Carroll University
Roger Nichols, University of Arizona
Paul Palmer, Texas A&I University
Al Parker, Riverside City College
Judith Parsons, Sul Ross State University
Neva Peters, Tarrant County Community College
James Prickett, Santa Monica College
Noel Pugash, University of New Mexico
Juan Gomez-Quiñones, University of California, Los Angeles
George Rable, Anderson College
Joseph P. Reidy, Howard University
Leonard Riforgiato, Pennsylvania State University
Randy Roberts, Purdue University
Mary Robertson, Armstrong State University
David Robson, John Carroll University
Sylvia Sebesta, San Antonio College
Herbert Shapiro, University of Cincinnati
David R. Shibley, Santa Monica College
Ellen Shockro, Pasadena City College
Kathryn Kish Sklar, State University of New York at Buffalo
James Smith, Virginia State University
John Snetsinger, California Polytechnic State University, San Luis Obispo
Tom Tefft, Citrus College
John A. Trickel, Richland College
Donna Van Raaphorst, Cuyahoga Community College
Morris Vogel, Temple University
Michael Wade, Appalachian State University
Jackie Walker, James Madison University

About the Authors

Gary B. Nash received his Ph.D. from Princeton University. He is currently Director of the National Center for History in the Schools at the University of California, Los Angeles, where he teaches colonial and revolutionary American history. Among the books Nash has authored are *Quakers and Politics: Pennsylvania, 1681–1726* (1968); *Red, White, and Black: The Peoples of Early America* (1974, 1982, 1992); *The Urban Crucible: Social Change, Political Consciousness, and the Origins of the American Revolution* (1979); and *Forging Freedom: The Black Urban Experience in Philadelphia, 1720–1840* (1988). His scholarship is especially concerned with the role of common people in the making of history. He wrote Part I and served as a general editor of this book.

Julie Roy Jeffrey earned her Ph.D. in history from Rice University. Since then she has taught at Goucher College. Honored as an outstanding teacher, Jeffrey has been involved in faculty development activities and curriculum evaluation. Jeffrey's major publications include *Education for Children of the Poor* (1978); *Frontier Women: The Trans-Mississippi West, 1840–1880* (1979, 1997); and *Converting the West: A Biography of Narcissa Whitman* (1991). She is the author of many articles on the lives and perceptions of nineteenth-century women. She has just finished a study of women in the abolitionist movement. She wrote Parts III and IV in collaboration with Peter Frederick and acted as a general editor of this book.

John R. Howe received his Ph.D. from Yale University. At the University of Minnesota, his teaching interests include early American politics and relations between Native Americans and whites. His major publications include *The Changing Political Thought of John Adams* (1966) and *From the Revolution Through the Age of Jackson* (1973). His major research currently involves a manuscript entitled "The Transformation of Public Life in Revolutionary America." Howe wrote Part II of this book.

Peter J. Frederick received his Ph.D. in history from the University of California, Berkeley. Innovative student-centered teaching in American history has been the focus of his career at California State University, Hayward, and since 1970 at Wabash College (1992–1994 at Carleton College). Recognized nationally as a distinguished teacher and for his many articles and workshops for faculty on teaching and learning, Frederick has also written several articles on life-writing and a book, *Knights of the Golden Rule: The Intellectual as Christian Social Reformer in the 1890s*. He coordinated and edited all the "Recovering the Past" and "The American People Gather ... " sections and coauthored Parts III and IV.

Allen F. Davis earned his Ph.D. from the University of Wisconsin. A former president of the American Studies Association, he is a professor of history at Temple University and Director of the Center for Public History.

He is the author of *Spearheads for Reform: The Social Settlements and the Progressive Movement* (1967) and *American Heroine: The Life and Legend of Jane Addams* (1973). He is coauthor of *Still Philadelphia* (1983), *Philadelphia Stories* (1987), and *One Hundred Years at Hull-House* (1990). He is currently working on a book on masculine culture in America. Davis wrote Part V of this book.

Allan M. Winkler received his Ph.D. from Yale. He is presently teaching at Miami University, where he chairs the History Department. His books include *The Politics of Propaganda: The Office of War Information, 1942–1945* (1978); *Modern America: The United States from the Second World War to the Present* (1985); *Home Front U.S.A.: America During World War II* (1986); and *Life Under a Cloud: American Anxiety About the Atom* (1993). His research centers on the connections between public policy and popular mood in modern American history. Winkler wrote Part VI of this book.

THE AMERICAN PEOPLE

A Colonizing People, 1492–1776

C O M P A R A T I V E   C H R O N O L O G I E S

Political and Diplomatic	Social and Economic	Cultural and Technological
1492		
1492 Spain completes expulsion of Moors and Jews	1492–1504 Columbus makes four voyages exploring the Americas	1500 Indian tribes of Southeast attain artistic peak
1493 Pope declares demarcation line in New World	1497–1585 French and English explore North America	1508 First New World sugar mill established in West Indies
1509–1547 Reign of Henry VIII in England	1498 Da Gama reaches India	1517 Luther launches the Reformation
1519–1521 Cortés conquers Aztec empire	1515–1565 Spanish explore southern parts of North America	
	1518–1530 European diseases decimate native populations in Mesoamerica	
	1521–1522 Magellan circumnavigates the earth	
1525		
1532–1535 Pizarro conquers Inca empire	1540–1542 Coronado explores the Southwest	1530s Calvin calls for further religious reforms
1558–1603 Reign of Elizabeth I in England	1545–1560 Bonanza silver strikes made in Mexico and Bolivia	1539 First printing press in New World established in Mexico City
1565 Spanish found St. Augustine in Florida	1550–1650 Price revolution in western Europe causes widespread distress	1564 Jacques LeMoyne paints first scenes of Indian life in New World
1575		
1585–1598 England colonizes Ireland	1616–1621 Decimation of Native Americans in New England by European diseases	1585 John White, member of Roanoke expedition, paints first scenes of Indian life in area of English settlement
1588 Spanish Armada attacks England	1617 First Virginia tobacco shipped to England	1612–1613 John Rolfe develops a tobacco hybrid suitable for export
1603–1625 Reign of James I in England	1619 First Africans brought to Virginia	
1607 Virginia Company of London settles Jamestown		
1620 Pilgrims establish colony at Plymouth		
1624 Dutch settle New Netherland		
1625		
1625–1649 Reign of Charles I in Enland	1625–1660 Slavery becomes backbone of labor force in English Caribbean	1636 Harvard College established
1630 Puritans emigrate to New England	1637 Pequot War in New England	1642 Massachusetts passes basic literacy law
1634 Settlement of Maryland begins	1650–1670 Judicial and legislative decisions solidify racial lines in southern colonies	1643 Roger Williams compiles first American dictionary of an Indian language
1642–1649 Civil war in England		1661 John Eliot's translation of the New Testament into Algonquian becomes first Bible printed in North America
1651 First Navigation Act		1662 Half-Way Covenant in Massachusetts
1660 Restoration of Stuart monarchy in England; Charles II installed		
1663 Carolina granted charter		
1664 English conquer New Netherland		

Political and Diplomatic	Social and Economic	Cultural and Technological

1675

Political and Diplomatic	Social and Economic	Cultural and Technological
1673–1683 French expand into Mississippi valley 1682 Quakers emigrate to Pennsylvania under proprietary charter to William Penn 1682 La Salle claims Louisiana for France 1688–1691 Revolts in American colonies inspired by overthrow of James II of England 1689–1697 King William's War 1702–1713 Queen Anne's War 1718 French settle New Orleans	1675–1677 King Philip's War in New England; war against Chesapeake tribes associated with Bacon's Rebellion 1690s South Carolinians begin rice cultivation 1690–1720 Most colonies enact slave codes 1692 Witchcraft trials and executions in Salem, Massachusetts 1697–1715 Colonial importations of slaves increase rapidly 1711–1715 Tuscarora and Yamasee wars in the Carolinas 1712 Slave revolt in New York City 1714–1720 Scots-Irish and German immigration begins 1715–1730 Volume of slave trade doubles	1690 First newspaper in colonies published (and quickly suppressed) in Boston 1693 William and Mary College founded 1701 Yale College founded 1721–1722 Inoculation against smallpox creates controversy in colonies

1725

Political and Diplomatic	Social and Economic	Cultural and Technological
1732 Georgia founded as colony for English paupers and buffer against Spanish Florida 1744–1748 King George's War 1756–1763 Seven Years' War 1764 Pontiac's Rebellion 1764–1765 Sugar, Stamp, and Currency acts 1767 Townshend duties 1773 Tea Act and Boston Tea Party 1774 Coercive Acts and meeting of First Continental Congress	1734–1760 Great Awakening in different regions of colonies 1739 Stono Rebellion in South Carolina 1741 Hysteria over suspected slave plot in New York City 1759–1761 Cherokee War against the English 1761–1765 Depression hits most colonies	1747 Benjamin Franklin publishes *Poor Richard's Almanack* in Philadelphia 1749 Franklin invents lightning rod 1752 First American hospital established in Philadelphia; Franklin's *Experiments and Observations in Electricity* published 1754 College of Philadelphia founded 1757 First streetlights in a colonial city installed in Philadelphia 1769 American Philosophical Society founded

1775

Political and Diplomatic	Social and Economic	Cultural and Technological
1775 Battles of Lexington and Concord; Meeting of Second Continental Congress 1776 Thomas Paine publishes *Common Sense*; Declaration of Independence	1775 Pennsylvania Abolition Society established	1775 Postal system established by Continental Congress

Three Worlds Meet

I n the late 1550s, a few years after Catholic King Philip II and Protestant Queen Elizabeth assumed the thrones in Spain and England, respectively, Opechancanough was born in Tsenacommacah. In the Algonquian language, the word *tsenacommacah* meant "densely inhabited land." Later, English colonizers would rename this place Virginia after their monarch, the virgin queen Elizabeth. Before he died in the 1640s, in the ninth decade of his life, Opechancanough had seen light-skinned, swarthy, and black-skinned newcomers from a half-dozen European nations and African kingdoms swarm into his land. Like thousands of other Native Americans, he was witnessing the early moments of European expansion across the Atlantic Ocean.

F. Maij

Opechancanough was only an infant when Europeans first reached the Chesapeake Bay region. A small party of Spanish had explored the area in 1561, but they found neither gold nor silver nor anything else of value. Upon departing, they took with them the brother of one of the local chieftains, who was a member of Opechancanough's clan. They left behind something of unparalleled importance in the history of contact between the peoples of Europe and the Americas: a viral infection that spread like wildfire through a population that had no immunity against it. Many members of Opechancanough's tribe died, although their casualties were light compared with those of other tribes that caught the deadly European diseases.

In 1570, when Opechancanough was young, the Spanish returned and established a Jesuit mission near the York River. Violence occurred, and before the Spanish abandoned the Chesapeake in 1572, they put to death a number of captured Indians, including a chief who was Opechancanough's relative. The Native Americans learned that Europeans, even when they came bearing the crosses of their religion, were a volatile and dangerous people.

Opechancanough was in his forties when three ships of fair-skinned settlers disembarked in 1607 to begin the first permanent English settlement in the New World. For several months, he watched his half brother Powhatan, high chief of several dozen loosely confederated tribes in the region, parry and fence with the newcomers. Then Powhatan sent him to capture the English leader John Smith and escort him to the Indians' main village. Smith was put through a mock execution but then released. He later got the best of Opechancanough, threatening him with a pistol, humiliating him in front of his warriors, and assaulting one of his sons, whom Smith "spurned like a dog."

Opechancanough nursed his wounds for years while Powhatan grew old and the English settlements slowly spread in the Chesapeake region. Then, in 1617, he assumed leadership of the Powhatan Confederacy. Two years later, a Dutch trader sold 20 Africans to the settlers after docking at Jamestown. Three years after that, Opechancanough led a determined assault on the English plantations that lay along the rivers and streams emptying into the bay. The Indians killed nearly one-third of the intruders. But they paid dearly in the retaliatory raids that the colonists mounted in succeeding years.

As he watched the land-hungry settlers swarm in during the next two decades, Opechancanough's patience failed him. Finally, in 1644, now in his eighties, he galvanized a new generation of warriors and led a final desperate assault on the English. It was a suicidal attempt, but the "great general" of the Powhatan Confederacy, faithful to the tradition of his people, counseled death over enslavement and humiliation. Though the warriors inflicted heavy casualties, they could not overwhelm the colonizers, who vastly outnumbered them. For two years, Opechancanough was kept prisoner by the Virginians. Nearly blind and "so decrepit that he was not able to walk alone," he was fatally shot in the back by an English guard in 1646.

The French, under Jean Ribault, discovering the River of May in Florida on May 1, 1564. Engraving by Theodore De Bry, 1591, after a painting by Jacques Le Moyne, who accompanied the expedition in 1564. (The Granger Collection, New York)

*O*ver a long lifetime, Opechancanough painfully experienced the meeting of people from three continents. His land was one of many that would be penetrated by Europeans over the next three centuries, as Christian civilization girdled the globe. On the Chesapeake Bay, this clash of cultures formed the opening chapter of what we know as American history. That history, in turn, was one scene in a much broader drama of European colonization and exploitation of many indigenous cultures thousands of miles from the Old World. The nature of this violent intermingling of Europeans, Africans, and Native Americans is an essential part of early American history. But to understand how the destinies of red, white, and black people became intertwined in Opechancanough's land, we must look at the precontact history and cultural foundations of life in the homelands of each of them.

The People of America Before Columbus

Thousands of years before the European voyages of discovery, the history of humankind in North America began. Nomadic bands from Siberia, hunting big game animals such as bison, caribou, and reindeer, began to migrate across a land bridge connecting northeastern Asia with Alaska. Geologists believe that this land bridge, perhaps 600 miles wide, existed most recently between 25,000 and 14,000 years ago, when massive glaciers locked up much of the earth's moisture and left part of the Bering Sea floor exposed. Ice-free passage through Canada was possible only briefly at the beginning and end of this period, however. At other times, melting glaciers flooded the land bridge and blocked foot traffic to Alaska. Paleoanthropologists remain divided on the exact timing, but the main migration apparently occurred between 12,000 and 14,000 years ago, although possibly much earlier.

Hunters and Farmers

For thousands of years, these early hunters trekked southward and eastward, following vegetation and game. In time, they reached the tip of South America and the eastern edge of North America, thousands of miles from their Asian homeland. Thus did people from the "Old World" discover the "New World" thousands of years before Columbus.

Archaeologists have excavated ancient sites of early life in the Americas, unearthing tools,

Migration Routes from Asia to the Americas

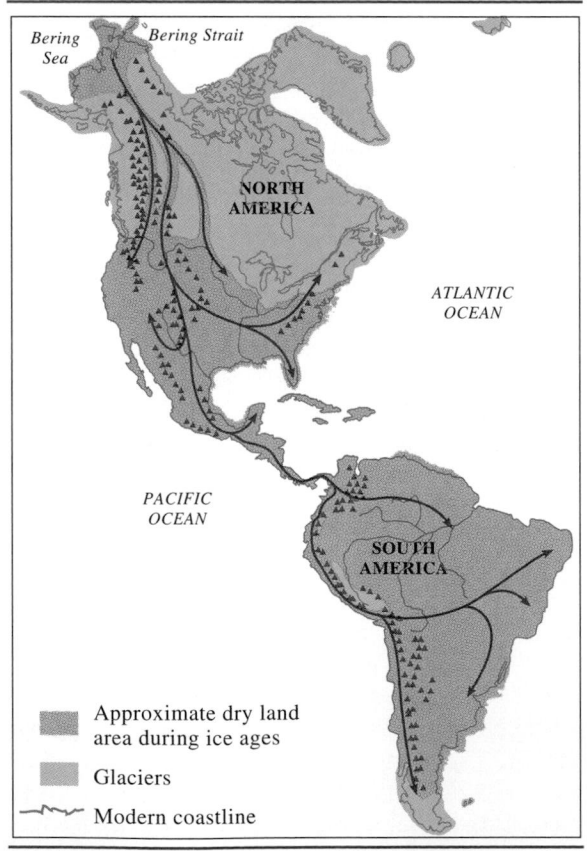

The red arrows indicate the general flow of migrating societies over thousands of years before Europeans reached the Americas. Based on archaeological evidence, these migratory patterns are necessarily tentative.

ornaments, and skeletal remains that can be scientifically dated. In this way, they have tentatively reconstructed the dispersion of these first Americans over an immense land mass. Although much remains unknown, this archaeological evidence suggests that as centuries passed and population increased, the earliest inhabitants evolved into separate cultures, organizing life and adjusting to a variety of environments in distinct ways. Europeans who rediscovered the New World thousands of years later would indiscriminately lump together the myriad societies they found. But by the 1500s, the "Indians" of the Americas were enormously diverse in the size and complexity of their societies, the languages they spoke, and their forms of social organization.

Archaeologists and anthropologists have charted several phases of "Native American" history. A long Beringian epoch ended about 14,000 years ago. From that time, a rich archaeological record indicates that the hunters had developed a new technology. Big-game hunters now flaked hard stones into spear points and chose "kill sites" where they slew whole herds of Pleistocene mammals. This more reliable food source allowed population growth, and nomadism began to give way to settled habitations or local migration within limited territories.

In another phase of evolution, the Archaic era, from about 10,000 to 2,500 years ago, great geological changes brought further adaptations to the land. As the massive glaciers of the Ice Age slowly retreated, a warming trend deprived vast areas from Utah to the highlands of Central America of sufficient water and turned them from grasslands into desert. The Pleistocene mammals were weakened by more arid conditions, but human populations ably adapted. They learned to exploit new sources of food, especially plant life. In time, a second technological breakthrough, the "agricultural revolution," occurred.

We have sometimes imagined that these early people lived in a primordial paradise where they lived in harmony with their surroundings. But recent archaeological evidence points to examples of environmental devastation that severely damaged the biodiversity of the Americas. The first wave of intruders coming across the Bering land bridge found a wilderness teeming with so-called megafauna: saber-toothed tigers, woolly mam-

moths, gigantic ground sloths, huge bison, and monstrous bear. But by about 10,000 years ago, these animals were almost extinct. Many anthropologists believe that native hunters engaged in "Pleistocene overkill" of the giant species. However, a massive shift of climate that deprived the huge beasts of their grazing environment was also a cause.

The depletion of the megafauna left the hemisphere with a much restricted catalogue of animals. Left behind were large animals such as elk, buffalo, bears, and moose. But the extinction of the huge beasts forced people to prey on new sources of food such as turkeys, ducks, and guinea pigs. Their reduced food supply may have gradually reduced their population.

Over many centuries in the Americas, salinization and deforestation put the environment under additional stress. For example, in what is today central Arizona, the Hohokam civilization collapsed hundreds of years ago, much like that in ancient Mesopotamia, when the irrigation system became too salty to support agriculture. At Arizona's Chaco Canyon, the fast-growing Anasazi denuded a magnificently forested region in their search for firewood and building materials. This, in turn, led to the erosion of rich soil that impoverished the region for the Anasazi.

When Native Americans learned to domesticate plant life, they began the long process of transforming their relationship to the physical world. Learning how to plant, cultivate, and harvest created a new relationship to natural forces that before had been ungovernable. Anthropologists believe that this process began independently in widely separated parts of the world—Africa, Asia, Europe, and the Americas—about 7,000 to 9,000 years ago. Though agriculture developed very slowly, everywhere it eventually brought dramatic changes in human societies.

Over the millennia, humans progressed from doorside planting of a few wild seeds to systematic clearing and planting of bean and maize fields. As the production of domesticated plant food ended dependence on gathering wild plants and pursuing game, settled village life began to replace nomadic existence. The increase in food supply brought about by agriculture triggered other major changes. As more ample food fueled population growth, large groups split off to form separate societies. Greater social and political complexity developed because not everyone was needed as before to secure the society's food supply. Men cleared the land and hunted game, and women planted, cultivated, and harvested crops. Many societies empowered religious figures, who organized the common followers, directed their work, and exacted tribute as well as worship from them. In return, the community trusted them to ward off hostile forces.

Everywhere in the Americas, regional trading networks formed. Along trade routes carrying commodities such as salt, obsidian rock for projectile points, and copper for jewelry also traveled technology, religious ideas, and agricultural practices. By the end of the Archaic period, about 500 B.C. (to use the Christian European method of dating), hundreds of independent kin-based

groups, like people in other parts of the world, had learned to exploit the resources of their particular area and to trade with other groups in their region.

Native Americans in 1600

The last epoch of pre-Columbian development, the post-Archaic phase, occurred during the 2,000 years before contact with Europeans. It involved a complex process of growth and environmental adaptation among many distinct societies—and crisis in some of them. In the American Southwest, for example, the ancestors of the present-day Hopi and Zuni developed carefully planned villages composed of large terraced multistoried buildings, each with many rooms. By the time the Spanish arrived in the 1540s, the indigenous Pueblo people were using irrigation canals, dams, and hillside terracing to bring water to their arid maize fields. In their agricultural techniques, their skill in ceramics, their use of woven textiles for clothing, and their village life, Pueblo society resembled that of peasant communities in many parts of Europe and Asia.

Far to the east were the mound-building societies of the Mississippi and Ohio valleys. When European settlers first crossed the Appalachian Mountains a century and a half after arriving on the continent, they were amazed to find hundreds of ceremonial mounds, some of them 70 feet high, and gigantic sculptured earthworks in geometric designs or in the shapes of huge humans, birds, or writhing serpents. Believing all "Indians" to be forest primitives, they reasoned that these were the remains of an ancient civilization that had found its way to North America—perhaps Phoenicians, survivors of the sunken island of Atlantis, or the Lost Tribes of Israel spoken of in European mythology.

The mound-building societies of the Ohio valley declined many centuries before Europeans reached the continent, perhaps because of attacks from other tribes or severe climatic changes that undermined agriculture. But about A.D. 600, another mound-building culture, based on intensive cultivation of beans, maize, and squash, began to flourish in the Mississippi valley. Its center, a city of perhaps 40,000, stood near present-day St. Louis. Great ceremonial plazas, flanked by a temple that rose in four terraces to a height of 100 feet, marked this first metropolis in America. This was the urban center of a far-flung Mississippi cul-

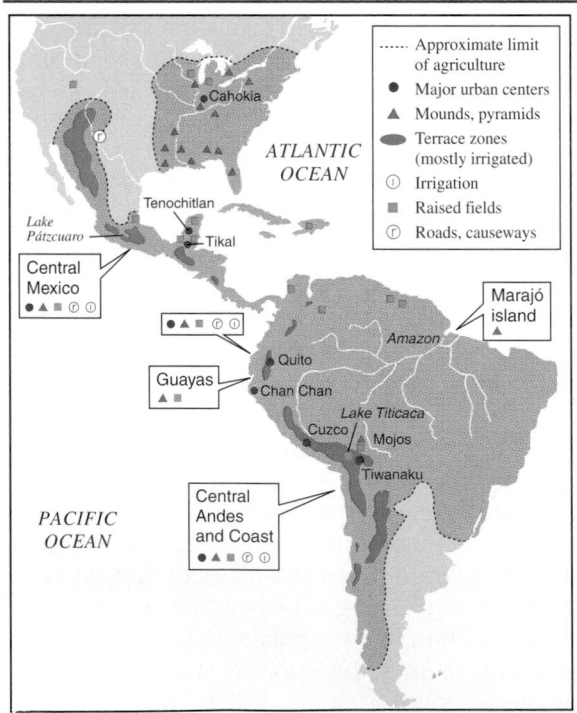

Pre-Columbian Societies of the Americas

Once described as nomadic hunter-gatherers, indigenous peoples in the Americas were agriculturalists and urban dwellers in many areas and populated the land as densely as did others in many other parts of the world.

ture that radiated out to encompass hundreds of villages from Wisconsin to Louisiana and from Oklahoma to Tennessee.

While the mound-building cultures of the continental heartlands mysteriously declined, their influence had already passed eastward to transform the woodlands societies along the Atlantic coastal plain. The numerous small tribes that settled from Nova Scotia to Florida never equaled the larger societies of the midcontinent in earthwork sculpture, architectural design, or development of large-scale agriculture. But they were far from the "savages" that the first European explorers described. They had added limited agriculture to their skill in exploiting natural plants for food, medicine, dyes, and flavoring and had developed food procurement strategies that used all the resources around them—cleared land, forests, streams, shore, and ocean.

Most of the eastern woodlands tribes lived in waterside villages. Locating their fields of maize near fishing grounds, they often migrated seasonally between inland and coastal village sites or situated themselves astride two ecological zones. In the Northeast, their birchbark canoes, light enough to be carried by a single man, gave them a means of trading and communicating over immense territories. In the Southeast, population was denser and social and political organization more elaborate.

As European exploration of the Americas drew near, the continent north of the Rio Grande contained at least 3 to 4 million people, of whom perhaps 500,000 lived along the eastern coastal plain and in the piedmont region accessible to the early European settlers. Though estimates vary widely, perhaps 40 to 60 million people lived in the entire hemisphere when Europeans first arrived. This contrasted with some 70 to 90 million in Europe about 1500 and about 50 to 70 million in Africa. The colonizers were not coming to a "virgin wilderness," as they often described it, but to a land inhabited for thousands of years by people whose village existence in many ways resembled that of the arriving Europeans.

In some important ways, however, Indian culture also differed from that of Europeans. Horses, for example, were not available to the native peoples of the New World as they developed their methods of farming, transportation, and warfare. Without draft animals such as the horse or ox, they had not developed wheeled vehicles or, for that matter, the potter's wheel, which also uses the wheel-and-axle principle. Many inventions—such as the technology for smelting iron, which had diffused widely in the Old World—had not crossed the ocean barrier to reach the New World. The opposite was also true: Valuable New World crops, such as corn and potatoes, which had been developed by Indian agriculturists, were unknown in the Old World before Columbus.

Contrasting World Views

Colonizing Europeans called themselves "civilized" and typically described the people they met in the Americas as "savage," "heathen," or "barbarian." The gulf separating people in Europe and North America was defined not only by their

One of the hundreds of symbolic mounds built by people of the Hopewell culture; this one, in the shape of a serpent, is near present-day Cincinnati. (National Museum of the American Indian, New York)

Archaeological Artifacts

The recovery of the past before there were extensive written records is the domain of archaeology. Virtually our entire knowledge of Indian societies in North America before the arrival of European colonizers is drawn from the work of archaeologists who have excavated the ancient living sites of the first Americans. Many Native Americans today strongly oppose this rummaging in the ancient ancestral places; they particularly oppose the unearthing of burial sites. But the modern search for knowledge about the past goes on.

Archaeological data have allowed us to overcome the stereotypic view of Native Americans as a primitive people whose culture was static for thousands of years before Europeans arrived in North America. This earlier view allowed historians to argue that the tremendous loss of Native American population and land accompanying the initial settlement and westward migration of white Americans was more or less inevitable. When two cultures, one dynamic and forward-looking and the other static and backward, confronted each other, historians have frequently maintained, the more advanced or "civilized" culture almost always prevailed.

Much of the elaborate early history of people in the Americas is unrecoverable. But many fragments of this long human history are being recaptured through archaeological research. Particularly important are studies that reveal how Indian societies were changing during the few centuries immediately preceding the European arrival in the New World. These studies give us a much better chance to interpret the seventeenth-century interaction of Native Americans and Europeans because they provide an understanding of Indian values, social and political organization, material culture, and religion as they existed when the two cultures first met.

One such investigation has been carried out over the last century at the confluence of the Mississippi and

A reconstructed view of Cahokia, the largest town in North America before European arrival, painted by William R. Iseminger. An estimated 50 million cubic feet of earth was used to construct the ceremonial and burial mounds. (Cahokia Mounds State Historic Site)

Missouri rivers near modern-day East St. Louis, Illinois. Archaeologists have found the center of a vast Mississippi culture that began about A.D. 600, reached its peak about 300 years before Columbus's voyages, and then declined through a combination of drought, dwindling food supplies, and internal tensions. Cahokia is the name given to the urban center of a civilization that at its height dominated an area as large as New York State. At the center of Cahokia stood one of the largest earth constructions built by ancient man anywhere on the planet. Its base covering 15 acres, this gigantic earthen temple rises in four terraces to a height of 100 feet, as tall as a ten-story modern office building. The imaginary drawing shown here indicates some of the dozens of smaller geometric mounds discovered near this major temple. Notice the outlying farms, a sure sign of the settled (as opposed to nomadic) existence of the people who flourished ten centuries ago in this region. How does this depiction of ancient Cahokia change your image of Native American life before the arrival of Europeans?

Pottery effigy vessels in the shape of human heads. (National Museum of the American Indian, New York)

By recovering artifacts from Cahokia burial mounds, archaeologists have pieced together a picture, still tentative, of a highly elaborate civilization along the Mississippi bottomlands. Cahokian manufacturers mass-produced salt, knives, and stone hoe blades for both local consumption and export. Cahokian artisans made sophisticated pottery, ornamental jewelry, metalwork, and tools. They used copper and furs from the Lake Superior region, black obsidian stone from the Rocky Mountains, and seashells from the Gulf of Mexico, demonstrating that the people at Cahokia were involved in long-distance trade. In fact, Cahokia was a crucial crossroads of trade and water travel in the heartland of North America.

The objects shown here, unearthed from graves by archaeologists, are an example of the culture of the Mississippi Mound Builders. The round-faced pottery bottles in the form of heads, each about 6 inches tall and wide, show a sense of humor in early Mississippi culture. Holes in the ears of the bottles once held thongs so that the objects could be hung or carried. Other objects, such as a kneeling woman found in Tennessee, had holes under the arms for a similar purpose. What other conclusions about Cahokian culture can you draw from figures such as these? Are there archaeological sites in your area that contain evidence of Native American civilization?

The fact that some graves uncovered at Cahokia contain large caches of finely tooled objects and other burial mounds contain many skeletons unaccompanied by any artifacts leads archaeologists to conclude that this was a more stratified society than those the first settlers encountered along the Atlantic seaboard. Anthropologists believe that some of the Mississippi culture spread eastward before Cahokia declined, but much mystery still remains concerning the fate and cultural diffusion of these early Americans.

material cultures, but also by how they viewed their relationship to the environment and how they defined social relations in their communities. Having evolved in complete isolation from each other, European and Indian cultures exhibited a wide difference in values.

Regarding the soil as a resource to be exploited for human benefit, Europeans believed that land should be privately possessed. Individual ownership of property became a fundamental concept, and an extensive institutional apparatus grew up to support it. Fences symbolized private property, inheritance became the mechanism for transmitting land from one generation to another within the same family, and courts gained the power to settle property disputes. Property was the basis not only of sustenance, but also of independence, material wealth, political status, and personal identity. The social structure directly mirrored patterns of land ownership, with a land-wealthy elite at the apex of the social pyramid and a mass of propertyless individuals forming the broad base.

Native Americans also had concepts of property, and tribes recognized territorial boundaries. But they believed that land was invested with sacred qualities and should be held in common. As one German missionary to the Delaware Indians explained their view in the eighteenth century, the Creator "made the Earth and all that it contains for the common good of mankind. Whatever liveth on the land, whatsoever groweth out of the earth, and all that is in the rivers and waters … was given jointly to all and everyone is entitled to his share."

Communal ownership sharply limited social stratification in most Indian communities. Accustomed to wide disparities of wealth, Europeans often found this remarkable. Observing the Iroquois of the eastern woodlands in 1657, a French Jesuit noted with surprise that they had no almshouses because "their kindness, humanity and courtesy not only makes them liberal with what they have, but causes them to possess hardly anything except in common. A whole village must be without corn, before any individual can be obliged to endure privation." Not all Europeans were acquisitive, competitive individuals. The majority were peasants scratching a subsistence living from the soil, living in kin-centered villages with little contact with the outside world, and exchanging goods and labor through barter. But in

Europe's urban centers, a wealth-conscious, ambitious individual who valued and sought wider choices and greater opportunities to enhance personal status was coming to the fore. In contrast, Native American traditions stressed the group rather than the individual. Holding land and other resources in common, Indian societies were usually more egalitarian and their members more concerned with personal valor than personal wealth.

Exceptions to this cultural system occurred in the highly developed and populous Aztec and Inca empires and, in North America, among a few tribes such as the Natchez. But on the eastern and western coasts of the continent and in the Southwest—the regions of contact in the sixteenth and seventeenth centuries—the European newcomers encountered a people whose cultural values differed strikingly from theirs.

European colonizers in North America also found disturbing the matrilineal organization of many tribal societies. Contrary to European practice, family membership among the Iroquois, for example, was determined through the female line. A typical family consisted of an old woman, her daughters with their husbands and children, and her unmarried granddaughters and grandsons. When a son or grandson married, he moved from this female-headed household to one headed by the matriarch of his wife's family. Divorce was also the woman's prerogative. If she desired it, she merely set her husband's possessions outside their dwelling door. Clans were composed of several matrilineal kin groups related by a blood connection on the mother's side. To Europeans, this was a peculiar and dangerous reversal of their sexual hierarchy in which men, from time immemorial, had been supreme.

In Native American societies, women also held subordinate positions, but not nearly to the extent found among European women. For example, European women, with rare exceptions, were entirely excluded from political affairs. By contrast, in Native American villages, again to take the Iroquois example, designated men sat in a circle to deliberate and make decisions, but the senior women of the village stood behind them, lobbying and instructing. The village chiefs were male, but they were named to their positions by the elder women of their clans. If they moved too far from

Indian Societies During the Period of Early European Settlement

The great number of Indian societies within the present-day boundaries of the United States—each with its own language—indicates the cultural diversity of the first peoples of North America at the time Europeans arrived.

the will of the women who appointed them, these chiefs were removed—or "dehorned." "Our ancestors," the Oneida chief Giod Peter explained, "considered it a great transgression to reject the counsel of their women, particularly the female governesses. Our ancestors considered them mistresses of the soil.... The women, they are the life of the nation."

The role of women in the tribal economy reinforced the sharing of power between male and female. Men were responsible for hunting, fishing, and clearing land, but women controlled the cultivation, harvest, and distribution of food. They were responsible for probably three-quarters of their family's nutritional needs. When the men were away on hunting expeditions, women directed village life. Europeans, imbued with the idea of male superiority and female subordination, perceived such a degree of sexual equality as

another mark of the uncivilized nature of tribal society.

In economic relations, Europeans and Indians differed in ways that sometimes led to misunderstanding and conflict. Over vast stretches of the continent, Indians had engaged in trading networks for centuries before Europeans arrived. This experience made it easy for them to engage in trade with arriving Europeans and incorporate new metal and glass trade items into their culture. But trade for Indian peoples was not only a way of acquiring desirable goods. It was also a way of preserving interdependence and equilibrium between individuals and communities. This principle of reciprocity displayed itself in elaborate ceremonies of gift giving and pipe smoking that preceded the exchange of goods. For Europeans, trade was an economic matter with the benefit of building good will between two parties, but the social and spiritual functions of trade were sharply limited in comparison with Indians.

In the religious beliefs of Native Americans, the English saw a final damning defect. Europeans built their religious life around the belief in a single god, written scriptures, a trained and highly literate clergy, and churches with structured ceremonies. Native American societies, sharing no literary tradition, expressed their religious beliefs in a less structured way. At the core of their religion was a belief that spiritual power, mysterious and supernatural, existed everywhere in nature. Believing that human life could be affected—positively or negatively—by the spiritual power in rocks, water, sun, moon, and animals, Indian people sought to conciliate the spirits in nature—even the spirits of the fish, beaver, and deer they hunted. Pueblo people, for example, living in arid lands where rainfall dictated their well-being, expressed their thanks for rain by performing frequent ritual dances.

For Europeans, the Indians' polytheism was pagan and devilish. Europeans understood that Indians had religious leaders called *shamans,* who used medicinal plants and magical chants to heal the sick and facilitated the people's quests to communicate with the spiritual world. But Europeans regarded the *shamans* as especially dangerous because they occupied powerful roles among a spiritually misled people. Their fear and hatred of infidels intensified by the Protestant Reformation, Europeans saw a holy necessity to convert—or destroy—these enemies of their God.

Africa on the Eve of Contact

Half a century before Columbus reached the Americas, a Portuguese sea captain, Antam Gonçalves, made the first European landing on the west coast of sub-Saharan Africa. If he had been able to travel the length and breadth of the immense continent, he would have encountered a rich variety of African states, peoples, and cultures. The notion of African "backwardness" and cultural impoverishment was a myth perpetuated after the slave trade had begun transporting millions of Africans to the New World. During the period of early contact with Europeans, Africa, like pre-Columbian America, was recognized as a diverse continent with a long history of cultural evolution.

The Kingdoms of Africa

The peoples of Africa, estimated at about 50 million in the fifteenth century, when Europeans began making extensive contact with them, lived in vast deserts, grasslands, and tropical forests. As in Europe and the Americas at that time, most people tilled the soil. Part of their skill in farming derived from the development of iron production, which may have begun in West Africa while Europe was still in the Stone Age. More efficient iron implements increased agricultural productivity, which in turn spurred population growth. The pattern was repeated in other parts of the world—the Americas, Europe, the Far East, and the Middle East—when the agricultural revolution began.

By the time Europeans reached the west coast of Africa, a number of large empires had risen there. The first was the kingdom of Ghana. It embraced an immense territory between the Sahara and the Gulf of Guinea and stretched from the Atlantic Ocean to the Niger River.

The development of large towns, skillfully designed buildings, elaborate sculpture and metalwork depicting humans and animals, long-distance commerce, and a complex political structure marked the Ghanaian kingdom from the sixth to eleventh centuries. A thriving caravan trade with Arab peoples across the Sahara to Morocco and Algeria brought extensive Muslim influence by the end of this period. By the eleventh century, the king of Ghana boasted an army of 200,000, maintained trading contacts as far east as Cairo and Baghdad, and was furnishing, through Muslim middlemen in North Africa, much of the gold supply for the Christian Mediterranean region.

An invasion of North African Muslim people beginning in the eleventh century introduced a period of religious strife that eventually destroyed the kingdom of Ghana. But in the same region arose the Islamic kingdom of Mali. Prospering through its control of the gold trade, Mali flourished until the early sixteenth century. Its city of Timbuktu contained a distinguished faculty of scholars to whom North Africans and even southern Europeans came to study. Traveling there in the 1330s, the Arab geographer Ibn-Battuta wrote admiringly of "the discipline of its officials and provincial governors, the excellent condition of public finance, and … the respect accorded to the decisions of justice and to the authority of the sovereign."

Other kingdoms such as Kongo, Songhay, and Benin had also been growing for centuries before Europeans reached Africa by water. In their towns, rivaling those of Europe in size, lived people skilled in metalworking, weaving, ceramics, architecture, and aesthetic expression. Codes of law, regional trade, and effective political organization all developed by the fifteenth century. Finding their way to Africa south of the Sahara, Europeans encountered not a backward area, but a densely settled region with an ancient history of long-distance trade and cultural exchange with other peoples.

Population growth and cultural development in Africa, as elsewhere in the world, proceeded at different rates in different regions. Ecological conditions and geography had a great deal to do with this. Where soil was rich, rainfall was adequate, and minerals were abundant, as in western Sudan, for instance, population grew and cultures changed rapidly. Where inhospitable desert or impenetrable jungle ruled, societies remained small and changed at a very slow rate. Isolation from other cultures retarded development, whereas contact with other regions encouraged change. For example, cultural innovation accelerated in East African Swahili-speaking societies facing the Indian Ocean after trading contacts began with the Eastern world in the ninth century. Around the same time, traders from the Arab world began to spread Muslim influence in West Africa.

The African Ethos

The many peoples of Africa, who were to supply at least two-thirds of all the immigrants who crossed the ocean to the Western Hemisphere in the three centuries after Europeans began colonizing there, came from a rich diversity of cultures. But most of them shared certain ways of life that differentiated them from Europeans.

As in Europe, the family was the basic unit of social organization. Unlike Europe, however, African societies were organized in a variety of kinship and political systems. In many African societies, as in

The city of Loanga, at the mouth of the Congo River on the west coast of Africa, was larger at the time of this drawing in the mid-eighteenth century than all but a few seaports in the British colonies in North America. (The Granger Collection, New York)

The art of sixteenth-century West Africa, much of it ceremonial, shows a high degree of aesthetic development. On the right is Gou, god of war, a metal sculpture from the Fan culture in Dahomey; above is a pair of antelope headdresses (worn by running a cord through holes in the base and tying them atop the head) carved of wood by the Bambara people of Senegambia. (Musée de l'Homme, Paris)

many Native American ones, the family was matrilineal. Property rights and political inheritance descended through the mother rather than the father. It was not the son of a chief who inherited his father's position but the son of the chief's sister. When a man married, his wife did not leave her family and take his name; the bridegroom left his family to join that of his bride.

West Africans believed in a supreme creator of the cosmos and in an assortment of lesser deities associated with natural forces such as rain, fertility, and animal life. Because these deities could intervene in human affairs, they were elaborately honored. Like most North American Indian societies, the peoples of West Africa held that spirits dwelt in the trees, rocks, and rivers around them, and hence they exercised care in the treatment of these natural objects.

In Africa, ancestors were also worshiped, for they mediated between the Creator and the living of the earth. Because the dead played such an important role for the living, relatives held elaborate funeral rites to ensure the proper entrance of a deceased relative into the spiritual world. The more ancient an ancestor, the greater was this person's power to affect the living; thus the "ancient ones" were devoutly worshiped. Deep family loyalty and regard for family lineage flowed naturally from this ancestor worship.

Social organization in much of West Africa by the time Europeans arrived was as elaborate as in fifteenth-century Europe. At the top of society stood the nobility and the priests, usually men of advanced age. Beneath them were the great masses of people. Most of them were farmers, but some worked as craftsmen, traders, teachers, and artists. At the bottom of society resided slaves. As in ancient Greece and Rome, they were "outsiders"—war captives, criminals, or sometimes people who sold themselves into servitude to satisfy a debt. The rights of slaves were restricted, and their opportunities for advancement were narrow. Nevertheless, as members of the community, they were entitled to protection under the law and allowed the privileges of education, marriage, and parenthood. Their servile condition was not permanent, nor was it automatically inherited by their children, as would be the fate of Africans enslaved in the Americas.

West African Cultures and Slaving Forts

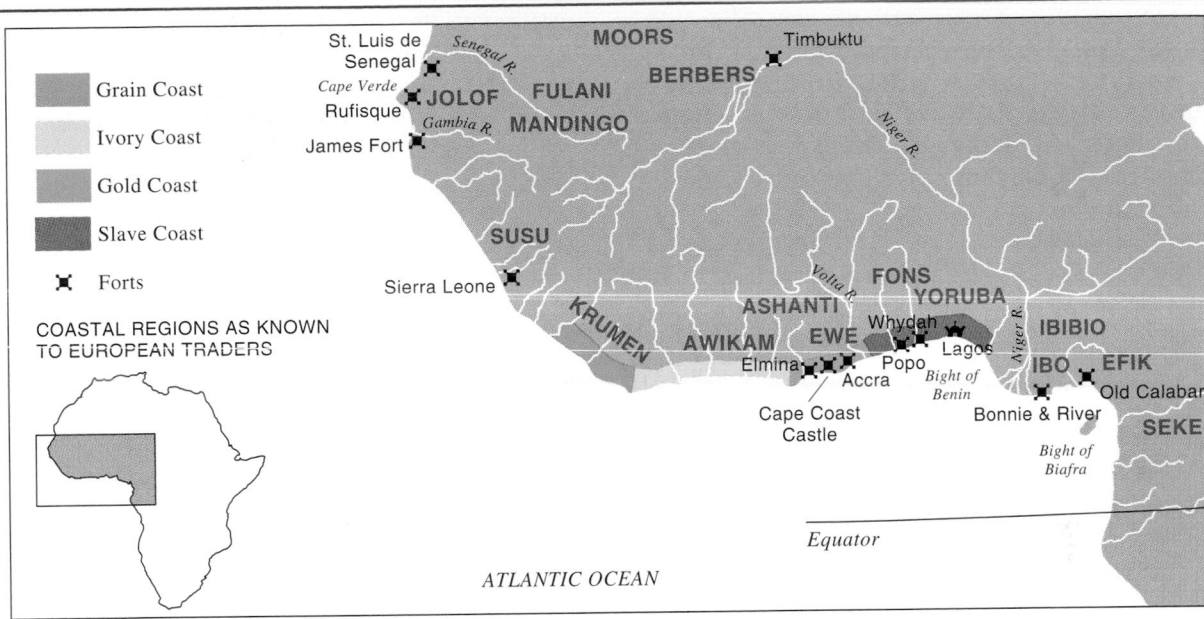

Europeans fought lustily for control of slaving forts on the West African coast, and many forts changed hands several times during the long period of the Atlantic slave trade.

Europe in the Age of Exploration

In the ninth century, about the time that the Mound Builders of the Mississippi valley were constructing their urban center at Cahokia and the kingdom of Ghana was rising in West Africa, western Europe was an economic and cultural backwater. The center of political power and economic vitality in the Old World had shifted eastward to Christian Byzantium, which controlled Asia Minor, the Balkans, and parts of Italy. The other dynamic culture of this age, Islam, had spread through the Middle East, spilled across North Africa, and penetrated Spain and West Africa south of the Sahara.

Over the next six centuries, an epic revitalization of western Europe occurred, creating the conditions that enabled its leading maritime nations vastly to extend their oceanic frontiers. Thence began a 400-year epoch of the militant expansion of European peoples and European culture into other continents. Only in the present century has this process of Europeanization been reversed, as colonized people have regained their autonomy and cultural identity through wars of national liberation.

The Rise of Europe

The rebirth of western Europe, which began around A.D. 1000, owed much to a revival of long-distance trading from Italian ports on the Mediterranean and the rediscovery of ancient knowledge that these contacts permitted. The once mighty cities of the Roman Empire had stagnated for centuries, but now Venice, Genoa, and other Italian ports began trading with peoples facing the Adriatic, the Baltic, and the North Sea. These new contacts brought wealth and power to the Italian commercial cities, which gradually evolved into merchant-dominated city-states that freed themselves from the rule of feudal lords in control of the surrounding countryside.

While merchants led the emerging city-states, western Europe's feudal system was gradually weakening. For centuries, feudal lords, not kings, had exercised the normal powers of the state—the power to tax, wage war, and administer the law. In the thirteenth and fourteenth centuries, however, kings began to reassert their political authority and to undertake efforts to unify their realms. One of their primary goals was to curb the power of the great lords who dominated entire regions and to force lesser nobles into dependence on and obedience to the crown.

The Black Death (bubonic plague) that devastated western Europe and Africa in 1348 and 1349 promoted the unification of old realms into early modern states. The plague killed one-third of the population, a blow from which Europe did not recover demographically for centuries. The nobilities with which monarchs had to contend were reduced in size, for the plague defied class distinction. Ironically, feudal lords treated their peasants better for a time because their labor, tremendously reduced by the plague, became more valuable.

Early developments in England led to a distinctive political system. In 1215, the English aristocracy curbed the powers of the king when they forced him to accept the Magna Carta. On the basis of this charter, a parliament composed of elective and hereditary members eventually gained the right to meet regularly to pass money bills. Parliament was thus in a position to act as a check on the crown, an arrangement unknown on the Continent. During the sixteenth century, the crown and Parliament worked together toward a more unified state, with the English kings wielding less political power than their European counterparts.

Economic changes of great significance also occurred in England during the sixteenth century. Members of the landed class began to combine their estates in order to practice more intensive and profitable agriculture. In this process, they threw peasant farmers off their plots, turning many of them into wage laborers. The formation of this working class was the crucial first step toward industrial development.

Continental Europe lagged behind England in two respects. First, it was far less affected by the move to consolidate, or "enclose," land. Part of the explanation lies in the values of continental aristocrats, who regarded the maximization of profit as unworthy of gentlemen. French nobles could lose their titles for commercial activities. Second, continental rulers were less successful in engaging the interests of their nobilities, and these nobles never shared governance with their king, as did English aristocrats through their participation in Parliament. In France, a noble faction assassinated Henry III in 1589, and the nobility remained disruptive for nearly another century. In Spain, the bloody expulsion of the Muslims and the Jews in 1492 strengthened the monarchy's hold, but regional cultures and leaders remained strong. The continental monarchs would thus warmly embrace doctrines of royal absolutism developed in the sixteenth century.

The New Monarchies and the Expansionist Impulse

In the second half of the fifteenth century, ambitious monarchs coming to power in France, England, and Spain sought social order and political stability in their kingdoms. Louis XI in France, Henry VII in England, Isabella of Castile, and Ferdinand of Aragon all created armies and bureaucratic state machinery strong enough to quell internal conflict, such as the English War of the Roses, and to raise taxes sufficient to support their regimes. In these countries, and in Portugal as well, economic revival and the reversal of more than a century of population decline and civil disorder nourished the impulse to expand beyond known frontiers. This impulse was also fed by Renaissance culture. Ushering in a new, more secular age, the Renaissance (Rebirth) encouraged freedom of thought, richness of expression, and an emphasis on human abilities. Beginning in Italy and spreading northward through Europe, the Renaissance peaked dramatically in the late fifteenth century when the age of exploration began.

The exploratory urge had two initial objectives: to circumvent Muslim traders by finding an eastward oceanic route to Asia and to tap the African gold trade at its source. Since the tenth century, Muslim middlemen in North Africa had brought the precious metal to Europe from Guinea. Now the possibility arose of bypassing these non-Christian traffickers. Likewise, Christian Europeans dreamed of eliminating Muslim traders from the commerce with Asia. Since 1291, when Marco Polo returned to Venice with tales of Eastern treasures—spices, silks, perfumes, drugs, and jewels—Europeans had bartered with the Orient.

But the difficulties of the long eastward overland route through the Muslim world kept alive the hopes of Christian Europeans that an alternative water route existed. Eventually, Europe's mariners would find that they could voyage to Cathay by both eastward and westward water routes, but this took two more centuries to discover.

Portugal seemed the least likely of the rising nation-states to lead the expansion of Europe outside its continental boundaries, yet it forged into the lead at the end of the fifteenth century. A poor and insignificant country of only one million inhabitants, Portugal had gradually overcome Moorish control in the twelfth and thirteenth centuries and, in 1385, had wrenched itself free of domination by neighboring Castile. Led by Prince Henry the Navigator, for whom trade was secondary to the conquest of the Muslim world, Portugal breached the geographical unknown. In the 1420s, Henry began dispatching Portuguese mariners to probe the unknown Atlantic "sea of darkness." His intrepid sailors were aided by important improvements in navigation, mapmaking, and ship design, all promoted by the prince.

Portuguese captains operated at sea on three ancient Ptolemaic principles: that the earth was round, that distances on its surface could be measured by degrees, and that navigators could "fix" their position on a map by measuring the position of the stars. The invention in the 1450s of the quadrant, which allowed a precise measurement of star altitude necessary for determining latitude, represented a leap forward from the chart-and-compass method of navigation. Equally important was the design of a lateen-rigged caravel, adapted from a Moorish ship design. Its triangular sails permitted ships to sail with a contrary wind, allowing them to beat southward along the African coast—a feat the square-rigged European vessels could never perform.

By the 1430s, the ability of Prince Henry's captains to break through the limits of the world known to Europeans had carried them to Madeira, the Canaries, and the Azores, lying off the coasts of Portugal and northwestern Africa. These were soon developed as the first European agricultural plantations, located on the Continent's periphery. From there, the Portuguese sea captains pushed farther south.

European Voyages of Exploration, 1487–1610

Within 100 years of da Gama's voyage to India around the Cape of Africa, European explorers had vastly expanded their knowledge of the world outside western Europe.

By the time of Prince Henry's death in 1460, Portuguese mariners had reached the west coast of Africa, where they began a profitable trade in ivory, slaves, and especially gold. By 1500, they had captured control of the African gold trade monopolized for centuries by North African Muslims. The gleaming metal now traveled directly to Lisbon by sea rather than by camel caravan across the Sahara to North African Muslim ports such as Tunis and Algiers. In 1497, Vasco da Gama became the first European to sail around the Cape of Africa, allowing the Portuguese to colonize the Indian Ocean and as far east as the Spice Islands and Canton by 1513. By forcing trade concessions in the islands and coastal states of the East Indies, the Portuguese unlocked the fabulous Asian treasure houses that since Marco Polo's time had whetted the appetites of Europe's seafarers.

Reaching the Americas

The marriage of Ferdinand and Isabella in 1469 united the independent states of Aragon and Castile and launched the Spanish nation into its golden age. Leading the way for Spain was an Italian sailor, Christopher Columbus. The son of a poor Genoese weaver, Columbus had married into a prominent family of Lisbon merchants and thus made important contacts at court.

Celebrated for hundreds of years as the intrepid explorer who initiated permanent contact between Europe and the Americas, Columbus is attacked by some today as the ruthless exploiter of Indian peoples and lands. But Columbus is best understood in the context of his own times—an age of great brutality and violence and also an age in which Catholic Spain was engaged in the final stages of expelling the Moorish people who had controlled southern Spain for centuries. Columbus's urge to explore was nourished by ideas and questions about the geographical limits of his world, and he was inspired by notions of contributing to the reconquest of Moorish Spain. The Latin inscription on the tomb of his monarchs, Isabella and Ferdinand, captures the mood of the era: "Overthrowers of the Mahometan sect and repressors of heretical stubbornness."

Like many sailors, Columbus had listened to sea tales about lands to the west. He may have heard Icelandic sagas about the voyages of Leif Eriksson and several thousand Norse immigrants who reached Newfoundland five centuries before. Other ideas circulated that the Atlantic Ocean stretched to India and eastern Asia. Could one reach the Indies by sailing west rather than by sailing east around Africa, as the Portuguese were attempting? Columbus hungered to know.

For nearly ten years, Columbus tried unsuccessfully to secure financial backing and royal sanction in Portugal for exploratory voyages. Many mocked his modest estimates of the distance westward from Europe to Japan. Finally, in 1492, Queen Isabella of Spain commissioned him, and he sailed west with three tiny ships and a crew of about 90 men. Strong winds, lasting ten days, blew the ships far into the Atlantic. There they were becalmed. In the fifth week at sea—longer than any European sailors had been out of the sight of land—mutinous rumblings swept through the crews. But Columbus pressed on. On the seventieth day, long after Columbus had calculated he would reach Japan, a lookout sighted land. On October 12, 1492, the sailors clambered ashore on a tiny island in the Bahamas, which Columbus named San Salvador (Holy Savior). Grateful sailors "rendered thanks to Our Lord, kneeling on the ground, embracing it with tears of joy."

Believing he had reached Asia, Columbus explored the island-speckled Caribbean for ten weeks. After landing on heavily populated islands that he named Hispaniola (shared today by Haiti and the Dominican Republic) and Cuba (which he thought was the Asian mainland), he set sail for Spain with cinnamon, coconuts, a bit of gold, and several kidnapped natives. While homeward bound, he penned a report of his discoveries. He believed that he had reached Asia and described its hospitable people, fertile soils, magnificent harbors, and gold-filled rivers.

Quickly printed and distributed throughout Europe, Columbus's report brought him financing between 1494 and 1504 for three much larger expeditions to explore the newfound lands. The second voyage, carrying over 1,200 Spanish in 17 ships, initiated the first extended contact between Europeans and Native Americans. In an ominous display of what was to come, Columbus's men captured some 1,600 Tainos on Hispaniola and carried 550 of them back to Spain as slaves in 1495. Only 350 survived the stormy voyage to Spain. Here began the Atlantic slave trade that would alter the history of the world, though it began in the reverse direction of what would soon become its dominant flow. Although at the time his discoveries seemed less significant than the Portuguese exploits in the South Atlantic, Columbus led Spain to the threshold of a mighty empire. He reaped few rewards, however, dying unnoticed and penniless in 1506. To the end, he believed that he had found the water route to Asia.

The expansion of Spain and Portugal into new areas of the world profoundly affected patterns of economic activity in Europe. Its commercial center now shifted away from the ports of the Mediterranean to the Atlantic ports facing the New World.

The New World also beckoned as a field of religious contest. The heavily populated Americas offered millions of potential Christian converts. But the Catholic-Protestant division within Christianity complicated Christian dreams of converting a "heathen" continent. The people of western Europe, at precisely the time they were unlocking the secrets of the new worlds to the east and west in the sixteenth century, were being torn by religious schisms that magnified the era's national rivalries.

Religious Conflict During the Reformation

At the heart of Europe's religious strife was a continental movement to cleanse the Christian church of corrupt practices and return it to the purer ways of "primitive" Christianity, as practiced by the early Christians. While criticism of the worldliness of the Catholic church mounted during the Renaissance, a German monk, Martin Luther, became the first to break successfully with Rome and initiate a Protestant Reformation of theology and practice. As Protestant sects multiplied, a Catholic Reformation grew up within the church, and the two groups began a long battle for the souls of Europeans.

Luther was preparing for a legal career in 1505 when a bolt of lightning nearly struck him during a violent thunderstorm. Trembling with fear, he vowed to become a monk. But in the religious order of Saint Augustine, he lost faith in the power of the age-old rituals of the church—prayer, the Mass, confession, pilgrimages to holy places, even crusades against Muslim infidels. He reasoned that salvation came through an inward faith, or "grace," that God conferred on those he chose. Good works, Luther believed, did not earn grace but were only the external evidence of grace won through faith. Luther had taken the revolutionary step of rejecting the church's elaborate hierarchy of officials, who presided over the rituals intended to guide individuals along the path toward salvation.

Luther's doctrine of private "justification by faith" did not immediately threaten the church. But in 1517, he openly attacked the sale of "indulgences" for sins by which the pope raised money for the building of St. Peter's in Rome. By purchasing indulgences, individuals believed they could reduce their time (or that of a deceased relative) in purgatory. Luther drew up 95 arguments against this practice and called on Christians to practice true repentance. The spread of printing, invented less than 70 years before, allowed the rapid circulation of his ideas. The printed word and the ability to read it were to become revolutionary weapons throughout the world.

Luther's cry for reform soon inspired Germans of all classes. He denounced five of the seven sacraments of the church, calling for a return to baptism and communion alone. He attacked the clergy for luxurious living and urged celibate prelates to marry. He railed against the "detestable tyranny of the clergy over the laity" and called for a priesthood of all believers. He urged people to seek faith individually by reading the Bible, which he translated into German and made widely available for the first time in printed form. Most dangerously, he called on the German princes to assume control over religion in their states, directly challenging the authority of Rome and further undermining the functions of its clergy.

The basic issue dividing Catholics and Protestants thus centered on the source of religious authority. To Catholics, religious authority resided in the organized Church, headed by the pope. To Protestants, the Bible was the sole authority, and access to God's word or God's grace did not require the mediation of the Church.

Building on Luther's redefinition of Christianity, John Calvin, a Frenchman, brought new intensity and meaning to the Protestant Reformation. In 1536, at age 26, he published a ringing appeal to

John Calvin (1509–1564), painted by Hans Holbein the Younger, is portrayed as a man of letters, books, and solemn religiosity. "What I have taught and written," wrote Calvin, "did not grow in my brain, but that I hold it from God." (The Granger Collection, New York)

down to the last detail so that all, whether saved or damned, would work for God's ends.

Calvinism, as a fine-tuned system of self-discipline and social control, was first put into practice in the 1550s in the city-state of Geneva, near the French border of Switzerland. Here the brilliant and austere leader established what he intended to be a model Christian community. A council of 12 elders drove nonbelievers from the city, rigidly disciplined daily life, and stripped the churches of every appeal to the senses—images, music, incense, and colorful clerical vestments. Religious reformers from all over Europe flocked to the new holy community, and Geneva soon became the continental center of the reformist Christian movement and a haven for refugee Protestant leaders. The city, wrote John Knox of Scotland in 1556, "is the most perfect school of Christ that ever was in the earth since the days of the apostles."

Calvin's radical program converted large numbers of people to Protestantism throughout Europe. Like Lutheranism, it recruited most successfully among the privileged classes of merchants, landowners, lawyers, and the nobility and among the rising middle class of master artisans and shopkeepers.

Sixteenth-century monarchs initially regarded attacks on the Catholic Church with horror. But many local princes adopted some version of the reformed faith. The most important monarch to break with Catholicism was Henry VIII of England. When Pope Clement VII refused him permission to divorce and remarry, Henry declared himself head of a Protestant (Anglican) Church. Although the Anglican Church retained many Catholic features, it moved further in a Protestant direction under Henry's son Edward. But when Mary, Henry's older Catholic daughter, came to the throne, she vowed to reinstate her mother's religion by suppressing Protestants. Her policy created Protestant martyrs, and many were relieved when she died in 1558, bringing Henry's younger Protestant daughter, Elizabeth, to the throne. During her long rule, the flinty Elizabeth helped create an Anglican Church that steered a middle course between the radicalism of Geneva and the Catholicism of Rome.

The countries most affected by the Reformation—England, Holland, and France—were slow in trying to colonize the New World, so Protestantism

every Christian to form a direct, personal relationship with God. By Calvin's doctrine, God had saved a few souls at random before Creation and damned the rest. Human beings were too depraved to know or alter this predestination, but good Christians must struggle to believe in their hearts that they were saved. Without mediation of ritual or priest but by "straight-walking," one was to behave as one of God's elect, the "saints." This radical theology, even more insistent on individual godliness than Luther's, spread among all classes throughout Europe.

Calvin proposed reformed Christian communities structured around the elect few. To remake the corrupt world and follow God's will, communities of "saints" must control the state, rather than the other way around. Elected bodies of ministers and dedicated laymen, called presbyteries, were to govern the church, directing the affairs of society did not gain an early foothold in the Americas. Catholicism in Spain and Portugal remained almost immune from the Protestant Reformation. Thus, even while under attack, Catholicism swept across the Atlantic almost unchallenged during the century after Columbus's voyages.

The Iberian Conquest of America

From 1492 to 1518, Spanish and Portuguese explorers opened up vast parts of Asia and the Americas to European knowledge. Yet during this age of exploration, only modest attempts at settlement were made, mostly by the Spanish on the Caribbean islands of Cuba, Puerto Rico, and Hispaniola. The three decades after 1518, however, became an age of conquest. In some of the bloodiest chapters in recorded history, the Spanish nearly exterminated the native peoples of the Caribbean islands, toppled and plundered the great inland empires of the Aztecs and Incas in Mexico and Peru, discovered fabulous silver mines, and built a westward oceanic trade of enormous importance to all of Europe. The consequences of this short era of conquest proved to be immense for the entire world.

Portugal, meanwhile, restricted by one of the most significant lines ever drawn on a map, concentrated mostly on building an eastward oceanic trade to southeastern Asia. In 1493, to settle a dispute, the pope had demarcated Spanish and Portuguese spheres of exploration in the Atlantic. Drawing a north-south line 100 leagues (about 300 miles) west of the Azores, the pope confined Portugal to the European side of the line. One year later, in the Treaty of Tordesillas, Portugal obtained Spanish agreement to move the line 270 leagues farther west. Nobody knew at the time that a large part of South America, as yet undiscovered by Europeans, bulged east of the new demarcation line and therefore fell within the Portuguese sphere. In time, Portugal would develop this region, called Brazil, into one of the most profitable areas of the New World.

The Spanish Onslaught

Within a single generation of Columbus's death in 1506, Spanish *conquistadores* explored, claimed, and conquered most of South America (except Brazil), Central America, and the southern parts of

The plan of Tenochtitlán, later Mexico City, is from the Latin edition of Cortés's "Second Letter," on his conquest of the Aztecs. Cortés's account was widely published in Europe, where Germans, French, and English were astounded to hear of such an extraordinary Aztec metropolis with floating gardens, causeways, and monumental architecture. (The Granger Collection, New York)

North America from Florida to California. Led by audacious explorers and military leaders, and usually accompanied by enslaved Africans, they established the authority of Spain and Catholicism over an area that dwarfed their homeland in size and population. They were motivated by religion, growing pride of nation, and dreams of personal enrichment. "We came here," explained one Spanish foot soldier in Cortés's legion, "to serve God and the king, and also to get rich."

In two bold and bloody strokes, the Spanish overwhelmed the ancient civilizations of the Aztecs and Incas. In 1519, Hernando Cortés set out with 600 soldiers from coastal Veracruz and marched over rugged mountains to attack Tenochtitlán (modern-day Mexico City), the capital of Montezuma's Aztec empire. At its height, centuries before, the ancient city in the Valley of Mexico had contained perhaps 200,000 people. But in 1521, following two years of tense relations between the Spanish and Aztecs, it fell before Cortés's assault. The Spanish use of horses and firearms provided an important advantage; so did a murderous smallpox epidemic in 1520 that felled thousands of Aztecs. The alliance of dissident natives oppressed by Montezuma's tyranny was also indispensable in overthrowing the Aztec ruler. From the Valley of Mexico, the Spanish extended their dominion over the Mayan people of the Yucatán and Guatemala in the next few decades.

In the second conquest, the intrepid Francisco Pizarro, marching from Panama through the jungles of Ecuador and into the towering mountains of Peru with a mere 168 men, most of them not even soldiers, toppled the Inca empire. Like the Aztecs, the populous Incas lived in a highly organized social system. But also like the Aztecs, they were riddled by smallpox and weakened by violent internal divisions. This ensured Pizarro's success in capturing their capital at Cuzco in 1533. From there, Spanish soldiers marched farther afield, plundering other gold- and silver-rich Inca cities. Further expeditions into Chile, New Granada (Colombia), Argentina, and Bolivia in the 1530s and 1540s brought under Spanish control an empire larger than any in the Western world since the fall of Rome.

By 1550, Spain had overwhelmed the major centers of native population throughout the Caribbean, Mexico, Central America, and the west coast of South America. Spanish ships carried gold, silver, dyewoods, and sugar east across the Atlantic and transported African slaves, colonizers, and finished goods west. In a brief half century, Spain had exploited the advances in geographical knowledge and marine technology made by its Portuguese rivals and brought into harsh but profitable contact with each other the people of three continents. The triracial character of the Americas was already firmly established by 1600.

For nearly a century after Columbus's voyages, Spain enjoyed almost unchallenged dominion over the fabulous hemisphere newly revealed to Europeans. Greedy buccaneers of various nations snapped at the heels of homeward-bound Spanish treasure fleets with cargoes of silver, but this was only a nuisance. France made gestures of contesting Spanish or Portuguese control by planting small settlements in Brazil and Florida in the mid-sixteenth century, but they were quickly wiped out. England remained island-bound until the 1580s.

Spanish and Portuguese Conquests in the Americas

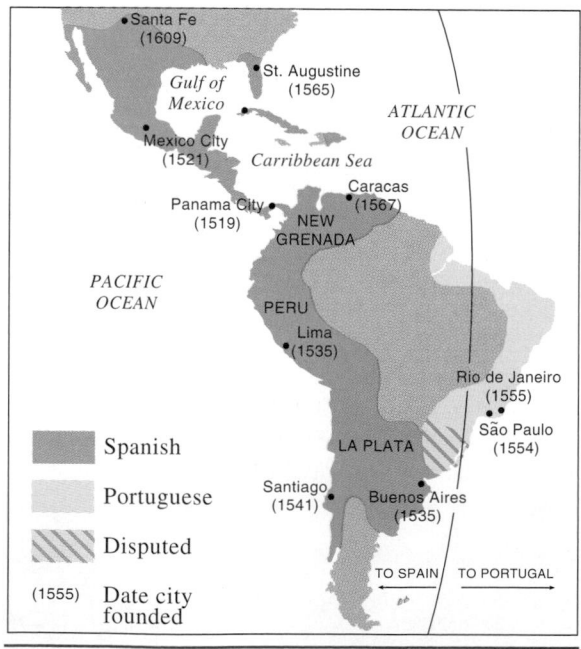

Never before the Spanish and Portuguese arrived in the Americas had such small numbers of people established their dominance over such a large and populous area.

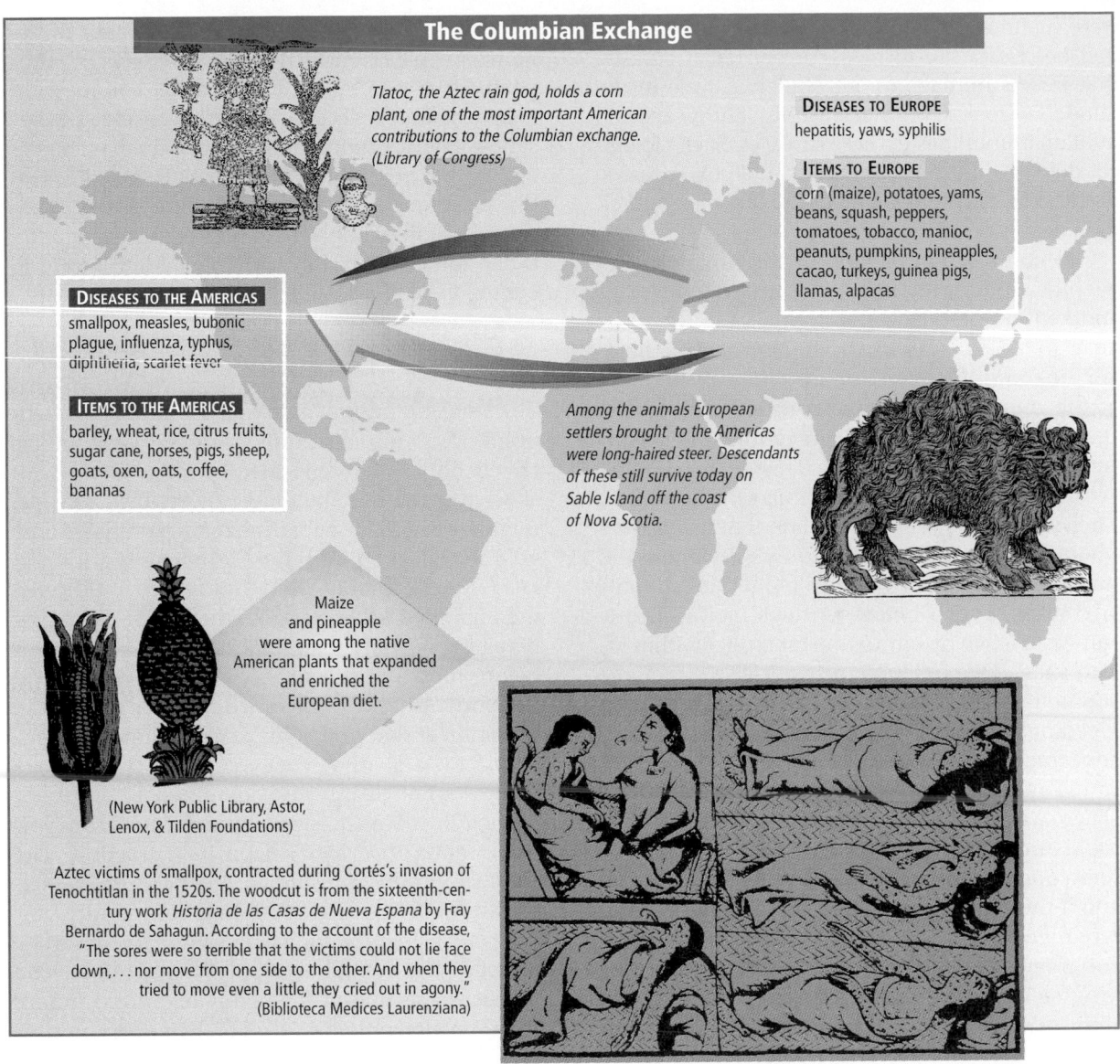

The Columbian Exchange

Tlatoc, the Aztec rain god, holds a corn plant, one of the most important American contributions to the Columbian exchange. (Library of Congress)

DISEASES TO EUROPE
hepatitis, yaws, syphilis

ITEMS TO EUROPE
corn (maize), potatoes, yams, beans, squash, peppers, tomatoes, tobacco, manioc, peanuts, pumpkins, pineapples, cacao, turkeys, guinea pigs, llamas, alpacas

DISEASES TO THE AMERICAS
smallpox, measles, bubonic plague, influenza, typhus, diphtheria, scarlet fever

ITEMS TO THE AMERICAS
barley, wheat, rice, citrus fruits, sugar cane, horses, pigs, sheep, goats, oxen, oats, coffee, bananas

Among the animals European settlers brought to the Americas were long-haired steer. Descendants of these still survive today on Sable Island off the coast of Nova Scotia.

Maize and pineapple were among the native American plants that expanded and enriched the European diet.

(New York Public Library, Astor, Lenox, & Tilden Foundations)

Aztec victims of smallpox, contracted during Cortés's invasion of Tenochtitlan in the 1520s. The woodcut is from the sixteenth-century work *Historia de las Casas de Nueva Espana* by Fray Bernardo de Sahagun. According to the account of the disease, "The sores were so terrible that the victims could not lie face down, . . . nor move from one side to the other. And when they tried to move even a little, they cried out in agony." (Biblioteca Medices Laurenziana)

Until the seventeenth century, only Portugal, which staked out important claims in Brazil in the 1520s, challenged Spanish domination of the New World.

The Great Dying

Spanish conquest of major areas of the Americas set in motion two of the most far-reaching processes in modern history. One involved microbes, the other precious metal. Spanish contacts with the natives of the Caribbean basin, central Mexico, and Peru in the early sixteenth century triggered the most dramatic and disastrous population decline ever recorded in the history of the world. The population of the Americas on the eve of European arrival had grown to an estimated 50 to 60 million or more. In some areas, such as central Mexico, the highlands of Peru, and certain Caribbean islands, population density exceeded that of most of Europe. But though they were less populous than the people of the Americas, the European colonizers had one extraordinary biological advantage over them. They were members of a population that for centuries had been exposed to nearly every lethal parasite that infects humans on an epidemic scale in the temperate zone. Over the centuries, Europeans had built up immunities to these diseases. Such biological defenses did not eliminate smallpox, measles, diphtheria, and other afflictions, but they limited their deadly power.

In contrast, the people of the Americas had been geographically isolated from these diseases and kept no domesticated animals that were the hosts of most diseases. Arriving Europeans therefore unknowingly encountered a huge component of the human race that was utterly defenseless against the "domesticated" infections the explorers, traders, and settlers carried inside their bodies.

The results were catastrophic. On Hispaniola, a population of about one million that had existed when Columbus arrived had only a few thousand survivors by 1530. Of some 15 million inhabitants in central Mexico before Cortés's arrival, nearly half were felled by murderous microbes within fifteen years. Demographic disaster also struck the populous Inca peoples of the Peruvian Andes, even speeding ahead of Pizarro's *conquistadores*. Smallpox "spread over the people as great destruction," an old Indian told a Spanish priest in the 1520s. "There was great havoc. Very many died of it. They could not stir, they could not change position, nor lie on one side, nor face down, nor on their backs. And if they stirred, much did they cry out.... And very many starved; there was death from hunger, [for] none could take care of [the sick]." Such terrifying sickness led many natives to believe that their gods had failed them, and this belief left them ready to acknowledge the greater power of the Christian God that Spanish priests proclaimed.

In most areas where Europeans intruded in the hemisphere for the next three centuries, the catastrophe repeated itself. Whether Protestant or Catholic, whether French, English, Spanish, or Dutch, whether male or female, every newcomer from the Old World participated accidentally in the spread of disease that typically eliminated, within a few generations, at least two-thirds of the native population. Millions of Native Americans who never saw a European died of European diseases, which swept like wildfire through densely populated regions.

The enslavement and brutal treatment of the native people intensified the lethal effects of European diseases. After their spectacular conquests of the Incas and Aztecs, the Spanish enslaved thousands of native people and assigned them work regimens that severely weakened their resistance to disease. Some priests like Bartolomé de Las Casas waged lifelong campaigns to reduce the exploitation of the Indians, but they had only limited power to control the actions of their colonizing compatriots.

Silver, Sugar, and Their Consequences

The small amount of gold that Columbus brought home from his explorations of the West Indies raised hopes that this metal, which along with silver formed the standard of wealth in Europe, might be found in the transatlantic paradise. Some gold was gleaned from the Caribbean islands and later from Colombia, Brazil, and Peru. But though men pursued it fanatically to the far corners of the hemisphere, more than three centuries would pass before they found gold in windfall quantities on the North American Pacific slope and in the Yukon. It was silver that proved most abundant—so plenteous, in fact, that when bonanza strikes were made in Bolivia in 1545 and then in northern Mexico in the next decade, much of Spain's New World enterprise focused on its extraction. The Spanish empire in America, for most of the sixteenth century, was a vast mining community.

Native people, along with some African slaves, provided the first labor supply for the mines. The Spaniards permitted the highly organized Indian societies to maintain control of their own communities but exacted from them huge labor drafts for mining. By imposing themselves at the top of a highly stratified social order that had previously been organized around tributary labor, the Spanish enriched themselves beyond the dreams of even the most visionary explorers. At Potosí, in Bolivia, 58,000 workers labored at elevations of up to 13,000 feet to extract the precious metal from a fabulous sugarloaf "mountain of silver." The town's population reached 120,000 by 1570, making it larger than any in Spain at the time. Thousands of other workers toiled in the mines of Zacatecas, Taxco, and Guanajuato. By 1660, they had scooped up more than 7 million pounds of

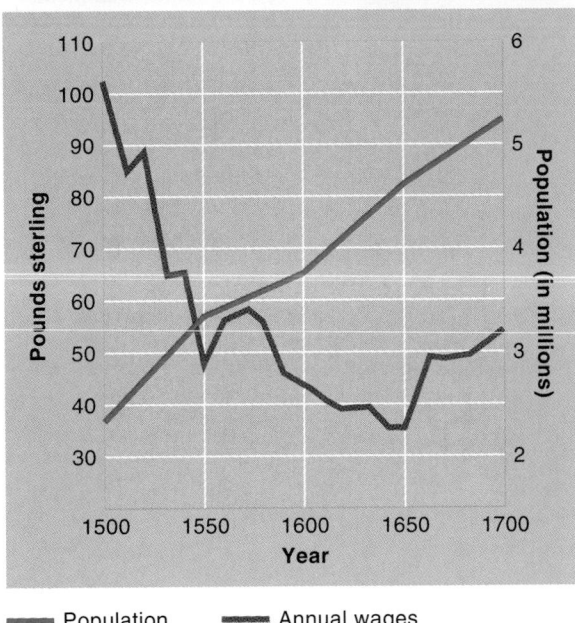

Real Wages and Population in England, 1500–1700

Population
Annual wages

In the 200 years after Columbus's voyages, the population of England more than doubled, while declining wages created increasing pressure to move to the Americas. Sources: Gary Walton and James Shepherd, *The Economic Rise of Early America* (1979); and D.C. Coleman, *The Economy of England, 1450–1750* (1977).

silver from the Americas, tripling the entire European supply.

The massive flow of bullion from the Americas to Europe triggered profound changes. It financed further conquests and settlement in Spain's American empire, spurred long-distance trading in luxury items such as silks and spices from the Far East, and capitalized agricultural development in the New World of sugar, coffee, cacao, and indigo. The bland diet of Europeans gradually changed as items such as sugar and spices, previously luxury articles for the wealthy, became accessible to ordinary people.

The enormous increase of silver in circulation in Europe after the mid-sixteenth century also caused a "price revolution." As the supply of silver increased faster than the volume of goods and services that Europeans could produce, the value of the metal declined. Put differently, prices rose. Between 1550 and 1600, they doubled in many parts of Europe and then rose another 50 percent in the next half century. Land-owning farmers got more for their produce,

and merchants thrived on the increased circulation of goods. But artisans, laborers, and landless agricultural workers (the vast majority of the population) suffered because their wages did not keep pace with rising prices. Skilled artisans, lamented one of the first English immigrants to America, "live in such a low condition as is little better than beggary."

Overall, the price revolution brought a major redistribution of wealth and increased the number of people in western Europe living at the margins of society. It thus built up the pressure to emigrate to the Americas, Europe's new frontier. At the same time, rising prices stimulated commercial development. Expansion overseas fed expansion at home and intensified changes toward capitalist modes of production already under way in the sixteenth century.

While the Spaniards organized their overseas empire around the extraction of silver from the highlands of Mexico, Bolivia, and Peru, the Portuguese staked their future on sugar production in the lowlands of Brazil. Spanish colonial agriculture supplied the huge mining centers, but the Portuguese, adapting techniques of cultivation worked out earlier on their Atlantic islands, produced sugar for the export market.

Whereas the Spanish mining operations rested primarily on the backs of the native labor force, the lowland Portuguese sugar planters scattered the indigenous people and replaced them with platoons of African slaves. By 1570, this regimented work force was producing nearly 6 million pounds of sugar annually; by the 1630s, output had risen to 32 million pounds per year. High in calories but low in protein, the sweet "drug food" revolutionized the tastes of millions of Europeans and caused the oceanic transport of millions of African slaves to the coast of Brazil and later to Colombia, Ecuador, and Peru.

From Brazil, sugar production jumped to the island-speckled Caribbean. Here, in the early seventeenth century, England, Holland, and France challenged Spain and Portugal for the riches of the New World. Once they secured a foothold in the West Indies, Spain's enemies stood at the gates of the Hispanic New World empire. This ushered in a long period of conflict "beyond the line"—where European treaties had no force. Through contraband trading with Spanish settlements, piratical

This 1823 lithograph by William Clark romanticizes gang labor in the sugar fields of the British West Indies by decorously clothing men and women in trousers, jackets, and skirts. In reality, enslaved Africans worked seminaked under the punishing sun. However, this depiction accurately reflects the use of female labor in the holing, planting, and harvesting of sugar cane. (By permission of The British Library)

attacks on Spanish treasure fleets, and outright seizure of Spanish-controlled islands, the Dutch, French, and English in the seventeenth century gradually sapped the strength of the first European empire outside of Europe.

Spain's Northern Frontier

The crown jewels of Spain's New World empire were silver-rich Mexico and Peru, with the islands and coastal fringes of the Caribbean representing lesser, yet valuable, gemstones. Distinctly third in importance were the northern borderlands of New Spain—the present-day Sun Belt of the United States. Yet the early Spanish influence in Florida, the Gulf region, Texas, New Mexico, Arizona, and California indelibly marked the history of the United States. Spanish control of the southern fringes of North America began in the early 1500s and did not end for three centuries, when Mexico wrested independence from Spain in 1821. Far outlasting Spanish rule were the plants and animals they introduced to North America, ranging from sheep, cattle, and horses to various grasses and weeds.

Spanish explorers began charting the southeastern region of North America in the early six-

teenth century, beginning with Juan Ponce de León's expeditions to Florida in 1515 and 1521 and Lucas Vasquez d'Ayllon's short-lived settlement at Winyah Bay in South Carolina in 1526. For the next half century, Spaniards planted small settlements along the coast as far north as the Chesapeake Bay where their temporary settlement included many enslaved Africans. The Spanish traded some with the natives, but the North American coast, especially Florida, was chiefly important to the Franciscan priests, who attempted to gather the local tribes into mission villages and convert them to Catholicism.

The Spanish made several attempts to bring the entire Gulf of Mexico region under their control. From 1539 to 1542, Hernando de Soto, a veteran of Pizarro's conquest of the Incas, led a military expedition deep into the homelands of the Creeks and Choctaws and explored westward from Tampa Bay across the Mississippi to Arkansas.

De Soto's expedition at first found receptive natives, but his men could not provide what the Spanish most wanted—gold. Pillaging Indian villages and seizing food supplies, de Soto's men cut a brutal swath as far north as North Carolina and as far west as Arkansas. Disease followed the Spanish explorers everywhere they went. Little could the

James Walker's Vaqueros in a Horse Corral *speaks beautifully of the Spanish origins of the cowboy American West. (Gilcrease Museum of American Art, Tulsa, OK)*

English know that their Spanish enemies were paving the way for them in North America's southeastern sector by spreading lethal microbes that devastated Indian societies and broke up the great chiefdoms of the lower South.

In 1559, Spaniards again marched northward from Mexico in an attempt to establish their authority in the lower Gulf region. Everywhere they went, they enslaved Indians and used them as provision carriers. In 1565, they sought to secure Florida. Building a fort at St. Augustine, they evicted their French rivals at Fort Caroline, 40 miles to the north. St. Augustine became the center of Spain's northeastern frontier, and Florida remained a Spanish possession for more than two centuries.

The Southwest became a more important region of early Spanish activity in North America. Francisco Vásquez de Coronado explored the region from 1540 to 1542, leading an expedition of several hundred Spanish soldiers, a number of Africans, and a baggage train of 1,300 friendly Indians, servants, and slaves. Coronado never found the Seven Cities of Cíbola, reported by earlier Spanish explorers to be fabulously decorated in turquoise and gold. But he opened much of Arizona, New Mexico, and Colorado to eventual Spanish control, happened upon the Grand Canyon, and probed as far north as the Great Plains. His interior explorations, together with the nearly simultaneous expedition of de Soto in the Southeast, established Spanish claims to the southern latitudes of North America and gave them contacts, often bloody, with the populous corn-growing Indian societies of the region.

The Southwest, like Florida and the Gulf region, proved empty of the fabled golden cities. In New Mexico, however, Franciscan priests tried to harvest souls rather than mine precious metals. They made no attempt to uproot the Rio Grande Pueblo people who they proselytized or even to contain them within mission walls. A half century after Coronado's exploratory intrusions, Juan de Onate led 400 Spanish soldiers and ten Franciscan friars up the Rio Grande in 1598 to find some 60,000 Pueblos gathered in scores of settled towns where they had practiced agriculture for centuries. For the next 80 years, the Franciscans tried to graft Catholicism onto Pueblo culture by building churches on the edges of ancient native villages. As long as the priests were content to overlay Indian culture with a veneer of Catholicism, they encountered little resistance because the Pueblos found advantage in Spanish military protection from their Apache enemies and valued access to mission livestock and grain during years of drought. It proved useful to profess the Christian faith while practicing traditional religion in the underground Pueblo ceremonial chambers called *kivas*.

England Looks West

By the time England awoke to the promise of the New World, the two Iberian powers were firmly entrenched there. But by the late sixteenth century, the conditions necessary to propel England overseas had ripened. During the seventeenth century, the English, as well as the Dutch and French, began overtaking their southern European rivals. The first challenge came in the Caribbean, where between 1604 and 1640, the English planted several small colonies producing tobacco and later sugar. Few guessed that some secondary and relatively unproductive settlements also being planted on the North American mainland would in time be among England's most prized possessions.

England Challenges Spain

England was the most backward of the European nations facing the Atlantic in exploring and colonizing the New World. Although far more numerous than the Portuguese, the English in the fifteenth century had little experience with long-distance trade and few contacts with cultures beyond their island aside from the French, against whom they had waged the Hundred Years' War (1337–1453). Only the voyages of John Cabot (the Genoa-born Giovanni Caboto) gave England any claim in the New World sweepstakes. But Cabot's

Under the leadership of Elizabeth I, here displayed in royal finery and resting her hand on the globe, England challenged and ultimately overturned Spain's domination of worldwide sea trade. Behind the placid face was a determined and sometimes ruthless ruler. (By kind permission of Marquess of Tavistock and Trustees of Bedford Estate)

voyages to Newfoundland and Nova Scotia a few years after Columbus's first voyage—the first northern crossing of the Atlantic since the Vikings—were never followed up.

At first, England's interest in the far side of the Atlantic centered primarily on fish. This high-protein food, basic to the European diet, was the gold of the North Atlantic. The early North Atlantic explorers found the waters off Newfoundland and Nova Scotia teeming with fish, not only the ordinary cod, but also the delectable salmon. But it was the fishermen of Portugal, Spain, and France, more than those of England, who began making annual spring trips to the offshore fisheries in the 1520s. Not until the end of the century would the French and English drive Spanish and Portuguese fishermen from the Newfoundland Banks.

Exploratory voyages along the eastern coast of North America hardly interested the English. It was for the French that Cartier and Verrazano sailed between 1524 and 1535. Looking for straits westward to India, through the northern land mass, which was still thought to be a large island, they made contact with many Indian tribes and charted the coastline from the St. Lawrence River to the Carolinas. They established the northern latitudes as a suitable place for settlement, but found nothing of immediate value to take home. The time had not yet arrived when Europeans would leave their homelands to resettle in America rather than go there merely to extract its riches.

Changes occurred in the late sixteenth century, however, that propelled the English overseas. The rising production of woolen cloth, a mainstay of the English economy, had sent merchants scurrying for new markets after 1550. Their success in establishing trading companies in Russia, Scandinavia, the Middle East, and India vastly widened England's commercial orbit and raised hopes that still other spheres could be developed. At the same time, population growth and rising prices depressed the existence of ordinary people and made them look to the transoceanic frontier for new opportunities.

Queen Elizabeth I, who ruled from 1558 to 1603, followed a cautious policy that did not include the promotion of overseas colonies. She favored Protestantism partly as a vehicle of national independence. Ambitious and talented, she had to contend with Philip II, king of Spain and her fervently Catholic brother-in-law, whose long reign nearly coincided with hers. Regarding Elizabeth as a Protestant heretic, Philip plotted incessantly against her. The pope added to Catholic-Protestant tensions in England by excommunicating Elizabeth in 1571 and absolving her subjects from paying her allegiance. This, in effect, gave them religious license to overthrow her.

The smoldering conflict between Catholic Spain and Protestant England broke into open flames in 1587. Two decades before, Philip II had sent 20,000 Spanish soldiers into his Netherlands provinces to suppress Protestantism. Then, in 1572, he had helped arrange the massacre of thousands of French Protestants. By the 1580s, Elizabeth was providing covert aid to the Protestant Dutch revolt against Catholic rule. Philip vowed to crush the rebellion and decided as well to launch an attack on England in order to wipe out this growing center of Protestant power.

Elizabeth fed the flames of the international Catholic-Protestant conflict in 1585 by sending 6,000 English troops to aid the Dutch Protestants. Three years later, Philip dispatched a Spanish armada of 130 ships carrying 30,000 men and 2,400 artillery pieces. Sails blazing with crusaders' crosses, the fleet set forth to conquer Elizabeth's England. For two weeks in the summer of 1588, a sea battle raged off the English coast. A motley collection of smaller English ships, with the colorful sea dog Francis Drake in the lead, defeated the Armada, sinking many of the lumbering Spanish galleons and then retiring as the legendary "Protestant wind" blew the crippled Armada into the North Sea.

The Spanish defeat prevented a crushing Catholic victory in Europe and brought a temporary stalemate in the religious wars. It also solidified Protestantism in England and brewed a fierce nationalistic spirit there. Shakespeare's love of "this other Eden, this demi-paradise" spread among the people; and with Spanish naval power checked, both the English and the Dutch found the seas more open to their rising maritime and commercial interests.

The Westward Fever

In the last decades of the sixteenth century, the idea of overseas expansion captured the imagination of important elements of English society. Urging them

on were two Richard Hakluyts, uncle and nephew. In the 1580s and 1590s, they devoted themselves to advertising the advantages of colonizing on the far side of the Atlantic. For nobles at court, colonies offered new baronies, fiefdoms, and estates. For merchants, the New World promised exotic produce to sell at home and a new outlet for English cloth and other goods. For the militant Protestant clergy, there awaited a continent filled with heathen people to be saved from both savagery and Catholicism. For the commoner, opportunity beckoned in the form of bounteous land, almost for the taking. In a number of pamphlets, the Hakluyts publicized the idea that the time was ripe for England to break the Iberian monopoly on the riches of the New World.

England mounted its first attempts at colonizing, however, in Ireland. In the 1560s and 1570s, the English gradually extended their control over the country through brutal military conquest. Ireland became a turbulent frontier for thousands of career-hungry younger sons of gentry families as well as landless commoners. Many of the leaders first involved in New World colonizing had served in Ireland, and many of their ideas of how to deal with a "savage" and "barbaric" people stemmed from their Irish experience.

The first English attempts at overseas settlement were small, feeble, and ill-fated. Whereas the Spanish encountered unheard-of wealth and scored epic victories over ancient and populous civilizations, the English at first met only failure in relatively thinly settled lands. Beginning in 1583, they mounted several unsuccessful attempts to settle Newfoundland. Other settlers, organized by Walter Raleigh, planted a settlement from 1585 to 1588 at Roanoke Island, off the North Carolina coast. They apparently perished in attacks by a local tribe after killing a tribal leader and displaying his head on a pike. Small groups of men sent out to establish a tiny colony in Guiana, off the South American coast, failed in 1604 and 1609, and another group that set down in Maine in 1607 lasted only a year. Even the colonies founded in Virginia in 1607 and Bermuda in 1612, although they would flourish in time, floundered badly for several decades.

English merchants, sometimes supported by gentry investors, undertook these first tentative efforts. They risked their capital hoping that small-scale ventures in North America might produce the

John White, governor of the second expedition to Virginia in 1587, rendered the first pictorial records of native life in the Americas. This watercolor of a tatooed noblewoman of Pomeiock shows her right arm resting in a chain of pearls or copper beads. Her young daughter holds a prized English doll in an Elizabethan dress. (Copyright The British Museum)

uncertainties of mixed farming, lumbering, and fishing on the North American mainland. In the 1620s and 1630s, most of the English capital invested overseas went into establishing tobacco colonies in a dusting of tiny Caribbean islands, including St. Christopher (1624), Barbados (1627), Nevis (1628), Montserrat (1632), and Antigua (1632).

Apart from the considerable financing required, the vital element in launching a colony was a suitable body of colonists. About 80,000 streamed out of England between 1600 and 1640, as economic, political, and religious developments pushed them from their homeland at the same time that dreams of opportunity and adventure pulled them westward. In the next 20 years, another 80,000 departed.

Economic difficulties in England prompted many to try their luck in the New World. The changing agricultural system, combined with population growth and the unrelenting increase in prices caused by the influx of New World silver, produced a surplus of unskilled labor, squeezed many small producers, and spread poverty and crime. By the late 1500s, the roads, wrote Richard Hakluyt, were swarming with "valiant youths rusting and hurtful for lack of employment," and the prisons were "daily pestered and stuffed full of them."

A generation later, beginning in 1618, the renewed European religious wars between Protestants and Catholics devastated the continental market for English woolen cloth, bringing unemployment and desperate conditions to the textile regions. Probably half the households in England lived on the edge of poverty, struggling for survival and subject to a punishing economic system in which they had no voice. "This land grows weary of her inhabitants," wrote John Winthrop of East Anglia, "so as a man, which is the most precious of all creatures, is near more vile among us than a horse or a sheep."

Religious persecution and political considerations intensified the pressure to emigrate from England in the early seventeenth century. How this operated in specific situations will be considered in the next chapter. The largest number of emigrants went to the West Indies. The North American mainland colonies attracted perhaps half as many, and the Irish plantations in Ulster and Munster still fewer. For the first time in their history, large numbers of English people were abandoning their island homeland to carry their destinies to new frontiers.

profits of their other overseas commercial ventures. They had little backing from the government, in subsidies, ships, or naval protection, though they had the blessing of their queen. The Spanish and Portuguese colonizing efforts were national enterprises, sanctioned, capitalized, and coordinated by the crown. The English colonies were private ventures, organized and financed by small partnerships of merchants who pooled their slender resources.

Not until these first merchant adventurers solicited the wealth and support of the prospering middle class of English society could colonization succeed. This support grew steadily in the first half of the seventeenth century, but even then, investors were drawn far more to the quick profits promised in West Indian tobacco production than to the

Anticipating North America

The early English settlers in North America were far from uninformed about the indigenous people of the New World. Beginning with Columbus's first description of the New World, published in several European cities in 1493 and 1494, reports and promotional accounts circulated among the participants in early voyages of discovery, trade, and settlement. This literature became the basis for anticipating the world that had been discovered beyond the setting sun.

Colonists who read or listened to these accounts probably held a split image of the native people. On the one hand, the Indians were depicted as a gentle people who eagerly received Europeans. Columbus had written of the "great amity toward us" that he encountered in San Salvador in 1492 and had described the Arawaks there as "a loving people" who "were greatly pleased and became so entirely our friends that it was a wonder to see." Verrazano, the first European to touch the eastern edge of North America, wrote optimistically about the native people in 1524. The natives, graceful of limb and tawny-colored, he related, "came toward us joyfully uttering loud cries of wonderment, and showing us the safest place to beach the boat."

This positive image of the Native Americans reflected both the friendly reception that Europeans often actually received and the European vision of the New World as an earthly paradise where war-torn, impoverished, or persecuted people could build a new life. The strong desire to trade with the native people also encouraged a favorable view because only a friendly Indian could become a suitable partner in commercial exchange.

A counterimage, of a savage, hostile Indian, however, also entered the minds of settlers coming to North America. Like the positive image, it originated in the early travel literature. As early as 1502, Sebastian Cabot had paraded in England three Eskimos he had kidnapped on an Arctic voyage. They were described as flesh-eating savages and "brute beasts" who "spake such speech that no man could understand them." Many other accounts portrayed the New World natives as crafty, brutal, loathsome halfmen, who lived, as Amerigo Vespucci put it, without "law, religion, rulers, immortality of the soul, and private property."

TIMELINE

	Pre-Columbian Epochs
12,000 B.C.	Beringian epoch ends
6000 B.C.	Paleo-Indian phase ends
500 B.C.	Archaic era ends
500 B.C.–	Post-Archaic era in North America
c. 1000	Norse seafarers establish settlements in Newfoundland
A.D. 1500	Kingdoms of Ghana, Mali, Songhay in Africa
1420s	Portuguese sailors explore west coast of Africa
1492	Christopher Columbus lands on Caribbean islands
	Spanish expel Moors (Muslims) and Jews
1494	Treaty of Tordesillas
1497–1585	French and English explore northern part of the Americas
1498	Vasco da Gama reaches India after sailing around Africa
1513	Portuguese explorers reach China
1515–1565	Spanish explore Florida and southern part of North America
1520s	Luther attacks Catholicism
1521	Cortés conquers the Aztecs
1530s	Calvin calls for religious reform
1533	Pizarro conquers the Incas
1540–1542	Coronado explores the Southwest
1558	Elizabeth I crowned queen of England
1585	Roanoke Island settlement
1588	English defeat the Spanish Armada
1603	James I succeeds Elizabeth I
1607	English begin settlement at Jamestown, Virginia
1680	Popé's revolt in New Mexico

The English had another reason for believing that all would not be friendship and amiable trading when they came ashore. For years they had read accounts of the Spanish experience in the Caribbean, Mexico, and Peru—and the story was not pretty. Many books described in gory detail the wholesale violence that occurred when Spaniard met Mayan, Aztec, or Inca. Accounts of Spanish cruelty, even genocide, were useful to Protestant pamphleteers, who labeled the Catholic Spaniards "hell-hounds and wolves." Immigrants embarking for North America wondered if similar violent confrontations did not await them.

Another factor nourishing negative images of the Indian stemmed from the Indians' possession of the land necessary for settlement. For Englishmen, rooted in a tradition of the private ownership of property, this presented moral and legal, as well as practical, problems. As early as the 1580s, George Peckham, an early promoter of colonization, had admitted that the English doubted their right to take the land of others. In 1609, Anglican minister Robert Gray wondered, "By what right can we enter into the land of these savages, take their rightful inheritance from them, and plant ourselves in their places, being unwronged or unprovoked by them?"

The problem could be partially solved by arguing that English settlers did not intend to take the Indians' land but wanted only to share it with them. In return, they would offer the natives the advantages of a more advanced culture and, most important, the Christian religion. This argument was heard repeatedly in succeeding generations. As the governing council in Virginia put it in 1610, the settlers "by way of merchandizing and trade, do buy of [the Indians] the pearls of earth, and sell to them the pearls of heaven."

A more ominous argument arose to justify English rights to native soil. By denying the humanity of the Indians, the English, like other Europeans, claimed that the native possessors of the land disqualified themselves from rightful ownership of it. "Although the Lord hath given the earth to children of men," one Englishman reasoned, "the greater part of it [is] possessed and wrongfully usurped by wild beasts and unreasonable creatures, or by brutish savages, which by reason of their godless ignorance and blasphemous idolatry, are worse than those beasts which are of the most wild and savage nature."

Defining the Native Americans as "savage" and "brutish" did not give the English arriving in Opechancanough's land the power to dispossess his people of their soil, but it armed them with a moral justification for doing so when their numbers became sufficient. Few settlers arriving in North America doubted that their technological superiority would allow them to overwhelm the indigenous people. For their part, people like Opechancanough probably perceived the arriving Europeans as impractical, irreligious, aggressive, and strangely intent on accumulating material wealth.

Conclusion

Converging Worlds

The English immigrants who began arriving on the eastern edge of North America in the early seventeenth century came late to a New World that other Europeans had been colonizing for more than a century. The first English arrivals, the immigrants to Virginia, were but a small advance wave of the large, varied, and determined fragment of English society that would flock to the western Atlantic frontier during the next few generations. Like Spanish, Portuguese, and French colonizers before them, they would establish new societies in the newfound lands in contact with the people of two other cultures—one made up of ancient inhabitants of the lands they were settling and the other composed of those brought across the Atlantic against their will. We turn now to the richly diverse founding experience of the English latecomers in the seventeenth century.

Recommended Reading

The People of America Before Columbus

Brian M. Fagan, *The Great Journey: The Peopling of Ancient America* (1987) and *Ancient North America: The Archaeology of a Continent* (1991); Kenneth Macgowan and Joseph A. Hester, Jr., *Early Man in the New World* (1983); Jesse Jennings, *The Prehistory of North America* (1968); Dean Snow, *The Archaeology of North America: American Indians and Their Origins* (1976); Nigel Davis, *The Aztecs* (1973); Marshall Sahlins, *Stone Age Economics* (1972); Philip Kopper, *The Smithsonian Book of North American Indians: Before the Coming of Europeans* (1986); Alvin M. Josephy, Jr., *America in 1492: The World of the Indian Peoples Before the Arrival of Columbus* (1992); Lynne Sebastian, *The Chaco Anasazi: Sociopolitical Evolution in the Prehistoric Southwest* (1994).

Africa on the Eve of Contact

Basil Davidson, *The African Genius* (1969); J. D. Fag, *A History of West Africa*, 5th ed. (1978); Paul Bohannan and Philip Curtin, *Africa and the Africans*, 2d ed. (1971); Richard Olaniyan, *African History and Culture* (1982); George E. Brooks, *Landlords and Strangers: Ecology, Society, and Trade in Western Africa, 1000–1630* (1993); Paul E. Lovejoy, *Transformations in Slavery: A History of Slavery in Africa* (1983); Roland Oliver and Anthony Atmore, *The African Middle Ages, 1400–1800* (1981).

Europe in the Age of Exploration

W. H. McNeill, *The Rise of the West* (1963); Ralph Davis, *The Rise of the Atlantic Economies* (1973); J. H. Parry, *The Age of Reconnaissance* (1963); Carlo M. Cipolla, *Guns, Sails, and Empires: Technological Innovations and the Early Phases of European Expansion, 1400–1700* (1966) and *Before the Industrial Revolution: European Society and Economy, 1000–1700* (1976); Eric Wolf, *Europe and the People Without History* (1982); J. H. Elliot, *The Old World and the New,*

1492–1650 (1970); William D. Phillips, Jr., and Carla Rahn Phillips, *The Worlds of Christopher Columbus* (1992).

The Iberian Conquest of America

James Lockhart and Stuart B. Schwartz, *Early Latin America* (1983); Alfred Crosby, Jr., *The Columbian Exchange: Biological and Cultural Consequences of 1492* (1972) and *Ecological Imperialism: The Biological Expansion of Europe, 900–1900* (1986); David E. Stannard, *American Holocaust: Columbus and the Conquest of the New World* (1992); R. C. Padden, *The Hummingbird and the Hawk: Conquest and Sovereignty in the Valley of Mexico, 1503–1541* (1962); Charles Gibson, *The Aztecs Under Spanish Rule* (1964) and *Spain in America* (1966); J. H. Elliot, *Imperial Spain, 1469–1716* (1963); J. H. Parry, *The Spanish Seaborne Empire* (1966); C. R. Boxer, *The Portuguese Seaborne Empire, 1415–1825* (1972); M. Leon Portilla, *The Broken Spears: The Aztec Account of the Conquest of Mexico* (1962).

England Looks West

Kenneth R. Andrews, *Trade, Plunder, and Settlement: Maritime Enterprise and the Genesis of the British Empire, 1480–1630* (1985); Carl Bridenbaugh, *Vexed and Troubled Englishmen, 1500–1642* (1968); De Lamar Jensen, *Reformation Europe, Age of Reform and Revolution* (1981); Peter Laslett, *The World We Have Lost* (1971); C. R. Elton, *England Under the Tudors* (1955); A. G. Dickens, *The English Reformation* (1964); Keith Wrightson, *English Society, 1580–1680* (1982); Peter Clark and Paul Slack, eds., *Crisis and Order in English Towns, 1500–1700* (1972); A. L. Rowse, *The Expansion of Elizabethan England* (1955); Nicholas P. Canny, *The Elizabethan Conquest of Ireland* (1976); David B. Quinn, *England and the Discovery of America, 1481–1620* (1974), *North America from Earliest Discovery to First Settlements: The Norse Voyages to 1612* (1977), and *Set Fair for Roanoke: Voyages and Colonies, 1584–1606* (1985); Karen Kupperman, *Roanoke: the Abandoned Colony* (1984).

Colonizing a Continent

$\mathcal{B}$y 1637, after five years in New England, John Mason knew both the prospects and perils of England's new overseas frontier. In his early thirties, Mason had emigrated from southeastern England. He was part of the flock of John Warham, a Puritan minister from the village of Dorchester. In Massachusetts, the group commemorated their origins by giving the name Dorchester to the area assigned to them. Here, six miles south of Boston, they built a simple church, assigned town lots and outlying farms, and began the work of serving their God in the wilderness of North America.

Like many Puritans, Mason had thrilled at the sight of southern New England's game-filled forests and fish-filled streams, the fields cleared and tilled by Algonquian agriculturists, the lush meadows available for grazing stock. Though the winters were inhospitable, it seemed this might be the Promised Land where Puritan refugees could plant their New World Zion. But Mason also recognized that these lands were not vacant. From the earliest days of the Pilgrim settlers at Plymouth in 1620, it was evident that the native occupiers of the region, whose claim went back a hundred generations, stood in the way of the Puritan "errand into the wilderness."

In the fall of 1636, Mason followed many of his Dorchester friends out of Massachusetts. Desirous of better land and restless with the political squabbling in the Massachusetts Bay Colony, the Dorchester settlers set out for the Connecticut River, 100 miles to the west. For 14 days, nipped by the frost of late autumn, they trekked wearily along Indian paths, carrying their meager possessions. At their journey's end, they founded the town of Windsor, on the west bank of the Connecticut.

Six months later, when his new village was no more than a collection of crude lean-tos, militia captain John Mason marched south against the Pequots. He owed his officership to military experience in the Netherlands, where thousands of English soldiers had gone in the 1620s to help the Protestant Dutch break the yoke of Catholic Spain in the Lowlands. Now he commanded several hundred men whom the fledgling Connecticut River towns had dispatched to drive the Pequots from the area. In the years before the English arrival, the powerful Pequots had formed a network of tributary tribes. Finding it impossible to placate the English as they swarmed into the Connecticut River valley, the Pequots chose resistance.

At dawn on May 26, 1637, Captain Mason and his troops approached a Pequot village on the Mystic River. Supported by Narragansett allies, the English slipped into the town. After a few scuffles in the half-light, Mason cried out, "We must burn them," and his men began torching the Pequot wigwams. Then they rushed from the fortified village. As flames engulfed the huts, the Pequots fled the inferno, only to be cut down with musket and sword by the English soldiers, who had ringed the community. Most of the terrified victims were noncombatants—old men, women, and children—for the Pequot warriors were preparing for war at another village about five miles away.

Before the sun rose, a major portion of the Pequot tribe had been exterminated. The resistance of the others crumbled when they learned the fate of their families. "It was a fearful sight to see them thus frying in the fire," wrote one Puritan, "and horrible was the stink and scent thereof; but the victory seemed a sweet sacrifice, and they gave the praise thereof to God, who had wrought so wonderfully for them." Mason himself wrote that God had "laughed at his enemies and the enemies of his people, . . . making them as a fiery oven."

Cecil Calvert grasping a map of Maryland held by his grandfather, the second Lord Baltimore; detail of a painting by Gerard Soest, court painter to Charles II. (Enoch Pratt Free Library, Baltimore)

C aptain John Mason was a God-fearing Puritan and a man highly esteemed by his fellow colonists. His actions at the Mystic River, just seven years after the great Puritan migration to New England had begun in 1630, testify that the European colonization of America involved a violent confrontation of two cultures. We often speak of the "discovery" and "settlement" of North America by English and other European colonists. But the penetration of the eastern edge of what today is the United States might more accurately be called the "invasion of America."

Yet mixed with violence was utopian idealism. In the New World, Puritans—and countless waves of immigrants who followed them—sought both spiritual and economic renewal. Settlement in America represented a chance to escape European war, despotism, material want, and religious corruption. The New World was a place to rescue humankind from the ruins of the Old World. This chapter reconstructs the manner of settlement and the character of immigrant life in six areas of early colonization: the Chesapeake Bay, southern New England, the French and Dutch area from the St. Lawrence River to the Hudson River, the Carolinas, Pennsylvania, and the Spanish toeholds on the southern fringe of the continent. A comparison of these various colonies will show how the colonizers' backgrounds, ideologies, goals, and modes of settlement produced distinctly different societies in North America in the seventeenth century.

The Chesapeake Tobacco Coast

In 1585, England gained a first foothold in a hemisphere dominated by Spanish and Portuguese colonizers. A reconnaissance expedition organized by Walter Raleigh, one of Queen Elizabeth's favorite courtiers, scouted the Carolina coast, surveyed Roanoke Island in Albemarle Sound, and then hastened homeward carrying two natives and a string of tales about rich soil, friendly Indians, and mineral wealth. A second voyage in 1585 and a third in 1587, composed of 91 men, 17 women, and 9 children, planted a small colony on Roanoke Island. But the enterprise failed. The voyages to Roanoke were too small and poorly financed to establish successful settlements. They served only as tokens of England's rising challenge to Spain in North America and as a source of valuable information for colonists later settling the area.

The Roanoke colony also failed resoundingly as the first sustained contact between English and Native American peoples. Although one member of the first expedition reported that "we found the people most gentle, loving, and faithful, void of all guile and treason," relations with the local tribes quickly soured and then turned violent. Charges flew back and forth, the English believing that the local Indians had stolen a silver cup and the Indians angered by English raids on their winter supply of corn. Aware of their numerical disadvantage and afraid of a coordinated attack against them, the English turned their muskets on a local leader to intimidate the natives with their superior technology. In 1591, when a relief expedition reached Roanoke, none of the settlers could be found.

It is likely that in spite of the Indians' Iron Age weaponry, these "lost colonists" of Roanoke succumbed to Indian attacks. It was an ominous beginning for England's overseas ambitions.

Jamestown

In 1607, a generation after the first Roanoke expedition, a group of merchants established England's first permanent colony in North America at Jamestown, Virginia. Under a charter from James I, they operated as a joint-stock company, an early form of a modern corporation that allowed them to sell shares of stock in their company and use the pooled investment capital to outfit and supply overseas expeditions. Although the king's charter to the Virginia Company of London began with a concern for bringing Christian religion to native people who "as yet live in darkness and miserable ignorance of the true knowledge of God," most of the settlers probably agreed with Captain John Smith, who emerged as their strongest leader. "We did admire," he wrote, "how it was possible such wise men could so torment themselves with such absurdities, making religion their colour, when all their aim was profit."

Profits in the early years proved elusive, however. Expecting to find gold and other minerals, anticipating a rewarding trade with Indians for beaver and deer skins, and, best of all, hoping to discover the fabled passage through the North American continent to China, the original investors and settlers received a rude shock. Rather than duplicating the remarkable success of the Spanish and Portuguese in Mexico, Peru, and Brazil, the early Virginia colonists died miserably of dysentery, malaria, and malnutrition. More than 900 settlers, mostly men, arrived in the colony between 1607 and 1609; only 60 survived.

Seeking occupational diversity, the Virginia Company sent French silk artisans, Italian glassmakers, and Polish potash burners to Jamestown. But one-third of the first three groups of immigrants were gold-seeking adventurers with unroughened hands, a proportion of gentlemen six times as great as in the English population. Many others were unskilled servants, some with criminal backgrounds, who "never did knowe what a days work was," observed John Smith. Both types adapted poorly to wilderness conditions, leaving Smith begging for "but thirty carpenters, husbandmen, gardeners, fishermen, and blacksmiths" rather than "a thousand such gallants as were sent to me, that would do nothing but complain, curse and despair, when they saw ... all things contrary to the report in England."

The Jamestown colony, in addition to its unproductive mix of settlers, was hampered by the common assumption that Englishmen could exploit the Indians of the region. Cortés and Pizarro had conquered the mighty Aztec and Inca empires with a few hundred soldiers and then turned the labor of thousands of natives to Spanish advantage. Why, the early settlers mused, should it not be so in Virginia?

But in the Chesapeake, the English found that the indigenous peoples were not densely settled and could not be easily subjugated. Contrary to expectations, no wealthy Indian empire lay waiting to be conquered. Nor could the Virginians mold the 20,000 Powhatan Indians of the region

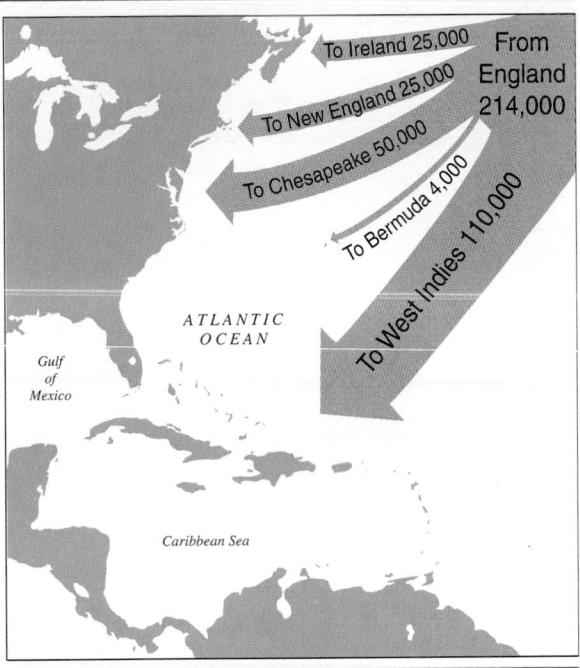

The Great English Migration, 1630–1660

To Ireland 25,000
To New England 25,000
To Chesapeake 50,000
From England 214,000
To Bermuda 4,000
To West Indies 110,000

ATLANTIC OCEAN

Gulf of Mexico

Caribbean Sea

The preponderance of English immigrants going to the West Indies was matched by the disproportionate number of enslaved Africans going to the same islands.

into a servile labor force, because, unlike the Spanish, the English settlers brought neither an army of *conquistadores* nor an army of priests to subdue the natives.

Instead, relations with some 40 small groups, united into a confederacy led by the able Powhatan, turned bitter almost from the beginning. Powhatan brought supplies of corn to the sick and starving Jamestown colony during the first autumn. However, John Smith, whose military experience in eastern Europe had schooled him in dealing with people he regarded as "barbarians," raided Indian corn supplies and tried to cow the local tribes by shows of force. In response, Powhatan withdrew from trade with the English and sniped at their flanks. Many settlers died in the "starving times" of the first years.

Despite these early failures, merchants of the Virginia Company of London poured more money and settlers into the venture. Understanding the

No one knows exactly what the Jamestown settlement looked like in its early years; this twentieth-century mural by Stanley King is a conjectured rendering based on archaeological evidence. New archaeological findings at the site of the Jamestown fort are adding to our knowledge of the first English Virginians. (National Park Service, Colonial National Historical Park)

Early Chesapeake Settlement

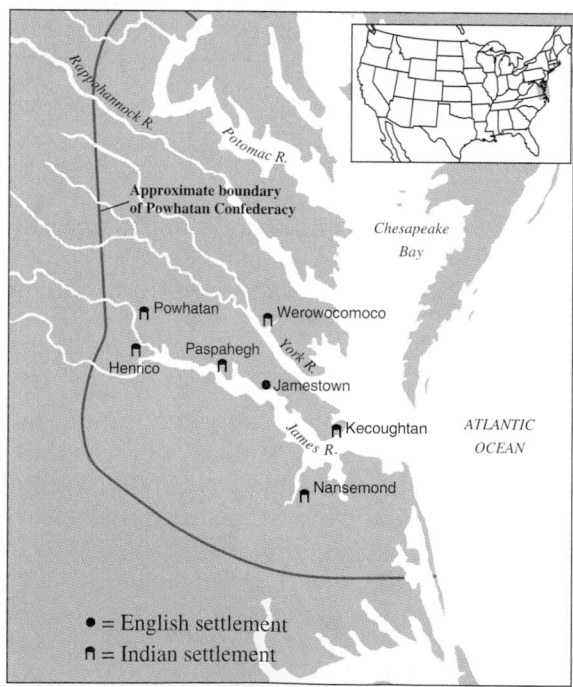

- = English settlement
n = Indian settlement

Only the major Indian villages in the early 1600s are indicated on this map. Note that the town sites are all oriented to the rivers—the source of both food and transportation.

need for ordinary farmers who could raise the food necessary to sustain the colony, they reorganized the company in 1609. They enticed many new settlers by promising free land at the end of seven years' labor for the company. In 1618, they sweetened the terms by offering 50 acres of land outright to anyone journeying to Virginia. To thousands of people on the margins of English society, such an offer seemed irresistible. More than 9,000 crossed the Atlantic between 1610 and 1622 to begin life anew in Virginia. Yet only 2,000 remained alive at the end of that period. "Instead of a plantation," wrote one English critic, "Virginia will shortly get the name of a slaughter house."

Sot Weed and Indentured Servants

The promise of free land lured a steady stream of settlers to Virginia, even though the colony proved a burial ground for most immigrants within a few years of arrival. Also crucial to the continued migration was the discovery that tobacco grew splendidly in Chesapeake soil. Frenchmen had first brought tobacco from Florida to Portugal in the 1560s. But it was Francis Drake's boatload of the "jovial weed" (so named for its intoxicating effect), procured in the West Indies in 1586, that popularized it among the upper class and launched a long history of addiction among Europeans.

Even James I's denunciation of smoking as "loathsome to the eye, hateful to the nose, harmful to the brain, and dangerous to the lungs" failed to halt the smoking craze. It proved to be Virginia's salvation. The planters shipped the first crop in 1617, and thereafter tobacco cultivation spread rapidly. Commanding the handsome price of three shillings per pound in England, tobacco allowed a profit sufficient for settlers to plant it even in the streets and marketplace of Jamestown. By 1624, Virginia was exporting 200,000 pounds of the "stinking weed"; by 1638, though the price had plummeted, the crop exceeded three million pounds. Tobacco became to Virginia in the 1620s what sugar was to the West Indies and silver to Mexico and Peru. In London, men gibed that Virginia was built on smoke.

While launching Virginia on an era of sustained growth, the cultivation of tobacco also obliged Virginia's planters to find a reliable supply of cheap labor. The "sot weed" required intensive care through the various stages of planting, weeding, thinning, suckering, worming, cutting, curing, and packing. To fill their need, planters recruited immigrants in England and Ireland and a scattering from Sweden, Portugal, Spain, Germany, and even Turkey and Poland. Such people, called indentured servants, willingly sold a portion of their working lives in exchange for free passage across the Atlantic. About four of every five seventeenth-century immigrants to Virginia—and later, Maryland—came in this status. Nearly three-quarters of them were male, and most of them were between 15 and 24 years old.

Many of the indentured servants came from the armies of the unemployed. Others were orphans, political prisoners, or common criminals swept out of jails and given a choice of transportation or the gallows. Some were of the "middling sort," younger sons unlikely to inherit a father's farm or shop, or young men eager to leave behind an unfortunate marriage. Others were drawn simply by the prospect of adventure in a "strange new land." But overwhelmingly, indentured servants had occupied the lower rungs of the social ladder in their place of origin.

Life for indentured servants often turned into a nightmare. Only a handful, perhaps one in 20, realized the dream of achieving freedom and

By the end of the 1600s, most young European males were addicted to tobacco. Like the young Dutchmen shown in this painting they practiced various tricks such as the "ring," "whiffle," "gulp," and "retention" as part of the smoking cult. (Adriaen Brouwer, "The Smokers," The Metropolitan Museum of Art, Bequest of Michael Friedsam, 1931, The Friedsam Collection)

acquiring land. If malarial fevers or dysentery did not quickly kill them, servants often succumbed to the brutal work routine harsh masters imposed. Even by the middle of the seventeenth century, when the starving times were only a memory, about half died during the first few years of "seasoning." Masters bought and sold their servants as property, gambled for them at cards, and worked them to death, because there was little motive for keeping them alive beyond their term of labor. "My Master Adkins," wrote one servant in 1623, "hath sold me for £150 like a damned slave." When servants neared the end of their contract, masters found ways to add time and were backed by courts controlled by the planter class.

Contrary to English custom, masters often put women servants to work at the hoe. Sexual abuse by masters was common. Servant women paid dearly for illegitimate pregnancies. The courts fined them heavily and ordered them to serve an extra year or two to repay the time lost during pregnancy and childbirth. They also deprived mothers of their illegitimate children, indenturing them out at an early age. For many servant women, marriage was the best release from this hard life. Many willingly accepted the purchase of their indenture by any man who suggested marriage.

Expansion and Indian War

As Virginia's population increased, spurred by the growth of tobacco production, violence mounted between white colonizers and the Powhatan tribes. In 1614, the sporadic hostility that had marred rela-

Robert Vaughan's scenes for John Smith's memoirs (1624) get some of the story right but are fanciful in some respects. Above, Smith takes the gigantic Powhatan by the scalplock. The close combat between Indians and Englishmen in the background is dramatic but hardly accurate. (From The Generall Historie of Virginia, 1624, *by Captain John Smith/Library of Congress)*

tions in the early years ended temporarily with the arranged marriage of Powhatan's daughter, the fabled Pocahontas, to planter John Rolfe. However, the profitable cultivation of tobacco created an intense demand for land. As more and more settlers pushed up the rivers that flowed into Chesapeake Bay, the local tribes worried that the previous abrasive and sometimes bloody contact might become a disastrous one.

In 1617, when Powhatan retired, the leadership of the Chesapeake tribes fell to Opechancanough. This proud and talented leader began building military strength for an all-out attack on his English enemies. The English murder of Nemattanew, a Powhatan war captain and religious prophet, triggered a fierce Indian assault on Good Friday in 1622 that dealt Virginia a staggering blow. More than one-quarter of the white population fell before the marauding tribesmen; the casualties in cattle, crops, and buildings were equally severe.

The devastating attack led to the bankruptcy of the Virginia Company. As a result, the king annulled its charter in 1624, and established a royal government, which allowed the elected legislative body established in 1619, the House of Burgesses, to continue lawmaking in concert with the royal governor and his council.

The Indian assault of 1622 fortified the determination of the surviving planters to pursue a ruthless new Indian policy. John Smith, writing from England two years later, noted the grim satisfaction that had followed the Indian attack. Many, he reported, believed that it "will be good for the plantation, because now we have just cause to destroy them by all means possible." Bolstered by instructions from London to "root out [the Indians] from being any longer a people," the Virginians adopted a policy of annual military expeditions against the native villages west and north of the settled areas. The "flood of blood," as the English poet John Donne called it, in 1622 had cost the colony dearly and doomed the Virginia Company of London. Yet it justified a policy of "perpetual enmity," even though several leaders admitted that the Indians had attacked in 1622 because of "our own perfidious dealing with them."

Population growth after 1630 and the recurrent need for fresh acreage by settlers who planted

Tobacco production involved indentured servants and slaves in a multistage work process as they planted, topped, suckered, cut, cured, stripped, and prized (packed into hogsheads) the leaf. Some of the stages are pictured here in a London book, The Culture of Tobacco. *(Arents Collection, New York Public Library, Astor, Lenox & Tilden Foundations)*

soil-exhausting tobacco intensified the pressure on Indian land. The tough, ambitious planters soon encroached on Indian territories, provoking war in 1644 and again in 1675. In each of these conflicts, the colonizers proved superior. Greatly outnumbering their opponents, they reduced the native population of Virginia to less than 1,000 by 1680. The Chesapeake tribes, Virginians came to believe, had little to contribute to the goals of English colonization; they were merely obstacles to be removed from the path of English settlement.

Proprietary Maryland

By the time Virginia had achieved commercial success in the 1630s, another colony on the Chesapeake took root. Rather than hoping for profit, the founder sought to establish a religious refuge for Catholics and a New World version of the English manorial countryside.

George Calvert, an English nobleman, designed and promoted Virginia's Chesapeake neighbor. Closely connected to the royal family, he had received a huge grant of land in Newfoundland in 1628, just three years after James I had elevated him to the peerage as Lord Baltimore. In 1632, Charles I, James's son, prepared to grant him a more hospitable domain of 10 million acres. Calvert named it Terra Maria after the king's Catholic wife, Queen Henrietta Maria. In English it became Maryland.

Catholics were an oppressed minority in England, and Lord Baltimore planned his colony as a place where they could start anew without fear of harassment. But knowing that he needed more than a small band of Catholic settlers, the proprietor planned to invite others as well. Catholics would never form a majority in his colony. They were quickly overwhelmed by Protestants who jumped at the offer of free land with only a modest

Population of the Chesapeake Colonies, 1610–1750

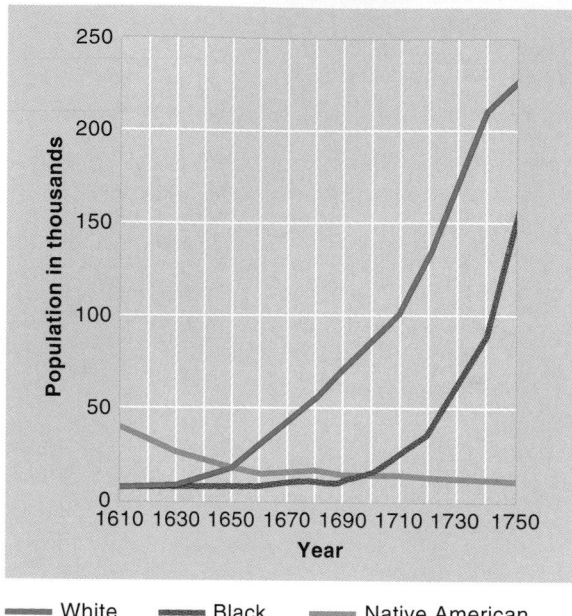

White   Black   Native American

As indicated in this chart, it was not until the 1690s, when Chesapeake planters began turning to Africa for their labor, that the black population in the Chesapeake colonies began to rise rapidly. Source: U.S. Bureau of the Census.

yearly fee to the proprietary family (a "quitrent") of two shillings per 100 acres.

Calvert died while the charter for his colony was being drawn up in 1632, leaving his 26-year-old son, Cecilius, to carry out his plans. The charter guaranteed the proprietor control over all branches of government, but young Calvert learned that his colonists could not be satisfied with fewer political liberties than they enjoyed at home or could find in other colonies. Hence, the Lords Baltimore were obliged to give up their charter-given right to initiate all colonial laws, subject only to the advice and consent of the people.

In land policy, Calvert's heirs found it impossible to carry out his plan for establishing feudalism in the woodlands of eastern North America. Arriving in 1634, immigrants blithely ignored his design of 6,000-acre manors for his relatives and 3,000-acre manors for lesser aristocrats, each to be ruled by provincial nobles and worked by flocks of serflike tenants. The newcomers took up their free land, imported as many indentured servants as

they could afford, maintained generally peaceful relations with local Indian tribes, began to grow tobacco on scattered riverfront plantations like their Virginia neighbors, and governed themselves locally as much as possible. In time, they created their own social hierarchy, not with assigned social roles but with status determined by the ability of some to rise above others in the competitive tobacco economy. Although Maryland grew slowly at first—in 1650, it had a population of only 600—it developed rapidly in the second half of the seventeenth century. By 1700, its population of 33,000 was half that of Virginia.

Daily Life on the Chesapeake

Though immigrants to the Chesapeake Bay region dreamed of bettering the life they had known in England, existence for most of them was dismally difficult. Only a minority could expect to marry and rear a family, because marriage had to be deferred until after the indenture was completed; also, there were three times more men than women. Once made, marriages were fragile. Either husband or wife was likely to succumb to disease within about seven years. The vulnerability of pregnant women to malaria frequently terminated marriages in the first few years, and death claimed half the children born before they reached adulthood. Few children could expect to have both parents alive while growing up. Grandparents were almost unknown.

In a society so numerically dominated by men, widowed women were prized and remarried quickly. Such conditions produced complex families, full of stepchildren and stepparents, half-sisters and half-brothers. In the common case of marriage between a widow and a widower, each with children from a previous marriage, the web of family life became particularly complex, and the tensions attending child rearing unusually thick.

The household of Robert Beverley of Middlesex County illustrates the tangled family relationships in this death-filled society. When Beverley married Mary Keeble in 1666, she was a 29-year-old widow who had borne seven children during her first marriage. At least four of them were still alive to join the household of their mother's new husband. They gained five half-brothers and half-sisters during their mother's 12-year marriage to Beverley. When Mary Keeble Beverley died at age

41, her husband quickly remarried a recent widow, Katherine Hone. Beverley's second wife brought her son into the household and in the next nine years produced four more children with Beverley before his death in 1687. Thus, between 1666 and 1687, Beverley had married two widows who bore him nine children and had been stepfather to the eight children his two wives had produced with previous husbands. Not one of these 17 children, from an interlocking set of four marriages, reached adulthood with both a living mother and father.

Plagued by such mortality, the Chesapeake remained, for most of the seventeenth century, a land of immigrants rather than a land of settled families. Social institutions such as churches and schools took root very slowly amid such fluidity. The large number of indentured servants further increased the instability of community life. Strangers in a household, they served their time and moved on. Other strangers, purchased as they clambered off boats fresh from England, replaced them.

The fragility of life in the tobacco-growing Chesapeake world showed clearly in the region's architecture. As in most New World colonies, the settlers at first erected only primitive huts and shanties, hardly more than windbreaks. After establishing crops, planters improved their habitats but still built ramshackle one-room dwellings. "Their houses," it was observed in 1623, "stand scattered one from another, and are only made of wood ... so as a firebrand is sufficient to consume them all." Even as Virginia and Maryland matured, cheaply built and cramped houses, usually no larger than 16 by 24 feet, remained the norm. Life was too uncertain, the tobacco economy too volatile, and the desire to invest every available shilling in field labor too great for men to build grandly. In England, solidly framed buildings erected on stone foundations had become the rule several centuries before. But throughout the Chesapeake, settlers erected "earthfast" flimsy cabins and houses directly on the ground or on posts.

Even by the early eighteenth century, most Chesapeake families were "pigg'd lovingly together," as one planter said, in a crude house without interior partitions. Eating, dressing, working, and loving all took place with hardly a semblance of privacy. For nearly two centuries, most ordinary Virginians and Marylanders lived in such quarters. "Like a flock of sheep in a fold," an eigh-

We think of the churches of the colonial South as handsome, steepled, red brick buildings, but this unpainted clapboard church is typical of the rudimentary buildings erected by early colonists in the Chesapeake region. (Harold Wickliffe Rose Papers, Yale University Library, New Haven, CT)

teenth-century traveler described the family he bedded down with, 16 to a room, on the Virginia frontier. Even prosperous planters did not begin constructing fully framed, substantial homesteads until a century after the colony was founded.

The crudity of life also showed in the household possessions of the Chesapeake colonists. Struggling farmers and tenants were likely to own only a straw mattress, a simple storage chest, and the tools necessary for food preparation and eating—a mortar and pestle to grind corn, knives for butchering, a pot or two for cooking stews and porridges, wooden trenchers and spoons for eating. Most ordinary settlers owned no chairs, no dressers, no plates or silverware. Among middling planters, the standard of living was raised only by possession of a flock mattress, coarse earthenware for milk and butter, a few pewter plates and porringers, a frying pan or two, and a few rough tables and chairs.

Even one of Virginia's wealthiest planters, the prominent Robert Beverley, had "nothing in and about his house but what was necessary ... good beds ... but no curtains, and instead of cane chairs, he hath stools made of wood." To be near the top of Chesapeake society meant to enlarge one's living

RECOVERING THE PAST

Houses

Homesteading is central to our national experience. For 300 years after the founding of the first colonies, most Americans were involved in taming and settling the land. On every frontier, families faced the tasks of clearing the fields, beginning farming operations, and building shelter for themselves and their livestock. The kinds of structures they built depended on available materials, their resources and aspirations, and their notions of a "fair" dwelling. The plan of a house and the materials used in its construction reveal much about the needs, resources, priorities, and values of the people who built it.

By examining archaeological remains of early ordinary structures and by studying houses that are still standing, historians are reaching new understandings of the social life of pioneering societies. Since the 1960s, archaeologists and architectural historians have been studying seventeenth-century housing in the Chesapeake Bay and New England regions. They have discovered a familiar sequence of house types—from temporary shanties and lean-tos to rough cabins and simple frame houses to larger and more substantial dwellings of brick and finished timber. This hovel-to-house-to-home pattern existed on every frontier, as sodbusters, gold miners, planters, and cattle raisers secured their hold on the land and then struggled to move from subsistence to success.

What is unusual in the findings of the Chesapeake researchers is the discovery that the second phase in the sequence—the use of temporary, rough-built structures—lasted for more than a century. Whereas many New Englanders had rebuilt and extended their temporary

William Boardman house, Saugus, Massachusetts, c. 1687; a floor plan of the house is shown at the right. (The Society for the Preservation of New England Antiquities)

46

clapboard houses into timber-framed, substantial dwellings by the 1680s, Chesapeake settlers continued to construct small, rickety buildings that had to be repaired continually or abandoned altogether every 10 to 15 years.

The William Boardman house, built around 1687, is an example of the "orderly, fair, and well-built" houses of late-seventeenth-century Massachusetts. Its plan shows a typical arrangement of space: the hall, used for cooking, eating, working, and socializing; the parlor; a sleeping room for the parents; and a lean-to for kitchen chores and activities such as dairying. The great central chimney warmed the main downstairs room. Upstairs were two rooms used for both storage and sleeping. As you examine the exterior of the building, note the materials that have been used and the arrangement and treatment of windows, doors, and chimney. What impression of the Boardman family might visitors have as they approached the house? What kind of privacy and comfort did the house provide for family members?

The second house is a typical reconstructed tobacco planter's house. It has some of the same features as the Boardman house, for both are products of an English building tradition. But there are some major differences between the two. In the Chesapeake house, the chimney is not built of brick, but of mud and wood; there is no window glass, only small shutters. The exterior is rough, unfinished planking. The placement of doors and windows and the overall dimensions indicate that this house has only one room downstairs and a loft above. The builders of this house clearly enjoyed less privacy and comfort than the Boardmans.

Historians have puzzled over this contrast between the architecture of the two regions. Part of the explanation may lie in the different climatic conditions and different immigration patterns of New England and the Chesapeake. In the southern region, disease carried off thousands of settlers in the early decades. The imbalance of men and women produced a stunted and unstable family life, hardly conducive to an emphasis on constructing fine homes. In New England, good health prevailed almost from the beginning, and the family was at the heart of society. It made more sense, in this environment, to make a substantial investment in larger and more permanent houses. Some historians argue, moreover, that the Puritan work ethic impelled New Englanders to build solid homes—a compulsion unknown in the culturally backward, "lazy" South.

Reconstructed Chesapeake planter's house, typical of such simply built and unpainted structures in the seventeenth century. (Photograph by Julie Roy Jeffrey)

Archaeological evidence combined with data recovered from land, tax, and court records, however, suggests another reason for the impermanence of housing in the Chesapeake region. Living in a labor-intensive tobacco world, it is argued, planters large and small economized on everything possible in order to buy as many indentured servants and slaves as they could. Better to live in a shanty and have ten slaves than to have a handsome dwelling and nobody to cultivate the fields. As late as 1775, the author of American Husbandry calculated that in setting up a tobacco plantation, five times as much ought to be spent on purchasing 20 black fieldhands as on the "house, offices, and tobacco-house."

Only after the Chesapeake region had emerged from its prolonged era of mortality and gender imbalance and a mixed economy of tobacco, grain, and cattle had replaced the tobacco monoculture did the rebuilding of the region begin. Excavated house sites indicate that this occurred in the period after 1720. New research is revealing that the phases of home building and the social and economic history of a society were closely interwoven. What do houses today reveal about the resources, economic livelihood, priorities, and values of contemporary Americans? Do class and regional differences in house design continue?

space to three or four rooms, to sleep more comfortably, to sit on chairs rather than squat on the floor, and to acquire such ordinary decencies as chamber pots, candlesticks, bed linen, a chest of drawers, and a desk. But only the affluent few could boast luxury items such as clocks, books, punch bowls, wine glasses, and imported furniture. Four generations elapsed in the Chesapeake settlements before the frontier quality of life slowly gave way to more refined living.

Massachusetts and Its Offspring

While some English settlers in the reign of James I (1603–1625) scrambled for wealth on the Chesapeake, others in England were seized by the spirit of religion. They looked to the wilds of North America as a place to build a tabernacle to God. The society they fashioned aimed at unity of purpose and utter dedication to reforming the corrupt world. American Puritanism would powerfully affect the nation's history, especially in planting the seeds of a belief in America's special mission in the world. Yet the "New England way" only partially prefigured the pathways of American development because Puritanism represented a visionary attempt to banish diversity on a continent where the arrival of streams of immigrants from around the globe was destined to become a primary phenomenon.

Puritanism in England

England had been officially Protestant since 1558. Many English in the late sixteenth century, however, thought the Church of England was still ridden with Catholic elements. Detesting such remnants of Catholicism as vestments and rituals that lingered on in the reign of Elizabeth (1558–1603), some voices demanded the end of every taint of "the Bishop of Rome and all his detestable enormities." Because they wished to purify the Church of England, they were dubbed Puritans.

The people attracted to the Puritan movement were not only religious reformers, but also men and women who hoped to find in religion an antidote to the changes sweeping over English society. Many feared for the future, as they witnessed the growth of turbulent cities, the increase of wandering poor, rising prices, and accelerating commercial activity. In general, they disapproved of the growing freedom from the restraints of gentry-dominated medieval institutions such as the church, guilds, and local government.

The concept of the individual operating as freely as possible, maximizing both opportunities and personal potential, is at the core of our modern system of beliefs and behavior. But many in England cringed at the crumbling of traditional restraints of individual action. They worried that individualistic behavior would undermine the notion of community—the belief that people were bound together by reciprocal rights, obligations, and responsibilities. Especially they decried the "degeneracy of the times," which they saw in the defiling of the Sabbath by maypole dancing, card playing, fiddling, bowling, and all the rest of the roistering and erotic behavior reflected in Shakespeare's dramatic portrayals of "Merrie England." Puritans vowed to reverse the march of disorder, wickedness, and disregard for community by imposing a new discipline. They intended not only to purify the Church of England, but to reform society as well.

One part of their plan was a social ethic stressing work as a primary way of serving God. Derived from the Calvinist concept of "calling," this emphasis on work made the religious quest of every member of society equally worthy. The labor of a mason was just as valuable in God's sight as that of a merchant, and so was his soul. The "work ethic" would banish idleness and impart discipline throughout the community. Second, Puritans organized themselves into religious congregations where each member hoped for personal salvation but also supported all others in their quest. Third, Puritans assumed responsibility for the "unconverted" people around them. They were convinced that others who could not find Christian truth in their hearts might have to be coerced and controlled, as in Calvin's Geneva. Religious reform and social vision were in this way interlocked.

When King James VI of Scotland succeeded the childless Elizabeth as James I of England in

1603, he spoke stridently for the divine right of the monarch and his own role as head of the church. Claiming responsibility only to God, James collided with the rising power of the Puritans. They had occupied the pulpits in hundreds of churches, gained control of several colleges at Oxford and Cambridge, and recruited large numbers to their cause. Translating their religious appeal into political power, the Puritans obtained many seats in Parliament and aggressively challenged the king's power. James responded by harassing them, removing dozens of Puritan ministers from their pulpits, and threatening many others. "I will harry them out of the land," he vowed, "or else do worse."

When Charles I succeeded to the throne in 1625, the situation worsened for Puritans. Determined to strengthen the monarchy and stifle dissent, the king summoned a new Parliament in 1628 and one year later adjourned this venerable body (which was the Puritans' main instrument of reform) when it would not accede to royal demands. The king then appointed William Laud, the bishop of London, to high office and turned him loose on the Puritans, whom Laud called "wasps" and the "most dangerous enemies of the state."

By 1629, when the king began ruling without Parliament, many Puritans were turning their eyes outward to Northern Ireland, Holland, the Caribbean islands, and, especially, North America. They were convinced that God intended them to carry their religious and social reforms beyond the reach of persecuting authorities. The state of the economy added to their discouragement about their homeland, for England was suffering a depression in the cloth trades, most severely in Puritan strongholds. To some distant shore, many Puritans decided, they would transport a fragment of English society and carry out the completion of the Protestant Reformation. As they understood history, God had assigned them a special task in his plan for the redemption of humankind.

Puritan Predecessors in New England

Puritans were not the first Europeans to reach the shores of New England. Fishermen of various European nations had been working the fishing banks off Newfoundland and drying the cod they caught on the coast of Cape Cod and Maine since the early 1500s. They frequently made contact with the Algonquian-speaking tribes of the area. A short-lived attempt at settlement on the coast of Maine had also been made in 1607. Seven years later, the aging Chesapeake war dog, John Smith, hired to hunt whales off the North American coast, coined the term "New England" after visiting the area. In his *Description of New England,* published in 1616, he excited considerable interest in the "Paradise of these parts."

No permanent settlement took root, however, until the Pilgrims—actually outnumbered in the expedition by non-Pilgrims—arrived in Plymouth in 1620. Unlike the Puritans who followed, these humble Protestant farmers did not expect to convert a sinful world. Rather, they wanted to be left alone to realize their radical vision of a pure and primitive life. Rather than reform the Church of England, they left it and hence were called Separatists. They had first fled from England to Amsterdam in 1608, then to Leyden when they found the commercial capital of Holland too corrupt, and, finally, in 1620, to North America.

When they arrived at the northern tip of Cape Cod in November of that year, the Pilgrims were weakened from the stormy nine-week voyage and ill-prepared for the harsh winter ahead. Misled by John Smith's glowing report of a warm, fertile country, they discovered instead a severe climate and a rockbound coast. By the following spring, half the Mayflower passengers were dead, including 13 of the 18 married women.

The survivors, led by the staunch William Bradford, settled at Plymouth. Squabbles soon erupted with local Indians, whom Bradford considered "savage and brutish men, which range up and down, little otherwise than the wild beasts." In 1622, they found themselves nearly overwhelmed by the arrival of 60 non-Pilgrims, sent out by the London Company, which had helped the Pilgrims finance their colony. For two generations, the Pilgrims tilled the soil and fished while trying to keep intact their religious vision. But with the much larger Puritan migration that began in 1630, the Pilgrim villages nestled on the shores of Cape Cod Bay became a backwater of the thriving, populous Massachusetts Bay Colony, which absorbed them in 1691.

Errand into the Wilderness

In 11 ships, about a thousand Puritans set out from England in 1630 for the Promised Land. They were the vanguard of a movement that by 1642 had brought about 18,000 colonizers to New England's shores. Led by John Winthrop, a talented Cambridge-educated member of the English gentry, they operated under a charter from the king to the Puritan-controlled Massachusetts Bay Company. The Puritans set about building their utopia with the fervor of people convinced they were carrying out a divine task. "God hath sifted a nation," wrote one Puritan, "that he might send choice grain into this wilderness."

Their intention was to establish communities of pure Christians who collectively swore a covenant with God to work for his ends. To accomplish this, the Puritan leaders agreed to employ severe means. Civil and religious transgressors must be rooted out and severely punished. Their emphasis was on homogeneous communities where the

John Winthrop was one of the lesser English gentry who joined the Puritan movement and in the 1620s looked westward for a new life. Always searching himself as well as others for signs of weakness, Winthrop was one of the Massachusetts Bay Colony's main leaders for many years. (American Antiquarian Society)

good of the group outweighed individual interests. "We must delight in each other, make others' conditions our own, rejoice together, mourn together, labor and suffer together," counseled Winthrop.

To realize their utopian goals, the Puritans willingly gave up freedoms that their compatriots sought. An ideology of rebellion in England, Puritanism in North America became an ideology of control. Much was at stake, for as Winthrop reminded the first settlers, "we shall be as a city upon a hill [and] the eyes of all people are upon us." That visionary sense of mission would help to shape a distinctive American self-image in future generations.

As in Plymouth and Virginia, the first winter tested the strongest souls. More than 200 of the first 700 settlers perished, and 100 others, disillusioned and sickened by the forbidding climate, returned to England the next spring. But Puritans kept coming. They "hived out" along the Back Bay of Boston, the port capital of the colony, along the rivers that emptied into the bay, south into what became Connecticut and Rhode Island a few years later, and north along the rocky Massachusetts coast.

Motivated by their militant work ethic and sense of mission, led by men experienced in local government, law, and the uses of exhortation, the Puritans thrived almost from the beginning. The early leaders of Virginia were soldiers of fortune or roughneck adventurers with predatory instincts, men who had no families or had left them at home. The ordinary Chesapeake settlers were mostly young men with little stake in English society who sold their labor to cross the Atlantic. In Massachusetts, the early leaders were university-trained ministers, experienced members of the lesser gentry, and men with a compulsion to fulfill what they knew was God's prophecy for New England. Most of the ordinary settlers came as freemen in families. Trained artisans and farmers from the middling rank of English society, they established tight-knit communities in which, from the outset, the brutal exploitation of labor rampant in the Chesapeake had no place.

An Elusive Utopia

The Massachusetts Bay Colony flourished at first. The Puritans built a sound economy based on agriculture, fishing, timbering, and trading for beaver furs with local Indians. Even before leaving

England, the directors of the Massachusetts Bay Company transformed their commercial charter into a rudimentary government and transferred the charter to New England. Once there, they laid the foundations of self-government. Free male Church members annually elected a governor and deputies from each town, who formed one house of a colonial legislature. The other house was composed of the governor's assistants, later to be called councillors. Consent of both houses was required to pass laws.

The Puritans also established the first printing press in the English colonies and planted the seed of a university, Harvard College, which opened its doors in 1636 for the training of prospective clergymen. The Puritan leaders also launched a brave attempt in 1642 to create a tax-supported school system so that all children might gain the "ability to read and understand the principles of religion and the capital laws of this country." In 1647, the government ordered every town with 50 families to establish an elementary school and every town with 100 families a secondary school as well, open to all who wished to take advantage of this education.

In spite of these accomplishments, the Puritan colony suffered many of the tensions besetting people bent on perfecting the human condition. Also, its inhabitants proved no better than their less religious countrymen on the Chesapeake in reaching an accommodation with the Native Americans. Surrounded by seemingly boundless land, the Puritans found it difficult to stifle acquisitive instincts and to keep families confined in compact communities. Restless souls looked to more distant valleys. "An over-eager desire after the world," wrote an early leader, "has so seized on the spirits of many as if the Lord had no farther work for his people to do, but every bird to feather his own nest." Others, remaining at the nerve center in Boston, agitated for broader political rights and even briefly ousted Winthrop as governor in 1635, when the colony's clergy backed the stiff-necked Thomas Dudley. After a few years, Governor Winthrop wondered if the Puritans had not gone "from the snare to the pit."

Winthrop's troubles multiplied in 1633 when Salem's Puritan minister, Roger Williams, began to voice disturbing opinions on church and government policies. Now the colony's leaders faced a contentious and visionary young man who argued that the Massachusetts Puritans were not truly pure because they would not completely separate themselves from the polluted Church of England (which most Puritans still hoped to reform). Williams also denounced mandatory worship, which he said "stinks in God's nostrils," and argued that government officials should not interfere with religious matters but confine themselves to civil affairs. "Coerced religion," he warned, "on good days produces hypocrites, on bad days rivers of blood." Later to be celebrated as the earliest spokesman for the separation of church and state, Williams seemed in 1633 to strike at the heart of the Bible commonwealth, whose leaders regarded civil and religious affairs as inseparable. Williams also charged the Puritans with illegally intruding on Indian land.

Winthrop and others spent two years plying Williams alternately with sweet reason and threats, but they could not quiet the determined young man. Convinced that he would split the colony into competing religious groups and undermine authority, the magistrates vowed to deport him to England. Warned by Winthrop, Williams fled southward through winter snow with a small band of followers to found Providence, a settlement on Narragansett Bay in what would become Rhode Island.

Even as they were driving Williams out, the Puritan authorities confronted another threat. This time it was a magnetic woman of extraordinary talent and intellect. Anne Hutchinson was as devoted a Puritan as any who came to the colony. Arriving in 1634 with her husband and seven children, she gained great respect among Boston's women as a practiced midwife, healer, and spiritual counselor. She soon began to discuss religion, suggesting that the "holy spirit" was absent in the preaching of some ministers. Before long Hutchinson was leading a movement labeled *antinomianism,* an interpretation of Puritan doctrine that stressed the mystical nature of God's free gift of grace while discounting the efforts the individual could make to gain salvation.

By 1636, Boston was dividing into two camps, those who followed the male clergy and those who cleaved to the theological views of a gifted though untrained woman with no official standing. Her followers included most of the community's malcontents—merchants who chafed under the price

Early New England

Maine and New Hampshire became the frontier to which New England settlers migrated when their towns and farmlands became too crowded.

controls the magistrates imposed in 1635, young people resisting the rigid rule of their elders, women disgruntled by male authority, and artisans who resented wage controls designed to arrest growing inflation. Hutchinson doubly offended the male leaders of the colony because she boldly stepped outside the subordinate position expected of women. "The weaker sex" set her up as a "priest" and "thronged" after her, wrote one male leader. Another described a "clamour" in Boston that "New England men ... usurp over their wives and keep them in servile subjection."

Determined to remove this thorn from their sides, the clergy and magistrates put Hutchinson on trial in 1637. After two long interrogations, they convicted her of sedition and contempt in a civil trial and banished her from the colony "as a woman not fit for our society." Six months later, the Boston church excommunicated her for preaching 82 erroneous theological opinions. She had "highly transgressed and offended and troubled the church," intoned the presiding clergyman, and "therefore in the name of our Lord Jesus Christ, I do cast you out and deliver you up to

Satan and account you from this time forth to be a heathen and a leper." In the last month of her eighth pregnancy, Hutchinson, with a band of supporters, followed the route of Roger Williams to Rhode Island, the catch basin for Massachusetts Bay's dissidents.

But ideas proved harder to banish than people. The magistrates could never enforce uniformity of belief. Neither could they curb the appetite for land. Growth, geographic expansion, and commerce with the outside world all eroded the ideal of integrated, self-contained communities filled with religious piety. Leaders never wearied of reminding Puritan settlers that the "care of the public must oversway all private respects." But they faced the nearly impossible task of containing land-hungry immigrants in an expansive region. By 1636, groups of Puritans had swarmed not only to Rhode Island, but also to Hartford and New Haven, where Thomas Hooker and John Davenport led new Puritan settlements in what became Connecticut.

New Englanders and Indians

The charter of the Massachusetts Bay Company proclaimed that the "principal end of this plantation" was "to win and incite the natives to the knowledge and obedience of the only true God and Saviour of mankind and the Christian faith." But the instructions that Governor John Winthrop carried from England reveal other Puritan thoughts about the native inhabitants. According to Winthrop's orders, all men were to receive training in the use of firearms, a reversal of the sixteenth-century English policy of disarming the citizenry in order to quell public disorders. New England magistrates prohibited Indians from entering Puritan towns and threatened to deport any colonist selling arms to an Indian or instructing one in their use.

Only sporadic conflict with local tribes occurred at first because disease had catastrophically struck the Native Americans of New England, who may have numbered 125,000 in 1600, and left much of their land vacant. English fishermen, stopping along the coast in 1616, triggered a ferocious outbreak of respiratory viruses and smallpox among a population with no immunity against European microbes. Entire towns of Indians died in an epidemic that wiped out three-quarters of

the population. Five years later, an Englishman exploring the area wrote that the Indians "died on heapes, as they lay in their houses" and described walking through a forest where human skeletons covered the ground.

When smallpox returned in 1633, killing thousands more natives, it again relieved pressure for land. The Puritans saw the disease as proof that God had intervened on their side, just when a flood of new settlers was causing trouble over rights to land. "Without this remarkable and terrible stroke of God upon the natives," reported the Charlestown settlers, "[we] would with much more difficulty have found room, and at far greater charge have obtained

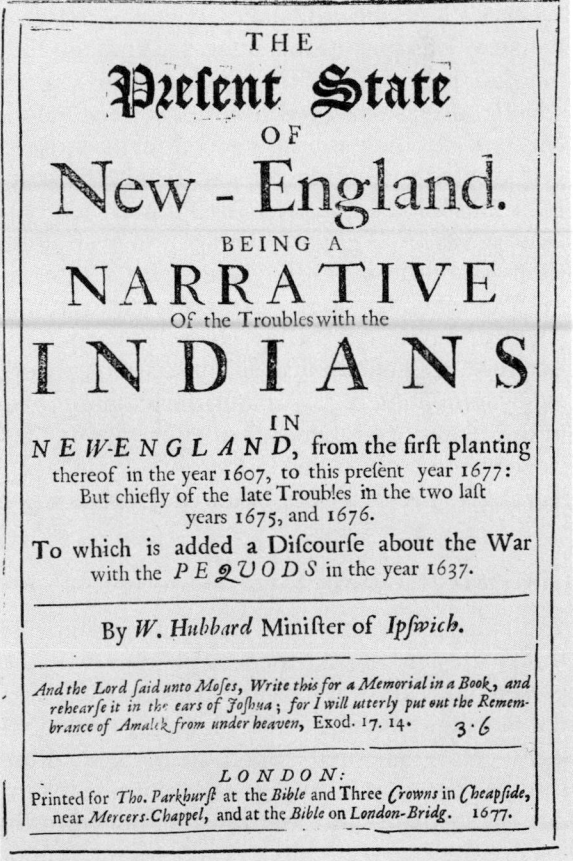

New England's leaders were always troubled by their difficult relations with the native inhabitants of the region. Histories of these tensions, like this one published in Boston and London in 1677, often appeared after Indian wars and usually defended the colonists' actions. (The New York Public Library)

and purchased land." Many surviving Indians welcomed the Puritans because they now had surplus land and through trade hoped to gain English protection against tribal enemies to the north.

The settler pressure for new land, however, soon reached into areas untouched by disease. When land hunger mingled with the Puritan sense of mission, it proved an explosive mix. To a people charged with messianic zeal, the heathen Indians represented a mocking challenge to the building of a religious commonwealth that would "shine as a beacon" back to decadent England. A failure to convert the natives to civility and Christianity would have represented a failure by the Puritans to control the land to which God had directed them. God, they knew, would answer this failure with his wrath.

Making the "savages" of New England strictly accountable to the ordinances that governed white behavior was part of this quest for fulfilling their mission. In this, the Puritans succeeded with the smaller, disease-ravaged tribes of eastern Massachusetts. But their attempts to control the stronger Pequots led to the bloody war in 1637 in which John Mason was a leader. The Puritan victory in that war assured English domination over all the tribes of southern New England except the powerful Wampanoags and Narragansetts of Rhode Island and removed the last obstacle to expansion into the Connecticut River valley. Missionary work, led by John Eliot, began among the remnant tribes in the 1640s. After a decade of effort, about 1,000 Indians had been settled in four "praying villages," learning to live according to the white man's ways.

The Web of Village Life

The village was the vital center of Puritan life. Unlike the Chesapeake tobacco planters, who dispersed along the streams and rivers of their area, the Puritans established small, tightly settled villages. Most pursued "open field" agriculture, trudging out from the village each morning to farm narrow strips of land that radiated out from the town. They grazed their cattle on common meadow and cut firewood on common woodland. Such a system recreated agricultural life in many parts of England.

In other towns, Puritans employed the "closed field" system of self-contained farms that they had known at home. But in either system, families lived close together in compact towns built around a common, where the meetinghouse and tavern were located. These small, communal villages kept families in close touch so that each could be alert not only to its own transgressions, but also to those of its neighbors. "In a multitude of counsellors is safety," Puritan ministers were fond of advising, and the little villages of 50 to 100 families perfectly served the need for moral surveillance, or "holy watching."

Determined to achieve godliness and communal unity, Puritans also prohibited single men and women from living by themselves, for this would put individuals beyond patriarchal authority and group observation. Left to themselves, men and women would stray from the path, for, as Thomas Hooker put it, "every natural man and woman is born full of sin, as full as a toad of poison." In Virginia, the planters counted the absence of restraint as a blessing. In New England, it was feared as the Devil.

At the center of every Puritan village stood the meetinghouse. These plain wooden structures, sometimes called "Lord's barns," gathered within them every soul in the village, not just once but twice a week—on the Lord's day and during midweek as well. No man stood higher in the community than the minister. He was the spiritual leader in these small, family-based, community-oriented settlements, which viewed life as a Christian pilgrimage.

The unique Puritan mixture of strict authority and incipient democracy, of hierarchy and equality, can be seen in the way the Massachusetts town distributed land and devised local government. Each town was founded by a grant of the colony's General Court, sitting in Boston. Only groups of Puritans who had signed a compact signifying their unity of purpose received settlement grants. "We shall by all means," read the town of Dedham's covenant, "labor to keep off from us such as are contrary minded, and receive only such unto us as may be probably of one heart with us."

After receiving a grant, townsmen met to parcel out land. They awarded individual grants according to the size of a man's household, his wealth, and his usefulness to the church and town. Such a system perpetuated existing differences in wealth and status. Yet some towns wrote language into their covenants that to the modern ear has an almost socialistic ring. "From each according to his

The similarity in settlement patterns between England and New England can be seen in a modern rendering of early seventeenth-century Rowley, Massachusetts (left, Reprinted by permission of David Grayson Allen, ©1981. All rights reserved), and a plan of Chelmsford, Essex, in 1591 (right, Essex Record Office, Essex, England)

ability to each as need shall require," read one. It was not socialism that the Puritans had in mind. Rather, they believed that the community's welfare transcended individual ambitions or accomplishments and that unity demanded limits on the accumulation of wealth. Every family should have enough land to sustain it, and prospering men were expected to use their wealth for the community's benefit, not for conspicuous consumption. Repairing the meetinghouse, building a school, aiding a widowed neighbor—such were the proper uses of wealth.

Having felt the sting of centralized power in Church and state, Puritans emphasized local exercise of authority. Until 1684, only male Church members could vote, and as the proportion of males who were Church members declined, so did the proportion of men who could vote. These voters elected selectmen, who allocated land, passed local taxes, and settled disputes. Once a year, all townsmen gathered for the town meeting, called later by Thomas Jefferson the "wisest invention ever devised by the wit of man for the perfect exercise of self-government." At the town meeting, the citizens selected town officers for the next year and decided matters large and small: Should the

playing of football in the streets be prohibited? Might Widow Thomas be allowed £10 for a kidney stone operation for her son? What salary should the schoolteacher be paid?

The appointment of many citizens to minor offices—surveyors of hemp, informers about deer, purchasers of grain, town criers, measurers of salt, fence viewers, and many others—bred the tradition of local government. Complaints about officialdom rarely grew into political bitterness in such a system. All officeholders were annually subject to electoral approval, and about one out of every ten adult males in many towns was selected each year for some office, large or small. In New England, nobody could acquire a reputation for sobriety and industry without finding himself elected to a local post.

The predominance of families also lent cohesiveness to Puritan village life. Strengthening this family orientation was the remarkably healthy environment of the Puritans' "New Israel." Whereas the germs carried by English colonizers devastated neighboring Indian societies, the effect on the newcomers of entering a new environment was the opposite. The low density of settlement prevented infectious diseases from spreading, and the isolation of the New England villages from the avenues of Atlantic commerce, along which diseases as well as cargo flowed, minimized biological hazards in the seventeenth century.

The result was a spectacular natural increase in the population and a life span unknown in Europe. At a time when the population of western Europe was barely growing—deaths almost equaled births—the population of New England, discounting new immigrants, doubled every 27 years. The difference was not a higher birthrate. New England women typically bore about seven children during the course of a marriage, but this barely exceeded the European norm. The crucial factor was that chances for survival after birth were far greater than in England because of the healthier climate and better diet. In most of Europe, only half the babies born lived long enough to produce children themselves. Life expectancy for the population at large was less than 40 years. In New England, nearly 90 percent of the infants born in the

seventeenth century survived to marriageable age, and life expectancy exceeded 60 years—longer than for the American population as a whole at any time until the early twentieth century. About 25,000 people immigrated to New England in the seventeenth century, but by 1700, they had produced a population of 100,000. By contrast, some 75,000 immigrants to the Chesapeake colonies had yielded a population of about 70,000 by the end of the century.

Women played a vital role in this family-centered society. In the household economies of the Puritan villages, the woman was not only wife, mother, and housekeeper, but also custodian of the vegetable garden; processor of salted and smoked meats, dairy products, and preserved vegetables; and spinner, weaver, and clothesmaker.

The presence of women and a stable family life strongly affected New England's regional architecture. As communities formed, the Puritans converted early economic gains into more substantial housing rather than investing in bound labor as in the Chesapeake colonies, where family formation was retarded and the economy unstable. Well-constructed one-room houses with sleeping lofts quickly replaced the early "wigwams, huts, and hovels." Families then added parlors and lean-to kitchens as soon as they could. Within a half century, New England immigrants accomplished a general rebuilding of their living structures, whereas the Chesapeake lagged far behind.

A final binding element in Puritan communities was the stress on literacy and education, eventually to become a hallmark of American society. Placing religion at the center of their lives, Puritans emphasized the ability to read catechisms, psalmbooks, and especially the Bible. Literacy could instill the basic precepts of life in all. "Thy life to mend, this book attend" went one verse in a children's schoolbook. In literacy, Puritans saw guarantees that they would not succumb to the savagery they perceived all around them in the new land. They also trusted that through education, they could preserve the central values of their struggle to redeem humankind in the North American wilderness.

An event in England in 1642 affected the future development of the New England colonies. King Charles I pushed his people into revolution by vio-

Population of the New England Colonies, 1620–1750

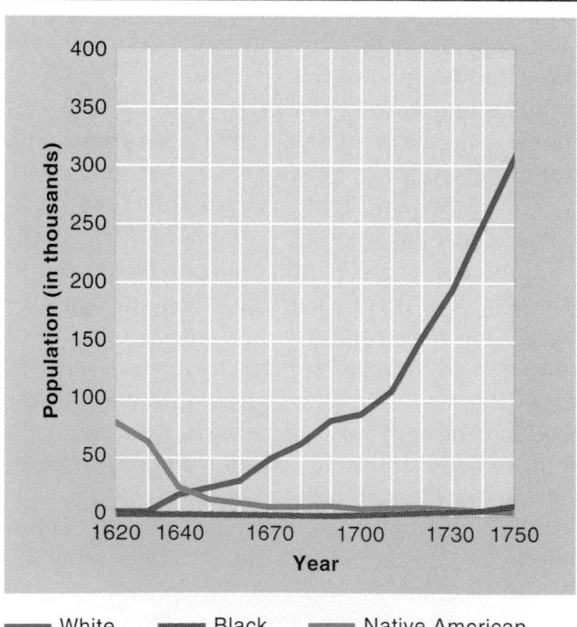

The far more rapid white population growth in New England than in the Chesapeake region reflected higher birthrates, a healthier environment, and a reliance on free labor. Source: U.S. Bureau of the Census.

Primers such as this with biblical themes served to instill religious values as well as literacy in the Puritan colonies. (American Antiquarian Society)

Noah did view
The old World & new

Young Obadias,
David, Josias,
All were pious.

Peter deny'd
His Lord, and cry'd.

Queen Esther sues,
And saves the Jews.

Young pious Ruth,
Left all for Truth.

Young Samuel dear
The Lord did fear.

lating the country's customary constitution and continuing earlier attacks against Puritans. The ensuing civil war climaxed with the trial and beheading of the king in 1649. Thereafter, during the so-called Commonwealth period (1649–1660), Puritans in England had the opportunity to complete the reform of religion and society at home. Migration to New England abruptly ceased.

The 20,000 English immigrants who had come to New England by 1649 were scattered from Maine to Long Island. Governor Winthrop of Massachusetts lamented the dispersion, and Roger Williams condemned the "depraved appetite" for new and better land. Yet, in a terrain so rock-strewn that its pastures were said to produce Yankee sheep with sharpened noses, it was natural that farmers should seek better plow land.

To combat the problems of dispersion, Puritan leaders established a broad intercolony political structure in 1643 called the Confederation of New England. Designed to coordinate government among the various Puritan settlements (Rhode Island was pointedly excluded) and especially to provide greater defense against the French, the Dutch, and the Indians, the pact bound together Massachusetts, Plymouth, the small colony of New Haven, and the river towns of Connecticut. This first American attempt at federalism managed to function fitfully for a generation, though Massachusetts, the strongest and largest member, often refused to abide by group decisions when they ran counter to its objectives.

Although the Puritans fashioned stable communities, developed the economy, and constructed effective government, their leaders, as early as the 1640s, complained that the founding vision of Massachusetts Bay was faltering. Material concerns seemed to transcend religious commitment; the individual prevailed over the community. In 1638, the General Court declared a day of humiliation and prayer to atone for the colony's "excess idleness and contempt of authority." A generation later, the synod of 1679—a convention of Puritan Churches—cried out that the "church, the commonwealth and the family are being destroyed by self-assertion." By this time, Puritans rarely mentioned the work of salvaging English Protestantism by example. Instead, they concentrated on keeping their children on the straight and narrow road.

Frequent complaints about moral laxness notwithstanding, New England had achieved economic success and political stability by the end of the seventeenth century. Towns functioned efficiently, poverty was uncommon, public education had been mandated, and family life was stable. If social diversity increased and the religious zeal of the founding generation waned, that was only to be expected. One second-generation Bay colonist put the matter bluntly. His minister had noticed his absence in church and found him late that day at the docks, unloading a boatload of cod. "Why were you not in church this morning?" asked the clergyman. Back came the reply: "My father came here for religion, but I came for fish."

From the St. Lawrence to the Hudson

The New Englanders were not the only European settlers in the northern region, for both France and Holland created colonies there. At the same time that Jamestown was founded, the French repeated their attempt to settle Canada, more successfully than in the 1540s.

France's America

Henry IV, the first strong French king in half a century, sent Samuel de Champlain to explore deep into the territory even before the English had obtained a foothold on the Chesapeake. Champlain established a small settlement in Port Royal, Acadia (later Nova Scotia), in 1604 and another at what would become the capital of New France, Quebec, in 1608. Already established French fish-drying stations in Newfoundland had initiated trading with Indians for furs, and Champlain's settlers hoped for easy profits on beaver. But the holders of the fur monopoly in France did not encourage emigration to the colony because settlement would reduce the forests from which the furs were harvested. New France therefore remained so lightly populated that English marauders easily seized and held Quebec from 1629 to 1632.

In 1609–1610, Champlain allied with the Algonquian Indians of the St. Lawrence region in attacking their Iroquois enemies to the south, earning their eternal enmity. This drove the Iroquois to trade furs for European goods with the Dutch on the Hudson River, and when the Iroquois exhausted the furs of their own territory, they turned north and west, determined to seize the forest-rich resources of the French-allied Hurons in the Great Lakes region and seize their rich forests.

When the fury of the Iroquois descended on them in the 1640s, the Hurons were a people already decimated by a decade of epidemics that had spread among them as they accepted Jesuit priests in their villages. In the "beaver wars" of the 1640s and 1650s, the Iroquois used Dutch guns to attack Huron parties carrying beaver pelts to the French. By mid-century, Iroquois attacks had scattered the Hurons, all but ending the French fur trade and reducing the Jesuit influence to a few villages of Christianized Hurons.

The bitterness bred in these years colored future colonial warfare, driving the Iroquois to ally with the English against the French. But for the time being, in the mid-seventeenth century, the English remained unhindered by the beleaguered French colonists, who numbered only about 400.

England Challenges the Mighty Dutch

By the mid-seventeenth century, the Chesapeake and New England regions each contained about 50,000 settlers. Between them lay the mid-Atlantic area controlled by the Dutch, who had planted a small colony named New Netherland at the mouth of the Hudson River in 1624 and in the next four decades had extended their control to the Connecticut and Delaware river valleys. To the south of the Chesapeake lay a vast territory where only the Spanish, on their mission frontier in Florida, challenged the power of Native American tribes.

These two areas, north and south of the Chesapeake, became strategic zones of English colonizing activity after the end of England's civil war in 1660 brought the restoration of the English monarchy. Commercial rival of the Dutch and religious and economic enemy of the Spanish, England moved to cement its claims on the North American coast.

Although for generations they had been the Protestant bulwarks in a mostly Catholic Europe, England and Holland became bitter commercial rivals in the mid-seventeenth century. By the time the Puritans arrived in New England, the Dutch had become the mightiest carriers of seaborne commerce in western Europe. By one contemporary estimate, Holland owned 16,000 of Europe's 20,000 merchant ships. The Dutch had also muscled in on Spanish and Portuguese transatlantic commerce, trading illegally with Iberian colonists who gladly violated their government's commercial policies in order to obtain cloth and slaves more cheaply.

By 1650, the Dutch had temporarily overwhelmed the Portuguese in Brazil, and soon their vast trading empire reached the East Indies, Ceylon, India, and Formosa. The best shipbuilders, mariners, and businessmen in western Europe,

Restoration Colonies: New York, the Jerseys, Pennsylvania, and the Carolinas

Old colonies

Restoration colonies

Later colonies

★ Provincial capitals

After founding the Restoration colonies from the 1660s to the 1680s, England's colonists claimed the entire seaboard between Spanish Florida and French Canada.

they validated the dictum of Sir Walter Raleigh that "whosoever commands the sea commands the trade; whosoever commands the trade of the world commands the riches of the world, and consequently the world itself."

In North America, the Dutch West India Company's New Netherland colony was small but profitable. Agents fanned out from Fort Orange (Albany) and New Amsterdam (New York City) into the Hudson, Connecticut, and Delaware river valleys. There they established a lucrative fur trade with local tribes by hooking into the sophisticated trading network of the Iroquois Confederacy, which stretched to the Great Lakes. The Iroquois welcomed the Dutch presence. The newcomers

were few in number, they did not have voracious appetites for land, and they were willing to exchange desirable goods for the pelts of animals that were abundant in the vast Iroquois territory. At Albany, the center of the Dutch-Iroquois trade, relations remained peaceful and profitable for several generations because both peoples admirably served each other's needs.

Although the Dutch never settled more than 10,000 people in their mid-Atlantic colonies, their commercial and naval powers were impressive. The Virginians learned as much in 1667 when brazen Dutch raiders captured 20 tobacco ships on the James River and confiscated virtually the entire tobacco crop for that year.

By 1650, England was ready to challenge Dutch maritime supremacy. Three times between 1652 and 1675, war broke out between the two Protestant competitors for control of the emerging worldwide capitalist economy. In the second and third wars, the Dutch colony on the Hudson River became an easy target for the English. They captured it in 1664 and then, after it fell to the Dutch in 1673, recaptured it almost immediately. By 1675, the Dutch had been permanently dislodged from the North American mainland. But they remained mighty commercial competitors of the English in Europe, Africa, the Far East, and the Caribbean.

New Netherland, where from the beginning Dutch, French Huguenots, Walloons from present-day Belgium, Swedes, Portuguese, Finns, English, refugee Portuguese Jews from Brazil, and Africans had commingled in a babel of languages and religions, now became New York. It was so named because Charles II made a proprietary grant of the territory, along with the former Dutch colonies on the Delaware River, to James, duke of York, his brother and heir to the English throne.

Under English rule, the former Dutch colonists retained much of their ethnic identity for several generations. They spoke their native language, worshiped in their Dutch Reformed Calvinist churches, and perpetuated Dutch architecture. In time, however, English immigrants overwhelmed the Dutch, and gradual intermarriage between the Dutch, the Huguenots, and the English—the three main groups—diluted ethnic loyalties. But New York retained its polyglot, religiously tolerant character, and its people never allowed religious concerns or utopian plans to interfere with the pragmatic conduct of business.

Proprietary Carolina: A Restoration Reward

In 1663, three years after he was restored to the throne taken from his father, Charles II granted a vast territory named Carolina to a group of men who had supported him when he was in exile. Its boundaries extended from ocean to ocean and from Virginia to central Florida. Within this miniature empire, eight proprietors, including several involved in Barbados sugar plantations, gained large powers of government and semifeudal rights to the land. For settling their royal reward, they constructed a system of government with both feudal and modern features. To lure settlers, they promised religious freedom and offered land free for the asking. Onto this generous land offer, they grafted plans for a semimedieval government that provided themselves, their deputies, and a small number of noblemen with a monopoly of political power.

The architects of Carolina, which included the brilliant young John Locke, were reacting to a generation of violence and radical social experiments during the English civil war (1642–1649). They intended their design for Carolina to bring social and political stability to the southern wilds of North America. A hereditary aristocracy of wealthy manor lords, they thought, would check boisterous small landholders.

However, the reality of settlement in Carolina bore faint resemblance to what the planters envisioned. The rugged sugar and tobacco planters who streamed in from Barbados and Virginia, where depressed economic conditions made a new beginning in Carolina seem attractive, claimed their 150 acres of free land (and additional acreage for each family member or servant they brought). But they ignored proprietary regulations about settling in compact rectangular patterns and reserving two-fifths of every county for an appointed nobility. In government, they also did as they pleased. Meeting in assembly for the first time in 1670, they refused to accept the proprietors' Fundamental Constitutions of 1667 and ignored the orders of the governor appointed in London. In shaping local government, the planters were guided mostly by their experience in the slave society of Barbados, whence most of them had come.

The Indian Debacle

Carolina was the most elaborately planned colony in English history but the least successful in achieving amicable relations with the natives. The proprietors in London had intended otherwise. Mindful of the violent encounters that had plagued other settlements, they projected a well-regulated Indian trade limited to their appointed agents. But the aggressive settlers from the West

Indies and the Chesapeake openly flouted proprietary policy. Those from Barbados, accustomed to exploiting African slave labor, saw that if the major tribes of the Southeast—the Cherokees, Creeks, and Choctaws—could be drawn into trade, the planters might reap vast wealth. The Spanish in Florida had done little to tap this potential gold mine; their main goal was to protect their territorial claim by establishing missions that gathered local Indians into a sedentary, agricultural life.

It was not the beaver that beckoned in the Indian trade, as in the North, but the deerskin, much desired in Europe for making warm and durable clothing. In the villages of the southeastern tribes, where natives farmed as well as hunted, the Carolina colonies found a people eager to obtain European trade goods. But what began as a trade for the skins of deer soon became a trade for the skins of Indians. To the consternation of the London proprietors, capturing Indians for sale in New England and the West Indies became the cornerstone of commerce in Carolina in the early years.

The Indian slave trade plunged Carolina into a series of wars. Local planters and merchants selected a tribe, armed it, and rewarded it handsomely for bringing in captives from another. Even strong tribes that allied for trade with the Carolinians found that after they had used English guns to enslave their weaker neighbors, they themselves were sometimes scheduled for elimination. The colonists justified the policy by claiming that "thinning the barbarous Indian natives" was necessary to make room for white settlement. The "thinning" was so thorough that by the early eighteenth century, the two main tribes of the coastal plain, the Westos and the Savannahs, were nearly extinct.

Early Carolina Society

Carolina's fertile land and warm climate convinced many that it was a "Country so delicious, pleasant, and fruitful that were it cultivated doubtless it would prove a second Paradize." Into the country came Barbadians, Swiss, Scots, Irish, French Huguenots, English, and even migrants from New England, New York, and New Jersey. But far from creating paradise, this ethnically and religiously diverse people clashed abrasively in an atmosphere of fierce competition, ecological exploita-

This painting of Mulberry Plantation in South Carolina shows the mansion house, built in 1708, and rows of slave huts constructed in an African style. Most enslaved Africans lived in far more primitive structures in the eighteenth century. (Gibbes Museum)

tion, brutal race relations, and stunted social institutions.

For the land-hungry white cattle raisers and rice growers of coastal South Carolina, the Indian slave trade had no direct benefits, because the profits flowed entirely to the merchants of Charleston, the main port and seat of government. They reaped important secondary advantages, however. As the Indian population of the coastal region fell sharply, expansion from the initial settlements around Charleston became easier. Along the twisting rivers that flowed to the coast, planters staked out claims and experimented with a variety of exotic crops, including sugar, indigo, tropical fruits, tobacco, and rice. It was this last that, after much experimentation, proved to be the staple crop on which a flourishing economy could be built.

The cultivation of rice required backbreaking labor to drain the swampy lowlands, build dams and levees, and hoe, weed, cut, thresh, and husk the crop. Many of the early settlers had experience with African slaves in Barbados, so their early reliance on slave labor came naturally to them. On widely dispersed plantations, black labor came to predominate. In 1680, four-fifths of South Carolina's population was white. But by 1720, when the colony had grown to 18,000, black slaves outnumbered whites two to one.

As in Virginia and Maryland, the low-lying areas of coastal Carolina were so disease-ridden that population grew only slowly in the early years. "In the spring a paradise, in the summer a hell, and in the autumn a hospital," remarked one traveler. Malaria and yellow fever, especially dangerous to pregnant women, were the twin killers that retarded population growth, and the scarcity of women further limited natural increase. Like the West Indies, the rice-growing region of Carolina was at first more a place to accumulate a fortune than to rear a family.

In the northern part of Carolina, mostly pine barrens along a sandy coast, a different kind of society emerged. Populated largely by small tobacco farmers from Virginia seeking free land, the Albemarle region developed a mixed economy of livestock grazing, tobacco and food production, and the mining of the pine forests for naval stores—turpentine, resin, pitch, tar, and lumber. In 1701, North and South Carolina became separate colonies, but their distinctiveness had emerged before that. Slavery took root only slowly in North Carolina, which was still 85 percent white in 1720. A land of struggling white settlers (called "Lubberland" by one prosperous Virginia planter), its healthier climate and settlement by families rather than by single men with servants and slaves gave it a greater potential for sustained growth. But in both North and South Carolina, several factors inhibited the growth of a strong corporate identity: the pattern of settlement, the ethnic and religious diversity, and the lack of shared assumptions about social and religious goals.

The Quakers' Peaceable Kingdom

Of all the utopian dreams imposed on the North American landscape in the seventeenth century, the most remarkable was that of the Quakers. During the English civil war, the Society of Friends, as the Quakers called themselves, had sprung forth as one of the many radical sects searching for a more just society and a purer religion. Their visionary ideas and their defiance of civil authority cost them dearly in fines, brutal punishment, and imprisonment. After Charles II and Parliament stifled radical dissent in the 1660s, they, too, sent many converts across the Atlantic. The society they founded in Pennsylvania foreshadowed more than any other colony the future religious and ethnic pluralism of the United States.

The Early Friends

Like their Puritan cousins, the Quakers regarded the English Protestant Church (called the Church of England) as corrupt and renounced its formalities and rituals, which smacked of Catholicism. They also foreswore all Church officials and institutions, persuaded that every believer could find grace through the "inward light," a spark of redemption that resided in every man and woman. By discarding the ideas of original sin and eternal predestination, the Quakers offered a radically liberating alternative to the reigning Calvinist doctrine.

Quakers were persecuted in England after their movement, led by George Fox and Margaret Fell, gathered momentum in the 1650s. Other Protestants regarded them as dangerous fanatics, for the Quakers' egalitarian doctrine of the light within elevated all lay people to the position of the clergy and denied the primary place accorded the Scriptures.

Garbing themselves in plain black cloth and practicing civil disobedience, the Quakers presented a threat to social hierarchy and order. They refused to observe the customary marks of deference, such as doffing one's hat to a superior, believing that in God's sight no social distinctions existed. They used the familiar *thee* and *thou* instead of the formal and deferential *you*, they resisted taxes supporting the Church of England, and they refused to sign witnesses' oaths on the Bible, regarding this as profane. They also shocked a world conditioned to violence by renouncing the use of force in human affairs and refused to perform militia service.

Quakers also affronted traditional views when they insisted on the spiritual equality of the sexes and the right of women to participate in church matters on an equal, if usually separate, footing with men. Quaker leaders urged women to preach and to establish separate women's meetings. Among Quakers who fanned out from England to preach the doctrine of the inward light, 26 of the first 59 to cross the Atlantic were women. All but four of them were unmarried or without their husbands and therefore living, traveling, and ministering outside the bounds of male authority.

Intensely committed to converting the rest of the world to their beliefs, the Quakers ranged westward to North America and the Caribbean in the 1650s and 1660s. Nearly everywhere, they were reviled, mutilated, imprisoned, and deported. Puritan Massachusetts warned them that their liberty in that colony consisted of "free liberty to keep away from us and such as will come to be gone as fast as they can, the sooner the better." Hungering to serve in what they called "the Lamb's War" (the crusade of the meek), the Quakers vowed to test the Puritans' resolve and kept coming.

The Bay Colony magistrates were desperate to eliminate this dangerous threat to religious conformity and civil authority. Finally, in 1659, they hanged two Quaker men on the Boston Common and threatened to hang Mary Dyer, an old woman who had followed Anne Hutchinson a quarter century before. Escorted from the colony, Mary Dyer returned the next year to defy the Massachusetts ban. Undaunted, she met her death at the end of a rope.

Early Quaker Designs

By the 1670s, the English Quakers were looking for a place in the New World to carry out their millennial dreams. In England, royal fears of a Catholic conspiracy led to severe religious repression of all dissenting groups in the late 1670s. Thousands of Quakers were jailed and fined heavily for practicing their faith.

Emerging as their leader in this dark period was William Penn, the son of Admiral Sir William Penn, who by capturing Jamaica from the Spanish in 1654 had placed in English hands one of the most productive sugar-growing sites in the world. Young William had been groomed for life in the English aristocracy, but he rebelled against his parents' designs for him in one of the professions. At age 23, he was converted by a spellbinding speech about the power of the Quaker inward light. After joining the Society of Friends in 1666, Penn devoted himself to their cause.

In 1674, Penn joined other Friends in establishing their own colony, on former Dutch territory, between the Hudson and Delaware rivers. They purchased the rights to the land, known as West Jersey, from Lord John Berkeley. Penn now helped fashion an extraordinarily liberal constitu-

tion for the budding Quaker colony. Legislative power and the authority to constitute courts were vested in an assembly chosen annually by virtually all free males in the colony. The laws also mandated the election of justices of the peace and local officeholders. Settlers were guaranteed freedom of religion and trial by jury. As Penn and the other trustees of the colony explained, "We lay a foundation for [later] ages to understand their liberty as men and Christians, that they may not be brought in bondage, but by their own consent; for we put the power in the people."

The last phrase, summing up the document, would have shocked anyone of property and power in England or America at the time. Most regarded "the people" as ignorant, dangerous, certain to bring society to a state of anarchy if entrusted with the right to rule themselves. Nowhere in the English world had ordinary citizens, especially those who owned no land, enjoyed such extensive privileges. Nowhere had a popularly elected legislature received such broad authority.

Despite these idealistic plans, West Jersey sputtered at first. Only 1,500 immigrants arrived in the first five years, and the colony for several decades was caught up in legal complications caused by the tangled claims to the land and government. The center of Quaker hopes lay across the Delaware River, where in 1681, Charles II granted William Penn a vast territory, almost as large as England itself. The grant extinguished a large royal debt to Penn's father, but the crown also benefited by getting the pesky Quakers out of England. To the Quakers' great fortune, the territory granted to Penn, the last unassigned segment of the eastern coast of North America, was also one of the most fertile.

Pacifism in a Militant World: Quakers and Indians

On the day Penn received his royal charter for Pennsylvania, he wrote a friend, "My God that has given it to me will, I believe, bless and make it the seed of a nation." The nation that Penn envisioned was unique among colonizing schemes. Penn intended to make his colony an asylum for the persecuted, a refuge from arbitrary state power. Puritans strove to nurture social homogeneity and religious uniformity, excluding all not of like mind.

Just as a deed finalized a land exchange to Europeans, the wampum belt signified an agreement to the Indians. This Lenape belt, made of leather and simple shell beads, is said to have been given to William Penn at the signing of the Treaty of Shackamaxon in 1682. (National Museum of the American Indian, New York)

In the Chesapeake and Carolina colonies, aggressive, nonidealistic men sought to exploit the region's resources. But Penn dreamed of inviting to his forest-filled colony people of all religions and national backgrounds and blending them together in peaceful coexistence. His state would claim no authority over the consciences of its citizens nor demand military service of them.

The Quakers who began streaming into Pennsylvania in 1682 quickly absorbed earlier Dutch, Finnish, and Swedish settlers. Primarily farmers, they fanned out from the capital city of Philadelphia. They participated in the government by electing representatives who initiated laws. Like colonists elsewhere, they avidly acquired land, purchasing it from Penn at reasonable rates. But unlike other colonizers, the Quakers practiced pacifism, holding the ethic of love and nonresistance embodied in the Sermon on the Mount as literally binding on them.

Even before arriving, Penn laid the foundation for peaceful relations with the Delaware tribe inhabiting his colony. He wrote to the Delaware chiefs: "The king of the Country where I live, hath given me a great Province; but I desire to enjoy it with your Love and Consent, that we may always live together as Neighbors and friends." In this single statement Penn dissociated himself from the entire history of European colonization in the New World and from the widely held negative view of Indians. Recognizing the Indians as the rightful owners of the land included in his grant, Penn pledged not to sell one acre until he had first purchased it from local chiefs. He also promised strict regulation of the Indian trade and a ban on the sale of alcohol.

The Quaker accomplishment is sometimes disparaged with the claim that there was little competition for land in eastern Pennsylvania between the natives and the newcomers. However, a comparison between Pennsylvania and South Carolina, both established after the restoration of Charles II to the English throne in 1660, shows the power of pacifism. A quarter century after initial settlement, Pennsylvania had a population of about 20,000 whites. Penn's peaceful policy had so impressed Native American tribes that Indian refugees began migrating into Pennsylvania from all sides. During the same 25 years, South Carolina had grown to only about 4,000 whites, but the area had become a cauldron of violence. Carolinians spread arms through the region to facilitate slave dealing, shipped some 10,000 members of local tribes off to New England and the West Indies as slaves, and laid waste to the Spanish mission frontier in Florida.

As long as the Quaker philosophy of pacifism and friendly relations with the Delawares and Susquehannocks held sway, interracial relations in the Delaware River valley contrasted sharply with those in other parts of North America. But ironically, the Quaker policy of toleration, liberal government, and exemption from military service attracted to the colony, especially in the eighteenth century, thousands of immigrants whose land hunger and disdain for Indians undermined Quaker trust and friendship. Germans and Scots-Irish flooded in, swelling the population to 31,000 by 1720. Neither of these groups shared Quaker idealism about racial harmony. Driven from their homelands by hunger and war, they pressed inland and, sometimes encouraged by the land agents of Penn's heirs, encroached on the lands of the local tribes. This created conflict with the natives who had sought sanctuary in Pennsylvania. By the mid-eighteenth century, a confrontation of displaced people, some red and some white, was occurring in Pennsylvania.

Edward Hicks painted Penn's Treaty with the Indians *in the nineteenth century. It is a romanticized version of the Treaty of Shackamaxon by which the Lenape chiefs ceded the site of Philadelphia to Penn. The treaty was actually made in 1682, but Hicks was correct in implying that the Lenape held Penn in high regard for his fair treatment of them. (National Gallery of Art, Washington, D.C.)*

Building the Peaceable Kingdom

Although Pennsylvania came closer to matching its founder's goals than any other European colony, Penn's dream of a society that banished violence, religious intolerance, and arbitrary authority never completely materialized. Nor was he able to convince people to settle in compact villages, which he believed necessary for his "holy experiment." The plain Quaker farmers scattered across the countryside and built simple farmsteads. Instead of agricultural villages with meetinghouses at their centers, as in New England, they created open country networks without any particular centers or boundaries. Yet a sense of common endeavor persisted.

Quaker farmers prized family life and emigrated almost entirely in kinship groups. This helped them maintain their distinctive identity. So did other practices such as allowing marriage only within their society, carefully providing land for their offspring, and guarding against too great a population increase (which would cause too rapid a division of farms) by limiting the size of their families.

Settled by religiously dedicated farming families and favored by rich grainlands, Pennsylvania's countryside blossomed. The colony's port capital of Philadelphia also grew rapidly. By 1700, it had overtaken New York City in population, and a half century later, it was the largest city in the colonies, bustling with a wide range of artisans, merchants, and professionals.

The Limits of Perfectionism

In spite of commercial success and peace with Native Americans, not all was harmonious in early Pennsylvania. Political affairs were often turbulent, in part, because of Pennsylvania's weak leadership. Penn was a much-loved proprietor, but he did not tarry long in his colony to guide its course. He returned to England in 1684, visited his colony briefly in 1700, and then left forever. The leadership vacuum he left was never filled.

A more important cause of disunity resided in the Quaker attitude toward authority. In England, balking at authority was almost a daily part of Quaker life. To be a Quaker was to refuse to bear arms, to disobey the law prohibiting nonconformists to hold religious services, to deny the Bible as revealed truth, to reject the traditional role assigned women, and to violate social custom obliging inferiors to defer to their superiors. The Quaker was the supremely "inner-directed" person, fired by an apocalyptic view of the world and bound to other Quakers by decades of persecution.

In Pennsylvania, the absence of persecution eliminated a crucial binding element. The factionalism that developed among them demonstrated that people never unify so well as when under attack. Rather than looking inward and banding together, they looked outward to an environment filled with opportunity. Their squabbling filled Penn with dismay. Why, he asked, were his settlers so "governmentish, so brutish, so susceptible to scurvy quarrels that break out to the disgrace of the Province?"

Meanwhile, Quaker industriousness and frugality led to such material success that after a generation, social radicalism and religious evangelicalism began to fade. As in other colonies, settlers discovered the door to prosperity wide open and surged across the threshold.

Where Pennsylvania differed from New England and the South was in its relations with Native Americans, at least for the first few generations. It also departed from the Puritan colonies in its immigration policy. Pennsylvania, it is said, was the first community since the Roman Empire to allow people of different national origins and religious persuasions to live together under the same government on terms of near equality. English, Highland Scots, French, Germans, Irish, Welsh, Swedes, Finns, and Swiss all settled in Pennsylvania. This ethnic mosaic was further complicated by a medley of religious groups, including Mennonites, Lutherans, Dutch Reformed, Quakers, Baptists, Anglicans, Presbyterians, Catholics, Jews, and a sprinkling of mystics. Their relations may not always have been friendly, but few attempts were made to discriminate against dissenting groups. Pennsylvanians thereby laid the foundations for the pluralism that was to become the hallmark of American society.

New Spain's Northern Frontier

Spain's frontier outposts in Florida and New Mexico, preceding all English settlements on the eastern seaboard, fell into disarray between 1680 and the early eighteenth century as the English colonies sank deep roots. Trying to secure a vast northern frontier with only small numbers of settlers, the Spanish relied on forced Indian labor. This reliance proved to be their undoing in Florida and New Mexico.

Popé's Revolt

During the 1670s, when the Franciscan priests developed a new zeal to root out traditional Indian religious ceremonies, the Pueblo people turned on

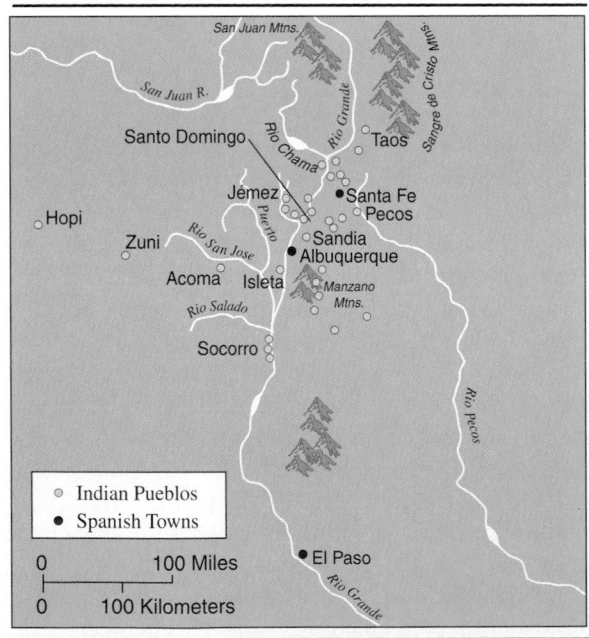

New Mexico in the Seventeenth Century

Dictated by geographical features, the route north from El Paso to Albuquerque followed the Rio Grande (like Interstate 25 today).

the Spanish intruders. In years of harsh rule, the Spanish had extracted tribute labor from the Pueblo people, who at the same time suffered the ravaging effects of European diseases. Both of these punishing long-term effects contributed to Pueblo alienation. But pushing the Pueblos to the edge was an assault on their religion. Launching a campaign to restrict native religious ceremonies in the 1670s, the Spanish friars began to seize the Pueblo *kivas* (deeply dug ceremonial religious chambers), forbid native dances, and destroy priestly Indian masks and prayer sticks. In August 1680, led by Popé, a much-persecuted medicine man from San Juan pueblo, about two dozen Pueblo villages scattered over several hundred miles rose up in fury, burning Spanish ranches and government buildings, systematically destroying Spanish churches, laying waste to Spanish fields, and killing half of the friars. As the Spanish governor in Santa Fe watched the church go up in flames, he reported his shock at the "scoffing and ridicule which the wretched and miserable Indian rebels made of the sacred things, intoning … prayers of the church with jeers."

Spanish settlers, soldiers, and friars streamed back to El Paso, abandoning their northern frontier in the Southwest for more than a decade. A new Spanish governor, the intrepid Diego de Vargas, regained Santa Fe in 1694 and gradually subdued most of the Pueblo people. Learning from Popé's rebellion, the Spanish declared a kind of cultural truce, easing their demands for Pueblo labor tribute and allowing certain Pueblo rituals in return for nominal acceptance of Christianity. Periodic tension and animosity continued, but for the Pueblo people, an accommodation with the Spanish was necessary because of their need for defense against their old enemies—the Navajos, Utes, and Apaches.

Decline of Florida's Missions

The Franciscan missions in Florida were as severely pummeled as those in New Mexico in the late seventeenth and early eighteenth centuries. Rapidly settling in South Carolina, the English were eager to use Indian allies to attack the Spanish Indian villages and sell the captives into slavery. The resentment of missionized Indians, wearying under demands on their labor, further weakened the tenuous Spanish hold on them. The

TIMELINE

1590	Roanoke Island colony fails
1607	Jamestown settled
1616–1621	Native American population in New England decimated by European diseases
1617	First tobacco crop shipped from Virginia
1619	First Africans arrive in Jamestown
1620	Pilgrims land at Plymouth
1622	Powhatan tribes attack Virginia settlements
1624	Dutch colonize mouth of Hudson River
1630	Puritan immigration to Massachusetts Bay
1632	Maryland grant to Lord Baltimore (George Calvert)
1633–1634	Native Americans in New England again struck by European diseases
1635	Roger Williams banished to Rhode Island
1636	Anne Hutchinson exiled to Rhode Island
1637	New England wages war against the Pequot people
1642–1649	English civil war ends great migration to New England
1643	Confederation of New England
1659–1661	Puritans hang three Quaker men and one Quaker woman on Boston Common
1660	Restoration of King Charles II in England
1663	Carolina charter granted to eight proprietors
1664	English capture New Netherland and rename it New York
	Royal grant of the Jersey lands to proprietors
1680	Popé's revolt in New Mexico
1681	William Penn receives Pennsylvania grant

attacks of Carolinians in the early 1680s destroyed a number of Spanish missions. When England and Spain went to war in 1701—called Queen Anne's War in the colonies—the Carolinians attacked St. Augustine by land and sea. By 1704, fifty Carolinians with hundreds of Creek allies invaded Florida. Burning mission villages to the ground, they slaughtered the Spanish friars and captured some 4,000 women and children to be sold as slaves. The Spanish mission frontier was thoroughly devastated with only St. Augustine remaining as a Spanish stronghold. No Spanish reconquest of the territory, as in New Mexico, would occur. From this time forward, English and French traders, with more attractive trade goods to offer, would have the main influence over Florida Indians.

Conclusion

The Achievement of New Societies

Nearly 200,000 immigrants who had left their European homelands reached the coast of North America in the seventeenth century. Coming from a variety of social backgrounds and spurred by different motives, they represented the rootstock of distinctive societies that would mature in the North American colonies of England, France, Holland, and Spain. For three generations, North America served as a social laboratory for religious and social visionaries, political theorists, fortune seekers, social outcasts, and, most of all, ordinary men and women seeking a better life than they had known in their European homelands.

Nearly three-quarters of them came to the Chesapeake and Carolina colonies. Most of them found this region a burial ground rather than an arena of opportunity. Disease, stunted family life, and the harsh work regimen imposed by the planters who commanded the labor of the vast majority ended the dreams of most who came. Yet population inched upward, and the bone and sinew of a workable economy formed. In the northern colonies, to which the fewest immigrants came, life was more secure. Organized around family and community, favored by a healthier climate, and motivated by religion and social vision, the Puritan and Quaker societies thrived. Utopian expectations were never completely fulfilled. But nowhere else in the Western world at that time could they even have been attempted. What did succeed was the rooting of agricultural life based on family farms and the establishment of locally oriented political institutions marked by widespread participation. Thus, as the seventeenth century progressed, the scattered settlements along the North American coast, largely isolated from one another, as well as a few inland French and Spanish settlements, pursued their separate paths of development.

Recommended Reading

The Chesapeake Tobacco Coast

Wesley F. Craven, *The Southern Colonies in the Seventeenth Century* (1949); Philip D. Morgan and Jean Russo, eds., *Colonial Chesapeake Society* (1989); Edmund S. Morgan, *American Slavery, American Freedom: The Ordeal of Colonial Virginia* (1975); Thad W. Tate and David L. Ammerman, eds., *The Chesapeake in the Seventeenth Century* (1979); David B. Quinn, ed., *Early Maryland in a Wider World* (1982); Gloria L. Main, *Tobacco Colony: Life in Early Maryland* (1982); Darrett

B. Rutman and Anita H. Rutman, *A Place in Time: Middlesex County, Virginia, 1650–1750* (1984); Karen Kupperman, *Settling with the Indians: The Meeting of English and Indian Cultures in America, 1580–1640* (1980); Alden Vaughan, *American Genesis: Captain John Smith and the Founding of Virginia* (1975); Kathleen M. Brown, *Good Wives, Nasty Wenches, and Anxious Patriarchs* (1996).

Massachusetts and Its Offspring

Christopher Hill, *Society and Puritanism in Pre-Revolutionary England*, 2d ed. (1967); Perry Miller, *Errand into the Wilderness* (1956); Alan Simpson, *Puritanism in Old and*

New England (1955); David Cressy, *Coming Over: Migration and Communication Between England and New England in the Seventeenth Century* (1987); David D. Hall, *Worlds of Wonder, Days of Judgment: Popular Religious Belief in Early New England* (1989); David G. Allen, *In English Ways* (1981); John Demos, *A Little Commonwealth* (1970); Kenneth Lockridge, *A New England Town* (1970); Philip Greven, Jr., *Four Generations* (1970); Stephen Innes, *Labor in a New Land* (1983); Darrett B. Rutman, *Winthrop's Boston* (1965); Edmund S. Morgan, *The Puritan Dilemma: The Story of John Winthrop* (1958); Richard S. Dunn, *Puritans and Yankees* (1962); Robert Middlekauff, *The Mathers* (1971); Roger Thompson, *Sex in Middlesex: Popular Mores in a Massachusetts County, 1649–1699* (1986); Stephen Innes, *Creating the Commonwealth: The Economic Culture of Puritan New England* (1995); Virginia D. Anderson, *New England's Generation: The Great Migration and the Formation of Society and Culture in the Seventeenth Century* (1991).

From the St. Lawrence to the Hudson

Robert C. Ritchie, *The Duke's Province: A Study of Politics and Society in Colonial New York, 1660–1691* (1977); Allen W. Trelease, *Indian Affairs in Colonial New York* (1960); Daniel K. Richter and James H. Merrell, eds., *Beyond the Covenant Chain: The Iroquois and Their Neighbors in Indian North America, 1600–1800* (1987); Oliver Rink, *Holland on the Hudson: An Economic and Social History of Dutch New York* (1986); Joyce Goodfriend, *Before the Melting Pot: Society and Culture in Colonial New York City, 1664–1730* (1992); Michael Kammen, *Colonial New York* (1975); Daniel K. Richter, *The Ordeal of the Longhouse: The Peoples of the Iroquois League in the Era of European Colonization* (1992); Bruce G. Trigger, *Children of the Aataentsic: A History of the Huron People, 1600–1664* (1976); James Axtell, *The Invasion Within: The Contest of Cultures in Colonial North America* (1985).

Proprietary Carolina

M. Eugene Sirmans, *Colonial South Carolina* (1966); Verner Crane, *The Southern Frontier, 1670–1732* (1929); Robert M. Weir, *Colonial South Carolina* (1983); Richard Waterhouse, *A New World Gentry: The Making of a Merchant and Planter Class in South Carolina, 1670–1770* (1989); Daniel C. Littlefield, *Rice and Slaves: Ethnicity and the Slave Trade in Colonial South Carolina* (1981).

The Quakers' Peaceable Kingdom

Frederick B. Tolles, *Meeting House and Counting House: The Quaker Merchants of Colonial Philadelphia* (1948); Edwin Bronner, *William Penn's "Holy Experiment"* (1962); Gary B. Nash, *Quakers and Politics: Pennsylvania, 1681–1726* (1968); Alan Tully, *William Penn's Legacy* (1977); J. William Frost, *The Quaker Family in Colonial America* (1972); Sharon V. Salinger, *"To Serve Well and Faithfully": Labor and Indentured Servitude in Pennsylvania* (1987); Sally Schwartz, *A Mixed Multitude: The Struggle for Toleration in Colonial Pennsylvania* (1987); Barry J. Levy, *Quakers and the American Family* (1988).

New Spain's Northern Frontier

John Francis Bannon, *The Spanish Borderlands Frontier, 1513–1821* (1970); David J. Weber, *The Spanish Frontier in North America* (1992); Ramon A. Gutierrez, *When Jesus Came, the Corn Mothers Went Away: Marriage, Sexuality, and Power in New Mexico, 1500–1846* (1991); Marvin T. Smith, *Archaeology of Aboriginal Culture Change in the Interior Southeast: Depopulation During the Early Historical Period* (1987).

Mastering the New World

Anthony Johnson, an African, arrived in Virginia in 1621 with only the name Antonio. Caught as a young man in the Portuguese slave-trading net, he had passed from one trader to another in the New World until he reached Virginia. There he was purchased by Richard Bennett and sent to work at Warrasquoke, Bennett's tobacco plantation situated on the James River. In the next year, Antonio was brought face to face with the world of triracial contact and conflict that would shape the remainder of his life. On March 22, 1622, the Powhatan tribes of tidewater Virginia fell on the white colonizers in a determined attempt to drive them from the land. Of the 57 people on the Bennett plantation, only Antonio and four others survived.

Antonio—anglicized to Anthony—labored on the Bennett plantation for some 20 years, slave in fact if not in law, for legally defined bondage was still in the formative stage. During this time, he married Mary, another African trapped in the labyrinth of servitude, and fathered four children. In the 1640s, Anthony and Mary Johnson gained their freedom after half a lifetime of servitude. Probably at this point they chose a surname, Johnson, to signify their new status. Already past middle age, the Johnsons began carving out a niche for themselves on Virginia's eastern shore. By 1650, they owned 250 acres, a small herd of cattle, and two black servants. In a world in which racial boundaries were not yet firmly marked, the Johnsons had entered the scramble of small planters for economic security.

By schooling themselves in the workings of the English legal process, carefully cultivating white patronage, and working industriously on the land, the Johnsons gained their freedom, acquired property, established a family, warded off contentious neighbors, and hammered out a decent existence. But by the late 1650s, as the lines of racial slavery tightened, the customs of the country began closing in on Virginia's free blacks.

In 1664, convinced that ill winds were blowing away the chances for their children and grandchildren in Virginia, the Johnsons began selling their land to white neighbors. The following spring, most of the clan moved north to Maryland, where they rented land and again took up farming and cattle raising. Five years later, Anthony Johnson died, leaving four children and his wife. The growing racial prejudice of Virginia followed Johnson beyond the grave. A jury of white men in Virginia declared that because Johnson "was a Negroe and by consequence an alien," the 50 acres he had deeded to his son Richard before moving to Maryland should be awarded to a local white planter.

Johnson's children and grandchildren, born in America, could not duplicate the modest success of the African-born patriarch. By the late seventeenth century, people of color faced much greater difficulties in extricating themselves from slavery. When they did, they found themselves forced to the margins of society. Anthony's sons never rose higher than tenant farmer or small freeholder. John Johnson moved farther north into Delaware in the 1680s, following a period of great conflict with Native Americans in the Chesapeake region. Members of his family married local Indians and became part of a triracial community that has survived to the present day. Richard Johnson stayed behind in Virginia. When he died in 1689, just after a series of colonial insurrections connected with the overthrow of James II in England, he had little to leave his four sons. They became tenant farmers and hired servants, laboring on plantations owned by whites. By now, in the early eighteenth century, slave ships were pouring Africans into Virginia and Maryland to replace white indentured servants, the backbone of the labor force for four generations. To be black had at first been a handicap. Now it became a fatal disability, an indelible mark of degradation and bondage.

Slave Deck of the Albanoz, watercolor done by a young naval officer in a Spanish slave ship captured by the *HMS Albanoz*. (National Maritime Museum, Greenwich, England)

*M*astering the North American environment involved several processes that would echo down the corridors of American history. Prominent among them were the molding of an African labor force and the gradual subjection of Native American tribes who contested white expansion. Both developments occurred in the lifetimes of Anthony and Mary Johnson and their children. Both involved a level of violence that made this frontier of European expansion not a zone of pioneer equality and freedom, but one of growing inequality and servitude.

This chapter surveys the fluid, conflict-filled era from 1675 to 1715, a time when five overlapping struggles for mastery occurred. First, in determining to build a slave labor force, the colonists struggled to establish their mastery over resistant African captives. Second, the settlers sought mastery over Native American tribes, both those that stood in the way of white expansion and those that were their trading and military partners. Third, the colonists resisted the attempts of English imperial administrators to bring them into a more dependent relationship. Fourth, within colonial societies, emerging elites struggled to establish their claims to political and social authority. Finally, the colonizers, aided by England, strove for mastery over French, Dutch, and Spanish contenders in North America.

African Bondage

For almost four centuries after Columbus's voyages to the New World, European colonizers forcibly transported Africans out of their homelands and used their labor to produce wealth in their colonies. Estimates vary widely, but the number of Africans brought to the New World was probably not less than 12 million. Millions more lost their lives while being marched from the African interior to coastal trading forts or during the passage across the Atlantic. Of all the immigrants who peopled the New World between the fifteenth and eighteenth centuries, the Africans were by far the most numerous, probably outnumbering Europeans two or three to one.

European slave traders carried a large majority of the slaves to the West Indies, Brazil, and Spanish America. Fewer than one out of every 20 reached North America, which remained a fringe area for slave traders until the eighteenth century. Yet those who came to the American colonies, about 10,000 in the seventeenth century and 350,000 in the eighteenth, profoundly affected the destiny of American society. In a prolonged period of labor scarcity, their labor and skills were indispensable to colonial economic development. Their African culture mixed continuously with that of their European masters. And the race relations that grew out of slavery so deeply marked society that the problem of race has continued ever since to be one of this nation's most difficult problems.

The Slave Trade

The African slave trade did not begin as a part of the colonization of the Americas, but rather as an attempt to fill a labor shortage in the Mediterranean world. As early as the eighth century, Arab and Moorish traders had driven slaves across Saharan caravan trails for delivery to Mediterranean ports. Seven centuries later, Portuguese merchants became the first European slave traders.

When Portuguese ship captains reached the west coast of Africa by water, they tapped into a slave-trading network that had operated in central and west Africa for many generations. Slaveholding was deeply rooted in African societies, where owning slaves was an important way of enhancing one's status and augmenting one's ability to produce wealth. However, slaves were employed in a wide variety of occupations, often serving as soldiers, administrators, and even occasionally as royal advisors.

Many Africans were relegated to slavery by judicial decree for crimes they had committed, but far more were victims of military enslavement, cap-

Europe's Contest for Control in 1660

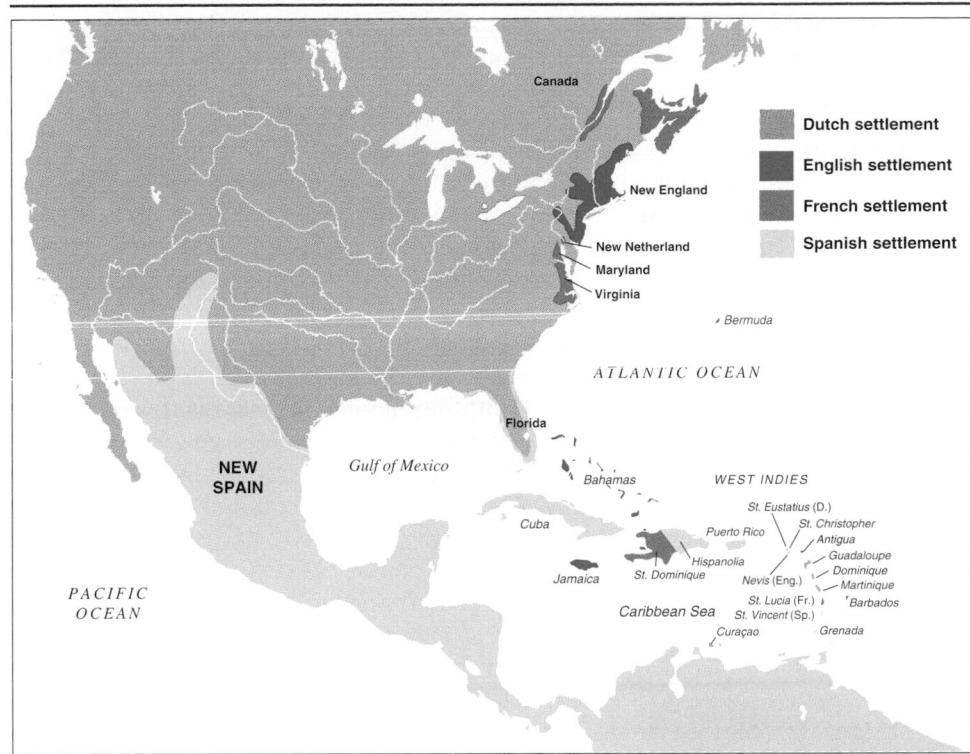

Canada

Dutch settlement
English settlement
French settlement
Spanish settlement

New England

New Netherland
Maryland
Virginia

Bermuda

ATLANTIC OCEAN

Florida

NEW SPAIN

Gulf of Mexico

Bahamas

WEST INDIES

St. Eustatius (D.)

Cuba

Puerto Rico
St. Christopher
Antigua
Guadaloupe
Dominique

Jamaica   St. Dominique   Hispaniola

Nevis (Eng.)   Martinique

St. Lucia (Fr.)   Barbados

Caribbean Sea   St. Vincent (Sp.)

Curaçao   Grenada

PACIFIC OCEAN

While the English clung to part of North America's eastern coast, they battled with their European rivals for control of the more valuable Caribbean.

tives in the wars between the numerous states of central and west Africa. For example, Songhay—the largest state in Africa in the 1500s—waged wars of territorial conquest recurrently, capturing slaves as it expanded its empire. The economy of the kingdom of Dahomey leaned heavily for several centuries on commerce in slaves. One former slave, Francisco Feliz de Sousa, came to own a fleet of slave ships. But the carrying trade was mainly in the hands of Europeans.

More than anything else, sugar transformed the African slave trade. For centuries, sugarcane had been grown in the Mediterranean countries to sweeten the diet of the wealthy. As sugar's popularity grew, the center of production shifted to Portuguese Madeira, an island off the coast of Africa. Here in the sixteenth century, a European nation for the first time established an overseas colony organized around slave labor. From Madeira, the cultivation of sugar spread to Portuguese Brazil and Spanish Santo Domingo. By the seventeenth century, with Europeans developing a taste for

sugar almost as insatiable as their craving for tobacco, they vied fiercely for possession of the tiny islands dotting the Caribbean and for control of the trading forts on the West African coast. African kingdoms, eager for European trade goods, warred against each other in order to supply the "black gold" demanded by white ship captains.

Many European nations competed for trading rights on the West African coast. In the seventeenth century, when about 1 million Africans were brought to the New World, the Dutch replaced the Portuguese as the major supplier. The English, meanwhile, hardly counted in the slave trade. Not until the 1690s, when they began their century-long rise to maritime greatness, did the English challenge the Dutch. But by the 1790s, the English were the foremost slave traders in Europe.

In the eighteenth century, European traders carried at least 6 million Africans to the Americas, probably the greatest forced migration in history. By this time African slave labor figured so importantly in the colonial world that one Englishman called slavery the "strength and the sinews of this western world."

Even the most vivid accounts of the slave trade cannot convey the pain and demoralization that accompanied the initial capture and subsequent march to slave-trading forts on the West African coast or the dreaded passage across the Atlantic. Olaudah Equiano, an eighteenth-century Ibo from what is now Nigeria, described how raiders from another tribe kidnapped him and his younger sister when he was only 11 years old. He passed from one trader to another while being marched to the coast. Many slaves attempted suicide or died from exhaustion or hunger on these forced marches. But Equiano survived. Reaching the coast, he encountered the next humiliation, confinement in barracoons, fortified enclosures on the beach where a surgeon from an English slave ship inspected him. Equiano was terrified by the light skins, language, and long hair of the English and

The pain of a slave coffle, where enslaved Africans were tied together with forked branches and bark rope, shows in this eighteenth-century print. About one-eighth of the slaves marched toward coastal holding pens were children. (The Mansell Collection)

was convinced that he "had got into a world of bad spirits and that they were going to kill me."

More cruelties followed. European traders often branded the African slaves they purchased with a hot iron to indicate which company had procured them. The next trauma came with the ferrying of slaves in large canoes to the ships anchored in the harbor. An English captain recounted the desperation of Africans who were about to lose touch with their ancestral homeland and embark on a vast unknown ocean. "The Negroes are so loath to leave their own country, that they have often leaped out of the canoes, boat and ship, into the sea, and kept under the water till they were drowned."

Conditions aboard the slave ships were miserable, even though the traders' goal was to deliver alive as many slaves as possible to the other side of the Atlantic. Equiano recounted the scene below decks, where manacled slaves were crowded together like corpses in coffins. "With the loathsomeness of the stench, and crying together, I became so sick and low that I was not able to eat, nor had I the least desire to taste anything." The refusal to take food was so common that ship captains devised special techniques to cope with slaves who were determined to starve themselves to death rather than reach the New World in chains. Slavers flogged their captives brutally and applied hot coals to their lips. If this did not suffice, they employed a specially devised mouth wrench to pry apart the jaws of resistant Africans for forced feeding.

The Atlantic passage usually took four to eight weeks. It was so physically depleting and psychologically wrenching that one of every seven captives died en route. Many others arrived in the Americas deranged or near death. In all, the relocation of any African may have averaged about six months from the time of capture to the time of arrival at the plantation of a colonial buyer. During this protracted personal crisis, the slave was completely cut off from the moorings of a previous life—language, family and friends, tribal religion, familiar geography, and status in a local community. Still awaiting these victims of the European demand for cheap labor was adaptation to a new physical environment, a new language, a new work routine, and a life of unending bondage for themselves and their children.

The Southern Transition to Black Labor

Although they were familiar with Spanish, Dutch, Portuguese, and French use of black slaves, English colonists on the mainland of North America turned only slowly to Africa to solve their labor problem. Like other Europeans, they first regarded Native Americans as the obvious source of labor. But European diseases ravaged native societies, and Indians, more at home in the environment than the white colonizers, proved difficult to subjugate. Indentured white labor proved the best way to meet the demand for labor during most of the seventeenth century. Beginning in 1619, a small number of Africans entered Virginia and Maryland to labor in the tobacco fields alongside white servants. But as late as 1671, when some 30,000 slaves toiled in English Barbados, fewer than 3,000 served in Virginia. They were still outnumbered there at least three to one by white indentured servants.

The transformation of the southern labor force from one in which many whites and a few black servants labored side by side to one in which black slaves performed most of the field labor began only in the last quarter of the seventeenth century. Three reasons explain this shift. First, the rising commercial power of England, at the expense of the Spanish and Dutch, swelled English participation in the African slave trade. Beginning in the 1680s, southern planters could purchase slaves more readily and cheaply than before. Second, the supply of white servants from England began drying up. Those who did arrive fanned out among a growing number of colonies. Finally, white servant unrest and a growing population of ex-servants who were landless, discontented, and potential challengers to established white planters led the southern elite to welcome a more pliable labor force. Consequently, by the 1730s, the number of white indentured servants had dwindled to insignificance. Black hands, not white, tilled and harvested Chesapeake tobacco and Carolina rice. Nothing had greater priority in starting a plantation than procuring slave labor. "If any one designs to make a plantation in this province," wrote Thomas Nairne from South Carolina in 1710, "the first thing to be done is, after having cut down a few trees, to split palisades or clapboards and therewith make small houses or huts to shelter the slaves."

In enslaving Africans, English colonists merely copied their European rivals in the New World. Making it all the more natural for American planters to adopt this labor system was the precedent their countrymen had set in the English West Indies. From the 1630s onward, the English imported Africans in droves in Barbados, Jamaica, and the Leeward Islands. Through brutal repression, they molded them into a sugar-producing, slave labor force. Human bondage would later become the subject of intense moral debate. But in the seventeenth century, all but a few whites readily accepted it.

Slavery in the Northern Colonies

Slavery never became the foundation of the northern colonial work force, for labor-intensive crops such as sugar and rice would not grow in colder climates. On the smaller family farms, household labor and occasional hired hands sufficed. Only in the cities, where slaves worked as artisans and domestic servants, and in a few scattered rural areas did slavery take substantial root.

Although the northern colonists employed few slaves, their economies were becoming enmeshed in the commercial network of the Atlantic basin, which depended on slavery and the slave trade. New England's merchants eagerly pursued profits in the slave trade as early as the 1640s, when their ships began supplying Barbados with Africans. By 1676, New England slavers were packing their holds with slaves from Madagascar, off the coast of East Africa, and transporting them 6,000 miles to the western side of the Atlantic. Rhode Island became so involved in the dirty business that by 1750 half the merchant fleet of Newport reaped profits from carrying human cargo. In New York and Philadelphia, building and outfitting slave vessels proved profitable.

New England's involvement in the international slave trade deepened with the growth of its seaports as centers for the distilling of rum—the "hot, hellish and terrible liquor." Made from West Indian sugar, rum became one of the principal commodities traded for slaves on the African coast. As the number of slaves to be fed in the Caribbean multiplied—from about 50,000 in 1650 to 500,000 in 1750—the West Indies became a

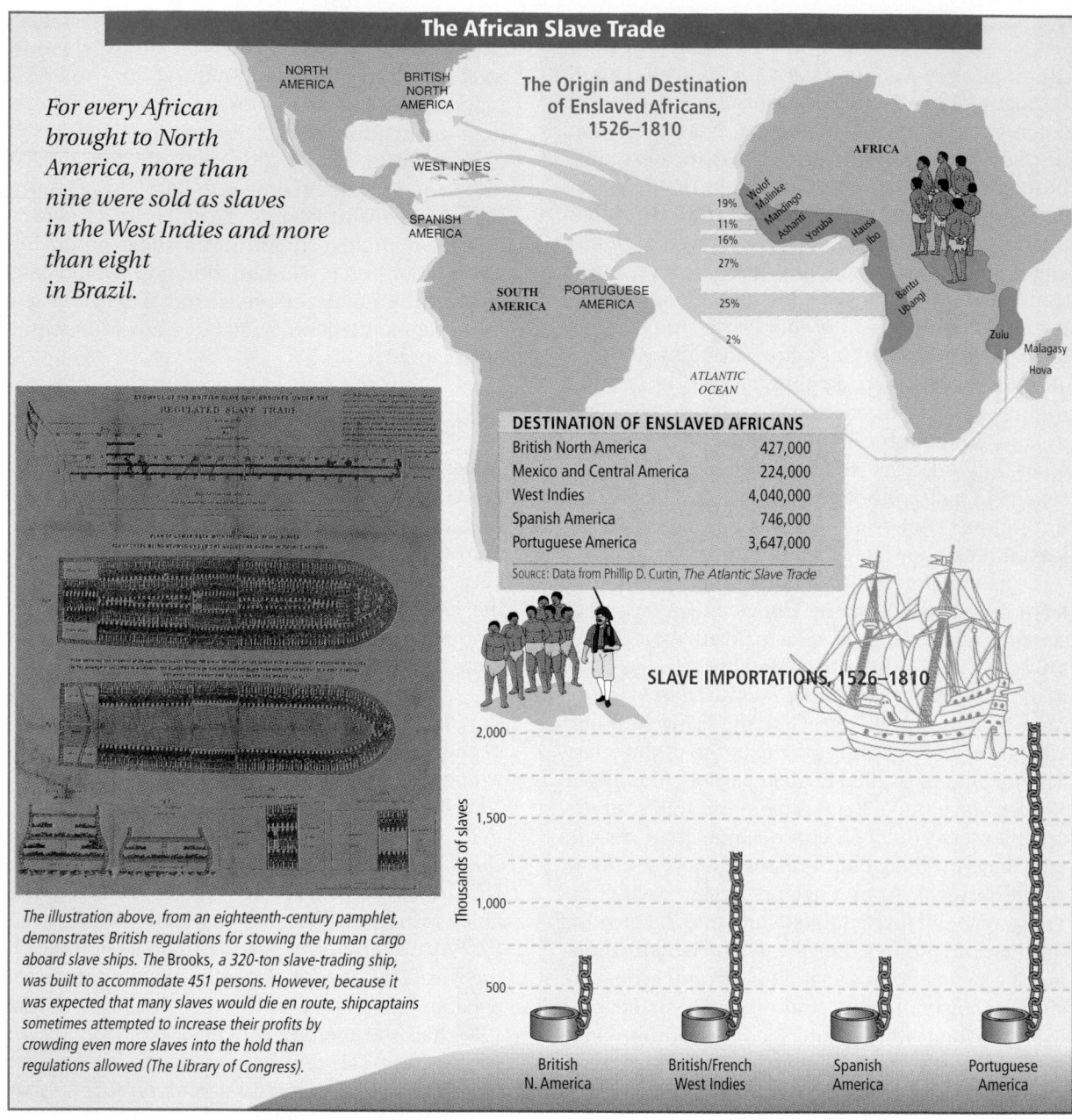

The African Slave Trade

The Origin and Destination of Enslaved Africans, 1526–1810

For every African brought to North America, more than nine were sold as slaves in the West Indies and more than eight in Brazil.

19%
11%
16%
27%
25%
2%

DESTINATION OF ENSLAVED AFRICANS

British North America	427,000
Mexico and Central America	224,000
West Indies	4,040,000
Spanish America	746,000
Portuguese America	3,647,000

SOURCE: Data from Phillip D. Curtin, *The Atlantic Slave Trade*

SLAVE IMPORTATIONS, 1526–1810

The illustration above, from an eighteenth-century pamphlet, demonstrates British regulations for stowing the human cargo aboard slave ships. The Brooks, a 320-ton slave-trading ship, was built to accommodate 451 persons. However, because it was expected that many slaves would die en route, shipcaptains sometimes attempted to increase their profits by crowding even more slaves into the hold than regulations allowed (The Library of Congress).

favorite market for the codfish hauled in by New England's extensive fishing fleet. Wheat from the middle colonies and barrel staves and hoops from North Carolina also fed into the slave-based West Indies economy. Hence, as the plantation South became most directly involved in an international system of racial exploitation, every other North American colony also participated in it.

The System of Bondage

The first Africans brought to the American colonies came as bound servants. They served for a number of years; then, like Anthony and Mary Johnson, many of them eventually gained their freedom. Once released, they could own land, hire out their labor, and move as they pleased. Their children, like those of white indentured servants, were born free. Gradually during the seventeenth century, Chesapeake planters began to draw tighter lines around the activities of black servants. By the 1640s, Virginia forbade blacks, free or bound, to carry firearms. In the 1660s, marriages between white women and black servants were called "shameful matches" and the "disgrace of our Nation." Bit by bit, white settlers strengthened the association between black skin and slave status.

By the mid-seventeenth century, most white colonists were convinced that perpetual bondage was the appropriate status for black servants. By the end of the century, when incoming Africans increased from a trickle to a torrent, even the small number of free blacks found themselves pushed to the margins of society. Slavery, which had existed for centuries in many societies as the lowest social status, was becoming in the Americas a racial caste reserved for those with black skin. Step by step, white society transformed the black servant from human being to chattel.

In this dehumanization of Africans, which the English largely copied from their colonial rivals, the key step was instituting hereditary lifetime service. Once servitude became perpetual, relieved only by death, the elimination of all other privileges followed quickly. When the slave condition of the mother legally fell on the black infant (not the case in other forms of slavery, such as in Africa), slavery became self-perpetuating, passing automatically from one generation to the next.

Slavery existed not only as a system of forced labor, but also as a pattern of human relationships eventually legitimated by law. By the early eighteenth century, most provincial legislatures were enacting laws for controlling black rights and activities. Borrowed largely from the statute books of England's Caribbean colonies, these "black codes" forced Africans into an ever more limited world. Slaves were forbidden to testify in court, engage in commercial activity, hold property, participate in the political process, congregate in public, travel without permission, or engage in legal marriage or parenthood. Nearly stripped of human status, they became defined as a form of property. Restraints on the master's freedom to deal with his slave property in any way he saw fit gradually disappeared.

Eliminating all slave rights had both pragmatic and psychological dimensions. Every black man and woman in chains was a potential rebel. So the rapid increase in the slave population brought anxious demands to bring slaves under strict control. The desire to stifle black rebelliousness mingled with a need to justify brutal behavior toward slaves by defining them as less than human. "The planters," wrote one Englishman in Jamaica, "do not want to be told that their Negroes are human creatures. If they believe them to be of human kind, they cannot regard them as no better than dogs or horses."

Defining slaves in nonhuman terms involved one of the great paradoxes of modern history. Many Old World immigrants imagined the Americas as a liberating and regenerating arena. Yet the opportunity to exploit its resources led to a historic world process by which masses of people were wrenched from their homelands and forced into a system of slavery that could be maintained only by increasing intimidation and brutality.

Slave Culture

The basic struggle for Africans toiling on plantations 5,000 miles from their homes was to create strategies for living as satisfactorily as possible despite horrifying treatment. The master hoped to convert the slave into a mindless drudge who obeyed every command and worked efficiently for his profit. But the attempt to cow slaves rarely succeeded completely. Masters could set the external boundaries of existence for their slaves, controlling physical location, work roles, diet, and shelter. But the authority of the master class impinged far less on how slaves established friendships, fell in love, formed kin groups, reared children, worshiped their gods, buried their dead, and organized their leisure time.

In these aspects of daily life, slaves in America drew on their African heritage to shape their existence to some degree. In doing so, they laid the foundations for an African American culture. At first, this culture had many variations because slaves came from many areas in Africa and lived under different conditions in the colonies. But

Africans as a Percentage of the Total Population in the British Colonies, 1650–1770

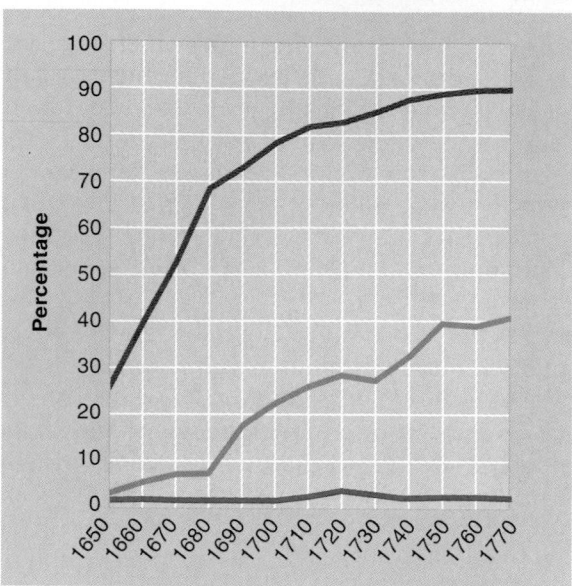

- ━━ British Caribbean colonies
- ━━ Southern British mainland colonies
- ━━ Northern British mainland colonies

Variations in the racial composition of Britain's American colonies led to distinct differences in cuisine, dress, language, music, and other cultural characteristics. Source: Robert W. Fogel and Stanley L. Engerman, *Time on the Cross* (Boston: Little, Brown, 1974), 21.

common elements emerged, led by developments in the South, where about 90 percent of American slaves labored in the colonial period.

The Growth of Slavery

In contrast to other areas of the New World, in North America, Africans reached a relatively healthy environment. The West Indies became a graveyard for both whites and blacks. In South America, tropical diseases swept away slaves like leaves in a windstorm. In the southern colonies, where the ghastly mortality of the early decades had subsided by the time Africans were arriving in large numbers, their chances for survival were much better. A simple comparison makes the point. Colonizers in Virginia and Jamaica each owned about 200,000 slaves in 1775. But to attain

that number, more than three times as many Africans had been imported into Jamaica as into Virginia during the eighteenth century. This environmental advantage, combined with a more even sex ratio, led to a natural increase in the North American slave population that was unparalleled elsewhere.

In 1675, about 4,000 slaves were scattered across Virginia and Maryland. Most were men. They toiled with their masters and a larger number of white indentured servants, clearing the land, planting, hoeing, and harvesting tobacco. A half century later, with the decline of white servitude, 45,000 slaves labored on Chesapeake plantations. By 1760, when the number of slaves exceeded 185,000, the Chesapeake plantations relied almost entirely on black labor. Although slave codes severely restricted the lives of slaves, the possibility for family life increased as the southern colonies matured. Larger plantations employed dozens and even hundreds of slaves, and the growth of roads and market towns permitted them greater opportunities to forge relationships beyond their own plantation. By the 1740s, a growing proportion of Chesapeake slaves were American-born, had established families, and lived in plantation outbuildings where from sundown to sunup they could fashion personal lives of their own.

In South Carolina, African slaves drew on agricultural skills they had practiced on the other side of the Atlantic and made rice the keystone of the coastal economy by the early eighteenth century. Their numbers increased rapidly, from about 4,000 in 1708 to 90,000 by 1760. Working mostly on large plantations in swampy lowlands, they endured the most life-sapping conditions on the continent. But in the coastal low country, they outnumbered whites three to one by 1760 and hence were able to maintain more of their African culture than slaves in the Chesapeake. South Carolina, one European observed in 1737, "looks more like a negro country than like a country settled by white people." Many slaves spoke Gullah, a "pidgin," or mixture of several African languages. They often gave African names to their children, names like Cudjoe, Cuffe, Quashey, and Phibbi. And they kept alive their African religious customs.

In the northern colonies, where no labor shortage existed and the climate did not allow the cultivation of staple crops, slaves made up less than 10 percent of the population. They typically worked as artisans, farmhands, or personal servants. Mingled among them were occasional Indian slaves. Whereas about two-thirds of all southern slaves worked on plantations with at least ten of their fellows by the 1720s, in the North, the typical slave labored alone or with only a few others. Living in the same house as the master, slaves adapted to European ways much faster than in the South, where the slave quarters were places for perpetuating African folkways. Slavery was also less repressive in the North than in the South. Slaves were more widely dispersed among the white population, and black-white contact was so extensive that African culture faded more quickly.

Slavery spread more extensively in the northern ports than across the countryside. Artisans found it profitable to invest in slaves whom they could work on a year-round basis. Ship captains purchased them for maritime labor. And an emerging urban elite of merchants, lawyers, and landlords displayed its wealth and status by employing slaves as liveried coachmen and house servants. By the beginning of the eighteenth century, more than 40 percent of New York City's households owned slaves. Even in Quaker Philadelphia, slaveholding increased sharply in the eighteenth century. Struggling white artisans resented slave workers for undercutting their wages, and the white citizenry felt threatened by potential black arsonists and rebels. Yet where labor demand was high, the desire for lifelong servants, who could be purchased for a mere two years of a free white laborer's wages, outweighed these reservations.

Resistance and Rebellion

While struggling to adapt to bondage in various regions of British America, slaves also resisted and rebelled in ways that constantly reminded their masters that slavery's price was eternal vigilance. Slaveowners preferred to interpret rebelliousness as evidence of the "barbarous, wild savage natures" of Africans, as a South Carolina law of 1712 phrased it. Some planters, like Virginia's Landon Carter, believed that "slaves are devils and to make them free is to set devils free." But from the African point of view, the struggle against enslavement was essential to maintaining meaning and dignity in a life of degrading toil.

"Saltwater" Africans, those fresh from their homelands, often resisted slavery fiercely. "You would really be surprised at their perseverance," wrote one observer. "They often die before they can be conquered." Commonly, this initial resistance took the form of escaping to the frontier to begin renegade settlements, to Indian tribes in the interior that sometimes offered refuge, or to Spanish Florida. Open rebellions, such as those in New York City in 1712 and at Stono, South Carolina, in 1739, mostly involved newly arrived slaves.

There was no North American parallel, however, for the massive slave uprisings that erupted periodically in the West Indies and Brazil. Nor was there an American parallel to the semistates in the South Atlantic sugar world, where runaway slaves built their own communities and resisted periodic assaults by colonial troops. Slaves had far better chances to mount successful rebellions in these areas because they vastly outnumbered their masters and, in the case of Brazil, could flee to the rugged interior to join unconquered Indian tribes. "The greater number of blacks which a frontier has," remarked one colonist, "and the greater the disproportion is between them and her white people, the more danger she is liable to."

In North America, slaves rarely outnumbered whites except in South Carolina, and the master class tried to cultivate tension between local Indians and slaves so that they would be a "check upon each other," as one worried planter explained. When rebellion did occur, white colonizers stopped at nothing to quell it. They tried to intimidate all slaves by torturing, hanging, dismembering, and even burning captured rebels at the stake. After an uprising was disclosed near Charleston, South Carolina, in 1739, for example, city officials tortured and hanged 50 blacks. Their decapitated heads, impaled on posts, gave warning to other potential insurrectionists. In New York City a year later, officials responded to a rumored insurrection by hanging 18 slaves and four white allies and burning 13 other slaves at the stake.

Open rebelliousness often gave way to more subtle forms of resistance as slaves learned English;

adjusted to the routines of shop, farm, and plantation; and began forming families. Dragging out the job, shamming illness, pretending ignorance, and breaking tools were strategies for avoiding physical exhaustion and also indirect forms of opposing slavery itself.

Slaves resisted more directly through truancy, arson directed against the master's barns and houses, crop destruction, pilfering to supplement their food supply, and direct assaults on masters, overseers, and drivers. Slave masters extracted labor and obedience from their slaves in an overall sense. If they had not, the slave system would have collapsed. But they did so only with difficulty. Masters learned that to push slaves too hard could be costly. One South Carolina planter drove his slaves late into the night cleaning and barreling a rice crop in 1732. When he awoke in the morning, he found his barn, with the entire harvest in it, reduced to ashes.

Black Religion and Family

Resistance and rebellion represented attacks on the institution of slavery. But the balance of power was always massively stacked against the slaves. Only the most desperate were willing to challenge the system directly. Of greater importance was the struggle of black slaves to find meaning and worth in their existence, no matter how brutal and discouraging the slave system that manacled them. In this quest, religion and family played a central role—one destined to continue far into the post-slavery period.

Africans brought a complex religious heritage to the New World. No amount of desolation or physical abuse could wipe out these deeply rooted beliefs. People enduring the daily travail that accompanied slavery typically turned for relief to their deepest emotional sources. Coming from cultures where the division between sacred and secular activities was less clear than in Europe, slaves made religion central to their existence. The black Christianity that emerged in the eighteenth century blended African religious practices with the religion of the master class. It laid the foundations for the black Church that later became the central institution in African American life.

Slave masters were not eager to see their slaves exposed to Christianity, because of its potentially dangerous notions of brotherhood and its prohibition against enslaving other Christians. Yet Christianity's emphasis on meekness and obedience might restrain black rebelliousness. Gradually in the eighteenth century, slaves gained exposure to Christianity. They used it both to light the spark of resistance and to find comfort from oppression.

The religious revival that began in the 1720s in the northern colonies and spread southward thereafter made important contributions to African American religion. Evangelicalism stressed personal rebirth, used music and body motion, and caught individuals up in an intense emotional

This eighteenth-century watercolor depicts slaves in South Carolina dancing the "juba," a West African dance. The gourdlike banjo and the twisted leather drumsticks are of African design, reflecting the cultural heritage of Africa transplanted to the American colonies. (Abby Aldrich Rockefeller Folk Art Center)

The physical appearance of Africans captured the imaginations of some American artists. John Singleton Copley's Head of a Negro *(left) (1777–78, Detroit Institute of Arts, Founders Society Purchase, Gibbs-Williams Fund) and John Greenwood's* Jersey Nanny *(right) (1748, Gift of Henry Lee Shattuck, Courtesy, Museum of Fine Arts, Boston) depicted two slaves in the eighteenth century.*

experience. The dancing, shouting, rhythmic clapping, and singing that came to characterize slaves' religious expression represented a creative mingling of West African and Christian religions.

Besides religion, the slaves' greatest refuge from their dreadful fate lay in their families. In West Africa, all social relations were centered in kinship lines, which stretched backward to include dead ancestors. Torn from their native societies, slaves placed great importance on rebuilding extended kin groups.

Most English colonies prohibited slave marriages. But in practice, domestic life was an area in which slaves and masters struck a bargain. Masters found that slaves would work harder if they were allowed to form families. Moreover, family ties stood in the way of escape or rebellion, for few slaves wanted to leave loved ones at the mercy of an angry master. For their part, slaves valued family life so highly that they were willing to risk almost everything to secure the right to marry and parent children.

Slaves fashioned a family life only with difficulty, however. The general practice of importing three male slaves for every two females stunted family formation. Female slaves, much in demand, married in their late teens, but males usually had to wait until their mid- to late twenties. As natural increase swelled the slave population in the eigh-

teenth century, however, the sex ratio became more even.

The sale of either husband or wife could abruptly sever their fragile union. Broken marriages were frequent, especially when a deceased planter's estate was divided among his heirs or his slaves were sold to his creditors to satisfy debts. Young children usually stayed with their mothers until about age 8; then they were frequently torn from their families through sale, often to small planters needing only a hand or two. Few slaves escaped separation from family members at some time during their lives.

White male exploitation of black women represented another assault on family life. How many black women were coerced or lured with favors into sexual relations with white masters and overseers cannot be known. But the sizable mulatto (racially mixed) population at the end of the eighteenth century indicates that the number was large. Interracial liaisons, frequently forced, were widespread, especially in the Lower South. In 1732, the *South-Carolina Gazette* called racial mixing an "epidemical disease." It was a malady that had traumatic effects on slave attempts to build stable relationships.

In some interracial relationships, the coercion was of a more subtle nature. In some cases, black women sought the liaison to gain advantages for themselves or their children. These unions nonetheless threatened both the slave community and the white plantation ideal. They bridged the supposedly unbridgeable gap between slave and free society and produced children who plagued whites because they did not fit into the separate racial categories that the colonists wished to maintain.

Despite such obstacles, slaves fashioned intimate ties as husband and wife, parent and child. If monogamous relationships did not last as long as in white society, much of the explanation lies in the conditions of slave life: the shorter life span of African Americans, the shattering of marriage through sale of one or both partners, and the call of freedom that impelled some slaves to run away.

Whereas slave men struggled to preserve their family role, many black women assumed a position in the family that differed from that of white women. Plantation mistresses usually worked hard in helping manage estates, but nonetheless the ideal grew that they should remain in the house to guard white virtue and set the standards for white culture. In contrast, the black woman remained indispensable to both the work of the plantation and the functioning of the slave quarters. She toiled in the fields and worked in the slave cabins. Paradoxically, black women's roles, which required constant labor, made them more equal to men than was the case of women in white society.

Above all, slavery was a set of power relationships designed to extract the maximum labor from its victims. Hence, it regularly involved cruelties that filled family life with tribulation. But slaves in America were unusually successful in establishing families because they lived in a healthier environment; toiled in less physically exhausting circumstances than slaves on sugar and coffee plantations; and were better clothed, fed, and treated than Africans in the West Indies, Brazil, and other parts of the hemisphere. In these more tropical areas, plantation owners imported large numbers of male slaves, literally worked them to death, and then purchased replacements from Africa. Family life in the American colonies brimmed over with uncertainty and sorrow, but slaves nonetheless made it the greatest monument to their will to endure captivity and eventually gain their freedom.

The Struggle for Land

In the same period that slavery gained a permanent foothold in North America, both New England and Virginia fought major wars against Native Americans. The desire for land, a cause of both wars, produced a similar conflict somewhat later in South Carolina. The conflicts brought widespread destruction to the towns of both colonizers and Indians, inflicted heavy human casualties, and left a legacy of bitterness on both sides. For the coastal tribes, it was a disastrous time of defeat and decline. For the colonists, the wars contributed to the turbulence of the late seventeenth and early eighteenth centuries. Sometimes, as in Virginia, Indian war overlapped with a struggle within white society for social and political control.

King Philip's War in New England

Following the Pequot War of 1637 in New England, the Wampanoags and Narragansetts, whose fertile land lay within the boundaries of Plymouth and Rhode Island, attempted to maintain their distance from the New England colonists. But the New Englanders coveted Indian territories. As they quarreled among themselves over provincial boundaries, they gradually reduced the Indians' land base.

By the 1670s, when New England's population had grown to about 50,000, younger Indians began brooding over their situation. Their leader, Metacomet (named King Philip by the English), was the son of Massasoit, the Wampanoag who had allied himself with the first Plymouth settlers in 1620. Metacomet had watched his older brother preside over the deteriorating position of his people after their father's death in 1661. A year later, Metacomet's brother died mysteriously while Plymouth officials questioned him about a rumored Indian conspiracy. As the Wampanoag leader, Metacomet faced one humiliating challenge after another.

In 1671, Plymouth forced Metacomet to surrender a large stock of guns and accept a treaty of submission acknowledging Wampanoag subjection to English law. Convinced that more setbacks would follow and humiliated by the discriminatory treatment of Indians brought before English

The Wampanoags led New England tribes in a tenacious campaign of resistance against the white settlers. Paul Revere engraved this picture of the Wampanoag chief Metacomet, called King Philip by the English. The musket held by Metacomet bespeaks the Indian adoption of European weaponry. (American Antiquarian Society)

courts, Metacomet began recruiting for a resistance movement.

The triggering incident of King Philip's War was the trial of three Wampanoags who were dragged before a Puritan court for an act of tribal revenge against John Sassamon, a Christianized Indian educated at Harvard. Sassamon was a man caught between two cultures. Though he had fled white society after his college years, he warned the Plymouth government in 1675 that the Wampanoags were preparing a general attack on the English settlements. When Sassamon was found murdered shortly afterward, Plymouth officials produced an Indian who claimed he had witnessed the murder and could identify the felons. As a result, three Wampanoags swung at the end of English ropes in June 1675.

The execution of the three tribesmen was the catalyst, but the root cause of the war that erupted was the rising anger of the young Wampanoag males. As would happen repeatedly in the next two centuries as Americans pushed westward, these younger Native Americans refused to imitate their fathers, who had watched the colonizers erode their land base and compromise their sovereignty. Rather than put themselves under white authority, they attempted a pan-Indian offensive against an intruder with far greater numbers and a much larger arsenal of weapons. For the young tribesmen, revitalization of their ancient culture through war became as important a goal as defeating the enemy.

In the summer of 1675, the Wampanoags unleashed daring hit-and-run attacks on villages in the Plymouth colony. By autumn, many New England tribes, including the powerful Narragansetts, had joined Metacomet's warriors. Towns all along the frontier reeled under Indian attacks. "We were too ready to think that we could easily suppress that flea," confessed John Eliot, who had worked to convert the Indians to Christianity, "but now we find that all the craft is in catching them, and that in the meantime they give us many a sore nip." By the time the first snow fell in November, mobile Indian warriors had laid waste to the entire upper Connecticut River Valley.

By March 1676, Metacomet's forces were attacking less than 20 miles from Boston and Providence. Assumptions about English military superiority faded. Desperate to reverse the course of the war, New England officials passed America's first draft laws. Evasion was widespread, however, with eligible men—all those between ages 16 and 60—"skulking from one town to another." Political friction among the New England colonies also hampered a united counteroffensive.

Metacomet's offensive faltered in the spring of 1676. Food shortages and disease sapped Indian strength, and the powerful Mohawks, with their own advantages in the fur trade to protect, refused to support the New England tribes. By summer, groups of Indians were surrendering, while some moved westward seeking shelter among other tribes. Metacomet fell in a battle near the Wampanoag village in Rhode Island where the war had begun. The head of this "hell-hound, fiend, serpent, caitiff and dog," as one colonial leader branded him, was carried triumphantly back to Plymouth, where it remained on display for 25 years.

At war's end, several thousand colonists and perhaps twice as many Indians lay dead. Of some 90 Puritan towns, 52 had been attacked and 13 completely destroyed by the "tawny serpents." Some 1,200 homes lay in ruins and 8,000 cattle were dead. The estimated cost of the war exceeded the value of all personal property in New England. Not for 40 years would the frontier advance beyond the line it had reached in 1675. Indian towns were devastated even more completely, including several of those inhabited by "praying Indians" who had converted to Christianity and allied with the whites. An entire generation of young men had been nearly annihilated. Many of the survivors, including Metacomet's wife and son, were sold into slavery in the West Indies.

Bacon's Rebellion Engulfs Virginia

While New Englanders fought local tribes in 1675 and 1676, the Chesapeake colonies became locked in a struggle involving both a war between the red and white populations and civil war within the colonizers' society. Before it ended, hundreds of whites and Indians lay dead in Virginia and Maryland, Virginia's capital of Jamestown lay smoldering, and English troops were crossing the Atlantic to suppress what the king labeled an outright rejection of his authority. This deeply tangled conflict was called Bacon's Rebellion after the headstrong Cambridge-educated planter Nathaniel Bacon, who arrived in Virginia at age 28.

Bacon and many other ambitious young planters detested the Indian policy of Virginia's royal governor, Sir William Berkeley. In 1646, at the end of the second Indian uprising against the Virginians, the Powhatan tribes had accepted a treaty granting them exclusive rights to territory north of the York River, beyond the limits of white settlement. Stable Indian relations suited the established planters, some of whom traded profitably with the Indians, but became obnoxious to new settlers arriving in the 1650s and 1660s. Nor did the harmonious conditions please the white indentured servants who had served their time and were hoping to find cheap frontier land.

Land hunger and dissatisfaction with declining tobacco prices, rising taxes, and lack of opportunity erupted into violence in the summer of 1675. A group of frontiersmen used an incident with a local tribe as an excuse to attack the Susquehannocks, whose rich land they coveted. Governor Berkeley denounced the attack, but few supported his position. He faced, he said, "a people where six parts of seven at least are poor, indebted, discontented, and armed."

Although badly outnumbered, the Susquehannocks prepared for war. Virginians girded themselves for the southern version of what they heard was occurring in New England. Rumors swept the colony that the Susquehannocks were offering large sums to western Indian nations to join in attacking the colonists. Some even said that King Philip had formed a confederacy with the Chesapeake tribes.

Thirsting for revenge, the Susquehannocks attacked during the winter of 1675–1676 and killed 36 Virginians. That spring, the hot-blooded Nathaniel Bacon became the frontiersmen's leader. Joined by hundreds of runaway servants and some slaves, he launched a campaign of indiscriminate warfare on friendly and hostile Indians alike. When Governor Berkeley refused to sanction these attacks, Bacon ignored his authority. The governor then declared Bacon a rebel and sent out 300 militiamen to drag him to Jamestown for trial. Bacon headed into the wilderness for "a more agreeable destiny" and recruited more followers, including many substantial planters. Frontier skirmishes with Indians had turned into civil war.

During the summer of 1676, Bacon's and Berkeley's troops maneuvered around each other, while Bacon's men continued their forays against local Indian tribes. In one bold move, Bacon and his followers captured the capital at Jamestown. They razed the statehouse, church, and other buildings and put Governor Berkeley to flight across Chesapeake Bay.

Virginians at all levels had chafed under Berkeley's rule. High taxes, an increase in the governor's powers at the expense of local officials, and the monopoly that Berkeley and his friends held on the Indian trade were especially unpopular. This opposition surfaced in the summer of 1676 as Berkeley's and Bacon's troops pursued each other through the wilderness. Berkeley tried to rally public support by holding new assembly elections and extending the vote to all freemen, whether they owned property or not. The new assembly promptly turned on the governor, passing a set of reform laws intended to make government more responsive to the common people and to end rapacious officeholding. The assembly also made legal the enslavement of Native Americans.

Time was on the governor's side, however. Having crushed the Indians, Bacon's followers began drifting home to tend their crops. Meanwhile, Berkeley's reports of the rebellion brought the dispatch of 1,100 royal troops from England. By the time they arrived, in January 1677, Nathaniel Bacon lay dead of swamp fever and most of his followers had melted back into the frontier. After Bacon's death in October 1676, Berkeley rounded up 23 rebel leaders and hanged them without benefit of civil trial.

Royal investigators who arrived in 1677 remarked on the genocidal mentality of Bacon's followers, whom they denounced as the "inconsiderate sort of men who so rashly and causelessly cry up a war and seem to wish and aim at an utter extirpation of the Indians." Even a royal governor could not restrain such men, bent on pursuing their hopes of land ownership and independence. To them, Indians were only "wolves, tigers, and bears," as Bacon charged, "which daily destroyed our harmless and innocent lambs."

The hatred of Indians bred into white society during the war became a permanent feature of Virginia life. A generation later, in 1711, the legislature spurned the governor's plea for quieting the Indian frontier with a program of educational missions and regulated trade. Instead, the legislators voted military appropriations of £20,000 "for extirpating all Indians without distinction of Friends or Enemys." The remnants of the once populous Powhatan Confederacy lost their last struggle for the world they had known. Now they moved farther west or submitted to a life on the margins of white society as tenant farmers, day laborers, or domestic servants.

After Bacon's Rebellion, an emerging planter aristocracy annulled most of the reform laws of 1676. But the war relieved much of the social tension among white Virginians. Newly available Indian land created fresh opportunities for small planters and former servants. Equally important, Virginians with capital to invest were turning from the impoverished rural villages of England and Ireland to the villages of West Africa to supply their labor needs. This halted the influx of poor white servants who, once free, had formed a discontented mass at the bottom of Chesapeake society. A racial consensus, uniting whites of different ranks in the common pursuit of a prosperous, slave-based economy, began to take shape.

North and south of Virginia, Bacon's Rebellion caused insurrectionary rumblings. Many of Bacon's compatriots took refuge after his death in North Carolina's Albemarle County, the "backside of Virginia." There they joined dissident tobacco farmers, who were distressed by recent Indian uprisings, export duties on tobacco, and quitrents controlled by a mercenary elite. Led by George Durant and John Culpeper, they drove the governor from office and briefly seized the reins of power.

In Maryland, Protestant settlers chafed under high taxes; quitrents; and officeholders regarded as venal, Catholic, or both. Declining tobacco prices and a fear of Indian attacks increased their touchiness. A month after Bacon razed Jamestown, insurgent small planters tried to seize the Maryland government. Two of their leaders were hanged for the attempt. In 1681, Josias Fendall and John Coode, "two rank Baconists" according to Lord Baltimore, led another abortive uprising. After their attempt to kidnap the Catholic proprietor failed, the authorities executed Fendall and banished Coode from the colony.

In all three southern colonies, the volatility of late-seventeenth-century life owed much to the region's peculiar social development. Where family formation was retarded by imbalanced sex ratios and fearsome mortality, and where geographic mobility was high, little social cohesion or attachment to community could grow. Missing in the southern colonies were the stabilizing power of mature local institutions, a vision of a larger purpose, and the presence of experienced and responsive political leaders.

An Era of Instability

A dozen years after the major Indian wars in New England and Virginia, a series of insurrections and a major witchcraft incident rumbled through colonial society. The rebellions were triggered by the

Tombstones

Historians have used funeral orations, gravestone designs and inscriptions, and handbooks on how to die to gain insight into early American culture. Tombstone markings—"graven images," they have been called—provide a particularly fascinating body of evidence. At first, Puritans in New England marked their graves only with wooden rails and posts. But in the 1670s, carved headstones filled with symbolic images began to appear, and they became a regular feature of New England graveyards after that. Hardly any Puritan family thereafter, one historian noted, was "ready to commit its loved ones to the cold earth without an appropriate cluster of symbols hovering protectively over the grave." How the symbols carved on tombstones changed tells much about how people's attitudes and values shifted. "There is no better place in all New England to stand face to face with the past," it has been said, "than in the old burying grounds."

The tombstone shown here shows vividly the intensity with which Puritans faced death. To die was to be called to final account by a just and merciful God, and the way one died gave evidence of one's self-discipline and faith. The scrolled pediment on this gravestone signifies the doorway between earthly life and spiritual rebirth through which Joseph Tapping's relatives hoped he passed. The grim winged skull represents the soul of the dying man in transition. This death's-head motif was widely used on seventeenth-century gravestones. It conveys much of the Puritans' intense concern that life is transitory (note the hourglass) and that salvation is not automatically granted to those who believe in Christ. This emphasis on life as a preparation for afterlife is reinforced by the Latin mottoes on the right side of the stone: *Vive memor loethi* ("Live mindful of death") and *Fugit hora* ("The hour flies"). At bottom center of the stone is an image of Time fending off Death as Death tries to snuff out the candle of Life. Note Father Time's symbols—the hourglass and scythe—in the background.

The Puritans' fixation on death has also been noted in the elaborate and expensive funerals

Joseph Tapping headstone, Boston, 1678. (From the Daniel and Jessie Lie Farber Collection of Gravestone Photographs, American Antiquarian Society)

they often conducted and in the content of funeral sermons and handbooks on how to die well. In a popular book on advice for the young, *Token for Children,* published first in England in 1671 and in an American edition in 1700, James Janeway described the "Joy and holy Triumph" of a 12-year-old girl's death. As a model of faith in God's mercy, without yielding to pride or certainty of salvation in her last hours, this young girl

> spake with a holy Confidence in the Lord's Love to her Soul, and was not in the least daunted when she spake of her Death, but seemed greatly delighted in the Apprehension of her nearness to her Father's House: And it was not long before she was fill'd with Joy unspeakable in believing.

Also obsessed with death, but with a less joyful view, was Michael Wigglesworth's *Day of Doom* (1662), an account of the Judgment Day in verse intended to reinvigorate Puritan spirituality. *Day of Doom* was New England's first best-seller. The verses reprinted here may suggest why.

By the second quarter of the eighteenth century, attitudes toward death were changing, as the gravestone iconography after about 1730 attests. The epitaphs stressing mortality appeared much less frequently, and the ever-present foreboding death's-head, shovels, and hourglass symbols of the seventeenth century began to be replaced by smiling cherubs, angels, natural objects, and sentimentalized willow and urn motifs.

Note the details shown here from an eighteenth-century gravestone compared to those on the Tapping stone. A winged image of Mrs. Betsy Shaw (Plymouth, Massachusetts, 1795) optimistically represents the flight of her soul heavenward. This romantic design tells us much about the secularization of New England society and the passing of the early Puritans' intense seriousness about their godly mission in America to redeem humankind. As the funerary handiwork of stonecarvers reveals, the Puritans' early providential self-

Betsy Shaw headstone, Plymouth, 1795. (From the Daniel and Jessie Lie Farber Collection of Gravestone Photographs, American Antiquarian Society)

image had been transformed. Less piety and morbid intro-spection, more worldliness and individual hopefulness had spread through the Puritan Holy Commonwealth. Can you point out how these changes are reflected on the Shaw and Tapping gravestones? What do the markings, inscriptions, and design of tombstones in cemeteries near you reveal about the changing experience and values of later Americans?

Day of Doom

Michael Wigglesworth (1662)

56

Now it comes in, and every sin unto men's
*   charge doth lay;*
It judgeth them and doth condemn, though all
*   the world say nay.*
It so stingeth and tortureth, it worketh such
*   distress,*
That each man's self against himself is forced
*   to confess.*

57

It's vain moreover for men to cover the least
*   iniquity;*

The Judge hath seen, and privy been to all
*   their villainy.*
He unto light and open sight the work of
*   darkness brings;*
He doth unfold both new and old, both known
*   and hidden things.*

58

All filthy facts and secret acts, however closely
*   done*
And long concealed, are there revealed before
*   the mid-day sun.*
Deeds of the night, shunning the light, which
*   darkest corners sought,*
To fearful blame and endless shame are there
*   most justly brought.*

59

And as all facts and grosser acts, so every word
*   and thought,*
Erroneous notions and lustful motion, are
*   unto judgment brought,*
No sin so small and trivial but hither it must
*   come,*
Nor so long past, but now at last it must
*   receive a doom. . . .*

188

The Judge is strong; doers of wrong cannot his
*   power withstand.*
None can be flight run out of sight nor 'scape out
*   of his hand.*
Sad is their state, for advocate to plead their
*   cause there's none—*
None to prevent their punishment, or misery
*   bemoan.*

189

O dismal day! wither shall they for help and
*   succor flee?*
To God above, with hopes to move their
*   greatest enemy?*
His wrath is great, whose burning heat no
*   floods of tears can slake:*
His word stands fast, that they be cast into the
*   burning lake.*

harbor, which held most of the governor's small contingent of red-coated royal troops. Andros escaped, disguised in women's clothing, but was quickly recaptured. Boston's ministers, along with merchants and former magistrates, led the rebellion, but city folk of the lower orders supplied the foot soldiers. For three years, an interim government ruled Massachusetts while the Bay colonists awaited a new charter and a royal governor.

Although Bostonians had dramatically rejected royal authority, which to them represented the "bloody Devotees of Rome" as well as arbitrary power, no internal revolution occurred. However, growing social stratification and the emergence of a political elite led to some disturbing effects. Some citizens challenged the traditional view that those at the top of society were the true guardians of the public interest. They argued that men of modest means but common sense might better be trusted with power. Anarchy was the word chosen by Samuel Willard, minister of Boston's Third Church, to tar the popular spirit he saw unloosed in Boston in the aftermath of Andros's ouster. But such egalitarian rumblings came to little.

Leisler's Rebellion in New York

In New York, the Glorious Revolution was similarly bloodless at first but far more disruptive. It was not necessary to overthrow royal government when news arrived of James II's abdication. It simply melted away. When a local militia captain, the German-born Jacob Leisler, appeared at Fort James at the lower tip of Manhattan, Governor Francis Nicholson made only a token show of resistance before quietly stepping down. Displacing the governor's "popishly affected dogs and rogues," Leisler established an interim government and ruled with an elected Committee of Safety for 13 months until a governor appointed by King William arrived.

Leisler's government enjoyed popularity among small landowners and urban laboring people. Most of the upper echelon, however, detested him. They remembered that he had come to New Amsterdam in 1660 as a common foot soldier of the Dutch West India Company and three years later had leapfrogged into the merchant class by marrying a wealthy widow. After the English took over the Dutch colony in 1664, he was often at odds with New Yorkers of the upper rank. "Up jump into the saddle hott brain'd Capt. Leisler," sneered one aristocrat after Leisler's takeover. Thereafter, the Leislerians were often labeled as people of "mean birth, and sordid education and desperate fortunes."

Such antipathy was returned in kind by lower- and middle-class Dutch inhabitants, who felt a smoldering resentment toward the town's English elite. Many Dutch merchants had readily adjusted to the English conquest of New Netherland in 1664, and many incoming English merchants had married into Dutch families. But beneath the upper class, where economic success softened ethnic friction, incidents of Anglo-Dutch hostility were common. The feeling rose in the 1670s and 1680s among ordinary Dutch families that the English were crowding them out of the society they had built.

The Glorious Revolution provided a spark to ignite this smoldering social conflict. Leisler shared Dutch hostility toward New York's English elite, and his sympathy for the common people, mostly Dutch, earned him the hatred of the city's oligarchy. Leisler freed imprisoned debtors, planned a town-meeting system of government for New York City, and replaced merchants with artisans in important official posts. By the autumn of 1689, Leislerian mobs were attacking the property of some of New York's wealthiest merchants. Two merchants, refusing to recognize Leisler's authority, were jailed.

Leisler's opponents, accustomed to controlling government, were horrified at the power of what they called the "rabble," the "tumultuous multitude." They believed that ordinary people had no right to rebel against authority or to exercise political power. When a new English governor arrived in 1691, the anti-Leislerians embraced him and charged Leisler and seven of his assistants with treason for assuming the government without royal instructions.

In the ensuing trial, Leisler and Jacob Milbourne, his son-in-law and chief lieutenant, were convicted of treason by an all-English jury and hanged. Leisler's popularity among the artisans of the city was evident when his wealthy opponents could find no carpenter in the city who would furnish a ladder to use at the scaffold. After his execution, peace gradually returned to New York, but for years provincial and city politics reflected the deep rift between Leislerians and anti-Leislerians.

Southern Rumblings

The Glorious Revolution also focused dissatisfactions in several southern colonies. Because Maryland was ruled by a Catholic proprietor, the Protestant majority predictably seized on word of the Glorious Revolution and used it for their own purposes. Lord Baltimore had returned to England in 1684. In 1688, when his instructions to his colony to honor William and Mary were delayed, leading officials and planters formed a Protestant Association. Seizing control of the government in July 1689, they vowed to cleanse Maryland of its popish hue and to reform a corrupt customs service, cut taxes and fees, and extend the rights of the representative assembly. John Coode, formerly a fiery Anglican minister who, as we have seen, had been involved in a brief rebellion in 1681, assumed the reins of government and held them until the arrival of Maryland's first royal governor in 1692.

In neighboring Virginia, the wounds of Bacon's Rebellion were still healing when word of the Glorious Revolution arrived. The fact that Virginia lived under the governorship of the Catholic Lord Howard of Effingham, who had installed a number of Catholic officials, made it easy for rumors to spread that a Catholic conspiracy was hatching. News of the revolution in England led a group of planters, who had suffered a prolonged drop in tobacco prices, to attempt an overthrow of the governor. The uprising quickly faded when the governor's council asserted itself and took its own measures to remove Catholics from positions of authority.

The Glorious Revolution brought political changes to several colonies. The Dominion of New England was shattered. Whereas Connecticut and Rhode Island were allowed to elect their own governors, Massachusetts and New Hampshire became royal colonies with governors appointed by the king. In Massachusetts, a new royal charter in 1691 eliminated Church membership as a voting requirement. The Maryland proprietorship was abolished (to be restored in 1715 when the Baltimore family became Protestant), and Catholics were barred from office. Everywhere the liberties of Protestant Englishmen were celebrated.

The Social Basis of Politics

Although the colonial insurrections associated with the Glorious Revolution sought primarily to overthrow arbitrary royal governors and foil papist plots (most of them imaginary), they revealed social and political tensions that accompanied the transplanting of English society to the North American wilderness. Still hardly beyond the frontier stage, the immature societies along the coast were fluid and competitive. They lacked the stable political systems and acknowledged leadership class thought necessary for maintaining social order.

The colonial elite tried, of course, to foster social and political stability. The best insurance of this, they believed, was the maintenance of a stratified society where children were subordinate to parents, women to men, servants to masters, and the poor to the rich. Only well-knit societies had coherence and balance, the upper echelon believed. Amid the barbarizing conditions of the New World, where anarchy lurked just beyond every threshold, it was especially vital to reproduce the social arrangements of the Old World.

Hence, in every settlement, leaders tried to maintain a system of social gradations and subordination. Puritans did not file into church on Sundays and occupy the pews in random fashion. Rather, the seats were "doomed," or assigned according to customary yardsticks of respectability—age, parentage, social position, wealth, and occupation. Even in fluid Virginia, lower-class people were hauled before courts for horse racing because this was a sport by law reserved for men of social distinction.

This social ideal proved difficult to maintain on North American soil, however. Regardless of previous rank, settlers rubbed elbows so frequently and faced such raw conditions together that those without pedigrees often saw little reason to defer to men of superior rank. "In Virginia," explained John Smith, "a plain soldier that can use a pickaxe and spade is better than five knights." Colonists everywhere learned that basic lesson. They gave respect not to those who claimed it by birth, but to those who earned it by deed.

Adding to the difficulty of reproducing a traditional social order in the colonies was the social fluidity in frontier society. A native elite gradually formed, but it had no basis, as in Europe, in legally defined and hereditary social rank. Planters and merchants, accumulating large estates, aped the English gentry by cultivating the arts, building fine houses, and acquiring symbols of respectability such as libraries, coaches, and racehorses. Yet their place was rarely secure. In the race to drag wealth from the resource-rich environment, new competitors nipped constantly at their heels.

Amid such social flux, the elite could never command general allegiance to the ideal of a fixed social structure. Ambitious men on the rise such as Nathaniel Bacon and Jacob Leisler, and thwarted men below them who followed their lead, rose up against the constituted authorities, though they almost certainly would not have dared to do so in their homelands. When they gained power during the Glorious Revolution, in every case only briefly, the leaders of these uprisings linked themselves with a tradition of English struggle against tyranny and oligarchical power. They vowed to make government more responsive to the ordinary people, who composed most of their societies.

In both North and South, this earned parvenu leaders the epithet "Masaniello" after the peasant fish seller of Naples who in 1647 had mobilized ordinary people against exploitation by the rich. Masaniello briefly controlled the city, momentarily stood the political order on its head, and became an Italian Robin Hood. In America, Bacon's Rebellion was likened to Masaniello's revolt by the royal governor. In New York, Leisler was labeled a local Masaniello by his wealthy enemies. In Maryland, John Coode proudly called himself a Chesapeake Masaniello. The comparisons were far from exact, but references to the Italian folk hero indicate that colonists from all ranks recognized that social relations in their competitive and open society were subject to violent alterations that violated the ideal of a fixed, orderly social system.

Witchcraft in Salem

The ordinary people in the colonies, for whom Bacon and Leisler tried to speak, could sometimes be misled, as the tragic events of the Salem witch hunts demonstrated. In Massachusetts, the deposing of Governor Andros left the colony in political limbo for three years, and this allowed what might have been a brief outbreak of witchcraft in the little community of Salem to escalate into a bitter and bloody battle to which the provincial government, caught in transition, reacted only belatedly.

On a winter's day in 1692, 9-year-old Betty Parris and her 11-year-old cousin Abigail Williams began to play at magic in the kitchen of a small house in Salem, Massachusetts. They enlisted the aid of Tituba, the slave of Betty's father, Samuel Parris, the minister of the small community. Tituba told voodoo tales handed down from her African past and baked "witch cakes." The girls soon became seized with fits and began making wild gestures and speeches. Soon other young girls in the village were behaving strangely. Village elders extracted confessions that they were being tormented by Tituba and two other women, one a decrepit pauper, the other a disagreeable hag.

What began as the innocent play of young girls turned into a ghastly rending of a farm community capped by the execution of 20 villagers accused of witchcraft. In the seventeenth century, people still took literally the biblical injunction "Thou shalt not suffer a witch to live." For centuries throughout western Europe, people had believed that witches followed Satan's bidding and could spread his evil to anyone he designated. Communities had accused and sentenced women far more often than men to death for witchcraft. In Massachusetts, more than 100 people, mostly older women, had been accused of witchcraft before 1692, and more than a dozen had been hanged.

In Salem, the initial accusations against three older women quickly multiplied. Within a matter of weeks, dozens had been charged with witchcraft, including several prominent members of the community. But formal prosecution of the accused witches could not proceed because neither the new royal charter of 1691 nor the royal governor to rule the colony had yet arrived. For three months, while charges spread, local authorities could only send the accused to jail without trial. When Governor William Phips arrived from England in May 1692, he ordered a special court to try the accused, but by now events had careened out of control.

Witch hangings, usually of women, were numerous in Europe as well as the colonies; this woodcut appeared in England's Grievance Discovered *(1655), a book on injustices in England's coal industry. Identified by letter in the picture are the hangman (A), town crier (B), sheriff (C), and magistrate (D).*

All through the summer, the court listened to testimony. By September it had condemned about two dozen villagers. The authorities hanged 19 of them on barren "Witches Hill" outside the town and crushed 80-year-old Giles Corey to death under heavy stones. The trials rolled on into 1693, but by then, colonial leaders, including many of the clergy, recognized that a feverish fear of one's neighbors, rather than witchcraft itself, had possessed the little village of Salem.

Many factors contributed to the hysteria. Among them were generational differences between older Puritan colonists and the sometimes less religiously motivated younger generation, old family animosities, population growth and pressures on the available farmland, and tensions between agricultural Salem Village and the nearby commercial center called Salem Town. An outbreak of food poisoning may also have caused hallucinogenic behavior. Probably nobody will ever fully understand the exact mingling of causes, but the fact that most of the individuals charged with witchcraft were women underscores the relatively weak position of women in Puritan society. The fact that the accusations of witchcraft kept spreading suggests the anxiety of this tumultuous era, marked by war, economic disruption, the political takeover of the colony by Andros and then his overthrow, and the erosion of the early generation's utopian vision.

Contending for a Continent

At the end of the seventeenth century, following an era of Indian wars and internal upheaval, the colonists for the first time confronted an extended period of international war. The long incipient struggle for mastery of the New World among four contending European powers—Holland, Spain, France, and England—now became more overt. North America was less an arena of armed rivalry among the European powers than were the sugar-rich islands of the Caribbean. Nonetheless, the global struggle for control of land and sea that erupted late in the seventeenth century—the beginning of nearly 100 years of conflict—reached to the doorsteps of those who thought that in immigrating to North America they had left war behind.

Anglo-French Rivalry

In 1661, the French king, Louis XIV, ushered in a new era for New France. Determined to make his country the most powerful in Europe, the king regarded North America and the Caribbean with renewed interest. New France's timber resources would build the royal navy, its fish would feed the growing mass of slaves in the French West Indies, and its fur trade, if greatly expanded, would fill the royal coffers.

Under the leadership of able governors such as Count Frontenac, New France grew in population, economic strength, and ambition in the late seventeenth century. In the 1670s, Louis Jolliet and Father Jacques Marquette, a Jesuit priest, explored an immense territory watered by the Mississippi and Missouri rivers, previously unknown to Europeans. A decade later, military engineers and priests began building forts and missions, one complementing the other, throughout the Great Lakes region and the Mississippi valley.

Visions of a mighty inland empire grew in the 1680s when René Robert de La Salle canoed down the Mississippi all the way to the Gulf of Mexico and planted a settlement in Texas at Matagorda Bay. The dream of connecting Canada and Louisiana by a chain of forts and trading posts would not be realized for another half century. But it was the French, with a colonial population of only 12,000, rather than the English, with colonies inhabited by 200,000, whom the Indian tribes permitted to settle in the interior of North America. Traders and missionaries from France were very different in Indian villages than land-hungry, expansionist English settlers.

The growth of French strength and ambitions brought New England and New France into deadly conflict for a generation, beginning in the late seventeenth century. Religious hostility overlaid commercial rivalry. Protestant New Englanders regarded Catholic New France as a satanic challenge to their divinely sanctioned mission. When the European wars began in 1689, precipitated by Louis XIV's territorial aggression in western and central Europe, armed conflict between England and France quickly extended into every overseas theater where the two powers had colonies. In North America, the battle zone was New York, New England, and eastern Canada.

In two wars, from 1689 to 1697 and 1701 to 1713, the English and French, while fighting in Europe, also sought to oust each other from the New World. The zone of greatest importance was the Caribbean, where slaves produced huge sugar fortunes. Both home governments understood that the importance of the North American colonies lay chiefly in supplying the timber and fish necessary to sustain the sugar-producing tropical economy of the West Indies. In the North American zone, problems of weather, disease, transport, and supply were so great that only irregular warfare was possible.

The English struck three times at the centers of French power—Port Royal, which commanded the access to the St. Lawrence River, and Quebec, the administrative center of New France. In 1690, during King William's War (1689–1697), their small flotilla captured Port Royal, the hub of Acadia (which was returned to France at the end of the war). The English assault on Quebec, however, failed disastrously. In Queen Anne's War (1701–1713), New England attacked Port Royal three times before finally capturing it in 1710. A year later, when England sent a flotilla of 60 ships and 5,000 men to conquer Canada, the land and sea operations foundered before reaching their destinations.

With European-style warfare miserably unsuccessful in America, both England and France attempted to subcontract military tasks to their Indian allies. Here was a new aspect of the meeting of cultures—the use of Native Americans as mercenaries in an international conflict. This policy occasionally succeeded, especially with the French, who gladly sent their own troops into the fray alongside Indian partners. The French and their Indian allies wiped out the frontier outpost of Schenectady, New York, in 1690; razed Wells, Maine, and Deerfield, Massachusetts, in 1703; and battered other towns along the New England frontier during both wars.

In retaliation, the Iroquois, supplied by the English, stung several French settlements and left New France "bewildered and benumbed" after a massacre near Montreal in 1689. Assessing their own interests, and too powerful to be dictated to by either France or England, the Iroquois sat out the second war in the early eighteenth century. Convinced that neutrality served their purposes better than acting as mercenaries for the English, they held to the principle that "we are a free

Visiting French Louisiana in 1735, Alexander de Batz painted members of the Illinois tribe who traded at New Orleans. Note the hatted African who apparently has been adopted by the Illinois. (Alexander De Batz, Desseins de Sauvages de Plusieurs Natims, 1735/ Peabody Museum, Harvard University)

people uniting ourselves to whatever sachem [chief] we wish."

The Results of War

The Peace of Utrecht in 1713, which ended the war, capped the century-long rise of England and the decline of Spain in the rivalry for the sources of wealth outside Europe. England, the big winner, received Newfoundland and Acadia (renamed Nova Scotia), and France recognized English sovereignty over the fur-rich Hudson Bay territory. France retained Cape Breton Island, controlling the entrance to the St. Lawrence River. In the Caribbean, France yielded St. Kitts and Nevis to England. In Europe, Spain lost its provinces in Italy and the last of its holdings in the Netherlands to the Austrian Habsburgs. Spain also surrendered Gibraltar and Minorca to the English and awarded England the lucrative privilege of supplying the Spanish empire in America with African slaves, a favor formerly enjoyed by the French Senegal Company.

The French were the big losers in these wars, but they did not abandon their ambitions in the New World. Soon after Louis XIV died in 1715, the Regency government of the duke of Orleans tried to regain lost time in America by mounting a huge expedition to settle Louisiana. Because France deported many undesirables to the colony and because the French aristocracy destroyed by wild speculation the stock that financed the project, few French immigrants joined the settlement of New Orleans thereafter. French colonies expanded only in the Caribbean, where by 1750, the islands of Hispaniola, Martinique, and Guadeloupe counted 46,000 whites and 250,000 slaves. Although the islands enriched a few, they strengthened the empire little, because slaves could not be armed and the islands were expensive to defend.

At the Peace of Utrecht in 1713, Spain retained—on paper—a vast empire in North America. However, its hold was very tenuous on the southern tier of the continent, and it had learned how easily its thinly peopled missions and frontier outposts could be crippled or destroyed by chafing Native Americans and invading English. In the first half of the eighteenth century, the Spanish settlements stagnated, suffering from Spain's colonial policy that regarded them as marginal, money-losing affairs worth the trouble only as essentially defensive outposts.

Spain's priority was not to expand its presence in North America, but to preserve what it had by keeping others away from it. That in itself would prove to be difficult, for this garrison mentality had to compete with the commercially minded English and French whose colonial population, especially the former's, was growing rapidly. Small, impoverished Spanish frontier outposts could do little to halt the expansion of British and French America.

Though England had rebuffed France after a generation of war, New England suffered grievously. In time, Nova Scotia would provide a new frontier for Puritan farmers. But the two wars between 1689 and 1713 struck hard at New England's economy. Massachusetts bore the brunt of the burden. Probably one-fifth of all able-bodied males in the colony participated in the Canadian campaigns, and of these, about one-quarter never lived to tell of the terrors of New England's first major experience with international warfare. At the end of the first war in 1697, one leader bemoaned

that Massachusetts was left "quite exhausted and ready to sink under the calamities and fatigue of a tedious consuming war." The war debt was £50,000 sterling in Massachusetts alone, a greater per capita burden than the national debt today.

At the end of the second conflict in 1713, war widows were so numerous that the Bay Colony faced its first serious poverty problem. In addition, wartime taxes had "much impoverished and enfeebled" the people, and price inflation had eaten deeply into the pocketbooks of most working families. Pamphleteers in New England's principal port wrote of the "present melancholy circumstances" and the "distressed state of the Town of Boston."

The colonies south of New England remained on the sidelines during most of the war. But war at sea between European rivals affected even those who sat out the land war. In Queen Anne's War, New York lost one of its best grain markets when Spain, allied with France, outlawed American foodstuffs in its West Indian colonies. The French

North American Cultural Regions

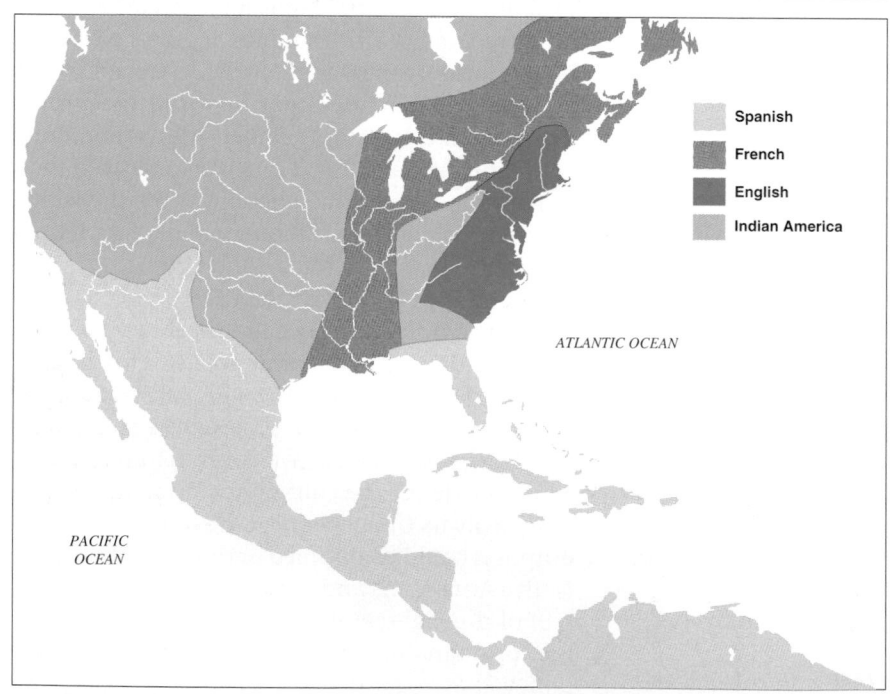

This map of European cultural regions in mid-eighteenth-century North America disguises the cultural influence of hundreds of Indian societies that lived among, between, and beyond the sparsely settled European settlements. Only along the eastern seaboard was European dominance secure.

navy plucked off nearly 30 New York merchant vessels, about one-quarter of the port's fleet, and disrupted the vital sea lanes between the mainland and the Caribbean, to the detriment of Philadelphia's grain merchants as well.

One lesson of war, to be repeated many times in succeeding generations, was that the burdens and rewards fell unevenly on the participants. Some lowborn men could rise spectacularly. William Phips, the twenty-sixth child in his family, had been a poor sheep farmer and ship's carpenter in Maine who seemed destined to go nowhere. Then he won a fortune by recovering a sunken Spanish treasure ship in the West Indies in 1687. For that feat, he was given command of the expedition against Port Royal in 1690. Victory there catapulted him to the governorship of Massachusetts in 1691, and thereafter his status was secure.

Other men, already rich, multiplied their wealth. Andrew Belcher of Boston, who had grown wealthy on provisioning contracts during King Philip's War in 1675 and 1676, combined patriotism with profit in King William's and Queen Anne's wars by supplying warships and outfitting the New England expeditions to Canada. As one of the favored recipients of the fruits of war, Belcher became a local titan, riding through Boston's crooked streets in London-built coaches, erecting a handsome mansion on State Street, and purchasing slaves to symbolize his rise to the pinnacle of New England society.

Most men, especially those who did the fighting, gained little, however, and many lost all. It was from the ranks of the least securely placed New Englanders—indentured servants, apprentices, recently arrived immigrants, unskilled laborers, fishermen, and ordinary farmers—that most troops were recruited or pressed involuntarily into service. Once in the army or navy, they died in numbers that seem staggering today. Fervent antipopery, dreams of glory, and promises of plunder from the commercial centers of French Canada lured most of them into uniform. Having achieved no place on the paths leading upward, they grasped at straws. A hefty percentage of those who sailed in the naval expeditions against Port Royal or plodded overland to attack Montreal and Quebec never lived even to collect their meager wages. None found the advertised booty, which turned out to be only a sugarplum dangled by military recruiters.

TIMELINE

1600–1700	Dutch monopolize slave trade
1619	First Africans imported to Virginia
1637	Pequot War in New England
1640s	New England merchants enter slave trade
	Virginia forbids blacks to carry firearms
1650–1670	Judicial and legislative decisions in Chesapeake colonies solidify racial lines
1651	Parliament passes first navigation act
1664	English conquer New Netherland
1673–1685	French expand into Mississippi valley
1675–1677	King Philip's War in New England
1676	Bacon's Rebellion in Virginia
1682	La Salle canoes down Mississippi River and claims Louisiana for France
1684	Massachusetts charter recalled
1688	Glorious Revolution in England, followed by accession of William and Mary
1689	Overthrow of Governor Andros in New England
	Leisler's Rebellion in New York
1689–1697	King William's War
1690s	Transition from white indentured servant to black slave labor begins in Chesapeake
1692	Witchcraft hysteria in Salem
1700	Spanish establish first mission in Arizona
1702–1713	Queen Anne's War
1713	Peace of Utrecht

Conclusion

Controlling the New Environment

By the second decade of the eighteenth century, the 12 English colonies on the eastern edge of North America had secured footholds in the hemisphere and erected the basic scaffolding of colonial life. With the aid of England, they had ousted the Dutch from their mid-Atlantic perch. They had fought the French to a draw and held their own against the Spanish. The coastal Indian tribes were reeling from disease and a series of wars that secured the colonists' land base along 1,000 miles of coastal plain. Though never controlling the powerful Indian tribes of the interior, the colonists had established a profitable trade with them. The settlers had overcome a scarcity of labor by copying the other European colonists in the hemisphere, who had linked the west coast of Africa to the New World through the ghastly trade in human flesh. Finally, the colonists had engaged in insurrections against what they viewed as arbitrary and tainted governments imposed by England.

The embryo of British America carried into the eighteenth century contained peculiarly mixed features. Still physically isolated from Europe, the colonists developed of necessity a large measure of self-reliance. Slowly, they began to identify themselves as the permanent inhabitants of a new land rather than as transplanted English, Dutch, or Scots-Irish. Viewing land and labor as the indispensable elements of a fruitful economy, they learned to exploit without apologies the land of one dark-skinned people and the labor of another. Yet even as they attained a precarious mastery in a triracial society, they were being culturally affected by the very people to which whose land and labor they laid claimed. Although utopian visions of life in America still reverberated in the heads of some, most colonists had awakened to the reality that life in the New World was a puzzling mixture of unpredictable opportunity and sudden turbulence, unprecedented freedom and debilitating wars, racial intermingling and racial separation. It was a New World in much more than geographic sense, for the people of three cultures who now inhabited it had remade it; and, while doing so, they were remaking themselves.

Recommended Reading

The Atlantic Slave Trade and the Beginnings of Slavery

Philip Curtin, *The Atlantic Slave Trade: A Census* (1969) and *The Rise and Fall of the Plantation Complex* (1990); Walter Rodney, *West Africa and the Atlantic Slave Trade* (1969); Patrick Manning, *Slavery and African Life: Occidental, Oriental, and African Slave Trades* (1990); Kwame Yeboa Daaku, *Trade and Politics on the Gold Coast, 1600–1720* (1970); Martin Kilson and Robert I. Rotberg, eds., *The African Diaspora* (1976); Basil Davidson, *The African Slave Trade* (1961); James A. Rawley, *The Transatlantic Slave Trade* (1981); John Thornton, *Africa and Africans in the Making of the Atlantic World, 1440–1680* (1992); Frank Tannenbaum, *Slave and Citizen* (1956); Carl N. Degler, *Neither Black nor White: Slavery and Race Relations in Brazil and the United States* (1971); H. Hoetink, *Slavery and Race Relations in the Americas* (1973); David B. Davis, *The Problem of Slavery in West-* *ern Culture* (1966); Richard S. Dunn, *Sugar and Slaves: The Rise of the Planter Class in the English West Indies, 1624–1713* (1972).

African Bondage and Slave Culture

Ira Berlin, "Time, Space, and the Evolution of Afro-American Society in British Mainland America," *American Historical Review,* 85 (1980); T. H. Breen and Stephen Innes, *"Myne Owne Ground": Race and Freedom on Virginia's Eastern Shore, 1640–1676* (1980); Peter H. Wood, *Black Majority: Negroes in South Carolina from 1670 Through the Stono Rebellion* (1974); Gerald Mullins, *Flight and Rebellion: Slave Resistance in Eighteenth-Century Virginia* (1972); Allan Kulikoff, *Tobacco and Slaves: The Development of Southern Cultures in the Chesapeake, 1680–1800*

(1986); Winthrop D. Jordan, *White over Black* (1968); Gwendolyn Midlo Hall, *Africans in Colonial Louisiana* (1992); Michael Mullin, *Africa in America: Slave Acculturation and Resistance in the American South* (1992); Mechal Sobel, *The World They Made Together: Black and White Relations in Eighteenth-Century Virginia* (1987); Marvin L. Michael Kay and Lorin Lee Cary, *Slavery in North Carolina, 1748–1775* (1995); Betty Wood, *Slavery in Colonial Georgia, 1730–1775* (1984); William Pierson, *Black Yankees: The Development of an African-American Subculture in Eighteenth-Century New England* (1988); Thomas J. Davis, *A Rumor of Revolt: The "Great Negro Plot" in Colonial New York* (1985).

Indian-White Relations

James Axtell, *The European and the Indian* (1981); David H. Corkran, *The Creek Frontier, 1540–1783* (1967); Wilcomb Washburn, *The Governor and the Rebel* (1957); Douglas Leach, *Flintlock and Tomahawk: New England in King Philip's War* (1958); Francis Jennings, *The Ambiguous Iroquois Empire* (1984); Calvin Martin, *Keepers of the Game: Indian-Animal Relationships and the Fur Trade* (1978); J. Leitch Wright, *The Only Land They Knew: The Tragic Story of the American Indians in the Old South* (1981); James H. Merrell, *The Indians' New World: Catawbas and Their Neighbors from European Contact through the Great Removal* (1989); Daniel Usner, Jr., *Indians, Settlers, and Slaves in a Frontier Exchange Economy: The Lower Mississippi Valley Before 1783* (1992); Gary B. Nash, *Red, White, and Black,* 3d ed. (1992).

The Glorious Revolution and the Era of Instability

David Lovejoy, *The Glorious Revolution in America* (1972); Jerome Reich, *Leisler's Rebellion* (1953); Paul Boyer and Steven Nissenbaum, *Salem Possessed: The Social Origins of Witchcraft* (1974); John P. Demos, *Entertaining Satan: Witchcraft and the Culture of Early New England* (1982); Carol F. Karlsen, *The Devil in the Shape of a Woman* (1987); Richard Weisman, *Witchcraft, Magic, and Religion in 17th–Century Massachusetts* (1984); Mary Beth Norton, *Founding Mothers and Fathers: Gendered Power and the Forming of American Society* (1996)

Contending for a Continent

A. H. Johns, *Storms Brewed in Other Men's Worlds: The Confrontation of Indians, Spanish, and French in the Old Southwest* (1975); Oakah L. Jones, Jr., *Los Paisanos: Spanish Settlers on the Northern Frontier of New Spain* (1979); W. J. Eccles, *The Canadian Frontier, 1534–1760* (1969), and *France in America* (1972); Richard White, *The Middle Ground: Indians, Empires, and Republics in the Great Lakes Region, 1650–1815* (1991); Charles Gibson, *Spain in America* (1966); Edward Spicer, *Cycles of Conquest: The Impact of Spain, Mexico, and the United States on the Indians of the Southwest, 1533–1960* (1962); D. W. Meinig, *The Shaping of America: Atlantic America, 1492–1800* (1986); John Francis Bannon, *The Spanish Borderlands Frontier, 1513–1821* (1970); David J. Weber, *The Spanish Frontier in North America* (1992); Ramon A. Gutierrez, *When Jesus Came, the Corn Mothers Went Away: Marriage, Sexuality, and Power in New Mexico, 1500–1846* (1992); and Stephen S. Webb, *The Governors-General: The English Army and the Definition of Empire, 1569–1681* (1979).

The Maturing of Colonial Society

As a youth, Devereaux Jarratt knew only the isolated life of the small southern planter. Born in 1733 on the Virginia frontier, he was the third son of an immigrant yeoman farmer. In New Kent County, where Jarratt grew up, class status showed in a man's dress, his leisure habits, his house, even in his religion. A farmer's "whole dress and apparel," Jarratt recalled later, "consisted in a pair of coarse breeches, one or two shirts, a pair of shoes and stockings, an old felt hat, and a bear skin coat." In a maturing colonial society that was six generations old by the mid-eighteenth century, such simple folk stepped aside and tipped their hats when prosperous neighbors went by. "A periwig, in those days," recollected Jarratt, "was a distinguishing badge of gentle folk," and when I saw a man riding the road, near our house, with a wig on, it would so alarm my fears … that, I dare say, I would run off, as for my life."

As the colonies grew rapidly after 1700, economic development brought handsome gains for some, opened modest opportunities for many, but produced disappointment and privation for others. Jarratt remembered that his parents "neither sought nor expected any title, honors, or great things, either for themselves or their children. They wished us all brought up in some honest calling that we might earn our bread, by the sweat of our brow, as they did." But Jarratt was among those who advanced. His huge appetite for learning was apparent to his parents when as a small child he proved able to repeat entire chapters of the Bible before he had learned to read. That earned him some schooling. But at age 8, when his parents died, he had to take his place behind the plow alongside his brothers. Then, at 19, Jarratt was "called from the ax to the quill" by a neighboring planter's timely offer of a job tutoring his children.

Tutoring put Jarratt in touch with the world of wealth and status. Gradually, he advanced to positions in the households of wealthy Virginia planters. His modest success also introduced him to the world of evangelical religion. In the eighteenth century, an explosion of religious fervor dramatically reversed the growing secularism of the settlers. Jarratt first encountered evangelicalism in the published sermons of George Whitefield, an English clergyman.

But it was later, at the plantation of John Cannon, "a man of great possessions in lands and slaves," that he personally experienced conversion under the influence of Cannon's wife. Jarratt later became a clergyman in the Anglican Church, which was dominated in the South by wealthy and dignified planters. But he never lost his religious zeal and desire to carry religion to the common people. In this commitment to spiritual renewal, he participated in the first mass religious movement to occur in colonial society.

Joseph Beekman Smith, *Wesley Chapel on John Street, New York City—1768* (detail), completed 1817–1844 (based on earlier sketches). (Old John Street United Methodist Church, New York)

Colonial North America in the first half of the eighteenth century was a thriving, changing set of regional societies that had developed from turbulent seventeenth-century beginnings. New England, the mid-Atlantic colonies, the Upper and Lower South, New France, and the northern frontier of New Spain were all distinct regions. Even within regions, diversity increased in the eighteenth century as incoming streams of immigrants, mostly from Africa, Germany, Ireland, and France, added new pieces to the emerging American mosaic.

Despite their bewildering diversity and lack of cohesion, the colonies along the Atlantic seaboard were affected similarly by population growth and economic development. Everywhere except on the frontier, class differences grew. A commercial orientation spread from north to south, especially in the towns, as local economies matured and forged links with the network of trade in the Atlantic basin. The exercise of political power of elected legislative assemblies and local bodies produced seasoned leaders, a tradition of local autonomy, and a widespread belief in a political ideology stressing the liberties that freeborn Englishmen should enjoy. All regions experienced a deep-running religious awakening that was itself connected to secular changes. All these themes will be explored as we follow the way in which scattered frontier settlements developed into mature provincial societies.

America's First Population Explosion

In 1680, some 150,000 colonizers clung to the eastern edge of North America. By 1750, they had swelled sevenfold to top one million. This growth rate, never experienced in Europe, staggered English policymakers. Perceptive observers understood that the gap between the population of England and its American colonies was closing rapidly. Benjamin Franklin's prediction in 1751—that before his grandchildren died, the colonies would outstrip the mother country in population—proved correct.

The population boom was fed from both internal and external sources. Among the white colonial population, a high marriage rate, large families, and lower mortality than in Europe prevailed by the 1720s. Natural increase accounted for much of the population boom in all the colonies and nearly all of it in New England, where immigrants arrived only in a trickle in the eighteenth century. The black population also began to increase naturally by the 1720s. American-born slaves, forming families and producing as many children as white families, soon began to outnumber slaves born in Africa.

The New Immigrants

While expanding through natural increase, the colonial population also received waves of new immigrants. They were not English, however. The last sizable group of settlers from England had arrived at the end of the seventeenth century. The eighteenth-century newcomers, who far outnumbered those emigrating before 1700, came overwhelmingly from Germany, Switzerland, Ireland, and Africa, and they were mostly indentured servants and slaves. Africans, who numbered about 15,000 in 1690, grew to 80,000 in 1730 and 325,000 in 1760. By the last date, when they composed one-fifth of the colonial population, their numbers were growing far more from natural increase than from importation. Of all the groups arriving in the eighteenth century, the Africans were the largest.

German-speaking settlers, about 90,000 strong, flocked to the colonies in the eighteenth century. Many were Protestant farmers of Swiss and French extraction, fleeing "God's three arrows"—famine, war, and pestilence. Drifting down the Rhine to Rotterdam, they crowded onto ships and began the long voyage to America. Once in the colonies, they hurried to areas where pro-

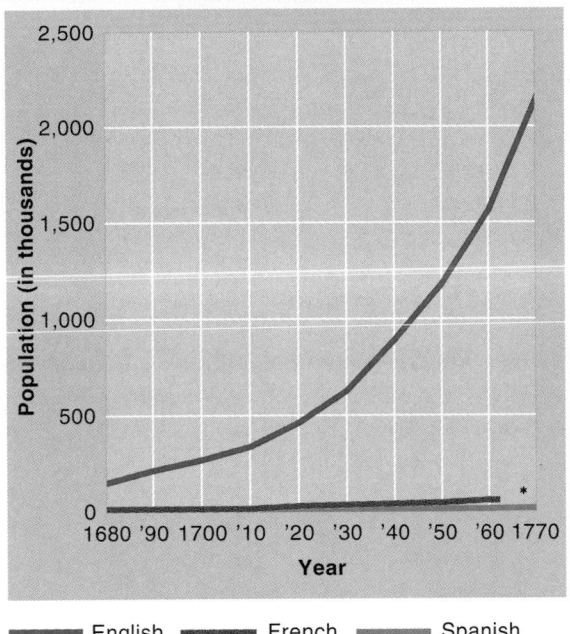

Population of European Colonies in North America, 1680–1770

Population (in thousands)

2,500
2,000
1,500
1,000
500
0

1680 '90 1700 '10 '20 '30 '40 '50 '60 1770
Year

——— English   ——— French   ——— Spanish

Whereas the French and Spanish populations in North America inched upward (the result of few arriving immigrants and a low birthrate in settlements dominated by males), the English and African American populations soared.

leys south into the Carolinas and Georgia. Occasionally mingling with the Germans, these Ulster families washed over the ridges of Appalachia until their appetite for land brought them face to face with the ancient occupiers of the land. No major Indian wars occurred between 1715 and 1754, but the frontier bristled with tension as the new settlers pushed westward.

In the enormous population growth occurring after 1715, the region southward from Pennsylvania witnessed the most spectacular increase. New England nearly tripled in population, but the middle and southern colonies quadrupled, though in the South the fast-growing slave population accounted for much more of the growth than in the mid-Atlantic. Pennsylvania, with its fertile lands and open door policy, grew fastest of all. Between 1720 and 1760, its population mushroomed from 30,000 to 180,000. Virginia, with a population of nearly 340,000 by 1760, remained by far the largest colony.

The social background of these new European immigrants differed substantially from their seventeenth-century predecessors. The early settlers included a number of men from the upper levels of the English social pyramid: university-trained Puritan ministers, sons of wealthy gentry, and merchants. In the eighteenth century, few such men arrived.

The seventeenth-century immigrants had also included many from the middle rungs of the English social ladder—yeomen farmers, skilled craftsmen, and shopkeepers. They formed the backbone of the provincial churches and participated actively in community politics. Through "shipboard mobility," they moved up a notch or two on the western side of the Atlantic. Many lived to see their sons enter the professions or embark on a mercantile career in a society with plenty of room at the top. Such people came rarely in the eighteenth century, for religious persecution had waned in England, and material conditions had improved.

Slaves and indentured servants made up most of the incoming human tide after 1713. The traffic in servants became a regular part of the commerce linking Europe and America. Shipowners made their profits fetching sugar, fish, furs, rice, tobacco, and forest products eastward. On the westbound voyages, plenty of room remained for human

moters promised them cheap and fertile land, low taxes, and freedom from military duty. Most settled between New York and South Carolina, with Pennsylvania claiming the largest number of them. Coming mostly in families, they turned much of the mid-Atlantic hinterland into a German-speaking region. Place names still mark their zone of settlement: Mannheim, New Berlin, and Herkimer, New York; Bethlehem, Ephrata, Nazareth, and Hanover, Pennsylvania; Hagerstown and Frederick, Maryland; Mecklenberg and New Hanover, North Carolina.

Outnumbering the Germans were the Protestant Scots-Irish. Several thousand from Northern Ireland arrived each year after the Peace of Utrecht in 1713 reopened the Atlantic sea lanes. Mostly poor farmers, they streamed into the same backcountry areas where Germans were settling, though more of them followed the mountain val-

Most German and Scots-Irish immigrants in the 1700s were farmers, and they quickly moved into the interior where land was cheapest and most available.

cargo after loading the less bulky textiles and manufactured products desired by colonists.

Shipboard conditions for servants worsened in the eighteenth century and were hardly better than aboard the slave ships. The wretchedness of the passage can be judged by the attempt at reform in the 1720s, when the British government required an increase in horizontal space to 6 feet by 18 inches per passenger, with no allowance for children.

Such attempts to reduce "tight packing" did little to improve shipboard life. Crammed between decks in stifling air, servants suffered from smallpox and fevers, rotten food, impure water, cold, and lice. "Children between the ages of one and seven seldom survive the sea voyage," bemoaned one German immigrant, "and parents must often watch their offspring suffer miserably, die, and be thrown into the ocean." One expedition of 3,000 Palatinate immigrants in 1717 lost 470 en route; on another, 250 succumbed shortly after reaching port. "I never see such parcels of poor wretches,"

one Virginia observer remarked of an incoming troop of servants in 1758, "some almost naked and what had clothes was as black as chimney sweepers and almost starved." The misery would be repeated thousands of times in the next two centuries. The shipboard mortality rate of about 15 percent in the colonial era made this the most unhealthy of all times to seek American shores.

Like indentured servants in the seventeenth century, the servant immigrants who poured ashore after 1715 came mostly from the lower ranks of society. As earlier, some were petty criminals, political prisoners, and the castoffs of the cities. Yet they were bold and ambitious souls. "Men who emigrate," an Englishman commented, "are from the nature of their circumstances, the most active, hardy, daring, bold and resolute spirits, and probably the most mischievous also."

Once ashore, most indentured servants, especially males, found the labor system harsh. Merchants sold them, one shocked Britisher reported

The communalistic Moravian immigrants who came to Pennsylvania in the 1740s dedicated themselves, like the Quakers, to peaceful relations with the Indians. The Prussian John Jacob Schmick and his Norwegian wife Johanna were missionaries to the Delawares. (Moravian Historical Society, Nazareth, PA)

in 1773, "as they do their horses, and advertise them as they do their beef and oatmeal." Facing cruel treatment, thousands of servants ran away. Advertisements for them filled the colonial newspapers alongside notices for escaped slaves. Servants knew the penalties if they were caught: whipping and additional service, usually reckoned at twice the time lost to the master, but sometimes calculated at a 5 to 1 or 10 to 1 ratio, as in Pennsylvania and Maryland. When war came in the mid-eighteenth century, hundreds of servants fled to the British army, not known for its kindly treatment of soldiers but preferable in many servants' eyes to four or five years under a harsh colonial master.

The goal of every servant was to secure a foothold on the ladder of opportunity. "The hope of buying land in America," a New Yorker noted, "is what chiefly induces people into America." However, many servants died before serving out their time. Others won freedom only to toil for years as poor day laborers and tenant farmers. Only a small proportion achieved the dream of becoming independent landholders. The indentured servants in the seventeenth-century Chesapeake world suffered fearful mortality rates, but those who survived often rose in society. Among the eighteenth-century servants, ironically, the chances of living long enough to complete the labor contract were much better, but the opportunity to climb into the propertied ranks became less favorable. The chief beneficiaries of the system of bound white labor were not the laborers but their masters.

Africans in Chains

Among the thousands of ships crossing the Atlantic in the eighteenth century, the ones fitted out as seagoing dungeons for slaves were the most numerous. The slave trade to the southern

Slaves Imported to North America, 1701–1775

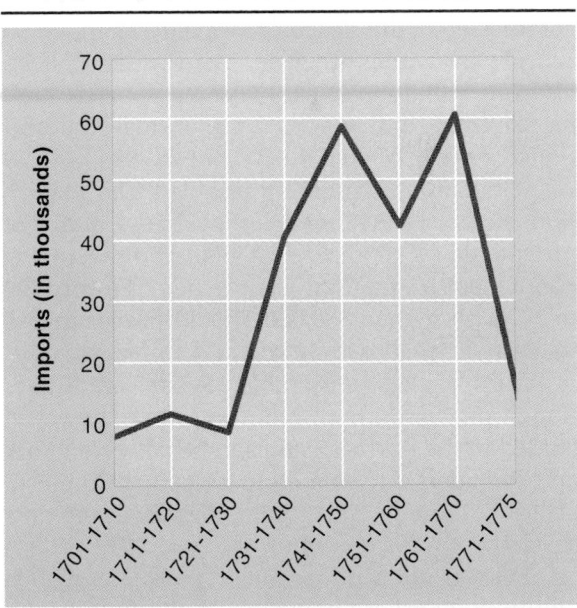

Overwhelmingly, Africans transported to the American colonies arrived from the 1730s to 1770s. Rapid natural increase, as well as importation, swelled the African population to about 500,000 by the outbreak of the American Revolution. Source: R. C. Simmons, *The American Colonies: From Settlement to Independence,* 1976.

New-Providence Township, Philadelphia County,
December 19th, 1772.

RUN AWAY from the sub-
scriber, living in the aforesaid
township, on Monday the fourteenth
instant, an indented Irish servant
man named BARNABAS KELLY,
about five feet three ~~inches high, and~~
twenty one years of ~~age,~~
blind and is near~~sighted in the~~
other, has long bla~~ck hair, which he~~
wears tied behind : Had on an old great~~coat, a~~
cut velvet jacket without buttons, a ~~new~~
and a white linen one without sleeves, ~~lea~~-
ther breeches, black stockings, and a ~~pair of pumps~~
with strings.   He took with him about Four or Five
Pounds in money, and his own and his master's part of
his indentures; also a grey HORSE, which trots mostly and paces a little.   Whoever will take up the said
servant, and secure him in any gaol, so that I may get
him again, shall have FORTY SHILLINGS, and
FORTY SHILLINGS more for the horse, and
reasonable charges, paid by
                    EDWARD ROBERTS.

TO BE SOLD,
The TIME of an *IRISH*
SERVANT GIRL,
WHO has about three years to serve. Enquire of
the Printers.

Like enslaved Africans, white indentured servants often fled the harsh conditions under which they labored. Advertisements for the recovery of runaway servants (right) filled the colonial newspapers. No explanation is given for the sale of the servant girl's time (left). Was her performance unsatisfactory? Did her master unexpectedly need cash? (Historical Society of Pennsylvania, Philadelphia)

colonies after the Peace of Utrecht expanded so sharply that within two generations what had been a society with many slaves became a society built on slavery. From 1690 to 1715, annual importations rarely exceeded 1,000, but in the next 15 years, the number probably doubled. The generation after 1730 witnessed the largest influx of African slaves in the colonial period, averaging about 5,000 a year. In the entire period from 1700 to 1775, more than 350,000 African slaves entered the American colonies.

Most of these miserable captives were auctioned off to southern planters. Some, however, landed in the northern cities, especially New York and Philadelphia. Merchants sold them there to artisans, farmers, and upper-class householders seeking domestic servants.

Even as the traffic in slaves peaked, religious and humanitarian opposition to slavery arose. A few individuals, mostly Quaker, had objected to slavery on moral grounds since the late seventeenth century. But the idea grew in the 1750s that slavery contradicted the Christian concept of brotherhood and the Enlightenment notion of the natural equality of all humans. Abolitionist sentiment was also fed by the growing belief that the master's authority "depraved the mind," as the Quaker John Woolman argued. An introspective tailor from New Jersey, Woolman dedicated his life in the 1750s to a crusade against slavery. He traveled thousands of miles on foot through the colonies to convince every Quaker slaveholder of his or her wrongdoing. Only a few hundred masters freed their slaves in the mid-eighteenth century, but men such as Woolman had nevertheless planted the seeds of abolitionism.

Beyond the Appalachians

By the mid-eighteenth century, the American colonists, though increasing rapidly in number, still occupied only a narrow strip of coastal plain in eastern North America. Of about 1.2 million settlers and slaves in 1750, only a tiny fraction lived farther than 100 miles from the shores of the

Atlantic. But between them and the Pacific Ocean lay rich soils in the river valleys of the Ohio and Mississippi and beyond that a vast domain that they had not even imagined. Beginning in the 1750s, westward-moving colonists in pursuit of more land would encounter four other groups already established to their west: the populous interior Native American tribes and smaller groups of French Americans, Spanish Americans, and African Americans. Changes already occurring among these groups would affect settlers breaching the Appalachian barrier and, in the third quarter of the eighteenth century, would even reach eastward to the original British settlements.

Cultural and Ecological Changes Among Interior Tribes

During the first half of the eighteenth century, the inland tribes proved their capacity to adapt to the contending European colonizers in their region while maintaining their political independence. Yet extensive contact with the French, Spanish, and English slowly transformed Indian ways of life in a manner that boded ill for the future.

The introduction of European trade goods, especially iron implements, textiles, firearms and ammunition, and alcohol, inescapably changed Indian lifeways. Subsistence hunting, limited to satisfying tribal food requirements, turned into commercial hunting, restricted only by the quantity of trade goods desired. Indian males, gradually exhausting the population of deer and beaver east of the Mississippi River, spent far more time away from the villages trapping and hunting, and the increased importance of this activity to tribal life undermined the matrilineal basis of society. Women were also drawn into the new economic activities. Once killed, the beaver, deer, marten, and fox had to be skinned and the pelts then scraped, dressed, trimmed, and sewn into robes. Among some tribes, the trapping, preparation, and transporting of skins became so time-consuming that they had to procure food resources from other tribes.

Involvement in the fur trade altered the traditional Native American belief that the destinies of humans and animals were closely linked, for both inhabited a spiritual world governed by a Great Creator. This imposed obligations on both hunters and animals. The hunter knew that he must never kill more animals than he needed and must treat their bodies with respect. The animals in return must not resist capture. When trappers and hunters declared all-out war on the beaver and other fur-bearing animals to provide pelts for the European traders who offered attractive trade goods, they began to ignore the age-old belief in a spiritual connection with the animal world.

In addition, the fur trade heightened intertribal tensions, often to the point of war. Conflict between tribes long preceded the arrival of Europeans, but trade frequently flowed between cooperating tribes. As fur traders of different nationalities competed for client tribes in the fur trade, the tribes were sucked into their patron's rivalry. Also, tribes came to depend on certain trade articles. When furs became depleted in their hunting grounds, they could maintain their trade only by conquering more remote tribes with fertile hunting grounds or by forcibly intercepting the furs of other tribes as they were carried to European trading posts. The introduction of European weaponry, which Indians quickly mastered, further intensified intertribal conflict.

Tribal political organization among the interior tribes also changed in the eighteenth century. Most tribes had earlier been loose confederations of villages and clans, each exercising local autonomy. The Creek, Cherokee, and Iroquois gave primary loyalty to the village, not to the tribe or confederacy. But trade, diplomatic contact, and war with Europeans required more coordinated policies. To deal effectively with traders and officials, the villages gradually adjusted to more centralized leadership.

Cherokee political organization in the eighteenth century illustrates the changes overcoming tribal societies. Early in the century, the nearly autonomous village formed the basic unit of political authority. But tension with Creek neighbors and intermittent hostilities with English traders and settlers pressed home the need for coordinated decision making. By 1750, the Cherokee had formed an umbrella political organization that under the leadership of Chief Old Hop gathered together the fragmented authority of the villages and formed a more centralized tribal "priest state."

When even this proved inadequate, warriors began to assume the dominant role in tribal councils, replacing the civil chiefs. By this process, the Cherokee reorganized their political structure so that dozens of scattered villages could amalgamate their strength.

While incorporating trade goods into their material culture and adapting their economies and political structures to new situations, the interior tribes held fast to tradition in many ways. Unimpressed with most settler practices, they saw little reason to replace what they valued in their own culture. When they observed the colonists' systems of law and justice, religion, education, family organization, and child rearing, Native Americans often concluded that their own ways were superior.

The Indians' refusal to accept the superiority of white culture frustrated English missionaries, eager to win Native Americans from "savage" ways. Some colonists understood that the white behavior observed by natives cast doubts on the notion that Indians were of an inferior race. A Carolinian admitted that "they are really better to us than we are to them. We look upon them with scorn and disdain, and think them little better than beasts in human shape, though if well examined, we shall find that, for all our religion and education, we possess more moral deformities and evils than these savages do."

Despite maintaining many cultural practices, the interior Indian tribes suffered from the commercial, diplomatic, and military contact with the British colonizers. Decade by decade, the fur trade spread epidemic diseases, raised the level of warfare, depleted their lands of game animals, and drew the Native Americans into a market economy where their trading partners gradually became trading masters.

France's Inland Empire

While the powerful Iroquois, Cherokee, Creek, and Choctaw tribes interacted with British colonists to their east, they also dealt with a growing French presence to their west. Between 1699 and 1754, the French developed a system of small forts, trading posts, and agricultural villages throughout the central area of the continent. The aim was to connect French Canada to the Gulf of Mexico and hence keep the settlers in the English colonies pinned to the seaboard. French success in this vast region hinged partly on shrewd dealing with the Indian tribes, which by their numbers retained sovereignty over the land but gradually succumbed to French diseases, French arms, and French-promoted intertribal wars.

At the same time, however, because France's interior empire was organized primarily as a military, trading, and missionizing operation, the French settlers arrived with few French women. This led to a long period when French males encountered Indians in a state of need—not only a need for trading partners, allies, and souls to be converted, but also as sexual consorts. From this need came the mingling of French and Indian peoples—what the French called *metissage*—in the vast North American interior. It was almost unthinkable for a French fur trader to do business without an Indian wife who could pave the way for his trading with the Ojibway, Menominee, or any other Great Lakes tribe.

Such interracial marriages, soon to be called "the custom of the country," were desired by the Indians as well as the French. Marital alliances created mutually beneficial social ties that cemented trade relations and military alliances. French traders were drawn into Indian kinship circles, making trade flow smoothly, while Indians gained protection against their enemies and access to provisions at the French trading posts. Though the French sometimes descended into fierce warfare with Indian peoples, the North American heartland was a cultural merging ground and a marrying ground as well as a trading ground and a battle ground.

For a full century after 1650, the French Jesuits and fur traders had been building a crescent of settlements and military posts extending down the St. Lawrence River basin, through the Great Lakes, and southward down the Mississippi Valley to the Gulf of Mexico. Even though thinly dotted with farming communities such as Kaskasia and Prairie du Chien, this vast French presence in the continent's heartland created an effective shield against the expansion-minded British to the east. As the French population grew to about 70,000 by 1750, they demonstrated uniquely how European settlers could coexist with Indian peoples by negotiating incessantly with Indian leaders, by respecting Indian ways of conducting trade, and—above all—by mingling so thoroughly with Indians that almost all French communities in North America's interior were mixed-race communities. French Louisiana, for example, had more mixed-race children and more white and black men who lived with Native Americans than any Anglo-American colony.

In 1718, the few hundred early French pioneers of the interior were suddenly inundated when France settled New Orleans at great cost by transporting almost 7,000 whites and 5,000 African slaves to the mouth of the Mississippi River. Disease rapidly whittled down these numbers, and an uprising of the powerful Natchez tribe in 1729 discouraged further French immigration. Most of the survivors settled around the little town of New Orleans in long, narrow plantations stretching from the Mississippi River to the endless cypress swamps. Slaves made wood products from cypress and pine for the West Indies and produced indigo, rice, and other crops for France. New Orleans merchants also received wheat from the little farming villages taking root in Illinois; bear oil and tobacco from settlements around the western post of Natchitoches; beef from herds in the Mobile valley; produce from the small upriver German village, Les Allemandes; and tens of thousands of deer skins and other pelts delivered annually by Indians for trade goods.

In its economy and society, New Orleans much resembled early Charleston, South Carolina. What distinguished the people of New Orleans from those of Charleston, however, was that the French knew nothing of representative political institutions. Ruled by a governor, a commissary and chief judge, and a small appointed council, the people had no elections or assembly, no newspapers or taxes. Because the French king paid dearly to keep the town's troops supplied, he would share power with no one, although he granted planters many favors. A mid-century English observer noted that the planter "is considered as a Frenchman venturing his life, enduring a species of banishment, and undergoing great hardships for the benefit of his country, for which reason he has great indulgence shown." This could not have been said of English planters in Georgia, South Carolina, or Virginia.

From its first introduction in Louisiana in 1719, French plantation slavery grew so that by 1765, blacks outnumbered whites. Most slaves and a majority of whites lived in the New Orleans area. The conditions of life for slaves differed little from the southern English colonies. In Louisiana, slaves also lived in simple cabins and worked under the sun and the lash in a master's fields and swamps. But the French had a paternalistic black legal code that gave slaves some protection in courts. When the Spanish took over the colony in 1769, they instituted their law guaranteeing slaves the right to buy freedom with money earned in their free time. Soon a large free black class emerged, headed by substantial people like Simon Calfat, who ran various enterprises, helped other slaves pay for their freedom, and headed the company of free black militia. When Americans acquired the colony in 1803, they suppressed freedom purchase and discouraged manumission.

Most blacks who lived outside the British colonies labored in New Orleans, but a few could be found pioneering elsewhere beyond the Appalachians. By the early eighteenth century, slaves who escaped Spanish, French, or English masters formed bands in the interior that allied them with Indian tribes. The Spanish settlers in Texas and California carried a few blacks with them. A supreme expression of the range of possibilities occurred just before the American Revolution when a free black of West Indian parentage, Jean-Baptiste Point Du Sable, with his Potawatom wife Kittihawa, set down the first settlement in what was to become Chicago. A few years later, the British army arrested Point Du Sable and his fellow pioneers as sympathizers with the American rebels.

Spain's America

In the first half of the eighteenth century, the Spanish still possessed by far the largest empire in the Americas. But in North America, the Spanish had great difficult defending their Florida mission network and military posts, while trying on a shoestring to counter the French expansion in the

French and Spanish Occupation of North America, to 1776

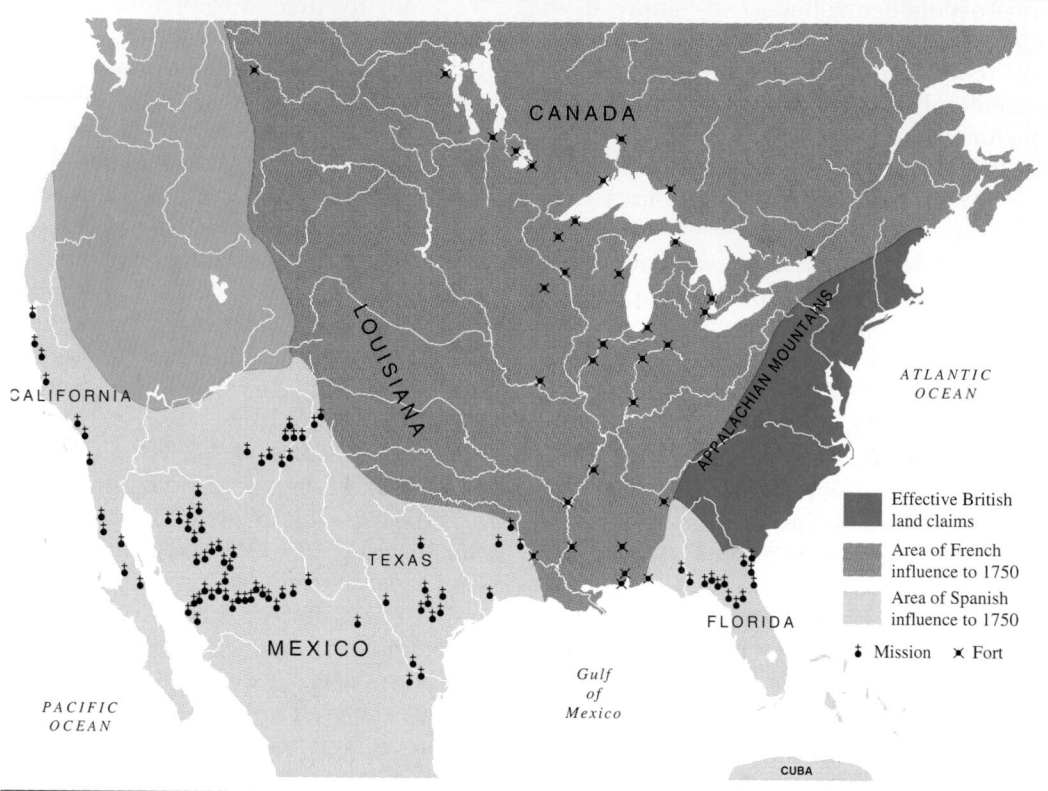

Although the Spanish and French settled only puny numbers of colonists in comparison to the English, they established themselves through trade and missionary activities over vast regions of North America.

Mississippi River watershed with military posts in Texas and New Mexico. Hispanics, mestizos, and detribalized Indians began to increase modestly in Texas, New Mexico, and California in the first half of the eighteenth century, but in fact they were falling farther and farther behind in relation to the English and French. The English in South Carolina were ten times as numerous as the Spanish in Florida by 1745, and the gap kept widening year by year. New Mexico's Hispanic population of about 10,000 at mid-century could defend the vast region only because no European challenger appeared.

As in New France, racial intermixture and social fluidity were more extensive in New Spain than in the English colonies. Precise counts of the various elements of society in these Spanish areas are rare because the Spanish never defined racial groups as distinctly as the English. The word *Spaniard* on a census might mean a white immi-

grant from Mexico or a part-Indian person who "lived like a Spaniard." Social mobility was considerable because the crown was willing to raise even a common person to the status of *hidalgo* (minor nobleman) as an inducement to settle in New Spain's remote northern frontier. Most of the immigrants became small ranchers, producing livestock, corn, and wheat for export to other Spanish provinces to the south.

The Native Americans of New Mexico were unusually successful in resisting Spanish domination. An early nineteenth-century Spanish investigator explained part of the reason by describing the *kivas* maintained by Pueblo people. These were "like impenetrable temples, where they gather to discuss mysteriously their misfortunes or good fortunes, their happiness or grief. The doors of these estufas are always closed to us." Through this secrecy, the Pueblos clung to their traditions better than most tribes.

The tribes of California were less successful in maintaining cultural cohesion. In the 1770s, the Spanish rapidly completed their western land and sea routes from San Diego to the new port of Yerba Buena (San Francisco) to block Russian settlement south of their base in northern California. The Spanish pioneers were Franciscan missionaries, accompanied by soldiers provided by the crown. The priests would choose a good location and then attract a few Indians to baptism by gifts and preaching. The priests settled "neophytes" next to the mission, which they helped build. When their relatives came to visit, priests induced them to stay as well. These Indians lived under an increasingly harsh regimen until they were reduced to a condition of virtual slavery. The California mission, with its extensive and profitable herds and grain crops, theoretically belonged to the Indian converts, but they did not enjoy the profits. Priests even hired them out to immigrant Spaniards. Ironically, the spiritual motives of the priests resulted in the same reduction and degradation of tribal Americans as elsewhere.

A Land of Family Farms

Population growth and economic development gradually transformed the landscape of eighteenth-century British America. Three variations of colonial society emerged: the farming society of the North, the plantation society of the South, and the urban society of the seaboard commercial towns. Although they shared some important characteristics, each was distinct.

Northern Agricultural Society

In the northern colonies, especially New England, tightknit farming families, organized in communities of several thousand people, dotted the landscape by the mid-eighteenth century. New Englanders staked their future on a mixed economy. They cleared forests for timber used in barrels, ships, houses, and barns. They plumbed the offshore waters for fish that fed both local populations and the ballooning slave population of the West Indies. And they cultivated and grazed as much of the thin-soiled, rocky hills and bottomlands as they could recover from the forest.

The farmers of the middle colonies—Pennsylvania, Delaware, New Jersey, and New York—set their wooden plows to much richer soils than New Englanders did. They enjoyed the additional advantage of settling an area cleared by Native Americans who had relied more on agriculture than New England tribes. Thus favored, mid-Atlantic farm families produced modest surpluses of corn, wheat, beef, and pork. By the mid-eighteenth century, New York and Philadelphia ships were carrying these foodstuffs not only to the West Indies, always a primary market, but also to areas that could no longer feed themselves—England, Spain, Portugal, and even New England.

In the North, the broad ownership of land distinguished farming society from every other agricultural region of the Western world. Although differences in circumstances and ability led gradually toward greater social stratification, in most communities, the truly rich and abjectly poor were few and the gap between them small compared with European society. Most men other than indentured servants lived to purchase or inherit a farm of at least 50 acres. With their family's labor, they earned a decent existence and provided a small inheritance for each of their children. Settlers valued land highly, for freehold tenure ordinarily guaranteed both economic independence and political rights.

Amid widespread property ownership, a rising population pressed against a limited land supply by the eighteenth century, especially in New England. Family farms could not be divided and subdivided indefinitely, for it took at least 50 acres (of which only a quarter could usually be cropped) to support a single family. In Concord, Massachusetts, for example, the founders had worked farms averaging about 250 acres. A century later, in the 1730s, the average farm had shrunk by two-thirds, as farm owners struggled to provide an inheritance for the three or four sons that the average marriage produced.

The decreasing fertility of the soil compounded the problem of dwindling farm size. When land had been plentiful, farmers planted crops in the same field for three years and then let it lie fallow in pasturage seven years or more until it regained its fertility. But on the smaller farms of the eighteenth century, farmers had reduced fallow time to only a year or two. Such intense use of the soil reduced crop yields, forcing farmers to plow marginal land or shift to livestock production. Such was the process that led Jaret Eliot, New England's first agricultural essayist, to refer to "our old land which we have worn out."

The diminishing size and productivity of family farms forced many New Englanders to move to the frontier or out of the area altogether in the eighteenth century. "Many of our old towns are too full of inhabitants for husbandry, many of them living on small shares of land," bemoaned one Yankee. In Concord, one of every four adult males migrated from town every decade from the 1740s on, and in many towns out-migration was even greater. Some drifted south to New York and Pennsylvania. Others sought opportunities as artisans in the coastal towns or took to the sea. More headed for the colony's western frontier or north into New Hampshire and the eastern frontier of Maine. Several thousand New England families migrated even farther north, to the Annapolis valley of Nova Scotia. Throughout New England after the early eighteenth century, most farmers' sons knew that their destiny lay elsewhere.

Wherever they took up farming, northern cultivators engaged in agricultural work routines that were far less intense than in the South. The growing season was much shorter, and the cultivation of cereal crops required incessant labor only during spring planting and autumn harvesting. This less burdensome work rhythm led many northern cultivators to fill out their calendars with intermittent work as clockmakers, shoemakers, carpenters, and weavers.

Changing Values

Boston's weather on April 29, 1695, began warm and sunny, noted the devout merchant Samuel Sewall in his diary. But by afternoon, thunder, lightning, and hailstones "as big as pistol and musket bullets" pummeled the town. Sewall dined that evening with Cotton Mather, New England's most prominent Puritan clergyman. Mather wondered why "more ministers' houses than others proportionately had been smitten with lightning." The words were hardly out of his mouth before hailstones began to shatter the windows of Sewall's house, "flying to the middle of the room or farther." Sewall and Mather fell to their knees and broke into prayer together "after this awful Providence."

These two third-generation Massachusetts Puritans understood that God was angry with them as leaders of a people whose piety and moral rectitude were being overtaken by worldliness. Even if farms were getting smaller and open land scarcer, growth and success had undermined early utopian dreams and made Massachusetts "sermon-proof," as one dejected minister put it.

In other parts of the North, the expansive environment and the Protestant emphasis on self-discipline and hard work were also breeding qualities that would become hallmarks of American culture: an ambitious outlook, individualistic behavior, and a love of material things. In Europe, most tillers of the soil expected little from life. With no frontier lands ripe for exploitation, impoverished peasant farmers viewed life not as a quest for achievement, but as a perpetual struggle against famine and disease. In America, starvation was almost unknown, and few obstacles held people back from uncharted expanses of land once they had overwhelmed the Native Americans. "Every man," one colonist remarked, "expects one day or another to be upon a footing with his wealthiest neighbor."

Commitment to religion, family, and community did not disappear in the eighteenth century. But fewer men and women saw daily existence as a preparation for the afterlife. They began to regard

A proud and prosperous Rhineland immigrant, Martin Van Bergen, had this mural painted over the mantelpiece of his New York farmhouse, giving us a rare view of a colonial farm. (New York State Historical Association, Cooperstown)

The wit and pragmatic wisdom of Boston-born Benjamin Franklin made his Poor Richard's Almanack *the most widely read book in the colonies after the Bible. (Historical Society of Pennsylvania, Philadelphia)*

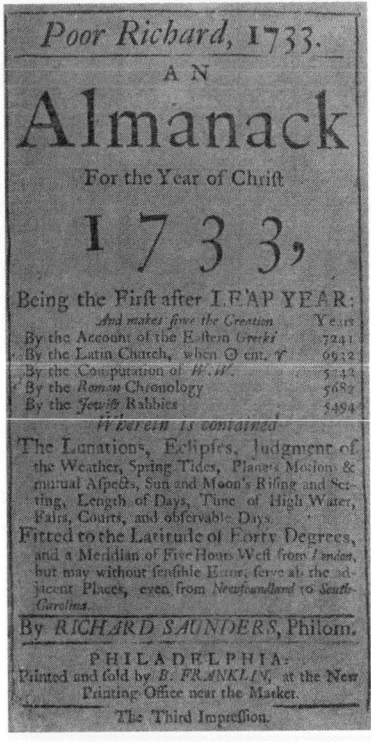

land not simply as a source of livelihood, but as a commodity to be bought and sold for profit. "Every man is for himself," sighed a Philadelphia leader only a generation after Penn had planted his "holy experiment." A few decades later, a New Yorker wrote that "the only principle of life propagated among the young people is to get money, and men are only esteemed according to what they are worth, that is, the money they are possessed of."

A slender almanac, written by the twelfth child of a poor Boston candlemaker, captured the new outlook with wit and charm. Born in 1706, Benjamin Franklin had climbed the ladder of success spectacularly. Running away from a harsh apprenticeship to an older brother when he was 16, he abandoned a declining Boston for a rising Philadelphia. By 23, he had learned the printer's trade and was publishing the *Pennsylvania Gazette.* Three years later, he began *Poor Richard's Almanack,* next to the Bible the most widely read book in the colonies.

Franklin spiced his annual almanac—the ordinary person's guide to weather and useful information—with quips, adages, and homespun philosophy. Eventually, this homely material added up to a primer for success published in 1747

as *The Way to Wealth.* "The sleeping fox gathers no poultry" and "Lost time is never found again," advised Poor Richard, emphasizing that time is money. "It costs more to maintain one vice than to raise two children," he counseled, advocating not morality, but practicality. "Sloth makes all things difficult but industry all easy," he assured his readers. Ever cocky, Franklin caught the spirit of the rising secularism of the eighteenth century. He embodied the growing utilitarian doctrine that the good is whatever is useful and the notion that the community is best served through individual self-improvement and accomplishment.

Women and the Family in Northern Colonial Society

In 1662, Elnathan Chauncy, a Massachusetts schoolboy, copied into his writing book that the soul "consists of two portions, inferior and superior; the superior is masculine and eternal; the feminine inferior and mortal." This lesson had been taught for generations on both sides of the Atlantic. It was part of a larger conception of a world, of God's design, that assigned degrees of status and stations in life to all individuals. In such a world, the place of women was, by definition, subordinate to that of men. From infancy, women were taught to be modest, patient, compliant. Regarded by men as weak of mind and large of heart, they existed for and through men. As daughters they were subject to their fathers, as wives to their husbands. John Winthrop reflected the common view that such submission was natural, and hence "a true wife accounts her subjection her honor."

European women usually accepted these narrowly circumscribed roles. Few complained, at least openly, that their work was generally limited to housewifery and midwifery. They remained silent about exclusion from the early public schools and laws that transferred to their husbands any property or income they brought into a marriage. Nor could women speak in their churches or participate in governing them (except in Quaker meetinghouses), and they had no legal voice in political affairs. Most women did not expect to choose a husband for love; parental guidance prevailed in a society in which producing legal heirs was the means of transmitting property. Once wed, women expected to remain so until death, for they could rarely obtain a divorce.

On the colonial frontier, women's lives changed in modest ways. In Europe, about one of ten women did not marry. But in the colonies, where men outnumbered women for the first century, a spinster was almost unheard of, and widows remarried with astounding speed. "A young widow with 4 or 5 children, who among the middling or inferior ranks of people in Europe would have little chance for a second husband," observed one Englishman, "is in America frequently courted as a sort of fortune." *Woman* and *wife* thus became nearly synonymous.

A second difference concerned property rights. Single women and widows in the colonies, as in England, could make contracts, hold and convey property, represent themselves in court, and conduct business. Under English common law, a woman forfeited these rights, as well as all property, when she married. In the colonies, however, legislatures and courts gave wives more control over property brought into marriage or left at their husbands' death. They also enjoyed broader rights to act for and with their husbands in business transactions. In addition, young colonial women slowly gained the right of consenting to a marriage partner—a right that came by default to the thousands of female indentured servants who completed their labor contracts and had no parents within 3,000 miles to dictate to them.

Although colonial society did not encourage or reward female individuality and self-reliance, women worked alongside their husbands in competent and complementary ways. Women had limited career choices and rights but broad responsibilities. The work spaces and daily routines of husband and wife overlapped and intersected far more than today. Farm women as well as men worked at planting, harvesting, and milking cows. Women also made candles and soap, butter and cheese, and smoked meat; they made cloth and sometimes marketed farm products. A merchant's wife kept shop, handled accounts when her husband voyaged abroad, and helped supervise the servants and apprentices. "Deputy husbands" and "yoke mates" were revealing terms used by New Englanders to describe eighteenth-century wives.

Women also figured importantly in neighborhood life. Within female networks, dictated by custom rather than by law, older women shaped the behavior of young women, aided the needy, and subtly affected menfolk, who held the formal reins of authority. In Church life, where they outnumbered men, women worked privately in their families to promote religion in outlying areas, to seat and unseat ministers, and to influence the community's moral life. Periodically, they appeared as visionaries and mystics. Schooled to believe that they were inferior and subordinate, women nonetheless operated within their families and localities to shape the world around them.

Women held vital responsibilities as midwives. Until the late eighteenth century, the "obstetrick art" was almost entirely in women's hands. Midwives such as Anne Hutchinson counseled pregnant women, delivered babies, supervised postpartum recovery, and participated in ceremonies of infant baptism and burial. Mrs. Phillips, an immigrant to Boston in 1719, who delivered more than 3,000 infants in her 42-year career, was a familiar figure as she hurried through the streets to attend the lying-in of about 70 women each year. Because colonial women were pregnant or nursing infants for about half their years between the ages 20 and 40 and because childbirth was a recurring and dangerous crisis, the circle of female friends and relatives who attended childbirth created strong networks of mutual assistance.

In her role as wife and mother, the eighteenth-century northern woman differed somewhat from her English counterpart. Whereas English women married in their mid-twenties, American women typically took husbands a few years earlier. This head start increased their childbearing years. Hence, the average colonial family included five children (two more typically died in infancy), whereas the English family contained fewer than three. Gradually, as the coastal plain filled up in the eighteenth century and older family farms were divided and subdivided among descendants of the early settlers, marriage age crept up and the number of children per family inched down.

Northern child-rearing patterns differed considerably. In the seventeenth century, stern fathers dominated Puritan family life, and few were reluctant to punish unruly children. "Better whip'd than damn'd," advised Cotton Mather, the minister who served as the Puritan conscience of New England. Many parents believed that breaking the young

Childbirth was an oft-repeated event in the lives of most colonial wives. In this portrait of the Cheney family, the older woman is a nanny or mother-in-law; the younger woman holding a baby is Mr. Cheney's second wife. (Anonymous, The Cheney Family, c. 1795, National Gallery of Art, Washington, D.C., Gift of Edgar William and Bernice Chrysler Garbisch)

child's will created a pious and submissive personality. In Quaker families, however, mothers played a more active role in child rearing. More permissive, they relied on tenderness and love rather than guilt to mold their children. Attitudes toward choosing a marriage partner also separated early Puritan and Quaker approaches to family life. Puritan parents usually arranged their children's marriages but allowed them the right to veto. Young Quaker men and women made their own matches, subject to parental veto.

Despite this initial diversity in child rearing, the father-dominated family of New England gradually declined in the eighteenth century. In its place rose the mother-centered family, in which affectionate parents encouraged self-expression and independence in their children. This "modern" approach, on the rise in Europe as well, brought the colonists closer to the methods of parenthood found among the coastal Native Americans, who initially had been widely disparaged for their lax approach to rearing their young.

Ecological Transformation

Wherever Europeans settled in the Americas, they brought with them animals, plant life, diseases, and ways of viewing the natural resources they found—all of which had enormous consequences for the ecosystems they were entering. In New Spain, the Spanish introduction of grazing animals—cattle, horses, pigs, sheep, and goats—profoundly altered the landscape. Breeding prolifically in an environment generally free of animal predators, pigs and cattle devoured the tall grasses and most palatable plant species. Within a half century, the domesticated animals left huge areas with little or no ground cover. In this rearranged landscape, new unwelcome plant species took hold—stinging nettles, nightshade, and dandelions.

In England's North American colonies, the rapid increase of settlers after 1715 had different environmental effects. Two were of special importance. First, the demand for wood—for building and heating houses, for producing the charcoal necessary for ironmaking, for shipbuilding and barrelmaking—led to a swift depletion of the forests near the coast. Just for heating and cooking, the typical northern farmhouse required an acre of trees each year. An iron furnace needed 20,000 acres of forest to produce a thousand tons of iron. A 40-acre field required 8,000 fence rails. With the population explosion of the eighteenth century, the price of firewood quickly rose as woodcutters ventured farther and farther inland.

Rapid and often wasteful harvesting of the forests had many effects. As the colonists chopped

The distribution of cultivated fields, dwellings, and commercial buildings in the tidewater landscape created "communities" without towns (rendered from historical and archaeological evidence). (From The Transformation of Virginia, 1740-1790 *by Rhys Isaac. Copyright © 1982 by the University of North Carolina Press. Published for the Institute of Early American History and Culture. Used by permission of the publisher.)*

down the forest canopy that had previously moderated the weather, the summers became hotter and the winters colder. In deforested areas, the snow melted sooner, and, as the winter's melting snow ran off more quickly, watersheds emptied faster. This, in turn, caused soil erosion and periods of drought.

A second ecological transformation occurred when animals brought by Europeans began to replace animals already in North America. European colonists were a livestock people, skilled in mixed farming and herding of domesticated cattle, horses, pigs, sheep, and goats. Such animals provided food, leather, fibers for clothmaking, and the sheer pulling and carrying power relied on by a people who had no other source of energy than their own muscles. Multiplying rapidly in a favorable environment, pigs and cattle "swarm like vermin upon the earth," reported one Virginia account as early as 1700. In some areas, the animals multiplied so rapidly and denuded the native grasses and shrubs so quickly that they actually ate themselves out of subsistence and began to die for lack of grazing land.

While European livestock filled the land, the native fur-bearing animals—beaver, deer, bear, wolf, raccoon, and marten—rapidly became extinct in the areas of settlement. Prized for their

skins, or hated as predators of domesticated animals, these species were hunted relentlessly as the colonists offered trade goods to Native Americans in exchange for pelts. One broken link in the ecological chain affected connecting links. For example, the dams and ponds of the beaver, which had been breeding grounds for many species of wild ducks, soon were drained and converted to meadows on which grazing cattle could live.

Animals prized for dinner table fare also quickly reached extinction along the East Coast. Wild turkeys were a rarity in Massachusetts by the 1670s. Deer disappeared by the early 1700s in settled areas. "Hunting with us exists chiefly in the tales of other times," wrote Yale's president in the late eighteenth century.

All these environmental changes were linked not only to the numbers of Europeans arriving in North America, but also to their ways of thinking about nature. Looking out over wooded hills and fertile valleys, transplanted Europeans could only imagine the possibility of raising valuable crops as if the ecosystem was composed of unconnected elements, each ripe for exploitation. Land, lumber, fish, and fur-bearing animals could be converted into sources of cash that would buy imported commodities that improved one's material condition. The New England writer Edward Johnson described the process perceptively as early as 1653: Who would have imagined, he mused, "that this wilderness should turn a mart for merchants in so short a space, Holland, France, Spain, and Portugal coming hither for trade?" Supplying these Europeans were the farmers, woodcutters, and fishermen who consigned to the marketplace huge portions of the ecosystem that in the world of Native Americans were all-important for sustaining life but were not part of a transoceanic system of commercial exchange.

Coming from homelands where land was scarce, the settlers viewed their ability to reap nature's abundance in North America as proof of their success. From their perspective, they were correct because in fact colonial agriculture was abundantly successful in terms of what the settlers obliged the land to yield up. Yet the "rage for commerce" and for an improved life produced wasteful practices on farms and in forests and fisheries. "The grain fields, the meadows, the forests, the cattle, etc.," wrote a Swedish visitor in the 1750s, "are treated with equal carelessness." Accustomed to the natural abundance once the native peoples had been driven from the land, and seeing no limits to the land that was available, the colonists embarked on ecologically destructive practices that over a period of many generations profoundly altered the natural world around them.

The Plantation South

Between 1680 and 1750, the white tidewater settlements of the southern colonies made the transition from a frontier society marked by a high immigration rate, a surplus of males, and an unstable social organization to a settled society composed mostly of native-born families. After 1715, Scots-Irish and German immigrants flooded into the backcountry of Virginia, the Carolinas, and Georgia, this last intended as a debtors' haven but designed in 1732 as a buffer between Spanish Florida and the Carolinas. But between the piedmont region and the ocean, a mature southern culture took form.

The Tobacco Coast

Tobacco production in Virginia and Maryland expanded rapidly in the seventeenth century, with exports reaching 25 million pounds annually during the 1680s. But war in Europe and the Americas for the two decades bridging the turn of the century drove up transportation costs and dampened the demand for tobacco. Stagnation in the tobacco market lasted from the mid-1680s until about 1715.

Yet it was in this period that the Upper South underwent a profound social transformation. First, slaves replaced indentured servants so rapidly that by 1730 the unfree labor force was overwhelmingly black. Second, the planters responded to the depressed tobacco market by diversifying their crops. They shifted some of their tobacco fields to grain, hemp, and flax; increased their herds of cattle and swine; and became more self-sufficient by developing local industries to produce iron, leather, and textiles. By the 1720s, when a profitable tobacco trade with France created a new period of prosperity, their economy was much more diverse and resilient than a generation before.

Third, the structure of the population changed rapidly. Black slaves grew from about 7 percent to more than 40 percent of the region's population between 1690 and 1750, and the drastic imbalance between white men and women disappeared. Families rather than single men now predominated. The earlier frontier society of white immigrants who mostly lived short and unrewarding lives as indentured servants grew into an eighteenth-century plantation society of native-born freeholder families.

Notwithstanding the influx of Africans, slave owning was far from universal. As late as 1750, a majority of families owned no slaves at all. Among slave owners, not more than one-tenth held more than 20 slaves. Nonetheless, the common goal was the large plantation where black slaves made the earth yield up profits to support an aristocratic life for their masters. As one Virginia minister observed, "the custom of the country is such that without slaves a man's children stand but a poor chance to marry in reputation."

The Chesapeake planters who acquired the best land and accumulated enough capital to invest heavily in slaves created a gentry life-style that set them apart from ordinary farmers such as Devereaux Jarratt's father. By the eighteenth century, the development of the northern colonies had produced prosperous farmers worth several thousand pounds. But such wealth paled by comparison with the estates of men such as Charles Carroll of Maryland and Robert "King" Carter and William Byrd of Virginia. These Chesapeake planters counted their slaves by the hundreds, their acres by the thousands, and their fortunes by the tens of thousands of pounds.

Ritual display of wealth marked southern gentry life. Racing thoroughbred horses and gambling on them recklessly, sometimes for purses of £100 (at a time when a laboring man earned £40 per year), became common sport for young gentlemen, who had often been educated in England. Planters began to construct stately brick Georgian mansions, some designed by imported English architects. These "greathouses," similar in style to the houses of English gentry, were filled with imported furniture, attended by liveried black slaves, and graced by formal gardens and orchards.

Some observers saw the cultivated aristocratic life-style as a veneer. "If a [man] has Money, Negroes, and Land enough," scoffed a Scottish newcomer, "he is a complete Gentleman. These hide all his defects, usher him into the best of company, and draw upon him the smiles of the fair Sex." Affected or not, the emerging Chesapeake planter elite controlled the county courts, officered the local militia, ruled the parish vestries of the Anglican Church, and made law in their legislative assemblies. To their sons, they passed the mantle of political and social leadership.

For all their social display, southern planter squires were essentially agrarian businessmen. They spent their days obtaining credit, dealing in land and slaves, scheduling planting and harvesting routines, conferring with overseers, disciplining slaves, and arranging leases with tenants. Cultivating tobacco was a particularly demanding enterprise and a highly personal one. Whereas other staple crops such as wheat and corn required intensive labor only during the planting and harvesting seasons, tobacco demanded the planter's attention throughout the year as the crop moved through the many stages of planting, transplant-

ing, topping, cutting, curing, and packing. A planter's reputation rose and fell with the quality of his crop, and so personalized was the culture of tobacco that planters stamped their hogsheads of leaf with their initials or emblem. "Question a planter on the subject," explained one observer, "and he will tell you that he cultivates such or such a kind [of tobacco], as for example, Colonel Carter's sort, John Cole's sort or [that of] some other leading crop master."

Planters' wives also shouldered many responsibilities. They superintended cloth production and the processing and preparation of food while ruling over households crowded with children, slaves, and visitors. An aristocratic veneer gave the luster of gentility to plantations from Maryland to North Carolina, but it could not disguise the fact that these were large working farms, often so isolated from one another that the planter and his wife lived a "solitary and unsociable existence," as one phrased it. With only infrequent contact with the outside world, they learned to be independent as they managed their own little communities of servants, slaves, and family members. Patriarchs on their estates, southern planters were "haughty and jealous of their liberties, impatient of restraint, and can scarcely bear the thought of being controlled by any superior power," noted Andrew Burnaby, a mid-eighteenth-century visitor.

The Rice Coast

The plantation economy of the Lower South in the eighteenth century rested on the production of rice and indigo. Rice exports surpassed 1.5 million pounds per year by 1710 and reached 80 million pounds by the eve of the Revolution. Indigo, a blue dye obtained from plants for use in textiles, became a staple crop in the 1740s after Eliza Lucas Pinckney, a wealthy South Carolina planter's wife, experimented successfully with its cultivation. Within a generation, indigo production had spread into Georgia. It soon ranked among the leading colonial exports.

The expansion of rice production transformed the swampy coastal lowlands. In the rice-producing region radiating out from Charleston, planters imported thousands of slaves after 1720; by 1740, slaves composed nearly 90 percent of the region's inhabitants. White population declined as wealthy planters left their estates in the hands of resident overseers. They wintered in cosmopolitan Charleston and summered in Newport, Rhode Island, their refuge from seasonal malaria along the rice coast. Rice converted the eighteenth-century Carolina coast into a tropical plantation regime similar to that of the sugar-producing West Indies. At mid-century, a shocked New England visitor described it as a society "divided into opulent and lordly planters, poor and spiritless peasants, and vile slaves."

Throughout the plantation South, the courthouse became a central gathering place for men. Court day brought together people of all classes. They came to settle debts, dispute land boundaries, sue and be sued. When court was over, a multitude lingered on, drinking, gossiping, and staging horse races, cockfights, wrestling matches, footraces, and fiddling contests. Competition and assertiveness lay at the heart of all these demonstrations of male personal prowess.

The church, almost always Anglican in the South before 1750, also became a center of community gathering. Philip Fithian described the animated socializing before worship, men "giving and receiving letters of business, reading advertisements, consulting about the price of tobacco and grain, and settling either the lineage, age, or qualities of favourite horses." Then, as the hour of service approached, people filed into church. Reaffirming the social gradation of their rank-conscious society, the lower and middling planters entered first. They stood attentively until the wealthy gentry, striding in together "in a body," took their pews at the front. After church, socializing continued, with young people strolling together and older ones extending invitations to Sunday dinner. The pious Sabbath atmosphere perpetuated in New England was little in evidence.

The Backcountry

While the southern gentry matured along the tobacco and rice coasts, settlers poured into the upland backcountry. As late as 1730, only hunters and Indian fur traders had known this vast expanse of hilly red clay and fertile limestone soils, stretching from Pennsylvania to Georgia. Over the next four decades, it attracted some 250,000 inhabitants, nearly half the southern white population.

Thousands of land-hungry German and Scots-Irish settlers spilled into the interior valleys running along the eastern side of the Appalachians. They squatted on land, lived tensely with neighboring Indians in a region where boundaries were shadowy, and created a subsistence society of small farms. Gradually acquiring slaves, this "mixed medley from all countries and the off scouring of America," as one colonist described them, pursued mixed farming and cattle raising. Their enclaves remained isolated from the coastal region for several generations, which helped these pioneers cling fiercely to the folkways they had known on the other side of the Atlantic.

The crudity of backcountry life appalled many visitors from the more refined seaboard. In 1733, William Byrd described a large Virginia frontier plantation as a "poor, dirty hovel, with hardly anything in

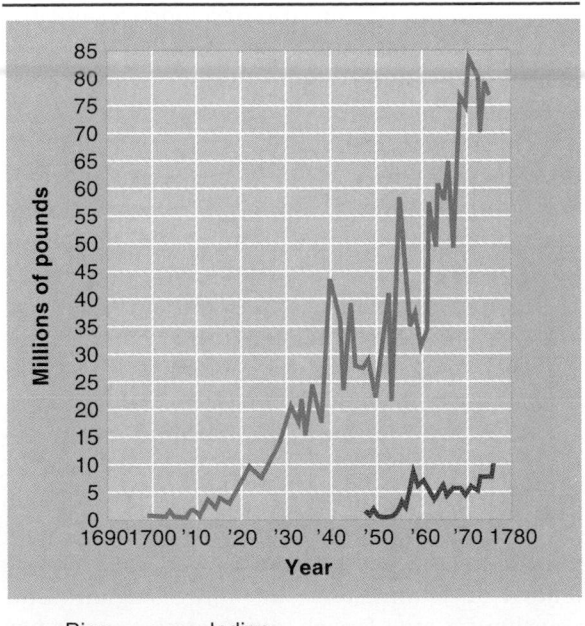

Rice and Indigo Exports from South Carolina and Georgia, 1698–1775

Just as Virginia had been built on tobacco, South Carolina and Georgia were built on rice. Much of it was sent to the West Indies to feed the huge population of enslaved Africans there. Source: U.S. Bureau of the Census.

it but children that wallowed about like so many pigs." Charles Woodmason, a stiff-necked Anglican minister who spent three years tramping between settlements in the Carolina upcountry, could hardly find words to express his shock. "Through the licentiousness of the people," he wrote, "many hundreds live in concubinage—swopping their wives as cattle and living in a state of nature more irregularly and unchastely than the Indians."

What Byrd and Woodmason were really observing was the poverty of frontier life and the lack of schools, churches, and towns. Most families plunged into the backcountry with only a few crude household possessions and farm tools, perhaps a pair of oxen, a few chickens and swine, and the clothes on their backs. They lived in rough-hewn log cabins—"cold cabins, unfloored and almost open to the sky," Woodmason observed— and planted their corn, beans, and wheat between the stumps of trees they had felled. Women toiled alongside men, in the fields, forest, and homestead. For a generation, these settlers endured a poor diet, endless work, and meager rewards.

By the 1760s, the southern backcountry had begun to emerge from the frontier stage. Small marketing towns such as Camden, South Carolina; Salisbury, North Carolina; Winchester, Virginia; and Fredericktown, Maryland, became centers of craft activity, Church life, and local government. Farms began producing surpluses for shipment east. Density of settlement increased, creating a social life known for harvest festivals, log-rolling contests, horse races, wedding celebrations, dances, and prodigious drinking bouts during which hard cider, whiskey, and apple and peach brandy flowed freely. Class distinctions remained narrow compared with the older seaboard settlements, as many backcountry settlements acquired the look of permanence.

Family Life in the South

As the South emerged from the early era of withering mortality and stunted families, male and female roles gradually became more physically and functionally separated. In most areas, the white gender ratio reached parity by the 1720s. Women lost the leverage in the marriage market that scarcity had provided earlier. With the growth of slavery, the work role of white women also changed. The wealthy planter's wife became the domestic manager in "the great house." In a description of his daughters' daily routine, William Byrd II pointed to the emerging female identity: "They are every day up to their elbows in housewifery, which will qualify them effectually for useful wives and if they live long enough for notable women."

The balanced sex ratio and the growth of slavery also brought changes for southern males. The planter's son had always been trained to operate in the world beyond the plantation-house doors. Learning horsemanship, the use of a gun, and the rhythms of agricultural life was as important a part of a young man's education as lessons with tutors such as Devereaux Jarratt. Ordering and disciplining slaves also became a part of the southern youth's education. Many had slaves of their own before reaching adulthood. Some planters worried that this would lead, as Thomas Jefferson would later write, to "odious peculiarities" in the character of southern men, because slavery involved a "perpetual exercise of the most boisterous passions" by white masters "nursed, educated, and daily exercised in tyranny." But bred to command, southern planters' sons also developed a self-confidence and authority that propelled many of them into leadership roles during the American Revolution.

On the small farms of the tidewater region and throughout the back settlements, women's roles closely resembled those of northern women. Women labored in the fields alongside their menfolk. "She is a very civil woman," noted an observer of a southern frontierswoman, "and shows nothing of ruggedness or immodesty in her carriage; yet she will carry a gun in the woods and kill deer and turkeys, shoot down wild cattle, catch and tie hogs, knock down beeves with an ax, and perform the most manful exercises as well as most men in those parts."

Marriage and family life were also more informal in the backcountry. With vast areas unattended by ministers of any religion and courthouses out of reach, most couples married or "took up" with each other in matches unsanctioned by state or Church. The arrival of an itinerant clergyman on horseback typically brought forth dozens of couples living in common-law marriage who asked to have vows performed and their children legitimized by baptism. Respectable clergymen saw the frontier settlers living in lascivious abandon. But the poor upcountry hunters and farmers were really only the first of many generations of pioneers who made do as best they could on the forest's edge, where the institutions of settled society had not yet arrived.

The Urban World of Commerce and Ideas

Only about 5 percent of the eighteenth-century colonists lived in towns as large as 2,500, and none of the commercial centers boasted a population greater than 16,000 in 1750 or 30,000 in 1775. Yet the urban societies were at the leading edge of social change. Almost all the alterations associated with the advent of "modern" life occurred first in the seaport towns and radiated outward to the villages, farms, and plantations of the hinterland. In the seaboard centers, the transition first occurred from a barter to a commercial economy, from a social order based on assigned status to one based on achievement, from rank-conscious and deferential politics to participatory and contentious politics, and from small-scale craftsmanship to factory production. In addition, the cities were the centers of intellectual life and the conduits through which European ideas flowed into the colonies.

Sinews of Trade

In the half century after 1690, Boston, New York, Philadelphia, and Charleston blossomed from urban villages into thriving commercial centers. This urban growth accompanied the development of the agricultural interior, to which the seaports were closely linked. As the colonial population rose and spread geographically, minor seaports such as Salem, Newport, Providence, Annapolis, Norfolk, and Savannah gathered 5,000 or more inhabitants.

Trade was indispensable to colonial economic life, and cities were trade centers. Through them flowed colonial export staples such as tobacco, rice, furs, wheat, timber products, and fish as well as the imported goods that colonists needed. The

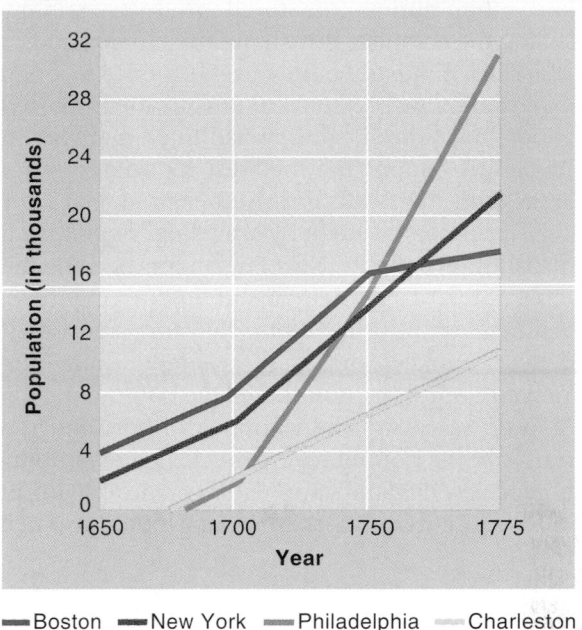

Urban Population Growth, 1650–1775

■Boston ■New York ■Philadelphia Charleston

By 1755, Boston had lost its lead as British North America's largest city. Plagued by costly wars and economic difficulties, its population leveled off, whereas that of other cities grew. Source: Gary B. Nash, *The Urban Crucible*, 1979.

imports included manufactured and luxury goods from England such as glass, paper, iron implements, and cloth; wine, spices, coffee, tea, and sugar from other parts of the world; and the human cargo to fill the labor gap. In these seaports, the pivotal figure was the merchant. Frequently engaged in both retail and wholesale trade, the merchant was also moneylender (for no banks yet existed), shipbuilder, insurance agent, land developer, and often coordinator of artisan production.

By the eighteenth century, the American economy was integrated into an Atlantic basin trading system that connected Great Britain, western Europe, Africa, the West Indies, and Newfoundland. The rulers of Great Britain, like those of other major trading nations of western Europe, pursued mercantilist trade policies. According to the principles of mercantilism, a country should strive to gain wealth by increasing its exports, levying duties on imports, regulating production and trade, and exploiting its colonies to its own advantage. The British followed these principles by controlling their colonies' trade, requiring their colonies to supply them with foodstuffs, lumber, and other nonmanufactured products, and by selling the colonists British manufactured goods.

The colonists could never produce enough exportable raw materials to pay for the imported goods they craved, so they had to earn credits in England by supplying the West Indies and other areas with foodstuffs and timber products. They also accumulated credit by providing shipping and distribution services. New Englanders became the most ambitious participants in the carrying trade. Sailing from Boston, Salem, Newport, and Providence, Yankee merchant seamen, manning Yankee-built ships, dominated the traffic along the Atlantic seaboard, the Caribbean trade, and the transatlantic commerce. A much higher proportion of New England's population made its living in maritime enterprise than in any other colonial region.

The Artisan's World

Though merchants stood first in wealth and prestige in the colonial towns, artisans were far more numerous. About two-thirds of urban adult males, slaves excluded, labored at handicrafts. By the mid-eighteenth century, the colonial cities contained scores of specialized "leather apron men," not only the proverbial butcher, baker, and candlestick maker, but also the carpenters and coopers (who made barrels); shoemakers and tailors; silver-, gold-, pewter-, and blacksmiths; mast and sail makers; masons, plasterers, weavers, potters; and many more. Handicraft specialization increased as the cities matured, but every artisan worked with hand tools, usually in small shops.

Work patterns for artisans were irregular, dictated by weather, hours of daylight, erratic delivery of raw materials, and shifting consumer demand. When ice blocked northern harbors, mariners and dockworkers endured slack time. If prolonged rain delayed the slaughter of cows in the country or made impassable the rutted roads into the city, the tanner and the shoemaker laid their tools aside. The hatter depended on the supply of beaver skins, which could stop abruptly if disease struck an Indian tribe or war disrupted the fur trade. Every urban artisan knew "broken days," slack

Most artisans thought of working under supervision as apprentices and journeymen as a temporary status because they aspired to self-employment. However, in a high-capital industry such as shipbuilding, most did not attain the status of master. (William Russell Birch, Preparation for War to Defend Commerce, 1800, Free Library of Philadelphia)

spells, and dull seasons. Ordinary laborers dreaded winter, for it was a season when cities had "little occasion for the labor of the poor," and firewood to heat even a small house could cost several months' wages.

Urban artisans took fierce pride in their crafts. While deferring to those above them, they saw themselves as the backbone of the community, contributing essential products and services. "Our professions rendered us useful and necessary members of our community," the Philadelphia shoemakers asserted; "proud of that rank, we aspired to no higher." This self-esteem and desire for community recognition sometimes jostled with the upper-class view of artisans as mere mechanics, part of the "vulgar herd."

In striving for respectability, artisans placed a premium on achieving economic independence. Every craftsman began as an apprentice, spending five or more teenage years learning the "mysteries of the craft" in the shop of a master "mechanick." After fulfilling his contract, the young artisan became a "journeyman." He sold his labor to a master craftsman and frequently lived in his house, ate at his table, and sometimes married his daughter. The journeyman hoped to complete within a few years the three-step climb from servitude to self-employment. After setting up his own shop, he could control his work hours and acquire the respect that came from economic independence. In trades requiring greater organization and capital, such as distilling and shipbuilding, the rise from journeyman to master proved impossible for many artisans. Nonetheless, the ideal of the independent craftsman prevailed.

In good times, urban artisans fared well. They expected to earn a "decent competency" and eventually to purchase a small house. But success was far from automatic, even for those following all of Poor Richard's advice about hard work and frugal living. An advantageous marriage, luck in avoiding illness, and the size of an inheritance were often the critical factors in whether an artisan moved up or down the ladder of success. In Philadelphia, about half the artisans dying in the first half of the eighteenth century left personal property worth between £50 and £200 sterling, signifying a comfortable standard of living. Another quarter left more than £200, often including slaves and indentured servants. New England's artisans did not fare so well, for their economy was weaker in the eighteenth century. But in all cities, artisans took pride in their life of productive labor. "The meanest [of them] thinks he has a right of civility from the greatest" person in the city, wrote one city dweller.

The Urban Social Structure

Population growth, economic development, and a series of wars that punctuated the period from 1690 to 1765 altered the urban social structure. Stately townhouses rose as testimony to the fortunes acquired in trade, shipbuilding, war contracting, and urban land development. This last may have been the most profitable of all. "It is almost a proverb," a Philadelphian observed in the 1760s, "that every great fortune made here within these 50 years has been by land." Some merchants amassed fortunes. A merchant's estate of £2,000 sterling was counted impressive in the early eighteenth century. Two generations later, some commercial titans had become North America's first millionaires by accumulating estates of £10,000 to £20,000 sterling.

The rise of Thomas Hancock, on whose fortune his less commercially astute nephew, John Hancock, would later construct a shining political career, provides a glimpse of how war could catapult an enterprising trader to affluence. Hancock, a minister's son, became a bookseller in Boston. An opportune marriage to the daughter of a prosperous merchant provided a toehold in commerce and enough capital to invest in several vessels. By 1735, Hancock had made enough money, much of it from smuggling tea, to build a mansion on Beacon Hill.

When war broke out with Spain in 1739, Hancock used his connections with the governor to obtain lucrative supply contracts for military expeditions to the Caribbean and Nova Scotia. He also invested heavily in privateers, who engaged in private warfare against enemy shipping and auctioned the enemy vessels they overpowered. When peace returned in 1748, all Boston witnessed what war had done for a well-connected merchant. The man who had sold books from a tiny shop on Drawbridge Street 15 years before now imported a four-horse chariot from London with the interior lined in scarlet and the doors emblazoned with a heraldic shield.

Alongside urban wealth grew urban poverty. From the beginning, every city had its disabled, orphaned, and widowed who required aid. But after 1720, poverty marred the lives of many more city dwellers. Many were war widows with numerous children and no means of support. Others were rural migrants seeking opportunities in the city. Some were recent immigrants, who found fewer chances for employment than earlier. Boston was hit especially hard. Its economy stagnated in the 1740s, and the taxpayers strained under the burden of paying for heavy war expenditures. The overseers of the poor groaned that their relief expenditures were double the outlays of any town of equal size "upon the face of the whole earth."

Burdened with mounting poor taxes, cities devised new ways of helping the needy. Rather than support the impoverished in their homes with "outrelief" payments, officials built large

Wealth Distribution in Colonial America

Percentage of wealth held by the richest 10% and the poorest 30% of the population in two cities and one rural area

Year	Richest 10%	Poorest 30%
Boston		
1684–1699	41.2	3.3
1700–1715	54.5	2.8
1716–1725	61.7	2.0
1726–1735	65.6	1.9
1736–1745	58.6	1.8
1746–1755	55.2	1.8
1756–1765	67.5	1.4
1766–1775	61.1	2.0
Philadelphia		
1684–1699	36.4	4.5
1700–1715	41.3	4.9
1716–1725	46.8	3.9
1726–1735	53.6	3.7
1736–1745	51.3	2.6
1746–1755	70.1	1.5
1756–1765	60.3	1.1
1766–1775	69.9	1.0
Chester County, Pennsylvania		
1693	23.8	17.4
1715	25.9	13.1
1730	28.6	9.8
1748	28.7	13.1
1760	29.9	6.3
1782	33.6	4.7

Source: Gary B. Nash, *The Urban Crucible*, 1979.

almshouses where the poor could be housed and fed more economically. Many of the indigent preferred "to starve in their homes," rather than leave their neighborhoods to suffer the discipline and indignities of the poorhouse. Boston's poor women also resisted laboring in the linen factory that was built in 1750 to enable them to contribute to their own support through spinning and weaving. Despite the warnings of Boston's ministers that "if any would not work, neither should they eat," they refused to leave their children at home to labor in America's first textile factory.

The increasing gap between the wealthy and the poor in the colonial cities was recorded in the eighteenth-century tax lists. The top 5 percent of taxpayers increased their share of the cities' taxable assets from about 30 to 50 percent between 1690 and 1770. The bottom half of the taxable inhabitants saw their share of the wealth shrink from about 10 to 4 percent. The urban middle classes, except in Boston, continued to make gains. But the growth of princely fortunes amid increasing poverty made some urban dwellers reflect that the conditions of the Old World seemed to be reappearing in the New.

The Entrepreneurial Ethos

As the cities grew, new values took hold. In the older, medieval, "corporate" view of society, economic life ideally operated according to what was equitable, not what was profitable. Citizens usually agreed that government should provide for the general welfare by regulating prices and wages, setting quality controls, licensing providers of service such as tavernkeepers and ferrymen, and supervising public markets where all food was sold. Such regulation seemed natural because a community was defined not as a collection of individuals, each entitled to pursue separate interests, but as a single body of interrelated parts where individual rights and responsibilities formed a seamless web.

In North America, as in Europe, new ideas about economic life gathered support. The subordination of private interests to the commonweal became viewed as a lofty but unrealistic ideal. Prosperity required the encouragement of acquisitive appetites rather than self-denial, for ambition would spur economic activity as more people sought more goods. According to the new view, if people were allowed to pursue their own material desires competitively, they would collectively form a natural, impersonal market of producers and consumers that would operate to everyone's advantage.

As the colonial port towns took their places in the Atlantic world of commerce, merchants became accustomed to making decisions according to the emerging commercial ethic that rejected traditional restraints on entrepreneurial activity. If wheat fetched 8 shillings a bushel in the West Indies but only 5 in Boston, a grain merchant felt justified in sending all he could purchase from local farmers to the more distant buyer. Indifferent to individuals and local communities, the new transatlantic market responded only to the invisible laws of supply and demand.

The tension between the new economic freedom and the older concern for the public good erupted only with food shortages or galloping inflation. Because the American colonies experienced none of the punishing famines that plagued Europe in this period, such crises occurred rarely, usually during war, when demand for provisions rose sharply.

Such a moment struck in Boston during Queen Anne's War. Merchant Andrew Belcher contracted to ship large quantities of wheat to the Caribbean, where higher prices would yield greater profit than in Boston. Ordinary neighbors, threatened with a bread shortage and angered that a townsman would put profit ahead of community needs, attacked one of Belcher's grain-laden ships in 1710. They sawed through the rudder and tried to run the vessel aground in order to seize the grain. Invoking the older ethic that the public welfare outweighed private interests, they took the law into their own hands. Even the grand jury, composed of substantial members of the community, hinted its approval of the violent action against Belcher by refusing to indict the rioters.

The two conceptions of community and economic life rubbed against each other for many decades. Urban merchants, shopkeepers, land speculators, and ambitious artisans—participants in England's rising commercial empire—cleaved more and more to the new economic formulas, although they continued to voice respect for the old precepts of the corporate community. The clergy continued to preach the traditional message: "Let no man seek his own, but every man another's wealth." But by the mid-eighteenth century, the pursuit of a profitable livelihood, not the social compact of the community, animated most city dwellers.

The American Enlightenment

Ideas about not only economic life but also the nature of the universe and improving the human condition reached across the Atlantic to the colonies. In the eighteenth century, an American version of the European intellectual movement called the Enlightenment occurred, and the cities became centers for disseminating these new ideas.

European thinkers, in what is called the Age of Reason, rejected the pessimistic Calvinist concept of innate human depravity, replacing it with the optimistic notion that a benevolent God had blessed humankind with the supreme gift of reason. Thinkers like John Locke, in his influential *Essay Concerning Human Understanding* (1689), argued that God had not predetermined the content of the human mind but furnished it with the capacity to acquire knowledge. All Enlightenment thinkers prized this acquisition of knowledge, for it allowed humankind to improve its condition. As the great scientific thinker Isaac Newton demonstrated, systematic investigation could unlock the secrets of the physical universe. Moreover, scientific knowledge could be applied to human institutions in order to improve society.

The scientific and intellectual advances of the seventeenth and eighteenth centuries encouraged a belief in "natural law" and debate about the "natural" rights of human beings. In Europe, French philosophers François Voltaire and Denis Diderot explored the issue of equality. From 1750 to 1772, Diderot published his *Encyclopedia,* which treated such topics as equality, liberty, reason, and rights. The ideas of the Enlightenment spread in Europe and the Americas and eventually found expression in movements for reform, democracy, and liberation—all of deep interest to those who were beginning to oppose slavery and the slave trade as abominations.

Though only a small number of educated colonists read the Enlightenment authors, they began in the eighteenth century to make significant contributions to the advancement of science. Naturalists such as John Bartram of Philadelphia ranged the eastern part of the continent gathering and describing American plants as part of the transatlantic attempt to classify all plant life into one universal system of classification. Professor

Sermons

Among seventeenth- and eighteenth-century colonists, sermons were the most popular form of reading other than the Bible and almanacs. Especially in New England, sermons came off the printing presses in great numbers and were far more common than books or political pamphlets. Usually consisting of 20 to 30 pages, sermons sold cheaply and could be easily passed from family to family. Sermon literature is therefore one of the most valuable sources for unearthing the history of pre-revolutionary North America.

Clergymen wrote sermons for numerous occasions. On days of fasting and thanksgiving, they urged their communities to behave righteously and keep the religious faith. At the funerals of important people, they delivered orations meant to inspire people to emulate the best qualities of the deceased. At hangings, they sermonized about the wages of sin. When colonial governments dispatched troops to fight against the French or Indians, they issued stirring calls for male courage in the face of the enemy. After earthquake, fire, drought, or military defeat, they explained the meaning of these calamities—usually in terms of the punishing hand of an angry God disappointed in his people. On Sunday after Sunday, ministers delivered sermons on a great variety of topics such as love, marriage, and child rearing; public and private morality; proper behavior for women, children, servants, and slaves; political and social controversies; war with European rivals and Native Americans; and, of course, religious controversy and religiosity itself. Thus, sermons are a record of a people's sense of their place in history, their values, their inner fears and insecurities, and their attitudes toward "others" in their communities such as Indians, enemies, and religious dissenters.

Precocious and prolific, Cotton Mather entered Harvard College at age 12 and went on to publish some 450 sermons, tracts, and books. He was the first American elected to England's Royal Society, the mother country's most important scientific organization. (Massachusetts Historical Society)

Fragments of two sermons are presented here. In the first, *A Sermon Preached After the Terrible Fire,* New England's most famous minister of the early 1700s, Cotton Mather, used the devastating fire of 1711 as an occasion to warn the citizens of Boston that they had strayed from the ways of piety and were being punished by God for their sins. In these passages, Mather was following a well-established practice of the clergy to issue *jeremiads*—laments that New Englanders were straying from the straight and narrow paths carved out by the pious founders of the Puritan colony of Massachusetts. Later in the sermon, however, Mather left clues about the social unrest occurring in Boston in 1711 during Queen Anne's War between the French and English. The unrest was caused by the shortages of bread and other provisions and by the profiteering of merchants that had left the city's poor in distress. This part of the sermon has an eerie resemblance to events in Los Angeles in 1992 during the riots over racial injustice. What social and ethical issues do you think need jeremiads by modern-day Mathers?

In the second sermon, Isaac Stiles of New Haven, Connecticut, tried to inspire the militia under the command of Colonel Nathan Whiting as it marched off to fight the French in the Seven Years' War in 1755. In *The Character and Duty of Soldiers,* Stiles condemned war as "one of the bitter fruits" that resulted from "the lusts of men, from pride, selfishness, malevolence, envy, avarice, etc." But Stiles soon moved on from these antiwar ponderings and focused on one of New England's most deeply held beliefs—that the Catholic French were the enemies not only of England, but of the Protestant God in whom New Englanders believed. His main purpose in the sermon was to inspire the troops with hatred of the French and convince them that their military expedition to Crown Point, on Lake Ticonderoga, was a divine mission with God on their side. The sermon tells us much about how colonial leaders tried to motivate their troops with religion in the middle of the eighteenth century. Take careful note of the incendiary language.

In what recent wars have American ministers (and politicians) used similar "sermonizing" to achieve nonreligious purposes? Do you think these are appropriate used of the sermon?

Both our State-house and the first-born of our meeting house are made a desolation; .... The great God has fired a couple of beacons, which call the whole province to take notice of them; and to consider how far they may be alarms to us in regard of our greatest interests. Unhappy we, oh! most unhappy! If after we have been so long incorrigible, we still refuse to receive correction. Oh! Let our behaviour be that of a people duly awakened by the consuming dispensations of God. If the fire will not awaken us, what will? God forbid that it should be said of us, "I have overthrown some of you by fire, and the rest of you are as a fire-brand pluck'd out of the burning, yet have ye not returned unto me," saith the Lord.

It is reported that when a consuming fire is raging there are thieves, who take that horrible occasion to seize and steal, and keep the goods that are saved out of the fire. The vilest sort of thieves that ever were heard of! ... To steal from any man at any time is a crying wickedness. But to steal from the neighbours at a time when the hand of God is upon them; to steal from the midst of the devouring flames, which the hand of God has kindled, I tell you truly 'tis a wickedness of a very prodigious elevation. O monstrous wretches! What have you done?

Segment from *A Sermon Preached After the Terrible Fire*

Be of good courage, and play the men for your people, and for the cities of your God; 'tis hopeful that you will be accessory to the humbling the price of France, the punishing the stout heart of their anti-christian, perfidious, and truce-breaking monarch and the glory of his high looks; scourging Canada, yea avenging of our Israel, and preventing the Romish faith its taking footing and gaining ground in this Protestant country. You are, I trust, in high spirits; full of the fury of the Lord, and resolved to do all that in you lies, in the defence of your dear country, sensible what numbers of blood-thirsty enemies are round about us on our borders ... whose tender mercies are cruelty and whose savage minds are continually whetted and exasperated against us by popish incendiaries.... Go out against them that in the name of the Lord we may cut 'em off or bring them to a better mind and to honourable and lasting terms of peace....

Segment from *The Character and Duty of Soldiers*

An ingenious lightning detector is shown (left) in Edward Fisher's portrait of Benjamin Franklin in 1763. Electricity from a violent thunderstorm, attracted by Franklin's famous lightning rod on top of his house, comes down through wire in glass tubes to set the two metal balls vibrating against each other with dramatic results. (The Granger Collection, New York) Franklin's global influence reached as far as Japan, as shown above in this Japanese electrical parlor game in 1813. (The Burndy Library, Dibner Institute for the History of Science and Technology)

John Winthrop III of Harvard made an unusually accurate measurement of the earth's distance from the sun. Standing above them all was Benjamin Franklin, whose spectacular (and dangerous) experiments with electricity, the properties of which were just becoming known, earned him an international reputation.

Franklin's true genius as a figure of the Enlightenment came, however, in his practical application of scientific knowledge. Among his inventions were the lightning rod, which nearly ended the age-old danger of fires when lightning struck wooden buildings; bifocal spectacles; and an iron stove that heated rooms—in an age when firewood was a major item in the household budget—far more efficiently than the open fireplace commonly used. Franklin also made his adopted home of Philadelphia a center of the American Enlightenment. He played a leading role in founding America's first circulating library in 1731, an artisans' debating club for "mutual improvement" through discussion of the latest ideas from Europe, and an intercolonial scientific association that would emerge in 1769 as the American Philosophical Society.

Though most colonists were not educated enough to participate actively in the American Enlightenment, the efforts of men such as Franklin exposed thousands, especially in the cities, to new currents of thought. This led to the growing sense that the colonists, blessed by their abundant environment, might truly inhabit the part of the world where the Enlightenment ideal of achieving a perfect society might be fulfilled.

The Great Awakening

Many of the social, economic, and political changes occurring in the eighteenth-century colonies converged in the Great Awakening, the first of many religious revivals that would sweep American society during the next two centuries. The timing, as well as the religious and social character of the Awakening, varied from region to region. But everywhere, this quest for spiritual renewal challenged old sources of authority and produced patterns of thought and behavior that helped fuel a revolutionary movement in the next generation.

Fading Faith

Colonial America in the early eighteenth century remained an overwhelmingly Protestant culture. The Puritan, or Congregational, Church dominated all of New England except Rhode Island. Anglicanism held sway in much of New York and throughout the South except the backcountry. In the mid-Atlantic and in the back settlements, a polyglot of German Mennonites, Dunkers, Moravians, and Lutherans; Scots-Irish Presbyterians; and English Baptists and Quakers mingled.

Yet these diverse groups commanded the allegiance of only about one-third of the colonists. Those who went to no church at all remained the majority. In many areas, ministers and churches were simply unavailable. In Virginia, the most populous colony, only 60 clergymen in 1761 served a population of 350,000—one parson for every 5,800 people.

In the eighteenth century, most colonial churches were voluntary or gathered ("congregated") groups, formed for reasons of conscience, not because of government compulsion. Catholics, Jews, and nonbelievers could not vote or hold office. But the persecution of Quakers and Catholics had largely passed, and some dissenting groups by 1720 had gained the right to use long-obligatory church taxes to support their own congregations.

The clergy often administered their congregations with difficulty. Anglicans and several German sects maintained close ties to mother churches across the Atlantic, whereas other denominations attempted to centralize authority. However, most efforts to tighten organization and discipline were ineffective. For example, Anglican ministers had to be ordained in England and make regular reports to the bishop of London. But once installed in Chesapeake parishes, Anglican priests faced wealthy planters who controlled the vestry (the local church's governing body), set the minister's salary, and drove out ministers who challenged

them too forcefully. In Connecticut, the Saybrook Platform of 1708 created a network, or "consociation," of Congregational Churches, but individual churches still preserved much of their autonomy.

Though governing their churches frustrated many clergymen, religious apathy was a far more pressing problem in the early eighteenth century. As early as the 1660s, the Congregational clergy of New England had attempted to return wandering sheep to the fold by adopting the Half-Way Covenant. It specified that children of church members, if they adhered to the "forms of godliness," might join the church even if they could not demonstrate that they had undergone a conversion experience. They could not, however, vote in church affairs or take communion.

Adopted in 1662, this compromise kept in the church many children of the founders, and they in turn could pass church membership on to their children. Some ministers took other measures to increase their flocks. Solomon Stoddard, for 60 years patriarch of the Congregational Church in Northampton, Massachusetts, gave communion to every professing Christian and used an emotional style of preaching to reap annual "harvests" of souls.

Despite compromises and innovations, most church leaders saw creeping religious apathy when they surveyed their towns. An educated clergy, its energies often drained by doctrinal disputes within denominations, appealed too much to the mind and not enough to the heart. In such a state, as one Connecticut leader remembered it, "the spirit of God appeared to be awfully withdrawn."

The Awakeners' Message

The Great Awakening was not a unified movement, but rather a series of revivals that swept different regions between 1720 and 1760 with varying degrees of intensity. The first stirrings came in the 1720s in New Jersey and Pennsylvania. Theodore Frelinghuysen, a Dutch Reformed minister, excited his congregation through emotional preaching. Avoiding theological abstractions, he concentrated on arousing a need to be "saved" among his parishioners. A neighboring Presbyterian, Gilbert Tennent, soon took up the Dutchman's techniques, with similar success.

THE AMERICAN PEOPLE GATHER

In Colonial Taverns

One of the few contemporary paintings of social activity in colonial taverns, this colorful portrayal of a tavern in Surinam, a Dutch island on the northeastern coast of South America, shows carousing sea captains. American ships went there frequently to trade illegally for shipments of sugar that were quickly transformed into rum—the alcohol of choice in many North American taverns. (John Greenwood, Sea Captains Carousing in Surinam, 1758, The Saint Louis Art Museum)

In the American colonies, people gathered in three main places: churches, courthouses, and taverns. Of the three, taverns attracted people on a daily basis, especially in towns, whereas churchgoing was a weekly duty and courthouse-going was customarily a monthly affair.

Taverns were centers of social, political, economic, and judicial activity. Following militia musters, men of all ages would mingle at the local tavern. Local political meetings, as well as state dinners, would meet at the public houses, as taverns were called. Merchants and retailers would gather at taverns to cut deals, settle bills, and even hold slave auctions. Local courts met quarterly in taverns in an era where courthouses had often not yet been built. Anyone wishing to see a traveler or visitor knew exactly where to find him—at the local tavern, for the public houses were also the eighteenth-century equivalent of today's hotels and motels. Every ordinary craftsman and farmer knew that by frequenting the closest tavern, he could put himself in touch with the world beyond his immediate neighborhood.

Seeking heat and light as well as alcoholic beverages and sociability, people of every colonial community repaired to the nearest tavern. In most towns, they didn't have to go far. One hardly had to turn a corner before finding a tavern. In Boston, for example, at least 177 taverns dispensed cheer by 1737—one tavern for every 20 adult males. In other cities, where the regulation of tavernkeepers was more lax, one could find one tavern for every ten adult males.

As centers of ritual and recreational life and as modes of communication, taverns were instrumental in promoting face-to-face contact, though mainly for men. When the community gathered in churches, the people assembled formally to listen and pray. By contrast, people gathering in taverns engaged in informal fellowship, which blurred the lines of social hierarchy as people of different occupations and status exchanged local news, gossiped, traded rumors, told tales, loosened their tongues and inhibitions, and exhibited their manliness and aggressiveness. Colonial ministers railed against tavern-haunting and excessive drinking, but most colonial Americans were sermon-proof when it came to limiting their tavern-going. Along the way, they began to erode the lines of authority that they had inherited from England.

In the coming of the American Revolution, the taverns were a vital part of a silent current that was converting ordinary people from postures of deference to postures of defiance. It was in taverns, especially in the cities, where the Revolution was spawned, that ordinary men learned to shed customary restraints on their political behavior. Lubricated by rum, ale, and other spirits, ordinary town dwellers heard the local news read aloud from newspapers, argued over English policies, and fortified their willingness to criticize, ridicule, and even plot against leaders to whom they had earlier deferred.

As colonial politics became more open and competitive, it became necessary by the 1760s for politicians to mingle with the swarm at the local tavern in order to win or hold office. The ambitious young John Adams, Harvard graduate though he was, learned that he had to learn the "arts of gain" if he wished to assume a leading role in the political arena. He had to "mix with the crowd in a tavern, in the meetinghouse, or the training field."

As the storm clouds gathered in the arguments about England's new imperial policies after the Seven Years' War, the taverns assumed a prominent role as the conduits and catchments of revolutionary rhetoric. In the local tavern, whether in Virginia, Pennsylvania, or Massachusetts, men pored over newspapers, pamphlets, and broadsides, read them aloud, and concocted strategies. Thus, the taverns became vehicles for organizing and focusing popular sentiment, the public stages for popular politics, and the bridges between the world of print and the oral culture of the unlettered. Without taverns, the people no doubt would have gathered elsewhere in the face of what they came to regard as British tyranny imposed on them. But the taverns, along with the spirituous beverages they dispensed, hastened the American people down the path toward independence. Throughout American history, taverns continued as a gathering place for political discussions, dissent, and drunkenness.

Frank H. Taylor, The Blue Anchor Tavern and Dock *(Library Company of Philadelphia)*.

Baptists, decried the growing materialism and deplored the new acceptance of self-interested behavior. He who was "governed by regard to his own private interest," Gilbert Tennent preached, was "an enemy to the public," for in true Christian communities, "mutual love is the band and cement." By learning to oppose authority and to take part in the creation of new churches, thousands of colonists unknowingly rehearsed for revolution.

Political Life

"Were it not for government, the world would soon run into all manner of disorders and confusions," wrote a Massachusetts clergyman early in the eighteenth century. "Men's lives and estates and liberties would soon be prey to the covetous and the cruel," and every man would be "as a wolf" to his neighbors. Few colonists, wherever they lived, would have disagreed. On both sides of the Atlantic, people believed that government protected life, liberty, and property.

A much less easily resolved matter was how political power should be divided—in England, between the English government and the American colonies, and within each colony. American colonists naturally drew heavily on inherited political ideas and institutions. These were almost entirely English because English charters sanctioned settlement, English governors ruled the colonies, and English common law governed the courts. But in a new environment, where they met unexpected circumstances, the colonists modified familiar political forms to suit their needs.

Structuring Colonial Governments

As in all societies, determining the source of political authority was fundamental. In England, the notion of the God-given supreme authority of the monarch was crumbling even before the planting of the colonies. In its place arose the belief that stable and enlightened government depended on balancing the interests of monarchy, aristocracy, and democracy. Each of these pure forms of government would degenerate into oppression if unleavened by the other two. Monarchy, the rule of one, would become despotism. Aristocracy, the rule of the few, would turn into corrupt oligarchy. Democracy, the rule of the many, would descend into anarchy or mob rule. The Revolution of 1688 in England, by thwarting the king's pretensions to greater power, seemed to most colonists a vindication and strengthening of a carefully balanced political system.

In colonial governments, political balance was achieved somewhat differently. The governor was the king's agent or, in proprietary colonies, the agent of the king's delegated authority. The council, composed of wealthy appointees of the governor in most colonies, was a pale equivalent of the English House of Lords. The assembly, elected by white male freeholders, functioned as a replica of the House of Commons. "The concurrence of these three forms of government," wrote a Bostonian in 1749, "seems to be the highest perfection that human civil government can attain to."

Bicameral legislatures developed in most of the colonies in the seventeenth century. The lower houses, or assemblies, represented the local interests of the people at large. The upper houses, or councils (which usually also sat as the highest courts), represented the nascent aristocracy. Except in Rhode Island and Connecticut, every statute required the governor's assent, and all colonial laws required final approval from the king's privy council. This royal check on colonial lawmaking operated imperfectly, however. Laws took months to reach England, and months more passed before word of their final approval or rejection returned. In the meantime, the laws set down in the colonies took force.

Behind the formal structure of politics stood the rules governing who could participate in the political process. In England since the fifteenth century, the ownership of land had largely defined electoral participation (women and non-Christians were uniformly excluded). Only those with property sufficient to produce an annual rental income of 40 shillings could vote or hold office. The colonists closely followed this principle, except in Massachusetts, where it took until 1691 to break the requirement of Church membership for suffrage. As in England, the poor and propertyless were

Colonial Foundations of the American Political System

1606	Virginia companies of London and Plymouth granted patents to settle lands in North America.
1619	First elected colonial legislature meets in Virginia.
1634	Under a charter granted in 1632, Maryland's proprietor is given all the authority "as any bishop of Durham" ever held—more than the king possessed in England.
1635	The council in Virginia deports Governor John Harvey for exceeding his power, thus asserting the rights of local magistrates to contest authority of royally appointed governors.
1643	The colonies of Massachusetts, Plymouth, Connecticut, and New Haven draw up articles of confederation and form the first intercolonial union, the United Colonies of New England.
1647	Under a charter granted in 1644, elected freemen from the Providence Plantations draft a constitution establishing freedom of conscience, separating church and state, and authorizing referenda by the towns on laws passed by the assembly.
1677	The Laws, Concessions, and Agreements for West New Jersey provide for a legislature elected annually by virtually all free males, secret voting, liberty of conscience, election of justices of the peace and local officeholders, and trial by jury in public so that "justice may not be done in a corner."
1689	James II deposed in England in the Glorious Revolution and royal governors, accused of abusing their authority, ousted in Massachusetts, New York, and Maryland.
1701	First colonial unicameral legislature meets in Pennsylvania under the Frame of Government of 1701.
1735	John Peter Zenger, a New York printer, acquitted of seditious libel for printing attacks on the royal governor and his faction, thus widening the freedom of the press.
1754	First congress of all the colonies meets at Albany (with seven colonies sending delegates) and agrees on a Plan of Union (which is rejected by the colonies and the English government).
1765	The Stamp Act Congress, the first intercolonial convention called outside England's authority, meets in New York.

excluded, for they lacked the "stake in society" that supposedly transformed unpredictable, ignorant creatures into thoughtful and responsible voters.

Whereas in England, the 40-shilling freehold requirement was intended to restrict the size of the electorate, in the colonies, because of the cheapness of land, it conferred the vote on a large proportion of adult males. Between 50 and 75 percent of the adult free males could vote in most colonies. As the proportion of landless colonists increased in the eighteenth century, however, the franchise slowly became more limited.

Though voting rights were broadly based, most men assumed that only the wealthy and socially prominent were entitled to hold positions of political power. Lesser men, it was held, ought to defer to their betters. Balancing this elitist conception of politics, however, was the notion that the entire electorate should periodically judge the performance of those they entrusted with political power and reject those who represented them inadequately. Unlike the members of the English House of Commons, who by the seventeenth century thought of themselves as representing the entire nation, the colonial representatives were expected to reflect the views of those who elected them locally. Believing this, their constituents judged them accordingly.

When were citizens entitled to defy those who ruled them? The answer to this vexing question followed English precedent: The people were justified in badgering their leaders, protesting openly, and, in extreme cases of abuse of power, assuming control in order to rectify the situation. The uprisings in the colonies associated with England's Glorious Revolution represented such moments when the deferential mass transformed itself into a purposeful crowd in order to overthrow those who trampled on their traditional English liberties.

The Crowd in Action

What gave special power to the common people when they assembled to protest oppressive authority was the general absence of effective police power. In the countryside, where most colonists lived, only the county sheriff, with an occasional deputy, insulated civil leaders from angry farmers. In the towns, police forces were still unknown. Only the sheriff, backed up by the night watch, safeguarded public order. As late as 1757, the night watch of New York was described as a "parcell of idle, drinking vigilant snorers, who never quelled any nocturnal tumult in their lives." In theory, the militia stood ready to suppress public disturbances, but both urban and rural crowds usually included many of the very people who composed the militia.

Agencies of law enforcement were weak, so the potential for political action outside formal legislative channels was never so great as in the colonial period. Crowd action, frequently effective, gradually achieved a kind of legitimacy. The assembled people became perceived as the watchdog of government, ready to chastise or drive from office those who violated the collective sense of what was right and proper.

Boston's impressment riot of 1747 vividly illustrates the people's readiness to defend their inherited privileges and the weakness of law enforcement. It began when Commodore Charles Knowles brought his Royal Navy ships to Boston for provisioning—and to replenish the ranks of mariners thinned by desertion. When Knowles sent press gangs out on a chill November evening with orders to fill the crew vacancies from Boston's waterfront population, they scooped up artisans, laborers, servants, and slaves, as well as merchant seamen from ships riding at anchor in the harbor.

But before the press gangs could hustle their victims back to the British men-of-war, a crowd of angry Bostonians seized several British officers, surrounded the governor's house, and demanded the release of their townsmen. When the sheriff and his deputies attempted to intervene, the mob mauled them. The militia, called to arms by the governor to "suppress the mob by force, and if need be to fire upon 'em with ball," refused to respond.

By dusk, a crowd of several thousand defied the governor's orders to disperse, stoned the windows of the governor's house, and dragged a royal barge from one of the British ships into the courtyard of his house, where they burned it amid cheers.

Enraged by the defiant Bostonians, Commodore Knowles threatened to bombard the town. Determined negotiations conducted during several days of further tumult averted a showdown. Finally, Knowles released the impressed Bostonians. After the riot, a young politician named Samuel Adams defended Boston's defiance of royal authority. The people, he argued, had a "natural right" to band together against press gangs that deprived them of their liberty. Local magnates who supported the governor in this incident were labeled "tools to arbitrary power."

The Growing Power of the Assemblies

Incidents such as the impressment riot of 1747 demonstrated the touchiness of England's colonial subjects. But a more gradual and restrained change—the growing ambition and power of the legislative assemblies—was far more important. For most of the seventeenth century, royal and proprietary governors had exercised greater power in relation to the elected legislatures than did the king in relation to Parliament. The governors could dissolve the lower houses and delay their sitting, control the election of their speakers, and in most colonies initiate legislation with their appointed councils. Colonial governors also had authority to appoint and dismiss judges at all levels of the judiciary and to create chancery courts, which sat without juries. Governors also controlled the expenditure of public monies and had authority to grant land to individuals and groups, which they sometimes used to confer vast estates on their favorites.

By the 1730s, royal governments had replaced many of the proprietary governments. In the seventeenth century, Virginia, Massachusetts, and New York had become royal colonies, with governors appointed by the crown. In the eighteenth century, royal government came to New Jersey (1702), South Carolina (1719), and North Carolina (1729).

Many of the royal governors were competent military officers or bureaucrats, but often they were simply recipients of patronage posts. They were rewarded for whom they knew, not what they had done or might accomplish. A few were psychologically damaged, like Sir Danvers Osborn, who committed suicide a week after arriving in New York in 1753. Many were corrupt. Some governors never took up their posts at all, preferring, like the earl of Orkney, Virginia's royal governor from 1705 to 1737, to pocket the salary and pay a part of it to other men who went to the colony as lieutenant governors. But most governors were not crazy, corrupt, or absent; they were merely mediocre.

In the eighteenth century, elected colonial legislatures challenged the swollen executive powers of these colonial governors. The governors lacked the extensive patronage power that in England enabled ministers of government to manipulate elections and buy off opposition groups. They could therefore contest but not prevent encroachments on their power. Bit by bit, the representative assemblies won new rights—to initiate legislation, to elect their own speakers, to settle contested elections, to discipline their membership, and to nominate provincial treasurers who controlled the disbursement of public funds. The most important gain of all was acquiring the "power of the purse"—the authority to initiate money bills, which specified how much money should be raised by taxes and how it should be spent.

Originally thought of as advisory bodies, the elected assemblies gradually transformed themselves into governing bodies reflecting the interests of the electorate. The Glorious Revolution had eroded royal power in England in the late seventeenth century. Thereafter, colonial executive power, an extension of royal power in the colonies, also gave ground to the ambitious legislative assemblies. Governors complained bitterly about the "levelling spirit" and "mutinous and disorderly behavior" of the assemblies, but they could not stop their rise.

Local Politics

Binding elected officeholders to their constituents became an important feature of the colonial political system. In England, the House of Commons was filled with representatives from "rotten boroughs," ancient places left virtually uninhabited by population shifts, and with men whose vote was in the pocket of the ministry because they had accepted crown appointments, contracts, or gifts. The American assemblies, by contrast, contained mostly representatives sent by voters who instructed them on particular issues and held them accountable for serving local interests.

Royal governors and colonial grandees who sat as councillors often deplored this localist, popular orientation of the people's representatives. The assemblies, sniffed one aristocratic New Yorker, were crowded with "plain, illiterate husbandmen [small farmers], whose views seldom extended farther than the regulation of highways, the destruction of wolves, wildcats, and foxes, and the advancement of the other little interests of the particular counties which they were chosen to represent." In actuality, the voters mostly sent merchants, lawyers, and substantial planters and farmers to represent them in the lower houses, and by the mid-eighteenth century in most colonies, these men had formed political elites. But it was true that they represented the local interests of their constituents. They prided themselves on doing so, for they saw themselves as bulwarks against oppression and arbitrary rule, which history taught them were most frequently imposed by monarchs and their appointed agents.

Local government was usually more important to the colonists than provincial government. In the North, local political authority generally rested in the towns. The New England town meeting decided a wide range of matters. In making decisions, the meeting strived for consensus, searching and arguing until it could express itself as a single unit. "By general agreement" and "by the free and united consent of the whole" were phrases denoting a decision-making process that sought participatory assent rather than a democratic competition among differing interests and points of view.

In the South, the county constituted the primary unit of government. No equivalent of the town meeting existed for placing local decisions before the populace. The planter gentry ruled the

When frontier farmers marched on Philadelphia in 1763 to demand more protection on the frontier, a miniature civil war almost broke out. Philadelphians had little use for the "Paxton Boys," who had murdered 20 harmless Christian Indians in retaliation for frontier raids. (The Library Company of Philadelphia)

county courts and the legislature, and substantial farmers served in minor offices such as road surveyor and deputy sheriff. At court sessions, usually convened four times a year, deeds were read aloud and then recorded, juries impaneled and justice dispensed, elections held, licenses issued, and proclamations read aloud. On election days, gentlemen treated their neighbors (on whom they depended for votes) to "bumbo," "kill devil," and other alcoholic treats. By the mid-eighteenth century, a landed squirearchy of third- and fourth-generation families had achieved political dominance.

The Spread of Whig Ideology

Whether in local or provincial affairs, a political ideology called Whig or "republican" had spread widely by the mid-eighteenth century. The canons of this body of thought, inherited from England, flowed from the belief that concentrated power

was historically the enemy of liberty and that too much power lodged in any person or group inevitably produced corruption and tyranny. The best defenses against concentrated power were balanced government, elected legislatures adept at checking executive authority, prohibition of standing armies (almost always controlled by tyrannical monarchs to oppress the people), and vigilance by the people in watching their leaders for telltale signs of corruption.

Much of this Whig ideology reached the people through the newspapers that began appearing in the seaboard towns in the early eighteenth century. The first was the *Boston News-Letter,* founded in 1704. By 1763, some 23 papers circulated in the colonies. Though limited to a few pages and published only once or twice a week, the papers passed from hand to hand and were read aloud in taverns and coffeehouses. In this way, their contents probably reached most households in the towns and a substantial minority of farmsteads in the countryside.

TIMELINE

1662	Half-Way Covenant in New England
1685–1715	Stagnation in tobacco market
1704	*Boston News-Letter,* first regular colonial newspaper, published
1713	Beginning of Scots-Irish and German immigration
1715–1730	Volume of slave trade doubles
1718	French settle New Orleans
1720s	Black population begins to increase naturally
1734–1736	Great Awakening begins in Northampton, Massachusetts
1735	Zenger acquitted of seditious libel in New York
1739–1740	Whitefield's first American tour spreads Great Awakening
	Slaves compose 90 percent of population on Carolina rice coast
1740s	Indigo becomes staple crop in Lower South
1747	Benjamin Franklin publishes first *Poor Richard's Almanack*
	Impressment riot in Boston
1760	Africans compose 20 percent of American population
1760s–1770s	Spanish establish California mission system
1769	American Philosophical Society founded at Philadelphia

By the 1730s, newspapers had become an important conduit of Whig ideology. Many of them reprinted material from English Whig writers who railed against corruption and creeping despotism in the reign of George II (1727–1760). Particularly popular were the essays of John Trenchard and Thomas Gordon, whose *Cato's Letters* and *Independent Whig* found their way into the private libraries of many colonists and were widely reprinted in the newspapers.

The new power of the press and its importance in guarding the people's liberties against would-be tyrants, such as abrasive royal governors, was vividly illustrated in the Zenger case in New York. Young John Peter Zenger, a printer's apprentice, had been hired in 1733 by the antigovernment faction of Lewis Morris to start a newspaper that would publicize the tyrannical actions of Governor William Cosby. In Zenger's *New-York Weekly Journal,* the Morris faction fired salvos at Cosby's interference with the courts and his alleged corruption in giving important offices to his henchmen. New Yorkers believed, said one essay published by Zenger, "that their LIBERTIES and PROPERTIES are precarious, and that SLAVERY is like to be tailed on them and their posterity if some things past are not amended."

This and other bruising indictments of the governor led to Zenger's arrest for seditious libel. He was rescued from an early end to his career by the brilliant defense of Andrew Hamilton, a Philadelphia lawyer hired by the Morris faction to convince the jury that Zenger was innocent of everything but trying to inform the people of attacks on their liberties. Although the jury acquitted Zenger, the libel laws remained very restrictive. But the acquittal did reinforce the notion that the government was the people's servant, and it brought home the point that public criticism could keep people with political authority responsible to the people they ruled. Such ideas about liberty and corruption, raised in the context of local politics, would shortly achieve a much broader significance.

Conclusion

America in 1750

The American colonies, robust and expanding, matured rapidly between 1700 and 1750. Transatlantic commerce linked them closely to Europe, Africa, and other parts of the New World. Churches, schools, and towns—the visible marks of the receding frontier—appeared everywhere. A balanced sex ratio and stable family life had been achieved throughout the colonies. Seasoned political leaders and familiar political institutions functioned from Maine to Georgia.

Yet the sinew, bone, and muscle of American society had not yet fully knit together. The ployglot population, one-fifth of it bound in chattel slavery and its Native American component still unassimilated and uneasily situated on the frontier, was a kaleidoscopic mixture of ethnic and religious groups. Its economy, while developing rapidly, showed weaknesses, particularly in New England, where land resources had been strained. The social structure reflected the colonizers' emergence from a frontier stage, but the consolidation of wealth by a landed and mercantile elite was matched by pockets of poverty appearing in the cities and some rural areas. Full of strength, yet marked by awkward incongruities, colonial America in 1750 approached an era of strife and momentous decisions.

Recommended Reading

Population Growth and Economic Development

John J. McCusker and Russell R. Menard, *The Economy of British America, 1607–1789* (1985); James A. Henretta and Gregory Nobles, *Evolution and Revolution: American Society: 1620–1820* (1986); Gary M. Walton and James F. Shepherd, *The Economic Rise of Early America* (1979); Edwin J. Perkins, *The Economy of Colonial America*, 2d ed. (1988); Stephanie G. Wolf, *Urban Village: Population, Community, and Family Structure in Germantown, Pennsylvania* (1977); R. J. Dickson, *Ulster Immigration to Colonial America, 1718–1775* (1966); Jon Butler, *The Huguenots in Colonial America* (1983); Ned Landsman, *Scotland and Its First American Colony* (1985); Bernard Bailyn, *Voyagers to the West: A Passage in the Peopling of America on the Eve of the American Revolution* (1986); Robert V. Wells, *The Population of the British Colonies in America Before 1776* (1975).

The Eighteenth-Century North

Richard Bushman, *From Puritan to Yankee* (1967); Christopher M. Jedrey, *The World of John Cleaveland: Family and Community in Eighteenth-Century New England* (1979); Daniel Vickers, *Farmers and Fishermen: Two Centuries of Work in Essex County, Massachusetts, 1630–1850* (1994); David W. Conroy, *In Public Houses: Drink and the Revolution of Authority in Colonial Massachusetts* (1995); Laurel T. Ulrich, *Good Wives: Image and Reality in the Lives of Women in Northern New England, 1650–1750* (1982); Cornelia Hughes Dayton, *Women before the Bar: Gender, Law, and Society in Connecticut, 1639–1789* (1995); Sung Bok Kim, *Landlord and Tenant in the Colony of New York: Manorial Society, 1664–1775* (1976); James Lemon, *The Best Poor Man's Country: A Geographical Study of Early Southeastern Pennsylvania* (1972); John L. Brooke, *The Heart of the Commonwealth: Society and Political Culture in Worcester County, Massachusetts, 1713–1861* (1989).

The Eighteenth-Century South

Paul G. E. Clemens, *The Atlantic Economy and Colonial Maryland's Eastern Shore: From Tobacco to Grain* (1980); Carville Earle, *The Evolution of a Tidewater Settlement System* (1975); Rhys Isaac, *The Transformation of Virginia, 1740–1790* (1982); Allan Kulikoff, *Tobacco and Slaves: The Development of Southern Culture in the Chesapeake, 1680–1800* (1986); T. H. Breen, *Tobacco Culture: The Mentality of the Great Tidewater Planters on the Eve of the Revolution* (1985); Daniel Blake Smith, *Inside the Great House: Planter Family Life in Eighteenth-Century Chesapeake Society* (1980); Julia C. Spruill, *Women's Life and Work in the Southern Colonies* (1938); Joyce E. Chaplin, *An Anxious Pursuit: Agricultural Innovation and Modernity in the Lower South, 1730–1815* (1993); Gregory Stiverson, *Poverty in the Land of Plenty: Tenancy in Eighteenth-Century Maryland* (1980).

The Developing Cities

Bernard Bailyn, *The New England Merchants in the Seventeenth Century* (1955); Gary B. Nash, *The Urban Crucible: Social Change, Political Consciousness, and the Origins of the American Revolution* (1979); Billy G. Smith, *The "Lower Sort": Philadelphia's Laboring People, 1750–1800* (1990); J. E. Crowley, *This Sheba Self: The Conceptualization of Economic Life in Eighteenth-Century America* (1974); Carl Bridenbaugh, *Cities in Revolt: Urban Life in America, 1743–1776* (1955); G. B. Warden, *Boston, 1687–1776* (1970); Esmond Wright, *Franklin of Philadelphia* (1986).

The Great Awakening and the American Enlightenment

Perry Miller, *From Colony to Province* (1953); Alan Heimert, *Religion and the American Mind: From the Great Awakening to the Revolution* (1966); Edwin Gaustad, *The Great Awakening in New England* (1957); Harry S. Stout, *The New England Soul: Preaching and Religious Life in Colonial New England* (1986); Patricia Tracy, *Jonathan Edwards, Pastor* (1979); Marilyn J. Westerkamp, *Triumph of the Laity: Scots-Irish Piety and the Great Awakening, 1625–1760* (1988); Frank J. Lambert, *"Pedlar in Divinity": George Whitefield and the Transatlantic Revivals* (1994); Patricia Bonomi, *Under the Cope of Heaven: Religion, Society, and Politics in Colonial America* (1986); Henry May, *The American Enlightenment* (1976); Lawrence A. Cremin, *American Education: The Colonial Experience, 1607–1783* (1970).

Colonial Politics

Bernard Bailyn, *The Origins of American Politics* (1968); Charles Sydnor, *American Revolutionaries in the Making: Political Practices in Washington's Virginia* (1965); Jack P. Greene, *The Quest for Power: The Lower Houses of Assembly in the Southern Royal Colonies, 1689–1776* (1963); Edward M. Cook, Jr., *The Fathers of the Towns: Leadership and Community Structure in Eighteenth-Century New England* (1976); William Pencak, *War, Politics, and Revolution in Provincial Massachusetts* (1981); Patricia Bonomi, *A Factious People: Politics and Society in Colonial New York* (1977); Robert Zemsky, *Merchants, Farmers, and River Gods: An Essay on Eighteenth-Century American Politics* (1971); Alan Tully, *Forming American Politics: Ideas, Interests, and Institutions in Colonial New York and Pennsylvania* (1994).

Bursting the Colonial Bonds

*I*n 1758, when he was 21 years old, Ebenezer MacIntosh of Boston laid down his shoemaker's awl and enlisted in the Massachusetts expedition against the French on Lake Champlain. The son of a poor Boston shoemaker who had fought against the French in a previous war, MacIntosh had known poverty all his life. Service against the French offered the hope of plunder or at least an enlistment bounty worth half a year's wages. One among thousands of colonists who fought against the "Gallic menace" in the Seven Years' War, MacIntosh contributed his mite to the climactic Anglo-American struggle that drove the French from North America.

But a greater role lay ahead for the poor Boston shoemaker. Two years after the Peace of Paris in 1763, England imposed a stamp tax on the American colonists. In the massive protests that followed, MacIntosh emerged as the street leader of the Boston crowd. In two nights of the most violent attacks on private property ever witnessed in America, a Boston crowd nearly destroyed the houses of two of the colony's most important officials. On August 14, they tore through the house of Andrew Oliver, a wealthy merchant and the appointed distributor of stamps for Massachusetts. Twelve days later, MacIntosh led the crowd in attacking the mansion of Thomas Hutchinson, a wealthy merchant who served as lieutenant governor and chief justice of Massachusetts. "The mob was so general," wrote the governor, "and so supported that all civil power ceased in an instant."

For the next several months, the power of the poor Boston shoemaker grew. Called "General" Mac-Intosh and "Captain-General of the Liberty Tree" by his townspeople, he soon sported a militia uniform of gold and blue and a hat laced with gold. Two thousand townsmen followed his commands on November 5, when they marched in orderly ranks through the crooked streets of Boston to demonstrate their solidarity in resisting the hated stamps.

Five weeks later, a crowd publicly humiliated stamp distributor Oliver. Demanding that he announce his resignation before the assembled citizenry, they marched him across town in a driving December rain. With MacIntosh at his elbow, he finally reached the "Liberty Tree," which had become a symbol of resistance to England's new colonial policies. There the aristocratic Oliver ate humble pie. He concluded his resignation remarks with bitter words, hissing sardonically that he would "always think myself very happy when it shall be in my power to serve the people."

"To serve the people" was an ancient idea embedded in English political culture, but it assumed new meaning in the American colonies during the epic third-quarter of the eighteenth century. Few colonists in 1750 held even a faint desire to break the connection with England, and fewer still might have predicted the form of government that 13 independent states in an independent nation might fashion. Yet in a whirlwind of events, 2 million colonists moved haltingly toward a showdown with mighty England. Little-known men like Ebenezer MacIntosh as well as his well-known and historically celebrated townsmen Samuel Adams, John Hancock, and John Adams were part of the struggle. Collectively, ordinary people such as MacIntosh influenced—and in fact sometimes even dictated—the revolutionary movement in the colonies. Though we read and speak mostly of a small group of "founding fathers," the wellsprings of the American Revolution can be fully discovered only among a variety of people from different social groups, occupations, regions, and religions.

A View of the Town of Concord (April 1775), attributed to Ralph Earle. (Courtesy Concord Museum, Concord, MA) his chapter addresses the tensions in late colonial society, the imperial crisis that followed the Seven Years' War (in the colonies often called the French and Indian War), and the tumultuous decade that led to the "shot heard round the world" fired at Concord Bridge in April 1775. It portrays the origins of a dual American Revolution. Ebenezer MacIntosh, in leading the Boston mob against crown officers and colonial collaborators who tried to implement a new colonial policy after 1763, helped set in motion a revolutionary movement to restore ancient liberties thought by the Americans to be under deliberate attack in England. This movement eventually escalated into the war for American independence.

But MacIntosh's Boston followers were also venting years of resentment at the accumulation of wealth and power by Boston's aristocratic elite. Behind every swing of the ax, every shattered crystal goblet and splintered mahogany chair, lay the fury of a Bostonian who had seen the city's conservative elite try to dismantle the town meeting, had suffered economic hardship, and had lost faith that opportunity and just relations still prevailed in his town. This sentiment, which called for the reform of a colonial society that had become corrupt, self-indulgent, and dominated by an elite, fed an idealistic commitment to reshape American society even while severing the colonial bond. As distinguished from the war for independence, this was the American Revolution.

The Climactic Seven Years' War

After a brief period of peace following King George's War (1744–1748), France and England fought the fourth, largest, and by far most significant of the wars for empire that had begun in the late seventeenth century. Known variously as the Seven Years' War, the French and Indian War, and the Great War for Empire, this global conflict in part represented a showdown for control of North America between the Atlantic Ocean and the Mississippi River. In North America, the Anglo-American forces ultimately prevailed in the Seven Years' War. This victory dramatically affected the lives of the great variety of people living in the huge region east of the Mississippi—English, German, and Scots-Irish settlers in the English colonies; French and Spanish colonizers in Canada, Florida, and interior North America; African slaves in a variety of settlements; and, perhaps most of all, the powerful Native American tribes of the interior.

War and the Management of Empire

After the Glorious Revolution of 1688, England began constructing a more coherent imperial administration. In 1696, a professional Board of Trade replaced the old Lords of Trade; the Treasury strengthened the customs service; and Parliament created overseas vice-admiralty courts, which functioned without juries to prosecute smugglers who evaded the trade regulations set forth in the Navigation Acts. Royal governors received greater powers and more detailed instructions and came under more insistent demands from the Board of Trade to enforce British policies. England was quietly installing the machinery of imperial management and a corps of colonial bureaucrats.

The best test of an effectively organized state was its ability to wage war. Four times between 1689 and 1763, England matched its strength against France, its archrival in North America and the Caribbean. These wars of empire had tremendous consequences for all involved—the home governments, their colonial subjects, and the Indian tribes that were drawn into the bloody conflicts.

We have already seen (in Chapter 3) how the Peace of Utrecht that ended Queen Anne's War (1702–1713) brought victor's spoils of great importance to England. The generation of peace that followed the Peace of Utrecht was really only a time-out between wars. Both England and France used the years until 1739 to strengthen their war-making capacity, to which productive and efficiently governed New World colonies made important contributions. Though known as a period of "salutary neglect," this was actually an era when king and Parliament increased their control over colonial affairs.

Parliament had already begun playing a more active role after the reign of Queen Anne (1702–1714) and continued to do so when weak, German-speaking King George I came to the throne. Concerned mainly with economic regulation, Parliament added new articles such as furs, copper, hemp, tar, and turpentine to the list of items produced in America that had to be shipped to England before being exported to another country. Parliament also curtailed colonial production of articles important to England's economy: woolen cloth in 1699, beaver hats in 1732, finished iron products in 1750. Most important, Parliament passed the Molasses Act in 1733. Attempting to stop the trade between New England and the French West Indies, where Yankee traders exchanged fish, beef, and pork for molasses to convert into rum, Parliament imposed a prohibitive duty of 6 pence per gallon on molasses imported from the French islands. This turned many of New England's largest merchants and distillers into smugglers and schooled them for a generation, along with their ship captains, crews, and allied waterfront artisans, in defying royal authority.

The generation of peace ended abruptly in 1739 when England declared war on Spain. The immediate cause of hostilities was the ear of an English sea captain, Robert Jenkins. He had been deprived of that appendage eight years before by Spanish authorities, who charged him with smuggling in the Spanish colonies. With encouragement from his government, Jenkins publicly displayed his severed ear in 1738 as a way of whipping up war fever against Spain, which English policymakers wanted to chasten for transferring certain commercial privileges from England to France.

The real cause of the war, however, was England's determination to continue its drive toward commercial domination of the Atlantic basin. Five years after the war with Spain began in 1739, it merged into a much larger conflict between England and France, in Europe called The War of Austrian Succession, that lasted until 1748. The scale of King George's War (1744–1748) far exceeded previous conflicts. As military priorities became paramount, the need increased for discipline within the empire. In addition, unprecedented military expenditures brought pressure to enlarge colonial revenues. England asked its West Indian and American colonies to share in the costs of defending—and extending—the empire and to tailor their behavior to the needs of the home country.

Outbreak of Hostilities

The tension between English and French colonists in North America, which reached back to the early seventeenth century, was intensified by the spectacular population growth of the English colonies: from 250,000 in 1700 to 1.25 million in 1750, and to 1.75 million in the next decade. Three-quarters of the increase came in the colonies south of New York. Such growth propelled thousands of land-hungry settlers toward the mountain gaps in the Appalachians in search of farmland.

Promoting this westward rush were fur traders and land speculators. The fur traders penetrated a French-influenced region, where they offered native trappers and hunters better prices and higher-quality goods than the French. In the 1740s and 1750s, speculators formed land companies to capitalize on the seaboard population explosion. Many of the future leaders of the Revolution were heavily involved in companies that raced to establish claims to millions of acres of western land. The farther west the settlement line moved, the closer it came to the western trading empire of the French and their Indian allies.

Colonial penetration of the Ohio valley in the 1740s established the first English outposts in the continental heartland. This challenged the French where their interest was vital. While the English controlled most of the eastern coastal plain of North America, the French had nearly encircled them to the west by building a chain of trading posts and forts along the St. Lawrence River, through the Great Lakes, and southward into the Ohio and Mississippi valleys all the way to New Orleans.

Challenged by the English, the French resisted. They attempted to block further English expansion by constructing new forts in the Ohio valley and by prying some tribes loose from their new English connections. The English, a French emissary warned a western tribe in the 1750s, "are much less anxious to take away your peltries than to become masters of your lands, and your blindness is so great that you do not perceive that the very hand that caresses you will scourge you like negroes and slaves, so soon as it will have got possession of your lands."

By 1755, the French had driven the English traders out of the Ohio valley and established forts as far east as the fork of the Ohio River, near present-day Pittsburgh. It was there, at Fort Duquesne, that the French smartly rebuffed an ambitious young Virginia militia colonel named George Washington, dispatched by his colony's government to expel them from the region.

Men in the capitals of Europe, not in the colonies, made the decision to force a showdown in the interior of North America. England's powerful merchants, supported by American clients, had been emboldened by English success in the previous war against the French. Now they argued that the time was ripe to destroy the French overseas trade. Convinced, the English ministry ordered several thousand troops to America in 1754; in France, 3,000 regulars embarked to meet the English challenge.

With war looming, the colonial governments attempted to coordinate their efforts. Representatives of seven colonies met with 150 Iroquois chiefs at Albany, New York, in June 1754. The twin goals were to woo the powerful Iroquois out of their neutrality and to perfect a plan of colonial union. Both failed. The Iroquois left the conference with 30 wagonloads of gifts but made no firm commitment to fight against the French. Benjamin Franklin designed a plan for an intercolonial government that would manage Indian affairs and defense and have the power to pass laws and levy taxes. But even the clever woodcut displayed in the *Pennsylvania Gazette* that pictured a chopped-up snake with the insignia "Join or Die" failed to overcome the long-standing jealousies that had thwarted previous attempts at intercolony cooperation. "Everyone cries a union is necessary," sighed Franklin, "but when they come to the manner and form of the union, their weak noodles are perfectly distracted."

With his British army and hundreds of American recruits, General Edward Braddock slogged his way across Virginia in the summer of 1755, each day cutting a few miles of road through forests and across mountains. A headstrong professional soldier who regarded his European battlefield experience as sufficient for war in the American wilderness, Braddock had contempt for the woods-wise French regiments and their stealthy Indian allies.

As Braddock neared Fort Duquesne, the entire French force and the British suddenly surprised one another in the forest. The French had 218 soldiers and militiamen and 637 Indian allies, while Braddock commanded twice that many men but few Indians. The initial bloody melee was a standoff. Then the French redeployed their Indian allies along both sides of the road in the trees. They poured murderous fire into Braddock's tidy lines of men, who could not see their enemies. Just before he fell, mortally wounded (perhaps by one of his own angry men), Braddock presumably learned that Indians were essential allies and were fully capable of pitched battle. Two-thirds of the British and Americans were killed or wounded, and Washington, his uniform pierced by four bullets, had two horses shot from beneath him. Although they had 1,000 men in reserve down the road, the Anglo-American force beat a hasty, ignominious retreat.

Throughout the summer, French-supplied Indian raiders put the torch to the Virginia and Pennsylvania backcountry. "The roads are full of starved, naked, indigent multitudes," observed one officer. One French triumph followed another during the next two years. The victory over Braddock's army had brought almost every tribe north of the Ohio River to the French side. Never was disunity within the English colonies so painfully evident. With its Indian allies, French Canada, only 70,000 inhabitants strong, had badly battered a million and a half colonists supported by the British army.

The turning point in the war came after the energetic William Pitt became England's prime minister in 1757. Proclaiming, "I believe that I can save this nation and that no one else can," he abandoned Europe as the main theater of action against the French and threw his nation's military might into the American campaign.

The forces dispatched by Pitt to America dwarfed all preceding commitments. About 23,000 British troops landed in America in 1757 and 1758, and the huge naval fleet that arrived in the latter year included 14,000 mariners. But even forces of this magnitude, when asked to engage the enemy in the forests of North America, were not necessarily sufficient to the task without Indian support, or at least neutrality. "A doubt remains not," proclaimed one English official in the colonies, "that the prosperity of our colonies on the continent will stand or fall with our interest and favour among them."

Tribal Strategies

Anglo-American leaders knew that in a war fought mainly in the northern colonies, the support of the Iroquois Confederacy and their tributary tribes was crucial. Iroquois allegiance could be secured in only two ways, through purchase or by a demonstration of power that would convince the tribes that the English would prevail with or without their assistance. The Iroquois understood that their interest lay in playing off one European power against the other. "To preserve the balance between us and the French," wrote a New York politician, "is the great ruling principle of modern Indian politics."

The first English stratagem for securing Iroquois support failed in 1754 when colonial negotiators heaped gifts on the Iroquois chiefs at the Albany Congress but received in return only tantalizing half-promises of support against the French. The second alternative fizzled because the English proved militarily inferior to the French in the first three years of the war. Hence, the westernmost of the Iroquois Six Nations, the Seneca, fought on the side of the French in the campaigns of 1757 and 1758, while the Delaware, a tributary tribe, harassed the Pennsylvania frontier.

In 1758, the huge English military buildup began to produce victories. The largest army ever assembled in North America to that point, some 15,000 British and American soldiers, including the Bostonian Ebenezer MacIntosh, suffered terrible casualties and withdrew from the field after attempting to storm Fort Ticonderoga on Lake Champlain in June 1758. Then the tide turned. Troops under Sir Jeffrey Amherst captured Louisbourg, on Cape Breton Island, and Fort Duquesne fell to an army of 6,000 led by General John Forbes. The resolute Pitt had mobilized the fighting power of the English nation and put more men in the field than existed in all of New France. The colonists, in turn, had put aside intramural squabbling long enough to overwhelm the badly outnumbered French.

The victories of 1758 finally moved the Iroquois away from neutrality. Added incentive to join the Anglo-American side came when the English navy bottled up French shipping in the St. Lawrence River, cutting the Iroquois off from French trade goods. By early 1759, foreseeing that the French were going down to defeat in North America, the Iroquois pledged 800 warriors for an attack on Fort Niagara, the strategic French trading depot on Lake Ontario. As always, their policy had been to assess the shifting military balance between rival European powers and to formulate their strategy accordingly.

Even dramatic Anglo-American victories did not always guarantee Indian support. In the South, backcountry skirmishes with the Cherokee from Virginia to South Carolina turned into a costly war from 1759 to 1761. In 1760, the Cherokee mauled a British army of 1,300 under Amherst. The following summer, a much larger Anglo-American force invaded Cherokee country, burning towns and food supplies. By this time, English control of the sea had interrupted the Indians' supply of French arms. Struggling against food shortages, lack of ammunition, and a smallpox epidemic, the Cherokee finally sued for peace.

Other Anglo-American victories in 1759, the "year of miracles," decided the outcome of the bloodiest war yet known in the New World. The capture of Fort Niagara, the critical link in the system of forts that joined the French inland empire with the Atlantic, was followed by the conquest of sugar-rich Martinique in the West Indies. The culminating stroke came with a dramatic victory at Quebec. Led by 32-year-old General James Wolfe, 5,000 troops scaled a rocky cliff and overcame the French on the Plains of Abraham. The

The storming of French Quebec in 1759 was the decisive blow in England's campaign to end the French domination of Canada and the lands west of the Appalachians. The heroic exploits of General James Wolfe made him a hero throughout England and the colonies. (A View of the Taking of Quebec, September 13, 1759/National Army Museum, London)

capture of Montreal late in 1760 completed the shattering of French power in North America. The theater of operations shifted to the Caribbean, where fighting continued, as in Europe, for three years longer. But in the American colonies, the old English dream of ridding the continent of the Gallic menace had finally come true.

Consequences of War

The strokes of a few diplomats' pens in 1762–1763 brought astounding changes to European and Indian peoples who for decades had been involved in dizzying complex and shifting relationships that alternated between conflict and cooperation over vast stretches of North American territory. The Spanish, who had tried to check the expansive French southern influence directed from Louisiana, now acquired New Orleans and all of the vast Louisiana territory west of the Mississippi. Although this could provide a buffer against English aspirations in the continent's heartland, Spain's king surrendered Spanish Florida to the British—a pragmatic decision because England agreed to compensate Spain with Havana, which the British had captured during the war.

For the interior Indian tribes, the Treaty of Paris ending the Seven Years' War in 1763 dealt a harsh blow. Unlike the coastal Native Americans, whose population and independence had ebbed rapidly through contact with the colonizers, the inland tribes had maintained their strength and sometimes even grown more unified through relations with settlers. Although they came to depend on European trade goods, Native Americans had turned this commercial connection to their advantage so long as more than one source of trade goods existed.

The Indian play-off system came to a crashing halt when the French ceded Canada and all territory east of the Mississippi, except for New Orleans, to England in the Treaty of Paris. For the interior tribes, only one source of trade goods remained. Two centuries of European rivalry for control of eastern North America ended abruptly. Iroquois, Cherokee, Creek, Ojibway, Shawnee, and scores of other interior tribes were now forced to adjust to this reality.

After concluding peace with the French, the English government launched a new policy in North America designed to separate Native Americans and colonizers by creating a racial boundary roughly following the crestline of the Appalachian Mountains from Maine to Georgia. The Proclamation of 1763 ordered the colonial governors to reserve all land west of the line for Indian nations.

White settlers already living beyond the Appalachians were charged to withdraw to the east.

Though well intended, this attempt to legislate interracial accord failed completely. Even before the proclamation was issued, the Ottawa chief Pontiac, concerned that the elimination of the French threatened the old treaty and gift-giving system, had gathered together many of the northern tribes that had aided the French assaults on the English forts during the Seven Years' War. Although Pontiac's pan-Indian movement to drive the British out of the Ohio valley collapsed in 1764, it served notice that the interior tribes would not passively watch the invasion of their lands after the French withdrawal from North America.

The English government could sternly command colonial governors to observe the Proclamation of 1763, but it could not enforce its policy. Staggering under an immense wartime debt, England decided to maintain only small army garrisons in America to regulate the interior. Nor could royal governors stop land speculators and settlers from privately purchasing land from trans-Appalachian tribes or from simply encroaching on their land. Under such circumstances, the western frontier seethed with tension after 1763.

Although the Seven Years' War marked an epic victory of Anglo-American arms over the French and redrew the map of North America, it also had important social and economic effects on colonial society. The war convinced the colonists of their growing strength, yet left them debt-ridden and weakened in manpower. The wartime economy spurred economic development and poured British capital into the colonies, yet rendered them more vulnerable to cyclic fluctuations in the British economy.

Military contracts, for example, brought prosperity to most colonies during the war years. Huge orders for ships, arms, uniforms, and provisions enriched northern merchants and provided good prices for farmers as well. Urban artisans enjoyed full employment and high wages, as tailors' needles flashed to meet clothing contracts, shoemakers stitched for an unprecedented demand for shoes, and bakers found armies clamoring for bread. Privateers—privately outfitted ships licensed by colonial governments to attack enemy shipping—enriched the fortunate few. On a single voyage in 1758, John MacPherson snared 18 French ships. The prize money was lavish enough to allow this son of a Scottish immigrant to pour £14,000 into creating a country estate outside Philadelphia, to which he retired in splendor.

The war, however, required heavy taxes and took a huge human toll. Privateering carried many fortune seekers to a watery grave, and the wilderness campaigns from 1755 to 1760 claimed thousands of lives. Garrison life brought wracking fevers (which claimed more victims than enemy weapons), and battlefield medical treatment was too primitive to save many of the wounded. Boston's Thomas Hancock accurately predicted at the beginning of the war that "this province is spirited to [send] every third man to do the work of the Lord." But the Lord's work was expensive. Thomas Pownall, assuming the governorship of Massachusetts in August 1757, found not the "rich, flourishing, powerful, enterprizing" colony he expected but a province "ruined and undone."

The magnitude of the human losses in Boston indicates the war's impact. The wartime muster lists show that nearly every working-class Bostonian tasted military service at some point during the long war. When peace came, Boston had a deficit of almost 700 men in a town of about 2,000 families. The high rate of war widowhood produced a feminization of poverty and required expanded poor relief for the maintenance of husbandless women and fatherless children.

Peace ended the casualties but also brought depression. The British forces in the American theater numbered about 40,000 at the conclusion of the North American campaigns. With their departure for the Caribbean in 1760, the economy slumped badly, especially in the coastal towns. "The tippling soldiery that used to help us out at a dead lift," mused a New York merchant, "are gone to drink [rum]in a warmer region, the place of its production."

The greatest hardships after 1760 fell on laboring people, although even some wealthy merchants went bankrupt. Those with the smallest wages had the thinnest savings to cushion them against hard times. How quickly their security could evaporate

The Year that Reshaped North America
North America After 1763

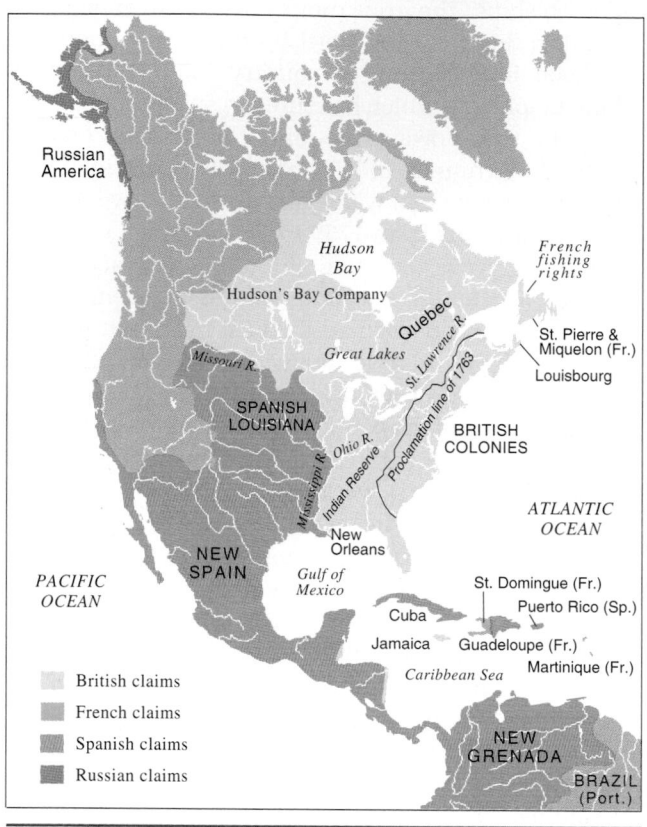

British claims
French claims
Spanish claims
Russian claims

At the Paris Peace Treaty in 1763, France surrendered huge claims west of the Mississippi River to Spain and east of the river to England. England also acquired Florida from Spain.

showed in Philadelphia, where early in the contractionary cycle many poor people, unable to pay their property taxes, were "disposing of their huts and lots to others more wealthy than themselves." The economic security of the middle sector of society also slipped, as established craftsmen and shopkeepers were caught between rising prices and reduced demand for their goods and services. A New York artisan expressed a common lament in 1762. Thankfully, he still had employment, he wrote in the *New-York Gazette*. But despite every effort at unceasing labor and frugal living, he had fallen into poverty and found it "beyond my ability to support my family … [which] can scarcely appear with decency or have necessaries to subsist." His situa-

tion, he added, "is really the case with many of the inhabitants of this city."

In spite of its heavy casualties and economic repercussions, the Seven Years' War paved the way, though not foreseen at the time, for a far larger conflict in the next generation. The legislative assemblies, for example, which had been flexing their muscles at the expense of the governors in earlier decades, accelerated their bid for political power. During wartime, knowing that their governors must obtain military appropriations, they extracted concessions as the price for raising revenues. The war also trained a new group of military and political leaders. In carrying out military operations on a scale unknown in the colonies and in shouldering heavier political responsibilities, men such as George Washington, Samuel Adams, Benjamin Franklin, Patrick Henry, and Christopher Gadsden acquired the experience that would serve them well in the future.

The Seven Years' War, in spite of the severe costs, left many of the colonists with a sense of buoyancy. New Englanders rejoiced at the final victory over the "Papist enemy of the North." Frontiersmen, fur traders, and land speculators also celebrated the French withdrawal, for the West now appeared open for exploitation. This "Garden of the World," trumpeted a Boston almanac publisher, was larger than France, Germany, and Poland combined, "and all well provided with rivers, a very fine wholesome air, a rich soil, … and all things necessary for the conveniency and delight of life." A new frontier now seemed to await those whom opportunity had passed by on the crowded seaboard.

The colonists also felt a new sense of their identity after the war. Surveying a world free of French and Spanish threats, they could not help but reassess the advantages and disadvantages of subordination to England. The colonists would soon discover, a French diplomat predicted at the war's end, "that they stand no longer in need of your protection. You will call on them to contribute towards supporting the burden which they have helped to bring on you; they will answer you by shaking off all dependence."

Although the American colonists inched toward thinking of themselves as a people capable of standing alone, the British viewed the matter differently at the end of the Seven Years' War. From their perspective, the colonists were unreliable and had fought poorly. Many royal army officers who had fought alongside the Americans had little but contempt for the "martial virtue" of the colonists. "He could take a thousand grenadiers to America," boasted one officer, "and geld all the males, partly by force and partly by a little coaxing."

The Crisis with England

George Grenville became the chief minister of England's 25-year-old king, George III, at the end of the Seven Years' War. He inherited a national debt that had billowed from £75 million to £145 million during the war and a nation of wearied taxpayers. To reduce the debt, Grenville proposed new taxes in England and others in America, where the colonists were asked to bear their share of running the empire. Grenville's particular concern was financing the 10,000 British regulars left in North America after 1763 to police French-speaking Canada and the frontier and to remind the unruly American subjects that they were still beholden to the crown. Grenville's revenue program initiated a rift between England and its colonies that a dozen years later would culminate in revolution.

Sugar, Currency, and Stamps

In 1764, Grenville pushed through Parliament several bills that in combination pressed hard against the economic system of the colonies. First came the Revenue Act (or Sugar Act) of 1764. While reducing the tax on imported French molasses from 6 to 3 pence per gallon, it added a number of colonial products to the list of commodities that could be sent only to England. It also required American shippers to post bonds guaranteeing observance of the trade regulations before loading their cargoes. Finally, it strengthened the vice-admiralty courts, where violators of the trade acts were prosecuted.

Many of the colonial legislatures grumbled about the Sugar Act because a strictly enforced duty of 3 pence per gallon on molasses pinched more than the loosely enforced 6-pence duty. But only New York objected that any tax by Parliament to raise revenue (rather than to control trade) violated the rights of overseas English subjects who were unrepresented in Parliament.

On the heels of the Sugar Act came the Currency Act. In 1751, Parliament had forbidden the New England colonies to issue paper money as legal tender, and now it extended that prohibition to all the colonies. In a colonial economy chronically short of hard cash, this constricted trade.

The move to tighten up the machinery of empire confused the colonists because many of the new regulations came from Parliament, which had heretofore been content to allow the king, his ministers, and the Board of Trade to run overseas affairs. In a world where history taught that power and liberty were perpetually at war, generations of colonists had viewed Parliament as a bastion of English liberty, the bulwark against despotic political rule. The Parliament on which colonial legislatures had modeled themselves now began to seem like a violator of colonial rights.

In protesting new parliamentary regulations, colonial leaders were hobbled by uncertainty concerning where Parliament's authority began and ended in administering the colonies. The colonists had always implicitly accepted parliamentary power overseas because it was easier to evade distasteful trade regulations than to contest this power. But the exact limits of that authority were vague.

After Parliament passed the Sugar Act in 1764, Grenville announced his intention to extend to America the stamp duties that had already been imposed in England. However, he gave the colonies a year to suggest alternative ways of raising revenue. The colonies objected strenuously to the proposed stamp tax, but none provided another plan. Knowing that colonial property taxes were slight compared with those in England, Grenville dismissed the petitions that poured in from the colonies and drove the bill through Parliament. The Stamp Act, effective November 1765, required revenue stamps on every newspaper, pamphlet, almanac, legal document, liquor license, college diploma, pack of playing cards, and pair of dice.

Colonial reaction to the Stamp Act ranged from disgruntled submission to mass defiance.

Household Inventories

Historians use probate records to examine social changes in American society. They include wills, the legal disposition of estates, and household inventories taken by court-appointed appraisers that detail the personal possessions left at death. Inventories have been especially valuable in tracing the transformation of colonial communities.

Like tax lists, inventories can be used to show changes in a community's distribution of wealth. But they are far more detailed than tax lists, providing a snapshot of how people lived at the end of their life. Inventories list and value almost everything a person owned—household possessions, equipment, books, clothes and jewelry, cash on hand, livestock and horses, crops and stored provisions. Hence, through inventories, we can measure the quality of life at different social levels. We can also witness how people made choices about investing their savings—in capital goods of their trade such as land, ships, and equipment; in personal goods such as household furnishings and luxury items; or in real property such as land and houses.

Studied systematically (and corrected for biases, which infect this source as well as others), inventories show that by the early 1700s, ordinary householders were improving their standard of living. Finished furniture such as cupboards, beds, tables, and chairs turn up more frequently in inventories. Pewter dinnerware replaces wooden bowls and spoons, bed linen makes an appearance, and books and pictures are sometimes noted.

Among an emerging elite before the Revolution, much more fashionable articles of consumption appear. The partial inventory of Robert Oliver, a wealthy merchant and officeholder living in a Boston suburb, is reproduced here. You can get some idea of the dignified impression Oliver wished to make by looking at his furniture and dishes and by noticing that he owned a mahogany tea table, damask linen, and a bed with curtains. The inventory further suggests the spaciousness of Oliver's house and shows how he furnished each room.

It is helpful when studying inventories to categorize the goods in the following way: those that are needed to survive (basic cooking utensils, for example); those that make life easier or more comfortable (enough plates and beds for each member of the family, for example); and those that make life luxurious (slaves, silver plates, paintings, mahogany furniture, damask curtains, spices, wine, and so forth). Oliver had many luxury goods as well as items that contributed to his use of leisure time and his personal enjoyment. Which items in his inventory do you think were needed only to survive comfortably? Which were luxuries? What other conclusions can you draw about the life style of rich colonial merchants like Oliver?

Beyond revealing a growing social differentiation in colonial society, the inventories help the historian understand the reaction during the Great Awakening to what many ordinary colonists regarded as sinful pride and arrogance displayed by the elite. By the 1760s, this distrust of affluence among simple folk had led to outright hostility toward men who surrounded themselves with the trappings of aristocratic life. Even the ambitious young John Adams, a striving lawyer, was shocked at what he saw at the house of a wealthy merchant in Boston. "Went over the House to view the Furniture, which alone cost a thousand Pound sterling," he exclaimed. "A seat it is for a noble Man, a Prince. The Turkey Carpets, the painted Hangings, the Marble Tables, the rich Beds with crimson Damask Curtains … are the most magnificent of any Thing I have ever seen."

Such a description takes on its full meaning only when contrasted with what inventories tell us about life at the bottom of society. The hundreds of inventories for Bostonians dying in the decade before the American Revolution show that fully half of them died with less than £40 personal wealth and one-quarter with £20 or less. The inventories and wills of Jonathan and Daniel Chandler of Andover, Massachusetts, show the material circumstances of less favored Americans who suffered from the economic distress afflicting New England since the 1730s. Note that Daniel Chandler, like Ebenezer MacIntosh, was a shoemaker. How do the possessions of these brothers compare with Oliver's partial inventory? An examination of these contrasting inventories helps explain the class tension that figured in the revolutionary experience.

Household Inventory of Jonathan Chandler (d. 1745)

Cash	£18p
Gun	1p
Psalmbook	8p
	£19p
Debts	£ 5p
Total	£14p

Household Inventory of Robert Oliver, Wealthy Merchant

Dorchester Jan.ry 11.th 1763.

Inventory of what Estates Real & Personall, belonging to Coll.o Robert Oliver [Esquire] late of Dorchester Deceased, that has been Exhibited to us the Subscribers, for Apprizement, Viz.t

In the Setting Parlour Viz.tt		£4.—.—
a looking Glass		0.6.0
a Small Ditto	@ 6/	3.12.—
12 Metzitens pictures Glaz'd		4.—.—
8 Cartoons D.o Ditto		—.4.—
11 small Pictures		—.10.—
4 Maps		—.10.—
1 Prospect Glass		—.4.—
2 Escutchons Glaz'd		—.6.—
1 pair small hand Irons		—.8.—
1 Shovel & Tongs		—.4.—
1 Tobacco Tongs		—.2.—
1 pair Bellowes		—.2.—
1 Tea Chest		—.1.—
2 Small Waters		1.—.—
1 Mehogony Tea Table		—.2.—
8 China Cups & Saucers		—.—.1
1 Earthen Cream Pott		—.—.4
1 Ditto. Sugar Dish		1.—.—
1 Black Walnut Table		0.6.—
1 Black Ditto Smaller		0.1.—
1 Round painted Table	@ 6/	2.2.—
7 Leather Bottom Chairs		1.3.—
1 Arm.d Chair Common		1.12.—
1 Black Walnut Desk		
1 pair Candlesticks snuffers & Stand Base Mettle		—.4.—
6 Wine Glasses 1 Water Glass		1.—.—
a parcell of Books		0.4.—
a Case with Small Bottles		22.1.5

In the Entry & Stair Case Viz.t	£0.10.—
17 pictures	0.10.0

In the Kitchen Chamber Viz.t		£4.—.—
a Bedstead & Curtains Compleat		5.—.—
a Bed Bolster & 2 pillows		0.1.—
a Under Bed & 1 Chair	@ 6/	0.48.—
2 Rugs & 1 Blankett		09.19.0

In the Dining Room Viz.t		£0.3.——
1 pair of andirons		0.7.——
7 Bass Bottoms Chairs		0.3.——
1 Large Wooden Table		0.1.——
1 Small Ditto Oak		0.6.——
1 Small looking Glass		0.6.——
1 Old Desk		0.2.——
1 Case with 2 Bottles		0.12.——
1 Warming pan		2.0.0

In the Marble Chamber Viz.t		£8.——
1 Bedstead & Curtains Compleat		8.——
1 feather Bed, Bolster & 2 pillows		2.8.——
1 Chest of Drawers		1.——
1 Burce Table	@ 6/	1.16.——
6 Chairs Leather'd Bottoms		—.6.——
1 Small dressing Glass		1.——
1 Small Carpett		—.18.——
1 White Cotton Counterpin		1.12.——
1 pair Blanketts		1.4.——
1 pair holland Sheets	@ 12s/p.r	1.16.——
3 pair Dowlases D.o New	@ 4/	0.14.——
3 pair & 1 Ditto Coarser	@ 3/	0.9.——
3 pair Cotton & Linnen D.o	@ 2/	0.8.——
4 pair Servants Ditto	@ 1/	0.4.——
4 Coarse Table Cloths	@ 1/	0.1.——
10 Ditto Kitchen Towels	@ 12/	3.—.——
5 Diaper Table Cloths	@ 18/	5.8.——
6 Damask Table Cloths	@ 3	0.12.——
4 N. England Diaper D.o	@ 2/	0.8.——
4 pair Linnen pillow Cases	@ 1/	0.5.——
5 Coarser Ditto	@ 6d	0.3.——
6 Diaper Towels	@ 2/	0.14.——
7 Damask Ditto	@ 2s/doz.n	3.6.——
2 doz.n & 9 Damask Napkins		0.1.——
1 Gauze Tea Table Cover		£43.13.0

Household Inventory of Daniel Chandler
(d. 1752), Shoemaker

Bible
Shoe knife
Hammer   Total £12
Last (shoe shaper)
Various notes

This wood engraving, published in 1829 in a history of the United States, recalls a New Hampshire riot in which townspeople lynched and stoned a stamp master in effigy. Cobblestones pried loose from the street seemed to provide the crowd's arsenal. (The Metropolitan Museum of Art, New York, Bequest of Charles Allen Munn)

and pensioners, and an enormous train of underlings and dependents"; they also warned of new measures designed to "suck the life blood" from the people and predicted that troops would be sent to "dragoon us into passive obedience." In many minds, the belief grew that the English were plotting "designs for destroying our constitutional liberties."

Troops indeed came. The attack on the customs officials brought a resolute response from England, where the government regarded the Bostonians' action as insubordinate and selfish. The ministry dispatched two regiments from England and two more from Nova Scotia. The intention was to bring the Bostonians to a proper state of subordination and make them an example to the rest of the colonies. Now cries went up against maintaining standing armies in peacetime, but radical Bostonians who proposed force to prevent the troops from landing got little support from delegates called to a special provincial convention. On October 1, 1768, red-coated troops marched into Boston without resistance.

After the troops occupied Boston, the colonists' main tactic of protest against the Townshend Acts became economic boycott. First in Boston and then in New York and Philadelphia, merchants and consumers adopted nonimportation and nonconsumption agreements. They pledged neither to import nor to use British articles. These measures promised to bring the politically influential English merchants to their aid, for half of British shipping was engaged in

commerce with the colonies, and one-quarter of all English exports were consumed there.

Many colonial merchants, however, especially those tied to the government's interest, had no intention of being bound by a community compact that had no force in law. They had to be persuaded otherwise by street brigades, usually composed of artisans who warmly supported nonimportation as a boon to home manufacturing. Crowd action welled up again in the seaports, as determined patriot bands attacked the homes and warehouses of offending merchants and "rescued" incoming contraband goods seized by zealous customs officials. When the southern colonies also adopted nonimportation agreements in 1768, a new step toward intercolonial union had been taken.

England's attempts to discipline its American colonies and oblige them to share the costs of governing an empire lay in shambles by the end of the 1760s. The employment of troops to restore order undermined the respect for the mother country on which colonial acceptance of its authority ultimately depended. American newspapers denounced new extensions of British authority. Colonial governors quarreled with their legislatures. Customs officials met with determined opposition and were widely accused of arbitrary actions and excessive zeal in enforcing the Navigation Acts. The Townshend duties had failed miserably, yielding less than £21,000 by 1770 while costing British business £700,000 through the colonial nonimportation movement.

Rather than quelling the disorder as King George III hoped, the occupation of Boston by British troops in 1768 increased tensions. In this engraving by Paul Revere, the troops are debarking at the Long Wharf. (Courtesy the Henry Francis du Pont Winterthur Museum)

In London, on March 5, 1770, Parliament repealed all the Townshend duties except the one on tea (which the new minister of state, Lord North, explained was retained "as a mark of the supremacy of Parliament and an efficient declaration of their right to govern the colonies"). On that same evening in Boston, British troops fired on an unruly crowd of heckling citizens. For months, Bostonians had been baiting the "lobsterbacks," as they dubbed the red-coated British soldiers. They hated them for competing with townspeople for menial jobs when off duty, as well as for their military presence. On this evening, a taunting crowd had first hurled insults and snowballs and then surged toward a sentry. After a squad of redcoats joined the sentry, someone cried, "Fire!" When the smoke cleared, five bloody bodies, including that of Ebenezer MacIntosh's brother-in-law, stained the snow-covered street. Bowing to furious popular reaction, Thomas Hutchinson, recently appointed governor, ordered the British troops out of town and arrested the commanding officer and the soldiers involved. They were later acquitted, with two young patriot lawyers, John Adams and Josiah Quincy, Jr., providing a brilliant defense.

In spite of the potential of the "Boston massacre" for galvanizing the colonies into further resistance, opposition to English policies, including economic boycotts, subsided in 1770. Popular leaders such as Samuel Adams in Boston and Alexander McDougall in New York, who had made names for themselves as the standard-bearers of American liberty, had few issues left to exploit. They were further handicapped by the end of the depression that had previously helped sow discontent. Yet the fires of revolution had been not extinguished, but merely damped.

The Growing Rift

From 1770 to 1772, relative quiet descended over the colonies. Not until June 1772 did England provide another inflammatory issue. Then, by announcing that it would pay the salaries of the royal governor and superior court judges in Massachusetts rather than allow the provincial legislature to continue supporting these positions, the crown created a new furor. Even though the measure saved the colony money, it was seen as a dangerous innovation because it undermined a right set forth in the colony's charter and hence was interpreted as a design to impose a despotic government on the colony. Judges paid from London, it was assumed, would respond to London.

Boston's town meeting protested loudly and created a Committee of Correspondence "to state the rights of the colonists ... and to communicate and publish the same to the several towns and to the world." Crown supporters called the committee "the foulest, subtlest, and most venomous serpent ever issued from the egg of sedition." By the end of 1772, another 80 towns in Massachusetts had created committees. In the next year, all but three colonies established Committees of Correspondence in their legislatures.

Samuel Adams was by now the leader of the Boston radicals, for the influence of laboring men like Ebenezer MacIntosh had been quietly reduced. Adams was an experienced caucus politicker, a skilled political journalist, and a man with deep roots among the laboring people despite his Harvard degree. He organized the working ranks through the taverns, clubs, and volunteer fire companies and also secured the support of wealthy merchants such as John Hancock, whose ample purse financed patriotic celebrations and feasts that kept politics on everyone's mind and helped build interclass bridges. In England, Adams became known as one of the most dangerous firebrands in America.

In 1772, a band of Rhode Island colonists gave Adams new material to work with when they attacked a royal warship. The British commander of the *Gaspee* was roundly hated for hounding the fishermen and small traders of Narragansett Bay. When his ship ran aground while pursuing a suspected smuggler, Rhode Islanders took their revenge. Clambering aboard the stranded vessel, they burned it to the waterline. Adding insult to injury, a Rhode Island court convicted the *Gaspee*'s captain of illegally seizing what he was convinced was smuggled sugar and rum. The government in London reacted with cries of high treason. Finding the lips of Rhode Islanders sealed regarding the identity of the arsonists, an investigating committee could do little. The event was tailor-made for Samuel Adams, who used it to "awaken the Ameri-

Paul Revere was not only a noted silversmith and political activist, but also a man who put art to work in the cause of revolutionary politics. This engraving became known throughout the colonies and convinced many people to involve themselves in what had been mainly New England's cause. The smiling British redcoats are reviled in verse: "While faithless P[resto]n and his savage Bonds, / With murd'rous Rancour stretch their bloody Hands, / Like fierce Barbarians grinning o'er their Prey, / Approve the Carnage and enjoy the Day." (American Antiquarian Society)

can colonies, which have been too long dozing upon the brink of ruin."

In early 1773, Parliament's passage of the Tea Act precipitated the final plunge into revolution. The act allowed the East India Company, which was on the verge of bankruptcy, to ship its tea directly to America. By eliminating English middlemen and English import taxes, this provided Americans with the opportunity to buy their tea cheaply from the company's agents in the colonies. Even with the small tax to be paid in the colonies, Indian tea would now undersell smuggled Dutch tea. The Americans would get inexpensive tea, the crown would derive a modest revenue, and the East India Company would obtain a new lease on life. The company soon had 600,000 pounds of tea in 2,000 chests ready for shipment to America.

Parliament monumentally miscalculated the American response. For several years, merchants in Philadelphia and New York had been flagrantly smuggling Dutch tea. As a consequence, imports of English tea in the two seaports plummeted from 500,000 pounds in 1768 to a mere 650 pounds in 1772. The merchants bitterly denounced the new act for giving the East India Company a monopoly on the American tea market. Other monopolies would follow, they predicted, and middlemen of all kinds would be eliminated. The colonists also objected that the government was shrewdly trying to gain implicit acceptance of Parliament's taxing power by offering tea at a new reduced rate. When Americans drank the taxed tea, they would also be swallowing the English right to impose taxes.

The colonists quickly demonstrated that their principles were not entirely in their pocketbooks. Mass meetings in the port towns soon forced the resignation of the East India Company's agents, and citizens vowed to stop the obnoxious tea at the water's edge.

Governor Hutchinson of Massachusetts brought the tea crisis to a climax. He decided that to yield once more to popular pressure would forever cripple English sovereignty in America. The popular party led by Samuel Adams had been urging the citizens to demonstrate that they were not yet prepared for the "yoke of slavery" by sending the tea back to England. Hutchinson's refusal to grant the tea ships clearance papers to return to England with their car-

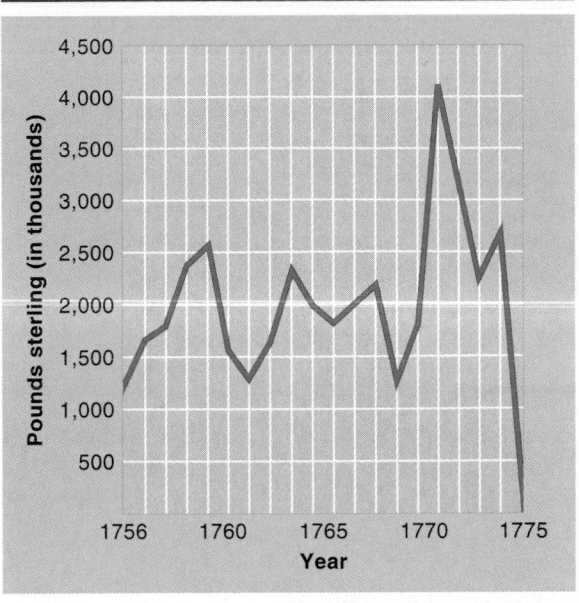

British Exports to North America, 1756–1775

The on-again, off-again American boycotts of British imports can be seen in this chart. The first big dip, from 1760 to 1762, was caused by the departure of the free-spending British army and navy from the North American theater during the Seven Years' War. Source: U.S. Bureau of the Census.

goes finally led to dramatic action. Buoyed by resolutions from surrounding towns, 5,000 Bostonians packed Old South Church on December 16, 1773. The meeting noisily passed resolutions urging the governor to clear the ships. But Hutchinson was not swayed by the Bostonians' determination to resist what they regarded as another affront to their liberties. "This meeting," despaired Samuel Adams, "can do no more to save the country."

At nightfall, a band of Bostonians, dressed as Indians, boarded the tea ships, broke open the chests of tea, and flung £10,000 worth of the East India Company's property into Boston harbor. George Hewes, a 31-year-old shoemaker, recalled how he had garbed himself as a Mohawk, blackened "face and hands with coal dust in the shop of a blacksmith," and joined men of all ranks in marching stealthily to the wharves to do their work.

Now the die was cast. Lord North, the king's chief minister, called the Bostonians "fanatics" and argued that the dispute was no longer about taxes but about whether England had any authority at all over the colonies. George III put it succinctly: "We must master them or totally leave them to themselves and treat them as aliens."

Thoroughly aroused, Parliament passed the Coercive Acts, a set of stern laws, which Bostonians promptly labeled the "Intolerable Acts." The acts closed the port of Boston to all shipping until the colony paid for the destroyed tea. They declared British soldiers and officials immune from local court trials for acts committed while suppressing civil disturbances. To hamstring the colony's truculent political assemblies, Parliament amended the Massachusetts charter to transform the council from an upper legislative chamber, elected by the lower house, to a body appointed by the governor. This stripped the council of its veto power over the governor's decisions.

The act also struck at local government by authorizing the governor to prohibit all town meetings except for one annual meeting in each town to elect local officers of government. Finally, General Thomas Gage, commander in chief of British forces in America, replaced Thomas Hutchinson as governor. "This is the day, then," declared Edmund Burke in the House of Commons, "that you wish to go to war with all America, in order to conciliate that country to this."

The English plan to strangle Massachusetts into submission and hope for acquiescence elsewhere in the colonies proved popular in England. Earlier, the colonies had gained supporters in Parliament for their resistance to what many regarded as attacks on their fundamental privileges. Now this support evaporated. After a decade of debating constitutional rights and mobilizing sentiment against what many believed was a systematic plot to enslave freeborn citizens, the Americans found their maneuvering room severely narrowed.

When the Intolerable Acts arrived in May 1774 aboard the *Harmony*, Boston's town meeting reacted belligerently. It dispatched a circular letter to all the colonies urging an end to trade with England. This met with faint support. But a second call, for a meeting in Philadelphia of delegates from all colonies, received a better response. The Continental Congress, as it was called, now began to transform a ten-year debate conducted by separate colonies into a unified American cause.

Fifty-five delegates from all the colonies except Georgia converged on Carpenter's Hall in Philadelphia in September 1774. The discussions centered not on how to prepare for a war that many sensed was inevitable, but on how to resolve differences that most delegates feared were irreconcilable. Overcoming sectional prejudices and hostilities was as important as the formal debates. New Englanders were especially eyed with suspicion for their reputed intolerance and self-interest. "We have numberless prejudices to remove here," wrote John Adams from Philadelphia. "We have been obliged to keep ourselves out of sight, and to feel pulses, and to sound the depths; to insinuate our sentiments, designs, and desires by means of

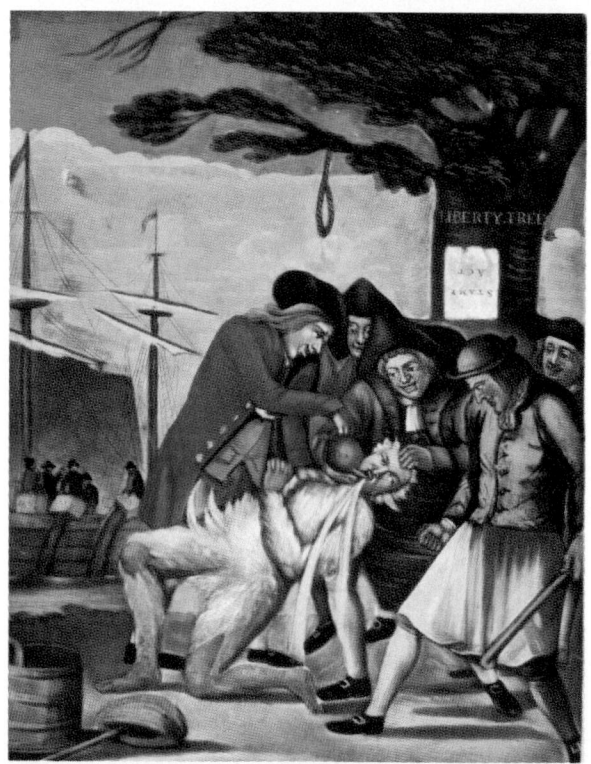

Public sentiment against the importation of tea and other British goods often found expression in a coat of tar and feathers applied to the bare skin of the offending importer. Note the symbols in The Bostonians Paying the Excise-Man: *the Liberty Tree with a hangman's noose and the overturned copy of the Stamp Act. In the background, Bostonians dump chests of tea into the harbor. (Library of Congress)*

other persons, sometimes of one province, and sometimes of another."

The Continental Congress was by no means a unified body. Some delegates, led by cousins Samuel and John Adams from Massachusetts and Richard Henry Lee and Patrick Henry of Virginia, argued for outright resistance to Parliament's Coercive Acts. Moderate delegates from the middle colonies, led by Joseph Galloway of Pennsylvania and James Duane of New York, urged restraint and further attempts at reconciliation. After weeks of debate, the delegates agreed to issue a restrained Declaration of Rights and Resolves. It attempted to define American grievances and to justify the colonists' defiance of English policies and laws by appealing to the "immutable laws of nature, the principles of the English constitution, and the several [colonial] charters and compacts" under which they lived. More concrete was the Congress's agreement on a plan of resistance. If England did not rescind the Intolerable Acts by December 1, 1774, a ban on all imports and exports between the colonies and Great Britain, Ireland, and the British West Indies would take effect. Some exceptions were made for the export of southern staple commodities in order to keep reluctant southern colonies in the fold.

By the time the Congress adjourned in late October, leaders from different colonies had learned of one another's conditions, measured one another's rhetoric and temperament, and transformed what had been primarily Boston's cause into a national movement. "Government is dissolved [and] we are in a state of nature," Patrick Henry argued dramatically. "The distinctions between Virginians, Pennsylvanians, New Yorkers, and New Englanders are no more. I am not a Virginian, but an American." Many of Henry's fellow delegates were a long way from converting their provincial identities to a national one, but in adjourning, the Congress agreed to reconvene in May 1775.

Even before the Second Continental Congress met, the fabric of government had been badly torn in most colonies. Revolutionary committees, conventions, and congresses, entirely unauthorized by law, were replacing legal governing bodies. Assuming authority in defiance of royal governors, who suspended truculent legislatures in many colonies, they often operated on instructions from mass meetings where the legal franchise was ignored. These extralegal bodies created and armed militia units, bullied merchants and shopkeepers refusing to conform to popularly authorized boycotts, levied taxes, operated the courts, and obstructed the work of English customs officials. By the end of 1774, all but three colonies defied their own charters by appointing provincial assemblies without royal authority. In the next year, this independently created power became evident in the nearly complete cessation of trade with England.

The Final Rupture

The final spark to the revolutionary powder keg was struck in early 1775. General Gage had assumed the governorship of Massachusetts 11 months earlier and occupied Boston with 4,000 troops—one for every adult male in the town. In April 1775, the government in London ordered Gage to arrest "the principal actors and abettors" of insurrection in Massachusetts. As a first step, he sent 700 redcoats out of Boston under cover of night to seize colonial arms and ammunition in nearby Concord. But Americans learned of the plan. When the troops reached Lexington at dawn, 70 "Minutemen"—townsmen available on a minute's notice—occupied the village green. In the skirmish that ensued, 18 Massachusetts farmers fell, eight of them mortally wounded.

Marching six miles west, the British entered Concord, where another firefight broke out. Withdrawing, the redcoats made their way back to Boston, harassed by militiamen firing from farmhouses and barns and from behind stone walls. Before the bloody day ended, 273 British and 95 Americans lay dead or wounded. News of the bloodshed swept through the colonies. Within weeks, thousands of men besieged the British troops in Boston. One colonist reported that wherever one traveled, "you see the inhabitants training, making firelocks, casting mortars, shells, and shot."

The outbreak of fighting vastly altered the debates of the Second Continental Congress, which assembled in Philadelphia in May 1775. The Congress had the same slim powers as its predecessor,

TO THE
Delaware Pilots.

WE took the Pleasure, some Days since, of kindly admonishing you *to do your Duty*; if perchance you should meet with the *(Tea,)* SHIP POLLY, CAPTAIN AYRES; a THREE DECKER which is hourly expected,

We have now to add, that Matters ripen fast here; and that *much is expected from those Lads who meet with the Tea Ship.*----There is some Talk of A HANDSOME REWARD FOR THE PILOT WHO GIVES THE FIRST GOOD ACCOUNT OF HER.----How that may be, we cannot *for certain* determine: But ALL agree, that TAR and FEATHERS will be his Portion, who pilots her into this Harbour.   And we will answer for ourselves, that, whoever is committed to us, as an Offender against the Rights of *America*, will experience the utmost Exertion of our Abilities; as

THE COMMITTEE FOR TARRING AND FEATHERING.

but it acquired awesome new responsibilities. Many delegates knew one another from the earlier Congress. But fresh faces appeared, including Boston's wealthy merchant, John Hancock; a tall, young planter-lawyer from Virginia, Thomas Jefferson; and the much-applauded Benjamin Franklin, who had arrived from London only four days before the Congress convened.

The Congress had no power to legislate or command; it could only request and recommend. Delegate John Adams worried that such a body could form a constitution "for a great empire," and "at the same time they have a country of 1,500 miles to fortify, millions to arm and train, a naval power to begin, an extensive commerce to regulate, numerous tribes of Indians to negotiate with, a standing army of 27,000 men to raise pay, victual, and officer."

Another 14 months elapsed before the Congress issued a formal declaration of independence, but the war with England—and a civil war in America—had already begun. Meeting in the statehouse in Philadelphia, where the king's arms hung over the entrance and the inscription on the tower bell read "Proclaim liberty throughout the land unto all the inhabitants thereof," the Second Congress set to work. It authorized a continental army of 20,000 and, partly to cement Virginia to the cause, chose George Washington as commander in chief. It issued a "Declaration of Causes of Taking-up Arms," sent the king an "Olive Branch Petition" humbly begging him to remove the obstacles to reconciliation, made moves to secure the neutral-

ity of the interior Indian tribes, issued paper money, erected a postal system, and approved plans for a military hospital.

While debate continued over whether the colonies ought to declare themselves independent, military action grew hotter. The hotheaded Ethan Allen and his Green Mountain Boys from eastern New York captured Fort Ticonderoga, controlling the Champlain valley, in May 1775. On New Year's Day in 1776, the British shelled Norfolk, Virginia. In March 1776, Washington's army forced the British to evacuate Boston. In spite of these acts of aggression, many members of the Congress dreaded a final rupture and still hoped for reconciliation with England. Such hopes crumbled at the end of 1775 when news arrived that the king, rejecting the Olive Branch Petition, had dispatched 20,000 additional British troops to quell the American insurrection and had proclaimed the colonies in "open and avowed rebellion." Those fatal words made all the Congress's actions treasonable and turned all who obeyed them into traitors.

By the time Thomas Paine's hard-hitting pamphlet *Common Sense* appeared in Philadelphia on January 9, 1776, members of the Congress were talking less gingerly about independence. Paine's blunt words and compelling rhetoric smashed through the remaining reserve. "O ye that love mankind! Ye that dare oppose not only the tyranny, but also the tyrant, stand forth!" wrote Paine. Within weeks, the pamphlet was in bookstalls all over the colonies. "The public sentiment which a few weeks before had shuddered at the tremen-

Steps on the Road to Revolution

1763	Treaty of Paris ends Seven Years' War between England and France; France cedes Canada to England.
	Proclamation of 1763 forbids white settlement west of Appalachian Mountains.
1764	Sugar Act sets higher duties on imported sugar, lower duties on molasses, and enlarges the power of vice-admiralty courts.
	Currency Act prohibits issuance of paper money by colonies.
1765	Stamp Act requires revenue-raising stamps purchased from British-appointed stamp distributors on printed documents.
	Stamp Act Congress meets in New York.
	Quartering Act requires colonies to furnish British troops with housing and certain provisions.
	Sons of Liberty formed in New York City and thereafter in many towns.
1766	Declaratory Act asserts Parliament's sovereignty over the colonies after repealing Stamp Act.
	Rent riots by New York tenant farmers.
1767	Townshend Revenue Acts impose duties on tea, glass, paper, paints, and other items.
	South Carolina Regulators organize in backcountry.
1768	British troops sent to Boston.
1770	British troops kill four and wound eight American civilians in Boston Massacre.
1771	Battle of Alamance pits frontier North Carolina Regulators against eastern militia led by royal governor.
1772	British schooner *Gaspee* burned in Rhode Island.
	Committee of Correspondence formed in Boston and thereafter in other cities.
1773	Tea Act reduces duty on tea but gives East India Company right to sell directly to Americans.
	Boston Tea Party dumps £10,000 of East India Company tea into Boston harbor.
1774	Coercive Acts close port of Boston, restrict provincial and town governments in Massachusetts, and send additional troops to Boston.
	Quebec Act attaches trans-Appalachian interior north of Ohio River to government of Quebec.
	First Continental Congress meets and forms Continental Association to boycott British imports.
1775	Battles of Lexington and Concord cause 95 American and 273 British casualties; Americans take Fort Ticonderoga.
	Second Continental Congress meets and assumes many powers of an independent government.
	Dunmore's Proclamation in Virginia promises freedom to slaves and indentured servants fleeing to British ranks.
	Prohibitory Act embargoes American goods.
	George III proclaims Americans in open rebellion.
1776	Thomas Paine publishes *Common Sense*.
	British troops evacuate Boston.
	Declaration of Independence.

dous obstacles, with which independence was envisioned," declared Edmund Randolph of Virginia, now "overleaped every barrier."

The Continental Congress continued to debate independence during the spring of 1776, even as the war became bloodier. While the delegates talked, men under arms acted. Washington's army forced the British to withdraw from Boston but an American assault on Quebec failed in May 1776. England embargoed all trade to the colonies and ordered the seizure of American ships. That convinced the Congress to declare its ports open to all countries. "Nothing is left now," Joseph Hewes of North Carolina admitted, "but to fight it out." It was almost anticlimactic when Richard Henry Lee introduced his congressional resolution on June 7 calling for a declaration of independence. After two days of debate, the Congress ordered a committee chaired by Jefferson to begin drafting the document.

Though it would become revered as the new nation's birth certificate, the declaration was not a highly original statement. It drew heavily on the addresses that the Congress had been issuing to justify American resistance, and it presented a theory of government that was embedded in the scores of pamphlets that had issued from the colonial presses over the previous decade. The ringing phrases that "all men are created equal, that they are endowed by their Creator with certain unalienable Rights, that among these are Life, Liberty and the pursuit of Happiness" were familiar in the writing of many pamphleteers, including John Adams, Thomas Paine, and James Wilson.

Jefferson's committee brought its handiwork before the Congress on June 28. The proposals were read and ordered to "lie on the table" until the following Monday, July 1. "This morning is assigned for the greatest debate of all," noted John Adams, when the Congress reconvened. "May Heaven prosper the new-born republic, and make it more glorious than any former republics have been." At the end of the day, nine colonies voted to adopt the declaration, two voted against, one delegation split, and one abstained. The next day, July 2, twelve delegations voted yes, with New York's abstaining, thus allowing the Congress to say that the vote for independence was unanimous. Two days more were spent cutting and polishing the document. The major change was the elimination of a long argument blaming the king for slavery in America.

On July 4, Congress sent the Declaration of Independence to the printer. Four days later, Philadelphians thronged to the statehouse to hear it read aloud. They huzzahed the reading, tore the king's arms from above the statehouse door, and later that night, amid cheers, toasts, and clanging church bells, hurled this symbol of more than a century and a half of colonial dependency on England into a roaring bonfire.

The Ideology of Revolutionary Republicanism

In the years after 1763, the colonists responded to a variety of ideas that gave meaning to the events and conditions they were experiencing. Most of these ideas were formally expressed, in

Liberty always had to struggle against power, as American colonists saw it; in this cartoon, England (power) forces Liberty (America in the form of a woman) to drink the "Bitter Draught" of tea. Uncompliant, America spits the tea into England's face while another corrupt Englishman peeks under her petticoat. (Massachusetts Historical Society)

hundreds of newspaper articles and pamphlets, by educated lawyers, clergymen, merchants, and planters, but some came from the middling and lower ranks of society in the form of broadsides, appeals in the newspapers, and even street demonstrations in which ordinary people carried out ideologically laden rituals of humiliation against their enemies such as tarring and feathering and burnings in effigy. Gradually, the colonists pieced together a political ideology, borrowed partly from English political thought, partly from the theories of the Enlightenment, and partly from their own experiences. Historians call this new ideology "revolutionary republicanism." But it is important to understand that because the colonists varied widely in interests and experiences, there was never a single coherent ideology to which they all subscribed.

A Plot Against Liberty

Many American colonists subscribed to the notion advanced by earlier English Whig writers that corrupt and power-hungry men were slowly extinguishing the lamp of liberty in England. The so-called country party represented by these Whig pamphleteers proclaimed itself the guardian of the true principles of the English constitution and opposed the "court" party representing the king and his appointees.

When the king's ministers began a new program for disciplining the empire after 1763, American Whig writers were intellectually prepared to view the new laws and policies as attacks on such traditional English liberties as balanced government, representative rights, and disestablishment of standing armies in peacetime. Even Parliament, traditionally the preserver of the people's rights against tyrannical executive power, seemed to threaten a despotism of its own in its alliance with the monarchy. Every ministerial policy and parliamentary act in the decade after the Stamp Act appeared as a subversion of English liberties. Most Americans regarded resistance to such blows against liberty as wholly justified.

The belief that England was carrying out "a deep-laid and desperate plan of imperial despotism ... for the extinction of all civil liberty," as the

Boston town meeting expressed it in 1770, spread rapidly in the next few years. By 1774, John Adams was writing of the "conspiracy against the public liberty [that] was first regularly formed and begun to be executed in 1763 and 1764." From London, America's favorite writer, Benjamin Franklin, described the "extreme corruption prevalent among all orders of men in this old rotten state." Another pamphleteer reached the conclusion that England was no longer "in a condition at present to suckle us, being pregnant with vermin that corrupt her milk and convert her blood and juices into poison."

Among many Americans, especially merchants, the attack on constitutional rights blended closely with the threats to their economic interests contained in the tough new trade policies. Merchants perceived a coordinated attack on their "lives, liberties, and property," as they frequently phrased it. If a man was not secure in his property, he could not be secure in his political citizenship, for it was property that allowed a man the independence to shape his identity.

Revitalizing American Society

The continuing crisis over the imperial relationship by itself inspired many colonists to resist impending tyranny. But the revolutionary mentality of others was also nourished by a belief that an opportunity was at hand to revitalize American society. They believed that the colonies had been undergoing a silent transformation and that the growing commercial connection with the decadent and corrupt mother country had injected deadly fluids into the American bloodstream. They worried about the luxury and vice they saw around them and came to believe that resistance to England would return American society to a state of civic virtue, spartan living, and godly purpose.

The fervent support of the patriot movement by much of the colonial clergy, especially in New England, and the clergy's importance in writing protest pamphlets helped give a high-toned moral character to colonial protest. As in most revolutionary movements, the notion of moral regeneration, of a societywide rebirth through battle against a corrupt enemy, ennobled the cause. Such appeals resonated most strongly in New England, where even so secular a man as John Adams groaned at the "universal spirit of debauchery, dissipation, luxury, effeminacy and gaming." But they also inspired people in areas that had been affected a generation before by the Great Awakening.

The growth of a revolutionary spirit among common people also owed much to the plain style of polemical writers such as Thomas Paine and Patrick Henry. Paine's *Common Sense* transformed the terms of the imperial argument by attacking monarchy itself. Its astounding popularity—it went through 25 editions in 1776 and sold more copies than any printed piece in colonial history—stemmed not only from its argument, but also from its style. Paine wrote for the common people, assuming their knowledge of nothing more than

the Bible. Using biblical imagery and plain language, he appealed to their Calvinist heritage and their belief in their providential destiny. After savagely attacking the king, whom he called "a royal brute," Paine appealed to millennial yearnings: "We have it in our power to begin the world over again. The birthday of a new world is at hand," if only the Americans would stand up for liberty, the goddess whom "Europe regards ... like a stranger, and England hath given ... warning to depart."

Paine avoided the elaborate legalistic style of most of the pamphlets written by lawyers and clergymen in the preceding decade. His language could be understood on the docks, in the taverns, on the streets, and in the farmyards. Many Whig leaders found his pungent language and egalitarian call for ending hereditary privilege and concentrated power too strong. They denounced the disheveled immigrant with "genius in his eyes" as a "crack-brained zealot for democracy" and a dan-

In Common Sense, *Thomas Paine dared to articulate, in plain but muscular language, the thoughts of rebellion and independence that others had only alluded to. Note that Paine did not put his name on the title page of* Common Sense, *though he was quickly identified as the author. (Library of Congress (left)/National Portrait Gallery, London (right))*

gerous man who appealed to "every silly clown and illiterate mechanic." But thousands who read or listened to *Common Sense* were radicalized by it, and came to believe that not only could independence be wrested from England but also a new social and political order could be created in North America.

The Turmoil of Revolutionary Society

The long struggle with England over colonial rights between 1764 and 1776 did not occur in a unified society. Social and economic change, which accelerated in the late colonial period, brought deep unrest and calls for reform from many quarters. By the end of the Seven Years' War, faith in the internal social systems of the colonies had waned among many colonists, just as allegiance to the mother country and to the British mercantile system had worn thin.

Many of the colonists who struggled for security in the aftermath of the Seven Years' War hoped that migration to frontier land would improve their fortunes. A flood of new immigrants from Ireland and Germany after the Treaty of Paris in 1763 added to the pressure to reach the trans-Appalachian river valleys. However, the western option involved much violence with Indian tribes unreceptive to encroaching settlers. So most colonists chose to work out their destinies at home or in other communities along the coastal plain to which they migrated in search of opportunity.

As agitation against English policy intensified, previously passive people took a more active interest in politics. In this charged atmosphere, the constitutional struggle with England spread quickly over its original boundaries into uncharted territory. Groups emerged—slaves, urban laboring people, backcountry farmers, evangelicals, women—who enunciated goals of their own that were sometimes only loosely connected to the struggle with England. The stridency and potential power of these groups raised for many upper-class leaders the frightening specter of a radically changed society. Losing control of

the protests they had initially led, many of them would abandon the resistance movement against England.

Urban People

Although the cities contained only about 5 percent of the colonial population, they formed the vital cores of revolutionary agitation. As centers of communications, government, and commerce, they led the way in protesting English policy, and they soon contained the most politicized citizens in America. Local politics could be rapidly transformed as the struggle against England became enmeshed with calls for internal reform.

In Philadelphia, for example, craftsmen had usually acquiesced in politics to the merchant and lawyer politicos before the Seven Years' War. But economic difficulties in the 1760s and 1770s led them to band together within their craft and their community. Artisans played a central role in forging a nonimportation agreement in 1768, calling public meetings, publishing newspaper appeals, organizing secondary boycotts against foot-dragging merchants, and ferreting out and tarring and feathering opponents to their policies. Cautious merchants complained that mere artisans had "no right to give their sentiments respecting an importation" and called the craftsmen a "rabble." But artisans, casting off their customary deference, forged ahead.

By 1772, artisans were filling elected municipal positions and insisting on their right to participate equally with their social superiors in nominating assemblymen and other important officeholders. They also began lobbying for reform laws. The craftsmen called for elected representatives to be more accountable to their constituents. Genteel Philadelphians muttered, "It is time the tradesmen were checked—they ought not to intermeddle in state affairs—they will become too powerful."

By 1774, working-class intermeddling in state affairs had taken a bold new step—the de facto assumption of governmental powers by committees called into being by the people at large. Craftsmen had first clothed themselves in such extralegal authority in policing the nonimportation agreement in 1769. Five years later, in response to the Intolerable Acts, they put forward a radical slate of candidates for a committee to enforce a new economic boycott. Their ticket drubbed one nominated by the city's conservative merchants.

The political mobilization and heightened consciousness of laboring Philadelphians continued as the impasse with England reached a climax in 1775. Many pacifist Quaker leaders of the city had abandoned politics by this time, and other conservative merchants had also concluded that mob rule had triumphed. Into the leadership vacuum stepped a group of radicals from the middling ranks: the fiery Scots-Irish doctor Thomas Young, who had agitated in Boston and Albany before migrating to Philadelphia; Timothy Matlack, a hardware retailer who was popular with the

Benjamin Rush, a young Philadelphia doctor, was one of the revolutionary radicals who wanted to reform American society as well as win independence. Among the reforms Rush promoted were abolishing slavery and establishing free public schools that would teach women as well as men. (Charles Willson Peale, Portrait of Benjamin Rush, 1783/The Henry Francis duPont Winterthur Museum)

lower class for matching his prize bantam cocks against those of New York's aristocratic James Delancy; James Cannon, a young schoolteacher; Benjamin Rush, whose new medical practice took him into the garrets and cramped rooms of the city's poor; and Thomas Paine, a recent immigrant seeking something better in America than he had found as an ill-paid excise officer in England.

The political support of the new radical leaders was centered in the 31 companies of the Philadelphia militia, composed mostly of laboring men, and in the extralegal committees now controlling the city's economic life. Their leadership helped overcome the conservatism of the regularly elected Pennsylvania legislature, which was resisting the movement of the Continental Congress toward independence. In addition, the new radical leaders demanded internal reforms: opening up opportunity; curbing the accumulation of wealth by "our great merchants" who were "making immense fortunes at the expense of the people"; abolishing the property requirement for voting; allowing militiamen to elect their officers; and imposing stiff fines, to be used for the support of the families of poor militiamen, on men who refused militia service.

Philadelphia's radicals never controlled the city. They always jostled for position with prosperous artisans and shopkeepers of more moderate views and with cautious lawyers and merchants. But mobilization among artisans, laborers, and mariners, in other cities as well as Philadelphia, became part of the chain of events that led toward independence. Whereas most of the patriot elite fought only to change English colonial policy, the populace of the cities also struggled for internal reforms and raised notions of how an independent American society might be reorganized.

Patriot Women

Women also played a vital role in the relentless movement toward revolution, and they drew upon revolutionary arguments to define their own goals. Women signed nonimportation agreements, harassed noncomplying merchants, and helped organize "fast days," during which communities prayed for deliverance from English oppression. But the women's most important role was in facilitating the economic boycott of English goods. The success of the nonconsumption pacts depended on substituting homespun cloth for English textiles on which colonists of all classes had always relied. From Georgia to Maine, women and children began spinning yarn and weaving cloth. "Was not every fireside, indeed a theatre of politics?" John Adams remembered after the war. Towns often vied patriotically with each other in the manufacture of cotton, linen, and woolen cloth, the women staging open-air spinning contests to publicize their commitment. In 1769, the women of tiny Middletown, Massachusetts, set the standard by weaving 20,522 yards of cloth, about 160 yards each.

After the Tea Act in 1773, the interjection of politics into the household economy increased as patriotic women boycotted their favorite drink. Newspapers carried recipes for tea substitutes and recommendations for herbal teas. In Wilmington, North Carolina, women paraded solemnly through the town and then made a ritual display of their patriotism by burning their imported tea. Many women could agree with one Rachel Wells: "I have done as much to carry on the war as many that set now at the helm of government."

Women's perception of their role was also changed by colonial protests and petitions against England's arbitrary uses of power. The more male leaders talked about England's intentions to "enslave" the Americans and England's callous treatment of its colonial "subjects," the more American women began to rethink their own domestic situations. The language of protest against England reminded many American women that they too were badly treated "subjects" of their husbands, who often dealt with them cruelly and exercised power over them arbitrarily. If there was to be independence, new laws must be passed, Abigail Adams reminded her husband John in March 1776. As they did their work, the male lawmakers should think about the rights of women and their enslavement by men. Choosing words and phrases that had been used over and over in the protests against England, she wrote: "Do not put such unlimited power into the hand of the husbands.... Put it out of the power of the vicious and the lawless to use us with cruelty and indignity," she insisted. "Remember, all men would be tyrants if they could." Borrowing directly from the republican ideology used to protest Parliament's attempts to tax the Americans, Abigail Adams warned that American women "will not hold ourselves bound by any laws in which we have no voice, or representation" and even promised that women would "foment a rebellion" if men did not heed their rightful claims.

As marketgoers and consumers, urban women played a crucial role in applying economic pressure on England during the prerevolutionary decade. This British cartoon, published in 1775, derisively depicts a group of North Carolina women signing an anti-tea agreement. (Library of Congress)

A Revolutionary People, 1775–1828

C O M P A R A T I V E   C H R O N O L O G I E S

Political and Diplomatic	Social and Economic	Cultural and Technological

1775

Political and Diplomatic	Social and Economic	Cultural and Technological
1776 Cherokee War; Declaration of Independence; British evacuate Boston and occupy New York	1775 Lord Dunmore's proclamation; Philadelphians organize first anti-slavery society	1776 Thomas Paine publishes *Common Sense*; Adam Smith publishes *Wealth of Nations*
1777 Burgoyne defeated at Saratoga; Washington's army encamps at Valley Forge	1780 Pennsylvania begins gradual abolition of slavery	1778 New Jersey Society for Promoting Agriculture
1778 Treaty of alliance with France; British peace commission fails	1781 Bank of North America	1780 American Academy of Arts and Sciences
1779 Sullivan's expedition against the Iroquois	1783 Massachusetts Supreme Court abolishes slavery	1781 Massachusetts Medical Society
1780 British capture Charleston	1784 Empress of China sails to Canton; Treaty of Fort Stanwix	1782 Crèvecoeur, *Letters from an American Farmer*; first Catholic parochial school established in Philadelphia
1781 Cornwallis surrenders to Washington at Yorktown; Articles of Confederation ratified; Robert Morris named superintendent of finance		1783 Noah Webster's *Spelling Book*
1782 British evacuate Savannah and Charleston		1784 Jefferson's *Notes on Virginia*
1783 Treaty of Paris with Great Britain ends Revolutionary War		

1785

Political and Diplomatic	Social and Economic	Cultural and Technological
1785 Congress adopts Land Ordinance; Jay-Gardoqui negotiations	1785 Treaty of Hopewell	1787 John Fitch launches first American steamboat; *Federalist Papers* published; Joel Barlow's, *Vision of Columbus*
1786 Annapolis convention	1786 Virginia statute of religious freedom	
1786–1787 Shays's Rebellion	1787 Free African School established in New York City	
1787 Northwest Ordinance; Constitutional Convention in Philadelphia	1789 Treaty of Fort Harmar	1789 State University of North Carolina begins instruction; Thanksgiving first celebrated as national holiday
1788 Constitution ratified	1790 Non-Intercourse Act regulates treaty-making by states; Samuel Slater's cotton mill	1790 Roman Catholic episcopate created; first federal patent issued
1789 George Washington inaugurated; French Revolution begins		1790s Second Great Awakening begins
1790 Congress adopts Hamilton's funding and assumption program; Hamilton's Reports on the Public Credit	1792 New York Stock Exchange established	1791 Anthracite coal discovered in Pennsylvania; first macadam road opens in Pennsylvania; Franklin's *Autobiography* published in France
1791 Bill of Rights becomes part of Constitution; first U.S. Bank established	179 Yellow fever epidemic hits Philadelphia	
1792 Washington reelected	1794 Battle of Fallen Timbers; Richard Allen establishes Bethel African Methodist Episcopal Church	1793 Eli Whitney perfects cotton gin
1793 Democratic-Republican societies founded; Washington issues Neutrality Proclamation; first Fugitive Slave Act; Citizen Genêt affair		1794 Charles Willson Peale establishes Philadelphia Museum
1794 Whiskey Rebellion		

Political and Diplomatic

1795 Jay's Treaty with Great Britain
1796 John Adams elected president
1797 XYZ affair
1798 Undeclared naval war with France; Alien and Sedition Acts; Naturalization Act; Virginia and Kentucky Resolutions
1800 Capital moves to Washington, D.C.
1801 Thomas Jefferson elected president; John Marshall named chief justice
1803 *Marbury* v. *Madison;* Louisiana Purchase
1803–1806 Lewis and Clark expedition
1804 Jefferson reelected

1806 Non-Importation Act
1807 Embargo Act; *Chesapeake-Leopard* affair
1808 James Madison elected president
1809 Non-Intercourse Act of 1809
1810 Macon's Bill No. 2
1812 West Florida annexed; Madison reelected; war declared against Britain
1814 Treaty of Ghent ends War of 1812
1814–1815 Hartford Convention

1816 Second U.S. Bank; first protective tariff; Monroe elected president
1819 *McCulloch* v. *Maryland;* Spain cedes East Florida
1820 Missouri Compromise; Monroe reelected
1822 Diplomatic recognition of Latin American republics
1823 Monroe Doctrine
1824 Henry Clay's "American System"; John Quincy Adams elected president; *Gibbons* v. *Ogden*

Social and Economic

1795 Treaty of Greenville
1796 Congress establishes Indian factory system
1800 Gabriel Prosser's Rebellion

1807 Congress prohibits slave trade
1808 John Jacob Astor founds American Fur Company
1809 Tecumseh forms confederation
1811 Battle of Kithtippecanoe
1813 Boston Manufacturing Company formed at Waltham, Massachusetts; Battle of the Thames
1814 Jackson defeats Creek Indians at Horseshoe Bend

1815 Battle of New Orleans
1817 American Colonization Society established
1818 First Seminole War
1819–1821 Financial panic and depression
1824 Bureau of Indian Affairs created; female weavers strike at Pawtucket, Rhode Island
1825 Erie Canal opens; Robert Owen begins New Harmony
1826 Sequoyah devises Cherokee alphabet
1827 Cherokee constitution established

Cultural and Technological

1799 Nathaniel Bowditch's, *Practical Navigator*
1800 Library of Congress established

1805–1809 Pike explores the West
1807 Robert Fulton launches steamboat *Clermont;* cast iron plow patented
1811 Construction begins on Cumberland Road
1812 Benjamin Rush's, *Diseases of the Mind*
1814 Francis Scott Key writes "The Star Spangled Banner"

1821 James Fenimore Cooper's, *The Spy;* Emma Willard founds New York Female Seminary at Troy, New York

A People in Revolution

Among the Americans wounded and captured at the Battle of Bunker Hill in the spring of 1775 was Lieutenant William Scott of Peterborough, New Hampshire. Asked by his captors how he had come to be a rebel, "Long Bill" Scott replied:

The case was this Sir! I lived in a Country Town; I was a Shoemaker, & got [my] living by my labor. When this rebellion came on, I saw some of my neighbors get into commission, who were no better than myself.... I was asked to enlist, as a private soldier. My ambition was too great for so low a rank. I offered to enlist upon having a lieutenant's commission, which was granted. I imagined my self now in a way of promotion. If I was killed in battle, there would be an end of me, but if my Captain was killed, I should rise in rank, & should still have a chance to rise higher. These Sir! were the only motives of my entering into the service. For as to the dispute between Great Britain & the colonies, I know nothing of it; neither am I capable of judging whether it is right or wrong.

Scott may have been trying to gain the sympathy of his captors, but people fought in America's Revolutionary War for reasons of fear and ambition as well as principle. We have no way of knowing whether Long Bill Scott's motives were typical. Certainly many Americans knew more than he about the colonies' struggle with England, but many did not.

In the spring of 1775, the Revolutionary War had just begun. So, as it turned out, had Long Bill's adventures. When the British evacuated Boston a year later, Scott was transported to Halifax, Nova Scotia. After several months' captivity, he managed to escape and make his way home to fight once more. He was recaptured in November 1776 near New York City, when its garrison fell to a surprise British assault. Again Scott escaped, this time by swimming the Hudson River at night with his sword tied around his neck and his watch pinned to his hat.

During the winter of 1777, he returned to New Hampshire to recruit his own militia company. It included two of his eldest sons. In the fall, he joined in the defeat of Burgoyne's army near Saratoga, New York, and later took part in the fighting around Newport, Rhode Island. When his light infantry company was ordered to Virginia in early 1778, Scott's health broke, and he was permitted to resign from the army. After only a few months of recuperation, however, he was at it again. During the last year of the war, he served as a volunteer on a navy frigate.

For seven years, the war held Scott in its harsh grasp. Scott's oldest son died of camp fever after six years of service. In 1777, Long Bill sold his New Hampshire farm, to meet family expenses. He lost a second farm in Massachusetts shortly afterward. After his wife died, he helplessly turned their youngest children over to his oldest son and set off to beg a pension or job from the government.

Long Bill's saga was still not complete. In 1792, he gained notoriety by rescuing eight people when their boat capsized in New York harbor. Three years later, General Benjamin Lincoln took Scott with him to the Ohio country, where they surveyed land that was opening for white settlement. At last he had a respectable job and even a small government pension as compensation for his nine wounds. But trouble would still not let him go. While surveying on the Black River near Sandusky, Scott and his colleagues contracted "lake fever." Though ill, he guided part of the group back to Fort Stanwix in New York, then returned for the others. It was his last heroic act. A few days after his second trip, on September 16, 1796, he died.

William Mercer, *Battle of Princeton*, c. 1786–1790. This somewhat stylized portrayal depicts the modest scale of many Revolutionary War battles. (Historical Society of Pennsylvania)

*A*merican independence and the Revolutionary War that accompanied it were not as hard on everyone as they were on Long Bill Scott, yet together they transformed the lives of countless Americans. The war lasted for seven years, longer than any other of America's wars until Vietnam nearly two centuries later. And unlike the nation's twentieth-century contests, it was fought on American soil, among the American people. It called men by the thousands from shops and fields, disrupted families, destroyed communities, spread diseases, and made a shambles of the economy.

While carrying on this struggle for independence, the American people also mounted a political revolution of profound importance. Politics and government were transformed in keeping with republican principles and the rapidly changing circumstances of public life. What did republican liberty entail? How should governmental power be organized? Who should be considered republican citizens? How democratic could American society safely be? These were among the questions with which the American people wrestled at the nation's beginning.

As the tempo of political activity increased under the pressures of war and revolution, people clashed repeatedly over such explosive issues as slavery, the separation of church and state, paper money and debt relief, the regulation of prices, and the toleration of political dissent. They argued as well over the design of new state constitutions and the shape of a new national government. Seldom has America's political agenda been more full, or more troubled.

The American Revolution dominated the lives of all who lived through it. But it had different consequences for men than for women, for black slaves than for their white masters, for Native Americans than for frontier settlers, for overseas merchants than for urban workers, for northern businessmen than for southern planters. Our understanding of the experience out of which the American nation emerged must begin with the Revolutionary War, for liberty came at a high cost.

The War for American Independence

Though the war began in Massachusetts in 1775, within a year the center of fighting had shifted to the middle states. After 1779, the primary theater was in the South. Why did this geographic pattern develop, what was its significance, and why did the Americans win?

The War in the North

For a brief time following Lexington and Concord, British officials thought of launching forays out from Boston into the surrounding countryside. They soon reconsidered, however, for the growing size of the continental army and the absence of significant Loyalist strength in the New England region urged caution. Even more important, the Americans' successful emplacement of artillery on the strategic Dorchester Heights overlooking the city made its continued occupation untenable. On March 7, 1776, the British commander, General William Howe, decided to evacuate.

People worried that Howe would set fire to the city as he departed. Fearing retaliation against Loyalist property and wishing not to destroy any lingering hopes of reconciliation, Howe spared the city from the torch. The town, however, had been treated badly enough. British officers had taken over the homes of John Hancock, James Bowdoin, and others, while Dragoons had used the Old South Meeting House as a riding school, after tearing out the pews. The Hollis Street church had served as barracks, and the Old North Church had been demolished for firewood. All around lay trampled gardens, uprooted trees, and filth. "Almost everything here, appears Gloomy and Melancholy," lamented one returning resident.

For a half dozen years after Boston's evacuation, British ships prowled the New England coast, confiscating supplies and attacking coastal towns. Yet away from the coast, there was little fighting at all. Most New Englanders had reason to be thankful for their good fortune.

After evacuating Boston, British officials established their military headquarters in New York City.

Their decision was strategically sound, for New York offered important advantages over Boston. It was more centrally located and its spacious harbor lay at the mouth of the Hudson River, the major water route northward into the interior. Control of New York would, in addition, ensure access to the abundant grain and livestock of the Middle Atlantic states. Finally, Loyalist sentiment ran deep among the inhabitants of the city and its environs.

In the summer of 1776, Washington moved his troops south from Boston, determined to challenge the British for control of New York City. It proved a terrible mistake. Outmaneuvered and badly outnumbered, he suffered defeat at the Battle of Long Island and then in Manhattan itself. By late October, the city was firmly in British hands. It would remain so until the war's end.

In the fall of 1776, King George III instructed his two chief commanders in North America, the brothers General William and Admiral Richard Howe, to make a final effort at reconciliation with the colonists. They carried authority to pardon all Americans who acknowledged allegiance to the king and to negotiate with any colony that dissolved its revolutionary committees. In early September, the Howes met with three delegates from the Congress on Staten Island, in New York harbor. The outcome was not long in doubt, for when the Howes demanded revocation of the Declaration of Independence before negotiations could begin, the Americans walked out. With that decision, all hope of reconciliation vanished.

For the next two years, the war swept back and forth across New Jersey and Pennsylvania. Reinforced by German mercenaries hired in Europe, the British moved virtually at will. Neither the state militias nor the continental army, weakened by losses, low morale, and inadequate supplies, offered serious opposition. At Trenton in December 1776 and again at Princeton the following month, Washington surprised the British and scored victories that prevented the Americans' collapse. For the rebels, however, survival remained the primary goal.

Because infantry weapons were often inaccurate at long distances, lines tended to form in close proximity where the weapons were deadly and where combat became intensely personal. (Henry Sandham, Dawn of Liberty, 1886/Lexington Historical Society)

Western Land Claims Ceded by the States, 1782-1802

Seven of the original states laid claim, based on their colonial charters, to lands west of the Appalachian Mountains. Eventually those states ceded their western claims to the Congress, thus making possible the creation of new states in the region.

west of the Appalachian Mountains that pitted states such as Virginia, South Carolina, and New York, which had western claims tracing back to their colonial charters, against states such as Maryland and New Jersey, which had none. In December 1778, the Maryland assembly announced that it would not ratify until all the western lands that were being "wrested from the common enemy by the blood and treasure of the thirteen states" had been ceded to the Congress. For several years, ratification hung in the balance while politicians and land speculators jockeyed for advantage. A break finally came in 1780 when New York and Virginia agreed to transfer their western lands to the Congress. Those decisions paved the way for Maryland's ratification in early 1781. Approval of the Articles was now assured.

The war, of course, did not wait during the struggle over ratification. The Continental Con-

gress managed the war effort as best it could, using the unratified Articles as a guide. Events, however, quickly proved the inadequacy of its powers, because it could do little more than pass resolutions and ask the states for support. If they refused, as they frequently did, the Congress could only protest and urge cooperation. Its ability to function was further limited by the stipulation that each state's delegation cast but one vote. On a number of occasions, disagreements within state delegations prevented them from voting at all. That could paralyze the Congress, because most important decisions required a nine-state majority.

As the war dragged on, Washington repeatedly criticized the Congress for its failure to support the army. Acknowledging its own ineffectiveness, the Congress in 1778 temporarily granted Washington extraordinary powers and asked him to manage the war on his own. In the end, the Congress survived because enough of its members realized that disaster would follow its collapse.

The War Moves South

As the war in the North bogged down in a costly stalemate, British officials adopted an alternative strategy: invasion and pacification of the South. Royal officials in the South encouraged the idea with reports that thousands of Loyalists would rally to the British standard. The southern coastline with its numerous rivers, moreover, offered maximum advantage to British naval strength. Then there were the slaves, that vast but imponderable presence in southern society. If they could be lured to the British side, the balance might tip in Britain's favor. In any case, the threat of slave rebellion would weaken white southerners' will to resist. Persuaded by these arguments, British policymakers made the southern states the primary theater of military operations during the final years of the war.

Georgia—small, isolated, and largely defenseless—was the initial target. In December 1778, Savannah, the state's major port, fell before a seaborne attack of 3,500 men. For nearly two years, the Revolution in the state virtually ceased. Encouraged by their success, the British turned to the Carolinas, with equally impressive results. On May 12, 1780, Charleston surrendered after a month's siege. At a cost of only 225 casualties, the British captured the entire 5,400-man American garrison. It was the costliest American defeat of the war.

After securing Charleston, the British quickly extended their control north and south along the coast. At Camden, South Carolina, the British commander Cornwallis, aided by a corps of mounted dragoons, killed nearly 1,000 Americans and captured 1,000 more, temporarily destroying the southern continental army. With scarcely a pause, the British pushed on into North Carolina. These successes, however, proved deceptive, for British officers quickly learned the difficulty of extending their lines into the interior. The distances were too large, the problems of supply too great, the reliability of Loyalist troops too problematic, and support for the Revolutionary cause among the people too strong.

In October 1780, Washington sent Nathanael Greene south to lead the continental forces. It was a fortunate choice, for Greene knew the region and the kind of war that had to be fought. Determined, like Washington, to avoid large-scale encounters, Greene divided his army into small, mobile bands. Employing what today would be called guerrilla tactics, he harassed the British and their Loyalist allies at every opportunity, striking by surprise and then disappearing into the interior. Nowhere was the war more fiercely contested than through the Georgia and Carolina countryside. Neither British nor American authorities could restrain the violence. Bands of private marauders, roving the land and seizing advantage from the war's confusion, compounded the chaos.

In time, the tide began to turn. At Cowpens, South Carolina, in January 1781, American troops under General Daniel Morgan won a decisive victory, suffering fewer than 75 casualties to 329 British deaths and taking 600 men prisoner. In March, at Guilford Court House in North Carolina, Cornwallis won, but at a cost that forced his retreat to safety at Wilmington, near the sea.

In April 1781, convinced that British authority could not be restored in the Carolinas while Virginia remained a supply and staging area for the rebels, Cornwallis moved north out of the Carolinas. With a force of 7,500, he raided deep into Virginia. In June, his forces sent Governor Jefferson and the Virginia legislature fleeing from Charlottesville into the mountains. But again Cornwallis found the costs of victory high, and again he turned toward the coast for protection and resupply. This time his goal was Yorktown, where he arrived on August 1.

As long as the British fleet controlled the waters of Chesapeake Bay, his position was secure. That advantage, however, did not last. In 1778, the French government, still smarting from its defeat by England in the Seven Years' War and buoyed by the American victory at Saratoga in 1777, had signed a treaty of alliance with the American Congress, promising to send its naval forces into the war. Initially, the French concentrated their fleet in the West Indies, where they hoped to seize some of the British sugar islands. After repeated American urging, however, the French finally sailed north, and on August 30, 1781, the French admiral, Comte

The tide of battle inthe South depended largely on British naval control of the coast and major riverways.

de Grasse, arrived off Yorktown. Reinforced by a second French squadron from the North, de Grasse established naval superiority in the region.

As Washington had foreseen, French entry turned the tide of war. Cut off from the sea and caught on a peninsula between the York and James rivers by 17,000 French and American troops, Cornwallis's fate was sealed. On October 17, 1781, he opened negotiations for surrender. Two days later, near the Virginia hamlet of Yorktown, Cornwallis surrendered to General Washington. While a military band played "The World Turned Upside Down" and hundreds of civilians looked on, nearly 7,000 British troops laid down their arms.

Learning the news of Yorktown in London a month later, Lord North, the king's chief minister, exclaimed, "Oh, God! It is all over." On February 27, 1782, the House of Commons voted against further support of the war. The next month Lord North resigned. In Philadelphia, citizens poured into the streets to celebrate while the Congress assembled for a solemn ceremony of thanksgiving. Sporadic fighting continued for another several months. It was not until November 1782 that the preliminary articles of peace were finally signed. But everyone knew after Yorktown that the war was over. Americans had won their independence.

Native Americans in the Revolution

The Revolutionary War involved more than Englishmen and colonists, for it drew in countless Native Americans as well. It could hardly have been otherwise, for the lives of all three peoples had been intimately connected since the first English settlements more than a century and a half before.

Though individual Indians still roamed the streets of America's port cities, by the time of the Revolution the coastal tribes were mostly gone, victims of white settlement and the ravages of European disease. Between the Appalachian Mountains and the Mississippi River, however, powerful tribes remained. The Iroquois Six Nations, formed into a confederation numbering 15,000 people, controlled the area from Albany, New York, to the Ohio country and dominated the "western tribes" of the Ohio Valley—the Shawnee, Delaware, Wyandotte, and Miami. In the Southeast, five tribes—the Choctaw, Chickasaw, Seminole, Creek, and Cherokee, 60,000 people in all—dominated the interior.

Though England's victory in the Seven Years' War had ended the Indians' "play-off game" and made them dependent on their sole Anglo-American trading partners, the interior tribes retained their distinctive ways of life. Far outnumbering the few white settlers that had pushed across the Appalachians, they remained more than a match, militarily and diplomatically, for the Anglo Americans. As the imperial crisis between England and its colonies deepened, whites and Indians eyed each other warily across this vast "middle ground."

When the Revolutionary War began, British and American officials urged neutrality on the Indians. The British, expecting the conflict to be short, wished to disrupt the interior as little as possible. The Americans worried about Indian attacks from the west while facing British power along the coast. The Native Americans, however, were too important militarily to ignore. By the spring of 1776, both sides were actively seeking Indian alliances.

Recognizing their immense stake in the imperial conflict, Native Americans up and down the interior debated their options. Alarmed by the westward advance of white settlement and eager

At Yorktown, Cornwallis asserted he was ill and sent a subordinate, Brigadier General Charles O'Hara, to yield the symbolic sword of surrender. (Library of Congress)

to take advantage of the colonists' troubles, a band of Cherokee, led by the warrior Dragging Canoe, launched a series of raids in July 1776 against white settlements in what is today eastern Tennessee. In a quick and devastating response, the Virginia and Carolina militias laid waste a group of Cherokee towns. Thomas Jefferson expressed satisfaction at the outcome. "I hope that the Cherokees will now be driven beyond the Mississippi," he wrote. "Our contest with Britain is too serious, and too great to permit any possibility of [danger] ... from the Indians."

During the winter of 1780–1781, American militias once more ravaged Cherokee towns. Though the Cherokee raided sporadically throughout the war, they never again mounted a sustained military effort against the rebels. Seeing what had become of their neighbors, the Creek stayed aloof. Their time for resistance would come in the early

Indian Battles and the War in the West, 1775-1783

Though most battles were fought along the coastal plain, the British and their Indian allies opened a second front far to the west.

nineteenth century, when white settlers began to push onto their lands.

In the Ohio country—home to the Shawnee and Delaware, the Wyandotte and the Miami—the struggle lasted longer. For several decades before the Revolution, explorers such as Daniel Boone had contested with the Shawnee and others for control of the region bordering the Ohio River. The Revolutionary War intensified these conflicts. In February 1778, George Rogers Clark led a ragtag body of Kentuckians through icy rivers and across 180 miles of forbidding terrain to attack an English outpost at Vincennes, in present-day Indiana. Though outnumbered nearly four to one by the 500 British regulars and their Indian allies, Clark fooled the fort's defenders into believing that his force was much larger. The British commander, convinced that he faced devastating losses against a superior force, surrendered without a shot. Skirmishes between England and the Indians on the one hand and marauding American forces on the other con-

tinued for several years, but Clark's victory tipped the balance in the war's western theater.

The Devastation of the Iroquois

To the northeast, a similar but even more deadly scenario unfolded. At a council in Albany, New York, in August 1775, representatives of the Iroquois Six Nations listened while American commissioners urged them to remain at home and keep the hatchet buried deep. "The determination of the Six Nations," replied Little Abraham, a Mohawk leader, "[is] not to take any part; but as it is a family affair, to sit still and see you fight it out." Iroquois neutrality, however, did not last long.

As the war spread throughout the Northeast in 1776, U.S. troops raided deep into Mohawk territory west of Albany. Alarmed, the British argued with words, rum, and trade goods that the Iroquois should join them against the rebels. At the Oswego Council in the summer of 1777, most of the Iro-

Mohawk chief Joseph Brant (Thayendanegea) played a major role in the Iroquois's decision to enter the war on the side of Britain. (The National Gallery of Canada, Ottawa)

quois abandoned neutrality and took up arms against the Americans. They did so at the urging of Joseph Brant, a Mohawk warrior who had visited England several years before and argued England's value as an ally against American expansion.

It was a fateful decision for Indians and whites alike. Over the next several years, the Iroquois and their English allies devastated large areas in central New York and Pennsylvania, destroying property and terrorizing the inhabitants. An officer of the Pennsylvania militia reported somberly, "Our country is on the eve of breaking up. There is nothing to be seen but disolation, fire & smoak."

The Americans' revenge came swiftly. During the summer of 1779, General John Sullivan led a series of punishing raids into the Iroquois country, burning the Iroquois villages, killing men, women, and children, and destroying fields of corn. His motto for the campaign was blunt: "Civilization or death to all American savages." By war's end, the

Iroquois had lost as many as a third of their people as well as countless towns. Their domination of the northeastern interior was permanently shattered.

Not all the Eastern Woodland tribes sided with England in the Revolutionary War. The Oneida and the Tuscarora, members of the Iroquois confederation, fought with the Americans, their decision driven by intertribal politics and effective diplomacy by emissaries of the Continental Congress. In New England, the Stockbridge, a small tribe surrounded by a sea of white settlements, contributed warriors and scouts, while farther to the south the Catawbas, similarly dependent on the Americans for trade and diplomacy, also signed on. The Indians who fought for American independence, however, reaped little benefit from their efforts. Though General Sullivan spared the Oneida and Tuscarora villages, the British and their Iroquois allies destroyed them in turn. And although a number of Indian warriors were compensated by grateful state governments once the war was over, tribes allied with the victorious American cause enjoyed no protection from the accelerating spread of white settlement.

At the peace talks that ended the Revolutionary War, the British ignored the interests of their Indian allies. They received neither compensation for their losses nor guarantees of their land, for the boundary of the United States was set far to the west, at the Mississippi River. Most Indians had had good reason for choosing England as their ally, because England had provided them with trade goods, arms, and markets for their furs. England, moreover, had offered protection against the expansionist Americans, as the Proclamation Line of 1763 had demonstrated. England, however, lost the war and so, as a consequence, did their Indian allies.

Negotiating Peace

In September 1781, formal peace negotiations began in Paris between the British commissioner, Richard Oswald, and the American emissaries, Benjamin Franklin, John Adams, and John Jay. The negotiations were complicated by the fact that several European countries, seeking to weaken Great Britain, had become involved. France had entered the war in February 1778. Eight months later, Spain declared war on England, though it declined to recognize American independence. Between 1780 and 1782, Russia, the Netherlands, and six other European countries joined in a League of Armed Neutrality aimed at protecting their maritime trade against British efforts to control it. America's Revolutionary War had quickly become internationalized. It could hardly have been otherwise, given England's centrality to the European balance of power and the long-standing competition between European powers for colonial dominance in North America.

Dependent on French economic and military support, the Congress instructed the American commissioners to follow the advice of Vergennes, the French foreign minister. As the treaty talks began, the American commissioners learned to their distress that Vergennes was prepared to let the exhausting war continue in order to weaken England and tighten America's dependence on France. Even more alarming, Vergennes suggested that the new nation's western boundary ought to be set no farther inland than the crest of the Appalachian Mountains. He hinted additionally that the British might retain areas they controlled at the war's end, a proposal that threatened to leave New York City and other coastal enclaves in British hands.

In the end, the American commissioners ignored their instructions and, without a word to Vergennes, arranged a provisional peace agreement with the British emissaries. It was fortunate that they did so, for the British were prepared to be generous. In the Treaty of Paris, signed in September 1783, England agreed to recognize American independence and set the western boundary of the United States at the Mississippi River. Moreover, Britain promised that U.S. fishermen would have the "right" to fish the waters off Newfoundland and that British forces would evacuate American territory "with all convenient speed" once hostilities had ceased. In return, the Congress agreed to recommend that the states restore the rights and property of the Loyalists. Both sides agreed that prewar debts owed the citizens of one country by the citizens of the other would remain valid. Each of these issues would trouble Anglo-American relations in the years immediately ahead, but for the moment it seemed a splendid outcome to a long and difficult struggle.

The Ingredients of Victory

How were the weak and disunited American states able to defeat Great Britain, the most powerful nation in the Atlantic world? Certainly the Dutch and French loans, war supplies, and military forces were crucially important. More decisive, though, was the American people's determination not to submit. Often the Americans were disorganized and uncooperative. Repeatedly, it seemed that the war effort was about to collapse as continental troops drifted away, state militias refused to march, and military supplies failed to materialize. Neither the Congress nor the states proved capable of providing consistent direction to the struggle. Yet as the war progressed, the people's estrangement from England deepened and their commitment to the "glorious cause" increased. To subdue the colonies, England would have had to occupy the entire eastern third of the continent, and that it could not do.

Even though state militias frequently refused to go beyond their own borders and after the first months of the war engaged in relatively few battles, they provided a vast reservoir of manpower capable of controlling the countryside, intimidating Loyalists, and harassing British forces. In the process, they occupied British troops that would otherwise have been free to engage the continental army.

The American victory owed much as well to the administrative and organizational talents of Washington. Against massive odds, he held the continental army together, often by the sheer force of his will. Facing inadequate supplies, low pay, high rates of turnover among the troops, ineffective support from the Congress, and lack of cooperation from the states, he created a military force capable of winning selected encounters and, more important, of surviving over time. Had he failed, the Americans could not possibly have defeated the British.

In the end, however, it is as accurate to say that Britain lost the war as that the United States won it. With vast economic and military resources, Britain enjoyed clear military superiority over the American states. Its troops were more numerous, better

John Jay, John Adams, and Benjamin Franklin (the three figures on the left in the unfinished painting by Benjamin West) meet with the British commissioners in Paris to negotiate preliminary conditions of peace. (Benjamin West, Commissioners of the Preliminary Peace Negotiations with Great Britain, c. 1783/Courtesy, The Henry Francis du Pont Winterthur Museum)

armed and supplied, and more professionally trained. Until the closing months of the contest, Britain enjoyed naval superiority as well. As a consequence, its forces moved up and down the coast virtually at will.

Britain, however, could not capitalize on its advantages. It had difficulty extending its command structures and supply routes across several thousand miles of ocean. Because information flowed erratically across the water, strategic decisions made in London were often based on faulty or outdated intelligence. Given the difficulties of supply, British troops often had to live off the land, thus reducing their mobility and increasing resentment among the Americans whose crops and animals they commandeered.

Faced with these circumstances, British leaders were often overly cautious. Burgoyne's attempt in 1777 to isolate New England by invading from Canada failed because Sir William Howe decided to attack Philadelphia rather than move northward up the Hudson River to join him. Similarly, neither Howe nor Cornwallis pressed his advantage in the central states during the middle years of the war,

when more aggressive action might have defeated and scattered the continental force.

Just as important, British commanders generally failed to adapt their battlefield tactics to the realities of the American war. They continued to fight in the European style, during specified times of the year and using set formations of troops deployed in formal battlefield maneuvers. Much of the American terrain, however, was rough and wooded, and thus better suited to the use of smaller units and irregular troops.

Washington and Greene were more flexible, often employing a patient strategy of raiding, harassment, and strategic retreat. Behind this strategy lay a willingness, grounded in necessity, to allow England control of considerable territory, especially along the coast. But it was based as well on the conviction that popular support for the Revolutionary cause would grow and that the costs of subduing the colonial rebellion would become greater than the British government could bear. As a much later American war in Vietnam would also reveal, a guerrilla force can win if it does not lose; a regular army loses if it does not consistently win.

The American strategy proved sound. As the war dragged on and its costs escalated, Britain's will began to waver. After France and Spain entered the conflict, Britain had to worry about Europe, the Caribbean, and even the Mediterranean as well as North America. Unrest in Ireland and massive London riots over food shortages prevented England from sending more troops to North America. As the cost in money and lives increased and prospects of victory diminished, political support for the war eroded. With the defeat at Yorktown, it collapsed. Britain's effort to hold onto its 13 North American colonies had failed.

The Experience of War

In terms of the loss of life and destruction of property, the Revolutionary War pales by comparison with America's more recent wars. How destructive could it have been when Franklin insisted that "Nothing terrifies enemies more than the deadly silent flight of a volley of arrows"? Yet modern comparisons are misleading, for by eighteenth-century terms, the War for American Independence was terrifying to the people caught up in it as well as destructive of lives and property.

Recruiting an Army

Estimates vary, but on the American side as many as 250,000 men may at one time or another have borne arms. That would amount to about one out of every two or three adult males.

Tens of thousands served in the state militias. At the time of independence, most state militias were not an effective fighting force. This was especially true in the South, where Nathanael Greene complained that the men came "from home with all the tender feelings of domestic life" and were not "sufficiently fortified ... to stand the shocking scenes of war, to march over dead men, [or] to hear without concern the groans of the wounded." Greene knew that fighting was neither pleasant nor often heroic.

The militia did serve as a convenient recruiting system, for men were already enrolled, and arrangements were in place for calling them into the field on short notice. This was of special importance during the early months of the war, before the continental army took shape. Given its grounding in local community life, the militia also served to legitimate the war among the people and secure their commitment to the Revolutionary cause. What better way, as well, to separate the Patriots from the Loyalists than by mustering the local company and seeing who turned out?

During the first year of the war, when enthusiasm ran high, men of all ranks—from the rich and middle classes as well as the poor—volunteered to fight the British. But as the war progressed and casualties increased, the army soon came to be filled with conscripts. Eventually, the war was transformed, as wars so often are, into a poor man's fight as wealthier men hired substitutes, and communities filled their quotas with strangers lured by the promise of enlistment bonuses. This social transformation was most evident in the continental army, where terms were longer, discipline stiffer, and battlefields more distant from the soldiers' homes.

For the poor and the jobless, whose ranks the war rapidly expanded, military bonus payments and the promise of board and keep proved attractive. But often the bonuses failed to materialize, and pay was long overdue. Moreover, life in the camps was harsh, and soldiers frequently heard from their wives of their families' distress at home. Faced with such trials, soldiers often became disgruntled and insubordinate. As the war progressed, Washington imposed harsher discipline on the continental troops in an effort to hold them in line.

Occasionally frustration spilled over into open revolt. In 1779, Sergeant Samuel Glover and a group of soldiers from the North Carolina line who had been unpaid for 15 months refused to obey the commands of their superior officer "until they had justice done them." Glover was executed for insubordination. His widow later apologized to the North Carolina assembly for her husband's conduct but asked sorrowfully, "What must the feeling of the man be who fought at Brandywine ... and at Stony Point and ... with poverty staring him full in the face, was denied his pay?" Poor soldiers, she

As this painting suggests, military recruiting was a community affair in the eighteenth century. What do you suppose the man with upraised arms is doing? What role might the women be playing in the recruitment process? (William T. Ranney & Charles F. Blauvelt, Recruiting for the Continental Army, c. 1857–59, oil on canvas, 53 3/4 × 82 1/4 in, Munson-Williams-Proctor Institute, Museum of Art, Utica, New York, Gift of T. Proctor Eldred)

protested, were "possessed of the same attachment and affection for their families as those in command."

Throughout the war, soldiers suffered from shortages of supplies. At Valley Forge during the terrible winter of 1777–1778, men hobbled about without shoes or coats. From the midst of that winter's gloom, Washington wrote, "There are now in this army 4,000 men wanting blankets, near 2,000 of which have never had one, altho' some of them have been 12 months in service." "I am sick, discontented, and out of humour," declared one despairing soul. "Poor food, hard lodging, cold weather, fatigue, nasty cloathes, nasty cookery, vomit half my time, smoked out of my senses. The Devil's in't, I can't Endure it. Why are we sent here to starve and freeze?"

The states possessed food and clothing enough but were often reluctant to strip their own people of wagons and livestock, blankets and shoes for use elsewhere. Moreover, mismanagement and difficulties in transportation stood in the way. Neither the state governments nor the Congress had the ability to administer a war effort of such magnitude. Wagon transport was slow and costly, and the British fleet made water transportation along the coast perilous. Though many individuals served honorably as supply officers, others took advantage of the army's distress. Washington commented bitterly on the "speculators, various tribes of money makers, and stock-jobbers of all denominations" whose "avarice and thirst for gain" threatened the country's ruin.

The Casualties of Combat

The death that soldiers dispensed to each other on the battlefield was intensely personal. Because of the limits of the weaponry—the effective range of muskets was little more than 100 yards—soldiers came virtually face to face with the men they killed. According to eighteenth-century military conventions, armies formed on the battlefield in ranks and fired in unison. After massed volleys, the lines often closed for hand-to-hand combat with knives and bayonets. Such encounters were powerfully etched in the memory of individuals who survived them. The partisan warfare in the South, with its emphasis on ambush and its cyclic patterns of revenge and counterrevenge, personalized combat even more. British officers, used to more dispassionate styles of warfare, were shocked at

Military Muster Rolls

In almost all of America's wars, patriotism has run high and bombastic rhetoric has inspired citizens to arms. The American Revolutionary War was no exception. But people fought for other than patriotic reasons, as the account of "Long Bill" Scott makes clear. It is always difficult to assess human motivations in something as complex as war. If we knew which Americans bore arms, however, it would help us understand why people fought and perhaps even understand what the war meant to them.

As we see in this chapter, the social composition of the revolutionary army changed markedly as the war went along. At the beginning, men from all walks of life and every class fought in defense of American liberty. Within a short time, however, that began to change. As the war lengthened and its costs increased, men who could afford to do so hired substitutes or arranged to go home, whereas men of less wealth and influence increasingly carried the burden of fighting. Many of them did so out of choice, for the army promised adventure, an escape from the tedium of daily life, a way to make a living, and even, as for "Long Bill" Scott, the chance to rise in the world. And so thousands of poorer men hired out to defend American liberty. Such a decision, of course, was more attractive to them because other opportunities were limited.

Enlistment lists of the continental army and the state militias offer one important source for studying the social history of the Revolutionary War. Although eighteenth-century records are imperfect by modern standards, recruiting officers did keep track of the men they signed up so that bounties and wages could be paid accurately. These lists usually give the recruit's name, age, occupation, place of birth, residence, and length of service.

Such lists exist for some of America's earliest wars. The muster rolls for New York City and Philadelphia during the Seven Years' War, for example, show that these two cities contributed 300 and 180 men per year, respectively, to the war effort. Most of the enlistees in that earlier war were immigrants—about 90 percent of New York's recruits and about 75 percent of Philadelphia's. Their occupations—mariner, laborer, shoemaker, weaver, tailor—

indicate that they came primarily from the lowest ranks of the working class. Many were former indentured servants and many others were servants running away from their masters to answer the recruiting sergeant's drum. In these Middle Atlantic port towns, successful, American-born artisans left the bloody work of bearing arms against the French to those beneath them on the social ladder. Enlistment lists for Boston, however, reveal that soldiers from that city were drawn from higher social classes.

A comparison of the Revolutionary War muster rolls from different towns and regions provides a view of the social composition of the revolutionary army and how it changed over time. It also offers clues to social conditions in different regions during the war and how they might have affected military recruitment.

The lists shown here of Captain Wendell's and Captain White's companies from New York and Virginia give "social facts" on 81 men. What kind of group portrait can you draw from the data? Some occupations, such as tanner, cordwainer, and chandler, may be unfamiliar, but they are defined in standard dictionaries. How many of the recruits come from middling occupations (bookkeeper, tobacconist, shopkeeper, and the like)? How many are skilled artisans? How many are unskilled laborers? What proportions are foreign and native-born? Analyze the ages of the recruits. What does that tell you about the kind of fighting force that was assembled? How do the New York and Virginia companies differ in terms of these social categories and occupations? How would you explain these differences?

To extract the full meaning of the soldiers' profile, you would have to learn more about the economic and social conditions prevailing in the communities from which these men are drawn. But already you have glimpsed how social historians are trying to go beyond the history of military strategy, tactics, and battles to understand the "internal" social history of the Revolutionary War.

How would social historians describe and analyze a more recent American war? What would a social profile of soldiers who fought in Vietnam, including their age, region, race, class, extent of education, and other differences, suggest to a social historian of this recent war?

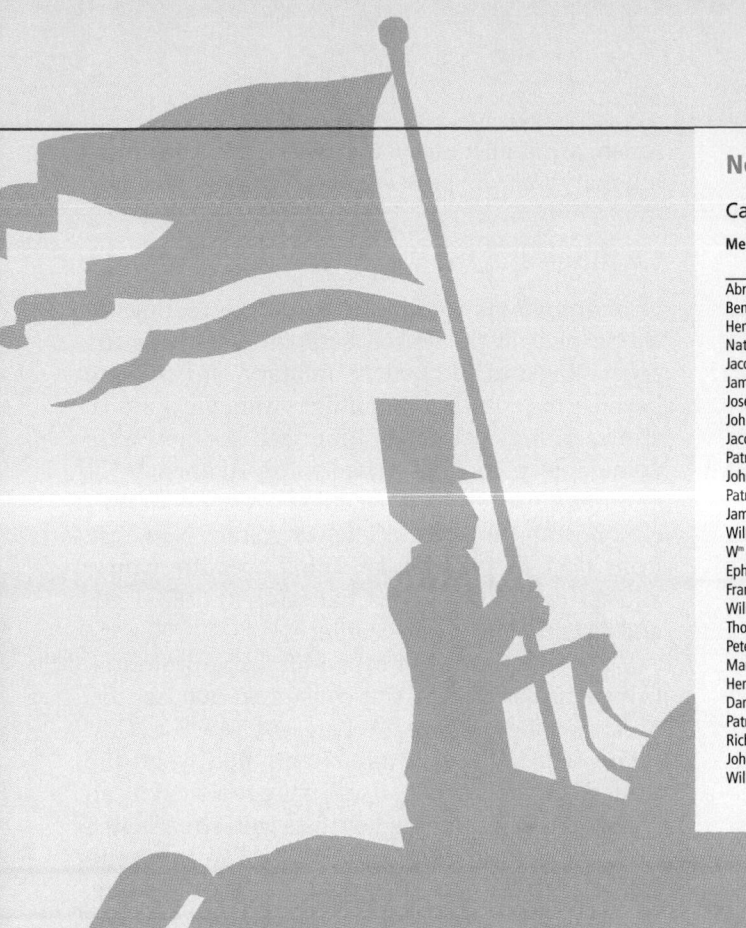

New York Line—1st Regiment

Captain John H. Wendell's Company, 1776–1777

Men's Names	Age	Occupation	Place of Birth	Place of Abode
Abraham Defreest	22	Yeoman	N. York	Claverack
Benjamin Goodales	20	do [ditto]	Nobletown	do
Hendrick Carman	24	do	Rynbeck	East Camp
Nathaniel Reed	32	Carpenter	Norwalk	Westchester
Jacob Crolrin	29	do	Germany	Bever Dam
James White	25	Weaver	Ireland	Rynbveck
Joseph Battina	39	Coppersmith	Ireland	Florida
John Wyatt	38	Carpenter	Maryland	
Jacob Reyning	25	Yeoman	Amsterdam	Albany
Patrick Kannely	36	Barber	Ireland	N. York
John Russell	29	Penman	Ireland	N. York
Patrick McCue	19	Tanner	Ireland	Scholary
James J. Atkson	21	Weaver	do	Stillwater
William Burke	23	Chandler	Ireland	N. York
Wᵐ Miller	42	Yeoman	Scotland	Claverack
Ephraim H. Blancherd	18	Yeoman	Ireland	White Creek
Francis Acklin	40	Cardwainer	Ireland	Claverack
William Orr	29	Cardwainer	Ireland	Albany
Thomas Welch	31	Labourer	N. York	Norman's Kill
Peter Gasper	24	Labourer	N. Jersey	Greenbush
Martins Rees	19	Labourer	Fishkill	Flatts
Henck Able	24	do	Albany	Flatts
Daniel Spinnie	21	do	Portsmouth	
Patrick Kelly	23	Labourer	Ireland	Claverack
Richᵈ James Barker	12	do	America	Rynbeck
John Patrick Cronkite	11			Claverack
William Dougherty	17		Donyal, Ireland	Schᵗʸ

Virginia Line—6th Regiment

Captain Tarpley White's Company, December 13th 1780

Name	Age	Trade	Where Born State or Country	Where Born Town or County	Place of Residence State or Country	Place of Residence Town or County
Win Balis, Serjt	25	Baker	England	Burningham	Virg.	Leesburg
Arthur Harrup"	24	Carpenter	Virg.	Southampton	"	Brunswick
Charles Caffatey"	19	Planter	"	Caroline	"	Caroline
Elisha Osborn"	24	Planter	New Jersey	Trenton	"	Loudon
Benj Allday	19	"	Virg.	Henrico	"	Pawhatan
Wm Edwards Senr	25	"	"	Northamberland	"	Northumberland
James Hutcherson	17	Hatter	Jersey	Middlesex	"	P. Willams
Robert Low	31	Planter	"	Powhatan	"	Powhatan
Cannon Row	18	Planter	Virg.	Hanover	Virg.	Louisa
Wardon Pulley	18	"	"	Southampton/	"	Hallifax
Richᵈ Bond	29	Stone Mason	England	Cornwell	"	Orange
Tho Homont	17	Planter	Virg.	Loudon	"	Loudon
Tho Pope	19	Planter	"	Southampton	"	Southampton
Tho Morris	22	Planter	"	Orange	"	Orange
Littlebury Overby	24	Hatter	"	Dinwiddie	"	Brunswick
James [Pierce]	27	Planter	"	Nansemond	"	Nansemond
Joel Counsil	19	Planter	"	Southampton	"	Southampton
Elisha Walden	18	Planter	"	P. Willliam	"	P. William
Wm Bush	19	S Carpenter	Virg.	Gloucester	Virg.	Glocester
Daniel Horton	22	Carpenter	"	Nansemond	"	Nansemond
John Soons	25	Weaver	England	Norfolk	"	Loudon
Mara Lumkin	18	Planter	Virg.	Amelia	"	Amelia
Wm Wetherford	27	Planter	"	Goochland	"	Lunenburg
John Bird	16	Planter	"	Southampton	"	Southampton
Tho Parsmore	22	Planter	England	London	"	Fairfax
Josiah Banks	27	Planter	Virg.	Gloucester	"	Gloucester
Richᵈ Roach	28	Planter	England	London	"	Culpeper
Joseph Holburt	33	Tailor	"	Middlesex	"	Federickbᵍ
Henry Willowby	19	Planter	Virg.	Spotsylvania	"	Spotsylvania
Thos Pearson	22	Planter		Pennsylvany	"	Loudon
Jno Scarborough	19	Planter	Virg.	Brunswick	"	Brunswick
Chas Thacker	21	Planter	"		"	
Nehemiah Grining	20	Planter	Virg.	Albemarle	Virg.	Albemarle
Ewing David	19	Planter	"	King Wᵐ	"	Brunswick
Isaiah Ballance	17	Shoemaker	"	Norfolk	"	Norfolk
Wm Alexander	20	Planter	Virg.	Northumblᵈ	Virgᵃ	Northumblᵈ
Wm Harden	26	Planter	"	Albemarle	"	Albemarle
John Ward	20	Sailor	England	Bristol	"	Northumblᵈ
Daniel Cox	19	Planter	Virg.	Sussex	"	Sussex
George Kirk	21	Planter	"	Brunswick	"	Brunswick
John Nash	19	Planter	"	Nothumlᵈ	"	Nothumblᵈ
Wm Edward, Jr.	19	Planter	"	Northlumlᵈ	"	Northumblᵈ
John Fry	20	Turner	"	Albemarle	"	Albemarle
Jno Grinning	25	Hatter	"	"	"	
Daniel Howell	30	Planter	"	Loudon	"	Loudon
Milden Green	25	Planter	"	Sussex	"	Sussex
Matthias Cane	32	Planter	"	Norfolk	"	Norfolk
Wm Mayo	21	Joiner	"	Dinwiddie	"	Dinwiddie
Jas Morgan	25	Shoemaker	England	Shropshire	"	Stafford
Mathew Carson	19	Planter	Pennsylvania	York	"	Berkly
Wm B[rown]	22	Planter	"		"	
Richᵈ Loyd	42	Planter	Virg.	Surry	"	Surry
Abram Foress	33	Planter	"	Gloster	"	Gloster
Wm White	19	Planter	"		"	

197

the "implacable ardor and revenge" with which the Americans fought.

The American fervor in battle is largely explained by the fact that this was a civil war. Not only did Englishmen fight Anglo Americans, but American Loyalists and Patriots fought each other as well. As many as 50,000 colonists fought for the king and engaged in some of the war's bitterest encounters. They figured importantly in Burgoyne's invasion from Canada and in the attacks on Savannah and Charleston. Benedict Arnold led a force of Loyalists on raids through the Connecticut and James river valleys, and Loyalist militia units joined Indian allies in destructive sweeps through central New York, Pennsylvania, and the backcountry of the Carolinas. Finally, American Patriots fervently believed that theirs was a struggle between irreconcilable principles of liberty and tyranny. In such a crusade, against such a threatening foe, nothing was to be spared that might bring victory.

Medical treatment, whether for wounds or diseases such as smallpox, dysentery, and typhus that raged through the camps, did little to help. Casualties poured into hospitals, often overcrowding them beyond capacity. Dr. Jonathan Potts, the attending physician at Fort George in New York, reported that "we have at present upwards of one thousand sick crowded into sheds & labouring under the various and cruel disorders of dysentaries, bilious putrid fevers and the effects of a confluent smallpox; to attend to this large number we have four seniors and four mates, exclusive of myself."

Surgeons, operating without anesthetics and with the crudest of instruments, threatened life as often as they preserved it. Few understood the causes and treatment of infection. Doctoring consisted mostly of bleeding, blistering, and vomiting (which was "deemed of excellent use, by opening and squeezing all the glands of the body, & then shaking from the nervous system, the contaminating poison"). One doctor reported "that we lost no less than from 10 to 20 of camp diseases, for one by weapons of the enemy."

How many soldiers actually died we do not know, for no one kept accurate records. But the most conservative estimate runs to over 25,000, a higher percentage of the total population than for any other American conflict except the Civil War. For the Revolutionary War soldier, death was an imminent reality.

Civilians and the War

Noncombatants also experienced the realities of war, especially in densely settled areas along the coast. England focused its military efforts there because the coastal communities were the political and economic centers of American life, and were vulnerable to England's naval power. At one time or another, British troops occupied every major port city: Boston for a year at the war's start, New York from 1777 to 1783, Philadelphia over the winter and spring of 1777–1778, Charleston in 1780–1781, and Savannah two years earlier.

The disruptions of urban life were profound. In September 1776, a fire consumed 500 houses, nearly a quarter of the dwellings, in New York City. About half the town's inhabitants fled when the British occupation began and were replaced by an almost equal number of Loyalists who streamed in from the surrounding countryside. Ten thousand British and German troops added to the crowding. Makeshift shelters of sailcloth and timber, patched together by the growing number of the poor, stretched along Broadway. An American officer somberly reported what he found as his troops entered New York at the war's end: "Close on the eve of an approaching winter, with an heterogeneous set of inhabitants, composed of almost ruined exiles, disbanded soldiery, mixed foreigners, disaffected Tories, and the refuse of the British army, we took possession of a ruined city."

In Philadelphia, the occupation was shorter and the disruptions less severe, but the shock of invasion was no less real. Elizabeth Drinker, living alone after local Patriots had exiled her Quaker husband, found herself the unwilling landlady of a British officer, Major Crammond, and his friends. The major's presence may have protected her from the plundering that went on all around. She was constantly anxious, however, confiding to her journal that "I often feel afraid to go to Bed." During the occupation, British soldiers frequently tore down fences for their campfires and confiscated food to supplement their own tedious fare. Even the Loyalists commented on the "dreadful consequences" of British occupation.

In September 1776, as American troops fought unsuccessfully for control of New York, nearly a quarter of the city was destroyed by a fire apparently set by a defiant Patriot woman. Not until the war ended did reconstruction and cleanup of the ruins begin. (Library of Congress)

Along the entire coastal plain, British landing parties descended without warning, capturing supplies and terrorizing the inhabitants. In 1780 and 1781, the British mounted a punishing attack along the Connecticut coast. Over 200 buildings in Fairfield were burned, and much of nearby Norwalk was destroyed. The southern coast, with its broad rivers, was even more vulnerable. In December 1780, Benedict Arnold ravaged the James River valley in Virginia, uprooting tobacco, confiscating slaves, and creating panic among the white population. Similar devastation befell the coasts of Georgia and the Carolinas.

Such punishing attacks sent civilians fleeing into the interior. During the first years of the war, the port cities lost nearly half their population, and inland communities strained to cope with the thousands of refugees who streamed into them. So many Boston refugees had crowded into Concord, Massachusetts, by July 1775 that they decided to hold a town meeting there! By March 1776, Concord's population had grown by 25 percent, creating major problems of housing, social order, and public health.

Not all the traffic was inland, away from the coast. In western New York, Pennsylvania, Virginia, and the Carolinas, frontier settlements collapsed in the face of British and Indian assaults. By 1783, the white population along the Mohawk River west of Albany, New York, had declined from 10,000 to 3,500. According to one observer, after nearly five years of warfare in Tryon County, 12,000 farms had been abandoned, 700 buildings burned, thousands of bushels of grain destroyed, nearly 400 women widowed, and perhaps 2,000 children orphaned.

Wherever the armies went, they generated a swirl of refugees, who spread vivid tales of the war's devastation. This refugee traffic, added to the constant movement of soldiers back and forth between army and civilian life, brought the war home to countless people who did not experience it at first hand. Disease followed the armies like an avenging angel, ravaging soldiers and civilians alike.

As they moved across the countryside, the armies lived off the land, commandeering the supplies they needed. During the desperate winter of 1777–1778, in an effort to protect the surrounding population, Washington issued an order prohibiting his troops from roaming more than a half mile from camp. In New Jersey, Britain's German mercenaries raised additional fears, particularly among women. In April 1777, a committee of the Congress, taking affidavits from women who had suffered rape, reported that it had "authentic information of many instances of the most indecent treatment, and actual ravishment of married and single women." Such was the nature of that "most irreparable injury," however, that the persons suffering it, "though perfectly innocent, look upon it as a kind of reproach to have the facts related and their names known." Whether the report had any effect is unknown.

The Loyalists

No Americans suffered greater losses than those who remained loyal to the crown. On September 8, 1783, Thomas Danforth, formerly a prosperous lawyer from Cambridge, Massachusetts, appeared in London before the King's Commission of Enquiry into the Losses and Services of the American Loyalists. Danforth was there to seek compensation for the losses he had suffered at the hands of the American revolutionaries. Like other Loyalists who appealed to the commission, Danforth began by explaining the consequences of his loyalty to the crown. Having devoted his whole life to "preparing himself for future usefulness," he now found himself "near his fortieth year, banished under pain of death, to a distant country, where he has not the most remote family connection ... cut off from his profession, from every hope of importance in life, and in a great degree from social enjoyments." Without the assistance of the British government, he would be forced to occupy "a station much inferior to that of a menial servant...."

The commission's response is unknown, but many of the several thousand Loyalists who appeared before it were reimbursed for about one-third of their losses. Though more than most Loyalist refugees ever received, this was meager compensation for the confiscation of house and property, expulsion from their communities, and the trauma of relocation in a distant and unfamiliar land.

Although we do not know how many colonists remained loyal to England, we do know that tens of thousands evacuated with British troops from New York, Charleston, and Savannah at the end of the war. At least as many slipped away to England,

Loyalists, or "Tories," as the Patriots called them, often suffered the indignities of tarring, feathering, and public humiliation for their loyalty to England. (Corbis-Bettmann)

Canada, or the West Indies while the fighting was still under way. Additional thousands who wished that independence had never come stayed on in the new nation and struggled to rebuild their lives. These are substantial numbers when set against the total American population, black and white, of about 2.5 million. The incidence of loyalism differed dramatically from region to region. There were fewest Loyalists in New England and most in and around New York City, where British authority was most stable.

Why did so many Americans remain loyal, often at the cost of personal danger and loss? Customs officers, members of the governors' councils, and Anglican clergymen—all appointed to office in the king's name—often remained with the crown. Loyalism was common as well among groups especially dependent on British authority—for example, settlers on the Carolina frontier who believed themselves mistreated by the planter elite along the coast; ethnic minorities, such as the Germans in the middle states, who feared domination by the Anglo-American majority; or tenants on some of the large estates along the Hudson River, who had struggled for years with their landlords over the terms of their leaseholds. For many Loyalists, the prospect of confronting English military power was sufficiently daunting, while others doubted the ability of a new, weak nation to survive in an Atlantic world dominated by competing empires, even if independence could be won.

But Loyalism often had a principled grounding as well, as Samuel Seabury made clear. "Every person owes obedience to the laws of the government," Seabury insisted, "and is obliged in honour and duty to support them. Because if one has a right to disregard the laws of the society to which he belongs, all have the same right; and then government is at an end." William Eddis wondered what kind of society independence would bring when revolutionary crowds showed no respect for the rights of Loyalist dissenters such as he. "If I differ in opinion from the multitude," he asked, "must I therefore be deprived of my character, and the confidence of my fellow-citizens; when in every station of life I discharge my duty with fidelity and honour?" Loyalists such as Eddis and Seabury claimed to support reason and the rule of law against revolutionary disorder. Given the Loyalists' adherence to monarchy with its values

of social hierarchy and political subordination, their loss weakened the forces of conservatism in America and facilitated the progress of revolutionary change.

Many who faced exile successfully established new lives in other parts of the empire. The majority settled in the Maritime Provinces of Canada. Those, such as Thomas Danforth, who made it to England often found themselves relegated to the fringes of English society, their financial affairs troubled, their futures uncertain.

African Americans and the Revolutionary War

American blacks were deeply involved in the Revolution. In fact, the conflict provoked the largest slave rebellion in American history prior to the Civil War. Once the war was under way, blacks found a variety of ways to turn events to their own advantage. For some, this meant applying revolutionary principles to their own lives and calling for their personal freedom. For others, it meant seeking liberty behind English lines or in the continent's interior.

During the prerevolutionary decade, as their white masters talked excitedly about liberty, increasing numbers of black Americans questioned their own oppression. In the North, some slaves petitioned legislatures to set them free. In the South, pockets of insurrection appeared. In 1765, more than 100 South Carolina slaves fled to the interior, where they tried to establish a colony of their own. The next year, slaves paraded through the streets of Charleston chanting "Liberty, liberty!"

In November 1775, Lord Dunmore issued a proclamation offering freedom to all Virginia slaves and servants, "able and willing to bear arms," who would leave their masters and join the British forces in Norfolk. Within weeks, 500 to 600 slaves had responded. Among them was Thomas Peters, from Wilmington, North Carolina.

Kidnapped from the Yoruba tribe in what is now Nigeria and brought to North America by a French slave trader, Peters had been purchased in Louisiana about 1760. He resisted enslavement so fiercely that his master sold him into the English colonies. By 1770, Peters belonged to William Campbell, an immigrant Scots planter on North

During the Revolutionary War, James Armistead Lafayette, a Virginia slave, served as a spy against the British for the French general Lafayette. In recognition of his service, the Virginia General Assembly granted him his freedom in 1786. (Valentine Museum, Richmond, VA)

Carolina's Cape Fear River. Here Peters toiled while the storm brewed between England and the colonies.

Peters's plans for his own declaration of independence may have ripened as a result of the rhetoric of liberty he heard around his master's house, for William Campbell had become a leading member of Wilmington's Sons of Liberty and talked excitedly about inalienable rights. By mid–1775, the Cape Fear region, like many areas from Maryland to Georgia, buzzed with rumors of slave uprisings. Importations of new slaves were banned, and patrols were dispatched to disarm all blacks in the area. In July, the state's revolutionary government imposed martial law when the British commander of Fort Johnston, situated at the mouth of the Cape Fear River near Wilmington, encouraged Negroes to "elope from their masters." When 20 British ships entered the Cape Fear River in March 1776 and disembarked royal troops, Peters seized the moment to redefine himself as a man, instead of William Campbell's property, and

escaped. Before long, he would fight with the British-officered Black Pioneers.

How many African Americans sought liberty behind British lines is unknown, but as many as 20 percent may have done so. In contrast to their white masters, blacks saw in England the promise of freedom, not tyranny. As the war dragged on, English commanders pressed blacks into service. A regiment of black soldiers, formed from Virginia slaves who responded to Dunmore's proclamation, marched into battle, their chests covered by sashes emblazoned with the slogan "Liberty to Slaves."

Some of the blacks who joined England achieved their freedom. At the war's end, several thousand were evacuated with the British to Nova Scotia, where they established their own settlements. Their reception by the white inhabitants, however, was generally hostile. By the end of the century, most had left Canada to found the free black colony of Sierra Leone on the west coast of Africa. Thomas Peters was a leader among them.

Many of the slaves who fled behind English lines, however, never won their freedom. In keeping with the terms of the peace treaty, hundreds were returned to their American owners. Several thousand others, their value as field hands too great to be ignored, were transported to the West Indies and the harsher slavery of the sugar plantations. England had not entered the war to abolish slavery.

Other blacks took advantage of the war's confusion to slip away from their masters in pursuit of a new life. Some sought refuge among the Indians in the interior. The Seminoles of Georgia and Florida generally welcomed black runaways and through intermarriage absorbed them into tribal society. The blacks' reception by the Cherokee and Creek, however, was more uncertain. Some were taken in, but others were returned to their white owners in return for bounties, and still others were held in slavelike conditions by new Indian masters. Numerous blacks made their way north, following rumors that slavery had been abolished there. Whatever their destination, thousands of African Americans acted to throw off the bonds of slavery.

Fewer blacks fought on the American side than on England's, in part because neither the

Congress nor the states were eager to see them armed. Faced with the increasing need for troops, however, the Congress and each of the states except Georgia and South Carolina eventually relented and pressed blacks into service. Of those who served the Patriot cause, many received the freedom they were promised. The patriotism of countless others, however, went unrewarded.

The Ferment of Revolutionary Politics

The Revolution altered people's lives in countless ways that reached beyond the sights and sounds of battle. No areas of American life were more powerfully changed than politics and government. Who among the American people would have a voice in revolutionary politics, and who would be excluded? How thoroughly would doctrines of political equality penetrate revolutionary politics, or how tenaciously would people cling to the more traditional belief that citizens should defer to their political leaders? And how would the new state governments balance the need for order and the security of property against the desire for democratic openness and accountability? These were some of the questions that had to be addressed.

There were other explosive issues complicating revolutionary politics and threatening to overwhelm both Congress and the states: controlling the Loyalist "menace," deciding whether to abolish slavery, arguing over religious freedom and the separation of church and state, apportioning taxes, regulating prices, issuing paper money and providing debt relief to desperate citizens. Seldom has American politics been more heated; seldom has it struggled with a more daunting agenda than during the years of the nation's founding.

Mobilizing the People

Under the pressure of revolutionary events, politics attracted people's attention like a magnet and absorbed their energies as never before. The politicization of American society was evident in the flood of printed material that streamed from American presses. While newspapers multiplied in number, pamphlets by the thousands fanned the political debate. Declared one contemporary in amazement, it was

> a spectacle ... without a parallel on earth.... Even a large portion of that class of the community which is destined to daily labor have free and constant access to public prints, receive regular information of every occurrence, [and] attend to the course of political affairs. Never ... were [political pamphlets] ... so cheap, so universally diffused, so easy of access.

Pulpits rocked with political exhortations as well. Religion and politics had never been sharply separated in colonial America, but the Revolution drew them more tightly together. Some believed that God intended revolutionary America as the place of Christ's Second Coming and that independence foretold that glorious day. Others of a less millennialist persuasion thought of America as a "New Israel," a covenanted people specially chosen by God to preserve liberty in a threatening world. Giving the metaphor a classical twist, Samuel Adams called on Bostonians to join in creating a "Christian Sparta."

In countless recruiting and election day sermons, Congregational, Presbyterian, and Baptist clergy exhorted the American people to repent the sins that had brought English tyranny upon them and urged them to rededicate themselves to God's law by fighting for American freedom. It was language that people nurtured in Puritan piety and the Great Awakening instinctively understood.

The belief that God sanctioned their Revolution strengthened Americans' resolve. It also encouraged them to identify national interest with divine intent, and thus offered convenient justification for whatever they believed necessary to do. This was not the last time Americans would make that dangerous equation.

By contrast, Loyalist clergy, such as Maryland's Jonathan Boucher, urged their parishioners to support the king as head of the Anglican Church. During the months preceding independence, as the local Committee of Safety interrupted worship to harass him, Boucher carried a loaded pistol into

Abigail Adams, like many women of the revolutionary generation, protested the contradiction in men's subordination of women while they extolled the principles of liberty and equality. (New York State Historical Association, Cooperstown)

numbers for his opponent. In no other state did women even temporarily secure the franchise.

Most women did not press for political equality, for the idea flew in the face of long-standing social convention, and its advocacy exposed a person to public ridicule. Some women did make the case, most often to each other or their husbands. "I cannot say, that I think you are very generous to the ladies," Abigail Adams chided her husband John. "For whilst you are proclaiming peace and good will to men, emancipating all nations, you insist upon retaining an absolute power over all wives." John consulted Abigail on many things but turned this admonition quickly aside. Not until the twentieth century would women secure the vote, that most fundamental attribute of citizenship.

Prior to independence, most women had accepted the principle that political debate fell outside the feminine sphere. The Revolution, however, significantly altered that attitude, for women felt the urgency of the revolutionary crisis as intensely as men. "How shall I impose a silence upon myself," wondered Anne Emlen in 1777, "when the subject is so very interesting, so much engrossing conversation & what every member of the community is more or less concerned in?" With increasing frequency, women wrote and spoke to each other about public events, especially as they affected their own lives. Declared Eliza Wilkerson of South Carolina during the British invasion of 1780, "None were greater politicians than the several knots of ladies, who met together. All trifling discourses of fashions, and such low chat was thrown by, and we commenced perfect statesmen."

As the war progressed, increasing numbers of women ventured their opinions publicly. A few, such as Esther DeBerdt Reed of Philadelphia, published essays explaining women's urgent need to contribute to the Patriot cause. In her 1780 broadside "The Sentiments of an American Woman," she declared that women wanted to be "useful," like "those heroines of antiquity, who have rendered their sex illustrious," and called on women to renounce "vain ornament" as they had earlier renounced English tea. The money no longer spent on clothing and hairstyles would be the "offering of the Ladies" to Washington's army. In Philadelphia, women responded by collecting $300,000 in continental currency from over 1,600 individuals. Refusing Washington's proposal that the money be mixed with general funds in the national treasury, they insisted on using it to purchase materials for shirts so that each soldier might know he had received a contribution directly from the women.

In the revolutionary context, even women's traditional roles took on new political meaning. With English imports cut off and the army badly in need of clothing, spinning and weaving assumed patriotic importance. Often coming together as Daughters of Liberty, women made shirts and other items of clothing. Charity Clarke, a New York teenager, acknowledged that she "felt Nationaly" as she knitted "stockens" for the soldiers. Though "heroines may not distinguish themselves at the head of an army," she informed an English cousin,

The outpouring of political broadsides issuing from American presses during the Revolutionary War gave evidence of women's activism as well as men's. This notice, dated 1770, calls for "tea-drinking ladies of New York" to reject the imported brew. (Library of Congress)

a "fighting army of amazons … armed with spinning wheels" would emerge in America. "These limbs," she concluded, "are armed with strength, the soul is fortified by virtue, and the love of liberty is cherished within this bosom."

The most traditional of female roles, the care and nurture of children, took on special political resonance during the revolutionary era. How could the republic be sustained once independence had been won? Only by a rising generation

of republican citizens schooled in the principles of public virtue and ready to assume the task. How would they be prepared? During their formative years by their "Republican Mothers," the women of the Revolution.

Women developed a variety of new connections with the public realm during the revolutionary years. Those connections, however, remained limited, for the assumption that politics and government were a male domain did not die easily. In time, further challenges to that assumption would come, and when they did, women would find guidance in the principles that the women of the Revolution had helped to define.

The Agenda of Revolutionary Politics

Revolutionary politics took different forms in different states, depending on the impact of the war, the extent of Loyalism, patterns of social conflict, and the disruptions of economic change. In Pennsylvania, political change ran deep, whereas in other states, such as Connecticut and Virginia, change was more muted. Everywhere, though, citizens struggled with a bewildering and often intractable array of issues that revealed the clash of conflicting ideologies, interests, and ambitions.

Separating Church and State

Among the most explosive issues was the proper relationship between church and state in a republican order. Prior to independence, Rhode Island, New Jersey, Pennsylvania, and Delaware had established full religious liberty. In the other colonies, however, one religious group had enjoyed the benefits of endorsement by the government and public tax support for its clergy. In those colonies, "dissenters" such as the Methodists and Baptists, growing in number among the lower classes of city and countryside and noisily pressing their case for religious liberty, were grudgingly tolerated by colonial authorities.

With independence, pressure built for severing church and state completely. Such pressure was fed by the belief that throughout history alliances between governmental and church

This nineteenth-century print says it gives "A Correct View of the Old Methodist Church in John Street, New York. The first erected in America. Founded A.D. 1768." Methodists and Baptists were among the "dissenting" groups pressing for full religious freedom during the revolutionary era. (The Metropolitan Museum of Art, Bequest of Edward W. C. Arnold, 1954. The Edward W. C. Arnold Collection of New York Prints, Maps and Pictures. (54.90.168))

authorities had been instruments of oppression, and that voluntary choice was the only safe basis for religious association.

In Massachusetts, Connecticut, and New Hampshire, the Congregationalists fought to retain their long-established privileges. To separate church and state, they argued, was to invite infidelity and disorder. Isaac Backus, the most outspoken of New England's Baptists, protested that "many, who are filling the nation with the cry of *liberty* and against *oppressors* are at the same time themselves violating that dearest of all rights, *liberty of conscience.*"

Massachusetts's new constitution guaranteed everyone the right to worship God "in the manner and season most agreeable to the dictates of his own conscience." But as Backus pointed out, it also empowered the legislature to require that towns tax their residents to support "the public worship of God." Though individuals could direct their taxes toward support of their own clergy, Backus argued that such official support should be ended completely. Religious toleration, he insisted, fell far short of true religious freedom.

During the decades following independence, New England's Congregational establishment continued to weaken. But not until the early nineteenth century—in Massachusetts not until 1833—were the laws linking church and state finally repealed.

In Virginia, the Baptists pressed their cause against the Protestant Episcopal Church, successor to the Church of England. The adoption in 1786 of Thomas Jefferson's Bill for Establishing Religious Freedom, rejecting all connections between church and state and removing all religious tests for public office, decisively settled the issue. Three years later, that statute served as a model for the First Amendment to the new federal Constitution.

Even most supporters of religious freedom, however, were not prepared to extend it universally. The people of Northbridge, Massachusetts, wanted to exclude "Roman Catholics, pagons, or Mahomitents" from public office. Disestablishment did not end religious discrimination. But it did firmly implant the principle of religious freedom in American law.

Loyalists and the Public Safety

Independence and the war raised troubling questions about the amount of freedom of speech and association that could be tolerated in a republican society, especially during such dangerous times. That issue affected most powerfully those colonists who remained loyal to England.

Emotions ran high between Patriots and Loyalists in revolutionary America. "The rage of civil discord," lamented one individual, "hath advanced among us with an astonishing rapidity. The son is armed against the father, the brother against the brother, family against family." In the midst of the Revolutionary War, security required stern measures against Loyalist counterrevolutionaries. More than security was involved, however, for the Patriots were also determined to exact revenge against those who had rejected the revolutionary cause.

During the war, each state enacted a series of laws designed to deprive Loyalists of the vote, confiscate their property, and banish them from their homes. In 1778, the Georgia assembly declared 117 persons guilty of treason, expelled them from the state on pain of death, and declared their possessions forfeit.

In 1776, the Connecticut assembly passed a remarkably punitive law threatening anyone who criticized either the assembly or the Continental Congress with immediate fine and imprisonment. Probably not more than a few dozen Loyalists actually died at the hands of the revolutionary regimes, but thousands found their livelihoods destroyed, their families ostracized, and themselves subject to physical attack.

Punishing Loyalists—or people accused of Loyalism, a distinction that was often unclear in the heat of political controversy—was a popular activity. Whereas some Patriots argued that the Loyalists, by their behavior, had put themselves outside the protection of American law, others worried that no one's rights would be safe when the rights of some were so clearly disregarded. Republics, after all, were supposed to be "governments of law, and not of men." Once that distinction disappeared, no one would be secure.

After the war ended and passions cooled, most states repealed their anti-Loyalist legislation. In the midst of the Revolution, however, no issue raised more clearly the difficult question of how to balance individual liberty against the needs of public security. That problem would return to trouble the nation in the years ahead.

Slavery Under Attack

The place of human slavery in a republican society also vexed the revolutionary generation. During the several decades preceding independence, the trade in human chattels had flourished. Though several northern colonies had abolished the slave trade, the 1760s had witnessed the largest importation of slaves in colonial history.

The Revolutionary War halted that trade almost completely. Though southern planters talked of replacing their lost chattels once the war ended, a combination of revolutionary principles, a reduced need for fieldhands in the depressed Chesapeake tobacco economy, the continuing natural increase among the slave population, and anxiety over black rebelliousness argued for the slave trade's extinction. By 1790, every state except South Carolina and Georgia had outlawed slave importations.

Termination of the slave trade had powerful implications, for it reduced the infusion of new Africans into the black population. This meant that an ever higher proportion of blacks was American-born, thus speeding the process of cultural transformation by which Africans became African Americans.

Slavery itself came under attack during the revolutionary era, with immense consequences for blacks and the nation's future. As the crisis with England heated up, catchwords such as *liberty* and *tyranny*, mobilized by colonists against British policies, reminded citizens that one-fifth of the colonial population was in chains. Samuel Hopkins, a New England clergyman, accosted his compatriots for "making a vain parade of being advocates for the liberties of mankind, while … continuing this lawless, cruel, inhuman, and abominable practice of enslaving your fellow creatures." Following independence, the attacks intensified.

In Georgia and South Carolina, where blacks outnumbered whites more than two to one, slavery escaped significant challenge. Committed to the doctrine of racial superiority and fearing the black majority, whites shuddered at the prospect of black freedom. Moreover, slave labor remained essential to the still prosperous rice economy. In response to the dangers generated by the war, whites wound the local slave codes even tighter.

In Virginia and Maryland, by contrast, whites argued openly whether slavery was compatible with republicanism, and in these states significant change did occur. The weakened demand for slave labor posed by the depressed tobacco economy facilitated the debate. Though neither state abolished slavery, both passed laws making it easier for owners to free their slaves without continuing to be responsible for their behavior. Moreover, increasing numbers of blacks purchased their own freedom or simply ran away. By 1800, more than one of every ten blacks in the Chesapeake region was free, a dramatic increase from 30 years before. The majority lived and worked in Baltimore, Richmond, and other towns, where they formed communities that became centers of an expanding African American society as well as havens for escaping slaves from the countryside. For blacks in the Chesapeake region, the conditions of life slowly changed for the better.

The most dramatic breakthrough occurred in the North. There slavery was either abolished or put on the road to gradual extinction. Abolition was possible in the North because slavery had neither the economic nor social importance that it did in the South. In most areas, blacks constituted no more than 4 percent of the population, nor were blacks so essential as a labor force.

Northern blacks joined in the attacks on slavery. Following independence, they eagerly petitioned state assemblies for their freedom. "Every Principle from which America has acted in the course of their unhappy difficulties with Great Britain," declared one group of Philadelphia blacks, "pleads stronger than a thousand arguments in favor of our petition." In 1780, the Pennsylvania assembly passed a law stipulating that all newborn blacks were to be free when they reached age 21. It was a cautious but decisive step. Other northern states adopted similar policies of gradual emancipation.

In scattered instances, free blacks participated actively in revolutionary politics. When the first draft of the Massachusetts constitution, explicitly excluding blacks and mulattoes from the franchise, was made public, William Gordon, a white clergyman, voiced his protest. "Would it not be ridiculous ... and unjust to exclude freemen from voting ... though otherwise qualified, because their skins are black?" he questioned. "Why not ... for being long-nosed, short-faced, or ... lower than five feet nine?" In the end, Massachusetts's constitution made no mention of race, and there, as well as in Pennsylvania and New York, African Americans occasionally cast their votes.

If civic participation by blacks was scattered and temporary in the North, it was almost totally absent in the South. With the brief exception of North Carolina, African Americans could neither vote nor enjoy such basic rights of citizenship as protection of their persons and property under the law. In the South, blacks remained almost entirely without political voice, except in the petitions against slavery and mistreatment that they pressed upon the state regimes. Even as freemen, blacks continued to encounter pervasive discrimination.

Still, remarkable progress had been made. Prior to the Revolution, slavery had been an accepted fact of northern life while after the Revolution, it no longer was. That change made a vast difference in the lives of countless black Americans. The abolition of slavery in the North increased the sectional divergence between North and South. The consequences of that divergence would become even more apparent in the nineteenth century. In addition, there now existed a coherent and publicly proclaimed antislavery argument, one closely linked in Americans' minds with the nation's founding. The first antislavery organizations had been created as well. Although another half century would pass before antislavery became a significant force in national politics, the groundwork for slavery's final abolition had been laid.

Politics and the Economy

The combined impact of independence and the Revolutionary War devastated the American economy. The cutoff of long-established patterns of overseas trade sent American commerce into a tailspin from which it did not recover for nearly 20 years. While English men-of-war prowled the coast, American ships rocked idly at empty wharves, New England's once booming shipyards grew quiet, and communities whose livelihood depended on the sea sank into depression. Virginia tobacco planters, their English markets gone and their plantations open to seaborne attack, struggled to survive. Farmers in the middle and New England states often prospered while hungry armies were nearby, but saw their profits plummet when the armies moved on.

As this Massachusetts broadside suggests, the lure of adventure and hope for quick profits enticed countless young men into dangerous but exciting service aboard American privateers. (American Antiquarian Society)

Exports and Imports, 1768–1783

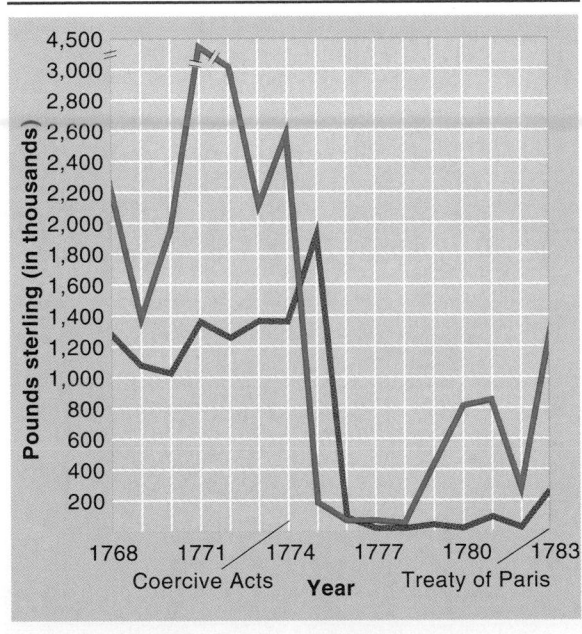

Nonimportation affected colonial commerce during the late 1760s and early 1770s, but American trade plummeted with the Coercive Acts and the outbreak of war. Source: U.S. Bureau of the Census.

Not everyone suffered from the effects of independence and the Revolutionary War. With British goods excluded from American markets and the wearing of homespun deemed patriotic, American artisans often prospered. (The familiar slogan "Buy American" has a long tradition.) Handsome profits, moreover, were to be made from government contracts by people enjoying the right political connections. Henry Knox, sometime merchant and commander of the continental artillery, observed that he was "exceedingly anxious to effect something in these fluctuating times, which may make … [me] easy for life." In the eighteenth century, as now, the boundary between private interest and public duty was often unclear.

But even as some prospered, countless others saw their affairs fall into disarray. Intractable issues such as price and wage inflation, skyrocketing taxation, and mushrooming debt set people

Wholesale Price Index, 1770–1789

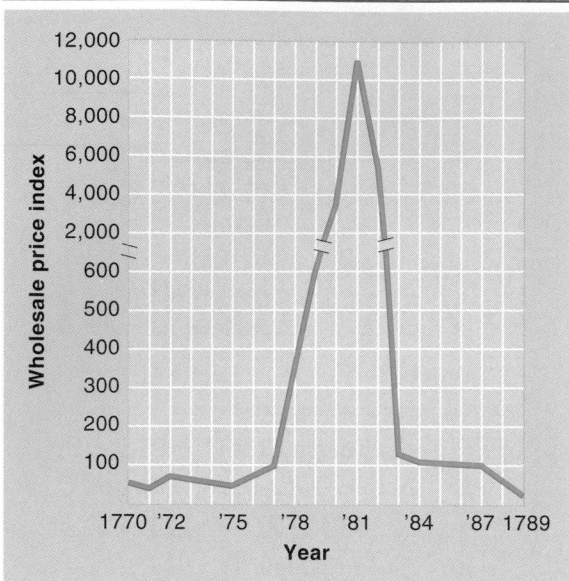

Note: 1850–1859 = 100

Prices skyrocketed as Congress and the state governments printed huge amounts of paper money in a desperate effort to cover the costs of the war. Source: U.S. Bureau of the Census.

sharply against each other. Heated debates arose over whether the states' war debts should be funded at face value or at some reduced rate. In support of full value were the states' creditors—merchants and other persons of wealth who had loaned the states money and had bought up large amounts of securities at deep discounts. These people spoke earnestly of upholding the public honor and giving fair return to those who had risked their own resources in the revolutionary cause. Opposed were common folk angered by the large profits of the speculators. No one, they argued, should reap personal advantage from public distress.

The issue of taxation, seared into Americans' consciousness by their troubles with England, generated even more heated controversy. As the costs of the war mounted, so did the burden of taxation. Between 1774 and 1778, Massachusetts levied a total of £408,976 in taxes, a dramatic increase over colonial days. Taxes, complained one anguished soul, equaled nearly one-third of the inhabitants' incomes. Massachusetts was not unique.

Lacking sufficient gold and silver to cover the escalating costs of war, Congress printed massive amounts of paper money, which, in spite of the printed pledge, rapidly depreciated in value. (Smithsonian Institution)

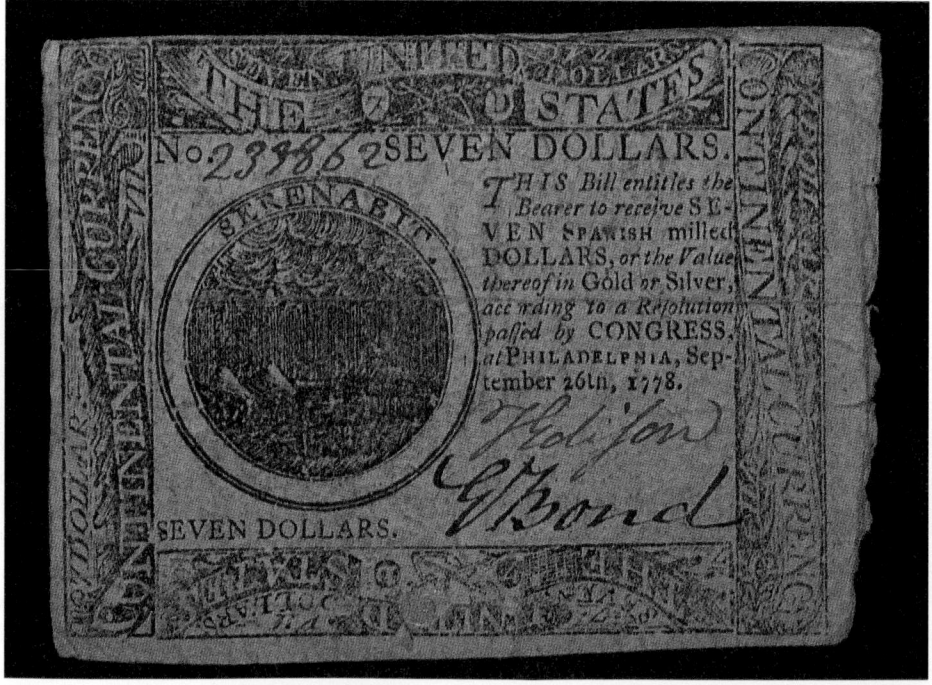

As taxes skyrocketed, so did clashes over tax policy. Farmers, artisans, and others of modest means argued that taxes should be payable in depreciated paper money or government securities rather than only in specie (gold or silver coin), as some state laws required. Lacking that kind of money, they faced the prospect of having their property foreclosed when they could not meet their obligations. Government officials responded that allowing payment in depreciated paper would deprive the government of critically needed revenue.

Controversy swirled as well around the states' efforts to control soaring prices. Each of the states experimented with price controls at one time or another. Seldom were such efforts effective; frequently, they generated political firestorms. In general, the poor and those not yet integrated into the market economy supported controls. Faced with escalating prices, they had difficulty making ends meet. They also believed that goods should carry a "just price," one deemed fair to buyer and seller alike. In keeping with these principles, a crowd in New Windsor, New York, in 1777 seized a shipment of tea bound for Albany and sold it for what they deemed a fair offering.

Merchants, shopkeepers, and others caught up in the commercial economy, however, believed that economic transactions should be regulated by the laws of supply and demand. "It is contrary to the nature of commerce," observed Benjamin Franklin, "for government to interfere in the prices of commodities." Attempts to regulate prices only created a disincentive to labor, which was "the principal part of the wealth of every country."

Disputes over paper money divided the American people as well. Faced with the uncontrollable escalation of wartime expenses, Congress and the states did what colonial governments had done before and American governments have done ever since: they printed money. In the first year of the war alone, they issued more than $400 million in various kinds of paper, and that was just the beginning. Only the citizens' willingness to accept such paper in their dealings with the government and each other supported its value. That willingness rapidly disappeared as the flood of paper

TIMELINE

1775 Lord Dunmore's proclamation to slaves and servants in Virginia

Iroquois Six Nations pledge neutrality

Continental Congress urges "states" to establish new governments

1776 British evacuate Boston and seize New York City

Declaration of Independence

Eight states draft constitutions

Cherokee raids and American retaliation

1777 British occupy Philadelphia

Most Iroquois join the British

Americans win victory at Saratoga

Washington's army winters at Valley Forge

1778 War shifts to the South

Savannah falls to the British

French treaty of alliance and commerce

1779 Massachusetts state constitutional convention

Sullivan destroys Iroquois villages in New York

1780 Massachusetts constitution ratified

Charleston surrenders to the British

Pennsylvania begins gradual abolition of slavery

1780s Virginia and Maryland debate abolition of slavery

Destruction of Iroquois Confederacy

1781 Cornwallis surrenders at Yorktown

Articles of Confederation ratified by states

1783 Peace treaty with England signed in Paris

Massachusetts Supreme Court abolishes slavery

King's Commission on American Loyalists begins work

increased. Congressional bills of credit that in 1776 were pegged against gold at the ratio of 1.5 to 1 had slipped five years later to 147 to 1. State currencies depreciated even more alarmingly. In 1780, New York exchanged its old currency for new at the rate of 128 to 1.

Such disastrous depreciation had ominous social consequences. James Lovell reported nervously that "sailors with clubs" paraded the streets of Boston "instead of working for paper." The upward spiral of prices was staggering. In Massachusetts, a bushel of corn that sold for less than a dollar in 1777 went for nearly $80 two years later, and in Maryland the price of wheat increased several thousandfold. In Boston, a crowd of women, angered by the escalating costs of food, tossed a merchant suspected of monopolizing commodities into a cart and dragged him through the city's streets while "a large concourse of men stood amazed."

With property values in disarray, it seemed at times as if the very foundations of society were coming unhinged. "The war," wrote Thomas Paine, has thrown property into channels where before it never was.... Monies in large sums ... enable ... [profiteers] to roll the snow ball of monopoly and forestalling ... [and] while these people are heaping up wealth ... the remaining part are jogging on in their old way, with few or no advantages.

The poor suffered most severely, for they were most vulnerable to losses in the purchasing power of wages and military pay. The poor, however, were not alone. Farmers and merchants, planters and artisans also faced the burden of growing debt and uncertainty.

Rarely has the American economy been in such disarray as at the nation's founding. There were no ready solutions to the problems of debt, taxation, price control, and paper money for such issues often exceeded the capacity of politics for compromise and resolution. Divisive and intractable, they continued to heighten political tensions through the 1780s.

Conclusion

The Crucible of Revolution

Independence and war redrew the contours of American life and changed the destinies of the American people. Though the Revolutionary War ended in victory, liberty had its costs. Lives were lost, property was destroyed, and local economies were deranged. The war altered relationships between Indians and whites, for it left the Iroquois and Cherokee severely weakened and opened the floodgates of western expansion. For African Americans, the Revolution had paradoxical results. It produced an ideology that decried slavery, generated efforts to end the slave trade, and marked the first general debate over abolishing the oppressive institution. Yet slavery was eradicated only where it was least important, in the North, while in the South, where slavery had the strongest hold, its future was guaranteed. In spite of the political ferment generated by the Revolution, women reaped few clear advantages. Though they participated in many revolutionary crowds and achieved enhanced status as "Republican Mothers," they were still denied the franchise, that critical index of full republican citizenship.

By 1783, a new nation had come into being where none had existed before, a nation based not on age-encrusted principles of monarchy and aristocratic privilege, but on the doctrines of republican liberty. That was the greatest change of all. The political transformations set in motion, however, generated angry disputes whose outcomes could be only dimly foreseen. Thomas Paine put the matter succinctly: "The answer to the question, can America be happy under a government of her own, is short and simple—as happy as she pleases; she hath a blank sheet to write upon." The years immediately ahead would determine whether America's republican experiment, launched with such hopefulness in 1776, would succeed.

Recommended Reading

The Revolutionary War

Don Higginbotham, *The War of Independence* (1983); Robert Middlekauff, *The Glorious Cause* (1982); John Shy, *A People Numerous and Armed* (1976); Ronald Hoffman and Peter Albert, eds., *Arms and Independence: The Military Character of the American Revolution* (1984); Charles Neimeyer, *America Goes to War: A Social History of the Continental Army* (1996).

Diplomacy

Richard Morris, *The Peacemakers: The Great Powers and American Independence* (1965); Jonathan Dull, *A Diplomatic History of the American Revolution* (1985); Reginald Horsman, *Diplomacy of the New Republic, 1776–1815* (1985); Ronald Hoffman and Peter Albert, eds., *Peace and the Peacemakers: The Treaty of 1783* (1986).

Indians and African Americans

Anthony Wallace, *The Death and Rebirth of the Seneca* (1969); Colin Calloway, *The American Revolution in Indian Country* (1995); Isabel Kelsey, *Joseph Brant, 1743–1807: Man of Two Worlds* (1984); James O'Donnell, *Southern Indians in the American Revolution* (1973); Tom Hatley, *The Dividing Paths: Cherokees and South Carolinians Through the Revolutionary Era* (1993); James Merrell, *The Indians' New World: Catawbas and Their Neighbors from European Contact Through the Era of Revival* (1989). Ira Berlin and Ronald Hoffman, eds., *Slavery and Freedom in the Age of the American Revolution* (1983); Gary B. Nash, *Race and Revolution* (1990); Sylvia Frey, *Water from the Rock; Black Resistance in a Revolutionary Age* (1991); David Brian Davis, *The Problem of Slavery in the Age of Revolution, 1770–1823* (1975); Sidney Kaplan, *The Black Presence in the Era of the American Revolution, 1770–1800* (1973).

Women and Loyalists

Linda Kerber, *Women of the Republic* (1980); Mary Beth Norton, *Liberty's Daughters* (1980); Joy Buel and Richard Buel, *The Way of Duty: A Woman and Her Family in Revolutionary America* (1984); Edith Gelles, *Portia: The World of Abigail Adams* (1992); Ronald Hoffman and Peter Albert, eds., *Women in the Age of the American Revolution* (1989). Robert Calhoon, *The Loyalists in Revolutionary America, 1760–1781* (1973); Mary Beth Norton, *The British-Americans: The Loyalist Exiles in England, 1774–1789* (1972); Bernard Bailyn, *The Ordeal of Thomas Hutchinson* (1974); Janice Potter, *Liberty We Seek: Loyalist Ideology in Colonial New York and Massachusetts* (1983).

Revolutionary Politics

Gordon Wood, *The Creation of the American Republic, 1776–1787* (1969) and *The Radicalism of the American Revolution* (1992); Robert Gross, *The Minutemen and Their World* (1976); Ronald Hoffman, et al., *An Uncivil War: The Southern Backcountry During the American Revolution* (1985); Edmund Morgan, *Inventing the People: The Rise of Popular Sovereignty in England and America* (1988); Thomas Doerflinger, *A Vigorous Spirit of Enterprise* (1986); Cathy Matson and Peter Onuf, *A Union of Interests: Political and Economic Thought in Revolutionary America* (1990); Al Young, ed., *Beyond the American Revolution: Explorations in the History of American Radicalism* (1993); Ronald Hoffman and Peter Albert, eds., *Religion in a Revolutionary Age* (1994); Rhys Isaac, *The Transformation of Virginia, 1740–1790* (1983); Ann Withington, *Toward a More Perfect Union; Virtue and the Formation of the American Republics* (1991); Jay Fliegelman, *Prodigals and Pilgrims: The American Revolution Against Patriarchal Authority, 1750–1800* (1982); Edward Countryman, *A People in Revolution: The American Revolution and Political Society in New York, 1760–1790* (1981).

Biographies

Pauline Meier, *The Old Revolutionaries: Political Lives in the Age of Samuel Adams* (1980); Norman Risjord, *Representative Americans: The Revolutionary Generation* (1980); Bernard Bailyn, *Faces of Revolution* (1991); Fawn Brodie, *Thomas Jefferson: An Intimate History* (1974); Claude Lopez and Eugenia Herbert, *The Private Franklin: The Man and His Family* (1975); Richard Beeman, *Patrick Henry* (1974).

Consolidating the Revolution

T imothy Bloodworth of New Hanover County, North Carolina, knew what the American Revolution was all about, for he had experienced it firsthand. A man of humble origins, Bloodworth had known poverty as a child. Lacking any formal education, he had worked hard and successfully during the middle decades of the eighteenth century as an innkeeper and ferry pilot, self-styled preacher and physician, blacksmith and farmer. By the mid–1770s, he owned nine slaves and 4,200 acres of land, considerably more than most of his neighbors.

His unpretentious manner and commitment to political equality earned Bloodworth the confidence of his community. In 1758, at the age of only 22, he was elected to the

North Carolina colonial assembly. Over the next three decades, he remained deeply involved in the political life of his home state.

When the colonies' troubles with England drew toward a crisis, Bloodworth spoke ardently of American rights and mobilized support for independence. In 1775, he helped form the Wilmington Committee of Safety. Filled with revolutionary fervor, he urged forward the process of republican political reform and, as commissioner of confiscated property for the district of Wilmington, pressed the attack on local Loyalists.

In 1784, shortly after the war ended, the North Carolina assembly named Bloodworth one of the state's delegates to the Confederation Congress. There he learned for the first time about the problems of governing a new nation. As the Congress struggled through the middle years of the 1780s with the intractable problems of foreign trade, war debt, and control of the trans-Appalachian interior, Bloodworth shared the growing conviction that the Articles of Confederation were too weak. He supported the Congress's call for a special convention to meet in Philadelphia in May 1787 for the purpose of considering matters necessary "to render the constitution of the federal government adequate to the exigencies of the Union."

Like thousands of other Americans, Bloodworth eagerly awaited the convention's work. And like countless Americans, he was stunned by the result, for the proposed constitution described a government that seemed to him designed not to preserve republican liberty but to endanger it.

Once again sniffing political tyranny on the breeze, Bloodworth resigned his congressional seat in August 1787 and hurried back to North Carolina to help organize opposition to the proposed constitution. Over the next several years, he worked tirelessly for its defeat.

Alarmed by the prospect of such a powerful central government, Bloodworth protested that "We cannot consent to the adoption of a Constitution whose revenues lead to aristocratic tyranny, or monarchical despotism, and open a door wide as fancy can point, for the introduction of dissipation, bribery and corruption to the exclusion of public virtue." Had Americans so quickly forgotten the dangers of consolidated power? he wondered. Were they already prepared to turn their backs on their brief experiment in republicanism?

A national government as strong as the one described in the proposed constitution, he feared, would remove power from the people's control, threaten political democracy, and destroy individual liberties. Alarmed by the provision that Congress "may at any time … make or alter" state regulations concerning elections as well as by the absence of explicit guarantees of trial by jury, Bloodworth demanded the addition of a federal bill of rights to protect individual liberties. Echoing the language of revolutionary republicanism, he warned the North Carolina ratifying convention that "Without the most express restrictions, Congress may trample on your rights. Every possible precaution should be taken when we grant powers," he continued, for "Rulers are always disposed to abuse them."

Bloodworth also feared the sweeping authority Congress would have to make "all laws which shall be necessary and proper" for carrying into execution "all other powers vested … in the government of the United States." That language, he insisted, "would result in the abolition of the state governments. Its sovereignty absolutely annihilates them."

In North Carolina, the arguments of Bloodworth and his Anti-Federalist colleagues carried the day. By a vote of 184 to 84, the ratifying convention declared that a bill of rights "asserting and securing from encroachment the great Principles of civil and religious Liberty, and the unalienable rights of the People" must be approved before North Carolina would concur. The convention was true to its word. Not until November 1789, well after the new government had gotten under way and Congress had forwarded a national bill of rights to the states for approval, did North Carolina, with Timothy Bloodworth's cautious endorsement, finally enter the new union.

Ratification of the U.S. Constitution by the states in 1788 not only brought into being a new and potentially more powerful national government, but also symbolized the often conflicting meanings of the American revolutionary era. (John Feingersh/Stock Boston)

*J*ust as Timothy Bloodworth knew the difficulties of achieving American independence, so he learned the problems of preserving American liberty once independence had been won. As a member of the Confederation Congress, Bloodworth confronted the continuing vestiges of colonialism: the patronizing attitudes of England and France, their continuing imperial ambitions in North America, and the republic's ongoing economic dependence on Europe. He also observed the Congress's inability to pay off the war debt, pry open foreign ports to American commerce, and persuade the states to join in a common tariff policy against England. As a southerner, Bloodworth was equally alarmed by the willingness of a congressional majority to forgo free navigation of the Mississippi River, deemed essential for development of the southern backcountry, in exchange for northern commercial advantages in Europe. Finally, he worried about political turmoil in the states as issues of taxation, debt, and paper money led discontented citizens openly to challenge public authority.

By 1786, Bloodworth, like countless other Americans, was caught up in an escalating debate between the Federalists, who believed that the Articles of Confederation were fatally deficient and must be replaced by a stronger national government, and the Anti-Federalists, who were committed to keeping government close to the people and were still deeply troubled by the dangers consolidated power posed to individual liberties.

That debate over the future of America's republican experiment came to a focus in the momentous Philadelphia convention of 1787, which produced not reform, but revolutionary change in the national government. With ratification of the new Constitution, the revolutionary era came to an end, and the American people opened a portentous new chapter in their history.

Struggling with the Peacetime Agenda

As the war ended, problems of demobilization and adjustment to the novel conditions of independence troubled the new nation. Whether the Confederation Congress could effectively deal with the problems of the postwar era remained unclear.

Demobilizing the Army

Demobilizing the army presented the Confederation government with some difficult moments, for when the fighting stopped, many of the troops refused to disband and go home until the Congress redressed their grievances. Trouble first arose in early 1783 when officers at the Continental army camp in Newburgh, New York, sent a delegation to the Congress to complain about arrears in pay and other benefits that the Congress had promised them during the dark days of the war. The Congress responded by calling for the army to disband. Almost immediately, an anonymous address circulated among the officers, attacking the "coldness and severity" of the Congress, calling on the offi-

cers to draw up "a last remonstrance," and hinting darkly at more direct action if their grievances were not met.

Several members of the Congress encouraged the officers' mutterings, hoping the crisis would add urgency to their own calls for a strengthened central government. Most, however, found this challenge to Congress's authority alarming. Washington moved quickly to calm the situation. Promising that the Congress would treat the officers justly, he counseled patience and urged his comrades not to tarnish the victory they had so recently won. His efforts succeeded, for the officers reaffirmed their confidence in the Congress and agreed to disband.

The officers were not the only ones to take action. In June, several hundred disgruntled continental soldiers and Pennsylvania militiamen gathered to express their frustrations in front of Philadelphia's Independence Hall, where both Congress and Pennsylvania's executive council were meeting. When the state authorities would not guarantee the Congress's safety, its members fled in confusion to Princeton, New Jersey. Once

Old Northwest Survey Patterns

The Land Ordinance passed by Congress in 1785 provided for townships divided into lots of 640 acres. Its purpose was to promote the rapid and orderly settlement of the Old Northwest.

there, they eased the tension by issuing the soldiers three months' pay and furloughing them until they could be fully discharged. By early November, the crisis was over, but the Congress's authority had been seriously damaged.

During the mid-1780s, the Congress shuffled between Princeton and Annapolis, Trenton and New York City, its transience visible evidence of its steadily eroding authority. A hot-air balloon, scoffed the *Boston Evening Herald,* would "exactly accommodate the itinerant genius of Congress," because it could then "float along from one end of the continent to the other … and when occasion requires … suddenly pop down into any of the states they please." The Congress had been criticized before, but never so mockingly.

Opening the West

The Congress was not without important accomplishments during the postwar years. Most notable were the two great land ordinances of 1785 and 1787. The first provided for the systematic survey and sale of the region west of New York and Pennsylvania and north of the Ohio River. The area was to be laid out in townships 6 miles square, which were in turn to be subdivided into lots of 640 acres each. Thus began the rectangular grid pattern of land survey and settlement that to this day characterizes the nation's Midwest and distinguishes it so markedly from the irregular settlement patterns of the older, colonial areas to the east.

Two years later, the Congress passed the Northwest Ordinance. It provided for the political organization of the same interior region, first under congressionally appointed officials, then under popularly elected territorial assemblies, and ultimately as new states to be incorporated into the Union "on an equal footing with the original states in all respects whatsoever." Together, these two pieces of legislation provided the legal mechanism for the nation's dramatic territorial expansion during the nineteenth century.

Both bills enjoyed broad political support, for they opened land to settlers and profits to speculators. The income from land sales, moreover, promised to help reduce the national debt. While permitting slave owners already living north of the

Ohio River to retain their chattels, the Ordinance of 1787 prohibited the importation of new slaves into the region. This made the area more attractive to white farmers from the Northeast who worried about their ability to compete with slave labor and were disinclined to live among blacks. Southern delegates in the Congress accepted the restriction because their constituents could look forward to slavery's expansion south of the Ohio. During the 1780s, the country's interior seemed large enough to accommodate everyone's needs.

Despite the Congress's success in providing a legal framework for settlement of the trans-Appalachian frontier, however, it could neither secure the removal of British troops from the western posts nor guarantee free navigation of the Mississippi. Nor was it able to clear the tribes of the Ohio region out of the white settlers' way. These failings led many Americans to question whether the Confederation government was capable of promoting the nation's westward expansion.

During the immediate postwar years, the Congress operated as if the Native Americans of the interior were "conquered" peoples. As allies of England, they had lost the war and thus came under the American government's control. The Treaty of Paris, which set the nation's western boundary at the Mississippi River, American officials insisted, gave the United States political sovereignty over the tribes east of the Mississippi as well as ownership of their land.

This "conquest theory" was fully consistent with white attitudes about Indian separateness and inferiority. Even the most sympathetic whites believed that Native Americans would have to become "civilized" and "Christianized" before they could coexist with white society. Many whites doubted that such "improvements" could take place at all, and argued that the Indians must simply be driven out of white settlers' way. George Washington gave blunt expression to the prevailing view. "The gradual extension of our settlements," he explained, "will as certainly cause the savage as the wolf to retire; both being beasts of prey though they differ in shape."

For a few years, the conquest strategy seemed to work. During the mid–1780s, the Congress imposed several important land treaties on the interior tribes, among them the Iroquois. Their

> ## "Utmost Good Faith" Clause from the Northwest Ordinance (1787)
>
> The following articles shall be considered as articles of compact between the original States and the people and States in the said territory and forever remain unalterable, unless by common consent, to wit:
>
> > The utmost good faith shall always be observed towards the Indians; their land and property shall never be taken from them without their consent; and, in their property, rights, and liberty, they shall never be invaded or disturbed, unless in just and lawful wars authorized by Congress, but laws founded in justice and humanity, shall from time to time be made for preventing wrongs being done to them, and for preserving peace and friendship with them.

numbers reduced and their confederation shattered, many of the Iroquois had fled into Canada. Pressed by the Congress and the New York government, those who remained deeded away most of their land. At the Treaty of Fort Stanwix in 1784, the first congressional treaty with an Indian tribe, the Six Nations made peace, ceded most of their lands to the United States, and retreated to small reservations. By the 1790s, little remained of the once imposing Iroquois domain but a few islands in a spreading sea of white settlement. On those islands, "slums in the wilderness" they have been called, the Iroquois struggled for survival against disease and poverty, their traditional lifeways gone, their self-confidence broken.

The Iroquois were not the only tribes to lose their land. In January 1785, representatives of the Wyandotte, Chippewa, Delaware, and Ottawa tribes relinquished claim to most of present-day Ohio.

Many of the treaties did not hold, however, because they were often exacted under the threat of force and generated widespread resentment. At Fort Stanwix, for example, negotiations were held at gunpoint, and hostages were taken to coerce the Indian delegates. Two years after the Fort Stanwix negotiations, the Iroquois openly repudiated the treaty, asserting that they were still sovereigns of their own soil and "equally free as ... any nation under the sun." The Revolution, moreover, left behind a legacy of bitterness among both Indians and whites: among Indians because they had suffered betrayal and defeat; among white Americans because the Indians had sided with England and thus threatened the Revolution's success. Such bitterness would trouble Indian-white relations for years to come.

By the mid-1780s, tribal groups above and below the Ohio River were actively resisting white expansion into the interior. In the summer of 1786, the Creek resumed hostilities in the backcountry of Georgia, while north of the Ohio, the Shawnee, Delaware, and Miami moved to strengthen their Western Confederacy and prepare for the defense of their common homeland. That fall, the confederacy rejected the whites' conquest theory, asserted that the Ohio River was

The symbolic figure of Columbia, often presented in the form of an Indian maiden embodying the innocence and freedom of the new republic, first became popular during the Revolution. This began to change as Americans moved west across the Appalachians. By the time this French engraving appeared in the early nineteenth century, Columbia was usually garbed in classical attire and had lost her Indian headdress. (Library of Congress)

the proper boundary between them and the United States, and insisted on a new treaty between the combined tribes of the confederacy and the United States. When white settlers continued to press into the region, Native Americans launched a series of devastating raids, bringing white settlement to a virtual halt. By 1786, the entire region from the Great Lakes to the Gulf of Mexico was embroiled in warfare. With the Continental army disbanded and the nation in no position to raise a new one, there was little that Congress could do.

The Congress's inability to open the interior to white settlement alarmed many Americans—speculators threatened with the loss of their investments, farmers wanting to leave the crowded lands of the East, revolutionary soldiers eager to start afresh on the rich soil of Kentucky and Ohio, and leaders such as Thomas Jefferson who believed that republican liberty depended on an expanding nation of yeoman farmers. With the Confederation Congress unable to act effectively, each of these groups found reason to question its adequacy.

Settling the interior, the indispensable land reserve for the fast-growing nation, involved relations with European nations as well. Here, too, the Congress proved ineffective.

In June 1784, Spain—still in possession of Florida, the Gulf Coast, and the trans-Mississippi West—closed the outlet of the Mississippi River at New Orleans to American shipping. Spain's action raised a storm of protest, especially among settlers in the West, who counted on the interior river system to float their produce downstream to outside markets. Land speculators from Virginia to South Carolina were aroused as well, for closure of the Mississippi would discourage development of the southern backcountry. Rumors spread, moreover, that Spanish agents were urging American frontiersmen to seek affiliation with Spain. Washington commented uneasily that throughout the West, settlers were "on a pivot." "The touch of a feather," he feared, "would turn them away."

For more than a year, Foreign Secretary John Jay negotiated with the Spanish ambassador to the United States, Don Diego de Gardoqui, in an effort to reopen the vital Mississippi River commercial outlet. When Gardoqui held firm, Jay switched tactics and offered to relinquish American claims to

British and Spanish Possessions in Eastern North America, 1783

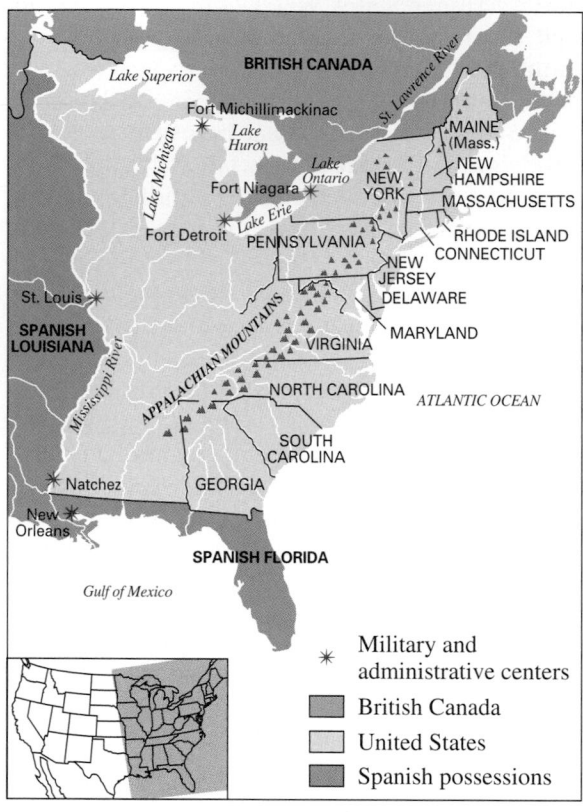

Military and administrative centers

British Canada

United States

Spanish possessions

Though victorious in its struggle for independence, the United States remained surrounded on three sides by British and Spanish possessions. North America continued to be a focus of European colonial ambitions after 1783.

free transit of the Mississippi in return for a new commercial treaty opening Spanish ports to American shipping. The northern states, excited at the prospect of Spanish trade, supported the bargain, but the southern states, angry at Jay's betrayal of their interests, refused. Thus stalemated, the Congress could take no action at all.

Wrestling with the National Debt

The Congress's inability to deal effectively with the massive war debt offered further evidence of the Confederation government's weakness. No one knew how large the public debt actually was at the war's end, but it probably stood at about $35 million. Much of the debt was held abroad by French and Dutch bankers. Not only was the Congress unable to make regular payment against the loan's principal, but it had to borrow additional money abroad simply to pay the accumulating interest. At home, things were no better. In response to the incessant demands of its creditors, the government could only delay and try to borrow more.

In 1781, the Congress appointed Robert Morris, a wealthy and influential Philadelphia merchant, superintendent of finance and gave him broad authority to deal with the nation's troubled affairs. Morris urged the states to stop issuing paper money and persuaded the Congress to demand that the states pay their requisitions in specie. In addition, he secured a Congressional charter for the Bank of North America and took steps to make federal bonds more attractive to investors.

Though Morris made considerable progress, the government's finances remained shaky. Lacking the power to tax, the Congress continued to depend on the states' willingness to meet their financial obligations. This arrangement, however, proved unworkable. Desperate for resources, the Congress, in October 1781, requested $8 million from the states. Two and a half years later, less than $1.5 million of that amount had come in. In January 1784, Morris resigned, partly in despair over the government's financial situation and partly to recoup his personal fortunes.

By 1786, total federal revenue amounted to no more than $370,000 a year, not a sufficient amount, as one official lamented, to provide for "the bare maintenance of the federal government [even] on the most economical establishment" and at a time of profound peace. "The crisis has arrived," declared a congressional committee, when Americans "must decide whether they will support their rank as a nation, by maintaining the public faith at home and abroad; or whether, for want of ... a general revenue ... they will hazard not only the existence of the Union, but of the great and invaluable privileges for which they have so arduously and so honorably contended."

Not all Americans were alarmed. Some pointed out approvingly that several state governments, having brought their own financial obligations under control, were beginning to assume responsibility for portions of the national debt. Others, however, saw that as additional evidence of the Congress's weakening condition and wondered how a government unable to maintain its credit could long endure.

Surviving in a Hostile Atlantic World

The Congress's difficulties in dealing with its creditors abroad and countering Spain's closure of the Mississippi River at home pointed to a broader problem in American foreign relations. Even after the United States had formally won independence, England, France, and Spain continued to threaten the new republic.

The Revolutionary War had dramatically transformed America's relationships with the outside world. England, once the nurturing "mother country," had become a tyrannical parent bent on enslaving its colonial children. Just as bewildering, France, long the mortal enemy of England and the colonies alike, had proven a vital ally. Yet France was at best an uncertain friend. With an empire of its own, France hardly approved of colonial rebellions. In addition, the French king and aristocracy regarded republicanism as deeply subversive. Finally, France's efforts to manipulate the peace process for its own advantage had provided the Americans with a hard lesson in the realities of power diplomacy.

Independence, moreover, did not end European imperial ambitions in North America. France had lost its North American possessions following the Seven Years' War (see Chapter Five), but before the century was over, it would gain title to most of the continent west of the Mississippi River. England's Union Jack continued to fly over eastern Canada, while English troops retained possession of strategic outposts on American soil—at Detroit, Michilimackinac, and Niagara. And as reaction to the Jay-Gardoqui affair made evident, Spain still conjured up grim memories of past New World conquests.

The reason for America's diplomatic troubles was clear: the country was new, weak, and republican in an Atlantic world dominated by strong, monarchical governments and divided into warring empires.

Nothing revealed more starkly the difficulties of national survival than the Congress's largely futile efforts to rebuild America's overseas commerce. A flourishing overseas trade, across the Atlantic to markets in England and down the coast to the Caribbean, had provided the foundation of colonial economic prosperity. As we have seen, the Revolutionary War brought American commerce virtually to a halt. Once the war was over, American traders eagerly sought to rebuild their overseas trade. It proved a difficult task because the Congress could give them little support.

When the war ended, familiar and highly desired English goods once again flooded American markets. Few American goods, however, flowed the other way. John Adams learned why. In 1785, he arrived in London as the first American minister to England. The Congress had assigned him the task of negotiating a commercial treaty, but he soon discovered how difficult that would be. After endless rebuffs, he wrote home in frustration that England had no intention of opening the empire's ports to American shipping. English officials testily reminded him that Americans had desired independence and must now live with its consequences. They pointed out, moreover, that British goods could command the American market without England's needing to grant trade concessions in return.

Although Americans enjoyed some success in their search for new commercial arrangements during the 1780s, progress was slow. Not only did England remain intractable, but also France and Spain gradually withdrew the trading privileges they had extended during the war and returned to their policy of maritime restrictions.

In an effort to rebuild American commerce, the Congress tried to secure the states' cooperation in a program of economic recovery. Its efforts, however, were unavailing. In 1784, it failed to obtain authorization from the states to regulate foreign commerce because each state wanted to channel its own trade for its own advantage. As a result, the Congress was unable to negotiate satisfactory commercial agreements abroad, and overseas trade continued to languish.

The result was deepening economic hardship. In Philadelphia, only 13 ships were built in 1786, one-third as many as just two years before. By the

RECOVERING THE PAST

Indian Treaties

During the 1780s, the new American government contracted its first treaties with Native Americans of the Trans-Appalachian interior, including the Wyandotte, the Delaware, and the Cherokee. The treaties were necessary to complete the peacemaking process at the end of the Revolutionary War, because most of the interior tribes had sided with England. The treaties were also intended to open Trans-Appalachia to white settlement.

The treaty texts, like the agreement between the Congress and the Cherokee signed at Hopewell in November 1785, presented here, tell us a great deal about the issues that lay at the center of Indian-white relations during the

---

Treaty with the Cherokee, 1785

Articles concluded at Hopewell, on the Keowee, between Benjamin Hawkins, Andrew Pickens, Joseph Martin, and Lachlan M'Intosh, Commissioners Plenipotentiary of the United States of America, of the one Part, and the Head-Men and Warriors of all the Cherokees of the other.

The Commissioners Plenipotentiary of the United States, in Congress assembled, give peace to all the Cherokees, and receive them into the favor and protection of the United States of America, on the following conditions:

Article I

The Head-Men and Warriors of all the Cherokees shall restore all the prisoners, citizens of the United States, or subjects of their allies, to their entire liberty: They shall also restore all the Negroes, and all other property taken during the late war from the citizens, to such person, and at such time and place, as the Commissioners shall appoint.

Article II

The Commissioners of the United States in Congress assembled, shall restore all prisoners taken from the Indians, during the late war, to the Head-Men and Warriors of the Cherokees, as early as is practicable.

Article III

The said Indians for themselves and their respective tribes and towns do acknowledge all the Cherokees to be under the protection of the United States of America, and of no other sovereign whosoever.

Article IV

The boundary allotted to the Cherokees for their hunting grounds, between the said Indians and the citizens of the United States, within the limits of the United States of America, is, and shall be the following [see map]....

Article V

If any citizen of the United States, or other person not being an Indian, shall attempt to settle on any of the lands westward or southward of the said boundary which are hereby allotted to the Indians for their hunting grounds, or having already settled and will not remove from the same within six months after the ratification of this treaty, such person shall forfeit the protection of the United States, and the Indians may punish him or not as they please....

Article VI

If any Indian or Indians, or person residing among them, or who shall take refuge in their nation, shall commit a robbery, or murder, or other capital crime, on any citizen of the United States, or person under their protection, the nation, or the tribe to which such offender or offenders may belong, shall be bound to deliver him or them up to be punished according to the ordinances of the United States; Provided, that the punishment shall not be greater than if the robbery or murder, or other capital crime had been committed by a citizen on a citizen.

Article VII

If any citizen of the United States, or person under their protection, shall commit a robbery or murder, or other capital crime, on any Indian, such offender or offenders shall be punished in the same manner as if the murder or robbery, or other capital crime, had been committed on a citizen of the United States; and the punishment shall be in presence of some of the Cherokees, if any shall attend at the time and place....

1780s. What major issues did the treaty of 1785 attempt to resolve? Why were these issues important to the Congress and the Native Americans?

A careful reading of the treaty language can also tell us much about the attitudes and values that white negotiators brought to the treaty-making process and provide hints of how that process functioned. Which phrases in the treaty reveal how the Congress's negotiators viewed their Cherokee counterparts? From the evidence of the treaty text, how would you characterize the treaty negotiations?

Most of the treaties arranged during the 1780s failed to last, and by the end of the decade Trans-Appalachia, both north and south of the Ohio River, was embroiled in Indian-white warfare. Why did these agreements prove so fragile?

Article VIII

It is understood that the punishment of the innocent under the idea of retaliation, is unjust, and shall not be practiced on either side, except where there is a manifest violation of this treaty; and then it shall be preceded first by a demand of justice, and if refused, then by a declaration of hostilities.

Article IX

For the benefit and comfort of the Indians, and for the prevention of injuries or oppressions on the part of the citizens or Indians, the United States in Congress assembled shall have the sole and exclusive right of regulating the trade with the Indians, and managing all their affairs in such manner as they think proper....

Article XI

The said Indians shall give notice to the citizens of the United States, of any designs which they may know or suspect to be formed in any neighboring tribe, or by any person whosoever, against the peace, trade or interest of the United States.

Article XII

That the Indians may have full confidence in the justice of the United States, respecting their interests, they shall have the right to send a deputy of their choice, whenever they think fit, to Congress.

Article XIII

The hatchet shall be forever buried, and the peace given by the United States, and friendship re-established between the said states on the one part, and all the Cherokees on the other, shall be universal; and the contracting parties shall use their utmost endeavors to maintain the peace given as aforesaid, and friendship re-established.

In witness of all and every thing herein determined, between the United States of America and all the Cherokees, we, their underwritten Commissioners, by virtue of our full powers, have signed this definitive treaty, and have caused our seals to be hereunto affixed.

Done at Hopewell, on the Keowee, this twenty-eighth of November, in the year of our Lord one thousand seven hundred and eighty-five.

Benjamin Hawkins,
And'w Pickens,
Jos. Martin,
Lach'n McIntosh,
Koatohee, or Corn Tassel of Toquo, his x mark,
Scholauetta, or Hanging Man of Chota, his x mark,
Tuskegatahu, or Long Fellow of Chistohoe, his x mark,
Ooskwha, or Abraham of Chilkowa, his x mark,
Kolakusta, or Prince of Noth, his x mark,
Newota, or the Gritzs of Chicamaga, his x mark,
Konatota, or the Rising Fawn of Highwassay, his x mark,
Tuckasee, or Young Terrapin of Allajoy, his x mark,
Toostaka, or the Waker of Oostanawa, his x mark,
Untoola, or Gun Rod of Seteco, his x mark,
Unsuokanail, Buffalo White Calf New Cussee, his x mark,
Kostayeak, or Sharp Fellow Wataga, his x mark,
Chonosta, of Cowe, his x mark,
Chescoonwho, Bird in Close of Tomotlug, his x mark,
Tuckasee, or Terrapin of Hightowa, his x mark,
Chesetoa, or the Rabbit of Tlacoa, his x mark....
Witness:
Wm. Blount,
Sam'l Taylor, Major.,
John Owen,
Jess. Walton,
Jno. Cowan, capt. comm'd't,
Thos. Gregg,4
W. Hazzard,
James Madison,
Arthur Cooley, Sworn interpreters.

Source: Charles Kapple, ed., *Indian Affairs: Laws and Treaties* (Washington, D.C.: U.S. Government Printing Office, 1904–1941), vol. 2, pp. 8–11.

This painting by Thomas Rossiter, done in the early nineteenth century, provides an imaginative portrayal of the Philadelphia convention, with George Washington presiding and a rising sun, symbolic of the new nation, shining behind him. (Independence National Historic Park Collection, Eastern National Parks and Monuments Association)

of democratic principles. Certainly, they believed more firmly than their Federalist opponents that if government was to be safe, it must be tied closely to the people.

Federalist spokesmen moved quickly to counter the Anti-Federalists' attack, for many of those criticisms carried the sanction of the revolutionary past. Their most important effort was a series of essays penned by James Madison, Alexander Hamilton, and John Jay and published in New York under the pseudonym Publius. *The Federalist Papers,* as they were called, were written to promote ratification in New York but were quickly reprinted by Federalists elsewhere.

Madison, Hamilton, and Jay moved systematically through the proposed Constitution, explaining its virtues and responding to the Anti-Federalists' attacks. In the process, they described a political vision fundamentally different from that of their Anti-Federalist opponents.

No difference was more dramatic than the Federalists' discussion of governmental power. Power, the Federalists now argued, was not the enemy of liberty, but its guarantor. Where government was not sufficiently "energetic" and "efficient" (these were favorite Federalist words), demagogues and disorganizers were able to do their nefarious work. It is far better, Hamilton wrote in *Federalist No. 26,* "to hazard the abuse of ... confidence than to embarrass the government and endanger the public safety by impolitic restrictions of ... authority."

The authors of the *Federalist Papers* also countered the Anti-Federalists' warning that a single, extended republic encompassing the country's economic and social diversity would lead inevitably to factional conflict and the end of republican liberty. Turning the Anti-Federalists' classic republican argument on its head, they explained that factional divisions were the inevitable accompaniment of human liberty. Wrote Madison in *Federalist No. 10:* "Liberty is to faction what air is to fire, an aliment without which it instantly expires." To suppress faction would require the destruction of liberty itself.

Earlier emphasis on public virtue as the guarantor of political order, the Federalists explained, had been naive, for most people would not consistently place the public good ahead of their own interests. Politics had to heed this harsh fact and provide for peaceful compromise among conflicting groups. That could be best accomplished by expanding the nation so that it included innumerable factions. Out of the clash and accommodation of multiple social and economic interests would emerge public order and the best possible approximation of the public good.

The Federalists' argument established the basic rationale for modern democratic politics, but it left the Anti's sputtering in frustration. Where in the Federalists' scheme was there a place for that familiar abstraction, the public good? What would become of public virtue in a system built on the notion of competing interests? In such a free market of competition, the

The eagle became an important symbol of the new nation appearing on water pitchers, whiskey bottles, flags, newspaper mastheads, and fabrics of all kinds. The flag also became an icon, although it had to be adapted frequently as new states entered the Union. (Quilt, National Gallery of Art, Index of American Design, Washington, D.C., Pine Chest, formerly in the Collection of The Henry Ford Museum and Greenfield Village)

Anti-Federalists warned, the wealthy and powerful would benefit, while ordinary folk would suffer.

As the ratification debate revealed, the Federalists and Anti-Federalists held sharply contrasting visions of the new republic. The Anti's remained much closer to the original republicanism of 1776, with its suspicion of power and wealth, its emphasis on the primacy of local government, and its fears of national development. They envisioned a decentralized republic filled with self-reliant citizens, limited in personal ambition and guided by public virtue, whose destiny was determined primarily by what happened in the states rather than the nation. Anxious about what the future might bring, they wanted to preserve their world much as it had been.

The Federalists, on the other hand, persuaded that America's situation had changed dramatically since 1776, eagerly embraced the idea of nationhood and looked forward with anticipation to the development of a rising "republican empire" based on commercial development and led by men of wealth and talent. Both Federalists and Anti-Federalists claimed to be heirs of the Revolution, yet they differed dramatically in their understanding of what that heritage entailed.

The Struggle over Ratification

No one knows with certainty what most Americans thought of the proposed Constitution, for no national plebiscite on it was ever taken. Probably no more than several hundred thousand people participated in the elections for the state ratifying conventions, and many of the delegates carried no binding instructions from their constituents on how they should vote. A majority of the people probably opposed the document, either out of indifference or alarm. Fortunately for the Federalists, they did not have to persuade most Americans; they needed only to gain majorities in nine of the state ratifying conventions, a much less formidable task.

They set about it with determination. As soon as the Philadelphia Convention adjourned, its members hurried home to organize the ratification movement in their states. In Delaware and Georgia, New Jersey and Connecticut, where the Federalists were confident of their strength, they pressed quickly for a vote. Where the outcome was uncertain, as in New York and Virginia, they delayed, hoping that word of ratification elsewhere would work to their benefit.

It took less than a year from the time the document left Congress to secure approval of the necessary nine states. Delaware, Pennsylvania, and New Jersey ratified first, in December 1787. Approval came a month later in Georgia and Connecticut. Massachusetts ratified in February 1788, but only after considerable political maneuvering. In an effort to woo Anti-Federalist delegates and persuade the uncommitted, Federalist leaders agreed to forward a set of amendments outlining a federal "bill of rights" along with notice of ratification. The strategy worked, for it brought Samuel Adams and John Hancock into line, and with them the crucial convention votes that they controlled.

Maryland and South Carolina were the seventh and eighth states to approve. That left New Hampshire and Virginia as the most likely candidates for the honor of being ninth and putting the Constitution over the top. There was determined opposition in both states. The New Hampshire convention met on February 13. Sensing that they lacked the necessary votes, the Federalists adjourned the convention until mid-June and worked feverishly to build support. When the convention reconvened, it took but three days to secure a Federalist majority. New Hampshire ratified on June 21.

Two massive gaps in the new Union remained—Virginia and New York. Clearly, the nation could not endure without them. In Virginia, Madison gathered support by promising that the new Congress would immediately consider a federal bill of rights. Other Federalists spread the rumor that Patrick Henry, most influential of the Anti-Federalist leaders, had changed sides. Henry angrily denied the charge, but his eloquence proved no match for the careful politicking of Madison and the others. On June 25, the Virginia convention voted to ratify by the narrow margin of ten votes.

The New York convention gathered on June 17 at Poughkeepsie, with the Anti-Federalist followers of Governor Clinton firmly in command. Hamilton worked for delay, hoping that news of the results in New Hampshire and Virginia would turn the tide. For several weeks, approval hung in the balance while the two sides maneuvered for support. On July 27, approval squeaked through, 30 to 27. That left two states still uncommitted. North Carolina (with Timothy Bloodworth's skeptical approval) finally

Ratification of the Constitution			
Votes of State Ratifying Conventions			
State	Date	For	Against
Delaware	December 1787	30	0
Pennsylvania	December 1787	46	23
New Jersey	December 1787	38	0
Georgia	January 1788	26	0
Connecticut	January 1788	128	40
Massachusetts	February 1788	187	168
Maryland	April 1788	63	11
South Carolina	May 1788	149	73
New Hampshire	June 1788	57	47
Virginia	June 1788	89	79
New York	July 1788	30	27
North Carolina	November 1789	194	77
Rhode Island	May 1790	34	32

ratified in November 1789. Rhode Island did not enter the Union until May 1790, more than a year after the new government had gotten under way.

The Social Geography of Ratification

A glance at the geographic pattern of Federalist and Anti-Federalist strength reveals their different sources of political support. Federalist strength was concentrated in areas along the coast and navigable rivers and was strongest in cities and towns.

Merchants and businessmen supported the Constitution most ardently. Enthusiasm also ran high among urban laborers, artisans, and shopkeepers—a surprising fact, given the Anti-Federalists' criticism of wealth and power and their emphasis on democratic political equality. City artisans and workers, after all, had been in the vanguard of political reform during the Revolution. But in the troubled circumstances of the late 1780s, they worried primarily about their livelihoods and believed that a stronger government could better promote overseas trade and protect American artisans from foreign competition.

On July 4, 1788, a grand procession celebrating the Constitution's ratification wound through the

Federalist and Anti-Federalist Areas, 1787–1790

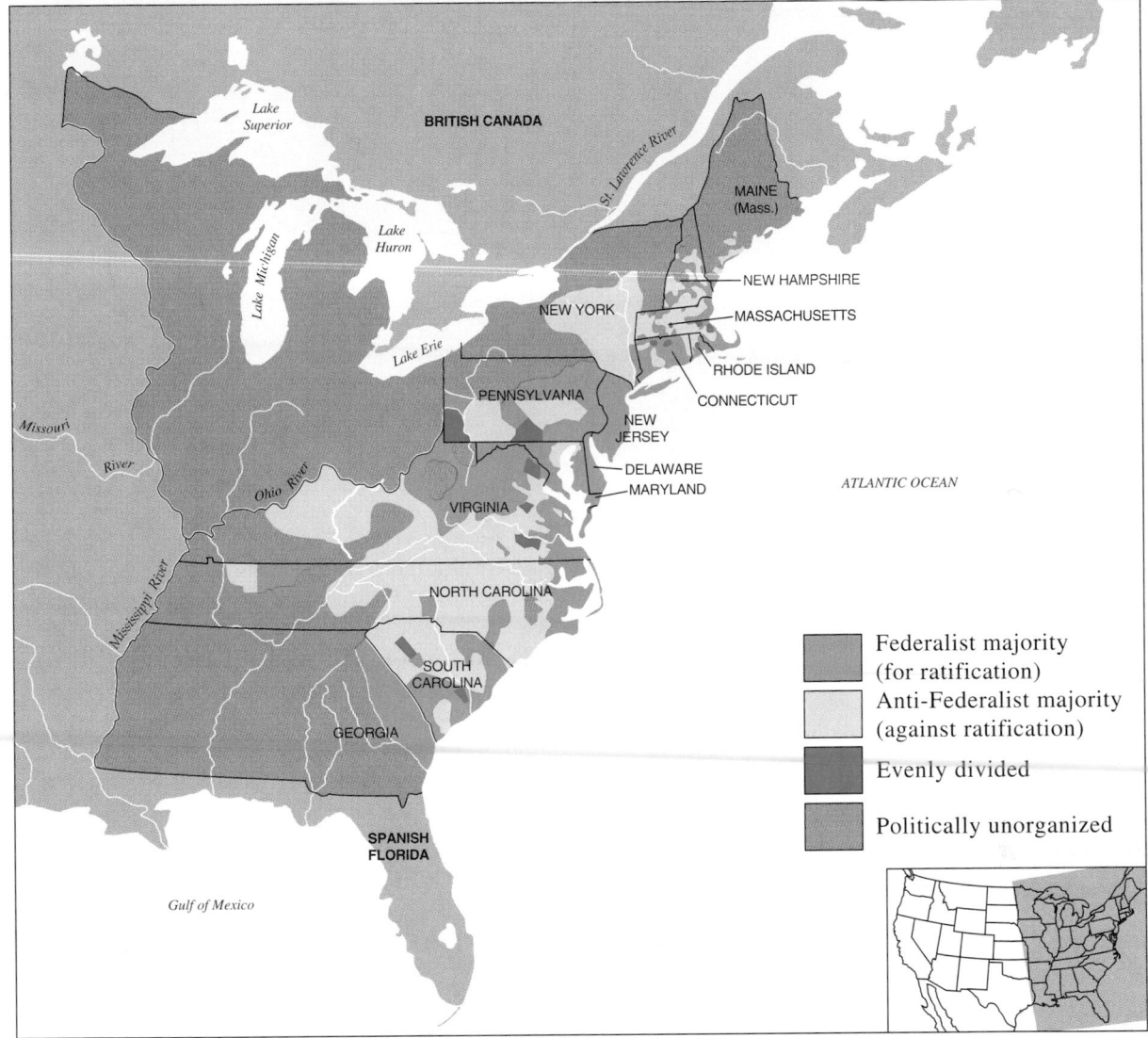

Distinct geographic patterns of Federalist and Anti-Federalist strength developed during the ratification debate. This map shows areas whose delegates to the state ratifying conventions voted for and against the Constitution.

streets of Philadelphia. Seventeen thousand strong, it graphically demonstrated working-class support for the Constitution. At the head of the line marched lawyers, merchants, and others of the city's elite, but close behind came representatives of virtually every trade in the city, from ship's carpenters to shoemakers, each with its own floats, flags, and mottoed banners. "May commerce flourish and industry be rewarded," declared the mariners and shipbuilders. "May the federal government revive our trade," exclaimed the bakers. "Home-brewed is best," insisted the maltsters.

For the moment, declared Benjamin Rush in amazement, "rank ... forgot all its claims. Hand in

The federal ship Hamilton *formed the centerpiece of a grand procession in New York City celebrating the successful ratification of the new Constitution.*

TIMELINE

1784 Treaty of Fort Stanwix with the Iroquois

Spain closes the Mississippi River to American navigation

1785 Treaty of Hopewell with the Cherokee

Land Ordinance for the Northwest Territory

Jay-Gardoqui negotiations

1786 Virginia adopts "Bill for Establishing Religious Freedom"

Annapolis Convention calls for revision of the Articles of Confederation

1786–1787 Shays's Rebellion

1787 Northwest Ordinance

Constitutional Convention

Federalist Papers published by Hamilton, Jay, and Madison

1788 Constitution ratified

hand marched merchants and sea-men, lawyers and artisans." Within a few years, political disputes would divide them once again. For the time being, however, people of all ranks joined in celebrating the new Constitution.

Though the Constitution also found support among commercial farmers and southern planters eager for profit and anxious about overseas markets, Federalist enthusiasm waned and Anti-Federalist sentiment increased in the interior. The centers of Anti-Federalism lay away from the coast in central New England, upstate New York, the Virginia Piedmont and southside, and in the western regions of the Carolinas. Among ordinary farmers living outside the market economy and immersed in the limited activities of their own localities, the republicanism of 1776 outweighed their interests in national affairs. The Federalists' vision of a strengthening "American empire" they found strange and alarming.

Why were the Federalists finally successful? The Anti-Federalists had only to arouse people's deep-seated fears of central government, and play on their local loyalties. The Federalists, by contrast, had to explain how republicanism had suddenly become compatible with a powerful national government and an expanding empire. Moreover, they faced the complicated task of coordinating ratification in the various states.

Their task was simplified by the widespread perception that the Articles needed strengthening. In light of the obvious troubles of the Confederation, the Federalists could argue that America's experiment in republican independence was doomed to failure unless dramatic action was taken. More than anything, however, the Federalists succeeded because of their determination and political skill. Most of the Revolution's major leaders were Federalists. Time and again these heroes spoke out for the Constitution, and time and again their support proved decisive. Their experience as army officers and as members of the Continental and Confederation Congresses caused them to identify with the nation and imagine what it might become. They brought their vision to the ratification process and asked others to share it. Altogether, it was an impressive political performance. With their success, the Federalists turned the American republic in a new and fateful direction.

Conclusion

Completing the Revolution

Only five years had passed between England's acknowledgment of American independence in 1783 and ratification of the new national Constitution, yet to many Americans it seemed far longer. At war's end, the difficulties of sustaining American liberty were evident. The experience of the next half decade added to them. Whether struggling to survive in a hostile Atlantic environment or trying to cope with economic distress and political turmoil at home, Americans continued to argue about their experiment in republicanism, above all about how democratic it could safely be, and to wonder whether it would actually work at all.

At the same time, the American people retained an immense reservoir of optimism about the future. Had they not defeated mighty England? Was not their revolution destined to change the course of history and preserve liberty for all mankind? Did not America's wonderfully rich interior contain a limitless promise of economic and social opportunity for all? Most Americans, still filled with the enthusiasm of their new beginning, answered with a resounding "Yes." Much would depend, of course, on their new Constitution and the government soon to be created under it. As the ratification debate subsided and Congress prepared for the transition, the American people looked eagerly and anxiously ahead.

Recommended Reading

The Articles of Confederation and the 1780s

Merrill Jensen, *The New Nation: A History of the United States During the Confederation, 1781–1789* (1950); H. James Henderson, *Party Politics in the Continental Congress* (1974); Jack Rakove, *The Beginnings of National Politics: An Interpretive History of the Continental Congress* (1979); Peter Onuf, *The Origins of the Federal Republic: Jurisdictional Controversies in the United States, 1775–1787* (1983); Jackson T. Main, *Political Parties Before the Constitution* (1973); Ronald Hoffman and Peter Albert, eds., *Sovereign States in an Age of Uncertainty* (1978); Peter Onuf, *Statehood and Union: A History of the Northwest Ordinance* (1987); David Szatmary, *Shays's Rebellion: The Making of an Agrarian Rebellion* (1980); Eric Foner, *Tom Paine and Revolutionary America* (1976); Patricia Watlington, *The Partisan Spirit: Kentucky Politics, 1779–1792* (1972).

The Constitution

Gordon Wood, *The Creation of the American Republic, 1776–1787* (1969); Richard Morris, *Witnesses at the Creation: Hamilton, Madison, Jay and the Constitution* (1985); Gary Wills, *Explaining America: The Federalist* (1981); Frederick W. Marks, III, *Independence on Trial: Foreign Affairs and the Making of the Constitution* (1973); Richard Beeman et al., eds., *Beyond Confederation: Origins of the Constitution and American National Identity* (1987); Jackson Main, *The Antifederalists: Critics of the Constitution, 1781–1788* (1961); Steven Boyd, *The Politics of Opposition: Antifederalists and the Acceptance of the Constitution* (1979); Robert Rutland, *The Ordeal of the Constitution: The Antifederalists and the Ratification Struggle of 1787–88* (1966); Patrick Conley and John Kaminski, eds., *The Constitution and the States* (1988); Forrest McDonald, *Novus Ordo Seclorum: The Intellectual Origins of the Constitution* (1985).

Creating a Nation

n October 1789, David Brown arrived in Dedham, Massachusetts. Born about 50 years before in Bethlehem, Connecticut, Brown served in the Revolutionary army. After the war was over, he shipped out on an American merchantman to see the world. His travels, as he later reported, took him to "nineteen different … Kingdoms in Europe, and nearly all the United States." For two years before settling in Dedham, he visited scores of Massachusetts towns, supporting himself as a day laborer while discussing the troubled state of public affairs with local townspeople.

Initially, the people of Dedham took little notice of Brown, but he soon made his presence felt. Though he had little formal schooling, he was a man of powerful opinions and considerable natural ability. His reading and personal experience had persuaded him that government was a conspiracy of the rich to exploit farmers, artisans, and other common folk, and he was quick to make his opinions known.

"The occupation of government," Brown declared bluntly in one of his numerous pamphlets, "is to plunder and steal." The object of his wrath was the central government recently established under the new national constitution. Though he could cite no evidence, he accused the leaders of government with engrossing the nation's western lands for themselves. "Five hundred [people] out of the union of five millions receive all the benefit of public property and live upon the ruins of the rest of the community." Brown warned that such policies would not last long, because no government could survive "after the confidence of the people was lost, for the people are the government."

In the highly charged political climate of the 1790s, Brown's radical language and exaggerated attacks on the new government's leaders brought a sharp response. In 1798, John Davis, the federal district attorney in Boston, issued a warrant for Brown's arrest on charges of sedition, while government-supported newspapers attacked him as a "rallying point of insurrection and disorder." Fearing arrest, Brown fled to Salem on the Massachusetts coast, but there he was caught and charged with intent to defame the government and aid the country's enemies. For want of $400 bail, he was clapped in prison.

In June 1799, Brown came before the U.S. Circuit Court, Justice Samuel Chase presiding. Chase was anything but judicious in his behavior. Persuaded that critics of the administration were also enemies of the republic, Chase was determined to make Brown an example of what the government's opponents could expect. Brown, confused and hoping for leniency, pleaded guilty. That made no difference to Chase, however.

Ignoring Brown's plea, he directed the federal prosecutor to "examine the witness . . . that the degree of his guilt might be duly ascertained." Before sentencing him, Chase demanded that Brown provide the names of his accomplices and a list of subscribers to his writings. When Brown refused, protesting that he would "lose all my friends," Chase sentenced him to a fine of $480 and 18 months in jail, no matter that Brown could not pay the fine and faced the prospect of indefinite imprisonment.

In rendering judgment, Chase castigated Brown for his "disorganizing doctrines and . . . falsehoods, and the very alarming and dangerous excesses to which he attempted to incite the uninformed part of the community." Not all citizens, Chase thought, should be allowed to comment so brashly on public affairs. For nearly two years, Brown languished in prison. Not until the Federalist party was defeated in the election of 1800 and the Jeffersonian Republicans had taken office was he freed.

Prior to 1799, when it moved to the new, permanent capital in the District of Columbia, the national government shared the State House in Philadelphia with the Pennsylvania assembly. This image of the state house yard suggests the government's smallness and informality during its earliest years. (William Birch, *The State House*, Philadelphia, 1800, Historical Society of Pennsylvania) avid Brown discovered how easy it was for critics of the government to get into trouble during the 1790s, a decade of extraordinary political controversy. Even though the Revolutionary War was long past, the debate over revolutionary principles and the struggle to define America's republican political order continued. As Benjamin Rush, Philadelphia physician and revolutionary patriot, explained: "The American War is over, but this is far from being the case with the American Revolution. On the contrary, nothing but the first act of the great drama is closed. It remains [for us] . . . to establish and perfect our new forms of government."

Efforts to perfect America's new governments proceeded differently in state and nation, for they differed markedly in leadership, public agenda, and the politics that surrounded them. In the states, government and its attendant politics remained close to the people. There the fires of political controversy, fanned to a white heat during the Revolution over economic issues, slavery, and the separation of church and state, continued to burn. Controversy swirled as well between the advocates of political democracy and defenders of a more conservative form of republican politics.

The new ingredient in American political life during the 1790s was the national government established under the new, federal Constitution. There had been no popular elections under the old Articles of Confederation, because members of the Confederation Congress had been appointed by the state legislatures. As we have seen, the Federalists had been careful at Philadelphia to buffer the new, national government against the passions of democracy so that it would support a continuing system of conservative, gentry-led politics. During the 1790s, such a system, setting Federalist supporters of President Washington's administration against Jeffersonian opponents, began to form in the new Congress.

Events, however, soon began to force together this politics of national elites and the rapidly evolving democratic politics in the states. As the 1790s progressed, controversy was fanned by Federalist economic policies, the French Revolution and the outbreak of European war, the internal security legislation imposed during John Adams's administration, and the election of 1800, which brought the Federalists' defeat and Thomas Jefferson's election to the presidency.

As political controversy increased, it caught up countless people like David Brown in its toils. By decade's end, it had become apparent how fragile, and at the same time how resilient America's new constitutional order could be.

Launching the National Republic

Once ratification of the Constitution was achieved, many Anti-Federalists seemed ready to give the new experiment a chance. They determined, however, to watch it closely for the first signs of danger. It was not many months before they sounded the alarm.

Beginning the New Government

On April 16, 1789, George Washington started north from Virginia toward New York City to be inaugurated as the first president of the United States. The Electoral College convened under the Constitution had unanimously elected him to the nation's highest office. Washington's feelings were mixed as he set forth. "I bade adieu to Mount Vernon, to private life, and to domestic felicity," he confided to his diary, "and with a mind oppressed with more anxious and painful sensations than I have words to express, set out for New York . . . with the best disposition to render service to my country in obedience to its call, but with less hope of answering its expectations." Events would soon show that he had good reason for such foreboding.

Washington's journey through the countryside resembled a royal procession, for he was the object of constant adulation along the way. In villages and towns, guns boomed their salutes, children danced in the streets, church bells pealed, and dignitaries toasted his arrival. On April 23, the president-elect and his entourage reached the New Jersey shore, where awaited an elegant barge, festooned with flowers and attended by 11 ship's captains. People crowded the shore as Washington climbed aboard and, accompanied by a flotilla of boats, was rowed across the harbor to New York City. There, throngs of citizens and newly elected members of Congress greeted the weary traveler. Over the streets of the city stretched gaily decorated arches. During the parade uptown to the governor's mansion, young women in white flowing robes preceded him, strewing flowers in his path. That night, bonfires illuminated the city.

Already the transition from the old Confederation Congress to the new government was under way. On October 2, the Congress had moved from its home in New York's City Hall so it could be redecorated for the new government. On October 10, the old Congress transacted its last official business and adjourned *sine die* after setting March 4, 1789, as the day for the new Congress to assemble.

Inaugural day was April 30. Shortly after noon, on a small balcony overlooking a Wall Street thronged with people, Washington took the oath of office. "It is done," exulted New York's chancellor, Robert Livingston. "Long live George Washington, President of the United States!" With the crowd roaring its approval and 13 guns booming in the harbor, the president bowed his way off the balcony and into Federal Hall. The rest of the day and late into the night, celebrations filled the air.

Though hopefulness and excitement surrounded the new government's beginning, those first weeks were not easy, for it was especially important that things begin on a proper footing. "Many things which appear of little importance in themselves and at the beginning," the president warned, "may have great and durable consequences from their having been established at the commencement of a new general government."

When Washington decided to address the first Congress, republican purists complained that it smacked too much of the English monarch's speech from the throne at the opening of Parliament. His appearance, moreover, confronted Congress with the question of how it should reply and thus opened the sensitive issue of whether titles should be used in a republican government. Some congressmen pointed out that state governors and foreign ambassadors carried the title of "Excellency" and argued that the American president should be more exalted than that. Vice President Adams proposed "His Most Benign Highness," while others offered the even gaudier suggestion: "His Highness, the President of the United States, and Protector of the Rights of the Same." Both proposals generated howls of outrage from those who thought titles had no place in a republic.

This imaginative scene of President-elect Washington's reception in Trenton, New Jersey, during his trip from Virginia to New York City for his first inauguration depicts the popular adulation that surrounded him, as well as the sharply different political roles of men and women. (Library of Congress)

President Washington took the oath of office on the balcony of the recently refurbished Federal Hall in New York City. Its cornice was emblazoned with the arms of the United States and its windows were topped with plaster friezes containing 13 arrows and an olive branch bound together. (Museum of the City of New York)

In the end, good sense prevailed, and Congress settled on the simple and now familiar "Mr. President," but not before the House and Senate had spent days debating the matter. During these early years, every decision seemed filled with significance, for people believed they were setting the direction of the new government for years to come. That belief gave special intensity to the politics of the time.

The Bill of Rights

Among the new government's first items of business was consideration of the constitutional amendments that several states had made conditions of their ratification. Though Madison, Hamilton, and others among the Federalists had argued that a national bill of rights was unnecessary, they were ready to keep their promise that such amend-

ments would be considered because it would reassure the fearful, weaken calls for a second constitutional convention, and build support for the new regime. "We have in this way something to gain," Madison observed, "and if we proceed with caution, nothing to lose."

After reviewing a variety of proposals offered by the states, Madison developed a set of specific propositions to place before Congress. After considerable debate, Congress reached agreement in September 1789 on 12 amendments and sent them on to the states for approval. By December 1791, 10 had been ratified. Those 10 became the national Bill of Rights. Among other things, they guaranteed freedom of speech, press, and religion; pledged the right of trial by jury and due process of law; forbade "unreasonable searches and seizures"; and protected individuals against self-incrimination in criminal cases. The Bill of Rights was the most important achievement of these early years, for it has protected individuals' basic, democratic rights throughout the nation's history.

The People Divide

During its first months in office, Washington's administration enjoyed almost universal support, both in Congress and among the people. The honeymoon did not last long, however, for within a year, criticism of the administration's policies began to mount. By the middle of the decade, opposition groups had come together in a political coalition known as the Jeffersonian Republicans. As they did, the administration's remaining supporters rallied under the name of Federalists.

Disagreement began at the seat of government in January 1790, when Secretary of the Treasury Alexander Hamilton submitted to Congress the first of several major policy statements, the "Report on the Public Credit." Seldom in the nation's history has a single official so dominated public affairs as Hamilton did during these first years. A man of extraordinary intelligence and ambition, Hamilton preferred to act behind the scenes, where he could shape events beyond the public eye. His instincts for locating and seizing the levers of political power were unerring.

Hamilton was an ardent proponent of America's economic development. Perhaps more clearly than anyone else among the nation's founders, he

Alexander Hamilton used both the office of secretary of the treasury and his personal relationship with President Washington to shape national policy during the early 1790s. (White House Collection)

foresaw the country's future strength and was determined to promote its growth. The United States, he was fond of saying, was a "Hercules in the cradle." Domestic manufacturing and overseas commerce were the ways to promote American development and build national strength. Competitive self-interest, whether of nations or of individuals, he thought the surest guide to behavior.

The proper role of the new government, Hamilton argued, was to promote economic enterprise. The people he most admired were men of wealth, ambitious entrepreneurs eager to tie their fortunes to America's rising empire. A close alliance between such people and government officials he regarded as essential to achieving American greatness.

If Hamilton's economic policies were liberal in looking forward to enhanced economic opportunity, his politics were profoundly conservative. He continued to be deeply impressed by the stability of the British monarchy and the confident governing style of the British upper class. At bottom, Hamilton distrusted the people, doubted their wisdom, and feared their purposes. "The people," he asserted, "are turbulent and changing; they

seldom judge or determine right." That stark belief guided his public career.

The Constitution that had emerged from the Philadelphia convention, Hamilton had thought not "high-toned" enough. But once it was ratified, he set out to give it proper direction. His opportunity came when Washington named him secretary of the treasury. Recognizing the potential importance of his office, he determined to use it to build the kind of nation he envisioned.

In his first "Report on the Public Credit," Hamilton recommended funding the remaining Revolutionary War debt by enabling the government's creditors to exchange their badly depreciated securities at face value for new interest-bearing government bonds. The foreign debt, held chiefly in France and the Netherlands, Hamilton set at $11.7 million. The domestic debt, including back interest, he fixed at $40.4 million. Second, he proposed that the federal government assume responsibility for the $21.5 million in remaining state war debts. By these actions, he hoped to stabilize the government's finances, establish its credit, build confidence in the new nation at home and abroad, and tie business and commercial interests firmly to the new administration.

The proposal to fund the foreign debt aroused little controversy, but Hamilton's plans for handling the government's domestic obligations generated immediate opposition. In the House of Representatives, James Madison, Hamilton's recent ally in the ratification process, protested the unfairness of funding depreciated securities at their face value, especially because speculators, anticipating Hamilton's proposals, had acquired most of them at a fraction of their initial worth. In addition, Madison and many of his southern colleagues knew that northern businessmen held most of the securities and that funding would bring little benefit to the South.

Hamilton was not impressed. The speculators, he observed, "paid what the commodity was worth in the market, and took the risks." They should therefore "reap the benefit." If his plan served the interests of the wealthy, that was exactly as he intended, for it would further strengthen the ties between wealth and national power. After a bit of grumbling, Congress endorsed the funding plan.

Federal assumption of the remaining state debts, another important part of Hamilton's program, aroused even greater criticism. States with

Patriotic Paintings

The questions that historians ask are limited only by their imagination and the historical evidence left behind for them to study. We have seen how historians use different kinds of written evidence, such as household inventories, and Indian treaties, as well as material artifacts like tombstones and house designs. They also study visual evidence such as paintings and sculpture, for these, too, can provide insight into the life and culture of the past. With the proper mixture of care and ingenuity, historians can tease surprising amounts of information out of materials that at first glance seem silent and unrewarding.

Paintings offer unique insights into the past. They can tell us about the development over time of artistic styles and techniques. They also offer a window into the past for social and cultural historians, for they reveal how people lived and looked and did their work, as well as what the landscape and home furnishings were like.

During the revolutionary era and the early national period, American artists employed painting and other visual arts to record the great events of the nation's founding. John Trumbull, for example, secured a commission from Congress in the early nineteenth century to prepare a series of historical canvasses. Grand in conception and scale, the four paintings that he completed—depicting the signing of the Declaration of Independence, the surrender of General Burgoyne at Saratoga and Lord Cornwallis at Yorktown, and Washington resigning his commission at the end of the war in 1783—now hang in the rotunda of the nation's Capitol in Washington, D.C. Explained Trumbull in a letter to Thomas Jefferson: "The greatest motive I [have] had ... for engaging in my pursuit of painting, has been the wish of commemorating the great events of our country's revolution."

The Founders were also popular subjects of the painter's brush. As a member of the Pennsylvania militia,

Charles Willson Peale carried paint kits and canvas along with his musket as he followed George Washington during the war. Before it was over, he had completed four portraits of the general.

Although Washington left the presidency in 1797 amid a storm of controversy, his death in 1799 generated a surge of public mourning. During the first year following his death, countless sermons and eulogies celebrated him as the "Father of his Country," a man "first in war, first in peace, and first in the hearts of his countrymen." Everywhere people organized memorial processions and decked themselves out in black crepe, gold mourning rings, and funeral medals. In New York, an enterprising bookseller named Mason Weems quickly published a best-selling biography of the great hero. Complete with invented accounts of the cherry tree episode and the story of Washington throwing a stone across the Rappahannock River, Weems's book went through 80 profitable editions over the next 100 years.

The Apotheosis of Washington, painted by an anonymous artist after an 1802 engraving by John Barralet and reproduced here, shows how Washington was mythologized during the years immediately following his death. Examine the painting carefully, for it is filled with a fascinating mixture of patriotic, religious, and cultural symbolism. Why is Washington depicted with his arms extended? Who is the woman standing at the left of the picture, and why are the children included? The bottom quarter of the picture is crowded with objects and human forms, each of them carefully chosen for what it might contribute to the painting's overall effect. Identify them and explain why they are there. Finally, why did the veneration of Washington in word and image take place?

Anonymous Chinese artisit, The Apotheosis of Washington, *after J. Barralet, 1802. (Peabody Essex Museum, Salem, MA, photo by Mark Sexton)*

251

the largest remaining unpaid obligations, such as Massachusetts, thought assumption a splendid idea. But others, such as Virginia and Pennsylvania, which had already retired much of their debt, were opposed. Critics also pointed out that assumption would strengthen the central government at the expense of the states, for wealthy individuals would now look to it rather than the states for a return on their investments. Moreover, with its increased need for revenue to pay off the accumulated debt, the federal government would have additional reason to exercise its newly acquired power of taxation. That was exactly what Hamilton intended.

Once again, Congress supported Hamilton's bill, in good measure because Madison and Jefferson approved it as part of an agreement to move the seat of government temporarily from New York to Philadelphia and then permanently to a special federal district on the Potomac River. Southerners hoped that locating the government away from northern commercial centers would enable them to control its development and keep it more closely aligned with southern, agrarian interests.

Opposition to the funding and assumption scheme, however, did not die. In December 1790, the Virginia assembly passed a series of resolutions, framed by that old republican Patrick Henry, warning that a monied aristocracy was taking control of the government, that southern agriculture was being subordinated to the interests of north-

ern commerce, and that the government's powers were expanding dangerously. Nothing in the Constitution, the assembly protested, authorized Congress to assume the states' debts. On hearing of the Virginia resolutions, Hamilton wrote privately to a friend that "This is the first symptom of a spirit which must either be killed, or will kill the Constitution." The contest for control of the new government was now vigorously joined.

As controversy grew, Hamilton introduced the second phase of his financial program in December 1790 by proposing a national bank capable of handling the government's financial affairs and pooling private investment capital for economic development. Though he was careful not to mention it publicly, he had the Bank of England and its ties with the royal government clearly in mind.

Congressional opposition to the bank came almost entirely from the South. Only one northern delegate voted against it. It seemed obvious that the bank would serve the needs of northern merchants and manufacturers far better than of southern agrarians. Still, in February 1791, Congress approved the bank bill.

Before signing it, Washington asked his cabinet for advice. Following the constitutional doctrine of "implied powers" (the principle that the government possessed the authority to make any laws "necessary and proper" for exercising the powers specifically granted to it), Hamilton argued that Congress could charter such a bank under its

While political conflict swirled around the new, national government, far in the interior towns such as Detroit were growing as service centers for the expanding white population. (Burton Historical Collection, Detroit Public Library)

power to collect taxes and regulate trade. Secretary of State Jefferson, however, disagreed and urged a presidential veto. He saw in Hamilton's argument a blueprint for the indefinite expansion of federal authority and urged instead that the government should be allowed only those powers specifically itemized in the Constitution. Because the Constitution said nothing at all about chartering banks, the bill was unconstitutional and should be rejected. Jefferson also opposed the bank because he feared the rapid development of commerce and domestic manufacturing that the bank was intended to promote. To Jefferson's distress, Washington followed Hamilton's advice and signed the bank bill into law.

In December 1790, in his second "Report on the Public Credit," Hamilton broached the issue of federal taxation by proposing a series of excise taxes, including one on the manufacture of distilled liquor. By this so-called Whiskey Tax, he intended to signal the government's intention to use its new taxing authority to increase federal revenue. The power to tax and spend, Hamilton knew, was the power to govern. The Whiskey Tax became law in March 1791.

The revolutionary generation found inspiration in the republican eras of ancient Greece and Rome. This bust of Thomas Jefferson, cast in the classical style, was completed in 1789 by the French sculptor Jean-Antoine Houdon. (Collection of The New-York Historical Society)

Finally, in his "Report on Manufactures," issued in December 1791, Hamilton called for a system of protective tariffs for American industry, bounties to encourage the expansion of commercial agriculture, and a network of federally sponsored internal improvements such as roadways and lighthouses. These were intended to stimulate commerce and bind the nation more tightly together. Neither the agrarian South nor northern seaport districts, however, wanted tariffs that might reduce trade and raise the cost of living. As a result, Congress never endorsed this report.

All the while, criticism of Hamilton's program continued to grow. In October 1791, opposition leaders in Congress established a newspaper, the *National Gazette,* and vigorously attacked the administration's program. Hamilton responded with a series of anonymous articles in the administration's paper, *The Gazette of the United States,* in which he attacked his cabinet colleague Jefferson, accused him (inaccurately) of having opposed the Constitution, and charged him (also inaccurately) of fomenting opposition to the government. Alarmed at the division within his administration, Washington pleaded for restraint.

Congressional criticism of Hamilton's policies reached a climax in January 1793 when Representative William Branch Giles of Virginia introduced a series of resolutions calling for an inquiry into the condition of the Treasury, accusing Hamilton of using the office for his own benefit, and urging censure of the secretary's conduct. Hamilton vigorously defended both his policies and his behavior and none of Giles's accusations passed the House. The month-long debate, however, showed just how bitter political discourse at the seat of government had become.

The debate was now spreading beyond the circle of governing officials in Philadelphia. Among ordinary Americans, Hamilton's financial program drew a mixed response. In northern towns and cities, artisans and other working people generally approved. Closely dependent on the expansion of commerce and manufacturing, they supported efforts to improve credit and stimulate economic development. With their own economic circumstances now improving, they seemed undisturbed by the special benefits that funding, assumption, and the bank brought to a few. Within several years, many of them would move into the Jeffersonian opposition, but for the moment, their support of the government was secure.

The Whiskey Rebellion

The farmers of western Pennsylvania provided the most dramatic expression of popular discontent with government policies. Their anger focused on the Whiskey Tax. Ever since the trouble with England 30 years before, Americans had been sensitive to taxation and suspicious of its connections with governmental power. The farmers of western Pennsylvania had special reason to dislike this particular tax. Their livelihood depended on their ability to transport surplus grain eastward across the mountains to market. To ship it in bulk was prohibitively expensive, so they distilled the grain and moved it in the more cost-efficient form of whiskey. Hamilton's tax threatened to make this practice unprofitable. They complained as well that people charged with evading the tax must stand trial in federal, rather than state court. The nearest federal court was hundreds of miles away, across the mountains, in Philadelphia.

The westerners' frustration went deeper than that, however, for they felt control of their own local affairs slipping away as they became increasingly caught up in an expanding market economy and a system of politics dominated by more populous and more commercialized areas to the east. In southern states like South Carolina, coastal planters were able to extend their control more easily over farmers of the interior because of their similar agricultural interests and shared racial alliance against blacks. In the more economically diverse and racially homogenous states to the north, however, conflicts between coastal and interior regions were sharper.

Hamilton cared little what the farmers thought either about the Whiskey Tax or local self-reliance. The government needed revenue, and the farmers would have to bear the cost. George Clymer, federal supervisor of revenue for Pennsylvania, was equally unsympathetic. Referring to the "moral and personal weakness" of "the lesser folk," Clymer publicly castigated the "sordid shopkeepers" who retailed Pennsylvania whiskey and the

"greatly depraved" farmers who produced it. The farmers resented the Federalists' arrogance as much as the tax and quickly made their resentment known.

Trouble was brewing by the summer of 1792 as angry farmers gathered in mass meetings across western Pennsylvania. In August, a convention at Pittsburgh drew up a series of resolutions denouncing the Whiskey Tax and declaring that the people would prevent its collection. Like opponents of the Stamp Act in 1765, they decided that repression would follow if resistance did not soon begin.

Alarmed by the convention's resolutions, Washington issued a proclamation warning against such "unlawful" gatherings and insisting that the Excise Tax be enforced. As tax collections began, the farmers took direct action.

In July 1794, federal marshal David Lennox, in company with John Neville, a local excise inspector, attempted to serve papers on several recalcitrant farmers near Pittsburgh. An angry crowd gathered and stood in the way. Soon 500 armed men surrounded Neville's home and demanded his resignation. Learning that Neville had left, they ordered the dozen soldiers trapped in the house to lay down their arms and come out. Fearing for their safety, the soldiers refused, and for several hours the two sides exchanged rifle fire. After several men had been wounded, the soldiers finally surrendered, whereupon Neville's house was put to the torch. Similar episodes involving angry crowds, the erection of liberty poles reminiscent of the Revolution, and the hoisting of banners bearing such slogans as "Liberty and No Excise. O Whiskey!" erupted across the state. At Parkinson's Ferry, a convention of over 200 delegates debated armed resistance and even talked about secession from the United States.

Alarmed that the protests might spread through the entire whiskey-producing backcountry from New York to Georgia, Washington ordered the insurgents home and called out troops from eastern Pennsylvania and surrounding states to restore order. For more than a year, Hamilton had been urging the use of force against the protesters. He viewed the insurrection not as evidence of an unjust policy needing change, but as a test of the administration's ability to govern. Suppressing the rebellion, Hamilton explained, "will … add to the

President Washington and Secretary of the Treasury Hamilton led a federal army of nearly 13,000 troops into the whiskey-producing region of western Pennsylvania in 1794. Rebelling farmers, protesting the government's excise tax on whiskey, dispersed as the army approached. (The Metropolitan Museum of Art, Gift of Edgar William and Bernice Chrysler Garbisch, 1963)

solidity of everything in this country." He eagerly volunteered to accompany the federal army west.

In late August, a force of nearly 13,000 men, larger than the average strength of the Continental army during the Revolutionary War, moved into western Pennsylvania. At its center was Colonel William McPherson's "Pennsylvania Blues," an upper-class, strongly Federalist cavalry regiment. At its head rode the president of the United States and the secretary of the treasury. Washington soon returned to Philadelphia, persuaded by his aides of the danger to his safety, but Hamilton pressed ahead. When later criticized for accompanying the army to Pittsburgh, he replied that he had "long since … learned to hold public opinion of no value." The battle that Hamilton had anticipated, however, never materialized, for as the federal army approached, the "Whiskey Rebels" dispersed, their two chief leaders fleeing across the Ohio River. The federal army managed to take 20 prisoners. Two were convicted of high treason and sentenced to death. Later, in a calmer mood, Washington pardoned them both.

As people quickly realized, the "Whiskey Rebellion" had never threatened the government's safety. "An insurrection was … proclaimed," Jefferson scoffed, "but could never be found." Hamilton was merely pursuing his "favorite purpose of strengthening government" under the "sanction of a name [Washington's] which has done too much good not to be sufficient to cover harm also." Even such an ardent Federalist as Fisher Ames was uneasy at the sight of federal troops marching against American citizens. Though a government "by overcoming an unsuccessful insurrection becomes stronger," he noted, "elective rulers can scarcely ever employ the physical force of a democracy without turning the moral force, or the power of public opinion, against the government." Americans would soon have additional reason to ponder Ames's warning.

The Republic in a Threatening World

Because the nation was so new and the outside world so threatening, issues of foreign policy generated extraordinary excitement during the 1790s. This was especially so after the tumultuous events of the French Revolution and the accompanying European war burst on the international scene. In the arguments over the revolution in France and

This scene of bustling commercial activity in New York City in 1797, reveals the benefits that expanded neutral trade brought to the nation's major seaports. (The New-York Historical Society)

its implications for the new American republic, the American people revealed once again how sharply they differed in values and beliefs.

The Promise and Peril of the French Revolution

France's revolution began in 1789 as an effort to reform an arbitrary monarchy weakened by debt and administrative decay. Pent-up demands for social justice, however, quickly outran the initial attempts at moderate, constitutional reform. By the early 1790s, France was embroiled in a genuinely radical, social revolution. In January 1793, the monarch, Louis XVI, was beheaded. While the rest of Europe watched in horrified fascination, the forces of revolution and reaction struggled for the nation's soul.

As the revolution extended its attack on the aristocracy, the monarchy, and the Catholic Church, conservatives across the Continent gathered in opposition, their fears fueled by the appeals of fleeing French aristocrats. Finding itself surrounded and facing assault by Austria and Prussia, France's revolutionary government launched a series of military thrusts into Belgium and Prussia, triggering a general declaration of war. By the end of 1793, Europe was locked in a deadly struggle between revolutionary France and a counterrevolutionary coalition led by Prussia and Great Britain.

For more than a decade, the French Revolution dominated European affairs. Before it was finished, it would transform the entire course of Western history. The revolution also cut like a plowshare through the surface of American politics, dividing Americans deeply against each other. Not only did it raise immediate threats to the nation's security, but it also captured people's imaginations and polarized the debate over what the future of democratic politics might be.

The outbreak of European war posed some thorny diplomatic problems for Washington's administration. According to international law, neutral nations could continue to trade with belligerent powers during times of war, as long as such trade did not involve goods directly related to the war effort. American merchants were eager to take advantage of that opportunity because it promised handsome profits. Within a few years of the war's beginning, American commerce was booming. For the first time since the Revolutionary War, prosperity returned to the nation's coastal cities. By 1800, American exports had more than doubled, and American ships were carrying an astonishing 92 percent of all commerce between America and Europe. Though the benefits were most evident in the port cities, they radiated out into the surrounding countryside, where the cargoes of agricultural and forest goods and the provisions required by the ships' crews were produced.

America's expanding commerce, however, posed serious problems as well, for both England and France, while seeking American goods for themselves, were determined to control American trade by stopping American ships headed for the other's ports and confiscating American cargoes. Neither country was willing to tie itself down with legal formalities when locked in such a deadly struggle.

America's relations with England were further complicated by its practice of impressing American sailors into service aboard ships of the Royal Navy to meet its growing demand for seamen. Washington faced the difficult problem of upholding the country's neutral rights and protecting its citizens without getting drawn into the European war.

The old French alliance of 1778 compounded the government's dilemma. If still in effect, it seemed to require the United States to aid France, much as France had assisted the American states a decade and a half before. Those sympathetic to the French cause argued that America's commitment still held. Others, however, fearing the consequences of American involvement and the political infection that closer ties with revolutionary France might bring, insisted that the old treaty had been dissolved when the French monarchy collapsed.

The American people's intense reaction to the European drama further complicated the situation. Though an ocean away, Americans followed France's revolution with fascination, for it seemed at first to be an extension of their own struggle for liberty. Even the swing toward genuine social revolution did not immediately dampen American enthusiasm.

By the mid-1790s, however, especially after France's revolutionary regime launched its attacks on organized Christianity, many Americans pulled back in alarm. What connection could there possibly be between the principles of 1776 and the chaos of revolutionary France? "There is a difference between the French and the American Revolution," insisted the *Gazette of the United States*, a staunchly Federalist newspaper. "In America no barbarities were perpetrated—no men's heads were stuck upon poles—no mangled ladies' bodies were carried thro' the streets in triumph. . . . Whatever blood was shed,

flowed gallantly in the field." The writer conveniently ignored the violence meted out by the supporters of monarchy in France, and betrayed a selective memory of America's own revolution. The differences in the two revolutions, though, were indeed profound.

For the Federalists, revolutionary France now symbolized social anarchy and threatened the European order on which they believed America's commercial and diplomatic well-being depended. With increasing vigor, they castigated the revolution, championed England as the defender of European civilization, and sought ways of linking England and the United States more closely together.

Many Americans, however, continued to support France. While decrying the revolution's excesses, they noted how deeply entrenched the forces of reaction had been and how difficult it was to root them out. Moreover, they believed that political liberty would ultimately emerge from the turmoil. Though Jefferson regretted the shedding of innocent blood, he thought it was necessary if true liberty was to be achieved. John Bradford, editor of the *Kentucky Gazette*, agreed. "Instead of reviling the French republicans as monsters," he wrote, "the friends of royalty in this country should rather admire their patience in so long deferring the fate of their perjured monarch, whose blood is . . . considered . . . atonement for the safety of many guilty thousands that are still suffered to remain in the bosom of France." In Bradford's judgment, England was not a bastion of order, but the defender of arbitrary privilege and despotism.

Citizen Genêt and the Democratic-Republican Societies

Popular associations known as the Democratic-Republican societies provided the most vocal, as well as the most popular support for revolutionary France. As early as 1792, ordinary citizens began to establish "constitutional societies" dedicated to "watching over the rights of the people, and giving an early alarm in case of governmental encroachments." During the government's first years, several dozen such societies, modeled after the Sons of Liberty of 30 years before and complete with Committees of Correspondence (see Chapter 5), had formed in opposition to Hamilton's financial program. The French Revolution now stoked the fires of democratic enthusiasm and stimulated the societies' growth.

The arrival in April 1793 of Citizen Edmund Genêt, minister from the French republic to the United States, provided the spark. Genêt landed first at Charleston, South Carolina, to a tumultuous reception. His instructions were to court popular support and negotiate a commercial treaty with Washington's administration. Immediately after his arrival, however, he began commissioning American privateers to prey on British shipping in the Caribbean and enlisting American seamen for expeditions against Spanish Florida, both clear violations of American neutrality.

As he traveled north toward Philadelphia, Genêt met enthusiastic receptions. His popularity soon led him beyond the bounds of diplomatic propriety. Despite a warning from Secretary of State Jefferson and in open defiance of diplomatic protocol, he urged Congress to reject Washington's recently issued neutrality proclamation and side with revolutionary France. That was the final straw. On August 2, the president demanded Genêt's recall, charging that his conduct threatened "war abroad and anarchy at home."

If Genêt had little success as a diplomat, he succeeded in fanning popular enthusiasm for revolutionary France. In June 1793, with his open encouragement, the largest and most influential of the new societies, the Democratic Society of Pennsylvania, was founded in Philadelphia. It called immediately for the formation of similar societies elsewhere to join in supporting France and promoting the "spirit of freedom and equality" at home. People across the land, it declared, should join the effort to "erect the temple of liberty on the ruins of palaces and thrones." Washington and his colleagues might wonder if that challenge was also aimed at them.

Although a full network of popular societies never developed, about 40 organizations scattered from Maine to Georgia sprang up during the next several years. Working people—mechanics, artisans, and laborers in the cities, small farmers and tenants in the countryside—provided the bulk of membership. Federalist critics derided them as "the lowest orders of mechanics, laborers ... dray-

men ... broken hucksters, and trans-Atlantic traitors." The societies' leaders were generally individuals of acknowledged respectability, such as doctors, lawyers, and tradesmen. All were united by a common dedication to what they called the "principles of '76" and a determination to preserve those principles against the "royalizing" tendencies of Washington's administration.

Lamenting the decline of egalitarianism at home, they organized public celebrations of the nation's birth, issued addresses to the people, and framed petitions to the president and Congress, almost all sharply critical of administration policies. Washington's proclamation of neutrality they labeled a "pusillanimous truckling to Britain, despotically conceived and unconstitutionally promulgated." Several of the societies openly urged the United States to enter the war on France's behalf. Declared the New York society: "We firmly believe that he who is an enemy to the French revolution cannot be a firm republican; and therefore ... ought not to be entrusted with the guidance of any part of the machine of government."

In western areas, local societies agitated against the continuing British occupation of the frontier posts around the Great Lakes and berated Spain for closing the Mississippi River. In the Northeast, they castigated England for its "piracy" against American shipping. In the Carolinas, they demanded greater representation for the growing backcountry in the state's assembly. And almost to a person, they protested the Excise Tax, opposed the administration's overtures to England, and demanded that public officials attend to the people's wishes.

Finally, they campaigned for a press free from the political control of Federalist "aristocrats." Declared William Manning, a Massachusetts farmer who had marched to the "Concord fight" in 1775 and who continued to praise the principles for which he had fought: "A labouring man may as well hunt for pins in a haymow as to try to collect the knowledge necessary for him to have from such promiscuous piles of contradictions" as appeared in the Federalist press.

President Washington and his supporters were incensed by the societies' support of Genêt and their criticism of the government. The "real design" of these "nurseries of sedition," thundered the staunch Federalist Fisher Ames, was to revolutionize America as the Jacobins had revolutionized France. Writing in the *Virginia Chronicle* of January 17, 1794, "Xantippe" berated Kentucky's Democratic Society as "that horrible sink of treason, that hateful synagogue of anarchy, that odious conclave of tumult, that frightful cathedral of discord, that poisonous garden of conspiracy, that hellish school of rebellion and opposition to all regular and well-balanced authority!" Such polemics illustrated how inflamed public discourse had become.

Jay's Controversial Treaty

Controversy over Jay's Treaty with England further heightened tensions at mid-decade. Alarmed by the deteriorating relations with England, Washington sent Chief Justice John Jay to London in the spring of 1794 with instructions to negotiate a wide range of troublesome issues carried over from the Revolutionary War. Ever since the American Revolution, tension had been building over the continued British occupation of the western posts and the failure of England to honor other clauses in the peace treaty of 1783. British interference with American neutral shipping and impressment of American seamen added to the rising tide of anti-English sentiment.

Early in 1795, Jay returned home with a treaty that resolved almost none of America's grievances. England finally agreed to vacate the western posts, but not for another year and then only if it had uninterrupted access to the fur trade on American soil south of the Great Lakes. Jay failed to secure compensation for American slaves carried off by the British at the end of the Revolutionary War. Nor would the British foreign minister offer guarantees against the future impressment of American seamen, compromise on the issue of neutral rights, or agree to open the British West Indies to American shipping.

When the terms of Jay's treaty were made public, they triggered an explosion of protest. The administration's pleas that the agreement headed off an open breach with England and was the best that could be obtained failed to pacify its critics. In New York City, Hamilton was stoned when he defended the treaty at a noonday mass meeting.

Cartoons became a powerful weapon in the superheated politics of the 1790s. This Jeffersonian cartoon lampoons William Cobbett, one of the Federalists' most acid-tongued pamphleteers who wrote under the pseudonym Peter Porcupine. While Columbia swoons, the English Lion urges Cobbett to "sow the seeds of discord." (Historical Society of Pennsylvania, Philadelphia)

The "rabble," sniffed a Federalist newspaper, attempted "to knock out Hamilton's brains to reduce him to an equality with themselves." Southern planters were angry because the agreement brought no compensation for their stolen slaves. Westerners complained that the British were not evacuating the posts, while merchants and sailors railed against Jay's capitulation on the West Indies trade and impressment. After a long and acrimonious debate, however, the Senate ratified the treaty by the narrowest of margins.

The administration made better progress on the still volatile issue of free transit out the mouth of the Mississippi River at New Orleans. In the Treaty of San Lorenzo, negotiated by Thomas Pinckney in 1795, Spain for the first time recognized the United States' boundaries under the peace treaty of 1783 (the Mississippi River to the west and the 31st parallel to the south) and thus gave up all claim to U.S. territory. Spain also granted free navigation of the Mississippi and the right of American merchants for the next three years to unload their goods on shore for transshipment. Even on that issue, however, the future remained uncertain.

By mid-decade, political harmony had disappeared as the American people divided sharply on virtually every important issue of foreign and domestic policy. Increasingly estranged from administration policy, Jefferson resigned as secretary of state in July 1793. He soon joined politicians such as Madison and Albert Gallatin of Pennsylvania in open opposition to the Federalist administration.

In September 1796, in what came to be called his Farewell Address, Washington announced that he would not accept a third term as president. He had long been contemplating retirement, for he was now 64 and was exhausted by the political controversy swirling around him. Even the Great Patriot was no longer immune to attack. The nadir of abuse had come in July in an open letter published in the Philadelphia *Aurora* by that old revolutionary, Thomas Paine. "As to you, sir," fumed Paine, "treacherous in private friendship ... and a hypocrite in public life, the world will be puzzled to decide, whether you are an apostate or an impostor; whether you have abandoned good principles, or whether you ever had any." Seldom

has an American president been subjected to such public abuse as was Washington during his final year in office.

The Political Crisis Deepens

By 1796, bitter controversy surrounded the national government. That controversy intensified during the last half of the 1790s until it seemed to threaten the very stability of the country.

The Election of 1796

The presidential election of 1796 reflected the political storms buffeting the nation. In 1792, Washington and Adams had been reelected with-

John Adams, Washington's vice president, won a narrow victory over Jefferson for the presidency in 1796. His administration foundered on conflicts over foreign policy abroad and the suppression of political dissent at home. (Adams National Historic Site/U. S. Department of the Interior, National Park Service)

out significant opposition. Four years later, the situation was vastly different.

With Washington out of the picture, the presidential contest quickly narrowed to John Adams and Thomas Jefferson. Both were now elder statesmen; Adams was 61 years old, and Jefferson was eight years his junior. Both had played distinguished roles during the Revolution when they had become friends and had earned each other's respect. They had shared first in the electrifying task of drafting the Declaration of Independence. During the 1780s, they had joined forces once again, this time in Europe where Adams served as first U.S. minister to Great Britain while Jefferson was minister to France. While abroad, they corresponded frequently and exchanged family visits. They came together a third time during the early 1790s, Adams as vice president (a position he described in frustration as "wholly insignificant") and Jefferson as Washington's first secretary of state.

Though they had worked closely together, Adams and Jefferson differed in many ways. Short, rotund, and fastidiously neat, Adams contrasted sharply in physical appearance with the tall and frequently disheveled Jefferson. At once intensely ambitious and deeply insecure about the judgments both of his contemporaries and of history, Adams struggled self-consciously to construct his public career. Jefferson, by contrast, charted his course more quietly and repeatedly sought the solace of private life.

They differed in intellect and vision as well. Jefferson's mind was more expansive and his interests far more encompassing. Politician and political theorist, he was also an avid naturalist, architect, and philosopher. Adams's interests were more tightly focused on legal and constitutional affairs.

By the mid-1790s, the two statesmen differed as well in their visions of what the national republic should be. Though fearing Hamilton's ambition and distrusting his infatuation with England, Adams was a committed Federalist. He believed in a vigorous national government, was appalled by the French Revolution, and longed for political discipline. Jefferson, while firmly supporting the Constitution, was alarmed by Hamilton's financial program, viewed France's revolution as a logical if chaotic extension of America's struggle for freedom, and sought to expand political democracy. By 1796, he had

become the vocal leader of an increasingly articulate political opposition, the Jeffersonian Republicans.

The election of that year bound Jefferson and Adams together in a deeply strained alliance. With Washington gone, Adams became the Federalists' candidate. Though Jefferson did not officially oppose Adams, his followers campaigned vigorously on Jefferson's behalf. In the election, Adams received 71 electoral votes and was declared president. Jefferson came in second with 68 and, as then specified in the Constitution, assumed the vice presidency. The narrowness of Adams's majority—his enemies gleefully reminded him that he was only a "President of three votes"—indicated the Federalists' weakness and the growing strength of the Jeffersonians.

Adams later recalled his inaugural day. "A solemn scene it was indeed, and it was made more affecting by the presence of the General [Washington], whose countenance was as serene and unclouded as the day. He seemed to enjoy a triumph over me. Methought I heard him say, 'Ay! I am fairly out and you fairly in! See which of us will be the happiest.'" The answer was not long in coming.

The War Crisis with France

Adams had no sooner taken office than he confronted a deepening crisis with France. Hoping to ease diplomatic relations between the two countries, he sent off a three-person commission to try to negotiate an accord.

When the commissioners arrived in Paris, three agents of the French foreign minister, Talleyrand, visited them and made it clear that the success of their mission depended on a prior loan to the French government and a $240,000 gratuity for the French agents themselves. The two staunchly Federalist commissioners, John Marshall and Charles Pinckney, indignantly rejected the demands and sailed home. The third commissioner, Elbridge Gerry, stayed behind, still hoping for an accommodation and alarmed by Talleyrand's intimation that if all three Americans left, France would declare war.

When Adams submitted a report to Congress on this so-called XYZ Affair, American opinion was outraged. The Federalists quickly took advantage of the political opening offered by the French

American anger over the XYZ Affair is shown in this cartoon depicting the American commissioners Gerry, Pinckney, and Marshall spurning the bribery demands of a five-headed monster symbolizing the French Directory. (Cinque-têtes, or the Paris Monster, c. 1798–1800/The Huntington Library, San Marino, CA)

blunder. Secretary of State Pickering urged an immediate declaration of war, while Federalist congressmen thundered against the insult to American honor and demanded action. "Millions for defense, but not one cent for tribute" became their rallying cry. Adams now found himself an unexpected hero. When he attended the theater in Philadelphia, audiences cheered themselves hoarse with shouts of "Adams and Liberty!" Caught up in the anti-French furor and emboldened by the petitions of support that flooded in from around the country, the president lashed out at "enemies" at home and abroad. The nation, he warned ominously, had never been in greater danger. "In the last extremity," he declared, "we shall find traitors who will unite with the invading enemy and fly within their lines." Emotions were further inflamed by the so-called Quasi War, a series of naval encounters between American and French ships on the high seas.

For the moment, the Republicans were in disarray. Publicly, they deplored the French government's behavior and pledged to uphold the nation's honor. But among themselves, they talked with alarm about the Federalists' intentions. They had good reason for concern, because the Federalists soon mounted a crash program to repel foreign invaders and roust out traitors in the country's midst.

The Alien and Sedition Acts

In May 1798, Congress created the Navy Department and called for the rapid development of a naval force to defend the American coast against French attack. In July, Congress unilaterally repealed the treaty of 1778, thus moving closer to an open breach with France. It followed that action by calling for the formation of a 10,000-man army.

(The Federalists' original goal had been 50,000 men.) The army's stated mission was to defend the country against an anticipated French invasion. The Jeffersonians, however, feared the army would be used for a different, domestic, and more partisan purpose. Given France's desperate struggle in Europe, its dispatch of troops to North America seemed inconceivable. The Jeffersonians, moreover, remembered the speed with which the Federalists had deployed military force against the Whiskey Rebels only a few years earlier.

As criticism of the army bill mounted, Adams had second thoughts. He was still enough of an old revolutionary to worry about the domestic dangers of standing armies. The navy, he believed, should be America's first line of defense, but the army alarmed him. "This damned army," he burst out, "will be the ruin of the country." He was further angered when some members of his party sought to put Hamilton at the head of the army. To the dismay of hard-line Federalists, Adams issued only a few of the officers' commissions that Congress had authorized. Without officers, the troops could not be mobilized.

Fearful of foreign subversion and aware that French immigrants were active in the Jeffersonian opposition, the Federalist-dominated Congress moved in the summer of 1798 to curb the flow of aliens into the country. The Naturalization Act extended from 5 to 14 years the residence requirement for citizenship, and the Alien Act authorized the president to expel all aliens that he judged "dangerous to the peace and safety of the United States." Imprisonment and permanent exclusion from citizenship awaited individuals who were warned to leave but refused to go. Another bill, the Alien Enemies Act, empowered the president in time of war to arrest, imprison, or banish the subjects of any hostile nation without specifying charges against them or providing opportunity for appeal. The Federalist Congressman Harrison Gray Otis explained that there was no need "to invite hordes of Wild Irishmen, nor the turbulent and disorderly of all parts of the world, to come here with a view to distract our tranquility."

The implications of these acts for basic political liberties were ominous enough, but the Federalists had not yet finished. In July 1798, Congress passed the Sedition Act, aimed directly at the Jeffersonian opposition. The bill made it a high misdemeanor, punishable by fine and imprisonment, for anyone, whether citizen or alien, to conspire in opposition to "any measure or measures of the government," or to aid "any insurrection, riot, unlawful assembly, or combination." Fines and imprisonment were provided as well for people who "write, print, utter, or publish … any false, scandalous and malicious writing" bringing the government, Congress, or the president into disrepute.

The Federalist moves stunned the Jeffersonians, for they threatened to smother all political opposition. The Federalists left no room for doubts on the matter. With an open declaration of war, predicted Congressman James Lloyd of Delaware, "traitors and sedition mongers who are now protected and tolerated, would … be easily restrained or punished." The Federalists now equated their own political domination with the survival of the nation.

Under the terms of the Alien Act, Secretary of State Pickering launched investigations intended to force the registration of all foreigners. The act's chilling effects were widespread. In July, Pickering noted approvingly that large numbers of aliens, especially people of French ancestry, were leaving the country. As prosecutions under the Sedition Act went forward, 25 people, among them David Brown of Dedham, were arrested. Fifteen were indicted, and ten were ultimately convicted, the majority of them Jeffersonian printers and editors.

Representative Matthew Lyon, a cantankerous, acid-tongued Jeffersonian recently elected from Vermont, soon learned the consequences, even for members of Congress, of political indiscretion. Born in Ireland, Lyon had come to America as a young indentured servant harboring undying enmity toward England and disrespect for privilege of all sorts. A veteran of the War for Independence, Lyon took his revolutionary principles seriously.

During a particularly heated debate over the Sedition Act, he spat in the face of a Federalist opponent, Roger Griswold of Connecticut (the "Spitting Lion," the Federalists called him derisively). Two weeks later, Griswold exacted revenge by caning Lyon on the House floor. Later that year, Lyon was hauled into court, fined $1,000, and sentenced to four months in prison. His crime? Making reference in a personal letter to President

Adams's "unbounded thirst for ridiculous pomp, foolish adulation, and selfish avarice."

Local Reverberations

Luther Baldwin of Newark, New Jersey, discovered how broadly the political crisis had spread among the people and how little it took to get into trouble with Federalist authorities. On July 27, 1798, President and Mrs. Adams passed through Newark on their way from Philadelphia to their home in Quincy, Massachusetts. As the nation's first couple moved along Broad Street around 11 o'clock that morning, they were greeted by the firing of cannon, the ringing of church bells, and the cheers of the citizenry.

Not all Newark's residents shared in the moment's enthusiasm. Luther Baldwin happened to be coming toward John Burnett's dram shop when one of the tavern's customers, noting that the cannon continued to fire after the president had passed by, observed, "There goes the President and they are firing at his a—." According to the *Newark Central of Freedom*, Baldwin, being "a little merry" with drink, replied that "he did not care if they fired thro' his a—." At that point, the Federalist tavern keeper cried out that Baldwin had spoken sedition and must be punished.

Within two months, a local grand jury indicted him, and the following year he was hauled before the federal Circuit Court, where he was convicted of speaking "seditious words tending to defame the President and Government of the United States," fined, assessed court costs, and committed to jail until both fine and fees were paid.

Baldwin's trial gave the local Jeffersonians a field day. The New York *Argus* confessed "astonishment . . . on hearing the peculiarity of the expressions for which so formal a trial was instituted. . . . Can the most enthusiastic Federalists and Tories suppose that those who are opposed to them would feel any justification in firing at such a disgusting target as the a–- of J. A.?" Local Jeffersonians, however, saw danger as well as humor in the Federalists' zealous overreaction. "When cognizance is taken of such a ridiculous expression," the *Argus* concluded, every Republican could see

the "extraordinary malignancy of the federal faction."

Passage of the Alien and Sedition Acts generated a firestorm of protest. The Virginia and Kentucky assemblies mounted a direct challenge to the Federalist laws. The Kentucky Resolutions, drafted by Jefferson and passed on November 16, 1798, declared that the national government had violated the Bill of Rights. Faced with the arbitrary exercise of federal power, the resolutions continued, each state "has an equal right to judge [of infractions] by itself . . . [and] the mode and measure of redress." Nullification (declaring a federal law invalid within a state's borders) was the "rightful remedy" for unconstitutional laws. The Virginia Resolutions, written by Madison and passed the following month, asserted that when the central government threatened the people's liberties, the states "have the right and are in duty bound to interpose for arresting the progress of the evil." It would not be the last time in American history that state leaders would claim authority to set aside a federal law.

The Kentucky and Virginia resolutions received little support elsewhere, and neither state actually attempted to obstruct enforcement of the Alien and Sedition Acts. Still, the resolutions indicated the depth of popular opposition to the Federalists' program. As the Federalists pressed ahead, some Jeffersonians prepared for open conflict. The Virginia assembly called for the formation of a state arsenal at Harpers Ferry, reorganization of the militia, and a special tax to pay for these preparations. In Philadelphia, Federalist patrols walked the streets to protect government officials from angry crowds. The turmoil prompted President Adams to smuggle arms into his residence as a precaution. As 1799 began, the country seemed on the brink of upheaval.

Within a year, however, the cycle turned again, this time decisively against the Federalists. The break came with Adams's dramatic decision to send a new emissary to France. From Europe, the president's son, John Quincy Adams, sent assurances that Talleyrand was now ready to negotiate an honorable accord. Alarmed at the political furor consuming the nation and fearful that war with France "would convulse the attachments of the country," Adams eagerly seized the opening. "The end of war is peace," Adams explained, "and peace was offered me." Moreover, he had concluded that his only chance of reelection lay in fashioning a peace coalition out of both parties.

When Adams told his cabinet of the new mission, they were enraged, for the Federalist war program depended for its legitimacy on the continuation of the French crisis. After Secretary of State Pickering repeatedly ignored the president's orders to send the new commissioners on their way, Adams dismissed him and personally ordered the commissioners to depart. By year's end, they had secured an agreement releasing the United States from the 1778 alliance and providing for the restoration of peaceful relations between the two nations.

The "Revolution of 1800"

As the election of 1800 approached, the Federalists were in disarray. They had squandered the political advantage handed them by France in 1798 and now, with peace a reality, stood before the nation charged with the unconstitutional exercise of federal power, the suppression of political dissent, and the intention of using the federal army against American citizens. The party, moreover, was bitterly divided. The Hamiltonians were furious at Adams's "betrayal" and demanded that he not seek reelection in 1800. When Adams did not withdraw, the Hamiltonians plotted his defeat.

Emotions were running high as the election approached. Fisher Ames berated the Federalists' opponents as "fire-eating salamanders" and "poison-sucking toads," while the Jeffersonians returned the abuse in kind. Both sides believed that the republic's survival depended on their own political triumph. This election, Jefferson declared, will "fix our national character" and "determine whether republicanism or aristocracy" will prevail. The Federalists saw the choice as between republicanism and "anarchy." In Virginia, rumors of a slave insurrection briefly interrupted the feuding, but the scare quickly passed and soon Federalists and Jeffersonians were at each others' throats once again.

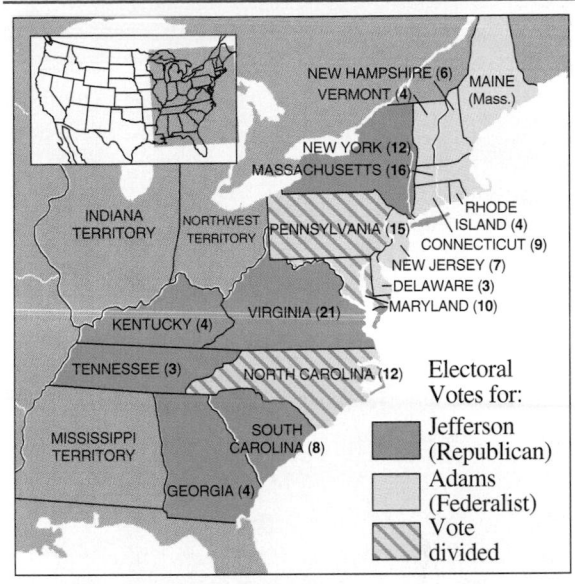

The Presidential Election of 1800

NEW HAMPSHIRE (6)
VERMONT (4)
MAINE (Mass.)
NEW YORK (12)
MASSACHUSETTS (16)
INDIANA TERRITORY
NORTHWEST TERRITORY
PENNSYLVANIA (15)
RHODE ISLAND (4)
CONNECTICUT (9)
NEW JERSEY (7)
DELAWARE (3)
MARYLAND (10)
VIRGINIA (21)
KENTUCKY (4)
TENNESSEE (3)
NORTH CAROLINA (12)
MISSISSIPPI TERRITORY
SOUTH CAROLINA (8)
GEORGIA (4)

Electoral Votes for:
Jefferson (Republican)
Adams (Federalist)
Vote divided

Though the federal government was little more than a decade old, the electoral vote in 1800 revealed the sectional divisions that already troubled national politics.

Though election day was tense throughout the nation, it passed without serious interruption, and as the results were tallied, it became clear that the Jeffersonians had handed the Federalists a decisive defeat. The two Republican candidates for president, Jefferson, the Republicans' first choice, and Aaron Burr, their other nominee, each had 73 electoral votes while Adams followed with 65.

Because of the tie vote, the election moved to the House of Representatives, as provided in the Constitution. There a deadlock quickly developed. In spite of considerable pressure from Jefferson's supporters, Burr refused to give way. The Federalist caucus decided to back Burr, believing him less dangerous than Jefferson and more sympathetic to Federalist principles. After a bitter struggle, the House finally elected Jefferson on the thirty-sixth ballot, ten states to four. (Seeking to prevent a recurrence of such a crisis, the new Congress soon passed and the states ratified the Twelfth Amendment, providing for separate Electoral College ballots for president and vice president.) The magnitude of the Federalists' defeat was even

Remembered later as the man who shot Alexander Hamilton in a duel in 1804, Aaron Burr came within a few votes of defeating Thomas Jefferson for the presidency in 1800. (Collection of The New-York Historical Society)

By 1800, presidential elections were generating increased popular interest, as evidenced by this textile banner celebrating Jefferson's victory. (Smithsonian Institution)

more evident in the congressional elections, where they lost their majorities in both House and Senate.

The election's outcome revealed the strong sectional divisions now evident in the country's politics. The Federalists remained dominant in New England because of regional loyalty to Adams, the importance of the area's commercial ties with England, and fears, fed by local ministers and politicians alike, that the Jeffersonians intended to import social revolution. From Maryland south, Jeffersonian control was almost as complete. In the middle states, the election was more closely contested because Federalists and Jeffersonians were more evenly balanced and issues of foreign and domestic policy cut across society in more complicated ways. In the years ahead, such sectional differences would continue to shape American politics.

The conflict between Federalists and Jeffersonians was deeply rooted as well in socioeconomic divisions among the American people. The Federalists were strongest among merchants, manufacturers, and commercial farmers located within easy reach of the coast—groups that had supported the Constitution in 1787 and 1788. "Here [in Connecticut] as everywhere," claimed one Federalist leader, "the men of talents, information, and property ... are found among the Federalists." In both New York City and Philadelphia, the Federalists were strongest in the wards where assessments were highest, houses largest, and addresses most fashionable.

By contrast, the Jeffersonian coalition included most of the old Anti-Federalists as well as agriculturalists in both North and South. As the election returns indicated, however, the Jeffersonians marshaled significant support in urban areas as well among workers and artisans, many of whom had once been staunch Federalists. The primary reason for their shift in political allegiance was illustrated by an episode that occurred in New York City in 1795.

Thomas Burke and Timothy Crady, two recent Irish immigrants, operated a ferry across the East River between lower Manhattan and Brooklyn. One day in early November, Gabriel Furman, a merchant and Federalist alderman, arrived on the Brooklyn shore a bit before the scheduled departure time. Impatient to get across, Furman instructed the ferrymen to leave early. When they refused, he upbraided the "rascals" for their disrespect and threatened to have them arrested. Crady was especially angered by the alderman's arrogance. He and Burke, Crady exploded, "were as good as any buggers," and he threatened to use his boathook on anyone who tried to arrest him.

When the ferry landed on the Manhattan shore, Furman had the two arrested, brandishing his cane at them as they were led off to jail, where they were charged with vagrancy. Their employer offered bail, but Furman refused to allow it, and so they remained 12 days in Bridewell prison awaiting trial.

Crady and Burke were eventually hauled before Mayor Varick and three other Federalist aldermen, sitting as the Court of General Sessions. The judges quickly decided to make examples of the two insolent Irishmen. "You rascals, we'll trim you," Varick allegedly said; "we'll learn you to insult men in office." The two ferrymen were not allowed to speak in their own behalf, nor were friendly witnesses permitted to testify. The magistrates found the two guilty on charges of insulting an alderman and threatening the constable, sentenced them to two months at hard labor, and ordered that 25 lashes be laid on Crady for good measure.

Within a month, the two ferrymen had bolted from jail and disappeared into Pennsylvania, never to be heard from again. The episode, however, was not yet over, for a young Jeffersonian lawyer named William Keteltas publicly castigated the "tyranny and partiality of the court" and concluded that Burke and Crady had been punished to "gratify the pride, the ambition and insolence of men in office." The authorities, he charged, acted to protect the mayor's reputation. But what, he asked, of the ferrymen's reputation?

When Keteltas was hauled before the authorities for his insolence, 2,000 citizens carried him through the streets chanting "The Spirit of '76" and waving a banner sardonically inscribed "What, you rascal, insult your superiors?"

In the politically charged setting of the 1790s, when the Revolution's legacy was still in dispute,

TIMELINE

1789	George Washington inaugurated as first president
	Outbreak of the French Revolution
1790	Slave trade outlawed in all states except Georgia and South Carolina
	Hamilton's "Reports on the Public Credit"
1791	Bill of Rights ratified
	Whiskey Tax and national bank established
	Hamilton's "Report on Manufactures"
1792	Washington reelected
1793	Outbreak of war in Europe
	Washington's Neutrality Proclamation
	Jefferson resigns from cabinet
	Controversy over Citizen Genêt's visit
1794	Whiskey Rebellion in Pennsylvania
1795	Controversy over Jay's Treaty with England
1796	Washington's Farewell Address
	John Adams elected president
1797	XYZ Affair in France
1798	Naturalization Act
	Alien and Sedition acts
	Virginia and Kentucky resolutions
1798–1800	Undeclared naval war with France
1799	Trials of David Brown and Luther Baldwin
1801	Jefferson elected president by House of Representatives

tensions between social privilege and democratic equality suffused American political life. Given the Jeffersonians' opposition to Federalist arrogance, support for revolutionary France, challenge to the Alien and Sedition Acts, and defense of religious liberty, those tensions worked steadily in the Jeffersonians' favor.

The political alignment evident in the election of 1800 resembled but did not duplicate the Federalist–Anti-Federalist division of 1787–1788. The Jeffersonian coalition was much broader than the Anti-Federalists' had been, for it included countless individuals, from urban workers to leaders such as Madison and Jefferson, who had supported the Constitution and had helped set the new government on its feet. Unlike the Anti-Federalists, the Jeffersonians were ardent supporters of the Constitution, but insisted that it be implemented consistently with political liberty and a strong dependence on the states. Far more than the Federalists, they also believed that government should be broadly accountable to the people. Nationally, the Jeffersonians now enjoyed a clear political majority. Their coalition would dominate American politics well into the nineteenth century.

 # Conclusion

Toward the Nineteenth Century

The election of 1800 was a remarkable outcome to more than a decade of political crisis. It had begun in the late 1780s with the intensifying debate over the Articles of Confederation and the movement toward a stronger central government. Then had come the heated contest over ratification of the new Constitution. Scarcely had the new government gotten under way than divisions began to form, first among political leaders in Congress but increasingly among the American people.

Hamilton's domestic policies generated the first outburst of political conflict but it was the French Revolution, the European war, Jay's Treaty, and the Federalists' war program that galvanized political energies and set the Federalists and Jeffersonians so adamantly against each other.

By 1800, the system of gentry-led politics centered in Congress and the more popular, democratic politics brewing in the states had drawn more closely together. The years immediately ahead would bring them into even more intimate political alignment, with dramatic consequences for the nation's future.

In the election of 1800, control of the federal government passed for the first time from one political party to another, not easily but peacefully and legally. "The Revolution of 1800," the Jeffersonians called it—"as real a revolution in the principles of our government as that of 1776 was in its form." The future would show whether the Jeffersonians were correct. But for the moment the crisis had passed, the Federalists had been defeated, and the government was in the hands of the Jeffersonians.

Recommended Reading

The Bill of Rights and Civil Liberties

Robert Rutland, *The Birth of the Bill of Rights, 1776–1791* (1983); Bernard Schwartz, *The Great Rights of Mankind* (1977); Leonard Levy, *Freedom of the Press from Zenger to Jefferson* (1966); James M. Smith, *Freedom's Fetters: The Alien and Sedition Laws and American Civil Liberties* (1956).

Party Politics at the Seat of Government

John Hoadley, *Origins of American Political Parties, 1789–1803* (1986); Richard Hofstadter, *The Idea of a Party System* (1970); John Nelson, Jr., *Liberty and Property: Political Economy and Policymaking in the New Nation, 1789–1812* (1987); John Zvesper, *Political Philosophy and Rhetoric: A*

Study of the Origins of American Party Politics (1977); Ralph Ketcham, *Presidents Above Party: The First American Presidency, 1789–1829* (1984); James Sharp, *American Politics in the Early Republic: The New Nation in Crisis* (1993); Stanley Elkins and Eric McKitrick, *The Age of Federalism* (1993).

Politics in the States

Norman Risjord, *Chesapeake Politics, 1781–1800* (1978); Charles Steffen, *The Mechanics of Baltimore: Workers and Politics in the Age of Revolution, 1763–1812* (1984); Ronald Schultz, *The Republic of Labor: Philadelphia Artisans and the Politics of Class, 1720–1830* (1993); Thomas Slaughter, *The Whiskey Rebellion: Frontier Epilogue to the American Revolution* (1986); Rachel Klein, *The Unification of a Slave State* (1990); Alan Taylor, *Liberty Men and Great Proprietors: The Revolutionary Settlement on the Maine Frontier, 1760–1812* (1990); Alfred Young, *The Democratic Republicans of New York: The Origins, 1763–1797* (1967); Richard Beeman, *Evolution of the Southern Backcountry* (1988).

Diplomacy and the French Revolution

Daniel Lang, *Foreign Policy in the Early Republic* (1985); William Stinchcombe, *The XYZ Affair* (1981); Albert Bowman, *The Struggle for Neutrality: Franco-American Diplomacy During the Federalist Era* (1974); Jerald Combs, *The Jay Treaty* (1970); Felix Gilbert, *To the Farewell Address: Ideas of Early American Foreign Policy* (1961).

Federalists Versus Jeffersonians

Joyce Appleby, *Capitalism and the New Social Order: The Republican Vision of the 1790s* (1984); Lance Banning, *The Jeffersonian Persuasion: The Evolution of a Party Ideology* (1978); Richard Kohn, *Eagle and Sword: The Federalists and the Creation of the Military Establishment in America, 1783–1802* (1975); Aleine Austin, *Matthew Lyon: "New Man" of the Democratic Revolution, 1749–1800* (1981); Merrill Peterson, *Adams and Jefferson: A Revolutionary Dialogue* (1976); John Howe, *The Changing Political Thought of John Adams* (1966).

CHAPTER 9

Society and Politics in the Early Republic

n May 1809, Mary and James Harrod gathered their five children, loaded a few belongings (tools, seeds for the summer planting, and several prized pieces of furniture) on a wagon, closed the door on their four-room cabin, fell in line with a dozen other families, and headed west from Spotsylvania County, Virginia, toward a new life in Kentucky. They left behind 10 acres of marginal upland, 15 years of wearying effort at trying to wring a modest living from it, and a family cemetery holding two of their other children and Mary's parents.

Beyond the Appalachian Mountains, 450 difficult miles ahead, lay additional hard work and uncertainty. Though central Kentucky where the Harrods would settle contained few Indian villages, powerful tribes from north and south of the Ohio River hunted there and fought for its control. They fought also against the growing tide of white settlers. The first years would be especially hard for James and Mary as they "opened up" the land, planted the first crops, and erected a cabin. They would be lonesome as well, for the Harrods would be unlikely to see even the chimney smoke from their nearest neighbors.

James and Mary were hopeful, though, and that sustained them as they trudged west. The land agent who had sold them their claim had promised rich, fertile soil that in time would support a good life. They looked forward as well to escaping Virginia's slave society with its arrogant planters and oppressed slaves. That was no place for poor whites to live. Just as important, Mary and James had shared in excited talk about new opportunities beyond the mountains and had agreed that it was time to join the swelling stream of migrants seeking new lives in the trans-Appalachian West. There they established themselves on their own plot of land, joined with their neighbors in fashioning a new community, and took responsibility for their own lives.

In April 1795, Ben Thompson started north from Queen Anne's County, Maryland, for New York City. Ben knew little beyond farming, but he was ambitious and when he arrived in New York he listened carefully to the ship's captains who talked about life at sea while they recruited men for their crews. Ben was lucky, for he arrived just as American overseas commerce, stimulated by renewed war in Europe, was entering a decade of unprecedented prosperity. Sailors were in demand, pay was good, and few questions were asked. For five years, Ben sailed the seas. Having enough of travel, he returned to New York and hired out as an apprentice to a ship's carpenter.

About the same time, Phyllis Sherman left her home in Norwalk, Connecticut. She also headed for New York, where she took a job as a maid in the household of one of the city's wealthy merchants. As fate would have it, Phyllis and Ben met, fell in love, and in the spring of 1802 were married.

There is little of note in this, except that Ben and Phyllis were former slaves and were married in the African Methodist Episcopal Zion Church. Ben had set aside his former slave name, Cato, as a sign of liberation, while Phyllis kept the name her master had given her. Ben was doubly fortunate, for he had purchased his freedom just as cotton production began to expand through the Chesapeake region. In another decade, he would have faced greater difficulty securing his independence. Phyllis had been freed as a child when slavery ended in Connecticut. As she grew up, she tired of living as a servant with her former owner's family and longed for the companionship of other blacks. She had heard that there were people of color in New York City, and she was correct. In 1800, it contained 6,300 African Americans, more than half of them free.

Though life in New York was better than either Ben or Phyllis had known before, it was hardly easy. They shared only marginally in the city's commercial prosperity. In 1804, they watched helplessly as yellow fever carried off their daughter and many of their friends. And while they found support in newly established African American churches and the expanding black community, they had to be on guard because slave ships still moved in and out of the port and slave catchers pursued southern runaways in the city's streets.

Detail from Thomas Coke Ruckle, *Fairview Inn or Three Mile House on Old Frederick Road* (near Baltimore), 1829. Country inns were places where people on the move bought supplies, exchanged goods, and secured information about the routes that lay ahead. (The Maryland Historical Society)

John Marshall, appointed chief justice of the United States by President Adams in 1801, served in that position for 34 years. Under his leadership, the Supreme Court established some of the most basic principles of American constitutional law. (Boston Antheneum)

should be left to the states because they were more closely attuned to the people's needs and could be held more closely accountable. In terms of domestic policy, the federal government did little more than deliver the mail, deal with the Indians on federal land, and administer the public domain. In addition to cutting government jobs, the Jeffersonians successfully reduced the national debt. From $83 million in 1801, the debt dropped to $57 million a decade later.

Not everything the Jeffersonians did was consistent with strict notions of a limited government. As the nation grew, so did pressures for a federal program of internal improvements, especially from the new states forming beyond the Appalachians that sought closer ties of trade and communication with the East. Before many years were out, the government responded by launching construction of several western routes, including the National Road (in 1811) connecting Cumberland, Maryland, with Wheeling, on the Ohio River. The states, however, continued to carry the major responsibility for internal improvements. Though the Jeffersonians may not have "revolutionized" the government as they claimed, they reduced its size and pointed it in a new direction.

Building an Agrarian Nation

The Jeffersonians did far more than reverse Federalist initiatives, for they worked vigorously to implement their own vision of an expanding, agrarian nation. That vision was mixed and inconsistent, for the Jeffersonian party embraced an array of often conflicting groups: southern patricians, such as Jefferson himself, determined to maintain a gentry-led, slavery-based agrarian order; lower- and middle-class southern whites committed to black servitude but ardent proponents of political equality among whites; northern artisans who brought to the Jeffersonian party an aversion to slavery (though not for the most part a commitment to racial equality) plus a fierce dedication to honest toil and their own economic advantage; western farmers devoted to self-sufficiency on the land; and northern intellectuals committed to the principle of political democracy.

Finally, the Jeffersonians sought ways to reduce the federal government's size even though it was tiny by modern standards. In 1802, it had fewer than 3,000 civilian employees, only 300 of them, including the cabinet and members of Congress, in Washington. That amounted to one federal public official for every 1,914 citizens, compared with one for approximately every 62 citizens today. Even so, Jefferson wrote his son-in-law that he was "hunting out and abolishing multitudes of useless offices, striking off jobs, etc., etc." In justification, Jefferson explained that the federal government was "charged with the external and mutual relations only of these states. The principal care of our persons, our property, and our reputation, constituting the great field of human concerns," he declared,

In time, this diversity would splinter the Jeffersonian coalition. For the moment, however, these groups found unity not only against their common Federalist enemies, but also in a set of broadly shared principles that guided Jeffersonian policies through the presidential administrations of Jefferson (1801–1808), James Madison (1809–1816), and James Monroe (1817– 1824).

The Jeffersonian Vision

Political liberty, the Jeffersonians believed, could survive only under conditions of broad economic and social equality. Their strategy centered on the independent, yeoman farmer—self-reliant, industrious, and yet filled with concern for the public good. Such people exemplified the qualities essential to democratic citizenship.

The Jeffersonian vision threatened to become clouded, however, because industriousness generated wealth, wealth bred social inequality, and inequality threatened to destroy the very foundation of a democratic society. The solution to that dilemma lay in rapid territorial expansion. Land, constantly expanding and readily available to the nation's yeoman citizens, would offer opportunity to a restless people, draw them out of the cities and off the crowded lands of the East, and preserve the social equality that democratic liberty required. The expansion of white settlement across the North American continent would delay, perhaps even prevent, the cyclical process of growth, maturity, and decay through which all past societies had moved.

Calls for expanding America's land base were strengthened by the somber arguments of an English clergyman and political economist named

Federal Revenues and Expenditures, 1790–1820 (in thousands of dollars)

Year	Revenues		Expenditures	
1790	Customs	4,399	Military	634
	Other	19	Interest on public debt	2,349
		4,418	Other	1,426
				4,409
1800	Customs	9,081	Military	6,010
	Internal revenue	809	Interest on public debt	3,375
	Other	793	Other	1,466
		10,683		10,851
1810	Customs	8,583	Military	3,948
	Internal revenue	7	Interest on public debt	2,845
	Sale on public lands	697	Other	1,447
	Other	793		8,240
		10,080		
1820	Customs	15,006	Military	7,018
	Internal revenue	106	Interest on public debt	5,126
	Sale on public lands	1,636	Other	9,324
	Other	2,769		21,468
		19,517		

Note: In constant dollars, the revenue of the federal government in 1993 was $1,148 trillion and its expenditures were $1,475 trillion.

Source: U.S. Bureau of the Census.

Presidential Elections, 1796–1820			
Year	Candidate	Party	Electoral Vote
1796	JOHN ADAMS	Federalist	71
	Thomas Jefferson	Democratic-Republican	68
	Thomas Pinckney	Federalist	59
	Aaron Burr	Democratic-Republican	30
	Minor Candidates		48
1800	THOMAS JEFFERSON	Democratic-Republican	73
	Aaron Burr	Democratic-Republican	73
	John Adams	Federalist	65
	Charles C. Pinckney	Federalist	64
	John Jay	Federalist	1
1804	THOMAS JEFFERSON	Democratic-Republican	162
	Charles C. Pinckney	Federalist	14
1808	JAMES MADISON	Democratic-Republican	122
	Charles C. Pinckney	Federalist	47
	George Clinton	Democratic-Republican	6
1812	JAMES MADISON	Democratic-Republican	128
	DeWitt Clinton	Federalist	89
1816	JAMES MONROE	Democratic-Republican	183
	Rufus King	Federalist	34
1820	JAMES MONROE	Democratic-Republican	231
	John Quincy Adams	Independent Republican	1

Note: Winner's names are in capital letters.

Thomas Malthus. In 1798, Malthus published an essay that jolted Europeans and Americans alike. Observing the growing population and increasingly crowded condition of his native England, Malthus argued, in characteristically stark language, that "the power of population" was "definitely greater than the power in the earth to produce subsistence for man." Enlightenment notions of a steadily improving quality of human life, he warned, were a delusion, for the future would be filled with increasing misery as human population outran its supply of food.

Jefferson took Malthus's warnings seriously but believed that the Englishman failed to understand how America's vast reservoir of land would enable its people to escape Europe's fate. "The differences of circumstance between this and the old countries of Europe," Jefferson explained, would produce a difference of result. "There … the quantity of food is fixed … [while] supernumerary births add only to mortality. Here the immense extent of uncultivated and fertile lands enables every one who will labor, to marry young, and to raise a family of any size. Our food, then, may increase geometrically with our laborers, and our births, however multiplied, become effective." Rapid and continuing territorial expansion was thus indispensable to the Jeffersonian vision of the nation's future.

Occupation of the West was essential as well to secure America's borders against continuing threats from England, France, and Spain. Finally, the Jeffersonians calculated that the creation of new, solidly Jeffersonian western states, committed to more democratic forms of politics, would strengthen their political control and assure the Federalists' demise.

The future would reveal that American exceptionalism, the notion that America could escape many of the woes that troubled Europe by expanding across the continent, was more limited than Jefferson imagined. And yet viewed from the perspective of the early nineteenth century, the Jeffersonians offered a compelling and hopeful vision of the nation's future.

The Windfall Louisiana Purchase

Efforts to secure the agrarian democracy by territorial expansion explain Jefferson's most dramatic accomplishment, his purchase of the Louisiana Territory in 1803.

In 1800, Spain ceded the vast trans-Mississippi region known as Louisiana to France. When Jefferson learned of the secret agreement, he was profoundly disturbed because it offered clear evidence that European nations still coveted North American territory. His fears were well grounded, for in October 1802, the Spanish commander at New Orleans, which Spain had retained, once again closed the Mississippi River to American commerce. Spain's action caused consternation in both Washington and the West.

In January 1803, the president sent his young associate James Monroe to Paris with instructions to purchase New Orleans and West Florida (which contained Mobile, the only good harbor on the Gulf Coast, and the mouths of several rivers that drained the southern interior). When Monroe arrived, he was surprised to find Talleyrand, the French foreign minister, prepared to sell all of Louisiana (though not West Florida). The recent black rebellion against French rule in Haiti and the renewed threat of war with England made Napoleon eager to concentrate French troops in Europe. In addition, he feared American designs on Louisiana and knew he would not be able to keep American settlers out. In April, the deal was struck. For $15 million, the United States obtained all of Louisiana, which was nearly 830,000 square miles, in one stroke nearly doubling the nation's size.

The Federalists reacted with alarm to news of the magnificent acquisition, fearing with good reason that the states to be carved from Louisiana would be staunchly Jeffersonian and worrying that a rapidly expanding frontier would "decivilize" the entire nation.

National expansion did not stop with Louisiana. In 1810, American adventurers fomented a revolt in Spanish West Florida, captured the fort at Baton Rouge, proclaimed an independent republic, and sought annexation by the United States. In May 1812, over vigorous Spanish objections, Congress annexed the region. In 1819, in the Adams-Onis Treaty, Spain ceded East Florida as well. As part of that agreement, the United States also extended its territorial claims beyond Louisiana to include the Pacific Northwest. These impressive accomplishments set the stage for the next and final surge of continental expansion during the 1840s.

In this 1803 panorama by Boqueto de Woiserie, the American eagle extends its wings over New Orleans following the Louisiana Purchase. (Chicago Historical Society)

Exploring the Trans-Mississippi West, 1804–1807

Louisiana Purchase, 1803

With the nation nearly doubled in size following the Louisiana Purchase, President Jefferson sent out exploring expeditions to map the region and lay visible claim to it.

Opening the Trans-Mississippi West

If America's vast domain was to serve the needs of the agrarian nation, it would have to be explored and prepared for white settlement. In the summer of 1803, Jefferson dispatched an expedition led by his personal secretary, Meriwether Lewis, and a young army officer named William Clark to explore the Far Northwest, make contact with the Native Americans there, open the fur trade, and bring back scientific information about the area. For nearly 2 ½ years, the intrepid band of explorers, assisted by the Shoshoni woman Sacajawea, made its way across thousands of miles of unmapped and hostile terrain—up the Missouri River, through the Rockies via the Bitterroot Valley and Lolo Pass, down the Columbia to the Pacific coast, and back again, finally reemerging at

St. Louis in September 1806. Lewis and Clark's journey established an American presence in the region, fanned American interest in the trans-Mississippi West, and demonstrated the feasibility of an overland route to the Pacific.

In 1805 and 1806, Lieutenant Zebulon Pike explored the sources of the Mississippi as far as Leech Lake in northern Minnesota. He followed that trek with an equally bold venture into the southern Rocky Mountains where he explored the peak that still bears his name. In the following decade, the government established a string of military posts from Fort Snelling, at the confluence of the Minnesota and Mississippi rivers, to Fort Smith on the Arkansas. Those forts were intended to secure the American frontier, promote the fur trade, and support white settlement.

Agricultural Productivity in 1800 and 1991				
	Wheat		Cotton	
	Worker-Hours per Acre	Yield per Acre	Worker-Hours per Acre	Yield per Acre
1800	56.0	15 bushels	185	147 pounds
1991	2.4	40 bushels	4.6	700 pounds

Source: U.S. Bureau of the Census.

The Jeffersonians' blueprint for an agrarian democracy also guided changes in federal land policy. Rather than viewing federal land as a resource used to generate government revenue, as the Federalists had done, the Jeffersonians wanted to speed its settlement. The Land Act of 1801 reduced the minimum required purchase from 640 to 320 acres, established a credit system, and offered 8 percent discounts for cash sales. Over the next year and a half, settlers, speculators, and land companies purchased nearly 400,000 acres of federal land, more than four times as much as during the entire 1790s.

During the 1820s, several additional principles were added to federal land policy, among them preemption, which enabled squatters to secure title to land simply by occupying it, and pricing graduation, whereby lands that did not readily sell were offered at discounted prices or were even given away. Though Jeffersonian land policy fostered widespread speculation and contributed to the Panic of 1819, it speeded the transfer of public land into private hands.

A Nation of Regions

During the early years of the republic, the vast majority of Americans drew their living from the land. In 1800, fully 83 percent of the labor force was engaged in agriculture; that figure had hardly changed a quarter of a century later. And yet people occupied the land in very different ways in different regions of the nation. While long-standing differences between the Northeast and the South persisted, an entirely new region of white settlement began to take shape beyond the Appalachians, in the nation's interior.

The Northeast

In the Northeast, a broad region stretching from eastern Pennsylvania and New Jersey through New England, family farms dominated the landscape. Because much of New England's land was poor, farmers there often turned their fields from tillage into pasture to take advantage of the greater profits to be made in dairying and livestock. On the richer agricultural lands of New York and Pennsylvania, by contrast, farmers cultivated their land intensively, planting it in grain year after year rather than following the customary practice of allowing worn-out fields to lie fallow and recover their fertility. Prior to American independence, the mid-Atlantic landscape had looked cluttered and unkempt, with wide areas still covered by timber, and with fallow lands lapsing back into brush. Fifty years later, however, the countryside looked increasingly clean and orderly, its carefully cultivated fields clearly marked by hedges or stone walls.

Farmers along the Hudson River in New York and in southeastern Pennsylvania produced an agricultural surplus, which they exchanged in nearby towns for commodities such as tea, sugar, window glass, and tools. As the term "surplus" indicates, however, most farmers marketed only what was left over after they had met their family's needs. "The great effort," reported a European traveler, "was for every farmer to produce anything he required within his own family; and he was

Maps

Of the several exploring ventures President Jefferson sent into the trans-Mississippi West, the Lewis and Clark expedition (1803–1806) was the most important. It proved the feasibility of an overland route to the Pacific, produced scientific information about the fauna and flora of the Far Northwest, established contact with the Native Americans of the area, and helped stimulate westward expansion. Many of the place names the explorers gave to rivers and other natural features are still in use today.

During their travels, Meriwether Lewis, William Clark, and others in their party kept extensive journals in which they recorded their experiences and observations. These journals provide a vivid account of the expedition, including information on the landscape through which the explorers passed and the people they encountered. The journals also reveal a great deal about the attitudes and expectations of the explorers themselves. As they moved across the continent, the explorers produced detailed trail maps as well. These cartographic records also tell us a great deal about the experience and perceptions of the explorers, as well as about the regions through which they passed.

Examine the map shown here. It is an example of the sketch maps that William Clark drew as the expedition made its way across the land. The map represents about a 30-mile stretch along the Missouri River in what is today west-central North Dakota. After the expedition was over, these detailed studies were used to prepare large, composite maps of the entire region that were far more accurate than any that had been made before.

Mapmaking has changed dramatically since Clark's early efforts. Over the years, as surveying technology and map design have changed, we have vastly improved our knowledge of the earth's topography, as well as our ability to represent the earth's rounded surface on a map's flat plane. Today, the most detailed and accurate maps are drawn from high-resolution photos taken by satellites.

To imagine Clark's mapmaking difficulties, as well as to appreciate his accomplishment, try this experiment. Without consulting anything but your own memory, try to draw a map of the region you passed through on your way to college. Include the major topographical and other interesting features on the route. Also indicate the groups of people you met or passed near. Alternatively, draw a map of the area around your hometown, including the major features, inhabitants, and travel routes. Make your map as accurate as possible to aid others who might depend on it for their own travels.

Now consider Clark's map carefully. How accurate do you suppose it is? How accurate would it have had to be in order to be useful? What does the map reveal about the explorers' rate of travel through this region? Why do you suppose they traveled along the winding course of the Missouri River rather than overland?

Cartographers, or mapmakers, have to decide what to include and what to omit from their maps. Those decisions depend on the purposes the map is intended to serve. Under what circumstances and for what purposes was Clark's map created? How many different kinds of information does it contain? What are its dominant features, and why are they emphasized? Imagine yourself in the role of Clark. As you observe your surroundings, what do you see but decide not to record on the map? How would a modern map of the same region differ?

Finally, think about the significance of the maps, written journals, and oral accounts generated by the Lewis and Clark expedition. How did they help change the map of the United States?

Lewis and Clark's map of the Missouri River, 1804.
(Joslyn Art Museum, Omaha, Nebraska)

was met from overseas. In 1803 alone, Georgia and South Carolina imported 20,000 new slaves, as southern planters and northern merchant suppliers rushed to fill the need before the slave trade ended in 1807. Much of the demand for agricultural labor, however, would be met by the internal slave trade that moved African Americans from the worn-out lands of the Chesapeake to the lush cotton fields of the Deep South.

Trans-Appalachia

A third region of settlement, west of the Appalachian Mountains, was forming as the nineteenth century began. New, raw, repeatedly embroiled in conflict between Indian inhabitants and white intruders, trans-Appalachia constituted a broad and shifting zone of cultural, economic, and military interaction between Native American and European-American peoples. It extended west from the Appalachian Mountains to the Mississippi River and south from the Great Lakes to the Gulf of Mexico. In 1790, scarcely 100,000 white settlers lived beyond the Appalachians. By 1810, their number had swollen to nearly a million; by 1820, fed by people like Mary and James Harrod, there were over a million more.

Dense forests made the overland trip into trans-Appalachia difficult under the best of circumstances. Even major routes were often little more than rough paths cut through the woods. (Charles Bodmer, Forest Scene on the Tobihanna, Alleghany Mountains, 1833/Joslyn Art Museum, Omaha, NE, Gift of The Enron Art Foundation)

They came by wagon along Zane's Trace and other tortuous, overland routes into Kentucky and Tennessee, and clambered aboard flatboats at Pittsburgh every spring when the water was high to float down the Ohio River to destinations at Wheeling, Cincinnati, and Louisville. The human tide seemed to grow with each passing year. "Genessee fever" brought thousands of settlers surging into the Genessee River country of western New York. "The woods are full of new settlers," wrote an amazed observer near Batavia, New York, in 1805. "Axes are resounding, and the trees literally falling around us as we passed." By 1812, some 200,000 souls lived in the western part of the state, where scarcely 30,000 whites had lived only 20 years before. "America is breaking up and going west!" exclaimed the British traveler Morris Birkbeck in wonder. At the time, it certainly seemed to be true.

Settlers were drawn by the promotions of speculators seeking their fortunes in the sale of western land. Between 1790 and 1820, land companies hawked vast areas of New York, Ohio, and Kentucky to prospective settlers such as James and Mary Harrod. The most extravagant ventures frequently failed, but many others succeeded, returning handsome profits to their investors. Individual settlers shared in the speculative fever, often going deeply into debt to buy extra land so they might sell it at a premium when population increased and land prices rose.

North of the Ohio River, settlement followed the grid pattern prescribed in the Land Ordinance of 1785, whereas south of the Ohio people distributed themselves more randomly across the land, much as their ancestors had done back east. Above the Ohio, mixed, free-labor agriculture took hold. In short order, towns such as Columbus and Cincinnati emerged to provide services and cultural amenities for the surrounding population. In Kentucky and Tennessee, free-labor agriculture also developed, but was soon challenged by the spread of slavery-based cotton.

As people continued to spill into the region, they established churches, schools, and even colleges (Transylvania University, founded in Lexington, Kentucky, in 1780, was the first college west of the Appalachians). Even so, trans-Appalachia retained a reputation for its rough and colorful

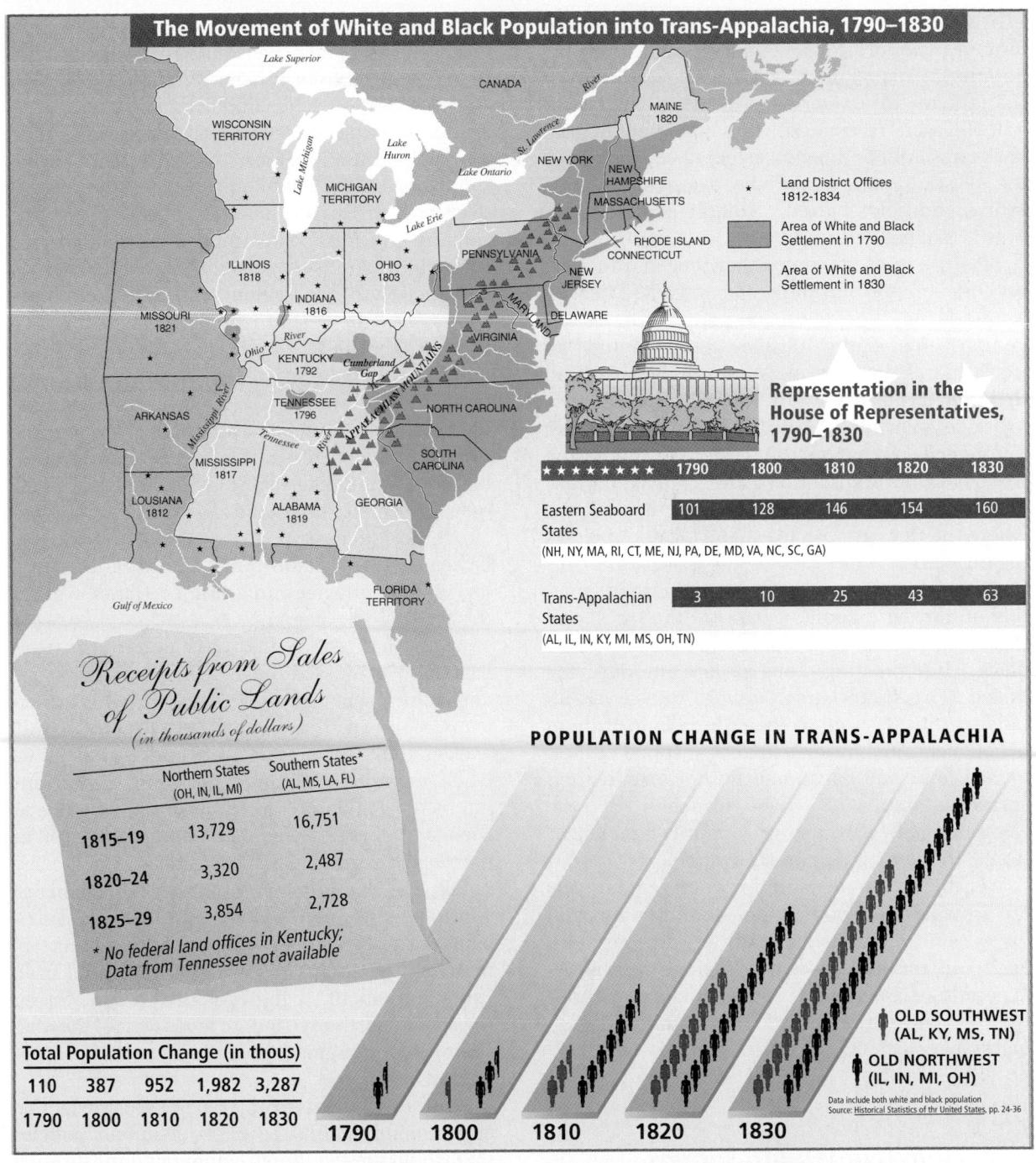

The Movement of White and Black Population into Trans-Appalachia, 1790–1830

Land District Offices 1812–1834 ★

Area of White and Black Settlement in 1790

Area of White and Black Settlement in 1830

Representation in the House of Representatives, 1790–1830

	1790	1800	1810	1820	1830
Eastern Seaboard States (NH, NY, MA, RI, CT, ME, NJ, PA, DE, MD, VA, NC, SC, GA)	101	128	146	154	160
Trans-Appalachian States (AL, IL, IN, KY, MI, MS, OH, TN)	3	10	25	43	63

Receipts from Sales of Public Lands
(in thousands of dollars)

	Northern States (OH, IN, IL, MI)	Southern States* (AL, MS, LA, FL)
1815–19	13,729	16,751
1820–24	3,320	2,487
1825–29	3,854	2,728

* No federal land offices in Kentucky; Data from Tennessee not available

Total Population Change (in thous)

110	387	952	1,982	3,287
1790	1800	1810	1820	1830

POPULATION CHANGE IN TRANS-APPALACHIA

1790 1800 1810 1820 1830

OLD SOUTHWEST (AL, KY, MS, TN)

OLD NORTHWEST (IL, IN, MI, OH)

Data include both white and black population
Source: Historical Statistics of the United States, pp. 24-36

ways. Life could be depressingly lonesome for families lost in the hollows of the Cumberland Mountains of eastern Tennessee. In the towns along the Ohio River, by contrast, boatmen and gamblers, con men and speculators gave civic life a raucous quality; and everywhere the transience, youthfulness, and predominant maleness of the population kept society unsettled.

The constant drama of migration and the grandeur of the natural surroundings stoked people's imaginations. No characters were more famous in popular folklore than western adventurers such as Daniel Boone. None was more colorful than the mythical riverman Mike Fink, "half man, half alligator," who could "whip his weight in grizzly bears." And nothing revealed more graphically the West's rawness than the eye-gouging, ear-biting, no-holds-barred, "rough and tumble" brawls that regularly erupted.

As the settlers came, they began the long process of transforming the region's heavily forested land. In the mountainous areas of western Pennsylvania, entire hillsides were denuded of trees that anxious travelers then dragged behind their wagons as makeshift brakes during the jolting rides downhill. Erroneously regarding the unforested "oak openings" scattered through the woods of Ohio and southern Michigan as "barren" and infertile, many farmers staked their claims where the trees grew thickest and set about clearing the land.

Farmers followed the long-established practice of cutting a girdle of bark off the trees, and then setting them on fire or leaving them to die in place while planting crops around the decaying hulks. "The scene is truly savage," observed an English traveler used to the orderly landscape of his own country. "Immense trees stripped of their foliage, and half consumed by fire extend their sprawling limbs … now bleached by the weather. …" By this method, a family could clear from 3 to 5 acres a year for cultivation.

The relentless demands for wood generated by the growing white population—for log cabins and barns, fences and fuel, potash and turpentine—added to the assault on the region's forests. As expanding areas of trans-Appalachia came under the farmers' plows, forests and wildlife increasingly gave way.

Indian-White Relations in the Early Republic

The years from 1790 to the end of the 1820s witnessed a dramatic turning point in Indian-white relations. As the era began, Native American tribes still controlled vast areas of the trans-Appalachian interior. North of the Ohio River, the Shawnee, Delaware, and Miami were allied in a western confederacy capable of mustering several thousand warriors. South of the Ohio lived five major tribal groups: the Cherokee, Creek, Choctaw, Chickasaw, and Seminole. Together, these southern tribes totaled nearly 60,000 people. By 1830, however, a decisive shift in the balance of power between Indians and European Americans had occurred throughout Trans-Appalachia as white settlers streamed into the region (carrying their black slaves with them south of the Ohio River) and occupied the land.

As the pressures of white expansion increased, tribal groups devised various strategies of resistance and survival. Many among the Cherokee followed a path of peaceful accommodation. Others, like the Shawnee and the Creek rose in armed resistance. Neither strategy was altogether successful, for by 1830, the Indians faced a future of continued acculturation, military defeat, or forced migration to lands west of the Mississippi River.

Less dramatic but no less important, these years also witnessed the sharply increased social and cultural separation of Indians and white Americans. As late as the 1780s, Native Americans still walked the streets of Boston and Philadelphia, while countless Indians and white Americans interacted regularly with each other, whether as friends or enemies, traders or workers, or even as marriage partners. By 1830, such contacts were much less common. East of the Appalachians, whites now regarded Indians as exotic curiosities, while west of the mountains the Indians' increasing confinement on reservations separated from white settlement, together with the first, forced removal of northern tribes to areas west of the Mississippi River, began a similar process of racial separation.

During the years from 1790 to 1830, the federal government established a set of Indian policies that would govern Indian-white relations through much of the nineteenth century. Intended in part to promote the eventual assimilation of Native Americans into white society, those policies in fact speeded the transfer of Indian land to white settlers and helped set the stage for a later and more dramatic policy of Indian removal.

The Initial Goals of Indian Policy

With the government's initial "conquest" theory rendered obsolete by the Indians' refusal to regard themselves as a conquered people (see Chapter 7), government officials shifted course by recognizing Indian rights to the land they inhabited and declaring that all future land transfers would come through treaty agreements.

Henry Knox, Washington's first secretary of war, laid out the government's new position in 1789. The Indians, he explained, "being the prior occupants of the soil, possess the right of the soil." It should not be taken from them "unless by their free consent, or by the right of conquest in case of just war." To dispossess them for other reasons "would violate the fundamental laws of nature and ... justice." Though Knox helped establish a more humane Indian policy, the acquisition of Indian land for white settlement remained the overarching goal.

The new treaty-based strategy proved effective. Native American leaders frequently agreed to cede land in return for trade goods, yearly annuity payments, and assurances that no further demands would be made on them. When tribal leaders proved reluctant, they often could be persuaded to cooperate by warnings about the inevitable spread of white settlement, or more tractable chieftains could be found. In these ways, vast areas of tribal land throughout the trans-Appalachian interior passed into the possession of white settlers.

Federal policy attempted to regulate the fur trade as well. Both Native Americans and whites found benefit in the trade. The Indians, in return for furs that they had in abundance, secured goods such as blankets, guns, rum, and ironware that they valued highly. White traders, by contrast, acquired valuable furs in exchange for relatively inexpensive trade items.

While the fur trade brought handsome profits to private companies such as John Jacob Astor's American Fur Company (1808), it often worked to the Indians' disadvantage. Trade goods frequently transmitted diseases such as measles and smallpox. Indians, moreover, often became dependent on the trade because it provided the only certain supplies of coveted goods such as rum and firearms. As the demand for furs and pelts increased, moreover, Native Americans frequently overtrapped their hunting grounds, forcing them to compete with other tribes for access to fresh sources of furs further to the west.

In 1796, in an effort to reduce fraud and the conflict it generated, Congress created a system of government trading posts, or "factories," where Indians could come for fair treatment. The system lasted until 1822, but never supplanted private traders as Congress had intended.

A third initial objective of federal Indian policy was to civilize and Christianize the Native Americans, then assimilate them into white society and accord them the blessings of democratic liberty. In the Trans-Appalachian West, where whites and Indians struggled directly against each other, most settlers regarded Indians as savages to be moved out of white settlement's way. In the East, however, clergymen and government officials displayed greater concern over the Native Americans' well-being. While uneasy over Indian "savagery," easterners admired the Native Americans' "bravery," "independence," and "simplicity of life," qualities that resembled American democratic virtues.

Although the assimilationists often cared deeply about the physical and spiritual fate of Native American people, they showed little sympathy for Indian culture, for they demanded that Native Americans give up their language, religion, dress, and extended family arrangements—that is, cease being Indian and adopt the ways of white society. Assimilation or continuing destruction were the alternatives posed by even the most benevolent whites.

Education and Christianization were the major instruments of assimilationist policy. After the Revolution, Moravians, Quakers, and Baptists launched mission efforts of their own or joined together in bodies such as the Society for Propagating the Gospel Among Indians (1787). Together, they sent scores of missionaries to live among the Indians, preach the Gospel, and teach the benefits of white civilization. Among them was John Stewart, a freeborn mulatto who was part Indian. From 1815 to his death in 1821, he preached to the Wyandotte near Sandusky, Ohio. Among the most selfless were Quaker missionaries who labored with the Iroquois in New York, attempting to inspire conversion and improve the conditions of Iroquois life. In spite of the missionaries' best

Indian Land Cessions, 1750–1830

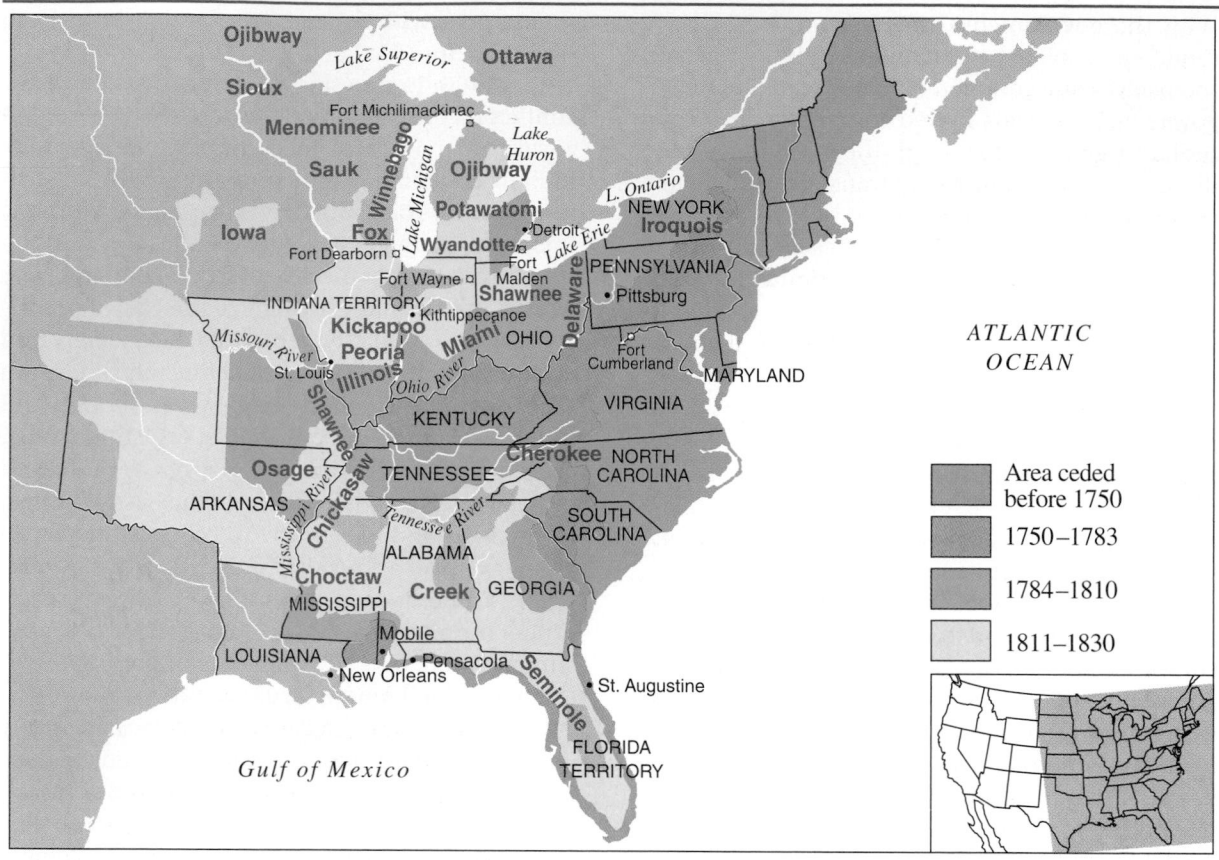

As white settlers streamed across the nation's interior, state and federal governments wrung land cessions from the Indians. By 1830, only the southeastern tribes still controlled significant areas of their ancestral land east of the Mississippi River. Labels in red indicate the major Native American groups of the Old Southeast and Old Northwest.

efforts, most Native Americans remained aloof, for the chasm between Christianity and their own religions was wide (see Chapter 1), and the missionaries' denigration of Indian culture was apparent.

Education was the other weapon of the assimilationists. In 1793, Congress appropriated $20,000 to promote literacy, agriculture, and vocational instruction. Because federal officials believed that Christianity and civilization necessarily went hand in hand, they encouraged missionaries to establish schools in which Indian children could be taught Christianity as well as reading, writing, and vocational skills.

The vast majority of Indian children never attended the mission schools. Among those who did, many stayed but a short while, they and their parents preferring the educational setting of family and tribal culture over the unfamiliar, culturally threatening environment of the schools.

Strategies of Survival: The Iroquois and the Cherokee

Faced with the steady loss of land and tribal autonomy, Native Americans devised various strategies of resistance and survival. Among the Iroquois, a prophet named Handsome Lake, who had fought with England during the Revolutionary War and who had succumbed to the despair of military defeat and reservation life, led his people through a process of religious renewal and cultural revitalization. In 1799, following a series of trance-like religious visions, he preached a combination of Indian and white ways that included temperance, peace, land retention, and the rituals of Gai-wiio, a new religion combining elements of Christianity and traditional Iroquois belief. His vision, providing a new definition of what it meant to be an Indian, offered hope and renewed pride for the Iroquois in the midst of their radically transformed lives.

Far to the south, the Cherokee followed a different path of accommodation. As the nineteenth century began, the Cherokee still controlled millions of acres in Tennessee, Georgia, and the western Carolinas. Their land base, however, was shrinking. By 1800, more than 40 Cherokee towns had already disappeared.

Southern state governments, responding to the aggressive demands of their white constituents for Indian lands, sought to undercut tribal autonomy. In 1801, the Tennessee legislature unilaterally expanded the boundaries of several counties to include Cherokee land and then claimed that the Indians fell under the authority of state law. As violence escalated along the borders between white and Indian settlements, state officials demanded that Native Americans accused of horse stealing and other crimes stand trial in state courts. The Cherokee, declaring that they had their own system of justice and distrusting the state courts with their all-white juries and exclusion of Indian testimony, rejected Tennessee's demands.

In Cherokee councils, a group of full-blood leaders called for armed resistance. Better to stand and fight, they argued, than follow the false path of accommodation. Others, however, including mixed-bloods such as John Ross, insisted that accommodation offered the best hope for survival. Following a bitter struggle for tribal control, the accommodationists won out.

Their first goal was to bring the tribe's scattered villages under a common government, the better to defend their freedom and prevent the further loss of land. In 1808, the Cherokee National Council adopted a written legal code combining elements of American and Indian law, and in July 1827, the Cherokee devised a written constitution patterned after those of nearby states. They accompanied it with a bold declaration of their standing as an independent nation holding full sovereignty over their lands. In 1829, the Cherokee government formalized the "blood law," making it an offense punishable by death for any member of

Sequoyah, who sat for this portrait in 1838, devised the Cherokee alphabet, which formed the basis for the first written Indian language in North America. (The Newberry Library, Chicago)

the tribe to transfer land to white ownership without the consent of tribal authorities.

Meanwhile, the process of social and cultural accommodation, encouraged by Cherokee leaders such as Ross and promoted by white missionaries and government agents, went forward. Missionaries opened a school for Cherokee youth on the Hiwanee River in 1804 and established a boarding school near present-day Chattanooga 12 years later. They stepped up their religious activities as well, baptizing Cherokee into the Christian faith.

As the Cherokee turned from their traditional hunting, gathering, and farming economy to settled agriculture, many of them moved from town settlements onto individual farmsteads. Others established sawmills, country stores, and blacksmiths' shops. In contrast to traditional Cherokee practices of sharing and the communal ownership of property, notions of private property took hold.

The majority of Cherokee people continued to inhabit crude log cabins and live a hand-to-mouth existence. Some, however, such as mixed-bloods like Joseph Vann who learned English and understood how to deal with white authorities, accumulated hundreds of acres of fertile land and scores of black slaves.

Since the mid-eighteenth century, the Cherokee had held a few runaway blacks in slavelike conditions. During the early nineteenth century, Cherokee slavery expanded and became more harsh. By 1820, there were nearly 1,300 black slaves in the Cherokee nation. A Cherokee law of 1824 forbade intermarriage with blacks. The accelerating spread of cotton cultivation increased the demand for slave labor among Cherokee as well as southern whites. As accommodation to white society increased, moreover, the ownership of slaves became a mark of social standing.

By 1820, the strategy of peaceful accommodation had brought clear rewards. Tribal government was stronger and the sense of Cherokee identity was reasonably secure. Before long, however, the Cherokee's success would prove their undoing, for as their self-confidence grew, so did the hostility of neighboring whites impatient to gain possession of their land. That hostility would soon erupt in a final campaign to remove the Cherokee from their land forever (see Chapter 13).

Patterns of Armed Resistance: The Shawnee and the Creek

Not all tribes of the interior proved so accommodating to white expansion. Faced with growing threats to their political and cultural survival, the Shawnee and Creek nations rose in armed resistance. Conflict was smoldering as the nineteenth century began; it burst into open flame during the War of 1812.

In the late 1780s, chieftains such as Little Turtle of the Miami and Blue Jacket of the Shawnee had led a series of devastating raids across Indiana, Ohio, and western Pennsylvania, creating panic among white settlers and openly challenging the federal government's control of the Old Northwest. After two federal efforts to quell the uprising had failed, President Washington determined to smash the Indians' resistance once and for all. In 1794, a federal army led by the old Revolutionary War general, Anthony Wayne, achieved a decisive victory over 2,000 Indian warriors in the Battle of Fallen Timbers. Shortly after, in the Treaty of Greenville, the assembled chiefs ceded the southern two-thirds of Ohio. That cession opened the heart of the Old Northwest to white control. In subsequent years, additional treaties further reduced the Indians' land base, driving the Shawnee and Delaware, the Miami and Wyandotte more tightly in upon each other.

By 1809, two Shawnee leaders, the brothers Tecumseh and Elskwatawa, the latter known to whites as "the Prophet," were traveling among the region's tribes warning of their common dangers and forging an alliance against the invading whites. They established headquarters at an ancient Indian town named Kithtippecanoe in northern Indiana. Soon it became a gathering point for Native Americans from across the region responding to the messages of cultural pride, land retention, and pan-Indian resistance presented by the Shawnee brothers.

Between 1809 and 1811, Tecumseh carried his message of Indian nationalism and military resistance south to the Creek and the Cherokee. His speeches rang with bitter denunciations of white Americans. "The white race is a wicked race," he told his listeners. "Since the days when the white race first came in contact with the red men, there has been a continual series of aggressions. The hunting grounds are fast disappearing, and they are driving the red men farther and farther to the west.... The only hope ... is a war of extermination against the paleface." The southern tribes refused to join, but by 1811, over 1,000 fighting men had gathered at Kithtippecanoe.

Alarmed by the Indians' growing militancy, the governor of the Indiana Territory, William Henry Harrison, surrounded the Indian stronghold with a force of 1,000 soldiers. He carried full authority to do whatever was necessary to secure the frontier. At dawn on November 7, 1811, 400 Indian warriors assaulted Harrison's lines. The battle raged for hours, and at day's end, the victorious Harrison counted over 150 warriors dead and countless others wounded. Before retiring to the territorial capital at Vincennes, he burned Kithtippecanoe to the ground.

Over the next several months, Tecumseh's followers, taking advantage of the recent outbreak of the War of 1812 between the United States and England and aided by British troops from Canada, carried out devastating raids across Indiana and southern Michigan. Together, they crushed American armies at Detroit and Fort Nelson and followed up with forays against Fort Wayne. The tide turned, however, at the Battle of the Thames near Detroit, for there Harrison inflicted a grievous defeat on a combined British and Indian force. Among those slain was Tecumseh.

The American victory at the Thames signaled the collapse of Tecumseh's confederacy and an end to Indian resistance in the Old Northwest. Beginning in 1815, American settlers surged once more across Ohio and Indiana, only now they pressed on into Illinois and Michigan. The balance of power in the Old Northwest had decisively shifted.

To the south, the Creek challenged white intruders with similar militancy. As the nineteenth century began, white settlers were pushing onto Creek lands in northwestern Georgia and central Alabama. Although some Creek leaders urged accommodation, others, called Red Sticks, prepared to fight. The embers of this smoldering conflict were fanned into flame by an aggressive Tennessee militia commander named Andrew Jackson. Citing Creek atrocities "which bring fresh to our recollection the influence . . . that raised the scalping knife and tomahawk against our defenseless women and children," Jackson in 1808 urged President Jefferson to endorse a campaign against the Creek. The Tennessee militia, Jackson reported, "pant for the orders of our government to punish a ruthless foe."

Bristling at their treatment by Georgia and Alabama, the Red Sticks carried out a series of frontier raids in the spring and summer of 1813, killing and scalping two white families and taking one woman captive. They capped their campaign with an assault on Fort Mims on the Alabama River, where they killed as many as 500 people, women and children among them. News of that tragedy raised bitter cries for revenge. The Tennessee legislature denounced the "horrid and inhuman murders" and called for proper "atonement," while frontier editors warned that "when the tomahawk and the scalping knife are drawn in the cabins of our peaceful and unsuspecting citizens, it is time, high time to prepare . . . for defense."

At the head of 5,000 Tennessee and Kentucky militia, augmented by Cherokee, Choctaw, and Chickasaw warriors eager to punish their traditional Creek enemies, Jackson launched his long-awaited attack. As he moved south, the ferocity of the fighting grew. David Crockett, one of Jackson's soldiers, later reported that the militia volunteers shot down the Red Sticks "like dogs." The Indians gave like measure in return.

The climactic battle of the Creek War came in March 1814 at Horseshoe Bend, on the Tallapoosa River in central Alabama. There, in the fortified town of Tohopeka, 1,000 Creek warriors made their stand against 1,400 state troops and 600 Cherokee allies. While American cannonfire raked the Creek defenses, the allied Cherokee crossed the river to cut off retreat. In the battle that followed, over 800 Native Americans died, more than in any other single battle in the history of Indian-white warfare.

Jackson followed up his victory with a scorched-earth sweep through the remaining Red Stick towns. With no hope left, Red Eagle, one of the few remaining Red Stick leaders, walked alone into Jackson's camp and addressed the American commander: "General Jackson, I am not afraid of you. I fear no man, for I am a Creek warrior. I have nothing to request in behalf of myself; you can kill me if you desire. But I come to beg you to send for the women and children of the war party, who are now starving in the woods. . . . I am now done fighting."

The Creek war was finished, and Jackson allowed Red Eagle and his followers to return home. But the general was not quite done. In August 1814 he exacted his final revenge by constructing Fort Jackson on the Hickory Ground, the most sacred spot of the Creek nation. Over the following months, he seized 22 million acres, nearly two-thirds of the Creek domain. Before his Indian-fighting days were over, Jackson would acquire for the United States, through treaty or military conquest, nearly three-fourths of Alabama and Florida, a third of Tennessee, and a fifth of Georgia and Mississippi.

Just as Tecumseh's death had signaled the end of Indian resistance in the North, so the Creek's defeat at Horseshoe Bend broke the back of Indian defenses in the South. With all possibility of armed resistance gone, the Native Americans of the Old Southwest gave way before the swelling tide of white settlement.

Perfecting a Democratic Society

Throughout our nation's history, the American people have launched a variety of reform movements aimed at achieving social justice and bringing the conditions of daily life into conformity with democratic ideals. The first of those reform eras occurred in the early nineteenth century.

The Revolutionary Heritage

The reform efforts were inspired by democratic ideals fostered during the Revolution and still fresh in countless Americans' minds. Preeminent among them was the principle of social equality. In part, this meant equality of opportunity, the notion that people should have a chance to rise as far as ability and ambition would carry them. Such an idea was attractive to social democrats, for it spoke of setting privilege aside and giving everyone an equal chance. Social conservatives could embrace it as well, for it could be used to justify the social inequalities that individual effort often produced. Social equality also had a powerful moral dimension, because it implied an equality of worth among individuals, no matter what their social standing might be. Though Americans generally accepted differences of wealth and social position, they were less willing to tolerate social pretension or the arrogant assumption that such differences made some people better than others.

The Evangelical Impulse

More than revolutionary principles lay behind the concern over social justice, for a complementary surge of evangelical religion inspired much of the reform impulse as well. Throughout our history, religion has been a major force in American public life. This was true during the years of the early republic, when a wave of Protestant religious enthusiasm known as the Second Great Awakening swept across the American nation. From its beginnings in the 1790s through much of the nineteenth century, and in settings as different as the Cane Ridge district of backwoods Kentucky and the sophisticated cities of the Northeast, Americans by the tens of thousands sought personal salvation and a sense of social belonging in the shared experience of religious enthusiasm.

Displayed most spectacularly among ordinary folk gathered in Methodist and Baptist camp meetings, the revivals reached across boundaries of class and race. And while spiritual outpourings erupted spontaneously in countless local communities, rough-hewn itinerant preachers, black as well as white, many of them theologically untrained but all of them afire with religious conviction, carried the Gospel message from place to place, in the process knitting networks of religious believers closely together.

In 1809, Benjamin Latrobe, principal architect of the new Capitol building in Washington, D.C., and shrewd observer of the American scene, visited a Methodist camp meeting on the Leesburg Road in northern Virginia, just outside the nation's capital. "As we came within a mile of the meeting ground," Latrobe reported, "we came upon parties of well dressed blacks of both sexes returning on foot towards the city, & of ill dressed white boys hurrying forward.... [Farther on] we could distinguish among the trees, half concealed by the underwood, houses, chaises, light waggons, hacks, & a crowd of men and women, in the midst of whom we presently arrived.... Crowds of negroes & mullatoes tastily dressed stood among the trees, & the groups looked as if any motives but religious ones had assembled them...."

Positioning himself at the head of the clearing, Latrobe watched and listened in fascination as "Mr. Bunn, a blacksmith of G[eorge] Town, one of the most eminent Preachers of the Methodists spoke [with] immense rapidity & exertion ... of the judgement to come." As Bunn proceeded, "a general groaning & shrieking was ... heard from all Quarters" while the preacher "threw out both his arms sideways at full length, & shook himself violently...." In several parts of the Camp, "women were shrieking" while under the stage on which Bunn held forth there erupted "an uncommon bustle & cry ... from some persons who were under conversion."

Every time Bunn pronounced "the stroke of grace," Latrobe continued, he brought his hands together so as to produce an astonishingly loud clap. "The stroke again," Bunn shouted, "and another stroke, and another ... and now it works, it works.... There it is, now she has it, glory! glory! glory!"

Though preaching and the salvation of souls were the central purposes of the camp meetings, Latrobe perceived that they ministered to a variety of other human needs as well. "The illumination of the woods, the novelty of a camp especially to the women and children, the dancing and singing, & the pleasure of a crowd, so tempting to the most fashionable," illustrated the powerful sense of social belonging that such gatherings provided.

Offering a simple message that ordinary folks could readily grasp, the Awakening emphasized the equality of all believers before God, held out the promise of universal salvation, and declared each individual to be responsible for his or her own soul. The power and inclusiveness of that message, driven home by the itinerant preachers, would be registered in the explosive growth of Methodist and Baptist Churches. By mid-century, they would surpass Presbyterians and Congregationalists as the largest religious denominations.

The Awakening had additional implications, for it called on believers to demonstrate their faith by going into the world to lift up the downtrodden and do good works. That religious impulse would provide much of the energy for later ante-bellum reforms such as temperance and abolition (see Chapter 12). Its influence was evident as well in earlier efforts at perfecting American society.

Patterns of Wealth and Poverty

In the early republic, as at other times in the nation's history, ideals jarred awkwardly against social reality. One source of that tension was the contrast between notions of democratic equality and the reality of social class distinctions.

As the nineteenth century began, women continued to hold far less property than men. For the large majority of black slaves, moreover, ownership of anything more than the smallest items of personal property was beyond reach. Though the condition of free blacks such as Ben and Phyllis was better, they, too, held little of the country's wealth.

Among white males, property was most broadly shared in rural areas of the North, where free labor and family-farm agriculture predominated, and least so in the South, where the planters' control of slave labor and the best land permitted them to monopolize the region's wealth. As we have seen, the class structure was sharply drawn in the port cities. The most even distribution of wealth existed on the edges of white settlement in Trans-Appalachia, but there it was an equality of want. As the frontier developed, differences in wealth appeared there as well.

Though America contained no destitute underclass (at least among its white citizens) such as could be found in the cities and countryside of Europe, poverty was real and was increasing. In the South, it was most evident among poor whites living on the sandy pine barrens of the backcountry. In the North, the port cities held growing numbers of the poor. Boston artisans and shopkeepers who together had owned 20 percent of the city's wealth in 1700, for example, held scarcely half as much a century later.

Recurring recessions hit the urban poor with particular force, and winter added to hard times as shipping slowed and jobs disappeared. During the winter of 1805, New York's Mayor DeWitt Clinton worried publicly about the fate—as well as the potentially disruptive behavior—of 10,000 impoverished New Yorkers, and asked the state legislature for help. During the winter of 1814–1815, relief agencies assisted nearly one-fifth of the city's population.

Even in rural New England and southeastern Pennsylvania, an underclass of transient and propertyless people was growing. The "strolling poor," they were called—men, and sometimes women, unable to secure land of their own and thus forced to roam the countryside searching for work.

Three other groups were conspicuous among the nation's poor. One consisted of old Revolutionary War veterans like Long Bill Scott, who had found poverty as well as adventure in the war. State and federal governments were peppered with petitions from grizzled veterans describing their misery and seeking relief. Women and children also suffered disproportionately from poverty. Annual censuses of almshouse residents in New York City from 1816 to 1821 consistently listed more women and children than men.

For every American who actually suffered poverty's effects, there were several others living just beyond its reach, their margin of safety alarmingly thin. Just how thin became clear during the depression of 1819–1822. Triggered by a financial panic created by the unsound practices of hundreds of newly chartered state banks, a deep depression settled over the land, generating bankruptcies and sending unemployment soaring. In upstate New York, the pay of turnpike workers sank from 75 to 12 cents a day. In Ohio, the governor reported in 1820 that "the greater part of our mercantile citizens are in a state of bankruptcy," while "the citizens of every class are … delinquent in discharging even the most trifling of debts." In the South, farms and plantations were abandoned as cotton and tobacco exports fell. By the early 1820s, the depression was lifting, but it left behind broken fortunes and shattered dreams.

Alleviating Poverty and Distress

Alleviating poverty was one goal of the early reformers. In New York City, private and public authorities established more than 100 charitable and relief agencies to aid orphans and widows, aged females and young prostitutes, immigrants and imprisoned debtors, juvenile delinquents and poverty-stricken seamen. Across the nation, a "charitable revolution" increased benevolent institutions from 50 in 1790 to nearly 2,000 by 1820. Most of these ventures drew a distinction between the "worthy poor," respectable folk who were victims of circumstance and merited assistance, and the "idle" or "vicious poor," who were deemed to lack character and who thus deserved their fate. Many Americans believed such distinctions were real and discoverable. No matter that a New York commission in 1823 found only 43 able-bodied adults (37 women and 9 men) among the 851 inmates of the city's almshouses or that another listing of supposed ne'er-do-wells included a variety of disabled Revolutionary War veterans, abandoned infants, and indigent immigrants recently arrived from Europe. New Yorkers had not yet connected pauperism with the changing conditions of urban life.

Poverty was not the only target of public and private reform. Municipal authorities and private charities also established orphanages for children, asylums for the insane, and hospitals for the sick. Most efforts were limited and short-lived, but they attested to the continuing strength of revolutionary and religious ideals, and provided a foundation for the more ambitious reform efforts that would come several decades later.

Women's Lives

Though women's lives were not markedly altered during these years, changes that helped set the stage for later, more dramatic breakthroughs did occur.

Divorce was one area where women achieved more equal treatment. When a neighbor asked John Backus, a silversmith in Great Barrington, Massachusetts, why he kicked and struck his wife, John replied that it was partly because his father had often treated his mother in the same way. We do not know whether John's mother tolerated such abuse, but his wife did not. She complained of cruelty and secured a divorce. Her determination was not unique, for more and more women were following her example.

The process of divorce was not easy, for most states allowed it only on the ground of adultery. South Carolina did not permit it at all. Moreover, women typically had to present detailed evidence of their husbands' infidelities and face the discomfort of an all-male court. Accusations of a wife's transgressions, by contrast, were more easily proven in court.

Still, divorce was becoming more available to women. In Massachusetts during the decade after independence, 50 percent more women than men filed for divorce, with almost exactly identical rates of success. Part of the explanation for the increase lay in the war's disruptions, which led large numbers of men to desert their families and thus encouraged their wives to take action. It seems just as certain, however, that women shared the values of individualism and equality and from them developed rising expectations of marriage.

Changes also occurred in women's education, reflecting a special concern for women's place in the new republic. Given women's special role as Republican Mothers, that is, as keepers of public morality and nurturers of future citizens, young women would have to prepare for the responsibilities that motherhood would bring. Judith Sargeant Murray, along with other women, demanded even more of women's education. In a series of essays published in the 1790s under the title *The Gleaner,* Murray criticized parents who "pointed their daughters" exclusively toward marriage and dependence. "I would give my daughters every

Female academies in the early republic provided young middle- and upper-class women with the knowledge and skills necessary for their roles as Republican Mothers. (Jacob Marling, The Crowning of Flora, *1816/The Chrysler Museum of Art, Norfolk, VA, Gift of Edgar William and Bernice Chrysler Garbisch 80.118.20)*

accomplishment which I thought proper," Murray wrote. "They should be enabled to procure for themselves the necessaries of life; independence should be placed within their grasp. A woman," she concluded, "should reverence herself."

Between 1790 and 1820, a number of female academies were established. Most, such as Susanna Rowson's Young Ladies Academy of Philadelphia, were located in northeastern cities. Timothy Dwight, the future president of Yale, opened his academy at Greenfield Hill in Connecticut to girls and taught them the same subjects he taught boys, at the same time and in the same room, but he was the exception. Most proposals for female education assumed that the curriculum should be different and less demanding than for boys. Though Benjamin Rush prescribed bookkeeping, reading, geography, vocal music ("because it soothes cares and is good for the lungs"), and history as proper elements of a girl's education, traditionalists such as the Boston minister John Gardiner were decidedly more conservative. Warning that intellectual activity would unsex women, he declared that "Women of masculine minds have generally masculine manners, and a

robustness of person ill calculated to inspire the tender passions." Even the most ardent supporters of female learning insisted that education was primarily important so that women might function more effectively within their traditional, domestic sphere. As Judith Sargeant Murray explained, the happiness of the nation was based on the happiness of families, and that depended in turn on "daughters of Columbia," educated women who would "fill with honor the parts allotted to them."

The evangelical impulse that caught so many women up in its enthusiasm and that did much to promote values of individualism and equality actually reduced women's roles in the evangelical churches. Whereas women had previously served as religious exhorters and participated actively in Baptist and Methodist church governance, they found themselves increasingly marginalized as those evangelical denominations grew in membership, strove to become more socially acceptable, and adopted the rigidly gendered rules that older denominations such as the Presbyterians and Congregationalists had always followed. Less frequently were Methodist and Baptist women welcomed as equal participants in matters of

At Agricultural Fairs

Though this Pennsylvania scene features cattle rather than merino sheep, it reveals the interests of farmers and more elegantly attired gentlemen in the commercial benefits of "scientific" livestock breeding. Note what appear to be plowing contests in the background. (John A. Woodside, A Country Fair in Pennsylvania, *1824, from the Collection of Harry T. Peters, Jr.)*

During the years of the early republic, men and women gathered together in a variety of settings to fashion a sense of common purpose, pursue their common goals, and improve their lives. Few occasions during these years touched the fabric of American life more closely than did agricultural fairs, precursors of the county fairs that have served as gathering places for the American people throughout the nation's history.

In the autumn of 1808, Elkanah Watson, a prosperous businessman turned gentleman farmer, led his two prize merino sheep onto the village common of Pittsfield, a small town hidden away in the Berkshire hills of western Massachusetts. His purpose, Watson explained, was to offer his sheep for public inspection and thus promote the improvement of local agriculture. "I have got completely infected with the Spanish Sheep mania," Watson observed, "& have made great efforts ... to promote a general diffusion of the breed by the Most Active Measures." "Merino-mad" Elkanah Watson was not alone in his fascination with this special breed of sheep, for reformers in the United States and Britain saw the promise of newfound agricultural prosperity in these fine-fleeced animals.

Watson's ambition encompassed more than merino sheep, however, for his goal was nothing less than the scientific transformation of American agriculture. Others shared Watson's sense of urgency. During the 1790s, leading citizens such as John Adams and Robert Livingston had created agricultural associations such as the Massachusetts Society for Promoting Agriculture and the New York Society for the Promotion of Agriculture, Manufactures, and the Arts. Recognizing that such elite societies with their genteel members, impressive agricultural libraries, and erudite publications had little relevance for the everyday lives of most American farmers, Watson founded a different kind of association, the Berkshire Agriculture Society in 1810. It was intended to be more "congenial to the genius of our country" by embracing "all the respectable farmers" and giving "direction to measures of general utility." Scarcely a year after its founding, the Berkshire Agriculture Society mounted its first agricultural fair. Thus was born an enduring American institution that mixed competition for the biggest watermelon, the heftiest hog, and the most appetizing apple pie with entertainment, the latest in scientific agriculture, and exhibitions of arts and crafts. Though himself a gentleman farmer of patrician demeanor, Watson was concerned about the backwardness of traditional agricultural practices and the isolated tedium of rural life. Part national visionary, part huckster, and part enthusiast for a scientifically based, commercially prosperous agriculture, Watson searched for ways to "excite a lively spirit of competition" and thus energize his rural neighbors. By appealing to the self-pride and patriotism of rural folk, as well as to their need for entertainment and common fellowship, Watson's efforts succeeded beyond his fondest hopes. Within a few years, rural folk by the thousands were converging on the annual Berkshire Fairs.

They gazed in wonder at the half-mile-long parade that announced the fair's beginning, a procession "splendid, novel, and imposing, beyond anything of the kind, ever exhibited in America." Led by a musical band, the parade included 69 oxen drawing a huge plow, members of the Agricultural Society marching in solemn array, mobile platforms carrying textile machinery and other instruments of local manufacturing, and ranks of rural artisans and mechanics displaying the banners and tools of their trades. Costumed marshals resplendent on prancing steeds signaled the parade's end.

Once assembled, country folk roamed the fairgrounds admiring the displays of farm animals and equipment, debating the latest in agricultural techniques, and cheering their favorites in foot races and plowing contests, while hawkers peddling a variety of gewgaws and medical nostrums added excitement to the occasion. There were limits to the activities that Watson's stern management allowed. "Innocent recreations will be permitted," he declared chastely, "but everything tending to immorality will be discountenanced." Still, there was plenty to provide entertainment and enlightenment for adults and children alike.

Elkanah Watson. Known as the father of country agricultural fairs, Watson combined a keen sense of self-promotion with an interest in scientific agriculture and rural community development. (The Granger Collection, New York)

In the afternoon, award presentations were held in the town church with engraved silver plates and ornate certificates arranged, communion-like, on a cloth-covered table in front of the pulpit. The purpose, as Watson explained, was "not only to excite an ardent spirit of emulation among the candidates," but also to "produce some tincture of envy, so as to call forth more extended efforts." As the winners stood proudly before the assembled throng, prizes in hand, the band struck up a national air, while "every countenance beamed with pleasure." In 1812, members of the Agricultural Society and their wives attended religious services where a minister invoked God's blessing on the festivities, a specially composed patriotic ode was read, and the gathering joined in a stirring agricultural hymn. In acknowledgment of women's contributions to the rural economy, the 1813 fair offered $60 in prizes for the most elegantly woven fabrics. Festivities concluded with an "Agricultural Ball," the attending women appropriately clothed in home-made gowns and the hall festooned with heads of wheat, artificial flowers, and boughs of hemlock. Every aspect of the occasion, noted Watson approvingly, contributed to "an interesting pastoral effect."

As word of the Pittsfield fair spread among rural Americans, scores of agricultural fairs, many of them supported by financial assistance from state governments, sprang up in counties from Maine to Virginia and as far west as Illinois. At once educational, social, recreational, ceremonial, and commercial in their purposes, agricultural fairs resonated with the values and concerns of ordinary Americans in the early years of the republic. In the years ahead, they would evolve into a distinctive American institution, the county fair, sites of some of the most participatory and profitable gatherings of the American people.

church discipline, while they were more often charged with "disorderliness" and condemned by their male brethren for "disobedience." Under siege was a once robust tradition of piety in which men and women discerned spiritual truth equally and ministered to each other's souls.

Race, Slavery, and the Limits of Reform

As we have seen (Chapter 7), the Revolution initiated the end of slavery in the northern states and raised challenges to its continued existence in the Upper South. As the new century began, however, antislavery sentiment was declining, while private manumission slowed as well. The reasons were several. The gradual abolition of slavery in the North soothed many consciences, while in the South, the spread of cotton increased the value of slave labor.

Equally important were two slave rebellions that generated intense alarm among American whites. Panic-stricken whites fleeing the Caribbean island of Santo Domingo in 1791 carried word to the North American mainland of the black Haitians' successful rebellion against a French colonial army of 25,000. The news spread terror through the South, where rumors abounded that Haitian incendiaries would soon be landing. Immediately, southern whites tightened their Black Codes, cut the importation of new slaves from the Caribbean, and sought out malcontents among their own chattels. Colonial rebellions were fine, but not when they set blacks against white authority.

Though the Haitian rebellion was not immediately successful, it began a long struggle that would create the first black republic in the Americas before Thomas Jefferson left the presidency.

A second shock followed in the summer of 1800, when another rebellion just outside Richmond, Virginia, was nipped in the bud. Gabriel Prosser, a 24-year-old slave, had devised a plan to arm 1,000 slaves for an assault on the city. Prosser and his accomplices were native-born African Americans who spoke English, worked at skilled jobs that gave them considerable personal freedom (and thus opportunity to lay their plans), and knew enough about American independence to speak confidently of freedom and equality. A drenching downpour delayed the attack, providing time for several black house servants (subsequently granted their freedom by the Virginia Assembly) to sound the alarm before the conspirators could act. No white lives were lost, but blacks paid a heavy price as alarmed whites exacted their revenge. Scores of slaves and free blacks were arrested, and 25 suspects, including Prosser, were hanged at the personal order of Governor James Monroe. The carnage saddened Thomas Jefferson. "There is strong sentiment that there has been hanging enough," he wrote to Monroe. "The other states and the world at large will forever condemn us if we … go one step beyond absolute necessity." In the midst of panic, however, necessity was hard to define.

In the early nineteenth century, antislavery appeals all but disappeared from the South. Even religious groups that had once denounced slavery now grew quiet. "A large majority of the people of the southern states," declared Congressman Peter Early of Georgia in 1806, "do not consider slavery as a crime. They do not consider it immoral to hold human flesh in bondage. Many deprecate slavery as an evil, as a political evil," he continued, "but not as a crime." White southerners at the time of the Civil War would be saying much the same thing.

In the North, sentiment was increasingly conciliatory toward slave owners. Most of slavery's critics assumed that private manumission was the only safe approach, that it should be gradual, and that freed blacks should be relocated to colonies in Africa. The American Colonization Society, founded in 1816, typified these attitudes. Many of its supporters, while detesting slavery, believed that the two races could not coexist together. Others were slaveholders who saw in colonization a convenient way of reducing the free black population and eliminating troublesome bondsmen. The Colonization Society never sent many blacks abroad, but it did help allay white anxieties.

During the half century following independence, strong and growing black communities appeared in the port cities. As the lives of Ben Thompson and Phyllis Sherman revealed, emancipation in the North and the increase of freedmen in the Upper South enabled increasing numbers of African Americans to leave their masters' homes and seek the companionship of other people of color in places such as Boston, New York, Philadelphia, and Baltimore. On the eve of independence, 4,000 slaves and a few hundred free blacks had

Blacks and Slavery, 1790–1820

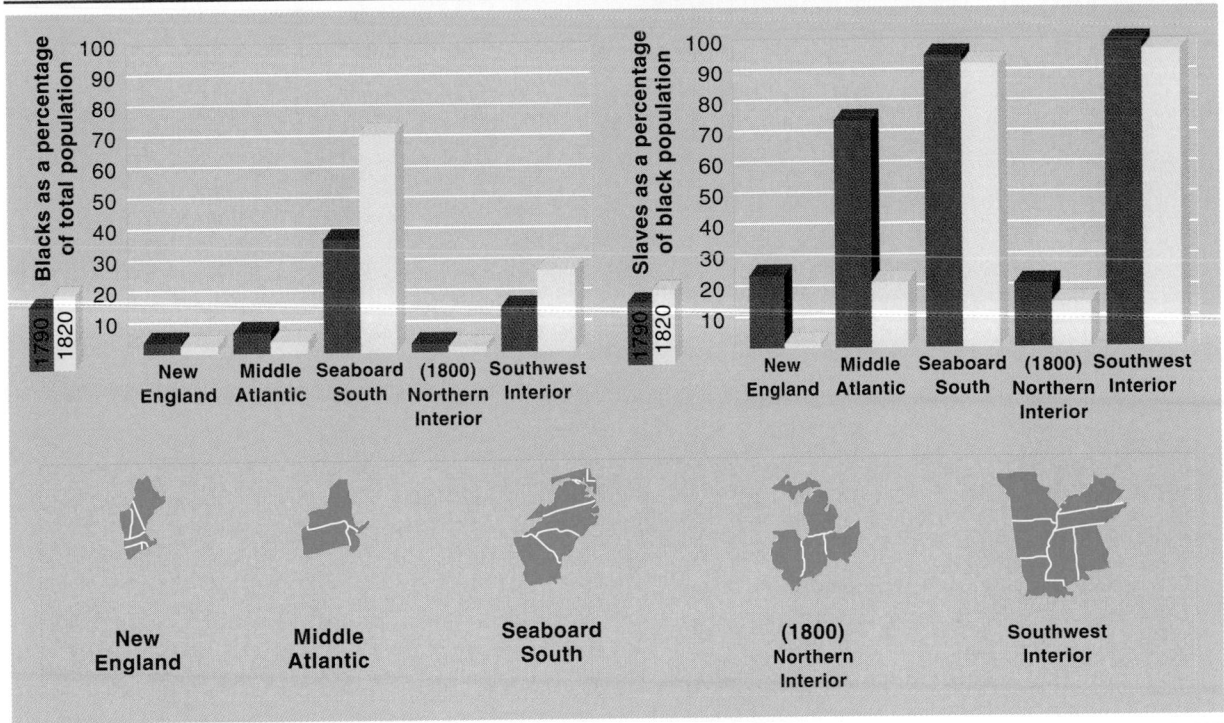

Though regions had differed in the importance of slavery and the number of blacks in their population as the Revolutionary War ended, those differences increased significantly over the next 30 years. Source: U.S. Bureau of the Census.

called the four port cities home; 50 years later, more than 30,000 African Americans did so.

The men who came sought employment as laborers or sailors, the women as domestics. There were hundreds like Alexander Giles, a free black Philadelphia seaman who had been born in 1777 in nearby Kent County, Delaware, and Randall Shepherd, who had made his way north from Nansemond County, Virginia, in 1798. The development of black neighborhoods reflected both white discrimination and blacks' ardent desire for their own communities. In rural areas, free blacks lived in isolation, as Phyllis Sherman had; in the port cities, black communities provided protection and greatly improved the chances of finding a marriage partner, establishing a family, and participating in the activities of community organizations.

Family formation was eased because many of the migrants were women, thus correcting a long-standing urban imbalance in the black population. Former slaves often created extended households that included relatives, friends, and boarders. As

circumstances allowed, single-family units were formed. By 1820, most blacks in the northern cities lived in autonomous households.

As their numbers grew, African Americans created an array of organizations independent of white control and capable of serving the needs of the black community. Schools provided education to black children excluded from white academies, mutual aid societies offered help to the down and out, and fraternal associations provided venues for fellowship and mutual support. It was black churches, however, that quickly emerged as the institutional cornerstones of black community life, a position they would continue to occupy throughout the nation's history.

Following the Revolution, growing numbers of free blacks joined integrated Methodist and Baptist congregations in cities such as Philadelphia and New York, drawn by their strongly biblical theology, enthusiastic forms of worship, and frequently stated opposition to slavery. As the numbers of black communicants grew, however, they found

In his watercolor of a black Methodist church meeting, Paul Svinin, a traveler from Russia, reveals his amazement at the physical emotion displayed by the worshipers. "African" churches and other organizations were rare before 1800 but grew steadily in the ensuing decades. (The Metropolitan Museum of Art, Rogers Fund, 1942 (42.95.19))

themselves segregated in separate church galleries, excluded from leadership roles, and even denied communion in white-dominated congregations. Whereas many black Christians were reluctant to withdraw from biracial congregations, others sought opportunity to control their own religious lives, first by forming their own churches within the Methodist and Baptist folds, and then by creating their own denominational structures.

In 1794, a small group of black Methodists led by Richard Allen, a slave–born, black itinerant preacher, organized the Bethel African American Methodist Church in Philadelphia. Originally established as an integral part of American Methodism, Allen's congregation moved toward separatism, first by requiring that only "Africans and descendants of the African race" be admitted to membership, and finally, in 1815, by rejecting denominational oversight altogether. A year later, the congregation joined with a similarly independent Negro Methodist congregation in Baltimore to form the African Methodist Episcopal Church—the first independent black denomination in the United States. Though never as numerous as black Methodists, black Baptists established their own separate churches during the early nineteenth century in places such as Boston (1805), Philadelphia (1810), New Orleans (1826), and St. Louis (1827).

Located in areas of densest black, urban settlement, these churches not only nurtured distinctive African American forms of Christian worship, but also provided education to black children via Sunday and day schools and burial sites for blacks excluded from other cemeteries. Equally important, black churches provided secure sites where the basic rituals of family and community life—marriages and birth announcements, funerals and anniversaries—could be celebrated, and where community norms could be enforced. By the 1830s, a rich cultural and institutional life had taken root in the black neighborhoods of American cities.

White hostility, however, remained a reality of black urban life. Slavery's abolition might actually have increased white enmity in the North, especially during hard times when free blacks competed with white laborers for employment. Working-class whites were unnerved as well by the growing black competition for cheap housing. Overt violence against free blacks was infrequent during the early decades of the century, but even so, blacks found themselves increasingly segregated in residence, employment, and social life. In the early republic, race as well as gender and class continued to separate Americans from each other and reveal the limits of America's emerging democratic faith.

A Foreign Policy for the New Nation

During the early decades of the nineteenth century, the Jeffersonians struggled to fashion a foreign policy appropriate for the expanding agrarian nation. They had several goals in mind: protecting American interests on the high seas, clearing America's western territories of foreign troops, and breaking free from the country's historic dependence on Europe. Those goals were not easily accomplished, yet by the 1820s, aided by changes taking place across the Atlantic, the Jeffersonians had fashioned a new relationship with Europe. In the Monroe Doctrine of 1823, they projected a momentous new role for the United States within the Americas as well.

Jeffersonian Principles

Jeffersonian foreign policy was based on the doctrine of "no entangling alliances" with Europe that Washington had articulated in his Farewell Address of 1796. In the Jeffersonians' minds, England was still the principal enemy, but France was now suspect as well. By the time the Jeffersonians took office, the French Revolution had run its course and ended in the consulate of Napoleon. Although some Jeffersonians still harbored hopes for French liberty, most were sobered by Napoleon's dictatorial rule.

Second, the Jeffersonians emphasized the importance of overseas commerce to the security and prosperity of the agrarian nation. Overseas trade provided markets for America's agricultural produce and fetched manufactured goods in return. While the Federalists had nurtured domestic manufacturing by offering tariff protection against European competition, the Jeffersonians hoped to keep large-scale manufacturing in Europe, because they feared the concentrations of wealth and the dependent working classes that domestic manufacturing would bring.

Maintaining peace was a third goal of the Jeffersonians' foreign policy because they feared war's effects on democratic liberty. Not only did war kill people and destroy property, but it also inflamed politics, stifled free speech, increased the public debt, and expanded governmental power.

While seeking peace, the Jeffersonians understood the dangers lurking throughout the Atlantic world and knew that protecting the nation's interests might require force. Between 1801 and 1805, Jefferson dispatched naval vessels to the Mediterranean to defend American commerce against the Barbary States (Algiers, Morocco, Tripoli, and Tunis). War, however, was to be regarded as a policy of last resort. The Jeffersonians' handling of the crisis leading into the War of 1812 against Great Britain illustrates how eagerly, and in this case how futilely, they sought to avoid conflict.

Struggling for Neutral Rights

After a brief interlude of peace, European war resumed in 1803. Once again Britain and France seized American shipping. Britain's overwhelming naval superiority made its attacks especially serious. Britain's continuing refusal to negotiate on issues of impressment, occupation of the Great Lakes fur-trading posts, and reopening the West

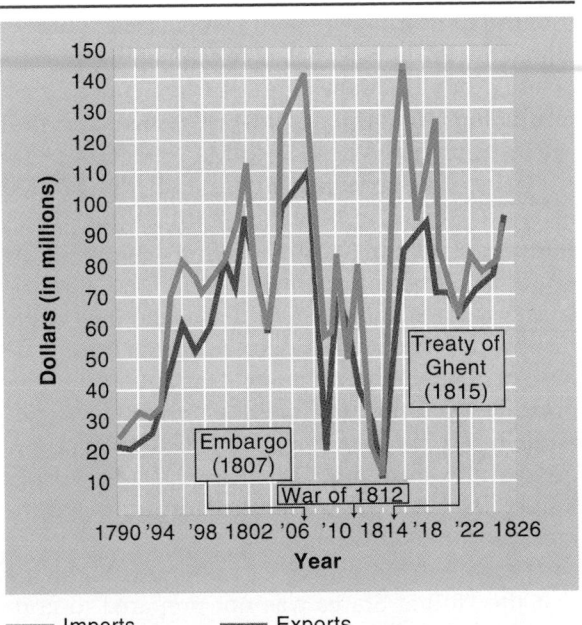

American Foreign Trade, 1790–1825

American overseas trade fluctuated dramatically as tensions with England and France ebbed and flowed. Source: U.S. Bureau of the Census.

The tranquillity of Crowninshield wharf in Salem, Massachusetts, gives evidence of the ships idled and docks emptied by Jefferson's embargo. (George Ropes, Crowninshield Wharf, 1805/The Essex Institute, Salem, Massachusetts)

Indian trade added to tension between the two nations.

In response to increasing British seizures of American shipping, Congress, in April 1806, passed the Non-Importation Act, prohibiting the importation of British goods that could be produced domestically or acquired elsewhere. A month later, Britain replied by declaring a blockade of the European coast. Threatened by Britain's action, Napoleon answered with the Berlin Decree, forbidding all commerce and communication with the British Isles.

Tension between Britain and the United States reached the breaking point in June 1807, when the British warship *Leopard* stopped the American frigate *Chesapeake* off the Virginia coast, claimed that four crew members were British deserters, and demanded that they be handed over. When the American commander protested that the crew members were Americans and refused, the *Leopard* opened fire, killing three men and wounding 18. After the *Chesapeake* limped back into port with the story, cries of outrage rang across the land.

Fearing the approach of war and recognizing that the United States was not prepared to confront Britain, Jefferson decided to withdraw American ships from the Atlantic. In December 1807, Congress passed the Embargo Act, forbidding all American vessels from sailing for foreign ports. It was one of Jefferson's most ill-fated decisions.

The embargo had relatively little effect. British shipping actually profited from the withdrawal of American competition, and British importers supplied their agricultural needs from Latin America. The embargo's domestic impact, however, was far-reaching. American exports fell 80 percent in a year, while imports dropped by more than half. New England was hardest hit. In ports such as Salem, Boston, and Providence, depression settled in as ships rocked idly at the wharves and thousands of workers went unemployed.

Up and down the coast, communities dependent on overseas commerce openly violated the embargo. Efforts to police it proved futile, for the government could not close off either the Atlantic coast or the long northern border across which large quantities of American goods were smuggled into Canada. In Plattsburgh, New York, on Lake Champlain, federal officials declared martial law and sent in troops in an effort to control the situation. The result was guerrilla skirmishing as local citizens fired on U.S. revenue boats and recaptured confiscated goods.

Throughout the largely Federalist Northeast, bitterness threatened to escalate into open rebellion. Connecticut's governor, in words reminiscent of the Virginia and Kentucky Resolutions, warned that whenever Congress exceeded its authority, the states were duty-bound "to interpose their protecting shield between the rights and liberties of the people and the assumed power of the general government."

In the election of 1808, the Federalists rebounded after nearly a decade's decline. James Madison handily succeeded Jefferson in the presidency, but the Federalist candidate, C. C. Pinckney, garnered 47 electoral votes. The Federalists made gains in Congress and recaptured several state legislatures as well.

Faced with the embargo's ineffectiveness abroad and its disastrous consequences at home, Congress repealed the measure in 1809. Over the next several years, Congress tried more limited trade restrictions aimed at reducing British and French attacks on American shipping. When these failed as well, war fever continued to mount.

The War of 1812

The loudest calls for war came from the West and the South. The election of 1810 had brought to Congress a new group of western and southern leaders, firmly Republican in their party loyalty, but impatient with the administration's bumbling policy and convinced of the need for tougher measures. The War Hawks, they were called, and an impressive group they proved to be: Henry Clay and Richard Johnson of Kentucky, John Calhoun and Langdon Cheves from South Carolina, Felix Grundy of Tennessee, and Peter Porter from western New York.

For too long, the War Hawks cried, the United States had tolerated Britain's presence on American soil, encouragement of Indian raids, and attacks on American commerce. Their language echoed as well with talk of territorial expansion, north into Canada and south into Spanish Florida. Most of all, these young, nationalistic War Hawks resented British arrogance and America's continuing humiliation. No government, they warned, could last unless it protected its people's interests and upheld the nation's honor. Nor could the Jeffersonian party survive unless it proved able to govern.

Responding to the growing pressure, President Madison finally asked Congress for a declaration of war on June 1, 1812. Opposition came entirely from the New England and Middle Atlantic states—ironically, the regions British policies affected most adversely—whereas the South and West voted solidly for war. Seldom had sectional alignments been more sharply drawn.

Seldom also had American foreign policy proved more ineffective. Madison decided to set economic coercion aside just as the British government, under increasing pressure to seek accommodation, suspended the European blockade. Three days later, unaware of Britain's action, the United States declared war.

The war itself was a curious affair. Britain successfully fended off several American forays into Canada. In spite of American braggadocio, Canada proved secure. As the war progressed, Britain launched a series of attacks across the Canadian border, along the Gulf Coast, and inland from the Atlantic. Once again, the British navy blockaded American coastal waters, while British landing parties launched punishing attacks up and down the East Coast. On August 14, a British force occupied Washington, torched the Capitol and the president's mansion (which became known as the White House after being repaired and whitewashed), and sent the president, Congress, and a panic-stricken American army fleeing into Virginia. Britain, however, did not press its advantage, for it was preoccupied with Napoleon's armies in Europe and wanted to end the American quarrel.

On the American side, emotions ran high among both the war's Federalist critics and Republican supporters. In Baltimore, on the night of June 22, 1812, a Republican crowd demolished the printing office of the *Federal-Republican,* a local Federalist newspaper. The attack reflected not only partisan politics, but also Republican working-class animosity toward Federalist "aristocrats" and the eagerness of working people to support the job-creating war. In late July, after copies of the *Federal-Republican* again appeared on Baltimore's streets, a crowd of more than 1,000 men and women once more surrounded the paper's office. Fifty armed Federalists were there to defend it. When the Federalist defenders opened fire, the crowd rolled up a cannon and sent a round of grapeshot into the building. Several people lay dead on both sides before the militia finally arrived to cart the Federalists off to the safety of jail.

The bloody encounter was not over yet, for on the following night, a crowd assembled in front of the city jail, brushed aside the mayor's pleas to disperse, and seized ten prisoners, including James Lingan, an old Revolutionary War general. The enraged mob beat Lingan and several others to death and left the bodies, stripped of their fine clothing, sprawling in the street.

The War of 1812

The War of 1812 scarcely touched the lives of most Americans, but areas around the Great Lakes, Lake Champlain, Chesapeake Bay, and the Gulf Coast witnessed significant fighting.

Though the Baltimore riots were not duplicated elsewhere, emotions continued to run high throughout the country. In Federalist-dominated New England, opposition to the war veered toward outright disloyalty. In December 1814, delegates from the five New England states met at Hartford, Connecticut, to debate proposals for secession. Cooler heads prevailed, but before adjourning, the Hartford Convention asserted the right of a state "to interpose its authority" against "unconstitutional" acts of the government. Now it was New England's turn to play with the nullification fire. As the war dragged on, Federalist fortunes soared in the Northeast, while elsewhere bitterness grew over New England's disloyalty.

The Hartford Convention

Resolved. That the following amendments of the constitution of the United States be recommended to the states....

First. Representatives and direct taxes shall be apportioned among the several states ... according to their respective numbers of free persons ... excluding Indians not taxed, and all other persons.

Second. No new state shall be admitted into the Union by Congress ... without the concurrence of two thirds of both houses.

Third. Congress shall not have power to lay any embargo on the ships or vessels of the citizens of the United States, in the ports or harbours thereof, for more than sixty days....

Fifth. Congress shall not make or declare war, or authorize acts of hostility against any foreign nation, without the concurrence of two thirds of both houses, except such acts of hostility be in defence of the territories of the United States when actually invaded.

Sixth. No person who shall hereafter be naturalized, shall be eligible as a member of the senate or house of representatives of the United States, nor capable of holding any civil office under the authority of the United States.

Seventh. The same person shall not be elected president of the United States a second time; nor shall the president be elected from the same state two terms in succession.

Before the war ended, American forces won several impressive victories, among them Commander Oliver Hazard Perry's defeat of the British fleet on Lake Erie in 1813. The most dramatic American triumph was Andrew Jackson's smashing victory in 1815 over an attacking British force at New Orleans. It had nothing to do with the war's outcome, however, for it occurred after preliminary terms of peace had already been signed.

Tiring of the contest and increasingly concerned about affairs in Europe, Britain's Foreign Secretary Lord Castlereagh offered to negotiate peace. Madison eagerly accepted, and on Christmas Eve in 1814, at Ghent, Belgium, the two sides reached agreement. The treaty resolved almost nothing, for it ignored impressment, blockades, neutral rights, and American access to Canadian fisheries. Britain did agree to evacuate the western posts, but other than that, the treaty simply ended the conflict, provided for an exchange of prisoners and the restoration of conquered territory, and called for several joint commissions to deal with the lingering disputes.

Still, the war left its mark on the American nation. It made Andrew Jackson a national hero and established him as a political leader of major importance. The American people, moreover, regarded the contest as a "Second War of American Independence" that finally secured the nation from outside interference.

Following 1815, the nation turned its energies primarily toward the task of internal development—occupying the continent, building the economy, and reforming American society. At the same time, European nations, increasingly occupied with their own internal problems of unification and economic change, began what would prove to be nearly a century free of general war. Finally, the focus of European colonialism was shifting toward Africa and Asia, and that diverted European attention from the Americas as well. In the past, European wars had drawn in the American people; in the twentieth century, they would do so again. For the remainder of the nineteenth century, however, that fateful link was broken.

The United States and the Americas

While disengaging from Europe, the Jeffersonians fashioned new policies for Latin America that would guide the nation's hemispheric relations for years to come. Although the American people had given little thought to Europe's Latin American colonies prior to 1800, they voiced their support when those colonies began their struggles for independence from Spain and Portugal in 1808. It was flattering to have leaders such as Simón Bolívar hold the United States up as a model for Latin American liberation, and North Americans were

A British cartoon shows President Madison spilling official papers as he flees the burning capital, while citizens react with sarcastic comments during the British attack on Washington in 1814. (Anne S. K. Brown Military Collection, Brown University Library)

happy to see European colonialism further weakened. What is more, independent nations in Latin America held out the promise of increased trade.

Though initially hesitant to recognize the newly independent governments of Colombia, Mexico, Chile, and Argentina, primarily for fear of disrupting delicate efforts then under way to secure Florida from Spain, President Monroe finally sent Congress a message proposing formal recognition of the new Latin American republics. Congress quickly agreed, and over the next several years, the United States established diplomatic relations with seven Latin American nations.

Trouble arose, however, in November 1822, when the Quadruple Alliance (France, Austria, Russia, and Prussia) talked of a plan to help Spain regain its American possessions. Prospects of a resurgent Spanish empire alarmed Great Britain as well as the United States, and in August 1823,

British Foreign Secretary George Canning broached the idea of Anglo-American cooperation to thwart Spain's intentions.

Secretary of State John Quincy Adams opposed the idea. Son of the former Federalist president, Adams had joined the Jeffersonian camp some years before as part of the continuing exodus from the Federalist party. In keeping with the new spirit of nationalism following the War of 1812 and his own suspicion of British intentions, Adams declared that the United States should not "come in as a cockboat in the wake of the British man-of-war." He urged independent action based on two principles: a sharp separation between the Old World and the New, and the United States' dominance in the Western Hemisphere.

Monroe agreed that the United States should issue its own policy statement. In his annual message of December 1823, he outlined a new Latin

American policy. Though known as the Monroe Doctrine, its content was of Adams's devising.

Monroe asserted four basic principles: (1) the American continents were closed to new European colonization, (2) the political systems of the Americas were separate from those of Europe, (3) the United States would consider as dangerous to its peace and safety any attempts to extend Europe's political influence into the Western Hemisphere, and (4) the United States would neither interfere with existing colonies in the New World nor meddle in the internal affairs of Europe.

When Monroe issued his doctrine, it had little effect, for the United States possessed neither the economic nor the military power to enforce it. By the end of the nineteenth century when the nation's might had increased, however, it would become clear what a fateful turning point in the history of the Americas Monroe's declaration had been.

Politics in Transition

For two decades following Jefferson's election in 1800, the Jeffersonian Republicans monopolized the presidency and dominated Congress, while the Federalist party, its reputation damaged by charges of disloyalty during the War of 1812 and its continu-

ing "aristocratic" image, gradually collapsed. By the late 1820s, however, the Jeffersonian ascendancy was at an end and the Federalist-Jeffersonian party system was in disarray.

As the old, gentry-based politics declined, a new, democratic system centered in the states emerged to take its place. It was in the states that governments acted decisively on people's lives, claimed their attention, and lured voters in extraordinary numbers to the polls. It was there that lingering vestiges of gentry elitism came under sharpest attack and assertions of political equality were most forcefully expressed. And it was in the states that a younger generation of political leaders, uninhibited by their elders' fear of party faction, first learned how to create sophisticated political parties capable of managing a new kind of democratic electoral politics. By the end of the 1820s, America stood poised on the threshold of a new political era.

Division Among the Jeffersonians

With the Federalists in disarray following the War of 1812, the Jeffersonian Republicans stood triumphant, their ranks swollen by fresh recruits in the East and the admission of new states in the West. The Jeffersonians' success, however, proved their undoing, for no single party could contain

Part street theater, part civic process, electoral politics generated excitement—at least for white males—during the early nineteenth century, as this Philadelphia scene reveals. (Historical Society of Pennsylvania, Philadelphia)

the nation's swelling diversity of economic and social interests, its increasing sectional differences, or the personal ambitions of a new generation of political leaders.

In response to growing pressures from the West and Northeast, as well as to nationalist sentiment stimulated by the War of 1812, Madison's administration launched a Federalist-like program of national development. In March 1816, President Madison signed a bill creating a second Bank of the United States (the first Bank's charter had expired in 1811), intended to stimulate economic expansion and regulate the loose currency-issuing practices of the country's countless state-chartered banks. At Madison's urging, the Congress, in December, also passed the first protective tariff in American history, a set of duties on imported woolen and cotton goods, iron, hats, and sugar.

The administration's program of national economic development drew sharp criticism from so-called Old Republicans, a group of southern politicians who regarded themselves as guardians of the Jeffersonian conscience. Speaking in opposition to the bank bill in 1816, Congressman John Randolph of Virginia warned that "the question is whether … the state governments are to be swept away; or whether we … still … regard their integrity and preservation as part of our policy." Over the following decade, the Old Republicans continued to sound the alarm, even as their numbers dwindled.

Madison also recommended the construction of a federally subsidized network of roads and canals to speed economic development and enhance national security. He warned of the need for a constitutional amendment authorizing such action, but Representatives John Calhoun and Henry Clay, unwilling to delay, pushed an internal improvements bill through Congress. True to his principles, Madison vetoed the bill, temporarily stopping the project. Schemes for federal programs of national development, however, would not die. By the early 1820s, Henry Clay and others, taking up the name National Republicans, were proposing an even more ambitious program of tariffs and internal improvements under the name the American System.

The Specter of Sectionalism

In spite of the surge of national spirit following the War of 1812, Federalist talk of disunion had revealed just how fragile national unity continued to be. Though Congressional debates over the tariff, internal improvements, and the national bank echoed with sectional tensions, it was the Missouri crisis of 1819–1820 that revealed just how deep-seated sectional rivalries had become.

The House of Representatives, depicted in this 1821 painting by Samuel F. B. Morse, later inventor of the telegraph, rang with debate over the Missouri Compromise and other explosive issues. (In the Collection of the Corcoran Gallery of Art)

Ever since 1789, politicians had labored to keep the explosive issue of slavery tucked safely beneath the surface of political life, for they recognized how quickly it could jeopardize national unity. Their fears were borne out in 1819 when Missouri applied for admission to the Union and raised anew the question of slavery's expansion. In the Northwest Ordinance of 1787, Congress had limited slavery north of the Ohio River while allowing its expansion to the south. But it had said nothing about slavery's place in the vast new territory west of the Mississippi River.

Seizing the opportunity to deal with that question, Senator Rufus King of New York demanded that Missouri prohibit slavery before entering the Union. His proposal triggered a fierce debate over Congress's authority to prevent the spread of slavery. Southerners were adamant that the trans-Mississippi West remain open to their slave property and were determined to maintain the Senate's equal balance between slave and free states. Already by 1819, the North's more rapidly growing population had given it a 105-to-81 advantage in the House of Representatives. Equality in the Senate offered the only sure protection of southern interests. Northerners, however, vowed to keep the trans-Mississippi West open to free labor, and that meant closing it to slavery.

For nearly three months, Congress debated the issue. During much of the time, free blacks listening intently to northern antislavery speeches filled the House gallery. "This momentous question," worried the aged Jefferson, "like a fire-bell in the night, [has] awakened and filled me with terror." Northerners were similarly alarmed. The Missouri question, declared the editor of the New York *Daily Advertiser,* "involves not only the future character of our nation, but the future weight and influence of the free states. If now lost—it is lost forever."

Missouri Compromise of 1820

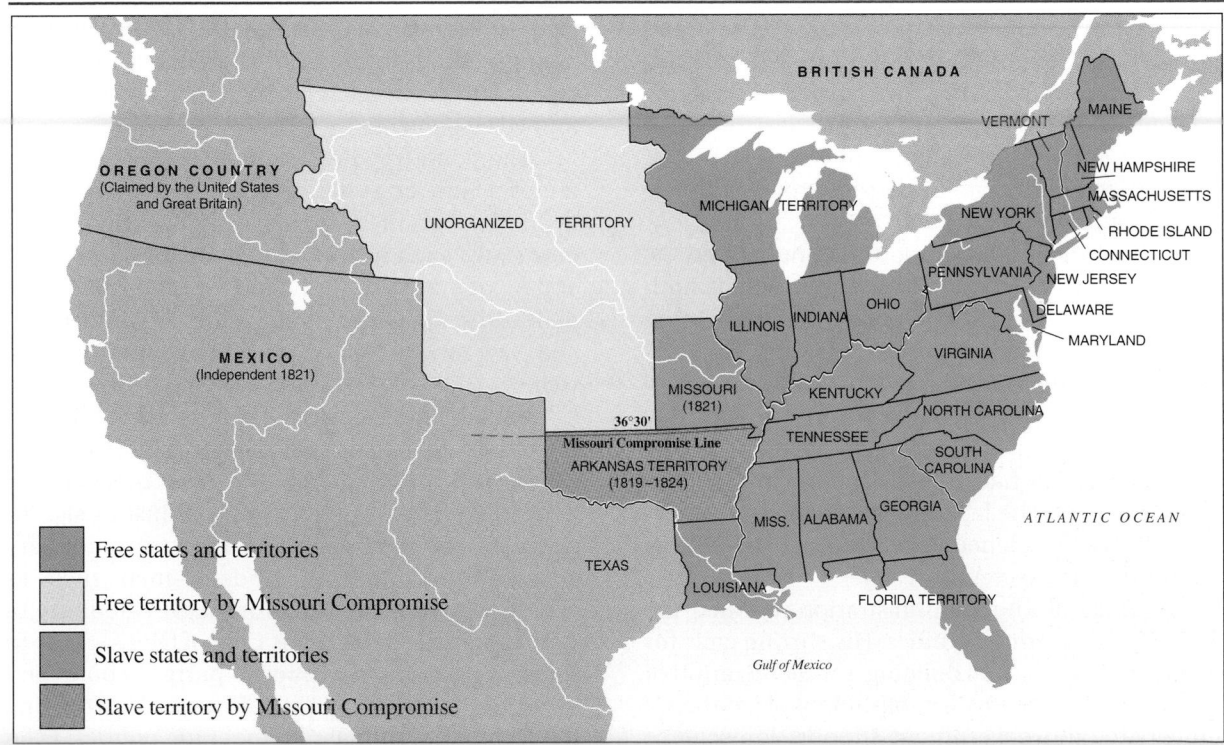

In the early nineteenth century, politicians struggled to contain the explosive issue of slavery's expansion. In 1820, they did so by balancing Missouri's admission as a slave state with Maine's as a free state, and drawing the Missouri Compromise line separating free territories from slave territories.

In the end, compromise prevailed. Missouri gained admission as a slave state, while Maine came in as a counterbalancing free state, and a line was drawn west from Missouri at latitude 36° 30' to the Rocky Mountains dividing the lands that would be open to slavery from those that would not. For the moment, the dangerous issue of slavery's expansion had been put to rest. It would not be long, however, before the problem of slavery's expansion would set North and South even more violently against each other.

Collapse of the Federalist-Jeffersonian Party System

The final collapse of the Federalist-Jeffersonian system of gentry politics came with the presidential election of John Quincy Adams in 1824. For the first time since 1800, when the "Virginia dynasty" of Jefferson, Madison, and Monroe began, there was competition for the presidency from every major wing of the Jeffersonian party. Of the five candidates, Adams of Massachusetts and Henry Clay of Kentucky advocated strong federal programs of economic development. William Crawford of Georgia and Andrew Jackson of Tennessee clung to traditional Jeffersonian principles of limited government, agrarianism, and states' rights. In between stood John Calhoun of South Carolina, just beginning his fateful passage from nationalism to southern nullification.

Attracting limited support, Calhoun withdrew to become the vice-presidential partner of both Adams and Jackson. When none of the remaining candidates received an electoral majority, the election, as in 1800, moved into the House of Representatives. There, an alliance of Adams and Clay supporters gave the New Englander the election, even though he had trailed Jackson in electoral votes, 84 to 99. The Jacksonians' charges of a "corrupt bargain" gained credence when Adams appointed Clay secretary of state.

Adams's ill-fated administration revealed the disarray in American politics. His stirring calls for federal road and canal building, standardization of weights and measures, establishment of a national university, and government support for science and the arts quickly fell victim to sectional conflicts, political factionalism, and his own open scorn for the increasingly democratic politics of the day.

Against the urging of his political advisers, Adams declined an invitation from the Maryland Agricultural Society to attend its annual cattle show, explaining in disgust that the President should stand above such efforts to court popular favor. In the political climate of the 1820s, such an attitude spelled political suicide. Within a year of his inauguration, Adams' administration had foundered. For the rest of his term, politicians jockeyed for position in the political realignment that was under way.

A New Style of Politics

As the old Federalist-Republican system of gentry politics collapsed, new political energies were stirring in the states. The most dramatic evidence of that was the surge of voter participation in state elections. Women, blacks, and Native Americans continued to be excluded, but white men flocked to the polls in unprecedented numbers. In the New Hampshire gubernatorial election of 1814, participation soared as high as 81 percent of eligible voters. On one occasion in Alabama, voter turnout topped 90 percent.

The flood of voters resulted in part from the removal of long-established, property-holding restrictions on the franchise. The constitutions of new states such as Indiana (1816), Illinois (1818), and Alabama (1819) provided for universal white, male suffrage. Older states such as Connecticut and New York abolished property requirements as well.

Equally important were the growing strength of democratic beliefs and the continuing drive of urban artisans and rural farmers to claim an increased share of political power. Just as significant was the emergence of a postrevolutionary generation of political leaders—men such as Martin Van Buren of New York, Levi Woodbury of New Hampshire, and Lewis Cass of Ohio—ready to set aside old worries about "party faction" and eager to make their political mark by perfecting the techniques of mass, democratic politics. Even some of the younger Federalists, learning from the

TIMELINE

1789	Knox's report on Indian affairs
1790s	Second Great Awakening begins
1794	Battle of Fallen Timbers
1795	Treaty of Greenville
1796	Congress establishes Indian Factory System
1800	Capital moves to Washington
1801	Thomas Jefferson elected president
	Judiciary Act
	New Land Act
1802	Judiciary Act repealed
1803	*Marbury* v. *Madison*
	Louisiana Purchase
1803–1806	Lewis and Clark expedition
1803–1812	Napoleonic wars resume
	British impress American sailors
1804	Jefferson reelected
1805–1807	Pike explores the West
1806	Non-Importation Act
1807	Embargo Act
	Chesapeake–Leopard affair
	Congress prohibits slave trade
1808	James Madison elected president
	Cherokee legal code established
1809	Tecumseh's confederacy formed
1811	Battle of Kithtippecanoe

1812	Madison reelected
	West Florida annexed
	War declared against Great Britain
1813	Battle of the Thames
1813–1814	Creek War
1814	Treaty of Ghent
	Battle of Horseshoe Bend
1814–1815	Hartford Convention
1815	Battle of New Orleans
	U.S. establishes military posts in trans-Mississippi West
1816	James Monroe elected president
	Second Bank of the United States chartered
1819	Adams-Onis Treaty with Spain
	Spain cedes East Florida to United States
	McCulloch v. *Maryland*
1819–1822	Bank panic and depression
1820	Land Act
	Missouri Compromise
1822	Diplomatic recognition of Latin American republics
1823	Monroe Doctrine proclaimed
1824	John Quincy Adams elected president
1827	Cherokee adopt written constitution

disastrous consequences of their elders' elitist behavior, changed their political ways. By the 1820s, successful politicians of every persuasion vied for voters' support through registration drives, party conventions, and popular campaigning. The antiparty, gentry-dominated politics of a generation before was increasingly a thing of the past.

Initially, the conduct of mass, democratic politics was most evident in state elections, for it was in the states that party techniques could be easily developed. Beginning in 1828, with the first election of Andrew Jackson to the presidency, however, the techniques of mass politics would be applied to presidential electioneering as well. When that happened, American politics would change forever.

Conclusion

The Passing of an Era

During the first quarter of the nineteenth century, Americans dramatically reshaped the social, geographic, and political dimensions of their republic. The nation's territory more than doubled in size. Safely in control of the federal government, the Jeffersonians labored to set it on a new and more democratic course. In the process, they fashioned domestic policies designed to promote the country's agrarian expansion and foreign policies that transformed the nation's relations with Europe and the Americas. They also sought, less successfully, to reconcile Native American rights with national growth.

By the end of the 1820s, American politics was no longer so clearly divided between a gentry-led politics situated at the seat of the national government and a more democratic form of politics centered in the states. As events would show, Andrew Jackson's election to the presidency in 1828 would represent the emergence of a new, unified system of democratic politics.

All these changes heralded the continued strengthening of a powerful democratic faith built around the values of equality, opportunity, and individual autonomy. Those values would continue to reverberate throughout the coming years.

During the 1820s, the American people turned from an earlier era of founding, when the national government was new and the outcome of their republican experiment seemed still uncertain, to a new era of rapid national development. That transition was dramatized on July 4, 1826, the fiftieth anniversary of American independence, when two of the last remaining Revolutionary patriarchs, John Adams and Thomas Jefferson, died within a few hours of each other. "The sterling virtues of the Revolution are silently passing away," mused George McDuffie of South Carolina, "and the period is not distant when there will be no living monument to remind us of those glorious days of trial." As those anniversary celebrations died away, the American people had reason to face the future with both confidence and concern.

Recommended Reading

Jeffersonians Versus Federalists

Drew McCoy, *The Elusive Republic* (1980); Noble Cunningham, *The Process of Government Under Jefferson* (1978); James Young, *The Washington Community, 1800–1828* (1966); Richard Buel, *Securing the Revolution* (1972); Merrill Peterson, *Thomas Jefferson and the New Nation* (1970); Ralph Ketcham, *James Madison: A Biography* (1990); Robert Shalhope, *John Taylor of Caroline: Pastoral Republican* (1980); Francis Stites, *John Marshall, Defender of the Constitution* (1981); Richard Ellis, *The Jeffersonian Crisis: Courts and Politics in the Young Republic* (1971); R. Kent Newmyer, *The Supreme Court Under Marshall and Taney* (1968).

Foreign Policy

Lawrence Kaplan, *"Entangling Alliances With None": American Foreign Policy in the Age of Jefferson* (1987); J. C. A. Stagg, *Mr. Madison's War* (1983); Ernest May, *The Making of the Monroe Doctrine* (1975); Burton Spivak, *Jefferson's English Crisis: Commerce, Embargo, and the Republican Revolution* (1974); Robert Rutland, *The Presidency of James Madison* (1990); J. Leitch White, Jr., *Britain and the American Frontier, 1783–1815* (1975).

Society and Economy in the Early Republic

Robert Wiebe, *The Opening of American Society: From the Adoption of the Constitution to the Eve of Disunion* (1984); Christopher Clark, *The Roots of Rural Capitalism: Western*

Massachusetts, 1780–1860 (1990); Stephen Hahn and Jonathan Prude, *The Countryside in the Age of Capitalist Transformation* (1985); Howard Rock et al., *American Artisans: Crafting Social Identity* (1995); James Lemon, *The Best Poor Man's Country: A Geographical Study of Early Southeastern Pennsylvania* (1972); Robert Doherty, *Society and Power: Five New England Towns, 1800–1860* (1977); Jeanne Boydston, *Home and Work: Housework, Wages, and the Ideology of Labor in the Early Republic* (1990); Jack Larkin, *Reshaping Everyday Life, 1790–1840* (1988); Anthony F. C. Wallace, *Rockdale: The Growth of an American Village in the Early Industrial Revolution* (1978); Jeremy Atack and Fred Bateman, *To Their Own Soil: Agriculture in the Antebellum North* (1987).

Trans-Appalachia and the West

Andrew Cayton, *The Frontier Republic: Ideology and Politics in the Ohio Country, 1780–1825* (1986); Malcolm Rohrbough, *The Trans-Appalachian Frontier* (1978); Robert Mitchell, ed., *Appalachian Frontiers: Settlement, Society, and Development in the Preindustrial Era* (1991); Donald Jackson, *Thomas Jefferson and the Stony Mountains: Exploring the West from Monticello* (1981); James Ronda, *Lewis and Clark Among the Indians* (1984); John Mack Faragher, *Daniel Boone: The Life and Legend of an American Pioneer* (1992); Wilma Dunaway, *The First American Frontier: Transition to Capitalism in Southern Appalachia, 1700–1860* (1995).

Native Americans and Indian Policy

Bernard Sheehan, *Seeds of Extinction: Jeffersonian Philanthropy and the American Indian* (1973); Wiley Sword, *President Washington's Indian War, 1790–1795* (1985); Gregory Dowd, *Spirited Resistance: The North American Indian Struggle for Unity, 1745–1815* (1992); William McLoughlin, *Cherokee Renascence in the New Republic* (1986); R. David Edmunds, *Tecumseh and the Quest for Indian Leadership* (1984); Richard White, *The Middle Ground: Indians, Empires, and Republics in the Great Lakes Region, 1650–1815* (1991); Richard Drinnon, *Facing West: The Metaphysics of Indian Hating and Empire Building* (1980); Francis Paul Prucha, *American Indian Policy in the Formative Years* (1970).

Perfecting American Society

Paul Conkin, *Cane Ridge: America's Pentecost* (1990); Nathan Hatch, *The Democratization of American Christianity* (1989);

John Boles, *The Great Revival, 1787–1805* (1972); Randolph Roth, *The Democratic Dilemma: Religion, Reform, and the Social Order in the Connecticut River Valley of Vermont, 1791–1850* (1987).

Jean Mathews, *Toward A New Society: American Thought and Culture, 1800–1830* (1990); Robert Cray, Jr., *Paupers and Poor Relief in New York City and Its Rural Environs, 1700–1830* (1988); Conrad Wright, *The Transformation of Charity in Post-Revolutionary New England* (1992); Raymond Mohl, *Poverty in New York, 1783–1825*; Michael Meranze, *Laboratories of Virtue: Punishment, Revolution, and Authority in Philadelphia, 1760–1835* (1996).

Nancy Cott, *The Bonds of Womanhood: "Women's Sphere" in New England, 1780–1835* (1977); Lee Chambers-Schiller, *Liberty, A Better Husband* (1984); Joan Jensen, *Loosening the Bonds: Mid-Atlantic Farm Women, 1750–1850* (1986); Cathy Davidson, *Revolution and the Word: The Rise of the Novel in America* (1986); Susan Juster, *Disorderly Women: Sexual Politics and Evangelicalism in Revolutionary New England* (1994); Laurel Thatcher Ulrich, *A Midwife's Tale: The Life of Martha Ballard, 1785–1812* (1990).

African Americans and Slavery

Gary B. Nash, *Forging Freedom: The Formation of Philadelphia's Black Community, 1720–1840* (1988); Gary B. Nash and Jean Soderlund, *Freedom by Degrees: Emancipation in Pennsylvania and Its Aftermath* (1991); Douglas Egerton, *Gabriel's Rebellion: The Virginia Slave Conspiracies of 1800 and 1802* (1993); Margaret Creel, *"A Peculiar People": Slave Religion and Community Culture Among the Gullahs* (1988); John Lofton, *Denmark Vesey's Revolt* (1983); Leonard Curry, *Free Blacks in Urban America, 1800–1850* (1981).

Political Realignment and the 1820s

Steven Watts, *The Republic Reborn: War and the Making of Liberal America, 1790–1820* (1987); Drew McCoy, *The Last of the Fathers: James Madison and the Republican Legacy* (1989); Ronald Formisano, *The Transformation of Political Culture: Massachusetts Parties, 1790s–1840s* (1983); Robert Remini, *Andrew Jackson and the Course of American Empire, 1767–1821* (1983); Mary Hargreaves, *The Presidency of John Quincy Adams* (1985).

An Expanding People, 1820–1877

COMPARATIVE CHRONOLOGIES

Political and Diplomatic	Social and Economic	Cultural and Technological
1820		
1820 Monroe reelected; Missouri Compromise	1822 Denmark Vesey slave conspiracy	1823 James Fenimore Cooper, *The Pioneers*
1823 Monroe Doctrine	1824 New Harmony founded	
1824 Clay's "American System"	1827 Mechanics' Union of Trade Association founded in Philadelphia	1824 Hudson River school of landscape painting
1825 John Quincy Adams chosen president by House of Representatives; Texas (Mexican territory) opened to settlement by United States citizens	1828 Tariff of Abominations	1825 Erie Canal completed
	1829 Workingmen's party founded in New York	1827 *Freedom's Journal* (first black newspaper)
1828 Andrew Jackson elected president		
1830		
1830 Webster-Hayne debate; Indian Removal bill	1830 Joseph Smith founds Mormon Church	1830 First commercial steam locomotive, *Tom Thumb*
1832 Jackson reelected; South Carolina nullification crisis; Black Hawk War	1831 Nat Turner's slave rebellion	1831 William Lloyd Garrison begins publishing *The Liberator*
1833 Force bill	1832 Jackson vetoes U.S. Bank charter	
1834 Whig party formed; Seminole Wars	1832–1836 U.S. Bank funds removed to state banks	1832 Samuel F. B. Morse invents telegraph
1836 "Gag rule"; Texas declares independence; battles of the Alamo and San Jacinto; Martin Van Buren elected president	1833 American Anti-Slavery Society founded; Oberlin College founded	1834 Cyrus McCormick patents reaper
	1834 Lowell mill girls strike; National Trades Union founded	1836 Ralph Waldo Emerson, *Nature*
	1836 Specie circular; Mount Holyoke Female Seminary founded	1837 Emerson, *The American Scholar*; John Deere invents first steel plow; George Catlin paints *Gallery of Indians*
1838 Cherokee removal	1837 Panic of 1837	
	1838–1844 Depression	1838 Morse code devised
		1839 Charles Goodyear produces vulcanized rubber
1840		
1840 William H. Harrison elected president; Liberty party formed	1840 Independent Treasury Act	1843 Edgar Allan Poe short stories
1841 Harrison dies; John Tyler becomes president	1840s Great migration to Oregon over Oregon Trail	1844 Morse sends first telegraph message
1842 Webster-Ashburton Treaty	1841 Brook Farm founded	1845 *Narrative of Frederick Douglass*
1844 James K. Polk elected president; boundary dispute over Oregon; Treaty of commerce and friendship with China	1847 Irish potato famine immigration	1846 Herman Melville, *Typee*; Elias Howe invents sewing machine
	1848 Oneida community founded; Women's rights convention, Seneca Falls, New York	
1845 United States annexes Texas	1849 California gold rush	
1846 Mexican-American War begins; Wilmot Proviso; Oregon boundary settled		
1848 Zachary Taylor elected president; Free-Soil party formed; Treaty of Guadalupe Hidalgo		

Political and Diplomatic

1850 Taylor dies; Millard Fillmore becomes president; Compromise of 1850
1852 Franklin Pierce elected president
1853 Gadsden Purchase
1854 Republican party formed; Know-Nothing party formed; Ostend Manifesto; Kansas-Nebraska Act
1855 William Walker overthrows Nicaraguan government
1856 James Buchanan elected president
1857 Dred Scott decision; Lecompton Constitution
1858 Lincoln-Douglas debates
1859 Raid on Harpers Ferry; John Brown hanged

Social and Economic

1851 Maine prohibition law; Fort Laramie Treaty; Women's Rights Convention meets in Ohio
1852 Massachusetts passes first school attendance law
1855 First oil business in United States
1857 Panic of 1857; German, Irish, British immigrants make up one-third to one-half the population of large cities

Cultural and Technological

1850 Nathaniel Hawthorne, *The Scarlet Letter*
1851 Melville, *Moby Dick*; Isaac Singer perfects sewing machine
1852 Harriet Beecher Stowe, *Uncle Tom's Cabin*; Otis invents passenger elevator
1854 Henry David Thoreau, *Walden*
1855 Walt Whitman, *Leaves of Grass*
1857 Central Park, New York, designed; *Atlantic Monthly* founded

1860 Abraham Lincoln elected president; South Carolina secedes
1861 Confederate States of America formed; Civil War begins; First Battle of Bull Run
1862 Battles of Shiloh, Bull Run, and Antietam
1863 Emancipation Proclamation; Battles of Gettysburg and Vicksburg
1864 Sherman's march through Georgia; Lincoln reelected
1865 Lee surrenders; Civil War ends; Lincoln assassinated; Andrew Johnson becomes president; Thirteenth Amendment
1866 Civil Rights Act
1868 Impeachment attempt against Johnson; Ulysses S. Grant elected president; Fourteenth Amendment

1860 Pony Express begins; the Great Lynn Shoe Strike
1861 First federal income tax
1862 Homestead Act; Morrill Land-Grant College Act; Morrill tariff
1864 Sand Creek, Colorado, massacre
1865 Freedmen's Bureau established; Union Stockyards opened in Chicago
1865–1866 Black codes
1867 Ku Klux Klan formed; urban population growth peaks

1861 Mathew Brady begins photographing Civil War
1863 Catharine Beecher's "Words of Comfort for a Discouraged House-keeper"; Steam engines become cheaper than water power
1864 Pullman creates sleeping car
1867 First elevated railway in New York City
1869 First transcontinental railroad completed

1870 Fifteenth Amendment
1870–1871 Force Acts
1872 Grant reelected
1875 Civil Rights Act
1877 Rutherford B. Hayes becomes president

1873 Financial panic and depression; growth of sharecropping and tenancy in the South; percentage of immigrants in large cities falls to less than one-third
1877 Great Railway Strike

1870s Black "exodusters" migrate to Kansas; geological surveys of Yellowstone, Grand Canyon
1876 Centennial Exhibition in Philadelphia

Currents of Change in the Northeast and the Old Northwest

For her first 18 years, Susan Warner was little touched by the far-reaching economic and social changes that were transforming the character of the country and her own city of New York. Whereas some New Yorkers toiled to make a living by taking in piecework and others responded to unsettling new means of producing goods by joining trade unions to agitate for wages that would enable them to "live as comfortable as others," Susan was surrounded by luxuries and privilege. Much of the year was spent in the family's townhouse in St. Mark's Place, not far from the home of the enormously rich real estate investor and fur trader John Jacob Astor. There Susan acquired the social graces and skills appropriate for a girl of her position and background. She had dancing and singing lessons, studied Italian and French, and learned the etiquette involved in receiving visitors and making calls. When hot weather made life in New York unpleasant, the Warners escaped to the cooler airs of Canaan, where they had a summer house. Like any girl of her social class, Susan realized that her carefree existence could not last forever. With her marriage, which she confidently expected some time in the future, would come significant new responsibilities as a wife and mother, but not the end of the comfortable life to which she was accustomed.

But it was not marriage and motherhood that disrupted the pattern of Susan's life but financial disaster. Sheltered as she had been from the far-reaching and unsettling economic and social changes of the early nineteenth century, Susan discovered that she, too, was at the mercy of forces beyond her control. Her father, heretofore so successful a provider and parent, lost most of his fortune during the financial Panic of 1837. Like others experiencing a sharp economic reversal, the Warners had to make radical adjustments. The fashionable home in St. Mark's Place and the pleasures of New York were exchanged for a more modest existence on an island in the Hudson River. Susan turned "housekeeper" and learned how to do tasks once relegated to others: sewing and making butter, pudding sauces, and johnny cake.

The change of residence and Susan's attempt to master domestic skills did not halt the family's financial decline. Prized possessions, including the piano and engravings, all symbols of the life the Warners had once taken for granted, eventually went up for auction. "When at last the men and the confusion were gone," Susan's younger sister, Anna, recalled, "then we woke up to life."

Waking up to life meant facing the necessity of making money. But what could Susan do to reverse sliding family fortunes? True, some women labored as factory operatives, domestics, seamstresses, or schoolteachers, but it was doubtful Susan could even imagine herself in any of these occupations. Her Aunt Fanny, however, had a suggestion that was more congenial to the genteel young woman. Knowing that the steam-powered printing press had revolutionized the publishing world and created a mass readership, much of it female, Aunt Fanny told her niece, "Sue, I believe if you would try, you could write a story." "Whether she added 'that . . . would sell,' I am not sure," recalled Anna later, "but of course that was what she meant."

Taking Aunt Fanny's advice to heart, Susan started to write a novel that would sell. She constructed her story around the trials of a young orphan girl, Ellen Montgomery. As Ellen suffered one reverse after another, she learned the lessons that allowed her to survive and eventually triumph over adversity: piety, self-denial, discipline, and the power of a mother's love. Entitled *The Wide, Wide World,* the novel was accepted for publication only after the mother of the publisher, George Putnam, read it and told her son, "If you never publish another book, you must make *The Wide, Wide World* available for your fellow men." A modest 750 copies were printed. Much to the surprise of the cautious Putnam, if not to his mother, 13 editions were published within two years. *The Wide, Wide World* became the first American novel to sell more than a million copies. It was one of the best-sellers of the century.

Long before she realized the book's success, Susan, always aware of the need to make money, was working on a new story. Drawing on her own experience of economic and social reversal, Susan described the spiritual and intellectual life of a young girl thrust into poverty after an early life of luxury in New York. Entitled *Queechy,* this novel was also a great success.

Though her fame as a writer made Susan Warner unusual, her books' popularity suggested how well they spoke to the concerns and interests of a broad readership. The background of social and financial uncertainty, with its sudden changes of fortune, so prominent in several of the novels, captured the reality and fears of a fluid society in the process of transformation. While one French writer was amazed that "in America a three-volume novel is devoted to the history of the moral progress of a girl of thirteen," pious heroines like Ellen Montgomery, who struggled to master their passions and urges toward independence, were shining exemplars of the new norms for middle-class women. Their successful efforts to mold themselves heartened readers who believed that the future of the nation depended on virtuous mothers and who struggled to live up to new ideals. Susan's novels validated their efforts and spoke to the importance of the domestic sphere. "I feel strongly impelled to pour out to you my most heartful thanks," wrote one woman. None of the other leading writers of the day had been able to minister "to the highest and noblest feelings of my nature *so much as yourself.*

This picture of an 1845 Fair suggests the cornucopia of goods made available in the early stages of industrialization. (B. J. Harrison, Fair of the American Institute at Niblo's Garden, 1845/Museum of the City of New York)

*S*usan Warner's life and her novels serve as an introduction to the far-reaching changes that this chapter explores. Between 1820 and 1860, as Susan Warner discovered, economic transformations in the Northeast and the Old Northwest reshaped economic, social, cultural, and political life. Though most Americans still lived in rural settings rather than in factory towns or cities, economic growth and the new industrial mode of production affected them through the creation of new goods, opportunities, and markets. In urban communities and factory towns, the new economic order ushered in new forms of work, new class arrangements, and new forms of social strife.

After discussing the factors that fueled antebellum growth, the chapter turns to the industrial world, where so many of the new patterns of work and life appeared. An investigation of urbanization reveals shifting class arrangements and values as well as rising social and racial tensions. Finally, an examination of rural communities in the East and on the frontier in the Old Northwest highlights the transformation of these two sections of the country. Between 1840 and 1860, industrialization and economic growth increasingly knit them together.

Economic Growth

Between 1820 and 1860, the American economy entered a new and more complex stage of development as it moved away from its reliance on agriculture as the major source of growth toward an industrial and technological future. In this period of general national expansion, real per capita output grew an average of 2 percent annually between 1820 and 1840 and slightly less between 1840 and 1860. This doubling of per capita income over a 40-year period suggests that many Americans were enjoying a rising standard of living.

Though expanding, the economy was also unstable, as the Warners discovered so dramatically. Periods of boom (1822–1834, mid-1840s–1850s) alternated with periods of bust (1816–1821, 1837–1843). As never before, Americans faced dramatic and recurrent shifts in the availability of jobs and goods and in prices and wages. Particularly at risk were working-class Americans, a third of whom lost their jobs during years of depression. Moreover, because regional economies were increasingly linked, problems in one area tended to affect conditions in others.

Factors Fueling Economic Development

What accounted for this new phase of growth and economic development? As the table suggests, the abundance of natural resources and an expanding population provided the raw materials and the human brawn and brains that supported growth

and transformation. Because the size of American families gradually shrank—in 1800, the average white woman bore seven children; by 1860, the number had declined to five—immigration from Europe (discussed in detail later in the chapter) played an important part in providing the new workers, new households, and new consumers so essential to economic development as well as the capital and technological ideas that helped to shape American growth.

Improved transportation played a key role in bringing about economic and geographic expansion. Early in the century, high freight rates discouraged production for distant markets and the exploitation of resources, and primitive transportation hindered western settlement. As one disgruntled Senate committee pointed out, "a coal mine may exist in the United States not more than ten miles from valuable ores of iron and other materials, and both of them be useless ... as the price of land carriage is too great to be borne by either." During the 1820s and 1830s, however, canal-building projects dramatically transformed this situation. The 363-mile-long Erie Canal, the last link in a chain of waterways binding New York City to the Great Lakes and the Northwest, was the most impressive of these new canals. The volume of goods and people it carried at low cost, the economic advantages it conferred on those within its reach (suggested by both the figure on inland freight rates and the table on page 323) prompted the construction of over 3,000 miles of canals by 1840, primarily in eastern and midwestern states.

Significant Factors Promoting Economic Growth, 1820–1860

Factor	Important Features	Contribution to Growth
Abundant natural resources	Acquisition of new territories (Louisiana Purchase, Florida, trans-Mississippi West); exploitation and discovery of eastern resources	Provided raw materials and energy vital to economic transformation
Substantial population growth	Increase from 9 million in 1820 to over 30 million in 1860—due to natural increase of population and, especially after 1840, to rising immigration; importance of immigration from Ireland, Germany	Provided workers and consumers necessary for economic growth; immigration increased diversity of work force with complex results, among them supply of capital and technological know-how
Transportation revolution	Improvement of roads; extensive canal building, 1817–1837; increasing importance of railroad construction thereafter; by 1860, 30,000 miles of tracks; steamboats facilitate travel on water	Facilitated movement of peoples, goods, and information; drew people into national economy market; stimulated agricultural expansion, regional crop specialization; decreased costs of shipping goods; strengthened ties between Northeast and Midwest
Capital investment	Investments by European investors and U.S. interests; importance of mercantile capital and banks, insurance companies in funneling capital to economic enterprises	Provided capital to support variety of new economic enterprises, improvements in transportation
Government support	Local, state, and national legislation; loans favoring enterprise; judicial decisions	Provided capital, privileges, and supportive climate for economic enterprises
Industrialization	New methods of producing goods, with and without involvement of machinery	Produced more numerous, cheaper goods for mass market; transformed classes and nature of work; affected distribution of wealth and individual opportunity

Even at the height of the canal boom, politicians, promoters, and others, impressed with Britain's success with railways, also supported the construction of railroads. Railroads, unlike canals that might freeze during the winter, were capable of operating all year-round. Nor did they need large amounts of water to operate, as canals did. They could be built almost anywhere, an advantage that encouraged Baltimore merchants, envious of New York's water link to the Northwest, to begin the Baltimore & Ohio Railroad in 1828.

Despite the interest in and advantages of railroads, there were technical problems to resolve; for example, the first trains jumped their tracks and spewed sparks, setting nearby fields ablaze. But such difficulties were quickly overcome. By 1840, there were 3,000 miles of track, most in the Northeast. Another 5,000 miles were laid during the 1840s, and by the end of the 1850s, total mileage soared to 30,000. Like the canals, the new railroads strengthened the links between the Old Northwest and the East.

Improved transportation had such a profound influence on American life that some historians use the term "transportation revolution" to refer to its impact. Canals and railroads bound the country together in a new way. They provided farmers, merchants, and manufacturers with cheap and reliable access to distant markets and goods and encouraged Americans to settle the frontier and cultivate virgin lands. The economic opportunities they opened fostered technological innovations that might increase

Inland Freight Rates

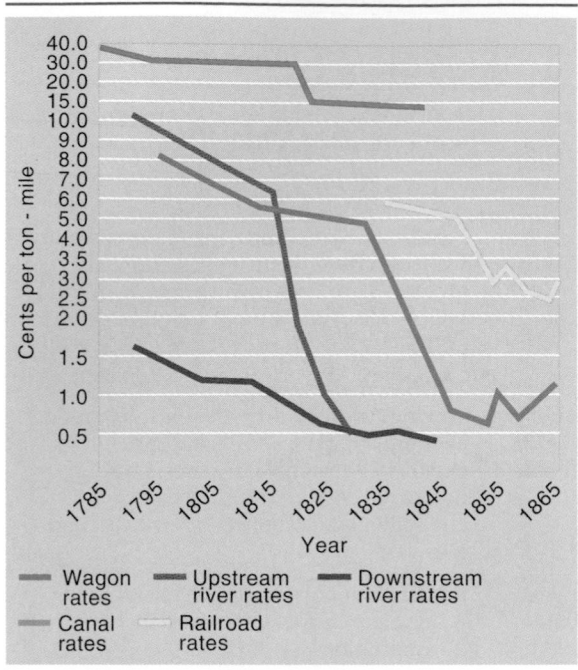

As this chart makes dramatically clear, the transportation revolution had a tremendous impact on the cost of shipping goods and materials to markets and factories.

production. Eventually, the strong economic and social ties the waterways and then the railways fostered between the Northwest and the East led people living in the two regions to share political outlooks.

Especially in terms of the pattern of western settlement, railroads exerted enormous influence. As the railroads followed—or led—settlers westward, their routes could determine whether a city, town, or even homestead survived. The railroad transformed Chicago from a small settlement into a bustling commercial and transportation center. In 1850, the city contained not 1 mile of track, but within five years, 2,200 miles of track serving 150,000 square miles terminated in Chicago.

The dramatic rise in railroad construction in the two decades before the Civil War contributed to faster economic growth after 1839. Goods, people, commercial information, and mail flowed ever more predictably, rapidly, and cheaply. In 1790, an order from Boston took two weeks to reach Philadelphia; in 1836, it took only 36 hours.

Improved transportation stimulated agricultural expansion and regional specialization. Farmers began to plant larger crops for the market, concentrating on those most suited to their soil and climate. By the late 1830s, the Old Northwest had become the country's granary, and New England farmers turned to dairy or produce farming. By 1860, American farmers were producing four to five

Mary Keys painted this picturesque view of the recently completed Erie Canal in 1832. Although her knowledge of perspective was limited, her picture reveals the canal's locks and the team that pulled the canal boat along. The 363-mile canal was the last link in a chain of waterways connecting New York to the Great Lakes and the Northwest. Irish immigrants who flooded into the country during the antebellum period provided the muscle power for the construction of the Erie Canal as well as many other transportation projects. One song sung by the laborers noted "such a great undertaking.... To dig through the vallies so level, through rocks for to cut a canal." (Munson-Williams-Proctor Institute Museum of Art, Utica, NY)

times as much wheat, corn, cattle, and hogs as they had in 1810. Their achievements meant plentiful, cheap food for American workers and more income for farmers to spend on the new consumer goods.

Capital and Government Support

Internal improvements, the exploitation of natural resources, and the cultivation of new lands all demanded capital. Much of it came from European investors. Between 1790 and 1861, over $500 million flowed into the United States from Europe. Foreign investors from Europe, adding to funds brought by immigrant families, financed as much

as a third of all canal construction and bought about a quarter of all railroad bonds.

American mercantile capital fueled growth as well. As Chapter 9 suggested, the merchant class prospered in the half century after the Revolution. Now merchants invested in schemes ranging from canals to textile factories. Many ventured into the production of goods and became manufacturers themselves.

Prosperous Americans eagerly sought opportunities to put their capital to work. Two New Yorkers, Arthur Bronson and Charles Butler, exemplify the speculative spirit nurturing economic development. Intrigued by the Northwest's investment

Growth of the Railroads, 1850–1860

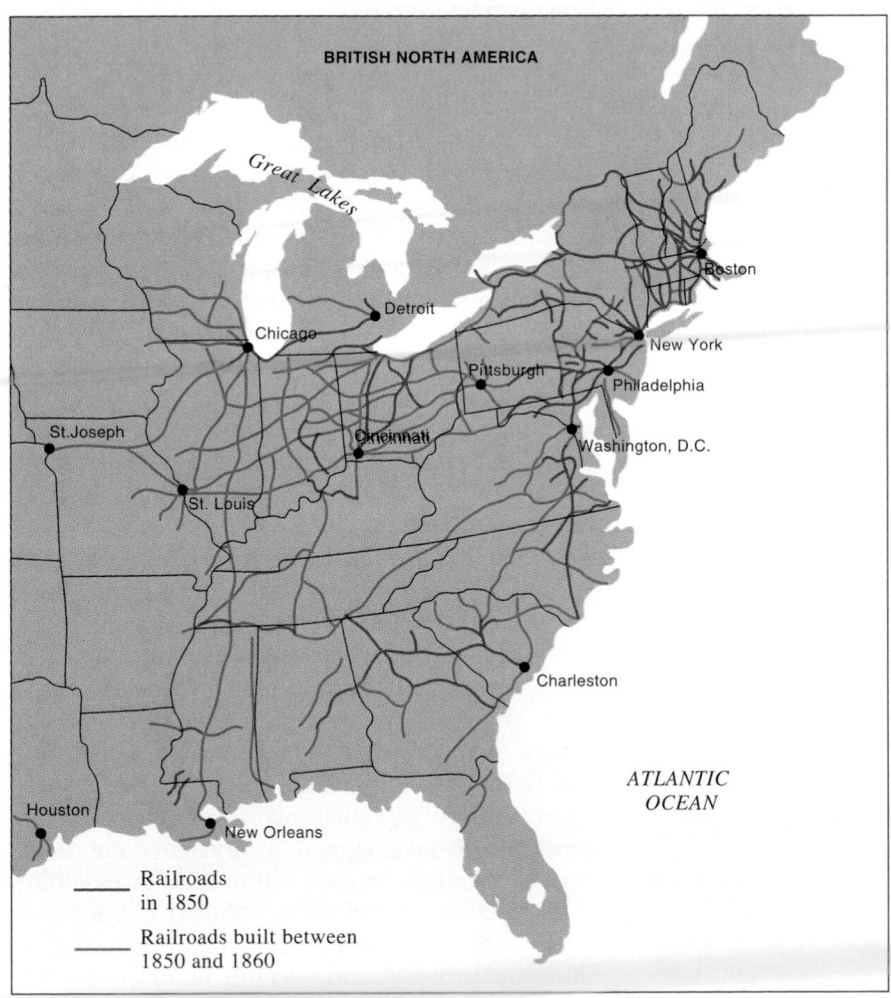

Railroads in 1850

Railroads built between 1850 and 1860

This map shows the tremendous surge of railroad building between 1850 and 1860 and the ways in which the railroad strengthened the ties between the Northeast and the Midwest. Notice that the railroad has crossed the Mississippi River. Because of the transportation revolution, almost the entire area east of the Mississippi was within a week's journey of New York City by 1860.

possibilities, Bronson and Butler made a careful tour of the region in 1833. They encountered "scenes, & things which we never dreamed of before leaving home, & which then should have revolted at." But despite primitive conditions, both men saw wonderful opportunities. Detroit, Butler concluded, 'is destined to be a very great city," and Chicago "presents one of the finest fields in America for industry & enterprise." Each man channeled funds into western projects. Bronson's investments ranged from Ohio banks to farmland in Wisconsin Territory, Illinois, Michigan, Ohio, and Indiana to real estate in Chicago and Detroit, all in addition to his holdings in New York ironworks and banks.

Bronson's investment in banks indicated his understanding of their role in stimulating economic growth. He also actively promoted life insurance companies, which, unlike commercial banks, lent money on a long-term basis. These financial institutions, he realized, served as intermediaries, funneling into economic enterprises the capital of people with neither the time nor the expertise to invest their money themselves.

Local and state government played their part by enthusiastically supporting economic growth. States often helped new ventures raise capital by passing laws of incorporation, by awarding entrepreneurs special privileges such as tax breaks or monopolistic control, by underwriting bonds for improvement projects, which increased their investment appeal, and by providing loans for internal improvements. New York, Pennsylvania, Ohio, Indiana, Illinois, and Virginia publicly financed almost 75 percent of the canal systems in their states between 1815 and 1860.

The national government also encouraged economic expansion by cooperating with states on some internal improvements, such as the National Road linking Maryland and Illinois. Federal tariff policy shielded American products, and the second U.S. Bank provided the financial stability investors required. So widespread was the enthusiasm for growth that the line separating the public sector from the private often became unclear.

The law also helped to promote aggressive economic growth. Judicial decisions created a new understanding of property rights. The case of *Palmer* v. *Mulligan,* decided by the New York State

Supreme Court in 1805, laid down the principle that property ownership included the right to develop property for business purposes. Land was increasingly defined as a productive asset for exploitation, not merely subsistence, as earlier judicial rulings had suggested.

Investors and business operators alike wanted to increase predictability in the conduct of business. Contracts lay at the heart of commercial relationships, but contract law hardly existed in 1800. A period of rapid development ensued. A series of important Supreme Court decisions between 1819 and 1824 established the basic principle that contracts were binding. In *Dartmouth College* v. *Woodward,* the Court held that a state charter could not be modified unless both parties agreed and declared in *Sturges* v. *Crowninshield* that a New York law allowing debtors to repudiate their debts was unconstitutional.

A New Mentality

As the discussion of the links between law and economic growth suggests, economic expansion depends on intangible factors as well as more obvious ones such as improved transportation. When a farmer decided to specialize in apples for the New York market rather than to concentrate on raising food for his family, he was thinking in a new way just as was Arthur Bronson when he invested in banks that would, in turn, finance a variety of economic enterprises. The entrepreneurial outlook, the *"universal desire,"* as one newspaper editor put it, *"to get forward,"* was shared by millions of Americans. By encouraging investment, new business and agricultural ventures, and land speculation, it played a vital role in antebellum economic development.

Europeans often recognized another intangible factor when they described Americans as energetic and open to change. As one Frenchman explained in 1834, "All here is circulation, motion, and boiling agitation. Experiment follows experiment; enterprise succeeds to enterprise." An American observer agreed. "Every man seems born with some steam engine within him, driving him into an incessant and restless activity of body and mind ... every head and every hand busy, with a thousand projects, and only one holiday—the 4th of July—working from morning till night with the most intense industry."

Others described an American mechanical "genius." The American was "a mechanic by nature," one Frenchman insisted. "In Massachusetts and Connecticut, there is not a labourer who had not invented a machine or tool." This observer exaggerated, because many American innovations drew on British precedents, but every invention attracted scores of imitators. In 1854, the government patent office issued 56 patents for harvesting implements and 39 for seed planters; the next year, it issued 40 for sewing machines.

Mechanically minded Americans prided themselves on developing efficient and productive tools and machines. The McCormick harvester, the Colt revolver, Goodyear vulcanized rubber products, and the sewing machine were developed, refined, and developed further. Such improvements cut labor costs and increased efficiency. By 1840, the average American cotton textile mill was about 10 percent more efficient and 3 percent more profitable than its British counterpart.

Although the shortage of labor in the United States stimulated technological innovations that replaced humans with machines, the rapid spread of education after 1800 also contributed to innovation and increased productivity. By 1840, most whites were literate. In that year, public schools nationwide were educating 38.4 percent of white children between the ages of 5 and 19.

The belief that education spurred economic growth helped foster enthusiasm for public education, particularly in the Northeast. The development of the Massachusetts common school illustrates the connections many saw between education and progress.

Although several states had decided to use tax monies for education by 1800, Massachusetts moved first toward mass education by mandating in 1827 that taxes pay the whole cost of the state's public schools. Several years later, the state set up a permanent elementary education fund and in 1836 forbade factory managers to hire children who had not spent 3 of the previous 12 months in school. Despite the legislation, the Massachusetts school system limped along. School buildings were often run-down, even unheated. Because school curricula were virtually nonexistent, students often lounged idly at their desks.

Under the leadership of Horace Mann, the reform of state education for white children began in earnest in 1837. Mann intended to regularize the operation of schools and attract more students to them. He and others pressed for graded schools, uniform curricula, and teacher training. Believing that the power of local districts over their schools presented a barrier against improvement, he sought to reduce local control. Mann's success inspired reformers everywhere. For the first time in American history, primary education became the rule for most children outside the South between 5 and 19. The expansion of education created a whole new career of schoolteaching, a career that mostly attracted young women.

Mann believed that education promoted inventiveness. It "had a market value." Businessmen often agreed. Prominent industrialists in the 1840s were convinced that education produced workers who could handle complex machinery without undue supervision and were superior employees—reliable, punctual, industrious, and sober. Manufacturers valued education not merely because of its intellectual content, but also because it encouraged habits essential to a disciplined and productive work force.

Ambivalence Toward Change

While supporting education as a means to economic growth, many Americans also firmly

White Secondary School Enrollment, 1840–1860*			
Percent of White Population between 5 and 19 Years of Age	1840	1850	1860
New England	81.4	76.1	73.8
Middle Atlantic	54.7	61.9	61.3
North Central	29.1	52.4	69.4
South Atlantic	16.2	29.7	31.4
South Central	13.4	31.0	38.6
Nationwide	38.4	50.4	57.0

*Note the regional differences in school enrollment and changes over time.
Source: Albert W. Niemi, *U.S. Economic History* (1975).

believed in its social value. They expected the public schools to mold student character and promote "virtuous habits" and "rational self-governing" behavior. Many school activities sought to instill good habits. Students learned facts by rote because memory work and recitation taught them discipline and concentration. Nineteenth-century schoolbooks reinforced classroom goals. "It is a great sin to be idle," children read in one 1830 text, and another encouragingly pointed out, "He who rises early and is industrious and temperate will acquire health and riches." A third warned of the consequences of ignoring the message: "Poverty is the fruit of idleness."

The concern with education and character indicates that as much as Americans welcomed economic progress, they also feared its results. The

much-heralded improvements in transportation that encouraged trade and emigration, for example, created anxieties that civilization might disintegrate as people moved far from their place of birth and from familiar institutions. Others worried that rapid change undermined the American family and would turn children into barbarians. Schools, which taught students to be deferential, obedient, and punctual, could counter the worst by-products of change. The schools served as much as a defense against change as they did its agents. Fear and confidence were two sides of the coin of economic transformation.

Other signs of cultural uneasiness appeared. In the eighteenth century, Benjamin Franklin emphasized the importance of hard work in his celebrated *Poor Richard's Almanack*. In the 1830s, popularizers restated Franklin's message. As the publishing revolution lowered costs and speeded the production of printed material, these authors poured out tracts, stories, and manuals on how to get ahead. Claiming that hard work and good character led to success, they touted the virtues of diligence, punctuality, temperance, and thrift. These habits probably did assist economic growth. Slothful workers are seldom productive. Industry and perseverance often pay off. But the success of early nineteenth-century economic ventures frequently depended on the ability to take risks, to think daringly. The emphasis these publicists gave to the safe but stolid virtues and to responsible behavior suggests their fear of social disintegration. Their books and tracts aimed to counter unsettling effects of change and ensure the dominance of middle-class values.

This photograph of the Emerson School for Young Ladies was taken sometime between 1840 and 1862. An examination of the way the classroom was organized— the relative position of students and teacher and the prominent role of the clock—begins to suggest the emphasis schools placed on obedience, deference, order, and punctuality. The varied clothing of the students also highlights the impact of the manufacturing revolution on everyday life. (The Metropolitan Museum of Art, Gift of I. N. Phelps Stokes, Edward S. Hawes, Alice Mary Hawes, Marion Augusta Hawes, 1937)

The Advance of Industrialization

Significant economic growth between 1820 and 1860 resulted from the reorganization of production. Before industrialization, individual artisans fashioned goods with hand tools. Many American families also fabricated necessary articles; as late as 1820, Americans made two-thirds of all their clothes at home.

Factory production moved away from this decentralized system of artisan or family-based manufacturing and reorganized work by breaking down the manufacture of an article into discrete steps. Initially, early manufacturers often relied on the putting-out system. Their strategy was to gain control of the raw materials from which goods were fashioned—leather in the case of shoes; cotton, flax, and wool for textiles—and arrangements for marketing the finished products. Some steps in the manufacturing process they farmed out to workers in shops and homes, paying them on a piecework basis, a practice that came to be called the "putting-out" system. Other steps they consolidated in their own central shops. Eventually, they centralized all the steps of production under one roof, where hand labor gradually gave way to power-driven machinery such as wooden "spinning jennies." Often they sought the help of British immigrants who had the practical experience and technical know-how no American possessed.

In 1789, William Ashley and Moses Brown, Rhode Island merchants, hired 21-year-old Samuel Slater, a former apprentice with an English cotton textile firm, to devise a water-powered, yarn-spinning machine. Slater did that, but he also developed a machine capable of carding, or straightening, the cotton fibers. Within a year, Ashley and Brown's spinning mill had begun operations in Pawtucket, Rhode Island. Its initial work force consisted of nine children, ranging in age from 7 to 12. Ten years later, their number had grown to over 100. As factory workers replaced artisans and home manufacturers, the volume of goods rose, and prices dropped dramatically. The price of a yard of cotton cloth fell from 18 to 2 cents over the 45 years preceding the Civil War.

The transportation improvements that provided the opportunity to reach large markets after 1820 encouraged the reorganization of the production process and the use of machinery. The simple tastes and rural character of the American people suggested the wisdom of manufacturing inexpensive everyday goods like cloth and shoes rather than luxuries for the rich.

Between 1820 and 1860, textile manufacturing became the country's leading industry. Textile mills sprang up across the New England and Middle Atlantic states, regions that contained swift-flowing streams to power the mills, capitalists eager to finance the ventures, children and women to tend the machines, and numerous cities and towns with ready markets for cheap textiles. Early mills were small affairs, containing only the machines for carding and spinning. The thread was then put out to home workers to be woven into cloth. The early mechanization of cloth production did not replace home manufacture but supplemented it.

Already under way, however, were experiments that would further transform the industry. Closeted in the attic of a Boston house in 1813, Francis Cabot Lowell, a merchant, and Paul Moody, a mechanic, worked to devise a power loom capable of weaving cloth. Lowell's study of mechanical looms during his earlier tour of English and Scottish cotton factories guided their work. Eventually, they succeeded, and the loom they devised was soon installed in a mill at Waltham, Massachusetts, capitalized at $300,000 by Lowell and his Boston Associates.

The most important innovation of the Waltham operation was Lowell's decision to bring all the steps of cotton cloth production together under one roof. The Waltham mill thus differed from mills in Rhode Island and Great Britain, where spinning and weaving were separate operations. Through this centralizing of the entire manufacturing process and work force in one factory, cloth for the mass market could be produced more cheaply and more profitably. In 1823, the Boston Associates expanded their operations to East Chelmsford on the Merrimack River, a town they renamed Lowell.

Most New England mills followed the Lowell system. In the Middle Atlantic states, the textile industry was more varied. Philadelphia became a center for fine textiles, and Rhode Island factories produced less expensive materials. Maryland manufacturers, like those in Philadelphia, focused on quality goods. The cumulative impact of the rise of the textile industry was to supplant the home production of cloth, even though some women would continue to spin and weave for their families for some years to come, and hand-loom weavers would survive for another generation. In the process, Americans were transformed from a people clad in earth-colored homespun into a nation decked out in gayer, more colorful clothing.

THE MANCHESTER PRINT WORKS, AT MANCHESTER, N. H.

Gleason's Pictorial, *one of the many modestly priced publications that the introduction of steam-powered printing presses put within reach of the reading public, pictures the Manchester Print Works in New Hampshire in 1854. Although the smokestacks spewing forth black clouds of smoke hint at the pollution that accompanied the industrial revolution, nineteenth-century viewers most likely were impressed by the dignified mill building and the seeming spacious surroundings. Men appear in the foreground, but over half the workers in this calico factory were female. (Library of Congress)*

Textile mills were an important component of the increasingly industrial character of the Northeast. The majority of the South's cotton still went to England, but an increasing share flowed to northeastern mills. Other manufacturing concerns, such as shoemaking, also contributed to the Northeast's economy. By 1860, fully 71 percent of all manufacturing workers lived in this region of the country. Still other important manufacturing operations reached west and south from New England. The processing of wheat, timber, and hides using power-driven machinery was common in most communities of 200 families or more. Although a third of them were clustered in Philadelphia, paper mills were widespread. The ironworking and metalworking industry stretched from Albany, New York, south to Maryland and west to Cincinnati.

✳ Environmental Consequences

Although canals, railroads, steamboats, and the growth of industry undergirded economic growth, their impact on the environment was far-reaching and often harmful. Steamboats and early railroads, for example, depended on wood for fuel. So, too, did the heating stoves that were keeping American

families warm. Armed with new steel axes, lumbermen and farmers kept up with the increased demand for wood, and the eastern forest and the wildlife that lived there rapidly disappeared. Better transportation, which encouraged western settlement, also promoted forest clearance as individual settlers cleared land for crops and cut wood for housing. Sawmills and milldams interfered with spawning habits of fish, clogged their gills with sawdust, and even changed the flow of rivers. The process of ecological change, spurred by the desire for wood, recurred as lumber companies and entrepreneurs moved from the East to exploit the forests of the Great Lakes and of the Gulf states.

As late as 1840, wood was the main source for the country's energy needs. But the high price of wood and the discovery of anthracite coal in Pennsylvania signaled the beginning of a shift to coal as the major source of power. While the East gradually regained some of its forest cover, the heavy use of coal resulted in air pollution. Steam engines and heating stoves poured out dirty fumes into the air. In New York City, one could see the evidence of pollution everywhere—in the gray cloud hanging over the city, in the smoke rising from its machine shops, refineries, and private houses, in the acrid smells and black soot that were a part of daily life.

Textile mills located along rivers and streams might present a prettier picture than the shops and refineries of New York, but they also adversely affected the environment. Dams and canals supporting industrial activities contributed to soil erosion. "Industrial operations," declared the Vermont fish commissioner in 1857, are "destructive to fish that live or spawn in fresh water.... The thousand deleterious mineral substances, discharged into rivers from metallurgical, chemical, and manufacturing establishments, poison them by shoals."

Some Americans were aware of the environmental consequences of rapid growth and change. Author James Fenimore Cooper had one of his characters in his novel *The Pioneers* condemn those who destroyed nature "without remorse and without shame." The popularity in the 1820s of a song with the lines "Woodman, / Spare that Tree / Touch not a single bough" suggested sympathy for that point of view. Yet most Americans accepted the changing environment as an inevitable part of progress.

Early Manufacturing

Industrialization created a more efficient means of producing more goods at much lower cost than had been possible in the homes and small shops of an earlier day. Philadelphian Samuel Breck's diary reveals some of the new profusion and range of goods. "Went to town principally to see the Exhibition of American Manufactures at the Masonic Hall," he noted in 1833. "More than 700 articles have been sent. Among this great variety, I distinguished the Philadelphia porcelains, beautiful Canton cotton, made at York in this state, soft and capacious blankets, silver plate, cabinet ware, marble mantels, splendid pianos and centre tables, chymical drugs, hardware, saddlery, and the most beautiful black broadcloth I ever saw."

The Impact of Industrialization

Two examples illustrate how industrialization transformed American life in both simple and complex ways. Before the nineteenth century, local printing shops depended on manual labor to produce books, newspapers, and journals. The cost of reading material was high enough to make a library a sign of wealth. Many literate families of moderate means had little in their homes to read other than a family Bible and an almanac.

Between 1830 and 1850, however, adoption and improvement of British inventions revolutionized the printing and publishing industries. Like other changes in production, the transformation of publishing involved not only technological, but also managerial and marketing innovations. A $2.5 million market in 1830, the book business quintupled by 1850.

As books and magazines dropped in cost and grew in number, far more people could afford them. Without this new mass market of readers, Susan Warner's literary success would hardly have been possible. But the implications of the changes in publishing went beyond best-sellers. The presence of inexpensive reading material inspired and nourished literacy. Easy access to reading material also encouraged a new sort of independence. No longer needing to rely solely on the words of the "better sort" for information, people could form their own views on the basis of what they read. At the same time, however, readers everywhere were exposed repeatedly to the mainstream norms, values, and ideas expressed in magazines and books. Even on the frontier, pioneer women could study inexpensive ladies' magazines and books of domestic advice or be inspired by the pious example of Ellen Montgomery in *The Wide, Wide World*. Their husbands could follow the latest political news, market prices, or theories about scientific farming while the children learned their letters and the moral lesson in McGuffey readers. The proliferation of printed matter had an enormous impact on people's stock of information, values, tastes, and use of leisure time.

Just as printed materials wrought great changes in American life, the making of inexpensive timepieces affected its pace and rhythms. Before the 1830s, when few Americans could afford a clock, it was difficult to make exact plans or to establish rigid schedules. But the production of timepieces soared in the 1830s, and by midcentury, inexpensive mass-produced ones could be found everywhere. Even on the frontier, "in

Kentucky, in Indiana, in Illinois, in Missouri, and here in every dell in Arkansas, and in cabins where there was not a chair to sit on," according to one observer, "there was sure to be a Connecticut clock." Free of nature's irregular divisions of the day, Americans could decide how to use their time and coordinate their activities. Clocks encouraged a more disciplined use of time and undergirded the economic changes taking place. Timepieces, for example, were essential for the successful operation of railroads, which ran on schedules.

Clocks also imposed a new rhythm in many workplaces. For some Americans, the clock represented a form of oppression rather than liberation. An early mill song put it directly: "The factory bell begins to ring / And we must all obey, / And to our old employment go / Or else be turned away."

A New England Textile Town

The process of industrialization and its impact on work and the work force are ably illustrated by Lowell, the "model" Massachusetts textile town, and Cincinnati, a bustling midwestern industrial center. Though there were similarities between the process of industrialization in these two communities, significant differences also existed. The example of Lowell points out the importance of women in the early manufacturing work force, whereas Cincinnati shows that industrialization was often an uneven and complex process.

Lowell was a new town, planned and built expressly for industrial purposes in the 1820s. Planners gave most attention to the shops, mills, and workers' housing, but the bustling town had a charm that prompted visitors to see it as a model factory community. In 1836, Lowell, with 17,000 inhabitants, aspired to become the "Manchester of America." It was the country's most important textile center.

By 1830, women composed nearly 70 percent of the Lowell textile work force, with men and children filling the remaining positions. The women who came to Lowell for jobs were the first women to labor outside their homes in large numbers. They were also among the first Americans to experience the full impact of the factory system.

Lowell's planners realized the difficulty of persuading men to leave farming for mill work, but saw that they might recruit unmarried women relatively cheaply for a stint. Unlike mill owners farther south, they decided not to depend on child labor. By hiring women who would work only until marriage, they hoped to avoid the depraved and depressed work force so evident in Great Britain.

In this 1832 painting, Lowell, Massachusetts, is shown as a dignified town set amidst rolling hills and fields. Its substantial appearance testified to the mill owners' desire to create a model community that would avoid the blight associated with English industrial towns. (New York Public Library, Astor, Lenox and Tilden Foundations)

New England factory communities, they hoped, because of their special arrangements, would become models for the world.

Working and Living in a Mill Town

At the age of 15, Mary Paul wrote to her father asking him "to consent to let me go to Lowell if you can." This young woman from Vermont was typical of those drawn to work in Lowell and other New England textile towns. As the planners had anticipated, the bulk of the work force was made up of young unmarried women. In 1830, more than 63 percent of Lowell's population was female, and most were between the ages of 15 and 29.

These women, from New England's middling rural families, came to the mills for a variety of reasons, but desperate poverty was not one of them. The decline of home manufacture deprived many women, especially daughters in farming families, of their traditional productive role. Mill work offered them the possibility of economic independence. As Sally Rice from Vermont explained, "I am almost nineteen years old. I must of course have something of my own before many more years have passed over my head. And where is that something coming from if I go home and earn nothing." Mill work paid women relatively well in the 1820s and 1830s. Domestic servants' weekly wages hovered around 75 cents, and seamstresses' 90 cents, whereas in the mid-1830s women could make between $2.40 and $3.20 a week in the mill. The lure of the "privileges" of the new environment also drew young women to Lowell.

Few considered their decision to come to Lowell a permanent commitment. Most young women were like Mary Paul and Sally Rice. They came to work for a few years, felt free to go home or

Studying this 1853 timetable for work in the Lowell mills reveals the long hours the operatives spent in the factories and the seasonal variations in work. Perhaps even more striking, the very organization of this timetable emphasizes the regimentation factory employment entailed. (Merrimack Valley Textile Museum)

TIME TABLE OF THE LOWELL MILLS,

Arranged to make the working time throughout the year average 11 hours per day.

TO TAKE EFFECT SEPTEMBER 21st., 1853,

The Standard time being that of the meridian of Lowell, as shown by the Regulator Clock of AMOS SANBORN, Post Office Corner, Central Street.

From March 20th to September 19th, inclusive.

COMMENCE WORK, at 6.30 A.M. LEAVE OFF WORK, at 6.30 P.M., except on Saturday Evenings.
BREAKFAST at 6 A.M. DINNER, at 12 M. Commence Work, after dinner, 12.45 P.M.

From September 20th to March 19th, inclusive.

COMMENCE WORK at 7.00 A.M. LEAVE OFF WORK, at 7.00 P.M., except on Saturday Evenings.
BREAKFAST at 6.30 A.M. DINNER, at 12.30 P.M. Commence Work, after dinner, 1.15 P.M.

BELLS.

From March 20th to September 19th, inclusive.

Morning Bells.	*Dinner Bells.*	*Evening Bells.*
First bell, ...4.30 A.M.	Ring out, ...12.00 M.	Ring out, ...6.30 P.M.
Second, 5.30 A.M.; Third, 6.20.	Ring in, ...12.35 P.M.	Except on Saturday Evenings.

From September 20th to March 19th, inclusive.

Morning Bells.	*Dinner Bells.*	*Evening Bells.*
First bell, ...5.00 A.M.	Ring out, ...12.30 P.M.	Ring out at . . . . .7.00 P.M.
Second, 6.00 A.M.; Third, 6.50.	Ring in, ...1.05 P.M.	Except on Saturday Evenings.

SATURDAY EVENING BELLS.

During APRIL, MAY, JUNE, JULY, and AUGUST, Ring Out at 6.00 P.M.
The remaining Saturday Evenings in the year, ring out as follows :

SEPTEMBER.	NOVEMBER.	JANUARY.
First Saturday, ring out 6.00 P.M.	Third Saturday ring out 4.00 P.M.	Third Saturday, ring out 4.25 P.M.
Second " " 5.45 "	Fourth " " 3.55 "	Fourth " " 4.35 "
Third " " 5.30 "		**FEBRUARY.**
Fourth " " 5.20 "	**DECEMBER.**	First Saturday, ring out 4.45 P.M.
OCTOBER.	First Saturday, ring out 3.50 P.M.	Second " " 4.55 "
First Saturday, ring out 5.05 P.M.	Second " " 3.55 "	Third " " 5.00 "
Second " " 4.55 "	Third " " 3.55 "	Fourth " " 5.10 "
Third " " 4.45 "	Fourth " " 4.00 "	**MARCH.**
Fourth " " 4.35 "	Fifth " " 4.00 "	First Saturday, ring out 5.25 P.M.
Fifth " " 4.25 "		Second " " 5.30 "
NOVEMBER.	**JANUARY.**	Third " " 5.35 "
First Saturday, ring out 4.15 P.M.	First Saturday, ring out 4.10 P.M.	Fourth " " 5.45 "
Second " " 4.05 "	Second " " 4.15 "	

YARD GATES will be opened at the first stroke of the bells for entering or leaving the Mills.

❖ *SPEED GATES commence hoisting three minutes before commencing work.*

Penhallow, Printer, Wyman's Exchange, 28 Merrimack St.

to school for a few months, and then returned to mill work. Once married—and the majority of women did marry—they left the mill work force forever.

New manufacturing work was regimented and exhausting. The day began at dawn or even earlier and ended about 7 in the evening. The standard schedule was 12 hours a day, six days a week, with only a half hour for breakfast and lunch. The clock tower atop the attractive four- to six-story brick mills symbolized the new control of work.

Within the factory, the organization of space facilitated production. In the basement was the waterwheel, the source of power. Above, successive floors were completely open, each containing the machines necessary for the different steps of cloth making: carding, spinning, weaving, and dressing.

This anonymous drawing shows a neatly dressed young woman carefully tending her machine. Her task, the most highly skilled in the textile factory, involved pulling warp threads through the harness and weave. A close examination reveals the repetitive nature of her work, but there is no hint of the tedium, noise, or other difficulties of millwork that the young women often mentioned in their letters. (Museum of American Textile History, North Andover, Massachusetts)

Elevators moved materials from one floor to another. On a typical floor, rows of machines stretched the length of the low room, tended by operatives who might watch over several machines at the same time. From his elevated desk at the end of the room, the overseer watched the workers. The male supervisor and two or three children roamed the aisles to survey the work and to help out. The rooms were noisy, poorly lit, and badly ventilated. Overseers, believing that humidity would prevent threads from breaking, often nailed the windows shut.

Although machines, not operatives, did the basic work of production, workers had to ensure that their machines worked properly. The lowest-paid women workers who watched over the spinning frames and drawing frames were responsible for piecing together broken yarn once the machines had automatically halted. The better-paid weavers made skillful interventions in the production process, repairing warp yarns and rapidly replacing shuttle bobbins when they ran out of yarn so that production would slow down for only a moment. "I can see myself now," recalled Harriet Robbins, "racing down the alley, between the spinning frames, carrying in front of me a bobbin-box bigger than I was … so as not to keep the spinning-frames stopped long."

Involving an adaptation to a completely new work situation, mill work also entailed an entirely new living situation for women operatives. The companies provided substantial quarters for their overseers and housing for male workers and their families. Hoping to attract respectable females to Lowell, the mill owners also constructed company boardinghouses where women workers had to live. Headed by female housekeepers, the boardinghouse maintained strict rules, including a 10 o'clock curfew. Owners wanted a respectable and well-rested work force. Little personal privacy was possible in the crowded 2- to 3½-story buildings. Normally, four or six women shared a small room, which contained little more than the double beds in which they slept together.

Amid such intimate working and living conditions, young women formed close ties with one another and developed a strong sense of community. Strong group norms dictated acceptable behavior, clothing, and speech and shared leisure activities at lectures, night classes, sewing and literary circles, and church. At work, experienced operatives initiated newcomers into the mysteries of tending machines, stood in for each other, and shared work assignments.

Female Responses to Work

Although mill work offered better wages than other occupations open to women, all female workers had limited job mobility. The small number staying in the mills for more than a few years did receive increases in pay and promotions to more responsible positions. A top female wage earner took home 40 percent more than a newcomer. But she never could earn as much as male employees, who at the top of the job ladder earned 200 percent more than men at the bottom. Because only men could hold supervisory positions, economic and job discrimination were an integral part of the early American industrial system.

Job discrimination generally went unquestioned, for most female operatives accepted sexual differences as part of life. But the sense of sisterhood, so much a part of the Lowell work experience, supported open protest, most of it focused against a system that workers feared was turning them into a class of dependent wage earners. Lowell women's critique of the new industrial order drew on both the sense of female community and the revolutionary tradition.

Trouble broke out when hard times hit Lowell in February 1834. Falling prices, poor sales, and rising inventories prompted managers to announce a 15 percent wage cut. This was their way of protecting profits—at the expense of their employees. The mill workers sprang into action. Petitions circulated, threatening a strike. Meetings followed. At one lunchtime gathering, the company agent, hoping to end the protests, fired an apparent ringleader. But, as the agent reported, "she declared that every girl in the room should leave with her," then "made a signal, and ... they all marched out & few returned the ensuing morning." The strikers roamed the streets appealing to other workers and visited other mills. In all, about a sixth of the town's work force turned out.

Though this work stoppage was brief and failed to prevent the wage reduction, it demonstrated women workers' concern about the impact of industrialization on the labor force. Strikers, taunted as unfeminine for their "amazonian display," refused to agree that workers were inferior to bosses. Pointing out that they were daughters of free men, strikers sought to link their protest to their fathers' and grandfathers' efforts to throw off the bonds of British oppression during the Revolution.

> *Let oppression shrug her shoulders,*
> *And a haughty tyrant frown,*
> *And little upstart Ignorance,*
> *In mockery look down.*
> *Yet I value not the feeble threats*
> *Of Tories in disguise,*
> *While the flag of Independence*
> *O'er our noble nation flies.*

The women viewed threatened wage reductions as an unjust attack on their economic independence and also on their claim to equal status with their employers. Revolutionary rhetoric that once held only political meaning took on economic overtones as Lowell women confronted industrial work.

During the 1830s, wage cuts, long hours, increased work loads, and production speedups, mandated by owners' desires to protect profits, constantly reminded Lowell women and other textile workers of the possibility of "wage slavery." In Dover, New Hampshire, 800 women turned out and formed a union in 1834 to protest wage cuts. In the 1840s, women in several New England states agitated for the ten-hour day, and petitions from Lowell prompted the Massachusetts legislature to hold the first government hearing on industrial working conditions.

The Changing Character of the Work Force

Most protest efforts met with limited success. The short tenure of most women mill workers prevented permanent labor organizations. Protests mounted in hard times often failed because mill owners could easily replace striking workers. Increasingly, owners found that they could do without the Yankee women altogether. The waves of immigration that deposited so many penniless foreigners in northeastern cities in the 1840s and 1850s created a new pool of labor. The newcomers were desperate for jobs and would accept lower wages than New England farm girls. Gradually, the Irish began to replace Yankee women in the mills. Representing only 8 percent of the Lowell work force in 1845, the Irish composed nearly half the workers by 1860.

As the example of Lowell suggests, the reality of massive immigration had a far-reaching effect on American life in the antebellum period. Immigration, of course, had been a constant part of the country's experience from the early seventeenth century. But it occurred on an unprecedented scale after 1845, the figure here makes clear. What had been a trickle in the 1820s—some 128,502 foreigners came to U.S. shores during that decade—became a torrent in the 1850s, with more than 2.8 million migrants to the United States. Although families and single women emigrated, the majority of the newcomers were young European men of working age.

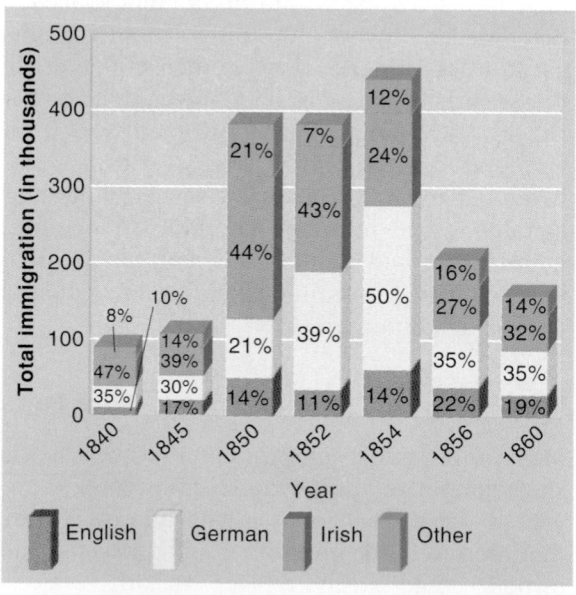

Immigration: Volume and Sources, 1840–1860

This chart captures the growing ethnic diversity of the country in the years before the Civil War. What is only implied is the element of religious diversity that immigration also introduced. Most of the Irish immigrants and half of the Germans were Roman Catholics. The presence of immigrants who differed so dramatically from Protestant Americans in background and culture contributed to the tensions of the period.

This vast movement of people, which began in the 1840s and continued throughout the nineteenth century, resulted from dramatic changes in European life: a population explosion between 1750 and 1845 and the introduction of new farming and industrial practices that undermined or ended traditional means of livelihood. Agricultural disaster also played a major role in uprooting the Irish from their homeland. Potatoes were the staple of the Irish diet. In 1845, a terrible blight attacked and destroyed the potato crop. Years of devastating famine followed. One million Irish starved to death between 1841 and 1851; another million and a half emigrated. Although not all chose the United States as their destination, the Irish were the most numerous of all newcomers to America in the two decades preceding the Civil War. They usually arrived almost penniless in eastern port cities without the skills needed for good jobs. With only their raw labor to sell, employers, as one observer noted, "will engage Paddy as they would a dray horse."

German immigrants, who made up the second largest group of newcomers during this period (1,361,506 arrived between 1840 and 1859), were not driven to the United States by the kind of desperate circumstances forcing the Irish to leave their homeland. Some even arrived with sufficient resources to go west and buy land. (The significance of this German midwestern presence is suggested by the fact that as late as 1940, German was one of the most common "street" languages in Minnesota.) Others had the training to join the urban working class as shoemakers, cabinetmakers, and tailors.

The arrival of so many non-British newcomers made American society more diverse than it had ever been. The consequences of this diversity were complex, as discussions in this and subsequent chapters will make clear. Because over half of the Irish and German immigrants were Roman Catholics, a religion long feared and disliked by Protestants, religious differences acerbated economic and ethnic tensions.

The impact of the Irish presence in Lowell was far reaching. As the ethnic makeup of the work force changed in the city, so did its gender composition. More men came to work in the mills. By 1860, some 30 percent of the Lowell workers were male. All these changes made the Yankee women expendable and increased the costs of going "against the mill."

It was easy for New England women to blame the Irish for declining pay and deteriorating conditions. Gender no longer unified women workers, not only because there were more men in the mills but also because Irish women and New England women had little in common. The Irish mill girl who started working as early as age 13 to earn money for her family's survival had a different perspective on work than the older Yankee woman who was earning money for herself. Segregated living conditions further divided the work force and undermined the likelihood of united worker actions in the 1850s.

Lowell itself changed as the Irish crowded into the city and New England women gradually left the mills. With owners no longer feeling the need to continue paternalistic practices, boardinghouses disappeared. A permanent work force, once a nightmare to owners, had become a reality by 1860, and Lowell's reputation as a model factory town faded away.

Factories on the Frontier

Cincinnati, a small Ohio River settlement of 2,540 in 1810, grew to be the country's third-largest industrial center by 1840. With a population of 40,382, it contained a variety of industries at different stages of development. Cincinnati manufacturers who turned out machines, machine parts, hardware, and furniture were quick to mechanize for increased volume and profits. Other trades like carriage making and cigar making moved far more slowly toward mechanization before 1860. Alongside these concerns, artisans like coopers, blacksmiths, and riverboat builders still labored in small shops, using traditional hand tools. The new and the old ways coexisted in Cincinnati, as they did in most manufacturing communities.

No uniform work experience prevailed in Cincinnati. The size of the shop, the nature of work, the skills required, and the rewards all varied widely. In 1850, most Cincinnati workers worked in small or medium-sized shops, but almost 20 percent labored in factories with over 100 employees. Some craftsmen continued to use a wide array of

skills as they produced goods in time-honored ways. Others used their skills in new factories, but they tended to focus on more specialized and limited tasks. In furniture factories, for example, machines did the rough work of cutting, boring, and planing, while some artisans worked exclusively as varnishers, others as carpenters, and still others as finishers. No single worker made a chair from start to finish. But all used some of their skills and earned steady wages. Though in the long run, machines threatened to replace them, these skilled factory workers often had reason in the short run to praise the factory's opportunities.

Less fortunate was the new class of unskilled factory laborers who performed limited operations at their jobs either with or without the assistance of machinery. In the meatpacking industry, for example, workers sat at long tables. Some cleaned the ears of the hogs, others scraped the bristles, others had the unenviable task of gutting the dead animals. Whereas owners in the industry profited from efficient new operations, workers received low wages and had little job security. Because they had no skills to sell, they were easily replaced and casually dismissed during business slowdowns.

The experience of Cincinnati's working women differed from that of their male counterparts. Cincinnati's large black community was so economically marginal, that a majority of black

Changing Occupational Distribution, 1820–1860*			
	1820	*1840*	*1860*
Agriculture	78.8%	63.1%	52.9%
Mining	0.4	0.6	1.6
Construction	—	5.1	4.7
Manufacturing	2.7	8.8	13.8
Trade	—	6.2	8.0
Transport	1.6	1.8	2.0
Service	4.1	5.0	6.4
Other	12.4	9.4	10.6

*The decline of agriculture and the increased involvement in industrial pursuits appear in this table.

Source: U.S. Bureau of the Census.

In 1848, an unknown photographer took this picture of Cincinnati. The prominence of steamboats in the picture suggests the role location and improvements in transportation played in the city's growth. Although the countryside is visible in the background, the rows of substantial commercial and industrial buildings make Cincinnati's status as a bustling urban center clear. (Public Library of Cincinnati and Hamilton County, Ohio)

women labored as washerwomen, cooks, or maids. Many white women were earning money as "out-workers" for the city's growing ready-to-wear clothing industry. Manufacturers purchased the cloth, cut it into basic patterns, and then contracted the work out to be finished by the women in small workshops or at home. Like many other urban women, Cincinnati women sought employment of this kind because they could not count on their husbands or fathers earning enough to support the family and because outwork allowed them to labor at home. Middle-class domestic ideology prescribed that home was the proper sphere for women, not the workplace. Many working men supported these views because they feared female labor would undercut their wages and destroy

order in the family. Outwork, then, allowed poor married women to supplement their family income while honoring social norms.

Paid by the piece, female outworkers were among the most exploited of Cincinnati's workers. Long days spent sewing in darkened rooms not only often failed to bring an adequate financial reward, but also led to health problems—ruined eyes and curved spines.

The successful marketing of sewing machines in the 1850s contributed to worsening working conditions and lower pay. The sewing machine made stitching easier, so the pool of potential workers increased and the volume of work that bosses expected grew. As tasks were further subdivided, work also became more monotonous. As one Cincinnati citizen observed, "as many as 17 hands" were employed on a single pair of pants.

Cincinnati employers claimed that the new industrial order offered great opportunities to most of the city's male citizens. Manufacturing work encouraged the "manly virtues" so necessary to the "republican citizen." Not all Cincinnati workers agreed. Like workers in Lowell and other manufacturing communities, Cincinnati's laborers rose up against their bosses in the decades before the Civil War.

The workingman's plight, as Cincinnati labor leaders analyzed it, stemmed from his loss of independence. Even though a manufacturing job provided a decent livelihood for some people, the new industrial order was changing the nature of the laboring class itself. A new kind of worker had emerged. Rather than selling the products of his skills, he had only his raw labor to sell. His "wage slavery," or dependence on wages, promised to be lifelong. The reorganization of work signaled the end of the progression from apprentice to journeyman to master and undermined traditional skills. Few workers could expect to rise to the position of independent craftsman. Most would only labor for others, just as slaves labored for their masters. Nor would wages bring to most that other form of independence, the ownership of shop and home. The expression "wage slavery" contained a deep truth about the changed conditions of many American workingmen.

Workers also resented the masters' attempts to control their lives. In the new factories, owners insisted on a steady pace of work and uninterrupted production. Artisans who were used to working in spurts, stopping for a few moments of conversation or a drink, disliked the new routines. Those who took a dram or two at work found themselves discharged. Even outside the workplace, manufacturers attacked Cincinnati's working-class culture. Crusades to abolish volunteer fire companies and to close down saloons, both attacked as nonproductive activities, suggested how little equality the Cincinnati worker enjoyed in an industrializing society.

The fact that workers' wages in Cincinnati, as in other cities, rose more slowly than food and housing costs compounded discontent over changing working conditions. The working class sensed it was losing ground at the very time the city's rich were visibly growing richer. In 1817, the top tenth of the city's taxpayers owned over half the wealth, whereas the bottom half possessed only 10 percent. In 1860, the share of the top tenth had increased to two-thirds, while the bottom half's share had shrunk to 2.4 percent. Cincinnati workers may not have known these exact percentages, but they could see growing social and economic inequality in the luxurious mansions the city's rich were building and in the spreading blight of slums.

In the decades before the Civil War, Cincinnati workers formed unions, turned out for fair wages, and rallied in favor of the ten-hour day. Like the Lowell mill girls, they cloaked their protest with the mantle of the Revolution. Striking workers staged parades with fifes and drums and appropriated patriotic symbols to bolster their demands for justice and independence. Although they did not see their bosses as a separate or hostile class, labor activists insisted that masters were denying workers a fair share of profits. This unjust distribution doomed them to economic dependency. Because the republic depended on a free and independent citizenry, the male workers warned that their bosses' policies threatened to undermine the republic itself.

Only in the early 1850s did Cincinnati workers begin to suspect that their employers formed a distinct class of parasitic "nonproducers." Although most strikes still revolved around familiar issues of better hours and wages, signs appeared of the more hostile labor relations that would emerge after the Civil War.

As elsewhere, skilled workers were in the forefront of Cincinnati's labor protest and union activities. But their victories proved temporary. Depression and bad times always harmed labor organizations and canceled out employers' concessions. Furthermore, Cincinnati workers did not readily unite to protest new conditions. The uneven pace of industrialization meant that these workers, unlike the Lowell mill women, had no common working experience. Moreover, growing cultural, religious, and ethnic diversity compounded differences in the workplace. By 1850, almost half the people in the city were foreign-born, most of them German, whereas only 22 percent had been in 1825.

As the heterogeneity of the American people increased, ethnic and religious tensions simmered. Immigrants, near the bottom of the occupational ladder, faced limited job choices and suspicion of their faith, habits, and culture. Protestant workers frequently felt that they had more in common with their Protestant bosses than with Catholic Irish or German fellow workers. These tensions exploded in Cincinnati in the spring of 1855. Americans attacked barricades erected in German neighborhoods, crying out death threats. Their wrath visited the Irish as well. Ethnic, cultural, and social differences often drove workers apart and concealed their common grievances. In many cases, disunity served economic progress by undermining workers' efforts for higher pay, shorter hours, and better working conditions, thus enabling businesses to maximize productivity and profits while minimizing the cost of labor.

Urban Life

Americans experienced the impact of economic growth most dramatically in the cities. In the four decades before the Civil War, the rate of urbanization in the United States was faster than ever before or since. In 1820, about 9 percent of the American people lived in cities (defined as areas containing a population of 2,500 or more). Forty years later, almost 20 percent of them did. Older cities like Philadelphia and New York mushroomed, while new cities like Cincinnati, Columbus, and Chicago sprang up "as if by enchantment." Although urban growth was not confined to the East, it was most dramatic there. By 1860, more than a third of the people living in the Northeast were urban residents, compared with only 14 percent of westerners and 7 percent of southerners. Although the majority of northerners still lived on farms or in small farm towns, the region was clearly urbanizing.

The Process of Urbanization

Three distinct types of cities—commercial centers, mill towns, and transportation hubs—emerged during these years of rapid economic growth.

Although the lack of water power limited industrial development, commercial seaports like Boston, Philadelphia, and Baltimore expanded steadily and developed diversified manufacturing to supplement the older functions of importing, exporting, and providing services and credit. New York replaced Philadelphia as the country's largest and most important city. The completion of the Erie Canal allowed New York merchants to gain control of much of the trade with the West. By 1840, they had also seized the largest share of the country's import and export trade.

Access to water power fueled the development of a second kind of city, exemplified by Lowell, Massachusetts; Trenton, New Jersey; and Wilmington, Delaware. Situated inland along the waterfalls and rapids that provided the power to run their mills, these cities burgeoned, as American industry, especially the production of textiles, expanded in the decades before the Civil War.

Between 1820 and 1840, one-quarter of the increase in urban population occurred west of the Appalachian Mountains, where a third type of city arose. Louisville, Cleveland, and St. Louis were typical of cities that had served as transportation service and distribution centers from the earliest days of frontier settlement. Chicago acted as "grand depot, exchange, counting-house, and metropolis" for its hinterlands. Like most of these western cities, Chicago was a commercial rather than an industrial center. In the 1850s, selling lumber to prairie farmers who needed it for fences and housing was one of Chicago's most significant commercial activities.

As the number of urban dwellers grew, their needs helped generate economic growth. City dwellers rarely had gardens or animals, so they had to purchase their food. This encouraged farmers to turn to commercial farming. Cities also provided a growing market for other products, including shoes, clothing, furniture, and carriages. The iron industry sold more than a half million cast-iron stoves yearly, mainly to city dwellers, and city governments purchased cast-iron pipes for sewers and the water supply and city merchants erected cast-iron buildings.

Until 1840, the people eagerly crowding into cities came mostly from the American countryside. Then ships began to spill their human cargoes into

Saint Louis is one example of the inland ports: you can see the bustle of urban life. Notice the prominent position the artist gave the church. (Chicago Historical Society)

seaboard cities, and a growing number of immigrants began their lives anew in the United States. Immigrants who could afford to leave the crowded port cities for the interior, many of them Germans and Scandinavians, did so. But the penniless had little choice but to remain in eastern cities and search for work there. By 1860, fully 20 percent of the people living in the Northeast were immigrants; in some of the largest cities, they and their children comprised more than half the population. The Irish, fleeing famine and poverty at home, were the largest foreign group in the Northeast.

A look at Philadelphia reveals the character, rhythms, rewards, and tensions of urban life during the antebellum period. The city was one of the giants of the age. An inland port, a bustling mercantile city, a center of shops producing textiles, metals, and a host of other products, Philadelphia stood second only to New York. Though William Penn's "green country town" boasted an attractive appearance and an orderly plan, the expanding nineteenth-century city merited little praise. Speculators interested only in profit relied on the grid pattern as the cheapest and most efficient way to divide land for development. They built monotonous miles of new streets, new houses, new alleys, with "not a single acre left for public use, either for pleasure or health," as merchant Samuel Breck observed.

Not all citizens enjoyed the benefits of urban life. Overwhelmed by rapid growth, city governments provided few of the services we consider essential today, and usually only to those who paid for them. Poor families devoted many hours to securing necessities that affluent citizens had at their fingertips. Water is a case in point. By 1801, Philadelphia had constructed a system of waterworks that drew water from the Schuylkill River, and then pumped it through wooden pipes to street hydrants. Only by paying a special fee could Philadelphians have water brought into their homes, so most of the city's residents went

Although this panoramic view of Philadelphia in about 1855 shows individual buildings and empty lots, it is the grid street pattern that stands out as the main feature of the city. By imposing the grid pattern on varied landscapes, Americans created similar types of urban spaces all over the country. This picture does not hint at the underside of Philadelphia life; its purpose seems to be to highlight the importance of the nation's second-largest city. (The Historical Society of Pennsylvania)

without. In the 1820s, the city expanded the water system by constructing the Fairmount water-works, but the more abundant supply of water again benefited those who could afford to pipe it into their homes.

In 1849, Isaac Parrish's report on the sanitary conditions in Philadelphia lamented some of the consequences. "There is … a general absence of bathing apparatus, and even of hydrants," he wrote, "in the houses of the poorer classes, and especially in confined courts and alleys of the populous districts of the city." An earlier inspection, carried out by Mathew Carey in 1837, had pointed to an even more basic problem: 253 persons crowded into 30 tenements without even one privy. The ability to pay for services determined not only comfort, but health.

Class Structure in the Cities

The drastic differences in the quality of urban life reflected social fluidity and the growing economic inequality that characterized Philadelphia and other American cities. In sharp contrast to the colonial period, the first half of the nineteenth century witnessed a dramatic rise in the concen-

tration of wealth in the United States. The pattern was most extreme in cities.

Because Americans believed that capitalists deserved most of their profits, the well-to-do profited handsomely from this period of growth, whereas workers lost ground. The merchants, brokers, lawyers, bankers, and manufacturers of Philadelphia's upper class gained control of more and more of the city's wealth. By the late 1840s, the wealthiest 4 percent of the population held about two-thirds of the wealth. The economic pattern was similar in other American cities, as the table on page 343 indicates. The houses of the city's elite were spacious and filled with new conveniences. Samuel Breck's house in 1839 was elegant and luxurious, with "parlours 14 feet high,… furnaces, water closet and shower and common bath up stairs, marble mantels and fireplaces in dressing rooms." Costing $22,500, Breck's "splendid house" represented the sum an ordinary Philadelphia textile factory operative might expect to earn in 75 years of work.

The widening gap between the upper class and the working class did not translate into mass suffering because more wealth was being generated. But the growing inequality hardened class

Wealth Distribution in Three Eastern Cities in the 1840s*			
Level of Wealth	Percentage of Population	Approximate Noncorporate Wealth Owned	Percentage Noncorporate Wealth
Brooklyn in 1841			
$50,000 or more	1	$10,087,000	42
$15,000 to $50,000	2	$14,000,000	17
$4,500 to $15,000	9	$15,730,000	24
$1,000 to $4,500	15	$12,804,000	12
$100 to $1,000	7	$11,000,000	4
Under $100	66	—	—
New York City in 1845			
$50,000 or more	1	$85,804,000	40
$20,000 to $50,000	3	$55,000,000	26
Boston in 1848			
$90,000 or more	1	$47,778,500	37
$35,000 to $90,000	3	$34,781,800	27
$4,000 to $35,000	15	$40,636,400	32
Under $4,000	81	$16,000,000	4

*Americans and foreign visitors often commented on the rough equality they believed characterized American life. Wealth distribution figures, although incomplete, suggest a different picture of American society.

Source: Edward Pessen, *Riches, Class, and Power Before the Civil War* (1973).

lines, nourished social tensions, and contributed to the labor protests of the antebellum period.

Between 1820 and 1860, a new working and middle class were in the process of formation in Philadelphia and elsewhere. As preindustrial ways of producing goods yielded to factory production and as the pace of economic activity quickened, some former artisans and skilled workers took advantage of newly created opportunities. Perhaps 10 to 15 percent of Philadelphians in each decade before the Civil War were able to improve their occupations and places of residence. They became businessmen, factory owners, mill supervisors, clerks, bookkeepers, engineers, or shopkeepers. Increasingly, membership in this middle class meant having a nonmanual occupation and a special place of work suited to activities that demanded brainpower rather than brawn. But as new opportunities opened up for some, downward occupational mobility increased. Former artisans or journeymen became part of a new class of permanent manual workers, dependent on wages for their livelihood. Fed by waves of immigrants, the lower class was growing at an accelerating rate. Moreover, within the working class itself, the percentage of unskilled wage earners living in poverty or on its brink increased from 17 to 24 percent between 1820 and 1860. At the same time, the proportion of craftsmen, once the heart of the laboring class, shrank from 56 to 47 percent.

The Urban Working Class

As with so much else in urban life, housing patterns reflected social and economic divisions. The poorest rented quarters in crowded, flimsily constructed shacks, shanties, and two-room houses. Because renters moved often, from one cramped lodging to another, it was difficult for them to create close-knit neighborhoods that might offer the fellowship and assistance to offset the harsh conditions of daily life.

Substantial houses fronting the main streets concealed the worst urban housing, which was in back alleys or even in backyards. Many visitors did not even realize slums lay behind the rows of brick housing, nor did they know of the uncollected garbage, privy runoffs, and fetid decay in the dark, unpaved alleys. In his diary, Philadelphia shopkeeper Joseph Sill left a description of living conditions at the bottom. "In the afternoon," he wrote, "Mrs. S & I went to the lowest part of the City to see some poor persons who had call'd upon us for Charity. We found one woman, with two children, & expecting soon to be confined, living in a cellar, part of which was unfloored, & exhibited much wretchedness; but it was tolerably clean. Her husband is a Weaver, & had his loom in the Cellar, but has only occasional work."

What the Sills witnessed during their visit to the weaver's family was not just poverty, but the transformation of working-class family life. Men could no longer be sure of supporting their wives and children, even when they were employed, and felt that they had lost much of their authority and power in the family. Some found their wives no longer subservient or seemingly careless with their hard-earned money. One woman angered her husband by failing to give a clear account of what she had done with the grocery money. "He said if she did not give him a full account … he would kill her or something like that." The squabble over grocery money ended in murder. This family was an extreme case, but family violence that spilled out onto the streets was not uncommon in working-class quarters.

Middle-Class Life and Ideals

Although the Sills ventured into the world of the working class, their life could not have been more different. Members of the new middle class like the Sills profited from the dramatic increase in wealth in antebellum America. They lived in pleasantly furnished houses, enjoying more peace, more privacy, and more comfort than the less affluent. Franklin stoves gave warmth in winter, and iron cookstoves made cooking easier. Conveniences like Astral lamps made it possible to read after dark. Bathing stands and bowls ensured higher standards of cleanliness. Rugs muffled sounds and kept in the heat.

Material circumstances were one badge of middle-class status, but there were others as well. The acceptance of certain norms and values also identified a person as a member of the new middle class. Genteel behavior and the careful observance of elaborate rules of etiquette (a gentleman was expected to back out of a parlor after making a call upon a lady), the appropriate clothes and conversation, an elegantly furnished parlor for the entertainment of visitors—all served to establish the standing of the members of a middle-class family.

New expectations about the roles of men and women, prompted partly by economic change, also shaped middle-class life. In the seventeenth and eighteenth centuries, the labor of men and women, adults and children, all contributed to the family's economic welfare. But improved transportation, new products, and the rise of factory production and large businesses changed the family economy. Falling prices for processed and manufactured goods like soap, candles, clothing, and even bread made it unnecessary for women, except on the frontier, to continue making these items at home.

As men increasingly involved themselves in a money economy, whether through commerce or market farming, women's and children's contributions to the family welfare became relatively less significant. Although middle-class women and children still worked in their homes as their husbands left to "bring home the bacon," they often neither produced vital goods nor earned money. Even the rhythm of their lives, oriented to housework rather than the demands of the clock, separated them from the bustling commercial world where their husbands now labored. By 1820, the notion that the sexes occupied separate spheres emerged to express the new reality. Men's sphere was the public world, whereas women's was the domestic.

Men were charged with the task of financial support, a responsibility that, as Susan Warner's family experience suggested, was a heavy one in a changing economy. Women's duties included working at home, not as producer, but as housekeeper. As a popular book, *Whisper to a Bride*, counseled readers, "For his sake ... acquaint thyself with the knowledge that appertaineth unto a wife and housekeeper. If thou art deficient in this knowledge, rest not, till thou hast acquired it. It cometh readily to an attentive mind, and groweth with experience."

The role of housekeeper had both pleasure and frustration built into it. Susan Warner's celebration of domestic life in her novels suggested the satisfactions derived from a cozy household. Yet it was sometimes impossible to achieve the new standards of cleanliness, order, and beauty. Catharine Beecher's "Words of Comfort for a Discouraged Housekeeper" listed just of a few of the problems—an inconvenient house, sick children, poor domestics—that undermined efforts to create a perfect harmonious home.

Although women were expected to become "systematic, neat and thorough" housekeepers, whatever the personal costs might be, they were also given more elevated responsibilities as moral and cultural guardians of their own families and, by extension, of society as a whole. Believing that women were innately pious, virtuous, unselfish, and modest (all characteristics that men lacked), publicists built on the argument developed during the revolutionary era. By training future citizens and workers to be obedient, moral, patriotic, and hardworking, mothers ensured the welfare of the republic. Just as important, they preserved important values in a time of rapid change. Because men had none of women's virtues and were daily caught up in the fast-paced world of business, wives were responsible for helping husbands cope with temptations and tensions. A wife was, in the words of one preacher, the "guardian angel" who "watches over" her husband's interests, "warns him against dangers, comforts him under trial; and by ... pious, assiduous, and attractive deportment, constantly endeavors to render him more virtuous, more useful, more honourable, and more happy."

This view, characterizing women as morally superior to and different from men, had important consequences for female life. Because women thought they had a unique nature and because their husbands spent much of their time away

This illustration, entitled "Maternal Instruction," from an 1845 issue of Godey's Lady's Book and Magazine *not only suggests the importance of the printing revolution in spreading the new middle-class norms, but also emphasizes the importance attached to women's role as guides for their children. (The Newberry Library, Chicago)*

from home working, friendship with other women often became central. Women felt that they shared more with one another than with men, even their husbands. Similar social experiences and perspectives made female friendships a source of comfort, security, and happiness.

Although the concept of domesticity seemed to confine women to their homes and to emphasize the private nature of family life, it actually prompted women to take on activities in the outside world. If women were the guardians of morality, why should they not carry out their tasks in the public sphere? "WOMAN," said Sarah Hale, editor of the popular magazine *Godey's Lady's Book*, was "God's appointed agent of *morality*." Such reasoning lay behind the tremendous growth of voluntary female associations in the early decades of the nineteenth century. Initially, most involved religious and charitable activities. Women supported orphanages, paid for and distributed religious tracts and Bibles, established Sunday schools, and ministered to the poor. The associations provided women with congenial companions and suitable tasks for their "moral character." Sometimes the women recognized special interests that men did not share. In the 1830s, as we shall see in Chapter 12, women added specific moral concerns like the abolition of slavery to their missionary and benevolent efforts. As these women took on more active and controversial tasks, they often clashed with men and with social conventions about "woman's place."

Domesticity described norms, not the actual conduct of middle-class women. Obviously, not all women were pious, disinterested, selfless, virtuous, cheerful, and loving. But these ideas, expressed so movingly by novelists like Susan Warner, influenced how women thought of themselves and promoted "female" behavior by encouraging particular choices. Domestic ideals helped many women make psychological sense of their lives. The new norms, effectively spread by the publishing industry, influenced rural and urban working women. The insistence on marriage and service to family discouraged married women from entering the work force. Those who had to work often bore a burden of guilt. Many took in poorly paid piecework so that they could remain at home. Though the new feminine ideal may have seemed noble to middle-class women in cities and towns, it created difficult tensions in the lives of working-class women.

As family roles were reformulated, a new view of childhood emerged. Working-class children still worked or scavenged for goods to sell or use at home, but middle-class children were no longer expected to contribute economically to the family. Middle-class parents now came to see childhood as a special stage of life, a period of preparation for adulthood. In a child's early years, mothers were to impart important values, including the necessity of behaving in accordance with gender prescriptions. Harsh punishments lost favor. As Catharine Beecher explained, "Affection can govern the human with a sway more powerful than the authority of reason or [even] the voices of conscience." Schooling also prepared a child for the future, and urban middle-class parents supported the public school movement.

Children's fiction, which poured off the printing presses, also socialized children. Stories pictured modest youngsters happily making the correct choices of playmates and activities, obeying their parents, and being dutiful, religious, loving, and industrious. Occasionally, as in *The Child at Home* (1833), the reader could discover the horrible consequences of wrongdoing. The young girl who refused to bring her sick mother a glass of water saw her promptly die. Heavy-handed moralizing made sure that children got the proper message.

The growing publishing industry helped spread new ideas about family roles and appropriate family behavior. Novels, magazines, etiquette and child-rearing manuals, and schoolbooks all carried the message from northern and midwestern centers of publishing to the South, to the West, and to the frontier. Probably few Americans lived up to the new standards established for the model parent or child, but the standards increasingly influenced them.

New notions of family life supported the widespread use of contraception for the first time in American history. Because children required so much loving attention and needed careful preparation for adulthood, many parents desired smaller families. The declining birthrate was evident first in the Northeast, particularly in cities and among the middle class. Contraceptive methods included abortion, which was legal in many states until 1860. This medical procedure terminated perhaps as many as a third of all pregnancies. Other birth control methods included coitus interruptus and abstinence. The success of these methods for family limitation suggests that many men and women adopted the new definitions of the female sex as naturally affectionate but passionless and sexually restrained.

Mounting Urban Tensions

The social and economic changes transforming U.S. cities in the half century before the Civil War produced urban violence on a scale never before witnessed in the United States, not even during the Revolution. Festering ethnic and racial tensions often triggered mob actions that lasted for days. American cities were slow to establish a modern police force (London had organized one in 1829).

Most still had the traditional constable-and-watch system. The night watch lit city streetlights and patrolled the streets to preserve order and arrest suspicious characters. During the day, constables investigated health hazards, carried out court orders, and apprehended criminals against whom complaints had been lodged. Neither group tried to prevent crimes or discover offenses. Neither wore uniforms. Certainly, neither was able to "prevent a tumult." Each chaotic event made the London model more attractive.

Racial tensions contributed to Philadelphia's disorders. An unsavory riot in August 1834 revealed other important sources of social antagonism as well as the inability of its police force to control disorder.

One hot August evening, several hundred white Philadelphians wrecked a building on South Street that contained the Flying Horses, a merry-go-round patronized by both blacks and whites. A general melee followed. As the *Philadelphia Gazette* reported, "At one time it is supposed that four or five hundred persons were engaged in the conflict, with clubs, brickbats, paving stones, and the materials of the shed in which the flying horses were kept." Spurred by the taste of blood, the white mob moved into the center of the crowded, racially mixed neighborhood, where they continued their orgy of destruction, looting, and intimidation of black residents. Similar mayhem followed on the next two nights. Intermittent rioting broke out the succeeding night as well, but the presence of 300 special constables, a troop of mounted militia, and a company of infantry prevented the violence from reaching the pitch of the previous nights.

An investigation following the riots revealed that the white mob had caused at least $4,000 of damage to two black churches and more than 36 private homes. At least one black had been killed, and numerous others had been injured. As one shocked eyewitness reported, "The mob exhibited more than fiendish brutality, beating and mutilating some of the old, confiding and unoffending blacks with a savageness surpassing anything we could have believed men capable of."

Many rioters bragged that they were "hunting the nigs." Riots, however, are complicated events, and this racial explanation does not reveal the range of causes underlying the rampage of violence and destruction. The rioters were young and generally of low social standing. Many were Irish. Some had criminal records. A number of those arrested, however, were from a "class of mechanics of whom better things are expected": weavers, house painters, a cabinetmaker, a carpenter, a blacksmith, and a plasterer. No professional people or businessmen seem to have been involved. Accompanying the rioters, however, were onlookers who egged the mob on. As one paper reported, these onlookers "countenanced" the operations of the mob "and in one or two instances coincided with their conduct by clapping." The rioters revealed that in the event of an "attack by the city police, they confidently counted" on the assistance of these bystanders.

The mob's composition hints at some of the reasons for participation. Many of the rioters were at the bottom of the occupational and economic ladder and competed with blacks for jobs. This was particularly true of the newly arrived Irish immigrants, who were attempting to replace blacks in low-status jobs. Subsequent violence against blacks suggested that economic rivalry was an important component of the riot. "Colored persons, when engaged in their usual vocations," the *Niles Register* observed, "were repeatedly assailed and maltreated.... Parties of white men have insisted that no blacks shall be employed in certain departments of labor."

If blacks threatened the dream of advancement of some whites, this was not quite the complaint of the skilled workers. These men were more likely to have experienced the negative impact of a changing economic system that was undermining the small-scale mode of production. The dream of a better life seemed increasingly illusory as their declining wages drew them closer to unskilled workers than to the middle class. Like other rioters, they were living in one of the poorest and most crowded parts of the city. Their immediate scapegoats were blacks, but for them, the real but intangible villain was the economic system itself. Trade union organizing and a general strike a year later would highlight the grievances of this group.

Urban expansion also figured as a factor in the racial violence. Most of the rioters lived either in the riot area or nearby. All had experienced the overcrowded and inadequate living conditions caused by the city's rapid growth. The racial tensions generated by squalid surroundings and social proximity go far to explain the outbreak of violence. The same area would later become the

Family Paintings

Although paintings are often admired and studied for artistic reasons alone, their value as historical documents should not be overlooked. In an age before the camera, paintings, sketches, and even pictures done in needlework captured Americans at different moments of life and memorialized their significant rituals. Paintings of American families in their homes, for example, reveal both an idealized conception of family life and the details of its reality. In addition, the paintings provide us with a sense of what the houses of the middle and upper classes (who could afford to commission art) were like.

Artists trained in the European tradition of realism painted family scenes and portraits, but so did many painters who lacked formal academic training, the so-called primitive artists. Their art was abstract in the sense that the artists tended to emphasize what they knew or felt rather than what they actually saw.

Some primitive artists were women who had received some drawing instruction at school. They often worked primarily for their own pleasure. Other artists were craftsmen, perhaps house or sign painters, who painted pictures in their leisure time. Some traveling house decorators made a living by making paintings and wall decorations. Many primitive paintings are unsigned, and even when we know the painter's identity, we rarely know more than a name and perhaps a date. Primitive artists flourished in the first three-quarters of the nineteenth century, eventually supplanted by the camera and inexpensive prints.

We see here a painting of the Sargent family done by an unknown artist around 1800. Though not an exact representation of reality, it does convey what the artist and the buyer considered important. Like any piece of historical evidence, this painting must be approached critically and carefully. Our questions focus on four areas: (1) the individual family members and their treatment, (2) the objects associated with each, (3) the implied or apparent relationship between family members, and (4) the domestic environment. The painting gives us an idealized version of what both the painter and the subjects felt ought to be as well as what actually was.

First, study the family itself. Describe what you see. How many family members are there, and what is each

Anonymous, The Sargent Family, *1800. (National Gallery of Art)*

one doing? What seems to be the relationship between husband and wife? Why do you think Mr. Sargent is painted with his hat on? Who seems to dominate the painting, and how is this dominance conveyed (positioning, attitude or facial expression, eye contact, clothing)? What can you conclude about different "spheres" and roles for men and women?

Why do you think the artist painted two empty chairs and included a ball and a dog in this scene of family life? What do these choices suggest about attitudes toward children and their upbringing? What seems to be the role of the children in the family? What does the painting suggest about how this family wished to be viewed? How do your conclusions relate to information discussed in this chapter?

Take a look at the room in which the Sargents are gathered. Make an inventory of the objects and furnishings in it. The room seems quite barren in comparison with present-day interiors. Why? Why do you think the chairs are placed near the window and door? What kind of scene does the window frame?

The *Family at Home,* painted by H. Knight in 1836, is a more detailed painting showing a larger family gathering almost 40 years later. Similar questions can be asked about this painting,, particularly in relationship to the different treatment of boys and girls and the positioning and objects associated with each sex. There are many clues about the different socialization of male and female children. The family's living room can be contrasted with the Sargent family's room to reveal some of the changes brought about by industrialization.

Finally, how do these nineteenth-century homes and sex roles differ from those in colonial New England and the Chesapeake?

H. Knight, The Family at Home, *1836. (Private collection)*

scene of race riots and election trouble and became infamous for harboring criminals and juvenile gangs. The absence of middle- or upper-class participants did not mean that these groups were untroubled during times of growth and change, but their material circumstances cushioned them from some of the more unsettling forces.

The city's police force proved unable to control the mob, thus prolonging the violence. Philadelphia, like other eastern cities, was in the midst of creating its police force. In 1833, a small force had been added to the constable-and-watch system. The new force was supposed to deter crime by walking the city streets. But the force's small size rendered it powerless in the face of the angry mob. Only continued rowdiness, violence, and riots would convince residents and city officials in Philadelphia (and in other large cities) to support an expanded, quasi-military, preventive, and uniformed police force. By 1855, most sizable eastern cities had established such forces.

Finally, the character of the free black community itself was a factor in producing those gruesome August events. Not only was the community large and visible, but it also had created its own institutions and its own elite. Whites resented "dressy blacks and dandy coloured beaux and belles" returning from "their proper churches." The mob vented its rage against black affluence by targeting the solid brick houses of middle-class blacks and robbing them of silver and watches. Black wealth threatened the notion of the proper social order held by many white Philadelphians and seemed unspeakable when whites could not afford life's basic necessities or lacked jobs.

The Black Underclass

Events in Philadelphia showed how hazardous life for free blacks could be. Although a small elite group of blacks emerged in Philadelphia and in other cities as well, most African Americans did not enjoy the rewards of economic expansion and industrial progress. Black men, often with little or no education, held transient and frequently dangerous jobs. Black women, many of whom headed their households because men were away working or had died, held jobs before and after marriage. In Philadelphia in 1849, almost half of the black women washed clothes for a living. Others took boarders into their homes and thereby added to their domestic chores.

Northern whites, like southerners, believed in black inferiority and depravity and feared black competition for jobs and resources. Although northern states had passed gradual abolition acts between 1780 and 1803 and the national government had banned slaves from entering new states to be formed out of the Northwest Territory, nowhere did any government extend equal rights and citizenship or economic opportunities to free blacks in their midst.

For a time in the early nineteenth century, some blacks living in the North were permitted to vote, but they soon lost that right. Beginning in the 1830s, in part because of the influx of fugitive slaves and manumitted blacks without property or jobs, Pennsylvania, Connecticut, and New Jersey disenfranchised blacks. New York allowed only those with three years' residence and property valued at $250 or more to vote. Only the New England states (with the exception of Connecticut), which had tiny black populations, preserved the right to vote regardless of color. By 1840, fully 93 percent of the northern free black population lived in states where law or custom prevented them from voting.

Other black civil rights were also restricted. In five northern states, blacks could not testify against whites or serve on juries. In most states, the two races were thoroughly segregated. Blacks increasingly endured separate and inferior facilities in railway cars, steamboats, hospitals, prisons, and other asylums. In some states, they could enter public buildings only as personal servants of white men. They sat in "Negro pews" in churches and took communion only after whites had left the church. Although most Protestant religious denominations in the antebellum period split into northern and southern branches over the issue of slavery, most northern Churches were not disposed to welcome blacks as full members.

As the Philadelphia riot revealed, whites were driving blacks from their jobs. In 1839, *The Colored American* blamed the Irish. "These impoverished and destitute beings … are crowding themselves into every place of business … and driving the poor colored American citizen out." Increasingly after 1837, these "white niggers" became coachmen, stevedores, barbers, cooks, house servants—all occupations blacks had once held.

Educational opportunities for blacks were also severely limited. Only a few school systems admitted blacks, in separate facilities. The case of Prudence Crandall illustrates the lengths to which northern whites would go to maintain racial segregation. In 1833, Crandall, a Quaker schoolmistress in Canterbury, Connecticut, announced that she would admit "young colored ladies and Misses" to her school. The outraged townspeople, fearful that New England would become the "Liberia of America," tried all sorts of persuasion and intimidation to induce Crandall to abandon her project.

Nonetheless, Crandall opened the school. Hostile citizens harassed and insulted students and teachers, refused to sell them provisions, and denied them medical care and admission to churches. Ministers preached against Crandall's efforts, and local residents poured manure in the school's well, set the school on fire, and knocked in walls with a battering ram. Crandall was arrested, and after two trials—in which free blacks were declared to have no citizenship rights—she finally gave up and moved to Illinois.

Crandall likely did not find the Old Northwest much more hospitable. The fast-growing western states were intensely committed to white supremacy and black exclusion. In Ohio, the response to talk of freeing the slaves was to pass "black laws" excluding them from the state. Said one Ohioan, "The banks of the Ohio would be lined with men with muskets to keep off the emancipated slaves." In 1829 in Cincinnati, where evidence of freedom papers and $500 bond were demanded of blacks who wished to live in the city, white rioters ran nearly 2,000 blacks out of town.

As an Indiana newspaper editor observed in 1854, informal customs made life dangerous for blacks. They were "constantly subject to insults and annoyance in traveling and the daily avocations of life; [and] are practically excluded from all social privileges, and even from the Christian communion." An Indiana senator proclaimed in 1850 that a black could "never live together equally" with whites because "the same power that has given him a black skin, with less weight or volume of brain, has given us a white skin with greater volume of brain and intellect." A neighboring politician, Abraham Lincoln of Illinois, would not have disagreed with this assessment.

Rural Communities

Although the percentage of families involved in farming fell from 72 to 60 percent between 1820 and 1860, Americans remained a rural people. Agriculture persisted as the country's most significant economic activity, and farm products still made up most of the nation's exports. The small family farm still characterized eastern and western agriculture.

Even though farming remained the dominant way of life, agriculture changed in the antebellum period. Vast new tracts of land came under cultivation in the West. Railroads, canals, and better roads pulled rural Americans into the orbit of the wider world. Some crops were shipped to regional markets; others, like grain, hides, and pork, stimulated industrial processing. Manufactured goods, ranging from cloth to better tools, flowed in return to farm families. Like city dwellers, farmers and their families read books, magazines, and papers that exposed them to new ideas. Commercial farming encouraged different ways of thinking and acting and lessened the isolation so typical before 1820.

Farming in the East

During the antebellum period, economic changes created new rural patterns in the Northeast. Marginal lands in New England, New York, and Pennsylvania, cultivated as more fertile lands ran out, yielded discouraging returns. Gradually, after 1830, farmers abandoned these farms, forest reclaimed farmland, and the New England hill country began a slow decline. By 1860, almost 40 percent of people who had been born in Vermont had left their native state. A popular song of the 1840s captured the pattern of flight. "Come, all ye Yankee farmers who wish to change your lot, / Who've spunk enough to travel beyond your native spot. / And leave behind the village where Pa and Ma do stay, / Come follow me, and settle in Michigan, yea, yea."

Farmers who did not migrate west had to transform their production. By the 1830s, eastern farmers, realizing that they could not compete with western grain, sought new agricultural opportunities created by better transportation and growing urban markets. One demand was for fresh milk. By the 1830s, some eastern cities had grown so large that milk was turning sour before it reached central marketplaces. As a result, several cities, including New York, started urban dairies, where cows often fed on garbage and slop from distilleries and breweries. When railroad lines extended into rural areas, however, farmers living as far away as Vermont and upper New York State discovered that they could ship cooled milk to urban centers. In 1842 and 1843, the Erie Railroad carried 750,000 gallons of milk to New York City. New dairy farmers eventually drove the unsavory city dairies out of business. City residents had fresher and cheaper milk and drank more of it as a result.

Urban appetites encouraged other farmers to cultivate fruit and vegetables. Every city was surrounded by farmers growing produce for urban consumption. Railroads also prompted farmers miles away to turn to specialized farming. Upper New York State farmers began to raise and ship apples, while New Jersey and Delaware farmers became famous for their peaches. Thus, in July 1837, a Boston housewife could buy at the central market a wide variety of fresh vegetables and fruits, ranging from peas, summer squash, and cauliflower to grapes, cherries, and raspberries. Cookbooks began to include recipes calling for fresh ingredients.

As northern farmers adopted new crops, they began to consider farming as a scientific endeavor. After 1800, northern farmers started using manure as fertilizer rather than disposing of it as a smelly nuisance. By the 1820s, some farmers were rotating their crops and planting new grasses and clover to restore fertility to the soil. These techniques recovered worn-out wheat and tobacco lands in Maryland and Delaware for livestock farming. Calculation began to replace "habit and prejudice ... the powerful opponents of improvement."

Farmers in the Delaware River valley were leaders in adopting new methods, but interest in scientific farming was widespread. By 1860, American farmers had developed thousands of special varieties of plants for local conditions. Many improvements resulted from experimentation, but farmers also enjoyed more and better information. New journals like the *New England Farmer,* the *Farmers' Register,* and the *Cultivator* informed readers of modern farming practices, fertilizers, scientific breeding, and methods for treating fruits and vegetables. Following New York's lead in 1819, many states established agricultural agencies to propagate new ideas. Although wasteful farming practices did not disappear, they became less characteristic of the Northeast. Improved farming methods contributed to increased agricultural output and helped reverse a 200-year decline in farm productivity in some of the oldest areas of settlement. The increased use of a tool called the cradle increased farmers' ability to harvest grain and made it possible to cultivate more acres than before. A "scientific" farmer in 1850 could often produce two to four times as much per acre as in 1820.

Farmers in the fertile area around Northampton, Massachusetts, illustrate the American farmer's adjustment to new economic conditions. As early as 1800, better roads, a turnpike, and stage routes reduced rural isolation. Canal improvements and then railroads strengthened new contacts. With markets ever more accessible, farmers began to change agricultural patterns. Rather than raising crops and animals for home use or for local barter, farmers started to cultivate crops "scientifically" in order to increase profits. Farming was becoming a business. At home, women found themselves freed from many of their traditional tasks. Peddlers brought goods to the door. The onerous duty of making cloth and clothing disappeared with the coming of inexpensive ready-made cloth and even ready-made clothes in the 1820s. Daughters liberated from the chores of home manufacturing went off to the mills or earned money by taking in piecework from local merchants.

As the rhythms of rural life in the Connecticut River valley quickened, attitudes also changed. Cash transactions replaced the exchange of goods. Country stores became more reluctant to accept

This 1856 print titled "Preparing for Market" shows the farm as a center of human and animal activity and suggest the shifts in eastern agriculture that took place in the East as competition from the Midwest stimulated farmers to raise new crops for the market. The rise of commercial farming also encouraged technological innovation. The McCormick reaper was patented in 1834. (Yale University Art Gallery, New Haven. CT/Mabel Brady Garvan Collection)

wood, rye, corn, oats, and butter as payment for goods instead of cash. Some farmers adopted the ethic of getting ahead, although their motive was not entrepreneurship but rather a desire to provide for family material comfort.

Traditional attitudes did not disappear completely, however. Some farmers contented themselves with making a living rather than chasing a profit. "Reason's whole pleasure, all the joys of sense / Lie in three words, health, peace and competence" remained their motto. The desire to just get along rather than becoming involved in the market economy helps explain why wealth inequality increased near Northampton, as it did elsewhere in the rural Northeast.

Frontier Families

Many people who left the North during these years headed for the expanding frontier. After the War of 1812, Americans flooded into the Old Northwest. Early communities dotted the Ohio River, the link to the South. Concentrating on corn and pork, settlers sent their products down the Ohio and Mis-

sissippi rivers to southern buyers. In 1820, less than one-fifth of the American population lived west of the Appalachians; by 1860, almost half did, and Ohio and Illinois had become two of the nation's most populous states.

By 1830, Ohio, Indiana, and southern Illinois were heavily settled, but Michigan, northern Illinois, Wisconsin, and parts of Iowa and Missouri were still frontier. Chicago had only 250 residents. Conditions were often primitive, as Charles Butler and Arthur Bronson discovered during their 1833 trip. Their hotel in Michigan City, Indiana, was "a small log house, a single room, which answered the purpose of drawing room, sitting room, eating room & sleeping room; in this room some eleven or twelve persons lodged in beds & on the floor."

During the 1830s, land sales and settlement boomed in the Old Northwest. Changes in federal land policy, which reduced both prices and the minimum acreage a settler had to buy, helped stimulate migration, as the figure here shows. Eastern capital also contributed to the boom with loans, mortgages, and speculative buying. Speculators frequently bought up large tracts of land

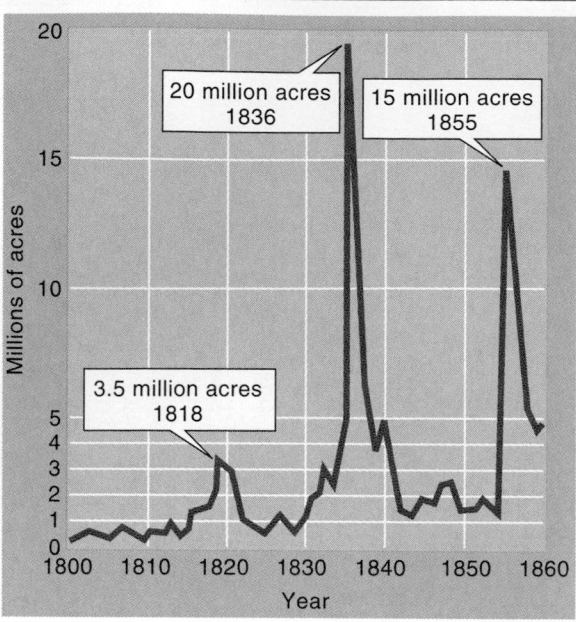

Western Land Sales, 1800–1860

20 million acres 1836

15 million acres 1855

3.5 million acres 1818

Millions of acres

Year

Note how changing federal policies encouraged western land sales.

from the government, and then subdivided them and sold parcels off to settlers.

Internal improvement schemes after 1830 also contributed to new settlement patterns and tied the Old Northwest firmly to the East. Erasmus Gest, who as a 17-year-old had worked on canal projects in Indiana, recalled the settlers' enthusiasm for improvements: "We Engineers were favorites with the People wherever we went."

Wheat for the eastern market rather than corn and hogs for the southern market became increasingly important with the transportation links eastward. Between 1840 and 1860, Illinois, southern Wisconsin, and eastern Iowa turned into the country's most rapidly growing grain regions. In the 1850s, these three states accounted for 70 percent of the increase in national wheat production.

Although the Old Northwest passed rapidly through the frontier stage between 1830 and 1860, its farming families faced severe challenges. Catharine Skinner, who moved from New York to Indiana with her husband when she was 24,

described her rigorous existence. "We are poor and live in the woods where deers roam plentifully and the wolf is occasionally heard," she wrote to her sister in 1849. "We are employed in honest business and trying to do the best we can; we have got 80 acres of land in the woods of Indiana, a very level country; we have got two acres cleared and fenced and four more pirty well under way; we have got about five acres of wheat in the ground; we raised corn enough for our use and to fat our pork … we have a cow so that we have milk and butter and plenty of corn bread but wheat is hard to be got in account of our not having mony."

The Skinners were typical. Western farms were small, for there were limits to what a family with hand tools could manage. A family with two healthy men could care for about 50 acres. In wooded areas, it took several years to get even that much land under cultivation, for only a few acres could be cleared in a year. The Skinners' target was to clear 10 acres during the first 12 months, if, as Catharine said, "health permit." At this rate, it could take ten years for settlers in forested areas to get a farm in full operation. On the prairies, the typical settler would need only half that time.

Catharine Skinner mentioned the shortage of money and described her family as "poor." Although money was in short supply in the Northwest, she probably overstated her family's poverty. It took capital to begin farming—a minimum initial investment of perhaps $100 for 80 acres of government land, $300 for basic farming equipment, and another $100 or $150 for livestock. To buy an already "improved" farm cost more, and free bidding at government auctions could drive the price of unimproved federal land far above the minimum price. Once farmers moved onto the prairies of Indiana and Illinois, they needed an initial investment of about $1,000, because they had to buy materials for fencing, housing, and expensive steel plows. If farmers invested in the new horse-drawn reapers, they could cultivate more land, but all their costs also increased.

Opportunities in the Old Northwest

It was possible to begin farming with less, however. Some farmers borrowed from relatives, banks, or insurance companies like the Ohio Life Insurance and Trust Company. Others rented land from farmers who had bought more acres than they could manage. Tenants who furnished their own seeds and animals could expect to keep about a third of the yield. Within a few years, some saved enough to buy their own farms. Even those without any capital could work as hired hands. Labor was scarce, so they earned good wages. In Indiana, German settler Jacob Schramm hired men "to help with heavy labors of lumbering and field work, ditch-digging, and so on." Five to ten years of frugal living and steady work for men like Schramm would bring the sum needed to get started.

Probably about a quarter of the western farm population consisted of young men laboring as tenants or hired hands. Although they stood on the bottom rung of the agricultural ladder, their chances of moving up and joining the rural middle class were favorable. Widespread ownership of land characterized western rural communities. Lucinda Easteen knew as much when she told her younger sister to come to Illinois, where "you can have a home of your own, but never give your hand or heart to a lazy man."

Rural communities, unlike the cities, had no growing class of propertyless wage earners, but inequalities nevertheless existed in the Old Northwest. In Butler County, Ohio, for example, 16 percent of people leaving wills in the 1830s held half the wealth. By 1860, the wealthiest 8 percent held half the wealth. In a Wisconsin frontier county in 1860, the richest tenth owned 40 percent of all property. Although wealth was not as concentrated in rural areas as in the cities, a few residents benefited more from rapid economic development than others.

Nevertheless, the Northwest offered many American families the chance to become independent producers and to enjoy a "pleasing competence." The rigors of frontier life faded with time. As Catharine Skinner wrote to her sister from her new Illinois home in 1850, "We here have meetings instead of hearing the hunters gun and the woo[d]man's ax on the sabbath."

Commercial farming brought new patterns of family life. As one Illinois farmer told his wife and daughter, "Store away your looms, wheels, [and] warping bars ... all of your utensils for weaving

TIMELINE

1805	*Palmer* v. *Mulligan*
1816	Second U.S. Bank
1817	New York Stock Exchange
1819	*Dartmouth College* v. *Woodward*
1820	Lowell founded by Boston Associates
	Land Act of 1820
	The expression "woman's sphere" becomes current
1824	*Sturges* v. *Crowninshield*
1824–1850	Construction of canals in the Northeast
1825–1856	Construction of canals linking the Ohio, the Mississippi, and the Great Lakes
1828	Baltimore & Ohio Railroad begins operation
1830	Preemption Act
1830s	Boom in the Old Northwest
	Increasing discrimination against free blacks
	Public education movement spreads
1833	Philadelphia establishes small police force
1834	Philadelphia race riots
	Lowell work stoppage
	Cyrus McCormick patents his reaper
1837	Horace Mann becomes secretary of Massachusetts Board of Education
1837–1844	Financial panic and depression
1840	Agitation for ten-hour day
1840s–1850s	Rising tide of immigration
1841	Distributive Preemption Act

cloth up in the loft. The boys and I can make enough by increasing our herds." Many farm families had money to spend on new goods. As early as 1836, the *Dubuque Visitor* was advertising the availability of ready-made clothing and "Calicoes, Ginghams, Muslins, Cambricks, Laces and Ribbands." The next year the *Iowa News* told of the arrival of "Ready Made Clothing from New York."

Agriculture and the Environment

Shifting agricultural patterns in the East and expanding settlement into the Old Northwest contributed to the changing character of the American landscape. As naturalist John Audubon mused in 1826, "a century hence," the rivers, swamps, and mountains "will not be here as I see them. Nature will have been robbed of many brilliant charms, the rivers will be tormented and turned astray from their primitive course, the hills will be levelled with the swamps, and perhaps the swamps will have become a mount surmounted by a fortress of a thousand guns." His sense of the consequences of the movement of peoples and the exploitation of land was shared by one French visitor who remarked that Americans would never be satisfied until they had subdued nature.

More than the subjugation of nature was involved, however. When eastern farmers changed their agricultural practices as they became involved in the market economy, their decisions left an imprint on the land. Selling wood and potash stimulated clearing of forests as did the desire for new tools, plow castings, threshing machines, or wagon boxes, which were produced in furnaces fueled by charcoal. As forests disappeared, so, too, did their wildlife. Even using mineral manures like gypsum or lime or organic fertilizers like guano to revitalize worn-out soil and increase crop yields meant the depletion of land elsewhere.

When farmers moved into the old Northwest, they used new steel plows, like the one developed in 1837 by Illinois blacksmith John Deere. Unlike older eastern plows, the new ones could cut through the dense, tough prairie cover. Deep plowing and the intensive cultivation of large cash crops had immediate benefits. But these practices could result in robbing the soil of necessary minerals like phosphorous, carbon, and nitrogen. When farmers built new timber houses as frontier conditions receded, they helped fuel the destruction of the country's forests.

Conclusion

The Character of Progress

Between 1820 and 1860, the United States experienced tremendous growth and economic development. Transportation improvements facilitated the movement of people, goods, and ideas. Larger markets stimulated both agricultural and industrial production. There were more goods and ample food for the American people. Cities and towns were established and thrived. Visitors constantly remarked on the amazing bustle and rapid pace of American life. The United States was, in the words of one Frenchman, "one gigantic workshop, over the entrance of which there is the blazing inscription 'NO ADMISSION HERE, EXCEPT ON BUSINESS.' "

Although the wonders of American development dazzled foreigners and Americans alike, economic growth had its costs. Expansion was cyclic, and financial panics and depression punctuated the era. Industrial profits were based partly on low wages to workers. Time-honored routes to economic independence disappeared, and a large class of unskilled, impoverished workers appeared in U.S. cities. Growing inequality characterized urban and rural life, prompting some labor activists to criticize new economic and social arrangements. But workers, still largely unorganized, did not speak with one voice. Ethnic, racial, and religious diversity divided Americans in new and troubling ways.

Yet a basic optimism and sense of pride also characterized the age. To observers, however, it frequently seemed as if the East and the Old Northwest were responsible for the country's achievements. During these decades, many noted that the paths between the East, Northwest, and South seemed to diverge. The rise of King Cotton in the South, where slave rather than free labor formed the foundation of the economy, created a new kind of tension in American life, as the next chapter will show.

Recommended Reading

Economic Change

Charles G. Sellars, *The Market Revolution: Jacksonian America, 1815–1848* (1991); Stuart Bruchey, *The Roots of American Economic Growth, 1607–1861* (1965); Albert W. Niemi, *U.S. Economic History: A Survey of the Major Issues* (1975); George R. Taylor, *The Transportation Revolution, 1815–1860* (1951); James A. Ward, *Railroads and the Character of America, 1820–1887;* Thomas C. Cochran, *Frontiers of Change: Early Industrialism in America* (1981); Nathan Rosenberg, *Technology and American Economic Growth* (1972); David J. Jeremy, *Transatlantic Industrial Revolution: The Diffusion of Textile Technology Between Britain and America, 1790–1830* (1981); David A. Hounshell, *From the American System to Mass Production, 1800–1832: The Development of Manufacturing Technology in the United States* (1984); Alfred D. Chandler, Jr., *The Visible Hand: Managerial Revolution in American Business* (1977); Robert F. Dalzell, Jr., *Enterprising Elite: The Boston Associates and the World They Made* (1987).

Laborers and Communities

Thomas Dublin, *Women at Work: The Transformation of Work and Community in Lowell, Massachusetts, 1826–1860* (1979) and, ed., *Farm to Factory: Women's Letters, 1830–1860* (1981); Alan Dawley, *Class and Community: The Industrial Revolution in Lynn* (1976); Mary H. Blewett, *Men, Women, and Work: Class, Gender, and Protest in the New England Shoe Industry, 1780–1910* (1988); Allen F. Davis and Mark H. Haller, eds., *The Peoples of Philadelphia: A History of Ethnic Groups and Lower-Class Life, 1790–1940* (1973); Steven J. Ross, *Workers on the Edge: Work, Leisure, and Politics in Industrializing Cincinnati, 1788–1890* (1985); Sean Wilentz, *Chants Democratic: New York City & The Rise of the American Working Class, 1788–1850* (1984); Richard B. Stott, *Workers in the Metropolis: Class, Ethnicity, and Youth in Antebellum New York City* (1990); Anthony F. C. Wallace, *Rockdale, The Growth of an American Village in the Early Industrial Revolution* (1978); Gary B. Nash, *Forging Freedom: The Formation of Philadelphia's Black Community, 1720–1840* (1988); Bruce Laurie, *Artisans into Workers: Labor in Nineteenth-Century America* (1989).

American Society

Alexis de Tocqueville, *Democracy in America* (1957 ed.); Edward Pessen, *Riches, Class, and Power Before the Civil War* (1973);. Stuart M. Blumin, *The Emergence of the Middle Class: Social Experience in the American City, 1760–1900* (1989); John F. Kasson, *Rudeness and Civility: Manners in Nineteenth-Century America* (1990); Elizabeth Blackmar, *Manhattan for Rent, 1785–1850* (1989); Russell Lynes, *The Domesticated Americans* (1957); Mary P. Ryan, *Cradle of the Middle Class: The Family in Oneida County, New York, 1790–1865* (1981); Karen Lystra, *Searching the Heart: Women, Men, and Romantic Love in Nineteenth-Century America* (1989); Christine Stansell, *City of Women: Sex and Class in New York, 1789–1860* (1986); Tamara K. Hareven, ed., *Family and Kin in Urban Communities, 1700–1930* (1977); Harvey J. Graff, *Conflicting Paths: Growing Up in America* (1995); Robert V. Wells, *Revolutions in Americans' Lives: A Demographic Perspective of the History of Americans, Their Families, and Their Society* (1982); Stephan Thernstrom, ed., *Harvard Encyclopedia of American Ethnic Groups* (1980).

Agricultural Change and the Frontier

Jeremy Atack and Fred Bateman, *To Their Own Soil: Agriculture in the Antebellum North* (1987); Christopher Clark, *The Roots of Rural Capitalism: Western Massachusetts, 1780–1860* (1992); Joan M. Jensen, *Loosening the Bonds: Mid-Atlantic Farm Women, 1750–1850* (1986); Robert Leslie Jones, *History of Agriculture in Ohio to 1880* (1983); Paul W. Gates, *The Farmer's Age: Agriculture, 1815–1860* (1960); Clarence Danhof, *Changes in Agriculture: The Northern United States, 1820–1870* (1969); John Denis Haeger, *The Investment Frontier: New York Businessmen and the Economic Development of the Old Northwest* (1981); Don H. Doyle, *The Social Order of a Frontier Community: Jacksonville, Illinois, 1825–1870* (1978); John Mack Faragher, *Sugar Creek: Life on the Illinois Prairies* (1986); Donald H. Parkerson, *The Agricultural Transition in New York State: Markets and Migration in Mid-Nineteenth Century America* (1995).

Slavery and the Old South

As a young slave boy, Frederick Douglass was sent by his master to live in Baltimore. When he first met his mistress, Sophia Auld, she appeared to be a "woman of the kindest heart and finest feelings." He was "astonished at her goodness" as she began to teach him to read. Her husband, however, ordered her to stop because Maryland law forbade teaching slaves to read. A literate slave was "unmanageable," utterly "unfit . . . to be a slave." From this episode Douglass learned to set inverse goals from Master Auld's wishes. "What he most dreaded, that I most desired . . . and the argument which he so warmly urged, against my learning to read, only served to inspire me with a desire and determination to learn."

In the seven years he lived with the Aulds, young Frederick used "various stratagems" to teach himself to read and write. In the narrative of his early life, written after his dramatic escape to the North, Douglass acknowledged that his master's "bitter opposition" had been as beneficial to him as Mrs. Auld's "kindly aid" in achieving his eventual freedom.

Most slaves did not, like Douglass, escape to freedom. But all were as inextricably tied to their masters as Douglass was to the Aulds. Nor could whites in antebellum America escape the pervasive influence of slavery. Otherwise decent people were often compelled by the "peculiar institution" to act inhumanely. After her husband's interference, Sophia Auld, Douglass observed, was transformed from an angel into a demon by the "fatal poison of irresponsible power." Her formerly tender heart turned to "stone" when she ceased teaching him. "Slavery proved as injurious to her," Douglass wrote, "as it did to me."

Such was also the case in Douglass's relationship with Mr. Covey, a slavebreaker to whom he was sent in 1833 to have his will broken. Covey succeeded for a time, Douglass reported, in breaking his "body, soul, and spirit" by brutal hard work and discipline. But one hot August day in 1833, the two men fought a long, grueling battle, which Douglass won. His victory, he said, "rekindled the few expiring embers of freedom, and revived within me a sense of my own manhood." Although it would be four more years before his escape to the North, the young man never again felt like a slave. The key to Douglass's successful resistance to Covey's power was not just his strong will, or even the magical root he carried in his pocket, but rather his knowledge of how to jeopardize Covey's reputation and livelihood as a slavebreaker. The oppressed survive by knowing their oppressors.

As Mrs. Auld and Covey discovered, as long as some people were not free, no one was free. Douglass observed, "You cannot outlaw one part of the people without endangering the rights and liberties of all people. You cannot put a chain on the ankle of the bondsman without finding the other end of it about your own necks." After quarreling with a house servant, one plantation mistress complained that she "exercises dominion over me—or tries to do it. One would have thought ... that I was the Servant, she the mistress." Many whites lived in constant fear of a slave revolt. A Louisiana planter recalled that he had "known times here when there was not a single planter who had a calm night's rest; they then never lay down to sleep without a brace of loaded pistols at their sides." In slave folktales, the clever Brer Rabbit usually outwitted the more powerful Brer Fox or Brer Wolf, thus reversing the roles of oppressed and oppressor.

Slavery, then, was an intricate web of human relationships as well as a labor system. After showing the economic growth and development of the Old South, in which slavery and cotton played vital roles, this chapter will emphasize the daily lives and relationships of masters and slaves who, like Douglass and the Aulds, lived, loved, learned, worked, and struggled with one another in the years before the Civil War.

The young Frederick Douglass, shown here in a photograph from about 1855, understood as well as any American the profound human, social, and political complexities and consequences of slavery. (New York Public Library, Schomburg Center for Research in Black Culture)

*P*erhaps no issue in American history has generated quite as many interpretations or as much emotional controversy as slavery. As American attitudes toward that institution have changed over the years, three interpretive schools have developed, each adding to our knowledge of the peculiar institution. The first saw slavery as a relatively humane and reasonable institution in which plantation owners took care of helpless, childlike slaves. The second depicted slavery as a harsh and cruel system of oppressive exploitation. The third, and most recent, interpretation described the slavery experience from the perspective of the slaves, who did indeed suffer brutal treatment in slavery yet nevertheless survived with integrity, self-esteem, and a sense of community and culture.

The first and second interpretive schools emphasized workaday interactions among masters and mostly passive, victimized slaves, while the third focused on the creative energies and agency of life in the slave quarters from sundown to sunup. In a unique structure, this chapter follows these masters and slaves through their day, from morning in the Big House through hot afternoon in the fields to the slave cabins at night. Although slavery was the crucial institution in defining the Old South, many other social groups and patterns contributed to the tremendous economic growth of the South from 1820 to 1860. We will look first at these diverse aspects of antebellum southern life.

Building the Cotton Kingdom

Many myths obscure our understanding of the vast region of the antebellum South. It was not a monolithic society filled only with large cotton plantations worked by hundreds of slaves. The realities of the South and slavery were much more complex. Large-plantation agriculture was dominant in the antebellum South, but most southern whites were not even slaveholders, much less large planters. Most southern farmers lived not in mansions, but in dark, cramped, two-room cabins. Cotton was a key cash crop in the South, but it was not the only crop grown there. Some masters were kindly, but many were not; some slaves were contented, but most were not.

There were many Souths, encompassing several geographic regions, each with different economic bases and social structures and each reflecting its own cultural and political values. The older Upper South of Virginia, Maryland, North Carolina, and Kentucky grew different staple crops from those grown in the newer, Lower or "Black Belt" South that stretched from South Carolina to eastern Texas. Within each state, moreover, the economies of flat coastal areas, inland upcountry forests, and pine barrens all differed. A still further diversity existed between these areas and the Appalachian highlands of northern Alabama and Georgia, eastern Tennessee and Kentucky, and western Virginia and North Carolina. Finally, the cultural and economic life of New Orleans, Savannah, Charleston, and Richmond differed dramatically from rural areas of the South.

Although the South was diverse, agriculture dominated its industry and commerce. In 1859, a Virginia planter complained about a neighbor who was considering abandoning his farm to become a merchant. "To me it seems to be a wild idea," the planter wrote in his diary, hoping that his friend would "give it up and be satisfied to farm." Southerners placed a high value on agricultural labor. Slavery was primarily a labor system intended to produce wealth for landowners. Although slavery in older areas was paternalistic, with masters and slaves owing mutual obligations to each other, increasingly it became a capitalistic enterprise intended to maximize productivity and profits.

Economic Expansion

In the 20 years preceding the Civil War, the South's economy grew slightly faster than the North's. Personal income in 1860 was 15 percent higher in the South than in the prosperous states of the Old Northwest. If the South had become an independent nation in 1860, it would have ranked as one of the wealthiest countries in the world in per capita income. One dramatic technological break-through, the cotton gin, was fundamental to this economic growth. The cotton gin had two momentous effects: first, it tied the southern economy to cotton production for a century; second, it allowed the expansion of slavery into vast new territories.

As we learned in Chapter 9, most cotton farmers planted "long-staple" cotton before the invention of Eli Whitney's cotton gin in 1793. After the cotton gin, the "short-staple" variety, which could grow anywhere in the South, predominated. But only large-plantation owners could afford to buy gins and purchase the fertile bottomlands of the Gulf states. Thus, the plantation system spread with the rise of cotton.

Because cotton could be grown all over the South after the perfection of the cotton gin, men rushed westward to fresh, fertile lands. Large-scale farming increased, demanding more and more slave labor. As a valuable capital resource, slaves received a degree of care and protection. But despite the abolition of slavery in the North and occasional talk of emancipation in the South, slavery became more deeply entrenched, seemingly a permanent part of southern life. Any doubts whispered about ending it could be dispelled by one word: cotton.

Although corn was a larger crop than cotton in total acreage, cotton was the largest cash crop and for that reason was called "king." In 1820, the South became the world's largest producer of cotton, and from 1815 to 1860, cotton represented more than half of all American exports. The economic growth spurred by cotton helped not only the South, but also the North and the Midwest. Northern merchants gained by shipping, insuring, and marketing southern cotton. Western farmers found a major market for their foodstuffs. Cotton was the mainstay of the southern economy, but it was also a crucial link in the national economy.

The supply of cotton from the South grew at an astonishing rate. Cotton production soared from 461,000 bales in 1817 to 1.35 million bales in 1840. A cotton "boom" started in 1849 when output

The Varied Economic Life in the South

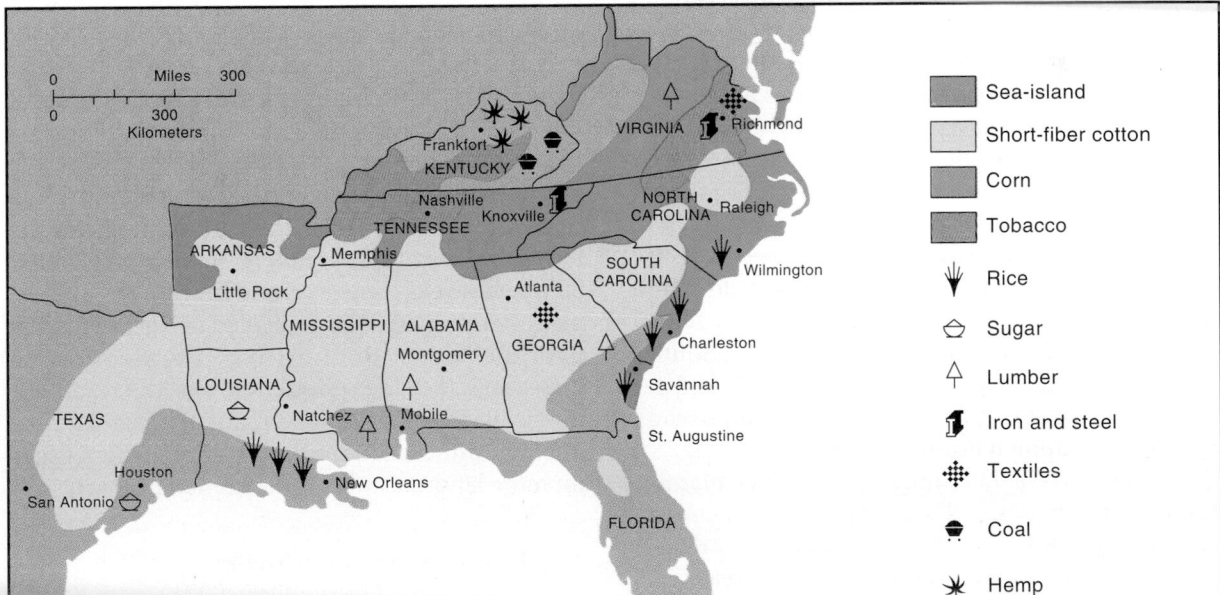

reached 2.85 million bales and continued until 1860, when production peaked at 4.8 million bales. In the period from 1817 to 1860, cotton production jumped over tenfold. This rapid growth was stimulated by world demand, especially from English textile mills. The availability of new lands, a self-reproducing supply of cheap slave labor, and low-cost steamboat transportation down the Mississippi River to New Orleans helped keep cotton king.

White and Black Migrations

Southerners migrated southwestward in huge numbers between 1830 and 1860 to grow more and more cotton. Seeking profits from the worldwide demand for cotton, they pushed the southeastern Indians and the Mexicans in Texas out of the way and were still moving into Texas as the Civil War began.

Southern cotton growers, like northern grain farmers, followed parallel migration paths westward. Whereas New Englanders moved into the upper Midwest, southerners migrated from the coastal states westward into the lower Midwest and the Lower South. By the 1830s, the center of cotton production had shifted from South Carolina and Georgia to Alabama and Mississippi. This process continued in the 1850s as southerners forged into Arkansas, Louisiana, and eastern Texas. As they moved, they carried their values and institutions, including slavery, with them. Usually, a father and his sons would go west first, find land and clear it, plant some corn, and begin to raise a cabin. Leaving the sons to finish, the father would return east, where his wife and daughters had been managing the farm, pack up the household, and bring it to the new home. Thus, in November 1835, one extended family of nearly 50 people left South Carolina for Alabama. "We bade adieu to friends," a daughter wrote, "and left the old homestead never to look upon it again."

Not only were these migrating southern families attracted by the pull of fresh land and cheap labor, but they also were pushed westward by deteriorating economic conditions and other pressures in the older Atlantic states. Beginning in the 1820s, the states of the Upper South underwent a long depression affecting tobacco and cotton prices.

Moreover, years of constant use had exhausted their lands, and families with numerous children struggled to give each child an inheritance or financial help to start a family or a career. In a society that valued land ownership, farm families had several choices. One was to move west. Another was to stay and diversify. Therefore, the older states of the Upper South continued to shift to grains, mainly corn and wheat. Because these crops required less labor than tobacco, slave owners, especially those with pressing debts, began to sell some of their slaves.

The internal slave trade from Virginia "down the river" to the Old Southwest thus became a multimillion-dollar "industry" in the 1830s. Between 1830 and 1860, an estimated 300,000 Virginia slaves were transported south for sale. One of the busiest routes was from Alexandria, Virginia, almost within view of the nation's capital, to a huge depot near Natchez, Mississippi. Although most southern states attempted occasionally to outlaw or control the traffic in slaves, these efforts were poorly enforced and usually short-lived. Besides, the reason for outlawing the slave trade was generally not humanitarian, but rather originated in a fear of a rapid increase in the slave population, especially of "wicked" slaves sent south because they were considered unmanageable. Alabama, Mississippi, and Louisiana all banned the importation of slaves after the Nat Turner revolt in Virginia in 1831 (described later in this chapter). But all three states permitted the slave trade again during the profitable 1850s.

Congress formally ended the external slave trade on January 1, 1808, the earliest time permitted by the Constitution. Enforcement by the United States was weak, however, and many thousands of blacks continued to be smuggled to North America until the end of the Civil War. The tremendous increase in the slave population was the result not of this illegal trade, however, but of natural reproduction, often encouraged by slave owners eager for more laborers and salable human property.

The Dependence on Slavery

The rapid increase in the number of slaves, from 1.5 million in 1820 to 4 million in 1860, paralleled the growth of the southern economy and its

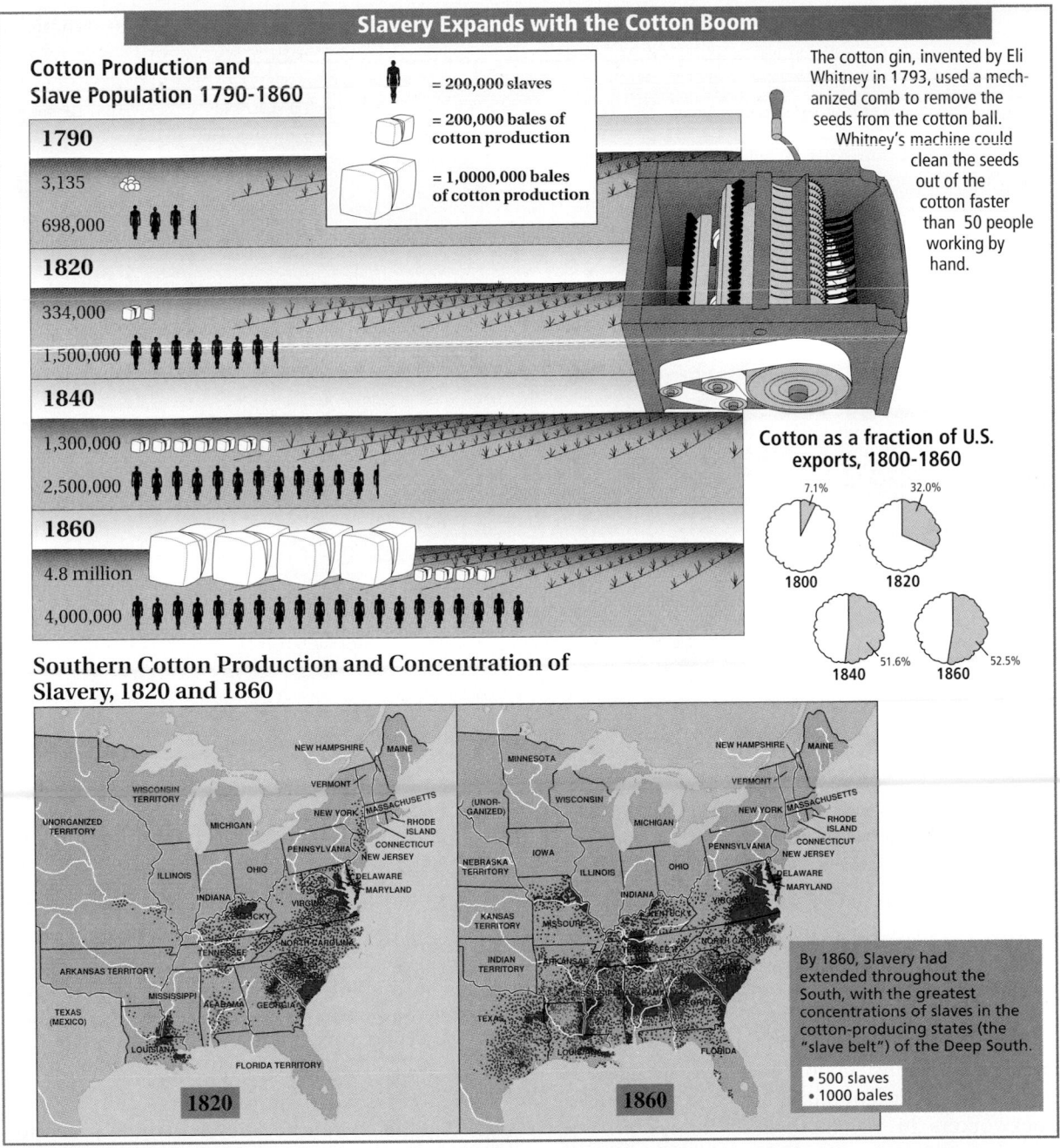

Slavery Expands with the Cotton Boom

Cotton Production and Slave Population 1790–1860

= 200,000 slaves
= 200,000 bales of cotton production
= 1,0000,000 bales of cotton production

1790 — 3,135 — 698,000
1820 — 334,000 — 1,500,000
1840 — 1,300,000 — 2,500,000
1860 — 4.8 million — 4,000,000

The cotton gin, invented by Eli Whitney in 1793, used a mechanized comb to remove the seeds from the cotton ball. Whitney's machine could clean the seeds out of the cotton faster than 50 people working by hand.

Cotton as a fraction of U.S. exports, 1800–1860
7.1% 1800 — 32.0% 1820 — 51.6% 1840 — 52.5% 1860

Southern Cotton Production and Concentration of Slavery, 1820 and 1860

1820   1860

By 1860, Slavery had extended throughout the South, with the greatest concentrations of slaves in the cotton-producing states (the "slave belt") of the Deep South.
• 500 slaves
• 1000 bales

dependence on the slave labor system. Economic growth and migration southwestward changed the geographic distribution of slaves, thus hindering the cause of abolition.

Although most slaves worked on plantations and medium-size farms, they could be found in all segments of the southern economy. In 1850, some 75 percent of all slaves were engaged in agricultural labor: 55 percent growing cotton, 10 percent tobacco, and 10 percent rice, sugar, and hemp. Of the remaining one-fourth, about 15 percent were domestic servants, and the remainder were in mining, lumbering, construction, and industry.

364   Part III   An Expanding People, 1820–1877

Population Patterns in the South: Whites, Slaves, and Free Blacks, by State, 1860

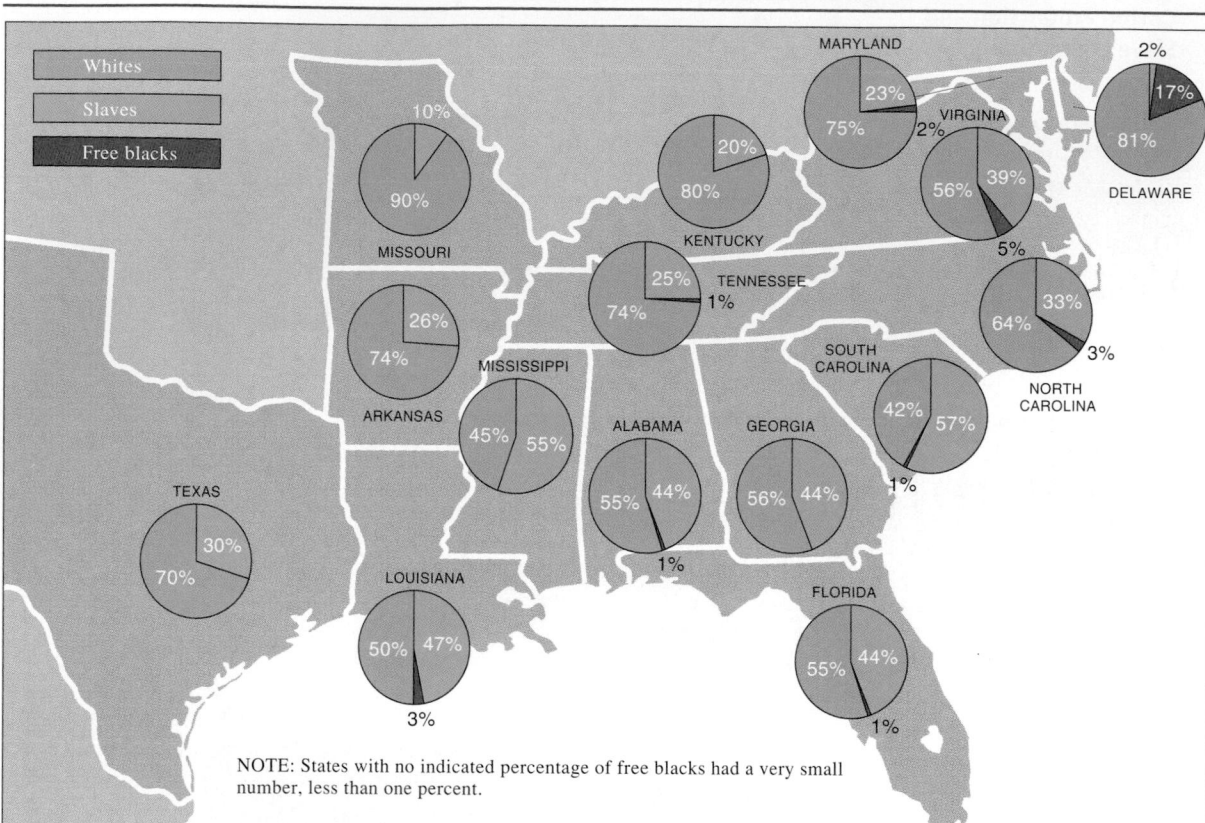

NOTE: States with no indicated percentage of free blacks had a very small number, less than one percent.

Note how the largest proportions of free blacks were in the older Upper South, and in Louisiana (mostly in New Orleans). Note also the two states with more slaves than whites.

The 300,000 slaves in 1850 who were not domestics or agricultural laborers worked as lumberjacks and turpentine producers in Carolina and Georgia forests; gold, coal, and salt miners in Virginia and Kentucky; boiler stokers and deckhands on Mississippi River steamships; toilers on road and railroad construction gangs in Georgia and Louisiana; textile laborers in Alabama cotton mills; dockworkers in Savannah and Charleston; and tobacco and iron workers in Richmond factories. A visitor to Natchez in 1835 observed slaves working as "mechanics, draymen, hostelers, labourers, hucksters, and washwomen, and the heterogeneous multitude of every other occupation, who fill the streets of a busy city—for slaves are trained to every kind of manual labour."

Masters also used slaves in the industrial sector. The Tredegar Iron Company of Richmond decided in 1847 to shift from white labor "almost exclusively" to slave labor in order to destroy the potential power of organized white workers to strike. Tredegar's decision, though local, had enormous future implications. Although black and white workers have sometimes been able to agree on class issues, racial animosities based on white perceptions of threats to their job security by black workers continue to this day.

Whether in iron factories, coal mines, or cotton fields, slavery was profitable as a source of labor and as a capital investment. In 1859, the average plantation slave produced $78 in cotton earnings for his master annually while costing only about $32 to be fed, clothed, and housed. Despite maintenance costs, debts from the purchase of land and more slaves, and the unstable price of cotton, the "crop value per slave" increased from about $15 in 1800 to $125 in 1860. Slaves were also a good investment. In 1844, a "prime field hand" sold for $600. A

Slaves were found not just on plantations doing agricultural labor, but in nearly every kind of labor in the South. These Virginia dockworkers were photographed about 1860 in Alexandria, Virginia, by Mathew Brady. (National Archives)

cotton boom beginning in 1849 raised this price by 1860 to $1800. A slave owner could prosper by buying slaves, working them for several years, and then selling them for a profit. The rising price of slaves reflected the optimism of the planter class.

The economic growth of the slaveholding South was impressive, but it was limited because of the dependence on slavery. Generally, agricultural growth leads to the rise of cities and industry, facilitating sustained economic growth. In the planter-dominated antebellum South, however, agricultural improvements did not lead to industrialization and urbanization. In 1860, the South had 35 percent of the country's population and only 15 percent of its manufacturing establishments. On the eve of the Civil War, 1 southerner in 14 was a city dweller, compared with 1 of every 3 people in the North. The South would continue its economic backwardness as long as whites with capital insisted on putting all their business energies toward cotton production.

Some southerners were aware of the dangers of following a single path to wealth. J. D. B. De Bow created a journal in 1846 dedicated to trade, commerce, and manufacturing. De Bow's *Review* called for greater economic independence in the South through the diversification of agriculture, the development of industry, and an improved transportation system. A believer in slavery, De Bow thought that slave labor could fuel the industrial revolution in the South. But the planter class had little enthusiasm for such plans. As long as money could be made through an agricultural slave system, plantation owners saw no reason to risk capital in new areas.

Slavery and Class in the South

Slavery was more than an economic institution, for it also served social purposes. Although the proportion of southern white families that owned slaves slowly declined from 40 to 25 percent as some families sold off their slaves to cotton planters, the ideal of slave ownership still permeated all classes and determined the hierarchical character of the southern social structure. At the top stood the planter aristocracy, much of it new wealth, elbowing its way among the old established families like the Byrds and Carters of Virginia. Some 10,000 rich families owned 50 or more slaves in 1860; about 3,000 of these owned over 100. Below them was a slightly larger group of small planters who held from 10 to 50 slaves. But the largest group, 70 percent of all slaveholders in

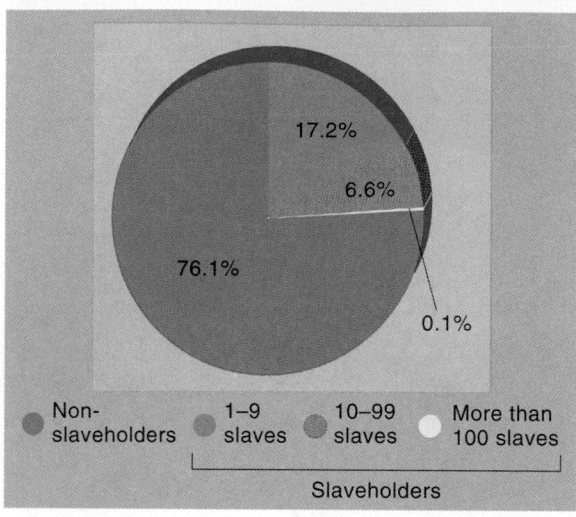

White Class Structure in the South, 1860

17.2%

6.6%

76.1%

0.1%

● Non-slaveholders   ● 1–9 slaves   ● 10–99 slaves   ○ More than 100 slaves

Slaveholders

In a pyramidal class structure, the richest southerners were those few with the largest number of slaves. As the chart shows, three-fourths of antebellum southerners held no slaves at all.

1860, comprised 270,000 middle-level farm families with fewer than ten slaves. The typical slaveholder worked a small family farm of about 100 acres with eight or nine slaves, perhaps members of the same family. The typical slave, however, was more likely to be in a group of 20 or more other slaves on a large farm or small plantation.

In 1841, a young white North Carolinian, John Flintoff, went to Mississippi to fulfill his dream of wealth and prestige. Beginning as an overseer managing an uncle's farm, he bought a "negro boy 7 years old" even before he owned any land. After several years of unrewarding struggle, Flintoff married and returned to North Carolina. There he finally bought 124 acres and a few more cheap, young blacks, and by 1860, he had a modest farm with several slaves growing corn, wheat, and tobacco. Although he never became as prosperous as he had dreamed, his son went to college, and his wife, he reported proudly, "has lived a Lady."

Slavery was a powerful force in the lives of middle-level farmers like John Flintoff, who had only a few slaves, and even for those who owned none. Upward economic mobility, social prestige, and political influence were determined by ownership of slaves. Many whites like John Flintoff hoped

to purchase one slave, perhaps a female who would bear children, and then climb the economic and social ladder of southern society. White southerners therefore supported slavery whether they owned slaves or not.

They also defended the institution because it gave them a sense of superiority over at least one group and a sense of kinship, if not quite equality, with other whites. Although there was always a small element of southern society that believed in emancipation, most southerners did not. A small Alabama farmer told a northern visitor in the 1850s that if the slaves were given their freedom, "they'd all think themselves just as good as we.... How would you like to hev a nigger feelin' just as good as a white man?" Another said that he wished "there warn't no niggers here" and did not know anybody who favored freeing them.

The Nonslaveholding South

Below Flintoff and other middling farmers lived the majority of white southerners, who owned no slaves but were equally, or even more, antiblack. Newton Knight, for example, worked a harsh piece of land cut out of the pines of southern Mississippi. He and his wife lived in a crude log cabin, scratching out their livelihood by growing corn and sweet potatoes and raising chickens and hogs. A staunch Baptist given to fits of violence, Knight had once killed a black.

The 75 percent of southern whites who, like Newton Knight and his family, owned no slaves were scattered throughout the South. Many were Scots-Irish. Most lived in the foothills of the mountains and worked generally poorer land than the large planters. They did not need to be near commercial centers because they were largely self-sufficient. Working together as a family, they raised mostly corn and wheat, hogs, enough cotton for their own clothes and a little cash, and subsistence vegetable crops. These farmers maintained a household economy, making soap, shoes, candles, whiskey, coarse textiles, and ax handles and trading hogs, eggs, small game, or homemade items for cash and other goods. They lived in two-room log houses separated by a "dog run." Cooperation with neighbors brightened the yeoman farmer's drab and isolated life. Families gathered at corn huskings and quilting parties, logrolling and wrestling matches, and political stump and revivalist camp meetings.

In many ways, the yeoman farmers were the solid backbone of the South. In 1860 in North Carolina, 70 percent of the farmers held fewer than 100 acres, whereas in Mississippi and Louisiana, reputedly large plantation states, more than 60 percent of the farms were under 100 acres. Fiercely proud of their independence, the yeoman farmers had a share of political power, voting overwhelmingly for Andrew Jackson. Although some resented the tradition of political deference to "betters," these farmers were not yet ready to challenge planters for political power. Yeoman farmers fought with the Confederacy during the Civil War; but some, like Newton Knight, refused to fight against the Union and ended up organizing a guerrilla band of Unionists in southern Mississippi.

Another little-known group of southern whites were the herdsmen who raised hogs and other livestock. Living among the plantations and small farms, they supplied bacon and pork to local slaveholders (who often thought hog growing was beneath their dignity) and drove herds of hogs to stockyards in Nashville, Louisville, and Savannah. The South raised two-thirds of the nation's hogs. In 1860, the value of southern livestock was $500 million, twice that of cotton. Although much of the corn crop fed the hogs, many herdsmen preferred to let their stock roam loose in the woods. As one South Carolinian explained, "We raise our hogs by allowing them to range in our woods, where they get fat … on acorns," which he and others considered a better diet for bacon and pork than corn. However valuable the total size of the hog business, individual hog herdsmen did not stand very high on the southern social ladder.

Below them were the poor whites of the South, about 10 percent of the population. Often sneeringly called "hillbillies," "dirt eaters," "crackers," or "poor white trash," they lived in isolated, inhospitable areas of the South, where they eked out a living from the poor soil of pine barrens, sand hills, and marshes. Although they grew a little corn and vegetables, their livelihood came mostly from fishing, hunting small game, and raising a few pigs. Some made corn whiskey, and many hired themselves out as farmhands for an average wage, with board, of about $14 per month. Because of poor diet and bad living conditions, these poor whites often suffered from diseases such as hookworm and malaria. This, and the natural debilitation of heat and poverty, led to their reputation as lazy, shiftless, and illiterate. An English visitor, Fanny Kemble, described them as "the most degraded race of human beings claiming an Anglo-Saxon origin that can be found on the face of the earth."

The poor whites were kept poor in part because the slave system allowed the planter class

Southern yeoman farm families lived self-sufficient lives of relative isolation. Gatherings such as this quilting party provided welcome social contact as well as the means to create a uniquely female American work of useful art. (Abby Aldrich Rockefeller Folk Art Center)

to accumulate a disproportionate amount of land and political power. High slave prices made entry into the planter class increasingly difficult, thus increasing class tensions within the South. Because the larger planters dominated southern life and owned the most slaves, an understanding of the character of slavery and the relationships between masters and slaves is best accomplished by looking at plantation life during a typical day from morning to night.

Morning: Master in the Big House

It is early morning in the South. Imagine four scenes. In the first, William Waller of Virginia and a neighbor are preparing to leave with 20 choice slaves on a long trip to the slave market in Natchez, Mississippi. Waller is making this "intolerable" journey, as he calls it, to sell some of his slaves in order to ease his heavy debts. Although he "loaths the vocation of slave trading," he must recover some money out of a "sense of duty" to see his family "freed from my bondage" of indebtedness. To ease his conscience, he intends to supervise the sale personally, thus securing the best possible deal not only for himself but also for his departing slaves.

On another plantation, owned by James Hammond of South Carolina, the horn blows an hour before daylight to awaken the slaves for work in the fields. Hammond rises soon after, ever aware that "to continue" as a wealthy master, he must "draw the rein tighter and tighter" to hold his slaves "in complete check." He is as good as his word, recommending that "in general 15 to 20 lashes will be sufficient flogging" for most offenses but that "in extreme cases," the punishment "must not exceed 100 lashes in one day."

On an Alabama plantation, Hugh Lawson is up early, writing a sorrowful letter to Susanna Clay, telling her of the death of a "devotedly attached and faithful" slave, Jim. "I feel desolate," Hugh writes, "my most devoted friend is gone and his place can never be supplied by another." As Lawson pens his letter, a female slave has already awakened and "walked across a frosty field in the early morning and gone to the big house to build a fire" for her mistress. As the mistress wakes up to a warming house, she says to the slave, a grown

woman responsible for the welfare of two families, "Well, how's my little nigger today?"

In a fourth household, this one a medium-size farm in upcountry Georgia, not far from Hammond's huge plantation, Charles Brock wakes up at dawn and joins his two sons and four slaves to work his modest acreage of grains and sweet potatoes, while Brock's wife and a female slave tend the cows that provide milk and butter. On small and medium-size family farms with five or fewer slaves, blacks and whites commonly worked together, as one observer noted, with the "axe of master and man [slave] falling with alternate strokes … [and] ploughing side by side."

As these diverse scenes suggest, slavery thoroughly permeated the lives of southern slaveholders. For the slaves, morning was a time for getting up and going to work. But for white slaveholders, morning involved contact with slaves in many ways: as burdens of figuring profit and loss, as objects to be kept obedient and orderly, as intimates and fellow workers, and as ever-present reminders of fear, hate, and uncertainty.

The Burdens of Slaveholding

Robert Francis Withers Allston (1801–1864) was a major rice planter in the Georgetown district of South Carolina, a low, swampy, mosquito-infested tidal area where four rivers empty into Winyah Bay. It was a perfect spot for growing rice, but so unhealthy that few whites wanted to live there. The death rate among slaves was appallingly high. In 1840, a total of 18,274 slaves toiled in the Georgetown district, but only 2,193 whites, many for only part of the year. Robert was the fifth generation of Allstons to live in this inhospitable land. By 1860, he owned seven plantations along the Peedee River, totaling some 4,000 acres, in addition to another 9,500 acres of pasture and timberland. He held nearly 600 slaves, 236 of whom worked at the home plantation, Chicora Wood. The total value of his land and slaves in the 1850s was approximately $300,000. Rich in land and labor, he nevertheless had large mortgages and outstanding debts.

Allston was an enlightened, talented, public-spirited man. Educated at West Point but also trained in the law, he did far more than practice agriculture. He served in the South Carolina state senate

Adele and Robert F. W. Allston shared the work and burdens of managing their rice plantations, while their slaves, many of them women, as seen in these drawings, planted rice seeds by covering them with their feet (as was done in Africa), and later carried the harvested rice to flatboats, where it was taken to the threshing yard. (Portraits, South Carolina Library, Columbia; Drawings, From Down by the Riverside, Charles Joyner, 1984, sketch by Alice R. Huger Smith, c. 1914)

for 24 years and as governor from 1856 to 1858. His political creed, he wrote in 1838, was one of "virtue and purity" based on "the principles of Thomas Jefferson." The core of his conviction was a "plain, honest, commonsense reading of the Constitution," which for Allston clearly meant the constitutionality of slavery and nullification and the illegitimacy of abolitionism and the United States Bank.

Allston also reflected Jefferson's humane side. He was an ardent reformer, advocating liberalization of South Carolina's poor laws; an improved system of public education open to rich and poor alike; humanitarian care of the deaf, blind, insane, and other disabled people; and the improvement of conditions on the reservations of the Catawba Indians. He was active in the Episcopal Church and gave money generously to support ministerial students.

In 1832, Allston married Adele Petigru, an equally enlightened and hardworking person. She participated fully in the management of the plantation and ran it while Robert was away on politics. In a letter to her husband, written in 1850, Adele demonstrated her diverse interests by reporting on family affairs and the children's learning, sickness among the slaves, the status of spring plowing, the building of a canal and causeway, her supervision of the bottling of some wine, and current politics. After Robert's death during the Civil War, she assumed control of the Allston plantations, which had been abandoned when Union troops moved through the area. Eventually, she had to sell most of the estate at auction, holding on only to Chicora Wood, which she managed with a daughter until her death in 1896.

State politics lured Robert from his land for part of each year, but he was by no means an absentee owner. Except when away to escape the worst periods of mosquitoes and heat, the Allstons were fully engaged in the operation of their plantations. Managing thousands of acres of rice required not only an enormous investment in labor and equipment, but also careful supervision of both the slaves and an elaborate irrigation system. Although Robert Allston's acreage and slave population were larger than those of most big planters and he grew rice rather than cotton, his concerns were typical.

Allston's letters frequently expressed the serious burdens of owning slaves. Although he was careful to distribute enough cloth, blankets, and shoes to his slaves and to give them sufficient rest, the sickness and death of slaves, especially young fieldworkers, headed his list of concerns. "I lost in one year 28 negroes," Allston complained, "22 of whom were task hands." He tried to keep slave families together, but sold slaves when necessary. In a letter to his son Benjamin, he expressed concern over the bad example set by a slave driver who was "abandon'd by his hands" because he had not worked with them the previous Sunday. In the same letter, Allston urged Benjamin to keep up the "patrol duty," less to guard against runaway slaves, he said, than to restrain the excesses of "vagabond whites." Clearly, the planter class felt a duty to control lower-class whites as well as black slaves.

Other planters shared Allston's concerns, seeing slavery as both a duty and a burden. A Louisiana planter, in financial difficulty, wrote how much he dreaded the "miserable occupation of seeing to negroes, and attending to their wants and sickness and to making them do their duty— and after all have no prospect of being paid for my trouble." Many planters insisted that they worked harder than their slaves to feed and clothe them and to make their lives "as comfortable as possible." Some accepted this as part of their responsibility, and others complained loudly. R. L. Dabney of Virginia exclaimed that "there could be no greater curse inflicted on us than to be compelled to manage a parcel of Negroes." Curse or not, Dabney and other planters profited from their burdens, a point they seldom admitted.

Their wives experienced other kinds of burdens. "The mistress of a plantation," wrote Susan Dabney Smedes, "was the most complete slave on it." Southern women were expected to adhere to the cult of domesticity both by improving their husbands' morals, which often meant restraining them from excessive cruelty toward slaves, and by beautifying their parlors. Moreover, plantation mistresses suffered under a double standard of morality. They were expected to act as chaste ladies, whereas their husbands had virtually unrestricted sexual access to slave women. "God forgive us, but ours is a monstrous system," Mary Boykin Chesnut wrote in her diary. "Like the patriarchs of old, our men live all in one house with their wives and their concubines; and the mulattoes one sees in every family partly

Agreement to Purchase Slaves, January 25, 1859

Robert Allston bought these slaves for his son, Benjamin, who was then 25 years old and taking charge of one of his father's many plantations, Guendalos. Note that in this (not unusual) case, slave families were kept together in the transaction.

Agreed to purchase from Dr. Forster Forty one Negroes of Mrs. Withers of the "remainder" from the Estate of the late Francis Withers, to be deliver'd in all this week at $500. Titles to Ben Allston his Bond and mine payable in 8, 10, 12 yrs. secured by mortgage of the property, viz

Price	No.	Name	Age	Remarks
$1,000	1	Andrew	38	yrs.
800	2	Serena	36	
400	3	Jos.	10	
300	4	Judy	8	
200	5	Henry	5	
1,000	6	Jack	30	
800	7	Patience	27	pregnant
400	8	Daniel	11	
300	9	Prince	9	
250	10	Phyllis	5	
200	11	Bess	3 ½	
800	12	James*	28	carpenter, Drinks, delicate
800	13	Hagar	24	pregnant, near time of delivery
200	14	Joe	39	carpenter and cooper
800	15	Levi	50	
500	16	Betsey†	40	delicate
400	17	Murria‡	18	
400	18	Toby	14	
$1,000	19	Paris	35	
800	20	Hannah	33	
800	21	Frank	16 ½	
500	22	William	14	
350	23	Caty	9	
300	24	Michael	6	
150	25	Eleanor	3 ½	
50	26	Dandy	1	
800	27	Strophon	50	
700	28	Lucy	18	
500	29	Judy	14	
1,000	30	Toney	38	an indifferent carpenter
800	31	Betty	35	
800	32	Daniel	16 ½	3 years with Bricklayers to mix mortar
200	33	Francis	4 ½	
100	34	Caesar	1 ½	
500	35	O Sary	50	cook and washer
1,000	36	Israel	31	
800	37	Esther	28	
100	38	William	1 ½	
800	39	Dinah	18 ½	
500	40	Quash	14 ½	
300	41	William	9	

*Has Epileptic attacks produced by drink, would be valuable if kept from drink.

†With this family there is the incumbrance of an old man of 80 years, father of Betsey.

‡Murria is half witted.

Note: Prices are from a second list, as are some of the remarks concerning individuals. The horizontal lines probably separate family groups.

Source: This and other material on the Allstons is from *The South Carolina Rice Plantation as Revealed in the Papers of Robert F. W. Allston*, ed., J. H. Easterby (1945).

resemble the white children. Any lady is ready to tell you who is the father of all the mulatto children in everybody's household but her own. Those, she seems to think, drop from the clouds."

Chesnut called the sexual dynamics of slavery "the sorest spot." There were others. Together with female slaves, plantation mistresses had to tend to the food, clothing, health, and welfare of not just their husbands and children, but the plantation slave population as well. Adele Allston, we saw, added plantation management to these duties. The son of a Tennessee slaveholder remembered his mother and grandmother as "the busiest women I ever saw." One woman, who spent the night sitting up to attend a slave birth, complained to a northern visitor: "It is the slaves who own me. Morning, noon, and night, I'm obliged to look after them, to doctor them, and attend to them in every way." The plantation mistress, then, served many roles: as a potential humanizing influence on men; as a tough, resourceful, responsible manager of numerous plantation affairs; as a coercer of slaves and perpetuator of the system; and sometimes as a victim herself.

Justifying Slavery

The behavior of Douglass's mistress, Sophia Auld, suggests that the institution of slavery pressured well-intentioned people, women and men alike, to act inhumanely. Increasingly attacked as immoral, slaveholders felt compelled to justify their institution. Until the 1830s, their defense explained slavery as a "necessary evil." After the abolitionists stepped up their attack in that decade, however, the justification shifted to defending slavery, in John C. Calhoun's words, as a "positive good." Various arguments were used: biblical, historical, constitutional, scientific, and sociological.

The biblical justification was based in part on the curse of Canaan, the son of Ham, who was condemned to eternal servitude because his father had looked on Noah's nakedness. Furthermore, in various places, both the Old and New Testaments admonished servants to obey their masters and accept their earthly lot. Southern apologists also cited historical arguments. Slavery had existed throughout history. In fact, the great ancient civilizations—Egypt, Greece, and Rome—had all built their strength and grandeur

in part on slave labor. No less an authority than Aristotle taught that in society, men of superior talents would become masters over those who were inferior.

A third argument justified slavery on legal grounds. Southerners pointed out that the United States Constitution did not forbid slavery. In fact, although slavery was not mentioned specifically, three passages in the original document clearly implied its constitutionality. First, slaves, called "all other Persons," were counted as three-fifths of a person for purposes of representation. Second, the overseas slave trade was protected from congressional abolition for 20 years. Third, the Constitution mandated the return of runaway slaves from one state to another.

A fourth justification was scientific. Until the 1830s, most white southerners believed that blacks were degraded not by nature but by environment, the special conditions and circumstances of African climate and American slavery. With the "positive good" defense in the 1830s, southern ethnologists increasingly argued that blacks had been created separately (a theory called "polygenesis") and were an inherently inferior race. Through a study of cranial shapes and sizes, called "niggerology" by one doctor, southern scientists maintained that in the black "the animal parts of the brain preponderate over the moral and intellectual, which explains why he is deficient in reason, judgement and forecast." Therefore, the destiny of the inferior Africans was to serve the superior Caucasians (the "Adamic race") in work. At best, the patriarchal slave system would domesticate uncivilized blacks. As Allston put it, "The educated master is the negro's best friend upon earth."

Allston's point suggested a paternalistic sociological defense of slavery. George Fitzhugh, a leading advocate of this view, argued that "the Negro is but a grown child and must be governed as a child." Therefore, he needed the paternal guidance, restraint, and protection of his white masters. What would happen, apologists asked, if the slaves were freed? Many southerners believed that chaos would ensue. Allston wrote that emancipation "cannot be contemplated," for it would lead to "giving up our beautiful country to the ravages of the black race and amalgamation with savages." Fitzhugh was a little less direct. He compared the treatment of southern slaves favorably with that of free blacks and of free laborers working in northern factories. These "wage slaves," he argued, worked as hard as slaves, yet with their paltry wages they had to feed, clothe, and shelter themselves. Southern masters took care of all these necessities. Emancipation, therefore, would be heartless and unthinkable, a burden to both blacks and whites.

Southern apologists for slavery faced the difficult intellectual task of justifying a system that ran counter to the main ideological directions of nineteenth-century American society: the expansion of individual liberty, mobility, economic opportunity, and democratic political participation. Moreover, the southern defense of slavery had to take into account the 75 percent of white families who owned no slaves and who envied those who did. Because of the potential for class antagonisms among whites, wealthy planters developed a justification of slavery that deflected class differences by maintaining that all whites were superior to all blacks but equal to one another. The theory of democratic equality among whites, therefore, was made consistent with racism and the holding of slaves.

However couched in the language of science, law, history, or religion, the underlying motive of these various justifications, though rarely admitted, was that slavery was profitable. As the southern defense of slavery intensified in the 1840s and 1850s, it aroused greater opposition from northerners and from slaves themselves. Although slavery was cruel in many ways, perhaps its worst feature was not physical but psychological: to be enslaved at all and barred from participation in a nation that put a high value on freedom and equality of opportunity. "One of the grossest frauds committed upon the down-trodden slave," Douglass wrote, was to encourage drunkenness during holidays so that slaves would be disgusted with freedom and would look forward to marching back to the fields.

Noon: Slaves in House and Fields

It is 2 o'clock on a hot July afternoon on the plantation. The midday lunch break is over, and the slaves are returning to their work in the fields. Lunch was the usual fare of cornmeal and pork.

The slaves return to work slowly and listlessly, not because of innate laziness, but because of a lack of stamina resulting from deficient diet and the suffocating heat and humidity. Douglass remembered that "we worked all weathers.... It was never too hot, or too cold" for toiling in the fields. Mary Reynolds of Louisiana recalled that she hated most having to pick cotton "when the frost was on the bolls," which made her hands "git sore and crack open and bleed."

Daily Toil

The daily work schedule for most slaves, whether in the fields or the Big House, was long and demanding. Aroused by a bell or horn before daybreak, they worked on an average day 14 hours in the summer and 10 hours in the winter. During harvest time, it was not uncommon to work for 18 hours. Depending on the size of the work force and the crop, the slaves were organized either in gangs or according to tasks. The gangs, usually of 20 to 25, worked their way along the cotton rows under the watchful eye and quick whip of a driver. Ben Simpson, a Georgia slave, remembered vividly how his master would use a "great, long whip platted out of rawhide" to hit a slave in the gang who would "fall behind or give out."

Under the task system, each slave had a specific task to complete daily. This system gave slaves the incentive to work hard enough to finish early, but it meant that the quality of their work was scrutinized constantly. An overseer's weekly report to Robert Allston in 1860 noted that he had "flogged for hoeing corn bad Fanny 12 lashes, Sylvia 12, Monday 12, Phoebee 12, Susanna 12, Salina 12, Celia 12, Iris 12." The black slave driver, George Skipwith, was no less rigorous in his expectations of work from fellow slaves. In 1847, he reported to his master that several slaves working under him "at a reasonable days work" should have plowed 7 acres apiece but had done only $1\frac{1}{2}$. Therefore, George proudly reported, "I gave them ten licks a peace upon their skins [and] I gave Julyann eight or ten licks for misplacing her hoe."

An average slave was expected to pick 130 to 150 pounds of cotton per day. The work on sugar and rice plantations was even harder. Sugar demanded constant cultivation and the digging of drainage ditches in snake-infested fields. At harvest time, cutting,

An Overseer's Report

W. Sweet to Adele Petigru Allston N[ightin]gale hall, 14th September, 1864.

Dear madam I comence my harvest on last saterday on Boath Plantations the weather is very fin for harvest so far I will Bring some Rice in to the Barn yard at N[ightin]gale hall to Day and at ganderloss to morrow. I think that I will make about 2 Barrels of Syrrup on Each Place I finish grinding at ganderloss to Day I will not finish at Nightingale hall until the last of next weeak. litle Dianah was confined with a boy child on the 9 I am very sorry to say to you that one of Prisilia children a boy name July Dide on 12th with fits a[nd] fever I have had a grea[t] deal of fever among the children But not much among the grone negroes. old Rose is Stil quite sick mr Belflowers sent toney to mee on friday last I have concluded to let toney wife stay whare she is for a while as I understand that she is Pregnant and will not Be much survice in the harvest if I am Rong for soe Doing Pleas let mee know. the negroes all sends thare love to you an family my self and family is very un well.

N[ightin]gale hall

8th September	all hands hoing Bancks and grinding shugar cain no sick
9th September	all hands hoing Bancks grind shugar cain no sick
10th September	all hands cu[tt]ing Rice grinding shugar cain no sick
12th September	all hands harvesting grinding shugar cain 3 women with sick children
13th September	all hands harvesting grinding shugar cain 3 women with sick children
14th September	all hands harvesting grinding shugar cain 1 woman with sick child

(Source: *The South Carolina Rice Plantation as Revealed in the Papers of Robert F. W. Allston,* ed., J. H. Easterby (1945).

stripping, and carrying the cane to the sugar house for boiling was exhausting. In addition, huge quantities of firewood had to be cut and carried. Working in the low-country rice fields was worse: Slaves spent long hours standing in water up to their knees.

House slaves, most of them women, had relatively easier assignments than the field slaves, though they were usually called on to help with the harvest. Their usual work was in or near the Big House as housemaids, cooks, seamstresses, laundresses, coachmen, drivers, gardeners, and mammies. Slaves did most of the artisanal work on the plantation; many became skilled carpenters, blacksmiths, stonemasons, weavers, mechanics, and millers. More intimacy between whites and blacks occurred near the house. House slaves ate and dressed better than their fellow slaves in the fields.

But there were also disadvantages. House slaves were watched more closely, were on call at all hours of the day and night, and were more often involved in personality conflicts in the white household. As one house servant put it, "We were constantly exposed to the whims and passions of every member of the family." This meant everything from assignment to petty jobs to insults, spontaneous angry whippings, and sexual assault.

The most feared punishment for a house slave, however, other than sale to the Deep South, was to be sent to the fields.

Slave Health

Although slave owners had an interest in keeping their slaves healthy by providing adequate care, slaves led sickly lives. Home was a crude one-room log cabin with a dirt floor; some such houses were well made, but most were full of cracks and holes. Pesky mosquitoes came in at night, making sleep difficult in the summer months. Most cabins had a fireplace for heat and cooking. Typical furnishings included a table, some stools or boxes to sit on, an iron pot and wooden dishes, and perhaps a bed. Some slaves slept on the ground on mattresses of corn shucks, using burlap bags for blankets. The cabins were crowded, with usually more than one family living in each. Slave clothing was shabby and uncomfortable. Usually, each man was issued two cotton shirts and two pairs of cotton or woolen pants each fall and spring and a pair of stout shoes once a year. Women were given cotton and woolen cloth twice a year with which to make their own and their children's clothes.

Studies on the adequacy of slave diet disagree, some showing that the food most slaves ate was deficient in calories and vitamins, others claiming that the energy value of the slave diet exceeded that of free whites in the general population. Compared with Latin American slavery, where the ratio of male slaves to white residents was much higher than in the United States, American slaves were well fed. Once a week, each slave was issued an average ration of a peck of cornmeal, 3 to 4 pounds of salt pork or bacon, some molasses, and perhaps some sweet potatoes. The main regimen, however, was "corn, at every meal, from day to day, and week to week." This bland fare was supplemented for some slaves, with the master's permission, by vegetables grown in a small garden and by fishing or hunting small game.

Most slaves, however, rarely enjoyed fresh meat, dairy products, fruits, or vegetables. To make up for these deficiencies, they sometimes stole from the master's kitchen, gardens, and barnyard. Such offenses were frequent, and just as frequently punished. A Louisiana planter told a neighbor, "I beg to regrets that two of my men have been found guilty of killing one of your calves," and another complained of many acts of theft committed by "famished negroes." Inadequate diet, moreover, led some slaves to become dirt eaters, which gave them worms and "swollen shiny skin, puffy eyelids, pale palms and soles." Others suffered regularly from skin disorders, cracked lips, and sore eyes. Many slaves, like poor whites, came down with vitamin deficiency diseases such as rickets, pellagra, beriberi, scurvy, and even mental illness.

Women slaves especially suffered weaknesses caused by vitamin deficiency, hard work, and disease, as well as those associated with the menstrual cycle and childbirth. Women were expected to do the same tasks in the fields as the men, in addition to cooking, sewing, child care, and traditional female jobs in the quarters when the fieldwork was finished. "Pregnant women," the usual rule stated, "should not plough or lift but must be kept at moderate work until the last hour" and were given a three-week recovery period after giving birth. But these guidelines were more often violated than honored. Infant mortality of slave children under 5 years of age was twice as high as for white children.

Life expectancy for American slaves was longer than for those in Latin America and the Caribbean, but not very high for either blacks or whites in the antebellum South (21.4 for blacks and 25.5 for whites in 1850). In part because of poor diet and climate, slaves were highly susceptible to epidemic diseases. Despite some resistance as a result of the sickle-cell trait, many slaves still contracted and died from malaria, yellow fever, cholera, and other diseases caused by mosquitoes or bad water, especially in the dangerous low-lying rice fields of the Georgia coast and the sugar fields of Louisiana. Slaves everywhere suffered and died from intestinal ailments in the summer and respiratory diseases in the winter. An average of 20 percent (and sometimes 50 to 60 percent) of the slaves on a given plantation would be sick at one time, and no overseer's report was complete without an account of sickness and the number of days of lost labor.

The relatively frequent incidence of whippings and other physical punishments aggravated the poor physical condition of the slaves. Many slaveholders offered rewards—a garden plot, an extra holiday, hiring oneself out, or passes—as inducements for faithful labor. For punishments, they would withhold these privileges rather than resort to the lash. But southern court records, newspapers, plantation diaries, and slave memoirs reveal that sadistic slave punishments were frequent and harsh.

The slave William Wells Brown reported that on his plantation, the whip was used "very frequently and freely" for inadequate or uncompleted work, stealing, running away, and even insolence and lying. Whippings ranged from 10 to 100 strokes of the lash, occasionally even more. Former slaves described a good owner as one who did not "whip too much" and a bad owner as one who "whipped till he'd bloodied you and blistered you." Slaveholders had many theories on the appropriate kind of lash to inflict sufficient pain and punishment without damaging a valuable laborer. Other forms of punishment included isolation and confinement in stocks and jails during leisure hours, chains, muzzling, salting lash wounds, branding, burning, and castration.

Nothing testifies better to the physical brutality of slavery than the advertisements for runaways that slaveholders printed in antebellum newspapers. In searching for the best way to describe the

Slaves survived nobly despite hard work, ill health, a deficient diet, and poor living conditions. Female slaves had a double burden of work and caring for their families, as seen below with the woman cooking in her cabin while her children peered out from the doorway. But female slaves also managed to develop networks of support while working, as seen to the left in the drawing of the three women winnowing rice. (left, From Down by the Riverside, Charles Joyner, 1984, sketch by Alice R. Huger Smith, c. 1914; right, Private Collection)

physical characteristics of a missing slave, slave owners unwittingly condemned their own behavior. One Mississippi slave had "large raised scars . . . in the small of his back and on his abdomen nearly as large as a person's finger." Another, a Georgia female, was "considerably marked by the whip." Still another, who according to his North Carolina master had a "remarkably bad temper," was described by the "marks of the lash upon his back." Slaves who were branded were even easier to identify in these advertisements. One fugitive, Betty, was described as recently "burnt . . . with a hot iron on the left side of her face." "I tried to make the letter M," her master admitted in his diary.

Slave Law and the Family

One can almost imagine Betty's master agonizingly applying his brand. Complicating master-slave relationships was the status of slaves as both human beings and property, a legal and psychological ambiguity the South never resolved. On the one hand, the slaves had names, personalities, families, and wills of their own. This required dealing with them as fellow humans. On the other hand, they were items of property, purchased and maintained to perform specific profit-making tasks. As a Kentucky court put the problem in 1836, "Although the law of this state considers slaves as property, . . . it recognizes their personal existence, and, to a qualified extent, their natural right."

This ambiguity led to confusion in the laws governing treatment of slaves. Until the early 1830s, some southern abolitionist activity persisted, primarily in the Upper South, and slaves had slight expectations that they might be freed, if not by state action, then by individual manumission. But along with this ray of hope, they suffered careless and often brutal treatment in matters of food, housing, work load, and punishments. This confusion changed with the threatening convergence in 1831 of Nat Turner's revolt and William Lloyd Garrison's publication of the abolitionist *Liberator*. After 1831, the South tightened up the slave system. Laws prohibiting manumission were passed, and the slaves' expectation of freedom other than by revolt or escape vanished. At the same time, laws protecting them from overly severe treatment were strengthened, and material conditions generally improved.

But whatever the law said, the practice was always more telling. Treatment varied with individual slaveholders and depended on their mood and other circumstances. This was especially true with regard to the slave family. Most planters, like Robert Allston, generally encouraged their slaves to marry and did all they could to keep families intact. They believed that families made black males more docile and less inclined to revolt or run away. But some masters failed to respect slave marriages or broke them up because of financial problems. This tendency was supported by southern courts and legislatures, which did not legally recognize slave marriages or the right to family unity. As a North Carolina supreme court justice said in 1853, "Our law required no solemnity or form in regard to the marriage of slaves."

Adding to the pain of forced breakup of the slave family was the sexual abuse of black women. Although the frequency of such abuse is unknown, the presence of thousands of mulattoes in the antebellum era is testimony to this practice. White men in the South abused black slave women in several ways: by offering gifts for sexual "favors," by threatening those who refused sex with physical punishment or the sale of a child or loved one, by purchasing concubines, and by outright rape. As Frederick Douglass put it, "the slave woman is at the mercy of the fathers, sons or brothers of her master."

Because of the need to obtain cheap additional slaves for the work force, slaveholders encouraged young slave women to bear children, whether married or not. If verbal prodding and inducements such as less work and more rations did not work, masters would choose mates and foist them on slave women. Massa Hawkins, for example, selected Rufus to live with 16-year-old Rose Williams, as she recalled many years later. She resisted the attempted liaison with unmistakable clarity: "I puts de feet 'gainst him and give him a shove and out he go on de floor 'fore he knew what I's doin'." When Rufus persisted, Rose took a poker and "lets him have it over de head." Hawkins then threatened Rose with a "whippin' at de stake" or sale away "from my folks." This was too much for her. "What am I's to do? So I 'cides to do as de massa wish and so I yields."

Unlike the case of Rose and Rufus, however, slaves usually chose their own mates on the basis of mutual attraction during an uneasy courtship complicated by the threat of white interferences. As among poor whites, premarital intercourse was frequent, but promiscuous behavior was rare. Most couples maintained affectionate, lasting relationships. This, too, led to numerous sorrows in slavery. Members of slave families had to witness the flogging or physical abuse of loved ones and were powerless to intervene. William Wells Brown remembered that "cold chills ran over me and I wept aloud" when he saw his mother whipped for being late into the fields for work. For this reason, some slaves preferred to marry a spouse from a plantation other than their own.

Although motherhood was the key event in a slave woman's life, bearing children and the double burden of work and family responsibilities challenged her resourcefulness. New mothers often had to choose between taking their babies into the fields to be fed or leaving them with others. Some masters would provide time off for nursing mothers, but the more common practice was for them to work in the fields with their newborn infants lying nearby, wrapped in cloth to protect them from the sun. Although children were sometimes denied proper physical care and emotional support by the absence of their parents during the working day, the slaves adapted. Women developed networks of mutual support, looking after one another's children; meeting together to sew, quilt, cook, or do laundry; and attending births, caring for the sick and dying, and praying together.

The most traumatic problem for slaves was the separation of families, a haunting fear rarely absent from slave consciousness. Although many slaveholders had both moral and economic reasons to maintain families, inevitably they found themselves destroying them. One study, compiling 30 years of data from three Deep South states, shows that masters dissolved one-third of all slave marriages. Even then, the slaves tried to maintain contact. When Abream Scriven informed his wife, Dinah, of his sale to a trader in New Orleans, he had no idea where he would be sold, but promised to "write and let you know where I am.... My Dear Wife for you and my Children my pen cannot Express the griffe I feel to be parted from you all." Two Missouri slave women, when told they might be sent to Texas, begged their master to reconsider, pleading that "to be separated from our husbands forever in this world would make us unhappy for life."

There was much basis in fact for the abolitionists' contention that slavery was a harsh, brutal system. However, two points need to be emphasized. First, although slavery was a barbarous institution that led otherwise decent human beings to commit inhumane acts, many slaveholders throughout the South were neither sadistic nor cruel, but did what they could to provide decent care and humane treatment for their slave laborers, out of both economic self-interest and Christ-

ian morality. Second, despite the travail of slavery, whether under relatively kind or cruel masters, the slaves endured with dignity, communal sensitivity, and even some joy. If daytime in the fields describes a view of slavery at its worst, nighttime in the quarters, as examined from the black perspective, reveals the slaves' survival powers and their capacity to mold an African American culture even under slavery.

Night: Slaves in Their Quarters

It is near sundown, and the workday is almost over. Some of the slaves begin singing the gentle spiritual "Steal Away to Jesus," and others join in. Or perhaps they sing "Dere's a Meeting Here Tonight." To the unwary overseer or master, the humming, soothing sound of the song suggests happy slaves, content with their earthly lot and looking forward to deliverance in heaven, "in the sweet bosom of Jesus." To the slaves, however, the songs are a signal that, as an ex-slave, Wash Wilson, put it, they are to "steal away to Jesus" because "dere gwine be a 'ligious meetin' dat night." When evening arrived on the plantation, after a hard day of work in the hot sun or in the Big House, the slaves returned to their own quarters. There, as Wilson said, "sometimes us sing and pray all night."

In the slave quarters, away from white masters, overseers, and the burdens of daily work, an elaborate black community helped the slaves make sense out of their lives. In family life, religion, song, dance, the playing of musical instruments, and the telling of stories, the slaves both described their experiences and sought release from hardship and suffering. However burdensome their lives from sunup to sundown, after work, the slaves experienced enjoyment and a sense of self-worth, hope, and group identity in their quarters.

Black Christianity

As suggested by the scene Wash Wilson described, Christian worship was an indispensable part of slave life in the quarters. The revivals of the early nineteenth century led to an enormous growth of

The breakup of families and friendships was an ever-present fear for slaves, who might be sold for purely economic reasons as well as in retribution for uncooperative behavior. In this painting of a slave market by an unidentified artist in the 1850s, note the varied colors of the African Americans (a sad light-skinned young woman in the center, a mulatto male in the right foreground staring longingly at her, and dark-skinned women clutching their children to the left) and the diverse social class of the whites (the suave merchant leaning back in a chair on the porch, nattily attired slave auctioneers and buyers, and a gaudily dressed lower-class overseer cracking the whip over the separation of child from mother). All southern social classes perpetuated slavery, and African Americans of all hues were victimized by it. (Anonymous American, Slave Market, c. 1860/The Carnegie Museum of Art, Gift of Mrs. W. Fitch Ingersoll)

Christianity among black Americans. Some independent black Baptist and Methodist Churches, especially in border states and cities, served both slaves and free blacks and occasionally even whites. These separate Churches had to steer a careful path to maintain their freedom and avoid white interference. But the vast majority of southern blacks were slaves, attending plantation missions set up by their masters.

Robert Allston built a prayer house for his slaves, reporting with pride that they were "attentive to religious instruction, and greatly improved in intelligence and morals." For the slaveholders, religion often represented a form of social control. Despite the presence of illiterate but eloquent slave preachers on the plantation, who frequently played a prominent role in administering baptisms, weddings, and funerals, white masters sought to direct the purposes of religion to their own ends. Black religious gatherings were usually forbidden unless white observers were present or white preachers led them. Whether in slave or white churches (where blacks sat in the back), preachers often delivered sermons from the text "Servants, obey your masters." These sermons emphasized the importance of work, obedience, honesty, and respect for the master's property. One former slave complained that "all that preacher talked about was for us slaves to obey our masters and not to lie and steal."

There were limits, however, to the effectiveness of white control. Although some slaves accommodated themselves to the master's brand of Christianity and patiently waited for heavenly deliverance, others rebelled and sought earthly liberty. Not far from Allston's plantation, several slaves were discovered (and imprisoned) for singing "We'll soon be free / We'll fight for liberty / When de Lord will call us home." Douglass had an illegal Sabbath school on one plantation, where he and others risked being whipped while learning about Christianity and how to read. "The work of instructing my dear fellow-slaves," he wrote, "was the sweetest engagement with which I was ever blessed."

In religious schools and meetings like these, the slaves created an "invisible" church. On Sunday morning, they sat dutifully through the master's service and waited for the "real meetin'," and "real preachin'," later that night. Sarah Fitzpatrick, an Alabama slave, recalled that the slaves wanted so much to "go to church by de'selves" that they were willing to sit through the "white fo'ks' …service in de mornin'." But when evening came, "a'ter dey clean up, wash de dishes, an' look a'ter ever'thing," the slaves would "steal away" to the nearby woods for their own service.

Long into the night, they would sing, dance, shout, and pray. "Ya' see," Sarah explained, "niggers lack ta shout a whole lot an' wid de white fo'ks al'round 'em, dey couldn't shout jes' lack dey want to." But at night they could, taking care to deaden the sound to keep the whites away. One method was to hang a curtain from the trees. Another, an African custom, was to turn over a pot to "catch the sound." Another African practice, the frenetic dancing of the ring shout, survived in adapted form. Dance, forbidden by Methodists, was transformed into the "ecstatic shout," praising the Lord. The religious ceremony itself, with its camp meeting features, relieved the day's burdens and expressed communal religious values. "At night," another ex-slave recalled with pride, "was when the darkies really did have they freedom of spirit."

Although many of the expressive forms were African, the message reiterated over and over in the invisible slave church was the Christian theme of suffering and deliverance from bondage. Slaves identified with the children of Israel and with the Exodus story, as well as with the suffering of Jesus and the inner turmoil of an unconverted "trebbled spirit." "We prayed a lot to be free," Anderson Edwards recalled, but the freedom the slaves sought was a complex blend of a peaceful soul and escape from slavery. Nothing illustrated both the communal religious experience and these mixed Christian themes of suffering and redemption better than slave spirituals.

The Power of Song

A group of slaves gathers in the dark of night in the woods behind their quarters to sing and shout together:

> *O brothers, don't get weary*
> *O brothers, don't get weary*
> *O brothers, don't get weary*
> *We're waiting for the Lord.*
> *We'll land on Canaan's shore*
> *We'll land on Canaan's shore*
> *When we land on Canaan's shore*
> *We'll meet forever more.*

Then, after moaning of being stolen from Africa and sold in Georgia, with families "sold apart," they sing:

> *There's a better day a-coming,*
> *Will you go along with me?*
> *There's a better day a-coming,*
> *Go sound the jubilee!*

Music was a crucial form of expression in the slave quarters on both secular and religious occasions. The slaves were adept at creating a song, as one slave woman recalled, "on de spurn of de moment." Jeanette Robinson Murphy described a process of spontaneous creation that, whether in rural church music or urban jazz, describes black music to this day. "We'd all be at the 'prayer house' de Lord's day," she said, when all of a sudden, perhaps even in the midst of a white preacher's sermon, "de Lord would come a-shinin' thoo dem pages and revive dis ole nigger's heart, and I'd jump up dar and den and holler and shout and sing and pat, and dey would all cotch de words and I'd sing it to some ole shout song I'd heard 'em sing from

After sundown, when the work was done, slaves often gathered in "hush arbors" deep in the woods away from the overseer's and master's interference. There they danced the "ring shout" and "praised de Lord" in ways that combined African and Christian forms of spiritual expression. This painting by John Antrobus shows a "Negro Burial." (The Historic New Orleans Collection)

Africa, and dey'd all take it up and keep at it, and keep a-addin' to it, and den it would be a spiritual."

Although the spirituals were composed for many purposes, they reiterated one basic Judeo-Christian theme: a chosen people, the children of God, were held captive in bondage but would be delivered. The titles and lyrics reveal the message: "We Are de People of de Lord," "To the Promised Land I'm Bound to Go," "Go Down, Moses," "Who Will Deliver Po' Me?" What they meant by deliverance was not always clear and often had a double meaning: freedom in heaven and freedom in the North. Where, exactly, was the desired destination of "Oh Canaan, sweet Canaan / I am bound for the land of Canaan"? Was it heaven? A vague symbol for freedom "anyplace else but here"? A literal reference to the terminus of the underground railroad? For different slaves, and at different times for the same person, it meant all of these.

"The songs of the slave," Douglass wrote, "represent the sorrows of his heart." Indeed, they often expressed the sadness of broken families and the burdens of work and were filled with images of trouble, toil, and homelessness. But they also expressed joy, triumph, and deliverance. Each expression of sorrow usually ended in an outburst of eventual affirmation and justice. "O nobody knows a who I am" resolved itself on "judgment morning" when one heard the "bells a-ringing in my soul." The sadness of "Nobody knows the trouble I've seen" was lightened by happening upon some juicy berries hanging down "just as sweet as

Music and dancing inspirited the slave community during the Easter and Christmas holidays, and at weddings and other family occasions. Although two white masters (in top hats) are seen here, often the slaves had the run of the plantation, especially during the holiday week between Christmas and New Year's Day (when work was light). (New York Public Library, Astor, Lenox and Tilden Foundations)

de honey in de comb." And the deep sorrow of "Sometimes I feel like a motherless chile," as terrible a situation as any person could endure, was transformed later in the song into "Sometimes I feel like / A eagle in de air.... / Gonna spread my wings an' / Fly, fly, fly."

Slave songs did not always contain hidden meanings. Sometimes slaves gathered simply for music, to play fiddles, drums, and other instruments fashioned by local artists in imitation of West African models. Some musicians were so talented that whites invited them to perform at ceremonies and parties. But most played for the slave community. Sacred and secular events such as weddings, funerals, holiday celebrations, family reunions, and a successful harvest were all occasions for a communal gathering, usually with music. So, too, was news of external events that affected their lives—a crisis in the master's situation, a change in the slave code, the outcome of a battle during the Civil War, or emancipation itself.

The Enduring Family

The role of music in births, weddings, funerals, and other milestones of family life suggests that the family was central to life in the slave quarters. Although the pain of sexual abuse and family separation was a real or potential part of the experience of all slaves, so was the hope for family continuity. The study of naming practices, for example, shows

that children were connected to large extended families. In the records of one plantation for the century from 1760 to the eve of the Civil War, some 175 men, women, and children were found to be linked by blood and marital ties, respecting taboos against marrying first cousins.

The benefits of family cohesion were those of any group: love, protection, education, moral guidance, the transmission of culture, and the provision of status, role models, and basic support. All of these existed in the slave quarters. As the slaves gathered together at the end of the working day, parents passed on to their children the family story, language patterns and words, recipes, folktales, religious and musical traditions, and strong impressions of strength and beauty. In this way, they preserved cultural traditions, which enhanced the identity and self-esteem of parents and children alike. Parents taught their children how to survive in the world and how to cope with life under slavery. As the young ones neared the age when they would work full time in the fields, their parents instructed them in the best ways to pick cotton or corn, how to avoid the overseer's whip, whom to trust and learn from, and ways of fooling the master.

Opportunities existed on many plantations for fathers, and mothers as well, to improve the welfare of the family by working extra to earn money to buy scarce items like sugar or clothing, by hunting and fishing to add protein to the diet, or by

Despite separation, sale, and sexual abuse by white masters, many slave families endured and provided love, support, and self-esteem to their members. This 1862 photograph shows five generations of a slave family, all born on the plantation of J. J. Smith of Beaufort, South Carolina. (Library of Congress)

seer in 1859 for raping his wife. Female slaves, too, risked the consequences of resistance to protect themselves or family members from harm. When Cherry Loguen was attacked by a knife-wielding, would-be rapist, she picked up a stick and knocked him out. And when an Arkansas overseer tried to make an example of a slave woman named Lucy, according to her son, "she jumped on him and like to tore him up."

Despite numerous incidents of mutual support, the love and affection that slaves had for each other was sometimes a liability. Many slaves, women especially, were reluctant to run away because they did not want to leave their families. Those who fled were easily caught because, as an overseer near Natchez, Mississippi, told a northern visitor, they "almost always kept in the neighborhood, because they did not like to go where they could not sometimes get back and see their families."

As these episodes suggest, violence, sexual abuse, and separation constantly threatened the stability of slave families. But despite these serious restraints, slave parents served as protectors, providers, comforters, transmitters of culture, and role models for their children. The slave family, though constantly endangered, played a crucial role in helping blacks adapt to slavery and achieve a sense of self-esteem.

Resistance and Freedom

Songs, folktales, and other forms of cultural expression enabled slaves to articulate their resistance to slavery. For example, Old Jim was going on a "journey" to the "kingdom," and, as he invited others to "go 'long" with him, he taunted his owner: "O blow, blow, Ole Massa, blow de cotton horn / Ole Jim'll neber wuck no mo' in de cotton an' de corn." From refusal to work, it was a short step to outright revolt. In another song, "Samson," the slaves clearly stated their determination to abolish the house of bondage: "An' if I had-'n my way / I'd tear the buildin' down! / ...And now I got my way / And I'll tear this buildin' down." Every hostile song, story, or event, like Douglass's victory over Covey, was an act of resistance by which the slaves asserted their dignity and gained a measure of freedom. Some escaped slavery altogether to

working a small garden to grow vegetables. J. W. C. Pennington proudly recalled helping his "father at night in making straw hats and willow-baskets, by which means we supplied our family with little articles of food, clothing and luxury."

Slaves were not always totally at the mercy of abusive masters and overseers. Occasionally, one family member could intervene to prevent the abuse of another. Harriet Jacobs successfully fended off her master's lustful advances partly by her own cleverness and sass ("I ... openly expressed my contempt for him"), and partly by threatening to use her free black grandmother's considerable influence in the community against him ("I told him that I must and would apply to my grandmother for protection"). That enraged but always stopped him.

When family intervention, emotional appeals for mercy, or the magic effects of the conjurer's bag of herbs hung around the neck did not work, some slaves resorted to physical force. In 1800, a slave called Ben shot and killed a white man for living with Ben's wife, and another slave killed an over-

Folktales

A frequent activity of family life in the slave quarters was telling stories. The folktale was an especially useful and indirect way in which older slaves could express hostility toward their masters, impart wisdom to the young, teach them how to survive, portray and mock their own weaknesses, and entertain themselves. Thus, folktales reveal to historians a great deal about the slaves' view of their experience.

Although the tales took many forms, perhaps the best known were the "Brer Rabbit" animal stories. The trickster rabbit, who existed originally in African folklore, was weak and careless, and was looked down on by the other animals. Like the slaves, he was a victim. But he was also clever, boastful, and full of mischief, and he knew how to use his cunning to outwit stronger foes, usually by knowing them better than they knew him, a psychological necessity for all who are oppressed.

In one story, the powerful Brer Tiger took all the water and food for himself during a time of famine, leaving the weaker animals miserable. Brer Rabbit, however, turned things around. He played on Brer Tiger's fears that he would be blown away by a "big wind," secretly manufactured by the rabbit. The tiger was so afraid of the wind (perhaps the winds of revolt?) that he begged Brer Rabbit to tie him "tightly" to a tree to keep from being blown away. Brer Rabbit was happy to oblige, after which all the creatures of the forest were able to share the cool water and juicy pears.

In another folktale, Brer Rabbit fell into a well, but then got out by tricking Brer Wolf into thinking it was better to be in the cool bottom of the well than outside where it was hot. As the wolf lowered himself down in one bucket, Brer Rabbit rose up in the other, laughingly saying as he passed Brer Wolf, "Dis am life; some go up and some go down." In these stories, the slaves vicariously

Tar Baby

Brer Wolf studied and studied to find a way to catch Brer Rabbit. He scratched his head, and he pulled his chin whiskers until by and by he said, "I know what I'll do. I'll make me a tar baby, and I'll catch that good-for-nothing rabbit."*

And so Brer Wolf worked and worked until he had made a pretty little girl out of tar. He dressed the tar baby in a calico apron and carried her up to the well, where he stood her up and fastened her to a post in the ground so that nobody could move her. Then Brer Wolf hid in the bushes and waited for Brer Rabbit to come for some water. But three days passed before Brer Rabbit visited the well again. On the fourth day, he came with a bucket in his hand. When he saw the little girl, he stopped and looked at her. Then he said, "Hello. What's your name? What are you doing here, little girl?"

The little girl said nothing.

This made Brer Rabbit angry, and he shouted at her, "You no-mannered little snip, you! How come you don't speak to your elders?"

The little girl still said nothing.

"I know what to do with little children like you. I'll slap your face and teach you some manners if you don't speak to me," said Brer Rabbit.

Still the little girl said nothing.

And then Brer Rabbit lost his head and said, "Speak to me, I say. I'm going to slap you." With that, Brer Rabbit slapped the tar baby in the face, and his right hand stuck.

"A-ha, you hold my hand, do you? Turn me loose, I say. Turn me loose. If you don't, I'm going to slap you with my left hand. And if I hit you with my left hand, I'll knock the daylights out of you."

But the little girl said nothing. So Brer Rabbit drew back his left hand and slapped the little girl in her face, bim, and his left hand stuck.

"Oh, I see. You're going to hold both my hands, are you? You better turn me loose. If you don't, I'm going to kick you. And if I kick you, it's going to be like thunder and lightning!" With that, Brer Rabbit drew back his right foot and kicked the little girl in the shins with all his might, blap! Then his right foot stuck.

"Well, sir, isn't this something? You better turn my foot loose. If you don't, I've got another foot left, and I'm going to kick you with it, and you'll think a cyclone hit you." Then Brer Rabbit gave that little girl a powerful kick in the shins with his left foot, blip! With that, his left foot stuck, and there he hung off the ground, between the heavens and the earth. He was in an awful fix. But he still thought he could get loose.

So he said to the little girl, "You've got my feet and my hands all stuck up, but I've got one more weapon, and that's my head. If you don't turn me loose, I'm going to butt you! And if I butt you, I'll knock your brains out." Finally then, Brer Rabbit struck the

*Tar was often spread on fences by masters to catch slaves who, out of hunger or mischief, would sneak into field and orchards to steal food. Tar stuck on the hands would betray the "guilty" slave.

outwitted their more powerful masters and even reversed roles, thus revealing much about their experience under slavery and their aspirations for freedom.

The accompanying excerpt is from perhaps the most famous animal tale, "The Tar Baby Tricks Brer Rabbit." This version is by William J. Faulkner, who, after he retired as minister and dean of men at Fisk University, gathered and recorded the folktales he had heard in his youth in South Carolina as told by an ex-slave, Simon Brown. Rev. Faulkner opposed telling the stories in dialect because he believed readers formed stereotyped judgments from the dialect and missed the significance of the tale itself. We enter the story as an angry Brer Wolf has decided on a plan to catch the lazy Brer Rabbit, who refused to help the wolf build a well and has been fooling him by drinking from the well while Brer Wolf was asleep.

When you have finished reading the story, ask yourself what you learned about slavery from this story. Did violence work for Brer Rabbit or did it only make things worse? What finally worked? How do you interpret the ending? Brer Rabbit is returned to the briar patch, "the place where I was born." But is the briar patch, with all its thorns, scratches, and roots, Africa or slavery? Or what?

Finally, reflect on the stories you heard as a child or now find yourself telling others. How do they express the realities, flaws, values, and dreams of the American people? The same question applies to the songs we sing, the art we make, the rhythms we move to, and the jokes we tell: What do they tell us about ourselves and our values? In answering these questions, we deepen the knowledge of our own history.

little girl a powerful knock on the foreheadwith his head, and it stuck, and there he hung. Smart old Brer Rabbit, he couldn't move. He was held fast by the little tar baby.

Now, Brer Wolf was hiding under the bushes, watching all that was going on. And as soon as he was certain that Brer Rabbit was caught good by his little tar baby, he walked over to Brer Rabbit and said, "A-ha, you're the one who wouldn't dig a well. And you're the one who's going to catch his drinking water from the dew off the grass. A-ha, I caught the fellow who's been stealing my water. And he isn't anybody but you, Brer Rabbit. I'm going to fix you good."

"No, sir, Brer Wolf, I haven't been bothering your water. I was just going over to Brer Bear's house, and I stopped by here long enough to speak to this little no-manners girl," said Brer Rabbit.

"Yes, you're the one," said Brer Wolf. "You're the very one who's been stealing my drinking water all this time. And I'm going to kill you."

"Please, sir, Brer Wolf, don't kill me," begged Brer Rabbit. "I haven't done anything wrong."

"Yes, I'm going to kill you, but I don't know how I'm going to do it yet," growled Brer Wolf. "Oh, I know what I'll do. I'll throw you in the fire and burn you up."

"All right, Brer Wolf," said Brer Rabbit. "Throw me in the fire. That's a good way to die. That's the way my grandmother died, and she said it's a quick way to go. You can do anything with me, anything you want, but please, sir, don't throw me in the briar patch."

"No, I'm not going to throw you in the fire, and I'm not going to throw you in the briar patch. I'm going to throw you down the well and drown you," said Brer Wolf.

"All right, Brer Wolf, throw me down the well," said Brer Rabbit. "That's an easy way to die, but I'm surely going to smell up your drinking water, sir."

"No, I'm not going to drown you," said Brer Wolf. "Drowning is too good for you." Then Brer Wolf thought and thought and scratched his head and pulled his chin whiskers. Finally he said, "I know what I'm going to do with you. I'll throw you in the briar patch."

"Oh, no, Brer Wolf," cried Brer Rabbit. "Please, sir, don't throw me in the briar patch. Those briars will tear up my hide, pull out my hair, and scratch out my eyes. That'll be an awful way to die, Brer Wolf. Please, sir, don't do that to me."

"That's exactly what I'll do with you," said Brer Wolf all happy-like. Then he caught Brer Rabbit by his hind legs, whirled him around and around over his head, and threw him way over into the middle of the briar patch.

After a minute or two, Brer Rabbit stood up on his hind legs and laughed at Brer Wolf and said to him, "Thank you, Brer Wolf, thank you. This is the place where I was born. My grandmother and grandfather and all my family were born right here in the briar patch."

And that's the end of the story.

Source: William J. Faulkner, *The Days When the Animals Talked*. Copyright © 1977 by William J. Faulkner. Used by permission of Modern Curriculum Press, Inc.

achieve such autonomy as was possible for free blacks in the antebellum South.

Forms of Black Protest

One way slaves protested the burdensome demands of continuous forced labor was in various "day-to-day" acts of resistance. These ranged from breaking tools to burning crops, barns, and houses, from stealing or destroying animals and food to defending fellow slaves from punishment, from self-mutilation to deliberate work slowdowns, and from poisoning masters to feigning illness. Two favorite techniques were to pretend sickness during periods when the overseers were driving the hardest and to misplace tools or deliberately leave them in the fields so that they would have to be "hunted all over the place when wanted."

Slave women, aware of their childbearing value, were adept at missing work on account of "disorders and irregularities," as a frustrated Virginia planter put it, "which cannot be detected by exterior symptoms." He went on to complain that "you dare not set her to work, and so she will lay up till she feels like taking the air again; and plays the lady at your expense." They established networks of support while winnowing and pounding rice or shucking corn, sharing miseries but also encouraging each other in private acts of subtle defiance and resistance such as ruining the master's meals and faking sickness.

Overseers also suffered from these acts of disobedience, for their job depended on productivity, which in turn depended on the goodwill of the slave workers. No one knew this better than the slaves themselves, who adeptly played on the frequent struggle between overseer and master. Often, the conflicts were ended by firing a bad overseer and hiring a more suitable replacement. Many slaveholders eventually resorted to using black drivers rather than overseers, but this created other problems.

The black slave drivers were "men between," charged with the tricky job of getting the master's work done without alienating fellow slaves or compromising their own values. Although some drivers were as brutal as white overseers, many became leaders and role models for other slaves. A common practice of the drivers was to appear to punish without really doing so. Solomon Northrup reported that he "learned to handle the whip with marvellous dexterity and precision, throwing the lash within a hair's breadth of the back, the ear, the nose, without, however, touching either of them." As he did this, the "punished" slave would howl in pretended pain and complain loudly to his master about his harsh treatment.

Another form of resistance was to run away. So many blacks ran off, that a southern doctor coined a new word, *drapetomania,* which meant "the disease causing negroes to run away." The typical runaway was a young male, who ran off alone and hid

Working with tools and machinery enabled slaves to engage in silent protests by misplacing tools or sabotaging equipment. Note the cotton press and gin in the background. Slave women were particularly adept at missing work by pretending to be sick. (Private Collection)

out in a nearby wood or swamp. He left to avoid a whipping or because he had just been whipped, to protest excessive work demands, or, as one master put it, for "no cause" at all. But there was a cause— the need to experience a period of freedom away from the restraints and discipline of the plantation. Many runaways would sneak back to the quarters at night for food, and after a few days, if not tracked down by hounds, they would return, perhaps to be whipped, but also perhaps with some concessions for better treatment in the future.

Some slaves left again and again. Remus and his wife Patty ran away from their master, James Battle, in Alabama. They were caught and jailed three times, but each time they escaped again. Battle urged the next jailer to "secure Remus well." Some runaways, called "Maroons," hid out for months and years at a time in communities of runaway slaves. Several Maroon colonies were located in the swamps and mountains of the South, especially in Florida, where Seminole and other Indians befriended them. In these areas, blacks and Indians, sharing a common hostility to local whites, frequently intermarried, though sometimes southeastern Indians were hired to track down runaway slaves.

The means of escape were manifold: forging passes, posing as master and servant, disguising one's sex, sneaking aboard ships, and pretending loyalty until taken by the master on a trip to the North. One slave even hid in a large box and had himself mailed to the North. The underground railroad, organized by abolitionists, was a series of safe houses and stations where runaway slaves could rest, eat, and spend the night before continuing. Harriet Tubman, who led some 300 slaves out of the South on 19 separate trips, was the railroad's most famous "conductor." It is difficult to know exactly how many slaves actually escaped to the North and Canada, but the numbers were not large. One estimate suggests that in 1850, about 1,000 slaves (out of over 3 million) attempted to run away, and most of them were returned. Nightly patrols by white militiamen, an important aspect of southern life, reduced the chances for any slave to escape and probably deterred many slaves from even trying to run away.

Other ways in which slaves sought their freedom included petitioning Congress and state legislatures, bringing suit against their masters that they were being held in bondage illegally, persuad-

ing masters to provide for emancipation in their wills, and purchasing their own freedom by hiring out to do extra work at night and on holidays.

Slave Revolts

The ultimate act of resistance, of course, was rebellion. Countless slaves committed individual acts of revolt. In addition, there were hundreds of conspiracies whereby slaves met to plan a group escape and often the massacre of whites. Most of these conspiracies never led to action, either because circumstances changed or the slaves lost the will to follow through or, more often, because some fellow slave— perhaps planted by the master—betrayed the plot. Such spies thwarted the elaborate conspiracies of Gabriel in Virginia in 1800 and Denmark Vesey in South Carolina in 1822. Gabriel and Vesey were both skilled, knowledgeable blacks who planned their revolts in hopes that larger events (a possible war with France in 1800 and the Missouri debates in 1820) would support their efforts. They planned to seize, respectively, Richmond and Charleston, but both were discovered and put down before the revolts could begin. Both resulted in severe reprisals by whites, including mass executions of leaders and the random killing of innocent blacks. The severity and intensity of the white response indicated the enormous fear southern whites had of a slave revolt.

Only a few organized revolts, in which slaves threatened white lives and property, ever actually took place. Latin American slaves challenged their masters more often than their North American counterparts. Weaker military control, easier escape to rugged interior areas, the greater imbalance of blacks to whites, and the continued dependence of Latin American slaveholders on the African slave trade for their supply of mostly male workers explain this pattern. Nearly 80 percent of the Africans imported into Brazil in the 1830s and 1840s were male, and as late as 1875, only one in six Brazilian slaves was recorded as married. The imbalance of males to females (156 to 100 in Cuba in 1860, for example, compared with a near one-to-one ratio in the United States) weakened family restraints on violent revolts.

The most famous slave revolt in North America, led by Nat Turner, occurred in Southampton County, Virginia, in 1831. Turner was an intelligent, skilled, unmarried, religious slave who had experienced many visions of "white spirits and black spirits engaged in battle." He believed that he was "ordained for some great purpose in the hands of the Almighty."

On a hot August night, Turner and a small band of fellow slaves launched their revolt. They intended, as Turner said, "to carry terror and devastation" throughout the country. They crept into the home of Turner's master, Joseph Travis, who Nat said was a "kind master" with "the greatest confidence in me," and killed the entire family. Before the revolt was finally put down, 55 white men, women, and children had been murdered and as many blacks killed in the aftermath. Turner hid in a hole in the woods for two weeks before he was apprehended and executed, but not before dictating a chilling confession to a white lawyer. The Nat Turner revolt was a crucial moment for southern whites. A Virginia legislator said that he suspected there was "a Nat Turner ... in every family." Rarely thereafter would slaveholders go to sleep without the Southampton revolt in mind.

The fact that Turner was an intelligent and trusted slave, with "no cause to complain" of his master's treatment, and yet led such a terrible revolt suggests again how difficult it is to generalize about slavery and slave behavior. Slaves, like masters, had diverse personalities and changeable moods, and their behavior could not be easily predicted. Sometimes humble and deferential, at other times obstinate and rebellious, the slaves made the best of a bad situation and did what they needed to do to survive and achieve a measure of self-worth.

Free Blacks: Becoming One's Own Master

No matter how well they coped with their bondage, the slaves obviously preferred freedom. As Frederick Douglass said of the slave, "Give him a bad master, and he aspires to a good master; give him a good master, and he wishes to become his own master." When Douglass himself had successfully forged a free black's papers as a seaman and sailed from Baltimore to become his own master in the North, he found "great insecurity and loneliness." Apart from the immediate difficulties of finding food, shelter, and work, he realized that he was a fugitive in a land "whose inhabitants are legalized kidnappers" who could at any moment seize and return him to the South. Apart from this fear, which haunted blacks in the North, what was life like for the 11 percent of the total African American population who in 1860 were not slaves?

Between 1820 and 1860, the number of free blacks in the United States doubled, from 233,500 to 488,000. This rise resulted from natural increase, successful escapes, "passing" as whites, purchasing of freedom, and a continuation of some manumissions despite legal restriction in most states after the 1830s. Some free blacks passed into the white population, and others migrated to Canada or the West Indies. The free African American population actually decreased from 13.2 percent in 1820 to a little more than 11 percent in 1860. Thus, the number of American blacks who were slaves grew faster than those who were free. More than half the free blacks lived in the South, most (85 percent in 1860) in the Upper South, where the total number of slaves had declined slightly.

Because free African Americans represented a constant reminder of freedom to slaves and feared reenslavement themselves, they were found least frequently in the Black Belt of the Lower South. They lived, rather, away from the dense plantation centers, scattered on impoverished rural farmlands and in small towns and cities. Still, fully one-third of the southern free African American population lived in cities or towns (compared to only 15 percent of whites and 5 percent of slaves). In part, because it took a long time to buy their freedom, they tended to be older, more literate, and lighter-skinned than other African Americans. In 1860, over 40 percent of free blacks were mulattoes (compared with 10 percent of the slaves). With strong leadership, Baltimore, Richmond, Charleston, New Orleans, and other southern cities developed vibrant African American communities, as free blacks formed churches, schools, and benevolent societies in the midst of white hostility and restrictions.

Most African Americans in the antebellum South were poor, laboring as farmhands, day laborers, or woodcutters. In the cities, they worked in factories and lived in appalling poverty. A few skilled jobs, such as barbering, shoemaking, and plastering, were reserved for black men; they were barred from more than 50 other trades. Women worked as cooks, laundresses, and domestics. The 15 percent of free African Americans who lived in the Lower South were divided into two distinct castes. Most were poor. But in New Orleans,

Charleston, and other southern cities, a small, mixed-blood class of free blacks emerged as an elite group, closely connected to white society and removed from the mass of poor blacks. A handful even owned land and slaves. One white observed that these blacks were "respectable" and enjoyed "their rights."

Most free blacks, however, had no such privileges. "We reside among you ... surrounded by the freest people and most republican institutions in the world," a Baltimore black paper said in 1826, pointing out that African Americans were not yet citizens: "Though we are not slaves, we are not free." Southern state laws seriously limited the mobility, rights, and opportunities of free blacks. In most states, they could not vote, bear arms, buy liquor, assemble, speak in public, form societies, or testify against whites in court. Nevertheless, the African American persistence to gather together and support each other in prayer meetings, back alleys, burial societies, and grocery stores was stronger than white efforts to impede it.

One reason urban whites sought to restrain African American contact was their fear of free black influence as they mixed with whites in working-class grogshops, gambling halls, and brothels. Richmond police closed one house of ill fame where "men and women of diverse colors ... con-

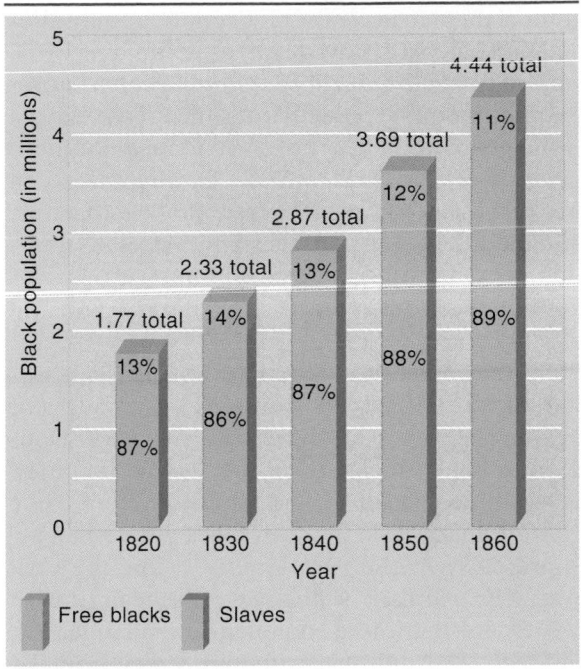

Growth of Black Population: Slave and Free, 1820–1860

Although the number of free African Americans doubled in size between 1820 and 1860, their proportion relative to the total black population actually decreased. This indicates that the institution of slavery seemed unlikely to be ended voluntarily by southerners.

Nat Turner's Revolt in 1831, the most famous American slave uprising, killed 55 whites in Southampton County, Virginia, before overwhelming white forces drove Turner to a hiding place in the woods. (Library of Congress)

gregate for most unhallowed purposes." Efforts were made to confine the free blacks to certain sections of the city or, increasingly by the 1850s, to compel them to leave the city, county, or state altogether. Those who stayed had trouble finding work, were required to carry licenses and freedom papers to be surrendered on demand, and often needed a white guardian to approve their actions. Southern whites were especially afraid of contact between free blacks and slaves, who often worked together, attended the same churches and places of entertainment in the city, occasionally got married, and developed strong bonds of mutual protection and identity.

The key institution in these developments was the African American Church. "As among our people generally," Martin Delaney wrote to Douglass in 1849, "the church is the Alpha and Omega of all things." Welcoming the freedom from white control, independent urban black churches grew enormously in the two decades before the Civil War. The African Methodist Episcopal Church (AME) in Baltimore doubled its membership between 1836 and 1856, with the overflow from the first congregation creating a second. By 1860, Bal-

timore had 15 African churches representing 5 different denominations. In Richmond the First African Church opened in 1841, soon followed by another; 20 years later, there were four! In the same period, 14 new black Baptist churches were founded in Virginia. These institutions not only performed the usual ritual functions and guarded moral discipline and community values, but also provided and promoted education, social insurance, self-help benevolent societies, picnics, concerts, and other forms of recreation.

The growth of African American churches resulted from the overflow of successful institutions, doctrinal differences, the vital role the urban church played in black community life, and conversions. White southerners were trapped by their need to convert Africans to Christianity and then not wanting them in their own churches. Besides, blacks were unwilling parishioners. As one Baptist observed about those forced to attend white churches: "the usual African resort is a loud, comfortable snoring nap."

Nor were African American Catholics left out. Baltimore and New Orleans had strong black Catholic adherents made up of Creoles, converts,

Churches for free blacks, rare before 1800, became a major source of social as well as religious activity by the 1840s. (Library of Congress)

former slaves, and refugees from Haiti. The first ordained African American priests were three Georgia sons, born of a mulatto slave mother and an Irish immigrant father, and educated at Holy Cross in the 1850s. But the next was three decades later. In the absence of African American priests, black sisterhoods took on special importance. The Sisters of the Holy Family and other communities of Catholic black women, begun in eastern cities, started schools and ministered to the aged and infirm as they spread with black Catholic communities westward to Louisville and St. Louis.

The African American churches not only were centers of vital urban black community activities, but also were springboards for activist black preachers seeking larger changes in American society. The Reverend J. C. Pennington, an escaped slave, attended lectures at Yale Divinity School (though denied the right to enroll or borrow books). Licensed to preach in 1838, he headed prominent black churches in New Haven, Hartford, and finally New York City. Pennington started several schools, was an abolitionist leader of the National Negro Convention movement (described in Chapter 12), and founded the Union Missionary Society in 1841, a black organization that focused on African missions and eventually merged with the American Missionary Society in 1846. Charles Bennett Ray was educated at Wesleyan University in Connecticut and, as minister of Bethesda Church in New York City for 20 years, was involved with the underground railroad and for four years was the editor of *The Colored American*. These and other black religious leaders prepared the way not only for Civil War, but also for an unprecedented further growth of African American Churches in the postwar years.

A young minister, Henry M. Turner, later an AME bishop, proudly proclaimed in the 1850s, "We, as a race, have a chance to be Somebody, and if we are ever going to be a people, now is the time." Turner's exhortations were heralded 20 years earlier by Maria Stewart, the first African American woman to give published public speeches. Stewart's religious conversion gave her the confidence to brave censure and ridicule in speaking out not only against slavery and northern racism, but also in opposition to those who cited St. Paul in defending the established order. "Did Saint Paul but know of our wrongs and depriva-

TIMELINE

1787	Constitution adopted with proslavery provisions
1793	Eli Whitney invents cotton gin
1800	Gabriel conspiracy in Virginia
1808	External slave trade prohibited by Congress
1820	South becomes world's largest cotton producer
1822	Denmark Vesey's conspiracy in Charleston
1830s	Southern justification of slavery changes from a necessary evil to a positive good
1831	Nat Turner's slave revolt in Virginia
1845	*Narrative of the Life of Frederick Douglass* published
1850s	Cotton boom
1851	Indiana state constitution excludes free blacks
1852	Harriet Beecher Stowe publishes best-selling *Uncle Tom's Cabin*
1860	Cotton production and prices peak

tions," Stewart said, "I presume he would make no objections to our pleading in public for our rights."

In part because free blacks were becoming more of a "people," they faced a crisis of extinction in the 1850s. Growing prosperity and the worsening conflict between North and South over slavery in the territories caused many white southerners to be even more concerned than usual with the presence of free blacks in their midst. North Carolina whites complained in 1852 that free blacks were "a perfect nuisance" because they attempted "in divers ways to equalize themselves with [the] white population." Pressures increased in the late 1850s, either to deport the free blacks or to enslave them. In the wake of increasing threats to their already precarious free status, some black leaders not surprisingly began to look more favorably on migration to Africa. That quest was interrupted, however, by the outbreak of the Civil War, rekindling in Douglass and others the "expiring embers of freedom."

Conclusion

Douglass's Dream of Freedom

Frederick Douglass eventually won his freedom by forging a free black sailor's pass and escaping through Chesapeake Bay to New York. In a real sense, he wrote himself into freedom. The *Narrative of the Life of Frederick Douglass,* "written by himself" in 1845, was a way both of exposing the many evils of slavery and of creating his own identity, even to the point of choosing his own name. Ironically, Douglass had learned to value reading and writing, we recall, from his Baltimore masters, the Aulds. This reminds us again of the intricate and subtle ways in which the lives of slaves and masters were tied together in the antebellum South. Our understanding of the complexities of this relationship is enhanced as we consider the variations of life in the Big House in the morning, in the fields during the afternoons, in the slave quarters at night, and in the degrees of freedom blacks achieved through resistance, revolt, and free status.

In a poignant moment in his *Narrative,* Douglass described his dreams of freedom as he looked out at the boats on the waters of Chesapeake Bay as a boy. Contrasting his own enslavement with the boats he saw as "freedom's swift-winged angels," Douglass vowed to escape: "This very bay shall yet bear me into freedom.... There is a better day coming." As we will see later, southern white planters also bemoaned their lack of freedom relative to the North and made their own plans to achieve independent status through secession. Meanwhile, as that struggle brewed beneath the surface of antebellum life, many other Americans were dismayed by various evil aspects in their society, slavery among them, and sought ways of shaping a better America. We turn to these other dreams in the next chapter.

Recommended Reading

Morning: Building the Cotton Kingdom: Masters, Mistresses, and the Social and Economic Life of the Old South

Orville Vernon Burton, *In My Father's House Are Many Mansions: Family and Community in Edgefield, South Carolina* (1985); Victoria E. Bynum, *Unruly Women: The Politics of Social and Sexual Control in the Old South* (1990); Catharine Clinton, *Plantation Mistress* (1983); Bruce Collins, *White Society in the Antebellum South* (1985); J. H. Easterby, ed., *The South Carolina Rice Plantation as Revealed in the Papers of Robert F. W. Allston* (1945); Clement Eaton, *The Growth of Southern Civilization* (1961); Drew Faust, *James Henry Hammond and the Old South: A Design for Mastery* (1982); Elizabeth Fox-Genovese, *Within the Plantation Household: Black and White Women of the Old South* (1988); John Hope Franklin, *The Militant South* (1966); George Fredrickson, *The Black Image in the White Mind: The Debate on Afro-American Character and Destiny, 1817–1914* (1971); Eugene Genovese, *The Slaveholder's Dilemma: Freedom and Progress in Southern Conservative Thought, 1820–1860* (1992); Suzanne Lebsock, *The Free Women of Petersburg: Status and Culture in a Southern Town, 1784–1860* (1984); James Oakes, *The Ruling Race: A History of American Slaveholders* (1982) and *Slavery and Freedom: An Interpretation of the Old South* (1990); Frank Owsley, *Plain Folk in the Old South* (1949);

William Stanton, *The Leopard's Spots: Scientific Attitudes Toward Race in America, 1815–1859* (1960); Steven Stowe, *Intimacy and Power in the Old South: Rituals in the Lives of the Planters* (1987); Harold Woodman, *Slavery and the Southern Economy* (1966); Gavin Wright, *The Political Economy of the Cotton South: Households, Markets, and Wealth in the Nineteenth Century* (1978).

Noon: The Institution of Slavery

John Blassingame, ed., *Slave Testimony* (1977); John B. Boles, *Black Southerners, 1619–1869* (1983); Paul David et al., *Reckoning with Slavery: A Critical Study of the Quantitative History of American Negro Slavery* (1976); Carl Degler, *Neither Black Nor White: Slavery and Race Relations in Brazil and the United States* (1971); Robert W. Fogel, *Without Consent or Contract: The Rise and Fall of American Slavery* (1989); Robert Fogel and Stanley Engerman, *Time on the Cross: The Economics of American Negro Slavery* (1974); Eugene Genovese, *Roll, Jordan, Roll: The World the Slaves Made* (1974); Herbert Gutman and Richard Sutch, *Slavery and the Numbers Game* (1975); Nathan I. Huggins, *Black Odyssey: The Afro-American Ordeal in Slavery* (1977); Peter Kolchin, *American Slavery, 1619–1877* (1993); Leslie Owens, *This Species of Property: Slave Life and Slave Culture in the Old*

South (1976); Ulrich B. Phillips, *American Negro Slavery* (1919) and *Life and Labor in the Old South* (1929); Willie Lee Rose, ed., *Documentary History of Slavery in North America* (1976); Kenneth Stampp, *The Peculiar Institution* (1956); Robert Starobin, *Industrial Slavery in the Old South* (1970); Richard Wade, *Slavery in the Cities* (1964).

Night: Black Culture and Community

William L. Andrews, *To Tell a Free Story: The First Century of Afro-American Autobiography, 1760–1865* (1986); John Blassingame, *The Slave Community*, rev. ed. (1979); Linda Brent, *Incidents in the Life of a Slave Girl* (1861); Frederick Douglass, *Narrative of the Life of Frederick Douglass* (1845); Dena J. Epstein, *Sinful Tunes and Spirituals: Black Folk Music to the Civil War* (1971); Jacqueline Jones, *Labor of Love, Labor of Sorrow: Black Women, Work, and the Family from Slavery to the Present* (1985); Charles Joyner, *Down by the Riverside: A South Carolina Slave Community* (1984); Herbert Gutman, *The Black Family in Slavery and Freedom, 1750–1925* (1976); James Oliver Horton, *Free People of Color: Inside the African-American Community* (1993); Lawrence Levine, *Black Culture and Black Consciousness: Afro-American Folk Thought from Slavery to Freedom* (1977); Albert Raboteau, *Slave Religion: The "Invisible Institution" in the Ante-bellum South* (1978); George Rawick, *From Sundown to Sunup: The Making of a Black Community* (1972); Sterling Stuckey, *Slave Culture: Nationalist Theory and the Foundation of Black America* (1987); Thomas L. Webber, *Deep Like Rivers: Education in the Slave Quarters, 1831–1865* (1978); Deborah Gray White, *Arn't I a Woman?* (1985).

Slave Resistance and Free Blacks

Herbert Aptheker, *Nat Turner's Slave Rebellion* (1966); Ira Berlin, *Slaves Without Masters: The Free Negro in the Antebellum South* (1976); Leonard Curry, *The Free Black in Urban America, 1800–1850: The Shadow of the Dream* (1981); Merton L. Dillon, *Slavery Attacked: Southern Slaves and Their Allies, 1619–1865* (1990) Frederick Douglass, *My Bondage and My Freedom* (1855) and *Life and Times of Frederick Douglass* (1881); Vincent Harding, *There Is a River: The Black Struggle for Freedom in America* (1981); Nathan I. Huggins, *Slave and Citizen: The Life of Frederick Douglass* (1980); Michael P. Johnson and James L. Roark, *No Chariot Down: Charleston's Free People of Color on the Eve of the Civil War* (1984) and *Black Masters: A Free Family of Color in the Old South* (1984); Norrece R. Jones, Jr., *Born a Child of Freedom, Yet a Slave: Mechanisms of Control and Strategies of Resistance in Antebellum South Carolina* (1990); John Lofton, *Denmark Vesey's Plot: The Slave Plot That Lit a Fuse to Fort Sumter* (1983); William S. McFeely, *Frederick Douglass* (1991).

Novel

Harriet Beecher Stowe, *Uncle Tom's Cabin* (1852).

Shaping America in the Antebellum Age

On November 19, 1836, as the second term of President Andrew Jackson neared its end, 30-year-old Marius Robinson and Emily Rakestraw were married near Cincinnati, Ohio. Two months after their wedding, he went on the road to speak against slavery and to organize abolitionist societies throughout Ohio. Emily stayed in Cincinnati to teach in a school for free blacks. During their ten-month separation, they exchanged affectionate letters that reflected their love and work.

Writing after midnight from Concord, Ohio, Marius complained of the "desolation of loneliness" he felt without her. Emily responded that she felt "about our separation just as you do" and confessed that her "womanish nature" did not much enjoy self-denial. In their letters, each imagined the "form and features" of the other and chided the other for not writing more often. Each voiced concern for the responsibilities and burdens of the other's work. Each expressed comfort and support, doubted his or her own abilities ("a miserable comforter I am"), and agreed that in their separation, as Marius put it, "we must look alone to God."

With such love for each other, what prompted this painful separation so early in their marriage? Emily wrote of their duty "to labor long in this cause so near and dear to us both," together if they could, but apart if so decreed by God. Marius, who had experienced a series of conversions inspired by the revivalist Charles G. Finney and his abolitionist disciple Theodore Dwight Weld, described the reason for their separation: "God and humanity bleeding and suffering demand our services apart." Thus motivated by a strong religious commitment to serve others, these two young reformers dedicated themselves to several social causes: the abolition of slavery, equal rights and education for free blacks, temperance, and women's rights.

Their commitments cost more than separation. When Emily went to Cincinnati to work with other young reformers, her parents disapproved. When she married Marius, who already had a reputation as a "rebel," her parents disowned her altogether. Emily wrote with sadness that her sisters and friends also "love me less ... than they did in by-gone days." Marius responded that he wished he could "dry your tears" and sought to heal the rift. Although Emily's family eventually accepted their marriage, there were other griefs. Teaching at the school in Cincinnati was demanding, and Emily could not get rid of a persistent cough. Furthermore, the white citizens of the city resented the school and the young abolitionists in their midst, treating them with contempt. Earlier in the year, Marius had escaped an angry mob by disguising himself and mingling with the crowd that came to sack the offices of a reformist journal edited by James G. Birney. Emily, meanwhile, tirelessly persisted in the work of "our school" while worrying about the health and safety of her husband on the road.

She had good reason for concern, for Marius's letters were full of reports of mob attacks, disrupted meetings, stonings, and narrow escapes. At two lectures near Granville, Ohio, he was "mobbed thrice, once most rousingly," as he faced crowds of "the veriest savages I ever saw," armed with clubs, cudgels, and intense hatred for those speaking against slavery. In June, he was dragged from the home of his Quaker host and beaten, tarred, and feathered. Never quite recovering his health, Marius spent half a year in bed, weak and dispirited. For nearly ten years after that, the Robinsons lived quietly on an Ohio farm, only slightly involved in the abolitionist movement. Despite the joyous birth of two daughters, they felt lonely, restless, and guilt-ridden, "tired of days blank of benevolent effort and almost of benevolent desires."

Marius and Emily Robinson, like other Americans, sought to find goodness and order in a society that seemed "everywhere unhinged." (Anonymous, Moving Day in the City, c. 1829/Mr. & Mrs. Screven Lorillard Collection, Photography by Eric Schaal, The Life History of the United States: The Sweep Westward, ©1963 Time-Life books, Inc.)

*T*he work of Emily and Marius Robinson represents one response by the American people to the rapid social and economic changes of the antebellum era described in Chapters 10 and 11. In September 1835, a year before the Robinsons' marriage, the *Niles Register* commented on some 500 recent incidents of mob violence and social upheaval. "Society seems everywhere unhinged, and the demon of 'blood and slaughter' has been let loose upon us.... [The] character of our countrymen seems suddenly changed." How did Americans adapt to these changes? In a world that seemed everywhere "unhinged" and out of control, in which old rules and patterns no longer provided guidance, how did people maintain some sense of control over their lives? How did they seek to shape their altered world? How could they both adopt the benefits of change and reduce the accompanying disruptions?

One way was to embrace the changes fully. Thus, some Americans became entrepreneurs in new industries; invested in banks, canals, and railroads; bought more land and slaves; and invented new machines. Others went west or to the new textile mills, enrolled in common schools, joined trade unions, specialized their labor in both the workplace and the home, and celebrated the practical benefits that resulted from modernization. Marius Robinson eventually went into life insurance, though he and Emily never fully abandoned their reformist efforts and idealism.

But many Americans were uncomfortable with the character of the new era. Some worried about the unrestrained power and selfish materialism symbolized by the slavemaster's control over his slaves. Others feared that institutions like the U.S. Bank represented a "monied aristocracy" capable of undermining the country's honest producers. Seeking positions of leadership and authority, these critics of the new order tried to shape a nation that retained the benefits of economic change without sacrificing humane principles of liberty, equality of opportunity, and community virtue. This chapter examines four ways in which the American people responded to change by attempting to influence their country's development: religious revivalism, party politics, utopian communitarianism, and social reform.

Religious Revival and Reform Philosophy

When the Frenchman Alexis de Tocqueville visited the United States in 1831 and 1832, he observed that he could find "no country in the whole world in which the Christian religion retains a greater influence over the souls of men than in America." What de Tocqueville was describing was a new and powerful religious enthusiasm among American Protestants. Fired by the power of religious rebirth, some discovered that religion provided them with moorings in a fast-changing world. Others were inspired by revivalism to refashion American society, working through new political parties to shape an agenda for the nation or through reform associations organized to eliminate a particular social evil. Although not all evangelicals agreed about politics or even about what aspects of American society needed to be reformed, religion was the lens through which they viewed contemporary events and through which they sought to effect change.

Finney and the Second Great Awakening

From the late 1790s until the late 1830s, a wave of religious revivals that matched the intensity of the Great Awakening in the 1730s and 1740s swept through the United States. The camp meeting revivals of the frontier at the turn of the century and the New England revivals sparked by Lyman Beecher took on a new emphasis and location after 1830. Led by the spellbinding Charles G. Finney, under whose influence Marius Robinson had been converted, revivalism shifted to upstate New York and the Old Northwest. Both areas had been experiencing profound economic and social changes, as the example of Rochester, New York, suggests.

This 1839 painting of a camp meeting captures the religious fervor that many Americans turned to in the face of social and economic upheavals. These mass conversions led some believers to individual salvation and others to social reform. (New Bedford Whaling Museum)

By the 1830s, Rochester, like Lowell and Cincinnati, was a rapidly growing American city. Located on the recently completed Erie Canal, it was a flour-milling center for the rich wheatlands of western New York. The canal changed Rochester from a sleepy little village of 300 in 1815 to a bustling commercial and milling city of nearly 20,000 inhabitants by 1830. As in other cities, economic growth affected relationships between masters and workers, distancing them both physically and psychologically. As the gulf widened, the masters' control over their laborers weakened. Saloons and unions sprang up in workingmen's neighborhoods, and workers became more transient, following the canal and other opportunities westward.

Prominent Rochester citizens therefore invited Charles Finney to come to town in 1830 to deliver some sermons. What followed was one of the most successful revivals of the Second Great Awakening. "You could not go upon the streets," a convert recalled, "and hear any conversation, except upon religion." Finney preached nearly every night and three times on Sundays, converting first the city's business elite, often through their wives, and then many workers. For six months, Rochester went through a citywide prayer meeting in which one conversion led to another.

The Rochester revival was part of the wave of religious enthusiasm in America that contributed to the tremendous growth of the Methodists, the Baptists, and other evangelical denominations in the first half of the nineteenth century. By 1844, for example, the Methodist church had become the largest denomination in America, with over a million members. To bring large masses of people to accept Christ as their savior, revivalist preachers deemphasized doctrine in favor of emotion, softening strict Calvinist tenets such as predestination, original sin, and limited atonement.

Unlike Jonathan Edwards, who believed that revivals were God's miracles, Finney understood that the human "agency" of the minister was crucial in causing a revival. He even published a do-it-yourself manual for other revivalists. Few, however, could match Finney's powerful preaching style. The hypnotic effect of his eyes and voice carried such power that he could dissolve an audience into tears. When he threw an imaginary brick at the Devil, people ducked. When his finger pointed the descent of a sinner into hell, people in the back row stood up to see the final disappearance. A former lawyer, Finney used logic as well as emotion to bring about conversions.

Many revivalists, especially in the South, sought individual salvation. American Catholics also caught the revival fervor in the 1830s. Scattered in small but growing numbers in eastern cities like Baltimore, Philadelphia, and New York and in western cities such as Cincinnati, St. Louis, Louisville, and New Orleans, Catholic leaders recognized that survival as a small and often despised religion depended on constant reinvigoration and evangelism. Focusing on the parish mission, energetic retreats and revivals gathered Catholics from miles around in order to preserve a religious heritage seriously threatened by life in Protestant America.

The Finney revivals differed from Catholic and southern revivalism because they insisted that conversion and salvation were not the end of religious experience but the beginning. Finney believed that humans were not passive objects of God's predestined plan, but moral free agents who could choose good over evil, convince others to do the same, and thereby eradicate sin from the world. Finney's idea of the "utility of benevolence" meant not only individual reformation, but also the commitment to do one's sacred duty in reforming one's society.

The Transcendentalists

No one knew this better than Ralph Waldo Emerson, a Concord, Massachusetts, essayist who was the era's foremost intellectual figure. Emerson's essays of the 1830s—"Nature," "American Scholar," and "Divinity School Address," among others—influenced the generation of reformist American intellectuals coming of age in mid-century and helped inspire artists and writers. The small but influential group of New England intellectuals who lived near Emerson were called Transcendentalists because of their belief that truth was found beyond experience in intuition. Casting off the European intellectual tradition, Emerson urged Americans to look inward and to nature for self-knowledge, self-reliance, and the spark of divinity burning within all people. "To acquaint a man with himself," he wrote, would inspire a "reverence" for self and others, which would then lead outward to social reform. "What is man born for," Emerson wrote, "but to be a Reformer?"

Inspired by self-reflection, the Transcendentalists asked troublesome questions about the quality of American life. They questioned not only slavery, an obvious evil, but also the obsessive competitive pace of economic life, the overriding concern for materialism, and the restrictive conformity of social life.

Although not considered Transcendentalists, Nathaniel Hawthorne and Herman Melville, two giants of mid-century American literature, also reflected these concerns in their fiction. Like Emerson, they were romantic in spirit, celebrating emotion over reason, nature over civilization, and virtue over self-interest. Hawthorne's great subject was the "truth of the human heart," which he portrayed as more authentic than the calculating minds of scientists and their schemes. In his greatest novel, *The Scarlet Letter* (1850), Hawthorne sympathetically told the story of a courageous Puritan woman's adultery and her eventual loving triumph over the narrowness of both cold intellect and intolerant social conformity.

Herman Melville dedicated his epic novel *Moby Dick* (1851) to Hawthorne. At one level, a rousing story of whaling on the high seas in pursuit of the great white whale, *Moby Dick* was actually an immense allegory of good and evil, bravery and weakness, innocence and experience. In Melville's other novels, he continued this sea voyage setting for making a powerful statement on behalf of the lowly seaman's claims for freedom and just social relations against the tyranny of the ship captain. Like Emerson, Hawthorne and Melville mirrored the tensions of the age as they explored issues of freedom and control.

When Emerson wrote, "Whoso would be a man, must be a nonconformist," he described his friend Henry David Thoreau. No one thought more deeply about the virtuous natural life than Thoreau. On July 4, 1845, he went to live in a small hut by Walden Pond, near Concord. There he planned to confront the "essential facts of life"—to discover who he was and how to live well. When Thoreau left Walden two years later, he protested against slavery and the Mexican War by refusing to pay his taxes. He went to jail briefly and wrote an essay, "On Civil Disobedience" (1849), and a book, *Walden* (1854), which are still considered classic statements of what one person can do to protest unjust laws and wars and live a life of principle.

The Political Response to Change

Although transcendentalism touched only a few elite New Englanders, perhaps as many as 40 percent of the American people were affected by the winds of evangelical Protestantism. Although economic, ethnic, and even regional factors played a part in shaping political loyalties, evangelical values and religious loyalties colored many people's understanding of the appropriate role of government and influenced their involvement in political activities. As politics became more a popular than an elite vocation, it was not surprising that religious commitments spilled over into the political sphere.

At the heart of American politics was the concern for the continued health of the republican experiment. As American society changed, so, too, did the understanding of what measures were necessary to maintain that health. In the late 1850s, a Maine newspaper warned that the preservation of the nation's freedom depended on the willingness of its citizens to go to the polls. It was, in fact, the "positive duty of every citizen of a Republic to vote." This insistence on voting as crucial to the well-being of the country was new. Before the 1820s, politics was primarily the business of the social and economic elite. Even though many states were removing voting restrictions in the early nineteenth century, the majority of white men did not trouble themselves with political matters. But the trauma of the Panic of 1819 and the spirited presidential campaigns for Andrew Jackson helped create widespread interest in politics. For many Americans, political participation became an important way of asserting and supporting important values and promoting their vision of the republic.

Changing Political Culture

The presidency of Andrew Jackson was a crucial factor in bringing politics to the center of many Americans' lives. Styling himself as the people's candidate in 1828, Andrew Jackson derided the Adams administration as corrupt and aristocratic and promised a more democratic political system with the interests of the people at its center. To this end, he told voters that he intended to "purify" and "reform the Government," purging all "who have been appointed from political considerations or against the will of the people." Unlike the 1990s, most Americans then believed the campaign rhetoric. Four times more men turned out to vote in the election of 1828 than had gone to the polls four years earlier. They gave Jackson a resounding

56 percent of their ballots. No other president in the century would equal that percentage of popular support.

Despite campaign rhetoric and his image as a democratic hero, Jackson was not personally very democratic, nor did the era he symbolized involve any significant redistribution of wealth. Jackson himself owned slaves, defended slavery, and condoned mob attacks on abolitionists like Marius Robinson in the mid–1830s. He disliked Indians and ordered the forcible removal of the southeastern Indian nations to west of the Mississippi River in blatant disregard of the treaty rights of the Cherokee and a Supreme Court decision that protected their Georgia lands. And belying promises of widening opportunity, the rich got richer during the Jacksonian era, and most farming and urban laboring families did not prosper.

But the nation's political life had changed in important ways. The old system of politics based on elite coalitions bound together by ties of family and friendship and dependent on the deference of voters to their "betters" largely disappeared. In its place emerged a competitive party system, begun early in the republic but now oriented toward widespread voter participation and state and local politics. Party organizations bent on mobilizing large numbers of citizens became key to political victory. The major parties grew adept at raising money, selecting and promoting candidates, and bringing voters to the polls. A new "democratic" style of political life emerged as parties sponsored conventions, rallies (much like evangelical revivals in their flavor and fervor), and parades to encourage political participation and identification. Party politics became a central preoccupation for many adult white males. In the North, even women turned out for political rallies and speeches and rode on floats at party parades.

A rough-and-ready style of political activity emerged as parties appealed to popular emotions, religious views, and ethnic prejudices. Party-subsidized newspapers regularly indulged in scurrilous attacks on political candidates. The language of politics became contentious and militaristic. Jackson's rhetoric exemplified the new trends. He described an opponent as an "enemy" who waged "war against the cause of the people." He reminded Americans that "those who are not for us are against us." Politicians pictured elections as

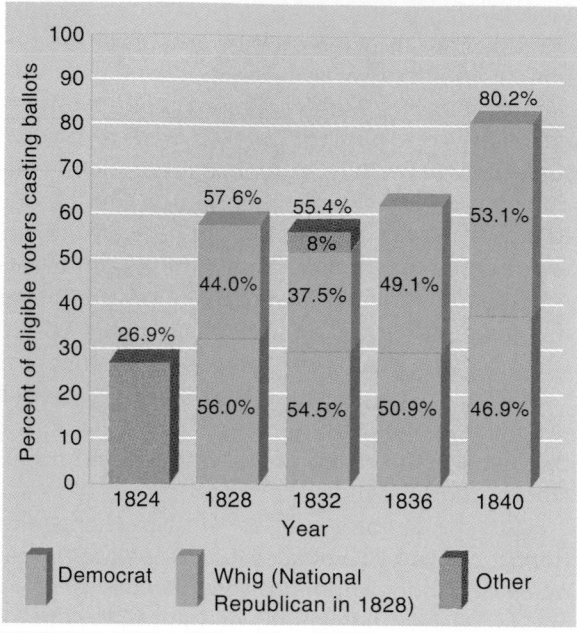

More Americans Vote for President, 1824–1840

The single-party system (Jeffersonian Democratic Republican) that existed in 1824 collapsed with the intense personal rivalries and ideological differences of the 1820s and 1830s. The emergence of a two-party system in the Jacksonian era dramatically increased (white male) voter participation to percentages far exceeding those of modern U.S. presidential elections.

battles or campaigns. Party leaders concerned themselves with the discipline of their party's "rank and file." Strong party identification was part of the new national political culture. James Buchanan complained in 1839 about a colleague who urged politicians "to rise above mere party, and to go for our country." Instead, Buchanan said, "in supporting my party, I honestly believe I am … promoting the interest of my country."

Jackson's Path to the White House

The early career of Andrew Jackson gave few hints of his future political importance. Orphaned at 14, young Jackson was rowdy, indecisive, and often in trouble. As a law student, he was "a most roaring, rollicking, game-cocking, horse-racing, card-playing, mischievous fellow." Despite these preoccupations, which also included dueling, Jackson passed the bar and set out at the age of 21 to seek his fortune in the West. Settling in the frontier town of

Nashville, the tall, redheaded young man built up a successful law practice in Tennessee and went on to become attorney general. Eventually, he became a substantial landowner and a prominent citizen of Nashville.

Jackson's national reputation stemmed mainly from his military exploits, primarily against American Indians. As major general of the Tennessee militia, he proved able and popular. Jackson's troops admired his toughness and nicknamed him "Old Hickory." His savage victory over the Creek nation in the South in 1813 and 1814 brought notoriety and an appointment as major general in the U.S. Army. But his victory over the British at New Orleans in 1815 and his image as a savior made him into a national hero. His tour of the country after the war suggested political ambitions. As early as 1817, resolutions supporting a Jackson bid for the presidency began to appear in several states.

Although Jackson's aggressive military forays into Spanish Florida in 1818 bothered rival politicians and added to his reputation for scandal, these actions increased his popularity and his interest in the presidency. Jackson recognized that his greatest appeal lay with ordinary people, whom he cultivated. At the same time, he realized the importance of effective political backing. Careful political maneuvering in Tennessee in the early 1820s brought him election as U.S. senator and nomination for the presidency in 1824.

In the 1824 election, Jackson won both the popular and the electoral votes, but lost in the House of Representatives to John Quincy Adams. When Henry Clay threw his support to Adams and was named secretary of state, Jackson condemned this deal as a "corrupt bargain." Soon after the 1824 election, a rumor surfaced in Washington that "a Party is forming itself to oppose Mr. Adams' administration." Jackson's loss convinced him of the importance of having an effective political organization. He felt confident of his strength in the West, and support by Adams's vice president, John C. Calhoun, helped him in the South. Jackson organized his campaign by setting up loyal committees and newspapers in many states and by encouraging efforts to undermine Adams and Clay.

The loose coalition promoting Jackson's candidacy, which began to call itself the Democratic party, was a mixed lot, drawing in politicians of diverse views from all sections of the country, including Martin Van Buren of New York. Jackson proved masterful in playing down his position on controversial issues. He concealed his dislike of banks and paper money and told supporters that he believed in a tariff that held to a "middle and just course," a position vague enough to offend no one. He did, however, make clear his intentions of reforming government by throwing out of office those who failed to represent the will of the people, promising to cleanse government of corruption and privileged interests.

The campaign between Jackson and Adams in 1828 degenerated into a nasty but entertaining contest. The Democrats organized barbecues, mass rallies, and parades to whip up enthusiasm. They gave out buttons and hats with hickory leaves attached. Amid the hoopla, few people discussed issues. Both sides engaged in slanderous personal attacks. Supporters of Adams and Clay, who called themselves National Republicans, claimed that Jackson was "an adulterer, a gambler, a cockfighter, a brawler, a drunkard, and a murderer." His wife, Rachel, was maligned as common and immoral.

The Jacksonians in turn charged Adams with bribing Clay for his support in 1824. They described him as a "stingy, undemocratic" aristocrat determined to destroy the people's liberties. Worse yet, Adams was an intellectual. Jackson, by contrast, was the hero of the Battle of New Orleans, a point underlined by an unprecedented campaign trip to celebrate the anniversary of his victory there. Jackson's campaign slogans emphasized the differences between himself as an energetic, military doer ("a man who can fight") and Adams as a weak, ineffectual thinker ("a man who can write"). "Who do you want," one slogan asked, "John Quincy Adams, who quotes law, or Andy Jackson, who makes law?" The question left little doubt as to how proud Americans would vote.

Jackson's supporters in Washington worked to ensure his election by devising a tariff bill to win necessary support in key states. Under the leadership of Van Buren, who hoped to replace Calhoun as Jackson's heir apparent, the Democrats in Congress put together enough votes to pass what opponents called the "Tariff of Abominations." The tariff arbitrarily raised rates to protect New England textiles, Pennsylvania iron, and some agricultural goods, thereby winning voters in those states where the Democrats needed more support. John Randolph of Virginia sneered that the tariff "referred to manufactures of no sort or kind but the manufacture of a President of the United States."

The efforts of Jackson and his party paid off as he won an astonishing 647,286 ballots, about 56 percent of the total. Organization, money, effective publicity, and a popular style of campaigning had brought the 60-year-old Jackson to the presidency. His inauguration, however, horrified many Americans. Washington was packed for the ceremonies. Daniel Webster noted that "persons have come five hundred miles to see General Jackson, and they really seem to think that the country is to be rescued from some dreadful danger." When Jackson appeared on the steps of the Capitol to take the oath of office, wild and unrestrained cheering broke out. Few in the crowd heard the short address or the oath, but many hoped to shake the new president's hand, and Jackson was all but mobbed as he tried to make his way to his horse.

The White House reception soon got completely out of hand. A throng of people, "from the highest and most polished, down to the most vulgar and gross," Justice Joseph Story observed, poured into the White House with muddy boots to overturn furniture in a rush for food and punch.

As depicted in the Robert Cruikshank lithograph, All Creation Going to the White House, *the first inauguration of Andrew Jackson in 1829 was the scene of wild festivities, a harbinger of the excesses in American life and politics in the ensuing years. (Library of Congress)*

Jackson was forced to leave by a side door. In an effort to stop the melee, the wine and ice cream were carried out to the lawn. The guests followed, many of them diving out through the windows. The inauguration, Story concluded, illustrated the "reign of King Mob." Another observer called it a "proud day for the people." These contrasting views on the events of the inauguration captured the essence of the Jackson era. For some, they symbolized the excesses of democracy; for others, they represented democratic fulfillment.

Old Hickory's Vigorous Presidency

Although Jackson had taken vague positions on important issues during the campaign, as president, he needed to confront many of them. His decisions, often controversial, helped sharpen what it meant to be a Democrat and what it meant to be Democracy's opponent.

A few key convictions—the principle of majority rule, the limited power of the national government, the obligation of the national government to defend the interests of the nation's average people against the machinations of the "monied aristocracy"—guided Jackson's political behavior as president. Because he saw himself as the people's most authentic representative (only the president was elected by all the people), Jackson intended to be an effective, vigorous executive. More than any previous president, Jackson used presidential power in the name of the people and justified his actions by popular appeals to the electorate.

Jackson asserted his power most dramatically through use of the veto. The six preceding presidents had used the veto only nine times, most often against measures that they had believed unconstitutional. Jackson, however, argued that he had "undoubted right ... to withhold ... assent from bills on other grounds than their constitutionality." In effect, he forced Congress to consider his position on legislative issues. In all, Jackson vetoed 12 bills during his eight years in office.

One of the abuses Jackson had promised to correct was what he described as an undemocratic and corrupt system of government officeholding. Too often "unfaithful or incompetent" men held on to their offices for years, making a mockery of the idea of representation. Jackson proposed to

throw these scoundrels out and to establish a system of rotation of office. Because the duties of public office were so "plain and simple," he argued, ordinary men were fit to govern.

Jackson's rhetoric was more extreme than his actions. He did not engage in wholesale replacement of officeholders with his own supporters. In the first year and a half of his presidency, he removed 919 officeholders of a total of 10,093, fewer than one in ten. Most of these were for good reason—corruption or incompetence. Nor were the new Democratic appointees especially plain, untutored, or honest; they were in fact much like their predecessors. Still, Jackson's rhetoric helped create a new kind of democratic political culture that would prevail for most of the nineteenth century.

His policy on internal improvements of roads, canals and other forms of transportation was less far-seeing. Like most Americans, Jackson recognized their economic importance and as president wished "to see them extended to every part of the country." But Jackson believed that the national government should not infringe on states' rights. When proposals for federal support for internal improvements seemed to rob local and state authorities of their proper function, he opposed them. In 1830, he vetoed the Maysville Road bill, which would have authorized the use of federal funds to build a road in Henry Clay's Kentucky. But projects of national significance, like the building of lighthouses or river improvements, were different matters. In fact, Jackson supported an annual average of $1.3 million in internal improvements while he was in office.

In a period of rapid economic change, tariffs were a matter of heated debate. New England and the Middle Atlantic states, the center of manufacturing operations, favored protective tariffs. But the South had long opposed such tariffs because they made it more expensive for southerners to buy manufactured goods from the North or abroad. In addition, they feared that high tariffs would lead to reductions in trade harmful to the export of southern cotton and tobacco. Feelings against the "Tariff of Abominations" ran particularly high in South Carolina. Some of that state's leaders saw the tariff as the prime cause of the economic depression that hung over their state (it actually stemmed from the opening of new fertile lands in the West). In addition, some worried that the federal government might eventually interfere with slavery, a frightening prospect in a state where slaves outnumbered whites.

Vice President Calhoun, a brilliant political thinker and opponent of the tariff, provided the appropriate theory to counteract the power of the federal government and to protect minority rights. "We are not a nation," he once remarked, "but a Union, a confederacy of equal and sovereign states." In 1828, the same year as the hateful tariff, Calhoun published an anonymous essay, *Exposition and Protest*, that presented the doctrine of nullification as a means by which southern states could protect themselves from harmful national action. He argued that when federal laws were deemed to overstep the limits of constitutional authority, a state had the right to declare that legislation null and void and to refuse to enforce it.

Two years later, Calhoun's doctrine was aired in a Senate debate over public land policy. South Carolina's Robert Hayne defined nullification and, in the name of liberty, urged western states to adopt the doctrine. In a speech spread over two days, Daniel Webster eloquently responded. The federal government, he maintained, was far more than an agent of the states. It was "made for the people, made by the people, and answerable to the people." No state legislature, therefore, could ever be sovereign over the people. Aware that nullification raised the specter of a "once glorious Union … drenched … in fraternal blood," Webster cried out in his powerful closing words that the appropriate motto for the nation was not "Liberty first and Union afterwards, but Liberty and Union, now and forever, one and inseparable!"

The drama was reenacted a month later at a Jefferson birthday dinner when President Jackson declared himself on the issue. Despite his support of states' rights, Jackson did not believe that any state had the right to reject the will of the majority or to destroy the Union. Knowing that the supporters of nullification hoped to use the gathering to win adherents, Jackson rose for a toast, held high his glass, and said, "Our Union—it must be preserved." Not to be outdone, Calhoun followed with his toast: "The Union—next to our liberty most dear." The split between them widened over personal as well as ideological issues, and in 1832 Cal-

This nearly 12-foot-high figurehead of "Old Hickory" carved by Laban S. Beecher for the frigate Constitution depicts Jackson's uncompromising and rigid policies as president. The nickname, after America's toughest hardwood, was earned in Jackson's early military career. The figurehead, though, was not tough enough to withstand an opponent of Jackson, who sawed off the head below the nose soon after it was mounted on the ship. (Museum of the City of New York)

houn resigned as vice president. Final rupture came in a collision over the tariff and nullification.

In 1832, following Jackson's recommendation of a "middle course" for tariff revisions, Congress modified the tariff of 1828 by retaining high duties on goods such as wool, woolens, iron, and hemp and lowering other rates to an earlier level. Many southerners felt injured. In a special convention later that year in South Carolina, the delegates adopted an Ordinance of Nullification, declaring that the offending tariffs of 1828 and 1832 were null and void in that state. Furthermore, the South Carolina legislature voted funds for a volunteer army and threatened secession if the federal government should try to force the state to comply.

South Carolina's actions represented a direct attack on the concepts of federal union and majority rule. Jackson responded with appropriate force. To the "ambitious malcontents" in South Carolina, as he called the nullifiers, he issued a proclamation that stated emphatically that "the laws of the United States must be executed.... Disunion by armed force is treason.... The Union will be preserved and treason and rebellion promptly put down."

Jackson's proclamation stimulated an outburst of patriotism and popular support all over the country. No other southern states supported nullification, and several state legislatures denounced it. South Carolina stood alone. Jackson asked Congress for legislation to enforce tariff duties (the Force Bill of 1833), and new tariff revisions, engineered by Henry Clay and supported by Calhoun, called for reductions over a ten-year period. South Carolina quickly repealed its nullification of the tariff laws but saved face by nullifying the Force Bill at the same time, an act that Jackson ignored. The crisis was over, but left unresolved were the constitutional issues it raised. Was the Union permanent? Was secession a valid way to protect minority rights? Debate on such questions would trouble Americans for three decades.

Jackson's Indian Policy

Although Jackson only threatened force on South Carolina, he used force on the southeastern Indians. His policy of forcible removal and relocation westward and on reservations defined white American practice toward the Native American Indians for the rest of the century. In the opening decades of the nineteenth century, the vast landholdings of the five "civilized nations" of the Southeast (the Cherokee, Choctaw, Chickasaw, Seminole, and Creek) had been seriously eroded by the pressures of land-hungry whites supported by successful military campaigns led by professional Indian fighters such as General Jackson. The Creeks lost 22 million acres in southern Georgia and central Alabama as a result of their defeat by Jackson at Horseshoe Bend in 1814. Land cessions to the government and private sales accounted for even bigger losses: Cherokee tribal holdings, for example, of more than 50 million acres in 1802 had dwindled to only 9 million 20 years later.

The trend was bolstered by a Supreme Court decision in 1823 declaring that Indians could occupy but not hold title to land in the United States. Recognizing that their survival was threatened, Indian nations acted to end the pattern. By 1825, the Creek, Cherokee, and Chickasaw had each resolved to restrict land sales to government agents. The Cherokee, who had already assimilated many elements of white culture including clothing, agricultural practices, and slaveholding (see Chapter 9), established a police force to prevent local leaders from selling off tribal lands. Indian determination to resist pressure confronted white resolve to gain these southern lands for cotton planting and mining. Jackson's election in 1828 boosted efforts to relocate the Indians west of the Mississippi.

In his first annual message to Congress in 1829, Jackson recommended removal of the southeastern tribes. Appealing at first more to sympathy than to force, Jackson argued that because the Indians were "surrounded by the whites with their arts of civilization," it was inevitable that the "resources of the savage" would be destroyed, dooming the Indians to "weakness and decay." Removal was justified, Jackson claimed, by both "humanity and national honor." He also endorsed the paramount right of state laws over the claims of either Indians or the federal government (thus contradicting his tariff policy).

The crisis soon came to a head in Georgia. In 1829, the Georgia legislature declared the Cherokee tribal council illegal and its laws null and void in Cherokee territories and announced that the state had jurisdiction over both the tribe and its lands. In the following year, the Cherokee were forbidden to defend their interests by bringing suits against whites into the Georgia courts or even by testifying in such cases. Without legal recourse on the state level, the Cherokee carried their protests to the Supreme Court. In 1832, Chief Justice Marshall supported their position in *Worcester* v. *Georgia*, holding that the Georgia law was "repugnant to the Constitution" and did not apply to the Cherokee nation.

Legal victory could not, however, suppress white land hunger. With Jackson's blessing, Georgians defied the Court ruling. By 1835, harassment, intimidation, and bribery had persuaded a minority of chiefs to sign a removal treaty. That year, Jackson informed the Cherokee, "You cannot remain where you are. Circumstances … render it impossible that you can flourish in the midst of a civilized community." Despite the president's pronouncement and the treaty, most Cherokee refused to leave their lands. Therefore, in 1837 and 1838, the U.S. Army searched out and seized the terrified Indians and gathered them in stockades before herding them west to the "Indian Territory" in Oklahoma. An eyewitness described how the Cherokee trek began:

> Families at dinner were startled by the sudden gleam of bayonets in the doorway and rose to be driven with blows and oaths along the weary miles of trail that led to the stockade. Men were seized in their fields, or going along the road, women were taken from their [spinning] wheels and children from their play. In many cases, on turning for one last look as they crossed the ridge they saw their homes in flames, fired by the lawless rabble that followed on the heels of the soldiers to loot and pillage.

The removal, the $6 million cost of which was deducted from the $9 million awarded the Cherokee for its eastern lands, brought death to perhaps a quarter of the 15,000 who set out. The Cherokee remember this event as the "Trail of Tears." Other southern and some northwestern tribes between 1821 and 1840 shared a similar fate. The Chickasaw suffered as high a death rate as the Cherokee during their removal, while such nations as the Seminole and the Sac and Fox fought to avoid deportation. Most nations were in the end removed. Although both Jackson and the Removal Act of 1830 had promised to protect and forever guarantee the Indian lands in the West, within a generation those promises, like others before and since, would be broken. Indian removal left the eastern United States open for the enormous economic expansion described in Chapter 10.

Jackson's Bank War and "Van Ruin's" Depression

As the (white) people's advocate, Jackson could not ignore the Second Bank of the United States, which had been chartered for 20 years in 1816. The fate of the bank was an issue generating intense feelings in a period of economic change. Jackson believed the bank threatened the people's liberties and called it a "monster." But the bank was not as irresponsible as Jacksonians imagined.

Guided since 1823 by the aristocratic Nicholas Biddle, the Philadelphia bank and its 29 branches performed many useful financial services and gen-erally played a responsible economic role in an expansionary period. As the nation's largest commercial bank, the U.S. Bank was able to shift funds to different parts of the country as necessary and to influence state banking activity. It restrained state banks from making unwise loans by insisting that they back their notes with specie (gold or silver coin) and by calling in its own loans to these institutions. The bank accepted federal deposits, made commercial loans, and bought and sold government bonds. Businessmen, state bankers needing credit, and nationalist politicians such as Webster and Clay, who were on the bank's payroll, all favored the bank.

Other Americans, however, led by the president, distrusted the bank. Businessmen and speculators in western lands resented the bank's careful control over state banking and wanted cheap, inflated money. Some state bankers, especially in New York and Baltimore, were jealous of the power and position of the Philadelphia bank. Southern and western farmers regarded the bank, which dealt with paper rather than landed property, as fundamentally immoral, and others thought it was unconstitutional and should be abolished.

Jackson had long opposed the U.S. Bank, both for personal reasons (a near financial disaster in his own past) and because he and his advisers believed it was the chief example of a special privilege monopoly that hurt the common man—farmers, craftsmen, and debtors. Jackson called the bank an "irresponsible power" and a threat to the Republic. Its power and financial resources, he thought, allowed the bank to become a "vast electioneering engine" with the "power to control the Government and change its character."

Aware of Jackson's persisting hostility, Clay and Webster persuaded Biddle to ask Congress to recharter the bank in 1832, four years ahead of schedule. They reasoned that in an election year, Jackson would not risk a veto. The bill to recharter the bank swept through Congress and landed on the president's desk one hot, muggy day in July. Many in his own party pressed for a "milk & water half way veto," which would make possible another attempt to recharter the bank at a less embarrassing time. But Jackson refused to listen. "The bank … is trying to kill me," he told Van Buren, "but I will kill it."

Jackson determined not only to veto the bill, but also to carry his case to the public. His veto message, which condemned the bank as undemocratic, un-American, and unconstitutional, was meant to stir up emotions among voters. He presented the bank as a dangerous monopoly that helped the rich by providing them with special privileges and harmed "the humble members of society … who have neither the time nor the means of securing … favors to themselves." He also pointed to the high percentage of foreign investors in the bank. Jackson's veto message turned the issue of rechartering the bank into a struggle between the people and the aristocracy. His oversimplified analysis made the bank into a symbol of all that was worrisome to many Americans in a time of change.

The furor over the bank helped to clarify party differences. In the election of 1832, the National Republicans, now becoming known as Whigs to show their opposition to "King Andrew," nominated Henry Clay. Biddle and the Whigs spent thousands of dollars trying to ensure Clay's election over Jackson, whom they labeled a "tyrant." Democratic campaign rhetoric pitted Jackson, the people, and democracy against Clay, the bank, and aristocracy. The Anti-Masons, the first third party in American political life and the first to hold a nominating convention, revealed real issues more clearly than the two major parties. The anti-Masonic movement, which began in upstate New York, expressed popular resentments against the elitist Masonic order (Jackson was a member) and other secret societies.

When the ballots were counted, Jackson had once again won handsomely, garnering 124,000 more popular votes than the combined total for Clay and the Anti-Mason candidate, William Wirt, who said of Jackson, "He may be President for life if he chooses."

Jackson interpreted the election as a victory for his bank policy and made plans to finish his war with Biddle. The bank still had four years before the charter expired. Jackson announced that "the hydra of corruption is only scotched, not dead" and declared that it must be killed. He and his advisers decided to weaken the bank by transferring $10 million in government funds to state banks. Although two secretaries of the treasury

balked at the removal request as financially unsound, Jackson persisted until he found one, Roger Taney, willing to remove the funds. And when Chief Justice John Marshall, a Whig, died in 1835, Jackson replaced him with Taney.

Jackson's war with Biddle and the bank had serious economic consequences. A wave of speculation in western lands and ambitious new state internal improvement schemes in the mid-1830s led to rising land prices and a flood of paper money. Even Jackson was concerned, and he determined to curtail irresponsible economic activity. In July 1836, he issued the Specie Circular, announcing that the government would accept only gold and silver in payment for public lands. Panicky investors rushed to change paper notes into specie, while banks started to call in loans. The result was the Panic of 1837. Although Jackson was blamed for this rapid monetary expansion followed by sudden deflation in the mid-1830s, international trade problems with Britain and China probably contributed more to the panic and to the ensuing seven years of depression than Jackson's erratic policies.

Whatever the primary cause, Jackson stuck his successor, Martin Van Buren, who was elected in 1836 over a trio of Whig opponents, with an economic crisis. Van Buren had barely taken the oath of office in 1837 when banks and businesses began to collapse. His term as president was marked by a depression so severe that it brought him the unfortunate nickname "Martin Van Ruin." As New York banks suspended credit and began calling in loans, an estimated $6 million was lost on defaulted debts. In 1838, a wealthy merchant and mayor of New York, Philip Hone, wrote in his diary that half his friends were deeply in debt. By 1840, he noted, his three grown sons were out of work and "business of all kinds [was] completely at a stand."

As Hone knew well, however, the laboring poor suffered most in a depression. By the fall of 1837, one-third of America's workers were unemployed, and thousands of others found only sporadic part-time work. For those fortunate enough to retain their jobs, wages fell by 30 to 50 percent within two years. Meanwhile, the price of necessities like flour, pork, and coal nearly doubled. As winter neared in late 1837, a journalist estimated that 200,000 in New York City were "in utter hopeless distress with no means of surviving the winter but those provided by charity." Not surprisingly, they took to the streets, demanding, "Bread! Meat! Rent! Fuel! Their prices must come down!" One worker told newspaperman Horace Greeley that most laborers called "not for the bread and fuel of charity, but for Work!"

The pride of workers was dampened as soup kitchens and bread lines grew faster than jobs. Moreover, the depression destroyed the trade union movement begun a decade earlier, leaving laboring families isolated and defenseless. Many employers hastened the process of killing trade unionism by imposing longer hours, cutting wages and piece rates, and dividing workers. One New England hat manufacturer offered to hire only those untouched by the "moral gangrene of Trades' Union principles." As the hardships of the depression grew worse, violence increased. In 1842, when Philadelphia textile employers lowered wages below subsistence levels, angry hand-loom weavers broke machinery, destroyed cloth, and wrecked the homes of Irish strikebreakers. Job competition, poverty, and ethnic animosities led to violent clashes in other eastern cities as well, as we saw in Chapter 10.

"How is it," a Philadelphia mechanic asked in 1837, that in a country as rich as the United States so many people were "pinched for the common necessaries of life . . . [and] bowed down with gloom and despair?" President Van Buren's responses to the social misery behind this question were sympathetic but limited and even made things worse. An executive order in 1840 declaring a ten-hour day for federal employees affected few workers. Despite inadequate measures, political participation, as well as church membership, reached new heights during the depression, as Americans sought to alleviate their "gloom and despair."

The Second American Party System

By the mid–1830s, a new two-party system and a lively participatory national political culture had emerged in the United States. The parties had taken shape amid the conflicts of Jackson's presidency and the religious fervor of the Second Great Awakening. Although both parties included wealthy and influential leaders and mirrored the growing diversity of a changing nation, the Democrats had the better claim that they were the party of the common man with strength in all sections of the country.

Whigs represented greater wealth than Democrats and were strongest in New England and in areas settled by New Englanders across the Upper Midwest. In an appeal to businessmen and manufacturers, Whigs generally endorsed Clay's American System, which meant that they favored a national bank, federally supported internal improvements, and tariff protection for industry. Many large southern cotton planters joined the Whig party because of its position on bank credit and internal improvements. Whigs ran almost evenly with Democrats in the South for a decade, and artisans and laborers belonged equally to each party. The difficulty in drawing clear regional or class distinctions between Whigs and Democrats suggests that other factors, such as ethnic, religious, and cultural background, also influenced party choice. Because each party offered its own vision of the good society and notions on the role of government in private lives, broad cultural and social perspectives helped to determine party affiliation.

In the Jeffersonian tradition, the Democrats espoused liberty and local rule. They wanted freedom from legislators of morality, from religious tyranny, from special privilege, and from too much government. For them, the best society was one in which all Americans were free to follow their own individual interests. Those who wanted to maintain religious or ethnic traditions found a home in the Democratic party. So, too, did many members of denominations that had suffered discrimination in the colonies and states that had had an established church. The Scots-Irish, German, French, and Irish Catholic immigrants, as well as free thinkers and labor organizers, tended to be Jacksonians. Although they zealously promoted their social vision, Democrats were less moralistic than Whigs. Especially on matters like temperance and slavery, their religious background generally taught the inevitability of sin and evil in the world. Therefore, Democrats sought to keep politics separate from moral issues.

By contrast, for many Whigs, the line between reform and politics was hazy. Indeed, politics seemed an appropriate arena for cleansing society

The Second American Party System		
	Democrats	Whigs
Leaders	Andrew Jackson John C. Calhoun Martin Van Buren Thomas Hart Benton	Henry Clay Daniel Webster John Quincy Adams William Henry Harrison
Political tradition	Republican party (Jefferson, Madison)	Federalist part (Hamilton, John Adams)
Major Political Beliefs		
	State and local autonomy Opposition to monopoly and privilege Low land prices and tariffs Freedom from government interference	National power Support for U.S. Bank, high tariff Internal improvement Broad government role in reforming America
Primary Sources of Support		
Region	South and West Upper Midwest	New England, Middle Atlantic,
Class	Middle-class and small farmers, northeastern urban laborers and artisans	Big southern planters and wealthy businessmen, pockets of middling farmers in Midwest and South, artisans
Ethnicity	Scots-Irish, Irish, French, German, and Canadian immigrants	English, New England old stock
Religion	Catholics, frontier Baptists and Methodists, free thinkers	Presbyterians, Congregationalists, Quakers, moralists, reformers

of sin. Calling themselves the party of law and order, most Whigs did not think Americans needed more freedom, but rather they needed to learn to use the freedom they already had. If all men were to vote, they required a "system of general education" that would teach them to use their political privileges. Old-stock New England Yankee Congregationalists and Presbyterians were usually Whigs. So were Quakers and evangelical Protestants, who believed that positive government action could change moral behavior and eradicate sin. Whigs supported a wide variety of reforms, such as temperance, antislavery, public education, and strict observance of the Sabbath, as well as government action to promote economic development.

Party identification played an increasingly large part in the lives of American men. The flamboyant new electioneering styles and techniques were designed to recruit new voters into the political process and to ensure continued loyalty. Party activities offered excitement, entertainment, and camaraderie. They offered a way to shape the changing world.

The election of 1840 illustrated the new style of political culture. Passing over Henry Clay, the Whigs nominated William Henry Harrison of Indiana, the aging hero of the Battle of Tippecanoe (Kithtippecanoe), fought nearly 30 years earlier. A Virginian, John Tyler, was nominated as vice-president to underline the regional diversity of the party. The Democrats had no choice but to renominate Van Buren, who conducted a quiet campaign. The Whig campaign, however, featured every form of popularized appeals for votes—barbecues, torchlight parades, songs, and cartoons. Political symbolism was exploited by posing Harrison (who lived in a mansion) in front of a rural log cabin with a barrel of hard cider. Jugs of cider and coonskin caps inscribed with clever slogans were lavishly dispensed to grateful voters.

The Whigs reversed conventional images by labeling Van Buren an aristocratic dandy and contrasting him with their simple candidate sitting in front of his cabin. Harrison reminded voters of General Jackson, and they swept him into office, 234 electoral votes to Van Buren's 60. In one of the largest turnouts in American history, over 80 percent of eligible voters marched to the polls. Commenting on the defeat, a Democratic party journal acknowledged that the Whigs had out-Jacksoned the Jacksonians: "We taught them how to conquer us."

Concern over the new politics outlasted Harrison, who died only a month after taking office. One man complained during the campaign that he was tired of all the hoopla over "the Old Hero. Nothing but politics … mass-meetings are held in every groggery." His comment about the combination of politics and drinking was especially telling. For many Americans, usually Whigs and often women, it was precisely the excesses of Jacksonian politics, most notably intemperance and the inherent violence of slavery, that led them to seek other ways than politics of imposing order and morality on American society. To gain a measure of control over their lives and reshape their changing world, the American people turned also to religion, social reform, and utopianism.

(Left) In the election of 1840, the Whigs "out-Jacksoned the Jacksonians" by playing to the popular political style of slogans, songs, and cider. They touted their candidate as a backwoodsy Indian fighter, the hero of the battle of Tippecanoe, who lived in a log cabin and drank hard cider. (Cincinnati Historical Society) (Below) Louisiana Democrats responded to the Whig use of the log cabin and cider campaign with this cartoon, titled the "Federal-Abolition-Whig Trap to Catch Voters In," which shows an unwary voter, a member of the "industrious laboring classes," being lured under the log cabin by the promise of hard cider. "Just let him get a taste," the text says, "and they come down at once upon him, hard and heavy, swig after swig, until they get him in a ranting way, shouting and bawling for Tip. and Ty." (Library of Congress)

Europeans' Travel Journals

The observations of Alexis de Tocqueville about American religion suggest that one source of recovering the American past is by reading the accounts of non-American visitors. In the 1830s and 1840s, a stream of Europeans came to the United States to see for themselves the development of American character and mass political participation in the age of Jackson. These notable visitors came from England, Scotland, France, Hungary, and the German states, as well as from Argentina and other newly independent nations in Latin America. On returning home, they wrote books about their travels, revealing their impressions of the character of the American people and institutions.

Obviously, these visitors did not all agree about the qualities they observed in Americans or whether the American style of democratic politics was a good or bad thing. Some saw the American people and their elected representatives as unsophisticated, uncultured, and undisciplined, less interested in the substance of a politician's speech, as Charles Dickens observed in 1842, than in "how long did he speak?" After a visit to Congress, Dickens described the dire condition of the handsome carpets in House chambers as a result of the prevalent habit of tobacco chewing and spitting by legislators. The Englishman noted the "universal disregard of the spittoon with which every honorable member is accommodated" and advised visitors not to look at the "squirted and dabbled upon" carpets or to pick up anything "with an ungloved hand." From many a European visitor's point of view, Americans were uncouth, violent, ill-mannered, more adept at handling a rifle than a fork.

Others, however, saw the United States as a model society that European nations should seek to imitate, whereas still others astutely observed the mixed, doubled-edged value of "democracy in America" for politics, the distribution of wealth, and personal character. Compare for example, the accounts of patriotism, property, and politics in America by three European visitors in the 1830s. Alexis de Tocqueville, a French aristocrat and probably the most famous of the European observers of American life, visited the United States in 1831–1832 and published his impressions and insights in *Democracy in America* in 1835. A British feminist, Harriet Martineau, traveled in the United States in the mid–1830s and published *Society in America* in 1837, the same year as the Czech, Francis Grund, visited America and wrote *The Americans in Their Moral, Social, and Political Relations.*,

All three celebrated democratic institutions in the United States, and all three explored the implications of democracy for individual freedom and equality of opportunity. But they did not come to the same conclusions. Summarize the major points of each observer and state their similarities and differences. What did they see as the most outstanding features of American life and politics? What did they note as the most dangerous flaws? Whether positive or negative in their overall assessment, how accurate and insightful do you think they were? Which one do you think was most perceptive in describing American life and politics and the character of the American people in the era of Andrew Jackson?

To what extent do these accounts still describe the American people and political styles a century and a half later? If you were to visit another society for several months, how accurate do you think you could be in assessing cultural values and

national character? To what extent would you, like these early visitors to the United States, reflect your own values and national and class background as you analyzed another culture? What questions would you ask?

Alexis de Tocqueville, 1835

In my opinion, the main evil of the present democratic institutions of the United States does not arise, as is often asserted in Europe, from their weakness, but from their irresistible strength. I am not so much alarmed at the excessive liberty which reigns in that country, as at the inadequate securities which one finds there against tyranny....

I do not say that there is frequent use of tyranny in America, at the present day; but I maintain that there is no sure barrier against it, and that the causes which mitigate the government there are to be found in the circumstances and the manners of the country, more than in its laws....

I know of no country in which there is so little independence of mind and real freedom of discussion as in America.... In America, the majority raises formidable barriers around the liberty of opinion: within these barriers, an author may write what he pleases; but woe to him if he goes beyond them.... He is exposed to continued obloquy and persecution. His political career is closed forever, since he has offended the only authority which is able to open to it. Every sort of compensation, even that of celebrity, is refused to him. Before publishing his opinions, he imagined that he held them in common with others; but no sooner has he declared them, than he is loudly censured by his opponents, whilst those who think like him, without having the courage to speak out, abandon him in silence. He yields at length, overcome by the daily effort which he has to make, and subsides into silence, as if he felt remorse for having spoken the truth.

Fetters and headsmen were the coarse instruments which tyranny formerly employed; but the civilization of our age has perfected despotism itself, though it seemed to have nothing to learn. Monarchs had, so to speak, materialized oppression: the democratic republics of the present day have rendered it as entirely an affair of the mind, as the will which it is intended to coerce. Under the absolute sway of one man, the body was attacked in order to subdue the soul; but the soul escaped the blows which were directed against it, and rose proudly superior. Such is not the course adopted by tyranny in democratic republics: there the body is left free, and the soul is enslaved. The master no longer says, "You shall think as I do, or you shall die"; but he says, "You are free to think differently from me, and to retain your life, your property, and all you possess; but you are henceforth a stranger among your people."

Harriet Martineau, 1837

One sunny October morning I was taking a drive, with my party, along the shores of the pretty Owasco Lake, in New York State, and conversing on the condition of the country with a gentleman who thought the political prospect less bright than the landscape. I had been less than three weeks in the country, and was in a state of something like awe at the prevalence of, not only external competence, but intellectual ability.

The striking effect upon a stranger of witnessing, for the first time, the absence of poverty, of gross ignorance, of all servility, of all insolence of manner, cannot be exaggerated in description. I had seen every man in the towns an independent citizen; every man in the country a land-owner. I had seen that the villages had their newspapers, the factory girls their libraries. I had witnessed the controversies between candidates for office on some difficult subjects, of which the people were to be the judges. With all these things in my mind, and with every evidence of prosperity about me in the comfortable homesteads which every turn in the road, and every reach of the lake, brought into view, I was thrown into a painful amazement by being told that the grand question of the time was "whether the people should be encouraged to govern themselves, or whether the wise should save them from themselves."

The confusion of inconsistencies was here so great as to defy argument; the patronage among equals that was implied; the assumption as to who were the wise; and the conclusion that all the rest must be foolish. This one sentence seemed to be the most extraordinary combination that could proceed from the lips of a republican. . . .

One of the most painful apprehensions seems to be that the poorer will heavily tax the richer members of society; the rich being always a small class. If it be true, as all parties appear to suppose, that rulers in general are prone to use their power for selfish purposes, there remains the alternative, whether the poor shall over-tax the rich, or whether the rich shall over-tax the poor: and, if one of these evils were necessary, few would doubt which would be the least.

But the danger appears much diminished on the consideration that, in the country under our notice, there are not, nor are likely to be, the wide differences in property which exist in old countries. There is no class of hereditary rich or poor. Few are very wealthy; few are poor; and every man has a fair chance of being rich. No such unequal taxation has yet been ordained by the sovereign people; nor does there appear to be any danger of it, while the total amount of taxation is so very small as in the United States, and the interest that every one has in the protection of property is so great.

A friend in the South, while eulogizing to me the state of society there, spoke with compassion of his northern fellow citizens, who were exposed to the risks of "a perpetual struggle between pauperism and property." To which a northern friend replied, that it is true that there is a perpetual struggle everywhere between pauperism and property. The question is, which succeeds. In the United States, the prospect is that each will succeed. Paupers may obtain what they want, and proprietors will keep that which they have.

Francis Grund, 1837

It often appeared to me as if the whole property of the United States was only held by the Americans in trust for their children, and that they were prepared to render a religious account of their stewardship. See with what willingness they labour to secure an independence to their children! —with what readiness they take a part in the national improvements of their country! —with what cheerfulness they quit an already fertilized soil and emigrate to the "far west" to make more room for their offspring! How ready they are to invest their fortunes in undertakings which can only benefit their progeny! Are these not proofs of a genuine patriotism? Is this not the most exalted love of country of which history furnishes us with a record? . . .

No class of society in the United States is opposed to republican institutions, as there is no political party whose permanent interests are opposed to the majority of the people. Neither is the policy of the United States likely to involve the country in a foreign war; and if in a national broil the republic should become a belligerent party, her political and geographical position is such, that she has little to fear from an enemy.

The Americans have kept good faith with all nations; and by the most unexampled economy discharged their national debt. Their credit is unrivalled; their honour unquestioned, and the most implicit confidence placed in their ability to fulfil their engagements. They have, thus far, received strangers with hospitality, and put no obstacles in the way of their progress. They have not monopolised a single branch of industry; but let foreigners and native citizens compete fairly for an equal chance of success. They have established liberty of conscience, and compelled no person to pay taxes for the support of ministers of a different persuasion from his own. They have abolished all hereditary privileges; but let all men start free and equal, with no other claims to preferment, than that which is founded on superiority of intellect. In short, they have made their country the market for talent, ingenuity, industry and every honest kind of exertion. It has become the home of all who are willing to rise by their own efforts, and contains within itself nearly half the enterprise of the world.

These are the true causes of the rapid growth of America, which, joined to her immense natural resources, must make her eventually the most powerful country on the globe. It is the principle of liberty, carried out in all its ramifications and details, which has produced these mighty results.

Perfectionist Reform and Utopianism

The Bible commanded humans, "Be ye therefore perfect even as your Father in heaven is perfect," and mid-nineteenth-century reformers, inspired by the Finney revivals, took the challenge seriously. Eventually, a perfected millennial era of 1,000 years of peace, harmony, and Christian brotherhood on earth would bring the Second Coming of Christ.

The perfectionist thrust in religion fit America's sense of itself as a redeemer nation chosen by God to reform the entire world. Religious commitment fused with patriotic duty. The motivating impulse to reform in the 1830s, then, had many deep-rooted causes. These included the Puritan idea of American mission; the secular examples of founding fathers like Benjamin Franklin to do good, reinforced by Republican ideology and romantic beliefs in the natural goodness of human nature; the social activist tendencies in Whig political ideology; anxiety over shifting class relationships and the need to achieve some control over one's life as a result of the socioeconomic changes of recent years; family influence and the desire of young people to choose careers of principled service; and the direct influence of the Finney revivals in the early 1830s.

The Dilemmas of Reform

Religious reformers and Whig politicians both faced timeless dilemmas about how best to effect change. Does one, for example, try to change attitudes first and then behavior, or the reverse? Which is more effective, to appeal to people's minds and hearts in order to change bad institutions, or to change institutions first, assuming that altered behavior will then change attitudes? Taking the first path, the reformer relies on education, on the moral suasion of sermons, tracts, literature, argument, and personal testimony. Following the second, the reformer acts politically and institutionally, seeking to pass laws, win elections, form unions, boycott tainted goods, and create or abolish institutions.

Reformers, moreover, have to decide whether to attempt to bring about limited, piecemeal practical change on a single issue or go for perfection. Should they improve on a partly defective system or tear down the entire system in order to build a utopian new one? Reformers must further decide whether to use or recommend force and whether to enter into coalitions with less principled potential allies. They also face the difficult challenge of making sure that their own attitudes and actions are thoroughly consistent with the principles of behavior they would urge on others, as Thoreau had demonstrated.

These challenging problems fill the lives of reformers with turmoil. Advocates of change in the status quo experience enormous pressures, recriminations, and economic or physical persecution from the majority. As Marius and Emily Robinson understood, promoting change has its costs. What is more, reformers invariably do not agree on appropriate ideology and tactics, so they

---

Motivations and Causes of Reform in America, 1830–1850

- Changing relationships between men and women, masters and workers as a result of the market economy, growth of cities, and increasing immigration
- Finney and other religious revivals in the Second Great Awakening
- Social activist and ethical impulses of the Whig party
- Psychological anxieties over shifting class and ethnic relationships
- Family traditions and youthful idealism
- Puritan and revolutionary traditions of the American mision to remake the world
- Republican ideology and Enlightenment emphasis on virtue and good citizenship
- Romantic literary influences such as Transcendentalism

end up quarreling with one another as well as with representatives of the established order they wish to change. Although reformers suffer pressure to conform and to cease questioning things, their duty to themselves, their society, and their God sustains their commitment.

Utopian Communities: Oneida and the Shakers

Thoreau tried to lead an ideal solitary life. Other reformers sought to create perfect communities. Emerson noted in 1840 that he hardly met a thinking, reading man who did not have "a draft of a new community in his waistcoat pocket." One way to redeem a flawed society, one that seemed to be losing the cohesion and traditional values of small community life, was to create miniature utopian societies. These would offer alternatives to a world characterized by factories, foreigners, flawed morals, and greedy entrepreneurship.

In 1831, as President Jackson and South Carolina neared their confrontation over the tariff and nullification, as Nat Turner planned his slave revolt in Virginia, and as the citizens of Rochester sought ways of controlling their workers' drinking habits, a young man in Putney, Vermont, heard Charles Finney on one of his whirlwind tours of New England. John Humphrey Noyes was an instant, if unorthodox, convert.

Noyes believed that the act of final conversion led to absolute perfection and complete release from sin. However spiritually blessed, Noyes's earthly happiness was soon sorely tested. In 1837, a woman he loved rejected both his doctrine and his marriage offer. Despondent, Noyes wrote a friend that "when the will of God is done on earth as it is in heaven there will be no marriage." Among those who were perfect, he argued, all men and women belonged equally to each other. For Noyes, complete sharing in family relationships was a step toward perfect cooperation, as was shared wealth in socioeconomic relationships. Others called his heretical doctrines "free love" and socialism. Noyes recovered from his unhappy love affair and married a loyal follower. When she delivered four stillborn children within six years, Noyes revised even further his unconventional ideas about sex.

In 1848, Noyes and 51 devoted followers founded a "perfectionist" community at Oneida, New York. Under his strong leadership, Oneida grew and prospered. Sexual life at the commune was subject to many regulations, including sexual restraint and male continence except under carefully prescribed conditions. In a system of planned reproduction, only certain spiritually advanced males (usually Noyes) were allowed to father children. Other controversial practices included communal child rearing, sexual equality in work, the removal of the competitive spirit from both work and play, and an elaborate program of "mutual criticism" at community meetings presided over by "Father" Noyes.

Though creating considerable tension, these unorthodox sexual and social rules gave Oneidans a sense of uniqueness. Wise economic decisions also bound community members in mutual prosperity. Forsaking the nostalgic agricultural emphasis that typified most other communes, Noyes opted for modern manufacturing. Oneida specialized at first in the fabrication of steel animal traps and later diversified into making silverware. Eventually abandoning religion to become a joint-stock company in which individual members held shares, Oneida thrived for many years and continues today as a silverware company.

Noyes greatly admired another group of communitarians, the Shakers, who also believed in perfectionism, the surrender of all worldly property to the community, and the devotion of one's labor and love to bringing about the millennial kingdom of heaven. But unlike the Oneidan experiments in reproduction, Shakers viewed sexuality as a sin and believed in absolute chastity, trusting in conversions to perpetuate their sect. Founded by an Englishwoman, Mother Ann Lee, who migrated to America in the late eighteenth century, Shaker conversions grew in the Second Great Awakening to a peak membership of around 6,000 souls by the 1850s. Centered at Mount Lebanon, New York, the Shakers established communities from Maine to Kentucky. They believed that God had a dual personality, male and female, and that Ann Lee was the female counterpart to the masculine Christ. The Shaker worship service featured frenetic dancing intended to release (or "shake") sin out through the fingertips. Shaker communities, some of which survived long into the twentieth century, were

In this sacred Shaker dance, sin is being shaken out of the body through the fingertips. Note the separation of women and men. (Shakertown at Pleasant Hill, Kentucky)

characterized by communal ownership of property, the equality of women and men, simplicity, and beautifully crafted furniture.

Other Utopias

In an era of disruptive economic and social change, over 100 utopian communities like Oneida and the Shaker colonies were founded. Some were religiously motivated; others were secular. Most were small and lasted only a few months or years. All eventually collapsed, though giving birth to significant social ideas.

Pietist German-speaking immigrants founded the earliest utopian communities in America, in order to preserve their language, spirituality, and ascetic lifestyle. The most notable of these were the Ephrata colonists in Pennsylvania, the Harmonists in Indiana, the Zoar community in Ohio, and the Amana Society in Iowa. Some antebellum utopian communities focused less on otherworldly contemplation than on the regeneration of this world. In 1840, Adin Ballou founded Hopedale in Massachusetts as a "miniature Christian republic" based on the ethical teachings of Jesus. Hopedale's newspaper, *The Practical Christian*, advocated temperance, pacifism, women's rights, and other reforms.

Other communities, founded on the secular principles of reason inherited from the Enlightenment, responded more directly to the social misery and wretched working conditions accompanying the industrial revolution. These communities differed from religious ones in assuming that evil came from bad environments rather than individual acts of sin. They consequently believed that altered environments rather than new morals would eliminate or reduce poverty, ignorance, intemperance, and other ugly by-products of industrialism.

Robert Owen was the best known of the secular communalists. A Scottish industrialist who saw firsthand the miserable lives of cotton mill workers, he envisioned a society of small towns—"Agricultural and Manufacturing Villages of Unity and Mutual Cooperation"—with good schools and healthy work for all citizens. Unemployment, poverty, and vice would be unknown in Owen's model communities. In 1824, he chose the abandoned Pietist community of Harmonists in Indiana as the site for his first town in America. He called it New Harmony. But problems rather than harmony prevailed. Overcrowding, lazy and uncooperative members, Owen's frequent absences, splintered goals, and financial mismanagement ruined New Harmony within three years.

Brook Farm, founded by two Concord friends of Emerson, Bronson Alcott and George Ripley, was an experiment in integrating "intellectual and manual labor." Residents would hoe in the fields and shovel manure for a few hours each day and then study literature and recite poetry. Although the colony lasted less than three years, it produced some notable literature in a journal, *The Dial*, edited by Margaret Fuller. Hawthorne lived at Brook Farm for a short time and wrote a novel, *The Blithedale Romance* (1852), that criticized the naive optimism of utopian communitarians.

Whether secular or religious, the utopian communities all failed for similar reasons. Americans seemed ill-suited to communal living and work responsibilities and were unwilling to share either their property or their spouses with others. Nor was celibacy greeted with much enthusiasm. Other recurring problems included unstable leadership, financial bickering, the hostility of local citizens toward sexual experimentation and other unorthodox practices, the indiscriminate admission of members, and a waning of enthusiasm after initial settlement. Emerson pinned the failure of the communities on their inability to confront the individualistic impulses of human nature. As he said of Brook Farm, "It met every test but life itself." That could serve as an epitaph for all the utopian communities.

Millerites and Mormons

If utopian communities failed to bring about the millennium, an alternative hope was to leap directly past the thousand years of peace and harmony to the Second Coming of Christ. William Miller, a shy farmer from upstate New York, became so absorbed with the idea of the imminent coming of Christ that he figured out mathematically the exact time of the event: 1843, probably in March. A religious sect, the Millerites, gathered around him to prepare for Christ's return and the Day of Judgment.

A mixture of excitement and fear grew as the day of the predicted return came closer. Some people gave away all their worldly belongings, neglected business, put on robes, and flocked to high hills and rooftops to be nearest the blessed event. When 1843 passed without the expected end, Miller and his followers recalculated and set a series of alternative dates. Each new disappointment diminished Miller's followers, and he died in 1848 a discredited man. But a small Millerite sect, the Seventh-Day Adventists, had already taken root and continues to this day.

Other groups that emerged from the same religiously active area of upstate New York were more successful. As Palmyra, New York, was being swept by Finney revivalism, young Joseph Smith, a recent convert, claimed to be visited by the angel Moroni. According to Smith, Moroni led him to golden tablets buried in the ground near his home. On these plates were inscribed more than 500 pages of *The Book of Mormon*, which described the one true church and a "lost tribe of Israel" missing for centuries. The book also predicted the appearance of an American prophet who would establish a new and pure kingdom of Christ in America. Smith published his book in 1830 and soon founded the Church of Jesus Christ of Latter-Day Saints (the Mormons). His visionary leadership attracted thousands of ordinary people trying to escape what they viewed as social disorder, religious impurity, and commercial degradation in the 1830s.

Smith and a steadily growing band of converts migrated successively to Ohio and Missouri and then back to Illinois, where they met ridicule, persecution, and violence. The hostility stemmed in part from their active missionary work, in part from their beliefs and support for local Indian tribes, and in part from rumors of unorthodox sexual practices.

Despite external persecution and internal dissension caused by Smith's strong leadership style, the Mormons prospered and increased. Converts from England and northern Europe added substantially to their numbers. By the mid–1840s, Nauvoo, Illinois, with a thriving population of nearly 15,000, was the showplace of Mormonism. Smith petitioned Congress for separate territorial status and ran for the presidency in 1844. This was too much for the citizens of nearby towns. Violence escalated and culminated in Smith's trial for treason and his murder by a mob. Under the brilliant leadership of Smith's successor, Brigham Young, the Mormons headed westward in 1846 in their continuing search for the "land of promise."

Reforming Society

The Mormons and the utopian communitarians had as their common goal, in Brigham Young's words, "the spread of righteousness upon the earth." Most people, however, preferred to spread righteousness in a practical way by focusing on a specific social evil rather than by embracing whole new religions or joining utopian colonies.

"We are all a little wild here," Emerson wrote in 1840, "with numberless projects of social reform." Mobilized in part by their increased participation in the political parties of Jacksonian America, the reformers created and joined all kinds of societies for social betterment. The reform ranks were swelled by thousands of women, stirred to action by the religious revivals and freed from domestic burdens by delayed marriage and smaller families. Organized in hundreds of voluntary societies, women such as Emily Rakestraw joined men such as Marius Robinson in directing their energies to numerous social issues. These included alcohol consumption; diet and health; sexuality; institutional treatment of the mentally ill, the disabled, paupers, and criminals; education; the rights of labor; slavery; and women's rights.

Temperance

On New Year's Eve in 1831, a Finney disciple, Theodore Dwight Weld, delivered a four-hour temperance lecture in Rochester. In graphic detail, he described the awful fate of those who refused to stop drinking and urged his audience not only to cease their tippling, but also to stop others. Several were converted to abstinence on the spot. The next day, Elijah and Albert Smith, the largest providers of whiskey in Rochester, rolled their barrels out onto the sidewalk and smashed them. Cheering Christians applauded as the whiskey ran out into Exchange Street.

Americans in the nineteenth century drank heavily. One man observed that "a house could not

Religion, Reform, and Utopian Activity, 1830–1850

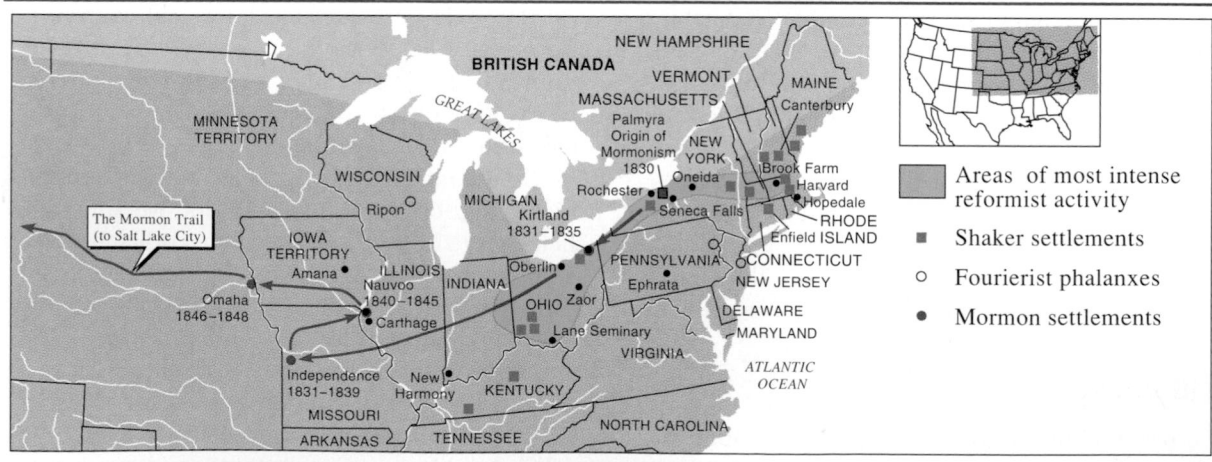

Reformist activity followed both religious revival areas and the Erie Canal into the growing states of the Old Northwest.

The temperance movement of the 1830s and 1840s used the tactics of religious revivalists to scare drinkers into taking the "teetotal" pledge. Who could resist this poignant 1846 portrayal of The Drunkard's Progress? *(Library of Congress)*

be raised, a field of wheat cut down, nor could there be a log rolling, a husking, a quilting, a wedding, or a funeral without the aid of alcohol." The corrosive effects of drinking were obvious: poverty, crime, illness, insanity, battered and broken families, and corrupt politics.

Early efforts at curbing alcohol consumption emphasized moderation. Forming local societies, groups of people agreed to limit how much they drank or to imbibe only beer and wine. Some societies even met in local taverns to toast their commitment to moderation. But under the influence of the Beecher and Finney revivals, the movement achieved better organization and clearer goals. The American Temperance Society, founded in 1826, was dedicated not just to moderation, but to total abstinence. Within a few years, thousands of local and state societies had formed, though some refused to prohibit drinking of hard cider and communion wine.

Temperance advocates copied successful revival techniques. Fiery lecturers expounded on the evil consequences of drink and urged group pressure on the weak-willed. Mass meetings were accompanied by a deluge of graphic and sometimes gory temperance tracts. Who would not cringe at descriptions of drinkers: "Some are killed instantly; some die a lingering, gradual death; some commit suicide in fits of intoxication; and some are actually burnt up." One "intemperate man," it was claimed, died when his "breath caught fire by coming in contact with a lighted candle." The accumulated pressure of both written and oral testimony, capped off by a sermon like Weld's, was intended to convince people to take the "teetotal" pledge.

By 1840, disagreements over goals and methods split the temperance movement into many separate organizations. In depression times, when jobs and stable families were harder to find than whiskey and beer, laboring men and women moved more by practical concerns than religious fervor joined the crusade. The Washington Temperance Society, founded in a Baltimore tavern in 1840, was enormously popular with unemployed young workers and grew to an estimated 600,000 members in three years. The Washingtonians, arguing that alcoholism was a disease rather than moral failure, changed the shape of the temperance movement. They replaced revivalist techniques with those of the new party politics by organizing parades, picnics, melodramas, and festivals to encourage people to take the pledge.

Tactics in the 1840s also shifted away from moral suasion to political action. Temperance societies lobbied for local option laws, which allowed communities to prohibit the sale, manufacture, and consumption of alcohol. The first such law in the nation was passed in Maine, in 1851. Fifteen other states followed with similar laws before the Civil War. Despite weak enforcement, the per capita consumption of alcohol declined dramatically in the 1850s. Interrupted by the Civil War, the movement did not reach its ultimate objective until passage of the Eighteenth Amendment to the Constitution in 1919.

The temperance crusade reveals the many practical motivations for Americans to join reform societies. For some, as in Rochester, temperance provided an opportunity for the Protestant middle classes to exert some control over laborers, immigrants, and Catholics. For perfectionists, abstinence was a way of practicing self-control and reaching moral perfection. For many women, the temperance effort was a respectable way to control the behavior of drunken men who beat wives and daughters. For many young men, especially after the onset of the depression of 1837, a temperance society provided entertainment, fellowship, and contacts to help their careers. In temperance societies as in political parties, Americans found jobs, purpose, support, spouses, and relief from the loneliness and uncertainty of a changing world.

Health and Sexuality

It was a short step from the physical and psychological ravages of drink to other potentially harmful effects on the body. Reformers were quick to attack excessive eating, use of stimulants of any kind, and, above all, the evils of too much sexual activity. Many endorsed a variety of special diets and exercise programs for maintaining good health. Some promoted panaceas for all ailments. One of these was hydropathy: clients sojourned at one of 70 special resorts for bathing and water purges of the body. Many of these resorts especially attracted women who not only found an escape from daily drudgery in the home, but also found cures for chronic and untreated urogenital infections. Other panaceas, including hypnotism, phrenology (the study of bumps on the head), and various "spiritualist" seances, sought to cure problems of the mind.

Another movement concerned sexual purity. In 1834, Sylvester Graham, a promoter of proper diet and hygiene, delivered a series of lectures on chastity, later published as a manual of advice. To those "troubled" by sexual desire, the inventor of the Graham cracker recommended taking "more active exercise in the open air" and using the "cold bath under proper circumstances." Women especially, not as "passionless" as the Victorian stereotype suggested, were advised to remain pure and to "have intercourse only for procreation." Although females learned to control sexuality for their own purposes, as we shall see, male "sexual purity" advocates urged sexual restraint to protect various male interests. One doctor argued that women ought not to be educated because blood needed for the womb would be diverted to the head, thus breeding "puny men."

The authors of antebellum "health" manuals advocated abstinence from sexual activity as vehemently as they recommended abstinence from alcohol. The body, they argued, was a closed energy system in which each organ had particular and limited functions to perform. Semen was to be saved for reproductive purposes and should not be used for pleasure in either masturbation or intercourse. Such use, maintained the manuals on sexual purity, would lead to enervation, disease, insanity, and death. Some argued further that the "expenditure" of sperm meant a loss of needed energy from the economy. To drain energy away from business to sex was both wasteful and contributory to Jacksonian social disorder.

Humanizing the Asylum

In their effort to restore order to American society, some reformers preferred to work not for private influence over individuals, but toward public changes in institutions. They wanted to transform such social institutions as asylums, almshouses, prisons, schools, and even factories. In many ways, Horace Mann, who led the struggle for common schools in Massachusetts (see Chapter 10), was a typical antebellum reformer. He blended dedicated idealism with a canny, practical sense of how to institutionalize educational improvements in one state: teacher training schools, higher teachers' salaries, and compulsory attendance laws.

Other reformers were less successful in achieving their goals. This was especially true of the treatment of society's outcasts. In the colonial era, the family or the local community cared for orphans, paupers, the insane, and even criminals. Beginning early in the nineteenth century, various states built asylums, houses of refuge, reform schools, jails, and other institutions to uplift and house social victims. In some of these institutions, such as prisons and almshouses, the sane and insane, children and hardened adult criminals were thrown together in terrible conditions. In 1843, Dorothea Dix, a frail New Englander, horrified the Massachusetts legislature with her famous report that imprisoned insane people in the state were subject to the "extremest state of degradation and misery." They were confined in "cages, closets, stalls, pens! Chained, naked, beaten with rods, and lashed into obedience!" Dix recommended special hospitals, or asylums, where the insane could be "humanly and properly controlled" by trained attendants.

Many perfectionist reformers like Dix believed that special asylums could reform society's outcasts. Convinced that bad institutions corrupted basically good human beings, they reasoned that reformed institutions could rehabilitate them. In 1853, Charles Loring Brace started a Children's Aid Society in New York City that was a model of change through effective education and self-help. Reformers like Dix and Brace, as well as Samuel Gridley Howe and Thomas Gallaudet, who founded institutions for the care and education of the blind and deaf, achieved remarkable results.

But all too often, results were disappointing. Prison reformers believed that a properly built and administered penitentiary could bring a hardened criminal "back to virtue." They argued intensely over the most appropriate structural design for

With strong religious roots, the frail Dorothea Dix tirelessly waged a courageous and creative campaign to improve conditions for the insane throughout the nation. "I encounter nothing which a determined will created by the necessities of the cause does not enable me to vanquish," she wrote, reflecting her irrepressible spirit on behalf of public support for humane hospitals for "hundreds of wailing, suffering creatures." (The Granger Collection, New York)

rehabilitating criminals. Some preferred the rectangular prison at Auburn, New York, with its tiny cells and common workrooms, whereas others pointed to the Pennsylvania star-shaped system, where each inmate was in solitary confinement, though in a fairly modern cell. Whichever system was preferred, prison reformers assumed that if "penitents" were put into isolated cells to study the Bible and reflect on their wrongdoing, they would eventually decide to become good citizens. In practice, many criminals simply went mad or committed suicide. The institutions built by well-intentioned reformers became dumping places for society's outcasts. By mid-century, American prisons and mental asylums had become sadly impersonal, understaffed, overcrowded institutions.

Working-Class Reform

Efforts to improve the institutional conditions of life in the United States were not all initiated and led by middle-class reformers on behalf of the less fortunate. For working-class Americans, the social institution most in need of transformation was the factory. Workers, many of whom were involved in other issues such as temperance, peace, and abolitionism, took it on themselves to improve their own lives. As labor leader Seth Luther told a meeting of New England mechanics and laborers, "We must take our business into our own hands. Let us awake." And awake they did, forming both trade unions and workingmen's parties as Andrew Jackson neared the presidency.

Between 1828 and 1832, dozens of workingmen's parties were formed, advocating such programs as free, tax-supported schools, free public lands in the West, equal rights for the poor, and the elimination of all monopolistic privilege. Trade union activity began in Philadelphia in 1827 as skilled workers organized journeymen carpenters, plasterers, printers, weavers, tailors, and other tradesmen. That same year, 15 unions combined into a citywide federation, a process followed in other cities. The National Trades Union, founded in 1834, was the first attempt at a national labor organization.

The trade unions fared better than the labor parties, in part because Jacksonian Democrats attracted many laboring men's votes and in part because trade union programs were more immediately practical. They included shorter hours, wages that would keep pace with rising prices, and ways (such as the closed shop) of warding off the competitive threat of cheap labor. In addition, both workers and their middle-class supporters called for the abolition of imprisonment for debt and of compulsory militia duty, both of which often cost workers their jobs; free public education; improved living conditions in workers' neighborhoods; and the right to organize. Discouraged by decisions of New York State courts, which denied the right to organize in 1835 and again in 1836, workers argued that unions were necessary to "resist the oppressions of avarice" and compared themselves to the Americans who dumped British tea in Boston harbor in 1773.

Thus strengthened by a Revolutionary tradition, by increasing political influence, and by a trade union membership of near 300,000, workers struck some 168 times between 1834 and 1836. Over two-thirds of the strikes were for higher wages or, as with the mill workers in Lowell, to avert wage cuts (see Chapter 10). The remaining strikes were for shorter hours. Identifying with the "blood of our fathers" shed on the battlefields of the American Revolution, Boston tradesmen struck in 1835 for a ten-hour day. They failed, but their attempt heralded the subsequent resurgence of a successful ten-hour-day movement in many states in the 1850s. The Panic of 1837 and the ensuing depression dashed the hopes and efforts of American workers. But the organizational work of the 1830s promised that the labor movement would reemerge with greater strength later in the century.

Abolitionism and Women's Rights

As American workers struggled in Lowell and other eastern cities for better wages and hours in 1834, Emily and Marius Robinson arrived in Cincinnati to fight for their causes. They had been attracted there, along with scores of other young idealists, by the newly founded Lane Seminary, a school to train abolitionist leaders. Financed by two wealthy New York brothers, Arthur and Lewis Tappan, Lane soon became a center of reformist activity. When nervous local residents persuaded President Lyman Beecher to crack down on the students, 40 "Lane rebels," led by Theodore Weld, fled to Oberlin in northern Ohio. As the Robinsons remained behind to marry and continue their reform work in southern Ohio, the group in the north turned Oberlin College into the first institution in the United States open equally to women and men, blacks and whites. Thus, the movements to abolish slavery and to grant equal rights to women and free blacks were joined.

These movements also united elements of both practical reform and utopian perfectionism. The goals of the struggle to abolish slavery and subtle forms of racism and sexism often seemed as distant and unrealizable as the millennium itself. Yet antislavery and feminist advocates persisted in their efforts to abolish what they believed were concrete, visible, institutionalized social wrongs. Whether seeking to eliminate coercion in the cotton fields or in the kitchen, they faced the dual challenge of pursuing distant and elusive goals while achieving practical changes in everyday life.

Tensions within the Antislavery Movement

Although the antislavery movement had a smaller membership than temperance reform, it revealed more clearly the difficulties of trying to achieve significant social change in America. As a young man of 22, William Lloyd Garrison passionately desired to improve, if not to perfect, the flawed world in which he lived. He was also ambitious and said that his name would "one day be known to the world." He was right. On January 1, 1831, eight months before Nat Turner's revolt, Garrison published the first issue of *The Liberator,* soon to become the leading antislavery journal in the United States. "I am in earnest," he wrote. "I will not equivocate—*AND I WILL BE HEARD.*" After first organizing the New England Anti-Slavery Society with a group of blacks and whites in a church basement in Boston, in 1833 Garrison and 62 others established the American Anti-Slavery Society.

Until Garrison's publication, most people opposed to slavery, other than blacks, had advocated gradual emancipation by individual slave owners. Many joined the American Colonizationist Society, founded in 1816, which sent a small number of manumitted slaves to Liberia, on the west coast of Africa. But these efforts proved inadequate and essentially racist in intent. Colonizationists seemed less interested in ending slavery (more new slaves were born in a week than were sent to Africa as free people in a year) than in ridding the country of free blacks.

Garrison opposed the moderation and gradualism of the colonizationists. "I do not wish to think, or speak, or write, with moderation," he wrote. "No! no! tell a man whose house is on fire to give a moderate alarm; tell him to moderately rescue his wife from the hands of the ravisher." For Garrison, compromise was unthinkable. There would be "no Union with slaveholders," he cried, condemning the Constitution that perpetuated slavery as "a covenant with death, an agreement with Hell." The American Anti-Slavery Society called for the immediate and total abolition of slavery. After his successful escape from slavery, Frederick Douglass agreed, saying, "Power concedes nothing without a demand. It never did and it never will." But the abolitionists did not always agree, splitting into factions over ideological differences among colonizationists, gradualists, and immediatists.

Abolitionists also differed over the tactics of ending slavery. Their primary method was moral suasion, by which they sought to convince slaveholders and their supporters that slavery was a sin. In an outpouring of sermons, petitions, resolutions, pamphlets, and speeches, abolitionists tried to overwhelm slaveholders with moral guilt to get them to free their slaves as an act of repentance. But as Marius wrote to Emily Robinson, "The spirit of slavery is not confined to the South." His Ohio trip suggests that northerners were equally guilty in providing the support necessary to maintain the slave system.

The abolitionists were unrestrained in their efforts. By 1837, they had flooded the nation with over a million pieces of antislavery literature. Their writing described slave owners as "mansteelers" who gave up all claim to humanity. A slaveholder, Garrison wrote, led a life "of unbridled lust,… of haughty domination, of cowardly ruffianism, of boundless dissipation, of matchless insolence, of infinite self-conceit, of unequalled oppression, of more than savage cruelty." In 1839, Weld published *American Slavery as It Is,* which described in gory detail every conceivable form of inhumane treatment of the slaves.

Other abolitionists preferred more direct methods than moral suasion. The main alternative lay in such political action as bringing antislavery petitions before Congress and forming third parties. Another tactic was to employ economic influence by boycotting goods made by slave labor. A fourth approach, although rare, was to call for slave rebellion, as did two northern blacks, David Walker in a pamphlet in 1829 and Henry Highland Garnet in a speech at a convention of black Americans in 1843.

Disagreement among abolitionists over tactics heightened ideological differences and helped to splinter the movement. Garrison's unyielding personal style and his commitment to even less popular causes such as women's rights offended many

At Minstrel Shows

The most popular form of entertainment for the American people in the antebellum period was the blackface minstrel show. Minstrelsy began in the late 1820s when an itinerant white actor, Thomas "Daddy" Rice, imitated the clumsy, hobbled dance steps of a crippled black stableman to standing-room audiences in New York's Bowery Theater. The main elements of the minstrel show as it developed in the 1830s and 1840s were in Rice's phenomenally popular rendition of "Jump Jim Crow" and other acts. He delighted white workingmen's audiences in northern cities by blacking his face with burnt cork (thus freeing himself from conventional norms) to perform rollicking songs, dances, and slapstick comedy that mocked stereotyped black characters.

By the 1840s and 1850s, the minstrel show had evolved into a troupe of several players who put on a variety show of earthy and sentimental songs (e.g., Stephen Foster airs such as "O Susannah" and "Away Down South"), eccentric dances, lewd female impersonations, musical skits, and scenes from plays such as *Uncle Tom's Cabin*, nearly always in blackface. A staple part of the show was a line of actors with a straight man in the middle flanked by outrageously dressed endmen, called Tambo and Bones, who shook tambourine and bone rhythm clackers while making rapid-fire wisecracks about sexuality, race, class, and other taboo topics. The negatively stereotyped blacks portrayed in the minstrels (such as those pictured here) included grotesquely big-lipped clownish women and men, sultry mulatto "yaller gals," large-hipped Mammies, asexual faithful "Old Darkies," homesick plantation runaways unable to cope with northern life, and urban dandies like "Zip Coon."

The American people gathered in a mania for minstrelsy that filled white needs and both reflected and shaped American values in the antebellum period. By performing in blackface, whites were able to express their ambivalent attraction and repulsion fantasies about African Americans. With material "borrowed" (i.e., stolen) from black culture, white actors both denigrated blacks and introduced northerners to black culture. The minstrels soothed white fears by making both slaves and free northern blacks acceptable to white audiences by minimizing and mocking their intelligence, sexuality, and capacity for rebellion. Although the skits, songs, and dances of the minstrels often featured southern plantation slaves as dim-witted, incompetent, happy-go-lucky clowns, the subtle message, sometimes represented in the pseudosuave but always humiliated northern black dandy ("Zip Coon") was one of reassuring northern urban workers that free blacks posed no threat to take either their women or their jobs.

(Harvard Theatre Collection)

Although the minstrels in the early years sometimes reflected abolitionist views of the evils of slavery, by the heyday of minstrelsy in the 1850s, the political tensions over slavery dramatized by the Fugitive Slave Act, publication of *Uncle Tom's Cabin,* and outbreaks of violence in Kansas, the minstrel shows minimized controversy by characterizing southern slaves as contented and happy. This further reassured whites, uniting them across socioeconomic lines and blunting the class conflict and occasional violence that existed in northern society. Minstrels continued to change to please their audiences in the late nineteenth century with the development of larger troupes, opulent extravaganzas, chorus girls, and even black minstrel troupes (in blackface). Eventually, the minstrels evolved into vaudeville, burlesque shows, and other forms of twentieth-century theater, including a strong tradition of black comedians such as Bert Williams, Redd Foxx, Bill Cosby, and Richard Pryor.

Zip Coon, 1833 (Harvard Theatre Collection)

abolitionists. In 1840, at its annual meeting in New York, intended as a unity convention to heal growing divisions, the American Anti-Slavery Society split into two groups. Several delegates walked out when a woman, Abby Kelley, was elected to a previously all-male committee. One group, which supported multiple issues and moral suasion, stayed with Garrison; the other followed James Birney and the Tappans into the Liberty party and political action on the single issue of slavery.

Class differences and race further divided abolitionists. Northern workers, though fearful of the potential job competition implicit in emancipation, nevertheless saw their "wage slavery" as similar to chattel slavery. Both violated fundamental republican values of freedom and equality. Strains between northern labor leaders and middle-class abolitionists, who minimized the seriousness of workingmen's concerns, were similar to those between white and black antislavery forces. Whites like Wendell Phillips decried slavery as a moral blot on American society, and blacks like Douglass were more concerned with the effects of slavery and discrimination on black people. Moreover, white abolitionists tended to see slavery and freedom as absolute moral opposites: A person was either slave or free. Blacks,

however, knew that there were degrees of freedom and that discriminatory restrictions on freedom existed for blacks in the North just as did relative degrees of servitude in the South.

Furthermore, black abolitionists themselves experienced prejudice, not just from ordinary northern citizens, but also from their white abolitionist colleagues. Many antislavery businessmen refused to hire blacks. The antislavery societies usually provided less than full membership rights for blacks, permitted them to do only menial tasks rather than form policy, and perpetuated black stereotypes in their literature. One free black, in fact, described a white abolitionist as one who hated slavery, "especially that slavery which is 1,000 to 1,500 miles away," but who hated even more "a man who wears a black skin."

The celebrated conflict between Garrison and Douglass reflected these tensions. The famous runaway slave was one of the most effective orators in the movement. But after a while, rather than simply describing his life as a slave, Douglass began skillfully to analyze abolitionist policies. Garrison warned him that audiences would not believe he had ever been a slave, and other whites told him to stick to the facts and let them take care of the philosophy.

This woodcut illustration of an abolitionist convention from Harper's Weekly *magazine in 1859 shows the mixture of both black and women delegates in the hall. The black man on the stage could be Frederick Douglass. (The Newberry Library, Chicago)*

Yᵉ ABOLITIONISTS IN COUNCIL—Yᵉ ORATOR OF Yᵉ DAY DENOUNCING Yᵉ UNION, MAY, 1859.

Douglass gradually moved away from Garrison's views, endorsing political action and sometimes even slave rebellion. Garrison's response, particularly when Douglass came out for the Liberty party, was to denounce his independence as "ungrateful ... and malevolent in spirit." In 1847, Douglass started his own journal, the *North Star,* later called *Frederick Douglass's Paper.* In it, he expressed his appreciation for the help of that "noble band of white laborers," but declared that it was time for those who "suffered the wrong" to lead the way in advocating liberty.

Moving beyond Garrison, a few black nationalists, like the fiery Martin Delany, totally rejected white American society and advocated emigration and a new destiny in Africa. Most blacks, however, agreed with Douglass to work to end slavery and discrimination in the United States. They believed that for better or worse, their home was America and not some distant land they had not known for generations.

These black leaders were practical. David Ruggles in New York and William Still in Philadelphia led black vigilance groups that helped fugitive slaves escape to Canada or to safe northern black settlements. Ministers, writers, and orators such as Douglass, Henry Highland Garnet, William Wells Brown, Samuel Cornish, Lewis Hayden, and Sojourner Truth lectured and wrote journals and slave narratives on the evils of slavery. They also organized a National Negro Convention Movement, which began annual meetings in 1830. These blacks met not only to condemn slavery, but also to discuss concrete issues of discrimination facing free blacks in the North.

Flood Tide of Abolitionism

Black and white abolitionists, however, agreed more than they disagreed and usually worked together well. They supported each other's publications. The first subscribers to Garrison's *Liberator* were nearly all black, and an estimated 80 percent of the readers of Douglass's paper were white. Weld and Garrison often stayed in the homes of black abolitionists when they traveled. Black and white "stations" cooperated on the underground railroad, too, passing fugitives on from hiding places in a black church to a white farmer's barn to a Quaker meetinghouse to a black carpenter's shop.

The two races worked together fighting discrimination as well as slavery. When David Ruggles was dragged from the "white car" of a New Bedford, Massachusetts, railway in 1841, Garrison, Douglass, and 40 other protesters organized what may have been the first successful integrated "sit-in" act of civil disobedience in American history. Blacks and whites also worked harmoniously in protesting segregated schools. After several years of joint boycotts and legal challenges in Massachusetts, in 1855, that state became the first to outlaw segregated public education. Almost exactly 100 years later, the Supreme Court would begin the desegregation of schools throughout the country.

White and black abolitionists were united perhaps most closely by defending themselves against the attacks of people who regarded them as dangerous fanatics bent on disrupting an orderly society. As abolitionists organized to rid the nation of slavery, they aroused many, northerners as well as southerners, who were eager to rid the nation of abolitionists. Mob attacks like the one on Marius Robinson in Ohio in 1836 occurred frequently in the mid-1830s. Abolitionists were stoned, dragged through streets, ousted from their jobs and homes, and reviled by northern mobs, often led or encouraged by leading citizens. Theodore Weld, known as "the most mobbed man in the United States," could hardly finish a speech without disruption. Douglass endured similar attacks, and Garrison was saved from a Boston mob only by being put in jail. In 1837, an antislavery editor in Illinois, Elijah Lovejoy, was murdered and his printing press destroyed.

Antiabolitionsts were as fervid as the abolitionists themselves and equally determined to publicize their cause. "I warn the abolitionists, ignorant and infatuated barbarians as they are," growled one South Carolinian, "that if chance shall throw any of them into our hands, they may expect a felon's death." One widely circulated book in 1836 described opponents of slavery, led by the "gloomy, wild, and malignant" Garrison, as "crack-brained enthusiasts" and "female fanatics" with "disturbed minds." President Jackson joined in, denouncing the abolitionists in his annual message in 1835 as "incendiaries" who deserved to have their "unconstitutional and wicked" activities broken up by mobs. The president went on to urge Congress to ban antislavery literature from the U.S. mails. A year later, southern Democratic congressmen, with the crucial support of Van Buren, succeeded in passing a "gag rule" to stop the flood of abolitionist petitions in Congress.

By the 1840s, despite factionalism and opposition, the antislavery movement had gained significant strength in American life. Many northerners, including many workers otherwise unsympathetic to the goal of ending slavery, decried the mob violence, supported the right of free speech, and denounced the South and its northern defenders as undemocratic. The gag rule, interference with the mails, and the killing of Lovejoy seemed proof of the growing pernicious influence of slave power. Former president John Quincy Adams, who had returned to Washington as a congressman, devoted himself for several years to the repeal of the gag rule, which he finally achieved in 1844. In this way, he kept the matter in the public eye until the question of slavery in the territories became the dominant national political issue of the 1850s (see Chapter 14). Meanwhile, black and white abolitionists continued their struggle, using many different tactics without knowing that the only one that would work, and indirectly at that, would be civil war.

Women's Rights

As a young teacher in Massachusetts in 1836, Abby Kelley circulated petitions for the local antislavery society. She came to reform from revivalism and in 1837 wrote, "'Tis a great joy to see the world grow better.... Indeed I think endeavors to improve mankind is the only object worth living for." A year later, she braved the threats of an angry crowd in Philadelphia by delivering an abolitionist speech to a convention of antislavery women. Her speech was so eloquent that Weld told her that if she did not join the movement full time, "God will smite you." Before the convention was over, a mob, incensed by both abolitionists and women speaking in public, attacked with stones and torches and burned the hall to the ground.

After a soul-searching year, Kelley left teaching to devote all her efforts to the antislavery movement and women's rights. When she married Stephen Foster, she retained her own name and went on lecture tours of the West while her husband stayed home to care for their daughter. Other young women were also defining unconventional new relationships while illustrating the profound difficulty of both fulfilling traditional roles and speaking out for change. Angelina and Sarah Grimké, two demure but outspoken Quaker sisters from Philadelphia who had grown up in slaveholding South Carolina, went to New England in 1837 to lecture to disapproving audiences on behalf of abolitionism and the rights of women. After the tour, Angelina married Theodore Weld and stopped her public speaking to show that she could also be a good wife and mother. At the same time, she and Sarah, who moved in with her, undertook the task of compiling most of the research and doing most of the writing for Weld's book attacking American slavery.

Young couples like the Robinsons, Kelley and Foster, and Grimké and Weld, while pursuing reform, also experimented with equal private relationships in an age that assigned distinctly unequal roles to husbands and wives. The cult of domesticity told women that their sphere was the home, where they served as guardians of piety and virtue, influencing their husbands and children to lead morally upright lives in a harsh, changing economic world. As one clergyman said, although women were not expected to "step beyond the threshold" of the home, their ethical influence would be "felt around the globe." Given moral responsibilities like this, it is not surprising that many women joined the perfectionist movement to cleanse America of its sins. Active in every reform movement, women discovered the need to improve their own condition.

To achieve greater personal autonomy in the antebellum era, American women pursued several paths. The choice depended on class, cultural background, and situation. Thus, in 1834, the Lowell textile workers went on strike to protest wage reductions while looking to marriage as an escape from mill work. Catharine Beecher argued that it was by accepting marriage and the home as a woman's sphere and by mastering domestic duties there that women could best achieve power

This marriage certificate from 1848, detailing the respective marital requirements of husband and wife, makes clear male dominance and female subservience ("the wife hath not power of her own body"). In that same year, however, women's rights activists began their long struggle for equality at Seneca Falls, New York. (Library of Congress)

and autonomy. In another form of "domestic feminism," American wives exerted considerable control over their own bodies by convincing their husbands to practice abstinence, coitus interruptus, and other forms of birth control.

Other women found an outlet for their role as moral guardians by attacking the sexual double standard. In 1834, a group of Presbyterian women formed the New York Female Moral Reform Society. Inspired by revivalism, they visited brothels and opened up a house of refuge in an effort to convert prostitutes to evangelical Protestantism. They went even further, seeking to limit men's sexual behavior by trying to close houses of prostitution and by publicly identifying men who visited them. Within five years, 445 auxiliaries of the Female Moral Reform Society had blossomed.

The Lowell mill workers and New York moral reformers generally accepted the duties—and attractions—of the cult of female domesticity. Other women, usually from upper-middle-class families, did not. They sought control over their lives by working directly for more legally protected equal rights with men. Campaigns to secure married women's control of their property and custody of their children involved many of them. Others, like Kelley and the Grimkés, labored in the abolitionist movement and garnered not only valuable experience in organizational tactics, but also a growing awareness of the striking similarities between the oppression of women and that of slaves. As they collected antislavery signatures and spoke out in churches and public meetings, they continually faced denials of their right to speak or act politically. American women "have good cause to be grateful to the slave," Kelley wrote, for in "striving to strike his iron off, we found most surely, that we were manacled *ourselves.*"

The more active women became in antislavery activities, the more hostility they encountered, especially from clergymen, who quoted the Bible to justify female inferiority and servility. Sarah Grimké was criticized once too often for her outspoken views. She struck back in 1837 with a series called *Letters on the Condition of Women and the Equality of the Sexes,* claiming that "men and

(Far Left) Elizabeth Cady Stanton (1815–1902) and (Left) Lucretia Mott (1793–1880) were the leaders of the 1848 gathering for women's rights at Seneca Falls, New York. "The acquaintance of Lucretia Mott, who was a broad, liberal thinker on politics, religion, and all questions of reform," Stanton wrote in her autobiography, "opened to me a new world of thought." (Sophia Smith Collection, Smith College, Northampton, Massachusetts)

women were created equal" and that "whatever is right for man to do, is right for woman." Arguing that men ought to be satisfied with 6,000 years of dominion based on a false interpretation of the creation story, Grimké concluded that she sought "no favors for my sex. I surrender not our claim to equality. All I ask of our brethren is, that they will take their feet from off our necks and permit us to stand upright on that ground which God designed us to occupy."

Male abolitionists were divided about women's rights. At the World Anti-Slavery Convention in 1840, attended by many American abolitionists, the delegates refused to let women participate. Two upstate New Yorkers, Elizabeth Cady Stanton and Lucretia Mott, were compelled to sit behind curtains and not even be seen, much less be permitted to speak. When they returned home, they resolved to "form a society to advocate the rights of women." In 1848, in Seneca Falls, New York, their intentions, though delayed, were fulfilled in one of the most significant protest gatherings of the antebellum era.

In preparing for the meeting, Mott and Stanton drew up a list of women's grievances. They discovered that even though some states had awarded married women control over their property, they still had none over their earnings. Modeling their "Declaration of Sentiments" on the Declaration of Independence, the women at Seneca Falls proclaimed it a self-evident truth that "all men and women are created equal" and that men had usurped women's freedom and dignity. A man, the Declaration of Sentiments charged, "endeavored in every way he could, to destroy [woman's] confidence in her own powers, to lessen her self-respect, and to make her willing to lead a dependent and abject life." The remedy was expressed in 11 resolutions calling for equal opportunities in education and work, equality before the law, and the right to appear on public platforms. The most controversial resolution called for women's "sacred right to the elective franchise." The convention approved Mott and Stanton's list of resolutions.

Throughout the 1850s, led by Stanton and Susan B. Anthony, women continued to meet in annual conventions, working by resolution, persuasion, and petition campaign to achieve equal political, legal, and property rights with men. The right to vote, however, was considered the cornerstone of the movement. It remained so for 72

TIMELINE

1824	New Harmony established
1825	John Quincy Adams chosen president by the House of Representatives
1826	American Temperance Society founded
1828	Calhoun publishes "Exposition and Protest"
	Jackson defeats Adams for the presidency
	Tariff of Abominations
1828–1832	Rise of workingmen's parties
1830	Webster-Hayne debate and Jackson-Calhoun toast
	Joseph Smith, *The Book of Mormon*
	Indian Removal Act
1830–1831	Charles Finney's religious revivals
1831	Garrison begins publishing *The Liberator*
1832	Jackson vetoes U.S. Bank charter
	Jackson reelected
	Worcester v. *Georgia*
1832–1833	Nullification crisis
1832–1836	Removal of funds from U.S. Bank to state banks
1833	Force Bill
	Compromise tariff
	Calhoun resigns as vice president
	American Anti-Slavery Society founded
1834	New York Female Moral Reform Society founded
	National Trades Union founded
	Whig party established

1835–1836	Countless incidents of mob violence
1836	"Gag rule"
	Specie circular
	Van Buren elected president
1837	Financial panic and depression
	Sarah Grimké, *Letters on the Equality of the Sexes*
	Emerson's "American Scholar" address
1837–1838	Cherokee "Trail of Tears"
1840	William Henry Harrison elected president
	American Anti-Slavery Society splits
	World Anti-Slavery Convention
	Ten-hour day for federal employees
1840–1841	Transcendentalists found Hopedale and Brook Farm
1843	Dorothea Dix's report on treatment of the insane
1844	Joseph Smith murdered in Nauvoo, Illinois
1846–1848	Mormon migration to the Great Basin
1847	First issue of Frederick Douglass's *North Star*
1848	Oneida community founded
	First women's rights convention at Seneca Falls, New York
1850	Nathaniel Hawthorne, *The Scarlet Letter*
1851	Maine prohibition law
	Herman Melville, *Moby Dick*
1853	Children's Aid Society established in New York City
1854	Thoreau, *Walden*
1855	Massachusetts bans segregated public schools

years of struggle until 1920, when passage of the Nineteenth Amendment made woman's suffrage part of the Constitution. The Seneca Falls convention was crucial in beginning the campaign for equal public rights. The seeds of gaining psycho- logical autonomy and self-respect, however, were sown in the struggles of countless women like Abby Kelley, Sarah Grimké, and Emily Robinson. The struggle for that kind of liberation continues today.

Conclusion

Perfecting America

Inspired by religious revivalism, advocates for women's rights and temperance, abolitionists, and other reformers carried on very different crusades from those waged by Andrew Jackson against Indians, nullificationists, and the U.S. Bank. In fact, Jacksonian politics and antebellum reform were often at odds. Most abolitionists and temperance reformers were anti-Jackson Whigs. Jackson and most Democrats repudiated the passionate moralism of reformers.

Yet both sides shared more than either side would admit. Reformers and political parties were both organized rationally. Both mirrored new tensions in a changing, growing society. Both had an abiding faith in change and the idea of progress yet feared that sinister forces jeopardized that progress. Whether ridding the nation of alcohol or the national bank, slavery or nullification, mob violence or political opponents, both forces saw these responsibilities in terms of patriotic duty. Whether inspired by religious revivalism or political party loyalty, both believed that by stamping out evil forces, they could shape a better America. In this effort, they turned to politics, religion, reform, and new life-styles. Whether politicians like Jackson and Clay, religious community leaders like Noyes and Ann Lee, or reformers like Garrison and the Grimkés, these antebellum Americans sought to remake their country politically and morally as it underwent social and economic change.

As the United States neared mid-century, slavery emerged as the most divisive issue. Against much opposition, the reformers had made slavery a matter of national political debate by the 1840s. Although both major political parties tried to evade the question, westward expansion and the addition of new territories to the nation would soon make avoidance impossible. Would new states be slave or free? The question increasingly aroused the deepest passions of the American people. For the pioneer family, who formed the driving force behind the westward movement, however, questions involving their fears and dreams seemed more important. We turn to this family and that movement in the next chapter.

Recommended Reading

Religious Revival and Reform

Robert Abzug, *Cosmos Crumbling: American Reform and the Religious Imagination* (1994); Richard J. Carwardine, *Evangelicals and Politics in Antebellum America* (1993); Jay P. Dolan, *Catholic Revivalism: The American Experience, 1830–1890* (1978); Clyde Griffen, *Their Brother's Keepers: Moral Stewardship in the United States, 1800–1865* (1960); Paul Johnson, *A Shopkeeper's Millennium: Society and Revivals in Rochester, New York, 1815–1837* (1978); William McLoughlin, *Modern Revivalism: From Charles G. Finney to Billy Graham* (1959) and *Revivals, Awakenings, and Reform: An Essay on Religion and Social Change in America* (1980); Richard Rabinowitz, *The Spiritual Self in Everyday Life: The Transformation of Personal Religious Experience in 19th Century New England* (1989); Mary Ryan, *Cradle of the Middle Class: The Family in Oneida County, New York, 1790–1865* (1981); Timothy Smith, *Revivalism and Social Reform* (1957); Alice Felt Tyler, *Freedom's Ferment* (1944); Ronald Walters, *American Reformers, 1815–1860* (1978); Bernard Weisberger, *They Gathered at the River* (1958).

Politics and Party in the Age of Jackson

Jean Baker, *Affairs of Party* (1983); Lee Benson, *The Concept of Jacksonian Democracy: New York as a Test Case* (1961); Donald B. Cole, *The Presidency of Andrew Jackson* (1993); Richard Ellis, *The Union at Risk: Jacksonian Democracy, States Rights, and the Nullification Crisis* (1987); Ronald

Formisano, *The Transformation of Political Culture* (1983); William Freehling, *Prelude to Civil War: The Nullification Controversy in South Carolina, 1816–1836* (1966); Daniel Howe, *The Political Culture of the American Whigs* (1980); Lawrence F. Kohl, *The Politics of Individualism: Parties and the American Character in the Jackson Era* (1989); Richard Latner, *The Presidency of Andrew Jackson: White House Politics, 1829–1837* (1979); Richard McCormick, *The Second Party System: Party Formation in the Jacksonian Era* (1966); John McFaul, *The Politics of Jacksonian Finance* (1972); Edward Pessen, *Jacksonian America: Society, Personality, and Politics*, rev. ed. (1979); Michael Paul Rogin, *Fathers and Children: Andrew Jackson and the Subjugation of the American Indian* (1975); Arthur Schlesinger, *The Age of Jackson* (1945); Charles Sellers, *The Market Revolution: Jacksonian America, 1815–1846* (1992); James Roger Sharp, *The Jacksonians Versus the Banks: Politics in the United States After the Panic of 1837* (1970); Thurman Wilkins, *Cherokee Tragedy: The Ridge Family and the Decimation of a People*, 2d ed. rev. (1986); Major L. Wilson, *The Presidency of Martin Van Buren* (1984).

Political Biography

Irving H. Bartlett, *Daniel Webster* (1978); Maurice G. Baxter, *One and Inseparable: Daniel Webster and the Union* (1984); Margaret Coit, *John P. Calhoun: American Portrait* (1950); Daniel B. Cole, *Martin Van Buren and the American Political System* (1984); Richard Current, *Daniel Webster and the Rise of National Conservatism* (1955); Clement Eaton, *Henry Clay and the Art of American Politics* (1957); John Niven, *John C. Calhoun and the Price of Union* (1988); Merrill O. Peterson, *The Great Triumvirate: Webster, Clay, and Calhoun* (1987); Robert Remini, *Life of Andrew Jackson* (1988), *Andrew Jackson and the Course of American Freedom, 1822–1832* (1981), and *Andrew Jackson and the Course of American Democracy* (1984); John William Ward, *Andrew Jackson: Symbol for an Age* (1955).

Utopian Communitarianism

Arthur Bestor, *Backwoods Utopias* (1950); Priscilla Brewett, *Shaker Communities, Shaker Lives* (1986); Fawn Brodie, *No Man Knows My History: The Life of Joseph Smith, Mormon Prophet* (1945); Maren Lockwood Carden, *Oneida: Utopian Community to Modern Corporation* (1969); Michael Fellman, *The Unbounded Frame: Freedom and Community in Nineteenth-Century American Utopianism* (1973); Robert Fogarty, ed., *American Utopianism* (1972); Lawrence Foster, *Women, Family, and Utopia: Communal Experiments of the Shakers, the Oneida Community, and the Mormons* (1991); Nathaniel Hawthorne, *The Blithedale Romance* (1852); William Kephart and William Zellner, *Extraordinary Groups: An Examination of Unconventional Life Styles*, 4th ed. (1991); Carol A. Kolmerten, *Women in Utopia: The Ideology of Gender in the American Owenite Communities* (1990); Perry Miller, ed., *The Transcendentalists* (1957); John Humphrey Noyes, *History of American Socialisms* (1870); Kenneth H. Winn, *Exiles in a Land of Liberty* (1989).

Temperance and Other Reforms

Susan Cayleff, *Wash and Be Healed: The Water-Cure Movement and Women's Health* (1987); Gerald Grob, *Mental Institutions in America: Social Policy to 1875* (1973); Stephen Nissenbaum, *Sex, Diet, and Debility in Jacksonian America: Sylvester Graham and Health Reform* (1980); Edward Pessen, *Most Uncommon Jacksonians: The Radical Leaders of the Early Labor Movement* (1967); W. J. Rorabaugh, *The Alcoholic Republic: An American Tradition* (1979); David Rothman, *The Discovery of the Asylum: Social Order and Disorder in the New Republic* (1971); Ian Tyrrell, *Sobering Up: From Temperance to Prohibition in Antebellum America, 1800–1860* (1979); Sean Wilentz, *Chants Democratic: New York City and the Rise of the American Working Class, 1788–1850* (1983).

Abolitionism and Women's Rights

Robert Abzug, *Passionate Liberator: Theodore Dwight Weld and the Dilemma of Reform* (1980); Barbara Berg, *The Remembered Gate—The Woman and the City, 1800–1860* (1978); Ellen DuBois, *Feminism and Suffrage: The Emergence of an Independent Women's Movement in America, 1848–1869* (1978); Lawrence Friedman, *Gregarious Saints: Self and Community in American Abolitionism, 1830–1870* (1982); Elisabeth Griffith, *In Her Own Right: The Life of Elizabeth Cady Stanton* (1984); Blanche Glassman Hersh, *The Slavery of Sex: Feminist Abolitionists in America* (1978); Gerda Lerner, *The Grimké Sisters from South Carolina: Rebels Against Slavery* (1967); Keith Melder, *Beginnings of Sisterhood: The American Woman's Rights Movement, 1800–1850* (1977); Jane A. Pease and William H. Pease, *They Who Would Be Free: Blacks' Search for Freedom, 1830–1861* (1974); Lewis Perry and Michael Fellman, eds., *Antislavery Reconsidered: New Perspectives on the Abolitionists* (1979); Benjamin Quarles, *Black Abolitionists* (1969); James Stewart, *Holy Warriors: The Abolitionists and American Slavery* (1976); Raymond Walters, *The Antislavery Appeal: American Abolitionism After 1830* (1976).

CHAPTER 13

Moving West

By the 1840s, the frontier was retreating across the Mississippi. As Americans contemplated the lands west of the great river, they debated the question of expansion. Some, like Michigan's senator Lewis Cass, saw the Pacific Ocean as the only limit to territorial expansion. Cass believed that the West represented not only economic opportunity for Americans, but also political stability for the nation as well. People crowded into cities and confined to limited territories endangered the Republic, he told fellow senators in a speech. But if they headed west to convert the "woods and forests into towns and villages and cultivate fields" and to extend the "dominion of civilization and improvement over the domain of nature," they would find rewarding personal opportunities that would ensure political and social harmony.

Cass's arguments supporting the righteousness and necessity of westward expansion were echoed again and again in the 1840s. Thousands of men seconded his sentiments by volunteering to join American forces in the war against Mexico in the summer of 1845. Largely untrained, dressed in fanciful uniforms, and called by names like Eagles, Avengers, and Tigers, the companies hurried south. But before long, these supporters of expansion saw the ugly side of territorial adventures: insects, bad weather, poor food, and unsanitary conditions. They discovered that such illnesses as the "black vomit" (yellow fever), dysentery, and diarrhea could kill more men than Mexican bullets. As a member of the American occupying army, Henry Judah also experienced the hostility of conquered peoples. In his diary, he reported, "It is dangerous to go out after night.... Four of our men were stabbed today." Not only, he wrote, was a man "by the name of Brown" stabbed in the back, but an "infernal villain cut his throat."

Like Henry Judah, Thomas Gibson, a captain of Indiana volunteers, also paid some of the costs of winning new territories. Less than a month after Cass's speech, he wrote to his wife, Mary, in Charlestown, Indiana. Although glad to report news of an American victory, he described a battlefield "still covered with [Mexican] dead" where "the stench is most horrible." Indiana friends had been killed, and Gibson himself had narrowly escaped. "The ball struck me a glancing blow on the head and knocked me down, but it did not harm me." As for the rest, the weather was foul, and so too was the food—"hard biscuit full of bitter black bugs."

Despite the harsh realities of war, Gibson did not challenge the enterprise. He bragged to Mary that "our little army could go out tomorrow in a fair field of battle and whip fifty thousand of the best Mexican troops that ever were on a field of battle. One thing is certain, we would be willing to try it."

Like other wives and family members at home, Mary was less interested in heroics than in the simple truth: Was Tommy dead or alive? As she anxiously awaited news, she wrote of her great hope: "May God bless you and send you home." Yet even with all her worries and prayers for the war's rapid conclusion, she could not escape the heady propaganda for national expansion. She had heard that Indiana soldiers had "shode themselves great cowards by retreating during battle," and she disapproved. "We all would rather you had stood like good soldiers," she told her husband.

This painting by Albert Bierstadt captures the majesty of the western landscape which dwarfs the Native Americans depicted in the foreground. (The Rocky Mountains, Lander's Peak, 1863, The Metropolitan Museum of Art, Rogers Fund, 1907 (07.123) Photograph by Geoffrey Clements)

*L*ewis Cass, Henry Judah, Thomas and Mary Gibson, and thousands of other Americans played a part in the nation's expansion into the trans-Mississippi West. The differences and similarities in their perspectives and in their responses to territorial growth unveil the complex nature of the western experience. Lewis Cass's speech illustrates the hold the West had on people's imagination and shows how some linked expansion to the American belief in individual opportunity and national progress. His reference to its riches reminds us of the gigantic contribution western resources made to national development and wealth. Yet his assumption that the West was vacant points to the costs of white expansion for Mexican Americans and Native Americans and the challenge non-Anglo groups would pose to the inclusiveness of American ideals. The Gibsons' letters show similar preconceptions and racial prejudices. They also portray the winning of the West on a human level: the anxieties, deprivation, enthusiasm, and optimism felt by those who fought for and settled in the West.

This chapter concerns movement into the trans-Mississippi West between 1830 and 1865. First, we will consider how and when Americans moved west, by what means the United States acquired the vast territories that in 1840 belonged to other nations, and the meaning of "Manifest Destiny," the slogan used to defend the conquest of the continent west of the Mississippi River. Then, we explore the nature of life on the western farming, mining, and urban frontiers. Finally, the chapter examines responses of Native Americans and Mexican Americans to expansion and illuminates the ways in which different cultural traditions intersected in the West.

Probing the Trans-Mississippi West

Until the 1840s, most Americans lived east of the Mississippi. The admission of new states between 1815 and 1840 symbolized the steady settlement of the eastern half of the continent. As frontier log cabins gave way to brick and clapboard houses, farmers cleared and planted land earlier settlers had ignored. Roads replaced tracks, and new churches, schools, stores, and banks attested to the march of settlement toward the Mississippi. By 1860, some 4.3 million Americans had moved west of the great river.

Foreign Claims and Possessions

With the exception of the Louisiana Territory, Spain held title to most of the trans-Mississippi region in 1815. For hundreds of years, explorers, soldiers, settlers, and missionaries had marched north from Mexico to explore and settle the lands lying beyond the Rio Grande and to spread Spanish culture to native peoples. Eventually, Spanish holdings included present-day Texas, Arizona, New Mexico, Nevada, Utah, western Colorado, California, and small parts of Wyoming, Kansas, and

Oklahoma. Spanish rulers had tried to keep foreigners out of its northern frontier areas, but increasingly, they found this policy difficult to enforce. When Mexico won its independence from Spain in 1821, it inherited this vast area with 75,000 Spanish-speaking inhabitants and numerous Native Americans living there. They also confronted the avid American appetite for expansion that Spain had tried to curb.

To the north of California was the Oregon country, a vaguely defined area extending from California to Alaska. Both Great Britain and the United States claimed the Oregon country on the basis of explorations in the late eighteenth century and fur trading in the early nineteenth. Joint occupation, agreed on in the Convention of 1818 and the Occupation Treaty of 1827, temporarily avoided settling the boundary question.

Early Interest in the West

Americans penetrated the trans-Mississippi West long before the great migrations of the 1840s and 1850s and were familiar with some of its people and terrains. Commercial goals fueled early interest as traders first sought beaver skins in Oregon territory and then bison robes prepared by the Plains tribes in the area around the upper Missouri River and its tributaries.

As early as 1811, Americans engaged in the fur trade in Oregon, and within ten years, fur trappers and traders were actively exploiting the resources of the Rocky Mountain region. Many of the men in the fur business married Indian women, thereby making valuable connections with Indian tribes involved in trapping. They and their wives occupied a cultural middle ground, adopting elements from both American and native ways of life. When the beaver was all but exterminated in the mid-1830s, some of the early traders and trappers acted as guides for Americans who would have little tolerance for the hybrid ways of the mountain men and their families.

Religious idealism also drew some Americans to the West. Two Presbyterian missionary couples, Marcus and Narcissa Whitman and Henry and Eliza Spalding, were among the first to travel to Oregon territory with help from fur traders. Like Methodist and Roman Catholic missionaries (sent from Europe), the Presbyterians hoped to convert Oregon Indians to Christianity. Their fervor drew strength from the fires of the Second Great Awakening and their conviction that without conversion, the Indians were doomed to everlasting torment in hell. Less successful initially in converting the Indians than their Catholic counterparts who were more tolerant of Indian culture, American missionaries also tried to teach Indians how to live like white people. Their missions became early outposts of Americanism.

In the Southwest, the collapse of the Spanish Empire in 1821 gave American traders an opportunity they had long sought. Each year, caravans from "the States" followed the Santa Fe Trail over the plains and mountains, loaded with weapons, tools, and brightly colored calicoes. New Mexico's 40,000 inhabitants proved eager buyers, exchanging precious metals and furs for manufactured goods. Eventually, some "Anglos" settled there. Their economic activities prepared the way for military conquest.

To the south, in Texas, land for cotton rather than trade or missionary fervor attracted settlers and squatters in the 1820s at the very time that the Hispanic population of 2,000 was adjusting to their country's new independence. The lure of cheap land drew more Americans to that area than to any other. By 1835, almost 30,000 Americans were living in Texas. As the largest group of Americans living outside the nation's boundaries at that time, their numbers dwarfed Tejanos.

On the Pacific, a handful of New England traders carrying sea-otter skins to China anchored in the harbors of Spanish California in the early nineteenth century. By the 1830s, as the near extermination of the animals ruined this trade, a commerce based on California cowhides and tallow developed. New England ships tied up in California ports while hides were collected from local ranches in exchange for clothes, boots, hardware, and furniture manufactured in the East.

Among the earliest easterners to settle in the trans-Mississippi West were tribes from the South and the Old Northwest whom the American government forcibly relocated in present-day Oklahoma and Kansas. Ironically, some of these eastern tribes acted as agents of white civilization by introducing cotton, the plantation system, black slavery, and schools. Other tribes triggered conflicts that weakened the western tribes with whom they came into contact. The Cherokee, Shawnee, and Delaware forced the Osages out of their Missouri and Arkansas hunting grounds, and tribes from the Old Northwest successfully claimed hunting areas long used by Kansas plains tribes. These disruptions foreshadowed white incursions later in the century.

The facts that much of the trans-Mississippi West lay outside U.S. boundaries and that the government had guaranteed Indian tribes permanent possession of some western territories did not curtail American economic or missionary activities. By the 1840s, a growing volume of published information fostered dreams of possession. Government reports by explorers Zebulon Pike and John C. Frémont, among others, provided detailed information about the interior, and guidebooks and news articles described the routes that such fur trappers as Jim Bridger, Kit Carson, and Jedediah Smith had mapped out. Going west was clearly possible. Lansford Hastings's *Emigrants' Guide to Oregon and California* (1845) provided not only the practical information that emigrants would need, but also the encouragement that heading for the frontier was the right thing to do.

In his widely read guide, Hastings minimized the importance of Mexican and British sovereignty. California, as a Mexican possession, presented a problem, he conceded, but Oregon did not. "So far from having any valid claim to any portion of it," Hastings argued, Great Britain "had no right even to occupy it." Furthermore, American settlers were already trickling into the Pacific Northwest, bringing progress with them. Surely the day could not be far distant, he wrote approvingly, "when genuine Republicanism and unsophisticated Democracy shall be reared up … upon the now wild shores, of the great Pacific," to replace "ignorance, superstition, and despotism."

Hastings's belief that Americans would obtain rights to foreign holdings in the West came true within a decade. In the course of the 1840s, the United States, through war and diplomacy, acquired Mexico's territories in the Southwest and on the Pacific (1,193,061 square miles, including Texas) as well as title to the Oregon country up to the 49th parallel (another 285,580 square miles). Later, with the Gadsden Purchase in 1853, the country incorporated another 29,640 square miles of Mexican territory.

Manifest Destiny

What explained the feverish desire to expand? Bursts of florid rhetoric accompanied territorial growth, and Americans used the slogan "Manifest Destiny" to justify and account for it. The phrase, coined in 1845 by John L. O'Sullivan, editor of the *Democratic Review,* referred to the conviction that the country's superior institutions and culture gave Americans a God-given right, even an obligation, to spread their civilization across the entire continent. Lewis Cass, Henry Judah, the Gibsons, Lansford Hastings, and most other Americans agreed.

This sense of uniqueness and mission was a legacy of early Puritan utopianism and the republicanism of the revolutionary era. By the 1840s, however, an argument for territorial expansion merged with the belief that the United States possessed a unique civilization. The successful absorption of the Louisiana Territory, rapid population growth, and advances in transportation, communication, and industry bolstered the idea of national superi-

ority and the notion that the United States could successfully absorb new territories. Publicists of Manifest Destiny proclaimed that the nation must.

Winning the Trans-Mississippi West

Manifest Destiny justified expansion but did not cause it. Concrete events in Texas triggered the national government's determination to acquire territories west of the Mississippi River. The Texas question originated in the years when Spain held most of the Southwest. Although some settlements such as Santa Fe, founded in 1609, were almost as old as Jamestown, the Spanish considered the sparsely populated and underdeveloped Southwest primarily a buffer zone for Mexico. The main centers of Spanish settlement were geographically distant from one another and thousands of miles from Mexico City. Although these northern borderlands formed a weak defensive perimeter of the Spanish Empire that was increasingly vulnerable as Spain weakened, their legal status was recognized internationally in the Transcontinental Treaty. Moreover, in its treaty negotiations with Spain in 1819, the United States, in return for Florida, accepted a southern border excluding Texas, to which the Americans had vague claims stemming from the Louisiana Purchase.

Annexing Texas, 1845

By the time the treaty was ratified in 1821, Mexico had won its independence from Spain but had scarcely had the opportunity to cope effectively with the borderlands, their people, and their problems or to develop powerful bonds of national identity. Mexicans soon had reason to wonder whether the American disavowal of any claim to Texas in the Transcontinental Treaty would last, for political leaders like Henry Clay began to cry out for "reannexation." Fear about American expansionism, fueled by several attempts to buy Texas and by continuing aggressive American statements, permeated Mexican politics.

In 1823, the Mexican government resolved to strengthen border areas by increasing population. To attract settlers, it offered land in return for token payments and pledges to become Roman

This 1872 painting by John Gast with its large goddesslike figure trailing telegraph lines, its parade of settlers, its depiction of technological progress captures the confidence of white Americans that the acquisition of the West was a positive and inevitable event. It also presents the conventional picture of the settlement of the frontier as a process generated by the movement of people from east to west. In fact, the West was also settled by emigrants moving from Mexico northward and by Indian tribes moving south.

Catholics and Mexican citizens. Stephen F. Austin, who gained rights to bring 300 families into Texas, was among the first of the American impresarios, or contractors, to take advantage of this opportunity. His call for settlers brought an enthusiastic response, as Mary Austin Holley recalled. "I was a young thing then, but 5 months married, my husband ... failed in Tennessee, proposed to commence business in New Orleans. I ready to go anywhere ... freely consented. Just then Stephen Austin and Joe Hawkins were crying up Texas—beautiful country, land for nothing, etc.—Texas fever rose then ... there we must go. There without much reflection, we did go." Like the Holleys, most of the American settlers came from the South, and some brought slaves. By the end of the decade, some 15,000 white Americans and 1,000 slaves lived in Texas, far outnumbering the 5,000 Tejano inhabitants.

Mexican officials soon questioned the wisdom of their invitation. Although Moses Austin, Stephen's father, converted to Roman Catholicism, few settlers gave signs of honoring their bargain with the Mexican government. Most remained far more American than Mexican. Some were malcontents who disliked Mexican laws and customs and limitations on their economic and commercial opportunities. In late 1826, a small group of them raised the flag of rebellion and declared the Republic of Fredonia. Although Stephen Austin and others assisted in putting down the brief uprising, American newspapers hailed the rebels as "apostles of democracy" and called Mexico an "alien civilization."

Mexican anxiety grew apace. Secretary of Foreign Relations Lucas Aláman accused American settlers of being advance agents of the United States. "They commence by introducing themselves into the territory which they covet," he told the Mexican Congress, "grow, multiply, become the predominant party in the population.... These pioneers excite ... movements which disturb the political state of the country ... and then follow discontents and dissatisfaction."

In 1829, the Mexican government altered its Texas policy. Determined to curb American influence, the government abolished slavery in Texas. The next year, it forbade further emigration from the United States, and officials began to collect customs duties on goods crossing the Louisiana

United States Territorial Expansion by 1860

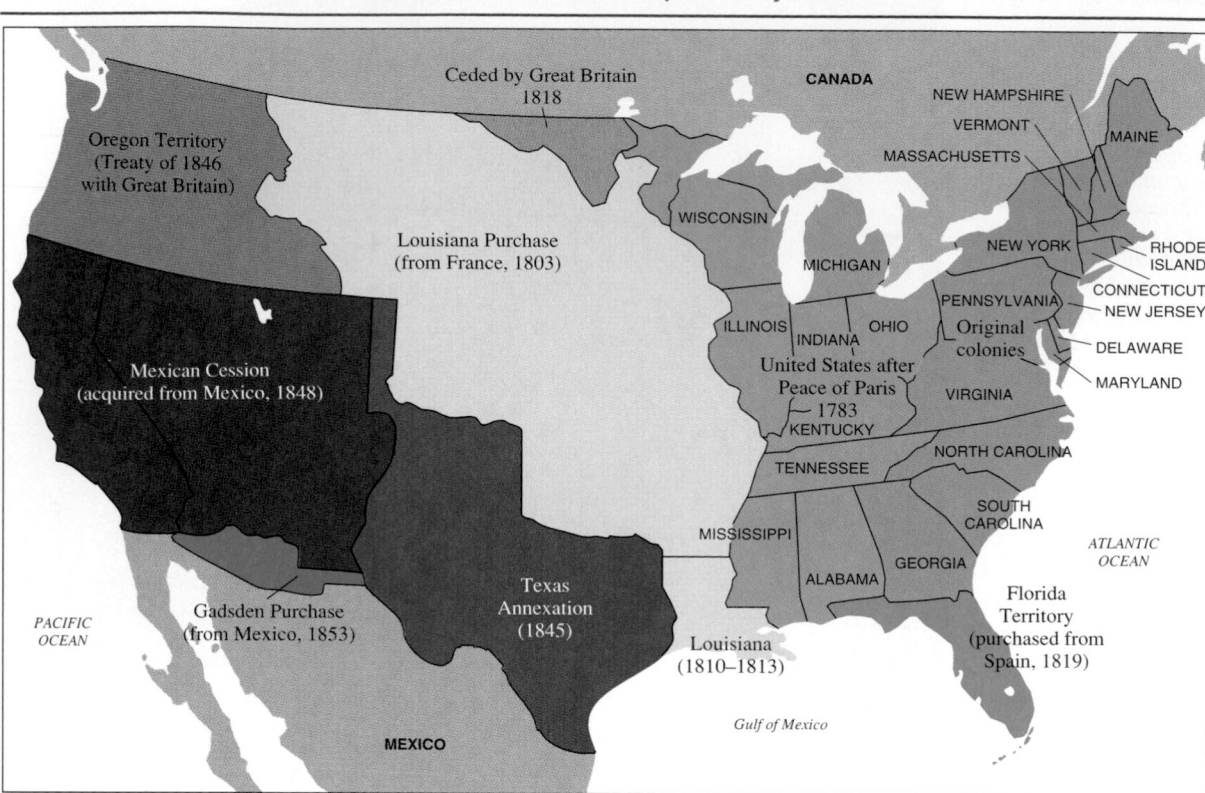

This map makes the rapidity of the acquisition of the Far West clear.

border. But little changed in Texas. American slave owners freed their slaves and then forced them to sign life indenture contracts. Emigrants still crossed the border and continued to outnumber Mexicans.

Tensions escalated to the brink of war. In October 1835, a skirmish between the colonial militia and Mexican forces signaled the beginning of hostilities. Sam Houston, onetime governor of Tennessee and army officer, became commander in chief of the Texas forces. Although Texans called the war with Mexico a revolution, a Vermont soldier perhaps more accurately observed, "It is in fact a rebellion."

Mexican dictator and general Antonio López de Santa Anna, hurried north to crush the rebellion with an army of 6,000 conscripts. Although he had a numerical advantage, many of his soldiers

were Mayan Indians who had been drafted unwillingly, spoke no Spanish, and were exhausted by the long march. Supply lines were spread thin. Nevertheless, Santa Anna and his men won the initial engagements of the war: the Alamo at San Antonio fell to him, taking Davy Crockett and Jim Bowie with it. So, too, did the fortress of Goliad, to the southeast.

As he pursued Houston and the Texans toward the San Jacinto River, carelessness proved Santa Anna's undoing. Although fully anticipating an American attack, the Mexican general and his men settled down to their usual siesta on April 21, 1836, without posting an adequate guard. As the Mexicans dozed, the Americans attacked. With cries of "Remember the Alamo! Remember Goliad!" the Texans overcame the army, captured its commander in his slippers, and won the war within 20 minutes. Their casualties numbered only 2, while 630 Mexicans lay dead.

With the victory at San Jacinto, Texas gained its independence. Threatened with lynching, Santa Anna saw little choice but to sign the treaty of independence setting the republic's boundary at the Rio Grande. When news of the disastrous events reached Mexico City, however, the Mexican Congress repudiated an "agreement carried out under the threat of death." Mexico maintained that Texas was still part of Mexico.

The new republic started off shakily. It was financially unstable, unrecognized by its enemy, rejected by its friends. Although Texans immediately sought admission to the Union, their request failed. Jackson, whose agent in Texas had reported that the republic was so weak that "her future security must depend more upon the weakness and imbecility of her enemy than upon her own strength," was reluctant to act quickly. Many northerners violently opposed annexation of

The Evolution of Texas

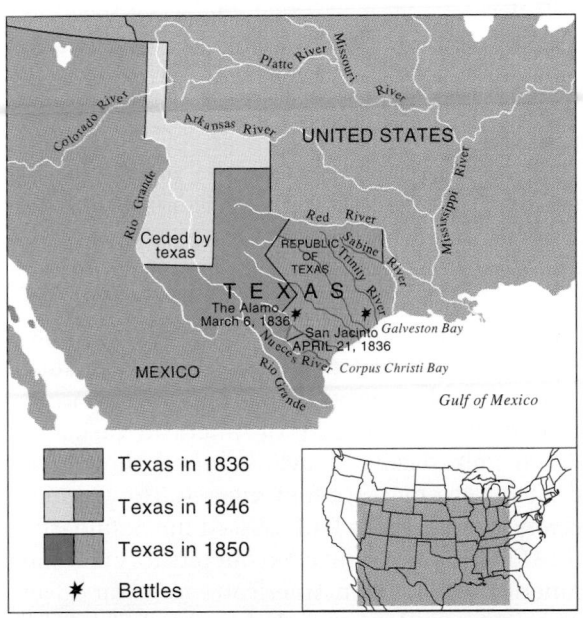

The results of continuing conflict with Mexico on the size and shape of Texas stand out clearly in this map. Note the location of the Neuces River, claimed by Mexico as the boundary between Texas and Mexico, and the Rio Grande, the boundary insisted on by Texans.

another slave state. The Union was precariously balanced, with 13 free and 13 slave states. Texas would upset that equilibrium in favor of the South. Petitions poured into Congress in 1837 opposing annexation, and John Quincy Adams repeatedly denounced the idea. Annexation was too explosive a political issue to pursue; debate finally died down and then disappeared.

For the next few years, the Lone Star Republic led a precarious existence. Mexico refused to recognize its independence, but could send only an occasional raiding party across the border. Texans skirmished with Mexican bands, did their share of border raiding, and suffered an ignominious defeat in an ill-conceived attempt to capture Santa Fe in 1841. Diplomatic maneuvering in European capitals for financial aid and recognition was only moderately successful. Financial ties with the United States increased, however, as trade grew and many Americans invested in Texas bonds and lands.

Texas became headline news again in 1844. "It is the greatest question of the age," an Alabama expansionist declared, "and I predict will agitate the country more than all the other public questions ever have." He was right. Although President John Tyler (who assumed office after Harrison's sudden death) reopened the question of annexation hoping that Texas would ensure his reelection, the issue exploded. It brought to life powerful sectional, national, and political tensions and demonstrated how divisive the questions connected to the expansion of slavery into the West could be. Southern Democrats insisted that the South's future hinged on the annexation of Texas. "Now is the time to vindicate and save our institutions," John C. Calhoun insisted. His supporters hoped that by exploiting the Texas issue, Calhoun would win the White House.

Other wings of the Democratic party capitalized more successfully on the issue, however. Lewis Cass, Stephen Douglas of Illinois, and Robert Walker of Mississippi vigorously supported annexation, not because it would expand slavery, a topic they carefully avoided, but because it would spread the benefits of American civilization. Their arguments, classic examples of the basic tenets of Manifest Destiny, put the question into a national context of expanding American freedom. So powerfully did they link

Texas to Manifest Destiny and avoid sectional issues that their candidate, James Polk of Tennessee, secured the Democratic nomination in 1844. Polk called for "the reannexation of Texas at the earliest practicable period" and the occupation of the Oregon Territory. Manifest Destiny had come of age.

Whigs tended to oppose annexation, fearing slavery's expansion and the growth of southern power with the addition of another slave state. They accused the Democrats of exploiting Manifest Destiny, more as a means of securing office than of bringing freedom to Texas.

The Whigs were right that the annexation issue would bring victory to the Democrats. Polk won a close election in 1844. But by the time he took the oath of office in March 1845, Tyler had resolved the question of annexation. In his last months in office, Tyler pushed through Congress a joint resolution admitting Texas to the Union. Unlike a treaty, which required the approval of two-thirds of the Senate and which Tyler had failed to win in 1844, a joint resolution needed only majority support. Nine years after its revolution, Texas finally became part of the Union. The agreement gave Texas the unusual right to divide into five states if it chose to do so.

War with Mexico, 1846–1848

When Mexico learned of Texas's annexation, it promptly severed diplomatic ties with the United States. It was easy for Mexicans to interpret the events from the 1820s on as part of a gigantic American plot to steal Texas. During the war for Texas independence, American papers, especially those in the South, had enthusiastically hailed the efforts of the rebels, while southern money and volunteers had aided the Texans in their struggle. Now that the Americans had gained Texas, would they want still more?

In his inaugural address in 1845, President Polk pointed out "that our system may easily be extended to the utmost bounds of our territorial limits, and that as it shall be extended the bonds of our Union, so far from being weakened will become stronger." What were those territorial limits? Did they extend into the territory the Mexican government considered as its own?

Polk, like many other Americans, failed to appreciate how the annexation of Texas humiliated Mexico and increased pressures on its government to respond belligerently. Aware of its weakness, the president anticipated that Mexico would grant his grandiose demands: a Texas bounded by the Rio Grande rather than the Nueces River 150 miles to its north, as well as California and New Mexico.

Even before the Texans could accept the long-awaited invitation to join the Union, rumors of a Mexican invasion were afloat. As a precautionary move, Polk ordered General Zachary Taylor to move "on or near the Rio Grande." By October 1845, Taylor and 3,500 American troops had reached the Nueces River. The positioning of an American army in Texas did not mean that Polk actually expected war. Rather, he hoped that a show of military force, coupled with secret diplomacy, would bring the desired concessions. In November, the president sent his secret agent, John L. Slidell, to Mexico City with instructions to secure the Rio Grande border and to buy Upper California and New Mexico. When the Mexican government refused to receive Slidell, an angry Polk decided to force Mexico into accepting American terms. He ordered Taylor south of the Rio Grande. To the Mexicans, who insisted that the Nueces River was the legitimate boundary, their presence constituted an act of war. Democratic newspapers and expansionists enthusiastically hailed Polk's provocative decision; the Whigs opposed it.

It was only a matter of time before an incident occurred to serve as the American justification for hostilities. In late April, the Mexican government declared a state of defensive war. Two days later, a skirmish broke out between Mexican and American troops, resulting in 16 American casualties. When Polk received Taylor's report, he quickly drafted a war message for Congress. The president claimed that Mexico had "passed the boundary of the United States . . . invaded our territory and shed American blood upon American soil." "War exists," he claimed, and, he added untruthfully, "notwithstanding all our efforts to avoid it, exists by act of Mexico."

Although Congress declared war, the conflict bitterly divided Americans. Many Whigs, including

Abraham Lincoln, questioned the accuracy of Polk's initial account of the events, and their opposition grew more vocal as time passed. Lincoln called the war one "of conquest brought into existence to catch votes." The American Peace Society revealed sordid examples of army misbehavior in Mexico, and Frederick Douglass accused the country of "cupidity and love of dominion." Many workers also were critical of the war.

Debate continued as American troops swept into Mexico and advanced toward the capital. Although the Mexicans were also fighting Indian tribes on their northern border, the government refused to admit defeat and negotiate an end to the hostilities. The war dragged on and on. The *American Review*, a Whig paper, proclaimed that the conflict was a "crime over which angels may weep." In 1847, a month after General Winfield Scott took Mexico City, Philadelphian Joseph Sills wrote in his diary, "There is a widely spread conviction ... that it is a wicked & disgraceful war."

Yet Polk enjoyed the enthusiastic support of expansionists. Thomas Gibson's men, like most other soldiers, were eager volunteers. Some expansionists even urged permanent occupation of Mexico. Illinois Democratic Senator Sidney Breese told the Senate, "The avowed objects of the war ... [were] to obtain redress of wrongs, a permanent and honorable peace, and indemnity for the past and security for the future." To secure these goals, Breese could even contemplate permanent occupation with "great ultimate good" to the United States, to Mexico, "and to humanity."

Inflated rhetoric did not win the war, however. In the end, chance helped draw hostilities to a close. Mexican moderates approached Polk's diplomatic representative, Nicholas Trist, who accompanied the American army in Mexico. In Trist's baggage were detailed, though out-of-date, instructions outlining Polk's requirements: the Rio Grande boundary, Upper California, and New Mexico. Although the president had lost confidence in Trist and had ordered him home in chains, Trist stayed in Mexico to negotiate an end to the war. Having obtained most of Polk's objectives, Trist returned to Washington to an ungrateful president. Apparently Polk had wanted more territory from Mexico for less money. Firing him from his job at the State Department, Polk denounced Trist as an "impudent and unqualified scoundrel."

This Currier & Ives print appeared in 1847 during the Mexican-American War. It shows the flight of the Mexican Army at the battle of Buena Vista. The fallen Mexicans so prominently placed in the foreground, the lines of fleeing and apparently frightened soldiers suggest the intent to convey to viewers the inferiority of the enemy against which the Americans were fighting. (Anne S. K. Brown Military Collection, Brown University Library)

California and New Mexico

Although Texas and Mexico dominated the headlines, Polk made it clear from the early days of his presidency that California and New Mexico were part of any resolution of the Mexico crisis. Serious American interest in California dated only from the late 1830s. A few Americans, mostly traders and shopkeepers, had settled in California during the 1820s and 1830s, but they constituted only a small part of the Spanish-speaking Californio population that had reached 3,200 by 1821. Many had married into Californio families and taken Mexican citizenship. But gradual recognition of California's fine harbors, its favorable position for the China trade, and the suspicion that other countries, especially Great Britain, had designs on the region nourished the conviction that it must become part of the United States.

In 1842, a comic dress rehearsal for rebellion occurred when a United States naval commodore, Thomas Catsby Jones, believing that war had broken out with Mexico, sailed into Monterey, forced the Mexican commander to surrender, and proclaimed California's annexation. When Jones learned of his error, he apologized and watched the Mexican flag hoisted once more. Yet the arrival of 1,500 American overland emigrants in a three-year period intensified the friction. These newcomers had little interest in blending into Californio society. They and their families wanted an American California. As one resident realized, "The American population will soon be sufficiently numerous to play the Texas game."

In 1845, Polk appointed Thomas Larkin, a successful American merchant in Monterey, as his confidential agent. Larkin had clear instructions should Californians decide to break with Mexico. "While the President will make no effort and use no influence to induce California to become one of the free and independent states of the Union," wrote Polk's secretary of state, James Buchanan, to Larkin, "yet if the people should desire to unite their destiny with ours, they would be received as brethren." Polk's efforts to purchase California suggested that he was sensitive to the fragility of American claims to the region. But Santa Anna, who bore the burden of having lost Texas, was in no position to sell. Thus, in 1846, a few armed American settlers rose up against Mexican "tyranny" and established the "Bear Flag Republic."

New Mexico was also on Polk's list. Ties with the United States began in the 1820s, when American traders began to bring their goods to Santa Fe. Economic profits stimulated American territorial appetites. As the oldest and largest Mexican group in North America (60,000 out of 75,000), however, New Mexicans had little desire for annexation. The unsuccessful attempt by the Texans to capture Santa Fe in 1841 and border clashes in the two following years did not enhance the attractiveness of their Anglo neighbors. But standing awkwardly in the path of westward expansion and further isolated from Mexico by the annexation of Texas in 1846, New Mexico's future as a Mexican province was uncertain.

In June 1846, shortly after the declaration of war with Mexico, the Army of the West, led by Colonel Stephen W. Kearney, left Fort Leavenworth, Kansas, for New Mexico. Kearney had orders to occupy Mexico's northern provinces and to protect the lucrative Santa Fe trade. Two months later, the army took Santa Fe without a shot, although one eyewitness noticed the "surly countenances" and the "wail of grief . . . above the din of our horses' tread." New Mexico's upper class, who had already begun to intermarry with American merchants and send some sons to colleges in the United States, readily accepted the new rulers. However, ordinary Mexicans and Pueblo Indians did not take conquest so lightly. After Kearney departed for California, resistance erupted in New Mexico. Californios also fought the American occupation force. Kearney was wounded, and the first appointed American governor of New Mexico was killed. In the end, however, superior American military strength won the day. By January 1847, both California and New Mexico were firmly in American hands.

The Treaty of Guadalupe Hidalgo, 1848

Negotiated by Trist and signed on February 2, 1848, the Treaty of Guadalupe Hidalgo dictated the fate of most people living in the Southwest. The United States absorbed the region's 75,000

The Mexican-American War

This map shows not only the movements of American troops during the Mexican-American War, but also the large area that was in dispute. The vast territorial acquisitions, the fruit of victory, are clear.

Spanish-speaking inhabitants and its 150,000 Native Americans and increased its territory by 529,017 square miles, almost a third of Mexico's extent. Mexico received $15 million and in 1853 would receive another $10 million for large tracts of land in southern Arizona and New Mexico (the Gadsden Purchase). In the treaty, the United States guaranteed the civil and political rights of former Mexican citizens and their rights to land and also agreed to satisfy all American claims against Mexico.

If the territorial gains were immense, some costs were equally huge: 13,000 American lives lost, mostly to diseases such as measles and dysentery, and $97 million expended for military operations. Although sporadic violence would continue for years in the Southwest as Mexicans protested

the new status quo, the war was over, and the Americans had won.

The Oregon Question, 1844–1846

Belligerence and war secured vast areas of the Southwest and California for the United States. In the Pacific Northwest, the presence of mighty Great Britain rather than the weak, crisis-ridden Mexican government suggested more cautious tactics. There diplomacy became the means for territorial gains. Despite the disputed nature of claims to the Oregon Territory, Polk assured the inauguration day crowd huddled under umbrellas that "our title to the country of Oregon is 'clear and unquestionable,' ...already our people are preparing to perfect that title by occupying it with their wives and children." Polk's words reflected American confidence that settlement carried the presumption of possession. But the British did not agree. As the London *Times* warned, "Ill regulated, overbearing, and aggressive ... [Polk's] pretensions amount, if acted upon, to the clearest *causa belli* which has yet arisen between Great Britain and the American Union."

Though the British considered the president's speech belligerent, Polk was correct in saying that Americans had not hesitated to settle the disputed territories. Between 1842 and 1845, the number of Americans in Oregon grew from 400 to over 5,000. Most located south of the Columbia River in the Willamette valley. By 1843, these settlers had written a constitution and soon after elected a legislature. At the same time, changing conditions set the stage for an eventual compromise. British interests in the area were declining as the near destruction of the beaver caused the fur trade to dwindle.

Attractive commercial opportunities elsewhere were opening up; New Zealand and other colonies lured English settlers away from the Pacific Northwest.

Polk's flamboyant posture and the expansive American claims made mediation difficult, however. The Democratic platform and the slogan that had helped elect Polk laid claim to a boundary of 54°40′. In fact, Polk was not willing to go to war with Great Britain for Oregon. Privately, he considered reasonable a boundary at the 49th parallel, which would extend the existing Canadian-American border to the Pacific and secure the harbors of Puget Sound for the United States. But Polk could hardly admit this to his Democratic supporters, who had so enthusiastically shouted "Fifty-four forty or fight" during the recent campaign.

Soon after his inaugural, Polk offered his compromise to Great Britain. But his tone offended the British minister, who rejected the offer at once. Polk compounded his error by gracelessly withdrawing the suggestion. In his year-end address to Congress in 1845, the president created more diplomatic difficulties. Urging the protection of American settlers in Oregon, he again publicly claimed that Oregon belonged to the United States. In addition, he asked Congress to give Britain the one-year notice required by previous agreements to terminate joint occupation there.

Discussions about Oregon occupied Congress for months in early 1846. Debate, however, gradually revealed deep divisions about Oregon and the possibility of war with Great Britain. Despite slogans, most Americans did not want to fight for Oregon and preferred to resolve the crisis diplomatically. As war with Mexico loomed, this task became more urgent.

The British, too, were eager to settle. In June 1846, the British agreed to accept the 49th-parallel boundary if Vancouver Island remained British. Polk took the unorthodox step of forwarding this proposal to the Senate for a preliminary response. Within days, the Senate overwhelmingly approved the compromise. Escaping some of the responsibility for retreating from slogans by sharing it with the Senate, Polk ended the crisis just a few weeks before the declaration of war with Mexico.

The Oregon Country

This map highlights the extravagant claims to Oregon voiced during the election of 1844 and the eventual boundaries established with Great Britain. The major trails that brought American settlers to the West suggest the population movements that lay behind the Oregon controversy.

As these events show, Manifest Destiny was an idea that supported and justified expansionist policies. It corresponded, at the most basic level, to what Americans believed, that expansion was both necessary and right. As early as 1816, American geography books pictured the nation's western boundary at the Pacific and included Texas. Poems, essays, and stories about winning the West, enlivened with illustrations of covered wagons and Indian fighters, were standard reading fare. Popular literature typically described Indians as a dying race that had failed in the basic tasks of cultivating the soil and conquering the wilderness. Mexicans were dismissed as "unjust and injurious neighbor[s]." Only whites could make the wilderness flower. Thus, as lands east of the Mississippi filled up, Americans automatically called on familiar ideas to justify expansion.

Going West

After diplomacy and war clarified the status of the western territories, Americans lost little time in moving there. What had been a trickle of emigrants became a flood. During the 1840s, 1850s, and 1860s, thousands of Americans left their homes for the frontier. By 1860, California alone had 380,000 settlers.

Some chose to migrate by sea. Although the trip was expensive, one could sail from Atlantic or Gulf Coast ports around South America to the West Coast or embark for Panama, cross the isthmus by land, and then continue by sea. Most emigrants, however, chose land routes. In 1843, the first large party succeeded in crossing the plains and mountains to Oregon. More followed. Between 1841 and 1867, some 350,000 traveled over the overland trails to California or to Oregon, while others trekked part of the way to intermediate points like Colorado and Utah.

The Emigrants

Most of the emigrants who headed for the Far West, where slavery was prohibited, were white and American-born. They came from the Midwest and the Upper South. A few free blacks made the trip as well. Pioneer Margaret Frink remembered seeing a "Negro woman ... tramping along through the heat and dust, carrying a cast iron black stove on her head, with her provisions and a blanket piled on top ... bravely pushing on for California." Emigrants from the Deep South usually selected Arkansas or Texas as their destination, and many took their slaves with them. By 1840, over 11,000 slaves toiled in Texas and 20,000 in Arkansas.

The many pioneers who kept journals during the five- to six-month overland trip captured the human dimension of emigrating. Their journals, usually their only contribution to the historical record, focused on day-to-day events and expressed some of the thoughts and emotions experienced on the long journey west. One migrant, Lodisa Frizzell, described her feelings at parting in 1852:

> Who is there that does not recollect their first night when started on a long journey, the well known voices of our friends still ring in our ears, the parting kiss feels still warm upon our lips, and that last separating word farewell! sinks deeply into the heart! It may be the last we ever hear from some or all of them, and to those who start ... there can be no more solemn scene of parting only at death.

Most emigrants traveled with family and relatives. Only during the gold rush years did large numbers, usually young men, travel independently. Migration was a family experience, mostly involving men and women from their late twenties to early forties. A sizable number of them had recently married. And for most, migration was a familiar experience. Like other geographically mobile Americans, emigrants to the Far West had earlier moved to other frontiers, often as children or as newlyweds. The difference was the vast distance to this frontier and the seemingly final separation from home.

Migrants' Motives

What led so many Americans to sell most of their possessions and embark on an unknown future thousands of miles away? Many believed that

Personal Diaries

Nineteenth-century journals kept by hundreds of ordinary men and women traveling west on the overland trails constitute a rich source for exploring the nature of the westward experience. They are also an example of how private sources can be used to deepen our understanding of the past. Diaries, journals, and letters all provide us with a personal perspective on major happenings. These sources tend to focus on the concrete, so they convey the texture of daily life in the nineteenth century, daily routines and amusements, clothing, habits, and interactions with family and friends. They also provide evidence of the varied concerns, attitudes, and prejudices of the writers, thus providing a test of commonly accepted generalizations about individual and group behavior.

Like any historical source, personal documents must be used carefully. It is important to note the writer's age, sex, class, and regional identification. Although this information may not be available, some of the writer's background can be deduced from what he or she has written. It is also important to consider for what purpose and for whom the document was composed. This information will help explain the tone or character of the source and what has been included or left out. It is, of course, important to avoid generalizing too much from one or even several similar sources. Only after reading many diaries, letters, and journals is it possible to make valid generalizations about life in the past.

Here we present excerpts from two travel journals of the 1850s. Few of the writers considered their journals to be strictly private. Often, they were intended as a family record or an infor-

mation for friends back home. Therefore, material of a personal nature has often been excluded. Nineteenth-century Americans referred to certain topics, such as pregnancy, only indirectly or not at all.

One excerpt comes from Mary Bailey's 1852 journal. Mary was 22 when she crossed the plains to California with her 32-year-old doctor husband. Originally a New Englander, Mary had lived in Ohio for six years before moving west. The Baileys were reasonably prosperous and were able to restock necessary supplies on the road west. The other writer, Robert Robe, was 30 when he crossed along the same route a year earlier than the Baileys, headed for Oregon. Robert was a native of Ohio and a Presbyterian minister.

As you read these excerpts, notice what each journal reveals about the trip west. What kinds of challenges did the emigrants face on their journey? Do these correspond to the picture you may have formed from novels, television, and movies? What kinds of work needed to be done, and who did it? Can you see any indication of a division of work based on sex? What kinds of interactions appear to have occurred between men and women on the trip? What does the pattern tell us about nineteenth-century society? How does the painting of the "emigrant train" reinforce the journal accounts of men's and women's roles?

Even these short excerpts suggest that men and women, as they traveled west, may have had different concerns and different perspectives on the journey. In what ways do the two accounts differ, and in what ways are they similar?

Journal of Robert Robe

[May] 19, [1851] *A fine day. The first spent in travelling on the plains of the Platte river.*

20. *Continue our journey up the Platte valley which I would judge to be here some 12 miles wide on this side of the river. The only game seen here are the antelope and wolf beside some wild fowl.*

21. *A rainy morning started early passed an old Pawnee village in ruins. The houses are constructed by placing timbers in forks and upon these without placing upright poles then rushes bound with [illegible] and finally earth. Chimney in center. Day became more & more rainy and wound up with a storm which beggared description.*

22. *Bluff approach the river—travelling less monotonous river finely skirted with timber.*

23. *Roads very muddy in afternoon. Today our wagon severed itself from our former companions & joined a company of Californians.*

24. *Before starting a trader direct from Ft. Kearney arrived at our camp. He informs us it is yet 25 miles thither. Travelling is by no means dangerous a waggon of provisions passing with only three guards. In the afternoon passed the entrance of the Independence Weston & St. Jo. roads. Emigrants became more numerous.*

25. *Passed Fort Kearney this morning and after a short drive encamped. Having conversed with some of the soldiers I find they consider life very monotonous.*

26. *Roads heavy—short drive—a storm.*

27. *High Bluffs on the opposite side of river approach and present a beautiful appearance. At night a fearful storm.*

28. *Roads heavy nothing singular.*

29. *Have arrived in the region abounding in Buffalo. At noon a considerable herd came in sight. The first any of us had ever seen. Thus now for the chase—the horsemen proved too swift in pursuit and frightened them into the Bluffs without capturing any—the footmen pursued however and killed three pretty good success for the first.*

30. *Nothing remarkable today.*

31. *Game being abundant we resolved to rest our stock and hunt today—Started in the morning on foot. Saw probably 1,000 Buffalo. Shot at several and killed one. Where ever we found them wolves were prowling around as if to guard them. Their real object is however no doubt to seize the calves as their prey. Saw a town of Prairie dogs, they are nearly as large as a gray squirrel. They bark fiercely when at a little distance but on near approach flee to their holes. Wherever they are we see numerous owls. After a very extensive ramble and having seen a variety of game we returned at sunset with most voracious appetites.*

June 1. *The Bluffs became beautifully undulating losing their precipitous aspect and the country further back is beautifully rolling prairie.*

2. *In the evening camped beside our old friends Miller and Dovey. They had met with a great loss this morning their 3 horses having taken fright at a drove of buffalo and ran entirely away. Some of our company killed more buffalo this evening & a company went in the night with teams to bring them in.*

3. *Spent the forenoon in an unsuccessful search for the above mentioned horses. In the afternoon pursued & caught our company after.*

4. *Crossed the south fork of the Platte at 2 P.M.*

Source: Pacific Northwest Quarterly 19 (January 1928): 52–63.

Journal of Mary Stuart Bailey

Wednesday, April 13, 1852

Left our hitherto happy home in Sylvania amid the tears of parting kisses of dear friends, many of whom were endeared to me by their kindness shown to me when I was a stranger in a strange land, when sickness and death visited our small family & removed our darling, our only child in a moment, as it were. Such kindness I can never forget....

Friday, 21st [May]

Rained last night. Slept in the tent for the first time. I was Yankee enough to protect myself by pinning up blankets over my head. I am quite at home in my tent. 12:00 Have traveled in the rain all day & we are stuck in the mud. I sit in the wagon writing while the men are at work doubling the teams to draw us out....

Sunday, 23rd.

Walked to the top of the hill where I could be quiet & commune with nature and nature's God. This afternoon I was annoyed by something very unpleasant & shed many tears and felt very unhappy....

Thursday, 4th [June]

Very cold this morning after the shower.... We stopped on the banks of the Platte to take dinner. I am sitting on the banks of the Platte with my feet almost in the water. Have been writing to my Mother. How I wish I had some of my own relations with me....

Sunday, 4th [July]

Started at 3 o'clock to find feed or know where it was. Had to go 4 or 5 miles off the road. Found water & good grass. Camped on the sand with sage roots for fuel. It is wintery, cold & somewhat inclined to rain, not pleasant.

Rather a dreary Independence Day. We speak of our friends at home. We think they are thinking of us....

Monday, 12th.

Stayed in camp another day to get our horse better. He is much improved. It is cold enough. Washed in the morning & had the sick headache in the afternoon....

Thursday, 12th [August]

Very warm. Slept until we stopped to take breakfast. Mr. Patterson starts as soon as light & stops in the heat of the day to rest the animals. We do not have much time to do anything except 4 or 5 hours in the middle of the day....

Friday, 17th [September]

Have been confined ever since Monday with ague in my face which is very much swollen. Have suffered very much. We are now in Carson Valley. Plenty of trees but the country is very barren.

Saturday, 18th.

Very pleasant, delightful weather. Feel much better today. We are not stirring this afternoon. We have heard to a great deal of suffering, people being thrown our on the desert to die & being picked up & brought to the hospital....

Tuesday, November 8th

Sacramento city has been nearly consumed. The Dr. has had all his instruments & a good deal of clothing burned, loss not exceeding $300. It really seems as though it was not right for us to come to California & lose so much. I do not think that we shall be as well off as at home.

Source: Sandra L. Myers, ed., Ho for California! Women's Overland Diaries from the Huntington Library *(San Marino, CA: Henry F. Huntington Library, 1980).*

Western Population Advance, 1830–1850

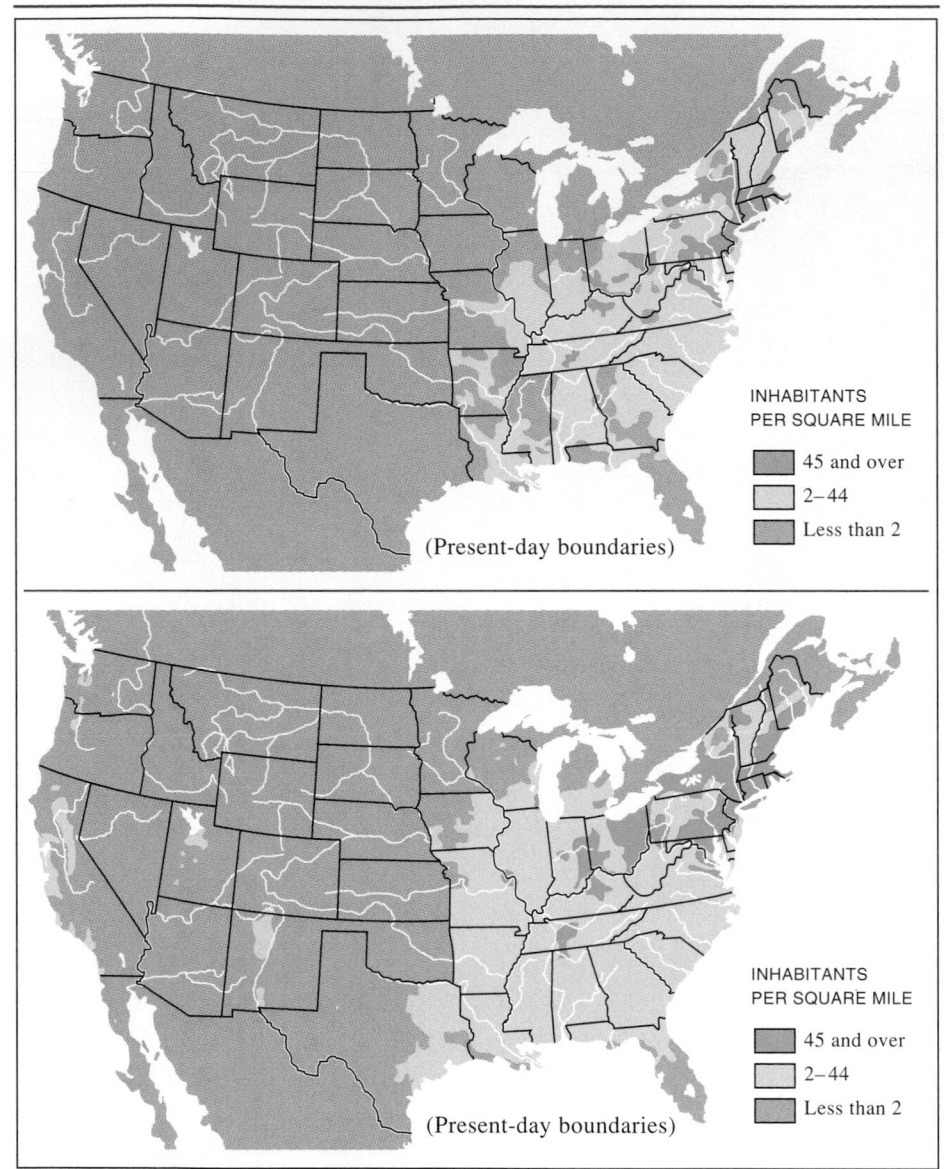

(Present-day boundaries)

INHABITANTS
PER SQUARE MILE

- 45 and over
- 2–44
- Less than 2

(Present-day boundaries)

INHABITANTS
PER SQUARE MILE

- 45 and over
- 2–44
- Less than 2

Within a 20-year period, as this map shows, the eastern half of the nation was almost completely settled while several areas of the trans-Mississippi West attracted immigrants.

frontier life would offer rich opportunities. A popular folk song expressed this widespread conviction:

Since times has been hard, I'll tell you sweetheart,
I've a notion to leave off my plow and my cart,
Away to Californy a journey pursue,
To double my fortunes as other men do.

The kinds of opportunities emigrants expected varied widely. Thousands sought riches in the form of gold. Others anticipated making their fortune as merchants, shopkeepers, and peddlers. Some intended to speculate in land, acquiring large blocks of public lands and then selling them later to settlers at a handsome profit. The possibility of professional rewards gained from practicing law or medicine on the frontier attracted still others.

Most migrants dreamed of bettering their life by cultivating the land. As one settler explained, "The motive that induced us to part with pleasant associates and dear friends of our childhood days, was to obtain from the government of the United States a grant of land that 'Uncle Sam' had promised." Federal and state land policies made the acquisition of land increasingly alluring. Preemption acts during the 1830s and 1840s gave "squatters" the right to settle public lands before the government offered them for sale and then allowed them to purchase these lands at the minimum price once they came on the market. At the same time, the amount of land a family had to buy shrank to only 40 acres. In 1862, the Homestead Act went further by offering 160 acres of government land free to citizens or future citizens over 21 who lived on the property, improved it, and paid a small registration fee. Oregon's land policy, which predated the Homestead Act, was even more generous. It awarded a single man 320 acres of free land and a married man 640 acres provided he occupied his claim for four years and made improvements.

Some emigrants hoped the West would restore them to health. Settlers from the Mississippi valley wished to escape the region's debilitating agues and fevers. Doctors advised those suffering the dreaded tuberculosis that the long out-of-doors trip and the western climate might cure them. Even invalids grasped at the advice offered by one doctor in 1850, who urged them to "attach themselves to the companies of emigrants bound for Oregon or Upper California."

Others pursued religious or cultural missions in the West. Missionary couples like David and Catherine Blaine, who settled in Seattle when it was a frontier outpost, determined to bring Protestantism and education west. Stirred by the stories they had heard of the "deplorable morals" on the frontier, they willingly left the comforts of home to evangelize and educate westerners. Still others, like the Mormons, made the long trek to Utah to establish a society in conformity with their religious beliefs.

Not everyone who dreamed of setting off for the frontier could do so, however. Unlike the

As the wagon cover and wooded landscape suggest, this emigrant was headed for Ohio during the 1840s. Often emigrants to the Far West had earlier migrated to other frontiers. It was thus no surprise that when they headed across the plains and prairies, they traveled in the same kinds of wagons that had served them before. (The Granger Collection, New York)

moves to earlier frontiers, the trip to the Far West involved considerable expense. The sea route, while probably the most comfortable, was the most costly. Guidebooks estimated that the trip around Cape Horn came to $600 per person. For the same sum, four people could make the overland trip. And if the emigrants sold their wagons and oxen at the journey's end, the final expenses might amount to only $220. Clearly, however, the initial financial outlay was considerable enough to rule out the trip for the very poor. Despite increasingly liberal land policies, migration to the Far West (with the exception of group migration to Utah) was a movement of middle-class Americans.

The Overland Trails

The trip started for most emigrants in the late spring when they left their homes and headed for

Overland Trails to the West

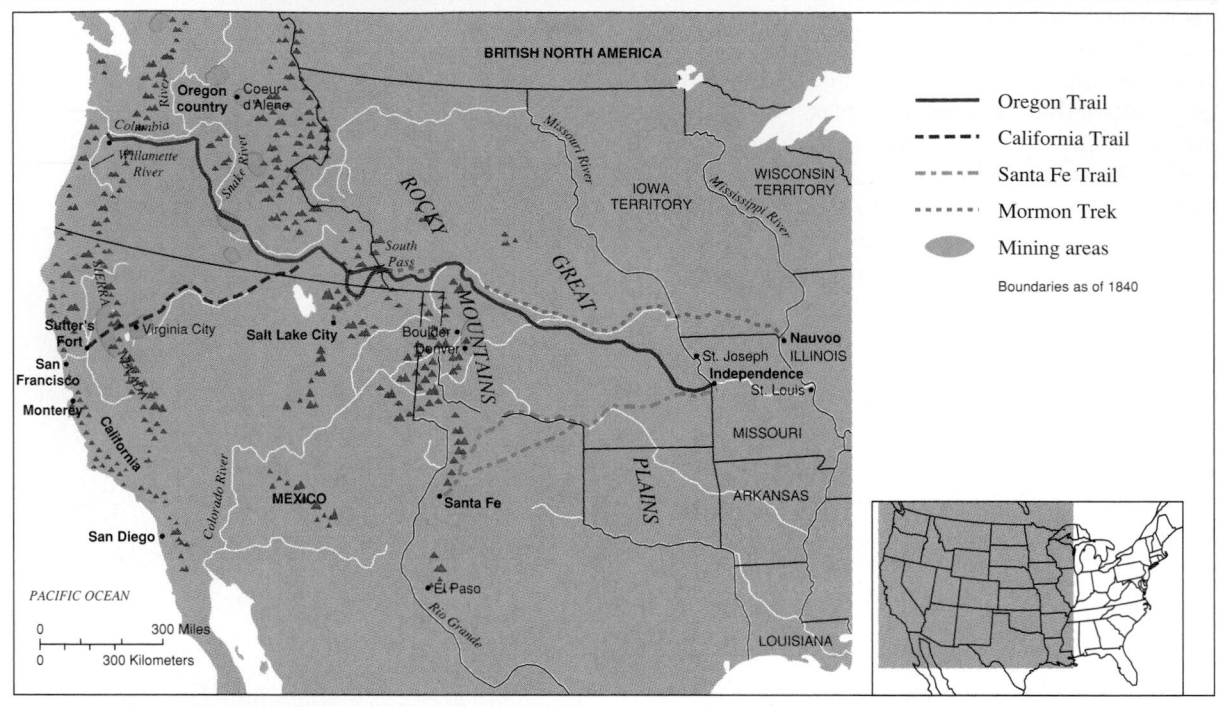

The various trails over which thousands of Americans traveled during the 1840s, 1850s, and 1860s are depicted on this map.

starting points in Iowa and Missouri: Council Bluffs, Independence, Westport, St. Joseph. There, companies of wagons gathered, and when grass was up for the stock, usually by the middle of May, they set out. Emigrant trains first followed the valley of the Platte River. Making only 15 miles a day, they slowly wound their way through the South Pass of the Rockies, heading for destinations in California or Oregon.

Emigrants found the first part of the trip novel and even enjoyable. The Indians, one woman noted, "proved better than represented"; some even helped emigrants cross rivers swollen by spring rains. The scenery, with its spring and early summer flowers, was new. Familiar chores were a challenge out in the open. The traditional division of labor known at home persisted. Generally, men did the "outdoor" work. They drove and repaired the wagons, ferried cattle and wagons across

rivers, hunted, and stood guard at night. Women labored at domestic chores, caring for children, cooking meals, and washing clothes. As they had at home, women procured small treats, trading with each other and with Indians for buffalo meat, fish, or moccasins. During travel, young children stayed out of the way in the wagons, while older brothers and sisters walked alongside and lent a hand to their elders. Many of the children later remembered the trip as an exciting adventure. Sometimes a day off from traveling provided a chance for fun. Wagon trains might stop to observe the Sabbath, allowing men and animals time to rest and women an opportunity to catch up on the laundry.

As the trip lengthened, difficulties multiplied. Cholera often took a heavy toll. Conflict with Indians became a problem only in the 1850s and made emigrants jumpy during the second half of the trip. (Between 1840 and 1860, Indians killed about 400 emigrants, most during the second half of the trip; the emigrants themselves killed at least that many Indians.) Traveling grew more arduous as deserts and mountains replaced rolling prairies.

Emigrants had to cross the final mountain ranges of the Sierras and the Cascades before the first snowfall, so there was a pressing need to push ever onward. Animals weakened by constant travel, poor feed, and bad water sickened, collapsed, and often died. As families faced the harsh realities of travel, they had to lighten their wagons by throwing out possessions lovingly brought from home. Food grew scarce.

The familiar division of responsibilities often broke down. Women found themselves driving wagons, loading them, even helping to drag them over rocky mountain trails. Their husbands worked frantically with the animals and the wagons as the time of the first snowfall drew closer. Tempers frayed among tired, overworked, and anxious families. Finally, five or six months after setting out, emigrants arrived, exhausted and often penniless, in Oregon or California. As one wrote on a September day in 1854, her journey had ended "which for care, fatigue, tediousness, perplexities and dangers of various kinds, can not be excelled."

The strains of the trip led some groups to draw up rules and elect officers. This did not prevent dissension, however. Many companies split because of arguments over the pace of travel or the number of rest stops or because some changed their minds about their eventual destination. Family harmony often collapsed under the strain of increased work loads, the irritations of travel, and crises of sickness and even death. Mary Power, who with her husband and three children crossed in 1853, revealed exasperation and depression in her journal: "I felt my courage must fail me, for there we were in a strange land, almost without anything to eat, [with] a team that was not able to pull an empty wagon." In a letter she was even more candid: "I felt as though myself and the little ones were at the mercy of a madman." Men, too, lost nerve as they confronted the hazards of travel. Oregon-bound John Minto described coming upon a father of four, "lying on his back upon a rock, taking the rain in his face, seemingly given up

all thought of manly struggle," while the cry of Indians sent some men in another train into their wagons to hide.

Living on the Frontier

When emigrants finally reached their destinations, their feelings ranged from acute disappointment to buoyant enthusiasm. But whether elated or depressed, they had no choice but to start anew. As they turned toward building a new life, they naturally drew on their experiences back East. "Pioneers though we are, and proud of it, we are not content with the wilds … with the idleness of the land, the rudely construct[ed] log cabin," one Oregon settler explained. "Pioneers are not that kind of folks."

The Agricultural Frontier

Pioneer farmers faced the urgent task of establishing their homesteads and beginning farming. First, the family had to locate a suitable claim. Clearing the land and constructing a crude shelter followed. Only then could crops be planted.

As farmers labored "to get the land subdued and the wilde nature out of it," they repeated a process that had occurred on earlier frontiers. Felling timber, pulling out native plants that seemed to have no value, and planting familiar crops began a transformation of the landscape (see Chapter 10). The results were often unanticipated. When they planted their crops, for example, farmers unknowingly introduced weeds whose seeds were mixed in with plant seeds from home. Some of the weeds, like the Canadian thistle, might do even better than the intended crops. Over time, the weeds could become much more than a nuisance to be pulled out of the ground. The Canadian thistle, for example, moved from field to pasture, where it gradually displaced grass and rendered the land useless for livestock grazing.

As they began their agricultural operations, emigrants did not recognize the ecological patterns that seem so clear to us today. The goal of taming nature was so central and the task so

This undated photograph of two emigrant wagons and their occupants gives a good idea of the family character of emigration and the limited space that was available for family possessions and items needed at the end of the trip. The presence of one adult male suggests that this picture depicts a Mormon husband, his two wives and their children on the way to Utah. (Denver Public Library, Western History Collection)

challenging that there was little time or inclination to question long-range consequences.

Because emigrants brought so few of their possessions west, the work of getting started was even more difficult than it would have been in the East. A young Oregon bride who set up housekeeping in the 1840s with only a stew kettle and three knives was not unusual. A letter from Sarah Everett to her sister-in-law in the East told the tale of hardship. Pleased with a gift of pretty trimmings, Sarah confessed, "I am a very old woman. My face is thin sunken and wrinkled, my hands bony and withered and hard—I shall look strangely I fear with your nice undersleeves and coquettish cherry bows." Sarah was 29 years old.

After months of intense interaction with other travelers, families were now alone on their claims. The typical frontier household consisted of parents with one to four children. Although frontier families might interact with nearby Indians, cultural biases made close friendships difficult. No wonder the pioneers often felt lonely and thought longingly of old friends. No wonder either that women helped men with their work and men assisted their wives in domestic chores such as washing.

For several years, such isolation was the rule. One pioneer remembered, "We were ... 'all told,' eleven families within a radius of six or eight miles, widely separated by our holdings and three hundred and twenty acres to each family. In those days anyone residing within twenty miles was considered a neighbor." But the isolation usually ended within a few years as most areas attracted new emigrants and old settlers seeking better claims.

As rural communities grew, settlers worked to establish schools, churches, and clubs. These organizations drew together people from different places and backgrounds and helped mold them into a new community. They also served to redefine acceptable forms of behavior and remind members of conventional standards and beliefs.

The determination to reestablish familiar institutions was most apparent in politics and law. In Oregon, for example, the pioneers set up a political system based on eastern models before the status of the territory was resolved. Before permanent schools or churches existed, men resumed the familiar political rituals of voting, electioneering, and talking politics. They were also going to court to resolve controversies and to ensure law and order. Although modern movies and novels suggest that violence was a part of everyday life on the frontier, this was not true on the farming frontier. Courts, rather than rough-and-ready vigilante groups, usually handled the occasional violence.

Setting up a common school system was more difficult and less urgent in the eyes of many frontier communities than beginning political life. Few settlers initially thought education important enough to tax themselves for permanent public schools. There were some schools, of course. But most operated sporadically and only for students who could pay at least part of the fees.

Various obstacles hindered organized religion. Although settlers often attended early church services no matter what the denomination, community growth proved a mixed blessing. When confirmed believers gathered in their own churches, they often discovered to their dismay that the congregation was too small to sustain the new church financially. Nor were converts plentiful, for many settlers had grown out of the habit of regular churchgoing. In early Seattle, Catherine and David Blaine were shocked. "Observation and experience have taught us since we left home," David remarked, "the unwelcome lesson that separation from gospel influences has rendered them quite indifferent to gospel truth." Catherine believed, "This is an awfully wicked country."

The chronic shortage of cash on the frontier retarded the growth of both schools and churches. Until farmers could send their goods to market, they had little cash to spare. Geographic mobility also contributed to institutional instability. Up to three-quarters of the population of a frontier county might vanish within a ten-year period as emigrants left to seek better land. Some farmed in as many as four locations until they found a satisfactory claim. Institutions relying on continuing personal and financial support suffered accordingly.

Yet even if their efforts to recreate familiar institutional life often faltered, settlers did not lose sight of their goals. Newspapers, journals, and books, which circulated early on the frontier, reinforced familiar values and norms and kept determination strong. As more and more settlers arrived, the numbers willing to support educational, religious, and cultural institutions grew. In the end, as one pioneer pointed out, "We have a telegraph line from the East, a daily rail road train, daily mail and I am beginning to feel quite civilized. And here ended my pioneer experience." Only 16 years had passed since she had crossed the Plains.

Although the belief in the frontier's special economic and social opportunities encouraged emigration, the dream was often illusory. Western society rapidly acquired a social and economic structure similar to that of the East. Frontier newspapers referred to leading settlers as the "better" sort, giving voice to an emerging world of social and economic distinctions. The appearance of workers for hire and tenant farmers also pointed to real economic differences and hinted at the difficulties those on the bottom would face as they tried to improve their situation.

Their widespread geographic mobility also indicates that many found it difficult to capitalize on the benefits of homesteading. Census data show that those who moved were generally less successful than the core of stable residents, who became the community's economic and social leaders. Of course, those on the move may have believed that fortune would finally smile on them at their next stop. But one wife was not so hopeful. When her husband announced that they were to move once again, she commented, "Perhaps I was not quite so enthusiastic as he. I seemed to have heard all this before."

The Mining Frontier

On the mining frontier, tales of prospectors who had reportedly struck it rich fueled the fantasies of fortune hunters. News of the discovery of gold in 1848 in California swept the country like "wildfire," according to one Missouri emigrant. Thousands raced to cash in on the bonanza. Within a year, California's population ballooned from 14,000 to almost 100,000. By 1852, that figure had more than doubled.

Like migrants to the agricultural frontier, the forty-niners were mostly young (in 1850, over half the people in California were in their twenties). Unlike pioneers headed for the rural frontier, however, the gold seekers were unmarried, predominantly male, and heterogeneous. Of those pouring into California in 1849, about 80 percent came from the United States, 8 percent from Mexico, and 5 percent from South America. The rest came from Europe and Asia. Few were as interested in settling the West as they were in extracting its precious metals and returning home rich.

Charles Nalil's 1856 painting Saturday Night at the Mines *creates a rather cozy picture of the men. But the presence of the bottle, the miners' rough clothing and beards, all show that the miners made little pretense of upholding eastern manners. Miners went west to get rich, not to advance civilization. (Stanford University Museum of Art, 12083, Gift of Jane Lathrop Stanford)*

California was the first and most dramatic of the western mining frontiers. But others sprang up. Rumors of gold propelled between 25,000 and 30,000 emigrants, many from California, to British Columbia in Canada in 1858. A year later, news of gold strikes in Colorado set off another frantic rush for fortune. Precious metals discovered in the Pacific Northwest early in the decade and in Montana and Idaho a few years later kept dreams alive and prospectors moving. In the mid-1870s, yet another discovery of gold, this time in the Black Hills of North Dakota, attracted hordes of fortune seekers.

The discovery of gold or silver spurred immediate, if usually short-lived, growth. In contrast to the agricultural frontier, where early settlers were isolated and the community expanded gradually, the mining frontier came to life almost overnight. Mining camps, ramshackle and often hastily constructed, soon housed hundreds or even thousands of miners and people serving them. Merchants, saloonkeepers, cooks, druggists, gamblers, and prostitutes hurried into boom areas as fast as prospectors. Usually, about half the residents of any mining camp were there to prospect the miners rather than the mines.

Given the motivation, character, and ethnic diversity of those flocking to boomtowns and the feeble attempts to set up local government in what were perceived as temporary communities, it was hardly surprising that mining life was often disorderly. Racial antagonism between American miners and foreigners, whom they labeled "greasers" (Mexicans), "chinks" (Chinese), "keskedees" (Frenchmen), and lesser "breeds," led to ugly riots and lynchings. Miners had few qualms about eliminating Indians and others who interfered with the race for riches. Fistfights, drunkenness, and murder occurred often enough to become part of the lore of the gold rush. Wrote one woman, "In the short space of twenty four days, we have had murders, fearful accidents, bloody deaths, a mob, whippings, a hanging, an attempt at suicide, and a fatal duel."

If mining life was usually not this violent, it tolerated behavior that would have been unacceptable farther east. Miners were not trying to recreate eastern communities, but to get rich. Married men, convinced of the raucous and immoral character of mining communities, hesitated to bring wives and families west. As one declared, "I would much prefer that a wife of mine should board in a respectable bawd house in the city of New York than live anywhere in the city of San Francisco."

Although the lucky few struck it rich or at least made enough money to return home with pride intact, miners' journals and letters reveal that many made only enough to keep going. Wrote one, "Everybody in the States who has friends here is always writing for them to come home. Now they all long to go home.... But it is hard for a man to leave ... with nothing.... I have no pile yet, but you can bet your life I will never come home until I have something more than when I started." The problem was that easily mined silver and gold deposits soon ran out. Although Chinese miners proved adept at finding what early miners overlooked, the remaining rich deposits lay deeply embedded in rock or gravel. Extraction required cooperative efforts, capital, technological experience, and expensive machinery. Eventually, mining became a corporate industrial concern, with miners as wage earners. As early as 1852, the changing nature of mining in California had transformed most of the shaggy miners into wage workers.

Probably 5 percent of early gold rush emigrants to California were women and children. Many of the women also anticipated getting "rich in a hurry." Because there were so few of them, the cooking, nursing, laundry, and hotel services women provided had a high value. When Luzena Wilson arrived in Sacramento, a miner offered to pay her $10 for a biscuit. That night, Luzena dreamt she saw "crowds of bearded miners striking gold from the earth with every blow of the pick, each one seeming to leave a share for me." Yet it was wearying work, and some wondered if the money compensated for the exhaustion. As Mary Ballou thought it over, she decided, "I would not advise any Lady to come out here and suffer to toil and fatigue I have suffered for the sake of a little gold." As men's profits shrank, so, too, did those of the women who served them.

Some of the first women to arrive on the mining frontier were prostitutes. They rejected the hard labor of cooking and washing that "respectable" women performed, hoping that the sex ratio would make their profession especially profitable. Prostitutes may have constituted as much as 20 percent of California's female population in 1850, and they probably vastly outnumbered other women in early mining camps. During boom days, they made good money and sometimes won a recognized place in society. But prostitutes always ran risks in a disorderly environment. They were more often the victims of murder and violence than the recipients of courtesy.

The Mexicans, South Americans, Chinese, and small numbers of blacks seeking their fortunes in California soon discovered that although they contributed substantially to California's growth, racial discrimination flourished vigorously in the land of golden promise. At first, American miners hoped to force foreigners out of the gold fields altogether. But an attempt to declare mining illegal for all foreigners failed. A high tax on foreign miners proved more successful. Thousands of Mexicans left the mines, while the Chinese found other jobs in San Francisco and Sacramento. As business stagnated in mining towns, however, white miners had second thoughts about the levy and reduced it. By 1870, when the tax was declared unconstitutional, the Chinese, who had paid 85 percent of it, had "contributed" $5 million to California for the right to prospect. The hostility that led to this legislation also fed widespread violence against the Chinese and Mexicans.

Black Americans found that their skin color placed them in a situation akin to that of foreigners. Deprived of the vote, forbidden to testify in civil or criminal cases involving whites, excluded from the bounties of the state's homestead law, blacks led a precarious existence. When news arrived of the discovery of gold in British Columbia in the late 1850s, hundreds of blacks as well as

This 1852 photograph of miners and the constructions they built on the American River hints at some of the environmental consequences of mining activity. The formal clothing of the woman contrasts sharply with that worn by the men and suggests that she has not forgotten the standards of civilized life. (California State Library)

thousands of Chinese left the state hoping that the Canadian frontier would be more hospitable than California.

Alluring as the mining frontier was, men's and women's fantasies of dazzling riches rarely came true. The ghost towns of the West testify to the typical pattern: boom, bust, decay, death. The empty streets and rotting buildings stood as symbols of dashed hopes and disappointed dreams. Also left behind were other physical signs recalling the presence and passing of the mining frontier. Mining operations left an indelible mark on the land. Forests were decimated to provide timber for the flumes miners constructed to divert rivers from their channels in the hopes of exposing rich gold deposits in the dry river beds. They built slurries and ditches and created mounds of debris that during floods or heavy rains oozed over fields and

choked rivers and streams. Consumed by visions of glittering metal, miners were blind to the realities of eroding soil, deforested mountains, diverted waterways, and silt.

It was difficult, however, to recognize some of the negative consequences of the discovery of gold, for it had many positive effects on the West as a whole. Between 1848 and 1883, California mines supplied two-thirds of the country's gold. Gold transformed San Francisco from a sleepy town into a bustling metropolis. It fueled the agricultural and commercial development of California and Oregon, as miners provided a market for goods and services. Gold built harbors, railroads, and irrigation systems not just in California and Oregon but all over the West. Though few people made large fortunes, both the region and the nation profited from gold.

This picture of the near ghost town of Ophir City, Nevada, taken in the 1870s, points to the way the mining frontier left its mark on the landscape and suggests the unstable nature of the mining frontier. (Denver Public Library, Western History Department)

The Mormon Frontier

In the decades before 1860, many emigrants heading for the Far West stopped to rest and buy supplies in Salt Lake City, the heart of the Mormon state of Deseret. There they encountered a society that seemed familiar and orderly, yet foreign and shocking. Visitors admired the attractively laid out town with its irrigation ditches, gardens, and tidy houses. But as they noted the decorous nature of everyday life, they gossiped about polygamy and searched for signs of rebellion in the faces of Mormon women. Emigrants who opposed slavery were fond of equating the position of the Mormon wife with that of the black slave. They were amazed that so few Mormon women seemed interested in escaping from the bonds of plural marriage.

Violent events had driven the Mormons to the arid Great Basin area. Joseph Smith's murder in 1844 marked no end to the persecution of his fol-

lowers. By the fall of 1846, angry mobs had chased the last of the "Saints" out of Nauvoo, Illinois. As they struggled to join their advance groups at temporary camps in Iowa, Smith's successor, Brigham Young, realized that flight from the United States represented the best hope for survival. The Saints must create the kingdom of God anew, somewhere in the West, far removed from the United States, that "Babylon" of corruption and injustice.

The Mexican-American war unexpectedly furthered Mormon plans. At first, most Mormons probably agreed with Hosea Stout, who was glad "to learn of the war," hoping it "might never end until the States were entirely destroyed, for they had driven us into the wilderness, and now were laughing at our calamities." But Brigham Young realized that war might provide capital needed for the new Mormon kingdom. By raising 500 Mormon young men for Kearney's Army of the West, Young acquired vital resources. The battalion's advance pay bought wagonloads of supplies

C. A. A. Christensen painted this picture of the Mormon Temple in Nauvoo, Illinois, in 1844. Despite the dignified and substantial nature of the building, which almost could be an academy or a New England church, the Mormons appeared to their neighbors to harbor unacceptable and un-American ideas. (Museum of Art, Brigham Young University)

for starving and sick Mormons strung out along the trail between Missouri and Iowa and helped finance the impending great migration.

Young selected the Great Basin area, technically part of Mexico, as the best site for his future kingdom. It was arid and remote, 1,000 miles from its nearest "civilized" neighbors. But if irrigated, Mormon leaders concluded it might prove as fertile as the fields and vineyards of ancient Israel.

In April 1847, Young led an exploratory expedition of 143 men, 3 women, and 2 children to this promised land. In late July, after reaching Salt Lake, Young exclaimed, "This is the place." Before returning to Iowa to prepare Mormons for the trip to Utah, he announced his land policy. Settlers would receive virtually free land on the basis of a family's size and its ability to cultivate it. After Young left, the expeditionary group followed his directions to construct irrigation ditches and begin planting.

The following months and years tested Young's organizational talents and his followers' cooperative abilities. By September 1847, fully 566 wagons and 1,500 of the Saints had made the arduous trek to Salt Lake City. Still more Mormons came the next year, inspired by visions of a new Zion in the West. Their trip was also a collective venture, planned and directed by Church leaders. By 1850, the Mormon frontier had attracted over 11,000 settlers. Missionary efforts in the United States and abroad, especially in Great Britain and Scandinavia, drew thousands of converts to the Great Basin. The Church emigration society and a loan fund facilitated the journey for many who could never have otherwise undertaken the trip. By the end of the decade, over 30,000 Saints lived in Utah, not only in Salt Lake City, but also in more than 90 village colonies Young had planned. Though hardship marked these early years, the Mormons thrived. As one early settler remarked, "We have everything around us we could ask."

Non-Mormon, or "Gentile," emigrants passing through Utah found much that was recognizable. The government had familiar characteristics. Most Mormons were farmers; many of them came originally from New England and the Midwest and shared many of the same customs and attitudes. But outsiders perceived profound differences, for the heart of Mormon society was not the individual farmer living on his own homestead, but the cooperative village.

Years of persecution had nourished a strong sense of group identity and acceptance of Church leadership. Organized by the Church leaders, who made the essential decisions, farming became a collective enterprise. All farmers were allotted land. All had irrigation rights, for water did not belong to individuals but to the community. During Sunday services, the local bishop might give farming instructions to his congregation along with his sermon. As Young explained, "I have looked upon the community of Latter-day Saints in a vision and beheld them organized as the great family of heaven, each person performing his several duties in his line of industry, working for the good of the whole more than for individual aggrandizement." In this vast communal effort, every Mormon was expected to work for success, men and women alike. "We do not believe in having any drones in the hive," one woman said tartly.

The Church was omnipresent in Utah; in fact, nothing separated Church and state. Despite familiar governmental forms, Church leaders occupied all important political posts. Brigham Young's Governing Quorum contained the high priests of the Church, who made both religious and political decisions.

When it became clear that Utah would become a territory, Mormon leaders drew up a constitution that divided religious and political power. But once in place, powers overlapped. As one Gentile pointed out, "This intimate connection of church and state seems to pervade everything that is done. The supreme power in both being lodged in the hands of the same individuals, it is difficult to separate their two official characters, and to determine whether in any one instance they act as spiritual or merely temporal officers."

The Treaty of Guadalupe Hidalgo officially incorporated Utah into the United States, but little affected political and religious arrangements. Brigham Young became territorial governor. Local bishops continued to act as spiritual leaders as well as civil magistrates in Mormon communities. Mormons had come to Utah to establish a kingdom rather than a republic. Their motives dictated the unique politicoreligious nature of the Utah experience.

Other aspects of the Mormon frontier were distinctive. Mormon policy toward the Indian tribes was remarkably enlightened. As one prominent Mormon pointed out, "It has been our habit to shoot Indians with tobacco and bread biscuits rather than with powder and lead, and we are most successful with them." After two expeditions against the Timpanagos and Shoshone in 1850, Mormons concentrated on converting rather than killing Native Americans. Mormon missionaries learned Bannock, Ute, Navajo, and Hopi languages in order to bring the faith to these tribes. They also encouraged Native Americans to ranch and farm.

Although most Gentiles could tolerate some of the differences they encountered on the Mormon frontier, few could accept polygamy and the seemingly immoral extended family structure that plural marriage entailed. Although Joseph Smith and other Church leaders had secretly practiced polygamy in the early 1840s, Brigham Young publicly revealed the doctrine only in 1852, when the Saints were safely in Utah. Smith believed that the highest or "celestial" form of marriage brought special rewards in the afterlife. Because wives and children contributed to these rewards, polygamy was a means of sanctification. From a practical standpoint, polygamy served to incorporate into Mormon society single female converts who had left their families to come to Utah.

Although most Mormons accepted the doctrine and its religious justification, some found it hard to follow. One woman called it a "great trial of feelings." Actually, relatively few families were polygamous. During the 40-year period in which Mormons practiced plural marriage, only 10 to 20 percent of Mormon families were polygamous. Few men had more than two wives. Because of the expense of maintaining several families and the personal strains involved, usually only the most successful and visible Mormon leaders practiced polygamy.

Polygamous family life was a far cry from the lascivious arrangement outsiders fantasized. Jealousy among wives could destroy the institution of plural marriage, so Mormon leaders minimized the role of romantic love and sexual attraction in courtship and marriage. Instead, they encouraged marriages founded on mutual attachment, with sex for the purposes of procreation rather than pleasure.

To the shock of outsiders, Mormon women did not consider themselves slaves, but rather highly regarded members of the Mormon community. Whether plural wives or not, they saw polygamy as the cutting edge of their society and defended it to the outside world. Polygamy was preferable to monogamy, which left the single woman without the economic and social protection of family life and forced some of them into prostitution, Brenda

Pratt explained. "Polygamy … tends directly to the chastity of women, and the sound health and morals … of their children."

Although they faced obvious difficulties, many plural wives found rewards in polygamy. Without the constant presence of husbands, they had an unusual opportunity for independence. Many treated husbands when they visited as revered friends; their children, not their spouses, provided them with day-to-day emotional satisfaction. Occasionally, plural wives lived together and shared domestic work, becoming close friends. As one such wife put it, "We three … loved each other more than sisters" and would "go hand in hand together down till eternity."

Although the Mormon frontier seemed alien to outsiders, it succeeded in terms of its numbers, its growing economic prosperity, and its group unity. Long-term threats loomed for this community, however, once the area became part of the United States. Attacks on Young's power as well as heated verbal denunciations of polygamy proliferated. Efforts began in Congress to outlaw polygamy. In the years before the Civil War, Mormons withstood these assaults on their way of life. But as Utah became more connected to the rest of the country, the tide would turn against them.

The Urban Frontier

Many emigrants went west not to claim farmland or to pan for gold, but rather to settle in cities like San Francisco, Denver, and Portland. There they hoped to find business and professional opportunities or, perhaps, the chance to make a fortune by speculating in town lots.

Cities were an integral part of frontier life and, in some cases, preceded agricultural settlement. Some communities turned into bustling cities as they catered to the emigrant trade. St. Joseph, Missouri, outfitted families setting out on the overland journey. Salt Lake City offered weary pioneers headed for California an opportunity to rest and restock. Portland was the destination of many emigrants and became a market and supply center for homesteaders.

Some cities grew so rapidly that they have been called "instant cities." San Francisco and Denver turned into cities almost overnight; in a mere 12 years, San Francisco's population zoomed from 812 to 56,802. The discovery of precious metals sent thousands of miners with diverse demands and desires to and through these places. And once the strike ran out, many miners returned to these cities to make a new start. Still other

Oregon City, pictured here in 1857, still has an unfinished appearance. But the presence of frame houses and town lots shows the determination of settlers to recreate familiar patterns of life in the West. (Oregon Historical Society)

places supplied frontier farmers and served as their markets. They only gradually acquired urban characteristics.

Commercial life bustled on the urban frontier, offering residents a wide range of occupations and services. As a Portland emigrant remarked in 1852, only a few years after that community's beginning, "In many ways life here ... was more primitive than it was in the early times in Illinois and Missouri. But in others it was far more advanced.... We could get the world's commodities here which could not be had then, or scarcely at all, in the interior of Illinois or Missouri."

Young, single men seeking their fortunes made up a disproportionate share of the urban population. Frontier Portland had more than three men for every woman. Predictably, urban life was often noisy, rowdy, and occasionally violent. The presence of so many young men could not help but affect urban family life. Mothers worried that their children would fall into bad company. Some attempted to reform the atmosphere by pressing for Sunday store closings or prohibition. Other women, of course, enjoyed all the attention that came with the presence of so many young men. As one observed with gusto, "There is plenty of men here. They cast sheeps eyes at Lib and Lucy's girl but have not popt the question yet." Eventually, the sex ratio became balanced, but as late as 1880, fully 18 of the 24 largest western cities had more men than women.

Although western cities began with distinctive characters, they soon resembled eastern cities. As a western publication boasted, "Transport a resident of an Eastern city and put him down in the streets of Portland, and he would observe little difference between his new surroundings and those he beheld but a moment before in his native city."

The history of Portland suggests the common pattern of development. In 1845, Portland was only a clearing in the forest, large enough for four streets and 16 blocks. Speculation in town lots was lively. By the early 1850s, Portland had grown into a small trading center with a few rough log structures and muddy tracks for streets. As farmers poured into Oregon, the city became a regional commercial center. More permanent structures were built, giving the city an "eastern" appearance.

This 1853 view of San Francisco reveals the rapid transformation of the city. Brick buildings, several stories high, with elaborate cornices, board sidewalks, kerosene street lamps, and the inevitable grid street pattern give San Francisco the appearance of an eastern city rather than a raw western community, only four years after the gold rush. (The Bancroft Library, University of California, Berkeley)

The belief that urban life in the West abounded with special opportunities initially drew many young men to Portland and other western cities. Many of them did not find financial success there. Opportunities were greatest for newcomers who brought assets with them. These residents became the elite of the community. By the 1860s, when the city's population had reached 2,874, Portland's Social Club symbolized the emergence of that city's elite. Portland's businessmen, lawyers, and editors controlled an increasing share of the community's wealth and set its social standards. Their elaborate parties, summer trips, and exclusive clubs showed how far Portland had come from its raw frontier beginnings.

Cultures in Conflict

Looking at westward expansion through the eyes of white emigrants provides only one view of the frontier experience. An entry from an Oregon Trail journal suggests other perspectives. On May 7, 1864, Mary Warner, a bride of only a few months, described a frightening event. That day, a "fine-looking" Indian had visited the wagon train and tried to buy her. Mary's husband, probably uncertain how to handle the situation, played along, agreeing to trade his wife for two ponies. The Indian generously offered three. "Then," wrote Mary, "he took hold of my shawl to make me understand to get out [of the wagon]. About this time I got frightened and really was so hysterical [that] I began to cry." Everyone laughed at her, she reported, though surely the Indian found the whole incident no more amusing than she had.

This ordinary encounter on the overland trail only begins to hint at the social and cultural differences separating white Americans moving west and the peoples with whom they came into contact. Confident of their values and rights, emigrants had little regard for those who had lived in the West for centuries and no compunction in seizing their lands. Many even predicted that the Indian race would disappear from the continent, a just reward for tribal "degeneracy."

Confronting the Plains Tribes

During the 1840s, white Americans, for the first time, came into extensive contact with the powerful Plains tribes, whose culture differed from that of the more familiar eastern Woodlands tribes. Probably a quarter million Native Americans occupied the area from the Rocky Mountains to the Missouri River and from the Platte River to New Mexico. Nearest the Missouri and Iowa frontier lived the "border" tribes—the Pawnee, Omaha, Oto, Ponca, and Kansa. These Indians, unlike other Plains tribes, lived in villages and raised crops, though they supplemented their diet with buffalo meat during the summer months. On the Central Plains lived the Brulé and Oglala Sioux, the Cheyenne, the Shoshone, and the Arapaho, aggressive tribes who followed the buffalo and often raided the border tribes. In the Southwest were the Comanche, Ute, Navajo, and some Apache bands, and the Kiowa, Wichita, Apache, and southern Comanche claimed northern and western Texas as their hunting grounds. Many of the southwestern tribes had adopted aspects of Spanish culture and European domestic animals like cattle, sheep, and horses.

Although there were differences between the Plains tribes, they shared certain characteristics. Most had adopted a nomadic way of life after the introduction of Spanish horses in the sixteenth century increased their seasonal mobility from 50 to 500 miles. Horses allowed Indian braves to hunt the buffalo with such success that tribes (with the exclusion of the border groups) came to depend on the beasts for food, clothing, fuel, teepee dwellings, and trading purposes. Because women were responsible for processing buffalo products, some men had more than one wife to tan skins for trading.

Mobility also increased tribal contact and conflict. War played a central part in the lives of the Plains tribes. No male became a fully accepted member of his tribe until he had proved himself in battle. But tribal warfare was not like the warfare of white men. Indians sought not to exterminate their enemies or to claim territory, but rather to steal horses and to prove individual prowess. They considered it braver to touch an enemy than to kill or scalp him. This pattern of conflict on the Plains discouraged political unity. Moreover, individual tribes were loosely organized. Chiefs enjoyed only limited authority over their followers. As Chief Low Horn, a Blackfoot, explained, chiefs "could not restrain their young men ... their young men were wild, and ambitious, in their turn to be braves and chiefs. They wanted by some brave act to win the favor of their young women, and bring scalps and horses to show their prowess."

Armed with guns, mounted on fast ponies, and skilled in warfare and raiding, the Plains tribes, though disunified, posed a fearsome obstacle to white expansion. They had signed no treaties with the United States and had few friendly feelings toward whites. Their contact with white soci-

Indian Tribes in 1840

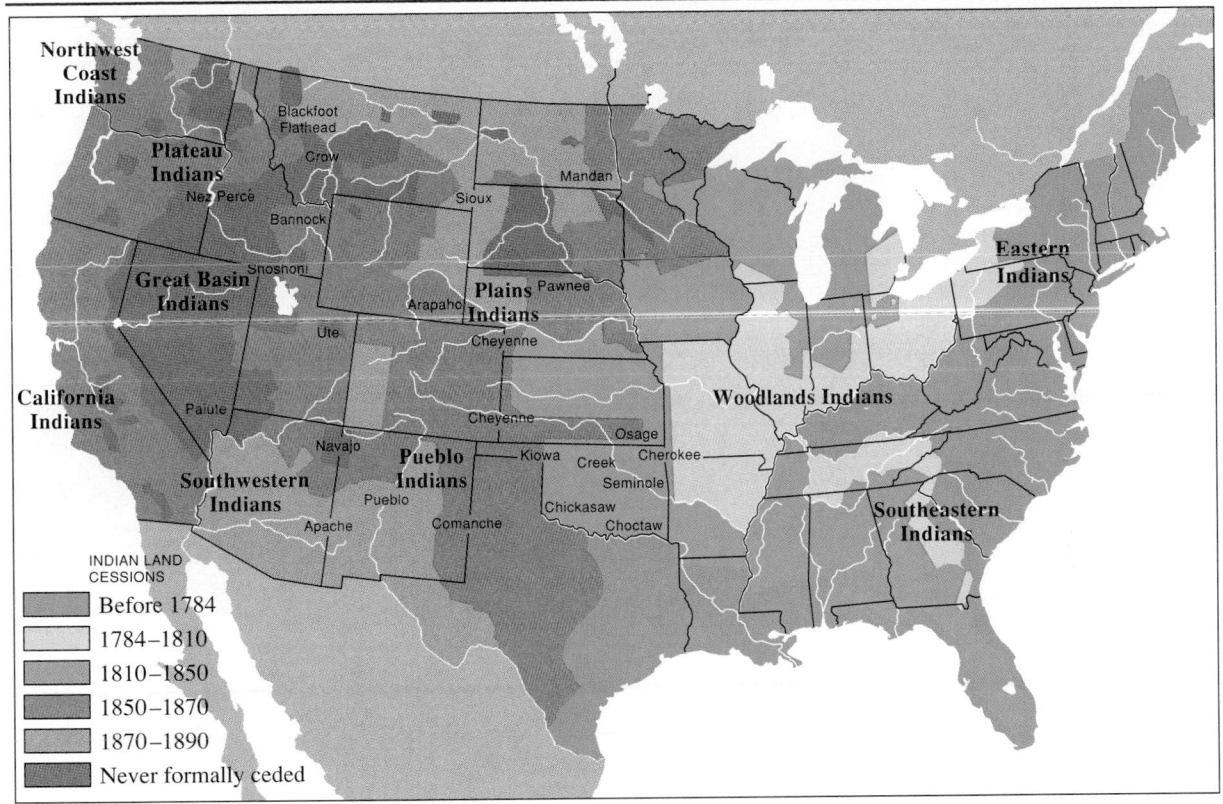

Although this map reveals the location of groups of Indian tribes in 1840, it presents too static a picture of tribal territories. Some of the Indian groups in the West had been forced across the Mississippi by events in the Midwest. What the map does make obvious, however, is the rapid pace of Indian land cessions in the nineteenth century.

ety had brought gains through trade in skins, but the trade had also brought alcohol and destructive epidemics of smallpox and scarlet fever.

When the first emigrants drove their wagons across the plains and prairies in the early 1840s, relations between Indians and whites were peaceable. But the intrusion of whites set in motion an environmental cycle that eventually drew the two groups into conflict. Indian tribes depended on the buffalo but respected this source of life. The Teton Sioux performed rituals to ensure a continuing supply of the animals, while hunters often ritualistically apologized to the Great Unseen Buffalo for slaughtering what the tribe needed. The grasses that nourished the buffalo also sustained the Indians' own ponies and the animals that supported horse traders like the Cheyenne.

Whites, however, fed their oxen and horses on the grass both the Indians' ponies and the buffalo needed. And they adopted the "most exciting sport," the buffalo hunt. As the great herds began to shrink, Native American tribes began to battle one another for hunting grounds and food. The powerful Sioux swooped down into the hunting grounds of their enemies and mounted destructive raids against the Pawnee and other smaller tribes. In an 1846 petition to President Polk, the Sioux explained that "for several years past the Emigrants going over the Mountains from the United States, have been the cause that Buffalo have in great measure left our hunting grounds, thereby causing us to go into the Country of Our Enemies to hunt, exposing our lives daily for the necessary subsistence of our wives and Children and getting killed on several occasions." Despite

Alfred Jacob Miller, like Albert Bierstadt, whose painting appears at the chapter's opening, was fascinated with the trans-Mississippi West. Miller's 1836 depiction of a Plains Indian throwing a lasso preceded the great wave of white migration that so disrupted native life. Most artists who sketched and painted scenes like the one here anticipated that native culture would disappear with the coming of the whites. (The Beinecke Rare Book and Manuscript Library, Yale University Library)

their difficulties, the Sioux had "all along treated the Emigrants in the most friendly manner, giving them free passage through our hunting grounds."

The Sioux requested compensation for damages caused by whites. When the president denied their request, they tried to extract taxes from the emigrants passing over their lands. Emigrants were outraged at what they considered Indian effrontery. After all, the United States had won these lands. Frontier newspapers printed letters denouncing the Sioux, demanding adequate protection for travelers and some chastening of the "savages." However, little was done to relieve the suffering of the tribes bearing the brunt of Sioux aggression, the dismay of the Sioux at the white invasion, or the fears of the emigrants themselves.

The discovery of gold in California, which lured over 20,000 across the Plains in 1849 alone, became the catalyst for federal action. The vast numbers of gold seekers and their animals wrought such devastation in the Platte valley that it rapidly became a wasteland for the Indians. The dreaded cholera that whites carried with them spread to the Indians, killing thousands.

To meet the crisis, government officials devised a two-pronged plan. The government would construct a chain of forts to protect emigrants and, simultaneously, call the tribes to a general conference. Officials expected that in return for generous presents, Indians would end tribal warfare and limit their movements to prescribed areas. They instructed tribes to select chiefs to speak for them at the conference.

The Fort Laramie Council, 1851

In 1851, the council convened at Fort Laramie. As many as 10,000 Indians, hopeful of ending the destruction of their way of life and eager for the promised presents, gathered at the fort. Tribal animosities simmered, however. Skirmishes occurred on the way to the fort, and the border tribes, fearful of the Sioux, declined to participate. The Comanche, Kiowa, and Apache also refused to come, because their enemies, the Sioux and the Crow, were to be there.

At the conference, whites told the gathered tribes that times had changed. In the past, "you had plenty of buffalo and game ... and your Great Father well knows that war has always been your favorite amusement and pursuit. He then left the question of peace and war to yourselves. Now, since the settling of the districts West ... by the white men, your condition has changed." There would be compensation for the destruction of their grass, timber, and buffalo and annual payments of goods and services. But in return, the tribes had to give up their rights of free movement. The government drew tribal boundaries, and chiefs made promises to stay within them. In most cases, some tribal lands were sold.

The Fort Laramie Treaty was the first agreement between the Plains tribes and the United States government. It expressed the conviction of whites that Indians must stay in clearly defined areas apart from white civilization.

But this system of isolation and its purported benefits were still in the future. During the conference, ominous signs appeared that more trouble would precede any "resolution" of Indian-white affairs. Sioux Chief Black Hawk told whites, "You have split the country and I do not like it." His powerful tribe refused to be restricted to lands north of the Platte, for south of the river lay their recently conquered lands. "These lands once belonged to the Kiowas and the Crows," one Sioux explained, "but we whipped those nations out of them and in this we did what the white men do when they want the lands of the Indians." The words suggested that Indians, despite agreements, would not willingly abandon their traditional way of life for confinement. In the following years, it would become evident that Americans and Sioux had conflicting interests south of the Platte. Elsewhere in the trans-Mississippi West, other tribes, like the fierce Navajo of New Mexico, also resisted white attempts to confine them.

Overwhelming the Mexicans

In the Southwest, in Texas, and in California, Americans encountered a Spanish-speaking population and Hispanic culture. Expansionist Lewis Cass expressed Americans' scorn for both. Speaking in a congressional debate on the annexation of New Mexico, Cass stated, "We do not want the people of Mexico, either as citizens or as subjects. All we want is a portion of territory ... with a population, which would soon recede, or identify itself with ours." Americans regarded Mexicans as lazy, ignorant, and cunning, the "dregs of society." Although Mexicans easily recognized such cultural arrogance, they lacked the numbers to fend off American aggression.

Although Anglo-Mexican interaction differed from place to place, few Anglos heeded the Treaty of Guadalupe Hidalgo's assurances that Mexicans would have citizens' rights and the "free enjoyment of their liberty and property." The greatest numbers of Spanish-speaking people lived in New Mexico, and, of all former Mexican citizens, they probably fared the best. Most were of mixed blood, living marginally as ranch hands for rich landowners or as farmers and herdsmen in small villages dominated by a *patron,* or headman. As the century wore on, Americans produced legal titles and took over lands long occupied by peasant farmers and stock raisers. But despite economic reversals, New Mexicans survived, carrying their rural culture well into the twentieth century.

Light-skinned, upper-class landowners fared better. Even before the conquest, rich New Mexicans had protected their future by establishing contracts with American businessmen and by sending their sons east to American schools. When the United States annexed New Mexico, this substantial and powerful class contracted strategic marriage and business alliances with the Anglo men who slowly trickled into the territory. During the 1850s, they maintained their influence and prestige and their American connections. Only rarely did they bother with the plight of their poor countrymen. Class outweighed ethnic or cultural considerations.

In Texas, the Spanish-speaking residents, only 10 percent of the population in 1840, shrank to a mere 6 percent by 1860. Although the upper class also intermarried with Americans, they lost most of their power, as Germans, Irish, French, and Americans poured into the state. Poor, dark-skinned Hispanics clustered in low-paying and largely unskilled jobs.

In California, the discovery of gold radically changed the situation for the Californios. In 1848, there were 7,000 Californios and about twice as many Anglos. By 1860, the Anglo population had ballooned to 360,000. Hispanic-Americans were hard-pressed to cope with the rapid influx of outsiders. At first, Californios and several thousand Mexicans from Sonora joined Anglos and others in the gold fields. But competition there fed antagonism and finally open conflict. Posters warned foreigners out of the gold fields. In Anglo eyes, one Hispanic was much like another, even if one claimed to be a Californio with political rights and another a Sonoran. Taxes and terrorism ultimately succeeded in forcing most Spanish speakers out of the mines and established the racial contours of the new California.

Other changes were even more disastrous. In 1851, Congress passed the Gwinn Land Law, supposedly a measure for validating Spanish and Mexican land titles. The law violated the pledge contained in a Statement of Protocol accompanying the Treaty of Guadalupe Hidalgo that stated the government "did not in any way" intend to annul the grants of lands made by Mexico, for it forced California landowners to defend what was already theirs and encouraged squatters to settle on land in the hopes that the Californios' titles would prove false. It took an average of 17 years to establish clear title to land. The process was slow and unfamiliar. As one woman explained, her mother had been "totally unprepared for the problems that came with American rule. Not only was the language foreign to her, but also the concept of property taxes, mortgages and land title regulations." Landowners found themselves paying American lawyers large fees, often in land, and borrowing at high interest rates to pay for court proceedings. A victory at court often turned into a defeat when legal

This painting presents an idyllic picture of the lives of the elite Mexican landowners. Their way of life would disappear with the arrival of hordes of American settlers. Both the former elite and more ordinary Mexicans would find themselves, in the words of Pablo la Guerra, "foreigners in their own land." (Charles Christian Nahl, The Fandango, *1873/Crocker Art Museum, E. B. Crocker Collection, Sacramento, California.)*

expenses forced owners to sell their lands to pay debts. In the South, where Anglos judged land less valuable than in the mining North, the process of dispossession was slower. But by the early 1860s, the ranching class there had also lost most of its extensive holdings and slid into relative poverty.

Working-class Hispanic-Americans became laborers for Anglo farmers or for mining and later railroad companies. They herded cattle on American ranches or dug irrigation ditches. Whatever their employment, Hispanic-Americans earned less and did more unpleasant jobs than Anglo workers. For them, the coming of the Anglos presented not opportunity, but a steadily deteriorating situation. By 1870, the average Hispanic-American worker's property was worth only about a third of its value of 20 years earlier. As newspaper editor and champion of the Mexican-American cause, Francisco Ramírez pointed out in the Los Angeles newspaper *El Clamor Publico* in 1856, "California has fallen into the hands of the ambitious sons of North America who will not stop until they have satisfied their passions, by driving the first occupants of the land out of the country, villifying their religion and disfiguring their customs."

Western movies and novels have played a large role in forming images of the nineteenth-century West. Cowboys, sheriffs, outlaws, and bandits gallop across screens and pages. One of these outlaws, a sombrero-clad rider, points to the reality of resistance to American expansion into the Southwest. The career of Tiburcio Vásquez, a notorious *bandido* in southern California, shows that some Hispanics felt that they could protest events only through violence:

> My career grew out of the circumstances by which I was surrounded.... As I grew to manhood I was in the habit of attending balls and parties given by the native Californians, into which the Americans, then beginning to become numerous, would force themselves and shove the native born men aside, monopolizing the dance and the women. This was about 1852. A spirit of hatred and revenge took possession of me. I had numerous fights in defense of my countrywomen. The officers were continually in pursuit of me. I believed we were unjustly and wrongfully deprived of the social rights that belonged to us.

TIMELINE

1803–1806	Lewis and Clark expedition
1818	Treaty on joint U.S.-British occupation of Oregon
1819	Spain cedes Spanish territory in United States and sets transcontinental boundary of Louisiana Purchase, excluding Texas
1821	Mexican independence
	Opening of Santa Fe Trail
	Stephen Austin leads American settlement of Texas
1821–1840	Indian removals
1830	Mexico abolishes slavery in Texas
1836	Texas declares independence
	Battles of the Alamo and San Jacinto
1840s	Emigrant crossings of Overland Trail
1844	James Polk elected president
1845	"Manifest Destiny" coined
	United States annexes Texas and sends troops to the Rio Grande
	Americans attempt to buy Upper California and New Mexico
1846	Mexico declares defensive war
	United States declares war and takes Santa Fe
	Resolution of Oregon question
1847	Attacks on Veracruz and Mexico City
	Mormon migration to Utah begins
1848	Treaty of Guadalupe Hidalgo
1849	California gold rush begins
1850	California admitted to the Union
1851	Fort Laramie Treaty
1853	Gadsden Purchase
1862	Homestead Act

Other Hispanics resorted to other tactics. In New Mexico, members of Las Gorras Blancas ripped up railroad ties and cut the barbed-wire fences of Anglo ranchers and farmers. The religiously oriented Penitentes tried to work through the ballot box. Ordinary men, women, and children resisted efforts to convert them to Protestantism and learned some of the skills they hoped would enable them to flourish in a changing culture while retaining many of their familiar customs and beliefs.

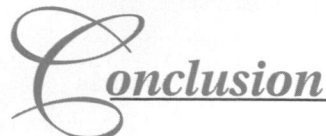

Conclusion

Fruits of Manifest Destiny

Like Lewis Cass, many nineteenth-century Americans were convinced that the country had merely gained western territories to which it was entitled. Although the process of acquiring the western half of the continent was swift, the prospect of winning the West loomed large in the imagination of the American people for many years. A number of western settlers became folk heroes. All white Americans could be thankful for the special opportunities, the new chance for success, that the West seemed to offer.

The expanding nation did gain vast natural wealth in the trans-Mississippi West. But only a small fraction of the hopeful emigrants heading for the frontier realized their dreams of success. And the move west had a dark side as Americans clashed with Mexicans and Native Americans in their drive to fulfill their "Manifest Destiny" and as the acquisition of new territories fueled the controversy over the future of slavery.

Recommended Reading

Overviews

Ray Allen Billington, *America's Frontier Heritage* (1966) and *The Far Western Frontier, 1830–1860* (1965); Patricia Nelson Limerick, *The Legacy of Conquest: The Unbroken Past of the American West* (1987); Lawrence H. Larson, *The Urban West at the End of the Frontier* (1978); David Hamer, *New Towns in the New World: Images and Perceptions of the Nineteenth-Century Frontier* (1990); William H. Troettner, *The West as America: Reinterpreting Images of the Frontier, 1820–1920* (1991); William Cronon, George Miles, and Jay Gitlin, eds., *Under An Open Sky: Rethinking America's Western Past* (1992).

Manifest Destiny and Its Fruits

Frederick Merk, *Manifest Destiny and Mission in American History* (1963); Norman A. Graebner, ed., *Manifest Destiny* (1968); Gene Brack, *Mexico Views Manifest Destiny, 1821–1846* (1975); Cecil Robinson, ed., *The View From Chapultepec: Mexican Writers on the Mexican-American War* (1989); Robert W. Johanssen, *To the Halls of Montezuma: The Mexican War in the American Imagination* (1985); Robert H. Ferrell, ed., *Monterrey Is Ours! The Mexican War Letters of Lieutenant Dana,*

1845–1847 (1990); David J. Weber, *The Mexican Frontier, 1821–1846* (1982); Neal Harlow, *California Conquered* (1982); Theodore J. Karamanski, *Fur Trade and Exploration: Opening the Far Northwest, 1821–1852* (1983); David Pletcher, *The Diplomacy of Annexation: Texas, Oregon, and the Mexican War* (1973); K. Jack Bauer, *Zachary Taylor* (1985); Ernest M. Lander, Jr., *Reluctant Imperialists: Calhoun, the South Carolinians, and the Mexican War* (1980); Anders Stephanson, *Manifest Destiny: American Expansionism and the Empire of Right* (1995).

Native Americans

George Pierre Castile, *North American Indians: An Introduction to the Chichimeca* (1979); Sylvia Van Kirk, *Many Tender Ties: Women in the Fur Trade Society, 1670–1870* (1983); Julie Roy Jeffrey, *Converting the West: A Biography of Narcissa Whitman* (1991); Jacqueline Peters, *Sacred Encounters: Father DeSmet and the Indians of the Rocky Mountain West* (1993); Theodore Stern, *Chiefs & Chief Traders: Indian Relations at Fort Nez Perces, 1818–1855* (1993); Robert A. Trennert, *Alternative to Extinction: Federal Indian Policy and the Beginnings of the Reservation System, 1846–1851* (1975); Peter Nabakov, ed., *Native American Testimony: An Anthol-*

ogy of Indian and White Relations (1978); David J. Wishart, *An Unspeakable Sadness: The Dispossession of the Nebraska Indians* (1994).

Frontier Society

Julie Roy Jeffrey, *Frontier Women: The Trans-Mississippi West, 1840–1880* (1979); Sandra Myres, ed., *Ho for California! Women's Overland Diaries from the Huntington Library* (1980); John Mack Faragher, *Women and Men on the Overland Trail* (1978); John D. Unruh, Jr., *The Plains Across: The Overland Emigrants and the Trans-Mississippi West, 1840–1860* (1979); Adolf E. Schroeder and Carla Schulz-Geisberg, eds., *Hold Dear, As Always: Jette, a German Immigrant Life in Letters* (1988); Rodman W. Paul, *California Gold: The Beginning of Mining in the Far West* (1974); Arrell Morgan Gibson, *Yankees in Paradise: The Pacific Basin Frontier* (1993); Laurie F. Maffly-Kipp, *Religion and Society in Frontier California* (1994); Peter G. Boag, *Environment and Experience: Settlement Culture in Nineteenth-Century Oregon* (1992); Dean L. May, *Three Frontiers: Family, Land, and Society in the American West, 1850–1900* (1994); William Loren Katz, *The Black West* (1971); Richard L. Bushman, *Joseph Smith and the Beginnings of Mormonism* (1984); Leonard Pitt, *The Decline of the Californios: A Social History of the Spanish-speaking Californians, 1846–1890* (1970); Robert J. Rosenbaum, *Mexicano Resistance in the Southwest: "The Sacred Right of Self-Preservation"* (1981); M. S. Meir and Feliciano Rivera, *The Chicanos: A History of Mexican-Americans* (1972); Albert Camarillo, *Chicanos in a Changing Society: From Mexican Pueblos to American Barrios in Santa Barbara and Southern California, 1848–1930* (1979); Alfredo Mirande and Evangeline Enriquez, *La Chicana: The Mexican-American Woman* (1979); Timothy M. Marovina, *Tejano Religion and Ethnicity: San Antonio, 1821–1860* (1995).

The Union in Peril

he autumn of 1860 was a time of ominous rumors and expectations. The election was held on November 6 in an atmosphere of crisis. In Springfield, Illinois, Abraham Lincoln, taking coffee and sandwiches prepared by the "ladies of Springfield," waited as the telegraph brought in the returns. By 1 A.M., victory was certain. He reported later, "I went home, but not to get much sleep, for I then felt, as I never had before, the responsibility that was upon me." And with good cause. He and the American people faced the most serious crisis since the founding of the Republic.

Lincoln won an unusual four-party election with only 39 percent of the popular vote. He had appealed almost exclusively to northern voters in a blatantly sectional campaign, defeating his three opponents by carrying every free state except New Jersey. Of the candidates, only Illinois Senator Stephen Douglas campaigned actively in every section of the country. For his efforts, he received the second-highest number of votes. Douglas's appeal, especially in the closing days of the campaign, was "on behalf of the Union," which he feared—correctly—was in imminent danger of splitting apart.

Other Americans sensed the mood of crisis that fall and faced their own fears and responsibilities. A month before the election, plantation owner Robert Allston wrote his oldest son, Benjamin, that "disastrous consequences" would follow from a Lincoln victory. Although his letter mentioned the possibility of secession, he dealt mostly with plantation concerns: a new horse, the mood of the slaves, ordering supplies from the city, instructions for making trousers on a sewing machine. After Lincoln's election, Allston corresponded with a southern colleague about the need for an "effective military organization" to resist "Northern and Federal aggression." In his shift from sewing machines to military ones, Robert Allston prepared for what he called the "impending crisis."

Frederick Douglass greeted the election of 1860 with characteristic optimism. Not only was this an opportunity to "educate ... the people in their moral and political duties," he said, but "slaveholders know that the day of their power is over when a Republican President is elected." But no sooner had Lincoln's victory been determined than Douglass's hopes turned sour. He noted that Republican leaders, in their desire to keep southern border states from seceding, sounded more antiabolitionist than antislavery. They vowed not to touch slavery in areas where it already existed, which included the District of Columbia, and they promised to enforce the hated Fugitive Slave Act and to put down slave rebellions. Slavery would, in fact, Douglass bitterly concluded, "be as safe, and safer" with Lincoln than with a Democrat.

Michael Luark, an Iowa farmer, was not so sure. Born in Virginia, Luark was a typically mobile nineteenth-century American. After growing up in Indiana, he followed the mining booms of the 1850s to Colorado and California before returning to the Midwest to farm. Luark sought a good living and resented all the furor over slavery. He could not, however, avoid the issue. Writing in his diary on the last day of 1860, Luark looked ahead to 1861 with a deep sense of fear. "Startling" political changes would occur, he predicted, perhaps even the "Dissolution of the Union and Civil War with all its train of horrors." He blamed abolitionist agitators, perhaps reflecting his Virginia origins. On New Year's Day, he expressed his fears that Lincoln would let the "most ultra sectional and Abolition" men disturb the "vexed Slavery question" even further, as Frederick Douglass wanted. But if this happened, Luark warned, "then farewell to our beloved Union of States."

Within four months of this diary entry, the guns of the Confederate States of America fired on a federal fort in South Carolina, and the Civil War began. Luark's fears, Douglass's hopes, and Lincoln's and Allston's preparations for responsibility all became realities. The explanation of the peril and dissolution of the Union forms the theme of this chapter.

George Caleb Bingham's *Stump Speaking* (1856) captures the democratic energy of politics at mid-century. Note the Lincolnlike figure sitting to the right. (The Boatmen's National Bank of St. Louis)

*S*uch a calamitous event as Civil War had numerous causes, large and small. The reactions of Allston, Douglass, and Luark to Lincoln's election suggest some of them: moral duties, sectional politics, growing apprehensions over emotional agitators, and a concern for freedom and independence on the part of blacks, white southerners, and western farmers. But as Douglass understood, by 1860, it was clear that "slavery is the real issue, the single bone of contention between all parties and sections. It is the one disturbing force, and explains the confused and irregular motion of our political machine."

This chapter analyzes how the momentous issue of slavery disrupted the political system and eventually the Union itself. We will look at how four major developments between 1848 and 1861 contributed to the Civil War: first, a sectional dispute over the extension of slavery into the western territories; second, the breakdown of the political party system; third, growing cultural differences in the views and life-styles of southerners and northerners; and fourth, intensifying emotional and ideological polarization between the two regions over losing their way of life and sacred republican rights at the hands of the other. A preview of civil war, bringing all four causes together, occurred in 1855–1856 in Kansas. Eventually, emotional events, mistrust, and irreconcilable differences made conflict inevitable. The election of Lincoln was the spark that touched off the conflagration of civil war, with all its "train of horrors."

Slavery in the Territories

Senator Lewis Cass (Chapter 13) was wrong when he confidently proclaimed that the western territories were areas of individual freedom where civilization would advance and political and social harmony would prevail. As many migrants and residents discovered, personal costs attended the American march westward. White migrations destroyed both the safety and the cultural integrity of Native Americans and Mexicans whose land stood in the way. They also brought Yankees and slaveholders into a costly collision.

The North and the South had managed to contain their differences over slavery, with only occasional difficulties, during the 60 years after the Constitutional Convention. Political compromise in 1787 had resolved the questions of the slave trade and how to count slaves for congressional representation. But although slavery threatened ("like a fireball in the night," Jefferson had said) to upset the uneasy sectional harmony in 1820, the Missouri Compromise had established a workable way of balancing the admission of free and slave states to the Union and had also defined a geographic line (36°30′) to determine future decisions. In 1833, compromise had defused South Carolina's

nullification of the tariff, and the gag rule in 1836 had kept abolitionist petitions to end slavery off the floor of Congress.

Each apparent resolution, however, raised the level of emotional conflict between North and South and put off an ultimate settlement of the slavery question to another time. One reason these compromises were temporarily successful was the existence of a two-party system with intersectional membership. Whigs and Democrats lived on both sides of the Mason-Dixon line. Party loyalties served as an "antidote," as Van Buren put it, to sectional allegiance. Whigs and Democrats expressed their differences over cultural and economic issues, sometimes passionately, but the volatile issue of slavery was largely kept out of political campaigns and congressional debates. This changed in the late 1840s, and the change would prove catastrophic to the Union.

Free Soil or Constitutional Protection?

When the war with Mexico broke out in 1846, it seemed likely that the United States would acquire new territories in the Southwest. Would they be slave or free? To an appropriations bill to pay for the war, David Wilmot, a congressman from Penn-

This 1848 painting by Richard Caton Woodville, titled War News from Mexico, *captures the mood of the period from the Mexican-American War through the Civil War; in towns across the country, outside of countless "American Hotels," the American people listened eagerly to the latest news in an era of steadily worsening political, socioeconomic, and constitutional crises. Separate from the men on the porch, but clearly a part of the picture, are a black father and daughter in rags; they await the war news with special interest, for black Americans would have most to lose by an outcome of the war that led to the expansion of slavery into the territories. (National Academy of Design, New York)*

sylvania, added a short amendment declaring that "neither slavery nor involuntary servitude shall ever exist" in any territories acquired from Mexico. The debates in Congress over the Wilmot Proviso were significant because legislators voted not as Whigs and Democrats, but as northerners and southerners.

A Boston newspaper prophetically observed that Wilmot's resolution "brought to a head the great question which is about to divide the American people." When the Mexican-American War ended, several solutions were presented to deal with this question of slavery in the territories. The first was the "free soil" idea of preventing any extensions of slavery. But did Congress have the power or right to do so? Two precedents suggested that it did. One was the Northwest Ordinance, which had prohibited the entry of slaves into states created in the Upper Midwest; the other was the Missouri Compromise.

Supporters of free soil had mixed motives. For some, slavery was a moral evil to be attacked and destroyed because it trampled on principles of liberty and equality. But for many northern white farmers looking to move westward, the threat of economic competition with an expanding system of large-scale slave labor was even more serious. Neither did they wish to compete for land with free blacks. As Wilmot put it, his proviso was intended to preserve the area for the "sons of toil, of my own race and own color." Other northerners supported the Wilmot Proviso as a means of restraining what seemed to them the growing political power and "insufferable arrogance" of the "spirit and demands of the Slave Power."

Opposed to the free-soil position were the arguments of Senator John C. Calhoun of South Carolina, expressed in several resolutions introduced in the Senate in 1847. Not only did Congress lack the constitutional right to exclude slavery from the territories, Calhoun argued, but it had a positive duty to protect it. The Wilmot Proviso, therefore, was unconstitutional, as was the Missouri Compromise, and any other federal act that prevented slaveholders from taking their slave property into the territories of the United States.

Economic, political, and moral considerations stood behind the Calhoun position. Many southerners hungered for new cotton lands in the West and Southwest, even in Central America and the Caribbean. Politically, southerners feared that northerners wanted to trample on their liberties, namely, the right to protect their institutions against abolitionism. Southern leaders saw the Wilmot Proviso as a moral issue that raised questions about basic republican principles. One congressman called it "treason to the Constitution," and Senator Robert Toombs of Georgia warned that if Congress passed the proviso, he would favor disunion rather than "degradation."

Popular Sovereignty and the Election of 1848

With such divisive potential, it was natural that many Americans sought a compromise solution to keep slavery out of politics. Polk's secretary of state, James Buchanan of Pennsylvania, proposed that the Missouri Compromise line be extended through the lands acquired from Mexico to the Pacific Ocean. This was a way of avoiding thorny questions concerning the morality of slavery and the constitutionality of congressional authority. "Popular sovereignty" was another way of begging these issues. This doctrine, as promulgated by Senator Lewis Cass, left the decision of whether to permit slavery in a territory to the local territorial legislature, an idea that appealed to the American democratic belief in local self-government. But popular sovereignty left many details unanswered, such as at what point in the process toward statehood a territorial legislature could decide to permit or forbid slavery. Cass preferred to leave such questions ambiguous, reasoning that both northern and southern politicians would conclude that popular sovereignty favored their interests.

The Democratic party, attracted to the idea that popular sovereignty could mean all things to all people, nominated Cass for president in 1848. He denounced abolitionists and the Wilmot Proviso, but otherwise avoided the issue of slavery. The Democrats, however, recognized the growing importance of sectional feeling by printing two campaign biographies of Cass, one for the South and one for the North.

The Whigs found an even better way to hold the party together by evading the slavery issue. Passing over Henry Clay, they nominated the Mexican-American War hero, General Zachary Taylor, a Louisiana slaveholder. Taylor compared himself to Washington as a "no party" man who was above politics. This was nearly the only thing he stood for. Southern Whigs supported Taylor because they thought he might understand the burdens of slaveholding, and northern Whigs were pleased that he took no stand on the Wilmot Proviso.

The evasions of the two major parties disappointed Calhoun, who tried to create a new unified southern party. His "Address to the People of the Southern States" rehearsed the history of northern attempts to destroy slavery. Threatening secession, Calhoun called for a united effort against further attempts to interfere with the southern right to extend slavery. But only 48 of 121 southern representatives signed the address, and his effort failed. Calhoun's argument, however, raised the specter of secession and disunion.

Warnings also issued from the North. A faction of Democrats in New York bolted the party to support Van Buren, a Cass foe for several years, for president. At first, the split had more to do with internal state politics than moral principles, but it soon involved the question of slavery in the territories. Disaffected "conscience" Whigs from Massachusetts, unhappy with a slaveholder as their party standard-bearer, were also interested in a third-party alternative. These groups met in Buffalo, New York, to form the Free-Soil party and nominate Van Buren as president. The platform of the new party, composed of an uneasy mixture of ardent abolitionists and opponents of free black mobility into western lands, pledged to fight for "free soil, free speech, free labor and free men."

General Taylor won the election easily, largely because defections from Cass to the Free-

Soilers cost the Democrats the electoral votes from New York and Pennsylvania. Although weakened, the two-party system survived, and purely sectional parties were prevented. The Free-Soilers helped elect local candidates opposed to the expansion of slavery, but received only about 10 percent of the popular vote and no electoral votes.

The Compromise of 1850

Although Taylor won the election by avoiding slavery issues, as president he could no longer do so. As he was inaugurated in 1849, four compelling issues faced the nation. The rush of some 80,000 unruly gold miners to California qualified that territory for admission to the Union. But California's entry as a free state would upset the balance between slave and free states in the Senate that had prevailed since 1820.

The unresolved status of the Mexican cession in the Southwest posed a second problem. The longer the area was left unorganized, the louder local inhabitants called for an application of either the Wilmot Proviso or the Calhoun doctrine of protecting the extension of slavery. The boundary between Texas and the New Mexico Territory was also in dispute, with Texas claiming lands all the way to Santa Fe. This increased northern fears that Texas might be divided into five or six slave states. The existence of slavery and one of the largest slave markets in North America in the nation's capital was a third problem, especially to abolitionists. Fourth, Southerners resented the lax federal enforcement of the Fugitive Slave Act of 1793. They called for a stronger act that would end the protection northerners gave runaway slaves as they fled along the underground railroad to Canada.

Although Taylor was a newcomer to politics (he had never even voted in a presidential election before 1848), he tried to tackle these problems in a statesmanlike, if evasive, manner. He thought he could sidestep the conflict over slavery in the territories by inviting California and New Mexico to apply immediately for statehood, presumably as free states. But it was not long before his efforts had alienated both southern supporters like Calhoun and mainstream Whig leaders like Clay and Webster.

Early in 1850, therefore, the old compromiser, Henry Clay, sought to regain control of the Whig party by proposing solutions to the divisive issues before the nation. With Webster's support, Clay introduced a series of resolutions in an omnibus package intended to settle these issues once and for all. The stormy debates, great speeches, and political maneuvering that followed provided a crucial and dramatic moment in American history. Yet despite some 70 speeches on behalf of the compromise, the Senate defeated Clay's Omnibus Bill. As new bills were proposed, the tired and disheartened 73-year-old Clay left Washington, hoping to regain his strength. He never did. Into the gap stepped a new compromiser, Senator Stephen Douglas of Illinois, who understood that Clay's resolutions had a better chance of passing if voted on individually rather than as a package. Under Douglas's leadership, and with the support of Millard Fillmore, who succeeded to the presidency upon Taylor's untimely death, a series of bills was finally passed.

The so-called Compromise of 1850 put Clay's resolutions, slightly altered, into law. First, California entered the Union as a free state, upsetting the balance of free and slave states, 16 to 15. Second, the territorial governments of New Mexico and Utah were organized by letting the people of those territories decide for themselves whether to permit slavery. The Texas–New Mexico border was settled in a compromise that denied Texas the disputed area. In turn, the federal government compensated Texas with $10 million to pay off debts owed to Mexico. Third, the slave trade, but not slavery itself, was abolished in the District of Columbia.

Fourth, the Fugitive Slave Act went into effect. This most controversial part of the compromise contained many provisions that offended northerners. One denied a jury trial to the alleged fugitive, establishing special commissioners to decide special cases. (A commissioner received $5 for setting a fugitive free, but $10 for returning a fugitive to his or her owner.) An especially repugnant provision compelled all northern citizens to assist in the enforcement of the act by hunting down runaway slaves and turning them in.

Senate Speeches

The history of average, anonymous Americans can be recovered in letters, diaries, folktales, and other nontraditional sources. But in times of political conflict with enormous implications for all Americans, as in the years before the Civil War, historians turn to more conventional sources such as congressional speeches. Recorded in the *Congressional Globe,* these speeches are a revealing means of recovering the substance, tone, and drama of political debate.

Despite the cynical view of American politics held by some European visitors, the mid–nineteenth century was an era of giants in the United States Senate: Daniel Webster, Henry Clay, Thomas Hart Benton, John C. Calhoun, William Seward, and Stephen Douglas. When Congress debated a major issue, such as the tariff, nullification, or the extension of slavery, large crowds would pack the Senate galleries. The speeches would then be quickly printed and widely distributed. These spectacular oratorical encounters provided mass entertainment and political instruction. Such was the case with the Senate speeches over the Compromise of 1850. The three principal figures early in the debates were Clay (Kentucky), Calhoun (South Carolina), and Webster (Massachusetts), each of whom delivered a great address crowning a long, distinguished career.

Born within five years of each other as the American Revolution was ending (1777–1782), each man began his political career in the House of Representatives in the War of 1812 era. Each served a term as secretary of state; in addition, Clay was speaker of the House and Calhoun secretary of war and vice-president. Each served for over a decade in the Senate (Clay, 13 years; Calhoun, 15 years; Webster, 19 years). Each was a party leader, Clay and Webster of the Whigs and Calhoun of the Democrats. During their 40 years of public service, they represented strong nationalistic positions as well as their various states and sections. All three were candidates for president between 1824 and 1844. All three spent most of their careers in the political shadow of Andrew Jackson, and all three had serious conflicts with him.

Many years of political and ideological conflict with each other not only sharpened their oratorical skills, but also led to mutual respect. Webster said of Calhoun that he was "the ablest man in the Senate. He could have demolished Newton, Calvin, or even John Locke as a logician." Calhoun said of Clay, "He is a bad man, but by god, I love him." And "Old Man Eloquent" himself, John Quincy Adams, said of Webster that he was "the most consummate orator of modern times."

It was therefore a momentous event when they each prepared speeches and met for one last encounter early in 1850. Clay was over 70 years old and in failing health, but he came out of retirement to try to keep the Union together. He defended his compromise proposals in a four-hour speech spread over two days, February 5 and 6. The Senate galleries were so packed that listeners were pushed into hallways and even into the rotunda of the Capitol. Copies of his speech were in such demand that over 100,000 were printed.

A month later, on March 7, the scene was repeated as Webster rose to join Clay in defending the compromise. Three days earlier, although too ill to deliver the speech himself, Calhoun had "tottered into the Senate" on the arm of a friend to hear James Mason of Virginia read his rejection of the compromise. Within a month, Calhoun was dead. Clay and Webster followed him to the grave two years later, and Senate leadership passed on to Seward, Douglas, and a new generation of Senate giants.

As you read the excerpts from each speech, try to imagine yourself sitting in the gallery overlooking the Senate floor, listening to each man and absorbing the drama of the moment. How do the oratorical styles differ? Which passages convey the most emotional power? Which speaker is most persuasive to you? Why? To what extent do the three agree on the fugitive slave issue?

John C. Calhoun

March 4, 1850

Having now, Senators, explained what it is that endangers the Union, and traced it to its cause, and explained its nature and character, the question again recurs—How can the Union be saved? To this I answer, there is but one way by which it can be—and that is—by adopting such measures as will satisfy the States belonging to the Southern section, that they can remain in the Union consistently with their honor and their safety....

But will the North agree to this? It is for her to answer the question. But, I will say, she cannot refuse, if she has half the love of the Union which she professes to have, or without justly exposing herself to the charge that her love of power and aggrandizement is far greater than her love of the Union. At all events, the responsibility of saving the Union rests on the North, and not on the South....

Henry Clay

February 5–6, 1850

I have seen many periods of great anxiety, of peril, and of danger in this country, and I have never before risen to address any assemblage so oppressed, so appalled, and so anxious; and sir, I hope it will not be out of place to do here, what again and again I have done in my private chamber, to implore of Him who holds the destinies of nations and individuals in His hands, to bestow upon our country His blessing, to calm the violence and rage of party, to still passion, to allow reason once more to resume its empire....

Mr. President, it is passion, passion-party, party, and intemperance—that is all I dread in the adjustment of the great questions which unhappily at this time divide our distracted country. Sir, at this moment we have in the legislative bodies of this Capitol and in the States, twenty old furnaces in full blast, emitting heat, and passion, and intemperance, and diffusing them throughout the whole extent of this broad land. Two months ago all was calm in comparison to the present moment. All now is uproar, confusion, and menace to the existence of the Union, and to the happiness and safety of this people....

Sir, when I came to consider this subject, there were two or three general purposes which it seemed to me to be most desirable, if possible, to accomplish. The one was, to settle all the controverted questions arising out of the subject of slavery.... I therefore turned my attention to every subject connected with this institution of slavery, and out of which controverted questions had sprung, to see if it were possible or practicable to accommodate and adjust the whole of them....

We are told now, and it is rung throughout this entire country, that the Union is threatened with subversion and destruction. Well, the first question which naturally rises is, supposing the Union to be dissolved, — having all the causes of grievance which are complained of, —How far will a dissolution furnish a remedy for those grievances? If the Union is to be dissolved for any existing causes, it will be dissolved because slavery is interdicted or not allowed to be introduced into the ceded territories; because slavery is threatened to be abolished in the District of Columbia, and because fugitive slaves are not returned, as in my opinion they ought to be, and restored to their masters. These, I believe, will be the causes; if there be any causes, which can lead to the direful event to which I have referred....

Mr. President, I am directly opposed to any purpose of secession, of separation. I am for staying within the Union, and defying any portion of this Union to expel or drive me out of the Union.

Daniel Webster

March 7, 1850

Mr. President: I wish to speak to-day, not as a Massachusetts man, nor as a Northern man, but as an American, and a member of the Senate of the United States....

I speak to-day for the preservation of the Union. "Hear me for my cause." I speak to-day, out of a solicitous and anxious heart, for the restoration to the country of that quiet and that harmony which make the blessing of this Union so rich, and so dear to us all.... I shall bestow a little attention, Sir, upon these various grievances existing on the one side and on the other. I begin with complaints of the South ... and especially to one which has in my opinion just foundation; and that is, that there has been found at the North, among individuals and among legislators, a disinclination to perform fully their constitutional duties in regard to the return of persons bound to service who have escaped into the free States. In that respect, the South, in my judgment, is right, and the North is wrong. Every member of every Northern legislature is bound by oath, like every other officer in the country, to support the Constitution of the United States; and the article of the Constitution which says to these States they shall deliver up fugitives from service is as binding in honor and conscience as any other article....

Where is the line to be drawn? What States are to secede? What is to remain American? What am I to be? An American no longer? Am I to become a sectional man, a local man, a separatist, with no country in common with the gentlemen who sit around me here, or who fill the other house of Congress? Heaven forbid! Where is the flag of the republic to remain? Where is the eagle still to tower? or is he to cower, and shrink, and fall to the ground?

The Compromise of 1850

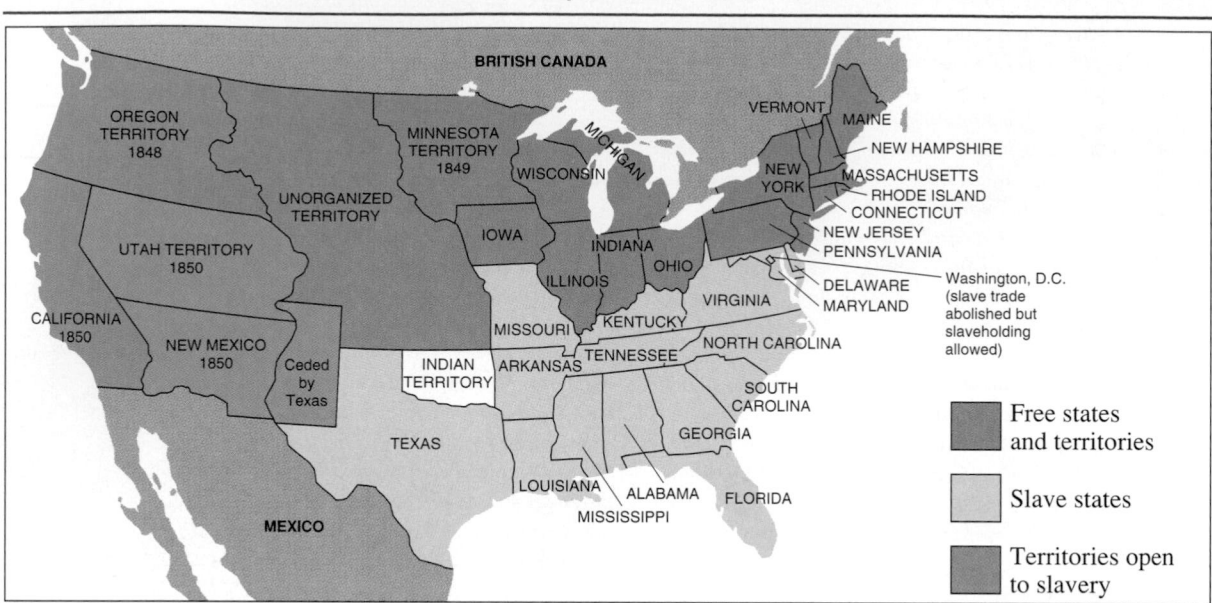

■	Free states and territories
□	Slave states
■	Territories open to slavery

"I have seen many periods of great anxiety, of peril, and of danger in this country," Henry Clay told the Congress in February of 1850, "and I have never before risen to address any assemblage so oppressed, so appalled, and so anxious." What followed were the debates that led eventually to the passage of his great compromise. Can you find three of the four major parts of the bill on the map?

Consequences of Compromise

The Compromise of 1850 was the last attempt to keep slavery out of politics. How well it succeeded in doing so is debatable. Voting behavior on the several bills varied, with legislators following sectional lines on some issues and party lines on others. Douglas had good reason to feel pleased, celebrating the acts of 1850 as a "final settlement" of the slavery question.

The Compromise of 1850, however, only delayed more serious sectional conflict. It added two new ingredients to American politics. The first hinted at the realignment of parties along sectional lines. Political leaders as different as Calhoun, Webster, Van Buren, and New York Senator William Seward all flirted with or committed themselves to new parties. Second, although repudiated by most ordinary citizens, ideas like secessionism, disunion, and a "higher law" than the Constitution entered more and more political discussions. Some people wondered whether the question of slavery in the territories could be compromised away the next time it arose.

Others were immediately upset. The new fugitive slave law angered many northerners because it brought the evils of slavery right into their midst. The owners of runaway slaves hired agents, labeled "kidnappers" in the North, to hunt down fugitives. In a few dramatic episodes, most notably in Boston, literary and religious intellectuals led mass protests to resist slave hunters' efforts to return alleged fugitives to the South. When Senator Webster supported the law, New England abolitionists denounced him as "indescribably base and wicked." Theodore Parker called the new law a "hateful statute of kidnappers," and Ralph Waldo Emerson said it was a "filthy law" that he would not obey.

Frederick Douglass would not obey it either. As a runaway slave himself, he was threatened with arrest and return to the South until friends overcame his objections and purchased his freedom. Douglass still risked harm by his strong defiance of

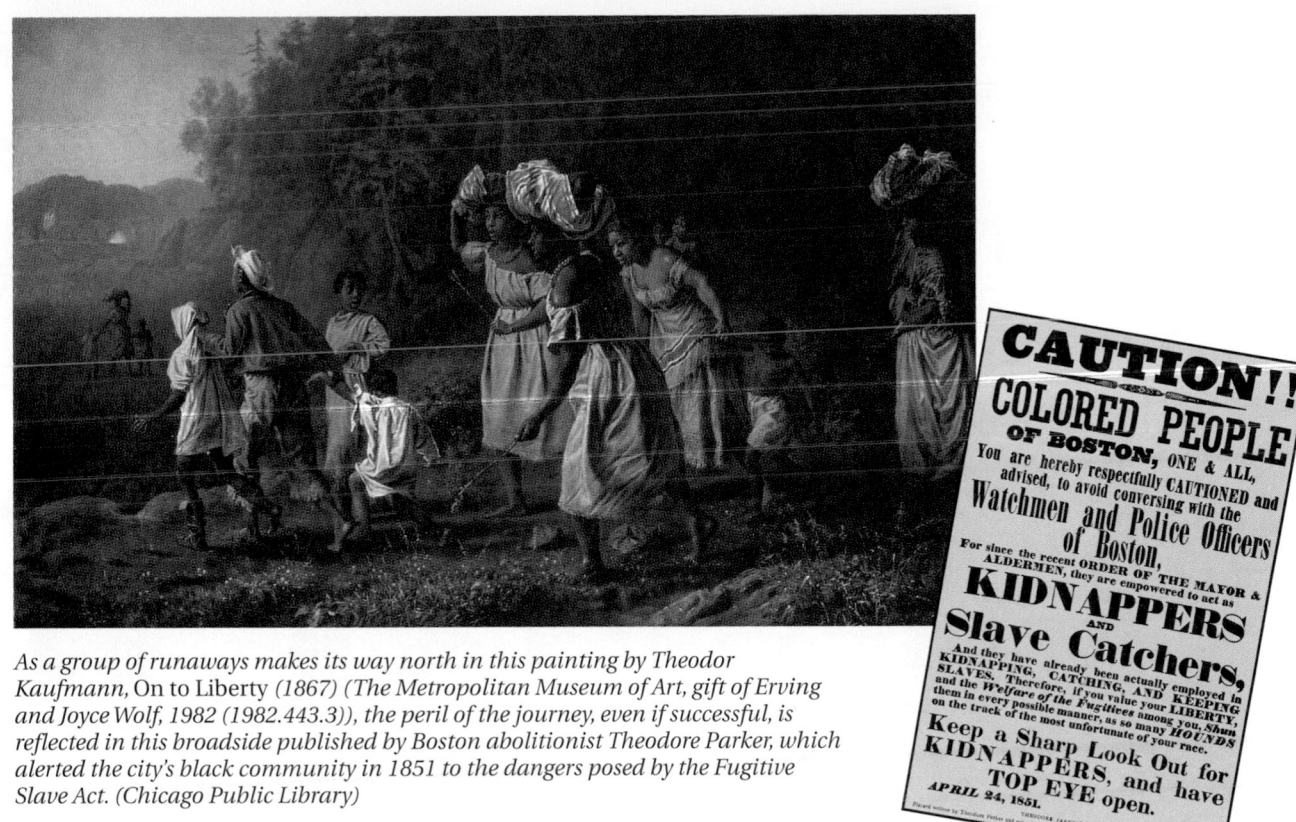

As a group of runaways makes its way north in this painting by Theodor
Kaufmann, On to Liberty *(1867) (The Metropolitan Museum of Art, gift of Erving
and Joyce Wolf, 1982 (1982.443.3)), the peril of the journey, even if successful, is
reflected in this broadside published by Boston abolitionist Theodore Parker, which
alerted the city's black community in 1851 to the dangers posed by the Fugitive
Slave Act. (Chicago Public Library)*

the Fugitive Slave Act. Arguing the "rightfulness of
forcible resistance," he urged free blacks to arm
themselves and even wondered whether it was jus-
tifiable to kill kidnappers. "The only way to make
the Fugitive Slave Law a dead letter," he said in
Pittsburgh in 1853, "is to make a half dozen or more
dead kidnappers." Douglass raised money for
black fugitives, hid runaways in his home, and
helped hundreds escape to Canada.

Other northerners, white as well as black,
increased their work for the underground railroad
in response to the fugitive slave law. Several states
passed "personal liberty laws" that prohibited the
use of state officials and institutions in the recovery of fugitive slaves. But most northerners complied with the law. Of some 200 blacks arrested in
the first six years of the law, only 15 were rescued,
and only 3 of these by force. Failed rescues, in fact,
had more emotional impact than successful ones.
In two cases in the early 1850s (Thomas Sims in

1851 and Anthony Burns in 1854), angry mobs of
abolitionists in Boston, reminiscent of the prerevolutionary days of the Tea Party, failed to prevent the
forcible return of blacks to the South. These celebrated cases aroused the antislavery emotions of
more northerners than the abolitionists had been
able to do in a thousand tracts and speeches.

But the spoken and written word also fueled
emotions over slavery in the aftermath of 1850. In
an Independence Day speech in 1852, Douglass
wondered, "What, to the American slave, is your
4th of July?" It was, he said, the day that revealed to
the slave the "gross injustice and cruelty to which
he is the constant victim." To a slave, the American
claims of national greatness were vain and empty;
the "shouts of liberty and equality" were "hollow
mockery,... mere bombast, fraud, deception,
impiety, and hypocrisy." Douglass's speeches, like
those of another ex-slave, Sojourner Truth, took on
an increasingly strident tone in the early 1850s.

The hypocrisy of the Fugitive Slave Act (part of the Compromise of 1850) and Henry Clay's mixed motives are the focus of this 1851 cartoon. Whites preach the "blessings of liberty" at a free black man they are holding back from freedom as Clay turns his back on the fugitive slave and talks to a northerner about the tariff. (Library of Congress)

At a women's rights convention in Akron, Ohio, in 1851, Truth made one of the decade's boldest statements for minority rights. The convention was attended by clergymen, who kept interrupting the proceedings to heckle female speakers. Up stood Sojourner Truth to speak in words still debated by historians. She pointed to her many years of childbearing and hard, backbreaking work as a slave, crying out in a repetitive refrain, "And ar'n't I a woman?" Referring to Jesus, she asked where he came from: "From God and a woman: Man had nothing to do with Him." Referring to Eve, she concluded, "If the first woman God ever made was strong enough to turn the world upside down all alone, these women together ought to be able to turn it back, and get it right side up again! And now they is asking to do it, the men better let them." Her brief speech silenced the hecklers.

As Truth spoke, another American woman, Harriet Beecher Stowe, was finishing a novel, *Uncle Tom's Cabin*, that would go far toward turning the world upside down and trying to right it again. As politicians were hoping the American people would forget slavery, Stowe's novel brought it to the attention of thousands. She gave readers an absorbing indictment of the horrors of slavery and its immoral impact on both northerners and southerners. Published initially in serial form, each month's chapter ended at a nail-biting dramatic moment. Readers throughout the North cheered Eliza's daring escape across the ice floes on the Ohio River, cried over Uncle Tom's humanity and Little Eva's death, suffered under the lash of Simon Legree, and rejoiced in the reuniting of black family members.

Although outraging the South when published in full in 1852, *Uncle Tom's Cabin* became one of the all-time best-sellers in American history. In the first year, over 300,000 copies were printed, and Stowe's novel was eventually published in 20 languages. When President Lincoln met Stowe in 1863, he is reported to have said to her, with a twinkle in his eye, "So you're the little woman who wrote the book that made this great war!"

Political Disintegration

The response to *Uncle Tom's Cabin* and the Fugitive Slave Act indicated that politicians had congratulated themselves too soon for saving the Republic in 1850. Political developments, not all dealing with slavery, were already weakening the ability of political parties—and ultimately the nation—to withstand the passions slavery aroused.

The Apathetic Election of 1852

Political parties, then and now, thrive on their ability to convince voters that their party stands for moral values and economic policies crucially different from those of the opposition. In the period between 1850 and 1854, these differences were blurred, thereby undermining party loyalty. First, both parties scrambled to convince voters that they had favored the Compromise of 1850. In addition, several states rewrote their constitutions and remodeled their laws in the early 1850s, standardizing many political and economic procedures. One effect of these changes was to reduce the number of patronage jobs available for party victors to dispense. Another effect was to regularize the process, begun in the 1830s, for securing banking, railroad, and other corporate charters, removing the role formerly played by the legislature. Both of these weakened the importance of the party in citizens' lives.

The third development that weakened parties was economic. For almost a quarter of a century, Whigs and Democrats had disagreed over such issues as the tariff, money and banking systems, and government support for internal improvements. But economic conditions im-

Changing Political Party Systems and Leaders

It is characteristic of American politics that when the two major parties fail to respond to the pressing issues of the day, third parties are born and major party realignment occurs. This happened in the 1850s over the issue of slavery and its extension into the territories, which resulted in the collapse of the Whigs and the emergence of the Republican party. Note that the "Republican" party begins in one tradition and ends up in the other. Is political realignment happening again in American politics?

First Party System: 1790s–1820s

REPUBLICAN	FEDERALIST
Jefferson	Hamilton
Madison	John Adams
Monroe	

Transition: 1824 and 1828

DEMOCRAT-REPUBLICAN	NATIONAL REPUBLICAN
Jackson	J. Q. Adams

Second Party System: 1830s–1850s

DEMOCRAT	WHIG
Jackson	Clay
Van Buren	Webster
Calhoun	W. H. Harrison
Polk	

Third Party System: 1856–1890s

DEMOCRAT	REPUBLICAN
Douglas	Lincoln
Pierce	Seward
Buchanan	Grant

proved markedly in the early 1850s. In a time of prosperity, party distinctions over economic policies seemed less important. An ample money supply made the revenues of a high tariff less necessary. Moreover, in the rush for railroad charters during the boom of the early 1850s, local connections were more important than national party politics.

Economic issues persisted, but the battles were fought at the local rather than national level. Thus Georgia voters in 1851 disagreed over commercial banking laws, taxes for internal improvements, and, as an Augusta newspaper put it, "the jealousies of the poor who owned no slaves, against the rich slaveholder." In Indiana, where Congressman George Julian observed that people "hate the Negro with a perfect if not a supreme hatred," legislators rewrote the state constitution in 1851, depriving blacks of the rights to vote, attend white schools, and make contracts. Those who could not post a $500 bond were expelled from the state, and an 1852 law made it a crime for blacks to settle in Indiana. In Massachusetts, temperance reform and a law limiting the working day to ten hours were hot issues. Fleeting political alliances developed around particular issues and local personalities. As a Baltimore businessman said, "The two old parties are fast melting away."

The election of 1852 illustrated the lessening significance of political parties. The Whigs nominated General Winfield Scott, another Mexican-American War hero, who they hoped would repeat Taylor's success four years earlier. With Clay and Webster both dead, party leadership had passed to Senator William Seward of New York, who wanted a president he could influence more successfully than the prosouthern Fillmore. Still, it took 52 ballots to nominate Scott over Fillmore, with serious costs to the party allegiance of southern Whigs. Democrats had their own problems deciding on a candidate. After 49 ballots, in which Cass, Douglas, and Buchanan each held the lead for a time, the party turned to the lackluster Franklin Pierce of New Hampshire as a compromise candidate.

The two parties offered little choice. Both played down issues so as not to widen intraparty divisions. Voter interest diminished. "Genl. Apathy is the strongest candidate out here," was the report from Ohio, while the Baltimore *Sun* remarked that "there is no issue that much interests the people." Democratic prospects were aided by thousands of new Catholic immigrants from Ireland and Germany. Eligible for naturalization and, therefore, the right to vote after only three years, they were influenced by party officials, usually Democrats, who bought their votes with bribes and drinks. Internal conflicts and defections seriously weakened the Whigs, and Pierce won easily, 254 to 42 electoral votes.

The Kansas-Nebraska Act

The Whig party's final disintegration came on a February day in 1854 when southern Whigs stood to support Stephen Douglas's Nebraska bill, thus choosing to be more southern than Whig. The Illinois senator had many reasons for introducing a bill organizing the Nebraska Territory (which included Kansas). As an ardent nationalist and chairman of the Committee on Territories, he was concerned for the continuing development of the West. As an Illinoisan in a period of explosive railroad building, he wanted the eastern terminus for a transcontinental railroad in Chicago rather than in rival St. Louis. This meant organizing the lands west of Iowa and Missouri.

Politics also played a role. Douglas wanted to recapture the party leadership he had held when he led the fight to pass the Compromise of 1850. He also harbored presidential ambitions. Although he had replaced Cass as the great advocate of popular sovereignty, which won him favor among northern Democrats, he needed the support of southern Democrats. Many southerners, especially slaveholders from Missouri, just east of the Nebraska Territory, opposed the organization of the territory unless it were open to slavery. The problem, as Douglas knew well, was that the entire Nebraska Territory lay north of the line where slavery had been prohibited by the Missouri Compromise.

Douglas's bill, introduced early in 1854, recommended using the principle of popular sovereignty in organizing the Kansas and Nebraska territories. This meant that inhabitants could vote slavery in, thereby violating the Missouri Compromise. Douglas reasoned, however, that the climate and soil of the prairies in Kansas and Nebraska would never support slavery-based agriculture, and the people would decide to be a free state. Therefore, he could win the votes he needed for the railroad without also getting slavery. His bill, then, ignored the Missouri Compromise, simply stating that the state or states created out of the Nebraska Territory would enter the Union "with or without slavery, as their constitution may prescribe at the time of their admission."

Douglas miscalculated. Northerners from his own party immediately attacked him and his bill as

SOLICITING A VOTE.

My honest friend, these men are interested parties, I have no further interest in this matter myself, than the inclination to "Serve my 'beloved' Country", My Family cannot subsist on less than 25,000 $ a year.

This is the "Ticket" for you, my good friend, I am 'Old Sam Houston" if elected I shall not only "lick all Europe" but all Creation" to boot.

There, there, go away, go away, don't worry the man, leave him to me, leave him to me!

My good Friend, allow me to pre—sent you this Ticket, I am 'Old Gen! Scott' you know me, I licked the British & the Mexicans, if elected I shall probably lick all Europe.

Webster.   Houston.   Douglas.   Scott.

In this 1852 political cartoon, a poor immigrant is accosted by Daniel Webster, Sam Houston, Stephen Douglas, and General Winfield Scott, each soliciting his vote. Partly to prevent such blatant political hustling, the American (Know-Nothing) party emerged, urging tighter restrictions on immigration and citizenship. (Library of Congress)

a "criminal betrayal of precious rights" and as part of a plot promoting his own presidential ambitions by turning free Nebraska over to "slavery despotism." The outrage among Whigs and abolitionists was even greater. Frederick Douglass branded the act a "hateful" attempt to extend slavery, the result of the "audacious villainy of the slave power."

But Stephen Douglas was a fighter. The more he was attacked, the harder he fought. Eventually his bill passed, but not without seriously damaging the political party system. What began as a railroad measure ended in reopening the question of slavery in the territories that Douglas and others had thought finally settled in 1850. What began as a way of avoiding conflict ended up in violence over whether Kansas would enter the Union slave or free. What began as a way of strengthening party lines over issues ended up destroying one party (the Whigs), planting deep, irreconcilable divisions in another (the Democrats), and creating two new ones (Know-Nothings and Republicans).

Expansionist "Young America"

The Democratic party was weakened in the early 1850s not only by the Kansas-Nebraska Act, but also by an ebullient, expansive energy that led Americans to adventures far beyond Kansas. As republican revolutions erupted in Europe in 1848, Americans greeted them as evidence that the American model of free republican institutions was the wave of the future. Those dedicated to the idea of this continuing national mission, which ironically included the spread of slavery, were called "Young America." An early expression of the spirit of Young America was the enthusiastic reception given the exiled Hungarian revolutionary Louis Kossuth while on a tour of the United States in 1851.

Pierce's platform in 1852 recalled the successful expansionism of the Polk years, declaring that the war with Mexico had been "just and necessary." Many Democrats took their overwhelming victory as a mandate to continue adding territory to the Republic. A Philadelphia newspaper in 1853 described the United States as a nation bound on the "East by sunrise, West by sunset, North by the Arctic Expedition, and South as far as we darn please." Southward expansion into Latin America looked most attractive.

Many of Pierce's diplomatic appointees were southerners interested in adding new cotton-growing lands to the national domain. As ambassador to Mexico, for example, Pierce sent James Gadsden of South Carolina to negotiate with Mexican President Santa Anna for the acquisition of large parts of northern Mexico. Gadsden failed to get all the land he wanted, but he did manage to purchase a strip of desert along the southwest border in order to build a transcontinental railroad linking the Deep South with the Pacific Coast.

The failure to acquire more territory from Mexico legally did not discourage expansionist Americans from pursuing illegal means. During the 1850s, Texans and Californians staged dozens of raids (called "filibusters") into Mexico. The most daring adventurer of the era was William Walker, a 100-pound Tennessean with a zest for danger and power. After migrating to southern California, Walker made plans to add slave lands to the country. In 1853, he invaded Lower California (the Baja Peninsula) with fewer than 300 men and declared himself president of the independent Republic of Sonora. Although eventually arrested and tried in the United States, he was acquitted after eight minutes of deliberation.

Back Walker went, invading Nicaragua two years later. He overthrew the government, proclaimed himself to have been elected dictator, and issued a decree legalizing slavery. When the Nicaraguans, with British help, acted to regain control of their country, the U.S. Navy rescued Walker. After a triumphant tour in the South, he tried twice more to conquer Nicaragua. Walker came to a fitting end in 1860 when he was captured and shot by a Honduran firing squad after invading that country.

Undaunted by failures in the Southwest, the Pierce administration looked to the acquisition of Cuba, a Spanish colony many Americans thought destined to be a part of their country. One expan-

In George Caleb Bingham's Verdict of the People *(after 1855), the American flag flies proudly over a happy throng celebrating the outcome of the political process. However, the process of deciding the Kansas-Nebraska Act marked the collapse of the Second Party System and moved the Union a step closer to disruption and civil war. Note the women on a hotel balcony in the upper right displaying a banner announcing (ironically?) "Freedom for Virtue." (Courtesy of the R.W. Norton Art Gallery, Shreveport, Louisiana)*

sionist even suggested that Cuba physically belonged to the United States because it had been formed by alluvial deposits from the Mississippi River. "What God has joined together let no man put asunder," he said. The acquisition of Cuba was necessary, many maintained, as an extension of America's Manifest Destiny and as an ideal place for expanding the slave-based economy of the southern states.

A decade earlier, the Polk administration had offered $10 million for Cuba, but Spain had refused the offer. Unsuccessful efforts were then made to foment a revolution among Cuban sugar planters, who would then request annexation by the United States. One Latin adventurer organized an invasion of Cuba, launched from New Orleans in 1850. When his attempt failed, he was executed, and hundreds of captured comrades were sent to Spain. The citizens of New Orleans rioted in protest, storming the Spanish consulate, which forced an embarrassed Congress to pay an indemnity. A few years later, a former governor of Mississippi, with the support of his friend, Secretary of War Jefferson Davis, planned to raise $1 million and 50,000 troops to invade the island. The proposed expedition, intended to carve Cuba into several new slave states, was aborted.

Although President Pierce did not support these illegal efforts, his administration did want Cuba. Secretary of State William Marcy instructed the emissary to Spain, Pierre Soulé, to offer $130 million for Cuba. If that failed, Marcy suggested stronger measures. In 1854, the secretary arranged for Soulé and the American ministers to France and England to meet in Belgium to consider options. The result was the Ostend Manifesto, a document intended to pressure Spain to sell Cuba to the United States. It also provides a fascinating glimpse of American expansionist attitudes.

The manifesto argued that Cuba "belongs naturally" to the United States. Both geographically and economically, the fortunes and interests of Cubans and southerners were so "blended" that they were "one people with one destiny." Trade and commerce in the hemisphere would "never be secure" until Cuba was part of the United States. Moreover, southern slaveholders feared that a slave rebellion would "Africanize" Cuba, like Haiti,

suggesting all kinds of "horrors to the white race" in the nearby southern United States. The American acquisition of Cuba was necessary, therefore, to "preserve our rectitude and self-respect."

If Spain refused to sell the island, the ministers threatened a revolution in Cuba with American support. If that should fail, the manifesto warned, "we should be justified in wresting it from Spain." Even Secretary Marcy was shocked when he received the document from Belgium, and he quickly rejected it. Like the Kansas-Nebraska Act, the Ostend Manifesto was urged by Democrats who advocated the expansion of slavery. The outraged reaction of northerners in both cases divided and further weakened the Democratic party.

Nativism, Know-Nothings, and Republicans

Foreign immigration damaged an already enfeebled Whig party and created concern among many native-born Americans. To the average hardworking Protestant American, the foreigners pouring into the cities and following the railroads westward spoke unfamiliar languages, wore funny clothes, drank alcohol freely in grog shops, and increased crime and pauperism. Moreover, they seemed content with a lower standard of living and would work for lower wages than American workers, thus threatening their jobs.

Still worse, these Irish and German immigrants were part of an unprecedented growth in the Catholic Church. By the 1850s, there were nearly 3 million Catholics in the United States, not only in eastern cities, but expanding westward into the Ohio Valley (Germans in Wheeling, Cincinnati, and St. Louis) and south along old French Canadian routes through Detroit, Green Bay, and Vincennes. A surprising and, to many, disturbing development was the Catholic success in converting Protestants. As one Catholic put it, it was "a time when great throngs of Americans began to flock to the Roman Catholic Church despite bitterly intense propaganda and overt opposition." Although overstated, two notable conversions in 1844 compelled Protestant Americans to take the threat seriously. Orestes Brownson, a lifelong Jacksonian democrat and spiritual seeker, moved successively through Congregationalism, Presbyterianism, Unitarianism, and Transcendentalism until finally converting to a Catholicism he argued was fully compatible with democracy. His disciple, the Methodist German immigrant, Isaac Hecker, converted to Catholicism two months earlier in 1844. Joining the Redemptorist order, Hecker served poor German immigrants and, with papal permission, shifted in the 1850s to the active recruiting of Protestants.

Led by the Redemptorists and Jesuits, over 400 parish mission revivals and retreats were held in the 1850s in an aggressive effort to convert urban American Protestants to Roman Catholicism. "All America can be reformed," one religious superior told a group of seminarians in 1856, calling them "instruments in the hands of God which He will use to effect a wonderful change—a spiritual revolution in this country." Sending their children to Catholic schools compounded the offenses against Protestants. Perhaps worst of all, many charged that Catholic immigrants corrupted American politics.

Most Catholics preferred the Democratic party out of traditional loyalties and because Democrats were less inclined than Whigs to interfere with religion, schooling, drinking, and other aspects of personal behavior. It was mostly former Whigs, therefore, who in 1854 founded the American party to oppose the new immigrants. Members

wanted a longer period of naturalization in order to guarantee the "vital principles of Republican Government" and pledged themselves never to vote for Irish Catholics for public office, because it was assumed that their highest loyalty was to the pope in Rome. They also agreed to keep information about their order secret. If asked, they would say, "I know nothing." Hence, they were dubbed the Know-Nothing party.

The Know-Nothings were overwhelmingly a party of the middle and lower classes, workers who worried about their jobs and wages and farmers and small-town Americans who worried about disruptive new forces in their lives. As one New Yorker put it in 1854, "Roman Catholicism is feared more than American slavery." It was widely believed that Catholics slavishly obeyed the orders of their priests, who represented a Church associated with European despotism. The opposition of the Catholic Church to the revolutionary movements of 1848 in Europe intensified the fears of many Protestant Americans that Catholic voters and the Catholic revivals deeply threatened their democratic order. The call to parish missions by Hecker, to "make Yankeedom the Rome of the modern world" confirmed their fears. In the 1854 and 1855 elections, the Know-Nothings gave anti-Catholicism a national political focus for the first time.

Although the nativists argued that papism would subvert freedom and other republican

The American (Know-Nothing) party campaign against the immigrants is dramatically shown in this cartoon of a whiskey-drinking Irishman and beer-barreled German stealing the ballot box while native-born Americans fight at the election poll in the background. (New York Public Library, Astor, Lenox & Tilden Foundations)

values, others maintained that the slave power of the South was the chief danger. No sooner had the debates over Nebraska ended than a group of ex-Whigs and Free-Soilers met and formed the nucleus of another new party, called the Republican party. Although concerned about southern expansionism, as reflected in the Kansas-Nebraska Act debates, the Ostend Manifesto, and plans to build a transcontinental railroad from the South to California on land acquired in the Gadsden Purchase, the party's first challenge was to respond to popular sentiments by mobilizing sectional fears and ethnic and religious concerns.

Composed almost entirely of northerners, former "conscience" Whigs, and disaffected Democrats, the Republican party combined four main elements. The first group, led by William Seward, Senators Charles Sumner of Massachusetts and Salmon P. Chase of Ohio, and Congressmen Joshua Giddings of Ohio and George Julian of Indiana, were fired by a moral fervor to prohibit slavery in the territories. They also sought to divorce the federal government from the support of slavery by freeing slaves in the District of Columbia, repealing the Fugitive Slave Act, and eliminating the internal slave trade. There were, however, limits to the idealism of most Republicans. A more moderate and larger group, typified by Abraham Lincoln of Illinois, opposed slavery in the western territories only, but would not interfere with it where it already existed. This group also indicated that it would not support efforts to achieve equal rights for northern free blacks.

Republicans were anti-Catholic as well as antislavery. This third element of the party, reflecting the traditional Whig reformist impulse, felt responsible for cleansing America of its sins of intemperance, impiety, parochial schooling, and other forms of immorality. Another sin included voting for Democrats, who were accused of catering to the "grog shops, foreign vote, and Catholic brethren" by combining the "forces of Jesuitism and Slavery."

The fourth element of the Republican party, a Whig legacy from the American System of Henry Clay, included those who wanted the federal government to promote commercial and industrial development and the dignity of labor. This fourth group, like the antislavery and anti-Catholic elements, had a strong ideological faith that a system of free labor led to progress. At the heart of both the new party and the future of America were hardworking, middle-class, mobile, free white laborers—farmers, small businessmen, and independent craftsmen. As the Springfield *Republican* said in 1856, the Republican party's strength came from "those who work with their hands, who live and act independently, who hold the stakes of

Year	Candidates	Party	Popular Vote	Electoral Vote
1852	FRANKLIN PIERCE	Democrat	1,601,474 (51%)	254
	Winfield Scott	Whig	1,386,578 (44%)	42
	John P. Hale	Free Soil	156,149 (5%)	0
1856	JAMES BUCHANAN	Democrat	1,838,169 (45%)	174
	John C. Frémont	Republican	1,335,264 (33%)	114
	Millard Fillmore	American	874,534 (22%)	8
1860	ABRAHAM LINCOLN	Republican	1,866,352 (40%)	180
	Steven A. Douglas	Democrat	1,375,157 (29%)	12
	John C. Breckinridge	Democrat	847,953 (18%)	72
	John Bell	Constitutional Union	589,581 (13%)	39

The Emerging Third Party System: Presidential Elections, 1852–1860

Note: Winners' names appear in capital letters.

home and family, of farm and workshop, of education and freedom—these as a mass are enrolled in the Republican ranks."

The strengths of the Republican and Know-Nothing (American) parties were tested in 1856. Which party could best oppose the Democrats? The American party nominated Fillmore, who had strong support in the Upper South and border states. The Republicans chose John C. Frémont, a Free-Soiler from Missouri with virtually no political experience. The Democrats nominated James Buchanan of Pennsylvania, commonly known as a "northern man with southern principles." Frémont's strength in the North helped him carry several free states, while Fillmore won only Maryland. Buchanan, taking advantage of the divided opposition, won the election, but with only 45 percent of the popular vote.

After 1856, the Know-Nothings died out, largely because Republican leaders cleverly redirected nativist fears—and voters—into their broader program, but also because Know-Nothing secrecy, hatreds, and occasional violent attacks on Catholic voters damaged their image. The Know-Nothings represented a powerful current in American politics that would return each time social and economic changes seemed to threaten the nation. It became convenient to label certain people "un-American" and seek to root them out. Thus, the Know-Nothing party disappeared after 1856, but nativism did not.

Kansas and the Two Cultures

However appealing nativist issues were for many Americans, the problem of slavery was the issue that would not disappear. As Democrats sought ways of expanding slavery and other American institutions westward across the Plains and south into Cuba in the mid-1850s, Republicans wanted to halt the advance of slavery to prove to the world, as Seward said, that the American "experiment in self-government" still worked. In 1854, Lincoln worried that it was slavery that "deprives our republican example of its just influence in the world." The specific cause of his concern was the

likelihood that slavery might be extended into Kansas as a result of the passage that year of Stephen Douglas's Kansas-Nebraska Act.

Competing for Kansas

During the congressional debates over the Kansas-Nebraska bill, Seward had accepted the challenge of slave-state senators to "engage in competition for the virgin soil of Kansas." The passage of the Kansas-Nebraska Act in 1854 opened the way for proslavery and antislavery forces to meet physically and to compete over whether Kansas would become a slave or free state. No sooner had the bill passed Congress than Eli Thayer founded the Massachusetts Emigrant Aid Society to recruit free-soil settlers to go to Kansas. From New York, Frederick Douglass called for "companies of emigrants from the free states ... to possess the goodly land." By the summer of 1855, about 1,200 New England colonists had migrated to Kansas.

One of the migrants was Julia Louisa Lovejoy, a Vermont minister's wife. As a Mississippi riverboat carried her into a slave state for the first time, she described the dilapidated plantation homes of the monotonous Missouri shore as reflecting the "blighting mildew of slavery." By the time Julia and her husband arrived in the Kansas Territory, she had concluded that the "inhabitants and morals" of slaveholding Missourians who had moved into Kansas were of an "*undescribably repulsive* and undesirable character." To Julia Lovejoy, northerners came to bring the "energetic Yankee" virtues of morality and economic enterprise to the drunken, unclean slaveholders of the Southwest.

Perhaps she had in mind David Atchison, Democratic senator from Missouri. Atchison believed that Congress had an obligation to protect slavery in the territories, thereby permitting Missouri slaveholders to move into Kansas. As early as 1853, he pledged himself "to extend the institutions of Missouri over the Territory at whatever sacrifice of blood or treasure." He described New England migrants as "negro thieves" and "abolition tyrants." He recommended to fellow Missourians that they defend their property and interests "with the *bayonet* and with *blood*" and, if need be, "to kill every God-damned abolitionist in the district."

Under Atchison's inflammatory leadership, secret societies sprang up in the Missouri counties adjacent to Kansas. They vowed to combat the Free-Soilers. One editor exclaimed that northerners came to Kansas "for the express purpose of stealing, running off and hiding runaway negroes from Missouri [and] taking to their own bed ... a stinking negro wench." It was not slaveholders but New Englanders, he said, who were immoral, uncivilized, and hypocritical. Rumors of 20,000 such Massachusetts migrants spurred Missourians to action. Thousands poured across the border late in 1854 to vote on whether to permit slavery in the territory. Twice as many ballots were cast as the number of registered voters, and in one polling place only 20 of over 600 voters were legal residents.

The proslavery forces overreacted to their fear of the New England migrants and their intentions. The permanent population of Kansas consisted primarily of migrants from Missouri and other border states who were more concerned with land titles than slavery. They opposed any blacks—slave or free—moving into their state. As one clergyman put it, "I kem to Kansas to live in a free state and I don't want niggers a-trampin' over my grave."

In March 1855, a second election was held to select a territorial legislature. The pattern of border crossings, intimidation, and illegal voting was repeated. Atchison himself, drinking "considerable whiskey" along the way, led a band of armed men across the state line to vote and frighten would-be Free-Soil voters away. Not surprisingly, a small minority of eligible voters elected a proslavery territorial legislature. Free-Soilers, meanwhile, staged their own constitutional convention in Lawrence and created a Free-Soil government at Topeka. It banned blacks from the state. The proslavery legislature settled first in Shawnee Mission and then in Lecompton, giving Kansas two governments.

The struggle shifted to Washington, where President Pierce, who could have nullified the illegal election, did nothing. Congress debated the wrongs in Kansas and sent an investigating committee, which further inflamed passions. Throughout 1855, the call to arms grew more strident. One proslavery newspaper invited southerners to bring their weapons and "send the scoundrels" from the North "back to whence they came, or ... to hell, it matters not which." In South Carolina, Robert Allston wrote his son Benjamin that he was "raising men and money ... to counteract the effect of the Northern hordes.... We are disposed to fight the battle of our rights ... on the field of Kansas."

Both sides saw Kansas as a holy battleground for their version of moral right. An Alabaman, Colonel Jefferson Buford, sold his slaves to raise money to hire an army of 300 men to fight for slavery in Kansas, promising free land to his recruits. A Baptist minister blessed their departure from Montgomery, promised them God's favor and gave each man a Bible. Northern Christians responded in kind. At Yale University, the noted minister Henry Ward Beecher presented 25 Bibles and 25 Sharps rifles to young men who would go fight for the Lord in Kansas. "There are times," he said, "when self-defense is a religious duty. If that duty was ever imperative it is now, and in Kansas." Beecher suggested that rifles would be of greater use than Bibles. Missourians dubbed them "Beecher's Bibles" and vowed, as one newspaper put it, "Blood for Blood!... for each drop spilled, we shall require one hundred fold!"

"Bleeding Kansas"

As civil war threatened in Kansas, a Brooklyn poet, Walt Whitman, heralded American democracy in his epic poem *Leaves of Grass* (1855). Whitman identified himself as the embodiment of average Americans "of every hue and caste,... of every rank and religion." Ebulliently, Whitman embraced urban mechanics, southern woodcutters, planters' sons, runaway slaves, mining camp prostitutes, and a catalog of others in his poetic celebration of "the word Democratic, the word En-Masse." At the same time, Whitman's faith in the American masses faltered in the mid–1850s. He worried that a knife plunged into the "breast" of the Union would bring on the "red blood of civil war."

As Whitman feared, blood flowed in Kansas. In May 1856, supported by a prosouthern federal marshall, a mob entered Lawrence, smashed the offices and presses of a Free-Soil newspaper, fired several cannonballs into the Free State Hotel, and destroyed homes and shops. Three nights later, motivated by vengeance and a feeling that he was

Led by Senator David Atchison, thousands of gun-toting Missourians crossed into Kansas in 1854 and 1855 in order to vote illegally for a proslavery territorial government. The ensuing bloodshed made Kansas a preview of the Civil War. (The Newberry Library, Chicago)

"Bleeding Kansas"

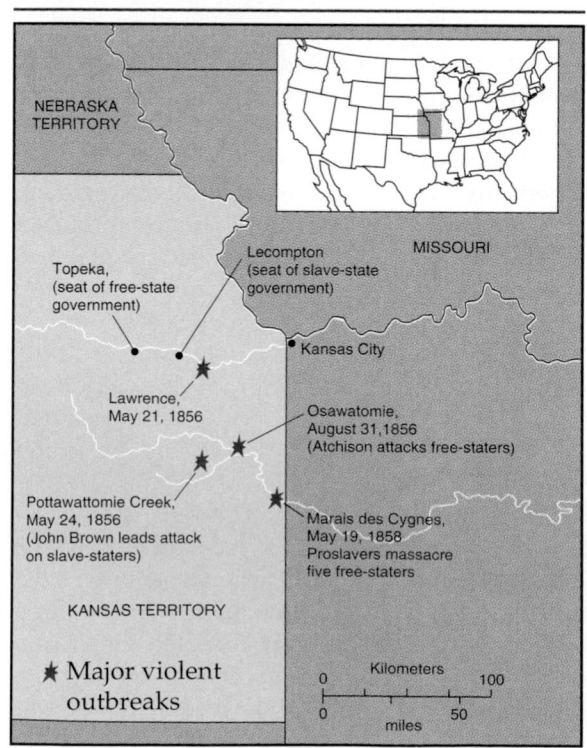

NEBRASKA TERRITORY

Topeka, (seat of free-state government)

Lecompton (seat of slave-state government)

MISSOURI

Kansas City

Lawrence, May 21, 1856

Osawatomie, August 31,1856 (Atchison attacks free-staters)

Pottawattomie Creek, May 24, 1856 (John Brown leads attack on slave-staters)

Marais des Cygnes, May 19, 1858 Proslavers massacre five free-staters

KANSAS TERRITORY

★ Major violent outbreaks

Kilometers
0   100
0   50
miles

doing God's will, John Brown led a small New England band, including four of his sons, to a proslavery settlement near Pottawatomie Creek. There they dragged five men out of their cabins and despite the terrified entreaties of their wives, hacked them to death with swords.

Violence also entered the halls of Congress. That same week, abolitionist Senator Charles Sumner delivered a tirade that became known as "The Crime Against Kansas." He lashed out at the "murderous robbers" and "incredible atrocities of the Assassins and ... Thugs" from the South. With nasty invective, he accused proslavery Senate leaders, especially Atchison and Andrew Butler of South Carolina, of cavorting with the "harlot, Slavery." Two days later, Butler's nephew, Congressman Preston Brooks, avenged the honor of his colleague by beating Sumner senseless with his cane as he sat at his Senate desk.

The sack of Lawrence, the massacre at Pottawatomie Creek, and the caning of Sumner set off a minor civil war, which historians have called "Bleeding Kansas." It lasted throughout the summer. Crops were burned, homes were destroyed, fights broke out in saloons and streets, and night raiders tortured and murdered their enemies. For residents like Charles Lines, who just wanted to farm his land in peace, it was impossible to remain neutral. Lines hoped his neighbors near Lawrence would avoid "involving themselves in trouble." But when proslavery forces seized a mild-mannered neighbor, bound him, tortured him, and left him to die, Lines joined the battle. He wrote to a friend that "blood must end in the triumph of the right."

Even before the bleeding of Kansas began, the New York *Tribune* warned, "We are two peoples. We are a people for Freedom and a people for Slavery. Between the two, conflict is inevitable." As the moral rhetoric and violence in Kansas demonstrated, competing visions of two separate cultures for the future destiny of the United States were at stake. Despite many similarities between the North and the South, the gap between the two sides widened as the hostilities of the 1850s increased.

Northern Views and Visions

The North saw itself, as Julia Lovejoy suggested, as a prosperous land of bustling commerce and expanding, independent agriculture. Northern farmers and workers were self-made free men who believed in individualism and democracy. The "free labor system" of the North, as both Seward and Lincoln often said, offered equality of opportunity and upward mobility. Both generated more wealth. Although the North contained many growing cities, northerners revered the values of the small towns that spread from New England across the Upper Midwest. These values included a respect for the rights of the people, tempered by the rule of law; individual enterprise, balanced by a concern for one's neighbors; and a fierce morality rooted in Calvinist Protestantism. Northerners would regulate morality—by persuasion if possible but by legislation if necessary—to remove the sins of irreligion, illiteracy, and intemperance from American society. It was no accident that the ideas of universal public education and laws against the sale and consumption of alcohol both began in New England.

Northerners valued the kind of republican government that guaranteed the rights of free men, enabling them to achieve economic progress. Specifically, this meant supporting government action to promote free labor, industrial growth, some immigration, foreign trade (protected by tariffs), and the development of railroads and free farm homesteads westward across the continent. Energetic mobility both westward and upward would dissolve state, regional, and class loyalties and increase the sense of nationhood. A strong Union could achieve national and even international greatness. These were the conditions, befitting a chosen people, that would, as Seward put it, spread American institutions around the world and "renovate the condition of mankind." These were also the ideological principles of the Republican party.

Only free men could achieve economic progress and moral society. Therefore, the worst sin in the northerner's view was the loss of one's freedom. Slavery was the root of all evil. It was, Seward said, "incompatible with all … the elements of the security, welfare, and greatness of nations." The South, then, represented the antithesis of everything that northerners saw as good. Southerners were unfree, backward, economically stagnant, uneducated, lawless, immoral, and out of harmony with the values and ideals of the nineteenth century. Julia Lovejoy's denunciation of slaveholding Missourians was mild. Her fellow migrants to Kansas described southerners as subhuman, unclean, and uncivilized. They were, as one put it, "drunken ourangoutans," "wild beasts" who drank whiskey, ate dirt, uttered oaths, raped slave women, and fought or dueled at the slightest excuse. In the popular language of the day, they were known as "Pukes."

The Southern Perspective

Epithets aside, southerners were a diverse people who, like northerners, shared certain broad values, generally those of the planter class. If in the North the values of economic enterprise were most important, southerners revered social values most. Like the English gentry they sought to emulate, they saw themselves as courteous, refined, hospitable, and chivalrous. By contrast, they saw northerners as coarse, ill-mannered, aggressive, materialistic "Yankees." In a society where one person in three was a black slave, racial distinctions and paternalistic relationships were crucial

These scenes illustrate the contrasting socioeconomic cultures of the antebellum North and South. Rochester, NY (top) in 1860 was a bustling industrial city, delivering manufactured goods to northern markets by canal boats and railroads, whereas the vital unit of southern commerce was the genteel individual plantation (bottom), with steamboats and flatboats carrying cotton and sugar to port cities for trade with Europe. (top: Stokes Collection, New York Public Library; bottom: Library of Congress)

A PLANTER'S HOUSE AND SUGAR PLANTATION, ON THE MISSISSIPPI RIVER.

in maintaining order and white supremacy. Fear of slave revolt was ever present. The South had five times more military schools than the North. Northerners educated the many for economic utility, but southerners educated the few for grace and character. In short, the South saw itself as a genteel, ordered society guided by the aristocratic code of the gentleman planter.

Southerners agreed with northerners that sovereignty in a republic rested in the people, who created a government of laws to protect life, liberty, and property. But unlike people in the North, southerners believed that the democratic principle of self-government was best preserved in local political units such as the state. Southerners were ready to fight to defend their sacred rights against any tyrannical encroachment on their liberty, as they had in 1776. They saw themselves, in fact, as true revolutionary patriots. Like northerners, southerners cherished the Union. But they preferred the loose confederacy of the Jeffersonian past to the centralized nationalism Seward kept invoking.

To southerners, Yankees were in too much of a hurry—to make money, to reform the behavior of others, to put dreamy theories (like racial equality) into practice. Two images dominated the South's view of northerners: either they were stingy, hypocritical, moralizing Puritans, or they were grubby, slum-dwelling, Catholic immigrants. A Georgia paper combined both images in an 1856 editorial: "Free society! we sicken at the name. What is it but a conglomeration of greasy mechanics, filthy operatives, small-fisted farmers, and moon-struck theorists?" These northerners, the paper said, "are devoid of society fitted for well-bred gentlemen."

Each side, then, saw the other threatening its freedom and infringing on its view of a proper republican society. Each saw the other imposing barriers to its vision for America's future, which included the economic systems described in Chapters 10 and 11. As hostilities increased, the views each section had of the other grew steadily more rigid and conspiratorial. Northerners saw the South as a "slave power," determined to foist the slave system on free labor throughout the land. Southerners saw the North as full of "black Republicanism," determined to destroy the southern way of life.

Polarization and the Road to War

Because of the national constituencies of the two major political parties, northern and southern cultural stereotypes and conspiratorial accusations had been largely held in check. But events in Kansas solidified the image of the Republicans as a northern party and seriously weakened the Democrats. Further events, still involving the question of slavery in the territories, soon split the Democratic party irrevocably into sectional halves: the Dred Scott decision of the Supreme Court (1857), the constitutional crisis in Kansas (1857), the Lincoln-Douglas debates in Illinois (1858), John Brown's raid in Virginia (1859), and Lincoln's election (1860). These incidents further polarized the negative images each culture held of the other and set the nation on the final road to civil war.

The Dred Scott Case

The events of 1857 reinforced the arguments of those who believed in a slave power conspiracy. Two days after James Buchanan's inauguration, the Supreme Court finally ruled in *Dred Scott* v. *Sandford*. The case had been pending before the Court for nearly three years, but the slave family of Dred Scott had been waiting longer for the decision. In 1846, Dred and Harriet Scott had filed suit in Missouri for their freedom. They argued that their master had taken them into Minnesota, Wisconsin, and other territories where the Missouri Compromise prohibited slavery, and therefore they should be freed. By the time the case reached the Supreme Court, the issue of slavery in the territories had become a heated political issue.

When the Court, which had a majority of southern judges, issued its decision, by a vote of 7 to 2, it made three rulings. First, because blacks were, as Chief Justice Roger Taney put it, "beings of an inferior order [who] had no rights which white men were bound to respect," Dred Scott was not a citizen and had no right to sue in federal courts. Justice Peter Daniel of Virginia was even more indelicate in his consenting opinion, saying that the "African Negro race" did not belong "to the family of nations," but rather was a subject for "commerce or traffic." The second ruling stated that the Missouri Compromise was unconstitutional because Congress did not have the power to ban slavery in a territory. And third, the fact that the Scotts had been taken in and out of free states did not affect their status. Despite two eloquent dissenting opinions, Dred and Harriet Scott remained slaves.

The implications of these decisions went far beyond the Scotts' personal freedom. The arguments about black citizenship infuriated many northerners. Frederick Douglass called the ruling "a most scandalous and devilish perversion of the Constitution, and a brazen misstatement of the facts of history." Many citizens worried about the few rights free blacks still held. Even more troublesome was the possibility hinted at in the decision that slavery might be permitted in the free states of the North, where it had long been banned. People who suspected a conspiracy were not calmed when Buchanan endorsed the Dred Scott decision as a final settlement of the right of citizens to take their "property of any kind, including slaves, into the common Territories . . . and to have it protected there under the Federal Constitution." Rather than settling the political issue of slavery in the territories, as Buchanan had hoped, the Dred Scott decision threw it back into American politics. It opened up new questions and increased sectional hostilities.

Douglas and the Democrats

The Dred Scott decision and Buchanan's endorsement fed northern suspicions of a slave power conspiracy to impose slavery everywhere. Events in Kansas, which still had two governments, heightened these fears. In the summer of 1857, Kansas had still another election, with so many irregularities that only 2,000 out of a possible 24,000 voters participated. They elected a proslavery slate of delegates to a constitutional convention meeting at Lecompton as a preparation for statehood. The convention decided to exclude free blacks from the state, to guarantee the property rights of the few slaveholders in Kansas, and to ask voters to decide in a referendum whether to permit more slaves.

The proslavery Lecompton constitution, clearly unrepresentative of the wishes of the majority of the people of Kansas, was sent to Congress for approval. Eager to retain the support of southern Democrats, Buchanan endorsed it. Stephen Douglas challenged the president's power and jeopardized his own standing with southern Democrats by opposing it. Facing reelection to the Senate from Illinois in 1858, Douglas needed to hold the support of the northern wing of his party. Congress sent the Lecompton constitution back to the people of Kansas for another referendum. This time they defeated it, which meant that Kansas remained a territory rather than becoming a slave state. While Kansas was left in an uncertain status, the larger political effect of the struggle was to split the Democratic party almost beyond repair.

No sooner had Douglas settled the Lecompton question than he faced reelection in Illinois. Douglas's opposition to the Lecompton constitution had restored his prestige in the North as an opponent of the slave power. This cut some ground out from under the Republican party claim that it was the only force capable of stopping the spread of southern power. Republican party leaders from the West, however, had a candidate who understood the importance of distinguishing Republican moral and political views from those of the Democrats.

Lincoln and the Illinois Debates

Although he was relatively unknown nationally and had not held elected office in several years, by 1858, Abraham Lincoln of Illinois had emerged to challenge William Seward for leadership of the Republican party. Lincoln's character was shaped on the midwestern frontier, where he had educated himself, developed mild abolitionist views, and dreamed of America's greatness.

Douglas was clearly the leading Democrat, so the Senate election in Illinois appeared to be a preview of the presidential election of 1860. The other Douglass, Frederick, observed that "the slave power idea was the ideological glue of the Republican party." Lincoln's handling of this idea would be crucial in distinguishing him from Stephen Douglas. The Illinois campaign featured a series of seven debates between Lincoln and Douglas in different cities. With a national as well as a local audience, the debates provided a remarkable opportunity for the two men to state their views on the heated racial issues before the nation.

Lincoln set a solemn tone when he accepted the Republican senatorial nomination in Chicago in June. The American nation, he said, was in a "crisis" and building toward a worse one. "A House divided against itself cannot stand. I believe this government cannot endure, permanently half *slave* and half *free*." Lincoln said he did not expect the Union "to be dissolved" or "the house to fall," but rather that "it will become *all* one thing, or *all* the other." Then he rehearsed the history of the South's growing influence over national policy since the Kansas-Nebraska Act, which he blamed on Douglas. Lincoln stated his firm opposition to the Dred Scott decision, which he believed part of a conspiracy involving Pierce, Buchanan, Taney, and Douglas. People like himself, who opposed this conspiracy, wished to place slavery, he said, on a "course of ultimate extinction."

In the ensuing debates with Douglas, Lincoln reiterated these controversial themes. He also expressed his views on race and slavery, formed from a blend of experience, principle, and politics. Although far from a radical abolitionist, in these debates, Lincoln skillfully staked out a moral position not only in advance of Douglas, but well ahead of his time.

Lincoln was also very much a part of his time. He believed that whites were superior to blacks and opposed granting specific equal civil rights to free blacks. He believed, furthermore, that the physical and moral differences between whites and blacks would "forever forbid the two races from living together on terms of social and political equality" and recommended "separation" and colonization in Liberia or Central America as the best solution to racial differences.

Lincoln, however, differed from most contemporaries in his deep commitment to the humane principles of the equality and essential dignity of all human beings, including blacks. Douglas, by contrast, arguing against race mixing in a blatant bid for votes, continually made racial slurs. Lincoln believed not only that blacks were "entitled to all the natural rights … in the Declaration of Independence," but also that they had many specific economic rights as well, like "the right to put into his mouth the bread that his own hands have earned." In these rights, blacks were, Lincoln said, "my equal and the equal of Judge Douglas, and the equal of every living man."

The overwhelming stress of leading the nation through the Civil War is evident in these two images of Abraham Lincoln. To the left is a portrait from 1860 (Chicago Historical Society) and on the right is an April 1865 photograph taken just before his assassination. (Library of Congress)

Unlike Douglas, Lincoln hated slavery. At Galesburg, he said, "I contemplate slavery as a moral, social, and political evil." In Quincy, he said that the difference between a Republican and a Democrat was quite simply whether one thought slavery wrong or right. Douglas was more equivocal and dodged the issue in Freeport by pointing out that slavery would not exist if favorable local legislation did not support it. Douglas's moral indifference to slavery was clear in his admission that he did not care if a territorial legislature voted it "up or down." A white supremacist, Douglas was democratic enough to want white people to be able to create whatever type of society they wanted. Republicans did care, Lincoln affirmed, sounding a warning that by stopping the expansion of slavery, the course toward "ultimate extinction" had begun. Although barred by the Constitution from doing anything about slavery where it already existed, Lincoln said that because Republicans believed slavery to be wrong, "we propose a course of policy that shall deal with it as a wrong."

What Lincoln meant by "policy" was not yet clear, even to himself. However, in the debates, he did succeed in affirming that the Republican party was the only moral and political force capable of stopping the slave power. It seems ironic now, though not at the time, that Douglas won the election. When he and Lincoln met again two years later, the order of their finish would be reversed. Elsewhere, in 1858, however, Democrats did poorly, losing 18 congressional seats to the Republicans.

John Brown's Raid

Unlike Lincoln, John Brown was prepared to act decisively against slavery. On October 16, 1859, he and a band of 22 men attacked a federal arsenal at Harpers Ferry, Virginia (now West Virginia). He hoped that the action might provoke a general uprising of slaves throughout the Upper South or at least provide the arms by which slaves could make their way to freedom. Although he seized the arsenal, federal troops soon overcame him. Nearly half his men were killed, including two sons. Brown himself was captured, tried, and hanged for treason. So ended a lifetime of failures.

In death, however, Brown was not a failure. His daring if foolhardy raid, and his impressively dignified behavior during his trial and speedy execution, unleashed powerful passions, further widening the gap between North and South. Northerners responded to his death with an outpouring of sympathy; memorial rallies, parades, and prayer meetings were held. Admirers wrote poems, songs, and speeches in Brown's honor. Thoreau compared him to Christ and called him an "angel of light." Abolitionist William Lloyd Garrison, though a pacifist, was moved to wish "success to every slave insurrection" in the South. Ministers called slave revolt a "divine weapon" and glorified Brown's treason as "holy."

Brown's raid, Frederick Douglass pointed out, showed that slavery was a "system of brute force" that would only be ended when "met with its own

The image of John Brown as martyr was memorialized in art as well as in song and story. This sentimental presentation, The Last Moments of John Brown, *was painted in 1884 by American genre artist Thomas Hovenden. (The Metropolitan Museum of Art, Gift of Mr. & Mrs. Carle Stoekel, 1987)*

In the aftermath of John Brown's raid, passions fed by fear were unleashed throughout the South against northern sympathizers, and vice versa. A year later, the editor of a Massachusetts newspaper who expressed Democratic, southern sympathies found himself the victim of the time-honored mob punishment of tarring and feathering. (The New York Public Library, Astor, Lenox & Tilden Foundations)

weapons." Southerners were filled with "dread and terror" over the possibility of a wave of slave revolts led by hundreds of imaginary John Browns and Nat Turners, and concluded that northerners would stop at nothing to free the slaves. This atmosphere of suspicion eroded freedom of thought and expression. A North Carolinian described a "spirit of terror, mobs, arrests, and violence" in his state. Twelve families in Berea, Kentucky, were evicted from the state for their mild abolitionist sentiments. A Texas minister who criticized the treatment of slaves in a sermon was given 70 lashes.

In response to the Brown raid, southerners also became more convinced, as the governor of South Carolina put it, that a "black Republican" plot in the North was "arrayed against the slaveholders." In this atmosphere of mistrust, southern Unionists lost their influence, and power became concentrated in the hands of those favoring secession. Only one step remained to complete the southern sense of having become a permanent minority within the United States: withdrawal to form a new nation. Senator Robert Toombs of Georgia, insistent that northern "enemies" were plotting the South's ruin, warned fellow southerners late in 1859, "Never permit this Federal government to pass into the traitorous hands of the black Republican party."

The Election of 1860

The conflict between Buchanan and Douglas took its toll on the Democratic party. When the nominating convention met in Charleston, South Carolina, a hotbed of secessionist sentiments, it met for a record ten days without being able to name a

The Presidential Election of 1860

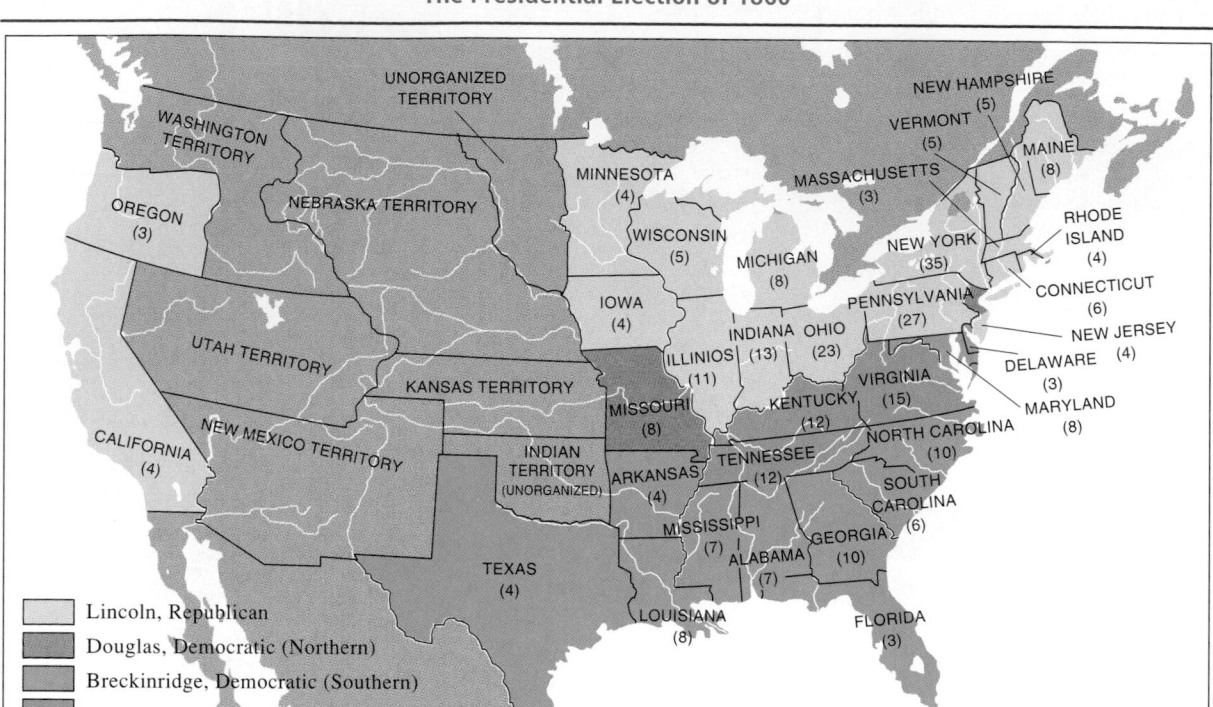

Lincoln, Republican
Douglas, Democratic (Northern)
Breckinridge, Democratic (Southern)
Bell, Constitutional Union

Lincoln's election, the first by a Republican, was on the basis of a totally northern sectional victory, and with only 40 percent of the popular vote.

presidential candidate. The convention went through 59 ballots, was disrupted twice by the withdrawal of southern delegates, and then adjourned for six weeks. Meeting again, this time in Baltimore, the Democrats acknowledged their irreparable division by naming two candidates in two separate conventions. Douglas represented northern Democrats, and John C. Breckinridge, Buchanan's vice president, carried the banner of the proslavery South. The Constitutional Union party, made up of former southern Whigs and border-state nativists, claimed the middle ground of compromise and nominated John Bell, a slave-holder from Tennessee with mild views.

With Democrats split in two and a new party in contention, the Republican strategy aimed at keeping the states carried by Frémont in 1856 and adding Pennsylvania, Illinois, and Indiana. Seward, the leading candidate for the nomination,

had been tempering his antislavery views to appear more electable. So had Abraham Lincoln, who seemed more likely than Seward to carry those key states. With some shrewd political maneuvering emphasizing Lincoln's "availability" as a moderate with widespread appeal, he was nominated by his party.

The Republican platform also reflected moderation, reducing attacks on slavery to oppose only its extension. Most of the platform spoke to the concerns of the several elements of the party: tariff protection, subsidized internal improvements, free labor, and a homestead bill. Above all, the Republicans, like southern Democrats, defended their view of what republican values meant for America's future. It did not include the kind of society of equal rights envisioned by Frederick Douglass. An English traveler in 1860 observed that in America "we see, in effect, two nations—one white and another black—growing up together within the same political circle, but never mingling on a principle of equality."

The Republican moderate strategy for electoral victory worked exactly as planned, as Lincoln swept the entire Northeast and Midwest. Although receiving less than 40 percent of the popular vote nationwide, his triumph in the North was decisive. Even a united Democratic party could not have defeated him. With victory assured, Lincoln finished his sandwich and coffee on election night in Springfield and prepared for his awesome new responsibilities. They came even before his inauguration.

The Divided House Falls

The Republicans overestimated the extent of Unionist sentiment in the South. They could not believe that the secessionists would prevail after Lincoln's victory. A year earlier, some southern congressmen had walked out in protest of the selection of an antislavery speaker of the House. A Republican leader, Carl Schurz, recalling this act, said that the southerners had taken a drink and then come back. After Lincoln's election, Schurz predicted, they would walk out, take two drinks, and come back again. He was wrong.

Secession and Uncertainty

On December 20, 1860, South Carolina seceded from the Union, declaring the "experiment" of putting people with "different pursuits and institutions" under one government a failure. By February 1, the other six Deep South states (Mississippi, Florida, Alabama, Georgia, Louisiana, and Texas) had seceded. A week later, delegates met in Montgomery, Alabama, created the Confederate States of America, adopted a constitution, and elected Jefferson Davis, a Mississippi senator and cotton planter, its provisional president. The divided house had fallen, as Lincoln had predicted it would. What was not yet certain, though, was whether the house could be put back together or whether disunion necessarily meant civil war.

The government in Washington had three options. The first was compromise, but the emotions of the time ruled out that possibility. Most proposed compromises were really concessions to the secessionist states. The second option, suggested by Horace Greeley, editor of the *New York Tribune*, was to let the seven states "go in peace," taking care not to lose the border states. But this was opposed by northern businessmen, who would lose profitable economic ties with the South, and by those who believed in an indissoluble Union. The third option was to compel secessionist states to return, which probably meant war.

Republican hopes that southern Unionism would assert itself and make none of these options necessary seemed possible in February 1861. The momentum toward disunion slowed, and no other southern states seceded. The nation waited and watched, wondering what Virginia and the border states would do, what outgoing President Buchanan would do, and what Congress would do. Prosouthern and determined not to start a civil war in the last weeks of his already dismal administration, Buchanan did nothing. Congress made some feeble efforts to pass compromise legislation, waiting in vain for the support of the president-elect. And as Union supporters struggled with secessionists, Virginia and the border states, like the entire nation, waited for Abraham Lincoln.

Frederick Douglass waited, too, without much hope. He wanted nothing less than the "complete and universal *abolition* of the whole slave system," as well as equal suffrage and other rights for free blacks. His momentary expectation during the presidential campaign, that Lincoln and the Republicans had the will to do this, had been thoroughly dashed. In November, the voters of New York State had defeated a referendum for black suffrage by more votes than a similar measure 14 years earlier. Moreover, Douglass saw northern politicians and businessmen "granting the most demoralizing concessions to the Slave Power."

In his despair, Douglass began to explore possibilities for emigration and colonization in Haiti, an idea he had long opposed. To achieve full freedom and citizenship in the United States

The Causes of the Civil War

Date	Issues and Events	Deeper, Underlying Causes of Civil War
1600s–1860s	Slavery in the South	Major underlying pervasive cause
1700s–1860s	Development of two distinct socioeconomic systems and cultures	Further reinforced slavery as fundamental socioeconomic, cultural moral issue
1787–1860s	States' rights, nullification doctrine	Ongoing political issue, less fundamental as cause
1820	Missouri Compromise (36°30′)	Background for conflict over slavery in territories
1828–1833	South Carolina tariff nullification crisis	Background for secession leadership in South Carolina
1831–1860s	Antislavery movements, southern justification	Thirty years of emotional preparation for conflict
1846–1848	War with Mexico (Wilmot Proviso, Calhoun, popular sovereignty)	Options for issue of slavery in territories

Date	Issues and Events	Specific Impact on the Road to War
1850	Compromise of 1850	Temporary and unsatisfactory "settlement" of divisive issue
1851–1854	Fugitive slaves returned and rescued in North; personal liberty laws passed in North; Harriet Beecher Stowe's *Uncle Tom's Cabin*	Heightened northern emotional reactions against the South and slavery
1852–1856	Breakdown of Whig party and national Democratic party; creation of a new party system with sectional basis	Made national politics an arena where sectional and cultural differences over slavery were fought
1854	Ostend Manifesto and other expansionist efforts in Central America	Reinforced image of Democratic party as favoring slavery
	Formation of Republican Party	Major party identified as opposing the extension of slavery
	Kansas-Nebraska Act	Reopened "settled" issue of slavery in the territories
1856	"Bleeding Kansas"; Senator Sumner physically attacked in Senate	Foretaste of Civil War (200 killed, $2 million in property lost) inflamed emotions and polarized North and South
1857	Dred Scott decision; proslavery Lecompton constitution in Kansas	Made North fear a "slave power conspiracy," supported by President Buchanan and the Supreme Court
1858	Lincoln-Douglas debates in Illinois; Democrats lose 18 seats in Congress	Set stage for election of 1860
1859	John Brown's raid and reactions in North and South	Made South fear a "black Republican" plot against slavery; further polarization and irrationality
1860	Democratic party splits in half; Lincoln elected president; South Carolina secedes from Union	Final breakdown of national parties and election of "northern" president; no more compromises
1861	Six more southern states secede by February 1; Confederate Constitution adopted February 4; Lincoln inaugurated March 4; Fort Sumter attacked April 12	Civil War begins

for all blacks, he said in January 1861, he would "welcome the hardships consequent upon a dissolution of the Union." In February, Douglass said, "Let the conflict come." He opposed all compromises, hoping that with Lincoln's inauguration in March it would "be decided, and decided forever, which of the two, Freedom or Slavery, shall give law to this Republic."

Lincoln and Fort Sumter

As Douglass penned these thoughts, Lincoln began a long, slow train ride from Springfield, Illinois, to Washington, writing and rewriting his inaugural address. Lincoln's quietness in the period between his election and his inauguration had led many to wonder if he were not weak and indecisive. He was not. Lincoln was firmly opposed to secession and to any compromises with the principle of stopping the extension of slavery. He would neither conciliate secessionist southern states nor force their return.

But Lincoln believed in his constitutional responsibility to uphold the laws of the land, and on this significant point, he would not yield. The focus of his attention was a federal fort in the harbor of Charleston, South Carolina. Major Robert Anderson, the commander of Fort Sumter, was running out of provisions and had requested new supplies from Washington. Lincoln would enforce the laws and protect federal property at Fort Sumter.

As the new president rose to deliver his inaugural address on March 4, he faced a tense and divided nation. Federal troops, fearing a Confederate attack on the nation's capital, were everywhere. Lincoln asserted his unequivocal intention to enforce the laws of the land, arguing that the Union was constitutionally "perpetual" and indissoluble. He reminded the nation that the "only substantial dispute" was that "one section of our country believes slavery is *right*, and ought to be extended, while the other believes it is *wrong*, and ought not to be extended." Still hoping to appeal to Unionist strength among southern moderates, Lincoln indicated that he would make no attempts to interfere with existing slavery or the law to return fugitive slaves.

TIMELINE

Year	Event
1832	Nullification crisis
1835–1840	Intensification of abolitionist attacks on slavery
	Violent retaliatory attacks on abolitionists
1840	Liberty party formed
1846	Wilmot Proviso
1848	Free-Soil party founded
	Zachary Taylor elected president
1850	Compromise of 1850, including Fugitive Slave Act
1850–1854	"Young America" movement
1851	Women's rights convention in Akron, Ohio
1852	Harriet Beecher Stowe publishes *Uncle Tom's Cabin*
	Franklin Pierce elected president
1854	Ostend Manifesto
	Kansas-Nebraska Act nullifies Missouri Compromise
	Republican and Know-Nothing parties formed
1855	Walt Whitman publishes *Leaves of Grass*
1855–1856	Thousands pour into Kansas, creating months of turmoil and violence
1856	John Brown's massacre in Kansas
	Sumner-Brooks incident in Senate
	James Buchanan elected president
1857	Dred Scott decision legalizes slavery in territories
	Lecompton constitution in Kansas
1858	Lincoln-Douglas debates
1859	John Brown's raid at Harpers Ferry
1860	Democratic party splits
	Four-party campaign
	Abraham Lincoln elected president
1860–1861	Seven southern states secede
1861	Confederate States of America founded
	Attack on Fort Sumter begins Civil War

Nearing the end of his address, Lincoln urged against rash actions and put the burden of initiating a civil war on the "dissatisfied fellow-countrymen" who had seceded. As if aware of the horrible events that might follow, he said in an eloquent conclusion:

> I am loath to close. We are not enemies, but friends. We must not be enemies. Though passion may have strained, it must not break our bonds of affection. The mystic chords of memory, stretching from every battlefield, and patriot grave, to every living heart and hearthstone, all over this broad land, will yet swell the chorus of the Union, when again touched, as surely they will be, by the better angels of our nature.

Frederick Douglass was not impressed with Lincoln's "honied phrases" and accused him of "weakness, timidity and conciliation." Also unmoved, Robert Allston wrote his son from Charleston, where he was watching the developing crisis over Fort Sumter, that the Confederacy's "advantage" was in having a "much better president than they have."

On April 6, Lincoln notified the governor of South Carolina that he was sending "provisions only" to Fort Sumter. No effort would be made "to throw in men, arms, or ammunition" unless the fort were attacked. On April 10, Jefferson Davis directed General P. G. T. Beauregard to demand the surrender of Fort Sumter. Davis told Beauregard to reduce the fort if Major Anderson refused.

On April 12, as Lincoln's relief expedition neared Charleston, Beauregard's batteries began shelling Fort Sumter, and the Civil War began. Frederick Douglass was about to leave for Haiti when he heard the news. He immediately changed his plans: "This is no time ... to leave the country." He announced his readiness to help end the war by aiding the Union to organize freed slaves "into a liberating army" to "make war upon ... the savage barbarism of slavery." The Allstons had changed places, and it was Benjamin who described the events in Charleston harbor to his father. On April 14, Benjamin reported exuberantly the "glorious, and astonishing news that Sumter has fallen." With it fell America's divided house.

Conclusion

The "Irrepressible Conflict"

Lincoln had been right. The nation could no longer endure half-slave and half-free. The collision between North and South, William Seward said, was not an "accidental, unnecessary" event, but an "irrepressible conflict between opposing and enduring forces." Those forces had been at work for many decades, but developed with increasing intensity after 1848 in the conflict over the question of the extension of slavery into the territories. Although economic, cultural, political, constitutional, and emotional forces all contributed to the developing opposition between North and South, slavery was the fundamental, enduring force that underlay all others, causing what Walt Whitman called the "red blood of civil war."

Recommended Reading

Overviews of the Imperiled Union and Crises of the 1850s

Bruce Collins, *The Origins of America's Civil War* (1981); Eric Foner, ed., *Politics and Ideology in the Age of the Civil War* (1980); James McPherson, *Ordeal by Fire: The Civil War and Reconstruction* (1982); Allen Nevins, *Ordeal of the Union*, Vols. 1 and 2 (1947); David Potter, *The Impending Crisis, 1848–1861* (1976); Richard Sewall, *A House Divided: Sectionalism and Civil War, 1848–1865* (1988); Kenneth Stampp, *The Imperilled Union: Essays on the Background of the Civil War* (1980); Kenneth Stampp, ed., *The Causes of the Civil War*, rev. ed. (1974); Mark Summers, *The Plundering Generation: Corruption and the Crisis of the Union, 1849–1861* (1987); Robert Swierenga, ed., *Beyond the Civil War Synthesis* (1975).

Compromises and Slavery in the Territories

Eugene Berwanger, *The Frontier Against Slavery: Western Anti-Negro Prejudice and the Slavery Extension Controversy* (1967); William W. Freehling, *The Road to Disunion: I. Secessionists at Bay, 1776–1854* (1990); Hamilton Holman, *Prologue to Conflict: The Crisis and Compromise of 1850* (1964); Robert W. Johanssen, *The Frontier, the Union, and Stephen A. Douglas* (1989) and *Stephen Douglas* (1973); Chaplain W. Morrison, *Democratic Politics and Sectionalism: The Wilmot Proviso* (1967); E. Smith, *The Presidencies of Zachary Taylor and Millard Fillmore* (1988); Geoffrey Wolff, *The Kansas-Nebraska Bill: Party, Section and the Origin of the Civil War* (1977).

Political Disintegration and Realignment

Eric Foner, *Free Soil, Free Labor, Free Men: The Ideology of the Republican Party Before the Civil War* (1970); Ronald Formisano, *The Birth of Mass Political Parties: Michigan, 1827–1861* (1971); William E. Gienapp, *The Origins of the Republican Party, 1852–1856* (1987); William E. Gienapp, Thomas B. Alexander, Michael F. Holt, Stephen E. Mazlish, and Joel H. Silbey, *Essays on American Antebellum Politics, 1840–1860* (1982); Michael Holt, *Forging a Majority: The Formation of the Republican Party in Pittsburgh, 1848–1860* (1969) and *The Political Crisis of the 1850s* (1978); Paul Kleppner, *The Third Electoral System, 1853–1892: Parties, Voters, and Political Cultures* (1979).

Kansas, Two Cultures, and the Emotions of Slavery Politics

Thomas B. Alexander, *Sectional Stress and Party Strength* (1967); William J. Cooper, *The South and the Politics of Slavery* (1978) and *Liberty and Slavery: Southern Politics to 1860* (1983); Donald Fehrenbacher, *Slavery, Law, and Politics: The Dred Scott Case in Historical Perspective* (1981); Thomas F. Gossett, *Uncle Tom's Cabin and American Culture* (1985); John McCardell, *The Idea of a Southern Nation: Southern Nationalists and Southern Nationalism, 1830–1861* (1979); James Rawley, *Race and Politics: "Bleeding Kansas" and the Coming of the Civil War* (1969); Richard Sewell, *Ballots for Freedom: Antislavery Politics in the United States, 1837–1865* (1976).

Lincoln and the Divided House: The Road to Civil War

William Barney, *The Road to Secession* (1972); Steven Channing, *Crisis of Fear: Secession in South Carolina* (1970); David H. Donald, *Lincoln* (1995); Don Fehrenbacher, ed., *Abraham Lincoln: A Documentary Portrait Through His Speeches and Writings* (1977); George Forgie, *Patricide in the House Divided: A Psychological Interpretation of Lincoln and His Age* (1979); Harry Jaffa, *Crisis of the House Divided: An Interpretation of the Lincoln-Douglas Debates* (1959); Mark E. Neely, *The Last Best Hope of Earth: Abraham Lincoln and the Promise of America* (1993); Roy Nichols, *The Disruption of American Democracy* (1948); Stephen Oates, *To Purge This Land with Blood: A Biography of John Brown* (1970) and *With Malice Toward None: The Life of Abraham Lincoln* (1982); Kenneth Stampp, *America in 1857: A Nation on the Brink* (1990) and *And the War Came* (1950).

The Union Severed

"W e cannot escape history," Abraham Lincoln reminded Congress in 1862. "We of this Congress and this administration will be remembered in spite of ourselves. No personal significance, or insignificance, can spare . . . us. The fiery trial through which we pass, will light us down, in honor or dishonor, to the latest generation." Lincoln's conviction that Americans would long remember him and other major actors of the Civil War was correct. Jefferson Davis, Robert E. Lee, Ulysses S. Grant—these are the men whose characters, actions, and decisions have been the subject of continuing discussion and analysis, whose statues and memorials dot the American countryside and grace urban squares. Whether seen as heroes or villains, great men have dominated the story of the Civil War.

Yet from the earliest days, the war touched the lives of even the most uncelebrated Americans. From Indianapolis, 20-year-old Arthur Carpenter wrote to his parents in Massachusetts begging for permission to enlist in the volunteer army: "I have always longed for the time to come when I could enter the army and be a military man, and when this war broke out, I thought the time had come, but you would not permit me to enter the service ... now I make one more appeal to you." The pleas worked, and Carpenter enlisted, spending most of the war fighting in Kentucky and Tennessee.

In that same year, in Tennessee, George and Ethie Eagleton faced anguishing decisions. Though not an abolitionist, George, a 30-year-old Presbyterian preacher, was unsympathetic to slavery and opposed to secession. But when his native state left the Union, George felt compelled to follow and enlisted in the 44th Tennessee Infantry. Ethie, his 26-year-old wife, despaired over the war, George's decision, and her own forlorn situation.

"Mr. Eagleton's school dismissed—and what for? O my God, must I write it? He has enlisted in the service of his country—to war—the most unrighteous war that ever was brought on any nation that ever lived. Pres. Lincoln has done what no other Pres. ever dared to do—he has divided these once peaceful and happy United States. And Oh! the dreadful dark cloud that is now hanging over our country—'tis enough to sicken the heart of any one.... Mr. E. is gone.... What will become of me, left here without a home and relatives, a babe just nine months old and no George."

Both Carpenter and the Eagletons survived the war, but the conflict transformed each of their lives. Carpenter had difficulty settling down. Filled with bitter memories of the war years in Tennessee, the Eagletons moved to Arkansas. Ordinary people such as Carpenter and the Eagletons are historically anonymous. Yet their actions on the battlefield and behind the lines helped to shape the course of events, as their leaders realized, even if today we tend to remember only the famous and influential.

Artist Winslow Homer captures a Union sharpshooter in one of his early paintings. (Portland Museum of Art, Maine. Gift of Barbro and Bernard Osher, 3.1993.3) or thousands of Americans, from Lincoln and Davis to Carpenter and the Eagletons, war was both a profoundly personal and a major national event. Its impact reached far beyond the four years of hostilities. The war that was fought to conserve two political, social, and economic visions ended by changing familiar ways of political, social, and economic life in both North and South. War was a transforming force, both destructive and creative in its effect on the structure and social dynamics of society and on the lives of ordinary people. This theme underlies this chapter's analysis of the war's three stages: the initial months of preparation, the years of military stalemate between 1861 and 1865, and, finally, resolution.

Organizing for War

The Confederate bombardment of Fort Sumter on April 12, 1861, and the surrender of Union troops the next day ended the uncertainty of the secession winter. The North's response to Fort Sumter was a virtual declaration of war as President Lincoln called for state militia volunteers to crush southern "insurrection." His action pushed several slave states (Virginia, North Carolina, Tennessee, Arkansas) off the fence and into the southern camp. Other states (Maryland, Kentucky, and Missouri) agonizingly debated which way to go. The "War Between the States" was now a reality.

Many Americans were unenthusiastic about the course of events. Southerners like George Eagleton only reluctantly followed Tennessee out of the Union. When he enlisted, he complained of the "disgraceful cowardice of many who were last winter for secession and war ... but are now refusing self and means for the prosecution of war." Robert E. Lee of Virginia was equally hesitant to resign his federal commission but finally decided that he could not "raise [a] hand against ... relatives ... children ... home." Whites living in the southern uplands (where blacks were few and slaveholders were heartily disliked and envied), yeomen farmers in the Deep South (who owned no slaves), and many residents of border states were dismayed at secession and war. Many would eventually join the Union forces.

In the North, large numbers had supported neither the Republican party nor Lincoln. Irish immigrants who feared the competition of free black labor and southerners now living in Illinois, Indiana, and Ohio harbored misgivings about the war. Indeed, northern Democrats at first blamed Lincoln and the Republicans almost as much as the southern secessionists for the nation's crisis.

Nevertheless, the days following Fort Sumter and Lincoln's call for troops saw an outpouring of support on both sides, fueled in part by relief at decisive action, in part by patriotism and love of adventure, in part by unemployment. Northern blacks and even some southern freedmen proclaimed themselves "ready to go forth and do battle," while whites like Carpenter enthusiastically flocked to enlist. In some places, workers were so eager to join up that trade unions collapsed. Sisters, wives, and mothers set to work making uniforms. A New Yorker, Jane Woolsey, described the drama of those early days "of terrible excitement."

> Outside the parlor windows the city is gay and brilliant with excited crowds, the incessant movement and music of marching regiments and all the thousands of flags, big and little, which suddenly came fluttering out of every window and door.... In our little circle of friends, one mother has just sent away an idolized son; another, two; another, four.... One sweet young wife is packing a regulation valise for her husband today, and doesn't let him see her cry.

The war fever produced so many volunteers that neither northern nor southern officials could handle the throng. Northern authorities turned aside offers from blacks to serve. Both sides sent thousands of white would-be soldiers home. The conviction that the conflict would rapidly come to a glorious conclusion fueled the eagerness to enlist. "We really did not think that there was going to be an actual war," remembered Mary Ward, a young Georgia woman. "We had an idea that when

In May 1861, the first Michigan Regiment mustered in Detroit before boarding the train to Washington. The people crowded in the square, on the porches of the "Rail-Road Hotel," and on rooftops suggest the patriotic enthusiasm of the send-off. As the picture shows, many women shared the fervor for the coming conflict. Thousands of them would be involved in war work at home or in army hospitals or camps. As one explained, "As the soldiers went from among us, there came the yearning wish to lessen somewhat the hardships of their lonely camp life, especially when sick in hospital or wounded." (Detroit Public Library)

our soldiers got upon the ground and showed, unmistakably that they were really ready and willing to fight ... the whole trouble would be declared at an end." Lincoln's call for 75,000 state militiamen for only 90 days of service, and a similar enlistment term for Confederate soldiers, supported the notion that the war would be short.

The Balance of Resources

Despite the bands, parades, cheers, and confidence, the outcome of the approaching civil conflict was much in doubt. Statistics of population and industrial development suggested that the North would win. But Great Britain had also enjoyed enormous statistical advantages in 1775 and yet had lost the War of American Independence. Many of the North's assets would become effective only with time. The military stalemate in 1861 and 1862 proved that in the short term, North and South were evenly matched.

In the North, state militia volunteers called up in April 1861 supplemented the small federal army of 16,000. Probably a quarter of the regular army officers, however, had followed Lee's example and resigned. The Confederate Army, authorized in March 1861, could count on the service of able military men like Robert E. Lee, Joseph E. Johnston, and Albert Sidney Johnston. Its president, Jefferson Davis, was an 1828 graduate of West Point.

The North's white population greatly exceeded that of the South, giving the appearance of a military advantage. Yet in the early days of war, the armies were not unevenly matched. Almost 187,000 Union troops bore arms in July 1861, while just over 112,000 men marched under Confederate colors. Even if numerically inferior, southerners believed that their population would prove the superior fighting force because it was more accustomed to outdoor life and the use of firearms. Many northerners feared that southerners were better natural warriors. True or not, slaves could carry on vital work behind the lines, freeing most adult white males to serve the Confederacy. Slavery, southerners thought, would prove to be a "tower of strength ... at the present crisis."

Resources for War: North Versus South

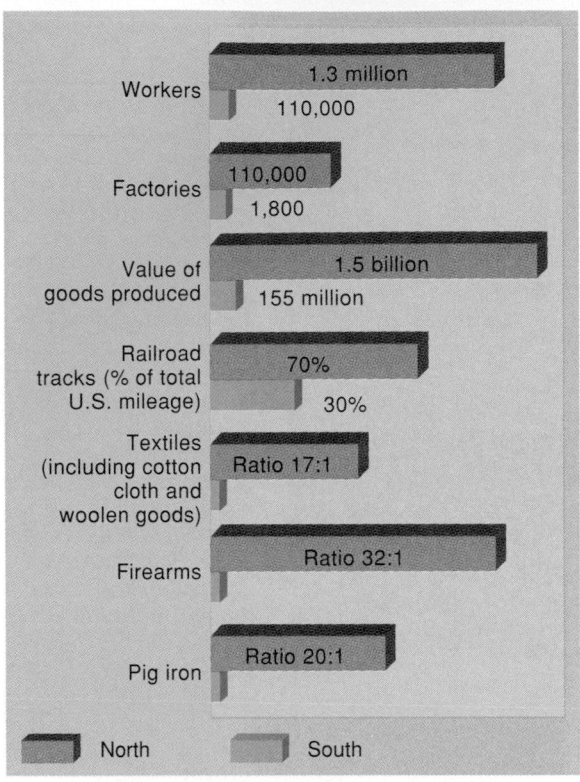

Workers	North: 1.3 million / South: 110,000
Factories	North: 110,000 / South: 1,800
Value of goods produced	North: 1.5 billion / South: 155 million
Railroad tracks (% of total U.S. mileage)	North: 70% / South: 30%
Textiles (including cotton cloth and woolen goods)	Ratio 17:1
Firearms	Ratio 32:1
Pig iron	Ratio 20:1

Legend: North / South

This chart shows the long-range advantages the North enjoyed in the war, but the length and destruction of the conflict suggest that the North was not able to capitalize on its strengths effectively to bring the war to a quick end.

The Union also enjoyed impressive economic advantages. In the North, 1 million workers in 110,000 manufacturing concerns produced goods valued at $1.5 billion annually, while 110,000 southern workers in 18,000 manufacturing concerns produced goods valued at only $155 million a year. The North had one factory for every southern industrial worker, and 70 percent of the nation's railroad tracks were in the North. Producing 17 times as much cotton cloth and woolen goods, 32 times as many firearms, and 20 times as much pig iron as the South, the North could clothe and arm troops and move them and their supplies on a scale that the South could not match. But to be effective, northern industrial resources had to be mobilized for war. That would take time, especially because the government did not intend to direct production. Furthermore, the depleted northern treasury made the government's first task the raising of funds to pay for military necessities.

The South traditionally depended on imported manufactured goods from the North and from Europe. If Lincoln cut off that trade, the South would face the enormous task of creating its industry almost from scratch. Moreover, its railroad system was organized to move cotton, not armies and supplies. Yet the agricultural South did have important resources of food, draft animals, and, of course, cotton, which southerners believed would secure British and French support. Finally, in choosing to wage a defensive war, the South could tap regional loyalty and would enjoy protected lines of supply and support.

Union forces, however, were embarked on an expensive and difficult war of conquest. Because many parts of the South raised cotton and tobacco rather than food crops, Union armies could not forage for necessary food and fodder. Supplying northern forces in the South presented significant logistic problems and dangers. Extended supply lines were always vulnerable to attack, rendering northern armies less mobile and secure than southern troops. The Union had to win a war of conquest and occupation. The South merely had to survive until its enemy tired and gave up.

The Border States

Uncertainty over the war's outcome and divided loyalties produced indecision in the border states. When the seven states of the Deep South seceded during the winter of 1860–1861, the border states adopted a wait-and-see attitude. Delaware identified with the Union camp, but the others vacillated. Their decisions were critically important to both North and South.

The states of the Upper South could provide natural borders for the Confederacy along the Ohio River, access to its river traffic, and vital resources, wealth, and population. The major railroad link to the West ran through Maryland and western Virginia. Virginia boasted the South's largest ironworks, and Tennessee was the region's principal source of grain. Missouri provided the road to Kansas and the West and was strategically placed to control Mississippi River traffic. It was

Secession of the Southern States

The map provides a chronology of secession and shows the geographical importance of the border states. The map also highlights the vulnerable position of Washington and explains many of Lincoln's actions in the early days of the war.

difficult to imagine the long- or short-term success of the Confederacy without the border states.

For the North, every border state that elected to remain loyal was a psychological triumph for the idea of Union. Nor was the North indifferent to the economic and strategic advantages of keeping the border states with the Union. Lincoln's call for troops precipitated decisions in several states, however. Between April 17 and May 20, 1861, Virginia, Arkansas, Tennessee, and North Carolina joined the Confederacy.

The significance of border state loyalty was soon dramatized in Maryland. Slave-owning tobacco and wheat planters from the state's southern counties and eastern shore favored secession. Confederate enthusiasts abounded in Baltimore. But in the western and northern parts of the state, small farmers, often of German background, opposed slavery and supported the Union cause.

On the morning of April 19, the 6th Massachusetts Regiment arrived in Baltimore headed for Washington. Because the regiment had to change railroad lines, the soldiers set out across the city on foot and in horsecars. As they marched through the streets, a mob of some 10,000 southern sympa-

thizers, flying Confederate flags, attacked them with paving stones, then bayonets and bullets. Finally, as a contemporary explained, the "patience of their commander was … exhausted. He cried out in a voice, which was heard even above the yells of the mob, 'Fire!' …A scene of bloody confusion followed." In the commotion, would-be secessionists burned the railroad bridges connecting Baltimore to the North and to the South. Washington found itself cut off from the rest of the Union, an island in the middle of hostile territory.

Lincoln took stern measures to secure Maryland. The president agreed temporarily to route troops around Baltimore. In return, the governor called the state legislature into session at Frederick, a center of Union sentiment in western Maryland. This action and Lincoln's swift violation of civil rights damped secessionist enthusiasm. Hundreds of southern sympathizers, including 19 state legislators and Baltimore's mayor, were arrested and languished in prison without trial. Although the chief justice of the United States, Roger B. Taney, challenged the legality of the president's action and issued a writ of habeas corpus for the release of John Merryman, a southern supporter, Lincoln ignored him. A month later, Taney ruled in *Ex parte Merryman* that if the public's safety was endangered, only Congress had the right to suspend a writ of habeas corpus. By then, Lincoln had secured Maryland for the Union.

Though Lincoln's quick and harsh response ensured Maryland's loyalty, he was more cautious elsewhere. Above all, he had to deal with slavery prudently, for any hasty action would push border states into the waiting arms of the Confederacy. Thus, when General John C. Frémont, in a burst of enthusiasm, issued an unauthorized declaration of emancipation in Missouri in August 1861, Lincoln revoked the order and recalled the general. As the president explained, he expected a chain reaction if certain key states left the Union. "I think to lose Kentucky is nearly the same as to lose the whole game. Kentucky gone, we cannot hold Missouri, nor, as I think, Maryland. These all against us, and the job on our hands is too large for us." In the end, after some fighting and much maneuvering, Kentucky and Missouri, like Maryland, stayed in the Union.

Challenges of War

The tense weeks after Fort Sumter spilled over with unexpected challenges. Neither North nor South could handle the floods of volunteers. Both faced enormous organizational problems as they readied for war. In the South, a nation-state had to be created and its apparatus set in motion. Everything from a constitution and governmental departments to a flag and postage stamps had to be devised. As one onlooker observed, "The whole country was new. Everything was to be done—and to be made."

In February 1861, the original seceding states sent delegates to Montgomery, Alabama, to begin work on a provisional framework and to select a provisional president and vice president. The delegates swiftly wrote a constitution, much like the federal constitution of 1787 except in its emphasis on the "sovereign and independent character" of the states and its explicit recognition of slavery. The provisional president, Jefferson Davis of Mississippi, tried to put together a geographically and politically balanced cabinet with a moderate face

for the outside world. He succeeded in creating a balanced cabinet, but it had few of his friends and, more serious, few men of political stature. As time passed, it turned out to be unstable as well. In a four-year period, 14 men held six positions.

Davis's cabinet appointees faced the formidable challenge of creating government departments from scratch. They had to hire employees and initiate administrative procedures with woefully inadequate resources. The president's office was in a hotel parlor. The Confederate Treasury Department was housed in a room in an Alabama bank "without furniture of any kind; empty ... of desks, tables, chairs or other appliances for the conduct of business." Treasury Secretary Christopher G. Memminger bought furniture with his own money; operations lurched forward in fits and starts. In those early days, when an army captain came to the treasury with a warrant from Davis for blankets, he found only one clerk. After reading the warrant, the clerk offered the captain a few dollars of his own, explaining, "This, Captain, is all the money that I will certify as being in the Confederate Treasury at this moment." Other departments faced similar difficulties.

Inheriting the federal government, Lincoln did not have to set up a postal system or decide whether laws passed before 1861 were valid. Without administrative experience, however, the new president, like his Confederate counterpart, faced organizational problems. Military officers and government clerks daily left the capital for the South. The treasury was empty. The Republicans had won their first presidential election, and floods of office seekers who had worked for Lincoln now thronged into the White House looking for rewards.

Nor could Lincoln, who did not know many of the "prominent men of the day," easily select a cabinet. Finally, he appointed important Republicans from different factions of the party to cabinet posts whether they agreed with him or not. Most were almost strangers to the president. Several scorned him as a bumbling backwoods politician. Treasury Secretary Salmon P. Chase actually hoped to replace Lincoln as president in four years' time. Soon after the inauguration, Secretary of State William Seward sent Lincoln a memo condescendingly offering to oversee the formulation of presidential policy.

Lincoln and Davis

A number of Lincoln's early actions illustrated that he was no malleable backcountry bumbler. As his Illinois law partner, William Herndon, pointed out, Lincoln's "mind was tough—solid—knotty—gnarly, more or less like his body." In his reply to Seward's memo, the president firmly indicated that he intended to run his own administration. After Sumter, he swiftly called up the state militias, expanded the navy, and suspended habeas corpus. He ordered a naval blockade of the South and approved the expenditure of funds for military purposes, all without congressional sanction, because Congress was not in session. As Lincoln told legislators later, "The dogmas of the quiet past are inadequate to the stormy present.... As our case is new, so must we think anew, and act anew ... and then we shall save our country." This willingness to "think anew" was a valuable personal asset, even though some critics called his expansion of presidential power despotic.

By coincidence, Lincoln and his rival, Jefferson Davis, were born only 100 miles apart in Kentucky. However, the course of their lives diverged radically. Lincoln's father had migrated north and eked out a simple existence as a farmer in Indiana and Illinois. Abraham had only a rudimentary formal education and was largely self-taught. Davis's family, however, had moved south to Mississippi and become cotton planters. Davis grew up in comfortable circumstances, went to Transylvania University and West Point, and fought in the Mexican-American War before his election to the U.S. Senate. In recognition of his social, political, and economic prominence, Davis served as secretary of war under Franklin Pierce (1853–1857). Tall and distinguished-looking, he appeared every inch the aristocratic southerner.

Although Davis had not been eager to accept the presidency, he had loyally responded to the call of the provisional congress in 1861 and worked tirelessly as the chief executive of the Confederacy until the war's end. His wife, Varina, observed that "the President hardly takes time to eat his meals and works late at night." Some contemporaries suggested that Davis's inability to let subordinates handle details explained this schedule. Others observed that he was sickly, reserved, humorless, too sensitive to criticism, and hard to get along with. But Davis, like Lincoln, found it necessary to "think anew." He reassured southerners in his inaugural address that his aims were conservative, "to preserve the Government of our fathers in spirit." Yet under the pressure of events, he moved toward creating a new kind of South.

Clashing on the Battlefield, 1861–1862

The Civil War was the most brutal and destructive conflict in American history. Much of the bloodshed resulted from changing military technology coupled with inadequate communications. By the opening of hostilities, the range of rifles had increased from 100 to 500 yards, in part owing to the new French minié bullet, which traveled with tremendous velocity and accuracy. The greater reach of the new rifles meant that it was no longer possible to position the artillery close enough to enemy lines to allow it to support an infantry charge. During the Civil War, then, attacking infantry soldiers faced a final, often fatal, dash of 500 yards in the face of deadly enemy fire.

As it became clear that infantry charges resulted in horrible carnage, military leaders increasingly valued the importance of the strong defensive position. Although Confederate soldiers criticized General Lee as "King of Spades" when he first ordered them to construct earthworks, the epithet evolved into one of affection as it became obvious that earthworks saved lives. Union commanders followed suit. By the end of 1862, both armies dug defensive earthworks and trenches whenever they interrupted their march.

War in the East

The war's brutal character only gradually revealed itself. The Union commanding general, 70-year-old Winfield Scott, at first pressed for a cautious, long-term strategy, known as the Anaconda Plan. Scott proposed weakening the South gradually through blockades on land and at sea until the northern army was strong enough for the kill. The excited public, however, hungered for action and quick victory. So did Lincoln, who knew that the longer the war lasted, the more embittered the South and the North would both become, making reunion ever more difficult. Under the cry of "Forward to Richmond!" 35,000 partially trained men led by General Irwin McDowell headed out from Washington in sweltering July weather.

On July 21, 1861, only 25 miles from the capital at Manassas Creek, or Bull Run, as it is also called, inexperienced northern troops confronted 25,000 raw Confederate soldiers commanded by Brigadier General P. G. T. Beauregard, a West Point classmate of McDowell's. Although sightseers, journalists, and politicians accompanied the Union troops, expecting only a Sunday outing, the encounter at Bull Run was no picnic. The course of battle swayed back and forth before the arrival of 2,300 fresh Confederate troops, brought by trains, decided the day. Union soldiers and sightseers fled toward Washington in terror and confusion. An English journalist, William Russell, described the troops as they poured into Washington on July 22:

> I saw a steady stream of men covered with mud, soaked through with rain ... pouring irregularly, without any semblance of order, up Pennsylvania Avenue toward the Capitol.... I perceived they belonged to different regiments ... mingled pell-mell together.... Hastily [I] ...ran downstairs and asked an officer ... a pale young man who looked exhausted to death and who had lost his sword ... where the men were coming from. "Where from? Well, sir, I guess we're all coming out of Virginny as far as we can, and pretty well whipped too.... I know I'm going home. I've had enough of fighting to last my lifetime."

"Pretty well whipped" the Union forces certainly were. Yet inexperienced Confederate troops had lost their chance to turn the rout into the quick and decisive victory they sought. As General Joseph E. Johnston pointed out, his men were disorganized, confused by victory, and not well enough supplied with food to chase the Union army back toward Washington.

In many ways, the Battle of Bull Run was prophetic. Victory would be neither quick nor easy.

In 1862, Lincoln met with his General in Chief George McClellan and posed for this stiff photograph. Although Lincoln's civilian status is clear in his clothing, his involvement in the military side of the war was great. (Library of Congress)

As the disorganization and confusion of both sides suggested, the armies were unprofessional. And it was becoming obvious that bravado would not win the war. Then, too, both sides faced problems with short-term enlistments. Finally, logistic problems connected with mass armies plagued both sides. The Civil War put more men in the field than any previous American engagement. Supplying and moving so many men and ensuring adequate communication, especially during battle, were tasks of an unprecedented kind. It was hardly surprising that the armies floundered trying to meet these logistic challenges.

Robert Allston, the prominent South Carolina rice planter, viewed the battlefield at Bull Run and decided it had been a "glorious tho bloody" day. For the Union, however, the loss at Bull Run was sobering. Replacing McDowell with 34-year-old General George McClellan, Lincoln began his search for a northern commander capable of winning the war. McClellan, formerly an army engineer, confronted the task of transforming the Army of the Potomac into a fighting force. Short-term militias went home. When Scott retired in the fall of 1861, McClellan became general in chief of the Union armies.

Eastern Theater of the Civil War, 1861–1862

Legend:
- ← Union movements
- ← Confederate movements
- ★ Union victory
- ★ Confederate victory
- ▓ Union
- ░ Confederate

The map reveals the military actions in the East during the early years of the war. Initially, military planners hoped to end the war quickly by capturing Richmond. They soon discovered that the Confederate army was too powerful to allow them an easy victory. Eventually, Lincoln decided to combine military pressure on Virginia with an effort in the West aimed at cutting the Confederacy in two.

McClellan had considerable organizational ability but no desire to be a daring leader on the battlefield. Convinced that the North must combine military victory with efforts to persuade the South to return to the Union, he sought to avoid unnecessary and embittering loss of life and property. He intended to win the war "by maneuvering rather than fighting."

In March 1862, pushed by an impatient Lincoln, McClellan finally led his army of 130,000 toward Richmond, now the Confederate capital. By late June, his army was close enough to hear Richmond's church bells pealing. But just as it seemed that victory was within grasp, Lee counterattacked and slowly drove the Union forces away from the city. Finally, orders came from Washington: Abandon the Peninsula campaign.

Other Union defeats followed in 1862 as commanders came and went. In September, the South

This dying horse, stripped of saddle and bridle, was the mount of a Confederate officer killed during the battle of Antietam. The stark character of the picture reveals the devastating nature of the Civil War battlefield. (Library of Congress)

took the offensive with a bold invasion of Maryland. But after a costly defeat at Antietam, in which more than 5,000 soldiers were slaughtered and another 17,000 wounded on the grisliest day of the war, Lee withdrew his army to Virginia. Victory eluded both sides. The war in the East was stalemated.

Trans-Mississippi Campaign of the Civil War

← Union movements

← Confederate movements

★ Union victory

The military movements in the trans-Mississippi West appear here. Union forces operating in the Mississippi Valley were attempting to separate Texas, Arkansas, and Louisiana from other southern states as part of an attempt to squeeze the Confederacy.

War in the West

The early struggle in the East focused on Richmond, the Confederacy's capital and one of the South's most important railroad, industrial, and munitions centers. But the East was only one of three theaters of action. Between the Appalachian Mountains and the Mississippi lay the western theater, the states of Kentucky, Tennessee, Mississippi, and Alabama. At its edge lay the Mississippi, with its vital river trade and its great port, New Orleans. Here both George Eagleton and Arthur Carpenter served. Beyond lay the trans-Mississippi West—Louisiana, Arkansas, Missouri, Texas, and the Great Plains—where Native American tribes joined the conflict on both sides.

In the western theater, the Union had two strategic objectives: the domination of Kentucky and eastern Tennessee, the avenues to the South and West, and control of the Mississippi River in order to split the South in two. Major campaigns sought strategic points along rivers and railroads.

It was in the western theater that Ulysses S. Grant rose to prominence. Working in his family's leather store in Illinois when the war broke out, Grant had lackluster military credentials. Although he had attended West Point and served creditably in the Mexican-American War, his career in the peacetime army was undistinguished and ended in resignation. But soon after Fort Sumter, Grant enlisted as a colonel in an Illinois militia regiment. Within two months, he was a brigadier general.

Grant's military genius consisted of an ability to see beyond individual battles to larger goals. In 1862, he realized that the Tennessee and Cumberland rivers were the paths for the successful invasion of Tennessee. A premature Confederate invasion of Kentucky allowed Grant to bring his forces into that state without arousing sharp local opposition. Assisted by gunboats, Grant was largely responsible for the capture of Fort Henry and Fort Donelson, key points on the rivers, in February 1862. His successes there raised fears among Confederate leaders that southern mountaineers, loyal to the Union, would rush to Grant's support.

Despite Grant's grasp of strategy, his army was nearly destroyed by a surprise Confederate attack at Shiloh Church in Tennessee. The North won this

This photograph taken at a field hospital in Virginia during a battle in the summer of 1862 shows surgeons trying to attend to the crowds of wounded lying on the ground. Many deaths resulted from inadequate care for the wounded and sick of both armies. Although there was initial resistance to the idea of women becoming nurses in such hospitals, the dreadful shortage of qualified medical men and the huge workload that they faced eventually resulted in allowing women nurses into hospitals. One described her first reaction to the scene that greeted her eyes. "A strange sense of suffocation oppressed me, as the air by which I was surrounded was filled with poisonous vapors, and for a few minutes I doubted my own strength." (Library of Congress)

battle, but victory proved enormously costly. In that two-day engagement, the Union suffered over 13,000 casualties, while 10,000 Confederates lay dead or wounded. More men fell in this single battle than in the American Revolution, the War of 1812, and the Mexican-American War combined. Because neither army offered sufficient care on the battlefield, untreated wounds caused many of the deaths. A full day after the battle had ended, nine-tenths of the wounded still lay in the rain. Many died of exposure; others drowned in the downpour. Those who survived the weather had infected wounds by the time they received medical attention. Though more successful than efforts in the East, such devastating Union campaigns failed to bring decisive results. Western plans were never coordinated with eastern military activities. Victories there did not force the South to its knees.

The war in the trans-Mississippi West was a sporadic, far-flung struggle for control of the manpower and natural resources of this vast area. California was one prize that lured both armies into the Southwest. Confederate troops from Texas held Albuquerque and Santa Fe briefly in 1862. Volunteer soldiers from the Colorado mining fields, joined by Mexican Americans and other soldiers, drove the Texas Confederates from New Mexico. A Union force recruited in California arrived after the Confederates were gone. They spent the remainder of the Civil War years fighting the Apache and the Navajo and with brutal competence crushed both Native American nations.

Farther east was another prize, the Missouri River, which flowed into the Mississippi River, bordered Illinois, and affected military campaigns in Kentucky and Tennessee. Initially, Confederate troops were successful here, as they had been in New Mexico. But in March 1862, at Pea Ridge in northern Arkansas, the balance tilted in favor of the Union. There the Union forces defeated a Confederate Army of 16,000 that included a brigade of Native Americans from the Five Civilized Nations. Missouri entered the Union camp for the first time in the war, and fierce guerrilla warfare continued in the region.

Naval Warfare

At the beginning of the war, Lincoln had decided to strangle the South with a naval blockade. But an effective blockade proved elusive. With no more than 33 ships, the Union navy tried to close up 189 ports along a 3,500-mile coastline. In 1861, the navy intercepted only about one blockade runner in ten and in 1862 one in eight. In the short run, the blockade did little damage to the South.

More successful were operations to gain footholds along the southern coast. In November 1861, a Union expedition took Port Royal Sound, where it freed the first slaves, and the nearby South Carolina sea islands. A few months later, the navy defeated a Confederate force on Roanoke Island, North Carolina. By gaining fueling stations and other important coastal points, the navy increased the possibility of making the blockade effective. The Union's greatest naval triumph in the early war years was the capture of New Orleans in 1862. The loss of the South's greatest port seriously weakened the Confederacy. The success of this amphibious effort stimulated other joint attempts to cut the South in two.

The Confederate leadership, recognizing that the South could not match the Union fleet, concentrated on developing new weapons like torpe-

does and formidable ironclad vessels, a concept already successfully tested by the French navy. Because the Union fleet consisted primarily of wooden ships, iron ships might literally crash through the Union blockade.

The *Merrimac* was one key to southern naval strategy. Originally a U.S. warship sunk as the federal navy hurriedly abandoned the Norfolk Navy Yard early in the war, the Confederates raised the vessel and covered it with heavy iron armor. Rechristened the *Virginia*, the ship steamed out of Norfolk in March 1862, heading directly for the Union ships blocking the harbor. Using its 1,500-pound ram and guns, the *Virginia* drove a third of the ships aground and destroyed the squadron's largest ships. Victory was short-lived. The next day, the *Virginia* confronted the *Monitor*, a newly completed Union iron vessel. Their duel was inconclusive, and the *Virginia* withdrew. It was burned during the evacuation of Norfolk that May. Southern attempts to buy ironclad ships abroad faded and with them southern hopes of evading the northern noose.

Though technological innovation failed to break the blockade, the Confederate Navy's policy of harming northern commerce brought some success. Confederate raiders, many of them built in England, wreaked havoc on northern shipping. In

This painting of the battle between the Confederate Virginia *(stubbornly called the* Merrimac *by northerners) and the Union* Monitor *captures the dramatic impact of the new iron ships. Both navies eventually used the innovative iron vessels. (Chicago Historical Society)*

its two-year career, the raider *Alabama* destroyed 69 Union merchant vessels valued at more than $6 million. But while such blows were costly to the North, they did not seriously damage its overall war effort.

Throughout the first two years of conflict, both sides achieved victories, but the war remained deadlocked. Although the South was far from being defeated, the North was as far from giving up or accepting southern independence. The costs of war, in manpower and supplies, far exceeded what either side had anticipated. The need to replace lost men and supplies thus loomed ever more serious at the end of 1862.

Cotton Diplomacy

Both sides in the Civil War realized that attitudes in Europe could be critical. European diplomatic recognition of the Confederacy would give the nation credibility in the eyes of the rest of the world. Furthermore, European loans and assistance might bring the South victory just as French and Dutch aid had helped the American colonies win their independence. If the European nations refused to recognize the South, however, the fiction of the Union was kept alive, undermining Confederate chances for long-term survival. The European powers, of course, consulted their own national interests. Neither England nor France, the two most important nations, wished to back the losing side. Nor did they wish to upset Europe's delicate balance of power by hasty intervention in American affairs. One by one, therefore, the European states declared a policy of neutrality.

Southerners were sure that cotton would be their trump card. English and French textile mills needed cotton, and southerners believed that their owners would eventually force government recognition of the Confederacy and an end to the North's blockade. But a glut of cotton in 1860 and 1861 left foreign mill owners oversupplied. As stockpiles dwindled, European industrialists found cotton in India and Egypt. The conviction that cotton was "the king who can shake the jewels in the crown of Queen Victoria" proved false.

Union Secretary of State Seward sought above all else to prevent diplomatic recognition of the Confederacy. The North had its own economic ties with Europe, so the Union was not as disadvantaged as southerners thought. Seward daringly threatened Great Britain with war if it interfered in what he insisted was an internal matter. Some called his boldness reckless, even mad. Nevertheless, his policy succeeded. Even though England allowed the construction of Confederate raiders in its ports, it did not intervene in American affairs in 1861 or 1862. Nor did the other European powers. Unless the military situation changed dramatically, the Europeans were willing to sit on the sidelines.

Common Problems, Novel Solutions

As the conflict dragged on into 1863, unanticipated problems appeared in both the Union and the Confederacy, and leaders devised novel approaches to solve them. War acted as a catalyst for changes that no one could have imagined in the heady spring days of 1861.

The problem of fighting a long war was partly monetary. Both treasuries had been empty initially, and the war proved extraordinarily expensive. Neither side considered trying to finance the war by imposing direct taxes. Such an approach violated custom and risked alienating support. Nevertheless, each side was so starved for funds that it initiated taxation on a small scale. Ultimately, taxes financed 21 percent of the North's war expenses (but only 1 percent of southern expenses). Both treasuries also tried borrowing. Northerners bought over $2 billion worth of bonds, but southerners proved reluctant to buy their government's bonds.

As in the American Revolution, the unwelcome solution was to print paper money. In August 1861, the Confederacy put into circulation $100 million in crudely engraved bills. Millions more followed the next year. Five months later, the Union issued $150 million in paper money, soon nicknamed "greenbacks" because of their color. Although financing the war with paper money was unexpected, the resulting inflation was not. Inflation was particularly troublesome in the Confederacy, but a "modest" 80 percent increase in food prices brought Union city families near starvation and contributed to urban unhappiness during the war.

Both sides confronted similar manpower problems as initial enthusiasm for the war evaporated. Soldiering, it turned out, was nothing like the militia parades and outings familiar to most American males. Young men were shocked at the deadliness of diseases that accompanied the army wherever it went and unprepared for the boredom of camp life. As one North Carolina soldier explained, "If anyone wishes to become used to the crosses and trials of this life, let him enter camp life." None was prepared for the vast and impersonal destruction of the battlefield, which made a mockery of values like courage and honor. It was with anguish that Robert Carter of Massachusetts saw bodies tossed into trenches "with not a prayer, eulogy or tear to distinguish them from so many animals." Those in the service longed to go home. The swarm of volunteers disappeared. Rather than fill their military quotas from within, rich northern communities began offering bounties of $800 to $1,000 to outsiders who would join up.

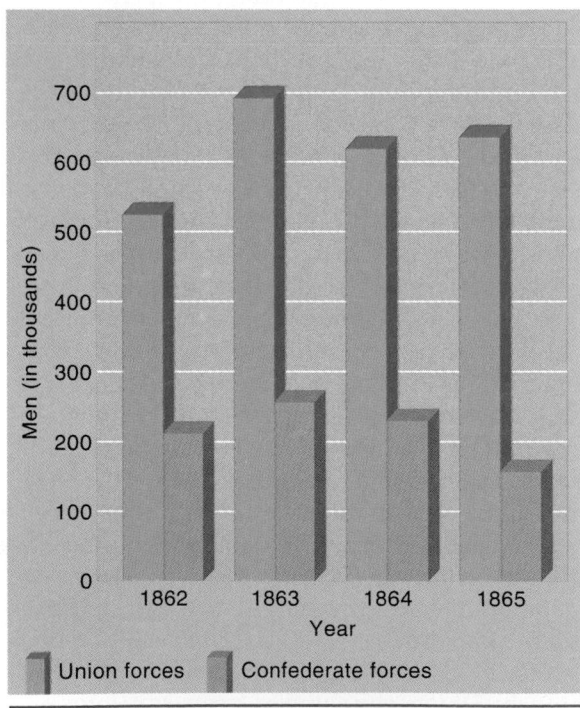

Men Present for Duty in the Civil War

The chart demonstrates the growing superiority of the North in terms of manpower and the impact of draft laws. After 1863, blacks, like native-born Americans and Irish and German immigrants, served in the armed forces.

Arthur Carpenter's letters give a good picture of life in the ranks and a young man's growing disillusionment with the war. As Carpenter's regiment moved into Kentucky and Tennessee in the winter of 1862, his enthusiasm for army life evaporated. "Soldiering in Kentucky and Tennessee," he complained, "is not so pretty as it was in Indianapolis. . . . We have been half starved, half frozen, and half drowned. The mud in Kentucky is awful." Soldiering often meant marching over rutted roads carrying 50 or 60 pounds of equipment with insufficient food, water, or supplies. One blanket was not enough in the winter. In the summer, stifling woolen uniforms attracted lice and other vermin. Poor food, bugs, inadequate sanitation, and exposure invited disease. Carpenter marched through Tennessee suffering from diarrhea and then fever. His regiment left him behind in a convalescent barracks in Louisville, which he fled as soon as he could. He feared the hospital at least as much as the sickness. "99 Surgeons out of a hundred," he wrote his parents, "would not know whether his patient had the horse distemper, lame toe, or any other disease."

Confederate soldiers, even less well supplied than their northern counterparts, complained similarly. In 1862, a Virginia captain described what General Lee called the best army "the world ever saw":

> During our forced marches and hard fights, the soldiers have been compelled to throw away their knapsacks and there is scarcely a private in the army who has a change of clothing of any kind. Hundreds of men are perfectly barefooted and there is no telling when they can be supplied with shoes.

In such circumstances, desertion was common. An estimated one of every nine men enlisting in the Confederate armies and one of every seven in the Union armies deserted.

As the manpower problems became critical, both governments resorted to the draft. Despite the sacrosanct notion of states' rights, the Confederate Congress passed the first conscription act in American history in March 1862. Four months later, the Union Congress also approved a draft measure. Both laws sought to encourage men already in the army to reenlist and to stimulate volunteers rather than to force men to serve. Ultimately, over 30 percent of the Confederate Army and 6 percent of the Union forces were draftees.

The Confederacy relied more heavily on the draft than the Union did because the North's initial manpower pool was larger and growing. During the war, 180,000 foreigners of military age poured into the northern states. Some came specifically to claim bounties and fight. Immigrants made up at least 20 percent of the Union army.

Necessary though they were, draft laws were very unpopular. The first Confederate conscription declared all able-bodied men between 18 and 35 eligible for military service but allowed numerous exemptions and the purchase of substitutes. Critics complained that the provision entitling every planter with more than 20 slaves to one exemption from military service favored rich slave owners. Certainly, the legislation fed class tension in the South and encouraged disloyalty and desertion among the poorer classes, particularly among southern mountaineers. The advice one woman shouted after her husband as he was dragged off to the army was hardly unique. "You desert again, quick as you kin.... Desert, Jake!" The law, as one southerner pointed out, "aroused a spirit of rebellion."

Northern legislation was neither more popular nor fair. The 1863 draft allowed the hiring of substitutes, and $300 bought an exemption from military service. Workers, already suffering from inflation, resented the ease with which moneyed citizens could avoid army duty. In July 1863, the resentment boiled over in New York City in the largest civil disturbance of the nineteenth century.

The three-day riot came only a month after a work stoppage on the New York waterfront. The process of selecting several thousand conscripts began on a weekend in early July. By Monday, workers opposed to the draft were parading through the streets. Several Irish members of the Black Joker Volunteer Fire Company whose names had been listed were determined to go further than peaceful protest by destroying draft records and the Enrollment Office. Events spun out of control as a mob also burned the armory, plundered the houses of the rich, and looted jewelry stores. Blacks, whom the Irish hated as economic competitors and the cause of the war, became special targets. Mobs shouting, "Vengeance on

These advertisements from a Virginia newspaper include two for substitutes, indicating the advantages money provided for those who wished to avoid military service. (Virginia Historical Society, Richmond)

every nigger in New York," beat and lynched blacks and even burned the Colored Orphan Asylum. More than 100 people died in the violence. There was much truth in the accusation that the war on both sides was a rich man's war but a poor man's fight.

Political Dissension, 1862

As the war continued, rumbles of dissension grew louder. On February 24, 1862, the *Richmond Examiner* summarized many southerners' frustration. "The Confederacy has had everything that was required for success but one, and that one thing it was and is supposed to possess more than anything else, namely Talent." As victory proved elusive, necessitating unpopular measures like the draft, criticism of Confederate leaders mounted. Jefferson Davis's vice president, Alexander Stephens of Georgia, became one of the administration's bitterest accusers. Public criticism reflected private disapproval. Wrote one southerner to a friend,

"Impeach Jeff Davis for incompetency & call a convention of the States.... West Point is death to us & sick Presidents & Generals are equally fatal."

Because the South had no party system, dissatisfaction with Davis and his handling of the war tended to be factional, petty, and personal. No party mechanism existed to channel or curb irresponsible criticism. Detractors rarely felt it necessary to offer programs in place of Davis's policies. Davis suffered personally from the carping comments of his detractors. More important, the Confederacy suffered. Without a party leader's traditional weapons and rewards, Davis had no mechanism to generate enthusiasm for his war policies.

Although Lincoln has since become a folk hero, at the time, many northerners derided his performance and eagerly looked forward to a new president in 1864. Peace Democrats, called Copperheads, claimed that Lincoln betrayed the Constitution and that working-class Americans bore the brunt of his policy of conscription. New York Democrats warned the city's Irish residents that freed blacks would "steal the work and bread of honest Irish." Immigrant workers in eastern cities and those who lived in the southern parts of the Midwest had little sympathy for abolitionism or blacks, and they supported the antiwar stance of the Copperheads. Even Democrats favoring the war effort found Lincoln arbitrary and tyrannical. Fearing his expansion of presidential power, they also worried that extreme Republicans would push Lincoln into making the war a crusade for the abolition of slavery. Some Republicans judged Lincoln indecisive and inept. William Herndon, his former law partner, was one of the many who lashed out against the president. "Does he suppose he can crush—squelch out this huge rebellion by pop guns filled with rose water?" he asked indignantly. "He ought to hang somebody and get up a name for will or decision."

Republicans split gradually into two factions. The moderates favored a cautious approach toward winning the war. They feared the possible consequences of emancipating the slaves, confiscating Confederate property, or arming blacks. The radicals, however, urged Lincoln to make emancipation a wartime objective. They hoped for a victory that would revolutionize southern social and racial arrangements. The reduction of the congressional Republican majority in the fall elections of 1862 made it imperative that Lincoln not only listen to both factions, but also to the Democratic opposition.

The Tide Turns, 1863–1865

Hard political realities as well as Lincoln's sense of the public's mood help explain why he delayed an emancipation proclamation until 1863. Like congressional Democrats, many northerners supported a war for the Union but not one for emancipation. Not only did many, if not most, whites see blacks as inferior, but they also suspected that emancipation would trigger a massive influx of former slaves who would steal white men's jobs and political rights. Race riots in New York, Brooklyn, Philadelphia, and Buffalo dramatized white attitudes. In Cincinnati, Irish dockworkers attacked blacks who were offering to work for less pay with the cry, "Let's clear out the niggers." Arthur Carpenter's evaluation of blacks was typical of many northern soldiers confronting blacks for the first time. In December 1861, he wrote to his parents:

> No one who has ever seen the nigger in all its glory on the southern plantations ... will ever vote for emancipation.... If emancipation is to be the policy of the war (and I think it will not) I do not care how quick the country goes to pot. The negro never was intended to be equal with the white man.

The Emancipation Proclamation, 1863

If the president moved too fast on emancipation, he risked losing the allegiance of people like Carpenter, offending the border states, and increasing the Democrats' chances for political victory. Moreover, he had at first hoped that pro-Union sentiment would emerge in the South and compel its leaders to abandon their rebellion. But if Lincoln did not move at all, he would alienate abolitionists and lose the support of radical Republicans, which he could ill afford.

For these reasons, Lincoln proceeded cautiously. At first, he hoped the border states would take the initiative. In the early spring of 1862, he urged Congress to pass a joint resolution offering federal compensation to states beginning a "gradual abolishment of slavery." Border state opposition killed the idea and indicated reluctance to believe, as Lincoln did, that the "friction and abrasion" of war would finally end slavery. Abolitionists and northern blacks, however, greeted Lincoln's proposal with a "thrill of joy."

That summer, Lincoln told his cabinet he intended to emancipate the slaves. Secretary of State Seward urged the president to delay any general proclamation until the North won a decisive military victory. Otherwise, he warned, Lincoln would appear to be urging racial insurrection behind the Confederate lines to compensate for northern military bungling.

Lincoln followed Seward's advice, using that summer and fall to prepare the North for the shift in the war's purpose. To counteract white racial fears of free blacks, he promoted various schemes for establishing free black colonies in Haiti and Panama. Seizing unexpected opportunities, he lay the groundwork for the proclamation itself. In August, Horace Greeley, the influential abolitionist editor of the New York *Tribune*, printed an open letter to Lincoln attacking him for failing to act on slavery. In his reply, Lincoln linked the idea of emancipation to military necessity. His primary goal, he wrote, was to save the Union:

> If I could save the Union without freeing any slave, I would do it; and if I could save it by freeing all the slaves, I would do it; and if I could do it by freeing some and leaving others alone, I would also do that. What I do about Slavery and the colored race, I do because I believe it helps to save this Union.

If Lincoln attacked slavery, then, it would be only because emancipation would save white lives, preserve the democratic process, and win the conflict for the Union.

In September 1862, the Union victory at Antietam gave Lincoln the opportunity to issue a preliminary emancipation proclamation. It stated that unless rebellious states (or parts of states in rebellion) returned to the Union by January 1, 1863, the president would declare their slaves "for-

ever free." Although supposedly aimed at bringing the southern states back into the Union, Lincoln never expected the South to lay down arms after two years of bloodshed. Rather, he was preparing northerners to accept the eventuality of emancipation on the grounds of necessity. Frederick Douglass greeted the president's action with jubilation. "We shout for joy," he wrote, "that we live to record this righteous decree."

Not all northerners shared Douglass's joy. In fact, the September proclamation probably harmed Lincoln's party in the fall elections. As one Democratic ditty put it:

> *"De Union!" used to be de cry—*
> *For dat we want it strong;*
> *But now de motto seems to be,*
> *"De nigger, right or wrong."*

Although the elections of 1862 weakened the Republicans' grasp on the national government, they did not destroy it. Still, cautious cabinet members begged Lincoln to forget about emancipation. His refusal demonstrated his vision and humanity, as did his efforts to reduce racial fears. "Is it dreaded that the freed people will swarm forth and cover the whole land?" he asked. "Are they not already in the land? Will liberation make them any more numerous? Equally distributed among the whites of the whole country, and there would be but one colored to seven whites. Could the one, in any way, greatly disturb the other?"

Finally, on New Year's Day, 1863, Lincoln issued the final Emancipation Proclamation as he had promised. It was an "act of justice, warranted by the Constitution upon military necessity." Thus, what had started as a war to save the Union now also became a struggle that, if victorious, would free the slaves. Yet the proclamation had no immediate impact on slavery. It affected only slaves living in the unconquered portions of the Confederacy. It was silent about slaves in the border states and in parts of the South already in northern hands. These limitations led Elizabeth Cady Stanton and Susan B. Anthony to establish the woman's Loyal National League to lobby Congress to emancipate all southern slaves.

Though the Emancipation Proclamation did not immediately liberate southern slaves from their masters, it had a tremendous symbolic

Frank Leslie's Illustrated Newspaper *showed this scene of Emancipation Day at Smith's Plantation, Port Royal, South Carolina. Black soldiers, some from the southern states, were accepted for combat duty in the Union army as the war progressed. Note that the officer of the First Carolina Volunteers is white and that the white people are seated on the stage, well above the crowds of African Americans. (January 24, 1863)*

importance. On New Year's Day, blacks gathered outside the White House to cheer the president and tell him that if he would "come out of that palace, they would hug him to death." They realized that the proclamation had changed the nature of the war. For the first time, the government had committed itself to freeing slaves. Jubilant blacks could only believe that the president's action heralded a new era for their race. More immediately, the proclamation sanctioned the policy of accepting blacks as soldiers into the military. Blacks also hoped that the news would reach southern slaves, encouraging them either to flee to Union lines or to subvert the southern war effort by refusing to work for their masters.

Diplomatic concerns also lay behind the Emancipation Proclamation. Lincoln and his advisers anticipated that the commitment to abolish slavery would favorably impress foreign powers. European statesmen, however, did not abandon their cautious stance toward the Union. The English prime minister called the proclamation "trash." But important segments of the English public who opposed slavery now came to regard any attempt to help the South as immoral. Foreigners could better understand and sympathize with a war to free the slaves than they could with a war to save the Union. In diplomacy, where image

is so important, Lincoln had created a more attractive picture of the North. The Emancipation Proclamation became the North's symbolic call for human freedom.

Unanticipated Consequences of War

The Emancipation Proclamation was but another example of the war's surprising consequences. Innovation was necessary for victory. In the final two years of the war, both North and South experimented on the battlefields and behind the lines in desperate efforts to conclude the conflict successfully.

One of the Union's experiments involved using black troops for combat duty. Blacks had offered themselves as soldiers in 1861 but had been turned away. They were serving as cooks, laborers, teamsters, and carpenters in the army, however, and composed as much as a quarter of the navy. But as white casualties mounted, so did the interest in black service on the battlefield. The Union government allowed states to escape draft quotas if they enlisted enough volunteers, and they allowed them to count southern black enlistees on their state rosters. Northern governors grew increasingly interested in black military service. One piece of doggerel reflected changing attitudes:

Some tell us 'tis a burnin' shame
To make the naygers fight;
And that the thrade of bein' kilt
Belongs but to the white:
But as for me, upon my soul!
So liberal are we here.
I'll let Sambo be murthered instead of myself
On every day in the year.

Beyond white self-interest lay the promises of the Emancipation Proclamation and the desire to prove blacks' value to the Union. Black leaders like Frederick Douglass pressed for military service. "Once let the black man get upon his person the brass letter, U.S., let him get an eagle on his button, and a musket on his shoulder and bullets in his pocket," Douglass believed, "there is no power on earth that can deny that he has earned the right to citizenship." By the war's end, 186,000 blacks (10 percent of the army) had served the Union cause, 134,111 of them escapees from slave states.

Enrolling blacks in the Union army was an important step toward citizenship and acceptance of blacks by white society. But the black experience in the army highlighted some of the obstacles to racial acceptance. Black soldiers, usually led by white officers, were second-class soldiers for most of the war, receiving lower pay ($10 a month as compared with $13), poorer food, often more menial work, and fewer benefits than whites. "If we are good enough to fill up white men's places and fight, we should be treated then, in all respects, the same as the white man," one black soldier

Newspaper engravings provided civilians with images of the conflict. This colored lithograph by Currier & Ives was produced a generation after the war, but it is very much like the journalistic images of the time. The picture shows a famous black regiment, the 54th Massachusetts, valiantly storming Fort Wagner, South Carolina. James Gooding, a member of the volunteer regiment and a free black from New Bedford, Massachusetts, described the assault. "We went at it, over the ditch and on to the parapet through a deadly fire; but we could not get into the fort. We met the foe on the parapet of Wagner with the bayonet—we were exposed to a murderous fire.... Mortal men could not stand such a fire, and the assault on Wagner was a failure." The experiences of the 54th form the basis for the movie, Glory. *(Library of Congress)*

Photography

The invention of photography in 1839 expanded the visual and imaginative world of nineteenth-century Americans. For the first time, Americans could visually record events in their own lives and see the images of people and incidents from far away. Photographs, of course, also expand the boundaries of the historian's world. As photographic techniques became simpler, more and more visual information about the nineteenth century was captured. Historians can use photographs to discover what nineteenth-century Americans wore, how they celebrated weddings and funerals, and what their families, houses, and cities looked like. Pictures of election campaigns, parades, strikes, and wars show the texture of public life. But historians can also study photographs, as they do paintings, to glean information about attitudes and norms. The choice of subjects, the way in which people and objects are arranged and grouped, and the relationships between people in photographs are all clues to the social and cultural values of nineteenth-century Americans.

Some knowledge of the early history of photography helps place the visual evidence in the proper perspective. The earliest type of photograph, the daguerreotype, was not a print, but the negative itself on a sheet of silver-plated copper. The first daguerreotype required between 15 and 30 minutes for the proper exposure. This accounts for the stiff and formal quality of many of these photographs. Glass ambrotypes (negatives on glass) and tintypes (negatives on gray iron bases), developed after the daguerreotype, were easier and cheaper to produce. But both techniques produced only one picture and required what to us would seem an interminable time for exposure.

A major breakthrough came in the 1850s with the development of the wet-plate process. In this process, the photographer coated a glass negative with a sensitive solution, exposed the negative (i.e., took the picture), and then quickly developed it. The new procedure required a relatively short exposure time of perhaps five seconds out of doors and one minute inside. Action shots, however, were still not feasible. The entire process tied the photographer to the darkroom. Traveling photographers carried their darkrooms with them. The advantage of the wet-plate process was that it was possible to make many paper prints from one negative, opening new commercial vistas for professional photographers.

Mathew Brady, a fashionable Washington photographer, realizing that the camera was the "eye of history,"

Mathew Brady, Confederate Captives, Gettysburg. *(National Archives)*

asked Lincoln for permission to record the war with his camera. He and his team of photographers left about 8,000 glass negatives, currently stored in the Library of Congress and the National Archives, as their record of the Civil War. Shown here are two photographs, one of three Confederate soldiers captured at Gettysburg, the other of the battlefield of Cold Harbor in Virginia.

In the first photograph, study and describe the three soldiers. How are they posed? What kind of clothes are they wearing? What about their equipment? What seems to be their physical condition? Using this photograph as evidence, what might you conclude about the southern soldier—his equipment, uniforms, shoes? How well fed do the men in the picture appear? What attitudes are conveyed through their facial expressions and poses? Finally, what kind of mood was the northern photographer trying to create? What might a northern viewer conclude about the South's war effort after looking at this picture?

The second picture was taken in April 1865, about a year after the battle at Cold Harbor. In the background, you can see two Union soldiers digging graves. In the foreground are the grisly remains of the battle. What do you think is the intent of the photograph? The choice of subject matter shows clearly that photography reveals attitudes as well as facts. What attitude toward war and death is conveyed in this picture? Why is the burial taking place a full year after the battle? What does this tell us about the nature of civil warfare? Notice that the soldiers ordered to undertake this ghastly chore are black, as was customary. What might this scene suggest about the experience of black soldiers in the Union army?

These photographs just begin to suggest what can be discovered from old photographs. Your local historical society and library probably have photograph collections available to you. In addition, at home or in a relative's attic you may find visual records of your family and its history.

Mathew Brady, Burial Party at Cold Harbor. *(Chicago Historical Society)*

on central direction and control. Many southerners denounced Davis as a tyrant and a despot because he recognized the need for the central government to take the lead. Despite the accusations, the Confederate Congress cooperated with him and established important precedents. In 1863, it enacted a comprehensive tax law and an impressment act that allowed government agents to requisition food, horses, wagons, and other necessary war materials, often for only about half their market price. These were prime examples of the central government's power to interfere with private property. Government impressment of slaves for war work in 1863 affected the very form of private property that had originally driven the South from the Union.

The Conscription Act of 1862 did not solve the Confederate Army's manpower problems. By 1864, the southern armies were only a third the size of the Union forces. Hence, in February 1864, an expanded conscription measure made all white males between the ages 17 and 50 subject to the draft. By 1865, the necessities of war had led to the unthinkable: arming slaves as soldiers. Black companies were recruited in Richmond and other southern towns. However, because the war soon ended, no blacks actually fought for the Confederacy.

In a message sent to Congress in November 1864, Davis speculated on some of the issues involved in arming slaves. "Should a slave who had served his country" be retained in servitude, he wondered, "or should his emancipation be held out to him as a reward for faithful service, or should it be granted at once on the promise of such service ...?" The war fought by the South to preserve slavery ended in the contemplation of emancipation.

Southern agriculture also changed under the pressure of war. Earlier, the South had imported food from the North, concentrating on the production of staples such as cotton and tobacco for market. Now, more and more land was turned over to food crops. Some farmers voluntarily shifted crops, but others responded only to state laws reducing the acreage permitted for cotton and tobacco cultivation. These measures never succeeded in raising enough food to feed southerners adequately. But they contributed to a dramatic decline in the production of cotton, from 4.5 million bales in 1861 to 300,000 bales in 1864.

The South had always depended on imported manufactured goods. Even though some blockade runners were able to evade the Union ships, the noose tightened after 1862. The Confederacy could not, in any case, rely on blockade runners to arm and equip the army. Thus, war triggered the expansion of military-related industries in the South. Here, too, the government played a crucial role. The war and navy offices directed industrial development, awarding contracts to private manufacturing firms like Richmond's Tredegar Iron Works and operating other factories themselves. The number of southerners working in industry rose dramatically. In 1861, the Tredegar Iron Works employed 700 workers; two years later, it employed 2,500, more than half of them black. The head of the Army Ordnance Bureau reflected on the amazing transformation. "Where three years ago we were not making a gun, pistol nor a sabre, no shot nor shell ... we now make all these in quantities to meet the demands of our large armies." At the end of the war, the soldiers were better supplied with arms and munitions than with food.

Although the war did not transform the southern class structure, relations between the classes began to change. The pressures of the struggle undermined the solidarity of whites, which was based on racism and supposed political unanimity. Draft resistance and desertion reflected growing alienation from a war perceived as serving only the interests of upper-class plantation owners. More and more yeoman families suffered grinding poverty as the men went off to war and government officials and armies requisitioned needed resources. A poor farmer from Georgia, Harlan Fuller, explained his family's situation in the spring of 1864. Fuller was 50 but now eligible for the draft. "I am liable at any time to be taken away from my little crops leaving my family almost without provisions & no hope of making any crop atal. I have sent six sons to the war & now the seventh enrolled he being the last I have no help left atal." This new poverty was an ominous hint of the decline of the yeoman farming class in postwar years.

The Victorious North

Although changes in the South were more noticeable, the Union's government and economy also responded to the demands of war. Like Davis, Lincoln was accused of being a dictator. Although he rarely tried to control Congress, veto its legislation, or direct government departments, Lincoln did use executive power freely. He violated the writ of habeas corpus by suspending the civil rights of over 13,000 northerners, who languished in prison without trials; curbed the freedom of the press because of supposedly disloyal and inflammatory articles; established conscription; issued the Emancipation Proclamation; and removed army generals. Lincoln argued that this vast extension of presidential power was temporarily justified because, as president, he was responsible for defending and preserving the Constitution.

Many of the wartime changes in government proved more permanent than Lincoln had imagined. The financial necessities of war helped revolutionize the country's banking system. Ever since Andrew Jackson's destruction of the Bank of the United States, state banks had served American financial needs. Treasury Secretary Chase found this banking system inadequate and chaotic and proposed to replace it. In 1863 and 1864, Congress passed banking acts that established a national currency issued by federally chartered banks and backed by government bonds. The country had a federal banking system once again.

The northern economy also changed under wartime demands. The need to feed soldiers and civilians stimulated the expansion of agriculture and new investment in farm machinery. With so many men off soldiering, farmers were at first short of labor. McCormick reapers performed the work of four to six men and farmers began to buy them. During the war, McCormick sold 165,000 of his machines. Northern farming, especially in the Midwest, was well on the way to becoming mechanized. Farmers not only succeeded in growing enough grain to feed civilians and soldiers, but also gathered a surplus to export as well.

The war also selectively stimulated manufacturing. Although it is easy to imagine that northern industry as a whole expanded during the Civil War, in fact, the war retarded overall economic growth. War consumed rather than generated wealth. Between 1860 and 1870, the annual rate of increase in real manufacturing value added was only 2.3 percent, in contrast with 7.8 percent for the years

between 1840 and 1860 and 6 percent for the period 1870 to 1900. Some important prewar industries, like cotton textiles, languished without a supply of southern cotton.

However, industries that produced for the war machine, especially those with advantages of scale, expanded and made large profits. Each year, the Union army required 1.5 million uniforms and 3 million pairs of shoes; the woolen and leather industries grew accordingly. Meatpackers and producers of iron, steel, and pocket watches all profited from wartime opportunities. Cincinnati was one city that flourished from supplying soldiers with everything from pork to soap and candles.

On the Home Front, 1861–1865

In numerous, less tangible ways, the war transformed northern and southern society. The very fact of conflict established a new perspective for most civilians. War news vied with local events for their attention. They read newspapers and national weekly magazines with a new eagerness. The use of the mails increased dramatically as they corresponded with faraway relatives and friends. Wrote one North Carolina woman, "I never liked to write letters before, but it is a pleasure as well as a relief now." Distant events became almost as real and vivid as those at home. The war helped make Americans less parochial, integrating them into the larger world.

For some Americans, like John D. Rockefeller and Andrew Carnegie, war brought army contracts and unanticipated riches. The New York *Herald* reported that New York City had never been "so gay,... so crowded, so prosperous," as it was in March 1864. Residents of Cincinnati noted people who "became suddenly immensely wealthy, and in their fine equipages, with liveried servants, rolled in magnificence along the city streets." In the South, blockade runners made fortunes slipping luxury goods past Union ships.

For the majority of Americans, however, war meant deprivation. The war effort gobbled up a large part of each side's resources, and ultimately ordinary people suffered. To be sure, the demand for workers ended unemployment and changed employment patterns. Large numbers of women and blacks entered the work force, a phenomenon

The dislocations caused by the war were many. These southerners, forced to leave their home by invading troops, have packed what few belongings they could transport and stand ready to evacuate their homestead. (Library of Congress)

that would be repeated in all future American wars. But whereas work was easy to get and wages appeared to increase, real income actually declined. Inflation, especially destructive in the South, was largely to blame. By 1864, eggs sold in Richmond for $6 a dozen; butter brought $25 a pound. Strikes and union organizing pointed to working-class discontent.

Low wages compounded the problem of declining income and particularly harmed women workers. Often forced into the labor market because husbands could save little or nothing from small army stipends, army wives and other women took what pay they could get. As more women entered the work force, employers cut costs by slashing wages. In 1861, the Union government paid Philadelphia seamstresses 17 cents per shirt. At the height of inflation, three years later, the government reduced the piecework rate to 15 cents. Private employers paid even less, about 8 cents a shirt. Working women in the South fared no better. War may have brought prosperity to a few Americans, North and South, but for most it meant trying to survive on an inadequate income.

Economic dislocation caused by the war reduced the standard of living for civilians. Shortages and hardships were severe in the South, which bore the brunt of the fighting. Most white southerners did without food, manufactured goods, and medicine during the war. Farming families who had no slaves to help with work in the fields fared poorly.

As one Georgia woman explained, "I can't manage a farm well enough [alone] to make a suporte." Conditions were most dismal in cities, where carts brought in vital supplies, because trains were reserved for military use. Hunger was rampant. Food riots erupted in Richmond and other cities; crowds of hungry whites broke into stores to steal food. The very cleanliness of southern cities pointed to urban hunger. As one Richmond resident noted, everything was so "cleanly consumed that no garbage or filth can accumulate."

Thousands of southerners who fled as Union armies advanced suddenly found themselves homeless. "The country for miles around is filled with refugees," noted an army officer in 1862. "Every house is crowded and hundreds are living in churches, in barns and tents." Caught up in the effort of mere survival, worried about what had happened to homes and possessions left behind and whether anything would remain when they returned, these southerners must have wondered if the cause was worth their sacrifices. Life was probably just as agonizing for those who chose to stay put when Union troops arrived. Virginia Gray, an Arkansas woman, wrote in her diary of her fear of the "Feds" and the turmoil they caused when they suddenly appeared and then disappeared.

White flight also disrupted slave life. Even the arrival of Union forces could prove a mixed blessing. White soldiers were unknown quantities, and as Carpenter's letter suggested, they might be hostile to blacks whom they were supposed to be liberating. One slave described the upsetting arrival of the Yankees at his plantation in Arkansas: "Them folks stood round there all day. Killed hogs ... killed cows.... Took all kinds of sugar and preserves.... Tore all the feathers out of the mattresses looking for money. Then they put Old Miss and her daughter in the kitchen to cooking." So frightened was this slave's mother that she hid in her bed, only to be roused by the lieutenant, who told her, "We ain't a-going to do you no hurt.... We are freeing you." But the next day, the Yanks were gone and the Confederates back. "Pa was 'fraid of both" and resolved the problem by hiding out in the cotton patch.

Wartime Race Relations

The journal kept by Emily Harris in South Carolina conveys some of the character of life behind the lines. She revealed not only the predictable story of shortages, hardships, and the psychological burdens of those at home, but also the subtle social changes the war stimulated. Emily and her husband David lived on a 500-acre farm with their seven young children and ten slaves. When David went to war, Emily had to manage the farm, even though David worried that she would be "much at a loss with the ... farm and the negroes."

Emily's early entries establish two themes that persist for the years she kept her diary. She was worried about how David would survive the "privation and hardships" of army life and was also anxious about her own "load of responsibilities." Her December 1862 entry provides a poignant picture of a wife's thoughts. "All going well as far as I can judge but tonight it is raining and cold and a soldier's wife cannot be happy in bad weather and during a battle." The dozens of tasks she had to do depressed her. "I shall never get used to being left as the head of affairs," she wrote in January 1863. "I am not an independent woman nor ever shall be." As time passed and the war went badly, the dismal news and mounting list of casualties heightened her concern about David's safety.

Her relations with her slaves compounded Emily's problems. As so many southerners discovered, war transformed the master-slave relationship. Because Emily was not the master David had been, her slaves gradually began to take unaccustomed liberties. At Christmas in 1864, several left the farm without her permission; others stayed away longer than she allowed. "Old Will" boldly requested his freedom. Worse yet, she discovered that her slaves had helped three Yankees who had escaped from prison camp.

The master-slave relationship was crumbling, and Emily reported in her journal the consequences for whites. "It seems people are getting afraid of negroes." Although not admitting to fear, she revealed that she could no longer control the blacks, who were increasingly unwilling to play a subservient role.

Understanding what was at stake, slaves, in their own way, often worked for their freedom. Said one later, "Us slaves worked den when we felt like it, which wasn't often." Emily's journal entry for February 22 confessed a "painful necessity." "I am reduced," she said, "to the use of a stick but the negroes are becoming so impudent and disrespectful that I cannot bear it." A mere two weeks later she added, "The Negroes are all expecting to be set free very soon and it causes them to be very troublesom."

Similar scenes occurred throughout the South. Insubordination, refusal to work, and refusal to accept punishment marked the behavior of black slaves, especially those who worked as fieldhands. Thousands of blacks (probably 20 percent of all slaves), many of them women who had been exploited as workers and as sexual objects, fled toward Union lines after the early months of the war. Their flight pointed to the changing nature of race relations and the harm slaves could do to the southern cause. Reflected one slaveowner, "The 'faithful slave' is about played out."

Women and the War

If Emily Harris's journal reveals that she was sometimes overwhelmed by her responsibilities and shocked by the changes in dealings with her slaves, it also illustrates how the war affected women's lives. Nineteenth-century ideology promoted women's domestic role and minimized their economic importance. But the war made it impossible for many women to live according to conventional norms of behavior. So many men on both sides had gone off to fight that women had to find jobs and had to carry on farming operations. During the war years, southern women who had no slaves to help with the farmwork and northern farm wives who labored without the assistance of husbands or sons carried new physical and emotional burdens.

Women also participated in numerous war-related activities. In both North and South, they entered government service in large numbers. In the North, hundreds of women became military nurses. Under the supervision of Drs. Emily and Elizabeth Blackwell; Dorothea Dix, superintendent of army nurses; and Clara Barton, northern women nursed the wounded and dying for low pay or even for none at all. They also attempted to improve hospital conditions by attacking red tape and bureaucracy. The diary of a volunteer, Harriet Whetten, revealed the activist attitude of many others:

> I have never seen such a dirty disorganized place as the Hospital. The neglect of cleanliness is inexcusable. All sorts of filth, standing water, and the embalming house near the Hospital.... No time had to be lost. Miss Gill and I set the contrabands at work making beds & cleaning.

Although men largely staffed southern military hospitals, Confederate women also played an important part in caring for the sick and wounded in their homes and in makeshift hospitals behind the battle lines. Grim though the work was, many women felt that they were participating in the real world for the first time in their lives.

Women moved outside the domestic sphere in other forms of volunteer war work. Some women gained administrative experience in soldiers' aid societies and in the United States Sanitary Commission. Many others made bandages and clothes, put together packages for soldiers at the front, and helped army wives and disabled soldiers find jobs. Fund-raising activities realized substantial sums. By the end of the war, the Sanitary Commission had raised $50 million for medical supplies, nurses' salaries, and other wartime necessities.

Many of the changes women experienced during war years ended when peace returned. Jobs in industry and government disappeared when the men came to reclaim them. Women turned over the operation of farms to returning husbands. But for women whose men came home maimed or not at all, the work had not ended. Nor had the discrimination. Trying to pick up the threads of their former lives, they found it impossible to forget what they had done to help the war effort. At least some of them were sure they had equaled their men in courage and commitment.

The Election of 1864

In the North, the election of 1864 brought some of the transformations of wartime into the political arena. The Democrats, seeking to regain power by capitalizing on war weariness, nominated General George McClellan for president. The party proclaimed the war a failure and demanded an armistice with the South. During the campaign, Democrats accused Lincoln of arbitrarily expanding executive power and denounced sweeping economic measures such as the banking bills. Arguing that the president had transformed the war from one for Union into one for emancipation, they tried to inflame racial passions by insinuating that if the Republicans won, a fusion of blacks and whites would result.

Although Lincoln easily gained the Republican renomination because of his tight control over party machinery and patronage, his party did not unite behind him. Lincoln seemed to please no one. His veto of the radical reconstruction plan for the South, the Wade-Davis bill, led to cries of "usurpation." The Emancipation Proclamation did not sit well with conservatives. In August 1864, a gloomy Lincoln told his cabinet that he expected to lose the election. As late as September, some Republicans actually hoped to reconvene the convention and select another candidate.

Sherman's capture of Atlanta in September 1864 and the march through Georgia to Savannah helped swing voters to Lincoln. In the end, Republicans had no desire to see the Democrats oust their party. Lincoln won 55 percent of the popular vote and swept the electoral college.

Why the North Won

In the months after Lincoln's reelection, the war drew to an agonizing conclusion. Sherman moved north from Atlanta to North Carolina, while Grant pummeled Lee's forces in Virginia. The losses Grant would sustain were staggering: 18,000 in the Battle of the Wilderness, over 8,000 at Spotsylvania, and another 12,000 at Cold Harbor. New recruits stepped forward to replace the dead. On April 9, 1865, Grant accepted Lee's surrender at Appomattox. Southern soldiers and officers were allowed to return home with their personal equipment after promising to remain there peaceably. The war was finally over.

Technically, the war was won on the battlefield and at sea. But Grant's military strategy succeeded because the Union's manpower and economic resources could survive staggering losses of men and equipment while the Confederacy's could not. As Union armies pushed back the borders of the Confederacy, the South lost control of territories essential for their war effort. Finally, naval strategy eventually paid off because the North could build enough ships to make its blockade work. In 1861, fully 90 percent of the blockade runners were slipping through the naval cordon. By the war's end, only half made it.

The South had taken tremendous steps toward meeting war needs. But despite the impressive growth of manufacturing and the increasing acreage devoted to foodstuffs, the southern army and the southern people were poorly fed and poorly clothed. As one civilian realized, "The question of bread and meat … is beginning to be regarded as a more serious one even than that of War." Women working alone or with disgruntled slaves on farms could not produce enough food. Worn-out farm equipment was not replaced. The government's impressment of slaves and animals cut production. The half million blacks who fled to Union lines also played their part in pulling the South down in defeat.

New industries could not meet the extraordinary demands of wartime, and advancing Union forces destroyed many of them. A Confederate officer in northern Virginia observed, "Many of our soldiers are thinly clothed and without shoes and in addition to this, very few of the infantry have tents. With this freezing weather, their sufferings are indescribable." Skimpy rations, only a third of a pound of meat for each soldier a day by 1864, weakened the Confederate force, whose trail was "traceable by the deposit of dysenteric stool" it left behind. By that time, the Union armies were so well supplied that soldiers often threw away heavy blankets and coats as they advanced.

The South's woefully inadequate transportation system also contributed to defeat. Primitive roads deteriorated and became all but impassable

This photograph showing an overturned train indicates the Confederate transportation breakdown caused by battle, sabotage, and simple wear and tear. Such damage led to food riots in southern cities and contributed to the defeat of the Confederacy. (Library of Congress)

without repairs. The railroad system, geared to the needs of cotton, not war, was inefficient. When tracks wore out or were destroyed, they were not replaced. Rails were too heavy for blockade runners to bother with, and as the Confederate railroad coordinator observed in 1865, "Not a single bar of railroad iron has been rolled in the Confederacy since the war, nor can we hope to do better." Thus, food intended for the army rotted awaiting shipment. Supplies were tied up in bottlenecks and soldiers went hungry. Food riots in southern cities pointed to the hunger, anger, and growing demoralization of civilians.

Ironically, measures the Confederacy took to strengthen its ability to win the war, as one Texan later observed, "weakened and paralyzed it." Eventually, the Confederacy could no longer "command and control its moral resources." Conscription, impressment, and taxes all contributed to resentment and sometimes open resistance. They fueled class tensions already strained by the poverty war brought to many yeoman farmers and led some of them to assist the invaders or to join the Union army. The proposal to use slaves as soldiers called into question the war's purpose. The many southern governors who refused to contribute men, money, and supplies on the scale Davis requested implicitly condoned disloyalty to the cause. The belief in states' rights and the sanctity of private property that gave birth to the Confederacy also helped kill it.

By the final months of the war, Jefferson Davis had recognized how dangerous opposition to governmental measures and defeatist attitudes were to the Confederacy's cause. "The malcontents, seizing on the restlessness consequent upon long and severe pressure," he pointed out, "have created a feeling hostile to the execution of the rigorous laws which were necessary to raise and feed our armies, then magnifying every reverse and prophesying ruin, they have produced public depression and sown the seeds of disintegration." But such realization did not result in any vigorous attempts to influence public opinion or to control internal dissent.

It is tempting to compare Lincoln and Davis as war leaders. There is no doubt that Lincoln's humanity, his awareness of the terrible costs of war, his determination to save the Union, and his eloquence set him apart as one of this country's most extraordinary presidents. Yet the men's personal characteristics were probably less important than the differences between the political and social systems of the two regions. Without the support of a party behind him, Davis failed to engender enthusiasm or loyalty. Even though the Republicans rarely united behind Lincoln, they uniformly wanted to keep the Democrats from office. Despite all the squabbles, Republicans tended to support Lincoln's policies in Congress and back in their home districts. Commanding considerable resources of patronage, Lincoln was able to line up federal, state, and local officials behind his party and administration.

Just as the northern political system provided Lincoln with more flexibility and support, its social system also proved more able to meet the war's extraordinary demands. Although both societies adopted innovations in an effort to secure victory, northerners were more cooperative, disciplined, and aggressive in meeting the organizational and production challenges of wartime. In the southern states, old attitudes, habits, and values impeded the war effort. Southern governors, wedded to states' rights, refused to cooperate with the Confederate government. North Carolina, the center of the southern textile industry, actually kept back most uniforms for its own regiments. At the war's end, 92,000 uniforms and thousands of blankets, shoes, and tents still lay in its warehouses. When Sherman approached Atlanta, Georgia's governor would not turn over the 10,000 men in the state army to Confederate commanders. Even slaveholders, whose property had been the cause for secession, resisted the impressment of their slaves for war work.

In the end, the Confederacy collapsed, exhausted and bleeding. Hungry soldiers received letters from their families revealing desperate situations at home. They worried and then slipped away. By December 1864, the Confederate desertion rate had passed 50 percent. Replacements could not be found. Farmers hid livestock and produce from tax collectors. Many southerners felt their cause was lost and resigned themselves to defeat. But some fought on till the end. One northerner described them as they surrendered at Appomattox:

> Before us in proud humiliation stood the embodiment of manhood: men whom neither toils and sufferings, nor the fact of death, nor disaster, nor hopelessness could bend from their resolve; standing before us now, thin, worn, and famished, but erect, and with eyes looking level into ours, waking memories that bound us together as no other bond.

The Costs of War

The long war was over, but the memories of that event would fester for years to come. About 3 million American men, a third of all free males between the ages of 15 and 59, had served in the army. Each would remember his own personal history of the war. For George Eagleton, who had worked in army field hospitals, the history was one of "Death and destruction! Blood! Blood! Agony! Death! Gaping flesh wounds, broken bones, amputations, bullet and bomb fragment extractions." Of all wars Americans have fought, none has been more deadly. The death rate during this war was over five times as great as the death rate during World War II. About 360,000 Union soldiers and another 258,000 Confederate soldiers died, about a third of them because their wounds were either improperly treated or not treated at all. Disease claimed more lives than combat. Despite the efforts of men like Eagleton and the women army nurses, hospitals could not handle the scores of wounded and dying. "Glory is not for the private soldier, such as die in the hospitals," reflected one Tennessee soldier, "being eat up with the deadly gangrene, and being imperfectly waited on."

Thousands upon thousands of men would be reminded of the human costs of war by the injuries they carried with them to the grave, by the missing limbs that marked them as Civil War veterans. About 275,000 on each side were maimed. Another 410,000 (195,000 northerners and 215,000 southerners) would recall their time in wretchedly overcrowded and unsanitary prison camps. The lucky ones would remember only the dullness and boredom. The worst memory was of those who rotted in prison camps, such as Andersonville in Georgia, where 31,000 Union soldiers were confined. At the war's end, over 12,000 graves were counted there.

Some Americans found it hard to throw off wartime experiences and adjust to peace. As Arthur Carpenter's letters suggest, he gradually grew accustomed to army life. War provided him with a sense of purpose. When it was over, he felt aimless. A full year after the war's end, he wrote, "Camp life agrees with me better than any other." Many others had difficulty returning to civilian routines and finding a new focus for life. Even those who adjusted successfully discovered that they looked at life from a different perspective. The experience of fighting, of mixing with all sorts of people from many places, of traveling far from home had lifted former soldiers out of their familiar local world and widened their vision. Fighting the war made the concept of national union real.

Unanswered Questions

What, then, had the war accomplished? On the one hand, death and destruction. Physically, the war devastated the South. Historians have estimated a 43 percent decline in southern wealth during the war years, exclusive of the value of slaves. Great cities like Atlanta, Columbia, and Richmond lay in ruins. Fields lay weed-choked and uncultivated. Tools were worn out. A third or more of the South's stock of mules, horses, and swine had disappeared. Two-thirds of the railroads had been destroyed. Thousands were hungry, homeless, and bitter about their four years of what now appeared a useless sacrifice. Over 3 million slaves, a vast financial investment, were free.

The Currier & Ives print, "The Soldier's Dream of Home," shows an idyllic homecoming and suggests the return to prewar roles would be smooth. In fact, not every soldier found that readjusting to civilian life was easy. Nor did all women who had become accustomed to directing family affairs want to give up their new responsibilities. Ironically, many would eventually look back to the wartime years with nostalgia. (Museum of the City of New York)

On the other hand, the war had resolved the question of union and ended the debate over the relationship of the states to the federal government. During the war, Republicans seized the opportunity to pass legislation that would foster national union and economic growth: the Pacific Railroad Act of 1862, which set aside huge tracts of public land to finance the transcontinental railroad; the Homestead Act of 1862, which was to provide yeoman farmers cheaper and easier access to the public domain; the Morrill Act of 1862, which established support for agricultural (land-grant) colleges; and the banking acts of 1863 and 1864.

The war had also resolved the issue of slavery, the thorny problem that had so long plagued American life. Yet uncertainties outnumbered certainties. What would happen to the former slaves? When blacks had fled to Union lines during the war, commanders had not known what to do with them. Now the problem became even more pressing. Were blacks to have the same civil and political rights as whites? In the Union army, they had been second-class soldiers. The behavior of Union forces toward liberated blacks in the South showed how deep the stain of racism went. One white soldier, caught stealing a quilt by a former slave, shouted, "I'm fighting for $14 a month and the Union"—not to end slavery. Would blacks be given land, the means for economic independence?

TIMELINE

1861 Lincoln calls up state militia and suspends habeas corpus

First Battle of Bull Run

Union blockades the South

1862 Battles at Shiloh, Bull Run, and Antietam

Monitor and *Virginia* battle

First black regiment authorized by Union

Union issues greenbacks

South institutes military draft

Pacific Railroad Act

Homestead Act

Morrill Land-Grant College Act

1863 Lincoln issues Emancipation Proclamation

Congress adopts military draft

Battles of Gettysburg and Vicksburg

Union Banking Act

Southern tax laws and impressment act

New York draft riots

Southern food riots

1864 Sherman's march through Georgia

Lincoln reelected

Union Banking Act

1865 Lee surrenders at Appomattox

Lincoln assassinated; Andrew Johnson becomes president

Congress passes Thirteenth Amendment, abolishing slavery

Ruins on Carey Street, Richmond, VA. (Library of Congress)

What would be their relations with their former owners?

What, indeed, would be the status of the conquered South in the nation? Should it be punished for the rebellion? Some people thought so. Should southerners keep their property? Some people thought not. There were clues to Lincoln's intentions. As early as December 1863, the president had announced a generous plan of reconciliation. He was willing to recognize the government of former Confederate states established by a group of citizens equal to 10 percent of those voting in 1860, as long as the group swore to support the Constitution and to accept the abolition of slavery. He began to restore state governments in three former Confederate states on that basis. But not all northerners agreed with his leniency, and the debate continued.

In his 1865 inaugural address, Lincoln urged Americans to harbor "malice towards none ... and charity for all." "Let us strive," he urged, "to finish the work we are in; to bind up the nation's wounds ... to do all which may achieve a just and lasting peace." Privately, the president said the same thing. Generosity and goodwill would pave the way for reconciliation. On April 14, he pressed the point home to his cabinet. His wish was to avoid persecution and bloodshed. That same evening, only five days after the surrender at Appomattox, the president attended a play at Ford's Theatre. There, as one horrified eyewitness reported,

> a pistol was heard and a man ... dressed in a black suit of clothes leaped onto the stage apparently from the President's box. He held in his right hand a dagger whose blade appeared about 10 inches long.... Every one leaped to his feet, and the cry of "the President is assassinated" was heard—Getting where I could see into the President's box, I saw Mrs. Lincoln ... in apparent anguish.

John Wilkes Booth, a southern sympathizer, had killed the president.

Conclusion

An Uncertain Future

As the war ended, many Americans grieved for the man whose decisions had so marked their lives for five years. "Strong men have wept tonight & the nation will mourn tomorrow," wrote one eyewitness to the assassination. Many more wept for friends and relations who had not survived the war, but whose actions had in one way or another contributed to its outcome. Perhaps not all Americans realized how drastically the war had altered their lives, their futures, their nation. It was only as time passed that the war's impact became clear to them. And it was only with time that they recognized how many problems the war had left unsolved. It is to these years of Reconstruction that we turn next.

Recommended Reading

Overviews

Peter J. Parrish, *The American Civil War* (1985); David Donald, *Liberty and Union* (1978); James McPherson, *Battle Cry of Freedom: The Civil War Era* (1988); Joseph T. Glatthatt, *Partners in Command: The Relationship between Leaders in the Civil War* (1994); Phillip S. Paludan, *"A People's Contest": The Union and the Civil War, 1861–1865* (1989); Emory M. Thomas, *The Confederate Nation, 1861–1865* (1979); Paul D. Escott, *After Secession: Jefferson Davis and the Failure of Confederate Nationalism* (1978); Robert F. Durden, *The Gray and the Black: The Confederate Debate on Emancipation* (1972); Paul D. Escott, *Many Excellent People* (1985); Malcolm C. McMillan, *The Disintegration of a Confederate State* (1986); David Gilchrist and W. David Lewis, eds., *Economic Change in the Civil War Era* (1965).

The Military Experience

T. Harry Williams, *The History of American Wars* (1981); Russell F. Weigley, *The American Way of War: A History of U.S. Military Strategy and Policy* (1973); Perry D. Jamieson, *Attack and Die: Civil War Tactics and the Southern Heritage* (1982); Richard E. Beringer, Herman Hattaway, Archer Jones, and William N. Still, Jr., *Why the South Lost the Civil War* (1986) and *The Elements of Confederate Defeat: Nationalism, War Aims, and Religion* (1988); Michael Barton, *Goodmen: The Character of Civil War Soldiers* (1981); Gerald F. Linderman, *Embattled Courage: The Experience of Combat in the American Civil War* (1987); Randall C. Jimerson, *The Private Civil War* (1988); Reid Mitchell, *The Vacant Chair: The Northern Soldier Leaves Home* (1993); Laurence M. Hauptman, *The Iroquois in the Civil War: From Battlefield to Reservation* (1993).

The Home Front

Eric Foner, *Politics and Ideology in the Age of Civil War* (1980); David Donald, *Lincoln* (1995); James Rawley, *The Politics of Union: Northern Politics During the Civil War* (1974); David E. Long, *The Jewel of Liberty: Abraham Lin-*

coln's Re-Election and the End of Slavery (1994); Joel Silbey, *A Respectable Minority: The Democratic Party in the Civil War Era* (1977); Cullom Davis et al., eds., *The Public and Private Lincoln: Contemporary Perspectives* (1979); John L. Thomas, ed., *Abraham Lincoln and the American Political Tradition* (1986); Michael Burlingame, *The Inner World of Abraham Lincoln* (1994); Glenn M. Lindend and Thomas J. Pressly, eds., *Voices From the House Divided* (1995); J. Matthew Gallman, *Mastering Wartime: A Social History of Philadelphia During the Civil War* (1990); Theodore J. Karamanski, *Rally 'Round the Flag: Chicago and the Civil War* (1993); Wayne K. Durrell, *War of Another Kind: A Southern Community in the Great Rebellion* (1990); Mary A. Decredico, *Patriotism for Profit: Georgia's Urban Entrepreneurs and the Confederate War Effort* (1990); Benjamin Quarles, *The Negro in the Civil War* (1968 ed.); Ira Berlin, ed., *Freedom: A Documentary History of Emancipation, 1861–1867*, Series I and II (1979, 1982); Barbara Jeanne Fields, *Slavery and Freedom on the Middle Ground* (1985); Clarence L. Mohr, *On the Threshold of Freedom* (1986); Leon F. Litwack, *Been in the Storm So Long: The Aftermath of Slavery* (1979); David W. Blight, *Frederick Douglass' Civil War* (1989); George M. Frederickson, *The Black Image in the White Mind* (1971); C. Vann Woodward, *American Counterpoint: Slavery and Racism in the North-South Dialogue* (1971); Elizabeth D. Leonard, *Yankee Women: Gender Battles in the Civil War* (1994); Wendy Hamand Venet, *Neither Ballots Nor Bullets: Women Abolitionists and the Civil War* (1991); John R. Brumgardt, ed., *Civil War Nurse: The Diary and Letters of Hannah Ropes* (1980); C. Vann Woodward and Elisabeth Muhlenfeld, eds., *Mary Chesnut's Civil War* (1981); Catherine Clinton, *Tara Revisited: Women, War, and the Plantation Legend* (1995); Phillip Shaw Paludan, *Victims: A True Story of the Civil War* (1981).

Novels

Stephen Crane, *The Red Badge of Courage* (any ed.); MacKinlay Kantor, *Andersonville* (1955).

The Union Reconstructed

n April 1864, one year before Lincoln's assassination, Robert Allston died of pneumonia. His daughter, Elizabeth, was left with a "sense of terrible desolation and sorrow" as the Civil War raged around her, and she and her mother took over the affairs of their many rice plantations. With Yankee troops moving through coastal South Carolina in the late winter of 1864–1865, Elizabeth's sorrow turned to "terror" as Union soldiers arrived seeking liquor, firearms, and hidden valuables. The Allston women endured an insulting search and then fled. In a later raid, Yankee troops encouraged the Allston slaves to take furniture and other household goods from the Big Houses, some of which the blacks returned when the Yankees were gone. But before they left, the Union soldiers, in their role as liberators, gave the keys to the crop barns to the semifree slaves.

When the war was over, Adele Allston took an oath of allegiance to the United States and secured a written order commanding the blacks to relinquish these keys. She and Elizabeth made plans to return in the early summer of 1865 to resume control of the family plantations, thereby reestablishing white authority. She was assured that although the blacks had guns and were determined to have the means to a livelihood, "no outrage has been committed against the whites except in the matter of property." But property was the key issue. Possession of the keys to the barns, Elizabeth wrote, would be the "test case" of whether former masters or their former slaves would control land, labor and its fruits, and even subtle aspects of interpersonal relations.

Not without some fear, Adele and Elizabeth Allston rode up in a carriage to their former home, Nightingale Hall, to confront their ex-slaves. To their surprise, a pleasant reunion took place. The Allston women greeted the blacks by name, inquired after their children, and caught up on the affairs of those with whom they had lived closely for many years. A trusted black foreman handed over the keys to the barns. This harmonious scene was repeated elsewhere.

But at Guendalos, a plantation owned by a son absent during most of the war fighting with the Confederate Army, the Allston women met a very different situation. As their carriage arrived and moved slowly toward the crop barns, a defiant group of armed ex-slaves lined both sides of the road, following the carriage as it passed by. Tension grew when the carriage stopped. A former black driver, Uncle Jacob, was unsure whether to yield the keys to the barns full of rice and corn, put there by black labor. Mrs. Allston insisted. As Uncle Jacob hesitantly began to hand the keys to her, an angry young man shouted out: "Ef yu gie up de key, blood'll flow." Uncle Jacob slowly slipped the keys back into his pocket.

The tension increased as the blacks sang freedom songs and brandished hoes, pitchforks, and guns in an effort to discourage anyone from going to town for help. Two blacks, however, left the plantation to find some Union military officers to come settle the issue of the keys, most likely on the side of the Allstons. As Adele and Elizabeth waited, word finally arrived that the Union officers, who were difficult to locate, would no doubt be found the next day and would come to Guendalos. The Allstons spent the night safely, if restlessly, in their house. Early the next morning, they were awakened by a knock at the unlocked front door. Adele slowly opened the door, and there stood Uncle Jacob. Without a word, he gave her the keys.

In this Winslow Homer painting, *A Visit from the Old Mistress,* imagine Adele Allston returning to her plantation to reunite with former slaves. What kind of new relationships would they form in the transformed world after a wrenching Civil War? (National Museum of American Art, Smithsonian Institution) he story of the keys reveals most of the essential human ingredients of the Reconstruction era. Despite defeat and surrender, southern whites were determined to resume control of both land and labor. Rebellion aside, the law, property titles, and federal enforcement were generally on the side of the original owners of the land. The Allston women were friendly to the blacks in a genuine but maternal way and insisted on the restoration of the deferential relationships that existed before the war. Adele and Elizabeth, in short, both feared and cared about their former slaves.

The black freedmen likewise revealed mixed feelings toward their former owners. At different plantations, they demonstrated a variety of emotions: anger, loyalty, love, resentment, and pride. Respect was paid to the person of the Allstons but not to their property and crops. The action of the blacks indicated that what they wanted was not revenge, but economic independence and freedom.

In this encounter between former slaves and their mistresses, the role of the northern federal officials is most revealing. The Union soldiers, literally and symbolically, gave the keys of freedom to the blacks, but did not stay around long enough to guarantee that freedom. Although encouraging the freedmen to plunder the master's house and take possession of the crops, in the crucial encounter, northern officials had disappeared. Understanding the limits of northern help, Uncle Jacob handed the keys to land and liberty back to his former owner. The blacks at Guendalos knew that if they wanted to ensure their freedom, they had to do it themselves.

The theme of this chapter is the story of what happened to the conflicting goals and dreams of three groups as they sought to form new social, economic, and political relationships during the Reconstruction era. Amid devastation and divisions of class and race, Civil War survivors sought to put their lives back together again. Victorious but variously motivated northern officials, defeated but defiant southern planters, and impoverished but hopeful black freedmen—all had strong needs and dreams. In no way could all fulfill their conflicting goals, yet each had to try. This situation guaranteed that the Reconstruction era would be divisive, leaving a mixed legacy of human gains and losses.

The Bittersweet Aftermath of War

"There are sad changes in store for both races," the daughter of a Georgia planter wrote in her diary early in the summer of 1865, adding, "I wonder the Yankees do not shudder to behold their work." In order to understand the bittersweet nature of Reconstruction, we must look at the state of the nation in the spring of 1865, shortly after the assassination of President Lincoln.

The United States in 1865

The "Union" was in a state of constitutional crisis in April 1865. The status of the 11 states of the former Confederate States of America was unclear. They had claimed the right to secede, were successful for a time, but finally had failed. The North had denied the South's constitutional right to secede but needed four years of civil war and over 600,000 deaths to win the point. Were the 11 states part of the Union or not? Lincoln's official position had been that the southern states had never left the Union, which was "constitutionally indestructible." As a result of their rebellion, they were only "out of their proper relation" with the United States. The president, therefore, as commander in chief, had the authority to decide on the basis for setting relations right and proper again.

Lincoln's congressional opponents argued that by declaring war on the Union, the Confederate states had broken their constitutional ties and reverted to a kind of prestatehood status like territories or "conquered provinces." Congress, therefore, which decided on the admission of new states, should resolve the constitutional issues

Conflicting Goals During Reconstruction

Victorious Northern ("Radical") Republicans

- Justify the war by remaking southern society in the image of the North
- Inflict political but not physical or economic punishment on Confederate leaders
- Continue programs of economic progress begun during the war: high tariffs, railroad subsidies, national banking
- Maintain the Republican party in power
- Help the freedmen make the transition to full freedom by providing them with the tools of citizenship (suffrage) and equal economic opportunity

Northern Moderates (Republicans and Democrats)

- Quickly establish peace and order, reconciliation between North and South
- Bestow on the southern states leniency, amnesty, and merciful readmission to the Union
- Perpetuate land ownership, free labor, market competition, and other capitalist ventures
- Promote local self-determination of economic and social issues, limit interference by the national government
- Provide limited support for black suffrage

Old Southern Planter Aristocracy (Ex-Confederates)

- Ensure protection from black uprising and prevent excessive freedom for former slaves
- Secure amnesty, pardon, and restoration of confiscated lands
- Restore traditional plantation-based, market-crop economy with blacks as cheap labor force
- Restore traditional political leaders in the states
- Restore traditional paternalistic race relations as basis of social order

New "Other South": Yeoman Farmers and Ex-Whigs (Unionists)

- Quickly establish peace and order, reconciliation between North and South
- Achieve recognition of loyalty and economic value of yeoman farmers
- Create greater diversity in southern economy: capital investments in railroads, factories, and the diversification of agriculture
- Displace the planter aristocracy with new leaders drawn from new economic interests
- Limit the rights and powers of freedmen; extend suffrage only to the educated few

Black Freedmen

- Secure physical protection from abuse and terror by local whites
- Achieve economic independence through land ownership (40 acres and a mule) and equal access to trades
- Receive educational opportunity and foster the development of family and cultural bonds
- Obtain equal civil rights and protection under the law
- Commence political participation through the right to vote

and assert its authority over the reconstruction process. In this conflict between Congress and the president was a powerful struggle between two branches of the national government. As has happened during nearly every war, the executive branch took on broad powers necessary for rapid mobilization of resources and domestic security. Many people believed, however, that Lincoln went far beyond his constitutional authority. As soon as the war was over, Congress sought to reassert its authority, as it would do after every subsequent war.

In April 1865, the Republican party ruled victorious and virtually alone. Although less than a dozen years old, the Republicans had made immense achievements in the eyes of the northern public. They had won the war, preserved the Union, and freed the slaves. Moreover, they had enacted most of the old Federalist-Whig economic programs on behalf of free labor and free enterprise: a high protective tariff, a national banking system, broad use of the power to tax and to borrow and print money, generous federal appropriations for internal improvements, the Home-

The United States in 1865: Crises at the End of the Civil War

- **Military Casualties**

  360,000 Union soldiers dead
  260,000 Confederate soldiers dead
  620,000 Total dead
  375,000 Seriously wounded and maimed
  995,000 Casualties nationwide in a total male population of 15 million (nearly 1 in 15)

- **Physical and Economic Crises**

  The South devastated, its railroads, industry, and some major cities in ruins, its fields and livestock wasted

- **Constitutional Crisis**

  Eleven ex-Confederate states not a part of the Union, their status unclear and future states uncertain

- **Political Crisis**

  Republican party (entirely of the North) dominant in Congress; a former Democratic slaveholder from Tennessee, Andrew Johnson, in the presidency

- **Social Crisis**

  Nearly 4 million black freedmen throughout the South facing challenges of survival and freedom, along with thousands of hungry demobilized white southern soldiers and displaced white families

- **Psychological Crisis**

  Incalculable stores of resentment, bitterness, anger, and despair throughout North and South

stead Act for western farmers, and an act to establish land-grant colleges to teach agricultural and mechanical skills. Alexander Hamilton, John Quincy Adams, and Henry Clay might all have applauded. Despite these achievements, the Republican party was still an uneasy grouping of former Whigs, Know-Nothings, Unionist Democrats, and antislavery idealists.

The Democratic party, by contrast, was in shambles. Republicans depicted southern Democrats as rebels, murderers, and traitors; northern Democrats as weak-willed, disloyal, and opposed to economic growth and progress. Nevertheless, it had been politically important in 1864 for the Republicans to show that the war was a bipartisan effort. A Jacksonian Democrat and Unionist from Tennessee, the tactless Andrew Johnson, had therefore been nominated as Lincoln's vice president. In April 1865, Johnson headed the government.

The United States in the spring of 1865 was a picture of stark economic contrasts. Northern cities hummed with productive activity, whereas southern cities lay in ruins. Northern factories pounded out railroad tracks and engines, steel,

textiles, farm implements, and building materials. Southern factory chimneys stood silent above the rubble. Roadways and railroad tracks laced the North, whereas in the South railroads and roads lay in ruins. Southern financial institutions were bankrupt, whereas northern banks flourished. Northern farms, under increasing mechanization, were more productive than ever before, and free farmers took pride that they had amply fed the Union army and urban workers throughout the war. They saw the Union victory as evidence of the superiority of free over slave labor. By contrast, southern farms and plantations, especially those that had lain in the path of Sherman's march, were like a "howling waste." Said one resident, "The Yankees came through . . . and just tore up everything."

Despite pockets of relative wealth, the South was largely devastated as soldiers demobilized and returned home in April 1865. Rare was the family, North or South, that had not suffered a serious casualty in the war. Missing limbs and suffering from hunger (a half-million southern whites faced starvation), the ragtag remains of the Confederate army experienced widespread sickness and social disorder as they traveled home. Yet, as a later southern writer, Wilbur Cash, explained, "If this war had smashed the Southern world, it had left the essential Southern mind and will … entirely unshaken." Many southerners wanted nothing less than to resist Reconstruction and restore their old world. The minority who had remained quietly loyal to the Union, however, dreamed of a postwar period not of defiance in upholding old values, but of reconciliation and the creation of new ones.

Whatever the extremes of southern white attitudes, the dominant social reality in the spring of 1865 was that nearly 4 million former slaves were on their own, facing the challenges of freedom. After an initial reaction of joy and celebration, expressed in jubilee songs, the freedmen quickly became aware of their continuing dependence on former owners. A Mississippi woman stated the uncertainty of her new status this way:

> I used to think if I could be free I should be the happiest of anybody in the world. But when my master come to me, and says—Lizzie, you is free! it seems like I was in a kind of daze. And when I would wake up in the morning I would think to myself, Is I free? Hasn't I got to get up before day light and go into the field of work?

For Lizzie and 4 million other blacks, everything—and nothing—had changed.

Hopes Among Freedmen

Throughout the South in the summer of 1865, there were optimistic expectations in the old slave quarters. As Union soldiers marched through Richmond, prisoners in slave-trade jails chanted: "Slavery chain done broke at last! Gonna praise God till I die!" The slavery chain, however, was not broken all at once but link by link. After Union soldiers swept through an area, Confederate troops would follow, or master and overseer would return, and the slaves learned not to rejoice too quickly or openly. "Every time a bunch of No'thern sojers would come through," recalled one slave, "they would tell us we was free and we'd begin celebratin'. Before we would get through somebody else would tell us to go back to work, and we would go." Another slave recalled celebrating emancipa-

Both white southerners and their former slaves suffered in the immediate aftermath of the Civil War, as illustrated by this engraving from Frank Leslie's Illustrated Newspaper. *(February 23, 1867)*

Many freed blacks, such as these young people photographed in Richmond, Virginia, gravitated to urban centers either to find work or to find family members. (Library of Congress)

tion "about twelve times" in one North Carolina county. So former slaves became cautious about what freedom meant.

Gradually, the freedmen began to express a vision of what life beyond bondage and the plantation might be like. The first thing they did to test the reality of freedom was to leave the plantation, if only for a few hours or days. "If I stay here I'll never know I am free," a South Carolina woman said, and off she went to work as a cook in a nearby town. Some former slaves cut their ties entirely, leaving cruel and kindly masters alike. Some returned to an earlier master, but others went to towns and cities to work and to find schools, churches, and association with other blacks, where they would be safe from whippings and retaliation.

Many freedmen left the plantation in search of members of their families. The quest for a missing spouse, parent, or child, sold away years before, was a powerful force in the first few months of emancipation. Advertisements detailing these sorrowful searches filled black newspapers. For those who found a spouse or who had been living together in slave marriages, freedom meant getting married legally. Wedding ceremonies involving many couples were common in the first months of emancipation. Legal marriage was important morally, but it also served such practical purposes as establishing the legitimacy of children and gaining access to land titles and other economic opportunities. Marriage also meant special

burdens for black women who took on the now familiar double role as housekeeper and breadwinner. For many newly married blacks, however, the initial goal was to create a traditional family life, resulting in the widespread withdrawal of women from plantation field labor.

Another way in which freedmen demonstrated their new status was by choosing surnames; names associated with the concept of independence, such as Washington, were common. As an indication of the mixed feelings the freedmen had toward their former masters, some would adopt their master's name, and others would pick "any big name 'ceptin' their master's." Emancipation changed black manners around whites as well. Masks were dropped, and old expressions of humility—tipping a hat, stepping aside, feigning happiness, addressing whites with titles of deference—were discarded. For the blacks, these were necessary symbolic expressions of selfhood; they proved that things were now different. To whites, these behaviors were seen as acts of "insolence," "insubordination," and "puttin' on airs."

However important were choosing names, dropping masks, moving around, getting married, and testing new rights, the primary goal for most freedmen was the acquisition of their own land. "All I want is to git to own fo' or five acres ob land, dat I can build me a little house on and call my home," a Mississippi black said. Only through economic independence, the traditional American goal of controlling

The Promise of Land: 40 Acres

Note the progression in the various documents in this chapter—from promised lands, to lands restored to whites (page 548), to work contracts (page 555), to semiautonomous tenant farms; freedom came by degrees to the freedmen.

To All Whom It May Concern

Edisto Island, August 15th, 1865

George Owens, having selected for settlement forty acres of Land, on Theodore Belab's Place, pursuant to Special Field Orders, No. 15, Headquarters Military Division of the Mississippi, Savannah, Ga., Jan. 16, 1865; he has permission to hold and occupy the said Tract, subject to such regulations as may be established by proper authority; and all persons are prohibited from interfering with him in his possession of the same.

By command of   R. SAXTON
                     Brev't Maj. Gen.,
                     Ass't. Comm.
                     S.C., Ga., and Fla.

one's own labor and land, could former slaves prove to themselves that emancipation was real.

During the war, some Union generals had placed liberated slaves in charge of confiscated and abandoned lands. In the Sea Islands off the coast of South Carolina and Georgia, blacks had been working 40-acre plots of land and harvesting their own crops for several years. Farther inland, most freedmen who received land were the former slaves of Cherokees and Creeks. Some blacks held title to these lands. Northern philanthropists had organized others to grow cotton for the Treasury Department to prove the superiority of free labor over slavery. In the Davis Bend section of Mississippi, thousands of ex-slaves worked 40-acre tracts on leased lands formerly owned by Jefferson Davis. In this highly successful experiment, they made profits sufficient to repay the government for initial costs, then lost the land to Davis's brother.

Many freedmen expected a new economic order as fair payment for their years of involuntary work on the land. "It's de white man's turn ter labor now," a black preacher in Florida told a group of fieldhands. Whites would no longer own all the land, he went on, "fur de Guverment is gwine ter gie ter ev'ry Nigger forty acres of lan' an' a mule." Other freedmen were willing to settle for less: One in Virginia offered to take only one acre of land— "Ef you make it de acre dat Marsa's house sets on." Another was more guarded, aware of how easy the power could shift back to white planters: "Gib us our own land and we take care ourselves; but widout land, de ole massas can hire us or starve us, as dey please." However cautiously expressed, the freedmen had every expectation, fed by the intensity of their dreams, that the promised "forty acres and a mule" was forthcoming. Once they obtained land, family unity, and education, they looked forward to civil rights and the vote.

The White South's Fearful Response

White southerners had equally mixed goals and expectations at the war's end. Yeoman farmers and poor whites stood side by side with rich planters in bread lines, as together they looked forward to the restoration of their land and livelihood. Suffering from "extreme want and destitution," as a Cherokee County, Georgia, resident put it, white south-

erners responded to the immediate postwar crises with feelings of outrage, loss, and injustice. "I tell you it is mighty hard," said one man, "for my pa paid his own money for our niggers; and that's not all they've robbed us of. They have taken our horses and cattle and sheep and everything." Others felt the loss more personally, as former slaves they thought were faithful or for whom they felt great affection suddenly left. "Something dreadful has happened dear Diary," a Florida woman wrote in May 1865. "My dear black mammy has left us.... I feel lost, I feel as if someone is dead in the house. Whatever will I do without my Mammy?"

A more dominant emotion than sorrow, however, was fear. The entire structure of southern society was shaken, and the semblance of racial peace and order that slavery had provided was shattered. Many white southerners could hardly imagine a society without blacks in bondage. It was the basis not only of social order, but of a lifestyle the larger slaveholders, at least, had long regarded as the perfect model of gentility and civilization. Having lost control of all that was familiar and revered, whites feared everything from losing their cheap labor supply to having to sit next to blacks on trains.

The mildest of their fears was the inconvenience of doing various jobs and chores they had rarely done before, like housework. A Georgia woman, Eliza Andrews, complained that it seemed to her a "waste of time for people who are capable of doing something better to spend their time sweeping and dusting while scores of lazy negroes that are fit for nothing else are lying around idle." Worse yet was the "impudent and presumin'" new manners of former slaves, as a North Carolinian put it, worrying, with others, that blacks wanted social equality.

The worst fears of southern whites were rape and revenge. Impudence and pretensions of social equality, some thought, would lead to legal intermarriage, which in turn would produce mulattoes, "Africanization," and the destruction of the purity of the white race. The presence of black soldiers touched off fears of violence and revenge. Although demobilization occurred rapidly after Appomattox, a few black militia units remained in uniform, parading with guns in southern cities.

The black codes, widespread violence against freedmen, and President Johnson's veto of the Civil Rights Bill gave rise to the sardonic question "Slavery Is Dead?" Note the irony of blind justice presiding over two violations of the freedmen's rights (described in the newspaper headings at the bottom on either side of a death's head encircled by "state right"). (The Newberry Library, Chicago)

Acts of violence by black soldiers against whites, however, were extremely rare.

Believing that their world was turned upside down, the former planter aristocracy tried to set it right again. Their goal was to restore the old plantation order and appropriate racial relationships. The key to reestablishing white dominance were the "black codes" that state legislatures passed in the first year after the end of the war. Many of the codes granted freedmen the right to marry, sue and be sued, testify in court, and hold property. But these rights were qualified. Complicated passages in the codes explained under exactly what circumstances blacks could testify against whites or own property (mostly they could not) or exercise other rights of free people. Some rights were denied, including racial intermarriage and the right to bear arms, possess alcoholic beverages, sit on trains except in baggage compartments, be on city streets at night, or congregate in large groups.

Many of the qualified rights guaranteed by the black codes— testimony in court, for example— were only passed to induce the federal government to withdraw its remaining troops from the South. This was a crucial issue, for in many places marauding groups of whites were assaulting and terrorizing virtually defenseless freedmen. In one small district in Kentucky, for example, a government agent reported in 1865:

> Twenty-three cases of severe and inhuman beating and whipping of men; four of beating and shooting; two of robbing and shooting; three of robbing; five men shot and killed; two shot and wounded; four beaten to death; one beaten and roasted; three women assaulted and ravished; four women beaten; two

women tied up and whipped until insensible; two men and their families beaten and driven from their homes, and their property destroyed; two instances of burning of dwellings, and one of the inmates shot.

Freedmen clearly needed protection and the right to testify in court against whites.

For white planters, the violence was another sign of social disorder that could be eased only by restoring a plantation-based society. More significantly, they needed the freedmen's labor. The crucial provisions of the black codes were thus intended to regulate the freedmen's economic status. "Vagrancy" laws provided that any blacks not "lawfully employed," which usually meant by a white employer, could be arrested, jailed, fined, or hired out to a man who would assume responsibility for their debts and future behavior. The codes regulated the work contracts by which black laborers worked in the fields for white landowners, including severe penalties for leaving before the yearly contract was fulfilled and rules for proper behavior, attitude, and manners. Thus, southern leaders sought to reestablish their dominance. Although thwarted in perpetuating slavery or even in a program for gradual emancipation, many southerners believed, like this Texan, that "we will be enabled to adopt a coercive system of labor." A Kentucky newspaper was more direct: "The tune … will not be 'forty acres and a mule,' but … 'work nigger or starve.'"

National Reconstruction

The black codes passed by southern legislatures supported these intentions. The question facing the national government in 1865 was whether it would use its power to support the black codes and the reimposition of racial intimidation in the South or to uphold the newly sought rights of the freedmen. Would the federal government side with the democratic reform impulse in American history, which stressed human rights and liberty, or with the forces emphasizing property, order, and self-interest? Although the primary drama of Reconstruction took place in the conflict between white landowners and black freedmen over land and labor in the South, the struggle over Recon-

struction policy among politicians in Washington played a significant role in the local drama, as well as the next century of American history.

The Presidential Plan

After an initially tough stand calling for punishment of the defeated Confederates for "treason," President Johnson soon adopted a more lenient policy. On May 29, 1865, he issued two proclamations setting forth his reconstruction program. Like Lincoln, he maintained that the southern states had never left the Union. His first proclamation continued Lincoln's policies by offering "amnesty and pardon, with restoration of all rights of property" to all former Confederates who would take an oath of allegiance to the Constitution and the Union of the United States. There were exceptions: ex-Confederate government leaders and rich rebels whose taxable property was valued at over $20,000. In this latter exception, Johnson revealed his old Jacksonian hostility to wealthy aristocratic planters and his preference for leadership by self-made yeoman farmers like himself. Any southerners not covered by the amnesty proclamation, however, could apply for special individual pardons, which Johnson granted to nearly all applicants. By the fall of 1865, only a handful remained unpardoned.

Johnson's second proclamation accepted the reconstructed government of North Carolina and laid out the steps by which other southern states could reestablish state governments. First, the president would appoint a provisional governor, who would call a state convention representing "that portion of the people of said State who are loyal to the United States." This included those who took the oath of allegiance or were otherwise pardoned. The convention should ratify the Thirteenth Amendment, which abolished slavery; void secession; repudiate all Confederate debts; and then elect new state officials and members of Congress.

Under this lenient plan, each of the southern states successfully completed Reconstruction and sent newly elected members to the Congress that convened in December 1865. Southern voters defiantly elected dozens of former officers and legislators of the Confederacy, including a few not yet pardoned. Some state conventions hedged on rati-

Promised Land Restored to Whites

Richard H. Jenkins, an applicant for the restoration of his plantation on Wadmalaw Island, S. C., called "Rackett Hall," the same having been unoccupied during the past year and up to the 1st of Jan. 1866, except by one freedman who planted no crop, and being held by the Bureau of Refugees, Freedmen and Abandoned Lands, having conformed to the requirements of Circular No. 15 of said Bureau, dated Washington, D. C., Sept. 12, 1865, the aforesaid property is hereby restored to his possession.

. . . The Undersigned, Richard H. Jenkins, does hereby solemnly promise and engage, that he will secure to the Refugees and Freedmen now resident on his Wadmalaw Island Estate, the crops of the past year, harvested or unharvested; also, that the said Refugees and Freedmen shall be allowed to remain at their present houses or other homes on the island, so long as the responsible Refugees and Freedmen (embracing parents, guardians, and other natural protectors) shall enter into contracts, by leases or for wages, in terms satisfactory to the Supervising Board.

Also, that the undersigned will take the proper steps to enter into contracts with the above described responsible Refugees and Freedmen, the latter being required on their part to enter into said contracts on or before the 15th day of February, 1866, or surrender their right to remain on the said estate, it being understood that if they are unwilling to contract after the expiration of said period, the Supervising Board is to aid in getting them homes and employment elsewhere.

fying the Thirteenth Amendment, and some asserted their right to compensation for the loss of slave property. No state convention provided for black suffrage, and most did nothing to guarantee civil rights, schooling, or economic protection for the freedmen.

Less than eight months after Appomattox, the southern states were back in the Union, the freedmen were returning to work for their former masters under annual contracts, and the new president seemed firmly in charge. Reconstruction of the southern states seemed to be over. But northern Republicans were far from satisfied with President Johnson's efforts. Georges Clemenceau, a young French newspaper reporter covering the war, wondered if the North, having made so many "painful sacrifices," would "let itself be tricked out of what it had spent so much trouble and perseverance to win."

Congressional Reconstruction

As they looked at the situation late in 1865, northern leaders painfully saw that almost none of their postwar goals—moral, political, or psychological—were being fulfilled. The South seemed far from reconstructed and was taking advantage of the president's program to restore the power of the prewar planter aristocracy. The freedmen were receiving neither equal citizenship nor economic

independence. And the Republicans were not likely to maintain their political power and stay in office. Would the Democratic party and the South gain by postwar elections what they had been unable to achieve by civil war?

A song popular in the North in 1866 posed the question: "Who shall rule this American Nation?"—those who would betray their country and "murder the innocent freedmen" or those "loyal millions" who had shed their "blood in battle"? The answer was obvious. Congressional Republicans, led by Congressman Thaddeus Stevens of Pennsylvania and Senator Charles Sumner of Massachusetts, thus asserted their own policies for reconstructing the nation. Although labeled "radicals," the vast majority of Republicans were moderates on the issues of the economic and political rights of the freedmen.

Rejecting Johnson's notion that the South had already been reconstructed, Congress asserted its constitutional authority to decide on its own membership and refused seats to the newly elected senators and representatives from the old Confederate states. Congress then established the Joint Committee on Reconstruction to investigate conditions in the South. Its report documented disorder and resistance and the appalling treatment and conditions of the freedmen. Even before the report was made final in 1866, Congress passed a civil rights bill to protect the fragile rights of the

A white mob burned this freedmen's school during the Memphis riot of May 1866. (Library Company of Philadelphia)

blacks and extended for two more years the Freedmen's Bureau, an agency providing emergency assistance at the end of the war. President Johnson vetoed both bills, arguing that they were unconstitutional and calling his congressional opponents "traitors."

Johnson's growing anger forced moderates into the radical camp, and Congress passed both bills over his veto. Both, however, were watered down by weakening the power of enforcement. Southern civil courts, therefore, regularly disallowed black testimony against whites, acquitted whites charged with violence against blacks, sentenced blacks to compulsory labor, and generally made discriminatory sentences for the same crimes. In this judicial climate, racial violence erupted with discouraging frequency.

In Memphis, for example, a race riot occurred in May 1866 that typified race relations during the Reconstruction period. In the months before the riot, local Irish policemen frequently unleashed unprovoked brutality on black Union soldiers stationed at nearby Fort Pickering. A Memphis newspaper suggested that "the negro can do the country more good in the cotton field than in the camp" and criticized what it called the "dirty, fanatical, nigger-loving Radicals of this city" who thought otherwise.

In this inflamed atmosphere, a street brawl erupted between the police and some recently discharged but armed black soldiers. After some fighting and an exchange of gunfire, the soldiers went back to their fort. That night, white mobs, led by prominent local officials (one of whom urged the mob to "go ahead and kill the last damned one of the nigger race"), invaded the black section of the city. With the encouragement of the Memphis police, the mobs engaged in over 40 hours of terror, killing, beating, robbing, and raping virtually helpless residents and burning houses, schools, and churches. When it was over, 48 people, all but two of them black, had died in the riot. The local Union army commander took his time intervening to restore order, arguing that his troops had a "large amount of public property to guard [and] hated Negroes too." A congressional inquiry found that in Memphis, blacks had "no protection from the law whatever."

A month later, Congress proposed to the states the ratification of the Fourteenth Amendment, the single most significant act of the Reconstruction era. The first section of the amendment sought to provide permanent constitutional protection of the civil rights of freedmen by defining them as citizens. States were prohibited from depriving "any person of life, liberty, or property, without due process of law," and all people were guaranteed the "equal protection of the laws." In Section 2, Congress granted black male suffrage in the South by making blacks whole people eligible to vote (thus canceling the Constitution's "three-fifths" clause).

States that denied this right would have their "basis of representation reduced" proportionally. Other sections of the amendment denied leaders of the Confederacy the right to hold national or state political office (except by act of Congress), repudiated the Confederate debt, and denied claims of compensation by former slave owners for their lost property.

President Johnson urged the southern states not to ratify the Fourteenth Amendment, and ten states immediately rejected it. Johnson then went on the campaign trail in the midterm election of 1866 to ask voters to throw out the radical Republicans. Vicious name calling and other low forms of electioneering marked this first political campaign since the war's end. The president exchanged insults with hecklers and lashed out against his opponents. Democrats in both the South and the North appealed openly to racial prejudice in calling for the defeat of those who had passed the Fourteenth Amendment. The nation would be "Africanized," they charged, with black equality threatening both the marketplace and the bedroom.

Republican campaigners, in turn, called Johnson a drunkard and a traitor. Bitter Civil War memories were revived as Republicans "waved the bloody shirt" in telling voters that Democrats were traitorous rebels or draft dodgers, whereas Republicans were courageous soldiers and patriotic saviors of the Union. Governor Oliver P. Morton of Indiana described the Democratic party as a "common sewer and loathsome receptacle, into which is emptied every element of treason ... inhumanity and barbarism which has dishonored the age." Although the electorate was moved more by self-interest on other issues than by the persuasive power of these speeches, the result of the election was an overwhelming victory for the Republicans. The mandate was clear. The presidential plan of reconstruction in the seceded states had not worked, and Congress must suggest another.

Therefore, early in 1867, three Reconstruction acts were passed. The first divided the southern states into five military districts in which military commanders had broad powers to maintain order and protect the rights of property and individuals. Congress also defined a new process for readmitting a state. Qualified voters, which included blacks and excluded unreconstructed rebels, would elect delegates to state constitutional conventions, which then would write new constitutions guaranteeing black suffrage. After the new voters of the states had ratified the constitutions, elections would be held to choose governors and state legislatures. When a state ratified the Fourteenth Amendment, its representatives to Congress would be accepted, thus completing readmission to the Union.

The President Impeached

At the same time that it passed the Reconstruction acts, Congress also approved bills to restrict the powers of the president and to establish the dominance of the legislative branch over the executive. The Tenure of Office Act, designed to prevent Johnson from removing the outspoken Secretary of War Edwin Stanton, limited the president's appointment powers. Other measures restricted his power as commander in chief. Johnson behaved exactly as congressional Republicans had anticipated, vetoing the Reconstruction acts, issuing orders to limit military commanders in the South, and removing cabinet and other government officials sympathetic to Congress's program. The House Judiciary Committee investigated, charging the president with "usurpations of power" and of acting in the "interests of the great criminals" who had led the southern rebellion. It was evident, however, that Johnson was guilty only of holding principles, policies, and prejudices different from those of congressional leaders, and moderate House Republicans defeated the impeachment resolutions.

In August 1867, Johnson finally dismissed Stanton and asked for Senate consent. When the Senate refused, the president ordered Stanton to surrender his office, which he refused, barricading himself inside. This time the House rushed impeachment resolutions to a vote, charging the president with "high crimes and misdemeanors" as detailed in 11 offenses while in office, mostly focusing on alleged violations of the Tenure of Office Act. The three-month trial in the Senate early in 1868 featured impassioned oratory. Radical Republicans declared the president "guilty of all, and infinitely more." Evidence was skimpy, however, that Johnson had committed any crime

Presidential Elections, 1864–1868				
Year	Candidate	Party	Popular Vote	Electoral Vote
1864	ABRAHAM LINCOLN	Republican	2,206,938 (55.0%)	212
	George B. McClellan	Democratic	1,803,787 (45.0%)	21
1868	ULYSSES S. GRANT	Republican	3,013,421 (52.7%)	214
	Horatio Seymour	Democratic	2,706,829 (47.3%)	80

Note: Winners' names are in capital letters.

that justified his removal. With seven moderate Republicans joining Democrats against conviction, the effort to find the president guilty as charged fell short of the two-thirds majority required by a single vote.

The moderate Republicans, satisfied with the changes wrought by the Civil War, may have feared the consequences of removing Johnson, for the next man in line for the presidency, Senator Benjamin Wade of Ohio, was a leading radical Republican. Wade had endorsed women's suffrage, rights for labor unions, and civil rights for blacks in both southern and northern states. As the moderate or regular Republicans gained strength in 1868 through their support of the presidential election winner, Ulysses S. Grant, radicalism lost much of its power within Republican ranks. Not for another 100 years would a president again face removal from office through impeachment.

Congressional Moderation

The impeachment crisis revealed that most Republicans were more interested in protecting themselves than the freedmen and in punishing Johnson rather than the South. Congress's political battle against the president was not matched by an idealistic resolve on behalf of the rights and welfare of the freedmen. As early as the state and local elections of 1867, it was clear that voters preferred moderate reconstruction policies. It is important to look not only at what Congress did during Reconstruction, but also at what it did not do.

With the exception of Jefferson Davis, Congress did not imprison Confederate leaders, and only one person, the commander of the infamous Andersonville prison camp, was put to death. Congress did not insist on a long-term probationary period before southern states could be readmitted to the Union. It did not reorganize southern local governments. It did not mandate a national program of education for the 4 million ex-slaves. It did not confiscate and redistribute land to the freedmen, nor did it prevent President Johnson from taking land away from freedmen who had gained possessory titles during the war. It did not, except indirectly, provide economic help to black citizens.

What Congress did do, and that only reluctantly, was grant citizenship and suffrage to the freedmen. At the end of the Civil War, northerners were no more prepared than southerners to make blacks equal citizens. Between 1865 and 1869, several states held referendums proposing black suffrage. Voters in Kansas, Ohio, Michigan, Missouri, Wisconsin, Connecticut, New York, and the District of Columbia (by a vote of 6,521 to 35!) all turned the proposals down. Only in Iowa and Minnesota (on the third try, and then only by devious wording) did northern whites grant the vote to blacks.

Black suffrage gained support, however, after the election of 1868, when General Grant, a military hero regarded as invincible, barely won the popular vote in several states. Congressional Republicans, who had twice rejected a suffrage amendment, took another look at the idea as a way of adding grateful black votes to party rolls. After a

Reconstruction Amendments		
Constitutional Seeds of Dreams Deferred for 100 Years (or More)		
Substance	Outcome of Ratification Process	Final Implementation and Enforcement
Thirteenth Amendment—Passed by Congress January 1865		
Prohibited slavery in the United States	Ratified by 27 states, including 8 southern states, by December 1865	Immediate, although economic freedom came by degrees
Fourteenth Amendment—Passed by Congress June 1866		
(1) Defined equal national citizenship; (2) reduced state representation in Congress proportional to number of disenfranchised voters; (3) denied former Confederates the right to hold office	Rejected by 12 southern and border states by February 1867; radicals made readmission depend on ratification; ratified in July 1868	Civil Rights Act of 1964
Fifteenth Amendment—Passed by Congress February 1869		
Prohibited denial of vote because of race, color, or previous servitude	Ratification by Virginia, Texas, Mississippi, and Georgia reqired for readmission; ratified in March 1870	Voting Rights Act of 1965

bitterly contested fight, repeated in several state ratification contests, the Fifteenth Amendment, forbidding all states to deny the vote to anyone "on account of race, color, or previous condition of servitude," became part of the Constitution in 1870. A black preacher from Pittsburgh observed that "the Republican party had done the Negro good, but they were doing themselves good at the same time."

Congress, therefore, gave blacks the vote but not the land, the opposite priority of what the freedmen wanted. Almost alone, Thaddeus Stevens argued that "forty acres ... and a hut would be more valuable ... than the ... right to vote." But Congress never seriously considered his plan to confiscate the land of the "chief rebels" and to give a small portion of it, divided into 40-acre plots, to the freedmen, for it went against deeply held beliefs of the Republican party and the American people in the sacredness of private property. Moreover, the idea of a large propertyless class of cheap black laborers attracted northern business inter-

ests concerned with the development of southern industry and with investing in southern land.

Although most Americans, in the North as well as the South, opposed confiscation and did not want blacks to become independent landowners, Congress passed an alternative measure. Proposed by George Julian of Indiana, the Southern Homestead Act of 1866 made public lands available to blacks and loyal whites in five southern states. But the land was of poor quality and inaccessible. No transportation, tools, or seed was provided, and most blacks who might have wanted to take advantage of the offer had only until January 1, 1867, to claim their land. But that was nearly impossible for most because they were under contract to white employers until that date. Only about 4,000 black families even applied for the Homestead Act lands, and fewer than 20 percent of them saw their claims completed. The record of white claimants was not much better. Congressional moderation, therefore, left the freedmen economically weak as they faced the challenges of freedom.

Women and the Reconstruction Amendments

One casualty of the Fourteenth and Fifteenth amendments was the goodwill of the women who had been petitioning and campaigning for suffrage for two decades. They had hoped that grateful male legislators would recognize their support for the Union effort during the war and the suspension of their own demands in the interests of the more immediate concerns of preserving the Union, nursing the wounded, and emancipating the slaves. During the war, for example, the Woman's Loyal League, headed by Elizabeth Cady Stanton and Susan B. Anthony, gathered nearly 400,000 signatures on petitions asking Congress to pass the Thirteenth Amendment. They were therefore shocked to see the wording of the Fourteenth Amendment, which for the first time inserted the word male in the Constitution in referring to a citizen's right to vote.

Stanton and Anthony campaigned actively against the Fourteenth Amendment, despite the pleas of those who, like Frederick Douglass, had long supported woman suffrage yet declared that this was "the Negro's hour." When the Fifteenth Amendment was proposed, they wondered why the word sex could not have been added to the "conditions" no longer a basis for denial of the vote. Largely abandoned by radical reconstructionists and abolitionist activists, they had few champions in Congress and their efforts were put off for half a century. Disappointment over the suffrage issue was one of several reasons that led to a split in the women's movement in 1869. Anthony and Stanton continued their fight for a national amendment for woman suffrage and a long list of other rights, and other women concentrated their hopes on securing the vote on a state-by-state basis.

Life After Slavery

Union army Major George Reynolds boasted to a friend late in 1865 that in the area of Mississippi under his command, he had "kept the negroes at work, and in a good state of discipline." Clinton Fisk, a well-meaning white who helped found a

The Freedmen's Bureau had fewer resources in relation to its purpose than any agency in the nation's history. Harper's Weekly *published this engraving of freedmen lining up for aid in Memphis in 1866. (Library of Congress)*

black college in Tennessee, told freedmen in 1866 that they could be "as free and as happy" working again for their "old master ... as any where else in the world." For many blacks, such pronouncements sounded familiar, reminding them of white preachers' exhortations during slavery to work hard and obey their masters. Ironically, though, both Fisk and Reynolds were agents of the Freedmen's Bureau, the crucial agency intended to ease the transition from slavery to freedom for the 4 million ex-slaves.

The Freedmen's Bureau

Never in American history has one small agency—underfinanced, understaffed, and undersupported—been given a harder task than was the Bureau of Freedmen, Refugees and Abandoned Lands. Its purposes and mixed successes symbolize, as well as those of any other institution, the tortuous course of Reconstruction.

The activities of the Freedmen's Bureau included issuing emergency rations of food and providing clothing and shelter to the homeless, hungry victims of the war; establishing medical care and hospital facilities; providing funds for transportation for the thousands of freedmen and white refugees dislocated by the war; helping blacks search for and put their families back together; and arranging for legal marriage ceremonies. The bureau also served as a friend in local civil courts to ensure that the freedmen got fair trials. Although not initially empowered to do so, the agency was responsible for the education of the ex-slaves. To bureau schools came many idealistic teachers from various northern Freedmen's Aid societies.

In addition to these many activities, the largest task of the Freedmen's Bureau was to serve as an employment agency, tending to the economic well-being of the blacks. This included settling them on abandoned lands and getting them started with tools, seed, and draft animals, as well as arranging work contracts with white landowners. As we shall see, in the area of work contracts, the Freedmen's Bureau served more to "reenslave" the freedmen as impoverished fieldworkers than to set them on their way as independent farmers.

Although some agents were idealistic young New Englanders eager to help slaves adjust to freedom, others were Union army officers more concerned with social order than social transformation. Working in a postwar climate of resentment and violence, Freedmen's Bureau agents were constantly accused of partisan Republican politics, corruption, and partiality to blacks by local white residents. But even the best-intentioned agents would have agreed with General O. O. Howard, commissioner of the bureau, in a belief in the traditional nineteenth-century American values of self-help, minimal government interference in the marketplace, the sanctity of private property, contractual obligations, and white superiority. The bureau's work served to uphold these values.

On a typical day, these overworked and underpaid agents would visit courts and schools in their district, supervise the signing of work contracts, and handle numerous complaints, most involving contract violations between whites and blacks or property and domestic disputes among blacks. One agent sent a man who had complained of a severe beating back to work with the advice, "Don't be sassy [and] don't be lazy when you've got work to do." Another, reflecting his growing frustrations, complained that the freedmen were "disrespectful and greatly in need of instruction." Although help-

ful in finding work for the freedmen, more often than not the agents found themselves defending white landowners by telling the blacks to obey orders, to trust their employers, and to sign and live by disadvantageous contracts.

Despite mounting pressures to support white landowners, personal frustrations, and even threats on their lives, the agents accomplished a great deal. In little more than two years, the Freedmen's Bureau issued 20 million rations (nearly one-third to poor whites), reunited families and resettled some 30,000 displaced war refugees, treated some 450,000 cases of illness and injury, built 40 hospitals and hundreds of schools, provided books, tools, and furnishings—and even some land—to the freedmen, and occasionally protected their economic and civil rights. Black historian W. E. B. Du Bois wrote an epitaph for the bureau that might stand for the whole of Reconstruction: "In a time of perfect calm, amid willing neighbors and streaming wealth," he wrote, it "would have been a herculean task" for the bureau to fulfill its many purposes. But in the midst of hunger, sorrow, spite, suspicion, hate, and cruelty, "the work of any instrument of social regeneration was . . . foredoomed to failure."

Economic Freedom by Degrees

The economic failures of the Freedmen's Bureau, symbolic of the entire congressional program, forced the freedmen into a new economic dependency on their former masters. Although the planter class did not lose its economic and social power in the postwar years, the character of southern agriculture went through some major changes. First, a land-intensive system replaced the labor intensity of slavery. Land ownership was concentrated into fewer and even larger holdings than before the Civil War. From South Carolina to Louisiana, the wealthiest tenth of the population owned about 60 percent of the real estate in the 1870s. Second, these large planters increasingly concentrated on one crop, usually cotton, and were tied into the international market. This resulted in a steady drop in food production (both grains and livestock) in the postwar period. Third, reliance on one-crop farming meant that a new credit system emerged whereby most farmers,

A Freedman's Work Contract

As you read this rather typical work contract defining the first economic relationship between whites and blacks in the early months of the postwar period, note the regulation of social behavior and deportment as well as work and "pay" arrangements. How different is this from slavery? As a freedman or woman, would you have signed such an agreement? Why or why not? What options did you have?

State of South Carolina
Darlington District
Articles of Agreement

This Agreement entered into between Mrs. Adele Allston Exect of the one part, and the Freedmen and Women of The Upper Quarters plantation of the other part Witnesseth:

That the latter agree, for the remainder of the present year, to reside upon and devote their labor to the cultivation of the Plantation of the former. And they further agree, that they will in all respects, conform to such reasonable and necessary plantation rules and regulations as Mrs. Allston's Agent may prescribe; that they will not keep any gun, pistol, or other offensive weapon, or leave the plantation without permission from their employer; that in all things connected with their duties as laborers on said plantation, they will yield prompt obedience to all orders from Mrs. Allston or his [*sic*] agent; that they will be orderly and quiet in their conduct, avoiding drunkenness and other gross vices; that they will not misuse any of the Plantation Tools, or Agricultural Implements, or any Animals entrusted to their care, or any Boats, Flats, Carts or Wagons; that they will give up at the expiration of this Contract, all Tools & c., belonging to the Plantation, and in case any property, of any description belonging to the Plantation shall be willfully or through negligence destroyed or injured, the value of the Articles so destroyed, shall be deducted from the portion of the Crops which the person or persons, so offending, shall be entitled to receive under this Contract.

Any deviations from the condition of the foregoing Contract may, upon sufficient proof, be punished with dismissal from the Plantation, or in such other manner as may be determined by the Provost Court; and the person or persons so dismissed, shall forfeit the whole, or a part of his, her or their portion of the crop, as the Court may decide.

In consideration of the foregoing Services duly performed, Mrs. Allston agrees, after deducting Seventy five bushels of Corn for each work Animal, exclusively used in cultivating the Crops for the present year; to turn over to the said Freedmen and Women, one half of the remaining Corn, Peas, Potatoes, made this season. He [*sic*] further agrees to furnish the usual rations until the Contract is performed.

All Cotton Seed Produced on the Plantation is to be reserved for the use of the Plantation. The Freedmen, Women and Children are to be treated in a manner consistent with their freedom. Necessary medical attention will be furnished as heretofore.

Any deviation from the conditions of this Contract upon the part of the said Mrs. Allston or her Agent or Agents shall be punished in such manner as may be determined by a Provost Court, or a Military Commission. This agreement to continue till the first day of January 1866.

Witness our hand at The Upper Quarters this 28th day of July 1865.

black and white, depended on local merchants for renting seed, farm implements and animals, provisions, housing, and land. These changes affected race relations and class tensions among whites.

This new system, however, took a few years to develop after emancipation. At first, most freedmen signed contracts with white landowners and worked in gangs in the fields as farm laborers very much as during slavery. Watched over by superintendents, who still used the lash, they toiled from sunrise to sunset for a meager wage and a monthly allotment of bacon and meal. All members of the family had to work to receive their rations. The freedmen resented this new form of semiservitude, preferring small plots of land of their own to grow vegetables and grains. Moreover, they wanted to be able to send their children to school and insisted on "no more outdoor work" for women. What the

Changes on the Barrow Plantation, 1860–1881

After refusing to accept labor contracts and a competitive gang system, the former slaves of David C. Barrow moved their households to 25 30-acre tenant farms, which they rented from the Barrow family in annual contracts requiring payment in cotton and other crops.

freedmen wanted, a Georgia planter correctly observed, was "to get away from all overseers, to hire or purchase land, and work for themselves."

Many blacks therefore broke contracts, ran away, engaged in work slowdowns or strikes, burned barns, and otherwise expressed their displeasure with the contract labor system. One white landowner expressed his frustration over having "to bargain and haggle with our servants about wages." In the Sea Islands and rice-growing regions of coastal South Carolina and Georgia, where slaves had long held a degree of autonomy, resistance was especially strong. On the Heyward plantations, near those of the Allstons', the freedmen "refuse work at any price," a Freedman's Bureau agent reported, and the women "wish to stay in the house or the garden all the time." The Allstons' former slaves also refused to sign their contracts, even when offered livestock and other favors, and in 1869, Adele Allston was forced to sell much of her vast landholdings.

Blacks' insistence on autonomy and land of their own was the major impetus for the change from the contract system to tenancy and sharecropping. As a South Carolina freedman put it, "If a man got to go crost de riber, and he can't git a boat, he take a log. If I can't own de land, I'll hire or lease land, but I won't contract." Families would hitch a team of mules to their old slave cabin to drag it to their assigned plot of land as far away from the Big House as possible. The sharecroppers were given seed, fertilizer, farm implements, and all necessary food and clothing to take care of their families. In return, the landlord (or a local merchant) told them what to grow and how much and took a share—usually half—of the harvest. The half retained by the cropper, however, was usually needed to pay for goods bought on credit (at huge interest rates) at the landlord's store. Thus, the sharecroppers were semiautonomous, but remained tied to the landlord's will for economic survival.

Under the tenant system, farmers had only slightly more independence. In advance of the harvest, a tenant farmer promised to sell his crop to a local merchant in return for renting land, tools,

Sharecroppers and tenant farmers, though more autonomous than contract laborers, remained dependent on the landlord for their survival. (Brown Brothers)

and other necessities. He was also obligated to purchase goods on credit (at higher prices than whites paid) against the harvest from the merchant's store. At "settling up" time, the income from the sale of the crop was matched with debts accumulated at the store. It was possible, especially after an unusually bountiful season, to come out ahead and eventually to own one's own land. But tenants seemed rarely to do so; they remained in debt at the end of each year and were then compelled to pledge the next year's crop. World cotton prices remained low, and whereas large landowners still enjoyed profits through their large scale of operation, sharecroppers rarely received much money. When they were able to pay off their debts, landowners frequently altered the loan agreements. Thus, a system of debt peonage replaced slavery, ensuring a continuing cheap labor supply to grow cotton and other staples in the South. Only a very few blacks became independent landowners—about 2 to 5 percent by 1880, but closer to 20 percent in some states by 1900.

These changes in southern agriculture affected yeoman and poor white farmers as well as the freedmen. This raised the threat, always troubling to the planter class, of a coalition between poor black and pro-Unionist white farmers. As a yeoman farmer in Georgia said in 1865, "We should tuk the land, as we did the niggers, and split it, and giv part to the niggers and part to me and t'other Union fellers." But confiscation and redistribution of land was no more likely for white farmers than for the freedmen. Whites, too, were forced to concentrate on growing staples, to pledge their crops against high-interest credit from local merchants, and to face the inevitability of perpetual indebtedness. In the upcountry piedmont area of Georgia, for example, the number of whites who worked their own land dropped from nine in ten before the Civil War to seven in ten by 1880. During the same period, the production of cotton doubled.

Larger planters' reliance on cotton meant fewer food crops, which necessitated greater dependence on local merchants for provisions. In 1884, Jephta Dickson of Jackson County, Georgia, purchased over $50 worth of flour, meal, meat, syrup, and peas and corn from a local store, an almost unthinkable situation 25 years earlier, when he would have needed to buy almost no food to supplement his homegrown fare. Fencing laws seriously curtailed the livelihood of poor whites

Albion Tourgée summed up the Reconstruction era in his novel *A Fool's Errand* (1879): "The spirit of the dead Confederacy was stronger than the mandate of the nation to which it had succumbed in battle."

Congress and President Grant did not totally ignore the violence in the South. Three Force acts, passed in 1870 and 1871, gave the president strong powers to use federal supervisors to make sure that citizens were not prevented from voting by force or fraud. The third act, known as the Ku Klux Klan Act, declared illegal secret organizations that used disguise and coercion to deprive others of equal protection of the laws. Congress created a joint committee to investigate Klan violence, which reported in 1872 in 13 huge volumes of horrifying testimony. Grant, who had supported these measures, delivered special messages to Congress proclaiming the importance of the right to vote, issued proclamations condemning lawlessness, and sent some additional troops to South Carolina. However, as reform Republicans realized that black voters supported Grant, they lost interest in defending those voters. Regular Republicans were also not very supportive, because many felt that they could do without black voters. Both groups were much more concerned with northern issues. In 1875, Grant's advisers told him that Republicans might lose important Ohio elections if he continued to protect blacks. Thus, he decided that year to reject appeals by Mississippi blacks that troops be stationed in their state to guarantee free elections. Grant declared instead that he and the nation "had tired of these annual autumnal outbreaks."

The success of the Mississippi Plan in 1875, imitated a year later in South Carolina and Louisiana, indicated that congressional reports and presidential proclamations did little to stop the reign of terror against black and white Republicans throughout the South. The Force acts were wholly inadequate and were themselves weakly enforced. Although there were hundreds of arrests, all-white juries were reluctant to find their fellow citizens guilty of crimes against blacks. The U.S. Supreme Court backed them. In two decisions in 1874, the Court threw out cases against whites found guilty of preventing blacks from voting and declared key parts of the Force acts unconstitutional. In Hamburg, South Carolina, in 1876, several blacks were killed in a riot that started in a courtroom when a white mob came to provide its own form of "justice" to some black militiamen who had been arrested for parading on Independence Day. Although the Ku Klux Klan's power was officially ended, the attitudes (and tactics) of Klansmen would continue long into the next century.

Reconstruction, Northern Style

The American people, like their leaders, were tired of battles over the freedmen and were shifting their attention to other matters than fulfilling idealistic principles. Frustrated with the difficulties of trying to transform an unwilling South and seemingly ungrateful blacks, the easiest course was to give blacks their citizenship and the vote and move on to something else. After the interruptions of the Civil War and its aftermath, Americans of increasing diversity were primarily interested in starting families, finding work, and making money. Thus, German immigrants were firing furnaces in new steel plants in Wheeling, West Virginia; Chinese men were pounding in railroad ties for the Central Pacific over the Sierra Nevada mountains and across the Nevada desert; female teachers were struggling to teach in one-room schoolhouses in Vermont for $23 a month; Mexican *vaqueros* were driving Texas cattle herds to Kansas; and Scandinavian families were battling heat, locusts, and railroad rates on farmsteads in the Dakotas.

At both the individual and national levels, Reconstruction, northern style, meant the continuation of the enormous economic revolution of the nineteenth century. Although failing to effect a smooth transition from slavery to freedom for ex-slaves, Republican northerners were able to accelerate and solidify their program of economic growth and industrial and territorial expansion.

As Klansmen met in dark forests to plan their next raid in North Carolina in 1869, the Central Pacific and Union Pacific railroads met at Promontory Point, Utah, linking the Atlantic and the Pacific by rail. As cotton production increased again in the postbellum South, so did the making of iron and steel in the North and the settlement of the mining, cattle, and agricultural frontiers in the West. But also, as black farmers were "haggling" over work contracts with white landowners in

These two scenes vividly contrast family life during Reconstruction in the North and South. For most white northerners, as shown in this 1868 Currier & Ives print, the end of the Civil War meant renewing the good life of genteel middle-class values. (Museum of the City of New York, The Harry T. Peters Collection) For many black freedmen, however, family life was constantly threatened by the intrusion of Klan violence. (The Granger Collection, New York)

Georgia, white workers were organizing and joining the National Labor Union in Baltimore. As Elizabeth and Adele Allston demanded the keys to their crop barns in the summer of 1865, the Boston Labor Reform Association was demanding that "our … education, morals, dwellings, and the whole Social System" needed to be "reconstructed." If the South would not be reconstructed, labor relations might be.

The years between 1865 and 1875 featured not only the rise (and fall) of Republican governments in the South, but also the spectacular rise of working-class activity and organization. Stimulated by the Civil War to improve working conditions in northern factories, such groups as trade unions, labor reform associations, and labor parties flourished, culminating in the founding of the National Labor Union in 1866. Before the depression of 1873, an estimated 300,000 to 500,000 American workers had enrolled in some 1,500 trade unions, the largest such increase in the nineteenth century. This growth would inevitably affect class tensions. In 1876, hundreds of

Novels

We usually read novels, short stories, and other forms of fiction for pleasure, for the enjoyment of plot, style, symbolism, and character development. "Classic" novels such as *Moby Dick, Huckleberry Finn, The Great Gatsby, The Invisible Man,* and *Beloved,* to name a few American examples, are not only written well, but also explore timeless questions of good and evil, of innocence and knowledge, or of noble dreams fulfilled and shattered. Often, we enjoy novels because we find ourselves identifying with one of the major characters. Through that person's problems, joys, relationships, and search for identity, we gain insights about our own.

We can also read novels as historical sources, for they reveal much about the attitudes, dreams, fears and ordinary everyday experiences of human beings in a particular historical period. They also show how people reacted to and felt about the major events of that era. The novelist, like the historian, is a product of time and place and has an interpretive point of view. Consider the two novels about Reconstruction quoted here. Neither is reputed for great literary merit, yet both reveal much about the various interpretations and impassioned attitudes of the post-Civil War era. *A Fool's Errand* was written by Albion Tourgée, a northerner; *The Clansman,* by Thomas Dixon, Jr., a southerner.

Tourgée was a young northern teacher and lawyer who fought with the Union army at several major battles during the Civil War. After the war, he moved to North Carolina, partly for health reasons and partly to begin a legal career. He became a judge and was an active Republican, supporting black suffrage and helping shape the new state constitution and the codification of North Carolina laws in 1868. With jurisdiction over eight counties, Tourgée earned a reputation as one of the fairest judges in the state. Because he boldly criticized the Ku Klux Klan for its campaign of terror against blacks, his life was threatened many times. When the fearless judge finally left North Carolina in 1879, he published an autobiographical novel about his experiences.

The "fool's errand" in the novel is that of the northern veteran, Comfort Servosse, who like Tourgée seeks to fulfill humane goals on behalf of both blacks and whites in post-Civil War North Carolina. His efforts are thwarted, however, by threats, intimidation, a campaign of violent "outrages"

against Republican leaders in the county, and a lack of support from Congress. Historians have verified the accuracy, down to the smallest details, of the events in Tourgée's novel. While exposing the brutality of the Klan, Tourgée features loyal southern Unionists, respectable planters ashamed of Klan violence, and even guilt-ridden poor white Klansmen who try to protect or warn intended victims.

In the year of Tourgée's death, 1905, another North Carolinian published a novel with a very different analysis of Reconstruction and its fate. Thomas Dixon was born during the Civil War. He was a lawyer, North Carolina state legislator, Baptist minister, lecturer, and novelist. *The Clansman,* subtitled *A Historical Romance of the Ku Klux Klan,* reflects turn-of-the-century attitudes most white southerners still had about Republican rule during Reconstruction. According to Dixon, once the "Great Heart" Lincoln was gone, a power-crazed, vindictive radical Congress, led by scheming Austin Stoneman (Thaddeus Stevens), sought to impose corrupt carpetbagger and brutal black rule by bayonet on a helpless South. Only through the inspired leadership and redemptive role of the Ku Klux Klan was the South saved from the horrors of rape and revenge.

Dixon dedicated *The Clansman* to his uncle, a Grand Titan of the Klan in North Carolina during the time when two crucial counties were being transformed from Republican to Democratic through intimidation and terror. No such violence shows up in Dixon's novel. When the novel was made the basis of D. W. Griffith's film classic, *Birth of a Nation,* in 1915, the novel's attitudes were firmly imprinted on the twentieth-century American mind.

Both novels convey the events and attitudes of the era by creating clearly defined heroes and villains. Both include exciting chase scenes, narrow escapes, daring rescues, and tragic, heart-rending deaths. Both include romantic subplots in which a young white southern man falls in love with a young white northern woman. In each novel, however, the author's primary purpose was to convey his views of the politics of Reconstruction. Examining brief excerpts is a poor substitute for reading the novels in their entirety. Notice the obvious differences of style and attitude in the descriptions of Uncle Jerry and Old Aleck.

A Fool's Errand

When the second Christmas came, Metta wrote again to her sister:

"The feeling is terribly bitter against Comfort on account of his course towards the colored people. There is quite a village of them on the lower end of the plantation. They have a church, a sabbath school, and are to have next year a school. You can not imagine how kind they have been to us, and how much they are attached to Comfort.... I got Comfort to go with me to one of their prayer-meetings a few nights ago. I had heard a great deal about them, but had never attended one before. It was strangely weird. There were, perhaps, fifty present, mostly middle-aged men and women. They were singing in a soft, low monotone, interspersed with prolonged exclamatory notes, a sort of rude hymn, which I was surprised to know was one of their old songs in slave times. How the chorus came to be endured in those days I can not imagine. It was—

'Free! free! free, my Lord, free!
An' we walks de hebben-ly way!'

"A few looked around as we came in and seated ourselves; and Uncle Jerry, the saint of the settlement, came forward on his staves, and said, in his soft voice,

"'Ev'nin', Kunnel! Sarvant, Missus! Will you walk up, an' hev seats in front?'

"We told him we had just looked in, and might go in a short time; so we would stay in the back part of the audience.

"Uncle Jerry can not read nor write; but he is a man of strange intelligence and power. Unable to do work of any account, he is the faithful friend, monitor, and director of others. He has a house and piece of land, all paid for, a good horse and cow, and, with the aid of his wife and two boys, made a fine crop this season. He is one of the most promising colored men in the settlement: so Comfort says, at least. Everybody seems to have great respect for his character. I don't know how many people I have heard speak of his religion. Mr. Savage used to say he had rather hear him pray than any other man on earth. He was much prized by his master, even after he was disabled, on account of his faithfulness and character."

The Clansman

At noon Ben and Phil strolled to the polling-place to watch the progress of the first election under Negro rule. The Square was jammed with shouting, jostling, perspiring negroes, men, women, and children. The day was warm, and the African odour was supreme even in the open air....

The negroes, under the drill of the League and the Freedman's Bureau, protected by the bayonet, were voting to enfranchise themselves, disfranchise their former masters, ratify a new constitution, and elect a legislature to do their will. Old Aleck was a candidate for the House, chief poll-holder, and seemed to be in charge of the movements of the voters outside the booth as well as inside. He appeared to be omnipresent, and his self-importance was a sight Phil had never dreamed. He could not keep his eyes off him....

[Aleck] was a born African orator, undoubtedly descended from a long line of savage spell-binders, whose eloquence in the palaver houses of the jungle had made them native leaders. His thin spindle-shanks supported an oblong, protruding stomach, resembling an elderly monkey's, which seemed so heavy it swayed his back to carry it.

The animal vivacity of his small eyes and the flexibility of his eyebrows, which he worked up and down rapidly with every change of countenance, expressed his eager desires.

He had laid aside his new shoes, which hurt him, and went barefooted to facilitate his movements on the great occasion. His heels projected and his foot was so flat that what should have been the hollow of it made a hole in the dirt where he left his track.

He was already mellow with liquor, and was dressed in an old army uniform and cap, with two horse-pistols buckled around his waist. On a strap hanging from his shoulder were strung a half-dozen tin canteens filled with whiskey.

TIMELINE

1865	Civil War ends
	Lincoln assassinated; Andrew Johnson becomes president
	Johnson proposes general amnesty and reconstruction plan
	Racial confusion, widespread hunger, and demobilization
	Thirteenth Amendment ratified
	Freedmen's Bureau established
1865–1866	Black codes
	Repossession of land by whites and freedmen's contracts
1866	Freedmen's Bureau renewed and Civil Rights Act passed over Johnson's veto
	Southern Homestead Act
	Ku Klux Klan formed
	Tennessee readmitted to Union
1867	Reconstruction acts passed over Johnson's veto
	Impeachment controversy
	Freedmen's Bureau ends
1868	Fourteenth Amendment ratified
	Impeachment proceedings against Johnson fail
	Ulysses Grant elected president
1868–1870	Ten states readmitted under congressional plan
1869	Georgia and Virginia reestablish Democratic party control
1870	Fifteenth Amendment ratified
1870s–1880s	Black "exodusters" migrate to Kansas
1870–1871	Force acts
	North Carolina and Georgia reestablish Democratic control
1872	General Amnesty Act
	Grant reelected president
1873	Crédit Mobilier scandal
	Panic causes depression
1874	Alabama and Arkansas reestablish Democratic control
1875	Civil Rights Act
	Mississippi reestablishes Democratic control
1876	Hayes-Tilden election
1876–1877	South Carolina, Louisiana, and Florida reestablish Democratic control
1877	Compromise of 1877; Rutherford B. Hayes assumes presidency and ends Reconstruction
1880s	Tenancy and sharecropping prevail in the South
	Disfranchisement and segregation of southern blacks begins

Congressional Reconstruction, long dormant, had ended. The election of 1876 sealed the conclusion.

As their nominee for president in 1876, the Republicans turned to a former governor of Ohio, Rutherford B. Hayes, partly because of his reputation for honesty, partly because he had been an officer in the Union army (a necessity for post-Civil War candidates), and partly because, as Henry Adams put it, he was "obnoxious to no one." The Democrats chose Governor Samuel J. Tilden of New York, who achieved national recognition as a civil service reformer in breaking up the corrupt Tweed ring.

Tilden won a majority of the popular vote and appeared to have enough electoral votes for victory. Twenty more electoral votes were disputed, all but one in the Deep South states of Louisiana, South Carolina, and Florida, where some federal troops still remained on duty and where Republicans still controlled the voting apparatus. Democrats, however, had applied various versions of the Mississippi Plan to intimidate voters. To resolve the disputed electoral votes, Congress created a special electoral commission consisting of five senators, five representatives, and five Supreme Court justices—eight of whom were Republicans and seven Democrats. The vote in each disputed case was eight to seven along party lines. Hayes was given all 20 votes, enough to win, 185 to 184.

Outraged Democrats threatened to stop the Senate from officially counting the electoral votes, thus preventing Hayes's inauguration. The country was in a state of crisis, and some Americans wondered if civil war might break out again. But unlike the 1850s, when passions over slavery erupted, this time a compromise was drawn between northerners and southerners mutually interested in modernization of the southern economy through capital investments. They focused on a Pacific railroad linking New Orleans with the West Coast. Northern investors wanted the government to help pay for the railroad, whereas southerners, who hoped that it would revive their economy, wanted northern dollars but not northern political influence. This meant no social agencies, no federal enforcement of the Fourteenth and Fifteenth amendments, and no military occupation, not even the small symbolic presence left in 1876.

As the inauguration date approached and newspapers echoed outgoing President Grant's call for "peace at any price," the forces of mutual self-interest concluded the "compromise of 1877." The Democrats agreed to suspend resistance to the counting of the electoral votes, and on March 2, Rutherford B. Hayes was declared president. In exchange for the presidency, Hayes ordered the last remaining troops out of the South, appointed a former Confederate general to his cabinet, supported federal aid to bolster economic and railroad development in the South, and announced his intentions to let southerners handle race relations themselves. He then went on a goodwill trip to the South, where he told blacks in an Atlanta speech that "your rights and interests would be safer if this great mass of intelligent white men were let alone by the general government." The message was clear: Hayes would not enforce the Fourteenth and Fifteenth amendments, thus initiating a pattern of executive inaction not broken until the 1960s. But the immediate crisis was averted, officially ending the era of Reconstruction.

 onclusion

A Mixed Legacy

In the 12 years between Appomattox and Hayes's inauguration, there were conflicts among the diverse dreams of victorious northern Republicans, defeated white southerners, and hopeful black freedmen. There was little chance that all could be realized, yet each group could point to a modest fulfillment of its goals. The compromise of 1877 cemented the reunion of South and North, thus providing new opportunities for economic development in both regions. The Republican party achieved its economic goals and preserved its political hold on the White House, though not Congress, until 1932. The ex-Confederate states were brought back into the Union, and southerners retained their firm control of southern lands and black labor, though not without struggle and some changes. To the extent that the peace of 1877 was preserved "at any price," that price was paid by the freedmen.

In 1880, Frederick Douglass summarized Reconstruction for the freedmen:

Our Reconstruction measures were radically defective.... To the freedmen was given the machinery of liberty, but there was denied to them the steam to put it in motion. They were given the uniform of soldiers, but no arms; they were called citizens, but left subjects; they were called free, but left almost slaves. The old master class ... retained the power to starve them to death, and wherever this power is held there is the power of slavery.

PART IV

An Industrializing People, 1865–1900

COMPARATIVE CHRONOLOGIES

Political and Diplomatic	Social and Economic	Cultural and Technological
1865		
1867 Alaska purchased	1866 National Labor Union founded	1860s Bessemer and open-hearth steel
1869–1874 Granger laws	1867 National Grange founded	processes introduced
	1868 Eight-hour day for federal	1865 Vassar College founded
	employees	1866 Atlantic cable laid
	1869 Prohibition party formed; Knights of	1867 First Horatio Alger novels pub-
	Labor formed	lished; first elevated railway in New
		York City
		1869 First transcontinental railroad link
		completed
1870		
1870 Wyoming Territory grants suffrage	1870 J. D. Rockefeller forms Standard Oil	1870 Thomas Edison invents stock ticker
to women	of Ohio	1872 Expansion of public schools and
1871 Tweed ring exposed; Indian Appro-	1871 Chicago fire	higher education begins
priation Act; Civil Service Commis-	1872 Yellowstone National Park estab-	1873 Mark Twain and Charles Dudley
sion created	lished; Montgomery Ward, first mail-	Warner coin the expression "Gilded
1872 Grant reelected	order house, opens	Age"
1873 "Salary Grab" Act	1873 Bethlehem Steel begins production	1874 Barbed wire patented; first electric
	1873–1879 Depression	streetcar runs in New York City
	1874 Women's Christian Temperance	
	Union founded; Greenback party	
	founded	
1875		
1875 Specie Resumption Act; United		1875 Wellesley College founded; first
States–Hawaii commercial treaty		running of Kentucky Derby
1877 Rutherford B. Hayes becomes pres-	1875–1876 Indian Wars in Black Hills	1876 Centennial Exposition in Philadel-
ident; *Munn* v. *Illinois;* Reconstruc-	1877 Nez Percé Indian uprisings; black	phia; Alexander Graham Bell
tion ends	exodusters to Kansas; railroad	invents telephone; first major base-
1878 Bland–Allison Act	strikes	ball league formed; Mark Twain,
		Adventures of Tom Sawyer
		1877 C. E. Hires begins making root beer
		1878 Timber and Stove Act
		1879 Henry George, *Progress and*
		Poverty; Edison perfects light bulb
1880		
1880 James A. Garfield elected		1880 Social Darwinism and Social Gospel
president		1881 Tuskegee Institute founded
1881 Garfield assassinated; Chester A.	1880s "New South"	1883 Brooklyn Bridge completed
Arthur becomes president	1882 Standard Oil Trust established	1884 W. D. Howells, *The Rise of Silas*
1882 Chinese Exclusion Act	1883–1885 Depression	*Lapham*
1883 Pendleton Civil Service Act	1884 Southern Farmers' Alliance founded	
1884 Grover Cleveland elected president		

Political and Diplomatic	Social and Economic	Cultural and Technological

1885

Political and Diplomatic	Social and Economic	Cultural and Technological
1886 *Wabash* v. *Illinois*	1885 "New immigration" begins	1888 Edward Bellamy, *Looking Backward*
1887 Dawes Severalty Act; Interstate Commerce Act	1886 American Federation of Labor founded; Haymarket Riot	1889 Andrew Carnegie, "The Gospel of Wealth"
1888 Benjamin Harrison elected president	1887 College Settlement House Association founded	
	1888 Colored Farmers' Alliance established	
	1889 Hull House founded	
	1889–1890 Ghost Dance; Battle of Wounded Knee	

1890

Political and Diplomatic	Social and Economic	Cultural and Technological
		1890 Alfred Thayer Mahan, *Influence of Sea Power upon History*
1890 Sherman Anti-Trust Act; Sherman Silver Purchase Act; McKinley Tariff	1890 Yosemite National Park established; General Federation of Women's Clubs founded; National American Women Suffrage Association formed	1890s Electric trolleys
1890s Jim Crow laws and disfranchisement attempts in the South		1891 Hamlin Garland, *Main-Travelled Roads*
1892 Populist party formed; Cleveland elected to second term	1892 Homestead strike; Sierra Club founded	1893 Stephen Crane, *Maggie: A Girl of the Streets;* World's Columbian Exposition in Chicago; City Beautiful movement
1893 Hawaiian coup by American sugar growers	1893 Anti-Saloon League founded	
	1893–1897 Depression	
	1894 Pullman strike; Coxey's march	

1895

Political and Diplomatic	Social and Economic	Cultural and Technological
1895 Cuban revolution; *United States* v. *E. C. Knight*		1895 Elizabeth Cady Stanton, *Woman's Bible*
1896 William McKinley elected president; *Plessy* v. *Ferguson*	1895 Booker T. Washington's "Atlanta Compromise" speech	1896 Charles Sheldon, *In His Steps*
1898 Sinking of the Maine; Spanish-American War; Treaty of Paris; annexation of Hawaii and the Philippines		1898 Charlotte Perkins Gilman, *Women and Economics*
1899–1900 Open Door notes		1899 John Dewey, *School and Society*
1899–1902 Filipino-American War		

The Realities of Rural America

n 1873, Milton Leeper, his wife Hattie, and their baby Anna climbed into a wagon piled high with their possessions and set out to homestead in Boone County, Nebraska. Once on the claim, the Leepers dreamed confidently of their future. Wrote Hattie to her sister in Iowa, "I like our place the best of any around here." "When we get a fine house and 100 acres under cultivation," she added, "I wouldn't trade with any one." But Milton had broken in only 13 acres when disaster struck. Hordes of grasshoppers appeared, and the Leepers fled their claim and took refuge in the nearby town of Fremont.

There they stayed for two years. Milton worked first at a store, and then hired out to other farmers. Hattie sewed, kept a boarder, and cared for chickens and a milk cow. The family lived on the brink of poverty, but never gave up hope. "Times are hard and we have had bad luck," Hattie acknowledged, but "I am going to hold that claim … there will [be] one gal that won't be out of a home." In 1876, the Leepers triumphantly returned to their claim with the modest sum of $27 to help them start over.

The grasshoppers were gone, there was enough rain, and preaching was only half a mile away. The Leepers, like others, began to prosper. Two more daughters were born and cared for in the comfortable sod house, "homely" on the outside, but plastered and cozy within. As Hattie explained, the homesteaders lived "just as civilized as they would in Chicago."

Their luck did not last. Hattie, pregnant again, fell ill and died in childbirth along with her infant son. Heartbroken, Milton buried his wife and child and left the claim. The last frontier had momentarily defeated him, although he would try farming in at least four other locations before his death in 1905.

The same year that the Leepers established their Boone County homestead, another family tried their luck in a Danish settlement about 200 miles west of Omaha. Rasmus and Ane Ebbesen and their 8-year-old son, Peter, had arrived in the United States from Denmark in 1868, lured by the promise of an "abundance" of free land "for all willing to cultivate it." By 1870, they had made it as far west as Council Bluffs, Iowa. There they stopped to earn the capital that would be necessary to begin farming. Rasmus dug ditches for the railroad, Ane worked as a cleaning woman in a local boardinghouse, and young Peter brought drinking water to thirsty laborers who were digging ditches for the town gas works.

Like the Leepers, the Ebbesens eagerly settled on their homestead and began to cultivate the soil. Peter later recalled that the problems that the family had anticipated never materialized. Even the rumors that the Sioux, "flying demons" in the eyes of settlers, were on the rampage proved false. The real problems the family faced were unexpected: rattlesnakes, prairie fires, and an invasion of grasshoppers. The grasshoppers were just as devastating to the Ebbesen farm as they had been to the Leeper homestead. But unlike the Leepers, the Ebbesens stayed on the claim. Although the family "barely had enough" to eat, they survived the three years of grasshopper infestation.

In the following years, the Ebbesens thrived. Rasmus had almost all the original 80 acres under cultivation and purchased an additional 80 acres from the railroad. A succession of sod houses rose on the land and finally even a two-story frame house, paid for with money Peter earned teaching school. By 1873, Rasmus and Ane were over 50 and could look with pride at their "luxurient and promising crop." But once more natural disaster struck, a "violent hailstorm … which completely devastated the whole lot."

The Ebbesens were lucky, however. A banker offered to buy them out, for $1,000 under what the family calculated was the farm's "real worth." But it was enough for the purchase of a "modest" house in town. Later, there was even a "dwelling of two stories and nine rooms … with adjacent park."

The flat landscape disappearing into the horizon, the picture of a hardworking and determined woman, suggest some of the geographical and physical realities of rural life in the West. (Harvey Dunn, The Homesteader's Wife, 1916/South Dakota Memorial Art Center Collection, Brookings)

*T*he stories of the Leepers and the Ebbesens, though different in their details and endings, hint at some of the problems confronting rural Americans in the last quarter of the nineteenth century. As a mature industrial economy transformed agriculture and shifted the balance of economic power permanently away from America's farmlands to the country's cities and factories, many farmers found it impossible to realize the traditional dream of rural independence and prosperity. Even bountiful harvests no longer guaranteed success. "We were told two years ago to go to work and raise a big crop; that was all we needed," said one farmer. "We went to work and plowed and planted; the rains fell, the sun shone, nature smiled, and we raised the big crop they told us to; and what came of it? Eight cent corn, ten cent oats, two cent beef and no price at all for butter and eggs—that's what came of it." Native Americans also discovered that changes in rural life threatened their values and dreams. As the Sioux leader Red Cloud told railroad surveyors in Wyoming, "We do not want you here. You are scaring away the buffalo."

This chapter explores the agricultural transformation of the late nineteenth century and highlights the ways in which rural Americans—red, white, and black—joined the industrial world and responded to new economic and social conditions. The rise of large-scale agriculture in the West, the exploitation of its natural resources, and the development of the Great Plains form a backdrop for the discussion of the impact of white settlement on western tribes and their reactions to white incursions. In an analysis of the South, the efforts of whites to create a "New South" form a contrast to the underlying realities of race and cotton. Although the chapter shows that discrimination and economic peonage characterized the lives of most black southerners during this period, it also describes the rise of new black protest tactics and ideologies. Finally, the chapter highlights the ways in which agricultural problems of the late nineteenth century, which would continue to characterize much of agricultural life in the twentieth century, led American farmers to become reformers and to form a new political party.

Modernizing Agriculture

Between 1865 and 1900, the nation's farms more than doubled in number as Americans eagerly took up virgin land west of the Mississippi River. In both newly settled and older areas, farmers raised specialized crops with the aid of modern machinery and relied on the expanding railroad system to send them to market. The character of agriculture became increasingly capitalistic. Farmers, as one New Englander pointed out, "must understand farming as a business; if they do not it will go hard with them."

Rural Myth and Reality

The number of Americans still farming the land suggested the vigor of a rural tradition that pictured the farmer as a central figure for the nation. In Thomas Jefferson's words, the farmer was the "deposit for substantial and genuine virtue" and therefore fundamental to the health of the republic.

The notion that the farmer and the farm life symbolized the essence of America persisted as the United States industrialized. The popularity of inexpensive Currier and Ives prints, like the one pictured here, testifies to the powerful appeal of an idealized view of country life. Other prints implied harmony between the new technological industrial world and rural America. Trains, representing the new order, chug peacefully through fertile farmlands, bringing progress and prosperity.

The prints obscured the reality of American agriculture. However much Americans wanted to believe that no tension existed between technological progress and rural life, it did. Farmers were slipping from their dominant position in the work force. In 1860, they represented almost 60 percent of the labor force; by 1900, less than 37 percent of employed Americans farmed. At the same time, farmers' contribution to the nation's wealth declined from a third to a quarter.

Nor were farmers the independent yeomen of the rural myth, for the industrial and urban world

This Currier and Ives print provides an idyllic view of rural life. Happy children greet hunters loaded down with game, while the woman of the family looks out from her cozy cabin at the cheerful sight. This image looked more to an idealized frontier past than to the reality of rural life after the Civil War. American agriculture was tied increasingly to national and international markets. Settlers on the Plains frontier lived in dugouts or shacks rather than in the cozy log cabin pictured here. (Museum of the City of New York, The Harry T. Peters Collection)

increasingly affected them. Reliable, cheap transportation allowed them to specialize. Farmers on the Great Plains now grew most of the country's wheat, whereas those in the Midwest replaced that crop with corn used to feed hogs and cattle. Eastern farmers turned to vegetable, fruit, and dairy farming. Some, like Milachi Dodge from New Hampshire, gave up farming altogether. As he explained, when his "boys came home" from the Civil War, "they did not want to work on a farm, and I sold my farm out." Cotton continued to dominate the economy of the South, although farmers also raised tobacco, wheat, and rice. In the Far West, grain, fruits, and vegetables predominated.

As farmers specialized in cash crops for national and international markets, their success depended increasingly on outside forces and demands. Bankers and loan companies provided capital to expand farm operations, middlemen stored and sometimes sold produce, railroads carried farm goods to market. A prosperous American economy put money into laborers' pockets for food purchases. Even international conditions affected the American farmer. After 1870, exports of wheat, flour, and animal products rose, with wheat becoming the country's chief cash crop.

Thus, the cultivation of wheat in Russia and Argentina meant fewer foreign buyers for American grain and the opening of the Canadian high plains in the 1890s added another competitor. When several European countries banned American pork imports between 1879 and 1883, fearing trichinosis, American stock raisers suffered.

Farming was becoming a modern business calling for particular attitudes and skills. "Watch and study the markets and the ways of marketmen [and] learn the art of 'selling well,'" one rural editor advised in 1887. "The work of farming is only half done when the crop is out of the ground."

Like other businesses of the post–Civil War era, farming stimulated technological innovation. Farmers increasingly desired and depended upon improved machinery Inventors and manufacturers met the demand. "It is no longer necessary for the farmer to cut his wheat with sickle or cradle, nor to rake it and bind it by hand; to cut his cornstalks with a knife and shock the stalks by hand; to thresh his grain with a flail," reported one observer. Harvesters, binders, and other new machines, pulled by work animals, performed such tasks.

These machines diminished much of the drudgery of farming life, making the production of crops easier, more efficient, and cheaper. Moreover, they allowed a farmer to cultivate far more land than possible with hand tools. By 1900, more than twice as much land was in cultivation as in 1860. But machinery was expensive, and many American farmers borrowed to buy it. In the decade of the 1880s, mortgage indebtedness grew 2 1/2 times faster than agricultural wealth.

New Farmers, New Farms

As farmers used machinery, brought new land into cultivation, raised specialized crops, and sent them to faraway markets, they operated much like other nineteenth-century businessmen. Some even became large-scale entrepreneurs. Small family farms still typified American agriculture, but vast mechanized operations devoted to the cultivation of one crop appeared, especially west of the Mississippi River. These farms with huge barns for storage of machinery and only a handful of other buildings had few gardens, trees, or outbuildings. No churches or villages interrupted the monotony of the new agricultural landscape.

The bonanza farms, established in the late 1870s on the northern plains, symbolized the trend to large-scale agriculture. Thousands of acres in size, these wheat farms required large capital investments; in fact, corporations owned many of them. Like factories, they depended on machinery, hired workers, and efficient managers. The North Dakota farm that Oliver Dalrymple operated for two Northern Pacific Railroad directors used 200 pairs of harrows and 125 seeders for planting and required 155 binders and 26 steam threshers for harvesting. At peak times, the farm's work force numbered 600 men. The results were impressive: 600,000 bushels of wheat harvested in 1882. Although bonanza farms were not typical, they dramatized the agricultural changes that were occurring everywhere on a smaller scale.

Overproduction and Falling Prices

Subscribing wholeheartedly to the rural myth Currier and Ives pictured so winningly, farmers only gradually realized that technology might backfire. As they cultivated more land with the help of machinery, they began to discover unanticipated consequences. Productivity rose 40 percent between 1869 and 1899. Almost every crop showed impressive statistical gains. But the yields for some crops like wheat were so large that the domestic market could not absorb them.

The prices farm products commanded steadily declined. In 1867, corn sold for 78 cents a bushel. By 1873, it had tumbled to 31 cents, and by 1889, to 23 cents. Wheat similarly plummeted from about $2 a bushel in 1867 to only 70 cents a bushel in 1889. Cotton profits also spiraled downward, the value of a bale depreciating from $43 in 1866 to $30 in the 1890s.

George Inness's Lackawanna Valley, *with the reclining figure in the foreground, the train, and puffing smokestacks in the background, suggests that there need be no conflict between technology and agriculture. (National Gallery of Art)*

Falling prices did not automatically hurt all farmers. Because the supply of money rose more slowly than productivity, all prices declined—by more than half between the end of the Civil War and 1900 (for a full discussion of the money issue, see Chapter 19). In a deflationary period, farmers were receiving less for their crops but also paying less for their purchases.

Deflation may have encouraged overproduction, however. To make the same amount of money, many farmers believed they had to raise larger and larger crops. As they did, prices fell even lower. Furthermore, deflation increased the real value of debts. In 1888, it took 174 bushels of wheat to pay the interest on a $2,000 mortgage at 8 percent. By 1895, it took 320 bushels. Falling prices thus had their greatest impact on farmers in newly settled areas who had borrowed heavily to finance their new operations.

Farming on the Western Plains, 1880s–1890s

Between 1870 and 1900, the acreage devoted to farming tripled west of the Mississippi as settlers flocked to the Great Plains (North and South Dakota, Kansas, Nebraska, Oklahoma, and Texas). In the mid-nineteenth century, emigrants had driven their wagons over the Plains believing the semiarid climate made them unsuited for cultivation. Views of the farming potential of this vast area changed after the Civil War, however. Railroads, town boosters, land speculators all needed settlers to make their investments in the Great Plains profitable. To lure settlers there, they launched extravagant promotional campaigns. "This is the sole remaining section of paradise in the western world," claimed one newspaper. "All the wild romances of the gorgeous orient dwindle into nothing when compared to the everyday realities of Dakota's progress." Addressing the fear that the Plains lacked adequate rain, the article promised, "All that is needed is to plow, plant and attend to the crops properly; the rains are abundant." The rainfall, above average for the region in the 1880s, lent strength to the claim of adequate moisture.

Late-nineteenth-century industrial innovations helped settlers overcome the natural obstacles that made farming on the plains so

Price of Wholesale Wheat Flour, 1865–1900

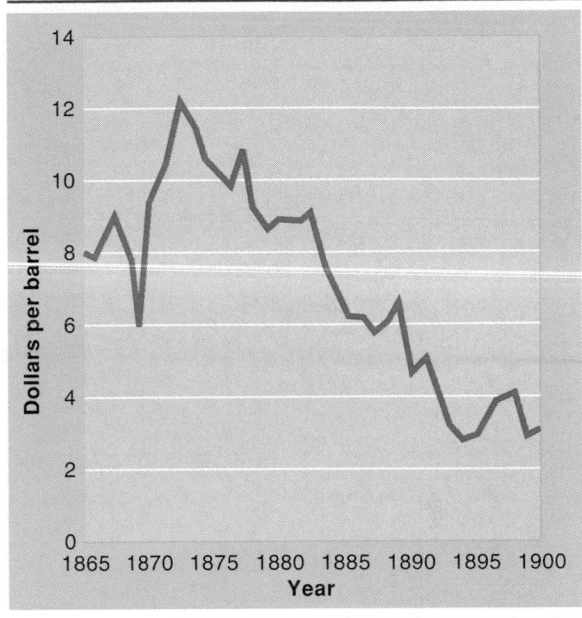

Note the plummeting price of wheat flour. Source: U.S. Bureau of the Census.

problematic at mid-century. Because there was so little timber for fencing or housing on the plains, early emigrants had chosen to settle elsewhere. But in the 1870s, Joseph Glidden developed barbed wire as a cheap alternative to timber fencing. During a visit to a country fair, Glidden had seen a simple wooden device with protruding points that was intended to keep animals away from fences. The device suggested the possibility of making fencing wire with similar protruding barbs. Before long, he and a partner were producing hundreds of miles of barbed wire fencing that could be used to enclose fields on the Plains. Other innovations overcame some of the remaining challenges to successful agriculture. Twine binders, which speeded up grain harvesting, reduced the threat of losing crops to the unpredictable weather. And mail-order steel windmills for pumping water from deep underground wells relieved water shortages by the 1890s.

In the first boom period of settlement, lasting from 1879 to the early 1890s, tens of thousands of eager families like the Leepers and Ebbesens moved onto the Great Plains and began farming. Some made claims under the Homestead Act,

Agricultural Productivity, 1800–1900				
Crop and Productivity Indicator	1800	1840	1880	1900
Wheat				
Worker-hours/acre	56	35	30	15
Yield/acre (bushels)	15	15	13	14
Worker-hours/100 bushels	373	233	152	108
Corn				
Worker-hours/acre	86	69	46	38
Yield/acre (bushels)	25	25	26	26
Worker-hours/100 bushels	344	276	180	147
Cotton				
Worker-hours/acre	185	135	119	112
Yield/acre (pounds of lint)	147	147	179	191
Worker-hours/bale	601	439	318	280

The astonishing gains in the productivity of wheat farmers points to the use of reapers that cut and bound the wheat and thrashers that knocked the grain off the stalks. The combine integrated both operations and also cleared and bagged the grain.

Source: U.S. Bureau of the Census.

which granted 160 acres to any family head or adult who lived on the claim for five years or who paid $1.25 an acre after six months of residence. Because homestead land was frequently less desirable than land held by railroads and speculators, however, most settlers bought land outright rather than taking up claims.

The costs of getting started were thus more substantial than the Homestead Act would suggest. Western land was cheap compared with farmland in the East, but an individual farmer was fortunate if he could buy a good quarter section for under $500. The costs of machinery would often reach $700. Although some farmers thought it made better economic sense to lease rather than buy land, many rented only because they lacked the capital to purchase land and set up operations. In 1880, some 20 percent of the Plains farmers were tenants, and this percentage rose over time.

Like the Ebbesens, many of the new settlers were immigrants, making the Great Plains the second most important destination for them. The most numerous arrived from Germany, the British Isles, and Canada. Many Scandinavians, Czechs, and Poles also moved to the new frontier. Unlike the single male immigrants flocking to American cities for work, these newcomers came with their families. From the beginning, they intended to put down roots in the new country.

Life on the Plains frontier often proved difficult. Wrote Miriam Peckham, a Kansas homesteader:

I tell you Auntie no one can depend on farming for a living in this country. Henry is very industrious and this year had in over thirty acres of small grain, 8 acres of corn and about an acre of potatoes. We have sold our small grain … and it come to $100; now deduct $27.00 for cutting, $16.00 for threshing, $19.00 for hired help, say nothing of boarding our help, none of the trouble of drawing 25 miles to market and 25 cts on each head for ferriage over the river and where is your profit. I sometimes think this a God forsaken country, the [grass]hopper hurt our corn and we have ½ a crop and utterly destroyed our garden. If one wants trials, let them come to Kansas.

Peckham's letter highlights the uncertainties of frontier life: the costs of machinery, the vagaries of crops and markets, the threat of pests and natural disasters, the shortage of cash. Unlike earlier emigrants to the Far West, who had to have the

Average Farm Acreage, 1860–1900					
Region	1860	1870	1880	1890	1900
Land in Farms (1,000 acres)					
United States	407,213	407,735	536,082	623,219	841,202
North Central	107,900	139,215	206,982	256,587	317,349
South	225,514	189,556	234,920	256,606	362,036
West	12,718	16,219	26,194	47,282	96,407
Northeast	61,082	62,744	67,986	62,744	65,409
Average Acreage per Farm (acres)					
United States	199	153	134	137	147
North Central	140	124	122	133	145
South	335	214	153	140	138
West	367	336	313	324	393
Northeast	108	104	98	95	97

This table shows the impact of bringing western lands into cultivation and highlights the regional differences in American agriculture.

Source: U.S. Bureau of the Census.

means to finance the six-month trip, many Plains pioneers took up their homesteads with only a few dollars in their pockets. Frontier diaries often revealed the marginality of early frontier operations, the loans from family in the East, the debts. Survival often depended on how well families managed to do during the crucial first years. If they succeeded in raising and selling their crops, they might accumulate the capital needed to continue. But if nature was harsh or their luck bad, or if they were unable to adjust to new conditions, the chances of failure were great.

Many settlers recoiled from a landscape without trees and the other natural markings that might make it familiar or provide a human scale. As one New England visitor observed, "It has been terrible on settlers, on the women especially, for there is no society and they get doleful and feel almost like committing suicide for want of society." This was the point many authors chose to emphasize. O. E. Rölvaag's novel *Giants in the Earth* (1927) depicts the wife of a Norwegian immigrant farmer driven to madness and death. Hamlin Garland's *Main-Travelled Roads* (1891), inspired by a "mood of resentment" after a visit to his mother

"on a treeless farm," pictures overworked, hopeless women whom the frontier defeats.

Life on the Plains was not always so discouraging, however. Willa Cather, who grew up in Nebraska, showed both the harshness and the appeal of the prairie in her novels. Alexandra Bergson, the main character of *O Pioneers!* (1913), loves the land: "It seemed beautiful to her, rich and strong and glorious." The thousands of letters and diaries that survive from the period also provide a more positive picture of farming life. One woman reflected on the way she had softened the harsh landscape. "Our flower garden was such a vision of beauty ... the dreary, desolate place was blossoming in all the gorgeous beauty that God has promised to those who try." Elam Bartholomew's diary shows a life filled with human contacts and social events. In 1880, only six years after he had settled in northern Kansas, Elam's journal reveals that 1,081 people stopped at his home. His wife served 783 meals to visitors. Trips to church, parties, sings, and neighborhood get-togethers brightened family life.

The Plains frontier required many adjustments. Scarce water and violent changes in temperature called for resourcefulness and new

The combination of graphics and text provided a persuasive message about the excellence of the Gold Medal Threshing-Machine. The picture gave prospective purchasers an idea of the machine's appearance and size, and the text emphasized its award-winning status and included testimonials about its performance. Manufacturers of farm machinery used many strategies, including mass advertising, to sell their products. In one Kansas county, farm families increased their spending for machinery by an average of 250 percent between 1870 and 1890. (Corbis-Bettmann)

modes of behavior. Without firewood, farmers learned to burn corncobs and twisted straw for warmth. The log cabin, long the symbol of frontier life, disappeared as inventive settlers discovered how to build houses of sod "bricks." Although from a distance such houses often looked like mounds of earth—"homely old things," as Hattie Leeper described them—they frequently had glass windows, wooden shingles, and even plastered interiors. Dark and gloomy to our eyes, they were comfortable, cozy, and practical for the settlers. Walls, 2 to 3 feet thick, kept out the scorching summer heat and fierce cold of winter, the moaning winds, and the prairie fires. The solidity of the sod house provided a welcome contrast to the impersonal power and scale of nature.

The first boom on the Great Plains halted abruptly in the late 1880s and early 1890s. Falling agricultural prices cut profits. Then, the unusual rainfall that had lured farmers into the semiarid region near the hundredth meridian vanished. A devastating drought followed. One farmer reported in 1890 that he had earned $41.48 from his wheat crop, yet his expenses for seed and threshing amounted to $56.00. The destitute survived on boiled weeds, a few potatoes, and a little bread and butter. Although cash was scarce on the frontier, credit had not been. Many farmers had accumulated debts they now could not repay.

This 1880 photo highlights the role of machine and animal power rather than human power during the wheat harvest. With more land under cultivation, there was a strong impetus to develop larger and/or more efficient harvesting machines. (Corbis-Bettmann)

In 1886, Solomon Butcher photographed the Rawding family in Custer County, Nebraska. The family posed with all their prized possessions in front of their sod house. Although the younger Rawdings are barefoot, the women have dressed carefully for the picture. Despite their neat attire, women of farm families like this one worked both in and outside of the house. Although their husbands often had machinery to help them with their tasks, except for the sewing machine and cookstove, farm women did their work without the help of mechanization. (Solomon D. Butcher Collection, Nebraska State Historical Society)

Thousands lost their farms to creditors. Some stayed on as tenants. Homesteaders like the Leepers gave up. By 1900, two-thirds of homesteaded farms had failed. Many homesteaders fled east. In western Kansas, the population declined by half between 1888 and 1892. The wagons of those who retreated bore the epitaph of their experience: "In God We Trusted: In Kansas We Busted."

Whether individual farmers remained on the Great Plains or retreated to more promising climates, collectively these new agricultural efforts had a significant long-term impact on the region's environment. When farmers removed sod to build their sod houses and broke the prairies with their plows in order to plant their crops, they were removing the earth's protective covering. The heavy winds so common on the prairies could lift exposed topsoil and carry it miles away. The deep plowing, which was essential for dry farming techniques introduced after the drought of the 1880s, worsened this situation. The dust bowl of the 1930s was the eventual outcome of these agricultural interventions. Other less obvious consequences of farming and settlement on the Great Plains included a lowering of the water table level as mail-order steel windmills provided the power for pumping water from deep underground. Far from the Plains, the pine forests around the Great Lakes fell to satisfy the settlers' need for wood and the railroads voracious appetite for railroad ties.

The Early Cattle Frontier, 1860–1890

In the mid-1870s, a clash between John Duncan, a cattleman, and Peter Schmidt, a German farmer, symbolized the meeting of the farming and cattle

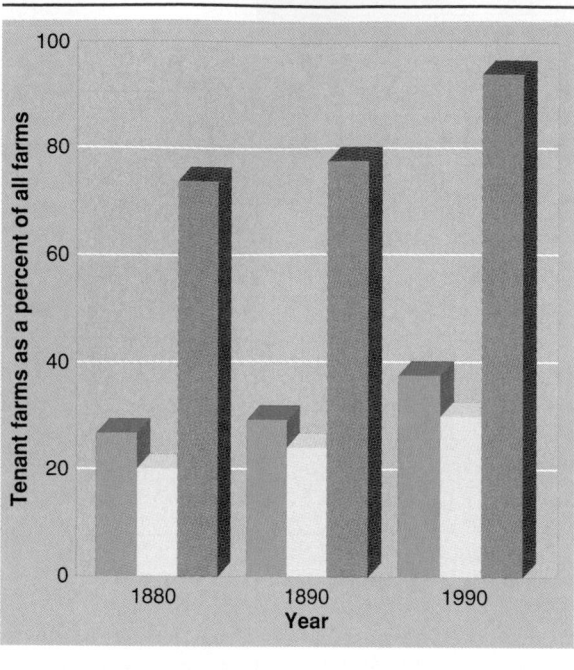

Percentage of Farms Operated by Tenants, 1880–1900

Legend: U.S. (total); West North Central (Plains); South (South Atlantic and East South Central)

The rise in tenancy, most pronounced in the South, suggests the problems American farmers were experiencing. Source: U.S. Bureau of the Census.

Dodge City, they could be loaded on railroad cars for slaughtering and packinghouses in cities like Chicago and Kansas City. Thus started the first cattle drives, celebrated in stories, movies, and television. In the late 1860s and 1870s, cowboys herded thousands of longhorns north with hefty profits for owners and investors.

Ranchers on the Great Plains, where grasses were ripe for grazing, bought some of the cattle and bred them with Hereford and Angus cows to create cattle able to withstand the region's severe winters. In the late 1870s and early 1880s, huge ranches appeared in eastern Colorado, Wyoming, and Montana and in western Kansas, Nebraska, and the Dakotas. These ventures, many owned by outside investors, paid off handsomely. Because the cattle could roam at will over the public domain, they cost owners little as they fattened up, but commanded good prices at the time of sale. The cowboys (a third of them Mexican and black) who herded the steers, however, shared few of the profits. Their meager wages of $25 to $40 a month were just enough to pay for a fling in the saloons, dance halls, and gambling palaces in Dodge City or Abilene when taking the cattle to market.

By the mid-1880s, the first phase of the cattle frontier was ending as farmers moved onto the Plains, bought up public lands once used for grazing, and fenced them in. But the struggle between cattle ranchers and farmers was only one factor in the cattle frontier's collapse. Eager for fat profits, ranchers overstocked their herds in the mid-1880s. European investors added to the rush of capital into herding. Hungry cattle ate everything in sight, then grew weak as grass became scarce. As was often the case on the Plains, the weather had a part to play. A winter of memorable blizzards followed the very hot summer of 1886. Cattle, usually able to forage for themselves during the winter months, could not dig through the deep snow to the grass and died from starvation. By spring, 90 percent of the cattle were dead. As one cattleman's journal observed, "An overstocked range must bleed when the blizzards sit in judgment." Frantic owners dumped their remaining cattle on the market, getting $8 or even less per animal.

frontiers. Duncan allowed his cattle to roam; some wandered onto Schmidt's property, devoured his corn, and destroyed his garden. Outraged at the damage, Schmidt ran the cattle off. For many years, such incidents had been rare, for few farmers were living on the Plains. As settlement increased in the 1880s and 1890s, they became more common.

Although cattle raising dated back to Spanish mission days, the commercial cattle frontier was an unexpected by-product of Union military strategy. During the war, the North had split the South and cut Texas off from Confederate cattle markets. By the war's end, millions of longhorns were roaming the Texas range. With the postwar burst of railroad construction came the means of turning these cattle into dollars. If Texas ranchers drove their steers north to towns like Abilene, Wichita, or

In the aftermath, the ranchers who remained stock raisers adopted new techniques. Experimenting with new breeds, they began to fence in

Frederick Remington captured the romantic aspect of the cattle frontier in this 1888 painting of a cowboy in the midst of a stampede. Although a substantial minority of cowboys in Texas and Oklahoma were black, most cowboys were white until the 1880s. Then owners, realizing they could pay Mexican Americans less, began to replace whites with Mexicans. (The Granger Collection, New York)

their herds and to feed them grain during the winter. Moreover, consumers were hungering for tender beef rather than the tough flesh of animals who roamed the land, and these new methods satisfied the market. Ranching, like farming, was becoming a modern business rather than the colorful adventure portrayed in popular culture.

Just as the plows and windmills of the agriculturist disrupted Plains ecology, so, too, did the herds of the cattle frontier. As one Texan realized, "Grass is what counts. It's what saves us all—as far as we get saved.... Grass is what holds the earth together." Seeing native species as either competing with cattle for nourishment or threatening them, ranchers hunted and killed antelope, elk, and wolves and other wildlife. When cattlemen

overstocked the range, their herds devoured the perennial grasses. In their place tough, less nutritious annual grasses sprang up, and sometimes even these grasses disappeared. Lands once able to support large herds of cattle eventually were transformed into deserts of sagebrush, weeds, and dust.

Cornucopia on the Pacific

When gold was discovered in California, Americans rushed west to find it. But as one father told his eager son, "Plant your lands; these be your best gold fields." He was right; with the completion of a national railroad system, farming eventually became California's greatest asset. But farming in California neither resembled the rural life Currier and Ives depicted nor fulfilled the dreams of the framers of the Homestead Act.

Although federal and state land policies supposedly promoted "homes for the homeless," little of California's land was actually homesteaded or developed as small family farms. When California entered the Union, Mexican ranchers had vast landholdings that never became part of the public domain. Because most Mexican-Americans impoverished themselves in legal efforts to establish the legitimacy of their claims, speculators eventually acquired much of their land. Consequently, small farmers needed substantial sums to buy land. As Charles Reed observed in 1869, "Land which but two years ago could have been bought ... for from $1 to $1.25 per acre cannot now be bought for less than $10 to $15 per acre."

By 1871, reformer Henry George described California as "not a country of farms but a country of plantations and estates." California farms were indeed substantially larger than farms in the rest of the country. In 1870, the average California farm was 482 acres, whereas the national average farm was only 153 acres. By 1900, farms of 1,000 acres or more made up two-thirds of the state's farmland. This landscape reflected the advent of large-scale farming. As one California visitor reported to the *New York Times* in 1887, "You go through miles and miles of wheat fields, you see the fertility of the land and the beauty of the scenery, but where are the hundreds of farm houses ... that you would see in Ohio or Iowa?"

Small farmers and ranchers did exist, of course, but they found it difficult to compete with large, mechanized operators using cheap migrant laborers, usually Mexican or Chinese. One wheat farm in the San Joaquin Valley was so vast that workers started plowing in the morning at one end of the 17-mile field, ate lunch at its halfway point, and camped at its end that night.

The value of much of California's agricultural land, especially the southern half of the Central Valley, depended on water. Many gold rush immigrants were stunned by the brown and yellow grasses, the parched earth. By the 1870s, however, water, land, and railroad companies, using the labor and expertise of Chinese workers, were taking on the huge costs of building dams, headgates, and canals. They passed on the costs of construction to settlers now eager to acquire hitherto barren lands along with water rights. By 1890, over a quarter of California's farms benefited from irrigation. The irrigation ditches were a fitting symbol of the importance of technology and a managerial attitude toward the land that characterized late-nineteenth-century agriculture, particularly in California.

Although grain was initially California's most valuable crop, it faced stiff competition from farmers on the Plains and in other parts of the world. Some argued that land capable of raising luscious fruits "in a climate surpassing that of Italy, is too valuable for the cultivation of simple cereals." But high railroad rates and lack of refrigeration limited the volume of fresh fruit and vegetables sent to market. As railroad managers in the 1880s realized the potential profit California's produce represented, they lowered rates and introduced refrigerated railroad cars. Fruit and vegetable production rose, benefiting from the agricultural expertise of Chinese laborers. In June 1888, fresh apricots and cherries successfully survived the trip from California to New York. Two years later, 9,000 carloads of navel oranges headed east. Before long, California fruit was available in London. Some travelers even began to grumble that the railroads treated produce better than people. Perhaps the complaint was true. The daily eastern express contained "two sleeping cars, two or three passenger cars, and twenty cars loaded with green fruit." The

comments highlighted the fact that successful agriculture in California depended on the railroad system, irrigation, and the use of machinery.

Exploiting Natural Resources

The perspective that led Americans to treat farming as a business was also evident in the ways in which they dealt with the country's abundant natural resources. Gold had been the precious metal originally drawing prospectors to California, but the discovery of some other precious materials—silver, iron, copper, coal, lead, zinc, tin—lured thousands west to Colorado, Montana, Idaho, Nevada as well as to states like Minnesota. The popular conception of the miner as a hardy forty-niner searching for loose placer deposits of gold captures the early days of mining. But it does not describe the reality of late-nineteenth-century mining that relied on machinery, railroads, engineers, and a large work force for the discovery and extraction of the earth's metals and minerals. Mining was a big business with high costs and a basic dynamic that encouraged rapid and thorough exploitation of the earth's resources.

The decimation of the nation's forests went hand in hand with large-scale mining and the railroads that provided the links to markets. Both railroads and mining depended on wood—railroads for wooden ties, mines for shaft timber and ore reduction. The impact of these demands is captured by the California State Board of Agriculture's estimate in the late 1860s that one-third of the state's forests had already disappeared.

When lumber companies cut down timber, they affected the flow of streams and destroyed the habitat supporting birds and animals. Like the activities of farmers and cattle owners, the companies that stripped the earth of its forest cover were also contributing to soil erosion. The idea that the public lands belonging to the federal government ought to be rapidly developed supported such exploitation of the nation's natural resources. Often, in return for royalties, the government leased parts of the public domain to companies who hoped to extract valuable minerals, not to own the land permanently. In other cases, companies bought land, but not always legally. In 1878,

This New Hampshire general store, photographed at the end of the nineteenth century, contains the wide variety of nonlocal products, including bananas, that better transportation made available. (Courtesy of The Vermont Historical Society)

Congress passed the Timber and Stone Act, which initially applied to Nevada, Oregon, Washington, and California. This legislation allowed the sale of 160-acre parcels of the public domain that were "unfit for cultivation" and "valuable chiefly for timber." Timber companies were quick to see the possibilities in the new law. They hired men willing to register for claims and then to turn them over to timber interests. By the end of the century, more than 3.5 million acres of the public domain had been acquired under the legislation, and most of it was in corporate hands.

The rapacious and rapid exploitation of resources combined with the increasing pace of industrialization to make some Americans uneasy. Many believed that forests played a part in causing rainfall and that their destruction would have an adverse impact on the climate. Others, like John Muir, lamented the destruction of the country's great natural beauty. In 1868, Muir came upon the Great Valley of California, "all one sheet of plant gold, hazy and vanishing in the distance ... one smooth, continuous bed of honey-bloom." He soon realized, however, that a "wild, restless agriculture" and "flocks of hoofed locusts, sweeping over the ground like a fire" would destroy this vision of loveliness. Muir became a conservation champion. He played a part in the creation of Yosemite National Park in 1890 and participated in a successful effort to allow President Benjamin Harrison to classify certain parts of the public domain as forest reserves (the Forest Reserve Act of 1891). In 1892, Muir established the Sierra Club. Conservation ideas were more popular in the East, however, than in the West, where the seeming abundance of natural resources and the profit motive diminished support.

The Second Great Removal

Black Elk, an Oglala Sioux, listened to a story his father had heard from his father.

> A long time ago ... there was once a Lakota [Sioux] holy man, called Drinks Water, who dreamed what was to be; and this was long before the coming of the Wasichus [white men]. He dreamed ... that a strange race had woven a spider's web all around the Lakotas. And he said: "When this happens, you shall live in square gray houses, in a barren land, and beside those square gray houses you shall starve."

Black Elk, pictured here on the left, was perceptive of the deleterious changes experienced by Indians during the latter part of the nineteenth century. Although Black Elk was one of the holy men of Oglala Sioux, he became a convert to Roman Catholicism in the early twentieth century. (Smithsonian Institution)

So great was the wise man's sorrow that he died soon after his strange dream. But Black Elk lived to see it come true.

As farmers settled the western frontier and became entangled in a national economy, they clashed with the Indian tribes who lived on the land. In California, disease and violence killed 90 percent of the Native American population in the 30 years following the gold rush. Elsewhere, the struggle among Native Americans, white settlers, the U.S. Army, and government officals and reformers was prolonged and bitter. Although some tribes moved onto government reservations with little protest, most tribes, including the Nez Percé in the Northwest, the Apaches in the Southwest, and the Plains Indians resisted the attempts to curb their way of life and to transform their culture.

Background to Hostilities

As Chapter 13 suggested, the lives of most Plains Indians revolved around the buffalo. Increased emigration to California and Oregon in the 1840s and 1850s disrupted tribal pursuits and animal migration patterns. Initially, the federal government tried, without much success, to persuade the Plains tribes to stay away from white wagon trains and white settlers. As Lone Horn, a Miniconjou chief, explained when American commissioners at the 1851 Fort Laramie Council asked him if he would be satisfied to live on the Missouri River, "When the buffalo comes close to the river, we come close to it. When the buffaloes go off, we go off after them."

During the Civil War, the eastern tribes that had been forced to relocate in Oklahoma divided. Some, especially the slaveholders, sided with the Confederacy, whereas other tribes remained loyal to the Union. After the war, however, all were lumped together and conveniently "treated as traitors." The federal government callously nullified earlier pledges and treaties, leaving Indians defenseless against further incursions on their lands. As settlers pushed into Kansas, the tribes living in Kansas were shunted into Oklahoma.

The White Perspective

When the Civil War ended, red and white men on the Plains were already at war. In 1864, the Colorado militia had massacred a band of friendly Cheyenne at Sand Creek, Colorado, despite the fact that Chief Black Kettle waved both a white flag of truce and an American flag. Militia leader John Chivington urged his men on. "Kill and scalp all, big and little." Before long, Cheyenne, Sioux, and Arapaho were responding in kind. The Plains wars had begun.

Although not all whites condoned the militia's butchery, the deliberations of the congressional commission authorized to make peace revealed a constricted vision of the future of Native Americans. The commission, which included the commander of the Army in the West, Civil War hero

General William T. Sherman, accepted as fact that the future of the West lay in an "industrious, thrifty, and enlightened population" of whites. All Native Americans, the commission believed, must relocate in one of two areas: the western half of present-day South Dakota and Oklahoma. There they would learn the ways of white society and agricultural and mechanical arts. Annuities, food, and clothes would placate the Indians and ease their transition from a "savage" to a "civilized" life.

At two major conferences in 1867 and 1868, Native American chiefs listened to these drastic proposals that spelled out the end of the traditional native life. Some agreed with the terms. Others like Satanta, a Kiowa chief, insisted, "I don't want to settle. I love to roam over the prairies." In any case, the agreements extracted were not binding, because no chief had authority to speak for his tribe. For its part, the U.S. Senate dragged its feet in approving the treaties. Supplies promised to Indians who settled in the arid reserved areas failed to materialize, and wildlife proved too sparse to support them. These Indians soon drifted back to their former hunting grounds.

As General Sherman had warned, however, "All who cling to their old hunting ground are hostile and will remain so till killed off." When persuasion failed, the U.S. Army adopted militant tactics. "The more we can kill this year," Sherman remarked, "the less will have to be killed the next war." In 1867, Sherman entrusted General Philip Sheridan with the duty of dealing with the tribes. Sheridan introduced winter campaigning, aimed at seeking out the Indians who divided into small groups during the winter and exterminating them.

The completion of the transcontinental railroad in 1869 added yet another pressure for "solving" the Indian question. Transcontinental railroads wanted rights-of-way through tribal lands and needed white settlers to make their operations profitable. They carried not only thousands of hopeful settlers to the West, but miners and hunters as well. Few thought Native Americans had any right to the lands whites wanted.

In his 1872 annual report, the commissioner for Indian affairs, Francis Amasa Walker, addressed the two fundamental questions troubling whites: how to prevent Indians from blocking white migration to and settlement in the Great Plains and what to do with Native Americans once they had been controlled. Because they could mount 8,000 warriors, Walker suggested buying off the "savages." With promises of food and gifts, he hoped to lure them onto reservations and there impose a "rigid reformatory discipline."

Coercion would be necessary, because Indians, according to Walker, were "unused to manual labor, and physically unqualified for it by the habits of the chase … without forethought and without self control … with strong animal appetites and no intellectual tastes or aspirations to hold those appetites in check." The grim reservations he proposed resembled prisons more than schools. Indians could not leave without permission and could be arrested if they tried to do so. Though Walker considered himself a "friend of humanity" and, like many reformers, wished to save the Indians from destruction, he says only one choice: "yield or perish."

The Tribal View

Native Americans defied such attacks on their ancient way of life and protested the wholesale violation of treaties. Black Elk remembered that in 1863, when he was only 3, his father had his leg broken in a fierce battle against the white men. "When I was older," he recalled,

> I learned what the fighting was about.… Up on the Madison Fork the Wasichus had found much of the yellow metal that they worship and that makes them crazy, and they wanted to have a road up through our country to the place where the yellow metal was; but my people did not want the road. It would scare the bison and make them go away, and also it would let the other Wasichus come in like a river. They told us that they wanted only to use a little land, as much as a wagon would take between the wheels; but our people knew better.

Black Elk's father and many others soon realized fighting was their only recourse. "There was no other way to keep our country." But "wherever

Indian Lands and Communities in the United States

The map shows a rich variety of Indian groups, state reservations (primarily in the East), and federal reservations in the West.

we went, the soldiers came to kill us, and it was all our country."

Broken promises fired Indian resistance. In 1875, the federal government allowed gold prospectors into the Black Hills, part of the Sioux reservation and one of their sacred places. Chiefs Sitting Bull, Crazy Horse, and Rain-in-the-Face led the angry Sioux on the warpath. At the Battle of Little Big Horn in 1876, they vanquished General George Custer. But their bravery and skill could not permanently withstand the power of the well-supplied, well-armed, and determined U.S. Army. Elsewhere, the pattern of resistance and ultimate defeat was repeated. In Texas, General Sherman vanquished Native American tribes, and in the Pacific Northwest, Nez Percé Chief Joseph surrendered in 1877.

The wholesale destruction of the buffalo was an important element in white victory. The animals were central to Indian life, culture, and reli-

gion. As one Pawnee chief explained, "Am afraid when we have no meat to offer, Great Spirit … will be angry & punish us." Although Plains Indians could be wasteful of buffalo in areas where the animals were abundant, white miners and hunters ultimately destroyed the herds. Sportsmen shot the beasts from train windows. Railroad crews ate the meat. Ranchers' cattle competed for grass. And demand for buffalo bones for fertilizer and hides for robes and shoes encouraged the decimation.

The slaughter, which had claimed 13 million animals by 1883, was in retrospect disgraceful. The Indians considered white men demented. "They just killed and killed because they like to do that," said one, whereas when "we hunted the bison … [we] killed only what we needed." But the destruction of the herds pleased whites determined to curb the movements of Native Americans. As Secretary of the Interior Columbus Delano explained in 1872, "I cannot regard the rapid disappearance of the game from its former haunts as a matter prejudicial to our management of the Indians." Rather, he said, "as they become convinced that they can no longer rely upon the supply of game for their support, they will return to the more reliable source of subsistence furnished at their agencies."

The Dawes Act, 1887

Changing federal policy aimed at ending Indian power and culture. In 1871, Congress ended the practice, in effect since the 1790s, of treating the tribes as sovereign nations. Other measures supplemented this attempt to undermine both tribal integrity and the prestige of tribal leaders, whom negotiators would no longer recognize as speaking for their tribes. The government urged tribes to replace tribal justice with a court system and extended federal jurisdiction to the reservations. Tribes were also warned not to gather for religious ceremonies.

The Dawes Severalty Act of 1887 pulled together the strands of federal Indian policy that emerged after the Civil War and set its course for the rest of the century. Believing that tribal bonds kept Indians in savagery, reformers intended to destroy them. As Theodore Roosevelt noted approvingly, the bill was a "mighty pulverizing engine to break up the tribal mass." Rather than allotting reservation lands to tribal groups, the act allowed the president to distribute these lands to individuals. By holding out the lure of private property, the framers of the bill hoped to destroy communal norms and encourage Indians to settle in one place and to farm as white men did. Those who accepted allotments would become citizens and presumably abandon any vestiges of their tribal identity. Although Indian agents explained that Native Americans opposed the Dawes Act, Congress, convinced that white people knew what was best for Indians, did not hesitate to legislate on their behalf.

The fact that speculators as well as reformers lobbied for the legislation betrayed another motive at work. Even if each Indian family head claimed a typical share of 160 acres, millions of "surplus" acres would remain for sale to white settlers. Within 20 years of the Dawes Act, Native Americans had lost 60 percent of their lands. The federal government held the profits from land sales "in trust" and used them for the "civilizing" mission.

The Ghost Dance: An Indian Renewal Ritual

By the 1890s, the grim reality of their plight made many Native Americans responsive to the message of Paiute prophet Wovoka. Although Wovoka did not urge Native Americans to strike out against whites, his revelations predicted that natural disasters would eliminate the white race. Dancing Indians would not only avoid this destruction, but also gain new strength as their ancestors and wild game returned to life. Wovoka's prophecies spread rapidly. Believers expressed their faith and hope through the new rituals of ghost or spirit dancing, hypnosis, and meditation. The more frequently they danced, the quicker whites would vanish.

Although Wovoka's prophecies discouraged hostile actions against whites, American settlers were uneasy. Indian agents tried to prevent the ghost dances and filed hysterical reports. "Indians are dancing in the snow and are wild and crazy.... We need protection, and we need it now." One agent determined that the Sioux medicine man Sitting Bull, who had strenuously opposed American expansion, was a leading troublemaker and determined to arrest him. In the confusion of arrest, Indian police killed Sitting Bull.

Bands of Sioux fled the reservation with the army in swift pursuit. In late December 1890, the army caught up with the Sioux at Wounded Knee Creek. Although the Sioux had raised a flag of truce, a scuffle as they were turning over their weapons led to a bloody massacre. Using the most up-to-date machine guns and Hotchkiss cannons, the army killed over 200 men, women, and children. An eyewitness described the desolate scene a few days later. "Among the fragments of burned tents ... we saw the frozen bodies lying close together or piled one upon another."

Thus arose the lament of Black Elk, who saw his people diminished, starving, despairing:

> Once we were happy in our own country and we were seldom hungry, for then the two-leggeds and the four-leggeds lived together like relatives, and there was plenty for them and for us. But then the Wasichus came, and

Magazines

Weekly and monthly magazines constitute a rich primary source for the historian, offering a vivid picture of the issues of the day and useful insights into popular tastes and values. With advances in the publishing industry and an increasingly literate population, the number of these journals soared in the years following the Civil War. In 1865, only 700 periodicals were published. Twenty years later there were 3,300. As the *National Magazine* grumbled, "Magazines, magazines, magazines! The newsstands are already groaning under the heavy load, and there are still more coming."

Some of these magazines were aimed at the mass market. *Frank Leslie's Illustrated Newspaper*, established in 1855, was one of the most successful. At its height, circulation reached 100,000. Making skillful use of pictures (sometimes as large as 2 by 3 feet and folded into the magazine), the weekly covered important news of the day as well as music, drama, sports, and books. Although Leslie relied more heavily on graphics and sensationalism than modern news weeklies, his publication was a forerunner of *Newsweek* and *Time*.

Another kind of weekly magazine was aimed primarily at middle- and upper-class readers. Editors like the oft-quoted Edwin Lawrence Godkin of *The Nation*, with a circulation of about 30,000, hoped to influence those in positions of authority and power by providing a forum for the discussion of reform issues. In contrast, *Scribner's* revealed a more conservative, middle-of-the-road point of view. Both magazines, however, exuded a confident, progressive tone characteristic of middle-class Americans.

Harper's Weekly was one of the most important magazines designed primarily for middle- and upper-class readers. Established in 1857, this publication continued in print until 1916. The success of *Harper's Weekly*, which called itself a "family newspaper," rested on a combination of its moderate point of view and an exciting use of illustrations and cartoons touching on contemporary events. The popular cartoons of Thomas Nast appeared in this magazine. In large part because of the use of graphics, in 1872, the circulation of *Harper's Weekly* reached a peak of 160,000.

Illustrated here is a page from the January 16, 1869, issue of *Harper's Weekly*. The layout immediately suggests the importance of graphics. Most of the page is taken up with the three pictures. The top and bottom pictures are wood engravings based on drawings by Theodore R. Davis, one of *Harper's* best-known illustrator-reporters. The center picture was derived from a photograph.

The story featured on this page concerns a victory of General George Custer in the war against the Cheyenne tribe that the U.S. Army was waging that winter. Davis had been a correspondent in the West covering Custer's actions in 1867. But when news of Custer's victory arrived, Davis was back in New York. He thus drew on his imagination for the two scenes reproduced on the next page. What kind of characterization of Native Americans does Davis give in the picture at the top of the page? What view of American soldiers does he suggest? At the bottom of the page, you can see soldiers slaughtering "worthless" horses while Cheyenne teepees burn in the background. Would the average viewer have any sympathy for the plight of the Cheyennes by looking at this picture? This "victory," in fact, involved the slaughter not only of horses but also of all males over age 8.

The editors' decision to insert a picture that had nothing to do with the incident being reported was obviously significant. As you can see, the subject is a white hunter who had been killed and scalped by Indians. What kind of special relationship were the editors suggesting by placing the picture of one dead white hunter in the center of a page that primarily covered a specific conflict between the Indians and the U.S. Army? How might the reader respond to the group of pictures as a whole? How do you? How does the text contribute to the overall view of the Indian-white relationship that the pictures suggest? By considering the choice of graphics and text, you can begin to discover how magazines provide insight, not only into the events of the day, but also into the ways magazines shaped the values and perspectives of nineteenth-century men and women.

CUSTER'S INDIAN SCOUTS CELEBRATING THE VICTORY OVER BLACK KETTLE. [Sketched by Thos. R. Davis.]

THE INDIAN WAR.

The Indian War, a continuation of Indian troubles that proved greater boons, then, better Indian wars extended over with the Cheyennes, Arrapahoes, Kiowas, Comanches, and was a few monopolies of the Commission the Powder River country was abandoned. This latter action was construed as the result of timidity on the part of the Government, and immediately the Sioux extended their depredations to the Pacific Railroad, on the Platte, while the Indians south of the Arkansas attempted to drive the whites out of the Smoky Hill country.

Last August the Cheyennes took the war path, and the valley of the Solomon and Solomon rivers became the theatre of a relentless savage war. It was at first supposed that the Cheyennes were about to attack a fort there for, but soon the mask was laid aside, and in less than a month one hundred whites fell victims to the tomahawk and scalping knife. The chiefs of the Arrapahoes had promised to

THE SCALPED HUNTER.—[Photographed by Wm. S. Soule.]

proceed to Fort Larned, get their annuities, and deliver withdraw to their reservations. Instead of fulfilling their promises, they began a series of depredations on the line between Fort Wallace and Denver, in Colorado Territory. The Kiowas and Comanches about the same time entered into an agreement at Fort Zarah, to remain at peace, and left with that impression fixed on the minds of those who represented the Government. The next information was that the Kiowas and Comanches had joined the Cheyennes and Arrapahoes. General Sheridan, taking the practical view of the condition of affairs within the limits of his department, at once transferred his head-quarters to the field, and commenced preparations for a determined war. General Sully's fight near that point, Forsyth's gallant fight on the Arrickaree fork of the Republican, Carpenter's and Graham's fight on the Beaver branch of the Republican, General Carr's decisive fight in the same vicinity, and General Cus-

CUSTER'S COMMAND SHOOTING DOWN WORTHLESS HORSES.—[Sketched by Thos. R. Davis.]

Harper's Weekly *delivers powerful messages about the Native Americans in its choice of illustrations. (The New York Public Library, Astor, Lenox & Tilden Foundations)*

595

they have made little islands for us ..., and always these islands are becoming smaller, for around them surges the gnawing flood of the Wasichus; ...dirty with lies and greed.

As Black Elk recognized, white Americans had finally defeated the western tribes. Once independent, proud, and strong, Native Americans suffered dependency, poverty, and social and cultural disorganization on the reservations, in grim Indian schools, and in the slums of America's cities.

The New South

Of all the nation's agricultural regions, the South was the poorest. In 1880, southerners' yearly earnings were only half the national average. But despite poverty and backwardness, some southerners during the late nineteenth century dreamed of making the agricultural South the rival of the industrial North.

The vision of a modern, progressive, and self-sufficient South had roots in the troubled decade of the 1850s. At that time, southern intellectuals and writers had argued that the South must throw off its dependence on the North and on cotton. "The smoke of the steam engine should begin to float over the cotton fields, and the hum of spindles and the click of looms make music on all our mountain streams," insisted the editor of the New Orleans *Picayune*.

Postwar Southerners Face the Future

Too few southerners had listened. Now, after the painful war and Reconstruction, the cry for regional self-sufficiency grew sharper. Publicists of the movement for a "New South" argued that southern backwardness did not stem from the war itself, as so many southerners wished to believe, but from basic conditions in southern life, a rural economy based on cotton foremost among them. The defeat only made clearer the reality of the nineteenth century. Power and wealth came not from cotton, but from factories, machines, and cities.

Henry Grady, editor of the Atlanta *Constitution* and the New South's most famous spokesman,

dramatized the need for change with his story of a southerner's funeral:

They buried him in the midst of a marble quarry; they cut through solid marble to make his grave; and yet a little tombstone they put above him was from Vermont. They buried him in the heart of a pine forest, and yet the pine coffin was imported from Cincinnati. They buried him within touch of an iron mine, and yet the nails in his coffin and the iron in the shovel that dug his grave were imported from Pittsburgh.... They put him away ... in a New York coat and a Boston pair of shoes and a pair of breeches from Chicago and a shirt from Cincinnati, leaving him nothing to carry into the next world with him to remind him of the country in which he lived and for which he fought for four years, but the chill of blood in his veins and the marrow in his bones.

Regional pride and self-interest dictated a new course. As Grady told a Boston audience in 1886, industrial advances would allow the South to match the North in another, more peaceful contest. "We are going to take a noble revenge," he said, "by invading every inch of your territory with iron, as you invaded ours twenty-nine years ago."

In hundreds of speeches, editorials, pamphlets, articles, and books, spokesmen for the New South tried to persuade fellow southerners of the need for change. Southerners must abandon prewar ideals that glorified leisure and gentility and adopt the ethic of hard work. To lure northern bankers and capitalists, New South advocates held out attractive investment possibilities. Because the South was short of capital, northern assistance was critically important. Thus, said one beckoning New South advocate, "the profits to be reaped from investments in the South ... appear to be fabulous." The South would be the "El Dorado of the next half century."

In a bid to attract manufacturers, several southern state governments offered tax exemptions and cheap labor based on leasing state prison convicts. Texas and Florida awarded the railroads land grants, and cities like Atlanta and Louisville mounted huge industrial exhibitions as incentives to industrial progress. Middle-class southerners increasingly accepted new entrepreneurial values. The most startling example of commitment to the vision of a New South may have come in 1886 when southern railroad companies decided to bring their tracks into line with the "standard" northern gauges. On a Sunday in May, 8,000 men equipped with sledgehammers and crowbars attacked the 2,000 miles of track belonging to the Louisville and Nashville Railroad Company and moved the western rail 3 inches to the east. On that same day, they also adjusted the iron wheels of 300 locomotives and 10,000 pieces of rolling stock to fit the new gauge.

During the late nineteenth century, northern money flowed south as dollars replaced the moral fervor and political involvement of the Civil War and Reconstruction years. In the 1880s, northerners increased their investment in the cotton industry sevenfold and financed the expansion of the southern railroad system. Northern capital helped southern cities to embark on an extended period of expansion. By 1900, some 15 percent of all southerners lived in cities, whereas only 7 percent had in 1860. (The national averages for these years were 40 and 20 percent, respectively.)

The city of Birmingham, Alabama, symbolized the New South. In 1870, the site of the future city was a peaceful cornfield. The next year, two northern real estate speculators arrived on the scene, attracted by the area's rich iron deposits. Despite a siege of cholera and the depression of the 1870s, Birmingham rapidly became the center of the southern iron and steel industry. By 1890, a total of 38,414 people lived in the city. Coke ovens, blast furnaces, rolling mills, iron foundries, and machine shops belched forth polluting smoke into the air where once there had been only fields. Millions of dollars of finished goods poured forth from the city's mills and factories, and eight railroad lines carried them away.

Other southern cities flourished as well. Memphis prospered from its lumber industry and the manufacturing of cottonseed products, and Richmond became the country's tobacco capital even as its flour mills and iron and steel foundries continued to produce wealth. Augusta, Georgia, was the "Lowell of the South," a leader in the emerging textile industry that blossomed in Georgia, North and South Carolina, and Alabama. Augusta's eight cotton mills employed about 2,800 workers, many of them women and children.

The Other Side of Progress

New South leaders, a small group of merchants, industrialists, and planters, bragged about the growth of the iron and textile industries and paraded statistics to prove the success of efforts to modernize. The South, one writer boasted, was "throbbing with industrial and railroad activity." But despite such optimism about matching or even surpassing the North's economic performance, the South made slow progress.

Older values persisted. Indeed, New South spokesmen paradoxically kept older chivalric values alive by romanticizing the recent past. "In the eyes of Southern people," one publication asserted, "all Confederate veterans are heroes." Loyalty to the past impeded full acceptance of a new economic order. It was significant that despite the interest in modernization, the southern school system lagged far behind that of the North.

Although new industries and signs of progress abounded, two of the new industries depended on tobacco and cotton, traditional crops long at the center of rural life. Moreover, the South did not better its position relative to the North. Whereas in 1860, the South had 17 percent of the country's manufacturing concerns, by 1904, it had only 15 percent. During the same period, the value of its manufactures grew from 10.3 percent of the total value of manufactures in the United States to only 10.5 percent. Commerce and government work still were responsible for urban growth, as they had been before the Civil War. The South's achievements were not insignificant during a period in which northern industry and cities rapidly expanded, but they could not make the South the equal of the North.

Moreover, the South failed to reap many benefits from industrialization. Southern businessmen like Richmond banker and railroad president John Skelton Williams hoped "to see in the South in the not distant future many railroads and business institutions as great as the Pennsylvania Railroad, the Mutual Life Insurance Company, the Carnegie Steel Company or the Standard Oil Company." This was not to happen. As in the antebellum period, the South remained an economic vassal of the North.

Southern businessmen grew in number, but with the exception of the American Tobacco Company, no great southern corporations arose. Instead, southerners worked for northern companies and corporations, which absorbed southern businesses or dominated them financially. By 1900, for example, five corporations directed three-quarters of the railroad mileage in the South (excluding Texas), and northern bankers controlled all five. Northerners also took over the southern steel industry.

As this happened, profits flowed north. "Our capitalists are going into your country," the Lowell *Manufacturers' Record* noted, "because they see a chance to make money there, but you must not think that they will give your people the benefit of the money they make. That will come North and enrich their heirs, or set up public libraries in our country towns." As dollars fled north, so, too, went the power to make critical decisions. In many cases, northern directors determined that southern mills and factories could handle only the early stages of processing, while northern factories finished the goods. Thus, southern cotton mills sent yarn and coarse cloth north for completion. Southern manufacturers who did finish their products, hoping to compete in the marketplace, found that railroad rate discrimination robbed their goods of any competitive edge.

Individual workers in the new industries may have found factory life preferable to sharecropping, but their rewards were meager. The thousands of women and children in factories were silent testimony to the fact their husbands and fathers could not earn sufficient wages to keep them at home. As usual, women and children earned lower wages than men. Justifying these policies, one Augusta factory president claimed that the employment of children was "a matter of charity with us; some of them would starve if they were not given employment.... Ours are not overworked. The work we give children is very light." Actually, many children at his factory were doing the same work as adults, for children's pay.

In general, all workers earned lower wages and worked longer hours in the South than elsewhere. Per capita income was the same in 1900 as it had been in 1860—and only half the national average. In North Carolina in the 1890s, workers were paid an average of 50 cents a day and toiled 70 hours a week. Black workers, who made up 6 percent of the southern manufacturing force in 1890 (but who were excluded from textile mills), usually had the worst jobs and the lowest wages.

Cotton Still King

Although New South advocates envisioned the South's transformation from a rural to an industrial society, they always recognized the need for agricultural change. "It's time for an agricultural revolution," Henry Grady proclaimed. "When we once decide that southern lands are fit for something else besides cotton, and then go to work in earnest to multiply and diversify our products and industries, independence and wealth will be the certain reward of our intelligent and industrious farmers."

The overdependence on "King Cotton" hobbled southern agriculture by making farmers the victims of faraway market forces and an oppressive credit system. Subdivide old cotton plantations into small diversified farms, Grady urged. Truck farming could produce "simply wonderful profits" and

> would give employment throughout the entire season, and at the end of it the fortunate farmer would have before him the assurance that diversified crops and a never-failing market alone afford, with no [fertilizer] ... bills to settle, and no liens past or to come to disturb his mind.

A new agricultural South with new class and economic arrangements did emerge, but it was not the one Grady and others envisioned. Despite the breakup of some plantations following the Civil War, large landowners proved resourceful in holding on to their property and in dealing with postwar conditions, as Chapter 16 showed. As they adopted new agricultural arrangements, former slaves sank into debt peonage.

White farmers on small and medium-size holdings fared only slightly better than black tenants and sharecroppers. Immediately after the war, high cotton prices tempted them to raise as much cotton as they could. Then prices began a disastrous decline, from 11 cents a pound in 1875 to less than 5 cents in 1894. "At the close of the war a 500 lb. bale of cotton would bring $100," a Cherokee

Black dockworkers load bales of cotton in this undated photograph, which is evidence not only of the kinds of jobs that free blacks could secure, but also of the continuing dominance of cotton in southern life. (Library of Congress)

County, Georgia, tenant complained in 1891, "and today it will bring $32.50." Yeoman farmers became entangled in debt. Each year, farmers found themselves buying supplies on credit from merchants so that they could plant the next year's crop and support their families until harvest time. In return, merchants demanded their exclusive business and acquired a lien (or claim) on their crops. But when farmers sold their crops at declining prices, they usually discovered that they had not earned enough to settle with the merchant, who had charged dearly for store goods and whose annual interest rates might exceed 100 percent. Each year, thousands of farmers fell further behind.

The story of S. R. Simonton was typical. Between 1887 and 1895, the South Carolina farmer spent $2,681 at T. G. Patrick's furnishing house. But he could manage to pay back only $687. Like many others, Simonton lost his land and became a tenant farmer. The number of tenants inched upward, whereas the number of small independent farmers fell. By 1900, over half the South's white farmers and three-quarters of its black farmers were tenants. Although tenancy was increasing all over rural America, nowhere did it rise more rapidly than in the Deep South.

These patterns had baneful results for individual southerners and for the South as a whole. Caught in a cycle of debt and poverty, few farmers could think of improving agricultural techniques or diversifying crops. In their desperate attempt to pay off debts, they concentrated on cotton, despite falling prices. "Cotton brings money, and money pays debt," was the small farmer's slogan. Landowners also pressured tenants to raise a market crop. Far from diversifying, as Grady had hoped, farmers increasingly limited the number of crops they raised. By 1880, the South was not growing enough food to feed its people adequately. Poor nutrition contributed to chronic bad health and sickness.

The Nadir of Black Life

Grady and other New South advocates painted a picture of a strong, prosperous, and industrialized South, a region that could deal with the troublesome race issue without the interference of any "outside power." Grady had few regrets over the end of slavery, which he thought had contributed to southern economic backwardness. Realizing that black labor would be crucial to the transformation he sought, he advocated racial cooperation.

But racial cooperation did not mean equality. Grady assumed that blacks were racially inferior and supported an informal system of segregation. "The negro is entitled to his freedom, his franchise, to full and equal legal rights," Grady wrote in 1883. But "social equality he can never have. He does not have it in the north, or in the east, or in the west. On one pretext or another, he is kept out of hotels, theatres, schools and restaurants."

By the time of Grady's death in 1889, a much harsher perspective on southern race relations was replacing his view. In 1891, at a national assembly of women's clubs in Washington, D.C., a black woman, Frances Ellen Watkins Harper, anticipated efforts to strip the vote from blacks and appealed to the white women at the meeting not to abandon black suffrage. "I deem it a privilege to present the negro," she said, "not as a mere dependent asking for Northern sympathy or Southern compassion, but as a member of the body politic who has a claim upon the nation for justice, simple justice." This claim, she continued, was for "protection to human life," for "the rights of life and liberty," and for relief from charges of ignorance and poverty. These were "conditions which men outgrow." Women, of all people, should understand this and not seek to achieve their own right to vote at the expense of the vote for black men. "Instead of taking the ballot from his hands, teach him how to use it, and add his quota to the progress, strength, and durability of the nation."

The decision by congressional leaders in 1890 to shelve a proposed act for protecting black civil rights and the defeat of the Blair bill providing federal assistance for educational institutions left black Americans vulnerable, as Frances Harper realized. The traditional sponsor of the rights of freedmen, the Republican party, left blacks to fend for themselves as a minority in the white South. The courts also abandoned blacks. In 1878, the Supreme Court declared unconstitutional a Louisiana statute banning discrimination in transportation. In 1882, the Court voided the Ku Klux Klan Act of 1871, deciding that the civil rights protections of the Fourteenth Amendment applied to states rather than to individuals. In 1883, the provisions of the Civil Rights Act of 1875, which assured blacks of equal rights in public places, were declared unconstitutional on the grounds that the federal government did not have the right to involve itself in the racial relations between individuals.

Northern leaders did not oppose these actions. In fact, northerners increasingly promulgated negative stereotypes, picturing blacks as either ignorant, lazy, childlike fools or as lying, stealing, raping degenerates. Obviously, they could not be left to themselves or given the same rights and freedoms whites enjoyed. Instead, blacks needed the paternal protection of the superior white race. These stereotypes filled the magazines and newspapers and were perpetuated in cartoons, advertisements, "coon songs," serious art and theater, and the minstrel shows that dominated northern entertainment.

The *Atlanta Monthly* in 1890 anticipated a strong current in magazine literature when it expressed doubts that this "lowly variety of man" could ever be brought up to the intellectual and moral standards of whites. Other magazines openly opposed suffrage as wasted on people too "ignorant, weak, lazy and incompetent" to make good use of it. *Forum* magazine suggested that "American Negroes" had "too much liberty." When this freedom was combined with natural "race traits" of stealing and hankering after white women, the *Forum* advised in 1893, black crime increased. Only lynching and burning would deter the "barbarous" rapist and other "sadly degenerated" Negroes corrupted since the Civil War by independence and too much education. The author concluded that the Negro question was "more vital" than gold, silver, or the tariff. Encouraged by northern public opinion, and with the blessing of Congress and the Supreme Court, southern citizens and legislatures sought to make blacks permanently second-class members of southern society.

In the political sphere, white southerners amended state constitutions to disenfranchise black voters. By various legal devices—the poll tax, literacy tests, "good character" and "understanding" clauses administered by white voter registrars, and all-white primary elections—blacks lost the right to vote. The most ingenious method was the "grandfather clause," which specified that only citizens whose grandfathers were registered to vote on January 1, 1867, could cast their ballots. This virtually excluded blacks. Although the Supreme Court outlawed such blatantly discriminatory laws as grandfather clauses, a series of other constitutional changes, beginning in Mississippi in 1890 and spreading to all 11 former Confederate states by 1910, effectively excluded the black vote. The results were dramatic. Louisiana, for example, contained 130,334 registered black voters in 1896. Eight years later, there were only 1,342.

In a second tactic in the 1890s, state and local laws legalized informal segregation in public facilities. Beginning with railroads and schools, "Jim Crow" laws were extended to libraries, hotels, restaurants, hospitals, asylums, prisons, theaters, parks and playgrounds, cemeteries, toilets, morgues, sidewalks, drinking fountains, and nearly every other place where blacks and whites might mingle. The Supreme Court upheld these laws in 1896 in *Plessy* v. *Ferguson* by declaring that "separate but equal" facilities did not violate the equal protection clause of the Fourteenth Amendment. The Court's decision opened the way for as many forms of legal segregation as the imaginations of southern lawmakers could devise.

Political and social discrimination made it ever more possible to keep blacks permanently confined to agricultural and unskilled labor and dependent on whites for their material welfare. In 1900, nearly 84 percent of black workers nationwide engaged in some form of agricultural labor as farmhands, overseers, sharecroppers, or tenant or independent farmers or in service jobs, primarily domestic service and laundry work. These had been the primary slave occupations. The remaining 16 percent worked in forests, sawmills, mines, and, with northward migration, in northern cities.

Gone were the skilled black tradesmen of slavery days. At the end of the Civil War, at least half of all skilled craftsmen in the South had been black. But by the 1890s, the percentage had decreased to less than 10 percent, as whites systematically excluded blacks from the trades. Such factory work as blacks had been doing was also reduced, largely in order to drive a wedge between poor blacks and whites to prevent unionization. In Greensboro, North Carolina, for example, where in 1870 some 30 percent of all blacks worked in skilled trades or factory occupations, by 1910, blacks in the skilled trades had been reduced to 8 percent, and not a single black worked in a Greensboro factory. The exclusion of blacks from industry prevented them from acquiring the skills and habits that would enable them to rise into the middle class as would many European immigrants and their children by the mid-twentieth century.

Blacks did not accept their declining position passively. In the mid-1880s, they enthusiastically joined the mass worker organization the Knights of Labor (discussed in Chapter 18), first in cities such as Richmond and Atlanta, and then in rural areas. As one South Carolina black explained, "We are [bound] to join something what will lead to better rights than we have." Blacks made up at least a third of the Knights' membership in the South. But southern whites feared that the Knights' policies of racial and economic cooperation might lead to social equality. "The forcing of a colored man among the white people here ... knocked me out of the order," reported one. The Charleston *News and Courier* warned of the dangers of "miscegenation" and the possibility that the South would be left "in the possession of ... mongrels and hybrids." As blacks continued to join it, whites abandoned the order in growing numbers. The flight of whites weakened the organization in the South, and a backlash of white violence finally smashed it.

Against this backdrop, incidents of lynchings and other forms of violence against blacks increased. On February 21, 1891, the *New York Times* reported that in Texarkana, Arkansas, a mob apprehended a 32-year-old black man, Ed Coy, charged with the rape of a white woman, tied him to a stake, and burned him alive. As Coy proclaimed his innocence to a large crowd, his alleged victim herself somewhat hesitatingly put the torch to his oil-soaked body. The *Times* report concluded that only by the "terrible death such as fire ... can inflict" could other blacks "be deterred from the commission of like crimes." Ed Coy was one of more than 1,400 black men lynched or burned alive during the 1890s. About a third were charged with sex crimes. The rest were accused of a variety of "crimes" related to not knowing their place: marrying or insulting a white woman, testifying in court against whites, having a "bad reputation."

At Buffalo Bill's Wild West Show

In the late nineteenth century, organized mass amusements, especially designed for leisure time, brought friends and strangers together as spectators not participants. These new leisure activities took the place of older rural pastimes like barn raisings and quilting bees that had often combined work with fun.

During the late 1880s and 1890s, Buffalo Bill's Wild West company thrilled audiences with a large-scale outdoor show, billed as "A DRAMATIC-EQUESTRIAN EXPOSITION OF LIFE ON THE PLAINS, WITH ACCOMPANYING MONOLOGUE AND INCIDENTAL MUSIC." Cody's extravaganza was the culmination of a variety of nineteenth-century entertainments capitalizing on the public's fascination with the West and the new hunger for mass entertainment.

In the post–Civil War era, new figures like the Indian scout and the cavalry officer joined the cast of familiar western characters. Bill Cody basked in the powerful appeal of his own past as an Indian scout and buffalo hunter, when he played himself in an 1872 stage melodrama entitled *Scouts of the Prairies*. Although critics lambasted the show, audiences loved it. In 1882, Cody helped organize the "Old Glory Blow Out," a Fourth-of-July celebration in North Platte, Nebraska, that featured riding, roping, and shooting contests as well as cowboys and authentic Indians (rather than, as in the melodrama, actors dressed in "tan-colored frocks and cambric pantalettes").

The following year, Buffalo Bill and his business partner pulled together the various strands of the western entertainments into "an original amusement enterprise" suitable for family audiences. They recruited a large cast of characters (Indians, Mexican *vaqueros,* former army scouts, sharpshooters, and cowboys) and collected hundreds of props (emigrant wagons, a stagecoach, horses, guns, and appropriate clothing). Although the show changed over the years, standard elements included band music, a spectacular parade including mounted Indians adorned with war paint and feathered bonnets, shooting and roping exhibitions, races, and several short dramas. One favorite featured a Pony Express "rider" who amazed viewers by successfully transferring himself and his mailbags from one galloping pony to another.

This poster captures the essence of many of the show's acts that showed noble white settlers or scouts repelling the attack of savage Indians. (The Granger Collection, New York)

This poster emphasizes the vivid and elaborate spectacles that attracted crowds to the new mass entertainments of the late nineteenth and early twentieth centuries. (The Granger Collection, New York)

Cody claimed his show depicted the West "as it was," that "the wigwam village, the Indian war-dance, the chant of the Great Spirit as it was sung on the Plains, the rise and fall of the famous tribes, were all pictured accurately." While many of the details were authentic, Buffalo Bill's Wild West show offered a particular interpretation of western life and reinforced a particular conception of the country's past. The show acknowledged the role of violence in winning the West, but the instigators of the violence in his portrayal were the Indians. White conquest was legitimated as an appropriate response to savagery; the bullet, as one program pointed out, was "the pioneer of civilization."

For the Indians working in the show, the experience was filled with ironies. Chief Sitting Bull toured with the show in 1885 (for $50 a week and a $125 bonus) and received both inaccurate publicity as the "slayer of General Custer" and the booing of American audiences. Yet he was pleased by the enthusiastic cheers of Canadian audiences and valued the presents Buffalo Bill presented to him when he left. For Kicking Bear, a Lakota Sioux, a European tour with Buffalo Bill was the means of avoiding exile for his part in the Ghost Dance movement. For the Indians who signed with Buffalo Bill, catering to white audiences was a means of escaping the bleak realities of reservation life.

The crowds who thronged to the show in cities all over the United States and Europe applauded the spectacle arranged for their amusement. As the St. Louis *Globe-Democrat* pointed out, "The most remarkable fact is that among so many thousands there were heard no grumbling nor expressions of dissatisfaction, and those who were present … have nothing but agreeable recollections of Buffalo Bill's Wild West." White Americans in the audience welcomed a vision of the past that accorded with their understanding of events. Attending the show was an exercise in patriotism—and in nostalgia. At the time of the show's greatest popularity, Americans were realizing that the frontier period was coming to an end. The show allowed them an opportunity to participate vicariously in an experience that was disappearing, to escape from the industrial and urban reality of the world outside the stadium.

court four or five years later, they often won their cases from judges suspicious of new federal authority. Between 1887 and 1906, a total of 16 cases made their way to the Supreme Court, which decided 15 of them in the railroads' favor. As one railroad executive candidly admitted, "There is not a road in the country that can be accused of living up to the rules of the Interstate Commerce Law."

The Southern Farmers' Alliance in the 1880s and 1890s

The Grange declined in the late 1870s as the nation recovered from depression. But neither farm organizations nor farm protest died. Depression struck farmers once again in the late 1880s and worsened as the 1890s began. Official statistics told the familiar, dismal story of falling prices for cereal crops grown on the plains and prairies. A bushel of wheat that had sold for $1 in 1870 was worth 60 cents in the 1890s. Kansas farmers, in 1889, were selling their corn for a mere 10 cents a bushel. The national currency shortage, which usually reached critical proportions at harvest time, helped push agricultural prices ever lower. And whereas prices declined, the load of debt climbed. Mortgage rates ranged between 18 and 36 percent, and shipping rates were high. It sometimes cost a farmer as much as one bushel of corn to send another one to market.

A Kansas farmer's letter reveals some of the human consequences of such trends:

> At the age of 52 years, after a long life of toil, economy and self-denial, I find myself and family virtually paupers. With hundreds of cattle, hundreds of hogs, scores of good horses, and a farm that rewarded the toil of our hands with 16,000 bushels of golden corn, we are poorer by many dollars than we were years ago. What once seemed a neat little fortune and a house of refuge for our declining years ... has been rendered valueless.

Under these pressures, farmers turned again to organization, education, and cooperation. The Southern Farmers' Alliance became one of the most important reform organizations of the 1880s as it launched an ambitious organizational drive, sending lecturers throughout the South and onto the western plains. Eventually, Alliance lecturers reached 43 states and territories, bringing their message to 2 million farming families and organizing a far-reaching agrarian network.

An article in their newspaper, the *National Economist,* pointed out some of the Alliance's fundamental beliefs. "The agricultural population of today is becoming rapidly aroused to the fact that agriculture, as a class, can only be rendered prosperous by radical changes in the laws governing money, transportation, and land." The economic and social position of farmers had slipped, even though as producers the farming class was critical to national well-being. The farmer's condition was, in the words of an Alliance song, a "sin," the result of the farmer's forgetting that "he's the man that feeds them all." Alliance lecturers proposed various programs that would help realize their slogan: "Equal rights to all, special privileges to none."

On the one hand, the Alliance experimented with buying and selling cooperatives in order to free farmers from the clutches of supply merchants, banks, and other credit agencies. Although these efforts often failed in the long run, they taught the value of cooperation to achieve common goals. On the other hand, the Alliance supported legislative efforts to regulate powerful monopolies and corporations, which they believed gouged the farmer. Many Alliance members also felt that increasing the money supply was critical to improving the position of farmers and supported a national banking system empowered to issue paper money.

The Alliance also called for a variety of measures to improve the quality of rural life: better public schools for rural children, state agricultural colleges, and an improvement in the status of women. "This order has the good sense, magnanimity and moral courage," declared Hattie Huntingdon of Louisiana, "to lay aside deeply-rooted prejudices handed down from the barbaric past and admit women into its fold and proclaim to the world that it believes in equal rights to all."

By 1890, rural discontent was spreading. In the Midwest, where farmers were prospering by raising hogs and cattle on cheap grain, and in the East, where farmers were growing fruit and vegetables for urban markets, discontent was muted. But that summer in Kansas, hundreds of farmers packed their families into wagons to set off for Alliance meetings or to parade in long lines through the streets of nearby towns and villages. Floats garnished with evergreens proclaimed that the farmers' new organization focused on live issues, not the dead ones Congress debated.

Similar scenes occurred through the West and the South. A farmer's wife, Zenobia Wheeless, captured the hopeful spirit of the protest in her letter to North Carolina Alliance leader Leonidas Polk. "We rode sixteen miles ... to hear Brother Tracy [an organizer from Texas]—started about sun-up and trotted all the way.... Brother Tracy's lecture was very interesting ... it seemed that all eyes were riveted upon him." Never had there been such a wave of organizational activity in rural America. In 1890, more than a million farmers counted themselves as Alliance members.

The Alliance network also included black farmers. In 1888, black and white organizers established the Colored Farmers' Alliance, headed by a white Baptist minister, R. M. Humphrey. The Colored Farmers' Alliance recognized that black and white farmers faced common economic problems and must cooperate to ameliorate their shared plight. Few initially confronted the fact that many southern cotton farmers depended on black labor and had a different perspective from blacks. In 1891, however, cotton pickers working on plantations near Memphis, Tennessee, went on strike. White posses chased the strikers, lynched 15 of them, and demonstrated that racial tensions simmered just below the surface.

The Ocala Platform, 1890

In December 1890, the National Alliance gathered in Ocala, Florida, to develop an official platform. Most delegates felt that the federal government had failed to address the farmers' problems. "Congress must come nearer the people or the people will come nearer the Congress," warned the Alliance's president. Both parties were far too subservient to the "will of corporation and money power."

The platform called for the direct election of U.S. senators. Alliance members supported lowering the tariff, a much debated topic in Congress, but their justification, emphasizing the need to reduce prices for the "poor of our land," had a radical ring. Their money plank went far beyond what any national legislator was likely to consider. Rejecting the notion that only gold had value or, indeed, that precious metals had to be the basis for currency, Alliance leaders boldly envisioned a new banking system controlled by the federal government. They demanded that the government take an active economic role by increasing the amount of money in circulation in the form of treasury notes and silver. More money would lead to inflation, higher prices, and a reduction in debt, they believed.

The platform also called for the creation of subtreasuries (federal warehouses) in agricultural regions where farmers could store their produce at low interest rates until market prices favored selling. To tide farmers over until that time, the federal government would lend farmers up to 80 percent of the current local price for their products. Thus, the plan would free farmers from the twin evils of the credit merchant and depressed prices at harvest time. Other demands included a graduated income tax and support for the regulation of transportation and communication networks. If regulation failed, the government was called on to take over both networks and run them for the public benefit.

In the context of late-nineteenth-century political life, almost all these planks represented radical departures from political norms. They demanded aggressive governmental action to assist the country's farmers at a time when the government favored big business (see Chapter 19). Even though a minority of farmers belonged to the Alliance, many Americans feared that the organization was capable of upsetting political arrangements.

The New York *Sun* reported that the Alliance had caused a "panic" in the two major parties. The Alliance's warning that the people would replace their representatives unless they were better represented was already coming true. Although the Alliance was not formally in politics, it had supported sympathetic candidates in the fall elections of 1890. A surprising number of these local and state candidates had won. Alliance victories in the West harmed the Republican party enough to cause President Harrison to refer to "our election disaster."

Before long, many Alliance members were pressing for an independent political party, as legislators who had courted Alliance votes conveniently forgot their pledges once elected. Alliance support did not necessarily bring action on issues of interest to farmers, or even respect.

One Texas farmer reported that the chairman of the state Democratic executive committee "calls us all skunks" and observed that "anything that has the scent of the plowhandle smells like a polecat" to the Democrats. On the national level, no one had much interest in the Ocala platform. As one North Carolinian observed, "I am not able to perceive any very great difference between the two parties."

Among the first to realize the necessity of forming an independent third party was Georgia's Tom Watson. "We are in the midst of a great crisis," he argued. "We have before us three or four platforms ... [and] the Ocala platform is the best of all three. It is the only one that breathes the breath of life." Watson also realized that electoral success in the South would depend on unity between white and black farmers.

The People's Party, 1892

In February 1892, the People's, or Populist, party was established, with almost 100 black delegates in attendance. Leonidas Polk, president of the Alliance and promoter of a political coalition between the South and the West, became the party's presidential candidate that fall. "The time has arrived," he thundered, "for the great West, the great South, and the great Northwest, to link their hands and hearts together and march to the ballot box and take possession of the government, restore it to the principles of our fathers, and run it in the interest of the people." But by the time the party met at its convention in July in Omaha, Polk had died. The party nominated James B. Weaver, Union army veteran from Iowa, as its presidential candidate, and James G. Field, a former Confederate soldier, for vice president.

The platform preamble, written by Ignatius Donnelly, a Minnesota farmer, author, and politician, caught much of the urgent spirit of the agrarian protest movement in the 1890s:

> We meet in the midst of a nation brought to the verge of moral, political and material ruin. Corruption dominates the ballot box, the legislatures, the Congress, and touches even the ermine of the bench. The people are demoralized.... The fruits of the toil of millions are

boldly stolen to build up colossal fortunes ... we breed two great classes—paupers and millionaires.

The charge was clear: "The controlling influences dominating the old political parties have allowed the existing dreadful conditions to develop without serious effort to restrain or prevent them."

The Omaha platform demands, drawn from the Ocala platform of 1890, were greatly expanded. They included more means of direct democracy (direct election of senators, direct primaries, the initiative, referendum, and the secret ballot) and several planks intended to enlist the support of urban labor (eight-hour workday, immigration restriction, and condemnation of the use of Pinkerton agents as an "army of mercenaries ... a menace to our liberties"). The People's party also endorsed a graduated income tax, the free and unlimited coinage of silver at a ratio of 16 to 1 (meaning that the U.S. Mint would have to buy silver for coinage at one-sixteenth the current official price of the equivalent amount of gold), and, rather than regulation, government ownership of railroads, telephone, and telegraph. "The time has come," the platform said, "when the railroad corporations will either own the people or the people must own the railroads."

The Populist party attempted to widen the nature of the American political debate by promoting a new vision of the government's role with respect to farmers' problems. But the tasks the party faced in attempting to win power were monumental. Success at the polls meant weaning the South away from the Democratic party, encouraging southern whites to work with blacks, and persuading voters of both parties to abandon familiar political ties. Nor were all Alliance members eager to follow their leaders into the third party. At the most basic level, the Populists had to create the political machinery necessary to function in the 1892 electoral campaign.

Despite these obstacles, the new party pressed forward. Unlike the candidates of the major parties in 1892, Benjamin Harrison and Grover Cleveland, Weaver campaigned actively. In the South, he faced rowdy audiences, rotten eggs, and rocks from hostile Democrats, who disapproved of attempts to form a biracial political coalition. The results of the campaign were mixed. Although Weaver won over a million popular votes (the first third-party candidate to do so), he carried only four states (Kansas, Colorado, Idaho, and Nevada) and parts of two others (Oregon and North Dakota), for a total of 22 electoral votes.

The attempt to break the stranglehold of the Democratic party on the South had failed. Democrats raised the cry of "nigger rule" and fanned racial fears. White farmers who viewed the alliance with blacks as one of necessity voted Democratic. Intimidation tactics and violence frightened off others.

Just as important, Weaver failed to appeal to city workers, who were suspicious of the party's antiurban tone and its desire for higher agricultural prices (which meant higher food prices). Nor did it appeal to people living east of the Mississippi or to farmers in the Great Lakes states. Their families enjoyed better farming weather, owed fewer debts, and were relatively prosperous. They saw little of value in the Omaha platform. Their disinterest was significant, for the growing population of the industrial northern cities, combined with the populous and prosperous Great Lake states, constituted an electoral majority by the 1890s.

Although the People's party failed to recruit a cross-section of American voters in 1892, it gained substantial support. Miners and mine owners in states like Montana and Colorado and in territories like New Mexico favored the demand for coinage of silver. Most Populists, however, were rural Americans in the South and West who stood outside the mainstream of American life. Economic grievances sharpened political discontent. But Populists were often no poorer or more debt-ridden than other farmers. They did tend to lead more isolated lives, however; often their farms were far from towns, villages, and railroads. They felt powerless to affect the workings of their political, social, and economic world. Thus, they responded to a party offering to act as their advocate.

Farmers who were better integrated into their world tended to believe they could work through existing political parties. In 1892, when thousands of farmers and others were politically and economically discontented, they voted for Cleveland and the Democrats, not the Populists.

TIMELINE

1860s	Cattle drives from Texas begin
1865–1867	Sioux Wars on the Great Plains
1867	National Grange founded
1869	Transcontinental railroad completed
1869–1874	Granger laws
1873	Financial panic triggers economic depression
1874	Barbed wire patented
1875	Black Hills gold rush incites Sioux War
1876	Custer's last stand at Little Big Horn
1877	*Munn* v. *Illinois*
	Bonanza farms in the Great Plains
1878	Timber and Stone Act
1880s	"New South"
1881	Tuskegee Institute founded
1883–1885	Depression
1884	Southern Farmers' Alliance founded
1886	Severe winter ends cattle boom
	Wabash v. *Illinois*
1887	Dawes Severalty Act
	Interstate Commerce Act
	Farm prices plummet
1888	Colored Farmers' Alliance founded
1890	Afro-American League founded
	Sioux Ghost Dance movement
	Massacre at Wounded Knee
	Ocala platform
	Yosemite National Park established
1890s	Black disenfranchisement in the South
	Jim Crow laws passed in the South
	Declining farm prices
1891	Forest Reserve Act
1892	Populist party formed
	Sierra Club founded
1895	Booker T. Washington's "Atlanta Compromise" address
1896	*Plessy* v. *Ferguson*

Yet the Populists did not lose heart in 1892, as Chapter 19 will show. Populist governors were elected in Kansas and North Dakota, and the party swept Colorado. It was obvious that the showing of the party in the South, where even Tom Watson lost his bid for a congressional seat, stemmed from violent opposition and fraud on the part of the Democrats. For example, returns in Richmond County, Georgia, revealed a Democratic majority of 80 percent in a total vote twice the size of the actual number of legal voters.

Conclusion

Farming in the Industrial Age

The late nineteenth century brought turbulence to rural America. The "Indian problem," which had plagued Americans for 200 years, was tragically solved for a while, but not without resistance and bloodshed. Few whites found these events troubling. Most were caught up in the challenge of responding to a fast-changing world. Believing themselves to be the backbone of the nation, white farmers brought Indian lands into cultivation, modernized their farms, and raised bumper crops. But success and a comfortable competency eluded many of them. Some, like Milton Leeper, never gave up hope or farming. Many were caught in a cycle of poverty and debt. Others fled to the cities, where they joined the industrial work force described in the next chapter. Many turned to collective action and politics. Their actions demonstrate that they did not merely react to events but attempted to shape them.

Recommended Reading

General

Gilbert C. Fite, *The Farmer's Frontier, 1865–1900* (1966); Rodman W. Paul, with Martin Ridge, *The Far West and the Great Plains in Transition, 1859–1900* (1988); William G. Robbins, *Colony & Empire: The Capitalist Transformation of the American West* (1994); Patricia N. Limerick, *Legacy of Conquest: The Unbroken Past of the American West* (1987); Donald Worster, *Rivers of Empire: Water, Aridity, and the Growth of the American West* (1985) and *An Unsettled Country: Changing Landscapes of the American West* (1994); Henry Nash Smith, *Virgin Land: The American West as Symbol and Myth* (1950); J. B. Jackson, *The Centennial Years, 1865–1976* (1972); Annette Kolodny, *The Land Before Her: Fantasy and Experience of the American Frontiers, 1630–1860* (1984); Paul W. Gates, *History of Public Land Law Development* (1978); Alan G. Bogue, *Money at Interest: The Farm Mortgage on the Middle Border* (1955).

Regions and Groups

Fred C. Luebke, ed., *Ethnicity on the Great Plains* (1980); Howard R. Lamar, *The Far Southwest, 1846–1880* (1963); Earl Pomeroy, *The Pacific Slope: A History of California, Oregon, Washington, Idaho, Utah, and Nevada* (1965); Carlos Schwantes, *The Pacific Northwest: An Interpretive History* (1989); Richard White, *Land Use, Environment, and Social Change: The Shaping of Island County, Washington* (1980); Sue Armitage and Elizabeth Jameson, eds., *The Women's West* (1987); Sarah Deutsch, *No Separate Refuge: Culture, Class, and Gender on an Anglo-Hispanic Frontier in the American Southwest, 1880–1940* (1987); David Montejano, *Anglos and Mexicans in the Making of Texas, 1831–1986* (1987).

Mining and Cattle Frontiers

R. W. Paul, *Mining Frontiers of the Far West, 1848–1880* (1963); William S. Greever, *Bonanza West: Western Mining Rushes* (1963); Malcolm Rohrbough, *Aspen: The History of a Silver Mining Town, 1879–1893* (1986); Paula Petrik, *No Step Backward: Women and Family on the Rocky Mountain Mining Frontier, Helena, Montana* (1987); Lewis Atherton, *The Cattle Kings* (1961); Robert R. Dykstra, *The Cattle Towns: A Social History of the Kansas Cattle Trading Centers* (1970); Joseph B. Frantz and Julian E. Choate, *The American Cowboy: The Myth and the Reality* (1968); Blake Allmendinger, *The Cowboy: Representations of Labor in an American Work Culture* (1992); Peter Iverson, *When Indians Became Cowboys: Native Peoples and Cattle Ranching in the American West* (1994).

Native Americans

William T. Hagan, *American Indians* (1979 ed.); Wilcomb E. Washburn, *The Indian in America* (1975); Ronald T. Takaki,

Iron Cages: Race and Culture in Nineteenth-Century America (1979); Francis P. Prucha, *American Indian Policy in Crisis: Christian Reformers and the Indians* (1976); Robert M. Utley, *The Indian Frontier of the American West* (1984) and *The Lance and the Shield: The Life and Times of Sitting Bull* (1993); Richard White, *The Roots of Dependency* (1983); Ralph K. Andrist, *The Long Death: The Last Days of the Plains Indians* (1964); John G. Neihardt, *Black Elk Speaks* (1932).

The New South

C. Vann Woodward, *The Origins of the New South, 1877–1913* (1951); Paul M. Gaston, *The New South Creed: A Study in Southern Mythmaking* (1970); Orville Vernon Burton and Robert C. McMath, Jr., eds., *Toward a New South?: Post–Civil War Southern Communities* (1982); Edward Royce, *The Origins of Southern Sharecropping* (1993); Lawrence H. Larsen, *The Rise of the Urban South* (1985); Morgan Kousser, *The Shaping of Southern Politics: Suffrage Restriction and the Establishment of the One-Party South* (1974); W. Fitzhugh Brundage, *Lynching in the New South; Georgia and Virginia, 1880–1930* (1993); William E. Montgomery, *Under Their Own Vine and Fig Tree: The African-American Church in the South. 1865–1900* (1993); Jacqueline Jones, *Labor of Love, Labor of Sorrow: Black Women, Work, and the Family from Slavery to the Present* (1985).

Populism

Lawrence Goodwyn, *The Populist Moment: A Short History of the Agrarian Revolt in America* (1978); Sheldon Hackney, *Populism to Progressivism in Alabama* (1969); Bruce Palmer, *"Men over Money": The Southern Populist Critique of American Capitalism* (1980); Peter H. Argersinger, *Populism and Politics: William Alfred Peffer and the People's Party* (1974); Steven Hahn, *The Roots of Southern Populism: Yeoman Farmers and the Transformation of the Georgia Upcountry, 1850–1890* (1983); Robert W. Larson, *Populism in the Mountain West* (1986); Jeffrey Ostler, *Prairie Populism: the Fate of Agrarian Radicalism in Kansas, Nebraska, and Iowa, 1880–1892* (1993); Robert C. McMath, *Populist Vanguard: A History of the Southern Farmers' Alliance* (1975).

Novels

Willa Cather, *My Antonia* (1918); O. E. Rölvaag, *Giants in the Earth* (1927).

The Rise of Smokestack America

y 1883, Thomas O'Donnell, an Irish immigrant, had lived in the United States for
over a decade. He was 30 years old, married, with two young children. His third
child had died in 1882, and O'Donnell was still in debt for the funeral. Money was
scarce, for O'Donnell was a textile worker in Fall River, Massachusetts, and not well educated. "I went to work when I was young," he explained, "and have been working ever
since." However, O'Donnell worked only sporadically at the mill. New machines needed "a
good deal of small help," and the mill owners preferred to hire man-and-boy teams.
Because O'Donnell's children were only 1 and 3, he often saw others preferred for day

work. Once, when he was passed over, he recalled, "I said to the boss ... what am I to do; I have got two little boys at home ... how am I to get something for them to eat; I can't get a turn when I come here.... I says, 'Have I got to starve; ain't I to have any work?'"

O'Donnell and his family were barely getting by, even though he worked with pick and shovel when he could. He estimated that he had earned only $133 the previous year. Rent came to $72. The family spent $2 for a little coal, but depended for heat on driftwood that O'Donnell picked up on the beach. Clams were a major part of the family diet, but on some days, there was nothing to eat at all.

The children "got along very nicely all summer," but it was now November, and they were beginning to "feel quite sickly." It was hardly surprising. "One has one shoe on, a very poor one, and a slipper, that was picked up somewhere. The other has two odd shoes on, with the heel out." His wife was healthy, but not ready for winter. She had two dresses, one saved for church, and an "undershirt that she got given to her, and ... an old wrapper, which is about a mile too big for her; somebody gave it to her."

O'Donnell was describing his family's marginal existence to a Senate committee that was gathering testimony in Boston in 1883 on the relations between labor and capital. As the senators heard the tale, they asked him why he did not go west. "It would not cost you over $1,500," said one senator. The gap between the worlds of the senator and the worker could not have been more dramatic. O'Donnell replied, "Well, I never saw over a $20 bill ... if some one would give me $1,500 I will go." Asked by the senator if he had friends who could provide him with the funds, O'Donnell sadly replied no.

The senators, of course, were far better acquainted with the world of comfort and leisure than with the poverty of families like the O'Donnells. From their vantage point, the fruits of industrial progress were clear. As the United States became a world industrial leader in the years after the Civil War, its factories poured forth an abundance of ever-cheaper goods ranging from steel rails and farm reapers to mass-produced parlor sets. These were years of tremendous growth and broad economic and social change. Manufacturing replaced agriculture as the leading source of economic growth between 1860 and 1900. By 1890, a majority of the American work force held nonagricultural jobs; over a third lived in cities. A rural nation of farmers was becoming a nation of industrial workers and city dwellers.

This anxious scene of a strike hints at the tensions between workers and owners during the industrial era. (Robert Koehler, The Strike (detail), 1886, Courtesy of District 1199, National Union of Hospital and Health Care Employees, RWDSW/AFL-CIO and Lee Baxandall)

*A*s O'Donnell's appearance before the senatorial committee illustrates, industrial and technological advances profoundly changed the nature of American life. For O'Donnell and others like him, the benefits of this transformation were hard to see. Although no nationwide studies of poverty existed, estimates suggest that perhaps half the American population was too poor to take advantage of the new goods of the age. Eventually, the disparity between the reality of life for families like the O'Donnell's and American ideals would give rise to attempts to improve conditions for working-class Americans, but it is unlikely that O'Donnell ever profited from such efforts.

This chapter examines the new order that resulted from the maturing of the American industrial economy. Focusing on the years between 1865 and 1900, it describes the rise of heavy industry, the organization and character of the new industrial workplace, and the emergence of big business. It then examines the locus of industrial life, the fast-growing city, and its varied people, classes, and social inequities. The chapter's central theme grows out of O'Donnell's story: As the United States built up its railroads, cities, and factories, its production and profit orientation resulted in the maldistribution of wealth and power. Although many Americans were too exhausted by life's daily struggles to protest new inequalities, strikes and other forms of working-class resistance punctuated the period. The social problems that accompanied the country's industrial development would capture the attention of reformers and politicians for decades to come.

The Texture of Industrial Progress

When Americans went to war in 1861, agriculture was the country's leading source of economic growth. Forty years later, manufacturing had taken its place. During these years, the production of manufactured goods outpaced population growth. By 1900, three times as many goods per person existed as in 1860. Per capita income increased by over 2 percent a year. But these aggregate figures disguise the fact that many people did not win any gains at all.

As American manufacturing progressed, new regions grew in industrial importance. From New England to the Midwest lay the country's industrial heartland. New England was still a center of light industry, and the Midwest continued to process natural resources. Now, however, the production of iron, steel, and transportation equipment joined the older manufacturing operations there. In the Far West, manufacturers concentrated on processing the region's natural resources, but heavy industry made strides as well. In the South, the textile industry put down roots by the 1890s, although the South as a whole was far less industrialized than either the North or the Midwest.

The Rise of Heavy Industry, 1880–1900

Although many factors contributed to the dramatic rise in industrial productivity, the changing nature of the industrial sector itself explains many of the gains. Manufacturers before the Civil War had concentrated either on producing textiles, clothing, and leather products or on processing agricultural and natural resources like grain, hogs, or lumber. Although these industries continued to be important, heavy industry, which produced goods like steel, iron, petroleum, and machinery, grew rapidly. The manufacturing of "producer's goods" (goods intended for other producers rather than consumers) provided the basis for economic growth. Farmers, who bought machinery for their farms; manufacturers, who installed new equipment in their factories; and railroads, which bought steel rails for their tracks—all contributed to rising productivity figures and encouraged the technological innovations that revolutionized production.

Technological innovations made possible the rise of heavy industries such as steel. Before the Civil War, the production of iron was slow and expensive. Skilled and highly paid workers turned iron ore into wrought iron, which farmers and mechanics could easily shape into tools and machines. But the iron was so soft that heavy trains wore out the iron rails within a few years. Demand for a more durable metal, especially for the railroads, supported the introduction of new technologies capable of producing hard steel. The Bessemer converter (named after its English inventor Henry Bessemer) transformed iron into steel by forcing air through the liquid iron, thus reducing the carbon (see the diagraphic). The process had the added advantage of reducing the need for so many skilled workers.

Dramatic changes in the steel industry resulted. Steel companies developed new forms of vertical organization that provided them with access to raw materials and markets and brought all stages of steel manufacturing, from smelting to rolling, into one mill. Production soared and prices fell. When Andrew Carnegie introduced the Bessemer process in his plant in the mid-1870s, the price of steel plummeted from $100 a ton to $50. In another two years, the price dropped to $40; by 1890, steel cost only $12 a ton.

In turn, the production of a cheaper, stronger, more durable material than iron created new goods, new demands, and new markets and stimulated further technological changes. Bessemer furnaces, geared toward making steel rails, did not produce steel appropriate for building. Experimentation with the open-hearth process that used very high temperatures in making steel resulted in a material used by bridge builders, engineers, architects, and even designers of subways. Proponents of a new foreign policy lobbied successfully for an expanded navy of steel vessels. Countless Americans bought steel in more humble forms: wire, nails, bolts, needles, and screws.

New sources of power facilitated the conversion of American industry to mass production. Because steam engines and coal were expensive, early manufacturers depended on water power. In 1869, about half the industrial power used came from water. With the opening of new anthracite coal deposits, however, the cost of coal dropped, and American industry rapidly shifted to steam. By 1900, steam engines accounted for 80 percent of the nation's industrial energy supply. Then, fostered by the inventiveness of Thomas Edison, who had created at Menlo Park an integrated process of

This 1876 lithograph gives a good idea of the industrial character of a mining operation on the Comstock in Colorado. The Sutro Tunnel, which extended three miles into the mountain, was an example of the technological and capital requirements of the mining industry. As this illustrations shows, wooden supports were used throughout the mine, linking industrial work with environmental damage. (The Bancroft Library, University of California, Berkeley)

organized research and development, and George Westinghouse, electricity began to replace coal as a power source.

The completion of a national transportation and communications network was central to economic growth. In 1860, most railroads were located in the East and the Midwest. From 1862 on, the federal and state governments vigorously promoted railroad construction with land grants from the public domain. Eventually, the railroads received over 180 million acres, an area about 1 1/2 times the size of Texas. Similarly, counties and cities donated land for stations and terminals, bought railroad stock, made loans and grants, and gave tax breaks to railroads.

With such incentives, the first transcontinental railroad was completed in 1869. A burst of railroad construction followed. Four additional transcontinental lines and miles of feeder and branch roads were laid down in the 1870s and 1880s and gave birth to the steel industry. By 1890, trains rumbled across 165,000 miles of tracks. As railroads crisscrossed the country, Western Union lines arose alongside them. Mass production and distribution depended on fast, efficient, and regular transportation. The completion of the national system both encouraged and supported the adoption of mass production and mass marketing.

Financing Postwar Growth

Such changes demanded huge amounts of capital and the willingness to accept financial risks. The creation of the railroad system alone cost over $1 billion by 1859 (the canal system's modest price tag was less than $2 million). The completion of the national railroad network required another $10 billion. British, French, and German investors saw American railroads as a good investment; ultimately, foreigners contributed a third of the sum needed to complete the system. Americans also eagerly supported new ventures and began to devote an increasing percentage of the national income to investment rather than consumption.

Although savings and commercial banks continued to invest their depositors' capital, investment banking houses like Morgan & Co. played a new and significant role in matching resources with economic enterprises. Investment bankers

marketed investment opportunities. They bought up blocks of corporate bonds (which offered set interest rates and eventually the repayment of principal) at a discount for interested investors and also sold stocks (which paid dividends only if the company made a profit). Because stocks were riskier investments than bonds, buyers were at first cautious. But when John Pierpont Morgan, a respected investment banker, began to market stocks, they became more popular. The market for industrial securities expanded rapidly in the 1880s and 1890s. Although some Americans feared the power of investment bankers and distrusted the financial market, both were integral to the economic expansion of the late nineteenth century.

Railroads: Pioneers of Big Business

As the nature of the American economy changed, big businesses became the characteristic form of economic organization. Big businesses, with large amounts of capital, could afford to build huge factories, buy and install the latest and most efficient machinery, hire hundreds of workers, and use the most up-to-date methods. The result was more goods at lower prices. Machines costing thousands of dollars mass-produced goods costing pennies.

The railroads were the pioneers of big business and a great modernizing force in America. After the Civil War, railroad companies expanded rapidly. In 1865, the typical railroad was only 100 miles long. Twenty years later, it was 1,000. In 1888, a medium-size Boston railroad company had three times as many employees and received six times as much income as the Massachusetts state government.

The size of railroads, the huge costs of construction, maintenance, and repair, and the complexity of operations required unprecedented amounts of capital and new management techniques. No single person could finance a railroad or hope to supervise its operations involving hundreds of miles of track and hundreds of employees. Nor could any one person resolve the thorny questions such a large enterprise raised. How should the operations and employees be organized? What were the long- and short-term needs of the railroad? What were proper rates? What share of the profits did workers deserve?

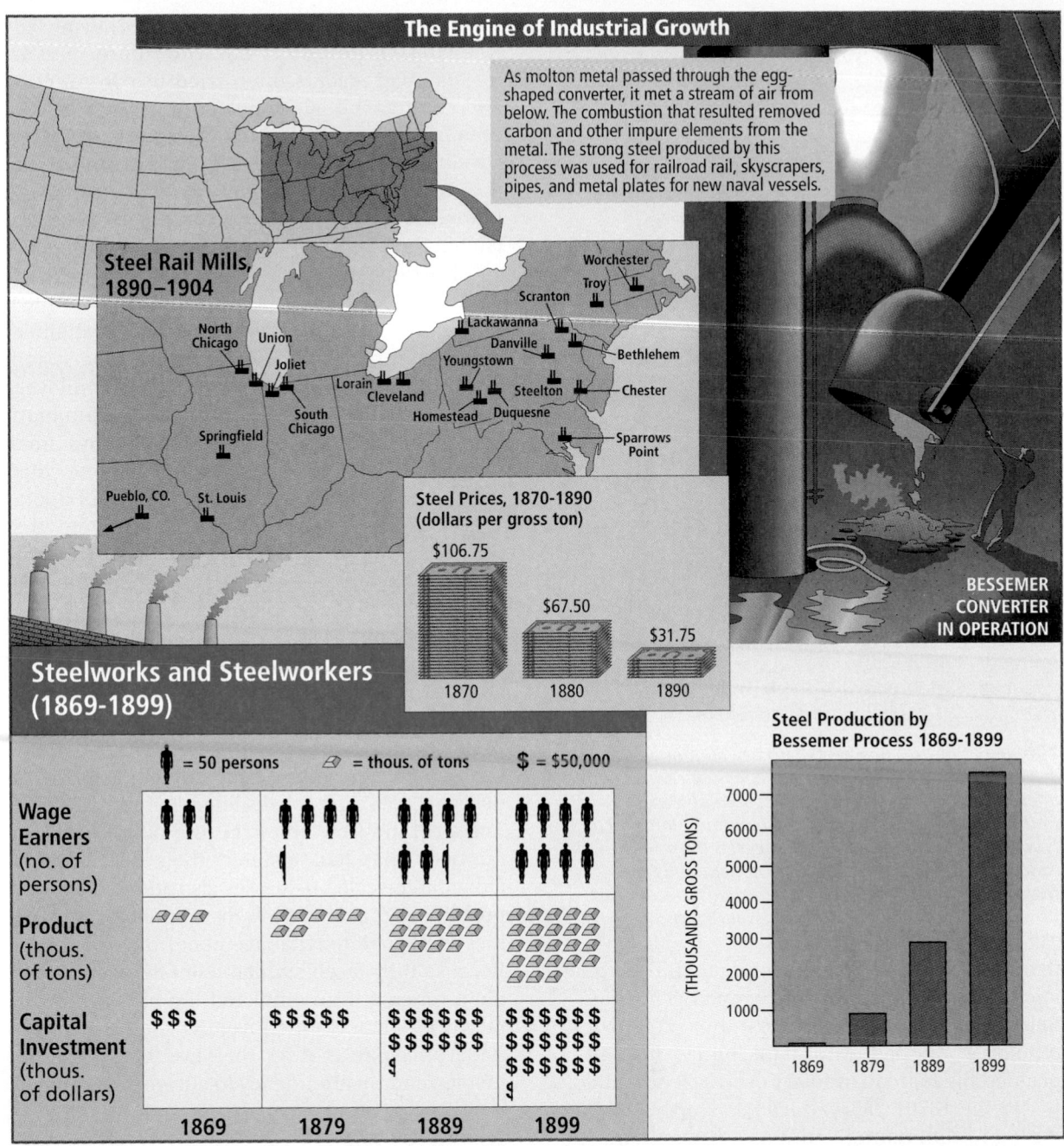

The Engine of Industrial Growth

As molton metal passed through the egg-shaped converter, it met a stream of air from below. The combustion that resulted removed carbon and other impure elements from the metal. The strong steel produced by this process was used for railroad rail, skyscrapers, pipes, and metal plates for new naval vessels.

BESSEMER CONVERTER IN OPERATION

Steel Rail Mills, 1890–1904

Steel Prices, 1870-1890 (dollars per gross ton)
$106.75 (1870), $67.50 (1880), $31.75 (1890)

Steelworks and Steelworkers (1869-1899)

🚶 = 50 persons   ◇ = thous. of tons $ = $50,000

Steel Production by Bessemer Process 1869-1899 (THOUSANDS GROSS TONS)

	1869	1879	1889	1899
Wage Earners (no. of persons)				
Product (thous. of tons)				
Capital Investment (thous. of dollars)				

Unlike small businesses with modest overhead costs, railroads faced high constant costs of maintaining equipment and lines. In addition, railroads carried a heavy load of debt, incurred to pay for construction and expansion. The burden of regular interest payments and expenses encouraged railroads to adopt aggressive business practices and to use their equipment as intensively as possible. If 20 cars were almost as expensive to pull as 25, why not haul 25? If lower rates would lure customers, why not offer them? Railroad freight charges dropped steadily during the last quarter of the century. When two or more lines competed for the same traffic, railroads often offered lower rates

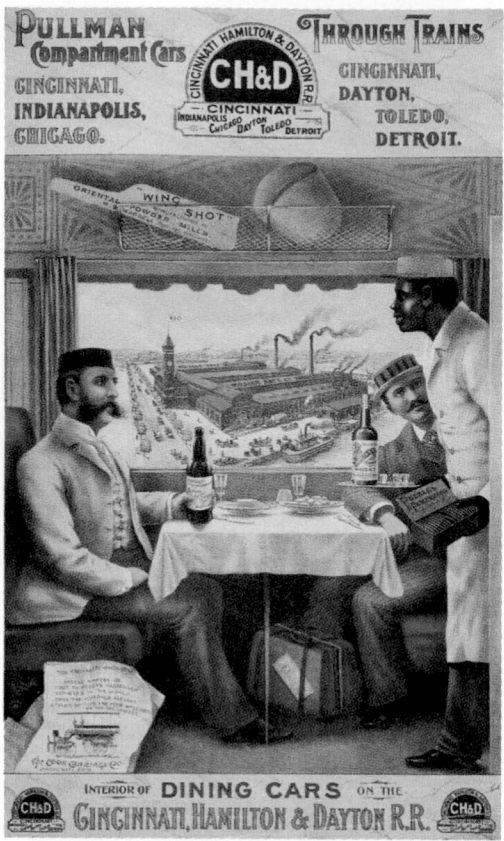

This depiction emphasizes the luxury, comfort, and attentive service (note the smiling black attendant who offers the diners cigars and drinks) available in a Pullman dining car. Through the window a large factory is visible. The image as a whole suggests the pride many Americans felt in industrial development and their realization of the importance of railroads to economic progress. (The Granger Collection, New York)

than their rivals or offered secret rebates (cheaper fares in exchange for all of a company's business). Rate wars helped customers, but they could plunge a railroad into bankruptcy. Instability plagued the railroad industry even as it expanded.

In the 1870s, railroad leaders sought stability through eliminating ruinous competition. As George Perkins of the Chicago, Burlington, and Quincy Railroad explained, "The struggle for existence and the survival of the fittest is a pretty theory, but it is also a law of nature that even the fittest must live." Railroad leaders established "pools," informal agreements that set uniform rates or divided up the traffic. Yet pools never completely succeeded. Too often, individual compa-

nies disregarded their agreements, especially when the business cycle took a downturn.

Railroad leaders often tried to control costs and counter the late-nineteenth-century pattern of falling prices by slashing their workers' wages. Owners justified this strategy by reasoning that they had taken all the business risks. As a result, railroads faced powerful worker unrest (described later in this chapter).

The huge scale and complexity of the railroads required new management techniques. In 1854, the directors of the Erie Railroad hired engineer and inventor Daniel McCallum to devise a system to make railroad managers and their employees more accountable. In his report, McCallum highlighted the differences between large and small organizations. In a small organization, one could pay personal attention to all the details of operation. But, McCallum argued, "any system that might be applicable to the business and extent of a short road would be found entirely inadequate to the wants of a long one."

McCallum's system, emphasizing division of responsibilities and a regular flow of information, attracted widespread interest, and railroads became pioneers in rationalized administrative practices and management techniques. Their procedures became models for other businesses in decision making, scheduling, and engineering. The steel industry emulated the practices of the railroads that had fostered their development. Other large-scale businesses also adopted the new procedures that effectively distributed responsibilities and separated management from operations. Because they faced similar economic conditions, big businesses also emulated the behavior of the railroads—their competitiveness, their attempts to underprice one another, their eventual interest in merger, and their tendency to cut workers' wages.

Growth in Other Industries

By the last quarter of the century, the textile, metal, and machinery industries equaled the railroads in size. In 1870, the typical iron and steel firm employed under 100 workers. Thirty years later, the average work force was four times as large. By 1900, more than 1,000 American factories had giant labor forces ranging between 500 and 1,000.

Almost 450 others employed more than 1,000 workers. Big business had come of age.

Business expansion was accomplished in one of two ways (or a combination of both). Some owners like steel magnate Andrew Carnegie integrated their businesses vertically. Vertical integration meant adding operations either before or after the production process. Even though he had introduced the most up-to-date innovations in his steel mills, Carnegie realized he needed his own sources of pig iron, coal, and coke. This was "backward" integration, away from the consumer, in order to avoid dependence on suppliers. When Carnegie acquired steamships and railroads to transport his finished products, he was integrating "forward," toward the consumer. Companies that integrated vertically frequently achieved economies of scale through more efficient management techniques.

Other companies copied the railroads and integrated horizontally by combining similar businesses. They did not intend to control the various stages of production, as was the case with vertical integration, but rather to gain a monopoly of the market in order to eliminate competition and to stabilize prices. Horizontal integration sometimes, though not always, brought economies and thus greater profits. The control over prices that monopoly provided did boost earnings.

John D. Rockefeller used the strategy of horizontal integration to gain control of the oil market. By a combination of astute and ruthless techniques, Rockefeller bought or drove out competitors of his Standard Oil of New Jersey. Although the company never achieved a complete monopoly, by 1898, it was refining 84 percent of the nation's oil. Rockefeller reflected, "The day of individual competition [in the oil business] ... is past and gone."

Rockefeller accurately characterized the new economic conditions. As giant businesses competed intensely, often cutting wages and prices, they absorbed or eliminated smaller and weaker producers. Business ownership became increasingly concentrated. In 1870, some 808 American iron and steel firms competed in the marketplace. By 1900, the number had dwindled to fewer than 70.

Like the railroads, many big businesses chose to incorporate. Although corporations were not new, most manufacturing firms were unincorporated in 1860. By 1900, corporations turned out two-thirds of the country's industrial goods.

Business gained many advantages by incorporating. Through the sale of stock, they could raise funds for their large-scale operations. The principle of limited liability protected investors, whereas the corporation's legal identity ensured its survival after the death of original and subsequent shareholders. Longevity suggested a measure of stability that heightened the attractiveness of a corporation as an investment.

The Erratic Economic Cycle

The transformation of the economy was neither smooth nor steady. Rockefeller, describing his years in the oil business as "hazardous," confessed that he did not know "how we came through them."

Two depressions, one from 1873 to 1879 and the other from 1893 to 1897, surpassed the severity of economic downturns before the Civil War. Collapsing land values, unsound banking practices, and changes in the supply of money had caused antebellum depressions. The depressions of the late nineteenth century, when the economy was larger and more interdependent, were industrial, intense, and accompanied by widespread unemployment, a phenomenon new to American life.

During expansionary years, manufacturers flooded markets with goods. The pattern of falling prices that characterized the postwar period and fierce competition between producers combined to encourage overproduction. When the market was finally saturated, sales and profits declined and the economy spiraled downward. Owners slowed production and laid off workers. Industrial workers, now an increasing percentage of the American work force, depended solely on wages for their livelihood. As they economized and bought less food, farm prices also plummeted. Farmers, like wage workers, cut back on purchases. Business and trade stagnated, and the railroads were finally affected. Eventually, the cycle bottomed out, but in the meantime, millions of workers lost employment, thousands of businesses went bankrupt, and many Americans suffered deprivation and hardship.

This 1896 picture of Chicago shows how the appearance of cities changed when structural steel became available for skyscrapers. Once the national rail system was complete, steel makers turned to new urban markets to maintain profits. (Chicago Historical Society)

Work in the industrial city was the prime attraction. Although urban jobs were often dirty, dangerous, and exhausting, so was farmwork. Moreover, by 1890, manufacturing workers were earning hundreds of dollars more a year than farm laborers. Some industrial workers, like miners in the Far West, earned even more. Part of the difference between rural and urban wages was eaten up by the higher cost of living in the city, but not all of it.

An intangible but important lure was the glitter of city life. Rural life was often monotonous and drab. The young man who saw Kansas City as a "gilded metropolis" filled with "marvels," a veritable "round of joy," found the excitement of urban life, its culture, its amusements dazzling. Shops, theaters, restaurants, churches, department stores, newspapers, ball games, and the urban throng all amazed young men and women who had grown up on farms and in small towns.

Novelists like Theodore Dreiser and Stephen Crane captured both the fascination and the dangers of city life. Writing in a style called *literary realism,* they examined social problems and cast their characters in carefully depicted local settings. Dreiser's novel *Sister Carrie* (1900) follows a typical country girl as she comes to Chicago. Carrie dreams of sharing Chicago's amusements and fantasizes a life of wealth, excitement, and ease. She finds, however, that the city's luxuries and pleasures are far beyond the reach of a mere factory employee. Only by taking lovers can she grasp the city's pleasures. Many readers were shocked that Dreiser never punished Carrie for her "sins."

In *Maggie: A Girl of the Streets* (1893), Stephen Crane's heroine did meet punishment at the story's end. As a young girl, Maggie retains her purity in the heart of New York's most appalling slums. Eventually, the city's pleasures lead to a loss of innocence. Maggie turns in despair to prostitution, and the reader is left at the novel's conclusion to guess whether Maggie has been murdered or commits suicide. Fascinating and yet repelling, the industrial city captured the imagination of American writers and American culture alike.

Southern blacks, often single and young, also fed the migratory stream into the cities. In the West and the North, blacks constituted only a tiny part of the population: 3 percent in Denver in the 1880s and 1890s, 2 percent in Boston. In southern cities, however, they were more numerous. About 44 percent of Atlanta's residents in the late nineteenth century were black, 38 percent of Nashville's. No matter where they were, however, the city offered them few rewards, little glamour, and many dangers.

The New Immigration, 1880–1900

In 1870, a "brokenhearted" Annie Sproul stole away from her parents' home in Londonderry, Ireland, to seek a new future in Philadelphia. She took all the money in the house, "leaving not the price of a loaf" behind. Probably the disgrace of a love affair prompted Annie's desperate flight, but the young woman was one of many who left their homelands in the nineteenth century in the hope of making a fortune in the New World. In the 40 years before the Civil War, 5 million immigrants poured into the United States; from 1860 to 1900, that volume almost tripled. Three-quarters of the newcomers stayed in the Northeast, and many of the rest settled in cities across the nation, where they soon outnumbered native-born whites. The American mosaic of differing cultures and races assumed new complexities.

As the flow of immigration increased, the national origin of immigrants shifted. Until 1880, three-quarters of the immigrants, often called the "old immigrants," hailed from the British Isles, Germany, and Scandinavia. Irish and Germans were the largest groups. Then the pattern slowly changed in ways that increased the ethnic and religious heterogeneity of the American people and changed the composition of the laboring class. By 1890, old immigrants composed only 60 percent of the total number of newcomers, and the "new immigrants" from southern and eastern Europe (Italy, Poland, Russia, Austria-Hungary, Greece, Turkey, and Syria) made up most of the rest. Italian Catholics and eastern European Jews were the most numerous, followed by Slavs.

Cheaper, faster, and better transportation facilitated the great tide of migration. Trains reached far into eastern and southern Europe. On transatlantic vessels, even steerage passengers could now expect a bed with blankets, cooked meals, and a communal washroom. But dissatisfaction with life at home was basic to the decision to migrate. Overpopulation, famine, and disease drove people to leave. "We could have eaten each other had we stayed," explained one Italian immigrant.

Efforts to modernize European economies also stimulated immigration. New agricultural techniques led landlords to consolidate their land, evicting longtime tenants. Younger European farmers traveled in increasingly wide circles searching for work. Some emigrated to cities elsewhere in Europe. Many set out for Canada or South America. The largest share went to the United States. Similarly, artisans and craftsmen whose skills were made obsolete by the introduction of machinery pulled up stakes and headed for the United States and other destinations. Government policies pushed others to leave. In eastern Europe, especially in Russia, the official persecution of

Immigration to the United States, 1870–1920

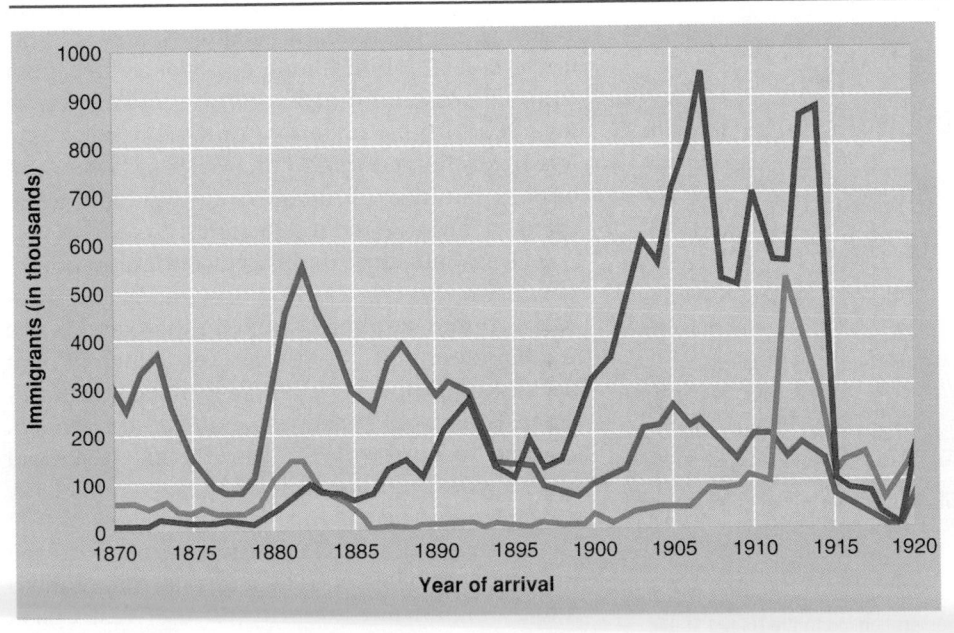

Immigrants (in thousands)

Year of arrival

—— Northern and western Europe   —— Southern and eastern Europe   —— Asia, Africa, and the Americas

This chart shows the changing pattern of immigration between 1870 and 1920. You can see the growing importance of immigration from southern and eastern Europe as well as a period of intensive immigration from China. Not only did newcomers make the United States more ethnically diverse, but more religiously diverse as well. The new European immigration contained large numbers of Jews and Roman Catholics. Source: U.S. Bureau of the Census.

minorities and the expansion of the draft for the czar's army led millions of Jewish families and others to emigrate.

Opportunity in the "golden land" of America also lured thousands to American shores. State commissioners of immigration and American railroad and steamship companies, eager for workers and customers, wooed potential immigrants. Friends and relatives wrote letters describing favorable living and working conditions and promising to help newcomers find work. American cities were great places for "blast frnises and Rolen milles," explained one unskilled worker." Often passage money or pictures of friends in alluringly fashionable clothes were slipped between the pages. The phenomenon of immigrants being recruited through the reports and efforts of their predecessors has come to be known as "chain migration."

Like rural and small-town Americans, Europeans came primarily to work. Most were young, single men, who, in contrast to pre–Civil War immigrants, had few skills. Jews, however, came most often in family groups, and women predominated among the Irish. When times were good and American industry needed large numbers of unskilled laborers, migration was heavy. When times were bad and letters warned that "work is dull all over … no work to be got except by chance or influence," numbers fell off. Immigrants hoped to earn enough money in America to realize their ambitions at home. A surprising number, perhaps as many as a third, eventually returned to their native lands.

Although the greatest influx of Mexicans would come in the twentieth century, Mexican laborers added to the stream of foreigners migrating to the United States. Like many European countries, Mexico was in the throes of modernization. Overpopulation and new land policies uprooted many inhabitants, including Gonzalo Plancarte. In the 1890s, Gonzalo and his father supported themselves by raising cattle in central Mexico. When the owner of the hacienda determined to turn his land over to producing goods for export, he ended the family's grazing privileges. The two men took to the road with their herd, but failed to find sufficient grazing for their animals. Eventually, they sold the cattle, and after his father died, a desperately poor Gonzalo headed north. In 1895, the construction of a railroad from the Texas border 900 miles into Mexico facilitated migration. Many of these newcomers found work in the Southwest and West, often on the railroads and in mines.

Overpopulation, depressed conditions, unemployment, and crop failures brought Asians, most of them from southern China, to the "Land of the Golden Mountains." "We were very much in debt because of the local warfare," explained one immigrant. "We planted each year, but we were robbed. We had to borrow. When news about the Gold Rush in California was spread by the shippers, my father decided to take the big chance."

Although only 264,000 Chinese came to the United States between 1860 and 1900, they constituted a significant minority on the West Coast. Most were unskilled male contract laborers who promised to work for a number of years and then

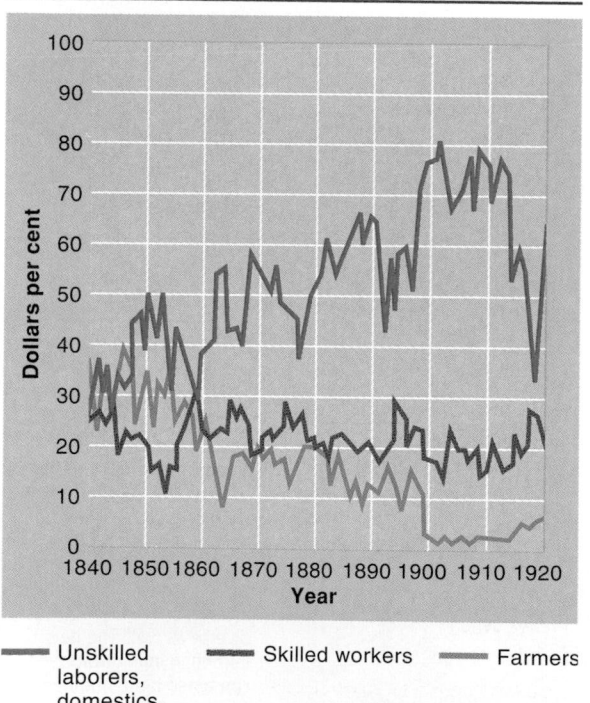

Working-Class Immigration, 1840–1920

Unskilled laborers, domestics, and farmhands — Skilled workers — Farmers

The large number of unskilled workers coming to the United States were responding to the need for unskilled labor during the second industrial revolution. Source: U.S. Bureau of the Census.

Although not one of the largest immigrant groups in the late nineteenth century, Chinese made up a sizable proportion of foreign workers in California. The overwhelming male nature of this immigration is apparent in this photograph. (Asian American Studies Library, University of Calilfornia, Berkeley)

return to their wives and families at home. They performed some of the hardest, dirtiest, and least desirable jobs in the West, including mining, railroad and levee construction, factory and laundry work. To serve these men, often away from their wives for years, contractors brought in Chinese women to serve as prostitutes. Virtually enslaved, some of these women were able to pay off the costs of their passage or escape from brothel life. But a Cantonese saying captured the sexual imbalance in the Chinese life: "pathetic the lonely bachelors stranded in a foreign land."

The Industrial City, 1880–1900

The late-nineteenth-century industrial city had new physical and social arrangements that attracted widespread comment. James Bryce, a Scottish visitor, noted that urban "monotony haunts one like a nightmare." Slums, which were not new, seemed disturbing because so many people lived in them. Yet these same cities also boasted of grand mansions, handsome business and industrial buildings, grandiose civic monuments, and acres of substantial middle-class homes.

By the last quarter of the nineteenth century, the jumbled arrangements of the antebellum walking city, whose size and configuration had been limited by the necessity of walking to work, disappeared. Where once substantial houses, businesses, and small artisan dwellings had stood side by side, central business districts emerged. Here were banks, shops, theaters, professional firms, and businesses. Few people lived downtown, although many worked or shopped there. Surrounding the business center were areas of light manufacturing and wholesale activity with housing for workers. Beyond these working-class neighborhoods stretched middle-class residential areas. Then came the suburbs, with "pure air, peacefulness, quietude, and natural scenery." Scattered throughout the city were pockets of industrial activity surrounded by crowded working-class housing.

This new pattern, with the poorest city residents clustered near the center, is familiar today. However, it reversed the early nineteenth-century urban form, when much of the most desirable housing was in the heart of the city. New living arrangements were also more segregated by race and class than those in the preindustrial walking city. Homogeneous social and economic neighborhoods emerged, and it became more unusual than before for a poor, working-class family to live near a middle- or upper-class family.

The changing urban geography reflected the dense development of the central business district, the rise of heavy industry, and improvements in transportation. Better transportation increasingly allowed middle- and upper-class residents to live away from their work and from grimy industrial districts.

The urban transportation revolution started modestly in the 1820s and 1830s with the horse-drawn omnibus. This slow-moving vehicle accommodated only 10 to 12 passengers. Its expensive fares obliged most people to live within walking distance of their work. In the 1850s, many cities introduced horse railways. Pulling cars over rails with as many as 25 passengers, horses could cover 5 to 6 miles an hour. The horse railways, which radiated from city centers like the spokes of a wheel, allowed the city to expand outward about 4 miles. The cost of a fare limited ridership to the middle and upper classes. The introduction of cable cars, trolley cars, and subways after 1880 further extended city boundaries and broadened residential choices for the middle class.

Neighborhoods and Neighborhood Life

Working-class neighborhoods clustered near the center of most industrial cities. Here lived newcomers from the American countryside and, because most immigrants settled in cities, crowds of foreigners as well.

Ethnic groups frequently chose to gather in particular neighborhoods, often located near industries requiring their labor. In Detroit in 1880, for example, 37 percent of the city's native-born families lived in one area, whereas 40 percent of the Irish inhabited the "Irish West Side." Over half the Germans and almost three-quarters of the Poles settled on the city's east side. Although such neighborhoods often had an ethnic flavor, with small specialty shops and foreign-language signs, they were not ethnic ghettos. Immigrants and native-born Americans often lived in the same neighborhoods, on the same streets, and even in the same houses. Toward the end of the century, when ethnic enclaves emerged, they were just that—enclaves within a neighborhood. Italians might live on one block, but Jews on the next.

Working-class neighborhoods were often what would be called slums today. They were crowded and unsanitary and had inadequate public services. Many workers lived in houses once occupied by middle- and upper-class residents, now divided and subdivided to accommodate more people than the original builders had intended. Others crowded into tenements, specially constructed to house as many families as possible. Outdoor privies, often shared by several families, were the rule. Water came from outdoor hydrants, and women had to carry it inside for cooking, washing, and cleaning. When there were indoor fixtures, they frequently emptied waste directly into unpaved alleys and courts served by inadequate sewage systems or none at all. Piles of garbage and waste stank in the

Downtown New York City in 1890 hosted a mixture of horse-drawn vehicles and the new "horseless carriages." (Brown Brothers)

summer and froze in the winter. Even when people kept their own living quarters clean, their outside environment was unsanitary and unhealthy. It was no surprise that urban death rates were so high. Only at the turn of the century did the public health movement, particularly the efforts to treat water supplies with germ-killing chemicals, begin to ameliorate these living conditions.

Not every working-class family lived in abject circumstances. Skilled workers might rent comfortable quarters, and a few even owned their own homes. A study of working-class families in Massachusetts found the family of one skilled worker living "in a tenement of five rooms in a pleasant and healthy locality, with good surroundings. The apartments are well furnished and [the] parlor carpeted." The family even had a sewing machine. But the unskilled and semiskilled workers were not so fortunate. The Massachusetts survey describes the family of an unskilled ironworker crammed into a tenement of four rooms,

> in an overcrowded block, to which belong only two privies for about fifty people. When this place was visited the vault had overflowed in the yard and the sink-water was also running in the same place, and created a stench that was really frightful.... The house inside, was badly furnished and dirty, and a disgrace to Worcester.

Drab as their neighborhoods usually were, working families created a community life that helped to alleviate some of the dreariness of their physical surroundings. The expense of moving around the city helped encourage a neighborhood and family focus. Long hours spent at work meant that precious free time was apt to be spent close to home.

A wide range of institutions and associations came to life in urban neighborhoods. Frequently, they were based on religious and ethnic ties. They made residents feel at home in the city yet at the same time often separated them from native-born Americans and other ethnic groups. Irish associational life, for example, focused around the Roman Catholic parish church, its Irish priest, and its many religious services, clubs and group activities. Catholicism had fused with nationalism in an Ireland dominated by Protestant English landlords. In the new country, it provided comfort and a shared

For the middle class, commuting to work from the suburbs became part of the daily routine. (Brown Brothers)

sense of identity. Irish nationalist organizations, ward politics, and Irish saloons gave men opportunities to meet, socialize, drink, and talk politics. Jews gathered in their synagogues, Hebrew schools, and Hebrew- and Yiddish-speaking literary groups. Germans had their family saloons and educational and singing societies. Although such activities may have slowed assimilation into American society and discouraged intergroup contact, they provided companionship, spiritual consolation, social life, and a bridge between life in the "old country" and life in America. Working-class men and women were far from mere victims of their environment. They found the energy, squeezed out the time, and even saved the money to support networks of social ties and associations.

Black Americans faced the most wretched living conditions of any group in the city. In the North, they often lived in segregated black neighborhoods. In southern cities, they gathered in back alleys and small streets. Many could afford only rented rooms.

However, a rich religious and associational life tempered the suffering. Black churches enjoyed phenomenal growth. Black members of mainline Protestant denominations separated from their white counterparts in order to establish autonomy and self-respect. The African Methodist Episcopal Church, with a membership of 20,000 in 1856, founded churches in every city and sizable town, and by 1900, claimed more than 400,000 members. Black worship continued to express the emotional exuberance that had characterized slave religion.

This photograph of a middle-class house in River Forest, Illinois, suggests the comfort available to those who could afford it and the ways in which suburban life shielded them from the squalor and ugliness of industrial life. (Culver Pictures)

Energetic preaching and expressive music helped make church-going a fulfilling spiritual experience. Often associated with churches were mutual-aid and benevolent societies that helped needy members of the community. Outreach activities also included support for black missionaries in Africa.

Some urban blacks in the late nineteenth century rose into the middle class. In spite of the heavy odds against them, they created the nucleus of professional and artistic life. Henry Ossawa Tanner gained international recognition as a painter and sculptor, black educators such as George Washington Williams wrote some of the first African American histories, and novelists such as Charles W. Chesnutt, William Wells Brown, and Paul Laurence Dunbar produced noteworthy novels and short stories.

Beyond working-class neighborhoods and pockets of black housing lay streets of middle-class houses. Here lived the urban lower middle class: clerks, shopkeepers, bookkeepers, salesmen, and small tradesmen. Their salaries allowed them to buy or rent houses with some privacy and comfort. Separate spaces for cooking and laundry work kept hot and often odorous housekeeping tasks away from other living areas. Many houses boasted up-to-date gas lighting and bathrooms. Outside, the neighborhoods were cleaner and more attractive than in the inner city. Residents could pay for garbage collection, gaslights, and other improvements.

Streetcar Suburbs

On the fringes of the city were houses for the substantial middle class and the rich, who made their money in business, commerce, and the professions or inherited family fortunes. Public transportation sped them downtown to their offices and then home. For example, Robert Work, a modestly successful cap and hat merchant, moved his family to a $5,500 house in West Philadelphia in 1865 and commuted more than 4 miles to work.

The 1880 census revealed his family's comfortable life-style. The household contained two servants, two boarders, his wife, and their eldest son, who was still in school. The Works' house had running hot and cold water, indoor bathrooms, central heating, and other modern conveniences of the age. Elaborately carved furniture, rugs, draperies, and lace curtains probably graced the downstairs, where the family entertained and gathered for meals. Upstairs, comfortable bedrooms provided a maximum of privacy for family members. The live-in servants, who did most of the housework, shared little of this space or privacy, however. They were restricted to the kitchen, the pantry, and bedrooms in the attic.

The Social Geography of the Cities

In industrial cities of this era, people were sorted by class, occupation, and race. The physical distances between upper- and middle-class neighborhoods and working-class neighborhoods meant that city dwellers often had little firsthand knowledge of people different from themselves. Ignorance led to distorted views and social disapproval. Middle-class newspapers unsympathetically described laboring men as "loafing" and criticized the "crowds of idlers, who, day and night, infect Main Street." Yet those "idlers" were often men who could not find work. The comments of a working-class woman to her temperance visitors in 1874 suggest the critical view from the bottom of society up: "When the rich stopped drinking, it would be time to speak to the poor about it."

The Life of the Middle Class

The sharp comments made by different classes of Americans suggest the economic polarization and social conflict that late-nineteenth-century industrialization spawned. Middle-class Americans found much to value in the new age: job and education opportunities, material comforts, and leisure time. Between 1865 and 1890, the average middle-class income had risen about 30 percent. Although the cost of living rose even faster than income, the difference was met by more family members' holding jobs and by taking in lodgers. By 1900, fully 36 percent of urban families owned their homes.

The expansion of American industry raised the living standard for increasing numbers of Americans, who were better able to purchase consumer products manufactured, packaged, and promoted in an explosion of technological inventions and shrewd marketing techniques. Among the still familiar products and brands invented or mass-produced for the first time in the 1890s were Del Monte canned fruits and vegetables, National Biscuit Company (Nabisco) crackers, Van Camp's pork and beans, Wesson oil, Lipton tea, Wrigley's Juicy Fruit chewing gum, Cracker Jacks, Tootsie Rolls, the Hershey bar, shredded wheat, Aunt Jemima pancake mix, Jell-O, Campbell's soup, Fig Newtons, Canada Dry ginger ale, Coca-Cola, Pepsi-Cola, and Michelob beer. Cooked chopped meat put between two pieces of bread was first sold (for 7 cents) and called a "hamburger" in 1899.

More time for recreation like bicycling or watching professional baseball and greater access to consumer goods signaled the power of industrialism to transform the lives of middle-class Americans. Once favored with greater buying power, middle-class Americans sought to organize efficient ways of producing, purchasing, and consuming the newfound wealth. American women, agents of the rise in consumer spending, were themselves often on display as stylish objects of leisure and ostentatious wealth.

Shopping for home furnishings, clothes, and other items became an integral part of many middle-class women's lives. A plentiful supply of immigrant servant girls relieved urban middle-class wives of many housekeeping chores, and smaller families lessened the burdens of motherhood. The realistic novelist William Dean Howells

This 1869 advertisement for a home washing machine shows an elegantly attired matron supervising her maids, who do the laundry in a well-equipped kitchen that includes a hot-water heater. Laundry was one of the most hated household chores, and even with this machine, wet clothes had to be put through a wringer. It was not until the 1930s that washers had the capacity to spin clothes dry. The arduous nature of laundering clothes accounted for the proliferation of laundries, often operated by the Chinese, in the nineteenth century. Although only a minority could afford washing machines in 1869, by 1941, a majority of American households owned a power-driven washer. (The Granger Collection, New York)

men's opposition to the new woman put limits on her emerging freedom.

Male Mobility and the Success Ethic

As middle-class women's lives were changing, so were men's. As the postwar economy expanded and the structure of American business changed, many new job opportunities opened up for middle-class men. The growing complexity of census classifications attests to some of them. Where once the census taker had noted only the occupation of "clerk," now were listed "accountant," "salesman," and "shipping clerk." As the lower ranks of the white-collar world became more specialized, the number of middle-class jobs increased.

To prepare for these new careers, Americans required more education. The number of public high schools in the United States increased from 160 in 1870 to 6,000 in 1900. By 1900, a majority of states and territories had compulsory school attendance laws.

Higher education also expanded in this period. The number of students in colleges and universities nearly doubled, from 53,000 in 1870 to 101,000 in 1900. Charles Eliot, president of Harvard from 1869 to 1909, led that university through a period of dynamic growth, introducing reforms such as higher faculty salaries and sabbatical leaves as well as the elective system of course selection for students. Harvard's growth reflected the rise of the university to a new stature in American life. As the land-grant state universities (made possible by the Morrill Act of 1862) continued to expand, generous gifts from wealthy businessmen helped found leading research universities such as Stanford, Johns Hopkins, and the University of Chicago.

These developments led to greater specialization and professionalism in education, medicine, law, and business. Before the Civil War, a Swedish pioneer in Wisconsin described a young mason who "laid aside the trowel, got himself some medical books, and assumed the title of doctor." But by the 1890s, with government licensing and the rise of professional schools, the word *career* began to take on its modern meaning. No longer were tradesman likely to read up on medicine and

become doctors. In this period, organizations like the American Medical Association and the American Bar Association were regulating and professionalizing membership. The number of law schools doubled in the last quarter of the century, and 86 new medical schools were founded in the same period. Dental schools increased from 9 to 56 between 1875 and 1900.

The need for lawyers, bankers, architects, and insurance agents to serve business and industry expanded career opportunities. Between 1870 to 1900, the number of engineers, chemists, metallurgists, and architects grew rapidly. As large companies formed and became bureaucratized, business required many more managerial positions. As the public sector expanded, new careers in social services and government opened up as well. Young professional experts with graduate training in the social sciences filled many of them. The professional disciplines of history, economics, sociology, psychology, and political science all date from the last 20 years of the nineteenth century.

The social ethic of the age stressed that economic rewards were available to anyone who fervently sought them. Many people argued that unlike Europe, where family background and social class determined social rank, in America, few barriers held back those of good character and diligent work habits. Anyone doubting this opportunity needed only to be reminded of the rise of two giants of industry. John D. Rockefeller had worked for a neighboring farmer and raised turkeys as a boy. Andrew Carnegie's mother was a washerwoman, and his father had worked himself to death in the mills within five years of reaching the United States. Both had risen spectacularly through their own efforts. Writers, lecturers, clergymen, and politicians zealously propagated the rags-to-riches tradition of upward mobility. Self-help manuals that outlined the steps to success for self-made men became widely available.

The best-known popularizer of the myth of the self-made man was Horatio Alger, Jr. Millions of boys read his 119 novels, with titles like *Luck and Pluck, Strive and Succeed,* and *Bound to Rise.* In a typical Alger novel, *Ragged Dick,* the story opens with the hero leading the low life of a shoeshine boy in the streets. Dressed in rags, he sleeps in packing crates and unwisely spends what little money he has on tobacco, liquor, gambling, and the theater. A chance opportunity to foil an attempt to cheat a gentleman results in the reward of a new suit of clothes for Dick. Before long, Dick aspires to become an office boy, "learn the business and grow up 'spectable." As he begins the process of becoming respectable, good fortune intervenes again. Dick is able to rescue a child who tumbles into the icy waters of the harbor. Her father completes the hero's transformation from Ragged Dick to Richard Hunter, Esq., by offering him a job as a clerk in his counting house. Although moralists pointed to virtuous habits as crucial in Alger's heroes, success often depended as much on luck as on pluck.

Unlimited and equal opportunity for upward advancement in America has never been as easy as the "bootstraps" ethic maintains. But the persistence of the success myth owes something to the fact that many Americans, particularly those who began well, did rise rapidly. Native-born, middle-class whites tended to have the skills, resources, and connections that opened up the most desirable jobs. Financier Jay Gould overstated the case in maintaining that "nearly every one that occupies a prominent position has come up from the ranks." In fact, the typical big businessman was a white, Anglo-Saxon Protestant from a middle- or upper-class family whose father was most likely in business, banking, or commerce.

Industrial Work and the Laboring Class

David Lawlor, an Irish immigrant who came to the United States in 1872, might have agreed with Jay Gould on the opportunities for mobility. As a child, he worked in the Fall River textile mills and read Horatio Alger in his free time. Like Alger's heroes, he went to night school and rose in the business world, eventually becoming an advertising executive.

But Lawlor's success was exceptional. Most working-class Americans labored long hours on dangerous factory floors, in cramped sweatshops, or in steamy basement kitchens for meager wages. As industrialization transformed the nature of work and the composition of the work force, tradi-

tional opportunities for mobility and even for a secure livelihood seemed to slip away from the grasp of many working-class Americans.

The Impact of Ethnic Diversity

Immigrants made up a sizable portion of the urban working class in the late nineteenth century. They formed 20 percent of the labor force and over 40 percent of laborers in the manufacturing and extractive industries. In cities, where they tended to settle, they accounted for more than half the working-class population.

The fact that more than half the urban industrial class was foreign and unskilled and often had only a limited command of English influenced industrial work, urban life, labor protest, and local politics. Eager for the unskilled positions rapidly being created as mechanization and mass production took hold, immigrants often had little in common with native-born workers or even with one another. Because of immigration, American working-class society was a mosaic of nationalities, cultures, religions, and interests, a patchwork where colors clashed as often as they complemented one another.

The ethnic diversity of the industrial work force helps explain its occupational patterns. Although every city offered somewhat different employment opportunities, generally occupation was related to ethnic background and experience.

At the top of the working-class hierarchy, native-born Protestant whites held a disproportionate share of well-paying skilled jobs. They were the aristocrats of the working class. Their jobs demanded expertise and training, as had been true of skilled industrial workers in the pre–Civil War period. But their occupations bore the mark of late-nineteenth-century industrialism. They were machinists, iron puddlers and rollers, engineers, foremen, conductors, carpenters, plumbers, mechanics, and printers.

Beneath native-born whites, skilled northern European immigrants filled most of the positions in the middle ranks of the occupational structure. The Germans, who arrived with training as tailors, bakers, brewers, and shoemakers, moved into similar jobs in this country, and Cornish and Irish miners secured skilled jobs in western mines. The

Status of Young People (12–20) by Ethnicity in Detroit in 1900

Ethnic Group	In School (%)	Working (%)	At Home (%)
Native white American[a]	54.7	40.4	4.9
	56.1	16.9	27.0
Black	50.0	50.0	0.0
	45.5	40.9	13.6
Irish	43.2	48.6	8.1
	43.2	39.8	17.0
German	30.5	59.5	10.0
	29.2	45.1	25.8
Polish	26.4	63.5	10.1
	26.15	6.2	17.6
Russian	53.3	30.0	16.7
	17.4	60.9	21.7

This table reveals the complex interaction of culture, ethnicity, economic circumstances, and gender.

[a]Born in the United States of two American-born parents.

Note: Percentage of boys is indicated in blue; percentage of girls is indicated in red.

Source: Olivier Zunz, *The Changing Face of Inequality* (1982).

market was an essential survival strategy for many working-class Americans. In 1880, one-fifth of the nation's children between the ages of 10 and 14 held jobs.

Child labor was closely linked to a father's income, which in turn depended on skill, ethnic background, and occupation. Immigrant families more frequently sent their young children out to work (and also had more children) than native-born families. Middle-class reformers sentimentalized childhood and thus disapproved of parents who put their children to work. As one investigator of working-class life reported, "Father never attended school, and thinks his children will have sufficient schooling before they reach their tenth year, thinks no advantage will be gained from longer attendance at school, so children will be put to work as soon as able." Reformers believed that such fathers condemned their children to future poverty by taking them out of school. Actually, sending children to work was a means of coping with the immediate threat of poverty, of financing the education of one of the children, or even of ensuring that children stayed near their family.

Women at Work

Many more young people over 14 were working for wages than was the case for children. Half of all Philadelphia's students had quit school by that age. Daughters as well as sons were expected to take positions, although young women from immigrant families were more likely to work than young American women. As *Arthur's Home Magazine* for women pointed out, a girl's earnings would help "to relieve her hard-working father of the burden of her support, to supply home with comforts and refinements, to educate a younger brother." By 1900, nearly 20 percent of American women were in the labor force.

Employed women earned far less than men. An experienced female factory worker might be paid between $5 and $6 a week, whereas an unskilled male laborer could make about $8. Discrimination, present from women's earliest days in the work force, persisted. Still, factory jobs were desirable because they often paid better than other kinds of work open to women.

Employment opportunities for women were narrow, and ethnic taboos and cultural traditions helped shape choices. About a quarter of working women secured factory jobs. Italian and Jewish women (whose cultural backgrounds virtually forbade their going into domestic service) clustered in the garment industry, and Poles and Slavs went into textiles, food processing, and meatpacking. In some industries, like textiles, women composed an important segment of the work force. But about 40 percent of them, especially those from Irish, Scandinavian, or black families, took jobs as maids, cooks, laundresses, and nurses.

Domestic service was arduous, with few machines to lighten the labor. A Minneapolis housemaid described an exhausting routine. "I used to get up at four o'clock every morning and work till ten P.M. every day of the week. Mondays and Tuesdays, when the washing and ironing was to be done, I used to get up at two o'clock and wash or iron until breakfast time." Nor could domestics count on much sympathy from their employers. "Do not think it necessary to give a hired girl as good a room as that used by members of the family," said one lady of the house. "She should sleep near the kitchen and not go up the front stairs or through the front hall to reach her room."

A servant received room and board plus $2 to $5 a week. The fact that so many women took domestic work despite the job's disadvantages speaks clearly of their limited opportunities.

The dismal situation facing working women drove some, like Rose Haggerty, into prostitution. Burdened with a widowed and sickly mother and four young brothers and sisters, Rose was only 14 when she started work at a New York paper bag factory. She earned $10 a month, but $6 went for rent. Her fortunes improved when a friend helped her buy a sewing machine. Rose then sewed shirts at home, often working as long as 14 hours a day, to support her family. Suddenly, the piecework rate for shirts was slashed in half. In desperation, Rose contemplated suicide. But when a sailor offered her money for spending the night with him, she realized she had an alternative. Prostitution meant food, rent, and heat for her family. "Let God Almighty judge who's to blame most," the 20-year-old Rose reflected, "I that was driven, or them that drove me to the pass I'm in."

Prostitution appears to have increased in the late nineteenth century, although there is no way of knowing the actual numbers of women involved. Probably most single women accepted the respectable jobs open to them. They tolerated discrimination and low wages because their families depended on their contributions. They also

These domestics, in their best clothes, pose with the symbol of their work in what appears to be the parlor. Although there is no way to ascertain the background of these young women, a majority of domestic servants were Irish or Irish American. Domestic work was often exhausting and provided little privacy or free time, but many women were attracted by the opportunity to live in a middle-class home and to have regular meals. In addition, domestic work often paid better than factory work. Still, some young women avoided service, explaining that, "It's freedom that we want when the day's work is done." (State Historical Society of Wisconsin, neg. #WHi (V22) 1387)

Congressional Hearings

Students of history can discover fascinating materials on nineteenth-century life by exploring the published records of the American political system. The *Congressional Globe,* the proceedings of the Senate and the House, privately published from 1833 to 1873, reveals the nature of congressional deliberations in an era when debate, such as that over the Compromise of 1850 in the Senate, was the focus of the national political process. After 1873, the government published these proceedings in the *Congressional Record.* The *Record* is not a literal transcription of debate, for members can edit their remarks, insert speeches, and add supporting materials. Still, it gives a good sense of the proceedings of both the Senate and the House.

Much of the serious work of government, past and present, takes place in congressional committees. One foreign observer called Congress "not so much a legislative assembly as a huge panel from which committees are selected." The committee system is almost as old as the constitutional system itself and is rooted in the Constitution's granting of the lawmaking power to Congress. From the start, Congress divided into assorted committees to gather information, enabling members to evaluate legislative proposals intelligently.

Two kinds of committees existed in the House and Senate. Standing committees had permanent responsibility for reviewing legislative proposals on a host of financial, judicial, foreign, and other affairs. By 1892, the Senate had 44 standing committees, and the House had 50. Select committees were temporary, often charged with investigating specific problems. In the late nineteenth century, congressional committees investigated such problems as Ku Klux Klan terrorism, the sweatshop system, tenement house conditions, and relations between labor and capital. In each case, extensive hearings were held.

Congressional hearings have become increasingly important sources of historical evidence in recent years. Hearings show the Senate and the House of Representatives in action as they seek to translate popular sentiment into law. But they also reveal public attitudes themselves as they record the voices of Americans testifying in committee halls. Because one function of legislative hearings is to enable diverse groups to express their frustrations and desires, they often contain the testimony of witnesses drawn from many different social and economic backgrounds. Included here is the partial testimony of a Massachusetts laborer who appeared before the Senate Committee on Education and Labor in 1883. Because working-class witnesses like this man usually left no other record of their experiences or thoughts, committee reports and hearings provide valuable insight into the lives and attitudes of ordinary people.

Hearings also reveal the attitudes and social values of committee members. Hence, caution is needed in the use of hearings. Witnesses often have vested interests and are frequently coached and cautious in what they communicate on the stand. Committee members often speak and explore questions for other reasons, usually political, than to illuminate issues.

Despite these limitations, committee hearings are rich sources of information. In this excerpt, what can you learn about the life of the witness testifying before the committee? In what way are the values of the committee members in conflict with those of the witness? Why is the chairman so harsh toward the witness? Is he entirely unsympathetic? Why do you think the questioner overemphasizes the relationship between moral beliefs and economic realities? What kind of social tensions does the passage reveal?

Have you observed any recent hearings of congressional investigating committees on television? Are moral behavior and hunger still topics of concern for Americans? How is the interaction between modern haves and have-nots similar to and different from those between this laborer and the committee members in 1883? Do ethical beliefs and economic realities still separate social classes?

Hearings on the Relations Between Labor and Capital

Q. You get a dollar a day, wages?—A. That is the average pay that men receive. The rents, especially in Somerville, are so high that it is almost impossible for the working men to live in a house.

Q. What rent do you pay?—A. For the last year I have been paying $10 a month, and most of the men out there have to pay about that amount for a house—$10 a month for rooms.

Q. For a full house, or for rooms only?—A. For rooms in a house.

Q. How many rooms?—A. Four or five.

Q. How much of your time have you been out of work, or idle, for the last full year, say?—A. I have not been out of work more than three weeks altogether, because I have been making a dollar or two peddling or doing something, when I was out of work, in the currying line.

Q. Making about the same that you made at your trade?—A. Well, I have made at my trade a little more than that, but that is the average.

Q. Are you a common drunkard?—A. No, sir.

Q. Do you smoke a great deal?—A. Well, yes, sir; I smoke as much as any man.

The CHAIRMAN. I want to know how much you have got together in the course of a year, and what you have spent your money for, so that folks can see whether you have had pay enough to get rich on.

The WITNESS. A good idea.

The CHAIRMAN. That is precisely the sort of idea that people ought to know. How much money do you think you have earned during this last year; has it averaged a dollar a day for three hundred days?

The WITNESS. I have averaged more than that; I have averaged $350 or $400. I will say, for the year.

Q. You pay $10 a month rent; that makes $120 a year?—A. Yes, sir.

The CHAIRMAN. I have asked you these questions in this abrupt way because I want to find out whether you have spent much for practices that might have been dispensed with. You say you smoke?

The WITNESS. Yes, sir.

Q. How much a week do you spend for that?—A. I get 20 cents worth of tobacco a week.

Q. That is $10.40 a year?—A. Yes, sir.

Q. And you say you are not a common drunkard?—A. No, sir.

Q. Do you imagine that you have spent as much more for any form of beer, or ale, or anything of that kind, that you could have got along without?—A. No, sir.

Q. How much do you think has gone in that way?—A. About $1 or $2.

Q. During the whole year?—A. Yes, sir.

Q. That would make $11.40 or $12.40—we will call it $12—gone for wickedness. Now, what else, besides your living, besides the support of your wife and children?—A. Well, I don't know as there is anything else.

Q. Can you not think of anything else that was wrong?—A. No, sir.

Q. Twelve dollars have gone for sin and iniquity; and $120 for rent; that makes $132?—A. Yes.

Q. How many children have you?—A. Two.

Q. Your family consists of yourself, your wife, and two children?—A. Yes.

Q. One hundred and thirty-two dollars from $400 leaves you $268, does it not?—A. Yes, sir.

Q. And with that amount you have furnished your family?—A. Yes, sir.

Q. You have been as economical as you could, I suppose?—A. Yes.

Q. How much money have you left?—A. Sixty dollars in debt.

Q. How did you do that?—A. I don't know, sir.

Q. Can you not think of something more that you have wasted?—A. No, sir.

Q. Have you been as careful as you could?—A. Yes, sir.

Q. And you have come out at the end of the year $60 in debt?—A. Yes, sir.

Q. Have you been extravagant in your family expenses?—A. No, sir; a man can't be very extravagant on that much money....

Q. And there are four of you in the family?—A. Yes, sir.

Q. How many pounds of beefsteak have you had in your family, that you bought for your own home consumption within this year that we have been speaking of?—A. I don't think there has been five pounds of beefsteak.

Q. You have had a little pork steak?—A. We had a half a pound of pork steak yesterday; I don't know when we had any before.

Q. What other kinds of meat have you had within a year?—A. Well, we have had corn beef twice I think that I can remember this year—on Sunday, for dinner.

Q. Twice is all that you can remember within a year?-A. Yes—and some cabbage.

Q. What have you eaten?—A. Well, bread mostly, when we could get it; we sometimes couldn't make out to get that, and have had to go without a meal.

Q. Has there been any day in the year that you have had to go without anything to eat?—A. Yes, sir, several days.

Q. More than one day at a time?—A. No.

Q. How about the children and your wife—did they go without anything to eat too?—A. My wife went out this morning and went to a neighbor's and got a loaf of bread and fetched it home, and when she got home the children were crying for something to eat.

Q. Have the children had anything to eat to-day except that, do you think?—A. They had that loaf of bread—I don't know what they have had since then, if they have had anything.

Q. Did you leave any money at home?—A. No, sir.

Q. If that loaf is gone, is there anything in the house?—A. No, sir; unless my wife goes out and gets something; and I don't know who would mind the children while she goes out.

This picture captures the destructiveness of the 1877 railroad strike. (Carnegie Library, Pittsburgh)

widespread working-class discontent. When Samuel M. Hotchkiss, Commissioner of the Connecticut Bureau of Labor Statistics, informally surveyed the state's workers in 1887, he was shocked by the "feeling of bitterness," the "distrust of employers," the "discontent and unrest." These sentiments exploded into strikes, sabotage, and violence, most often linked to demands for higher wages and shorter hours.

Nineteenth-century strike activity underwent important changes, however, as the consciousness of American workers expanded. In the period of early industrialization, discontented laborers rioted in their neighborhoods rather than at their workplaces. The Lowell protests of the 1830s (Chapter 10) were not typical. Between 1845 and the Civil War, however, strikes at the workplace began to replace neighborhood riots. Although workers showed their anger against their employers by turning out and often calling for higher wages, they had only a murky sense that the strike

could be a weapon to force employers to improve working conditions.

As industrialization transformed work and an increasing percentage of the work force entered factories, collective actions at the workplace spread. Local and national unions played a more important role in organizing protest, conducting 60 percent of the strikes between 1881 and 1905. As working-class leaders realized more clearly the importance of collective action in dealing with their opponents and perceived that transportation had knit the nation together, they also tried to coordinate local and national efforts. By 1891, more than one-tenth of the strikes called by unionized workers were sympathy strikes. Coordination between strikers employed by different companies improved as workers tried to order capitalism by making the same wage demands. Finally, wages among the most highly unionized workers became less of an issue. Workers sought more humane conditions. Some attempted to end subcontracting and the degradation of skills. Others, like the glassblowers, struggled to enforce work rules. Indeed, by the early 1890s, over one-fifth of strikes involved the rules governing the workplace.

Labor Organizing, 1865–1900

The Civil War experience colored labor organizing in the postwar years. As one working-class song pointed out, workers had borne the brunt of that struggle.

> *You gave your son to the war*
> *The rich man loaned his gold*
> *And the rich man's son is happy to-day,*
> *And yours is under the mold.*

Now workers who had fought to save the Union argued that wartime sacrifices justified efforts to gain justice and equality in the workplace.

Labor leaders quickly realized the need for national as well as local organizations to protect the laboring class against "despotic employers." In 1866, several craft unions and reform groups formed the National Labor Union (NLU). Claiming 300,000 members by the early 1870s, the organization supported a range of causes including temperance, women's rights, and the establishment of cooperatives to bring the "wealth of the land" into "the hands of those who produce it," thus ending "wage slavery."

The call for an eight-hour day reveals some of the basic assumptions of the organized labor movement. Few workers saw employers as a hostile class or felt it necessary to overturn the economic system. But they did believe bosses were often dangerous tyrants whose time demands threatened to turn citizens into slaves. The eight-hour day would curb the power of owners and allow workers the time to cultivate the qualities necessary for republican citizenship.

Many of the NLU's specific goals survived, although the organization did not. An unsuccessful attempt to create a political party and the depression of 1873 decimated the NLU and many local unions as well. Survival and the search for a job took precedence over union causes.

The Knights of Labor and the AFL

As the depression wound down, a new mass organization, the Noble and Holy Order of the Knights of Labor, rose to national importance. Founded as a secret society in 1869, the order became public and national when Terence V. Powderly, an Irish American, was elected Grand Master Workman in 1879. The Knights of Labor sought "to secure to the workers the full enjoyment of the wealth they create." Because the industrial system denied workers their fair share as producers, the Knights of Labor proposed to mount a cooperative system of production alongside the existing system. "There is no reason," Powderly believed, "why labor cannot, through cooperation, own and operate mines, factories and railroads." Cooperative efforts would give workers the economic independence necessary for citizenship, and an eight-hour day would provide them with the leisure for moral, intellectual, and political pursuits.

The Knights of Labor opened its ranks to all American "producers," defined as all contributing members of society—skilled and unskilled, black and white, men and women. Only the idle and the corrupt (bankers, speculators, lawyers, saloonkeepers, and gamblers) were to be excluded. Membership was even open to sympathetic merchants and manufacturers. In fact, many shopkeepers joined the order and advertised their loyalty as "friend of the workingman."

This inclusive membership policy meant that the Knights potentially had the power of great numbers. The organization grew in spurts, attracting miners between 1874 and 1879 and skilled urban tradesmen between 1879 and 1885. Masses of unskilled workers joined thereafter.

Although Powderly frowned on using the strike as a labor weapon, the organization reaped the benefits of grass-roots strike activity. Local struggles proliferated after 1883. In 1884, unorganized workers of the Union Pacific Railroad walked off the job when management announced a wage cut. Within two days, the company caved in, and the men joined the Knights of Labor. The next year, a successful strike against the Missouri Pacific Railroad brought in another wave of members. Then, in 1886, the Haymarket Riot in Chicago led to such a growth in labor militancy that in that single year, the membership of the Knights of Labor ballooned from 100,000 to 700,000.

The "riot" at Haymarket was, in fact, a peaceful protest meeting connected with a lockout at the McCormick Reaper Works. When the Chicago police arrived to disperse the crowd, a bomb exploded. Seven policemen were killed. Although no one knows who planted the bomb, eight anarchists were tried and convicted. Three were executed, one committed suicide, and the others served prison terms. Overheated newspaper accounts put the blame on "long-haired, wild-eyed, bad-smelling, atheistic, reckless foreign wretches, who never did an honest hour's work in their lives."

Labor agitation and turbulence spilled over into politics. In 1884 and 1885, the Knights of Labor lobbied to secure a national contract labor law that would demand work contracts and state laws outlawing the use of convict labor. The organization also pressed successfully for the creation of a federal Department of Labor. As new members poured in, however, direct political action became increasingly attractive. Between 1885 and 1888, the Knights of Labor sponsored candidates in 200 towns and cities in 34 states and 4 territories. They achieved many electoral victories. In Waterloo, Iowa, a bank janitor ousted a successful attorney to become the town's mayor. Despite local successes, no national labor party emerged. But in the 1890s, the Knights cooperated with the Populists in their attempt to reshape American politics and society.

Despite the dramatic surge in membership, the Knights of Labor could not sustain their momentum as the voice for the American laboring people. Employers, alerted by the Haymarket riot, determined to break the power of the organization. A strike against Jay Gould's southwestern railroad system in 1886 failed, tarnishing the Knights' reputation. Consumer and producer cooperatives fizzled; the policy of accepting both black and white workers led to strife and discord in the South. The two major parties proved adept at co-opting labor politicians. As labor politicians became respectable, they left the rank and file to fend for themselves.

The failure of national leaders paralleled the failure of local leadership. Powderly was never able to unify or direct his diverse following. His concern

with general reform issues and political action dissatisfied members pressing for better wages and work conditions. Nor could Powderly control the militant elements who opposed him. Local, unauthorized strike actions were often ill-considered and violent. Lawlessness helped neither the organization nor its members. By 1890, the membership had dropped to 100,000, although the Knights continued to play a role well into the 1890s.

In the 1890s, the American Federation of Labor (AFL), founded in 1886, replaced the Knights of Labor as the nation's dominant union. The history of the Knights pointed up the problems of a national union that admitted all who worked for wages, but officially rejected strike action in favor of the ballot box and arbitration. The leader of the AFL, Samuel Gompers, had a different notion of effective worker organization. Gompers's experience as head of the Cigarmakers' Union in the 1870s and as a founder of the Federation of Organized Trades and Labor Unions in 1881 convinced him that skilled workers should put their specific occupational interests before the interests of work-

This handbill in both German and English denouncing the "atrocious action of the police" highlights the importance of immigrants in the labor movement.

ers as a whole. By so doing, they could control the supply of skilled labor and keep wages up.

Gompers organized the AFL as a federation of skilled trades—cigar makers, iron molders, iron-workers, carpenters, and others—each one autonomous, yet linked through an executive council to work together for prolabor national legislation and mutual support during boycott and strike actions. Gompers was a practical man. He repudiated the notion of a cooperative common-wealth and dreams of ending the wage system, accepting the fact that workers "are a distinct and practically permanent class of modern society." Thus, he focused on immediate, realizable "bread and butter" issues, particularly higher wages, shorter hours, industrial safety, and the right to organize.

Although Gompers rejected direct political action as a means of obtaining labor's goals, he did believe in the value of the strike. He told a congressional hearing in 1899 that unless working people had "the power to enter upon a strike, the improvements will all go to the employer and all the injuries to the employees." A shrewd organizer, he knew from bitter experience the importance of dues high enough to sustain a strike fund through a long, tough fight.

Under Gompers's leadership, the AFL grew from 140,000 in 1886 to nearly one million by 1900. Although his notion of a labor organization was elitist, he succeeded in steering his union through a series of crises, fending off challenges from socialists on his left and corporate opposition to strikes from his right. But there was no room in his organization for the unskilled or for blacks, in whom he claimed to see an "abandoned and reckless disposition."

The AFL made a brief and halfhearted attempt to unionize women in 1892. Hostile male attitudes constituted a major barrier against organizing women. Men resented women as co-workers and preferred them to stay in the home. The AFL stood firmly for the principle that "the man is the provider" and that women who work in factories "bring forth weak children." The Boston Central Labor Union declared in 1897 "the demand for female labor an insidious assault upon the home.... It is the knife of the assassin, aimed at the family circle." Change was slow in coming. In 1900, the International Ladies' Garment Workers Union (ILGWU) was established. Although women were

the backbone of the organization, men dominated the leadership.

Working-Class Setbacks

Despite the growth of working-class organizations, workers lost many of their battles with management. Some of the more spectacular clashes reveal why working-class activism often ended in defeat and why so many workers lived precariously on the edge of poverty.

In 1892, silver miners in Coeur d'Alene, Idaho, went on strike when their employers installed machine drills in the mines, reduced skilled workers to shovelmen, and announced a wage cut of a dollar a day. The owners, supported by state militiamen and the federal government, successfully broke the strike by using scabs, but not without armed fighting. Several hundred union men were arrested, herded into huge bull pens, and eventually tried and found guilty of a wide variety of charges. Out of the defeat emerged the Western Federation of Miners (WFM), whose chief political goal was an eight-hour law for miners. The pattern of struggle in Coeur d'Alene was followed in many subsequent strikes.

Determined mine owners characteristically met strikes by shutting off credit to union men, hiring strikebreakers and armed guards, and paying spies to infiltrate unions. Violence was frequent, and confrontations usually ended with the arrival of state militia, the erection of bull pens, incarceration or intimidation of strikers and their local sympathizers, legal action, and elaborate blacklisting systems. In spite of this, the WFM won as many strikes as it lost.

The Homestead and Pullman Strikes of 1892 and 1894

The most serious setback to labor occurred in 1892 at the Homestead steel mills near Pittsburgh, Pennsylvania. Andrew Carnegie had recently purchased the Homestead plant and put Henry Clay Frick in charge. Together, they wanted to eliminate the Amalgamated Association of Iron, Steel, and Tin Workers, which threatened to increase its organization of the steel industry. After three months of stalemated negotiations over a new wage contract, Frick issued an ultimatum. Unless the union accepted wage decreases, he would lock them out and replace them. As the deadline passed, Frick erected a formidable wood and barbed wire fence around the entire plant, with searchlight and sentry stands on it, and hired 300 armed Pinkerton agents to guard the factory. As they arrived on July 6, they engaged armed steelworkers in a daylong gun battle. Several men on both sides were killed, and the Pinkertons retreated.

Frick telegraphed Pennsylvania's governor, who sent 8,000 troops to crush both the strike and the union. Two and a half weeks later, Alexander Berkman, a New York anarchist sympathetic to the plight of the oppressed Homestead workers, attempted to assassinate Frick. The events at Homestead dramatized the lengths to which both labor and capital would go to achieve their ends.

Observing these events, Eugene Victor Debs of Terre Haute, Indiana, for many years an ardent

In this 1892 engraving of the Homestead strikers surrendering, done for Harper's Weekly, *the sympathy of the artist lies with the detectives in the foreground. The strikers appear as an unruly crowd in the distance, whereas the detectives' kindly faces are highlighted. (Library of Congress)*

organizer of railroad workers, wrote, "If the year 1892 taught the workingmen any lesson worthy of heed, it was that the capitalist class, like a devilfish, had grasped them with its tentacles and was dragging them down to fathomless depths of degradation." Debs saw 1893 as the year in which organized labor would "escape the prehensile clutch of these monsters." But 1893 brought a new depression and even worse challenges and setbacks for labor. Undaunted, Debs succeeded in combining several of the separate railroad brotherhoods into a united American Railway Union (ARU). Within a year, over 150,000 railroadmen joined the ARU, and Debs won a strike against the Great Northern Railroad, which had attempted to slash workers' wages.

Debs faced his toughest crisis at the Pullman Palace Car Company in Chicago. Pullman was a model company town where management controlled all aspects of workers' lives. "We are born in a Pullman house, fed from the Pullman shop, taught in the Pullman school, catechized in the Pullman church, and when we die we shall be buried in the Pullman cemetery and go to the Pullman hell," said one worker wryly.

Late in 1893, as the depression worsened, Pullman cut wages by one-third and laid off many workers, but made no reductions in rents or prices in the town stores. Forced to pay in rent what they could not recover in wages, working families struggled to survive the winter. Some parents kept their children home from school because they had no shoes or coats and could keep warm only in bed. Those still at work suffered speedups, intimidating threats, and further wage cuts. Desperate and "without hope," the Pullman workers joined the ARU in the spring of 1894 and went out on strike.

In late June, after Pullman refused to submit the dispute to arbitration, Debs led the ARU into a sympathy strike in support of the striking Pullman workers. Remembering the ill-fated railroad strike of 1877, Debs advised his lieutenants to "use no violence" and "stop no trains." Rather, he sought to boycott trains handling Pullman cars throughout the West. As the boycott spread, the General Managers Association, which ran the 24 railroads centered in Chicago, came to the Pullman's support, convinced that "we have got to wipe him [Debs] out." After hiring some 2,500 strikebreakers, the GMA appealed to the state and federal governments for military and judicial support in stopping the strike.

Governor Richard Altgeld of Illinois, sympathizing with the workers and believing that local law enforcement was sufficient, opposed the use of federal troops. But Richard Olney, a former railroad lawyer and U.S. attorney general, persuaded President Cleveland that only federal troops could restore law and order. On July 2, Olney obtained a court injunction to end the strike as a "conspiracy in restraint of trade." Two days later, Cleveland ordered federal troops in to support the injunction and crush the strikers.

Violence now escalated rapidly. Local and federal officials hired armed guards, and the railroads paid them to help the troops. Within two days, strikers and guards were fighting bitterly, freight cars were burned, and over $340,000 worth of railroad property was destroyed. The press reported "Unparalleled Scenes of Riot, Terror and Pillage" and "Frenzied Mobs Still Bent on Death and Destruction." As troops poured into Chicago, the violence worsened, leaving scores of workers dead.

Debs's resources were near an end unless he could enlist wider labor support. "Capital has combined to enslave labor," he warned other labor groups. "We must all stand together or go down in hopeless defeat." When Samuel Gompers refused his support, the strike collapsed. Debs and several other leaders were arrested for the contempt of the court injunction of July 2 and found guilty. A lifelong Democrat, Debs soon became a confirmed socialist. His arrest and the defeat of the Pullman strike provided a deathblow to the American Railway Union. In 1895, the Supreme Court upheld the legality of using an injunction to stop a strike and provided management with a powerful weapon to use against unions in subsequent years. Most unions survived the difficult days of the 1890s, but the labor movement emerged with distinct disadvantages in its conflicts with organized capital.

Although in smaller communities strikes against outside owners might receive support from the local middle class, most labor conflicts ran up against the widespread middle- and upper-class conviction that unions and their demands were un-American. Many people claimed to accept the idea of worker organizations, but they would not concede that unions should participate in making economic or work decisions. Most employers violently resisted union demands as infringements of their rights to make production decisions, to hire and fire, to lock workers out, to hire scabs, or to reduce wages in times of depression. The sharp competition of the late nineteenth century, combined with a pattern of falling prices, stiffened employers' resistance to workers' demands. State and local governments and the courts frequently supported them in their battles to curb worker activism.

The severe depressions of the 1870s and 1890s also undermined working-class activism. Workers could not focus on union issues when survival itself was in question. They could not afford union dues or turn down offers of work, even at wages below union standards. Many unions collapsed during hard times. Of the 30 national unions in 1873, fewer than one-third managed to survive the depression.

A far more serious problem was the reluctance of most workers to organize even in favorable times. In 1870, less than one-tenth of the industrial work force belonged to unions, about the same as on the eve of the Civil War. Thirty years later, despite the expansion of the work force, only 8.4 percent (mostly skilled workers) were union members.

Why were workers so slow to join unions? Certainly, diverse work settings and ethnic differences made it difficult for workers to recognize common bonds. Moreover, many unskilled workers sensed that labor aristocrats did not have their interest at heart. Said one Cleveland Pole, "The [union] committee gets the money, 'Bricky' Flannigan [a prominent Irish striker] gets the whiskey, and the Polack gets nothing."

Moreover, many native-born Americans still clung to the tradition of individualism. "The sooner working-people get rid of the idea that somebody or something is going to help them," one Massachusetts shoemaker declared, "the better it will be for them." Others continued to nourish dreams of escaping from the working class and entering the ranks of the middle class. The number of workers who started their own small businesses attests to the power of that ideal, which prevented an identification with working-class causes.

The comments of an Irish woman highlight another important point. "There should be a law … to give a job to every decent man that's out of work," she declared, "and another law to keep all them I-talians from comin' in and takin' the bread out of the mouths of honest people." The ethnic and religious diversity of the work force made it difficult to forge a common front. No other industrial country depended so heavily on immigrants for its manufacturing labor force. The lack of common cultural traditions and goals created friction and misunderstandings. In addition, immigrants clustered in certain jobs and were insulated from other workers, both foreign-born and American. Skill differences related to ethnic group membership also clouded common class concerns.

The perspective of immigrant workers contributed to their indifference to unions and to tension with native-born Americans. Many foreigners planned to return to their homeland and had limited interest in changing conditions in the United States. Moreover, because their goal was to work, they took jobs as scabs. Much of the violence that accompanied working-class actions erupted when owners brought in strikebreakers. Some Americans blamed immigrants for both low wages and failed worker actions. Divisions among workers were often as bitter as those between strikers and employers. When workers divided, employers benefited.

The tension within laboring ranks appeared most dramatically in the anti-Chinese campaign of the 1870s and 1880s as white workers in the West began to blame the Chinese for economic hardships. A meeting of San Francisco workers in 1877 in favor of the eight-hour day exploded into a rampage against the Chinese. In the following years, angry mobs killed Chinese workers in Tacoma, Seattle, Denver, and Rock Springs, Wyoming. "The Chinese must go! They are stealing our jobs!" became a rallying cry for American workers.

Hostility was also expressed at the national level with the Chinese Exclusion Act of 1882. The law, which had the support of the Knights of Labor in the West, prohibited the immigration of both skilled and unskilled Chinese workers for a ten-year period. It was extended in 1892 and made permanent in 1902. Although both middle- and working-class Americans supported sporadic efforts to cut off immigra-

tion, working-class antipathy exacerbated the deep divisions that undermined worker unity.

At the same time, many immigrants, especially those who were skilled, did support unions and cooperate with native-born Americans. Irish Americans played important roles in the Knights of Labor and the AFL. British and Germans also helped build up the unions. Often ethnic bonds served labor causes by tying members to one another and to the community. For example, in the 1860s and 1870s, as the Molders' Union in Troy, New York, battled with manufacturers, its Irish membership won sympathy and support from the Irish-dominated police force, the Roman Catholic Church, fraternal orders, and public officials.

The importance of workers' organizations lay not so much in their successful struggles and protests as in the implicit criticism they offered of American society. Using the language of republicanism, many workers lashed out at an economic order that robbed them of their dignity and humanity. As producers of wealth, they protested that so little of it was theirs. As members of the working class, they rejected the middle-class belief in individualism and social mobility.

The Balance Sheet

Except for skilled workers, most laboring people found it impossible to earn much of a share in the material bounty industrialization created. Newly arrived immigrants especially suffered from low pay and economic uncertainty. Long hours on the job and the necessity of walking to and from work left workers little free time. Family budgets could include, at best, only small amounts for recreation. Even a baseball game ticket was a luxury.

Yet this view of the harshness of working-class life partly grows out of our own standards of what is acceptable today. Because so few working-class men or women recorded their thoughts and reactions, it is hard to know just what they expected or how they viewed their experiences. But culture and background influenced their perspectives. The family tenement, one Polish immigrant remarked, "seemed quite advanced when compared with our home" in Poland. American poverty was preferable to Russian pogroms. A ten-hour job in the steel

This photograph of a store in San Francisco's Chinatown suggests that even though many of the immigrants originally planned to return home, many stayed and created a lively culture in this country. The presence of only men in the picture highlights the male character of the Chinese immigration. (Collection University of Oregon Library)

mill might be an improvement over dawn-to-dusk farmwork that brought no wages.

Studies of several cities show that nineteenth-century workers achieved some occupational mobility. One worker in five in Los Angeles and Atlanta during the 1890s, for example, managed to climb into the middle class. Most immigrant workers were stuck in ill-paid, insecure jobs, but their children ended up doing better. The son of an unskilled laborer might move on to become a semi-skilled or skilled worker as new immigrants took the jobs at the bottom. Second-generation Irish made progress, especially in the West and the Midwest. Even in Boston, 40 percent of the children of Irish immigrants obtained white-collar jobs.

Mobility, like occupation, was related to background. Native-born whites, Jews, and Germans rose more swiftly and fell less often than Irish, Italians, or Poles. Cultural attitudes, family size, education, and group leadership all contributed to different ethnic mobility patterns. Jews, for example, valued education and sacrificed to keep children in school. By 1915, Jews represented 85 percent of the free City College student body in

New York City, 20 percent of New York University's student body, and one-sixth of those studying at Columbia University. With an education, they moved upward. The Slavs, however, who valued a steady income over mobility and education, took their children out of school and sent them to work at an early age. This course of action, they believed, not only helped the family, but gave the child a head start in securing reliable, stable employment. The southern Italian proverb "Do not make your child better than you are" suggests the value Italians placed on family rather than individual success. Differing attitudes and values led to different aspirations and career patterns.

Two groups enjoyed little mobility. African Americans were largely excluded from the industrial occupational structure and restricted to unskilled jobs. Unlike immigrant industrial workers, they did not have the opportunity to move to better jobs as new unskilled workers took the positions at the bottom. A study in Los Angeles suggests that Hispanic residents made minimal gains. Their experiences elsewhere may have been much the same.

TIMELINE

1843–1884	"Old immigration"
1844	Telegraph invented
1850s	Steam power widely used in manufacturing
1859	Value of U.S. industrial production exceeds value of agricultural production
1866	National Labor Union founded
1869	Transcontinental railroad completed
	Knights of Labor organized
1870	Standard Oil of Ohio formed
1870s–1880s	Consolidation of continental railroad network
1873	Bethlehem Steel begins using Bessemer process
1873–1879	Depression
1876	Alexander G. Bell invents telephone
	Thomas Edison establishes his "invention factory" at Menlo Park, New Jersey
1877	Railroad workers hold first nationwide industrial strike
1879	Thomas Edison invents incandescent light
1882	Chinese Exclusion Act
1885–1914	"New immigration"
1886	American Federation of Labor founded
	Haymarket Riot in Chicago
1887	Interstate Commerce Act
1890	Sherman Anti-Trust Act
1892	Standard Oil of New Jersey formed
	Coeur d'Alene strike
	Homestead steelworkers strike
1893	Chicago World's Fair
1893–1897	Depression
1894	Pullman railroad workers strike
1900	International Ladies' Garment Workers Union founded
	Corporations responsible for two-thirds of U.S. manufacturing

Although occupational mobility was limited for immigrants, other kinds of rewards often compensated for the lack of success at the workplace. Home ownership loomed important for groups like the Irish, for in their homeland, home ownership had been all but impossible. Ownership of a home also allowed a family to earn extra income by taking in boarders and provided some protection against the uncertainties of industrial life and the coming of old age. The Irish also proved adept politicians and came to dominate big-city government in the late nineteenth century. Their political success opened up city jobs, particularly in the police force, to the Irish. In 1886, one-third of Chicago's police force was Irish-born; many more were second-generation Irish Americans. The Irish were also successful in the construction industry and dominated the hierarchy of the Catholic Church. Irish who did not share this upward mobility could nevertheless benefit from ethnic connections and take pride in their group's achievements.

Likewise, participation in social clubs and fraternal orders compensated in part for lack of advancement at work. Ethnic associations, parades, and holidays provided a sense of identity and security that offset the limitations of the job world.

Moreover, a few rags-to-riches stories always encouraged the masses who struggled. The family of John Kearney, in Poughkeepsie, New York, for example, achieved modest success. After 20 years as a laborer, John started his own business as a junk dealer and even bought a simple house. His sons started off in better jobs than their father. One became a grocery store clerk, later a baker, a policeman, and, finally, at the age of 40, an inspector at the waterworks. Another was an iron molder, and the third son was a post office worker and eventually the superintendent of city streets. If this success paled next to that of industrial giants like Andrew Carnegie and John D. Rockefeller, it was still enough to keep the American dream alive.

Conclusion

The Complexity of Industrial Capitalism

The rapid growth of the late nineteenth century made the United States one of the world's industrial giants. Many factors contributed to the "wonderful accomplishments" of the age. They ranged from sympathetic government policies to the rise of big business and the emergence of a cheap industrial work force. But it was also a turbulent period. Many Americans benefited only marginally from the new wealth. Some of them protested by joining unions, by walking out on strike, or by initiating on-the-job actions. Most lived their lives more quietly and never had the opportunity that Thomas O'Donnell did of telling their story to others. But middle-class Americans began to wonder about the O'Donnells of the country. It is to their concerns, worries, and aspirations that we now turn.

Recommended Reading

Industrialism and Economic Growth

Stuart Bruchey, *Growth of the Modern American Economy* (1975); Alfred W. Niemi, *U.S. Economic History: A Survey of the Major Issues* (1975); Robert L. Heilbroner, *The Economic Transformation of America* (1977); Samuel P. Hays, *The Response to Industrialism, 1885–1914* (1957); Robert Wiebe, *The Search for Order, 1877–1920* (1967); Glenn Porter, *The Rise of Big Business, 1860–1910* (1973); Olivier Zunz, *Making America Corporate, 1870–1929* (1990); Alfred D. Chandler, Jr., *The Visible Hand: The Managerial Revolution in American Business* (1977); Louis Galambos and Barbara Barron Spence, *The Public Image of Big Business in America* (1975); James D. Norris, *Advertising and the Transformation of American Society, 1865–1920* (1990); Thomas P. Hughes, *American Genius* (1989); Thomas J. Misa, *A Nation of Steel* (1995).

Urban Life

Sam Bass Warner, Jr., *Streetcar Suburbs: The Process of Growth in Boston, 1870–1900* (1962); Gunther Barth, *The Rise of Modern City Culture in Nineteenth-Century America* (1980); David Goldfield, *Cotton Fields and Skyscrapers: Southern City and Region* (1989); William Cronon, *Nature's Metropolis: Chicago and the Great West* (1991); Carl Smith, *Urban Disorder and the Shape of Belief: the Great Chicago Fire, the Haymarket Bomb, and the Model Town of Pullman* (1993); James Borchert, *Alley Life in Washington: Family, Community, Religion, and Folklife in the City, 1850–1970* (1980); David Nasaw, *Going Out: The Rise and Fall of Public Amusements* (1993); William E. Montgomery, *Under Their Own Fig Tree* (1993).

Work and Workers

Thomas J. Archdeacon, *Becoming American: An Ethnic History* (1983); Alan M. Kraut, *The Huddled Masses: The Immigrant in American Society, 1880–1921* (1982); Peter Jones and Melvin G. Holli, eds., *Ethnic Chicago* (1981); Kerby A. Miller, *Emigrants and Exiles: Ireland and the Irish Exodus to North America* (1985); Mark Wyman, *Round Trip to America: The Immigrants Return to Europe, 1880–1930* (1993); Herbert G. Gutman, *Work, Culture, and Society in Industrializing America* (1976); David M. Gordon, Richard Edwards, and Michael Reich, *Segmented Work, Divided Workers: The Historical Transformation of Labor in the United States* (1982); Daniel Nelson, *Managers and Workers: Origins of the New Factory System in the United States, 1880–1920* (1975); David T. Rodgers, *The Work Ethic in Industrial America* (1978); David Montgomery, *Workers' Control in America: Studies in the History of Work, Technology, and Labor Struggles* (1970) and *The Fall of the House of Labor: The Workplace, The State, and American Labor Activism, 1865–1925* (1987); James Whiteside, *Regulating Danger: The Struggle for Mine Safety in the Rocky Mountain Coal Industry* (1990); Daniel J. Walkowitz, *Worker City, Company Town: Iron and Cotton-Worker Protest in Troy and Cohoes, New York, 1855–84* (1978); Theodore Hershberg, ed., *Philadelphia: Work, Space, Family, and Group Experience in the Nineteenth Century* (1981); Nell Irvin Painter, *Standing at Armageddon in the United States, 1877–1919* (1987); Leon Fink, *Workingmen's Democracy: The Knights of Labor and American Politics* (1983); Alice Kessler-Harris, *Out to Work: A History of Wage-earning Women in the United States* (1982); Julie Matthaei, *An Economic History of Women in America: Women's Work, the Sexual Division of Labor, and the Development of Capitalism* (1982); David M. Katzman, *Seven Days a Week: Women and Domestic Service in Industrializing America* (1978); Gary Scharnhorst, *Horatio Alger, Jr.* (1980); Stephan Thernstrom, *Poverty and Progress: Social Mobility in a Nineteenth Century City* (1964) and *The Other Bostonians: Poverty and Progress in the American Metropolis, 1880–1970* (1973); Clyde Griffen and Sally Griffen, *Natives and Newcomers: The Ordering of Opportunity in Mid-Nineteenth-Century Poughkeepsie* (1978); Michael P. Weber, *Social Change in an Industrial Town: Patterns of Progress in Warren, Pennsylvania, from the Civil War to World War I* (1976); Thomas Kessner, *The Golden Door: Italian and Jewish Immigrant Mobility in New York City, 1880–1915* (1977); Ronald Takaki, *A Different Mirror: A History of Multicultural America* (1993).

Novels

Theodore Dreiser, *Sister Carrie* (1900); Stephen Crane, *Maggie: A Girl of the Streets* (1893); Abraham Cahan, *The Rise of David Levinsky* (1917); Thomas Bell, *Out of This Furnace* (1976 ed.).

Politics and Reform

At the start of his best-seller *Looking Backward* (1888), Edward Bellamy likened the American society of his day to a huge stagecoach. Dragging the coach along sandy roads and over steep hills were the "masses of humanity." While they strained desperately "under the pitiless lashing of hunger" to pull the coach, at the top sat the favored few, riding well out of the dust in breezy comfort. The fortunate few, however, were constantly fearful that they might lose their seats from a sudden jolt, fall to the ground, and have to pull the coach themselves.

Bellamy's famous coach allegory introduced a utopian novel in which the class divisions and pitiless competition of the nineteenth century were replaced by a classless, caring, cooperative new society. Economic anxieties and hardships were supplanted by satisfying labor and leisure. In place of the coach, all citizens in the year 2000 walked together in equal comfort and security under a huge umbrella over the sidewalks of the city. Bellamy's outlook on American life was a middle-class reformist one. His book had enormous appeal, not only because of his humane economic analysis, but also because he clothed it in the form of a novel, complete with futuristic technological wonders, such as television and credit cards, a double-dream trick ending, and a love story.

The novel opens in 1887. The hero, Julian West, a wealthy Bostonian, falls asleep worrying about the effect local labor struggles might have on his upcoming wedding. When he wakes up, it is the year 2000. In the new society, he discovers, through his genial guide, Dr. Leete, that all citizens live in material comfort and happiness. Utopia had been achieved peacefully through the development of one gigantic trust, owned and operated by the national government. All citizens between 21 and 45 work in an industrial army with equalized pay and work difficulty. Retirement after age 45 is devoted to hobbies, reading, culture, and such minimal political and judicial leadership as is needed in a society without crime, poverty, graft, vice, lawyers, or war.

Bellamy's treatment of the role of women in the world of 2000 reflected his own era's struggle with changing gender and class relationships. On the one hand, new laborsaving gadgets relieved women of housework, and they served, like men, in the industrial army. Women married not for dependence, but for love and could even initiate romantic relationships. On the other hand, the women Bellamy portrayed were still primarily responsible for shopping, supervision of domestic and aesthetic matters, and nurturing the young. In a special women's division of the industrial army, they worked shorter hours in "lighter occupations." The purpose of equality of the sexes and more leisure, the novel made clear, was to enable women to cultivate their "beauty and grace" and, by extension, to feminize culture and politics.

Bellamy's book was popular with educated middle-class Americans, who were attracted by his vision of a society in which humans were both morally good and materially well off. Readers were intrigued not only by all that was new, but also by how much of the old society was preserved. The traditional male view of woman's place and purpose was one example. But Bellamy also retained such familiar values as individual taste and incentive, private property, and rags-to-riches presidents. Like most middle-class Americans of his day, he disapproved of European socialism. Although the collectivist features of Bellamy's utopia were socialistic, he and his admirers called his system "nationalism." This appealed to a new generation of Americans who had put aside Civil War antagonisms to embrace the greatness of a growing, if now economically divided, nation. In the early 1890s, with Americans buying nearly 10,000 copies of *Looking Backward* every week, over 160 Nationalist clubs were formed to crusade for the adoption of Bellamy's ideas.

Although this 1892 painting by John Klir shows the outcome of a "Lost Bet" in the election that year, note the ethnic, racial, and class diversity of the street crowds, momentarily united in enjoyment of the humiliated loser pulling his victorious opponent (and a wagon full of American flags). Will a more diverse America hold together? (Library of Congress)

$\mathcal{T}$he inequalities of wealth described in Bellamy's coach scene reflected a political life in which many participated, but only a few benefited. The wealthiest 10 percent, who rode high on the social coach, dominated national politics, whereas untutored bosses held sway in governing cities. Except for token expressions of support, national political leaders ignored the cries of factory workers, immigrants, farmers, African Americans, Native Americans, and other victims of the vast transformation of American industrial, urban, and agrarian life in the late nineteenth century. But as the century drew to a close, middle-class Americans like Bellamy, as well as labor, agrarian, and ethnic leaders themselves, proposed various reforms. Their concern was never more appropriate than during the depression of the mid-1890s, a social upheaval in real life that mirrored the worst features and fears of Bellamy's fictional coach.

In this chapter, we will examine American politics at the national and local level from the end of Reconstruction to the 1890s, a period that for the most part bolstered the rich and neglected the corrosive human problems of urban industrial life. Then we will look at the growing social and political involvement of educated middle-class reformers who, despite their distaste for mass politics, now acted to effect change both locally and nationally. We will conclude with an account of the pivotal importance of the 1890s, highlighted by the Populist revolt, the depression of 1893–1897, and the election of 1896. In an age of strong national identity and pride, the events of the 1890s shook many comfortable citizens out of their apathy and began the reshaping of American politics.

Politics in the Gilded Age

In a satirical book in 1873, Mark Twain, with Charles Dudley Warner, used the expression "Gilded Age" to describe the political corruption of Grant's presidency. The phrase, with its suggestion of shallow glitter, has come to characterize social and political life in the last quarter of the nineteenth century. Ironically, although Gilded Age politics was tainted by corruption and tinted by more color than substance, the period was one of high party vitality. Politicians avoided fundamental issues in favor of the politics of mass entertainment—pomp, parades, penny beer, pennants, and the prattle of three-hour speeches. As a result, voter participation in national elections between 1876 and 1896 hovered at an all-time high of 73 to 82 percent of all registered voters.

Behind the glitter of Gilded Age politics, though, occurred two gradual changes that would greatly affect twentieth-century politics. The first was the development of a professional bureaucracy. In congressional committees and executive branch offices, elite specialists and experts emerged as a counterfoil to the perceived dangers of majority rule represented by high voter participation, especially by new immigrants. How else,

New England poet James Russell Lowell wondered, could the culturally "better" classes temper the excesses of equality "when interpreted and applied politically by millions of newcomers alien to our traditions?" Second, after a period of close elections and party stalemate based on Civil War divisions between Democrats and Republicans, new issues and concerns fostered a party realignment in the 1890s.

Politics, Parties, Patronage, and Presidents

American government in the 1870s and 1880s clearly supported the interests of riders at the top of the coach. Although some modern observers think the national government should have tackled problems like poverty, unemployment, and trusts, few nineteenth-century Americans would have agreed. They mistrusted organized power and believed in harmony of interests and laissez-faire, a doctrine that argued that all would benefit from an economic life free of government interference. After the traumas of the Civil War era, when a strong centralized state pursued high moral causes, late-nineteenth-century political leaders favored a period of governmental passivity. This would permit the continuing pursuit of industrial expansion and wealth. As Republican leader Roscoe Conkling explained, the primary role of government was "to clear the way of impediments and dangers, and leave every class and every individual free and safe in the exertions and pursuits of life."

The Gilded Age, Henry Adams observed, was the most "thoroughly ordinary" period in American politics since Columbus. "One might search the whole list of Congress, Judiciary, and Executive during the twenty-five years 1870–95 and find little but damaged reputation." Few eras of American government were as corrupt as this one, and Adams was especially sensitive to this decline in the quality of democratic politics. His autobiography, *The Education of Henry Adams* (1907), contrasted the low political tone of his own age with the exalted political morality of the days of grandfather John Quincy Adams and great-grandfather John Adams.

As a result of the weak Johnson and Grant presidencies, Congress emerged in the 1870s as the dominant branch of government. With power in the committee system, the moral quality of congressional leadership was typified by men such as James G. Blaine and Roscoe Conkling. Despite a scandal in which he was paid for supporting favors to railroads and then lied about it afterward, Blaine was probably the most popular Republican politician of the era. A man of enormous charm, intelligence, wit, and ability, he served his country as senator from Maine and twice as secretary of state and was a serious contender for the presidency in every election from 1876 to 1892.

Blaine's intraparty foe, Roscoe Conkling, was even more typical. The *New York Times* described him as "a man by whose career and character the future will judge of the political standards of the present." A stalwart Republican who controlled the rich patronage jobs of the New York customhouse, Conkling spent most of his career in patronage conflicts with fellow party leaders. He quarreled even more with liberal Republican civil service reformers, who believed that government jobs should be dispersed for expertise and merit rather than party loyalty. Conkling could imagine no other purpose of politics and accused these genteel "mugwump" reformers of wanting the jobs for themselves. "Their real object is office and plunder." Fittingly, his career ended when he resigned from the Senate in a patronage dispute with President Garfield. Though he served in Congress for over two decades, Conkling never drafted a bill. His career was unharmed, for legislation was not Congress's primary purpose.

In 1879, a student of legislative politics, Woodrow Wilson, expressed his disgust with the degradation of Gilded Age politics in eight words: "No leaders, no principles; no principles, no parties." Little differentiated the two major parties. They diverged not over principles, but patronage, not over issues, but the spoils of office. At stake in elections were not laws, but the thousands of government jobs at the disposal of the winning candidate and his party. In a shrewd analysis of the American political system in the late nineteenth century, an English observer, Lord James Bryce, concluded that the most cohesive force in American politics was the "desire for office and for office as a means of gain." The two parties, like two bottles of liquor, Bryce said, bore different labels, yet "each was empty."

The clear ideological party positions taken during the Civil War and Reconstruction had all but disappeared. The Republican party frequently reminded voters of its role in winning the Civil War and preserving the Union. Republican votes still came from northeastern Yankee industrial interests and from New England migrants across the Upper Midwest. The main support for Democrats still came primarily from southern whites, northern workers, and Irish Catholic and other urban immigrants. For a few years, Civil War and Reconstruction issues generated party differences. But after 1876, on national issues at least, party labels did indeed mark "empty" bottles.

One reason for avoiding issues in favor of bland platforms and careful campaigning was that the two parties were evenly matched. In three of the five presidential elections between 1876 and 1892, a mere 1 percent of the vote separated the two major candidates. In 1880, for example, James Garfield defeated his Democratic opponent, General Winfield Hancock, a Reconstruction moderate and Union war hero, by only 7,018 votes. In 1884, Grover Cleveland squeaked by James G. Blaine by a popular vote margin of 48.5 to 48.2 percent. In two elections (1876 and 1888), the electoral vote winner had fewer popular votes. Further evidence of political stalemate was that only twice, and for only two years, did one party control the White House and both houses of Congress. Although all the presidents in the era except Cleveland were Republicans, the Democrats controlled the House of Representatives in eight of the ten sessions of Congress between 1875 and 1895. As a result, political interest shifted away from Washington to states and cities.

Lord Bryce titled one of the chapters of his book on American politics "Why Great Men Are Not Chosen Presidents." Gilded Age presidents were an undistinguished group. Like Washington, D.C., itself, they played only a minor role in national life, especially when compared with industrial entrepreneurs like Carnegie and Rockefeller. None of them—Rutherford B. Hayes (1877–1881), James Garfield (1881), Chester A. Arthur (1881–1885), Grover Cleveland (1885–1889 and 1893–1897), and Benjamin Harrison (1889–1893)—served two consecutive terms. None

was strongly identified with any particular issue. None has been highly regarded by historians.

Although Cleveland was the only Democrat in the group, he differed little from the Republicans. On his election in 1884, financier Jay Gould sent him a telegram stating his confidence that "the vast business interests of the country will be entirely safe in your hands." When Cleveland violated the expectation that presidents should not initiate ideas by devoting his entire annual message in 1887 to a call for a lower tariff, Congress listened politely and did nothing. Voters turned him out of office a year later.

Most Americans expected their presidents to take care of party business by rewarding the faithful with government positions. The scale of patronage was enormous. Garfield complained of having to dispense thousands of jobs as he took office in 1881, worrying, he said, "whether A or B should be appointed to this or that office." He is remembered primarily for being shot early in his administration by a disappointed office seeker. He

Presidential Elections, 1872–1892				
Year	Candidate	Party	Popular Vote	Electoral Vote
1872	ULYSSES S. GRANT	Republican	3,596,745 (56%)	286
	Horace Greeley	Democrat	2,843,446 (44%)	0*
1876	Samuel J. Tilden	Democrat	4,284,020 (51%)	184
	RUTHERFORD B. HAYES	Republican	4,036,572 (48%)	185
1880	JAMES A. GARFIELD	Republican	4,449,053 (48.5%)	214
	Winfield S. Hancock	Democrat	4,442,035 (48.1%)	155
	James B. Weaver	Greenback-Labor	308,578	0
1884	GROVER CLEVELAND	Democrat	4,911,017 (48.5%)	219
	James G. Blaine	Republican	4,848,334 (48.2%)	182
		Minor parties	325,739 (3.3%)	0
1888	Grover Cleveland	Democrat	5,540,050 (48.6%)	168
	BENJAMIN HARRISON	Republican	5,444,337 (47.9%)	233
		Minor parties	396,441 (3.5%)	0
1892	GROVER CLEVELAND	Democrat	5,554,414 (46%)	277
	Benjamin Harrison	Republican	5,190,802 (43%)	145
	James B. Weaver	Populist	1,027,329 (9%)	22

A British observer of American politics, James Bryce, said in 1888 that "the American usually votes with his party, right or wrong, and the fact that there is little distinction of view between the parties makes it easier to stick to your old friends." American voters stayed with their "old friends," as this table of the evenly matched presidential elections of the Gilded Age shows. Except for 1872, the popular vote was never wider than 3 percent and in three elections was less than 1 percent.

*Greeley died before the electoral college met.

Note: Winners' names appear in capital letters

achieved heroic stature only by hanging on for 2 1/2 months before he died. Garfield's successor, Chester Arthur, was so closely identified with Conkling's patronage operation that when the shooting of the president was announced, a friend said with shocked disbelief, "My God! Chet Arthur in the White House!"

National Issues

Arthur surprised his doubters by proving himself a capable and dignified president, responsive to the growing demands for civil service reform. Four issues were important at the national level in the Gilded Age: the tariff, currency, civil service, and government regulation of railroads (see Chapter 18). In confronting these issues, legislators tried to serve both their own self-interest and the national interest of an efficient, productive economy. Two additional issues, Indian "reform" and African American rights, were submerged in these interests (see Chapter 18).

The tariff was one issue where party, as well as regional attitudes toward the use of government power, made some difference. Republicans believed in using the state to support business interests and stood for a high protective tariff. A nation demonstrated its "intelligence," one orator said, by using law to promote a "dynamic and progressive" society. The tariff would protect American businessmen, wage earners, and farmers from the competition and products of foreign labor. By contrast, Democrats stressed that a low tariff exemplified the "economic axiom ... that the government is best which governs least." High tariffs falsely substituted the aims and actions of the state for those that should come from "individual initiative" and were a tax on consumers.

Although Democrats were identified with a low-tariff position and Republicans with a high one, in reality there was little consistency in either party's stand. In practice, politicians accommodated local interests in tariff adjustments. Democratic senator Daniel Vorhees of Indiana explained, "I am a protectionist for every interest which I am sent here by my constituents to protect."

Tariff revisions were bewilderingly complex as legislators catered to these many special interests. As one senator knowingly said, "The contest over a revision of the tariff brings to light a selfish strife which is not far from disgusting." Most tariffs included a mixture of higher and lower rates that

Although the tariff protectionist Harrison defeated Cleveland in 1888 (the results were reversed in 1892), all Gilded Age presidents were essentially "preservers" rather than innovators. None had approached the greatness of Washington, Lincoln, and the other Republican presidents hovering over Harrison and Morton in this illustration. (Library of Congress)

defied understanding. The federal government depended on tariffs and excise taxes (primarily on tobacco and liquor) for most of its revenue, so there was little chance that the tariff would be abolished or substantially lowered. Moreover, the surpluses produced by the tariff during the Gilded Age helped the parties finance patronage jobs as well as government programs.

The question of money was even more complicated. During the Civil War, the federal government had circulated paper money (greenbacks) that could not be exchanged for gold or silver. In the late 1860s and 1870s, politicians debated whether the United States should return to a metallic standard, which would allow paper money to be exchanged for specie. Proponents of a hard-money policy supported either withdrawing all paper money from circulation or making it convertible to specie. They opposed increasing the volume of money because they thought it would lead to higher prices. Greenbackers, who advocated soft money, argued that there was not enough currency in circulation for an expanding economy and urged increasing the supply of paper money. An inadequate money supply, they believed, led to falling prices and an increase in interest rates, which harmed farmers, industrial workers, and all people in debt.

Hard-money interests had more power and influence. In 1873, Congress demonetized silver. In 1875, it passed the Specie Resumption Act, gradually retiring greenbacks from circulation and putting the nation firmly on the gold standard. But as large supplies of silver were discovered and mined in the West, pressure was resumed for increasing the money supply by coining silver. Soft-money advocates pushed for the unlimited coinage of silver in addition to gold. A compromise of sorts was reached in 1878 with passage of the Bland-Allison Act requiring the Treasury to buy between $2 and $4 million of silver each month and to coin it as silver dollars. Despite the increase in money supply, the period was not inflationary, but prices fell, disappointing the supporters of soft money. Their response was to push for more silver, a move that continued the controversy into the 1890s.

The issue of civil service reform was, Henry Adams observed, a "subject almost as dangerous in political conversation in Washington as slavery itself in the old days before the war." The worst feature of the spoils system was that parties financed themselves by assessing holders of patronage jobs, often as much as 1 percent of their annual salaries. Reformers, most of whom were genteel white American-born Protestants, pressed for competitive examinations, allegedly to ensure the creation of a professional, honest, nonpartisan permanent civil service. But they were motivated as well by a desire to provide "barriers against the invasion of modern barbarism and vulgarity," as Harvard culture guardian Charles Eliot Norton put it, describing the threat of dividing the spoils of office among immigrants and their urban political machine bosses.

Civil service reform had first been raised during the Grant administration, but little was accomplished. Garfield's assassination, however, created enough public support to force Congress to take action. The Pendleton Act of 1883 established a system of merit examinations covering about one-tenth of federal offices. Gradually, more bureaucrats fell under its coverage, but parties became no more honest. As campaign contributions from government employees dried up, parties turned to other financial sources. In 1888, record corporate contributions helped elect Benjamin Harrison.

The Lure of Local Politics

The fact that the major parties did not disagree substantially on issues like money and civil service does not mean that nineteenth-century Americans found politics dull or uninteresting. In fact, far more eligible voters turned out in the late nineteenth century than at any time since. The 78.5 percent average turnout to vote for president in the 1880s contrasts sharply with the near–50 percent of eligible Americans who vote in the 1980s and 1990s.

What explains the amazing nineteenth-century turnout? Americans were drawn to the polls in part by the fun and games of party parades, buttons, and banners, but also by the lure of local issues. For example, Iowa corn farmers turned out to vote for state representatives who favored curbing the power of the railroads to set high grain-shipping rates. But emotional issues of

Women, often targets of drunken male violence, campaigned for temperance as well as for equal rights. Here Victoria Claflin Woodhull reads a suffrage proposal to the House Judiciary Committee in 1871. If denied the vote, she vowed that women "mean secession, and on a thousand times grander scale than was that of the South. We are plotting a revolution; we will overthrow this bogus Republic and plant a government of righteousness in its stead." (Library of Congress)

race, religion, nationality, and life-style often overrode economic self-interest. While Irish Catholics in New York sought political support for their parochial schools, third-generation, middle-class American Protestants from Illinois and Connecticut voted for laws that would compel attendance at public schools. Nashville whites supported laws that established segregated railroad cars and other public facilities. Milwaukee German brewery workers voted against local temperance laws because they valued both their jobs and their beer. Ohio and Indiana Protestant farmers, by contrast, believing they were protecting social order and morality against hard-drinking Catholic immigrants, pushed for temperance laws.

The influx of the new immigrants, especially in the mushrooming cities, played a large role in stimulating political participation. As traditional ruling groups, usually native-born, left local government for business, where they found more money and status, urban bosses stepped in. Their power to control city government rested on an ability to deliver the votes of poor, uneducated immigrants. In return for votes, bosses like "Big Tim" Sullivan of New York and "Hinky Dink" Kenna of Chicago operated informal welfare systems. They handed out jobs and money for rent, fuel,

and bail. Sullivan gave new shoes as birthday presents to all poor children in his district, as well as turkeys to poor families at Thanksgiving. Above all, party bosses provided a personal touch in a strange and forbidding environment. As one boss explained, "I think that there's got to be in every ward somebody that any bloke can come to—no matter what he's done—and get help."

New York City's Tammany Hall boss, George Washington Plunkitt, perfected the relationship of mutual self-interest with his constituents. The favors he provided in return for votes ranged from attending weddings and funerals to influencing police and the courts. His clients included not only Jewish brides, Italian mourners, and burned-out tenants, but also job seekers, store owners, saloonkeepers, and madams, all of whom needed favors. State party leaders were no less effective than urban bosses in mobilizing voters. An Indiana Republican state chairman appointed 10,000 district workers in 1884 responsible for discovering the "social and political affiliation" of every single voter.

Party leaders also won votes by making political participation exciting. Nineteenth-century campaigns were punctuated by parades, rallies, and oratory. Campaign buttons, handkerchiefs, songs, and other paraphernalia generated color and excitement in political races where substantive issues were not at stake. In the election of 1884, for example, emotions ran high over the moral lapses of the opposition candidate. The Democrats made much of Blaine's record of dishonesty, chanting in election eve parades and rallies: "Blaine! Blaine! James G. Blaine! / Continental liar from the state of Maine!" Republicans, in turn, learning of an illegitimate child fathered by Grover Cleveland, answered with their own chant: "Ma! Ma! Where's my pa? / Gone to the White House, Ha! Ha! Ha!" Cleveland won, in part because a Republican clergyman unwisely called the Democrats the party of "rum, Romanism, and rebellion" on election eve in New York. The remark backfired, and the Republicans lost both New York, which should have been a safe state, and the election.

The response of voters in New York in 1884 demonstrated that local and ethnocultural issues rather than national and economic questions explained party affiliation and political behavior. New Mexico politics, for example, was marked for 20 years by the corrupt land grabs of the Santa Fe ring, a small group of Anglo-Protestant Republican bankers, lawyers, and politicians who exploited anti-Mexican and anti-Catholic sentiments. The ring controlled judges, legislators, and the business interests of the state, as well as some Spanish-speaking voters. In the late 1880s, outraged Mexican tenant farmers resorted to violence, a tactic that the ring manipulated to dispossess Mexicans, Indians, and even white squatters from enormous tracts of land. The New Mexico events showed the power of race and religion in local politics.

Voters may have been cool toward the tariff and civil service, but they expressed strong interest in temperance, anti-Catholicism, compulsory school attendance and Sunday laws, aid to parochial schools, racial issues, restriction of immigration, and "bloody shirt" reminders of the Civil War.

Party membership reflected voter interest in these important cultural, religious, and ethnic questions. Midwestern Scandinavians and Lutherans, for example, tended to be Republicans, as were northerners who belonged to Protestant denominations. These groups believed in positive government action. Because the Republican party

had proved its willingness in the past to mobilize the power of the state to reshape society, people who wished to regulate moral and economic life were attracted to it. Catholics and various immigrant groups found the Democratic party more to their liking because it opposed government efforts to regulate morals. Said one Chicago Democrat, "A Republican is a man who wants you t' go t' church every Sunday. A Democrat says if a man wants t' have a glass of beer on Sunday he can have it."

These differences caused spirited local contests, particularly over prohibition. Many Americans considered drinking a serious social problem. Annual consumption of brewery beer had risen from 2.7 gallons per capita in 1850 to 17.9 in 1880. Although this increase could have been the result of changes in drinking habits, many people feared that alcoholism was on the increase. Certainly, the number of saloons ballooned. In one city, saloons outnumbered churches 31 to 1. Statistics like these shocked those who believed that drinking would destroy the American character, corrupt politics, and lead to poverty, crime, and unrestrained sexuality. Women especially supported temperance because they were often the targets of violent drunken men. Rather than trying to persuade individuals to give up drink, as the temperance movement had done earlier in the century, many now sought to make drinking a crime.

The battle in San Jose, California, illustrates the strong passions such efforts aroused. In the 1870s, temperance reformers put on the ballot a local option referendum to ban the sale of liquor in San Jose. Women, using their influence as guardians of morality, erected a temperance tent, where they held conspicuous daily meetings. Despite denunciations from some clergymen and heckling from some of the town's drinkers, the women refused to retreat to their homes. On election eve, a large crowd appeared at the temperance tent, but a larger one turned up at a proliquor rally. In the morning, women roamed the streets, urging men to adopt the referendum. Children were marched around to the polls and saloons, singing, "Father, dear father, come home with me now." By afternoon, the mood grew ugly, and the women were harassed and threatened by drunken men. The prohibition proposal lost by a vote of 1,430 to 918.

Similarly, emotional conflicts occurred in the 1880s at the state level over other issues, especially education. In Iowa, Illinois, and Wisconsin, Republicans sponsored laws mandating that children attend "some public or private day school" where instruction was in English, an early but not the last nativist movement for English-only education. The intent of these laws was to undermine parochial schools, which taught in the language of the immigrants. In Iowa, where a state prohibition law was passed as well, the Republican slogan was "A schoolhouse on every hill, and no saloon in the valley." Confident in their cause, Protestant Iowa Republicans proclaimed that "Iowa will go Democratic when hell goes Methodist." It went Republican. But in Wisconsin, a law for compulsory school attendance was so strongly anti-Catholic that it backfired. Many voters, disillusioned with Republican moralism, shifted to the Democratic party. Campaigns like these both reflected and nourished ethnic tension and helped draw the middle class into a more active engagement with politics.

Middle-Class Reform

Generally unexcited by tariffs and the money question, middle-class Americans were moved by moral issues such as education and temperance. Moreover, many were frightened into overcoming their aversion to politics by the corruption of urban life and the violent polarizing labor upheavals of the 1880s. Although most middle-class Americans were not reformers, nearly all worried about the social consequences of their absence from political discourse and saw the value of the sophisticated and moral thinking they could bring to national life.

Frances Willard and the Women's Christian Temperance Union (WCTU) is an example. As president of the WCTU from 1879 until her death in 1898, Willard headed the largest women's organization in the country. Most WCTU members were churchgoing, white Protestant women who, like Willard, supported temperance because they believed drunkenness caused poverty and family violence. But after 1886, the WCTU reversed its position, seeing drunkenness as a result of poverty, unemployment, and bad labor conditions. Willard

Frances Willard typified the middle-class reformer's effort to apply both Christian principles and organizational skill to solving social problems. Her goal was nothing less than "to influence those strongholds of power, the national Congress, State Legislatures and Municipal Councils." (Corbis-Bettmann)

joined the Knights of Labor in 1887 and by the 1890s had influenced the WCTU to extend its programs in a "do-everything" policy to alleviate the problems of workers, particularly women and children.

The Gospel of Wealth

Frances Willard called herself a Christian socialist because she believed in applying the ethical principles of Jesus to economic life. For Willard and many other educated middle-class reformers, Christianity called for a cooperative social order designed to reduce inequalities of wealth. But for most Americans in the Gilded Age, Christianity supported the competitive individualistic ethic that justified the lofty place of those who had won the race to the top.

This ethic was endorsed by prominent ministers and others, who preached sermons and wrote treatises emphasizing the moral superiority of the wealthy and justifying social class arrangements. Episcopal Bishop William Lawrence wrote that it was "God's will that some men should attain great wealth." Philadelphia Baptist preacher Russell Conwell's famous sermon "Acres of Diamonds," delivered 6,000 times to an audience estimated at 13 million, praised riches as a sure sign of "godliness" and stressed the power of money to "do good."

Industrialist Andrew Carnegie expressed the ethic most clearly. In an article, "The Gospel of Wealth" (1889), Carnegie celebrated the benefits of better goods and lower prices that resulted from competition, arguing that "our wonderful material development" outweighed the harsh costs of competition. The concentration of wealth in the hands of a few leading industrialists, he concluded, was "not only beneficial but essential to the future of the race." Those most fit would bring order and efficiency out of the chaos of rapid industrialization. Carnegie's defense of the new economic order in his article and in a book, *Triumphant Democracy* (1886), found as many supporters as Bellamy's *Looking Backward*. Partly, this was because Carnegie insisted that the rich were obligated to spend some of their wealth to benefit their "poorer brethren." Carnegie built hundreds of libraries, most still operating in large and small towns throughout the United States. In later years, the philanthropist turned his attentions to other projects, including world peace.

Carnegie's ideas about wealth were drawn from an ideology known as social Darwinism, based on the work of Charles Darwin, whose famous *Origin of Species* was published in 1859. Darwin had concluded that plant and animal species had evolved through a process of natural selection. In the struggle for existence, some species managed to adapt to their environment and survived. Others failed to adapt and perished. Herbert Spencer, an English social philosopher, adopted these notions of the "survival of the fittest" and applied them to human society. Progress, Spencer said, resulted from relentless competition in which the weak failed and were eliminated whereas the strong climbed to the top. He believed that "the whole effort of nature is to get rid of such as are unfit, to clear the world of them, and make room for better."

When Spencer visited the United States in 1882, leading men of business, science, religion, and politics thronged to honor him with a lavish banquet at Delmonico's restaurant in New York City. Here was the man whose theories justified their amassed fortunes because they were men of "superior ability, foresight, and adaptability." Spencer warned against any interference in the economic world by tampering with the natural laws of selection. The select at the dinner heaped their praise on Spencer as founder of not only a new sociology, but also a new religion.

Spencer's American followers, like Carnegie and William Graham Sumner, a professor of political economy at Yale, familiarized the American public with the basic ideas of social Darwinism. They emphasized that poverty was the inevitable consequence of the struggle for existence and that attempts to end it were pointless, if not immoral. Although Sumner's emotional hero was the middle-class "forgotten man" like his father, his writings defended the material accumulations of the wealthy. To take power or money away from millionaires, Sumner scoffed, was "like killing off our generals in war." It was "absurd," he wrote, to pass laws permitting society's "worst members" to survive or to "sit down with a slate and pencil to plan out a new social world."

The scientific vocabulary of social Darwinism injected scientific rationality into what often seemed a baffling economic order. Sumner and Spencer argued that underlying laws of political economy, like those governing the natural world, dictated economic affairs. Social Darwinists also believed in the superiority of the Anglo-Saxon race, which they maintained had reached the highest stage of evolution. Their theories were used to justify race supremacy and imperialism as well as the monopolistic efforts of American businessmen. Railroad magnate James J. Hill said that the absorption of smaller railroads by larger ones was the industrial analogy of the victory in nature of the fit over the unfit. John D. Rockefeller, Jr., told a YMCA class in Cleveland that "the growth of a large business is merely a survival of the fittest." Like the growth of a beautiful rose, "the early buds which grow up around it" must be sacrificed. This was, he said, "merely the working out of a law of nature and a law of God."

The luxury of a fashionable home full of ornate fine art was accessible to anyone who worked hard, according to advocates of the Gospel of Wealth and social Darwinism. Successful families like the Vanderbilts, they said, represented humanity's "fittest" element. Contrast this opulent scene with those of the middle- and lower-class families pictured in Chapters 17 and 18. (Courtesy of the Biltmore Estate, Asheville, NC)

Others questioned this rosy outlook. Brooks Adams, brother of Henry, wrote that social philosophers like Spencer and Sumner were "hired by the comfortable classes to prove that everything was all right." Fading aristocratic families like the Adamses, who were being displaced by a new industrial elite, may have felt a touch of envy and loss of status. They succeeded, however, in suggesting that social change was not as closed as the social Darwinists claimed.

Reform Darwinism and Pragmatism

A number of intellectual reformers directly challenged the gloomy social Darwinian notion that nothing could be done to alleviate poverty and injustice. With roots in antebellum abolitionism, women's rights, and other crusades for social justice, men like Wendell Phillips, Frederick Douglass, and Franklin Sanborn and women like Elizabeth Cady Stanton and Susan B. Anthony transferred their reform fervor to postbellum issues. Sanborn, for example, an Emersonian transcendentalist, founded the American Social Science Association in 1865 to "treat wisely the great social problems of the day." As the Massachusetts inspector of charities in the 1880s, he earned a reputation as the "leading social worker of his day."

A new group of reformers, however, went beyond charity work to suggest both specific social remedies and a professionalized body of social scientific research to support them. Henry George, who was not a social scientist, nevertheless observed that wherever the highest degree of "material progress" had been realized, "we find the deepest poverty." George's book, *Progress and Poverty* (1879), was an early statement of the contradictions of American life. With Bellamy's *Looking Backward*, it was the most influential book of the age, selling 2 million copies by 1905. George admitted that economic growth had produced wonders, but pointed out the social costs and the loss of Christian values. His remedy was to break up land-holding monopolists who profited from the increasing value of their land and rents they collected from those who actually did the work. He proposed a "single tax" on the unearned increases in land value received by landlords. In 1886, on a United Labor party ticket supported by workers, clergymen, and middle-class reformers, George ran well but unsuccessfully for mayor of New York City.

Henry George's solution may seem overly simple, but his religious tone and optimistic faith in the capacity of humans to effect change appealed to many middle-class intellectuals. Some went beyond George to develop social scientific models that justified reform energy rather than inaction. A sociologist, Lester Frank Ward, and an economist, Richard T. Ely, both found examples of cooperation in nature and demonstrated that competition and laissez-faire had proved both wasteful and inhumane. These reform Darwinists urged instead an economic order marked by caring cooperation and social regulation.

Two pragmatists, John Dewey and William James, established a philosophical foundation for reform. James, a professor at Harvard, argued that while environment was important, so was human will. People could influence the course of human events. "What is the 'cash value' of a thought, idea, or belief?" James asked. What was its result? "The ultimate test for us of what a truth means," he suggested, was in the consequences of a particular idea, in "the conduct it dictates." He made it clear that the expression of human sympathies and the aversion to both economic and international war was moral conduct with the most ethical consequences.

James and young social scientists like Ward and Ely gathered statistics documenting social wrongs and rejected the social determinism of Spencer and Sumner. They argued that the application of intelligence and human will could change the "survival of the fittest" into the "fitting of as many as possible to survive." Their position encouraged educators, economists, and reformers of every stripe, giving them an intellectual justification to struggle against the misery and inequalities of wealth found in many sectors of their society.

Settlements and Social Gospel

Jane Addams understood the gap between progress and poverty. She saw it in the streets of Chicago in the winter of 1893. For some time, she had been aware that life in big cities for working-class families was bitter and hard. "The stream of laboring people goes past you," she wrote, and "your heart sinks with a sudden sense of futility." Born in rural Illinois,

Addams founded Hull House in Chicago in 1889 "to aid in the solution of the social and industrial problems which are engendered by the modern conditions of life in a great city."

Vida Scudder, too, "felt the agitating and painful vibrations" of the depression. This young professor of literature at Wellesley College returned from study at Oxford resolved to do something to alleviate the suffering of the poor. She and six other Smith College graduates formed an organization of college women in 1889 to work in settlement houses.

Like Addams and Scudder, other middle-class activists worried about social conditions, particularly the degradation of life and labor in America's cities, factories, and farms. They were mostly professionals—lawyers, ministers, teachers, journalists, and academic social scientists. Influenced by European social prophets like Karl Marx, Leo Tolstoy, and Victor Hugo and by Americans such as Emerson, Whitman, George, and Bellamy, most turned to the ethical teachings of Jesus for inspiration in solving social problems.

The message they began to preach in the 1890s was highly idealistic, ethical, and Christian. They preferred a society marked by cooperation rather than competition, where self-sacrifice rather than self-interest held sway and, as they liked to say, where people were guided by the "golden rule rather than the rule of gold." Like Frances Willard, they meant to apply the ethics of Jesus to industrial and urban life in order to bring about the kingdom of heaven on earth. Some preferred to put their goals in more secular terms; they spoke of radically transforming American society. Most, however, worked within existing institutions. As middle-class intellectuals, they tended to stress an educational approach to problems. But they were also practical, involving themselves in an effort to make immediate, tangible improvements by running for public office, crusading for legislation, mediating labor disputes, and living in poor neighborhoods.

The settlement house movement typified the blend of idealism and practicality characteristic of middle-class reformers in the 1890s. Addams opened Hull House, and Scudder started Denison House in Boston. A short time later, on New York's Lower East Side, Lillian Wald opened her "house on Henry Street." The primary purpose of the settlement houses was to help immigrant families, especially women, adapt Old World rural styles of childbearing and child care, housekeeping, and cooking to the realities of urban living in America. This meant launching day nurseries, kindergartens, boarding rooms for working women, and classses in sewing, cooking, nutrition, health care, and English. The settlements also frequently organized sports clubs and coffeehouses for young people as a way of keeping them out of saloons.

A second purpose of the settlement house movement was to provide college-educated women with meaningful work at a time when they faced professional barriers and to allow them to preserve the strong feelings of sisterhood they had experienced at college. Settlement house workers, Scudder wrote, were like "Early Christians" in their renunciation of worldly goods and dedication to a life of service. Living in a settlement was in many ways an extension of woman's traditional role as nurturer of the weak. A third goal was to gather data exposing social misery in order to spur legislative action, such as developing city building codes for tenements, abolishing child labor, and improving safety conditions in factories. Hull House, Addams said, was intended in part "to investigate and improve the conditions in the industrial districts of Chicago."

The settlement house movement, with its dual emphasis on the scientific gathering of facts and spiritual commitment, nourished the new academic study of sociology, first taught in divinity schools. Many organizations were founded to blend Christian belief and academic study in an attempt to change society. One was the American Institute of Christian Sociology, founded in 1893 by Josiah Strong, a Congregational minister, and economist Richard T. Ely. Similar organizations were the Christian Social Union, the Church Association for the Advancement of the Interests of Labor, and the Society of Christian Socialists.

These organizations viewed the purpose of religion as collective redemption rather than individual salvation, as exhorted by Dwight Moody in a wave of urban revivals in the 1870s. The revivals appealed to lower-class rural folk who were either drawn to the city by expectant opportunities or pushed there by economic ruin. Supported by businessmen who felt that religion would make workers and immigrants more docile, revivalists battled sin through individual conversion. The revivals helped

Many of the settlement houses included public health clinics, like this one at Vida Scudder's Denison House in Boston. Settlement house work, Scudder wrote, fulfilled "a biting curiosity about the way the Other Half lived, and a strange hunger for fellowship with them." (Schlesinger Library, Radcliffe College)

nearly to double Protestant Church membership in the last two decades of the century. Although some urban workers drifted into secular faiths like socialism, most remained conventionally religious.

In the 1890s, many Protestant ministers immersed themselves in the Social Gospel movement, which tied salvation to social betterment. Like the settlement house workers, these religious leaders sought to make Christianity relevant to industrial and urban problems. In Columbus, Ohio, Congregational minister Washington Gladden advocated collective bargaining and various forms of corporate profit sharing in books such as *Working Men and Their Employers, Social Salvation,* and *Applied Christianity.* A young Baptist minister in the notorious Hell's Kitchen area of New York City, Walter Rauschenbusch, raised an even louder voice. Often called on to conduct funeral services for children killed by the airless, diseased tenements and sweatshops, Rauschenbusch unleashed scathing attacks on the selfishness of capitalism and church ignorance of socioeconomic issues. His progressive ideas for social justice and a welfare state were later published in two landmark Social

Gospel books, *Christianity and the Social Crisis* (1907) and *Christianizing the Social Order* (1912).

Perhaps the most influential book promoting social Christianity was a best-selling novel, *In His Steps,* published in 1897 by Charles Sheldon. The novel portrayed the dramatic transformations in business relations, tenement life, and urban politics made possible by the work of a few community leaders who resolved to base all their actions on a single question: "What would Jesus do?" For a minister, this meant seeking to "bridge the chasm between the church and labor." For the idle rich, it meant settlement house work and reforming prostitutes. For landlords and factory owners, it meant taking action to improve living and working conditions for tenants and laborers. Although streaked with naive sentimentality characteristic of much of the Social Gospel, Sheldon's novel prepared thousands of influential middle-class Americans for progressive civic leadership after the turn of the century.

Reforming the City

The crucial event in *In His Steps* was a city election pitting moral middle-class reformers against seedy saloon interests and corrupt urban political machines. No late-nineteenth-century institution needed reforming as much as urban government. The president of Cornell University described American city governments as "the worst in Christendom—the most expensive, the most inefficient, and the most corrupt." A Philadelphia committee found "inefficiency, waste, badly paved and filthy streets, unwholesome and offensive water, and slovenly and costly management" to have been the rule for years. New York and Chicago were even worse.

Rapid urban growth overburdened city leaders. Population increase and industrial expansion created new demands for service. Flush toilets, thirsty horses pulling street railways, and industrial users of water, for example, all exhausted the capacity of municipal waterworks built for an earlier age. As city governments struggled to respond to new needs, they raised taxes and incurred vast debts. This combination of rapid growth, indebtedness, and poor services, coupled with the influx of new immigrants, prepared fertile ground for graft and "bossism."

The rise of the boss was directly connected to the growth of the city. As immigrant voters appeared, traditional native-born ruling groups left city government for business, where more money and status beckoned. Into the resulting power vacuum stepped the boss. In an age of urban expansion, bosses dispensed patronage jobs in return for votes and contributions to the party machine. They awarded street railway, gas line, and other utility franchises and construction contracts to local businesses in return for kickbacks and other favors. They also passed on tips to friendly real estate men about the location of projected city improvements. Worse yet, the bosses received favors from the owners of saloons, brothels, and gambling clubs in return for their help with police protection, bail, and influence with the courts. These institutions were vital to the urban economy and played an important role in easing the immigrants' way into American life. For many young women, prostitution was a means of economic survival. For men, the saloon was the center of social life, as well as a place for cheap meals and information about work and aid to his family.

Bossism deeply offended middle-class urban reformers, who were unkindly dubbed "goo-goos" for their insistence on purity and good government. They opposed not only graft and vice, but also the perversion of democracy by the exploitation of ignorant immigrants. As one explained, the immigrants "follow blindly leaders of their own race, are not moved by discussion, and exercise no judgment of their own." Indeed, he concluded, they were "not fit for the suffrage."

The programs of urban reformers were similar in most cities. They not only worked for the "Americanization" of immigrants in public schools (and opposed parochial schooling), but also formed clubs or voters' leagues to discuss the failings of municipal government. They delighted in making spectacular exposures of electoral irregularities and large-scale graft. These discoveries led to strident calls for ousting the mayor, often an Irish Catholic, and replacing him with an Anglo-Saxon Protestant reform candidate.

Political considerations pervaded every reform issue. Many Anglo-Saxon men favored prohibition partly to remove ethnic saloon owners from politics and supported woman suffrage in part to gain a middle-class political advantage

New York City's William "Boss" Tweed (the heavyset man to the left) was head of the corrupt Tammany ring, which typified bossism in its cynical disregard for morality and truth. In Thomas Nast's famous cartoon "Who Stole the People's Money?" the answer is " 'Twas Him."

against male immigrant voters. Most urban reformers could barely hide their distaste for the "city proletariat mob," as one put it. They proposed to replace the bosses with expert city managers, who would bring honest professionalism to city government. They hoped to make government less costly and thereby lower taxes. One effect of their emphasis on cost efficiency was to cut services to the poor. Another was to disfranchise working-class and ethnic groups, whose political participation depended on the old ward-boss system.

Not all urban reformers were elitist managerial types. Samuel Jones, for example, both opposed the boss system and had a passionate commitment to democratic political participation by the urban immigrant masses. An immigrant himself, Jones was a self-made man in the rags-to-riches mold. Beginning in poverty in the oil fields of Pennsylvania, he worked his way up to the ownership of several oil fields and a factory in Toledo, Ohio. Once successful, however, Jones espoused a different ethic from Carnegie's "Gospel of Wealth." Jones described himself as a "Golden Rule man," converted by a combination of firsthand contact with the "piteous appeals" of people put out of work by the depression and by his reading of Emerson, Whitman, Tolstoy, and the New Testament.

In 1894, Jones resolved that he would "apply the Golden Rule as a rule of conduct" in his factory. He instituted an eight-hour day for his employees. In addtion, he gave them $2 minimum wage per day (50 to 75 cents higher than the Toledo average for ten hours), a cooperative insurance program, and an annual 5 percent Christmas dividend. He hired ex-criminals and outcasts that no one else would employ and plastered the Golden Rule all over his factory walls. Anticipating various twentieth-century industrial reforms, Jones created a company cafeteria, where he offered a hot lunch for 15 cents, a Golden Rule park for workers and their families, employee music groups, and a Golden Rule Hall, where he invited social visionaries to speak.

In 1897, Jones decided to extend his notions of cooperation and brotherhood to city government, much as Hazen Pingree had been doing in nearby Detroit. Running as a maverick Republican, Jones was elected to an unprecedented four terms as mayor of Toledo. In office, he advocated municipal ownership of natural gas, street railways, and other utilities; public works jobs and housing for the unemployed; more civic parks and playgrounds; and free municipal baths, pools, skating rinks, sleigh rides, vocational education, and kindergartens.

Few of these reforms were implemented, yet Jones's unorthodox ideas and behavior incurred the wrath of prominent citizens in Toledo. As a pacifist, he did not believe in violence or coercion of any kind and took away policemen's sidearms and heavy clubs. When he sat as judge in police court, he regularly dismissed most cases of petty theft and drunkenness brought before him, charging that the accused were victims of an unjust social order and that only the poor went to jail for such crimes. He refused to advocate closing the saloons or brothels, and when prostitutes were brought before him, he usually dismissed them after fining every man in the room 10 cents—and himself a dollar—for permitting prostitution to exist. The crime rate in Toledo, a notoriously sinful city, decreased during his tenure, and Jones was adored by the plain people. When he died in 1904, nearly 55,000 people, "tears streaming down their faces," filed past his coffin.

The Struggle for Woman Suffrage

Women served, in Jane Addams's phrase, as "urban housekeepers" in the settlement house and good government movements, which reflected the tension many women felt between their public and private lives, between their obligations to self, family, and society. This tension was not usually expressed openly. A few women writers, however, began to vent the frustrations and restraints of middle-class domestic life. In her novel *The Awakening* (1899), Kate Chopin portrayed a young woman who, in awakening to her own sexuality and life's possibilities beyond being a "mother-woman," defied conventional expectations of woman's role. Her sexual affair and eventual suicide prompted a St. Louis newspaper to say of the novel that it was "too strong drink for moral babes and should be labeled 'poison.'"

Some middle-class women, Addams and Scudder, for example, avoided marriage altogether, preferring the supportive relationships found in the female settlement house community. "Married life looks to me ... terribly impoverished for women," a Smith College graduate observed, declaring that "most of my deeper friendships have been with women." A few women boldly advocated free love or, less openly, formed lesbian relationships. Although most preferred traditional marriages and chose not to work outside the home, the generation of women that came of age in the 1890s married less—and later—than any other in American history.

One way women reconciled the conflicting pressures between their private and public lives, as well as deflected male criticism, was to see their work as maternal. Addams called Hull House the "great mother breast of our common humanity." Frances Willard told Susan B. Anthony in 1898 that "government is only housekeeping on the broadest scale," a job men had botched, thus requiring women's saving participation. One of the leading female organizers of coal workers was "Mother" Jones, and the fiery feminist anarchist Emma Goldman titled her monthly journal *Mother Earth*. By using maternal, nurturant language to describe their work, women furthered the very arguments used against them. Many, of course, remained economically dependent on men, and all women still lacked the essential rights of citizenship. How could they be municipal housekeepers if they could not yet even vote?

In the years after the Seneca Falls Convention in 1848, women's civil and political rights advanced very slowly. Although in several western states women received the right to vote in municipal and school board elections, only the territory of Wyoming, in 1869, had granted full political equality before 1890. Colorado, Utah, and Idaho enfranchised women in the 1890s, but no other states granted suffrage until 1910. This slow pace was in part the result of an antisuffrage movement led by an odd combination of ministers, saloon interests, and men threatened in various ways by women's voting rights. "Equal suffrage," said a Texas senator, "is a repudiation of manhood."

In the 1890s, leading suffragists reappraised the situation. The two wings of the women's rights movement, split since 1869, combined in 1890 as the National American Woman Suffrage Association (NAWSA). Although Elizabeth Cady Stanton and Susan B. Anthony continued to head the association, they were both in their seventies, and effective leadership soon passed to younger, more moderate women. The new leaders concentrated on the single issue of the vote rather than dividing their energies among the many causes Stanton and Anthony had espoused. Moderate leaders

The young Jane Addams was one of the college-educated women who chose to remain unmarried and pursue a career as an "urban housekeeper" and social reformer, serving immigrant families in the Chicago neighborhood near her Hull House. (The University of Illinois at Chicago, The University Library, Jane Addams Memorial Collection)

were also embarrassed by Stanton's *Woman's Bible* (1895), a devastating attack on the religious argument against woman suffrage. At the NAWSA convention in 1896, despite the pleas of Anthony not to "sit in judgment" on her good friend, a resolution renouncing any connection with Stanton's book passed by a vote of 53 to 41.

Changing leadership meant a shift from principled to expedient arguments for the suffrage. Since 1848, suffragists had made their argument primarily from principle, citing, as Stanton argued at a congressional hearing in 1892, "our republican idea, individual citizenship." But Stanton's leadership was on the wane, and the younger generation shifted to three expedient arguments. The first was that women needed the vote to pass self-protec-tion laws that would guard them against rapists, state age-of-consent laws, and unsafe industrial work. The second argument, Addams's notion of urban housekeeping, pointed out that political enfranchisement would further women's role in cleaning up morals, tenements, saloons, factories, and corrupt politics.

The third expedient argument reflected urban middle-class reformers' prejudice against non-Protestant newcomers to the city. As immigrant men arrived in America, local machine bosses saw to it that they would be able to vote. Suffragists argued that educated, native-born American women should be given the vote to counteract the undesirable influence of ignorant, illiterate, and immoral male immigrants. In a speech in Iowa in 1894, Carrie Chapman Catt, who would succeed Anthony as president of NAWSA in 1900, argued that the "Government is menaced with great danger ... in the votes possessed by the males in the slums of the cities," a danger that could be averted only by cutting off that vote and giving it instead to women. In the new century, under the leadership of women like Catt, suffrage would finally be secured.

The Pivotal 1890s

For years, many Americans have mistakenly called the last decade of the nineteenth century the "gay nineties." This phrase suggests mustached baseball players and sporty Gibson girls, the glitter of newly lighted electric streetcars and shop windows, and the opulent dinners of rich entrepreneurs. The 1890s was, indeed, a decade of sports and leisure, the electrification of the city, and the enormous wealth of the few. But for many more Americans, it was also a decade of dark tenement misery, grinding work or desperate unemployment, and poverty. As we have seen in Chapters 17 and 18, the early 1890s were marked by Populism and protesting farmers; Wounded Knee and the "second great removal" of Native Americans; lynchings, disfranchisement, and the "nadir of black life"; and the "new immigration," a changing workplace, and devastating labor defeats at Coeur d'Alene, Homestead, and Pullman.

The 1890s, far from gay, were years of contrasts and crises. The obvious contrast, as Bellamy had

The contrasts between rich and poor and the threat of social upheaval are dramatically illustrated in this turn-of-the-century work, called "From the Depths." (Culver Pictures)

anticipated, was between the rich and the poor. As the Populist Omaha platform put it, "We breed two great classes—paupers and millionaires." Supreme Court Justice John Harlan saw a "deep feeling of unrest" everywhere among people worrying that the nation was in "real danger from ... the slavery that would result from aggregations of capital in the hands of a few." And Populist "Sockless" Jerry Simpson bluntly called the crisis a struggle between two sides: "the robbers and the robbed." On the one side, Simpson saw "the allied hosts of monopolies, the money power, great trusts, and railroad corporations, who seek the enactment of laws to benefit them and impoverish the people." On the other, he put those "who produce wealth and bear the burdens of taxation. Between these two there is no middle ground."

Simpson was wrong about the absence of a middle ground, but the gap was indeed huge between the angry Kansas orator Mary E. Lease, who in 1890 said, "What you farmers need to do is to raise less corn, and more Hell," and the wealthy Indianapolis woman who told her husband, "I'm going to Europe and spend my money before these crazy people take it." The pivotal nature of the 1890s hinged on this feeling of polarizing unrest and upheaval as the nation underwent the traumas of change. America was transforming itself from a rural to an urban society and experiencing the pressures of rapid industrialization and accompanying changes in the workplace and on farms. Moreover, the new immigration from Europe and the northward, westward, and cityward internal migrations of blacks and farmers added to the "great danger" against which Carrie Catt warned. The depression of 1893 widened the gap between rich and poor and accelerated the demands for reform. Government bureaucratic structures began to adapt to the needs of governing a complex specialized society, and Congress slowly shifted away from laissez-faire in order to confront national problems.

Republican Legislation in the Early 1890s

Harrison's election in 1888 was accompanied by Republican control of both houses of Congress. Though by no means reformers, the Republicans moved forward in the first six months of 1890 with legislation in five areas: pensions for Civil War veterans and their dependents, trusts, the tariff, the money question, and rights for blacks. The Dependent Pensions Act, providing generous support of $160 million a year for Union veterans and their dependents, sailed through Congress.

The Sherman Anti-Trust Act also passed easily, with only one nay vote. The bill declared illegal "every contract, combination ... or conspiracy in restraint of trade or commerce." Although the bill was vague and not really intended to break up large corporations, the Sherman Act was an initial attempt to restrain large business combinations. But in *United States* v. *E. C. Knight* (1895), the Supreme Court ruled that the American Sugar Refining Company, which controlled more than 90 percent of the nation's sugar-refining capacity, was not in violation of the Sherman Act, which the Court said applied only to commerce, not manufacturing.

A tariff bill introduced in 1890 by Ohio Republican William McKinley generated more controversy. McKinley's bill was an attempt to make good the Republican stance on protection by raising tariff rates to higher levels than ever before. Despite heated opposition from agrarian interests, whose products were generally not protected, the bill passed the House and, after nearly 500 amendments, was passed by the Senate as well.

Silver was even trickier. Recognizing the appeal of free silver to agrarian debtors and the new Populist party, Republican leaders feared their party might be destroyed by the issue. Senator Sherman proposed a compromise measure that momentarily satisfied almost everyone. The Sherman Silver Purchase Act ordered the Treasury to buy 4.5 million ounces of silver monthly and to issue Treasury notes for it. Silverites were pleased by the proposed increase in the money supply. Opponents felt they had averted the worst—free coinage of silver. The gold standard remained secure.

Republicans were also prepared to confront violations of the voting rights of southern blacks in 1890. President Harrison told the editor of the New York *Tribune,* "I feel very strong upon the question of a free ballot." Political considerations paralleled moral ones. Since 1877, the South had become a Democratic stronghold, where party victories could be traced to fraud and intimidation of black Republican voters. "To be a Republican ... in the South," one Georgian noted, "is to be a foolish martyr." Republican legislation, then, would honor old commitments to the freedmen and improve party fortunes in the South. An elections bill, proposed by Massachusetts Senator Henry Cabot Lodge, was intended to ensure African American voter registration and fair elections. A storm of disapproval from Democrats greeted the measure, which they labeled the "Force Bill." Cleveland called it a "dark blow at the freedom of the ballot," and the Mobile *Daily Register* claimed that it "would deluge the South in blood." Senate Democrats delayed action with a filibuster.

Meanwhile, Republican leaders, in order to secure passage of the McKinley Tariff, bargained away the elections bill. The ploy marked the end of major party efforts to protect African American voting rights in the South until the 1960s. In a second setback for black southerners, the Senate defeated a bill to provide federal aid to schools in the South, mostly black, that did not receive their fair share of local and state funds. These two failed measures were the last gasp of the Republican party's commitment to the idealistic principles of Reconstruction. "The plain truth is," said the New York *Herald,* "the North has got tired of the negro," foreshadowing a similar abandonment of concern in the 1980s and 1990s.

The legislative efforts of the summer of 1890, impressive by nineteenth-century standards, fell far short of solving the nation's problems. Trusts grew more rapidly after the Sherman Act than before. Union veterans were pleased by their pensions, but southerners were incensed that Confederate veterans were not covered. Others regarded the pension measure as extravagant and labeled the 51st Congress the "billion-dollar Congress." Despite efforts to please farmers, many still viewed tariff protection as a benefit primarily for eastern manufacturers. Farm prices continued to decline, and gold and silver advocates were only momentarily silenced. African American rights were put off to another time. Polarizing inequalities of wealth remained. Nor did Republican legislative activism lead the Republicans to a "permanent tenure of power," as party leaders had hoped. Voters abandoned the GOP in droves in the 1890 congressional elections, dropping the number of Republicans in the House from 168 to 88.

Two years later, Cleveland won a presidential rematch with Harrison. His inaugural address underlined the lesson he drew from Republican legislative activism in 1890. "The lessons of paternalism ought to be unlearned," he said, "and the better lesson taught that while the people should ... support their government, its functions do not include the support of the people."

The Depression of 1893

Cleveland's philosophy of government soon faced a difficult test. No sooner had he taken office than began one of the worst depressions ever to grip the American economy, lasting from 1893 to 1897. The severity of the depression was heightened by the growth of a national economy and economic interdependence. The depression started in Europe and spread to the United States as overseas buyers

Major Legislative Activity of the Gilded Age

In the table, notice the kinds of issues dealt with at the different levels: mostly money, tariff, immigration, and civil service legislation at the national level and "hot button" social and value issues in the states and localities.

Date	National
1871	Civil Service Commission created
1873	Coinage Act demonetizes silver
	"Salary Grab" Act (increased salaries of Congress and top federal officials) partly repealed
1875	Specie Resumption Act retires greenback dollars
1878	Bland-Allison Act permits partial coining of silver
1882	Chinese Exclusion Act
	Federal Immigration Law restricts certain categories of immigrants and requires head tax of all immigrants
1883	Standard time (four time zones) established for the entire country
	Pendleton Civil Service Act
1887	Interstate Commerce Act sets up Interstate Commerce Commission
	Dawes Act divides Indian tribal lands into individual allotments
1890	Dependent Pension Act grants pensions to Union army veterans
	Sherman Anti-Trust Act
	Sherman Silver Purchase Act has government buy more silver
	McKinley Tariff sets high protective tariff
	Federal Elections bill to protect black voting rights in South fails in Senate
	Blair bill to provide support for education defeated
1891	Immigration law gives federal government control of overseas immigration
1893	Sherman Silver Purchase Act repealed
1894	Wilson-Gorman Tariff lowers duties slightly
1900	Currency Act puts United States on gold standard

	State and Local
1850s–1880s	State and local laws intended to restrict or prohibit consumption of alcoholic beverages
1871	Illinois Railroad Act sets up railroad commission to fix rates and prohibit discrimination
1874	Railroad regulatory laws in Wisconsin and Iowa
1881	Kansas adopts statewide prohibition
1882	Iowa passes state prohibition amendment
1880s	Massachusetts, Connecticut, Rhode Island, Montana, Michigan, Ohio, and Missouri all pass local laws prohibiting consumption of alcohol
	Santa Fe ring dominates New Mexico politics and land grabbing
1889	New Jersey repeals a county-option prohibition law of 1888
	Laws in Wisconsin and Illinois mandate compulsory attendance of children at schools in which instruction is in English
	Kansas, Maine, Michigan, and Tennessee pass antitrust laws
1889–1890	Massachusetts debates bill on compulsory schooling in English
1899–1902	Eleven ex-Confederate states amend state constitutions and pass statutes restricting the voting rights of blacks
1890–1910	Eleven ex-Confederate states pass segregation laws
1891	Nebraska passes eight-hour workday law
1893	Colorado adopts woman suffrage
1894–1896	Woman suffrage referenda defeated in Kansas and California

cut back on their purchases of American products. Shrinking markets abroad soon crippled American manufacturing. Moreover, many foreign investors, worried about the stability of American currency after passage of the Sherman Silver Purchase Act, dumped some $300 million of their securities in the United States. As gold left the country to pay for these securities, the nation's supply of money declined. At the same time, falling prices hurt farmers, many of whom discovered that it cost more to raise their crops and livestock than they could recover in the market. Workers fared no better, as wages fell faster than the price of food and rent.

The collapse in 1893 was also caused by serious overextensions of the economy at home, especially in railroad construction. Farmers, troubled by falling prices, planted more and more crops, hoping somehow that the market would pick up. As the realization of overextension spread, confidence faltered, and then gave way to financial panic. When the stock market crashed early in 1893, investors frantically sold their shares, companies plunged into bankruptcy, and disaster spread. People rushed to exchange paper notes for gold, reducing gold reserves and confidence in the economy even further. Banks called in their loans, which by the end of the year led to 16,000 business bankruptcies and 500 bank failures.

The decrease in available capital and diminished buying power of rural and small-town Americans (still half the population) forced massive factory closings. Within a year, an estimated 3 million Americans—20 percent of the work force—were unemployed. Suddenly, people began to look fearfully at the presence of tramps wandering from city to city looking for work. "There are thousands of homeless and starving men in the streets," one young man reported from Chicago, indicating that he had seen "more misery in this last week than I ever saw in my life before."

As in Bellamy's coach image, the misery of the many was not shared by the few, which only increased discontent. While unemployed men foraged in garbage dumps for food, the wealthy gave lavish parties sometimes costing $100,000. At one such affair, diners ate their meal while seated on horses; at another, many guests proudly proclaimed that they had spent over $10,000 on their attire. While poor families shivered in poorly heated tenements, the very rich built million-dollar summer resorts at Newport, Rhode Island, or grand mansions on New York's Fifth Avenue and Chicago's Gold Coast. While Lithuanian immigrants walked or rode streetcars to Buffalo steel factories to work, wealthy men skimmed across lakes and oceans in huge pleasure yachts. J. P. Morgan owned three, one with a crew of 85 sailors.

Nowhere were these inequalities more apparent than in Chicago during the World's Columbian Exposition, which opened on May 1, 1893, five days before plummeting prices on the stock market began the depression. The Chicago World's Fair was designed, as President Cleveland said in an opening-day speech, to show off the "stupendous results of American enterprise." When he pushed an ivory telegraph key, he started electric current that unfurled flags, spouted water through gigantic fountains, lit 10,000 electric lights, and powered huge steam engines, 37 in one building alone. For six months, some 27 million visitors strolled around the White City, admiring its wide lagoons, white plaster buildings modeled on classical styles, and exhibit halls filled with inventions. Built at a cost of $31 million, the fair celebrated the marvelous mechanical accomplishments of American enterprise and of an aesthetic "City Beautiful" movement to make cities more livable.

But as well-to-do fairgoers sipped pink champagne, men, women, and children in the immigrant wards of Chicago less than a mile away drank contaminated water, crowded into packed tenements, and looked in vain for jobs. The area around Jane Addams's Hull House was especially disreputable, with saloons, gambling halls, brothels, and pawnshops dotting the neighborhood. "If Christ came to Chicago," a British journalist, W. T. Stead, wrote in a book of that title in 1894, this would be "one of the last precincts into which we should care to take Him." Stead's book showed readers the "ugly sight" of corruption, poverty, and wasted lives in a city with 200 millionaires and 200,000 unemployed men.

Despite the magnitude of despair during the depression, national politicians and leaders were reluctant to respond. Only mass demonstrations forced city authorities to provide soup kitchens

The depression of 1893 accentuated contrasts between rich and poor. While well-to-do children enjoyed the giant Ferris wheel and other midway attractions at the Chicago World's Columbian Exposition (left) (Chicago Historical Society), slum children played in filthy streets nearby (below). (Library of Congress)

and places for the homeless to sleep. When an army of unemployed led by Jacob Coxey marched into Washington in the spring of 1894 to press for some form of public work relief, its leaders were arrested for stepping on the grass of the Capitol. Cleveland's reputation for callous disregard for citizens suffering from the depression worsened later that summer when he sent federal troops to Chicago to crush the Pullman strike.

The president focused his efforts on tariff reform and repeal of the Silver Purchase Act, which he blamed for the depression. Although repeal was ultimately a necessary measure to establish business confidence, in the short run, all Cleveland accomplished was to worsen the financial crisis, focus attention further on silver as a panacea, and hurt his conservative wing of the Democratic party. With workers, farmers, and wealthy silver

miners alienated, in the midterm elections of 1894, voters abandoned the Democrats in droves, giving both Populists and Republicans high hopes for electoral success in 1896.

The Crucial Election of 1896

The campaign of 1896, waged during the continuing depression, was one of the most critical in American history. Known as the "battle of the standards," the election was fought in part over the ratio of gold and silver as the standard national currency. Although Cleveland was in disgrace for ignoring depression woes, few leaders in either major party thought the federal government was responsible for alleviating the suffering of the people. But unskilled Slavic workers tending Pennsylvania blast furnaces, unemployed Polish meatpackers in Chicago, railway firemen in Terre Haute, Italian immigrant women in New Haven tenements, and desperate white and black tenant farmers in Georgia all wondered where relief might be found. Would either major party respond to the pressing human needs of the depression? Would the People's party succeed in setting a new national agenda for politics? Or would the established order prevail? These questions were raised and largely resolved in the election of 1896.

As the election approached, Populist leaders focused on the issues of silver and whether to fuse with one of the major parties by agreeing on a joint ticket. But fusion required abandoning much of the Populist platform, thus weakening the party's distinctive character. Under the influence of silver mine owners, many Populists became convinced that the hope of the party lay in a single-issue commitment to the free and unlimited coinage of silver at the ratio of 16 to 1. James Weaver expected both parties to nominate gold candidates, which would send disappointed silverites to the Populist standard.

In the throes of the depression in the mid-1890s, silver took on enormous importance as the symbol of the many grievances of downtrodden Americans. Popular literature captured the rural, moral dimensions of the silver movement. Although William Harvey's highly popular *Coin's Financial School* (1894) was more timely, L. Frank Baum's *Wonderful Wizard of Oz* (1900), written as a "modernized fairy tale," has had an enduring claim on the hearts of all Americans. Read carefully, one sees in Baum's classic the defense of rural values (Kansas, Auntie Em, the uneducated but wise scarecrow, and the goodhearted tin woodsman) and Populist policies (the wicked witch of the East and the magical silver shoes in harmony with the yellow brick road, in "Oz"—ounces).

The Republicans, holding their convention first, nominated William McKinley on the first ballot. A congressman from 1877 to 1891 and twice

In his 1896 campaign, William McKinley periodically spoke to visitors gathered at his home, flailing free silver and flaunting the flag. His landslide electoral victory represented Americans' endorsement of the Republican party as the party of prosperity, tariff protection, thriving factories, and the gold standard. (The Granger Collection, New York)

Political Campaign Artifacts

Historians recover the past, as we have seen, not only through the printed words in books, diaries, magazines, tax lists, and government documents, but also through such visual records as paintings, photographs, and buildings. All material objects recovered from the past, in fact, help historians understand how people lived and what they valued and thought. The products of the human experience include everything from tools to toys, farm implements to furniture, and cooking pots to clothes. Historians have learned from archaeologists and anthropologists that every object, or artifact, no matter how trivial, tells something about people's lives. We call such objects *material culture*.

Consider, for example, how material culture can provide insight into the political life of the past. Political historians tend to examine party platforms, campaign speeches, public opinion, and congressional and public voting behavior. But the study of material artifacts, such as those generated by the campaign of 1896, can also reveal much about the values and issues of American political life. The fervor of that political contest led to the production of thousands of lapel studs, pins, and other articles intended to influence American voters to cast their ballot for either Bryan or McKinley. Cloth campaign ribbons, bandannas, shirts, teacups, and even McKinley soap dolls were produced. Items such as teacups, silver spoons, and pillows were designed for the women of the family, suggesting that even though they did not vote, party leaders and manufacturers believed that women influenced men's votes.

Bryan campaign artifacts.
(Courtesy Rodger Fischer)

Shown here are examples of buttons, badges, and stickpins produced during the campaign of 1896. Study the artifacts supporting Bryan's candidacy. What do they show about the ideological aspects of the Democratic campaign? What issues are voters reminded of? In what way are the artifacts supporting McKinley similar to or different from the Democratic ones? Do you see any specific attempts to refute the free-silver argument? How do Republican artifacts deal with the money question? Can you find any evidence of a specific appeal to different groups of Americans? If so, which ones? Again, make a comparison between these artifacts and the ones manufactured by the Democrats. What general statements might you make about the campaign on the basis of these material remains? What would the buttons, bumper stickers, and other objects of the 1996 presidential election tell future historians about the parties and issues of that political campaign?

McKinley campaign artifacts. (Courtesy Michael Kelly)

William Jennings Bryan, surprise nominee at the 1896 Democratic Convention, was a vigorous proponent of the "cause of humanity." His nomination threw the country into a frenzy of fear and the Populist party into a fatal decision over "fusion." (Library of Congress)

governor of Ohio, McKinley was happily identified with the high protective tariff that bore his name. Republicans were quick to cite the familiar argument that prosperity depended on the gold standard and protection and blamed the depression on Cleveland's attempt to lower the tariff. The excitement of the Democratic convention in July contrasted with the staid, smoothly organized Republican one, a pattern to be repeated throughout most of the twentieth century. Cleveland had already been repudiated by his party, as state after state elected convention delegates pledged to silver. Gold Democrats, however, had enough power left to wage a close battle for the platform plank on money.

The surprise nominee of the convention was an ardent young silverite, William Jennings Bryan, a 36-year-old congressman from Nebraska. Few saw him as presidential material, but as a member of the Resolutions Committee, Bryan arranged to give the closing argument for a silver plank himself. His dramatic speech swept the convention for silver and ensured his own nomination. "I come to speak to you," Bryan cried out, "in defense of a cause as holy as the cause of liberty—the cause of humanity." At the conclusion of what was to become one of the most famous political speeches in American history, Bryan attacked the "goldbugs" and promised,

> Having behind us the producing masses of this nation ... and toilers everywhere, we will answer their demand for a gold standard by saying to them: "You shall not press down upon the brow of labor this crown of thorns, you shall not crucify mankind upon a cross of gold."

As he spoke, Bryan stretched out his arms as if on a cross, and the convention exploded with applause.

The Presidential Election of 1896

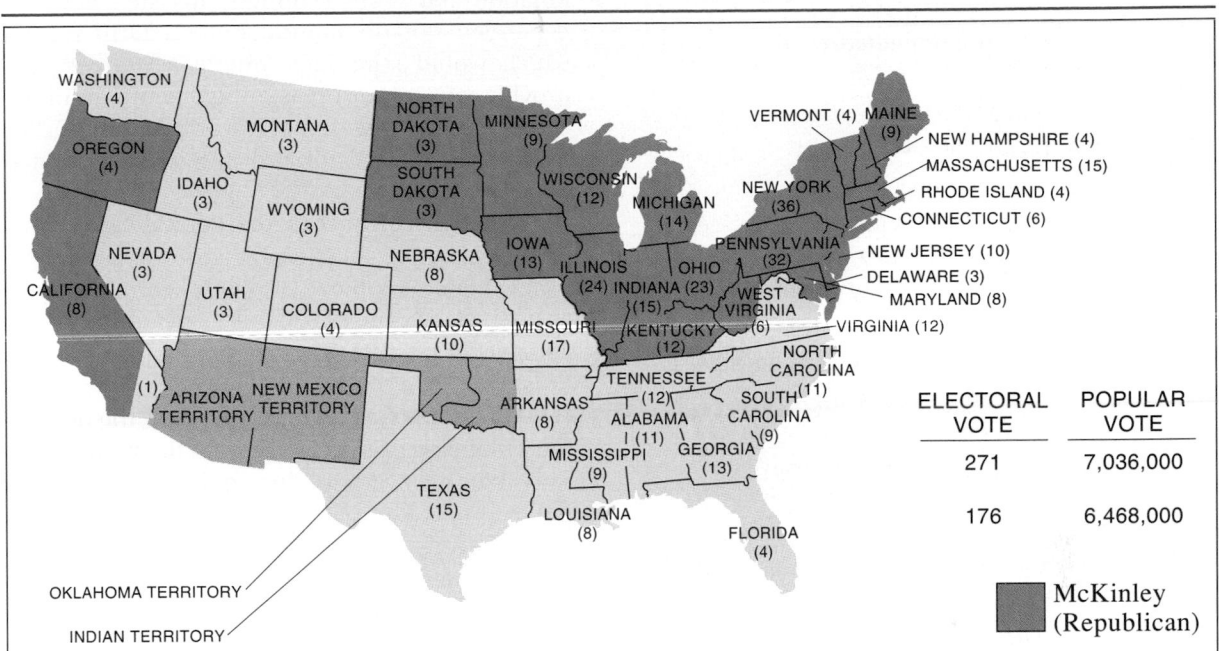

ELECTORAL VOTE	POPULAR VOTE
271	7,036,000
176	6,468,000

■ McKinley (Republican)

□ Bryan (Democratic)

In his sweep of the densely populated urban Northeast and Midwest, McKinley beat Bryan by the largest popular vote margin since 1872. In his cabled congratulations, the first ever by a loser, Bryan, ever the "democrat," said: "We have submitted the issues to the American people and their will is law." Note that California's nine electoral votes (few compared to today) were split. As was then legal, one elector, from the Imperial Valley bordering the Arizona Territory, voted for Bryan and the Democrats.

Populist strategy lay in shambles with the nomination of a Democratic silver candidate. Some party leaders favored fusion with the entire Democratic ticket. Antifusionists were outraged, in part because the Democratic vice-presidential candidate, Arthur Sewall, was an East Coast banker and a hard-money man. An unwise compromise was achieved when the Populist convention nominated Bryan but instead of Sewall chose Populist Tom Watson of Georgia as his running mate. The existence of two silverite slates damaged Bryan's electoral hopes.

During the campaign, McKinley stayed at his home in Canton, Ohio, where some 750,000 admirers came to visit him, helped by low excursion rates offered by the railroads. Republican strategy featured an unprecedented effort to reach voters through a highly sophisticated mass-media campaign, heavily financed by such major corporations as Standard Oil and the railroads. Party leaders hired thousands of speakers to support McKinley and distributed over 200 million pamphlets to a voting population of 15 million. The literature, distributed in 14 languages, was designed to appeal to particular national, ethnic, regional, and occupational groups. To all these people, McKinley was advertised as the "advance agent of prosperity."

From his front porch in Canton, McKinley responded to Bryan's challenge by aiming his appeal not only at the business classes, but also at unemployed workers, to whom he promised a "full dinner pail." He also spoke about the money issue, declaring that "our currency today is ... as good as

TIMELINE

1873	Congress demonetizes silver
1875	Specie Resumption Act
1877	Rutherford B. Hayes becomes president
1878	Bland-Allison Act
1879	Henry George, *Progress and Poverty*
1880	James A. Garfield elected president
1881	Garfield assassinated; Chester A. Arthur succeeds to presidency
1883	Pendleton Civil Service Act
1884	Grover Cleveland elected president
	W. D. Howells, *The Rise of Silas Lapham*
1887	College Settlement House Association founded
1888	Edward Bellamy, *Looking Backward*
	Benjamin Harrison elected president
1889	Jane Addams establishes Hull House
	Andrew Carnegie promulgates "The Gospel of Wealth"
1890	General Federation of Women's Clubs founded
	Sherman Anti-Trust Act
	Sherman Silver Purchase Act
	McKinley Tariff
	Elections bill defeated
1890s	Wyoming, Colorado, Utah, and Idaho grant woman suffrage
1892	Cleveland elected president for the second time; Populist party wins over a million votes
	Homestead steel strike
1893	World's Columbian Exposition, Chicago
1893–1897	Financial panic and depression
1894	Pullman strike
	Coxey's march on Washington
1895	*United States* v. *E. C. Knight*
1896	Charles Sheldon, *In His Steps*
	Populist party fuses with Democrats
	William McKinley elected president
1897	"Golden Rule" Jones elected mayor of Toledo, Ohio
	Economic recovery begins

gold." Free silver, he maintained, would lead to inflation and more economic disaster. Recovery depended not on money, but on tariff reform, which would stimulate American industry and provide jobs—"not open mints for the unlimited coinage of the silver of the world," he said, "but open mills for the full and unrestricted labor of American workingmen."

In sharp contrast to the Republican stay-at-home policy, Bryan took his case to the people. Three million people in 27 states heard him speak as he traveled over 18,000 miles, giving as many as 30 speeches a day. Bryan's message was simple. Prosperity would return with free coinage of silver. Government policies should attend to the needs of the producing classes rather than the vested interests that believed in the gold standard. "That policy is best for this country," Bryan proclaimed, "which brings prosperity first to those who toil." But his rhetoric favored rural toilers. "The great cities rest upon our broad and fertile prairies," he had said in the "Cross of Gold" speech. "Burn down your cities and leave our farms, and your cities will spring up again as if by magic; but destroy our farms and the grass will grow in the streets of every city in the country." Urban workers were little inspired by this rhetoric, nor were immigrants impressed by Bryan's prairie moralizing.

To influential easterners, the brash young Nebraskan represented a threat to social harmony. Theodore Roosevelt wrote that "this silver craze surpasses belief. Bryan's election would be a great calamity." A Brooklyn minister declared that the Democratic platform was "made in Hell." One newspaper editor said of Bryan that he was just like Nebraska's Platte River: "six inches deep and six miles wide at the mouth." Others branded him a "madman" and an "anarchist." The New York *Mail* wrote that "no wild-eyed and rattle-brained horde of the red flag ever proclaimed a fiercer defiance of law, precedent, order, and government."

With such intense interest in the election, it was predictable that voters would turn out in record numbers. In key states like Illinois, Indiana, and Ohio, 95 percent of those eligible to vote went to the polls. When the voting was over, McKinley had won 271 electoral votes to Bryan's 176. Millionaire Mark Hanna jubilantly wired McKinley: "God's in his heaven, all's right with the world." Bryan had been defeated by the largest popular majority since Grant trounced Greeley in 1872.

Although Bryan won over 6 million votes (47 percent of the total), more than any previous Democratic winner, he failed to carry the Midwest. Nor could he make large inroads into the votes of the urban middle classes and industrial masses, who had little confidence that the Democrats could stimulate economic growth or cope with the problems of industrialism. McKinley's promise of a "full dinner pail" was more convincing than the untested formula for free silver. Northern laborers feared that inflation would leave them even poorer than they already were, because they believed that prices and rents would rise faster than their wages, and Catholic immigrants distrusted the Protestantism of the Populists. Farmers in the established Great Lakes states enjoyed prosperous years and felt less discontented than farmers in other regions. But chance also played a part in Bryan's defeat. Bad wheat harvests in India, Australia, and Argentina drove up grain prices in the world market. Many of the complaints of American farmers evaporated amid rising farm prices.

The New Shape of American Politics

The landslide Republican victory marked the end of the political stalemate that had characterized American politics since the end of the Civil War. Republicans lost their identification with the politics of piety and strengthened their image as the party of prosperity and national greatness, which gave them a party dominance that lasted until the 1930s. The Democrats, under Bryan's leadership until 1912, took on the mantle of populist moralism, but were largely reduced to a sectional party, reflecting narrow southern views on money, race, and national power. The 1896 election demonstrated that the Northeast and Great Lakes states had acquired so many immigrants that they now controlled the entire nation's political destiny. Populists, demoralized by fusion with a losing campaign, fell apart and disappeared. Within the next 20 years, however, many Populist issues were taken over and adopted by politicians of the major parties.

Another result of the election of 1896 was a change in the pattern of political participation. Because the Republicans were so dominant, few states had vigorous two-party political battles. There seemed less and less reason to continue party activities aimed at bringing out large numbers of voters. Likewise, individual voters had less and less motivation to cast a ballot, especially because election results were so often a foregone conclusion. Many black voters in the South, moreover, were disfranchised, and middle-class good government reformers succeeded in reducing the high voter turnout achieved by urban party bosses. Thus, the tremendous rate of political participation that had characterized the nineteenth century since the Jackson era gradually declined. In the twentieth century, political involvement among poorer Americans lessened considerably, a phenomenon unique among western industrial countries.

McKinley had promised that Republican rule meant prosperity, and as soon as he took office, the economy recovered. Discoveries of gold in the Yukon and the Alaskan Klondike increased the money supply, thus thwarting silver mania until the early 1930s. Industrial production returned to full capacity. In a tour of the Midwest in 1898, McKinley spoke to cheering crowds about the hopeful economic picture. "We have gone from industrial depression to industrial activity," he told citizens of Clinton, Iowa, who burst into enthusiastic applause.

McKinley's election marked not only the return of an era of economic health, but also the emergence of the executive as the preeminent focus of the American political system. Just as McKinley's campaign set the pattern for the extravagant efforts to win office that have dominated modern times, his conduct as president foreshadowed the nature of the twentieth-century presidency. McKinley rejected traditional views of the president as the passive executor of laws, instead playing an active role in dealing with Congress and the press. His frequent trips away from Washington showed an increasing regard for public opinion. Some historians regard McKinley as the first modern president in his emphasis on the role of the chief executive in contributing to industrial growth and national power. As we shall see in Chapter 20, he began the transformation of the presidency into a potent force, not only in domestic life, but in world affairs as well.

Conclusion

Looking Forward

This chapter began with Edward Bellamy's imaginary look backward from the year 2000 at the grim economic realities and unresponsive politics of American life in the late nineteenth century. McKinley's triumph in 1896 indicated that in a decade marked by depression, Populist revolt, and cries for action to close the inequalities of wealth—represented by Bellamy's coach—the established order remained intact and politics remained as unresponsive as ever. Calls for change did not necessarily lead to change. But in the areas of personal action and the philosophical bases for social change, intellectual middle-class reformers like Edward Bellamy, Henry George, William James, Jane Addams, "Golden Rule" Jones, and many others were showing the way to progressive reforms in the new century. More Americans were able to look forward to the kind of cooperative, caring, and cleaner world envisioned in Bellamy's utopian novel.

As the year 1900 approached, people took a predictably intense interest in what the new century would be like. Henry Adams, still the pessimist, saw an ominous future, predicting the explosive and ultimately destructive energy of unrestrained industrial development, symbolized by the "dynamo" and other engines of American power. Such forces, he warned, would overwhelm the gentler, moral forces represented by art, woman, and religious symbols like the Virgin. But others were more optimistic, preferring to place their confidence in America's historic role as an exemplary nation, demonstrating to the world the moral superiority of its economic system, democratic institutions, and middle-class Protestant values. Surely the new century, most thought, would see not only the continued perfection of these values and institutions, but also the spread of American influence throughout the world. Such confidence resulted in foreign expansion by the American people even before the old century had ended. We turn to that in the next chapter.

Recommended Reading

Politics in the Gilded Age

John Allswang, *Bosses, Machines, and Urban Voters* (1977); Charles W. Calhoun, *The Gilded Age: Essays on the Origins of Modern America* (1996); Sean Dennis Cashman, *America and the Gilded Age: From the Death of Lincoln to the Rise of Theodore Roosevelt* (1984); Harold U. Faulkner, *Politics, Reform and Expansion, 1890–1900* (1959); John A. Garraty, *The New Commonwealth, 1877–1890* (1968); Samuel P. Hays, *The Response to Industrialism, 1885–1914* (1957); Richard Jensen, *The Winning of the Midwest: Social and Political Conflict, 1888–1896* (1971); Morton Keller, *Affairs of State: Public Life in Late Nineteenth Century America* (1977); Paul Kleppner, *The Cross of Culture: A Social Analysis of Midwestern Politics, 1850–1900* (1970) and *The Third Electoral System, 1853–1892: Parties, Voters, and Political Cultures* (1979); H. Wayne Morgan, *From Hayes to McKinley: National Party Politics, 1877–1896* (1969); Nell I. Painter, *Standing at Armageddon in the United States, 1877–1919* (1987); William Riordon, *Plunkitt of Tammany Hall* (1963); Robert Wiebe, *The Search for Order, 1877–1920* (1967); R. Hal Williams, *Years of Decision: American Politics in the 1890s* (1978); Richard E. Welch, Jr., *The Presidencies of Grover Cleveland* (1988).

Middle-Class Reform and Reformers

Jane Addams, *Twenty Years at Hull House* (1910); Ruth Bordin, *Frances Willard: A Biography* (1986) and *Women and Temperance: The Quest for Power and Liberty, 1873–1900* (1981); Paul Boyer, *Urban Masses and Moral Order in America, 1820–1920* (1978); Mina Carson, *Settlement Folk: Social Thought and the American Settlement Movement, 1885–1930* (1990); Susan Curtis, *A Consuming Faith: The Social Gospel and Modern American Culture* (1991); Allen F. Davis, *American Heroine: The Life and Legend of Jane Addams* (1973) and *Spearheads for Reform: The Social Settlements and the Progressive Movement, 1890–1914* (1967); Robert Fogarty, *All Things New: American Communes and Utopian Movements, 1860–1914* (1990); Margaret Forster, *Significant Sisters: The Grassroots of Active Feminism* (1984); Peter J. Frederick, *Knights of the Golden Rule: The Intellectual as Christian Social Reformer in the 1890s* (1976); Richard Hofstadter, *Age of Reform: From Bryan to F.D.R.* (1955); Melvin G. Holli, *Reform in Detroit: Hazen S. Pingree and Urban Politics* (1969); Aileen Kraditor, *The Ideas of the Woman's Suffrage Movement, 1890–1920* (1965); Ralph Luker, *The Social Gospel in Black and White: American Racial Reform, 1885–1912* (1991); Arthur Mann, *Yankee Reformers in an Urban Age: Social Reform in Boston, 1880–1900* (1954); Daphne Pata, ed., *Looking Backward, 1988–1888: Essays on Edward Bellamy* (1988); Kathryn Kish Sklar, *Florence Kelly and the Nation's Work: The Rise of Women's Political Culture, 1830–1900* (1995); John Sproat, *"The Best Men": Liberal Reformers in the Gilded Age* (1968); John L. Thomas, *Alternative America: Henry George, Edward Bellamy, Henry Demarest Lloyd and the Adversary Tradition* (1983); Ronald C. White and Charles Howard Hopkins, *The Social Gospel: Religion and Reform in Changing America* (1976).

Cultural Life, Thought, and Literature of the Late Nineteenth Century

Edward Bellamy, *Looking Backward* (1888); Burton J. Bledstein, *The Culture of Professionalism: The Middle Class and the Development of Higher Education in America* (1976);

Mark C. Carnes and Clyde Griffen, eds., *Meanings for Manhood: Constructions of Masculinity in Victorian America* (1990); John Cawelti, *Apostles of the Self-Made Man: Changing Concepts of Success in America* (1965); Kate Chopin, *The Awakening* (1899); Theodore Dreiser, *Sister Carrie* (1900); Peter Filene, *Him/Her/Self: Sex Roles in Modern America*, 2d ed. (1986); Richard Hofstadter, *Social Darwinism in American Thought* (1955); William Dean Howells, *A Hazard of New Fortunes* (1889) and *The Rise of Silas Lapham* (1885); Bruce Kuklick, *The Rise of American Philosophy: Cambridge, Massachusetts, 1860–1930* (1977); T. Jackson Lears, *No Place of Grace: Antimodernism and the Transformation of American Culture, 1880–1920* (1981); H. Wayne Morgan, *Unity and Culture: The United States, 1877–1890* (1971); Frank Norris, *The Octopus* (1901); Sheila Rothman, *Woman's Proper Place: A History of Changing Ideals and Practices, 1870 to the Present* (1978); Alan Trachtenberg, *The Incorporation of America: Culture and Society in the Gilded Age* (1982); Mark Twain and Charles D. Warner, *The Gilded Age* (1873); Irvin G. Wyllie, *The Self-Made Man in America* (1954); Larzer Ziff, *The American 1890s: Life and Times of a Lost Generation* (1966).

Depression Politics, Populism, and the Election of 1896

Gene Clanton, *Populism: The Humane Preference in America, 1890–1900* (1991); Robert F. Durden, *The Climax of Populism: The Election of 1896* (1965); Paul Glad, *McKinley, Bryan and the People* (1964); Lawrence Goodwyn, *Democratic Promise: The Populist Movement in America* (1976); Charles Hoffman, *The Depression of the Nineties: An Economic History* (1970); Samuel McSeveney, *The Politics of Depression: Political Behavior in the Northeast, 1893–1896* (1972); David P. Thelen, *The New Citizenship: Origins of Progressivism in Wisconsin, 1885–1900* (1972).

CHAPTER 20

Becoming a World Power

n January 1899, the United States Senate was locked in a dramatic debate over whether to ratify the Treaty of Paris concluding the recent war with Spain over Cuban independence. At the same time, American soldiers uneasily faced Filipino rebels across a neutral zone around the outskirts of Manila, capital of the Philippines. Until recent weeks, the Americans and Filipinos had been allies, together defeating the Spanish to liberate the Philippines. The American fleet under Admiral George Dewey had destroyed the Spanish naval squadron in Manila Bay on May 1, 1898. Three weeks later, an American ship brought from exile the native Filipino insurrectionary leader Emilio Aguinaldo to lead rebel forces on land while U.S. gunboats patrolled the seas.

At first, the Filipinos looked on the Americans as liberators. Although the intentions of the United States were never clear, Aguinaldo believed that, as in Cuba, the Americans had no territorial ambitions. They would simply drive the Spanish out and then leave themselves. In June, therefore, Aguinaldo declared the independence of the Philippines and began setting up a constitutional government. American officials pointedly ignored the independence ceremonies. When an armistice ended the war in August, American troops denied Filipino soldiers an opportunity to liberate their own capital city and shunted them off to the suburbs. The armistice agreement recognized American rights to the "harbor, city, and bay of Manila," while the proposed Treaty of Paris gave the United States the entire Philippine Island archipelago.

Consequently, tension mounted in the streets of Manila and along 14 miles of trenches separating American and Filipino soldiers. Taunts, obscenities, and racial epithets were shouted across the neutral zone. Barroom skirmishes and knifings pervaded the city at night; American soldiers searched houses without warrants and looted stores. Their behavior was not unlike that of the English soldiers in Boston in the 1770s.

On the night of February 4, 1899, Privates William Grayson and David Miller of Company B, 1st Nebraska Volunteers, were on patrol in Santa Mesa, a Manila suburb surrounded on three sides by insurgent trenches. The Americans had orders to shoot any Filipino soldiers found in the neutral area. As the two Americans cautiously worked their way to a bridge over the San Juan River, they heard a Filipino signal whistle, answered by another. Then a red lantern flashed from a nearby blockhouse. The two froze as four Filipinos emerged from the darkness on the road ahead. "Halt!" Grayson shouted. The native lieutenant in charge answered, "Halto!," either mockingly or because he had similar orders. Standing less than 15 feet apart, the two men repeated their commands. After a moment's hesitation, Grayson fired, killing his opponent with one bullet. As the other Filipinos jumped out at them, Grayson and Miller shot two more. Then they turned and ran back to their own lines shouting warnings of attack. A full-scale battle followed.

The next day, Commodore Dewey cabled Washington that the "insurgents have inaugurated general engagement" and promised a hasty suppression of the insurrection. The outbreak of hostilities ended the Senate debates. On February 6, the Senate ratified the Treaty of Paris, thus formally annexing the Philippines and sparking a war between the United States and Filipino nationalists.

In a guerrilla war similar to those fought later in the twentieth century in Asia and Central America, Filipino nationalists tried to undermine the American will by hit-and-run attacks. American soldiers, meanwhile, remained in heavily garrisoned cities and undertook search-and-destroy missions to root out rebels and pacify the countryside. The Filipino-American War lasted until July 1902, three years longer than the Spanish-American War that caused it and involving far more troops, casualties, and monetary and moral costs.

Dewey at Manila Bay, May 1, 1898 (painting by Rufus Zogbaum): American Expansionism Triumphant. (Courtesy of The Vermont State House)

*H*ow did all this happen? What brought Private Grayson to "shoot my first nigger," as he put it, halfway around the world in distant Asia? For the first time in history, regular American soldiers found themselves fighting outside North America. The "champion of oppressed nations," as Aguinaldo said, had turned into an oppressor nation itself, imposing the American way of life and American institutions on faraway peoples against their will.

The war in the Philippines marked a critical transformation of America's role in the world. Within a few years at the turn of the century, the United States acquired an empire, however small by European standards, and established itself as a world power. In this chapter, we will review the historical dilemmas of America's role in the world, especially those of the expansionist nineteenth century. Then we will examine the motivations for the intensified expansionism of the 1890s and how they were manifested in Cuba, the Philippines, and elsewhere. Finally, we will look at how the fundamental patterns of modern American foreign policy were established for Latin America, Asia, and Europe in the early twentieth century. Throughout this discussion, we will see that the tension between idealism and self-interest that has permeated America's domestic history has guided its foreign policy as well.

Steps Toward Empire

The circumstances that brought Privates Grayson and Miller from Nebraska to the Philippines originated deep in American history. As early as the Puritan migration from England to Massachusetts Bay in the seventeenth century, Americans faced the dilemma of how to do good in a world that does wrong. John Winthrop sought to set up a "city on a hill" in the New World, a model community of righteous living for others in the world to behold and imitate. "Let the eyes of the world be upon us," Winthrop said, and that wish, reaffirmed during the American Revolution, became a permanent goal of American policy toward the outside world.

America as a Model Society

Nineteenth-century Americans continued to believe in the nation's special mission. The Monroe Doctrine in 1823 pointed out moral differences between the monarchical, arbitrary governments of Europe and the free republican institutions of the New World. As Spanish colonies in South and Central America followed the American revolutionary model, Monroe warned Europe to stay out. In succeeding decades, a number of distinguished European visitors came to study

"democracy in America," to see for themselves the "great social revolution" at work (see Chapter 12). They found widespread democracy, representative and responsive political and legal institutions, a religious commitment to the notion of human perfectibility, unlimited energy, and the ability to apply unregulated economic activity and inventive genius to produce more things for more people.

The model seemed irresistible. In a world that was evil, Americans believed that they stood as a transforming force for good. Many others agreed. The problem was how a nation committed to isolationism was to do the transforming. One way was to encourage other nations to observe and imitate the good example set by the United States. Often, however, other nations preferred their own society or were attracted to competing models of modernization, such as socialism, as frequently happened in the twentieth century. This implied the need for a more aggressive foreign policy.

Americans have rarely simply focused on perfecting the good example at home, waiting for others to copy it. This requires patience and passivity, two traits not characteristic of Americans. Rather, throughout history, the American people have actively and sometimes forcefully imposed their ideas and institutions on others. The interna-

Clustered in trenches against Filipino nationalists, American soldiers in the faraway Philippine Islands in 1899 were a harbinger of twentieth-century wars to come. (Library of Congress)

tional crusades of the United States, well intentioned if not always well received, have usually been motivated by a mixture of idealism and self-interest. Hence, the effort to spread the exemplary American model to an imperfect world has been both a blessing and a burden, both for others and for the American people themselves.

Early Expansionism

A consistent expression of continental expansionism marked the first century of American independence. Jefferson's purchase of the Louisiana Territory in 1803 and the grasping for Florida and Canada by War Hawks in 1812 signaled an intense American interest in territorial growth. Although the United States remained "unentangled" in European affairs for most of the century, as both Washington and Jefferson had advised, the American government and people were much entangled elsewhere. To the Cherokee, Seminole, Lakota, Apache, Cheyenne, and other Native American nations, the United States was far from isolationist. Nor did the Canadians,

the Spanish in Florida, or Mexicans in Texas and California consider the Americans nonexpansionist. Until mid-century, the United States pursued its "Manifest Destiny" (see Chapter 13) by expanding across the North American continent. But in the 1850s, Americans began to look beyond their own continent. This trend was marked most significantly by Commodore Perry's visit to Japan, the expansion of the China trade, and various expeditions into the Caribbean in search of more cotton lands and a canal connecting the two oceans.

Lincoln's secretary of state, William Seward, accelerated these outward thrusts. During the Civil War, Seward was preoccupied with preventing the Confederacy from receiving foreign aid and diplomatic recognition. But once the war ended, he revived his vision of an America that would hold a "commanding sway in the world." Although restrained in his territorial ambitions, Seward believed that the United States was destined to exert commercial domination "on the Pacific ocean, and its islands and continents." His goal was that from markets, raw materials, and trade would come the "regeneration of ... the East."

Toward this end, Seward purchased Alaska from Russia in 1867 for $7.2 million. He also acquired a coaling station in the Midway Islands near Hawaii, where missionaries and merchants were already active, and thus paved the way for American commercial expansion in Korea, Japan, and China. Moreover, he advocated the annexation of Cuba and other islands of the West Indies and tried to negotiate a treaty securing an American-built canal through the isthmus of Panama. Seward dreamed of "possession" of the entire North and Central American continent and ultimately "control of the world." Although his larger dreams went unrealized, his interest in expansion into the Caribbean persisted among business interests and politicians after Cuba's attempted revolt against Spain in 1868.

Expansion After Seward

In 1870, foreshadowing the Philippine debates 30 years later, supporters of President Grant tried to force the Senate to annex Santo Domingo (Hispaniola), an island near Cuba. They cited the strategic importance of the Caribbean and argued forcefully for the economic value of raw materials and markets that the addition of Santo Domingo would bring. Senatorial opponents responded that expansionism violated the American principle of self-determination and government by the consent of the governed. They pointed out, moreover, that the native peoples of the Caribbean were brown-skinned, culturally inferior, non-English-speaking, and therefore unassimilable. Finally, they suggested that expansionism might involve foreign entanglements, necessitating a large and expensive navy, growth in the size of government, and higher taxes. The Senate rejected the treaty to annex Santo Domingo.

Although reluctant to add territory outright, American interests in Latin America and Asia were eager for commercial dominance. A number of statesmen asserted the United States' influence in these areas. President Hayes said in 1880 that despite a treaty with England pledging joint construction and control of a canal across either Panama or Nicaragua, he was certain that if such a canal were built, it would be "under American con-

trol" and would be considered "virtually a part of the coast line of the United States." But nothing came of diplomatic efforts with Nicaragua to smooth the way for an American-built canal except Nicaraguan suspicions of U.S. intentions.

In 1881, Secretary of State James G. Blaine sought to convene a conference of American nations to promote hemispheric peace and trade. Although motivated mostly by his presidential ambitions, his effort nevertheless led to the first Pan-American Conference eight years later. The Latin Americans may have wondered what Blaine intended, for in 1881 he intervened in three separate border disputes in Central and South America, in each case at the cost of goodwill and trust.

Ten years later, relations with Chile were harmed when several American sailors on shore leave were involved in a barroom brawl in Valparaiso. Two Americans were killed and several others injured. American pride was also injured, and President Benjamin Harrison sent an ultimatum calling for a "prompt and full reparation." After threats of war, Chile complied.

Similar incidents occurred as American expansionists pursued Seward's goals in the Pacific. In the mid-1870s, American sugar-growing interests in the Hawaiian Islands were strong enough to place whites in positions of influence over the native monarchy. In 1875, they obtained a reciprocity treaty admitting Hawaiian sugar duty-free to the United States. When the treaty was renewed and approved in 1887, the United States also gained exclusive rights to build a naval base at Pearl Harbor on the island of Oahu.

Native Hawaiians resented the growing influence of American sugar interests, especially as they turned to Japanese immigrants to replace Hawaiians (many of whom were killed by white diseases) in the sugarcane fields. Between 1885 and 1924, 200,000 Japanese workers, pursuing "huge dreams of fortune … across the ocean," migrated to Hawaii and nearly another 200,000 went to the West Coast of the United States.

In 1891, the strongly nationalist Queen Liliuokalani assumed the throne in Hawaii and promptly abolished the constitution, seeking to establish control over whites in the name of "Hawaii for the Hawaiians." In 1893, with the help of U.S.

gunboats and marines, sugar planters, fearful of losing influence and of the queen's turning to Japan for political support, staged a palace coup (a revolution later called one "of sugar, by sugar, for sugar") and sought formal annexation by the friendly Harrison administration. But before final Senate ratification could be achieved, Grover Cleveland, who opposed imperial expansion, returned to the presidency for his second term and stopped the move. He was, however, unable to remove the white sugar growers from power in Hawaii. They waited patiently for a more desirable time for annexation, which came during the war in 1898.

Moving ever closer toward the fabled markets of the Far East, the United States acquired a naval station at Pago Pago in the Samoan Islands in 1878. However, it had to share the port with Great Britain and Germany. In an incident in 1889, American and German naval forces almost fought each other, but a typhoon wiped out both navies and ended the crisis. Troubles in the Pacific also occurred in the late 1880s over the American seizure of several

Canadian ships in seal fur and fishing disputes in the Bering Sea. This issue was settled only by the British threat of naval action and with the ruling of an international arbitration commission, which ordered the United States to pay damages.

The United States confronted the English closer to home as it sought to replace Britain as the most influential nation in Central American affairs. In 1895, a boundary dispute between Venezuela and British Guiana threatened to bring British intervention against the Venezuelans. President Cleveland, in need of a popular political issue to deflect attention from the depression, discovered the political value of a tough foreign policy by defending a weak sister American republic against the British bully. He asked Secretary of State Richard Olney to send a message to Great Britain. Olney's note, which was stronger than Cleveland had intended, invoked the Monroe Doctrine, declared the United States as "practically sovereign on this continent," and demanded British acceptance of international arbitration to

Iolani Palace, former home of Queen Liliuokalani, was the scene of annexation ceremonies in 1898, when Hawaii became a U.S. territory. "We need Hawaii just as much as and a good deal more than we did California," President McKinley said. "It is manifest destiny." (Library of Congress)

settle the dispute. The British ignored the note, and war threatened. Although England was the United States' chief rival for economic influence in the Caribbean, both sides eventually realized that war between them would be an "absurdity." The dispute was settled by agreeing to an impartial American commission to settle the boundary.

These increasing conflicts in the Caribbean and the Pacific signaled the rise of American presence beyond the borders of the United States. Yet, as of 1895, the nation had neither the means nor a consistent policy for enlarging its role in the world. The diplomatic service was small, inexperienced, and unprofessional. Around the world, American emissaries kept sloppy records, issued illegal passports, involved themselves in petty local issues and frauds, and exhibited insensitive behavior toward indigenous cultures. Not until the 1930s did a U.S. embassy official in Beijing speak Chinese. The U.S. Army, numbering about 28,000 men in the mid-1890s, ranked thirteenth in the world, behind that of Bulgaria. The navy, dismantled after the Civil War and partly rebuilt under President Arthur, ranked no higher than tenth and included many ships powered by dangerously outdated boilers. These limited and backward instruments of foreign policy could not support the aspirations of an emerging world power, especially one whose rise to power had come so quickly.

Expansionism in the 1890s

In 1893, the historian Frederick Jackson Turner wrote that for three centuries, "the dominant fact in American life has been expansion." Turner observed that the "extension of American influence to outlying islands and adjoining countries" indicated that expansionism would continue. Turner's observations struck a responsive chord in a country that had always been restless, mobile, and optimistic. With the western American frontier closed, Americans would surely look for new frontiers, for mobility and markets as well as for morality and missionary activity. The motivations for the expansionist impulse of the late 1890s resembled those that had prompted people to settle the New World in the first place: greed, glory,

and God. We will examine expansionism as a reflection of profits, patriotism, piety (moral mission), and politics.

Profits: Searching for Overseas Markets

Albert Beveridge of Indiana bragged in 1898 that "American factories are making more than the American people can use; American soil is producing more than they can consume. Fate has written our policy for us; the trade of the world must and shall be ours." Americans like Beveridge believed in the dream of Seward, Blaine, and others to establish a commercial empire in the islands and adjoining countries of the Caribbean Sea and the Pacific Ocean. With a strong belief in free enterprise and open markets for investing capital and selling products, American businessmen saw huge profits beckoning in the heavily populated areas of Latin America and Asia. They also believed it essential to get their share of these markets to stay competitive with European countries. The attraction was enhanced by the availability in those lands of abundant raw materials such as sugar, coffee, fruits, oil, rubber, and minerals.

Understanding that an increase in commerce required a stronger navy and coaling stations and colonies, business interests began to shape diplomatic and military strategy. As Senator Orville Platt of Connecticut said in 1893, "A policy of isolation did well enough when we were an embryo nation, but today things are different." By 1901, the economic adviser for the State Department described overseas commercial expansion as a "natural law of economic and race development."

Not all businessmen in the 1890s agreed that commercial expansion backed by a vigorous foreign policy was desirable. Some preferred traditional trade with Canada and Europe rather than risky new ventures in Asia and Latin America. Securing colonies and developing faraway markets and investment opportunities not only would require initially high expenses, but also might involve the United States in wars with commercial rivals or native peoples in distant places. Some businessmen, furthermore, thought it more important in 1897 to secure recovery from the depression than little islands in Asia.

But the decrease in domestic consumption during the depression also encouraged businessmen to expand into new markets to sell surplus goods. The tremendous growth of American industrial and agricultural production in the post–Civil War years made expansionism an attractive alternative to drowning in overproduction. Many businessmen preferred new markets to cutting prices, which would redistribute wealth by allowing the lower classes to buy excess goods, or to laying off workers, which would increase social unrest. Thus, many reasons, not least the fear of overproduction and a desire to remain competitive in international markets, convinced hesitant businessmen to expand. They were led by the newly formed National Association of Manufacturers, which emphasized in 1896 "that the trade centres of Central and South America are natural markets for American products."

Despite the depression of the 1890s, products spewed from American factories at a staggering rate. The United States moved from fourth in the world in manufacturing in 1870 to first in 1900, doubling the number of factories and tripling the value of farm output, mainly cotton, corn, and wheat. The United States led the world not only in railroad construction (206,631 miles of tracks in 1900, four times more than in 1870), but also in agricultural machinery and mass-produced technological products such as sewing machines, electrical implements, telephones, cash registers, elevators, and cameras. Manufactured goods grew nearly fivefold between 1895 and 1914.

Correspondingly, the total value of American exports tripled, jumping from $434 million in 1866 to nearly $1.5 billion in 1900. By 1914, exports had risen to $2.5 billion, a 67 percent increase over 1900. The increased trade continued to go mainly to Europe rather than Asia. In 1900, for example, only 3 to 4 percent of U.S. exports went to China and Japan. Nevertheless, interest in Asian markets grew, especially as agricultural production continued to increase and prices remained low. Farmers dreamed of selling their surplus wheat to China. James J. Hill of the Great Northern Railroad promoted their hopes by printing wheat cookbooks in various Asian languages and distributing them in the Far East, hoping to fill his westward-bound

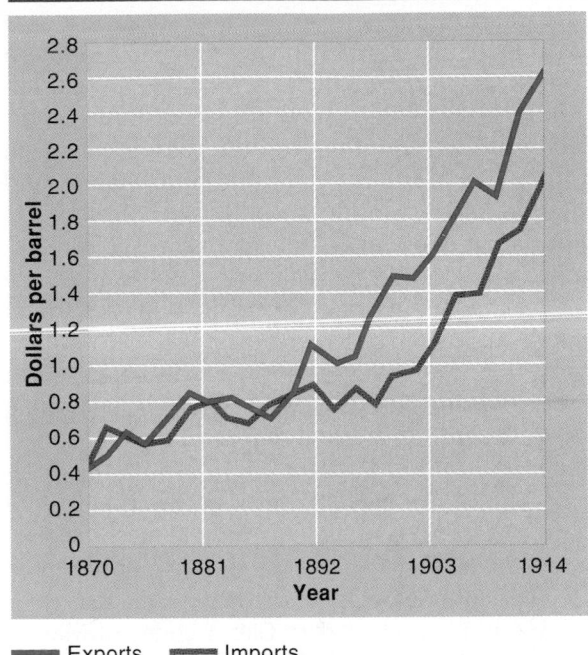

American Foreign Trade, 1870–1914

Exports   Imports

After a rather gradual increase in trade through the boom-and-bust cycles of the 1870s and 1880s, and an actual dip during the depression of 1893–1895, note the spectacular increases during the Republican era of Presidents McKinley, Roosevelt, and Taft. Source: U.S. Bureau of the Census.

boxcars and merchant ships with wheat and other grains.

Investment activity followed a similar pattern. American direct investments abroad increased from about $634 million to $2.6 billion between 1897 and 1914. Although investments were largest in Britain, Canada, and Mexico, the potential of Asia and Central America received the most attention. Central American investment increased from $21 million in 1897 to $93 million by the eve of World War I, mainly in mines, railroads, and banana and coffee plantations. At the turn of the century came the formation and growth of America's biggest multinational corporations—the United Fruit Company, Alcoa Aluminum, Amalgamated Copper, Du Pont, American Tobacco, and others. Although slow to respond to investment and market opportunities abroad, these companies soon supported an aggressive foreign policy and the expansion of America's role in the world.

Patriotism: Asserting National Power

American interest in investments, markets, and raw materials abroad reflected a determination not to be left out of the international competition among European powers and Japan for commercial spheres of influence and colonies in Asia, Africa, and Latin America. England, France, and Germany were frequently on the verge of war as they scrambled for colonies as a measure of economic worth and national glory. In 1898, a State Department memorandum stated that "we can no longer afford to disregard international rivalries now that we ourselves have become a competitor in the world-wide struggle for trade." The national state, then, had a role in supporting commercial interests.

More Americans, however, saw national glory and greatness as legitimate motivations for expansionism. In the late 1890s, a group of men centered on Assistant Secretary of the Navy Theodore Roosevelt and Senator Henry Cabot Lodge of Massachusetts emerged as highly influential leaders of a changing American foreign policy. These vigorous and intensely nationalistic young men successfully shifted official policy from "continentalism" to what Lodge called the "large policy." By 1899, Assistant Secretary of State John Bassett Moore wrote that the United States had finally moved "into the position of what is commonly called a world power.... Where formerly we had only commercial interests, we now have territorial and political interests as well." Roosevelt agreed that economic interests should take second place to questions of what he called "national honor."

The writings of Alfred Thayer Mahan, a naval strategist and author of several books on the importance of sea power to national greatness, greatly influenced the new foreign policy elite. Mahan argued that in a world of Darwinian struggle for survival, national power depended on naval supremacy, control of sea lanes, and vigorous development of domestic resources and foreign markets. He advocated colonies in both the Caribbean and the Pacific, linked by a canal built and controlled by the United States. Strong nations, Mahan wrote, had a special responsibility to dominate weak ones. In a world of constant "strife," where "everywhere nation is arrayed against nation," it was imperative that Americans begin "to look outward." National pride and glory would surely follow.

Advocates of expansionism urged enlarging the U.S. Navy, part of which is pictured here in 1892. The armored warship Maine, *which would explode and sink in Havana harbor before the outbreak of the Spanish-American War, is shown in the middle foreground. (The New York Public Library, Astor, Lenox & Tilden Foundations)*

Piety: The Missionary Impulse

As Mahan's and Roosevelt's statements suggest, a strong sense of duty and the missionary ideal of doing good for others also motivated expansionism. A statesman once boasted that "with God's help, we will lift Shanghai up and up, ever up, until it is just like Kansas City." Richard Olney agreed, saying in 1898 that "the mission of this country is … to forego no fitting opportunity to further the progress of civilization." Motivated by America's sense of itself as a model nation, such statements sometimes rationalized the exploitation and oppression of weaker peoples. Although the European countries had their own justifications for imperialism, Americans such as Roosevelt, Lodge, and Mahan all would have agreed with the following summary of expansionist beliefs:

> Certain nations are more civilized than others. These nations are peopled by those who are white, Anglo-Saxon, Protestant, and English-speaking. They enjoy free enterprise and republican political institutions, meaning representative government, shared power, and the rule of law. Further evidence of the civilized nature of such nations includes their advanced technological and industrial development, large middle classes, and high degree of education and literacy. The prime examples in the world are England, Germany, and the United States.

> In the natural struggle for existence, the races and nations that survive and prosper, such as these, prove their fitness and superiority over others. The United States, as a matter of history, geographic location, and political genius, is so favored and fit that God has chosen it to take care of and uplift less favored peoples. This responsibility cannot be avoided. It is a national duty, or burden—the "white man's burden"—that civilized nations undertake to bring peace, progressive values, and ordered liberty to the world.

These ideas, widespread in popular thought, described America's providential sense of itself. As a missionary put it in 1885, "The Christian nations are subduing the world in order to make mankind free." Josiah Strong, a Congregational minister, was one of the most ardent advocates of American missionary expansionism. Although his book *Our Country* (1885) focused on internal threats to American social order, in a long chapter titled "The Future of the Anglo-Saxon Race," Strong made his case for an outward thrust. He argued that in the struggle for survival among nations, the United States had emerged as the center of Anglo-Saxonism and was "divinely commissioned" to spread the blessings of political liberty, Protestant Christianity, and civilized values over the earth. "This powerful race," he wrote, "will move down upon Mexico, down upon Central and South America, out upon the islands of the sea, over upon Africa and beyond." In a cruder statement of the same idea, Albert Beveridge said in 1899 that God had prepared English-speaking Anglo-Saxons to become the "master organizers of the world to establish and administer governments among savages and senile peoples."

If not so crudely, missionaries carried similar Western values to non-Christian lands around the world. China was a favorite target. The number of American Protestant missionaries in China increased from 436 in 1874 to 5,462 in 1914. The largest increase came in the 1890s. Although the missionaries were not as effective as they had hoped to be, the estimated number of Christian converts in China jumped from 5,000 in 1870 to nearly 100,000 in 1900. This tiny fraction of the Chinese population included many young reformist intellectuals who absorbed Western ideas in Christian mission colleges and went on to lead the Revolution of 1912 that ended the Manchu dynasty. Economic relations between China and the United States increased at approximately the same rate as missionary activity. The number of American firms in China grew from 50 to 550 between 1870 and 1930, while trade increased 1,500 percent.

Politics: Manipulating Public Opinion

These figures suggest how economic, religious, moral, and nationalistic motivations became interwoven in American expansionism in the late 1890s. Although less significant than the other motives, politics also played a role. For the first time in American history, public opinion over international issues loomed large in presidential politics. The psychological tensions and economic hardships of the depression of the 1890s jarred national self-confidence. Foreign adventures and the glories of expansionism provided an emotional release from domestic turmoil and promised to restore patriotic pride—and maybe even win votes.

This process was helped by the growth of a highly competitive popular press, the penny daily newspaper, which brought international issues before a mass readership. When several newspapers in New York City, notably William Randolph Hearst's *Journal* and Joseph Pulitzer's *World,* competed to see which could stir up more public support for the Cuban rebels in their struggle for independence from Spain, politicians ignored the public outcry at their peril. Daily reports of Spanish atrocities in 1896 and 1897 kept public moral outrage constantly before President McKinley as he considered his course of action. His Democratic opponent, William Jennings Bryan, entered the fray. Although in principle a pacifist, he, too, advocated United States intervention in Cuba on moral grounds of a holy war to help the oppressed. Bryan even raised a regiment of Nebraska volunteers to go off to the war, but the Republican administration kept him far from battle and therefore far from the headlines.

Politics, then, joined profits, patriotism, and piety in motivating the expansionism of the 1890s. These four impulses interacted to influence the Spanish-American War, the annexation of the Philippine Islands, and the foreign policy of President Theodore Roosevelt.

Cuba and the Philippines

Lying 90 miles off the southern tip of Florida, Cuba had been the object of intense American interest for a half century. Although successful in thwarting American adventurism in Cuba in the 1850s, Spain was unable to halt the continuing struggle of the Cuban people for relief from exploitive labor in the sugar plantations, even after slavery itself ended, and for a measure of autonomy. The most recent uprising, which lasted from 1868 to 1878, had raised tensions between Spain and the United States; it also whetted the Cuban appetite not just for reforms but for complete independence.

The Road to War

When the Cuban revolt flared up anew in 1895, the Madrid government again failed to implement reforms but instead sent General "Butcher" Weyler with 50,000 troops to quell the disturbance. When Weyler began herding rural Cuban citizens into "reconcentration" camps, Americans were outraged. An outpouring of sympathy swept the nation, especially as reports came back of the horrible suffering in the camps, with thousands dying of malnutrition, starvation, and disease. Sensationalist newspapers in the United States, competing for readers, stirred up sentiment with pages of bloody stories of atrocities. "The old, the young, the weak, the crippled—all are butchered without mercy," wrote the New York *World.*

The Cuban struggle appealed to a country convinced of its role as protector of the weak and defender of the right of self-determination. One editorial deplored Spanish "injustice, oppression, extortion, and demoralization," while describing the Cubans as heroic freedom fighters "largely inspired by our glorious example of beneficent free institutions and successful self-government." Motivated by genuine humanitarian concern and a sense of duty, many Americans held Cuba rallies to raise money and food for famine relief. They called for land reforms, and some advocated armed intervention, but neither President Cleveland nor President McKinley wanted a war over Cuba.

Self-interested motives also played a role. For many years, Americans had noted the profitable resources and strategic location of the island. American companies had invested extensively in Cuban sugar plantations. By 1897, trade with Cuba reached $27 million per year. Appeals for reform had much to do with ensuring a stable environment for further investments, as well as for the protection of sugar fields against the ravages of civil war.

The election of 1896 diverted attention from Cuba to the issues of free silver and jobs, but only temporarily. A new government in Madrid recalled Weyler and seemed ready to grant a degree of self-government to the Cubans. But these concessions were halfhearted. Conditions worsened in the reconcentration camps, and the American press kept the plight of the Cuban people before the public. McKinley, eager not to

United States Territorial Expansion to 1900

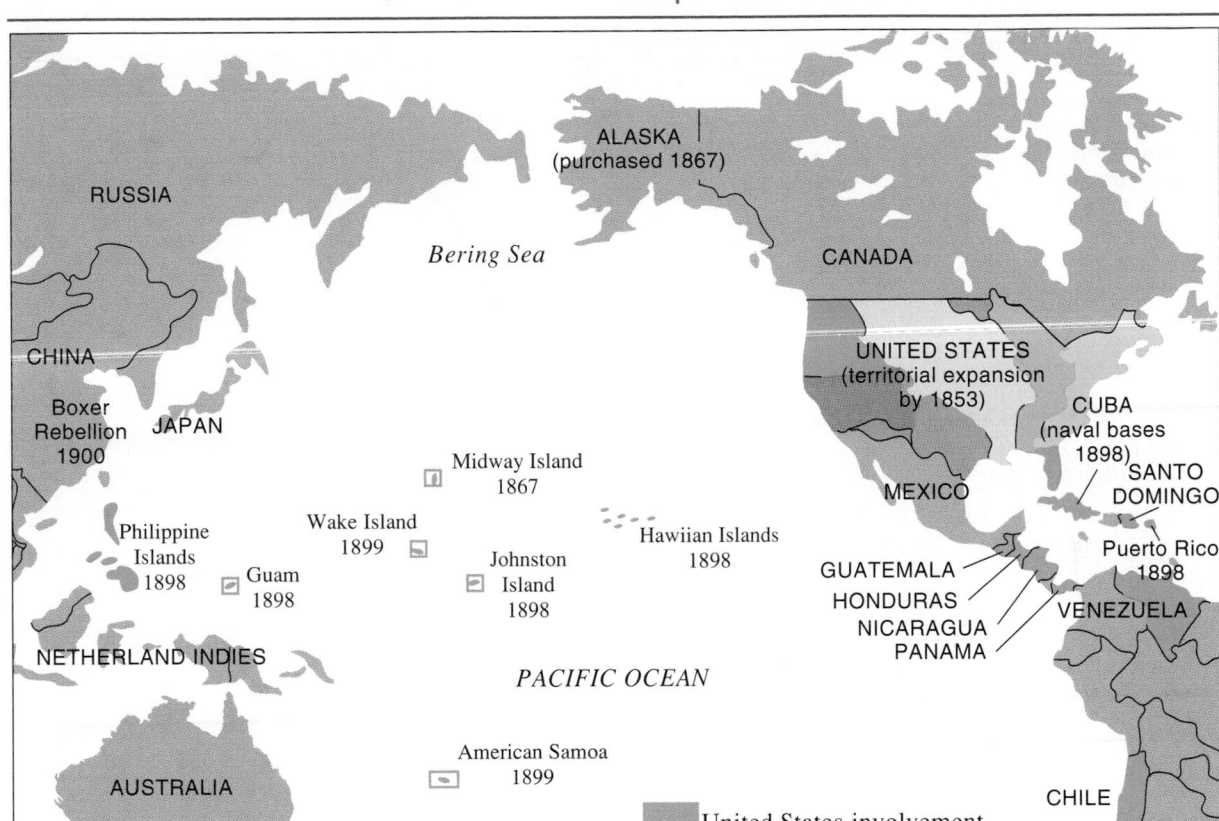

Compare this map with the one on U.S. territorial expansion to 1860 on page 438 (represented in miniature in the U.S. portion of this map).

take any action that might upset business recovery from the depression, skillfully resisted the pressure for war. But his skill could not control Spanish misrule or Cuban aspirations for freedom. The fundamental causes of the war—Spanish intransigence in the face of persistent Cuban rebellion and American sugar interests and sympathies for the underdog—were seemingly unstoppable.

Events early in 1898 sparked the outbreak of hostilities. Rioting in Havana intensified both Spanish repression and American outrage. As pressures for war increased, a letter from the Spanish minister to the United States, Depuy de Lôme, calling McKinley a "weak" hypocritical politician, was intercepted by spies and made public. The American populace became enraged as Hearst's New

York *Journal* called De Lôme's letter "the worst insult to the United States in its history."

A second event was more serious. When the rioting broke out, the U.S. battleship *Maine* was sent to Havana harbor to protect American citizens. Early in the evening on February 15, a tremendous explosion blew up the *Maine*, killing 262 men. American advocates of war, who assumed Spanish responsibility, called immediately for intervention. Newspaper publishers offered rewards for discovery of the perpetrators of the crime and broadcast slogans like "Remember the *Maine*! To hell with Spain!"

Assistant Secretary of the Navy Theodore Roosevelt, who had been preparing for war for some time, said that he believed the *Maine* had been sunk "by an act of dirty treachery on the part of the

Remembering the Maine, *citizens decorated its mast in observance of the second anniversary of its sinking in Havana harbor. Secretary of the Navy John Long, on returning to his office to discover that Assistant Secretary Roosevelt had cabled Admiral Dewey to prepare for war in the aftermath of the* Maine *explosion, wrote in his diary, "I find that Roosevelt has come very near causing more of an explosion than happened to the* Maine*." (The Granger Collection, New York)*

Spaniards" and that he would "give anything if President McKinley would order the fleet to Havana tomorrow." When the president did not, Roosevelt privately declared that McKinley had "no more backbone than a chocolate éclair" and continued to ready the navy for action. Although an official board of inquiry concluded that an external submarine mine caused the disaster, probably a faulty boiler or some other internal problem set off the explosion, a possibility even Roosevelt later conceded.

After the sinking of the *Maine*, Roosevelt took advantage of Secretary of the Navy John D. Long's absence from the office one day to send a cable to Commodore George Dewey, commander of the United States' Pacific fleet at Hong Kong. Roosevelt's message ordered Dewey to fill his ships with coal and, "in the event" of a declaration of war with Spain, to sail to the Philippines and make sure "the Spanish squadron does not leave the Asiatic coast." Roosevelt wrote in his diary that night that "the Secretary is away and I am having immense fun running the Navy."

Roosevelt's act was not impetuous, as Long thought, but consistent with naval policies he had been urging on his more cautious superior for more than a year. As early as 1895, the navy had formulated plans for attacking the Philippines. Influenced by Mahan and Lodge, Roosevelt wanted to enlarge the navy, whose growth had been restricted for years. He also believed that the United States should construct an interoceanic canal, acquire the Danish West Indies (the Virgin Islands), annex Hawaii outright, and oust Spain from Cuba. As Roosevelt told McKinley late in 1897, he was putting the navy in "the best possible shape" for "when war began." His order to Dewey, then, reflected a well-thought-out strategy to implement the "large policy" necessary for the advance of civilization.

The public outcry over the *Maine* drowned out McKinley's efforts to calm the populace and avoid war. The issues had become highly political, especially with midterm elections in the fall and a presidential race only two years away. Fellow

Republican Senator Lodge warned McKinley that "if war in Cuba drags on through the summer with nothing done we shall go down to the greatest defeat ever known." McKinley hoped that the Madrid government would make the necessary concessions in Cuba and sent some tough demands in March. But the Spanish response was delayed and inadequate, refusing to grant full independence to the Cubans.

On April 11, 1898, President McKinley sent an ambiguous message to Congress that seemed to call for war. Two weeks later, Congress authorized the use of troops against Spain and passed a resolution recognizing Cuban independence, actions amounting to a declaration of war. In a significant additional resolution, the Teller Amendment, Congress stated that the United States had no intentions of annexing Cuba, guaranteeing the Cubans the right to determine their own destiny. Senator George F. Hoar of Massachusetts, who later assailed the United States for its war against the Filipinos, declared that intervention in Cuba would be "the most honorable single war in all history," undertaken without "the slightest thought or desire of foreign conquest or of national gain or advantage."

"A Splendid Little War"

As soon as war was declared, Theodore Roosevelt resigned his post in the Navy Department and prepared to lead a cavalry unit in the war. African-American regiments as well as white headed to Tampa, Florida, to be shipped to Cuba. One black soldier, noting the stark differences in the southern reception of the segregated regiments, commented, "I am sorry that we were not treated with much courtesy while coming through the South." Blacks were especially sympathetic to the Cuban people's struggle. As one soldier wrote in his journal, "Oh, God! at last we have taken up the sword to enforce the divine rights of a people who have been unjustly treated." On arriving in Puerto Rico, a white soldier wrote that it was a "wonderful sight how the natives respect us." As the four-month war neared its end in August, John Hay wrote Roosevelt that "it has been a splendid little war; begun with the highest motives, carried on with magnificent intelligence and spirit."

It was a "splendid" war also because compared with the long, bloody Civil War or even the British fight with the Boers in South Africa going on at the same time, the war with Spain was short and relatively easy. Naval battles were won almost without return fire. At both major naval engagements, Manila Bay and Santiago Bay, only two Americans died, one of them from heat prostration while stoking coal. The islands of Guam and Puerto Rico were taken virtually without a shot. Only 385 men died from Spanish bullets, but over 5,000 succumbed to tropical diseases.

The Spanish-American War was splendid in other ways, as letters from American soldiers suggest. One young man wrote that his comrades were all "in good spirits" because oranges and coconuts were so plentiful and "every trooper has his canteen full of lemonade all the time." Another wrote his mother that he found Cuba not only cooler, but better than Texas in many ways: "Our money is worth twice as much as Spanish money. We do not want for anything." And another wrote his brother that he was having "a lot of fun chasing Spaniards."

But for many men, the war was anything but splendid. One soldier wrote that "words are inadequate to express the feeling of pain and sickness when one has the fever. For about a week every bone in my body ached and I did not care much whether I lived or not." Another wrote:

> One of the worst things I saw was a man shot while loading his gun. The Spanish Mauser bullet struck the magazine of his carbine, and ... the bullet was split, a part of it going through his scalp and a part through his neck.... He was a mass of blood.

The "power of joy in battle" that Teddy Roosevelt felt "when the wolf rises in the heart" was not a feeling all American soldiers shared. Roosevelt's brush with death at Las Guásimas and his celebrated charge up Kettle Hill near Santiago, his flank protected by African-American troops, made 3-inch headlines and propelled him toward the New York governor's mansion in Albany. "I would rather have led that charge," he said later, "than served three terms in the U.S. Senate." Nonetheless, no one did as much during the war as Roosevelt to

The celebrated charge of "Teddy's Rough Riders" up Kettle Hill, shown in this heroic picture (left) (The Granger Collection, New York), was made possible (and safe) because Spanish resistance was neutralized by African-American troops like these from the 9th U.S. Cavalry (right). (Library of Congress)

advance not only his political career, but also the cause of expansion and national glory.

The Philippines Debates and War

Roosevelt's ordering Dewey to Manila initiated a chain of events that led to the annexation of the Philippines. The most crucial battle of the Spanish-American War occurred on May 1, 1898, when Dewey destroyed the Spanish fleet in Manila Bay and cabled McKinley for additional troops. The president said later that when he received Dewey's cable, he was not even sure "within two thousand miles" where "those darned islands were." Actually, McKinley had approved Roosevelt's policies and knew what course of action to pursue. He sent twice as many troops as Dewey had asked for and began the process of shaping American public opinion to accept the "political, commercial [and] humanitarian" reasons for annexing all 7,000 Philippine islands. The Treaty of Paris gave the United States all of them in exchange for a $20 million payment to Spain.

The treaty was sent to the Senate for ratification during the winter of 1898–1899. Senators for and against annexation hurled arguments at each other across the floor of the Senate as American soldiers hurled oaths and taunts across the neutral zone at Aguinaldo's insurgents near Manila. Private Grayson's encounter, as we have seen, led to the passage of the treaty in a close Senate vote and began the Filipino-American War and the debates over what to do with the Philippines. These debates took place in a wider arena than the Senate, as the entire nation joined the argument. At stake were two very different views of foreign policy and of America's vision of itself. After several months of quietly seeking advice and listening to public opinion, McKinley finally recommended annexation.

Many Democrats supported the president out of fear of being labeled disloyal. At a time when openly racist thought flourished in the United States, fellow Republicans confirmed McKinley's arguments for annexation, adding even more insulting ones. Filipinos were described as childlike, savage, stunted in size, dirty, and backward. Unflattering comparisons were made to blacks and Native Americans, and policies were proposed befitting the inferior condition in which white Americans saw the Filipinos. "The country won't be pacified," a Kansas veteran of the Sioux wars told a reporter, "until the niggers are killed off like the Indians." Roosevelt called Aguinaldo a "renegade Pawnee" and said that the Filipinos had no right "to administer the country which they happen to be occupying." The attitudes favoring annexation, therefore, asserted Filipino inferiority

The Spanish-American War

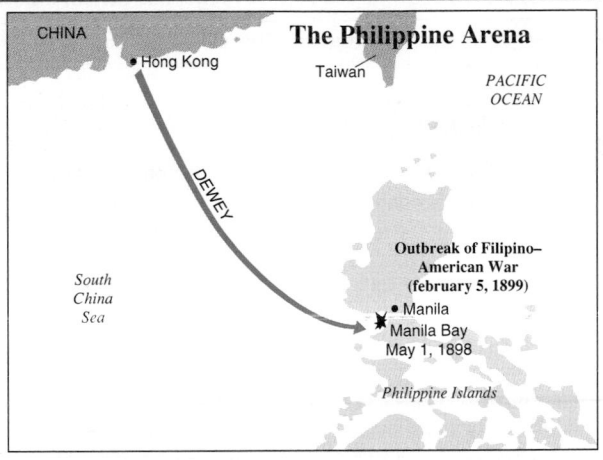

Refer to the first map in this chapter (on page 699) to see how far apart these two war zones were; as a result, American foreign policy was forever transformed.

and incapacity for self-rule while also reflecting America's proud sense of itself in 1900 as a nation of civilized order and progress.

Other Americans were not so positive about such "progress." A small but vocal group organized in the Anti-Imperialist League vigorously opposed war and annexation. Many felt displaced by the younger generation of modern expansion-

ists. By attacking imperialism, the anti-imperialists struck out against the forces of modernism that they felt threatened their elite social position. They included a cross-section of American dignitaries: ex-Presidents Harrison and Cleveland, Samuel Gompers and Andrew Carnegie, William James, Jane Addams, Mark Twain, and many others.

President McKinley's Annexation Argument

In a speech to a group of expansionist Methodist ministers and missionaries in 1900, President McKinley explained his reasons for recommending annexation of the Philippines. His statement summarizes most of the reasons for expansionism. It also offers a fascinating glimpse into the inner process of presidential decision making (or at least of a president who later sought to justify a decision).

The truth is I didn't want the Philippines and when they came to us as gift from the gods, I did not know what to do about them.... And one night it came to me this way—(1) that we could not give them back to Spain—that would be cowardly and dishonorable; (2) that we could not turn them over to France or Germany—our commercial rivals in the Orient—

that would be bad business and discreditable; (3) that we could not leave them to themselves—they were unfit for self-government—and they would soon have anarchy and misrule over there worse than Spain's was; and (4) that there was nothing left for us to do but to take them all, and to educate the Filipinos, and uplift and civilize and Christianize them, and by God's grace do the very best we could by them, as our fellowmen for whom Christ also died. And then I went to bed, and went to sleep, and slept soundly, and the next morning I sent for the chief engineer of the War Department (our mapmaker), and I told him to put the Philippines on the map of the United States, and there they are, and there they will stay while I am President!

Senator Hoar's Statement Against Imperialism

In one of the strongest anti-imperialist statements, Senator George F. Hoar of Massachusetts, who had called the war in Cuba "honorable," described the war in the Philippines in the following way.

> We changed the Monroe Doctrine from a doctrine of eternal righteousness and justice, resting on the consent of the governed, to a doctrine of brutal selfishness looking only to our own advantage. We crushed the only republic in Asia. We made war on the only Christian people in the East. We converted a war of glory to a war of shame. We vulgarized the American flag. We introduced perfidy into the practice of war. We inflicted torture on unarmed men to extort confession. We put children to death. We devastated provinces. We baffled the aspirations of a people for liberty.

The major anti-imperialist arguments pointed out how imperialism in general and annexation in particular contradicted American ideals. First, the annexation of territory without immediate or planned steps toward statehood was unprecedented and unconstitutional. Second, to occupy and govern a foreign people without their consent violated the ideals of the Declaration of Independence. A third argument was that social reforms needed at home demanded American energies and money before foreign expansionism. "Before we attempt to teach house-keeping to the world," one writer put it, we needed "to set our own house in order."

Not all anti-imperialist arguments were so noble. Some were practical or downright racist. One position alleged that because the Filipinos were nonwhite, Catholic, and inferior in size and intelligence, they were unassimilable. Annexation would lead to miscegenation and contamination of Anglo-Saxon blood. Senator Ben Tillman of South Carolina argued that although whites could "walk on the necks of every colored race," he still opposed "incorporating any more colored men into the body politic." The practical argument suggested that once in possession of the Philippines, the United States would have to defend them, possibly even acquiring more territories. This would require higher taxes and bigger government in order to build and support the navy that holding such possessions demanded. Some saw the Philippines as a burden that would require American troops to fight distant Asian wars.

The last argument became fact when Private Grayson's encounter started the Filipino-American War. Before it was over in 1902, some 126,500 American troops served in the Philippines, 4,234 died there, and 2,800 more were wounded. The cost was $400 million. Filipino casualties were much worse. In addition to the 18,000 killed in combat, an estimated 200,000 Filipinos died of famine and disease as American soldiers burned villages and destroyed crops and livestock in order to disrupt the economy and deny rebel fighters their food supply. General Jacob H. Smith ordered his troops to "kill and burn and the more you kill and burn, the better you will please me." Atrocities on both sides increased with the frustrations of a lengthening war, but the American "water cure" and other tortures were especially brutal.

As U.S. treatment of the Filipinos during the war became more and more like Spanish mistreatment of the Cubans, the hypocrisy of American behavior became even more evident. This was especially true for black American soldiers who fought in the Philippines. They identified with the dark-skinned insurgents, whom they saw as tied to the land, burdened by debt, and pressed by poverty like themselves. They were also called "nigger" from morning to night. "I feel sorry for these people," a sergeant in the 24th Infantry wrote. "You have no idea the way these people are treated by the Americans here."

The war starkly exposed the hypocrisies of shouldering the white man's burden. On reading a report that 8,000 Filipinos had been killed in the first year of the war, Carnegie wrote a letter, dripping with sarcasm, congratulating McKinley for "civilizing the Filipinos.... About 8,000 of them have been completely civilized and sent to Heaven. I hope you like it." Another writer penned a devastating one-liner: "Dewey took Manila with the loss of one man—and all our institutions." One of the most active anti-

Bringing "civilization" to the Filipinos, American soldiers stand guard over captured guerrillas in 1899. Finley Peter Dunne quipped, "Twud be a disgrace f'r to lave befure we've pounded these frindless an' ongrateful people into insinsibility." (Library of Congress)

imperialists, Ernest Howard Crosby, wrote a parody of Rudyard Kipling's "White Man's Burden," which he titled "The Real 'White Man's Burden'":

> *Take up the White Man's burden.*
> *Send forth your sturdy kin,*
> *And load them down with Bibles*
> *And cannon-balls and gin.*
> *Throw in a few diseases*
> *To spread the tropic climes,*
> *For there the healthy niggers*
> *Are quite behind the times.*
>
> *They need our labor question, too.*
> *And politics and fraud—*
> *We've made a pretty mess at home,*
> *Let's make a mess abroad.*

The anti-imperialists failed either to prevent annexation or to interfere with the war effort. However prestigious and sincere, they had little or no political power. They were seen as an older, conservative, elite group of Americans opposed to the kind of dynamic progress represented by Teddy Roosevelt and other expansionists. They were out

of tune with the period of exuberant national pride, prosperity, and promise.

Expansionism Triumphant

By 1900, Americans had ample reason to be patriotic. Within a year, the United States had acquired several island territories, thereby joining the other great world powers. But several questions arose over what to do with the new territories. What was their status? Were they colonies? Would they be granted statehood or would they develop gradually from colonies to constitutional parts of the United States? Moreover, did the indigenous peoples of Hawaii, Puerto Rico, Guam, and the Philippines have the same rights as American citizens on the mainland? Were they protected by the U.S. Constitution? The answers to these difficult questions emerged in a series of Supreme Court cases, congressional acts, and presidential decisions.

Although slightly different governing systems were worked out for each new territory, the solution in each was to define its status somewhere between subject colony and candidate for statehood. Territorial status came closest. The native people were usually allowed to elect their own legislature for internal lawmaking, but had governors and other judicial and administrative officials appointed by the American president. A provincial governor, George Curry, was subsequently made governor of the New Mexico Territory, a step indicating that both the Philippines and New Mexico remained somewhere between colonies and equal states. The first full governor of the Philippines, McKinley appointee William Howard Taft, effectively moved the Filipinos toward self-government. Final independence did not come until 1946, however, and elsewhere the process was equally slow.

The question of constitutional rights was resolved by deciding that Hawaiians and Puerto Ricans, for example, would be treated differently from Texans and Oregonians. In the "insular cases" of 1901, the Supreme Court ruled that these people would achieve citizenship and constitutional rights only when Congress said they were ready. To the question "Does the Constitution follow the flag?" the answer, as Secretary of State Elihu Root put it, was, "Ye-es, as near as I can make out the Constitution follows the flag—but doesn't quite catch up with it."

McKinley's resounding defeat of Bryan in 1900 clearly revealed the optimistic, nationalistic spirit of the American people. Bryan's intentions to make imperialism the "paramount issue" of the campaign

This 1900 campaign poster for McKinley makes a compelling case that four years of Republican party leadership had brought prosperity and humanity both at home and abroad. Note not only that McKinley and Roosevelt have wrapped themselves in the American flag, but also the dramatic contrasts after four years of Republican rule compared to the condition of the United States and Cuba when the Democrats left office in 1896. (Culver Pictures)

failed, in part because the country strongly favored annexation of the Philippines. A rising sense of nationhood made the Filipino-American War a popular one, and it was politically unwise to risk being branded a traitor by opposing it. In the closing weeks of the campaign, Bryan and the Democrats shied away from imperialism and the war as a "paramount issue" and focused more on economic issues—trusts, the labor question, and free silver.

But Bryan fared no better on those issues. Prosperity returned with the discovery of gold in Alaska, and cries for reform fell on deaf ears. The McKinley forces rightly claimed that under four years of Republican rule, more money, jobs, thriving factories, and manufactured goods had been created. Moreover, McKinley pointed to the tremendous growth in American prestige abroad. Spain had been kicked out of Cuba, and the American flag flew in many places around the globe. It had been a triumphant four years. As a disappointed Tom Watson put it, noting the end of the Populist revolt with the war fervor over Cuba, "The Spanish war finished us. The blare of the bugle drowned out the voice of the reformer."

He was more right than he knew. Within one year, the active expansionist Theodore Roosevelt went from assistant secretary of the navy to colonel of the Rough Riders to governor of New York. For some Republican politicos, who thought he was too vigorous, unorthodox, and independent, this quick rise to prominence as McKinley's potential rival came too fast. One way to eliminate Roosevelt politically, or at least slow him down, they thought, was to make him vice president, which they did at the Republican convention in 1900. But six months into McKinley's second term, the president was shot and killed by an anarchist, the third presidential assassination in less than 40 years. "Now look," exclaimed party boss Mark Hanna, who had opposed putting Roosevelt on the ticket; "that damned cowboy is President of the United States!"

Theodore Roosevelt's Energetic Diplomacy

At a White House dinner party in 1905, a guest told a story about visiting the Roosevelt home when Teddy had been a baby. "You were in your bassinet, making a good deal of fuss and noise," the guest reported, "and your father lifted you out and asked me to hold you." Secretary of State Elihu Root looked up from his plate and asked, "Was he hard to hold?" Whether true or not, the story reveals much about President Roosevelt's principles and policies on foreign affairs. As president from 1901 to 1909, and as the most dominating American personality for the 15 years between 1897 and 1912, Roosevelt made much fuss and noise about the activist role he thought the United States should play in the world. As he implemented his policies, he often seemed "hard to hold." Roosevelt's energetic foreign policy in Latin America, Asia, and Europe paved the way for the vital role of the United States as a world power.

Foreign Policy as Darwinian Struggle

Roosevelt's personal principles and presidential policies went together. He was an advocate of both individual physical fitness and collective national strength. As an undersized, weak young boy who suffered humiliating drubbings by schoolmates, he undertook a rigorous program of strengthening his body through boxing and other exercise. During summers spent on his ranch in the North Dakota Badlands, Roosevelt learned to value the "strenuous life" of the cowboy. He read Darwin and understood that life among humans, as in nature, was a constant struggle for survival.

Roosevelt extended his beliefs about strenuous struggle from individuals to nations. His ideal was a "nation of men, not weaklings." To be militarily prepared and to fight well were the tests of racial superiority and national greatness. "All the great masterful races," he said, "have been fighting races." Although he believed in Anglo-Saxon superiority, he admired—and feared—Japanese military prowess. Powerful nations, like individuals, Roosevelt believed, had a duty to cultivate qualities of vigor, strength, courage, and moral commitment to civilized values. In practical terms, this meant developing natural resources, building large navies, and being ever prepared to fight. "I never take a step in foreign policy," he wrote, "unless I am assured that I shall be able eventually to carry out my will by force."

Although known for his advice to "speak softly and carry a big stick," Roosevelt often not only

The "big stick" became a memorable image in American diplomacy as Teddy Roosevelt sought to make the United States a policeman not only of the Caribbean basin, but also of the whole world. "As our modern life goes on," Roosevelt said, "and the nations are drawn closer together for good and for evil, and this nation grows in comparison with friends and rivals, it is impossible to adhere to the policy of isolation." (Puck, 1901)

wielded a large stick, but spoke loudly as well. In a speech in 1897, he used the word *war* 62 times, saying that "no triumph of peace is quite so great as the supreme triumphs of war." But despite his bluster, Roosevelt was usually restrained in the exercise of force. He won the Nobel Peace Prize in 1906 for helping end the Russo-Japanese War. The purpose of the big stick and the loud talk was to preserve order and peace in the world. "To be prepared for war," he said, "is the most effectual means to promote peace."

Roosevelt divided the world into civilized and uncivilized nations, the former usually defined as Anglo-Saxon and English-speaking. The civilized nations had a responsibility to "police" the uncivilized, not only maintaining order, but also spreading superior values and institutions. This "international police power," as Roosevelt called it, was the "white man's burden." As part of this burden, civilized nations sometimes had to fight wars against the uncivilized, as the British did against the Boers in South Africa

and the Americans did in the Philippines. These wars were justified because the victors bestowed the blessings of culture and racial superiority on the vanquished.

A war between two civilized nations, however, as between Germany and England, would be wasteful and foolish, upsetting order in the world. Above all, Roosevelt believed in the balance of power. Strong, advanced nations like the United States had a duty to use their power to preserve order and peace. The United States had "no choice," Roosevelt said, but to "play a great part in the world." Americans could no longer "avoid responsibilities" that followed from "the fact that on the east and west we look across the waters at Europe and Asia." The 1900 census had recently shown that the United States, with 75 million people, was much more populous than Great Britain, France, or Germany. All these nations had many colonies in Asia and Africa, so it seemed time for Americans to exercise a greater role in world affairs.

As Roosevelt looked across the oceans, he developed a highly personal style of diplomacy. Rather than relying on the Department of State, he preferred face-to-face contact and personal exchange of letters with foreign ambassadors, ministers, and heads of state. Roosevelt made foreign policy while horseback riding with the German ambassador or while discussing history with the ambassador from France. A British emissary observed that Roosevelt had a "powerful personality" and a commanding knowledge of the world. As a result, ministries from London to Tokyo respected both the president and the power of the United States.

When threat of force failed to accomplish his goals, Roosevelt used direct personal intervention as a third-party mediator. "In a crisis the duty of a leader is to lead," he said. Congress was too slow and deliberate to play a significant role in foreign affairs. When he wanted Panama, Roosevelt bragged later, "I took the Canal Zone" rather than submitting a long "dignified State Paper" for congressional debate on a suitable policy. And while Congress debated his actions, he was fond of pointing out, the building of the canal across Panama began. Roosevelt's energetic executive activism in foreign policy set a pattern followed by nearly every twentieth-century American president.

Taking the Panama Canal

In justifying the intervention of 2,600 American troops in Honduras and Nicaragua in 1906, Philander Knox, secretary of state from 1909 to 1913, said, "We are in the eyes of the world, and because of the Monroe Doctrine, held responsible for the order of Central America, and its proximity to the Canal makes the preservation of peace in that neighborhood particularly necessary." The Panama Canal was not yet finished when Knox spoke, but it had already become a vital cornerstone of United States policy in the region.

Three problems had to be surmounted to fulfill the long-sought goal of an interoceanic connection. First, an 1850 treaty bound the United States to build a canal jointly with Great Britain.

But in 1901, John Hay, secretary of state between 1901 and 1905, convinced the British to cancel the treaty in exchange for an American guarantee that the canal, once built, would be "free and open to the vessels of commerce and of war of all nations." A second problem was where to build the canal. After considering a long but technically easy route through Nicaragua, American engineers settled on the shorter but more rugged path across the isthmus of Panama, where a French firm, the New Panama Company, had already begun work.

The third problem was that Panama was a province of Colombia and thus could not negotiate with the United States. The Colombian government was unimpressed with the share of a likely settlement the Americans would provide in buying up the New Panama Canal Company's $40 million in assets. Indeed, in 1903, the Colombian senate rejected a treaty negotiated by Hay, but mostly on nationalistic, not financial, grounds. Roosevelt, angered by this rebuff, called the Colombians "Dagoes" and "foolish and homicidal corruptionists" who tried to "hold us up" like highway robbers.

Aware of Roosevelt's fury, encouraged by hints of American support, and eager for the economic benefits the building of a canal would bring, Panamanian nationalists in 1903 staged a revolution led by several rich families and a Frenchman, Philippe Bunau-Varilla of the New Panama Canal Company. The Colombian army, dispatched to quell the revolt, was deterred by the presence of an American warship; local troops were separated from their officers, who were bought off. The bloodless revolution occurred on November 3; the next day, Panama declared its independence. On November 6, the United States officially recognized the new government in Panama. Although Roosevelt did not formally encourage the revolution, it would not have occurred without American money and support.

On November 18, Hay and Bunau-Varilla signed a treaty establishing the American right to build and operate a canal through Panama and to exercise "titular sovereignty" over the 10-mile-wide Canal Zone. The Panamanian government protested the treaty, to no avail, and a later government called it the "treaty that no Panamanian

(Above) In 1903, despite protests from the Panamanian government, the United States acquired the right to begin the enormous engineering feat of building the Panama Canal. (Library of Congress)

(Right) A year later, a cartoonist showed the American eagle celebrating "his 128th birthday" with wings spanning the globe from Panama to the Philippines. In a prophetic anticipation of American overexpansion in the twentieth century, the eagle says, "Gee, but this is an awful stretch." (The Granger Collection, New York)

signed." Roosevelt, in his later boast that he "took the canal," claimed that his diplomatic and engineering achievement, completed in 1914, would "rank ... with the Louisiana Purchase and the acquisition of Texas."

Policeman of the Caribbean

As late as 1901, the Monroe Doctrine was still regarded, according to Roosevelt, as the "equivalent to an open door in South America." To the United States, this meant that although no nation had a right "to get territorial possessions," all nations had equal commercial rights in the Western Hemisphere south of the Rio Grande. But as American investments poured into Central America and Caribbean islands, that policy changed to one of the primary right of the United States to dominant influence in the lands of the Caribbean basin. Order was indispensable for profitable economic activity.

This change was demonstrated in 1902, when Germany and Great Britain seized several Venezuelan gunboats and blockaded Venezuela's

ports to force the government to pay defaulted debts. Roosevelt was especially worried that German influence would replace the British. He insisted that the European powers accept arbitration of the disputed financial claims and threatened to "move Dewey's ships" to the Venezuelan coast to enforce his intentions. The crisis passed, largely for other reasons, but Roosevelt's threat of force made very clear the paramount presence and self-interest of the United States in the Caribbean.

After the Spanish were expelled from Cuba, the United States supervised the island under Military Governor General Leonard Wood until 1902, when the Cubans elected their own congress and president. The United States honored Cuban independence, as it had promised to do in the Teller Amendment. But through the Platt Amendment, which Cubans reluctantly attached to their constitution in 1901, the United States obtained many economic rights in Cuba, a naval base at Guantanamo Bay, and the right of intervention if Cuban sovereignty were ever threatened. Newspapers in Havana assailed this violation of their newfound independence. One cartoon, titled "The Cuban Calvary," showed a figure representing the "Cuban people" crucified between two thieves, Wood and McKinley.

American policy intended to make Cuba a model of how a newly independent nation could achieve orderly self-government with only minimal guidance. Cuban self-government, however, was shaky. When in 1906 an internal political crisis threatened to plunge the infant nation into civil war, Roosevelt expressed his fury with "that infernal little Cuban republic." At Cuba's request, he sent warships to patrol the coastline and special commissioners and troops "to restore order and peace and public confidence." As he left office in 1909, Roosevelt proudly proclaimed that "we have done our best to put Cuba on the road to stable and orderly government." The road was paved with sugar. U.S. trade with Cuba increased from $27 million in the year before 1898 to an average of

$43 million per year during the following decade. Along with economic development, American political and even military involvement in Cuban affairs continued throughout the century.

The pattern repeated itself throughout the Caribbean region. The Dominican Republic, for example, suffered from unstable governments and economic ill health. In 1904, as a revolt erupted, European creditors pressured the Dominican government for payment of $40 million in defaulted bonds. With the presence of its warships to discourage European intervention, the United States took over the collection of customs in the republic. Two years later, the United States intervened in Guatemala and Nicaragua, where American bankers controlled nearly 50 percent of all trade, the first of several interventions in those Central American countries in the twentieth century.

Roosevelt clarified his policy that civilized nations should "insist on the proper policing of the

United States Involvement in Central America and the Caribbean, 1898–1939

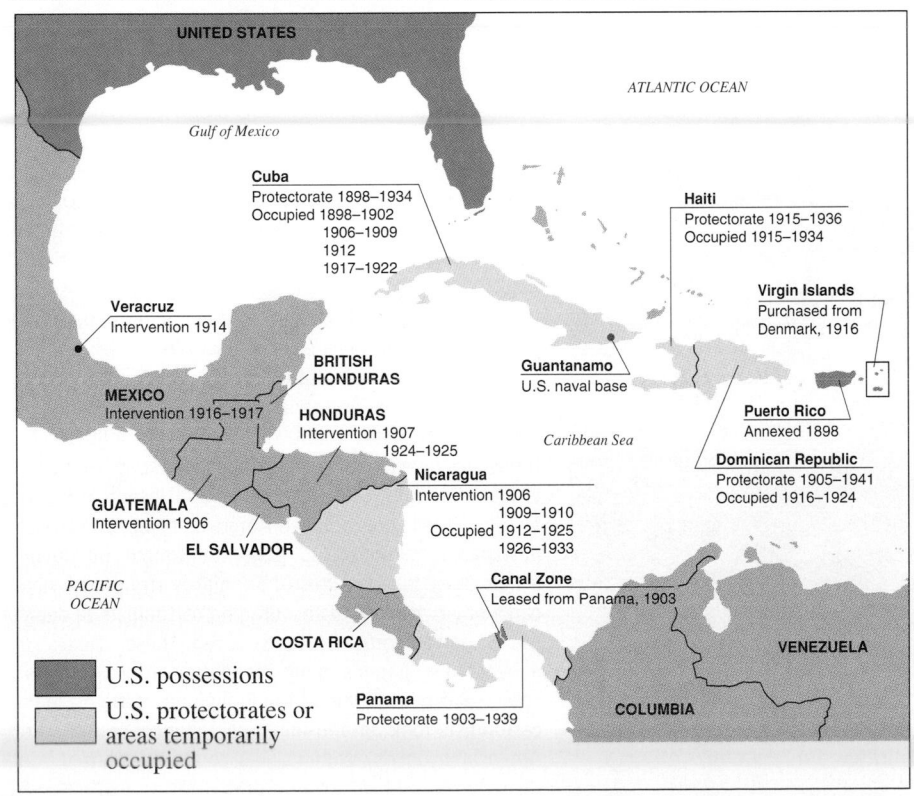

Can you update the location of further interventions in Central America and the Caribbean since the 1950s?

Political Cartoons

One of the most enjoyable ways of recovering the values and attitudes of the past is through political cartoons. Ralph Waldo Emerson once said, "Caricatures are often the truest history of the times." A deft drawing of a popular or unpopular politician can freeze ideas and events in time, conveying more effectively than columns of type the central issues of the day and creating an immediate response in the viewer. It is this freshness that makes caricatures such a valuable source when attempting to recover the past. Cartoonists are often at their best when they are critical, exaggerating a physical feature of a political figure or capturing public sentiment against the government.

The history of political cartoons in the United States goes back to Benjamin Franklin's "Join or Die" cartoon calling for colonial cooperation against the French in 1754. But political cartoons were rare until Andrew Jackson's presidency. Even after such cartoons as "King Andrew the First" in the 1830s, they did not gain notoriety until the advent of Thomas Nast's cartoons in *Harper's Weekly* in the 1870s. Nast drew scathing cartoons exposing the corruption of William "Boss" Tweed's Tammany Hall, depicting Tweed and his men as vultures and smiling deceivers.

"Liberty Halts American Butchery in the Philippines," from Life, 1899.

"The Spanish Brute Adds Mutilation to Murder," by Grant Hamilton, in Judge, July 9, 1898. (Culver Pictures)

"Stop them damn pictures," Tweed ordered. "I don't care so much what the papers write about me. My constituents can't read. But, damn it, they can see pictures." Tweed sent some of his men to Nast with an offer of $100,000 to "study art" in Europe. The $5000-a-year artist negotiated up to a half million dollars before refusing Tweed's offer. "I made up my mind not long ago to put some of those fellows behind bars," Nast said, "and I'm going to put them there." His cartoons helped drive Tweed out of office.

The emergence of the United States as a world power and the rise of Theodore Roosevelt gave cartoonists plenty to draw about. An impetus to political cartoons was given by the rise of cheap newspapers such as William Randolph Hearst's *Journal* and Joseph Pulitzer's *World.* When the Spanish-American War broke out, newspapers whipped up public sentiment by having artists draw fake pictures of Spaniards stripping American women at sea and encouraging cartoonists to depict the "Spanish brute." Hearst used these tactics to increase his paper's daily circulation to one million copies. But by the time of the Philippines debates, many cartoonists took an anti-imperialist stance, pointing out American hypocrisy. Within a year, cartoonists shifted from depicting "The Spanish Brute Adds Mutilation to Murder" (1898) to "Liberty Halts American Butchery in the Philippines" (1899). The cartoons are very similar in condemning "butchery" of native populations, but the target has of course changed. Although Uncle Sam as a killer is not nearly as menacing as the figure of Spain as an ugly gorilla, both cartoons share a similarity of stance, the blood-covered swords, and a trail of bodies behind.

When Theodore Roosevelt rose to the presidency, cartoonists rejoiced. His physical appearance and personality made him instantly recognizable, a key factor in the success of a political cartoon. His broad grin, eyeglasses, and walrus mustache were the kind of features that fueled the cartoonist's imagination. A man of great energy, Roosevelt's style was as distinctive as his look. Other factors, such as the "Rough Rider" nickname, the symbol of the "big stick," and policies like "gunboat diplomacy" made Teddy the perfect target for political cartoons.

To understand and appreciate the meaning of any cartoon, certain facts must be ascertained, such as the date, artist, and source of the cartoon; the particular historical characters, events, and context depicted in it; the significance of the caption; and the master symbols employed by the cartoonist. The two remaining cartoons, "Panama or Bust" (1903) and "For President!" (1904), were both printed in American daily newspapers. Aside from the context and meaning of each cartoon, which should be obvious, note how the cartoonists use familiar symbols from Roosevelt's life and American history to underline the ironic power of their point. How many can you identify, and how are they used?

"Panama or Bust," from the New York Times, *1903.*

L. C. Gregg in the Atlanta Constitution.

FOR PRESIDENT!

"For President!" by L. C. Gregg, in the Atlanta Constitution, *1904.*

world" in his annual message in 1904. The goal of the United States, he said, was to have "stable, orderly and prosperous neighbors." A country that paid its debts and kept order "need fear no interference from the United States." A country that did not, but rather committed "chronic wrong-doing" and loosened the "ties of civilized society," would require the United States to intervene as an "international police power." This doctrine became known as the Roosevelt Corollary to the Monroe Doctrine. Whereas Monroe's doctrine had warned European nations not to intervene in the Western Hemisphere, Roosevelt's corollary justified American intervention. Starting with a desire to protect property, loans, and investments, the United States often interceded in these countries to maintain order. This meant supporting the brutal regimes of wealthy elites who owned most of the land, suppressed the poor and efforts for reform, and acted as surrogates of American policy.

After 1904, the Roosevelt Corollary was invoked in several Caribbean countries. Intervention usually required the landing of U.S. Marines to counter the threat posed by political instability and bankruptcy to American economic interests: railroads, mines, and the production of sugar, bananas, and coffee. Occupying the capital and major seaports, U.S. Marines, bankers, and customs officials usually remained for several years, until they were satisfied that stability had been reestablished. Roosevelt's successors, William Howard Taft and Woodrow Wilson, pursued the same interventionist policy. Later presidents, most recently Ronald Reagan (Grenada and Nicaragua), George Bush (Panama), and Bill Clinton (Haiti) would do likewise.

Opening the Door to China

Throughout the nineteenth century, American relations with China were restricted to a small but profitable trade. The British, in competition with France, Germany, and Russia, took advantage of the weak, crumbling Manchu dynasty by making trade treaties with China. These gave access to treaty ports and most-favored-nation trading privileges in various spheres of influence throughout the country. After 1898, Americans with dreams of

exploiting the seemingly unlimited markets of China wanted to join the competition and enlarge their share. The United States, too, wanted favorable commercial rights and a place to sell surplus goods. Moral interests, however, including many missionaries, reminded Americans of their revolutionary tradition against European imperialism. They made clear their opposition to crass U.S. commercial exploitation of a weak nation and supported the preservation of China's political integrity against continuing interference by the European powers.

American attitudes toward the Chinese people reflected this confusion of motives. Some Americans held an idealized view of China as the center of Eastern wisdom and saw a "special relationship" between the two nations. But the dominant American attitude viewed the Chinese as heathen, exotic, backward, and immoral. The Exclusion Act of 1882 and the riots in western states against Chinese workers in the 1870s and 1880s reflected this negative stereotype. The Chinese, in turn, regarded the United States with a mixture of curiosity, resentment, suspicion, and disdain, as well as with admiration for a potential, if arrogant ally.

The annexation of Hawaii, Samoa, and the Philippines in 1898–1899 convinced Secretary of State Hay that the United States should announce its own policy for China. The result was the Open Door notes of 1899–1900, which became the cornerstone of U.S. policy in Asia for half a century. The first note, focusing on customs collection issues, opened a door for American trade by declaring the principle of equal access to commercial rights in China by all nations. The second note, addressing Russian movement into Manchuria, called on all countries to respect the "territorial and administrative integrity" of China. This second principle opened the way for a larger American role in Asia, offering China protection from foreign invasions and preserving a balance of power in the Far East.

An early test of this new role came during the Boxer Rebellion in 1900. The Boxers were a society of young traditionalist Chinese in revolt against both the Manchu dynasty and the growing Western presence and influence in China. During the summer of 1900, fanatical Boxers killed some 242 missionaries and other foreigners and besieged the western quarter of Peking. Eventually, an international military force of 19,000 troops, including some 3,000 Americans sent from the Philippines, marched on Peking to end the siege.

The American relationship with China was plagued by the exclusionist immigration policy. Despite the barriers and riots, Chinese workers kept coming to the United States, entering illegally through Mexico and British Columbia. In 1905, Chinese nationalists at home boycotted American goods and called for a change in immigration policy. Roosevelt, who had a low opinion of the Chinese as a "backward" people, bristled with resentment and sent troops to the Philippines as a threat. Halfheartedly, he also asked Congress for a modified immigration bill, but nothing came of it.

Despite exclusion and insults, the idea that the United States had a unique guardian relationship with China persisted into the twentieth century. Japan had ambitions in China, so this created a rivalry between Japan and the United States, testing the American commitment to preserve the Open Door in China and the balance of power in Asia. Economic motives in Asia, however, proved to be less significant. Investments there developed very slowly, as did the dream of the "great China market" for American grains and textiles. Although textile exports to China increased from $7 to nearly $24 million in a decade, the China trade always remained larger in imagination than in reality.

Japan and the Balance of Power

Because of population pressures on the limited land mass of Japan, as well as war and the quest for economic opportunities, Japanese immigration to the United States dramatically increased around the turn of the century. Coming first as unmarried males working on western railroads and in Pacific Coast canneries, mines, and logging camps, immigrants from Japan increased from 25,000 in the 1890s to 125,000 between 1901 and 1908. Like the earlier Chinese immigrants, they were met with nativist hostility and discrimination. Japanese workers were barred from factory jobs and shunted off to agricultural labor in California fields and orchards. In 1906, the San Francisco school board, claiming that Japanese children were "crowding the whites out of the schools," segregated them into separate schools and asked Roo-

sevelt to persuade Japan to stop the emigration of its people. Though the Japanese were insulted, they agreed to limit the migration of unskilled workers to the United States in a gentleman's agreement signed in 1907. In return, the segregation law was repealed, but not without costs in relations between the two nations.

Roosevelt also relied on the use of diplomacy and negotiation in his effort to balance Asian powers against one another. The Boxer Rebellion of 1900 left Russia with 50,000 troops in Manchuria, the strongest nation in eastern Asia. Roosevelt's admiration for the Japanese as a "fighting" people and valuable factor in the "civilization of the future" contrasted with his low respect for the Russians, whom he described as "corrupt," "treacherous," and "incompetent." As Japan moved into Korea, and Russia into Manchuria, Roosevelt hoped that each would check the growing power of the other.

Because of increasing Russian strength, Roosevelt welcomed news in 1904 that Japan had

The United States' imperial role in China is supported in this cartoon showing President McKinley and Uncle Sam leading the charge against the Boxer Rebellion in 1900. What do you think is the point of view of the cartoonist? (The Granger Collection, New York)

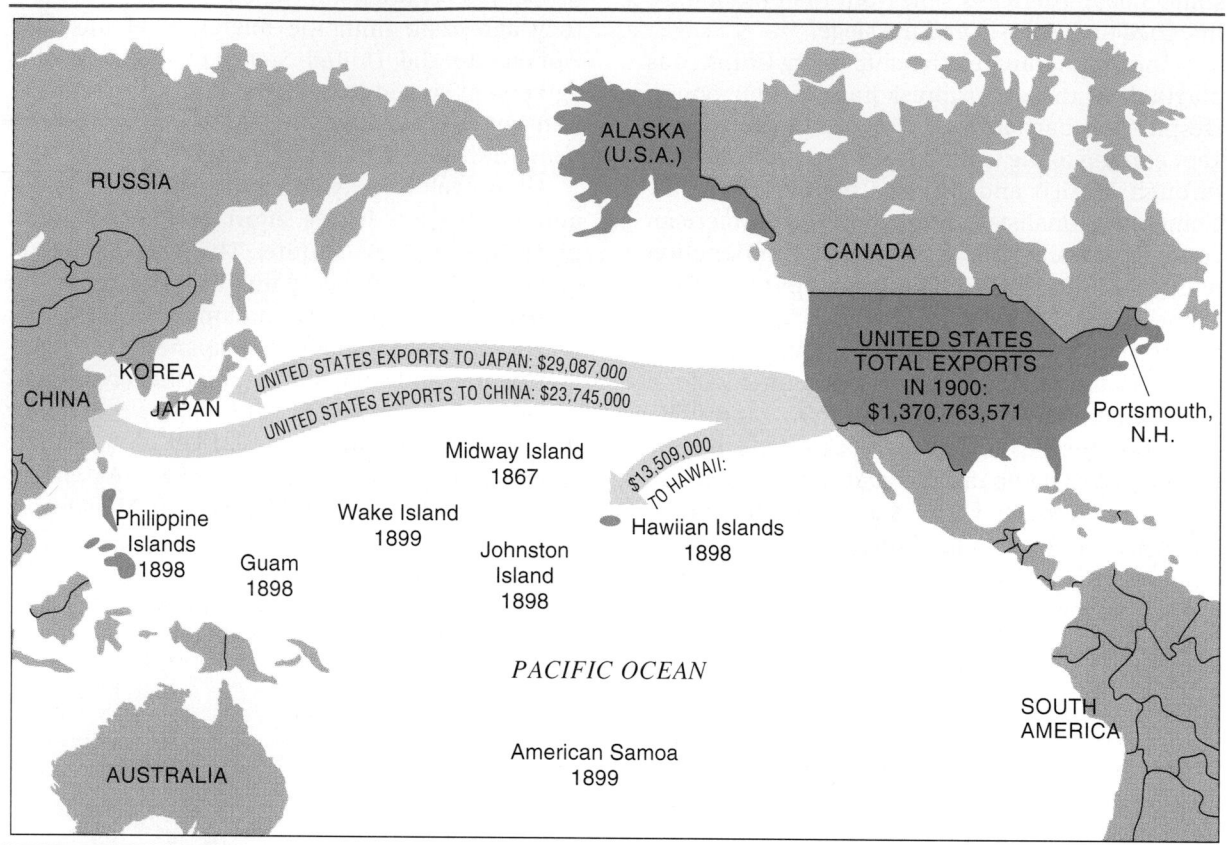

United States Involvement in Asia, 1898–1909

What major twentieth-century events have followed the acquisition of territories in the Pacific and the development of intensified trade with East Asian countries?

launched a successful surprise attack on Port Arthur in Manchuria, beginning the Russo-Japanese War. He was "well pleased with the Japanese victory," he told his son, "for Japan is playing our game." But as Japanese victories continued, many Americans worried that Japan might play the game too well, shutting the United States out of Far Eastern markets. Roosevelt shifted his support toward Russia. When the Japanese expressed interest in an end to the war, the American president was pleased to exert his influence.

Roosevelt's goal was to achieve peace and leave a balanced situation. "It is best," he wrote, that Russia be left "face to face with Japan so that each may have a moderative action on the other." The negotiations and resulting treaty were carried out in the summer of 1905 near Portsmouth, New

Hampshire. No single act better symbolizes the new posture of American power and presence in the world than the signing of a peace treaty ending a war in Manchuria between Russia and Japan halfway around the globe in New Hampshire!

The Treaty of Portsmouth actually left Japan dominant in Manchuria and established the United States as the major balance to Japan's power. Almost immediately, the Japanese developed a naval base at Port Arthur, built railroads, and sought exclusive rights of investment and control in the Chinese province. In part because of his lack of respect for the Chinese, Roosevelt willingly recognized Japan's "dominance in Manchuria," as well as its control in Korea. But in return, in the Root-Takahira Agreement of 1908, he received Japan's promise to honor U.S. control in the Philippines and to make no further encroachments into China.

These agreements over territorial divisions barely covered up the tensions in Japanese-American relations. Some Japanese were angry that they had not received in the Portsmouth Treaty the indemnities they had wanted from Russia, and they blamed Roosevelt. American insensitivity to the immigration issue also left bad feelings. In Manchuria, U.S. Consul General Willard Straight aggressively pushed an anti-Japanese program of financing capital investment projects in banking and railroads. This policy, later known as "dollar diplomacy" under Roosevelt's successor, William Howard Taft, like the pursuit of markets, was larger in prospect than results. Nevertheless, the United States was in Japan's way, and rumors of war circulated in the world press.

It was clearly time for Roosevelt's version of the "big stick." In 1907, he told Secretary of State Root that he was "more concerned over the Japanese situation than almost any other. Thank Heaven we have the navy in good shape." Although the naval buildup had begun over a decade earlier, under Roosevelt, the U.S. Navy had developed into a formidable force. From 1900 to 1905, outlays to the Navy rose from $56 to $117 million. Such a naval spending binge was without precedent in peacetime. In 1907, to make it clear that "the Pacific was as much our home waters as the Atlantic," Roosevelt sent his new, modernized "Great White Fleet" on a goodwill tour around the world. The first stop was the Japanese port of Yokohama. Although American sailors were greeted warmly, the act may have stimulated navalism in Japan, which came back to haunt the United States in 1941. But for the time being, the balance of power in Asia was preserved.

Preventing War in Europe

The United States was willing to stretch the meaning of the Monroe Doctrine to justify sending Marines and engineers to Latin America and the Navy and dollars to Asia. Treaties, agreements, and the protection of territories and interests entangled the United States with foreign nations from Panama and the Dominican Republic to the Philippines and Manchuria. Toward Europe, how-

President Roosevelt stands proudly between Russian and Japanese representatives as they negotiated an end to the Russo-Japanese War in 1905 in, of all places, Portsmouth, New Hampshire. No image better captured the expanding role of the United States in global affairs than this photograph of Teddy Roosevelt helping to negotiate the end of war fought in Manchuria halfway around the world from the East Coast of the United States. (Corbis-Bettmann)

ever, the traditional policies of neutrality and nonentanglement continued.

The most powerful nations of the world were European. Roosevelt, therefore, believed that the most serious threats to world peace and civilized order lay in the relationships among Germany, Great Britain, and France. He established two fundamental policies toward Europe that would define the U.S. role throughout the century. The first was to make friendship with Great Britain the cornerstone of U.S. policy. As Roosevelt told King Edward VII in 1905, "In the long run the English people are more apt to be friendly to us than any other." Second, the crucial goal of a neutral power like the United States was to prevent the outbreak of a general war in Europe among strong nations. Toward this end, Roosevelt depended on his personal negotiating skills and began the practice of summit diplomacy.

It is difficult now to think of England as anything other than the most loyal friend of the United

Theodore Roosevelt with Kaiser Wilhelm II of Germany. The Kaiser mistook his shared interests with the American statesman as evidence of American alliance with German interests, but TR's interventions countered imperialistic German policies and so helped maintain peace in Europe. (Archive Photos/Levick)

States outside North America. Yet throughout most of the nineteenth century, England was America's chief enemy and commercial rival. From the War of 1812 to the Venezuelan border crisis of 1895, conflict with Great Britain developed in squabbles over old debts and trade barriers, disputes over Canadian borders and fishing jurisdictions, and British interference in the American Civil War.

The Venezuelan crisis and a number of other events at the turn of the century shocked the United States and England into an awareness of their mutual interests. Both nations appreciated the neutrality of the other in their respective wars shouldering the white man's burden against the Filipinos and the Boers. Roosevelt supported British imperialism because he favored the dominance of the "English-speaking race" and believed that England was "fighting the battle of civilization." Furthermore, both nations worried about growing German power in Europe, Africa, and the Far East. As German naval power increased, England had to bring its fleet closer to home. Friendly allies were needed to police parts of the world formerly patrolled by the British navy. England therefore concluded a mutual-protection treaty with Japan in 1902 and willingly let the Americans police Central America and the Caribbean Sea.

Similarities of language and cultural traditions, as well as strategic self-interest, drew the two countries together. Roosevelt's personal style fur-

thered the connection. He was clearly and unashamedly pro-British, and his most intimate circle of friends included many Englishmen. Although Roosevelt sometimes criticized English policies, his British bias was never in doubt. He knew, as he wrote to Lodge in 1901, that the United States had "not the least particle of danger to fear" from England and that German ambitions and militarism represented the major threat to peace in Europe. As Roosevelt left the presidency in 1909, one of his final acts was to proclaim the special American friendship with Great Britain.

German Kaiser Wilhelm II often underestimated the solidity of Anglo-American friendship and thought that Roosevelt was really pro-German, an error the American president skillfully used. He cultivated the Kaiser to make him think they were friends sharing mutual interests. Wilhelm, therefore, sought Roosevelt's support on several diplomatic issues between 1905 and 1909. In each case, Roosevelt flattered the Kaiser while politely rejecting his overtures. The relationship gave Roosevelt a unique advantage in influencing affairs in Europe to prevent the outbreak of war.

The Moroccan crisis in 1905 and 1906 is illustrative. European powers competed for colonies and spheres of influence in Africa as well as in Asia. Germany in particular resented French dominance along the North African coast in Morocco and feared the recent Anglo-French entente. The

TIMELINE

1823	Monroe Doctrine
1857	Trade opens with Japan
1867	Alaska purchased from Russia
1870	Failure to annex Santo Domingo (Hispaniola)
1875	Sugar reciprocity treaty with Hawaii
1877	United States acquires naval base at Pearl Harbor
1878	United States acquires naval station in Samoa
1882	Chinese Exclusion Act
1889	First Pan-American Conference
1890	Alfred Mahan publishes *Influence of Sea Power upon History*
1893	Hawaiian coup by American sugar growers
1895	Cuban revolt against Spanish
	Venezuelan boundary dispute
1896	Weyler's reconcentration policy in Cuba
	McKinley-Bryan presidential campaign
1897	Theodore Roosevelt's speech at Naval War College
1898 January	De Lôme letter
February	Sinking of the battleship *Maine*
April	Spanish-American War
	Teller Amendment
May	Dewey takes Manila Bay
July	Annexation of Hawaiian Islands
August	Americans liberate Manila; war ends
December	Treaty of Paris; annexation of the Philippines
1899	Senate ratifies Treaty of Paris
	Filipino-American War begins
	American Samoa acquired
1899–1900	Open Door notes
1900	Boxer Rebellion in China
	William McKinley reelected president
1901	Supreme Court insular cases
	McKinley assassinated; Theodore Roosevelt becomes president
1902	Filipino-American War ends
	U.S. military occupation of Cuba ends
	Platt Amendment
	Venezuela debt crisis
1903	Panamanian revolt and independence
	Hay-Bunau-Varilla Treaty
1904	Roosevelt Corollary
1904–1905	Russo-Japanese War ended by treaty signed at Portsmouth, New Hampshire
1904–1906	United States intervenes in Nicaragua, Guatemala, and Cuba
1905–1906	Moroccan crisis
1906	Roosevelt receives Nobel Peace Prize
1907	Gentleman's agreement with Japan
1908	Root-Takahira Agreement
1909	U.S. Navy ("Great White Fleet") sails around the world
1911	United States intervenes in Nicaragua
1914	Opening of the Panama Canal
	World War I begins
1916	Partial home rule granted to the Philippines

Kaiser precipitated a crisis in the summer of 1905 by delivering a bellicose speech in Casablanca, Morocco, intended to split the British and French and to force an opening of commercial doors in Morocco. In this endeavor, he sought help from Roosevelt. The French were outraged at Wilhelm's boldness, and war threatened. Roosevelt intervened, arranging a conference in Algeciras, Spain, to avert conflict. The treaty signed in 1906 prevented war and settled the issues of commerce and police administration in Morocco favorably for the French.

Roosevelt's successful countering of meddlesome German policies continued, as did his efforts in preventing war. At the Hague conference on disarmament in 1907, the Kaiser sought an agreement to reduce British naval supremacy, a superiority Roosevelt thought "quite proper." The German emperor also tried to promote German-Chinese-American entente to balance the Anglo-Japanese Treaty in Asia. Roosevelt rebuffed all these efforts. While on a European tour in 1910, the retired American president was warmly entertained and celebrated by Wilhelm, who continued to misunderstand him. Roosevelt, meanwhile, kept on urging his English friends to counter the German naval buildup in order to maintain peace in Europe.

In 1911, Roosevelt wrote that there would be nothing worse than that "Germany should ever overthrow England and establish the supremacy in Europe she aims at." German interest "to try her hand in America," he thought, would surely follow. To avert such horrors, Roosevelt's policy for Europe included cementing friendship with England and, while maintaining official neutrality, using diplomacy to prevent hostilities among European powers. The relationship between Great Britain and Germany continued to deteriorate, however, and by 1914, a new American president, Woodrow Wilson, would face the terrible reality that Roosevelt had skillfully sought to prevent. When World War I finally broke out, no American was more eager to fight on the British side against the Germans than the leader of the Rough Riders.

Conclusion

The Responsibilities of Power

Since the earliest settlements at Massachusetts Bay, Americans had struggled with the dilemma of how to do good in a world that did wrong. The realities of power in the 1890s brought increasing international responsibilities. Roosevelt said in 1910 that because of "strength and geographical situation," the United States had itself become "more and more, the balance of power of the whole world." This ominous responsibility was also an opportunity to extend American economic, political, and moral influence around the globe.

As president in the first decade of the twentieth century, Roosevelt established aggressive American policies toward the rest of the world. The United States dominated and policed Central America and the Caribbean Sea to maintain order and protect its investments and other economic interests. In the Far East, Americans marched through Hay's Open Door with treaties, troops, navies, and dollars to protect the newly annexed Philippine Islands, to develop markets and investments, and to preserve the balance of power in Asia. In Europe, the United States sought to remain neutral and uninvolved in European affairs and at the same time to cement Anglo-American friendship and prevent "civilized" nations from going to war.

How well these policies worked would be seen later in the twentieth century. Whatever the particular judgment, the fundamental ambivalence of America's sense of itself as a model "city on a hill," an example to others, remained. As widening involvements around the world—the Filipino-American War, for example—painfully demonstrated, it was increasingly difficult for the United States to be both responsible and good, both powerful and loved. The American people thus learned to experience both the satisfactions and burdens, both the profits and costs, of the missionary role.

Recommended Reading

American Expansionism: Moving Toward Empire

Robert Beisner, *From the Old Diplomacy to the New, 1865–1900* (1975); Charles Campbell, *The Transformation of American Foreign Relations, 1865–1900* (1976); John Dobson, *Reticent Expansionism: The Foreign Policy of William McKinley* (1988); Lewis Gould, *The Presidency of William McKinley* (1980); David Healy, *U.S. Expansion: Imperialist Urge in the 1890s* (1970); Walter La Feber, *The New Empire: An Interpretation of American Expansion, 1860–1898* (1963); Ernest May, *Imperial Democracy: The Emergence of America as a Great Power* (1961); H. Wayne Morgan, *America's Road to Empire: The War with Spain and Overseas Expansion* (1965); Milton Plesur, *America's Outward Thrust, 1865–1890* (1971); Emily Rosenberg, *Spreading the American Dream: American Economic and Cultural Expansion, 1890–1945* (1982); Rubin Weston, *Racism in U.S. Imperialism: The Influence of Racial Assumptions on American Foreign Policy, 1893–1946* (1972); William Widenor, *Henry Cabot Lodge and the Search for an American Foreign Policy* (1980).

The Spanish-American War and the Philippines

Robert Beisner, *Twelve Against Empire: The Anti-Imperialists, 1898–1900* (1975); James C. Bradford, ed., *Crucible of Empire: The Spanish-American War and Its Aftermath* (1993); Frank Freidel, *The Splendid Little War* (1958); Willard Gatewood, Jr., *Black Americans and the White Man's Burden* (1975) and *"Smoked Yankees" and the Struggle for Empire: Letters from Negro Soldiers, 1898–1902* (1971); Stanley Karnow, *In Our Image: America's Empire in the Philippines* (1989); Gerald Linderman, *The Mirror of War: American Society and the Spanish-American War* (1974); Glenn A. May,

Social Engineering in the Philippines: The Aims, Execution, and Impact of American Colonial Policy, 1900–1913 (1980); Stuart Creighton Miller, *"Benevolent Assimilation": The American Conquest of the Philippines, 1899–1903* (1982); John L. Offner, *An Unwanted War: The Diplomacy of the United States and Spain over Cuba, 1895–1898* (1992); David Trask, *The War with Spain in 1898* (1981); Richard Welch, *Response to Imperialism: The United States and the Philippine-American War, 1899–1902* (1979); Leon Wolff, *Little Brown Brother: How the United States Purchased and Pacified the Philippine Islands at the Century's Turn* (1961).

Roosevelt's Energetic Foreign Policy and Relations with Asia and the Caribbean

Howard Beale, *Theodore Roosevelt and the Rise of America to World Power* (1956); Roger Daniels, *Asian Americans: Chinese and Japanese in the United States Since 1850* (1988); Raymond Esthus, *Theodore Roosevelt and the International Rivalries* (1970); Michael Hunt, *The Making of a Special Relationship: The United States and China to 1914* (1983); Walter La Feber, *Inevitable Revolutions: The United States in Central America* (1983) and *The Panama Canal* (1978); Frederick Marks II, *Velvet on Iron: The Diplomacy of Theodore Roosevelt* (1979); David McCullough, *The Path Between the Seas: The Creation of the Panama Canal, 1870–1914* (1977); Dana Munro, *Intervention and Dollar Diplomacy in the Caribbean, 1900–1920* (1964); Charles E. Neu, *An Uncertain Friendship: Theodore Roosevelt and Japan, 1906–1909* (1967); Ronald Takaki, *Strangers from a Different Shore: A History of Asian Americans* (1989); Marilyn B. Young, *The Rhetoric of Empire: American China Policy, 1895–1901* (1968).

A Modernizing People, 1900–1945

COMPARATIVE CHRONOLOGIES

Political and Diplomatic	Social and Economic	Cultural and Technological
1900		
1900 William McKinley reelected president	1901 United States Steel Corporation organized	1901 Frank Norris, *The Octopus*
1901 McKinley assassinated; Theodore Roosevelt becomes president; Socialist Party of America founded	1902 Anthracite coal strike	1903 Wright brothers make first heavier-than-air flight
	1903–1910 Muckrakers attack social evils and corruption	1904 Lincoln Steffens, *The Shame of the Cities*
1904 Roosevelt reelected	1905 Industrial Workers of the World (IWW) organized	1906 Upton Sinclair, *The Jungle*
1906 Hepburn Act; Meat Inspection Act; Pure Food and Drug Act	1907 Panic caused by business failures; gentlemen's agreement stops emigration of Japanese laborers to United States	1908 Frank Lloyd Wright designs Robie House in Chicago
1908 William Howard Taft elected president	1908 *Muller* v. *Oregon*	1909 First Model T Ford produced
	1909 National Association for the Advancement of Colored People (NAACP) founded	
1910		
1910 Mann Act	1911 Triangle Shirtwaist Company fire	1910 Jane Addams, *Twenty Years at Hull House*
1912 Woodrow Wilson elected president	1913 Federal Reserve System established; Department of Labor separated from Department of Commerce	1911 Frederick Taylor, *The Principles of Scientific Management*
1913 Sixteenth Amendment provides for an income tax; Seventeenth Amendment provides for direct election of senators	1914 Clayton Act	1913 First assembly line at Ford Motor Company; Armory Show, New York
1914 World War I begins in Europe	1917 Literacy test for new immigrants established; Espionage Act	1914 Panama Canal completed
1915 *Lusitania* sunk	1918–1919 Influenza epidemic	1915 D. W. Griffiths produces *Birth of a Nation*
1916 Wilson reelected	1919 United States becomes creditor nation for first time	1916 Margaret Sanger organizes New York Birth Control League
1917 United States declares war on Germany and Austria-Hungary		
1918 War ends in Europe		
1919 Senate defeats League of Nations Treaty; Eighteenth Amendment establishes prohibition		
1920		
1920 Warren G. Harding elected president; Nineteenth Amendment provides for woman suffrage	1921 Sheppard-Towner Act; Immigration limited to 3 percent of each nationality in country in 1910	1920 First commercial radio broadcast, WWJ Detroit
1921 Washington Naval Conference	1924 Immigration limited to 2 percent of each nationality in country in 1890	1922 Sinclair Lewis, *Babbitt*
1923 Harding dies; Calvin Coolidge becomes president; Teapot Dome scandal	1925 A&W Root Beer becomes first fast-food franchise	1925 Scopes trial
1924 Coolidge reelected	1929 Stock market crash heralds Great Depression	1926 Langston Hughes, *Weary Blues*
1928 Herbert Hoover elected president		1927 Charles Lindbergh flies solo to Paris; Sacco and Vanzetti executed; *The Jazz Singer*, first feature-length talking movie
		1929 William Faulkner, *The Sound and the Fury*

Political and Diplomatic	Social and Economic	Cultural and Technological

1930

Political and Diplomatic	Social and Economic	Cultural and Technological
1932 Franklin D. Roosevelt elected president	1932 Bonus March	1934–1938 Radar developed by Army Signal Corps and U.S. Navy
1933 TVA and CCC created; NIRA and AAA	1933 Twenty-first Amendment ends prohibition	1935 Walt Disney releases *Flowers and Trees,* his first movie in color
1935 Social security and WPA established	1934 Indian Reorganization Act	1935–1936 WPA artists' and writers' projects
1936 Roosevelt reelected	1935 Committee for Industrial Organization (CIO) formed	1936 Margaret Mitchell, *Gone with the Wind*
1937 Wagner-Steagall Act	1936 United Auto Workers hold sit-down strike at General Motors plant	1938 Orson Welles's radio broadcast "The War of the Worlds"; nylon and fiberglass developed
1939 World War II begins in Europe	1938 Fair Labor Standards Act	1939 John Steinbeck, *The Grapes of Wrath;* New York World's Fair; first scheduled television broadcast

1940

Political and Diplomatic	Social and Economic	Cultural and Technological
1940 Roosevelt reelected for third term	1941 Roosevelt outlaws discrimination in defense industries	1942 Jet plane first tested in United States
1941 Japanese attack Pearl Harbor; Japan and Germany declare war on United States	1942 Congress of Racial Equality (CORE) founded	1943 Wendell Willkie, *One World*
1942 Allies invade North Africa	1944 Bretton Woods Conference	1944 First electronic calculator; Serviceman's Readjustment Act ("GI Bill")
1943 Italy surrenders		
1944 Normandy invasion; Roosevelt reelected for fourth term		

The Progressives Confront Industrial Capitalism

Frances Kellor, a young woman who grew up in Ohio and Michigan, received her law degree in 1897 from Cornell University and became one of the small but growing group of professionally trained women. Deciding that she was more interested in solving the nation's social problems than in practicing law, she moved to Chicago, studied sociology, and trained herself as a social reformer. Kellor believed passionately that poverty

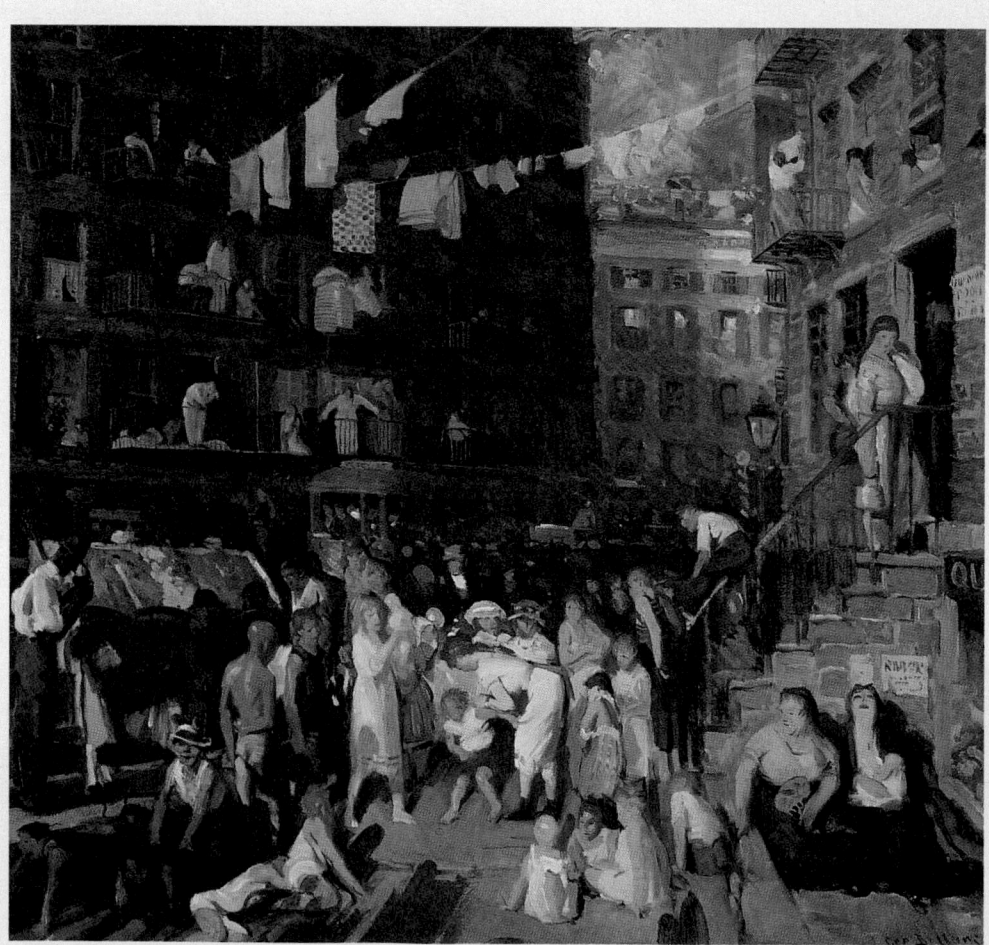

and inequality could be eliminated in America. She also had the progressive faith that if Americans could only hear the truth about the millions of people living in urban slums, they would rise up and make changes. She was one of the experts who provided the evidence to document what was wrong in industrial America.

Like many progressives, Kellor believed that environment was more important than heredity in determining ability, prosperity, and happiness. Better schools and better housing, she thought, would produce better citizens. Even criminals, she argued, were simply victims of environment. Kellor demonstrated that poor health and deprived childhoods explained the only differences between criminals and college students. If it were impossible to define a criminal type, then it must be possible to reduce crime by improving the environment.

Kellor was an efficient professional. Like the majority of the professional women of her generation, she never married but devoted her life to social research and social reform. She lived for a time at Hull House in Chicago and at the College Settlement in New York, centers not only of social research and reform, but also of lively community. For many young people, the settlement, with its sense of commitment and its exciting conversation around the dinner table, provided an alternative to the nuclear family or the single apartment.

While staying at the College Settlement, Kellor researched and wrote a muckraking study of employment agencies, published in 1904 as *Out of Work*. She revealed how employment agencies exploited immigrants, blacks, and other recent arrivals in the city. Kellor's book, like the writing of most progressives, spilled over with moral outrage. But Kellor went beyond moralism to suggest corrective legislation at the state and national levels. Kellor became one of the leaders of the movement to Americanize the immi-

grants pouring into the country in unprecedented numbers. Between 1899 and 1920, over 8 million people came to the United States, most from southern and eastern Europe. Many feared that this flood of immigrants threatened the very basis of American democracy. Kellor and her co-workers represented the side of progressivism that sought state and federal laws to protect the new arrivals from exploitation and to establish agencies and facilities to educate and Americanize them. Another group of progressives, often allied with organized labor, tried to pass laws to restrict immigration. Kellor did not entirely escape the ethnocentrism that was a part of her generation's world view, but she did maintain that all immigrants could be made into useful citizens.

Convinced of the need for a national movement to push for reform legislation, Kellor helped to found the National Committee for Immigrants in America, which tried to promote a national policy "to make all these people Americans," and a federal bureau to organize the campaign. Eventually, she helped establish the Division of Immigrant Education within the Department of Education. A political movement led by Theodore Roosevelt excited her most. More than almost any other single person, Kellor had been responsible for alerting Roosevelt to the problems the immigrants faced in American cities. When Roosevelt formed the new Progressive party in 1912, she was one of the many social workers and social researchers who joined him. She campaigned for Roosevelt and directed the Progressive Service Organization, to educate voters in all areas of social justice and welfare after the election. After Roosevelt's defeat and the collapse of the Progressive party in 1914, Kellor continued to work for Americanization. She spent the rest of her life promoting justice, order, and efficiency and trying to find ways for resolving industrial and international disputes.

George Bellows, *Cliff Dwellers,* 1913. Bellows was one of many talented artists who migrated from the Midwest to New York early in the century. In this painting he captures some of the life and excitement in a tenement district on a hot summer night. To Bellows this was romantic; to the progressive reformers it was a problem to be solved. (Los Angeles County Museum of Art, Los Angeles County Funds) rances Kellor's life illustrates two important aspects of progressivism, the first nation-wide reform movement of the modern era: first, a commitment to promote social justice, to assure equal opportunity, and to preserve democracy; and second, a search for order and efficiency in a world complicated by rapid industrialization, immigration, and spectacular urban growth. But no one person can represent all facets of so complex a movement. Borrowing from populism and influenced by a number of reformers from the 1890s, progressivism reached a climax in the years from 1900 to 1914. Like most American reform movements, the progressive movement did not plot to overthrow the government; rather, it sought to reform the system in order to assure the survival of the American way of life.

This chapter traces the important aspects of progressivism. It examines the social justice movement, which sought to promote reform among the poor and to improve life for those who had fallen victim to an urban and industrial civilization. It surveys life among workers, a group the reformers sometimes helped but often misunderstood. Then it traces the reform movements in the cities and states, where countless officials and experts tried to reduce chaos and promote order and democracy. Finally, it examines progressivism at the national level during the administrations of Theodore Roosevelt and Woodrow Wilson, the first thoroughly modern presidents.

The Social Justice Movement

Historians write of a "progressive movement," but actually there were a number of movements, some of them contradictory, but all focusing on the problems created by a rapidly expanding urban and industrial world. Some reformers, often from the middle class, sought to humanize the modern city. They hoped to improve housing and schools and to provide a better life for the poor and recent immigrants. Others were concerned with the conditions of work and the rights of labor. Still others pressed for changes in the political system to make it more responsive to their interests. Progressivism had roots in the 1890s, when many reformers were shocked by the devastation caused by the depression of 1893, and they were influenced by reading Henry George's *Progress and Poverty* (1879) and Edward Bellamy's *Looking Backward* (1888). They were also influenced by the Social Gospel movement, which sought to build the kingdom of God on earth by eliminating poverty and promoting equality (see Chapter 19).

The Progressive World View

Intellectually, the progressives were influenced by the Darwinian revolution. They believed that the world was in flux, and they rebelled against the fixed and the formal in every field. One of the philosophers of the movement, John Dewey, wrote that ideas could become instruments for change. William James, in his philosophy of pragmatism, denied that there were universal truths; ideas should be judged by their usefulness. Most of the progressives were environmentalists who were convinced that environment was much more important than heredity in forming character. Thus, if one could build better schools and houses, one could make better people and a more perfect society. Yet even the more advanced reformers thought in racial and ethnic categories. They believed that some groups could be molded and changed more easily than others. Thus, progressivism did not usually mean progress for blacks.

In many ways, progressivism was the first modern reform movement. It sought to bring order and efficiency to a world that had been transformed by rapid growth and new technology. Yet elements of nostalgia infected the movement as reformers tried to preserve the handicrafts of a preindustrial age and to promote small-town and farm values in the city. The progressive leaders were almost always middle class, and they quite consciously tried to teach their middle-class values to the immigrants and the working class. Often, the progressives seemed more interested in control than in reform; frequently, they betrayed a sense of paternalism toward those they tried to help.

The progressives were part of a statistics-minded, realistic generation. They conducted surveys, gathered facts, wrote reports about every conceivable problem, and usually had faith that their reports would lead to change. Their urge to document and to record came out in haunting photographs of young workers taken by Lewis Hine, in the stark and beautiful city paintings by John Sloan, and in the realist novels of Theodore Dreiser and William Dean Howells.

The progressives were optimistic about human nature, and they believed that change was possible. In retrospect, they may seem naive or bigoted, but they wrestled with many social questions, some of them old but fraught with new urgency in an industrialized society. What is the proper relation of government to society? In a world of large corporations, huge cities, and massive transportation systems, how much should the government regulate and control? How much responsibility does society have to care for the poor and needy? The progressives could not agree on the answers, but for the first time in American history, they struggled with the questions.

The Muckrakers

One group of writers who exposed corruption and other evils in American society were labeled "muckrakers" by Theodore Roosevelt. Not all muckrakers were reformers—some merely wanted to profit from the scandals—but the reformers learned from their techniques of exposé.

In part, the muckrakers were a product of the journalistic revolution of the 1890s. Nineteenth-century magazines such as *Atlantic, Century,* and *Scribner's* had small, highly educated audiences. The new magazines, among them *American, McClure's,* and *Cosmopolitan,* had slick formats, carried more advertising, and sold more widely. Several had circulations of more than 500,000 in 1910. Competing for readers, editors eagerly published the articles of investigative reporters who

John Sloan (1871–1951) was one of the leading members of the "ashcan" school, a group of artists who experimented with new techniques and tried to document ordinary scenes. Sloan's realistic depictions of the city, such as this 1914 painting, Backyards, Greenwich Village, *shocked Americans just as much as the progressive era reports on child labor, prostitution, and poor housing. (Collection Whitney Museum of American Art, New York)*

wanted to tell the public what was wrong in American society.

Lincoln Steffens, a young California journalist, wrote articles for *McClure's* exposing the connections between respectable urban businessmen and corrupt politicians. When published in 1904 as *The Shame of the Cities,* Steffens's account became a battle cry for people determined to clean up the graft in city government. Ida Tarbell, a teacher turned journalist, had grown up in western Pennsylvania, almost next door to the first oil well in the United States. She published several successful books before turning her attention to the Standard Oil Company and John D. Rockefeller. Her outraged exposé, based on years of research, revealed Rockefeller's ruthless ways and his unfair business practices.

After Steffens and Tarbell achieved popular success, many others followed. Ray Stannard Baker exposed the railroads. David Graham Phillips revealed the alliance of politics and business in *The Treason of the Senate* (1906). Robert Hunter, a young settlement worker, shocked Americans in 1904 with his book *Poverty:* setting the poverty line at $460 for a family of five, he found 10 million people living below that level. Realistic fiction also mirrored such concerns. Upton Sinclair's novel *The Jungle* (1906) described the horrors of the Chicago meatpacking industry, and Frank Norris in *The Octopus* (1901) dramatized the railroads' stranglehold on the farmers.

Working Women and Children

Nothing disturbed the social justice progressives more than the sight of children, sometimes as young as 8 or 10, working long hours in dangerous and depressing factories. Young people had worked in factories since the beginning of the industrial revolution, but that did not make the practice any less repugnant to the reformers. "Children are put into industry very much as we put in raw material," Jane Addams objected, "and the product we look for is not better men and women, but better manufactured goods."

Florence Kelley was one of the most important leaders in the crusade against child labor. Kelley had grown up in an upper-class Philadelphia family and graduated from Cornell in 1882, like Addams and Kellor she was a member of the first generation of college women. When the University of Pennsylvania refused her admission as a graduate student because she was a woman, she went to the University of Zurich in Switzerland. There she married and became a socialist. The marriage failed, and some years later, Kelley moved to Chicago with her children, became a Hull House resident, and poured her considerable energies into the campaign against child labor. A friend described her as "explosive, hot-tempered, determined ... a smoking volcano that at any moment would burst into flames." When she could find no attorney in Chicago to argue child labor cases against some of the prominent corporations, she went to law school, passed the bar exam, and argued the cases herself.

Although Kelley and the other child labor reformers won a few cases, they quickly recognized the need for state laws if they were going to have any real influence. Child labor was an emotional issue. Many businesses made large profits by employing children, and many legislators and government officials, remembering their own rural childhoods, argued that it was good for the children's character to work hard and take responsibility. Reformers, marshaling their evidence about the tragic effects on growing children of long working hours in dark and damp factories, pressured the Illinois state legislature into passing an anti–child labor law. A few years later, however, the state supreme court declared the law unconstitutional.

Judicial opposition was one factor leading reformers to the national level in the first decade of the twentieth century. Florence Kelley again led the charge. In 1899, she had become secretary of the National Consumers League, an organization that enlisted consumers in a campaign to lobby elected officials and corporations to ensure that products were produced under safe and sanitary conditions. It was not Kelley, however, but Edgar Gardner Murphy, an Alabama clergyman, who suggested the formation of the National Child Labor Committee. Like many other Social Gospel ministers, Murphy believed that the church should reform society as well as save souls. He was appalled by the number of young children working in southern textile mills, where they were exposed to great danger and condemned to "compulsory ignorance" (because they dropped out of school).

The National Child Labor Committee, headquartered in New York, drew up a model state child labor law, encouraged state and city campaigns, and coordinated the movement around the country. Although two-thirds of the states passed some form of child labor law between 1905 and 1907, many had loopholes that exempted a large number of children, including newsboys and youngsters who worked in the theater. The committee also supported a national bill introduced in Congress by Indiana Senator Albert Beveridge in 1906 "to prevent the employment of children in factories and mines." The bill went down to defeat. However, the child labor reformers convinced Congress in 1912 to establish a children's bureau in the Department of Labor. Despite these efforts, compulsory school attendance laws did more to reduce the number of children who worked than federal and state laws, which proved difficult to pass and even more difficult to enforce.

The crusade against child labor was a typical social justice reform effort. Its origins lay in the moral indignation of middle-class reformers. But reform went beyond moral outrage as reformers gathered statistics, took photographs documenting the abuse of children, and used their evidence to push for legislation first on the local level, then in the states, and eventually in Washington.

Like other progressive reform efforts, the battle against child labor was only partly successful. Too many businessmen, both small and large, were profiting from employing children at low wages. Too many politicians and judges were reluctant to regulate the work of children or adults because work seemed such an individual and personal matter. And some parents, who often desperately needed the money their children earned in the factories, opposed the reformers and even broke the law to allow their children to work.

The reformers also worried over the young people who got into trouble with the law, often for pranks that in rural areas would have seemed harmless. They feared for young people tried by adult courts and thrown into jail with hardened criminals. Almost simultaneously in Denver and Chicago, reformers organized juvenile courts, where judges had the authority to put delinquent youths on probation, take them from their families and make them wards of the state, or assign them to an institution. The juvenile court often helped

Nothing tugged at the heartstrings of the reformers more than the sight of little children, sullen and stunted, working long hours in factory, farm, and mine. These children, breaker boys who spent all day sorting coal in western Pennsylvania, were carefully posed by documentary photographer Lewis Hine while he worked for the National Child Labor Committee in 1911. (Records of the Children's Bureau, The National Archives, Office of the Chief Signal Officer)

prevent young delinquents from adopting a life of crime. Yet the juvenile offender was frequently deprived of all rights of due process, a fact that the Supreme Court finally recognized in 1967, when it ruled that children were entitled to procedural rights when accused of a crime.

Closely connected with the anti–child labor movement was the effort to limit the hours of women's work. It seemed inconsistent to protect a girl until she was 16 and then give her the "right to work from 8 A.M. to 10 P.M., 13 hours a day, 78 hours a week for $6." Florence Kelley and the National Consumers League led the campaign. It was foolish and unpatriotic, they argued, to allow the "mothers of future generations" to work long hours in dangerous industries. "Adult females," a Pennsylvania superior court stated, "are so constituted as to be unable to endure physical exertion and exposure."

The most important court case on women's work came before the U.S. Supreme Court in 1908. Josephine Goldmark, a friend and co-worker of Kelley's at the Consumers League, wrote the brief for *Muller* v. *Oregon* that her brother-in-law, Louis Brandeis, used when he argued the case. The Court upheld the Oregon ten-hour law largely because Goldmark's sociological argument detailed the danger and disease that factory women faced. Brandeis opposed laissez-faire legal concepts, arguing that the government had a special interest in protecting the health of its citizens. Most states fell into line with the Supreme Court decision and passed protective legislation for women, though many companies found ways to circumvent the laws. Even the work permitted by the law seemed too long to some women. "I think ten hours is too much for a woman," one factory worker stated. "I have four children and have to work hard at home. Make me awful tired. I would like nine hours. I get up at 5:30. When I wash, I have to stay up till one or two o'clock."

By contending that "women are fundamentally weaker than men in all that makes for endurance: in muscular strength, in nervous energy, in the powers of persistent attention and application," the reformers won some protection for women workers. But their arguments that women were weaker than men would eventually be used to reinforce gender segregation of the work force for the next half century.

In addition to working for protective legislation for working women, the social justice progressives also campaigned for woman suffrage. Unlike some supporters who argued that middle-class women would offset the ignorant and corrupt votes of immigrant men, these social reformers supported votes for all women. Addams argued that urban women not only could vote intelligently, but also needed the vote to protect, clothe, and feed their families. Women in an urban age, she suggested, needed to be municipal housekeepers. Through the suffrage, they would ensure that elected officials provided adequate services—pure water, uncontaminated food, proper sanitation, and police protection. The progressive insistence that all women needed the vote helped to push woman suffrage toward the victory that would come during World War I.

Much more controversial than either votes for women or protective legislation was the movement for birth control. Even many advanced progressives could not imagine themselves teaching immigrant women how to prevent conception, especially because the Comstock Law of 1873 made it illegal to promote or even write about contraceptive devices.

Margaret Sanger, a nurse who had watched poor women suffer from too many births and even die from dangerous illegal abortions, was one of the founders of the modern American birth control movement. Middle-class Americans had limited family size in the nineteenth century through abstinence, withdrawal, and abortion, as well as through the use of primitive birth control devices, but much ignorance and misinformation remained, even among middle-class women. Sanger obtained the latest medical and scientific European studies and in 1914 explained in her magazine, *The Woman Rebel,* and in a pamphlet, *Family Limitation,* that women could separate sex from procreation. She was promptly indicted for violation of the postal code and fled to Europe to avoid arrest.

Birth control remained controversial, and in most states illegal, for many years. Yet Sanger helped to bring the topic of sexuality and contraception out into the open. When she returned to the United States in 1921, she founded the American Birth Control League, which became the Planned Parenthood Federation in 1942.

Home and School

The reformers believed that better housing and education could transform the lives of the poor and create a better world. Books such as Jacob Riis's *How the Other Half Lives* (1890) horrified them. With vivid language and haunting photographs, Riis had documented the overcrowded tenements, the damp, dark alleys, and the sickness and despair that affected people who lived in New York's slums. Reformers had been trying to improve housing for the poor for years. They had constructed model tenements and housing projects and had sent "friendly visitors" to the residents to collect the rent and to teach them how to live like the middle class. Riis labored to replace New York's worst slums with parks and playgrounds.

In the first decade of the twentieth century, the progressives took a new approach toward the housing problems. They collected statistics, conducted surveys, organized committees, and constructed exhibits to demonstrate the effect of urban overcrowding. Then they set out to pass tenement house laws in several cities, but the laws were often evaded or modified. In 1910, they organized the National Housing Association, and some of them looked ahead to federal laws and even to government-subsidized housing.

The housing reformers combined a moral sense of what needed to be done to create a more just society with practical ability to organize public opinion and get laws passed. They also took a paternalistic view toward the poor. Many reformers disapproved of the clutter and lack of privacy in immigrant tenements. One reformer's guide, *How to Furnish and Keep House in a Tenement Flat,* recommended "wood-stained and uncluttered furniture surfaces, iron beds with mattresses, and un-upholstered chairs.... Walls must be painted not papered. Screens provide privacy in the bedrooms; a few good pictures should grace the walls." But often immigrant family ideals and values differed from those of the middle-class reformers. The immigrants actually did not mind the clutter

Overcrowded tenement housing depressed and angered the reformers. This carefully posed photograph, taken in New York in 1910 by Jacob Riis, illustrates not only poor living conditions, but also unusual neatness for such overcrowded conditions. (Museum of the City of New York)

Documentary Photographs

Lewis Hine, Carolina Cotton Mill, *1908. (George Eastman House)*

As we saw in Chapter 15, photographs are a revealing way of recovering the past visually. But when looking at a photograph, especially an old one, it is easy to assume that it is an accurate representation of the past. Photographers, however, like novelists and historians, have a point of view. They take their pictures for a reason and often to prove a point. As one photographer remarked, "Photographs don't lie, but liars take photographs."

To document the need for reform in the cities, progressives collected statistics, made surveys, described settlement house life, and even wrote novels. But they discovered that the photograph was often more effective than words. Jacob Riis, the Danish-born author of *How the Other Half Lives* (1890), a devastating exposure of conditions in New York City tenement house slums, was also a pioneer in urban photography. Others had taken pictures of dank alleys and street urchins before, but Riis was the first to photograph slum conditions with the express purpose of promoting reform. At first he hired photographers, but then he bought a camera and taught himself how to use it. He even tried a new German flash powder to illuminate dark alleys and tenement rooms in order to record the horror of slum life.

Riis made many of his photographs into lantern slides and used them to illustrate his lectures on the need for housing reform. Although he was a creative and innovative photographer, his pictures were often far from objective. His equipment was awkward, his film slow. He had to set up and prepare carefully before snapping the shutter. His views of tenement ghetto streets and poor children now seem like clichés, but they were designed to make Americans angry, to arouse them to reform.

Another important progressive photographer was Lewis Hine. Trained as a sociologist, like Riis, he taught himself photography. Hine used his camera to illustrate his lectures at the Ethical Culture School in New York. In 1908, he was hired as a full-time investigator by the National Child Labor Committee. His haunting photographs of children in factories helped convince many Americans of the need to abolish child labor. Hine's children were appealing human beings. He showed them eating, running, working, and staring wistfully out factory windows. His photographs avoided the pathos that Riis was so fond of recording, but just as surely they documented the need for reform.

Another technique that the reform photographer used was the before-and-after shot. The two photographs shown here of a one-room apartment in Philadelphia early in the century illustrate how progressive reformers tried to teach immigrants to imitate middle-class manners. The "before" photograph shows a room cluttered with washtubs, laundry, cooking utensils, clothes, tools, even an old Christmas decoration. In the "after" picture, much of the clutter has been cleaned up. A window has been installed to let in light and fresh air. The wallpaper, presumably a haven for hidden bugs and germs, has been torn off. The cooking utensils and laundry have been put away. The woodwork has been stained, and some ceremonial objects have been gathered on a shelf.

What else can you find that has been changed? How well do you think the message of the photographic combi-nations like this one worked? Would the immigrant family be happy with the new look and condition of their room? Could anyone live in one room and keep it so neat?

As you look at these, or any photographs, ask yourself: What is the photographer's purpose and point of view? Why was this particular angle chosen for the picture? And why center on these particular people or objects? What does the photographer reveal about his or her purpose? What does the photographer reveal unintentionally? How have fast film and new camera styles changed photography? On what subjects do reform-minded photographers train their cameras today?

The reality of one-room tenement apartments (above) contrasted with the tidiness that reformers saw as the ideal (right). (Temple University Libraries/Urban Archives)

and lack of privacy. Despite the reformers' efforts to separate life's functions into separate rooms, most immigrants still crowded into the kitchen and hung religious objects rather than "good pictures" on the walls.

Ironically, many middle-class women reformers who tried to teach working-class families how to live in their tenement flats had never organized their own homes. Often they lived in settlement houses, where they ate in a dining hall and never had to worry about cleaning, cooking, or doing laundry. Some of them, however, began to realize that the domestic tasks expected of women of all classes kept many of them from taking their full place in society. Charlotte Perkins Gilman, author of *Women and Economics* (1898), dismantled the traditional view of "woman's sphere" and sketched an alternative. Suggesting that entrepreneurs ought to build apartment houses designed to allow women to combine motherhood with careers, she advocated shared kitchen facilities and a common dining room, a laundry run by efficient workers, and a roof-garden day nursery with a professional teacher.

Gilman, who criticized private homes as "bloated buildings, filled with a thousand superfluities," was joined by a few radicals in promoting new living arrangements. Most Americans, however, of all political persuasions continued to view the home as sacred space where the mother ruled supreme and created an atmosphere of domestic tranquillity for the husband and children.

Next to better housing, the progressives stressed better schools as a way to produce better citizens. Public school systems were often rigid and corrupt. Far from producing citizens who would help transform society, the schools seemed to reinforce the conservative habits that blocked change. A reporter who traveled around the country in 1892 discovered mindless teachers who drilled pupils through repetitious rote learning. A Chicago teacher advised her students, "Don't stop to think; tell me what you know." When asked why the students were not allowed to move their heads, a New York teacher replied, "Why should they look behind when the teacher is in front of them?"

Progressive education, like many other aspects of progressivism, opposed the rigid and the formal in favor of flexibility and change. John Dewey was the key philosopher of progressive education. Having grown up in Vermont, he tried throughout his life to create a sense of the small rural community in the city. In his laboratory school at the University of Chicago, he experimented with new educational methods. He replaced the school desks, which were bolted down and always faced the front, with seats that could be moved into circles and arranged in small groups. The movable seat, in fact, became one of the symbols of the progressive education movement.

Dewey insisted that the schools be child-centered, not subject-oriented. Teachers should teach children rather than teach history or mathematics. Dewey did not mean that history and math should not be taught, but that those subjects should be related to the students' experience. Students should learn by doing. They should actually build a house, not just study how others constructed houses. Students should not just learn about democracy; the school itself should operate like a democracy.

Dewey also maintained, somewhat controversially, that the schools should become instruments for social reform. But like most progressives, Dewey was never quite clear whether he wanted the schools to help the students adjust to the existing world or to turn out graduates who would change the world. Although he wavered on that point, the spirit of progressive education, like the spirit of progressivism in general, was optimistic. The schools could create more flexible, better-educated, more understanding adults who would go out to improve society.

Crusades Against Saloons, Brothels, and Movie Houses

Given their faith in the reforming potential of healthy and educated citizens, it was logical that most social justice progressives opposed the sale of alcohol. Some came from Protestant homes where the consumption of liquor was considered a sin, but most favored prohibition for the same reasons they opposed child labor and favored housing reform. They saw eliminating the sale of alcohol as part of the process of reforming the city and conserving human resources.

Americans did drink great quantities of beer, wine, and hard liquor, and the amount they consumed rose rapidly after 1900, peaking between 1911 and 1915. An earlier temperance movement had achieved some success in the 1840s and 1850s (see Chapter 12), but only three states still had prohibition laws in force. The modern anti-liquor movement was spearheaded in the 1880s and 1890s by the Women's Christian Temperance Union and after 1900 by the Anti-Saloon League and a coalition of religious leaders and social reformers. During the progressive era, temperance forces had considerable success in influencing legislation. Seven states passed temperance laws between 1906 and 1912.

The reformers were appalled to see young children going into saloons to bring home a pail of beer for the family and horrified by tales of alcoholic fathers beating wives and children. But most often progressives focused on the saloon and its social life. Drug traffic, prostitution, and political corruption all seemed linked to the saloon. "Why should the community have any more sympathy for the saloon … than … for a typhoid-breeding pool of filthy water, … a swarm of deadly mosquitoes, or … a nest of rats infected with bubonic plague?" an irate reformer asked.

Although they never quite understood the role alcoholic drinks played in the social life of many ethnic groups, Jane Addams and other settlement workers appreciated the saloon's importance as a neighborhood social center. Addams started a coffeehouse at Hull House in an attempt to lure the neighbors away from the evils of the saloon. In his study *Substitutes for the Saloon*, Raymond Caulkins, a young social worker, suggested parks, playgrounds, municipal theaters, and temperance bars as replacements for the saloons, where so many men gathered after work.

The progressives never found an adequate substitute for the saloon, but they set to work to pass local and state prohibition laws. As in many other progressive efforts, they joined forces with diverse groups to push for change. Their combined efforts led to victory on December 22, 1917, when Congress sent to the states for ratification, a constitutional amendment prohibiting the sale, manufacturing, or importing of intoxicating liquor within the United States. The spirit of sacrifice for the war effort facilitated its rapid ratification.

In addition to the saloon, the progressives saw the urban dance hall and the movie theater as threats to the morals and well-being of young people, especially young women. The motion picture, invented in 1889, developed as an important form of entertainment only during the first decade of the twentieth century. At first, the "nickelodeons," as the early movie theaters were called, appealed mainly to a lower-class and largely ethnic audience. In 1902, New York City had 50 theaters; by 1908, there were over 400 showing 30-minute dramas and romances.

Not until World War I, when D. W. Griffith produced long feature films, did the movies begin to attract a middle-class audience. The most popular of these early films was Griffith's *The Birth of a Nation* (1915), a blatantly racist and distorted epic of black debauchery during Reconstruction. Many early films were imported from France, Italy, and Germany; because they were silent, it was easy to use subtitles in any language. But one did not need to know the language, or even be able to read, to enjoy the action. That was part of the attraction of the early films. Many had plots that depicted premarital sex, adultery, and violence, and, unlike later films, many attacked authority and had tragic endings. *The Candidate* (1907) showed an upper-class reform candidate who gets dirt thrown at him for his efforts to clean up the town. The film *Down with Women* (1907) showed well-dressed men denouncing woman suffrage and the incompetence of the weaker sex, but throughout the film, only strong women are depicted. In the end, when the hero is arrested, a woman lawyer defends him.

Some of the films stressed slapstick humor or romance and adventure; others bordered on pornography. The reformers objected not only to the plots and content of the films, but also to the location of the theaters, near saloons and burlesque houses, and to their dark interiors. "In the dim auditorium which seems to float on the world of dreams … an American woman may spend her afternoon alone," one critic wrote. "She can let her fantasies slip through the darkened atmosphere to the screen where they drift in rhapsodic amours with handsome stars." It was these fantasies, in addition to the other things they imagined were going on in the dark, that disturbed the reformers. But for young immigrant women, who made up the bulk of the audience at most urban movie theaters, the films provided rare exciting moments in their lives. One daughter of strict Italian parents remarked, "The one place I was allowed to go by myself was the movies. I went to the movies for

At Amusement Parks

In the first two decades of the twentieth century, the construction of amusement parks marked the rise of a new, mass, urban culture and the commercialization of leisure. The first and the most famous of the amusement parks was Coney Island built near New York City in 1897, but virtually every city had its own park—Revere Beach near Boston; Willow Grove near Philadelphia; Cedar Point near Sandusky, Ohio; Electric Park in Kansas City; Venice Park near Los Angeles; Belmont Park in San Diego; and Playland in San Francisco—over 2,000 parks before World War I. The parks featured Ferris Wheels (made popular at the 1893 Chicago World's Fair) roller coasters, cyclones, shoot the chutes, and other rides. There were also concerts, restaurants, dance halls, and an endless variety of games, all contained within an exotic architecture of minarets, arches, and towers.

The amusement parks were made possible by a trolley and electric interurban transportation system that could move large numbers of people inexpensively to the city's edge where the parks were always located. Electrification was vital, not only to run the trolleys, but also the roller coasters and other rides, and to turn the parks into fantasy lands at night—25,000 light bulbs illuminated Luna Park at Coney Island.

Millions of people flocked to amusement parks early in the century. Twenty million visited Coney Island in one year, three million came to Willow Grove, and more than a million and a half to the three parks in Kansas City. They came from all walks of life. Even the typical worker, who made perhaps $600 a year and labored six days a week, was beginning to get a half-day off on Saturday and other

days off (without pay) during the summer when the parks were open. Some trolleys only charged five cents and that often included entrance into the park. Few parks charged more than ten cents for admission, so a great many workers could go at least a few times a year. Most rides cost ten cents and there was always the temptation to spend more than one could afford, but many women came hoping to find a man to "treat" them to a ride or a hot dog. Middle-class families made up a large part of the crowd, but there were also groups of young people, clerks, salesmen and saleswomen, secretaries, and telephone operators seeking a release from their work routines.

An imposing and colorful arch with plaster carvings and thousands of lights announced to the visitors that they were leaving the world of reality and entering a world of fantasy and make-believe. The rides, from the frightening roller coaster to the "tickler," which had circular cars that spun round and round as they careened down a ramp, all encouraged physical contact. The rides, according to one observer, provided people "a chance to wonder, a chance to shudder, and a chance to be scared out of their wits." The hidden jets at the "Blowhole Theater" blew off men's hats and lifted women's skirts. The Tunnel of Love and many other rides went through dark, winding passages, allowing plenty of opportunity for touching. "The men like it because it gives them a chance to hug the girls," one manager decided.

Picture postcards, which became popular in the United States after 1907, depicted some of the exciting attractions at the amusements parks and allowed visitors to write to friends: "Having a wonderful time; wish you were here." Turkish minarets help create an exotic atmosphere at Wonderland Park, Revere Beach, Massachusetts.

Most parks were near the ocean or a lake so beaches and swim attire added to the informality and to the chance for unsupervised encounters with strangers. The entire atmosphere of fantasy and play and sexual titillation encouraged people of all ages to act a little silly, to give up the sober seriousness of their work lives.

Yet exuberance had its limits. Most parks prohibited alcohol, tried to keep out undesirable types, and enforced an informal dress code. All parks, even in the North, prohibited blacks from entering through the gates. Still there was a greater mingling of people from diverse class and ethnic backgrounds than at any other place in American life, more than at clubs, labor unions, saloons, churches, or theaters. Many progressive reformers did not approve of the casual fun and the exuberant fantasy world of this new kind of urban entertainment. They preferred more structured and controlled forms of play. But for millions of Americans, carefully supervised recreation was no match for the enticements of the amusement park.

The parks declined after 1920, unable to compete with the automobile and the motion picture. Yet during the first two decades of the twentieth century, these precursors of Disneyland, Great America, and other theme parks provided casual and unstructured amusement for heterogeneous crowds of American people.

The whip and crazy house slide attract a big and well-dressed crowd at Long Beach, California.

Mary Pickford, one of the stars of the silent movies, played the heroine in a film that outraged the reformers because it dealt with the subject of unwed motherhood. (The Everett Collection)

fun. My parents wouldn't let me go anywhere else, even when I was twenty-four."

Saloons, dance halls, and movie theaters all seemed dangerous to progressives interested in improving life in the city, because all appeared to be somehow connected with the worst evil of all, prostitution. Campaigns against prostitution had been waged since the early nineteenth century, but they were nothing compared with the progressives' crusade to wipe out what they called the "social evil." All major cities and many smaller ones appointed vice commissions and made elaborate studies of prostitution. The reports, which often ran to several thick volumes, were typical progressive documents. Compiled by experts, they were filled with elaborate statistical studies and laced with moral outrage.

The progressive antivice crusade attracted many kinds of people, for often contradictory reasons. Racists and immigration restrictionists maintained that inferior people—blacks and recent immigrants, especially those from southern and eastern Europe—became prostitutes and pimps. Social hygiene progressives published vivid accounts of prostitution as part of their campaign to fight ignorance and prudery about sex. A number of women reformers joined the campaign and argued for a single sexual standard for men

and women. Others worried that prostitutes would spread venereal disease to unfaithful husbands, who would pass it on to unsuspecting wives and unborn babies, eventually wiping out humanity. Most progressives, however, stressed the environmental causes of vice. They viewed prostitution, along with child labor and poor housing, as evils that education and reform could eliminate.

Most progressive antivice reformers stressed the economic causes of prostitution. "Is it any wonder," the Chicago Vice Commission asked, "that a tempted girl who receives only six dollars per week working with her hands sells her body for twenty-five dollars per week when she learns there is a demand for it and men are willing to pay the price?" "Do you suppose I am going back to earn five or six dollars a week in a factory," one prostitute asked an investigator, "when I can earn that amount any night and often much more?"

Despite all their reports and all the publicity, the progressives failed to end prostitution and did virtually nothing to address its roots in poverty. They wiped out a few red-light districts, closed a number of brothels, and managed to push a bill through Congress (the Mann Act of 1910) that prohibited the interstate transport of women for immoral purposes. Perhaps more important, in several states, they got the age of consent for women raised, and in 20 states, they made the Wassermann test for syphilis mandatory for both men and women before a marriage license could be issued.

The Worker in the Progressive Era

Progressive reformers sympathized with industrial workers who struggled to earn a living for themselves and their families. The progressives sought protective legislation—particularly for women and children—unemployment insurance, and workers' compensation. But often they had little understanding of what it was really like to sell one's strength by the hour. For example, they supported labor's right to organize at a time when labor had few friends, yet often opposed the strike as a weapon against management. And neither organized labor nor the reformers, individually or in shaky partnership, had power over industry. Control was in the hands of the owners and managers, and they were determined to strengthen their grip on the workplace as the nature of industrial work was being transformed.

Adjusting to Industrial Labor

John Mekras arrived in New York from Greece in 1912 and traveled immediately to Manchester, New Hampshire, where he found a job in the giant Amoskeag textile mill. He did not speak a word of English. "The man who hands out the jobs sent me to the spinning room," he later remembered. "There I don't know anything about the spinning. I'm a farmer.... I don't know what the boss is talking about." Mekras didn't last long at the mill. He was one of the many industrial workers who had difficulty adjusting to factory work in the early twentieth century.

Many workers, whether they were from Greece, from eastern Europe, from rural Vermont, or from Michigan, confronted a bewildering world based on order and routine. Unlike farm or craft work, factory life was dominated by the clock, the bell tower, and the boss. The workers continued to resist the routine and pace of factory work, and they subtly sabotaged the employers' efforts to control the workplace as they had done in an earlier period (see Chapters 10 and 18). They stayed at home on holidays when they were supposed to work, took unauthorized breaks, and set their own informal productivity schedules. Often they were fired or quit. In the woolen industry, the annual turnover of workers between 1907 and 1910 was more than 100 percent. In New York needleworker shops in 1912 and 1913, the turnover rate was over 250 percent. Overall in American industry, one-third of the workers stayed at their jobs less than a year.

This industrial work force, still composed largely of immigrants, had a fluid character. Many migrants, especially those from southern and eastern Europe, expected to stay only for a short time and then return to their homeland. "Italians come to America with the sole intention of accumulating money," one Italian-American writer complained in 1905. "Their dreams, their only care is the bundle of money ... which will give them, after 20 years of deprivation, the possibility of having a mediocre standard of living in their native coun-

try." Many men came alone—70 percent in some years. They saved money by living in a boarding-house. In 1910, two-thirds of the workers in Pittsburgh made less than $12 a week, but by lodging in boardinghouses and paying $2.50 a month for a bed, they could save perhaps one-third of their pay. "Here in America one must work for three horses," one immigrant wrote home. "The work is very heavy, but I don't mind it," another wrote; "let it be heavy, but may it last without interruption."

About 40 percent of those who immigrated to America in the first decade of the twentieth century returned home, according to one estimate. In years of economic downturn, such as 1908, more Italians and Austro-Hungarians left the United States than entered it. For many immigrants, the American dream never materialized. But these reluctant immigrants provided the mass of unskilled labor that American industry exploited and sometimes consumed much the way other Americans exploited the land and the forests. The great pool of immigrant workers meant profits for American industry.

The nature of work continued to change in the early twentieth century as industrialists extended late-nineteenth-century efforts to make their factories and their work forces more efficient, productive, and profitable. In some industries, the introduction of new machines revolutionized work and eliminated highly paid skilled jobs. Glassblowing machines invented about 1900, for example, replaced thousands of glassblowers or reduced them from craftsmen to workers. Power-driven machines, better-organized operations, and, finally, the moving assembly line, perfected by Henry Ford, transformed the nature of work and turned many laborers into unskilled tenders of machines.

Coal miner John Brophy recalled his father's pride in his work as a miner. "The skill with which you undercut the vein, the judgment in drilling the coal after it has been undercut and placing the exact amount of explosive so that it would do an effective job of breaking the coal from the solid ... indicated the quality of his work." But by the beginning of the twentieth century, undercutting machines and the mechanization of mining operations diminished miners' pride and independence.

The influence of the machine was uneven, having a greater impact in some industries than in

This famous 1907 photograph, The Steerage, *by Alfred Stieglitz, is usually used to depict the horrors of steerage and the immigrants' hope for a better life in America. It is actually a picture of a ship returning to Europe, so it is more accurately an image of the failure of the American dream, though many immigrants only intended to stay a few years, earn some money, and then return to their homeland. (Philadelphia Museum of Art, Gift of Carl Zigrosser)*

others. Although some skilled weavers and glass-blowers were transformed into unskilled operators, the introduction of the machines themselves created the need for new skilled workers. In the auto industry, for example, the new elite workers were the mechanics and tool and die men who kept the assembly line running. Although these new skilled artisans survived, the trend toward mechanization was unstoppable, and even the most skilled workers were eventually removed from making decisions about the production process.

More than machines changed the nature of industrial work. The principles of scientific management, which set out new rules for organizing work, were just as important. The key figure was Frederick Taylor, the son of a prominent Philadelphia family. Taylor had a nervous breakdown while at a private school. When his physicians prescribed manual labor as a cure, he went to work as a laborer at the Midvale Steel Company in Philadelphia. Working his way up rapidly while studying engineering at night, he became chief engineer at the factory in the 1880s. Later he used this experience to rethink the organization of industry.

Taylor was obsessed with efficiency. He emphasized centralized planning, systematic analysis, and detailed instructions. Most of all, he studied all kinds of workers and timed the various components of their jobs with a stopwatch. "The work of every workman is fully planned out by the management at least one day in advance," Taylor wrote in 1898, "and each man receives in most cases complete written instructions, describing in detail the task which he is to accomplish, as well as the means to be used in doing the work."

Many owners enthusiastically adopted Taylor's concepts of scientific management, seeing an opportunity to increase their profits and to take firmer control of the workplace. As Taylor himself explained, scientific management meant the "deliberate gathering in on … management's side of all of the great mass of traditional knowledge, which in the past has been in the heads of the workmen, and in the physical skill and knack of the workman which he has acquired through years of experience." Not surprisingly, many workers resented the drive for efficiency and control. "We don't want to work as fast as we are able to," one machinist remarked. "We want to work as fast as we think it comfortable for us to work."

Union Organizing

The progressive reformers had little understanding of the revolution going on in the factory. Samuel Gompers, head of the American Federation of Labor, however, was quick to recognize that Taylorism would reduce workers to "mere machines." Under his guidance, the AFL prospered during the progressive era. Between 1897 and 1904, union membership grew from 447,000 to over 2 million, with 3 out of every 4 union members claimed by the AFL. By 1914, the AFL alone had over 2 million members. Gompers's "pure and simple unionism" was most successful among coal miners, railroad workers, and the building trades. As we saw in Chapter 18, Gompers ignored the growing army of unskilled and immigrant workers and concentrated on raising the wages and improving the working conditions of the skilled craftsmen who were members of unions affiliated with the AFL.

For a time, Gompers's strategy seemed to work. Several industries negotiated with the AFL as a way of avoiding disruptive strikes. But cooperation was short-lived. Labor unions were defeated in a number of disastrous strikes, and the National Association of Manufacturers (NAM) launched an aggressive counterattack. NAM and other employer associations provided strikebreakers, used industrial spies, and blacklisted union members to prevent them from obtaining other jobs.

The Supreme Court came down squarely on management's side, ruling in the Danbury Hatters case in 1908 that trade unions were subject to the Sherman Anti-Trust Act. Thus, union members themselves could be held personally liable for money lost by a business during a strike. Courts at all levels sided overwhelmingly with employers. They often declared strikes illegal and were quick to issue restraining orders, making it impossible for workers to interfere with the operation of a business.

Although many social justice progressives sympathized with the working class, they spent more time promoting protective legislation than strengthening organized labor. Often cast in the role of mediators during industrial disputes, they found it difficult to comprehend what life was really like for people who had to work six days a week.

Working women and their problems aroused more sympathy among progressive reformers than the plight of working men. The number of women working outside the home increased steadily during the progressive era, from over 5 million in 1900 to nearly 8.5 million in 1920. But few belonged to unions—only a little over 3 percent in 1900—and the percentage declined by half by 1910 before increasing a little after that date with aggressive organizing in the textile and clothing trades.

Although the AFL had hired Mary Kenney as an organizer in the 1890s and accepted a few women's unions into affiliation, the policy of Gompers and the other labor leaders was generally to oppose organizing women workers (see Chapter 18). "The demand for female labor," one leader announced, "is an insidious assault upon the home. It is the knife of the assassin, aimed at the family circle."

Yet of necessity, women continued to work to support themselves and their families. Many upper-class women reformers tried to help these working women in a variety of ways. The settlement houses organized day-care centers, clubs, and classes, and many reformers tried to pass protective legislation. Tension and misunderstanding often cropped up between the reformers and the working women, but one organization in which there was genuine cooperation was the Women's Trade Union League. Founded in 1903, the league was organized by Mary Kenney and William English Walling, a socialist and reformer, but it also drew local leaders from the working class, such as Rose Schneiderman, a Jewish immigrant cap maker, and Leonora O'Reilly, a collar maker. The league established branches in most large eastern and midwestern cities and served for more than a decade as an important force in helping to organize women into unions. The league forced the AFL to pay more attention to women, helped out in time of strikes, put up bail money for the arrested, and publicized the plight of working women.

Garment Workers and the Triangle Fire

Thousands of young women, most of them Jewish and Italian, were employed in the garment industry in New York City. Most were between 16 and 25; some lived with their families, and others lived alone or with a roommate. They worked a 56-hour, 6-day week and made about $6 for their efforts. New York was the center of the garment industry, with over 600 shirtwaist (blouse) and dress factories employing more than 30,000 workers.

Like other industries, garment manufacturing had changed in the first decade of the twentieth century. Once conducted in thousands of dark and dingy tenement rooms, now all the operations were centralized in large loft buildings in lower Manhattan. These buildings were an improvement over the sweating labor of the tenements, but many were overcrowded, and they had few fire escapes or safety features. In addition, the owners applied scientific management techniques in order to increase their profits, making life miserable for the workers. Most of the women had to rent their sewing machines and even had to pay for the electricity they used. They were penalized for mistakes or for talking too loudly. They were usually supervised by a male contractor who badgered and sometimes even sexually harassed them.

In 1909, some of the women went out on strike to protest the working conditions. The International Ladies' Garment Workers Union (ILGWU) and the Women's Trade Union League supported them. But strikers were beaten and sometimes arrested by unsympathetic policemen and by strikebreakers on the picket lines. At a mass meeting held at Cooper Union in New York on November 22, 1909, Clara Lemlich, a young shirtwaist worker who had been injured on the picket line and was angered by the long speeches and lack of action, rose and in an emotional speech in Yiddish demanded a general strike. The entire audience pledged its agreement. The next day, all over the city, the shirtwaist workers went out on strike.

"The uprising of the twenty thousand," as the strike was called, startled the nation. One young worker wrote in her diary, "It is a good thing, that strike is. It makes you feel like a grown-up person." The Jews learned a little Italian and the Italians a little Yiddish so that they could communicate. Many social reformers, ministers, priests, and rabbis urged the strikers on. Mary Dreier, an upper-class reformer and president of the New York branch of the Women's Trade Union League, was arrested for marching with the strikers. A young state legislator, Fiorello La Guardia, later to become a congressman and mayor of New York, was one of the many public officials to aid the strikers.

The shirtwaist workers won, and in part, the success of the strike made the garment union one of the most powerful in the AFL. But the victory was limited. Over 300 companies accepted the union's terms, but others refused to go along. The young women went back to work amid still oppressive and unsafe conditions. That became dramatically obvious on Saturday, March 25, 1911, when a fire broke out on the eighth floor of the ten-story loft building housing the Triangle Shirtwaist Company near Washington Square in New York. There had been several small fires in the factory in previous weeks,

The Triangle fire shocked the nation, and dramatic photographs, such as this candid shot showing bodies and bystanders waiting for more young women to jump, helped stimulate the investigation that followed. (Brown Brothers)

so no one thought much about another one. But this one was different. Within minutes, the top three floors of the factory were ablaze. Many exit doors were locked. The elevators broke down. There were no fire escapes. Forty-six women jumped to their deaths, some of them in groups of three and four holding hands. Over 100 died in the flames.

Shocked by the Triangle fire, the state legislature appointed a commission to investigate working conditions in the state. One investigator for the commission was a young social worker, Frances Perkins, who in the 1930s would become secretary of labor. She led the politicians through the dark lofts, filthy tenements, and unsafe factories around the state to show them the conditions under which young women worked. The result was state legislation limiting the work of women to 54 hours a week, prohibiting labor by children under 14, and improving safety regulations in factories. One supporter of the bills in Albany was a young state senator named Franklin Delano Roosevelt.

The investigative commission was a favorite progressive tactic. When there was a problem, reformers often got a city council, a state legislature, or the federal government to appoint a commission. If they could not find a government body to give them a mandate, they made their own studies. They brought in experts, compiled statistics, and published reports.

The federal Industrial Relations Commission, created in 1912 to study the causes of industrial unrest and violence, conducted one of the most important investigations. As it turned out, the commission spent most of its time exploring a dramatic and tragic incident of labor-management conflict in Colorado, known as the Ludlow Massacre. A strike broke out in the fall of 1913 in the vast mineral-rich area of southern Colorado, much of it controlled by the Colorado Fuel and Iron Industry, a company largely owned by the Rockefeller family. It was a paternalistic empire where workers lived in company towns and sometimes in tent colonies. They were paid in company scrip and forced to shop at the company store. When the workers, supported by the United Mine Workers, went on strike demanding an eight-hour day, better safety precautions, and the removal of armed guards, the company refused to negotiate. The strike turned violent, and in the spring of 1914, strikebreakers and

national guardsmen fired on the workers. Eleven children and two women were killed in an attack on a tent city near Ludlow, Colorado.

The Industrial Relations Commission called John D. Rockefeller, Jr., to testify and implied that he was personally guilty of the murders. The commission decided in its report that violent class conflict could be avoided only by limiting the use of armed guards and detectives, by restricting monopoly, by protecting the right of the workers to organize, and, most dramatically, by redistributing wealth through taxation. The commission's report, not surprisingly, fell on deaf ears. Most progressives, like most Americans, denied the commission's conclusion that class conflict was inevitable.

Radical Labor

Not everyone accepted the progressives' faith in investigations and protective labor legislation. Nor did everyone approve of Samuel Gompers's conservative tactics or his emphasis on getting better pay for skilled workers. A group of about 200 radicals met in Chicago in 1905 to form a new union as an alternative to the AFL. They called it the Industrial Workers of the World (IWW) and talked of one big union. Like the Knights of Labor in the 1880s, the IWW would welcome all workers: the unskilled, and even the unemployed, women, African Americans, Asians, and all other ethnic groups.

Daniel De Leon of the Socialist Labor party attended the organizational meeting, and so did Eugene Debs. Debs, who had been converted to socialism after the Pullman strike of 1894, had already emerged by 1905 as one of the outstanding radical leaders in the country. Also attending was Mary Harris Jones, who dressed like a society matron but attacked labor leaders "who sit on velvet chairs in conferences with labor's oppressors." In her sixties at the time, everyone called her "Mother" Jones. She had been a dressmaker, a Populist, and a member of the Knights of Labor. During the 1890s, she had marched with miners' wives on the picket line in western Pennsylvania. She was imprisoned and denounced, but by 1905, she was already a legend.

Presiding at the Chicago meeting was "Big Bill" Haywood. He had been a cowboy, a miner, and a prospector. Somewhere along the way, he had lost an eye and mangled a hand, but he had a booming voice and a passionate commitment to the workers. "This is the Continental Congress of the working class," he announced, adopting the rhetoric of the American Revolution. "We are here to confederate the workers of this country into a working-class movement that shall have for its purpose the emancipation of the working class from the slave bondage of capitalism." Denouncing Gompers and the AFL, he talked of class conflict. "The purpose of the IWW," he proclaimed, "is to bring the workers of this country into the possession of the full value of the product of their toil."

The IWW remained a small organization, troubled by internal squabbles and disagreements. Debs and De Leon left after a few years. Haywood dominated the movement, which played an important role in organizing the militant strike of textile workers in Lawrence, Massachusetts, in 1912 and the following year in Paterson, New Jersey, and Akron, Ohio. The IWW had its greatest success organizing itinerant lumbermen and migratory workers in the Northwest. But in other places, especially in times of high unemployment, the Wobblies, as they were called, helped the unskilled workers vent their anger against their employers.

Many American workers still did not feel, as European workers did, that they were engaged in a perpetual class struggle with their capitalist employers. Some immigrant workers, intent on earning enough money to go back home, had no time to join the conflict. Most of those who stayed in the United States were consoled by the promises of the American dream. Thinking they might secure a better job or move up into the middle class, they avoided organized labor militancy. They knew that even if they failed, their sons and daughters would profit from the American way. The AFL, not the IWW, became the dominant American labor movement. But for a few, the IWW represented a dream of what might have been. For others, its presence, though small and largely ineffective, meant that perhaps someday a European-style, working-class movement might develop in America.

Reform in the Cities and States

The reform movements of the progressive era usually started at the local level, then moved to the state, and finally to the nation's capital. Progressivism in the cities and states had roots in the depression and discontent of the 1890s. The reform banners called for more democracy, more power for the people, and legislation regulating railroads and other businesses. Yet often the professional and business classes were the movement's leaders. They intended to bring order out of chaos and to modernize the city and the state during a time of rapid growth.

Municipal Reformers

American cities grew rapidly in the last part of the nineteenth and the first part of the twentieth centuries. New York, which had a population of 1.2 million in 1880, grew to 3.4 million by 1900 and 5.6 million in 1920. Chicago expanded even more dramatically, from 500,000 in 1880 to 1.7 million in 1900 and 2.7 million in 1920. Los Angeles was a town of 11,000 in 1880, but multiplied ten times by 1900, and then increased another five times, to more than a half million, by 1920.

The spectacular and continuing growth of the cities caused problems and created a need for housing, transportation, and municipal services. But it was the kind of people who were moving into the cities that worried many observers. Americans from the small towns and farms continued to throng to the urban centers, as they had throughout the nineteenth century, but immigration produced the greatest surge in population. Fully 40 percent of New York's population and 36 percent of Chicago's was foreign-born in 1910; if one included the children of the immigrants, the percentage approached 80 percent in some cities. The new immigrants from eastern and western Europe, according to Francis Walker, the president of MIT, were "beaten men from beaten races, representing the worst failures in the struggle for existence." They seemed to threaten the American way of life and the very tenets of democracy.

Fear of the city and its new inhabitants motivated progressive municipal reform efforts. Urban problems seemed to have reached a crisis stage. The twentieth-century reformers, mostly middle-class citizens like those in the nineteenth, wanted to regulate and control the sprawling metropolis, restore democracy, reduce corruption, and limit the power of the political bosses and their immigrant allies. When these reformers talked of restoring power to the people, they usually meant ensuring control for people like themselves. The chief aim of municipal reform was to make the city more organized and efficient for the business and professional classes who were to control its workings.

Municipal reform movements varied from city to city. In Boston, the reformers tried to strengthen the power of the mayor, break the hold of the city council, and eliminate council corruption. They succeeded in removing all party designations from city election ballots, and they extended the term of the mayor from two to four years. But to their chagrin, in the election of 1910, John Fitzgerald, grandfather of John F. Kennedy and foe of reform, defeated their candidate. In other cities, the reformers used different tactics, but they almost always conducted elaborate studies and campaigned to reduce corruption.

The most dramatic innovation was the replacement of both mayor and council with a nonpartisan commission of administrators. This innovation began quite accidentally when a hurricane devastated Galveston, Texas, in September 1900. In one of the worst natural disasters in the nation's history, over 6,000 people died. The existing government was helpless to deal with the crisis, so the state legislature appointed five commissioners to run the city during the emergency.

The idea spread to Houston, Dallas, and Austin and to cities in other states. It proved most popular in small to medium-size cities in the Midwest and the Pacific Northwest. By World War I, more than 400 cities had adopted the commission form. Dayton, Ohio, went one step further: After a disastrous flood in 1913, the city hired a city manager to run the city and to report to the elected council. Government by experts was the perfect symbol of what most municipal reformers had in mind.

The commission and the expert manager did not replace the mayor in most large cities. One of the most flamboyant and successful of the progressive mayors was Tom Johnson of Cleveland. Johnson had made a fortune by investing in utility and railroad franchises before he was 40. But Henry George's *Progress and Poverty* so influenced him that he began a second career as a reformer. After serving in Congress, he was elected mayor of Cleveland in 1901. During his two terms in city hall, he managed to reduce transit fares and to build parks and municipal bath houses through-

out the city. Johnson also broke the connection between the police and prostitution in the city by promising the madams and the brothel owners that he would not bother them if they would be orderly and not steal from their customers or pay off the police.

His most controversial move, however, was to advocate city ownership of the street railroads and utilities (sometimes called municipal socialism). "Only through municipal ownership," he argued, "can the gulf which divides the community into a small dominant class on one side and the unorganized people on the other be bridged." Johnson was defeated in 1909 in part because he alienated many powerful business interests, but one of his lieutenants, Newton D. Baker, was elected mayor in 1911 and carried on many of his programs. Cleveland was one of many cities that began to regulate municipal utilities or to take them over from the private owners.

The way much of municipal reform and the progressive social justice movement was closely tied to religion, especially to the Protestant Social Gospel movement, can be illustrated by The Men and Religion Forward Movement. Led by the YMCA, The Federal Council of Churches, and a coalition of Protestant agencies, The Men and Religion Forward Movement conducted a whirlwind campaign in 1911–1912, not only to reform the cities, but also to bring men back into the churches. Believing that religion, like much of American life, had become too effeminate, too dominated by women, the leaders of the movement tried to bring "3,000,000 missing men" back to Christianity. Teams of men consisting of Social Gospel ministers and lay experts fanned out across the country, stopping a week in each city. They held rallies and revival meetings; they met with clergy, labor leaders, and urban reformers. They tried to stimulate an interest in the churches and at the same time to wipe out child labor, slum housing, gambling dens, and houses of prostitution. They also tried to promote cleaner streets and better government. One of the leaders of the movement, Raymond Robins, had been a settlement worker and a co-worker with Jane Addams in many reform crusades in Chicago. When the Men and Religion Forward campaign was finished, he moved directly to work for Theodore Roosevelt and the Progressive Party. The movement failed to bring a great many men back to religion, and it did not appreciably improve the cities, but it does suggest how religion and politics became intertwined during the progressive era.

City Beautiful

In Cleveland, both Tom Johnson and Newton Baker promoted the arts, music, and adult education. They also supervised the construction of a civic center, a library, and a museum. Most other American cities during the progressive era set out to bring culture and beauty to their centers. They were influenced at least in part by the great, classical White City constructed for the Chicago World's Fair of 1893 and by the grand European boulevards such as the Champs-Élysées in Paris.

The architects of the "city beautiful movement" preferred the impressive and ceremonial architecture of Rome or the Renaissance for libraries, museums, railroad stations, and other public buildings. The huge Pennsylvania Station in New York was modeled after the imperial Roman baths of Caracalla, and the Free Library in Philadelphia was an almost exact copy of a building in Paris. The city beautiful leaders tried to make the city more attractive and meaningful for the middle and upper classes. The museums and the libraries were closed on Sundays, the only day the working class could possibly visit them.

The social justice progressives, especially those connected with the social settlements, were more concerned with neighborhood parks and playgrounds than with the ceremonial boulevards and grand buildings. Hull House established the first public playground in Chicago. Jacob Riis, the housing reformer, and Lillian Wald of the Henry Street Settlement campaigned in New York for

Cities grew so rapidly that they often ceased to work. This 1909 photograph shows Dearborn Street looking south from Randolph in Chicago. Horse-drawn vehicles, streetcars, pedestrians, and even a few early autos clogged the intersection and created the urban inefficiency that angered municipal reformers. (Chicago Historical Society)

small parks and for the opening of schoolyards on weekends. Some progressives looked back nostalgically to their rural childhoods and desperately tried to get urban children out of the city in the summertime to rural camps. But they also tried to make the city more livable as well as more beautiful.

Most progressives had an ambivalent attitude toward the city. They feared it, and they loved it. Some saw the great urban areas filled with immigrants as a threat to American democracy, but one of Tom Johnson's young assistants, Frederic C. Howe, wrote a book called *The City: The Hope of Democracy* (1905). Hope or threat, the progressives realized that the United States had become an urban nation and that the problems of the city had to be faced.

Reform in the States

The progressive movements in the states had many roots and took many forms. In some states, especially in the West, progressive attempts to regulate railroads and utilities were simply an extension of populism. In other states, the reform drive bubbled up from reform efforts in the cities. Most states passed laws during the progressive era designed to extend democracy and give more authority to the people. Initiative and referendum laws allowed citizens to originate legislation and to overturn laws passed by the legislature, and recall laws gave the people a way to remove elected officials. Most of these "democratic" laws worked better in theory than in practice, but their passage in many states did represent a genuine effort to remove special privilege from government.

Much progressive state legislation concerned order and efficiency, but many states passed social justice measures as well. Maryland enacted the first workers' compensation law in 1902, paying employees for days missed because of job-related injuries. Illinois approved a law aiding mothers with dependent children. Several states passed anti–child labor bills, and Oregon's ten-hour law restricting women's labor became a model for other states.

The states with the most successful reform movements elected strong and aggressive governors: Charles Evans Hughes in New York, Hoke Smith in Georgia, Hiram Johnson in California, Woodrow Wilson in New Jersey, and Robert La Follette in Wisconsin. After Wilson, La Follette was the most famous and in many ways the model progressive governor. Born in a small town in Wisconsin, he graduated from the University of Wisconsin in 1879 and was admitted to the bar. Practicing law during the 1890s in Madison, the state capital, he received a large retainer from the Milwaukee Railroad and defended the railroad against both riders and laborers who sued the company.

The depression of 1893 hit Wisconsin hard. More than a third of the state's citizens were out of work, farmers lost their farms, and many small businesses went bankrupt. At the same time, the rich seemed to be getting richer. "Men are rightly feeling that a social order like the present, with its enormous wealth side by side with appalling poverty, ... cannot be the final form of human society," a Milwaukee minister announced. As grass-roots discontent spread, a group of Milwaukee reformers attacked the giant corporations and the street railways. Several newspapers joined the battle and denounced special privilege and corruption. Everyone could agree on the need for tax reform, railroad regulation, and more participation of the people in government.

La Follette, who had had little interest in reform, took advantage of the general mood of discontent to win the governorship in 1901. It seemed ironic that La Follette, who had once taken a retainer from a railroad, owed his victory to his attack on the railroads. But La Follette was a shrewd politician. He used professors from the University of Wisconsin, in the capital, to prepare reports and do statistical studies. Then he worked with the legislature to pass a state primary law and an act regulating the railroads. "Go back to the first principles of democracy; go back to the people" was his battle cry. The "Wisconsin idea" attracted the attention of journalists like Lincoln Steffens and Ray Stannard Baker, and they helped to popularize the "laboratory of democracy" around the country. La Follette became a national figure and was elected to the Senate in 1906.

The progressive movement did improve government and make it more responsible to the people in states like Wisconsin. For example, the railroads were brought under the control of a railroad commission. But by 1910, the railroads no longer complained about the new taxes and restrictions. They had discovered that it was to their advantage to make their operations more efficient, and often they were able to convince the commission that they should raise rates or abandon the operation of unprofitable lines. Progressivism in the states, like progressivism everywhere, had mixed results. But the spirit of reform that swept the country was real, and progressive movements on the local level did eventually have an impact on Washington, especially during the administrations of Theodore Roosevelt and Woodrow Wilson.

Theodore Roosevelt and the Square Deal

President William McKinley was shot in Buffalo, New York, on September 6, 1901, by Leon Czolgosz, an anarchist. McKinley died eight days later, making Theodore Roosevelt, at 42, the youngest man ever to become president. The nation mourned its fallen leader, and in many cities, anarchists and other radicals were rounded up for questioning.

No one knew what to expect from Roosevelt. Some politicians thought he was too radical, but a few social justice progressives remembered his suggestion that the soldiers fire on the strikers during the 1894 Pullman strike. Nonetheless, under his leadership, progressivism reshaped the national political agenda. Although early progressive reformers had attacked problems that they saw in their own communities, they gradually understood that some problems could not be solved at the state or local level. The emergence of a national industrial economy had spawned conditions that demanded national solutions.

Progressives at the national level turned their attention to the workings of the economic system. They scrutinized the operation and organization of the railroads and other large corporations. They examined the threats to the natural environment. They reviewed the quality of the products of American industry. As they fashioned legislation to remedy the flaws in the economic system, they vastly expanded the power of the national government.

A Strong and Controversial President

Roosevelt came to the presidency with considerable experience. He had run unsuccessfully for mayor of New York, served a term in the New York state assembly, spent four years as a United States civil service commissioner, and served two years as the police commissioner of New York City. His exploits in the Spanish-American War brought him to the public's attention, but he had also been an effective assistant secretary of the navy and a reform governor of New York. While police commissioner and governor, he had been influenced by a number of progressives. Jacob Riis, the housing reformer, became one of his friends and led him on nighttime explorations of the slums of New York City. Roosevelt had also impressed a group of New York settlement workers with his genuine concern for human misery, his ability to talk to all kinds of people, and his willingness to learn about social problems.

But no one was sure how he would act as president. He came from an upper-class family and had associated with the important and the powerful all over the world. He had written a number of books and was one of the most intellectual presidents since Thomas Jefferson. But none of these things assured that he would be a progressive in office.

Roosevelt loved being president. He called the office a "bully pulpit," and he enjoyed talking to the people and the press. His appealing personality and sense of humor made him a good subject for the new mass-market newspapers and magazines. The American people quickly adopted him as their favorite. They called him "Teddy" and named a stuffed bear after him. Sometimes his exuberance got a little out of hand. On one occasion, he took a foreign diplomat on a nude swim in the Potomac River. You have to understand, another observer remarked, that "the president is really only six years old."

Roosevelt was much more than an exuberant 6-year-old. He was the strongest president since Lincoln. By revitalizing the executive branch, reorganizing the army command structure, and mod-

Theodore Roosevelt was a dynamic public speaker who used his position to influence public opinion. Despite his high-pitched voice, he could be heard at the back of the crowd in the days before microphones. Note the row of reporters decked out in their summer straw hats writing their stories as the President speaks. (Brown Brothers)

ernizing the consular service, he made many aspects of the federal government more efficient. He established the Bureau of Corporations, appointed independent commissions staffed with experts, and enlisted talented and well-trained men to work for the government. "TR," as he became known, called a White House conference on the care of dependent children, and in 1905, he even summoned college presidents and football coaches to the White House to discuss ways to limit violence in football. He angered many social justice progressives by not going far enough. In fact, on one occasion, Florence Kelley was so furious with him that she walked out of the Oval Office and slammed the door. But he was the first president to listen to the pleas of the progressives and to invite them to the White House. Learning from experts like Frances Kellor, he became more concerned with social justice as time went on.

Dealing with the Trusts

One of Roosevelt's first actions as president was to attempt to control the large industrial corporations. He took office in the middle of an unprecedented wave of business consolidation. Between 1897 and 1904, some 4,227 companies combined to form 257 large corporations. U.S. Steel, the first billion-dollar corporation, was formed in 1901 by joining Carnegie Steel with its eight main competitors. In one stroke, the new company controlled two-thirds of the market, and J. P. Morgan made $7 million for supervising the operation.

The Sherman Anti-Trust Act of 1890 had been virtually useless in controlling the trusts, but a new outcry from muckrakers and progressives called for regulation. Some even demanded the return to the age of small business. Roosevelt opposed neither bigness nor the right of businessmen to make money. "Our aim is not to do away with corporations," he remarked in 1902; "on the contrary, these big aggregations are the inevitable development of modern industrialism." But he thought some businessmen arrogant, greedy, and irresponsible. "We draw the line against misconduct, not against wealth," he said.

To the shock of much of the business community, he directed his attorney general to file suit to dissolve the Northern Securities Company, a giant railroad monopoly put together by James J. Hill and financier J. P. Morgan. Morgan came to the White House to tell Roosevelt, "If we have done anything wrong, send your man to my man and they can fix it up." Roosevelt was furious, and he

Business Mergers, 1895–1905

Business mergers did decline during the Roosevelt years, but they did not cease entirely and they even rose again during his second term. Source: U.S. Bureau of the Census.

was determined to let Morgan and other businessmen know that they could not deal with the president of the United States as just another tycoon.

The government won its case and proceeded to prosecute some of the largest corporations, including Standard Oil of New Jersey and the American Tobacco Company. However, Roosevelt's antitrust policy did not end the power of the giant corporations or even alter their methods of doing business. More disturbing to consumers, it did not force down the price of kerosene, cigars, or railroad tickets. But it did breathe some life into the Sherman Anti-Trust Act, and it increased the role of the federal government as regulator. It also caused large firms such as U.S. Steel to diversify in order to avoid antitrust suits.

Roosevelt sought to strengthen the regulatory powers of the federal government in other ways. He steered the Elkins Act through Congress in 1903 and the Hepburn Act in 1906, which together increased the power of the Interstate Commerce Commission (ICC). The first act eliminated the use of rebates by railroads, a method that many large corporations had used to get favored treatment. The second act broadened the power of the ICC and gave it the right to investigate and enforce

rates. Opponents in Congress weakened both bills, however, and the legislation neither ended abuses nor satisfied the farmers and small businessmen who had always been the railroads' chief critics.

Roosevelt firmly believed in corporate capitalism. He detested socialism and felt much more comfortable around business executives than labor leaders. Yet he saw his role as mediator and regulator. His view of the power of the presidency was illustrated in 1902 during the anthracite coal strike. Led by John Mitchell of the United Mine Workers, the coal miners went on strike to protest low wages, long hours, and unsafe working conditions. In 1901, a total of 513 coal miners had died in industrial accidents. The mine owners refused to talk to the miners. They hired strikebreakers and used private security forces to threaten and intimidate the workers. George F. Baer of the Reading Railroad articulated the most extreme form of the employers' position. He argued that workingmen had no right to strike or to say anything about working conditions.

> The rights and interests of the laboring man will be protected and cared for, not by the labor agitators, but by the Christian man to whom God in His infinite wisdom has given the control of the property interests of the country, and upon the successful management of which so much depends.

Although Roosevelt had no particular sympathy for labor, he would certainly not have gone as far as Baer. In the fall of 1902, however, schools began closing for lack of coal, and it looked like many citizens would suffer through the winter. Coal, which usually sold for $5 a ton, rose to $14. Roosevelt called the owners and representatives of the union to the White House even though the businessmen protested that they would not deal with "outlaws." Finally, the president appointed a commission that included representatives of the union as well as the community. Within weeks, the miners went back to work with a 10 percent raise.

Meat Inspection and Pure Food and Drugs

Roosevelt's first major legislative reform began almost accidentally in 1904 when Upton Sinclair, a 26-year-old muckraking journalist, started research on the Chicago stockyards. Born in Baltimore, Sinclair had grown up in New York, where he wrote dime novels to pay his tuition at City College. He was converted to socialism by his reading and by his association with a group of idealistic young writers in New York. Though he knew little about Chicago, he was driven by a desire to expose the exploitation of the poor and oppressed in America. He boarded at the University of Chicago Settlement while he did research, conducted interviews, and wrote the story that would be published in 1906 as *The Jungle.*

Sinclair's novel told of the Rudkus family, who emigrated from Lithuania to Chicago filled with ambition and hope. But the American dream failed for them. Sinclair documented exploitation in his fictional account, but his description of contaminated meat drew more attention. He described spoiled hams treated with formaldehyde and sausages made from rotten meat scraps, rats, and other refuse. Hoping to convert his readers to socialism, Sinclair instead turned their stomachs and caused a public outcry for better regulation of the meat-packing industry.

Selling 25,000 copies in its first six weeks, *The Jungle* disturbed many people, including Roosevelt, who, it was reported, could no longer enjoy his breakfast sausage. Roosevelt ordered a study of the meatpacking industry and then used the report to pressure Congress and the meatpackers to accept a bill introduced by Albert Beveridge, the progressive senator from Indiana.

In the end, the Meat Inspection Act of 1906 was a compromise. It enforced some federal inspection and mandated sanitary conditions in all companies selling meat in interstate commerce. The meatpackers defeated a provision that would have required the dating of all meat. Some of the large companies supported the compromise bill because it gave them an advantage in their battle with the smaller firms. But the bill was a beginning. It illustrates how muckrakers, social justice progressives, and public outcry eventually led to reform legislation. It also shows how Roosevelt used the public mood and manipulated the political process to get a bill through Congress. Many of the progressive reformers were disappointed with the final result, but Roosevelt was always willing to settle for half a loaf rather than none at all. Ironically, the Meat Inspection Act

Collier's, *one of the popular muckraking magazines, tried to alert the public to the dangerous drugs in patent medicines in this 1912 cover story. Magazines such as* Collier's, *with circulations approaching 1 million, had an immense influence during the progressive era. (The Granger Collection, New York)*

restored the public's confidence in the meat industry and helped the industry increase its profits.

Taking advantage of the publicity that circulated around *The Jungle,* a group of reformers, writers, and government officials supported legislation to regulate the sale of food and drugs. Americans consumed an enormous quantity of patent medicines, which they purchased through the mail, from traveling salesmen, and from local stores. One article pointed out in 1905:

Gullible Americans will spend this year some seventy-five million dollars in the purchase of patent medicines. In consideration of this sum it will swallow huge quantities of alcohol, an appalling amount of opiates and narcotics, a wide assortment of varied drugs ranging from powerful and dangerous heart depressants to insidious liver stimulants; and, far in excess of all other ingredients, undiluted fraud. For fraud exploited by the skillfulest of advertising bunco men is the basis of the trade.

Many packaged and canned foods contained dangerous chemicals and impurities. One popular remedy, Hosteter's Stomach Bitters, was revealed on analysis to contain 44 percent alcohol. Coca-Cola, a popular soft drink, contained a small amount of cocaine, and many medicines were laced with opium. Many people, including women and children, became alcoholics or drug addicts in their quest to feel better. The Pure Food and Drug Act, which passed Congress on the same day in 1906 as the Meat Inspection Act, was not a perfect bill, but it corrected some of the worst abuses, including eliminating the cocaine from Coca-Cola.

Conservation Versus Preservation

Although Roosevelt was pleased with the new legislation for regulating the food and drug industries, he always considered his conservation program his most important domestic achievement. An outdoorsman, hunter, and amateur naturalist since his youth, he announced soon after he became president that the planned protection of the nation's forests and water resources would be one of his most vital concerns. Using his executive authority, he more than tripled the land set aside for national forests, bringing the total to more than 150 million acres.

Because he had traveled widely in the West, Roosevelt understood, as few easterners did, the problems created by limited water in the western states. In 1902, with his enthusiastic support, Congress passed the Newlands Act, named after Francis Newlands, its most ardent advocate from the arid state of Nevada. The National Reclamation Act (as it was officially called) set aside the proceeds from the sale of public land in sixteen western states to pay for the construction of irrigation projects in those states. Although it tended to help big farmers more than small producers, the Newlands Act federalized irrigation for the first time.

More important than conservation bills passed during Roosevelt's presidency, however, were his efforts to raise the public consciousness about the need to save the nation's natural resources. He convened a White House Conserva-

tion Conference in 1908 that included among its delegates most of the governors and representatives of 70 national organizations. A direct result of the conference was Roosevelt's appointment of a National Conservation Commission charged with making an inventory of the natural resources in the entire country. To chair the commission Roosevelt appointed Gifford Pinchot, probably the most important conservation advocate in the country.

A graduate of Yale, Pinchot had studied scientific forestry management in Germany and France before becoming the forest manager of the Vanderbilt's Biltmore estate in North Carolina. In 1898, he was appointed chief of the United States Division of Forestry, and in 1900, he became the head of the Bureau of Forestry in the Department of Agriculture. An advocate of selective logging, fire control, and limited grazing on public lands, he became a friend and adviser to Roosevelt.

Pinchot's conservation policies pleased many in the timber and cattle industries; at the same time, they angered those who simply wanted to exploit the land. But his policies were denounced by the followers of John Muir, who believed passionately in preserving the land in a wilderness state. Muir had founded the Sierra Club in 1862 and had led a successful campaign to create Yosemite National Park in California. With his shaggy gray beard, his rough blue work clothes, and his black slouch hat, Muir seemed like an eccentric to many, but thousands agreed with him when he argued that to preserve the American wilderness was a spiritual and psychological necessity for overcivilized and overstimulated urban dwellers. Muir was one of the leaders in a "back-to-nature" movement at the turn of the century. Many middle-class Americans took up hiking, camping, and other outdoor activities, and children joined the Boy Scouts (founded in 1910) and the Camp Fire Girls (1912).

The conflicting conservation philosophies of Pinchot and Muir were most dramatically demonstrated by the controversy over Hetch-Hetchy, a remote valley deep within Yosemite National Park. It was a pristine wilderness area, and Muir and his followers wanted to keep it that way. But in 1901, the mayor of San Francisco decided the valley would make a perfect place for a dam and reservoir to supply his growing city with water for decades to come. Muir argued that wilderness soon would be scarcer than water and more important for the moral strength of the nation. Pinchot, on the other hand, maintained that it was foolish to pander to the aesthetic enjoyment of a tiny group of people when the comfort and welfare of the great majority was at stake.

The Hetch-Hetchy affair was fought out in the newspapers and magazines as well as in the halls of Congress, but in the end, the conservationists won out over the preservationists. Roosevelt and Congress sided with Pinchot and eventually the dam was built, turning the valley into a lake. But the debate over how to use the nation's land and water would continue throughout the twentieth century.

Progressivism for Whites Only

Like most of his generation, Roosevelt thought in stereotyped racial terms. He believed that blacks and Asians were inferior, and he feared that massive migrations from southern and eastern Europe threatened the Anglo-Saxon role. But Roosevelt was a politician, so he made gestures of goodwill to most groups. He even invited Booker T. Washington to the White House in 1901, though many southerners viciously attacked the president for his breach of etiquette. Roosevelt also appointed several qualified blacks to minor federal posts, notably Dr. William D. Crum to head the Charleston, South Carolina, customs house in 1905.

At other times, however, Roosevelt seemed insensitive to the needs and feelings of black Americans. This was especially true in his handling of the Brownsville, Texas, riot of 1906. Members of a black army unit stationed there, angered by discrimination against them, rioted one hot August night. Exactly what happened no one was sure, but one white man was killed and several wounded. Waiting until after the midterm elections of 1906, Roosevelt ordered all 167 members of three companies dishonorably discharged. It was an unjust punishment for an unproven crime, and 66 years later, the secretary of the army granted honorable discharges to the men, most of them by that time dead.

The progressive era coincided with the years of greatest segregation in the South, but even the most advanced progressives seldom included blacks in their reform schemes. Hull House, like most social settlements, was segregated, although

Jane Addams more than most progressives struggled to overcome the racist attitudes of her day. She helped found a settlement that served a black neighborhood in Chicago, and she spoke out repeatedly against lynching. Addams also supported the founding of the National Association for the Advancement of Colored People (NAACP) in 1909, the most important organization of the progressive era aimed at promoting equality and justice for blacks.

The founding of the NAACP is the story of cooperation between a group of white social justice progressives and a number of courageous black leaders. Even in the age of segregation and lynching, blacks in all parts of the country—through churches, clubs, and schools—sought to promote a better life for themselves. In Boston, William Monroe Trotter used his newspaper to oppose Washington's policy of accommodation. In Chicago, Ida Wells-Barnett, a large woman with flashing eyes, launched a one-woman crusade against lynching, organized a women's club for blacks, and founded the Negro Fellowship League to help black migrants.

The most important black leader who argued for equality and opportunity for his people was W. E. B. Du Bois. As discussed in Chapter 17, Du Bois differed dramatically with Booker T. Washington on the proper position of blacks in American life. Whereas Washington advocated vocational education, Du Bois argued for the best education possible for the most talented tenth of the black population. Whereas Washington preached compromise and accommodation to the dominant white society, Du Bois increasingly urged aggressive action to assure equality.

Denouncing Washington for accepting the "alleged inferiority of the Negro," Du Bois called a meeting of young and militant blacks in 1905. They met in Canada, not far from Niagara Falls, and issued an angry statement. "We want to pull down nothing but we don't propose to be pulled down," the platform announced. "We believe in taking what we can get but we don't believe in being satisfied with it and in permitting anybody for a moment to imagine we're satisfied." The Niagara movement, as it came to be called, was small, but it was soon augmented by a group of white liberals concerned with violence against blacks and race riots in Atlanta and even in Springfield, Illinois, the home of Abraham Lincoln. Jane Addams joined the

Tuskegee Institute followed Booker T. Washington's philosophy of black advancement through accommodation to the white status quo. Here students study white American history, but most of their time was spent on more practical subjects. This photo was taken in 1902 by Frances Benjamin Johnson, a pioneer woman photographer. (Library of Congress)

new organization, as did Oswald Garrison Villard, grandson of abolitionist William Lloyd Garrison.

In 1910, the Niagara movement combined with the NAACP, and Du Bois became editor of its journal, *The Crisis.* He toned down his rhetoric, but he tried to promote equality for all blacks. The NAACP was a typical progressive organization, seeking to work within the American system to promote reform. But to Roosevelt and many others who called themselves progressives, the NAACP seemed dangerously radical.

William Howard Taft

After two terms as president, Roosevelt decided to step down. "I believe in a strong executive," he

remarked in 1908. "I believe in power, but I believe that responsibility should go with power, and that it is not well that the strong executive should be a perpetual executive." But he soon regretted his decision. He was only 50 years old and at the peak of his popularity and power. Because the United States' system of government provides little creative function for former presidents, Roosevelt decided to travel and to go big-game hunting in Africa. But before he left, he hand-picked his successor.

William Howard Taft, Roosevelt's personal choice for the Republican nomination in 1908, was a distinguished lawyer, federal judge, and public servant. Born in Cincinnati, he had been the first civil governor of the Philippines and Roosevelt's secretary of war. After defeating William Jennings Bryan for the presidency in 1908, he quickly ran into difficulties. In some ways, he seemed more progressive than Roosevelt. His administration instituted more suits against monopolies in one term than Roosevelt had in two. He supported the eight-hour workday and legislation to make mining safer and urged the passage of the Mann-Elkins Act in 1910, which strengthened the ICC by giving it more power to set railroad rates and extending its jurisdiction over telephone and telegraph companies. Taft and Congress also authorized the first tax on corporate profits. He also encouraged the process that eventually led to the passage of the federal income tax, which was authorized under the Sixteenth Amendment, ratified in 1913. That probably did more to transform the relationship of the government to the people than all other progressive measures combined.

Taft's biggest problem was his style. He was a huge man, weighing over 300 pounds. Rumors circulated that he had to have a special oversize bathtub installed in the White House. Easily made fun of, the president wrote ponderous prose and spoke uninspiringly. He also lacked Roosevelt's political skills and angered many of the progressives in the Republican party, especially the midwestern insurgents led by Senator Robert La Follette of Wisconsin. Many progressives were annoyed when he signed the Payne-Aldrich Tariff, which midwesterners thought left rates on cotton and wool cloth and other items too high and played into the hands of the eastern industrial interests.

Even Roosevelt was infuriated when his successor reversed many of his conservation policies and fired Chief Forester Gifford Pinchot, who had attacked Secretary of the Interior Richard A. Ballinger for giving away rich coal lands in Alaska to mining interests. Roosevelt broke with Taft, letting it be known that he was willing to run again for president. This set up one of the most exciting and significant elections in American history.

The Election of 1912

Woodrow Wilson won the Democratic nomination for president in 1912. Born two years before Roosevelt, Wilson came from a very different back-

ground and would be cast in opposition to the former president during most of his political career. Wilson was the son and grandson of Presbyterian ministers. Growing up in a comfortable and intellectual southern household, he very early seemed more interested in politics than in religion. After graduating from Princeton University in 1879, he studied law at the University of Virginia and practiced law briefly before entering graduate school at the Johns Hopkins University in Baltimore. Soon after receiving his Ph.D. he published a book, *Congressional Government* (1885), that established his reputation as a shrewd analyst of American politics. He taught history briefly at Bryn Mawr College near Philadelphia and at Wesleyan in Connecticut before moving to Princeton. Less flamboyant than Roosevelt, he was an excellent public speaker with the power to convince people with his words.

In 1902, Wilson was elected president of Princeton University, and during the next few years, he established a national reputation as an educational leader. Wilson had never lost interest in politics, however, so when offered a chance by the Democratic machine to run for governor of New Jersey, he took it eagerly. In his two years as governor, he showed courage as he quickly alienated some of the conservatives who had helped elect him. Building a coalition of reformers, he worked with them to pass a direct primary law and a workers' compensation law. He also created a commission to regulate transportation and public utility companies. By 1912, Wilson not only was an expert on government and politics, but had also acquired the reputation of a progressive.

Roosevelt, who had been speaking out on a variety of issues since 1910, competed with Taft for the Republican nomination, but Taft, as the incumbent president and party leader, was able to win it. Roosevelt then startled the nation by walking out of the convention and forming a new political party, the Progressive party. The new party would not have been formed without Roosevelt, but the party was always more than Roosevelt. It appealed to progressives from all over the country who had become frustrated with the conservative leadership in both major parties.

Many social workers and social justice progressives supported the Progressive party

Major Parties in the Presidential Election of 1912

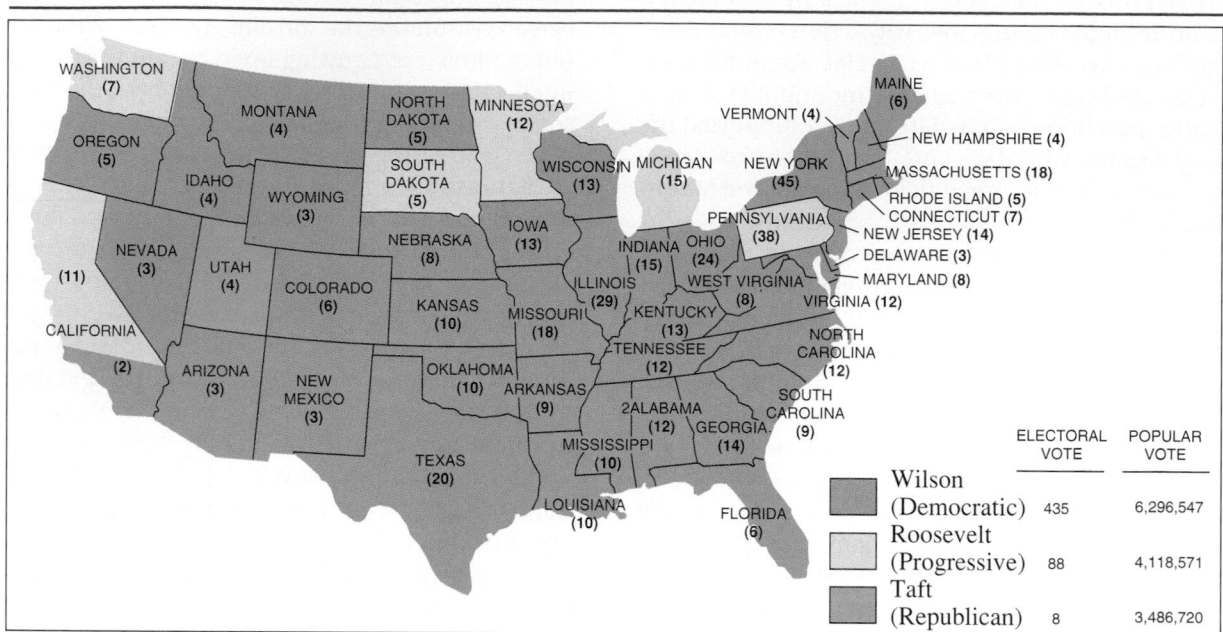

	ELECTORAL VOTE	POPULAR VOTE
Wilson (Democratic)	435	6,296,547
Roosevelt (Progressive)	88	4,118,571
Taft (Republican)	8	3,486,720

Even though Roosevelt ran one of the most successful third-party campaigns in American history, the American electoral system made it almost impossible for him to win. But Taft's overwhelming defeat was humiliating for an incumbent president. Notice how much of the electoral vote was concentrated in states east of the Mississippi.

because of its platform, which contained provisions they had been advocating for years. The Progressives supported an eight-hour day, a six-day week, the abolition of child labor under age 16, and a federal system of accident, old age, and unemployment insurance. Unlike the Democrats, the Progressives also endorsed woman suffrage. "Just think of having all the world listen to our story of social and industrial injustice and have them told that it can be righted," one social worker exclaimed.

Most supporters of the Progressives in 1912 did not realistically think they could win, but they were convinced that they could organize a new political movement that would replace the Republican party, just as the Republicans had replaced the Whigs after 1856. To this end, Progressive leaders, led by Kellor, set up the Progressive Service, designed to apply the principles of social research to educating voters between elections.

The Progressive convention in Chicago seemed to many observers more like a religious revival meeting or a social work conference than a political gathering. The delegates sang "Onward Christian Soldiers," "The Battle Hymn of the Republic," and "Roosevelt, Oh Roosevelt" (to the tune of "Maryland, My Maryland"). They waved their bandannas, and when Jane Addams rose to second Roosevelt's nomination, a large group of women marched around the auditorium with a banner that read "Votes for Women." The Progressive cause "is based on the eternal principles of righteousness," Roosevelt announced. "In the end the cause itself shall triumph."

The enthusiasm for Roosevelt and the Progressive party was misleading, for behind the unified facade lurked many disagreements. Roosevelt had become more progressive on many issues since leaving the presidency. He even attacked the financiers "to whom the acquisition of untold millions is the supreme goal of life, and who are too often utterly indifferent as to how these millions are obtained." But he was not as committed to social reform as some of the delegates. Perhaps the most divisive issue was the controversy over seating black delegates from several southern states. A number of social justice progressives fought hard to include a plank in the platform supporting equality for blacks and for seating the black delegation. Roosevelt, however, thought he had a realistic chance to carry several southern states, and he was not convinced that black equality was an important progressive issue. In the end, no blacks sat with the southern delegates, and the platform made no mention of black equality.

The political campaign in 1912 became a contest primarily between Roosevelt and Wilson, with Taft, the Republican candidate and incumbent, ignored by most reporters who covered the campaign. On one level, the campaign became a debate over political philosophy, the proper relationship of government to society in a modern industrial age. Roosevelt borrowed some of his ideas from a book, *The Promise of American Life* (1909), written by Herbert Croly, a young journalist. But he had also been working out his own philosophy of government. He spoke of the "new nationalism." In a modern industrial society, he argued, large corporations were "inevitable and necessary." What was needed was not the breakup of the trusts, but a strong president and increased power in the hands of the federal government to regulate business and industry and to ensure the rights of labor, women and children, and other groups. The government should be the "steward of the public welfare." He argued for using Hamiltonian means to assure Jeffersonian ends, for using strong central government to guarantee the rights of the people.

Wilson responded with a slogan and a program of his own. Using the writings of Louis Brandeis, he talked of the "new freedom." He emphasized the need for the Jeffersonian tradition of limited government with open competition. He spoke of the "curse of bigness" and argued against too much federal power. "If America is not to have free enterprise, then she can have freedom of no sort whatever." "What I fear is a government of experts," Wilson declared, implying that Roosevelt's New Nationalism would lead to regulated monopoly and even collectivism.

The level of debate during the campaign was impressive, making this one of the few elections in American history when important ideas were actually discussed. It also marked a watershed for

political thought for liberals who rejected Jefferson's distrust of a strong central government. It is easy to exaggerate the differences between Roosevelt and Wilson. There was some truth in the charge of William Allen White, the editor of the Emporia *Gazette* in Kansas, when he remarked, "Between the New Nationalism and the New Freedom was that fantastic imaginary gulf that always had existed between Tweedle-dum and Tweedle-dee." Certainly, in the end, the things that Roosevelt and Wilson could agree on were more important than the issues that divided them. Both Roosevelt and Wilson urged reform within the American system. Both defended corporate capitalism, and both opposed socialism and radical labor organizations such as the IWW. Both wanted to promote more democracy and to strengthen conservative labor unions. Both were very different in style and substance from the fourth candidate, Eugene Debs, who ran on the Socialist party ticket in 1912.

Debs, in 1912, was the most important socialist leader in the country. Socialism has always been a minority movement in the United States; it had its greatest success in the first decade of the twentieth century. Thirty-three cities including Milwaukee, Wisconsin; Reading, Pennsylvania; Butte, Montana; Jackson, Michigan; and Berkeley, California, chose socialist mayors. Socialists Victor Berger from Wisconsin and Meyer London from New York were elected to Congress. The most important socialist periodical, *Appeal to Reason*, published in Girard, Kansas, increased its circulation from about 30,000 in 1900 to nearly 300,000 in 1906. Socialism appealed to a diverse group. In the cities, some who called themselves socialists merely favored municipal ownership of street railways. Some reformers, such as Florence Kelley and William English Walling, joined the party because of their frustration with the slow progress of reform. The party also attracted many recent immigrants, who brought with them a European sense of class and loyalty to socialism.

A tremendously appealing figure and a great orator, Debs had run for president in 1900, 1904, and 1908, but in 1912, he reached much wider audiences in more parts of the country. His message differed radically from that of Wilson or Roosevelt. Unlike the progressives, socialists argued for fundamental change in the American system. The Socialist party is "organized and financed by the workers themselves," Debs announced, "as a means of wresting control of government and industry from the capitalists and making the working class the ruling class of the nation and the world." Debs polled almost 900,000 votes in 1912 (6 percent of the popular vote), the best showing ever for a socialist in the United States. Wilson received 6.3 million votes, Roosevelt a little more than 4 million, and Taft 3.5 million. Wilson garnered 435 electoral votes, Roosevelt 88, and Taft only 8.

Woodrow Wilson and the New Freedom

Wilson was elected largely because Roosevelt and the Progressive party split the Republican vote. But once elected, Wilson became a vigorous and aggressive chief executive who set out to translate his ideas about progressive government into legislation. Wilson was the first southerner elected president since Zachary Taylor in 1848 and only the second Democrat since the Civil War. Wilson, like Roosevelt, had to work with his party, and that restricted how progressive he could be. But he was also constrained by his own background and inclinations. Still, like Roosevelt, Wilson became more progressive during his presidency.

Tariff and Banking Reform

Wilson was not as charismatic as Roosevelt. He had a more difficult time relating to people in small groups, but he was an excellent public speaker who dominated through the force of his intellect. He probably had an exaggerated belief in his ability to persuade and a tendency to trust his own intuition too much. Ironically, his early success in getting his legislative agenda through Congress contributed to the overconfidence that would get him into difficulty later in foreign affairs. But his ability to push his legislative program through Congress during his first two years in office was matched only by Franklin Roosevelt

during the first months of the New Deal and by Lyndon Johnson in 1965.

Within a month of his inauguration, Wilson went before a joint session of Congress to outline his legislative program. He recommended reducing the tariff to eliminate favoritism, freeing the banking system from Wall Street control, and restoring competition in industry. By appearing in person before Congress, he broke a precedent established by Thomas Jefferson. First on Wilson's agenda was tariff reform. The Underwood Tariff, passed in 1913, was not a free-trade bill, but it did reduce the schedule for the first time in many years.

Attached to the Underwood bill was a provision for a small and slightly graduated income tax, which had been made possible by the passage of the Sixteenth Amendment. It imposed a modest rate of 1 percent on income over $4,000 (thus exempting a large portion of the population), with a surtax rising to 6 percent on high incomes. The income tax was enacted to replace the money lost from lowering the tariff. Wilson seemed to have no interest in using it to redistribute wealth in America.

The next item on Wilson's agenda was reform of the banking system. A financial panic in 1907 had revealed the need for a central bank, but few people could agree on the exact nature of the reforms. The progressive faction of the Democratic party, armed with the findings of the Pujo Committee's investigation of the money trust, argued for a banking system and a currency controlled by the federal government. The congressional committee, led by Arsène Pujo of Louisiana, had revealed a massive consolidation of banks and trust companies and a system of interlocking directorates and informal arrangements that concentrated resources and power in the hands of a few firms such as the J. P. Morgan Company. But talk of banking reform raised the specter among conservative Democrats and the business community of socialism, populism, and the monetary ideas of William Jennings Bryan.

The bill that passed Congress was a compromise. In creating the Federal Reserve System, it was the first reorganization of the banking system since the Civil War. The bill provided for 12 Federal Reserve banks and a Federal Reserve Board appointed by the president. The bill also created a flexible currency, based on Federal Reserve notes, that could be expanded or contracted as the situation required. The Federal Reserve System was not without its flaws, as later developments would show, and it did not end the power of the large eastern banks; but it was an improvement, and it appealed to the part of the progressive movement that sought order and efficiency.

Despite these reform measures, Wilson was not very progressive in some of his actions during his first two years in office. In the spring of 1914, he failed to support a bill that would have provided long-term rural credit financed by the federal government. He opposed a woman suffrage amendment, arguing that the states should decide who could vote. He also failed to support an anti–child labor bill after it had passed the House. Most distressing to some progressives, he ordered the segregation of blacks in several federal departments.

Booker T. Washington had remarked on Wilson's election, "Mr. Wilson is in favor of the things which tend toward the uplift, improvement, and advancement of my people, and at his hands we have nothing to fear." But when southern Democrats, suddenly in control in many departments, began dismissing black federal officeholders, especially those "who boss white girls," Wilson did nothing. When the NAACP complained that the shops, offices, rest rooms, and lunchrooms of the Post Office and Treasury departments and the Bureau of Engraving were segregated, Wilson replied, "I sincerely believe it to be in their [the blacks'] best interest."

Moving Closer to a New Nationalism

How to control the great corporations in America was a question Wilson and Roosevelt debated extensively during the campaign. Wilson's solution was the Clayton Act, submitted to Congress in 1914. The bill prohibited a number of unfair trading practices, outlawed the interlocking directorate, and made it illegal for corporations to purchase stock in other corporations if this tended to reduce competition. It was not clear how the government would enforce these provisions and ensure the competition that Wilson's New

Woman suffrage advocates, dressed fashionably in their long skirts and hats, gathered in Washington in 1913 to try to convince Congress and President Wilson to support a suffrage amendment. (Corbis-Bettmann)

Freedom doctrine called for, but the bill became controversial for another reason.

Labor leaders protested that the bill had no provision exempting labor organizations from prosecution under the Sherman Anti-Trust Act. When a section was added exempting both labor and agricultural organizations, Samuel Gompers hailed it as labor's Magna Carta. It was hardly that, because the courts interpreted the provision so that labor unions remained subject to court injunctions during strikes despite the Clayton Act.

More important than the Clayton Act, which both supporters and opponents realized was too vague to be enforced, was the creation of the Federal Trade Commission (FTC), modeled after the ICC, with enough power to move directly against corporations accused of restricting competition. The FTC was the idea of Louis Brandeis, but Wilson accepted it even though it seemed to move him more toward the philosophy of New Nationalism.

The Federal Trade Commission and the Clayton Act did not end monopoly, and the courts in the next two decades did not increase the government's power to regulate business. The suc-

cess of Wilson's reform agenda appeared minimal in 1914, but the outbreak of war in Europe and the need to win the election of 1916 would influence him in becoming more progressive in the next years.

Neither Wilson nor Roosevelt satisfied the demands of the advanced progressives. Most of the efforts of the two progressive presidents were spent trying to regulate economic power rather than to promote social justice. Yet the most important legacy of these two fascinating and powerful politicians was their attempts to strengthen the office of president and the executive branch of the federal government. The nineteenth-century American presidents after Lincoln had been relatively weak, and much of the federal power had resided with Congress. The progressive presidents reasserted presidential authority, modernized the executive branch, and began the creation of the federal bureaucracy, which has had a major impact on the lives of Americans in the twentieth century.

Both Wilson and Roosevelt used the presidency as a bully pulpit to make pronouncements,

Presidential Elections of the Progressive Era				
Year	Candidate	Party	Popular Vote	Electoral Vote
1900	WILLIAM MCKINLEY	Republican	7,218,039 (51.7%)	292
	William Jennings Bryan	Democratic, Populist	6,358,345 (45.5%)	155
1904	THEODORE ROOSEVELT	Republican	7,628,834 (56.4%)	336
	Alton B. Parker	Democratic	5,084,401 (37.6%)	140
	Eugene V. Debs	Socialist	402,460 (3.0%)	0
1908	WILLIAM H. TAFT	Republican	7,679,006 (51.6%)	321
	William J. Bryan	Democratic	6,409,106 (43.1%)	162
	Eugene V. Debs	Socialist	420,820 (2.8%)	0
1912	WOODROW WILSON	Democratic	6,296,547 (41.9%)	435
	Theodore Roosevelt	Progressive	4,118,571 (27.4%)	88
	William H. Taft	Republican	3,486,720 (23.2%)	8
	Eugene V. Debs	Socialist	897,011 (6.0%)	0
1916	WOODROW WILSON	Democratic	9,129,606 (49.4%)	277
	Charles E. Hughes	Republican	8,538,221 (46.2%)	254
	Allan L. Benson	Socialist	585,113 (3.2%)	0

Note: Winners' names appear in capital letters.

create news, and influence policy. For example, both presidents called White House conferences and appointed committees and commissions. Roosevelt strengthened the Interstate Commerce Commission and Wilson created the Federal Trade Commission, both of which were the forerunners of many other federal regulatory bodies. And by breaking precedent and actually delivering his annual message in person before a joint session of Congress, Wilson symbolized the new power of the presidency.

More than the increased power of the executive branch changed the nature of politics. The new bureaus, committees, and commissions brought to Washington a new kind of expert, trained in the universities, at the state and local level, and in the voluntary organizations. Julia Lathrop, a co-worker of Jane Addams at Hull House, was one such expert. Appointed by President Taft in 1912 to become chief of the newly created Children's Bureau, she was the first woman ever appointed to such a position. She used her post not only to work for better child labor laws, but also to train a new generation of women experts who would take their positions in state, federal, and private agencies in the 1920s and 1930s. Other experts emerged in Washington during the progressive era to influence policy in subtle and important ways. The expert, the commission, the statistical survey, and the increased power of the executive branch were all legacies of the progressive era.

TIMELINE

1901 McKinley assassinated; Theodore Roosevelt becomes president

Robert La Follette elected governor of Wisconsin

Tom Johnson elected mayor of Cleveland

Model tenement house bill passed in New York

U.S. Steel formed

1902 Anthracite coal strike

1903 Women's Trade Union League founded

Elkins Act

1904 Roosevelt reelected

Lincoln Steffens writes *The Shame of the Cities*

1905 Frederic C. Howe writes *The City: The Hope of Democracy*

Industrial Workers of the World formed

1906 Upton Sinclair writes *The Jungle*

Hepburn Act

Meat Inspection Act

Pure Food and Drug Act

1907 Financial panic

1908 *Muller* v. *Oregon*

Danbury Hatters case

William Howard Taft elected president

1909 Herbert Croly writes *The Promise of American Life*

NAACP founded

1910 Ballinger-Pinchot controversy

Mann Act

1911 Frederick Taylor writes *The Principles of Scientific Management*

Triangle Shirtwaist Company fire

1912 Progressive party founded by Theodore Roosevelt

Woodrow Wilson elected president

Children's Bureau established

Industrial Relations Commission founded

1913 Sixteenth Amendment (income tax) ratified

Underwood Tariff

Federal Reserve System established

Seventeenth Amendment (direct election of senators) passed

1914 Clayton Act

Federal Trade Commission Act

AFL has over 2 million members

Ludlow Massacre in Colorado

Conclusion

The Limits of Progressivism

The progressive era was a time when many Americans set out to promote reform because they saw poverty, despair, and disorder in the country transformed by immigration, urbanism, and industrialism. The progressives, unlike the socialists, however, saw nothing fundamentally wrong with the American system. Progressivism was largely a middle-class movement that sought to help the poor, the immigrants, and the working class. Yet the poor were rarely consulted about policy, and many groups, especially African Americans, were almost entirely left out of reform plans. Progressives had an optimistic view of human nature and an exaggerated faith in statistics, commissions, and committees. They talked of the need for more democracy, but they often succeeded in promoting bureaucracy and a government run by experts. They believed there was a need to regulate business, promote efficiency, and spread social justice, but these were often contradictory goals. In the end, their regulatory laws tended to aid business and to strengthen corporate capitalism, while social justice and equal opportunity remained difficult to achieve. By contrast, most of the industrialized nations of western Europe, especially Germany, Austria, France, and Great Britain, passed legislation during this period providing for old-age pensions and health and unemployment insurance.

Progressivism was a broad, diverse, and sometimes contradictory movement that had its roots in the 1890s and reached a climax in the early twentieth century. It began with many local movements and voluntary efforts to deal with the problems created by urban industrialism and moved to the state and finally the national level. Women played important roles in organizing reform, and many became experts at gathering statistics and writing reports. Eventually they began to fill positions in the new agencies in the state capitals and in Washington. Neither Theodore Roosevelt nor Woodrow Wilson was an advanced progressive, but during both their administrations, progressivism achieved some success. Both presidents strengthened the power of the presidency, and both promoted the idea that the federal government had the responsibility to regulate and control and to promote social justice. Progressivism would be altered by World War I, but it survived, with its strengths and weaknesses, to affect American society through most of the twentieth century.

Recommended Reading

General Accounts

John D. Buenker, John C. Burnham, and Robert Crunden, *Progressivism* (1977); Gabriel Kolko, *The Triumph of Conservatism* (1963); Arthur S. Link and Richard L. McCormick, *Progressivism* (1983); Robert Wiebe, *The Search for Order, 1877–1920* (1967); Richard Hofstadter, *The Age of Reform* (1955); Alan Dawley, *Struggle for Justice: Social Responsibility and the Liberal State* (1991).

The Progressive Impulse

Paul Boyer, *Urban Masses and Moral Order in America, 1820–1920* (1978); Robert M. Crunden, *Ministers of Reform* (1982); Peter Conn, *The Divided Mind: Ideology and Imagination in America, 1890–1927* (1983); David Noble, *The Progressive Mind, 1890–1917* (1970); Morton White, *Social Thought in America* (1949); Robert B. Westbrook, *John Dewey and American Democracy* (1991); Susan Curtis, *Consuming Faith: The Social Gospel and Modern American Culture* (1991); George Cotkin, *Reluctant Modernism: American Thought and Culture, 1880–1900* (1992).

A Diversity of Progressive Movements

Allen F. Davis, *Spearheads for Reform: The Social Settlements and the Progressive Movement* (1967); Walter I. Trattner, *Cru-*

sade for Children (1970); William L. O'Neill, *Divorce in the Progressive Era* (1963); Ruth Rosen, *The Lost Sisterhood* (1982); Mark T. Connelly, *The Response to Prostitution in the Progressive Era* (1980); Lary May, *Screening Out the Past: The Birth of Mass Culture and the Motion Picture Industry* (1980); Daniel Levine, *Poverty and Society: The Growth of the American Welfare State in International Perspective* (1988); James T. Klopenberg, *Social Democracy and Progressivism in European and American Thought* (1986); James H. Timberlake, *Prohibition and the Progressive Movement* (1963); Louis Filler, *The Muckrakers* (1976); David P. Thelen, *The New Citizenship* (1972); Bradley R. Rice, *Progressive Cities* (1977); Dewey Grantham, *Southern Progressivism* (1983); Aileen S. Kraditor, *The Ideas of the Woman Suffrage Movement, 1890–1920* (1965); August Meier, *Negro Thought in America, 1880–1915* (1963); Samuel P. Hays, *Conservation and the Gospel of Efficiency* (1959); Frederick Turner, *Rediscovering America: John Muir in His Time and Ours* (1985); David Brody, *Workers in Industrial America* (1980); Alice Kessler-Harris, *Out to Work* (1983); Rivka Shpak Lissak, *Pluralism and Progressivism* (1989); Ellen Fitzpatrick, *Endless Crusade: Women Social Scientists and Progressive Reform* (1990); Robyn Muncy, *Creating a Female Dominion in American Reform, 1890–1935* (1991); John F. Kasson, *Amusing the Million: Coney Island at the Turn of the Century* (1978); David Nasaw, *Going Out: The Rise and Fall of Public Amusements* (1993); Kathy Peiss, *Cheap Amusements: Working Women and Leisure in Turn of the Century New York* (1986).

National Politics

John Morton Blum, *The Progressive Presidents* (1980); John Milton Cooper, Jr., *The Warrior and the Priest* (1983); Arthur S. Link, *Woodrow Wilson and the Progressive Era* (1954); George E. Mowry, *The Era of Theodore Roosevelt* (1958); Paolo E. Coletta, *The Presidency of William Howard Taft* (1973); Nick Salvatore, *Eugene V. Debs* (1982); David P. Thelen, *Robert LaFollette and the Insurgent Spirit* (1976).

Fiction

Fiction from the period include Theodore Dreiser, *Sister Carrie* (1900), a classic of social realism; Upton Sinclair, *The Jungle* (1906), a novel about the meatpacking industry and the failure of the American dream; David Graham Phillips, *Susan Lenox* (1917), an epic of slum life and political corruption; and Charlotte Perkins Gilman, *Herland* (1915), the story of a female utopia.

The Great War

On April 7, 1917, the day after the United States officially declared war on Germany, Edmund P. Arpin, Jr., a young man of 22 from Grand Rapids, Wisconsin, decided to enlist in the Army. The war seemed to provide a solution for his aimless drifting. It was not patriotism that led him to join the Army, but his craving for adventure and excitement. A month later, he was at Fort Sheridan, Illinois, along with hundreds of other eager young men, preparing to become an Army officer. He felt a certain pride and sense of purpose, and especially a feeling of comradeship with the other men, but the war was a long way off.

Arpin finally arrived with his unit in Liverpool on December 23, 1917, aboard the *Leviathan,* a German luxury liner that the United States had interned when war was declared and pressed into service as a troop transport. In England, he discovered that American troops were not greeted as saviors. Hostility against the Americans simmered partly because of the previous unit's drunken brawls. Despite the efforts of the United States government to protect its soldiers from the sins of Europe, drinking seems to have been a preoccupation of the soldiers in Arpin's outfit. Arpin also learned something about French wine and women, but he spent most of the endless waiting time learning to play contract bridge.

Arpin saw some of the horror of war when he went to the front with a French regiment as an observer, but his own unit did not engage in combat until October 1918, when the war was almost over. He took part in the bloody Meuse-Argonne offensive, which helped end the war. But he discovered that war was not the heroic struggle of carefully planned campaigns that newspapers and books described. War was filled with misfired weapons, mix-ups, and erroneous attacks. Wounded in the leg in an assault on an unnamed hill and awarded a Distinguished Service Cross for his bravery, Arpin later learned that the order to attack had been recalled, but word had not reached him in time.

When the armistice came, Arpin was recovering in a field hospital. He was disappointed that the war had ended so soon, but he was well enough to go to Paris to take part in the victory celebration and to explore some of the famous Paris restaurants and nightclubs. In many ways, the highlight of his war experiences was not a battle or his medal, but his adventure after the war was over. With a friend, he went absent without leave and set out to explore Germany. They avoided the military police, traveled on a train illegally, and had many narrow escapes, but they made it back to the hospital without being arrested.

Edmund Arpin was in the Army for two years. He was one of 4,791,172 Americans who served in the Army, Navy, or Marines. He was one of the 2 million who went overseas, and one of the 230,074 who were wounded. Some of his friends were among the 48,909 who were killed. When he was mustered out of the Army in March 1919, he felt lost and confused. Being a civilian was not nearly as exciting as being in the Army and visiting new and exotic places.

In time, Arpin settled down. He became a successful businessman, married, and reared a family. A member of the American Legion, he periodically went to conventions and reminisced with men from his division about their escapades in France. Although the war changed their lives in many ways, most would never again feel the same sense of common purpose and adventure. "I don't suppose any of us felt, before or since, so necessary to God and man," one veteran recalled.

A 1918 painting of German and American wounded and exhausted soldiers after the Meuse-Argonne offensive captures some of the horror and pathos of war. (Harvey Dunn, Argonne, 1918/Smithsonian Institution) or Edmund P. Arpin, Jr., the Great War was the most important event of a lifetime. Just as war changed his life, so, too, did it alter the lives of most Americans. Trends begun during the progressive era accelerated. The power and influence of the federal government increased. Not only did the war promote woman suffrage, prohibition, and public housing, but it also helped to create an administrative bureaucracy that blurred the lines between public and private, between government and business—a trend that would continue throughout the twentieth century.

In this chapter, we examine the complicated circumstances that led the United States into the war and share the wartime experiences of American men and women overseas and at home. We will study not only military actions, but also the impact of the war on domestic policies and on the lives of ordinary Americans, including the migration of African Americans into northern cities. The war left a legacy of prejudice and hate and raised the basic question: could the tenets of American democracy, such as freedom of speech, survive participation in a major war? The chapter concludes with a look at the idealistic efforts to promote peace at the end of the war, and the disillusion that followed. The Great War thrust the United States into the role of leadership on the world scene, but many Americans were reluctant to accept that role.

The Early War Years

Few Americans expected the Great War that erupted in Europe in the summer of 1914 to affect their lives or alter their comfortable world. When a Serbian student terrorist assassinated Archduke Franz Ferdinand of Austria-Hungary in Sarajevo, the capital of the province of Bosnia, a place most Americans had never heard of, it precipitated a series of events leading to the most destructive war the world had ever known.

The Causes of War

Despite Theodore Roosevelt's successful peacekeeping attempts in the first decade of the century (see Chapter 20), relationships among the European powers had not improved. Intense rivalries for empire turned minor incidents in Africa, Asia, or the Balkans into events that threatened world peace. A growing sense of nationalism and pride in being French or British or German was fanned by a popular press, much the way Hearst's *Journal* and Pulitzer's *World* had increased American patriotism in the years before the Spanish-American War. National rivalry, especially between Great Britain and Germany, led to military competition and a race to build bigger battleships.

As European nations armed, they drew up a complex series of treaties. Austria-Hungary and Germany (the Central Powers) became military allies, and Britain, France, and Russia (the Allied Powers) agreed to assist one another in case of attack. Despite peace conferences and international agreements, many promoted by the United States, the European balance of power rested precariously on layers of treaties that barely obscured years of jealousy and distrust.

The incident in Sarajevo destroyed that balance. The leaders of Austria-Hungary determined to punish Serbia for the assassination. Russia mobilized to aid Serbia. Germany, supporting Austria-Hungary, declared war on Russia and France. England hesitated, but when Germany invaded Belgium in order to attack France, England declared war and the slaughter began.

Despite much evidence to the contrary, many intelligent people on both sides of the Atlantic believed that education, science, social reform, and negotiation had replaced all-out war as a way of solving international disputes. "It looks as though we are going to be the age of treaties rather than the age of wars, the century of reason rather than the century of force," a leader of the American peace movement had declared only two years before. But as news of the German invasion of Belgium and reports of the first bloody battles began to reach the United States in late summer, it seemed to most Americans that madness had replaced reason. Europeans "have reverted to the condition of savage tribes roaming the forests and

European Alignments, 1914

Allied Powers

Central Powers

Neutral countries

Joined Allied Powers
(year in parentheses)

Joined Central Powers
(year in parentheses)

FINLAND

NORWAY SWEDEN

RUSSIA

North Sea

Baltic Sea

DENMARK

GREAT NETHERLANDS
BRITAIN

IRELAND

GERMANY

ATLANTIC OCEAN

BELGIUM LUXEMBOURG

FRANCE AUSTRIA-HUNGARY

ROMANIA
(1916) *Black Sea*

SWITZERLAND

MONTENEGRO SERBIA

BULGARIA
(1915)

ITALY
(1915)

*Corsica
(France)*

ALBANIA

OTTOMAN
EMPIRE

PORTUGAL
(1916) SPAIN

*Sardinia
(Italy)*

GREECE

*Balearic
Islands
(Spain)* *Mediterranean Sea*

*Sicily
(Italy)*

MOROCCO
(France) ALGERIA
(France) TUNISIA
(France)

The Great War had an impact on all of Europe, even on the few countries that managed to remain neutral. Russia left the war in 1917, the same year that the United States joined the fight.

falling upon each other in a fury of blood and carnage," the *New York Times* announced.

The American sense that the nation would never succumb to the barbarism of war, combined with the knowledge that the Atlantic Ocean separated Europe from the United States, contributed to a great sense of relief after the first shock of the war began to wear off. Woodrow Wilson's official proclamation of neutrality on August 4, 1914, reinforced the belief that the United States had no major stake in the outcome of the war and would stay uninvolved. The president was preoccupied with his own personal tragedy. His wife, Ellen Axson Wilson, died of Bright's disease the day after his proclamation. Two weeks later, still engulfed by his own grief, he urged all Americans to "be neutral

in fact as well as in name, ... impartial in thought as well as in action." The United States, he argued, must preserve itself "fit and free" in order to do what "is honest and disinterested ... for the peace of the world." But it was obvious that it was going to be difficult to stay uninvolved, at least emotionally, with the battlefields of Europe.

American Reactions

Many social reformers despaired when they heard the news from Europe. Even during its first months, the war seemed to deflect energy away from reform. "We are three thousand miles away from the smoke and flames of combat, and have not a single regiment or battleship involved," remarked John Haynes Holmes, a liberal New York minister. "Yet who in the United States is thinking of recreation centers, improved housing or the minimum wage?" Settlement worker Lillian Wald responded to the threat of war by helping to lead 1,500 women in a "woman's peace" parade down Fifth Avenue. Jane Addams of Hull House helped to organize the Woman's Peace party. Drawing on traditional conceptions of female character, she argued that women had a special responsibility to work for peace and to speak out against the blasphemy of war because women and children suffered most in any war, especially in a modern war where civilians as well as soldiers became targets.

Although many people worked to promote an international plan to end the war through mediation, others could hardly wait to take part in the great adventure. Hundreds of young American men, most of them students or recent college graduates, volunteered to join ambulance units, to take part in the war effort without actually fighting. Among the most famous of them were Ernest Hemingway, John Dos Passos, and E. E. Cummings, who later turned their wartime adventures into literary masterpieces. Others volunteered for service with the French Foreign Legion or joined the Lafayette Escadrille, a unit of pilots made up of well-to-do American volunteers attached to the French army. Many of these young men were inspired by an older generation who pictured war as a romantic and manly adventure. One college president talked of the chastening and purifying effect of armed conflict, and Theodore Roosevelt projected an image of war that was something like a football game where red-blooded American men could test their idealism and manhood.

Alan Seeger, a graduate of Harvard in 1910, was one of those who believed in the romantic and noble purpose of the war. He had been living in Paris since 1912, and when the war broke out, he quickly joined the French Foreign Legion. For the next two years, he wrote sentimental poetry, articles, and letters describing his adventures. "You have no idea how beautiful it is to see the troops undulating along the road … with the captains and lieutenants on horse back at the head of the companies," he wrote his mother. When Seeger was killed in 1916, he became an instant hero. Some

The war in Europe appealed to the sense of adventure in many young American men. However, as in all wars, the women they left behind found it hard to say good-bye. (National Archives)

called him "America's Rupert Brooke," after the gallant British poet who died early in the war.

Many Americans visualized war as a romantic struggle for honor and glory because the only conflict they remembered was the "splendid little war" of 1898. For them, war meant Theodore Roosevelt leading the charge in Cuba and Commodore Dewey destroying the Spanish fleet in Manila harbor without the loss of an American life. Many older Americans recalled the Civil War, but the horrors of those years had faded, leaving only the memory of heroic triumphs. As Oliver Wendell Holmes, the Supreme Court justice who had been wounded in the Civil War, remarked, "War, when you are at it, is horrible and dull. It is only when time has passed that you see that its message was divine."

The reports from the battlefields, even during the first months of the war, should have indicated that the message was anything but divine. This would be a modern war in which men died by the thousands, cut down by an improved and efficient technology of killing.

The New Military Technology

The German Schlieffen plan called for a rapid strike through Belgium to attack Paris and the French army from the rear. However, the French stopped the German advance at the Battle of the Marne in September 1914, and the fighting soon bogged down in a costly and bloody routine. Soldiers on both sides dug miles of trenches and strung out barbed wire to protect them. Thousands died in battles that gained only a few yards or nothing at all. Rapid-firing rifles, improved explosives, incendiary shells, smokeless bullets, and tracer bullets all added to the destruction. Most devastating of all, however, was the improved artillery, sometimes mounted on trucks and directed by spotters using wireless radios, that could fire over the horizon and hit targets many miles behind the lines.

The technology of defense, especially the machine gun, neutralized the frontal assault, the most popular military tactic since the American Civil War. As one writer explained: "Three men and a machine gun can stop a battalion of heroes." But the generals on both sides continued to order their men to charge to their almost certain deaths.

The war was both a traditional and a revolutionary struggle. It was the last war in which cavalry was used and the first to employ a new generation of military technologies. By 1918, airplanes, initially used only for observation, were creating terror below with their bombs. Tanks made their first tentative appearance in 1916, but it was not until the last days of the war that this new offensive weapon began to neutralize the machine gun. Poison gas, first used in 1914, added a new element of fear to a war of already unspeakable horror. But then military technicians on both sides developed the gas mask, allowing the defense to counter the new offensive weapon.

Despite the reports of carnage from the battlefields, some Americans could hardly wait to join the fighting. Theodore Roosevelt and his friend Leonard Wood, the Army chief of staff, led a movement to prepare American men for war. Wood was determined that upper-class and college-educated men be ready to lead the nation into battle. In 1913, he established a camp for college men at Plattsburgh, New York, to give them some experience with military life, with order, discipline, and command. By 1915, thousands had crowded into the camp; even the mayor of New York enrolled. The young men learned to shoot rifles and to endure long marches and field exercises. But most of all, they associated with one another. Gathered around the campfire at night, they heard Wood and other veterans tell of winning glory and honor on the battlefield. In their minds at least, they were already leading a bayonet charge against the enemy, and the enemy was Germany.

Difficulties of Neutrality

Despite Wilson's efforts to promote neutrality, most Americans favored the Allied cause. About 8 million Austrian Americans and German Americans lived in the United States, and some supported the cause of the Central Powers. They viewed Kaiser Wilhelm II's Germany as a progressive parliamentary democracy. The anti-British sentiment of some Irish Americans led them to take sides not so much for Germany as against England. A few Swedish Americans distrusted Russia so vehemently that they had difficulty supporting the Allies. A number of American scholars, physicians, and intellectuals fondly remembered studying in Germany. To them, Germany meant great universities and cathedrals, music and culture. It also represented social planning, health insurance, unemployment compensation, and many programs for which the progressives had been fighting.

For most Americans, however, the ties of language and culture tipped the balance toward the Allies. After all, did not the English-speaking people of the world have special bonds and special responsibilities to promote civilization and ensure justice in the world? American connections with the French were not so close, but they were even more sentimental. The French, everyone remembered, had supported the American Revolution, and the French people had given the Statue of

Liberty, the very symbol of American opportunity and democracy, to the United States.

Other reasons made real neutrality nearly impossible. The fact that export and import trade with the Allies was much more important than with the Central Powers favored the Allies. Wilson's advisers, especially Robert Lansing and Edward House, openly supported the French and the British. Most newspaper owners and editors had close ethnic, cultural, and sometimes economic ties to the British and the French. The newspapers were quick to picture the Germans as barbaric Huns and to accept and embellish the atrocity stories that came from the front, some of them planted by British propaganda experts. Gradually for Wilson, and probably for most Americans, the perception that England and France were fighting to preserve civilization from the forces of Prussian evil replaced the idea that all Europeans were barbaric and decadent. But the American people were not yet willing to go to war to save civilization. Let France and England do that.

Woodrow Wilson also sympathized with the Allies for practical and idealistic reasons. He wanted to keep the United States out of the war, but he did not object to using force to promote diplomatic ends. "When men take up arms to set other men free, there is something sacred and holy in the warfare," he had written. Moreover, Wilson believed that by keeping the United States out of the war, he might control the peace. The war, he hoped, would show the futility of imperialism and would usher in a world of free trade in products and ideas. The United States had a special role to play in this new world and in leading toward an orderly international society. "We are the mediating nation of the world [and] we are therefore able to understand all nations."

Remaining neutral while maintaining trade with the belligerents became increasingly difficult. Remaining neutral while speaking out about the peace eventually became impossible. The need to trade and the desire to control the peace finally led the United States into the Great War.

World Trade and Neutrality Rights

The United States was part of an international economic community in 1914 in a way that it had not been a hundred years earlier during the Napoleonic Wars. The outbreak of war in the summer of 1914 caused an immediate economic panic in the United States. On July 31, 1914, the Wilson administration closed the stock exchange to prevent the unloading of European securities and panic selling. It also adopted a policy discouraging loans by American banks to belligerent nations. Most difficult was the matter of neutral trade. Wilson insisted on the rights of Americans to trade with both the Allies and the Central Powers, but Great Britain instituted an illegal naval blockade, mined the North Sea, and began seizing American ships, even those carrying food and raw materials to Italy, the Netherlands, and other neutral nations. The first crisis that Wilson faced was whether or not to accept the illicit British blockade. To do so would be to surrender one of the rights he supported most ardently, the right of free trade.

Wilson eventually backed down and accepted British control of the sea. His conviction that the destinies of the United States and Great Britain were intertwined outweighed his idealistic belief in free trade and caused him to react more harshly to German violations of international law than he did to British violators. Consequently, American trade with the Central Powers declined between 1914 and 1916 from $169 million to just over $1 million, whereas with the Allies it increased during the same period from $825 million to over $3 billion. At the same time, the United States government eased restrictions on private loans to belligerents. In March 1915, the House of Morgan loaned the French government $50 million, and in the fall of 1915, the French and British obtained an unsecured loan of $500 million from American banks. With dollars as well as sentiments, the United States gradually ceased to be neutral.

Germany retaliated against British control of the seas with submarine warfare. The new weapon, the U-boat (*Unterseeboot*), created unprecedented problems. Nineteenth-century international law obligated a belligerent warship to warn a passenger or merchant ship before attacking, but the chief advantage of the submarine was surprise. Rising to the surface to issue a warning would have meant being blown out of the water by an armed merchant ship.

On February 4, 1915, Germany announced a submarine blockade of the British Isles. Until Britain gave up its campaign to starve the German population, the Germans would sink even neutral ships. Wilson warned Germany that it would be held to "strict accountability" for illegal destruction of American ships or lives.

In March 1915, a German U-boat sank a British liner en route to Africa, killing 103 people, including one American. How should the United States respond? Wilson's advisers could not agree. Robert Lansing, a legal counsel at the State Department, urged the president to issue a strong protest, charging a breach of international law. William Jennings Bryan, the secretary of state, argued that an American traveling on a British ship was guilty of "contributory negligence" and urged Wilson to prohibit Americans from traveling on belligerent ships in the war zone. Wilson never did settle the dispute, for on May 7, 1915, a greater crisis erupted. A German U-boat torpedoed the British luxury liner *Lusitania* off the Irish coast. The liner, which was not armed but was carrying war supplies, sank in 18 minutes. Nearly 1,200 people, including many women and children, drowned. Among the dead were 128 Americans. Suddenly Americans confronted the horror of total war fought with modern weapons, a war that killed civilians, including women and children, just as easily as it killed soldiers.

The tragedy horrified most Americans. Despite earlier warnings by the Germans in American newspapers that it was dangerous to travel in war zones, the same newspapers denounced the act as "mass murder." Some called for a declaration of war. Wilson and most Americans had no idea of

The sinking of the Lusitania *shocked Americans and illustrated the complexity and horror of modern warfare. In the days before radio, most Americans received their news through the newspapers. New York had fifteen daily papers in 1915, and all produced "Extra" editions to announce such dramatic events as the sinking of the* Lusitania. *(New York Tribune, May 8, 1915)*

going to war in the spring of 1915, but the president refused to take Bryan's advice and prevent further loss of American lives by simply prohibiting all Americans from traveling on belligerent ships. Instead, he sent a series of protest notes demanding reparation for the loss of American lives and a pledge from Germany that it would cease attacking ocean liners without warning.

Bryan resigned as secretary of state over the tone of the notes and charged that the United States was not being truly neutral. Some denounced Bryan as a traitor, but others charged that if the United States really wanted to stay out of the war, Bryan's position was more logical, consistent, and humane than Wilson's. The president replaced Bryan with Robert Lansing, who was much more eager than Bryan to oppose Germany, even at the risk of war.

The tense situation eased late in 1915. After a German U-boat sank the British steamer *Arabic,* which claimed two American lives, the German ambassador promised that Germany would not attack ocean liners without warning (the *Arabic* pledge). But the *Lusitania* crisis caused an outpouring of books and articles urging the nation to prepare for war. The National Security League, the most effective of the preparedness groups, called for a bigger Army and Navy, a system of universal military training, and "patriotic education and national sentiment and service among the people of the United States."

Organizing on the other side were a group of progressive reformers who formed the American Union Against Militarism. They feared that those urging preparedness were deliberately setting out to destroy liberal social reform at home and to promote imperialism abroad.

Wilson sympathized with the preparedness groups to the extent of asking Congress on November 4, 1915, for an enlarged and reorganized Army. The bill met great opposition, especially from southern and western congressmen, but the Army Reorganization Bill that Wilson signed in June 1916 increased the regular Army to just over 200,000 and integrated the National Guard into the defense structure. Few Americans, however, expected those young men to go to war. One of the most popular songs of 1916 was "I Didn't Raise My Boy to Be a Soldier." Even before American soldiers

arrived in France, however, Wilson used the Army and the Marines in Mexico and Central America.

Intervening in Mexico and Central America

Woodrow Wilson came to office in 1913 planning to promote liberal and humanitarian ends, not only in domestic policies, but also in foreign affairs. Wilson had a vision of a world purged of imperialism, a world of free trade, but a world where American ideas and American products would find their way. Combining the zeal of a Christian missionary with the conviction of a college professor, he spoke of "releasing the intelligence of America for the service of mankind" and of enriching the world "with the products of our mines, our farms, and our factories, with the creations of our thought and the fruits of our character." With his secretary of state, William Jennings Bryan, Wilson denounced the "big stick" and "dollar diplomacy" of the Roosevelt and Taft years. Yet in the end, Wilson's administration used force more systematically than those of his predecessors. The rhetoric was different, yet just as much as Roosevelt, Wilson tried to maintain stability in the countries to the south in order to promote American economic and strategic interests.

At first, Wilson's foreign policy seemed to reverse some of the most callous aspects of dollar diplomacy in Central America. Bryan signed a treaty with Colombia in 1913 that agreed to pay $5 million for the loss of Panama and virtually apologized for the Roosevelt administration's treatment of Colombia. The Senate, not so willing to admit that the United States had been wrong, refused to ratify the treaty.

The change in spirit proved illusory. After a disastrous civil war in the Dominican Republic, the United States offered in 1915 to take over the country's finances and police force. But when the Dominican leaders rejected a treaty making their country virtually a protectorate of the United States, Wilson ordered in the Marines. They took control of the government in May 1916. Although Americans built roads, schools, and hospitals, people resented their presence. In neighboring Haiti, the situation was different, but the results were similar. The Marines landed at Port-au-

Prince in the summer of 1915 to prop up a pro-American regime. In Nicaragua, the Wilson administration kept the Marines sent by Taft in 1912 to keep the pro-American regime of Adolfo Díaz in place and acquired the right, through treaty, to intervene at any time to preserve order and protect American property. Except for a brief period in the mid–1920s, the Marines remained until 1933.

Wilson's policy of intervention ran into greatest difficulty in Mexico, a country that had been ruled by dictator Porfirio Díaz, who had long welcomed American investors. By 1910, more than 40,000 American citizens lived in Mexico, and more than $1 billion of American money was invested in the country. Americans controlled 75 percent of the mines, 70 percent of the rubber, and 60 percent of the oil. In 1911, however, Francisco Madero, a reformer who wanted to destroy the privileges of the upper classes, overthrew Díaz. Two years later, Madero was deposed and murdered by order of Victoriano Huerta, the head of the army. This was the situation when Wilson became president.

To the shock of many diplomats and businessmen, Wilson refused to recognize the Huerta government. Everyone admitted that Huerta was a ruthless dictator, but diplomatic recognition, the exchange of ambassadors, and the regulation of trade and communication had never meant approval. In the world of business and diplomacy, it merely meant that a particular government was in power. But Wilson set out to remove what he called a "government of butchers." "The United States Government intends not merely to force Huerta from power," he wrote to a British diplomat, "but also to exert every influence it can to secure Mexico a better government under which all contracts and business concessions will be safer than they have ever been."

At first, Wilson applied diplomatic pressure. Then, using a minor incident as an excuse, he asked Congress for power to involve American troops if necessary. Few Mexicans liked Huerta, but they liked even less the idea of North American interference. Hence, they rallied around the dictator. As it had in 1847, the United States landed troops at Veracruz. Angry Mexican mobs destroyed American property wherever they could find it. Wilson's action outraged many Europeans and Latin Americans as well as Americans.

A British cartoon pokes fun at the American president and his wavering policy toward Mexico. (Library of Congress)

Wilson's military intervention succeeded in forcing Huerta out of power, but a civil war between forces led by Venustiano Carranza and those led by General Francisco "Pancho" Villa ensued. The United States sent arms to Carranza, who was considered less radical than Villa, and Carranza's soldiers defeated Villa's. When an angry Villa led what was left of his army in a raid on Columbus, New Mexico, in March 1916, Wilson sent an expedition commanded by Brigadier General John Pershing to track down Villa and his men. The strange and comic scene developed of an American Army charging 300 miles into Mexico unable to catch the retreating villain. Not surprisingly, given the history of Mexican-American relations, the Mexicans feared that Pershing's army was planning to occupy northern Mexico. Even Carranza shot off a bitter note to Wilson, accusing him of threatening war, but Wilson refused to withdraw the troops. Tensions rose. An American patrol attacked a Mexican garrison, with loss of life on both sides. Just as war seemed inevitable, Wilson agreed to recall the troops and to recognize the Carranza government. But this was in January 1917, and if it had not been for the growing crisis in Europe, it is likely that war would have resulted.

The tragedy was that Wilson, who idealistically wanted the best for the people of Mexico and Central America and who thought he knew exactly what they needed, managed to intervene too often and too blatantly to protect the strategic and economic interests of the United States. In the process, his policy alienated one-time friends of the United States. His policies would contribute to future difficulties in both Latin America and Europe.

The United States Enters the War

A significant minority of Americans opposed going to war in 1917, and that decision would remain controversial when it was reexamined in the 1930s. But once involved, the government and the American people made the war into a patriotic crusade that influenced all aspects of American life.

The Election of 1916

American political campaigns do not stop even in times of international crisis. As 1915 turned to 1916, Wilson had to think of reelection as well as of preparedness, submarine warfare, and the Mexican campaign. At first glance, the president's chances of reelection seemed poor. He had won in 1912 only because Theodore Roosevelt and the Progressive party had split the Republican vote. If supporters of the Progressives in 1912 returned to the Republican fold, Wilson's chances were slim indeed. Because the Progressive party had done very badly in the 1914 congressional elections, Roosevelt seemed ready to seek the Republican nomination.

Wilson was aware that he had to win over voters who had favored Roosevelt in 1912. In January 1916, he appointed Louis D. Brandeis to the Supreme Court. The first Jew ever to sit on the High Court, Brandeis was confirmed over the strong opposition of many legal organizations. His appointment pleased the social justice progres-

sives because he had always championed reform causes. They made it clear to Wilson that the real test for them was whether or not he supported the anti–child labor and workers' compensation bills pending in Congress.

In August, Wilson put heavy pressure on Congress and obtained passage of the Workmen's Compensation Bill, which gave some protection to federal employees, and the Keatings-Owen Child Labor Bill, which prohibited the shipment in interstate commerce of goods produced by children under 14 and in some cases under 16. This bill, later declared unconstitutional, was a far-reaching proposal that for the first time used federal control over interstate commerce to dictate the conditions under which businesspeople could manufacture products.

To attract farm support, Wilson pushed for passage of the Federal Farm Loan Act, which created 12 Federal Farm Loan banks to extend long-term credit to farmers. Urged on by organized labor as well as by many progressives, he supported the Adamson Act, which established an eight-hour day for all interstate railway workers. Within a few months, Wilson reversed the New Freedom doctrines he had earlier supported and brought the force of the federal government into play on the side of reform. The flurry of legislation early in 1916 provided one climax to the progressive movement. The strategy seemed to work, for progressives of all kinds enthusiastically endorsed the president.

The election of 1916, however, turned as much on foreign affairs as on domestic policy. The Republicans ignored Theodore Roosevelt and nominated instead the staid and respectable Charles Evans Hughes, a former governor of New York and future Supreme Court justice. Their platform called for "straight and honest neutrality" and "adequate preparedness." In a bitter campaign, Hughes attacked Wilson for not promoting American rights in Mexico more vigorously and for giving in to the unreasonable demands of labor. Wilson, on his part, implied that electing Hughes would guarantee war with both Mexico and Germany and that his opponents were somehow not "100 percent Americans." As the campaign progressed, the peace issue became more and more important, and the cry "He kept us out of war" echoed through every Democratic rally. It was a slogan that would soon seem strangely ironic.

The election was extremely close. In fact, Wilson went to bed on election night thinking he had lost the presidency. The election was not finally decided until the Democrats carried California (by fewer than 4,000 votes). Wilson won by carrying the West as well as the South.

Deciding for War

Wilson's victory in 1916 seemed to be a mandate for staying out of the European war. But the campaign rhetoric made the president nervous. He had tried to emphasize Americanism, not neutrality. As he told one of his advisers, "I can't keep the country out of war. They talk of me as though I were a god. Any little German lieutenant can put us into war at any time by some calculated outrage."

People who supported Wilson as a peace candidate applauded in January 1917 when he went before the Senate to clarify the American position on a negotiated settlement of the war. The German government had earlier indicated that it might be willing to go to the conference table. Wilson outlined a plan for a negotiated settlement before either side had achieved victory. It would be a peace among equals, "a peace without victory," a peace without indemnities and annexations. The peace agreement Wilson outlined contained his idealistic vision of the postwar world as an open marketplace, and it could have worked only if Germany and the Allies were willing to settle for a draw.

The German government refused to accept a peace without victory, probably because early in 1917, the German leaders thought they could win. On January 31, 1917, the Germans announced that they would sink on sight any ship, belligerent or neutral, sailing toward England or France. A few days later, in retaliation, the United States broke diplomatic relations with Germany. But Wilson—and probably most Americans—still hoped to avert war without shutting off American trade. As goods began to pile up in warehouses and American ships stayed idly in port, however, pressure mounted to arm American merchant ships. An intercepted telegram from the German foreign secretary, Arthur Zimmermann, to the German minister in Mexico increased anti-German feeling. If war broke out, the German minister was to offer Mexico the territory it had lost in Texas, New Mexico, and Arizona in 1848. In return, Mexico would join Germany in a war against the United States. When this telegram was released to the press on March 1, 1917, many Americans demanded war against Germany. Wilson still hesitated.

As the country waited on the brink of war, news of revolution in Russia reached Washington. That event would prove as important as the war itself. The March 1917 revolution in Russia was a spontaneous uprising of the workers, housewives, and soldiers against the government of Tszar Nicholas II and its inept conduct of the war. The army had suffered staggering losses at the front. The civilian population was in desperate condition. Food was scarce, and the railroads and industry had nearly collapsed. At first, Wilson and other Americans were enthusiastic about the new republic led by Alexander Kerensky. The overthrow of the feudal aristocracy seemed in the spirit of the American Revolution. Kerensky promised to continue the struggle against Germany. But within months, the revolution took a more extreme turn. Vladimir Ilyich Ulyanov, known as Lenin, returned from exile in Switzerland and led the radical Bolsheviks to victory over the Kerensky regime in November 1917.

Lenin, a brilliant lawyer and revolutionary tactician, was a follower of Karl Marx (1818–1883). Marx was a German intellectual and radical philosopher who had described the alienation of the working class under capitalism and predicted a growing split between the proletariat (the unpropertied workers) and the capitalists. Lenin extended Marx's ideas and argued that capitalist nations eventually would be forced to go to war over raw materials and markets. Believing that capitalism and imperialism went hand in hand, Lenin, unlike Wilson, argued that the only way to end imperialism was to end capitalism. The new Soviet Union, not the United States, was the model for the rest of the world to follow; communism, Lenin predicted, would eventually dominate the globe. The Russian Revolution posed a threat to Wilson's vision of the world and to his plan to bring the United States into the war "to make the world safe for democracy."

More disturbing than the first news of revolution in Russia, however, was the situation in the North Atlantic, where German U-boats sank five American ships between March 12 and March 21, 1917. Wilson no longer hesitated. On April 2, he urged Congress to declare war. His words conveyed a sense of mission about the United States' entry into the war, but Wilson's voice was low and somber. "It is a fearful thing," he concluded, "to lead this great, peaceful people into war, into the most terrible and disastrous of all wars." The war resolution swept the Senate 82 to 6 and the House of Representatives 373 to 50.

Once war was declared, most Americans forgot their doubts. Young men rushed to enlist;

Recruiting posters helped to create a sense of purpose and patriotism, and often used pictures of attractive women to make their point. To be a soldier was to be a real man; to avoid service was to be something less than a man. (The Granger Collection, New York)

women volunteered to become nurses or to serve in other ways. Towns were united by patriotism.

A Patriotic Crusade

Not all Americans applauded the declaration of war. Some pacifists and socialists opposed the war, and a black newspaper, *The Messenger,* decried the conflict. "The real enemy is War rather than Imperial Germany," wrote Randolph Bourne, a young New York intellectual. "We are for peace," Morris Hillquit, a socialist leader, announced. "We are unalterably opposed to the killing of our manhood and the draining of our resources in … a pursuit which begins by suppressing the freedom of speech and press and public assemblage, and by stifling legitimate political criticism." "To whom does war bring prosperity?" Senator George Norris of Nebraska asked on the Senate floor.

> Not to the soldier, … not to the broken hearted widow, … not to the mother who weeps at the death of her brave boy. … War brings no prosperity to the great mass of common patriotic citizens. We are going into war upon the command of gold. … I feel that we are about to put the dollar sign on the American flag.

For most Americans in the spring of 1917, the war seemed remote. A few days after the war was declared, a Senate committee listened to a member of the War Department staff list the vast quantities of materials needed to supply an American army in France. One of the senators, jolted awake, exclaimed, "Good Lord! You're not going to send soldiers over there, are you?"

To convince senators and citizens alike that the war was real and that American participation was just, Wilson appointed a Committee on Public Information, headed by George Creel, a muckraking journalist from Denver. The Creel Committee launched a gigantic propaganda campaign to persuade the American public that the United States had gone to war to promote the cause of freedom and democracy and to prevent the barbarous hordes from overrunning Europe and eventually the Western Hemisphere.

The patriotic crusade soon became stridently anti-German and anti-immigrant. Most school districts banned the teaching of German, a "language that disseminates the ideals of autocracy, brutality and hatred." Anything German became suspect. Sauerkraut was renamed "liberty cabbage," and German measles became "liberty measles." Many families Americanized their German surnames. Several cities banned music by German composers from symphony concerts. South Dakota prohibited the use of German on the telephone, and in Iowa, a state official announced, "If their language is disloyal, they should be imprisoned. If their acts are disloyal, they should be shot." Occasionally, the patriotic fever led to violence. The most notorious incident occurred in East St. Louis, Illinois, which had a large German population. A mob seized Robert Prager, a young German American, in April 1918, stripped off his clothes, dressed him in an American flag, marched him through the streets, and lynched him. The eventual trial led to the acquittal of the ringleaders on the grounds that the lynching was a "patriotic murder."

The Wilson administration, of course, did not condone domestic violence and murder, but heated patriotism led to irrational hatreds and fears of subversion. Suspect were not only German Americans, but also radicals, pacifists, and anyone who raised doubts about the American war efforts or the government's policies. In New York, the black editors of *The Messenger* were given 2 ½-year jail sentences for the paper's article "Pro-Germanism Among Negroes." The Los Angeles police ignored complaints that Mexicans were being harassed because after learning of the Zimmermann telegram, they believed that all Mexicans were pro-German. In Wisconsin, Senator Robert La Follette, who had voted against the war resolution, was burned in effigy and censured by the faculty of the University of Wisconsin. At a number of universities, professors were dismissed, sometimes for as little as questioning the morality or the necessity of America's participation in the war.

On June 15, 1917, Congress, at Wilson's behest, passed the Espionage Act, which provided imprisonment of up to 20 years or a fine of up to $10,000, or both, for people who aided the enemy or who "willfully cause … insubordination, disloyalty, mutiny or refusal of duty in the military … forces

of the United States…." The act also authorized the postmaster general to prohibit from the mails any matter he thought advocated treason or forcible resistance to United States laws. The act was used to stamp out dissent, even to discipline anyone who questioned the administration's policies. Using the act, Postmaster General Albert S. Burleson banned the magazines *American Socialist* and *The Masses* from the mails.

Congress later added the Trading with the Enemy Act and a Sedition Act. The latter prohibited disloyal, profane, scurrilous, or abusive remarks about the form of government, flag, or uniform of the United States. It even prohibited citizens from opposing the purchase of war bonds. In the most famous case tried under the act, Eugene Debs was sentenced to ten years in prison for opposing the war. In 1919, the Supreme Court upheld the conviction, even though Debs had not explicitly urged the violation of the draft laws. Not all Americans agreed with the decision, for while still in prison, Debs polled close to one million votes in the presidential election of 1920. Ultimately, the government prosecuted 2,168 people under the Espionage and Sedition acts and convicted about half of them. But these figures do not include the thousands informally persecuted and deprived of their liberties and their right of free speech.

A group of amateur loyalty enforcers, called the American Protective League, cooperated with the Justice Department. League members often reported nonconformists and anyone who did not appear 100 percent loyal. People were arrested for criticizing the Red Cross or a government agency. One woman was sentenced to prison for writing, "I am for the people and the government is for the profiteers." Ricardo Flores Magon, a leading Mexican-American labor organizer and radical in the Southwest, was sentenced to 20 years in prison for criticizing Wilson's Mexican policy and violating the Neutrality Acts. In Cincinnati, a pacifist minister, Herbert S. Bigelow, was dragged from the stage where he was about to give a speech, taken to a wooded area by a mob, bound and gagged, and whipped. The attorney general of the United States, speaking of opponents of government policies, said, "May God have mercy on them for they need expect

Government Propaganda

All governments produce propaganda. Especially in time of war, governments try to convince their citizens that the cause is important and worthwhile even if it means sacrifice. Before the United States entered the war, both Great Britain and Germany presented their side of the conflict through stories planted in newspapers, photographs, and other devices. Some historians argue that the British propaganda depicting the Germans as barbaric Huns who killed little boys and Catholic nuns played a large role in convincing Americans of the righteousness of the Allied cause.

When the United States entered the war, a special committee under the direction of George Creel did its best to persuade Americans that the war was a crusade against evil. The committee organized a national network of "four-minute men," local citizens with the proper political views, who could be used to whip up a crowd into a patriotic frenzy. These local rallies, enlivened by bands and parades, urged people of all ages to support the war effort and buy war bonds. The Creel Committee also produced literature for the schools, much of it prepared by college professors who volunteered their services. One pamphlet, titled *Why America Fights Germany,* described in lurid detail a possible German invasion of the United States. The committee also used the new technology of motion pictures, which proved to be the most effective propaganda device of all.

There is a narrow line between education and propaganda. As early as 1910, Thomas Edison made films instructing the public about the dangers of tuberculosis, and others produced movies that demonstrated how to avoid everything from typhoid to tooth decay. However, during the war, the government quickly realized the power of the new medium and adopted it to train soldiers, instill patriotism, and help the troops avoid the temptations of alcohol and sex.

After the United States entered World War I, the Commission of Training Camp Activities made a film called *Fit to Fight* that was shown to almost all male servicemen. It was an hour-long drama following the careers of five young recruits. Four of them, by associating with the wrong people and through lack of willpower, caught venereal disease. The film interspersed a simplistic plot with grotesque shots of men with various kinds of venereal disease. The film also glorified athletics, especially football and boxing, as a substitute for sex. It emphasized the importance of patriotism and purity for America's fighting force. In one scene, Bill Hale, the only soldier in the film to remain pure, breaks up a peace rally and beats up the speaker. "It serves you right," the pacifist's sister remarks, "I'm glad Billy punched you."

Fit to Fight was so successful that the government commissioned another film, *The End of the Road,* to be shown to women who lived near military bases. The film is the story of Vera and Mary. Although still reflecting progressive attitudes, the film's message is somewhat different from that of *Fit to Fight.* Vera's strict mother tells her daughter that sex is dirty, leaving Vera to pick up "distorted and obscene" information about sex on the street. She falls victim to the first man who comes along and contracts a venereal disease. Mary, in contrast, has an enlightened mother who explains where babies come from. When

Liberty Bond propaganda. (The Granger Collection, New York)

Mary grows up, she rejects marriage and becomes a professional woman, a nurse. In the end, she falls in love with a doctor and gets married. *The End of the Road* has a number of subplots and many frightening shots of syphilitic sores. Several illustrations show the dangers of indiscriminate sex. Among other things, the film preached the importance of science, sex education, and the need for self-control.

What do the anti-VD films tell us about the attitudes, ideas, and prejudices of the World War I period? What images do they project about men, women, and sex roles? Would you find the same kind of moralism, patriotism, and fear of VD today? How have attitudes toward sex changed? Were you shown sex education films in school? Were they like these? Who sponsored them? What can historians learn from such films? Does the government produce propaganda today?

Scene from Fit to Fight. *(War Department, Commission on Training Camps)*

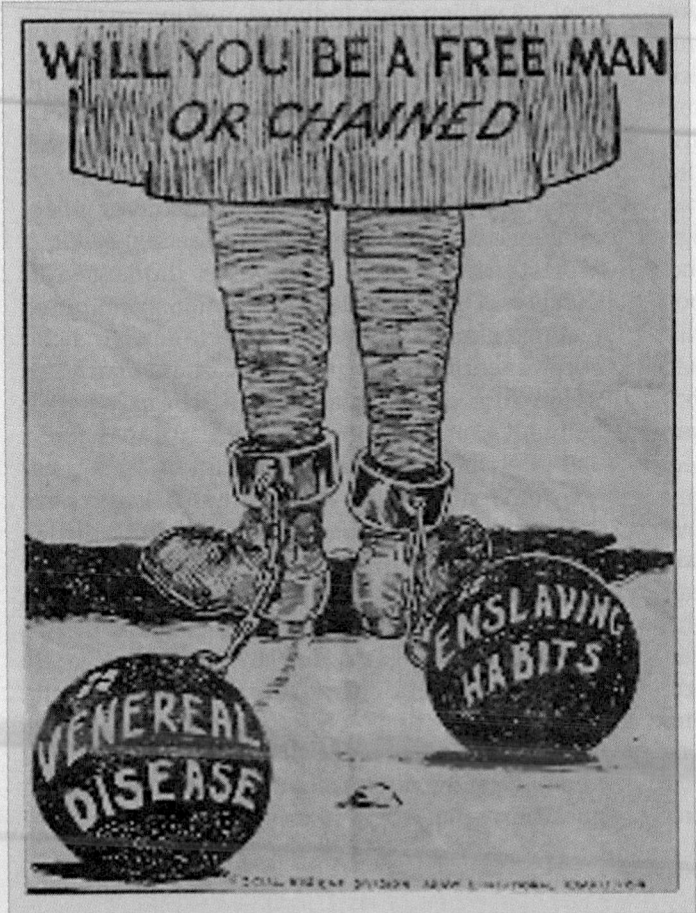

Anti-VD poster issued by the U.S. Commission on Training Camp Activities. (Army Educational Commission)

779

For many social justice progressives who had fought hard, long, and frustrating battles trying to humanize the industrial city, the very fact that suddenly people in high places were listening and approving programs was stimulating. "Enthusiasm for social service is epidemic," one social worker wrote in the summer of 1917:

> [A] luxuriant crop of new agencies is springing up. We scurry back and forth to the national capital; we stock offices with typewriters and new letterheads; we telephone feverishly regardless of expense, and resort to all the devices of efficient "publicity work."
> …It is all very exhilarating, stimulating, intoxicating.

One of the best examples of the progressives' influence on wartime activities was the Commission on Training Camp Activities, set up early in the war to solve the problem of mobilizing, entertaining, and protecting American servicemen at home and abroad. Chairman of the commission was Raymond Fosdick, a former settlement worker. He appointed a number of experts from the Playground Association, the YMCA, and social work agencies. They set out to organize community singing and baseball, establish post exchanges and theaters, and even provide university extension lectures to educate the servicemen. The overriding assumption was that the military experience would help produce better citizens, people who would be ready to vote for social reform once they returned to civilian life.

The Commission on Training Camp Activities also incorporated the progressive crusades against alcohol and prostitution. The Military Draft Act prohibited the sale of liquor to men in uniform and gave the president power to establish zones around military bases where prostitution and alcohol would be prohibited. Some military commanders protested, and at least one city official argued that prostitutes were "God-provided means for the prevention of the violation of innocent girls, by men who are exercising their 'God-given passions.'" Yet the commission, with the full cooperation of the Wilson administration, set out to wipe out sin, or at least to put it out of the reach of servicemen. "Fit to fight" became the motto. "Men must live straight if they would shoot straight," one official announced. It was a typical progressive effort combining moral indignation with the use of the latest scientific prophylaxis. The commissioners prided themselves on having eliminated by 1918 all the red-light districts near the training camps and producing what one person called "the cleanest army since Cromwell's day." When the boys go to France, the secretary of war remarked, "I want them to have invisible armour to take with them. I want them to have armour made up of a set of social habits replacing those of their homes and communities."

France tested the "invisible armour." The government, despite hundreds of letters of protest from American mothers, decided that it could not prevent the soldiers from drinking wine in France, but it could forbid them to buy or accept as gifts anything but light wine and beer. If Arpin's outfit is typical, the soldiers often ignored the rules.

Sex was even more difficult to regulate in France than liquor. Both the British and the French armies had tried to solve the problem of venereal disease by licensing and inspecting prostitutes. Clemenceau, the French premier, found the American attitude toward prostitution difficult to comprehend. On one occasion, he accused the Americans of spreading disease throughout the French civilian population and graciously offered to provide the Americans with licensed prostitutes. General Pershing considered the letter containing the offer "too hot to handle." So he gave it to Fosdick, who showed it to Baker, who remarked, "For God's sake, Raymond, don't show this to the President or he'll stop the war." The Americans never accepted Clemenceau's offer, and he continued to be baffled by the American progressive mentality.

Suffrage for Women

In the fall of 1918, while American soldiers were mobilizing for the final offensive in France and hundreds of thousands of women were working in factories and serving as Red Cross and Salvation Army volunteers near the army bases, Woodrow Wilson spoke before the Senate to ask its support of woman suffrage, which he maintained was "vital to the winning of the war." Wilson had earlier opposed the vote for women. His positive statement at this late date was not important, but his voice was a welcome addition to a rising chorus of support for an amendment to the Constitution that would permit the female half of the population to vote.

Not everyone favored woman suffrage. Many people still argued that the vote would make women less feminine, more worldly, and less able to perform their primary tasks as wives and mothers. The National Association Opposed to Woman Suffrage argued that it was only radicals who wanted the vote and declared that woman suffrage, socialism, and feminism were "three branches of the same Social Revolution."

Carrie Chapman Catt, an efficient administrator and tireless organizer, devised the strategy that finally secured the vote for women. Catt, who grew up in Iowa, joined the Iowa Woman Suffrage Association at age 28 shortly after her first husband died. Before remarrying, she insisted on a legal agreement giving her four months a year away from her husband to work for the suffrage cause. In 1915, she became president of the National American Woman Suffrage Association (NAWSA), the organization founded in 1890 and based in part on the society organized by Elizabeth Cady Stanton and Susan B. Anthony in 1869.

Catt coordinated the state campaigns with the office in Washington, directing a growing army of dedicated workers. The Washington headquarters sent precise information to the states on ways to pressure congressmen in local districts. In Washington, they maintained a file on each congressman and senator. "There were facts supplied by our members in the states about his personal, political, business and religious affiliations; there were reports of interviews; ... there was everything that could be discovered about his stand on woman suffrage."

The careful planning began to produce results, but a group of more militant reformers, impatient with the slow progress, broke off from NAWSA to form the National Woman's Party (NWP) in 1916. This group was led by Alice Paul, a Quaker from New Jersey, who had participated in some of the suffrage battles in England. Paul and her group picketed the White House, chained themselves to the fence, and blocked the streets. They carried banners that asked, "MR. PRESIDENT, HOW LONG MUST WOMEN WAIT FOR LIBERTY?" In the summer of 1917, the government arrested more than 200 women and charged them with "obstructing the sidewalk." It was just the kind of publicity the militant group

sought, and it made the most of it. Wilson, fearing even more embarrassment, began to cooperate with the more moderate reformers.

The careful organizing of the NAWSA and the more militant tactics of the NWP both contributed to the final success of the woman suffrage crusade. The war did not cause the passage of the Nineteenth Amendment, but it did accelerate the process. Fourteen state legislatures petitioned Congress in 1917 and twenty-six in 1919, urging the enactment of the amendment. Early in 1919, the House of Representatives passed the suffrage amendment 304 to 90, and the Senate approved by a vote of 56 to 25. Fourteen months later, the required 36 states had ratified the amendment, and women at last had the vote. "We are no longer petitioners," Catt announced in celebration. "We are not wards of the nation, but free and equal citizens." But the achievement of votes for women would not prove the triumph of feminism, nor the signal for the beginning of a new reform movement, that the women leaders believed at the time.

Planning for Peace

Woodrow Wilson turned U.S. participation in the war into a religious crusade to change the nature of international relations. It was a war to make the world safe for democracy—and more. On January 8, 1918, in part to counteract the Bolshevik charge that the war was merely a struggle among imperialist powers, he announced his plan to organize the peace. Called the Fourteen Points, it argued for "open covenants of peace openly arrived at," freedom of the seas, equality of trade, the self-determination of all peoples. But his most important point, the fourteenth, called for an international organization, a "league of nations," to preserve peace.

The Paris Peace Conference

Late in 1918, Wilson announced that he would head the American delegation in Paris, revealing his belief that he alone could overcome the forces of greed and imperialism in Europe and bring peace to the world. Wilson and his entourage of college professors, technical experts, and advisers set sail for Paris on the *George Washington* on

December 4, 1918. Secretary of State Lansing, Edward House, and a number of other advisers were there; conspicuously missing, however, was Henry Cabot Lodge, the most powerful man in the Senate, or any other Republican senator.

This would prove a serious blunder, for the Republican-controlled Senate would have to approve any treaty negotiated in Paris. It is difficult to explain Wilson's lack of political insight, except that he disliked Lodge intensely and hated political bargaining and compromise. Preferring to announce great principles, he had supreme confidence in his ability to persuade and to get his way by appealing to the people.

Wilson's self-confidence grew during a triumphant tour through Europe before the conference. The ordinary people greeted him like a savior who had brought the tragic war to an end. The American president had greater difficulty convincing the political leaders at the peace conference of his genius or his special grace. In Paris, he faced the reality of European power politics and ambitions and the personalities of David Lloyd George of Great Britain, Vittorio Orlando of Italy, and Georges Clemenceau of France.

Though Wilson was more naive and more idealistic than his European counterparts, he was a clever negotiator who won many concessions at the peace table, sometimes by threatening to go home if his counterparts would not compromise. The European leaders were determined to punish Germany and enlarge their empires. Wilson, however, believed that he could create a new kind of international relations based on his Fourteen Points. He achieved limited acceptance of the idea of self-determination, his dream that each national group could have its own country and that the people should decide in what country they wanted to live.

The peacemakers carved the new countries of Austria, Hungary, and Yugoslavia out of what had been the Austro-Hungarian Empire. In addition, they created Poland, Czechoslovakia, Finland, Estonia, Latvia, and Lithuania, in part to help contain the threat of bolshevism in eastern Europe. France was to occupy the industrial Saar region of Germany for 15 years with a plebiscite at the end of that time to determine whether the people wanted to become a part of Germany or France. Italy gained the port city of Trieste, but not the neigh-boring city of Fiume with its largely Italian-speaking population. Dividing up the map of Europe was difficult at best, but perhaps the biggest mistake that Wilson and other major leaders made was to give the small nations little power at the negotiating table and to exclude Soviet Russia entirely.

Wilson won some points at the peace negotiations, but he also had to make major concessions. He was forced to agree that Germany should pay reparations (later set at $56 billion), lose much of its oil- and coal-rich territory, and admit to its war guilt. He accepted a mandate system, to be supervised by the League of Nations, that allowed France and Britain to take over portions of the Middle East and allowed Japan to occupy Germany's colonies in the Pacific. He acquiesced when the Allies turned Germany's African colonies into "mandate possessions" because they did not want to allow the self-determination of blacks in areas they had colonized.

This was not a "peace without victory," and the sense of betrayal the German people felt would later have grave repercussions. Wilson also did not win approval for freedom of the seas or the abolition of trade barriers, but he did gain endorsement for the League of Nations, the organization he hoped would prevent all future wars. The League consisted of a council of the five great powers, elected delegates from the smaller countries, and a World Court to settle disputes. But the key to collective security was contained in Article 10 of the League covenant, which pledged all members "to respect and preserve against external aggression the territorial integrity" of all other members.

Women for Peace

While the statesmen met at Versailles to sign the peace treaty hammered out in Paris and to divide up Europe, a group of prominent and successful women—lawyers, physicians, administrators, and writers from all over the world, including many from the Central Powers—met in Zurich, Switzerland. The American delegation was led by Jane Addams and included Florence Kelley of the National Consumers League; Alice Hamilton, a professor at Harvard Medical School; and Jeannette Rankin. As congresswoman from Montana (one of the few states where women could vote),

The Big Four in December 1919: Italy's Orlando, Britain's Lloyd George, France's Clemenceau, and the United States' Wilson. (The Granger Collection, New York)

Rankin had voted against the war resolution in 1917. Some of the women who gathered at Zurich had met in 1915 at The Hague, in the Netherlands, to propose an end to the war through mediation. Now they met amid the devastation of war to promote a peace that would last. At their conference, they formed the Women's International League for Peace and Freedom. Electing Addams president of the new organization, they denounced the harsh peace terms, which called for disarmament of only one side and exacted great economic penalties against the Central Powers. Prophetically, they predicted that the peace treaty would result in the spread of hatred and anarchy and "create all over Europe discords and animosities which can only lead to future wars."

Hate and intolerance were legacies of the war. They were present at the Versailles peace conference, where Clemenceau especially wanted to humiliate Germany for the destruction of French lives and property. Also hanging over the conference was the Bolshevik success in Russia. Lenin's vision of a communist world order, led by workers, conflicted sharply with Wilson's dream of an anti-imperialist, free-trade, capitalist world. The threat of revolution seemed so great that Wilson and the Allies sent American and Japanese troops into Russia in 1919 to attempt to defeat the Bolsheviks and create a moderate republic. But by 1920, the troops had failed in their mission. They withdrew, but Russians never forgot the event, and the threat of bolshevism remained.

Wilson's Failed Dream

Probably most Americans supported the concept of the League of Nations in the summer of 1919. A few, like former senator Albert Beveridge of Indiana, an ardent nationalist, denounced the League as the work of "amiable old male grannies who, over their afternoon tea, are planning to denationalize America and denationalize the nation's manhood." But 33 governors endorsed the plan. Yet in the end, the Senate refused to accept American membership in the League. The League of Nations treaty, one commentator has suggested, was killed by its friends and not by its enemies.

First there was Lodge, who had earlier endorsed the idea of some kind of international peacekeeping organization but who objected to Article 10, claiming that it would force Americans to fight the wars of foreigners. Chairman of the Senate Foreign Relations Committee, Lodge, like Wilson, was a lawyer and a scholar as well as a

TIMELINE

1914 Archduke Ferdinand assassinated; World War I begins

United States declares neutrality

American troops invade Mexico and occupy Veracruz

1915 Germany announces submarine blockade of Great Britain

Lusitania sunk

Arabic pledge

Marines land in Haiti

1916 Army Reorganization Bill

Expedition into Mexico

Wilson reelected

Workmen's Compensation Bill

Keatings-Owen Child Labor Bill

Federal Farm Loan Act

National Women's Party founded

1917 Germany resumes unrestricted submarine warfare

United States breaks relations with Germany

Zimmermann telegram

Russian Revolution

United States declares war on Germany

War Revenue Act

Espionage Act

Committee on Public Information established

Trading with the Enemy Act

Selective Service Act

War Industries Board formed

1918 Sedition Act

Flu epidemic sweeps nation

Wilson's Fourteen Points

American troops intervene in Russian Revolution

1919 Paris peace conference

Eighteenth Amendment prohibits alcoholic beverages

Senate rejects Treaty of Versailles

1920 Nineteenth Amendment grants woman suffrage

politician. But in background and personality, he was very different from Wilson. A Republican senator since 1893, he had great faith in the power and prestige of the Senate. He disliked all Democrats, especially Wilson, whose idealism and missionary zeal infuriated him.

Then there was Wilson, whose only hope of passage of the treaty in the Senate was a compromise to bring moderate senators to his side. But Wilson refused to compromise or to modify Article 10 to allow Congress the opportunity to decide whether the United States would support the League in time of crisis. Angry at his opponents, who were exploiting the disagreement for political advantage, he stumped the country to convince the American people of the rightness of his plan. The people did not need to be convinced. They greeted Wilson much the way the people of France had. Traveling by train, he gave 37 speeches in 29 cities in the space of three weeks. When he described the graves of American soldiers in France and announced that American boys would never again die in a foreign war, the people responded with applause.

After one dramatic speech in Pueblo, Colorado, Wilson collapsed. His health had been failing for some months, and the strain of the trip was too much. He was rushed back to Washington, where a few days later he suffered a massive stroke. For the next year and a half, the president was incapable of running the government. Protected by his second wife and his closest advisers, Wilson became irritable and depressed and unable to lead a fight for the League. For a year and a half, the country limped along without a president.

After many votes and much maneuvering, the Senate finally killed the League treaty in March 1920. Had the United States joined the League of Nations, it probably would have made little difference in the international events of the 1920s and 1930s. Nor would American participation have prevented World War II. The United States did not resign from the world of diplomacy or trade, nor did the United States with that single act become isolated from the rest of the world. But the rejection of the League treaty was symbolic of the refusal of many Americans to admit that the world and America's place in it had changed dramatically since 1914.

Conclusion

The Divided Legacy of the Great War

For Edmund Arpin and many of his friends, who left small towns and urban neighborhoods to join the military forces, the war was a great adventure. For the next decades, at American Legion conventions and Armistice Day parades, they continued to celebrate their days of glory. For others who served, the war's results were more tragic. Many died. Some came home injured, disabled by poison gas, or unable to cope with the complex world that had opened up to them.

In a larger sense, the war was both a triumph and a tragedy for the American people. The war created opportunities for blacks who migrated to the North, for women who found more rewarding jobs, and for farmers who suddenly discovered a demand for their products. But much of the promise and the hope proved temporary.

The war provided a certain climax to the progressive movement. The passage of the woman suffrage amendment and the use of federal power in a variety of ways to promote justice and order pleased reformers, who had been working toward these ends for many decades. But the results were often disappointing. Once the war ended, much federal legislation was dismantled or reduced in effectiveness and votes for women had little initial impact on social legislation.

The Great War marked the coming of age of the United States as a world power, but the country seemed reluctant to accept the new responsibility. The war stimulated patriotism and pride in the country, but it also increased intolerance. With this mixed legacy from the war, the country entered the new era of the 1920s.

Recommended Reading

General Accounts

James Toll, *The Origins of the First World War* (1984); Frank Freidel, *Over There: The Story of America's First Great Overseas Crusade* (1964); Daniel M. Smith, *The Great Departure: The United States and World War I, 1914–1919* (1965); Ellis W. Hawley, *The Great War and the Search for Modern Order* (1979); Barbara W. Tuchman, *The Guns of August* (1962); Martin Gilbert, *The First World War: A Complete Account* (1994).

Diplomacy and Peace

D. F. Cline, *The United States and Mexico* (1953); P. Edward Haley, *Revolution and Intervention* (1970); C. C. Clemenden, *The United States and Pancho Villa* (1961); Robert H. Ferrell, *Woodrow Wilson and World War I* (1985); Ernest R. May, *The World War and American Isolation* (1966); N. Gordon Levin, Jr., *Woodrow Wilson and World Politics* (1968); Christopher Lasch, *The American Liberals and the Russian Revolution* (1962); C. Roland Marchand, *The American Peace Movement and Social Reform* (1973); Charles DeBenedetti, *Origins of the Modern Peace Movement* (1978).

The Battlefield Experience and Beyond

Edward M. Coffman, *The War to End All Wars: The American Military Experience in World War I* (1968); Lawrence Stallings, *The Doughboys: The Story of the AEF, 1917–1918* (1963); Arthur D. Barbeau and Florette Henri, *The Unknown Soldiers: Black American Troops in World War I* (1974); John

Ellis, *The Social History of the Machine Gun* (1975); Paul Fussell, *The Great War and Modern Memory* (1975); Michael C. C. Adams, *The Great Adventure: Male Desire and the Coming of World War I* (1990); Dorothy Goldman, *Women Writers and the Great War* (1995).

The War at Home

David M. Kennedy, *Over Here: The First World War and American Society* (1980); Maurine W. Greenwald, *Women, War, and Work* (1980); Carol S. Gruber, *Mars and Minerva: World War I and the Uses of Higher Learning in America* (1975); Donald Johnson, *The Challenge to American Freedoms: World War I and the Rise of the American Civil Liberties Union* (1963); Frederick C. Luebke, *Bonds of Loyalty: German-Americans and World War I* (1974); Florette Henri, *Black Migration: Movement Northward, 1900–1920* (1975); Michael I. Isenberg, *War on Film* (1981); Stanley Cooperman, *World War I and the American Novel* (1970); Ronald Schaffer, *America in the Great War: The Rise of the War Welfare State* (1991).

Fiction

Erich Maria Remarque highlights the horror of the war in his classic *All Quiet on the Western Front* (1929); John Dos Passos describes the war as a bitter experience in *Three Soldiers* (1921); and Ernest Hemingway portrays its futility in *A Farewell to Arms* (1929).

CHAPTER 23

Affluence and Anxiety

*J*ohn and Lizzie Parker were black sharecroppers who lived in a "stubborn, ageless hut squatted on a little hill" in central Alabama. They had two daughters, one age 6, the other already married. The whole family worked hard in the cotton fields, but they had little to show for their labor. One day in 1917, Lizzie straightened her shoulders and declared, "I'm through. I've picked my last sack of cotton. I've cleared my last field."

Like many southern African Americans, the Parkers sought opportunity and a better life in the North. World War I cut off the flow of immigrants from Europe, and suddenly there was a shortage of workers. Some companies sent special trains into the South to recruit

African Americans. John Parker signed up with a mining company in West Virginia. The company offered free transportation for his family. "You will be allowed to get your food at the company store and there are houses awaiting for you," the agent promised.

The sound of the train whistle seemed to promise better days ahead for her family as Lizzie gathered her possessions and headed north. But it turned out that the houses in the company town in West Virginia were little better than those they left in Alabama. After deducting for rent and for supplies from the company store, almost no money was left at the end of the week. John hated the dirty and dangerous work in the mine and realized that he would never get ahead by staying there. Instead of venting his anger on his white boss, he ran away, leaving his family in West Virginia.

John drifted to Detroit, where he got a job with the American Car and Foundry Company. It was 1918, and the pay was good, more than he had ever made before. After a few weeks, he rented an apartment and sent for his family. For the first time, Lizzie had a gas stove and an indoor toilet, and Sally, who was now seven, started school. It seemed as if their dream had come true. John had always believed that if he worked hard and treated his fellow man fairly, he would succeed.

Detroit was not quite the dream, however. It was crowded with all kinds of migrants, attracted by the wartime jobs at the Ford Motor Company and other factories. The new arrivals increased the racial tension already present in the city. Sally was beaten up by a gang of white youths at school. Even in their neighborhood, which had been solidly Jewish before their arrival, the shopkeeper and the old residents made it clear that they did not like blacks moving into their community. The Ku Klux Klan, which gained many new members in Detroit, also made life uncomfortable for the blacks who had moved north to seek jobs and opportunity. Suddenly the war ended, and almost immediately John lost his job. Then the landlord raised the rent, and the Parkers were forced to leave their apartment for housing in a section just outside the city near Eight Mile Road. The surrounding suburbs had paved streets, wide lawns, and elegant houses, but this black ghetto had dirt streets and shacks that reminded the Parkers of the company town where they had lived in West Virginia. Lizzie had to get along without her bathroom. Here there was no indoor plumbing and no electricity, only a pump in the yard and an outhouse.

The recession winter of 1921–1922 was particularly difficult. The auto industry and the other companies laid off most of their workers. John could find only part-time employment, while Lizzie worked as a domestic servant for white families. Because no bus route connected the black community to surrounding suburbs, she often had to trek miles through the snow. The shack they called home was freezing cold, and it was cramped because their married daughter and her husband had joined them in Detroit.

Lizzie did not give up her dream, however. With strength, determination, and a sense of humor, she kept the family together. In 1924, Sally entered high school. By the end of the decade, Sally had graduated from high school, and the Parkers finally had electricity and indoor plumbing in the house, though the streets were still unpaved. Those unpaved streets stood as a symbol of their unfulfilled dream. The Parkers, like most of the African Americans who moved north in the decade after World War I, had improved their lot, but they still lived outside Detroit—and, in many ways, outside America.

The movies, illegal liquor, the stock market, and the new jazz dances all appear in Thomas Hart Benton's painting of the pleasures of urban life in the 1920s. (City Activities with Dance Hall, 1930, Courtesy Maurice Segoura Gallery, New York)

Bartolomeo Vanzetti and Nicola Sacco, immortalized in paintings by Ben Shahn, became important symbols for liberals fighting prejudice in the 1920s. (Bartolomeo Vanzetti and Nicola Sacco, (1931–32). Tempera on paper over composition board, 10-1/2 × 14-1/2". (Gift of Abby Aldrich Rockefeller Photograph © 1997 The Museum of Modern Art, New York)

two were executed in the electric chair on August 23, 1927. But the case and the cause would not die. On the fiftieth anniversary of their deaths in 1977, Governor Michael Dukakis of Massachusetts exonerated Sacco and Vanzetti and cleared their names.

Religious Intolerance

The KKK and well-publicized cases like Sacco-Vanzetti touched a relatively small number of people, but a general spirit of intolerance permeated the decade and influenced the lives of millions. In Dearborn, Michigan, Henry Ford published anti-Semitic diatribes in the *Dearborn Independent* and many country clubs and resort hotels prohibited Jews from even entering the doors. Unable to frequent the fashionable resorts, Jews built their own in the Catskills in New York State, Long Branch in New Jersey, and other areas. Many colleges, private academies, and medical schools had Jewish quotas, some openly and others informally, and many suburbs explicitly limited residents to "Christians." Catholics, too, were prohibited from many fashionable and fraternal organizations as well as many country clubs, but unlike Jews, Catholics created their own

schools and colleges. Few Catholics even tried to enroll in the elite colleges where bias against Catholics and Catholicism remained. There had always been a great deal of prejudice and intolerance in the United States, but during the decade of the 1920s, much of that intolerance was made more fixed and formal.

A Prospering Economy

Although the decade after World War I was a time of intolerance and anxiety, it was also a time of industrial expansion and widespread prosperity. After recovering from a postwar depression in 1921 and 1922, the economy took off. Fueled by new technology, more efficient planning and management, and innovative advertising, industrial production almost doubled during the decade, and the gross national product rose by an astonishing 40 percent. A construction boom created new suburbs around American cities, and a new generation of skyscrapers transformed the cities themselves. However, the benefits of this prosperity fell unevenly on the many social groups forming American society.

The Rising Standard of Living

Signs of the new prosperity appeared in many forms. Millions of sturdy homes and apartments were built and equipped with the latest conveniences. The number of telephones installed nearly doubled between 1915 and 1930. Plastics, rayon, and cellophane altered the habits of millions of Americans, and new products, such as cigarette lighters, reinforced concrete, dry ice, and Pyrex glass, created new demands unheard of a decade before.

Perhaps the most tangible sign of the new prosperity was the modern American bathroom. For years, the various functions we associate with the bathroom were separated. There was an outhouse or privy, a portable tin bathtub filled with water heated on the kitchen stove, and a pitcher and washbasin in the bedroom. Hotels and the urban upper class began to install cast-iron bathtubs and primitive flush toilets in the late nineteenth cen-

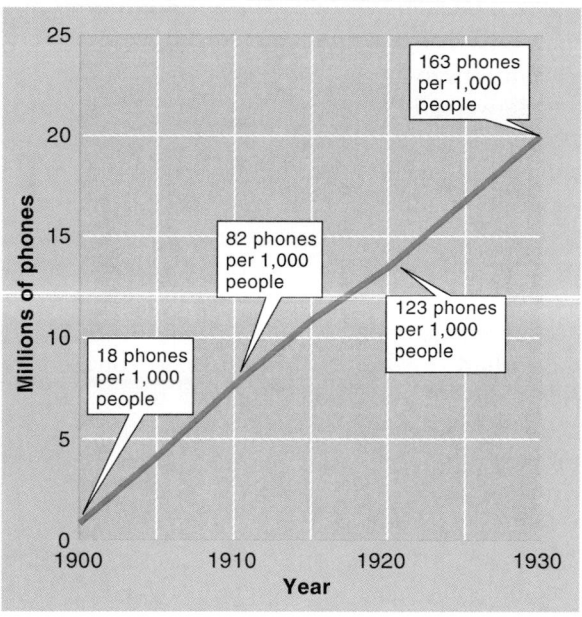

Telephones in Use, 1900–1930

163 phones per 1,000 people

82 phones per 1,000 people

123 phones per 1,000 people

18 phones per 1,000 people

Millions of phones

Year

The telephone, though still a primitive instrument in the 1920s, changed business practices, social life, and even dating customs for the middle class. Source: U.S. Bureau of the Census.

tury, but not until the early 1920s did the enameled tub, toilet, and washbasin become standard. By 1925, American factories turned out 5 million enameled bathroom fixtures annually. The bathroom, with unlimited hot water, privacy, and clean white fixtures, symbolized American affluence.

In sharp contrast to the nineteenth century, Americans had more leisure time. Persistent efforts by labor unions had gradually reduced the 60-hour workweek of the late nineteenth century to a 45-hour week. Paid vacations, unheard of in the nineteenth century, also became prevalent. In 1916, only 16 of 389 establishments studied provided paid vacations; by 1926, some 40 percent of 250 companies gave their workers at least one week of vacation with pay.

The American diet also improved during the decade. The consumption of cornmeal and potatoes declined, but the sale of fresh vegetables increased by 45 percent. Health improved and life expectancy increased. But Americans did not share the advantages of better health and more leisure evenly. A white male born in 1900 had a life

expectancy of 48 years and a white female of 51 years. By 1930, these figures had increased to 59 and 63 years, respectively. For a black male born in 1900, however, the life expectancy was only 33 years, and for the black female, 35 years. These figures increased to 48 and 47 by 1930, but the discrepancy remained.

Yet almost all Americans benefited to some extent from the new prosperity. Some took advantage of expanding educational opportunities. In 1900, only one in ten young people of high school age remained in school. By 1930, that number had increased to six in ten, and much of the improvement came in the 1920s. In 1900, only 1 college-age person in 33 attended an institution of higher learning; by 1930, the ratio was 1 in 7. Over 1 million people were enrolled in the nation's colleges.

The Rise of the Modern Corporation

The structure and practice of American business were transformed in the 1920s. After a crisis created by the economic downturn of 1920–1922, business boomed until the crash of 1929. Mergers increased during the decade at a rate greater than at any time since the end of the 1890s—there were more than 1,200 mergers in 1929 alone—creating such giants as General Electric, General Motors, Sears Roebuck, Du Pont, and U.S. Rubber. These were not monopolies but oligopolies (industry domination spread among a few large firms). By 1930, the 200 largest corporations controlled almost half the corporate wealth in the country. Large businesses also diversified during the decade. GE and Westinghouse began to produce household appliances and radios; Du Pont moved into plastics, paints, dyes, and film.

Perhaps the most important business trend of the decade was the emergence of a new kind of manager. No longer did family entrepreneurs make decisions relating to prices, wages, or output. Alfred P. Sloan, Jr., an engineer who reorganized General Motors, was a prototype of the new kind of manager. He divided the company into components, freeing the top managers to concentrate on planning new products, controlling inventory, and integrating the whole operation. Marketing and advertising became as important as production, and many businesses began to spend more money on research. The new manager often had a large staff, but owned no part of the company. He was usually an expert at cost accounting and analyzing data. Increasingly, he was a graduate of one of the new business colleges.

Continuing and extending the trends started by Frederick Taylor before World War I, the new managers tried to keep employees working efficiently, but they used more than the stopwatch and the assembly line. They introduced pensions, recreation facilities, cafeterias, and, in some cases, paid vacations and profit-sharing plans. The managers were not being altruistic, however; "welfare capitalism" was designed to reduce worker discontent and to discourage labor unions.

Planning was the key to the new corporate structure, and planning often meant a continuation of the business-government cooperation that had developed during World War I. Experts from philanthropic foundations, the National Bureau of Economic Research, and the U.S. Department of Commerce worked together hoping that they could provide a middle ground between collectivism and laissez-faire economy. All the planning and the new managerial authority failed to prevent the economic collapse of 1929, but the modern corporation survived the depression to exert a growing influence on American life in the 1930s and after.

Electrification

The 1920s also marked the climax of the "second industrial revolution." During the late nineteenth century, American industry had primarily manufactured goods intended for other producers. In the first quarter of the twentieth century, as industries like coal, textiles, and steel stabilized or declined, new manufacturing concerns that produced rubber, synthetic fabrics, chemicals, and petroleum arose. They focused on goods for consumers, such as silk stockings, washing machines, and cars.

Powering the second industrial revolution was electricity—a form of energy that rapidly replaced steam power after 1900. In the previous two decades, inventors such as Thomas A. Edison and George Westinghouse had developed generators for producing electric current and methods for transmitting it and using it to drive machinery. Edison's illuminating company opened the first commercial power station in New York in 1882; by the end of the century, more than 3,000 stations were supplying businesses and homes with electricity. Meanwhile, Edison's most famous invention, the electric light bulb, was rapidly replacing gas lanterns in homes and on streets.

Between 1900 and 1920, the replacement of steam power by electricity worked as profound a change as had the substitution of steam power for water power after the Civil War. In 1902, electricity supplied a mere 2 percent of all industrial power; by 1929, fully 80 percent derived from electrical generators. Less than one of every ten American homes was supplied with electricity in 1907, but more than two-thirds were by 1929. Powered by electricity, American industries reached new heights of productivity. By 1929, the work force was turning out twice as many goods as a similarly sized work force had ten years before.

Electricity brought dozens of gadgets and laborsaving devices into the home. Washing machines and electric irons gradually reduced the drudgery of washday for women, and vacuum cleaners, electric toasters, and sewing machines lightened housework. But the new machines still needed human direction and did not reduce the time the average housewife spent doing housework. For many poor urban and rural women, the traditional female tasks of carrying water, pushing, pulling, and lifting went on as they had for centuries. In many ways, the success of the electric revolution increased the contrast in American life. The "Great White Ways" of the cities symbolized progress, but they also made the darkness of slums and hamlets seem even more forbidding.

Automobile Culture

Automobile manufacturing, like electrification, underwent spectacular growth in the 1920s. The automobile was one major factor in the postwar economic boom. It stimulated and transformed the petroleum, steel, and rubber industries. The auto forced the construction and improvement of streets and highways and caused the spending of millions of dollars on labor and concrete. In 1925, the secretary of agriculture approved the first uniform numbering system for the nation's highways, but it was still an adventure to drive from one city to another.

The auto created new suburbs and allowed families to live many miles from their work. The filling station, the diner, and the tourist court became familiar and eventually standardized objects on the American scene. Traffic lights, stop signs, billboards, and parking lots appeared. Hitching posts and watering troughs became rarer, and gradually the garage replaced the livery stable. The auto changed the look of the American landscape and threatened the environment as well. Oil and gasoline contaminated streams, and piles of old tires and rusting hulks of discarded cars became a familiar sight along the highways. At the same time, the emissions from thousands and then millions of internal combustion engines polluted the air. But there was no turning back. The age of the auto had replaced the age of the horse.

The auto changed American life in other ways. It led to the decline of the small crossroads store as well as many small churches because the rural family could now drive to the larger city or town. The tractor changed methods of farming. Trucks replaced the horse and wagon and altered the marketing of farm products. Buses began to eliminate the one-room school, because it was now possible to transport students to larger schools. The automobile allowed young people for the first time to escape the chaperoning of parents. It was hardly the "house of prostitution on wheels" that one judge called it, but it did change courting habits in all parts of the country.

Gradually, as the decade progressed, the automobile became not just transportation, but a sign of status. Advertising helped create the impression that it was the symbol of the good life, of sex, freedom, and speed. The auto in turn transformed advertising and design. It even altered the way products were purchased. By 1926, three-fourths of the cars sold were bought on some kind of deferred-payment plan. Installment credit, first tried by a group of businessmen in Toledo, Ohio, in 1915 to sell more autos, was soon used to promote sewing machines, refrigerators, and other consumer products. "Buy now, pay later" became the American way.

The United States had a love affair with the auto from the beginning. There were 8,000 motor vehicles registered in the country in 1900, and nearly a million in 1912. But only in the 1920s did the auto come within the reach of middle-class consumers. In 1929, Americans purchased 4.5 million cars, and by the end of that year, nearly 27 million were registered. Automobile culture was a mass movement.

The auto industry, like most American businesses, went through a period of consolidation in the 1920s. In 1908, more than 250 companies were manufacturing automobiles in the United States. By 1929, only 44 remained.

Many men contributed to the development and production of the auto—William Durant organized General Motors; Charles Kettering, an engineering genius, developed the electric self-starter; and Ransom E. Olds built the first mass-produced, moderately priced, light car. Above all the others loomed a name that would become synonymous with the automobile itself—Henry Ford.

Ford had the reputation of being a progressive industrial leader and a champion of the common people. As with all men and women who take on symbolic significance, the truth is less dramatic than the stories. Ford is often credited with inventing the assembly line. In actuality it was the work of a team of engineers. But the Ford Motor Company was the first organization to perfect the moving assembly line and mass-production technology. Introduced in 1913, the new method reduced the time it took to produce a car from 14 hours to an hour and a half. It was the perfect application of Frederick Taylor's system of breaking down each operation into its components, applying careful timing, and integrating the laborer with the machine. The product of the carefully planned system was the Model T, the prototype of the inexpensive family car.

In 1914, Ford startled the country by announcing that he was increasing the minimum pay of the Ford assembly-line worker to $5 a day (almost twice the national average pay for factory workers). Ford was not a humanitarian. He wanted a dependable work force and understood that skilled workers were less likely to quit if they received good pay. Ford was one of the first to appreciate that workers were consumers as well as producers and that they might buy Model T Fords. But work in the Ford factory had its disadvantages. Work on the assembly line was repetitious and numbing. "You could drop over dead" one worker recalled, "and they wouldn't stop the line." And when the line closed down, as it did periodically, the workers were released without compensation.

Henry Ford was not an easy man for whom to work. One newspaper account in 1928 called him "an industrial fascist—the Mussolini of Detroit." He ruthlessly pressured his dealers and used them to

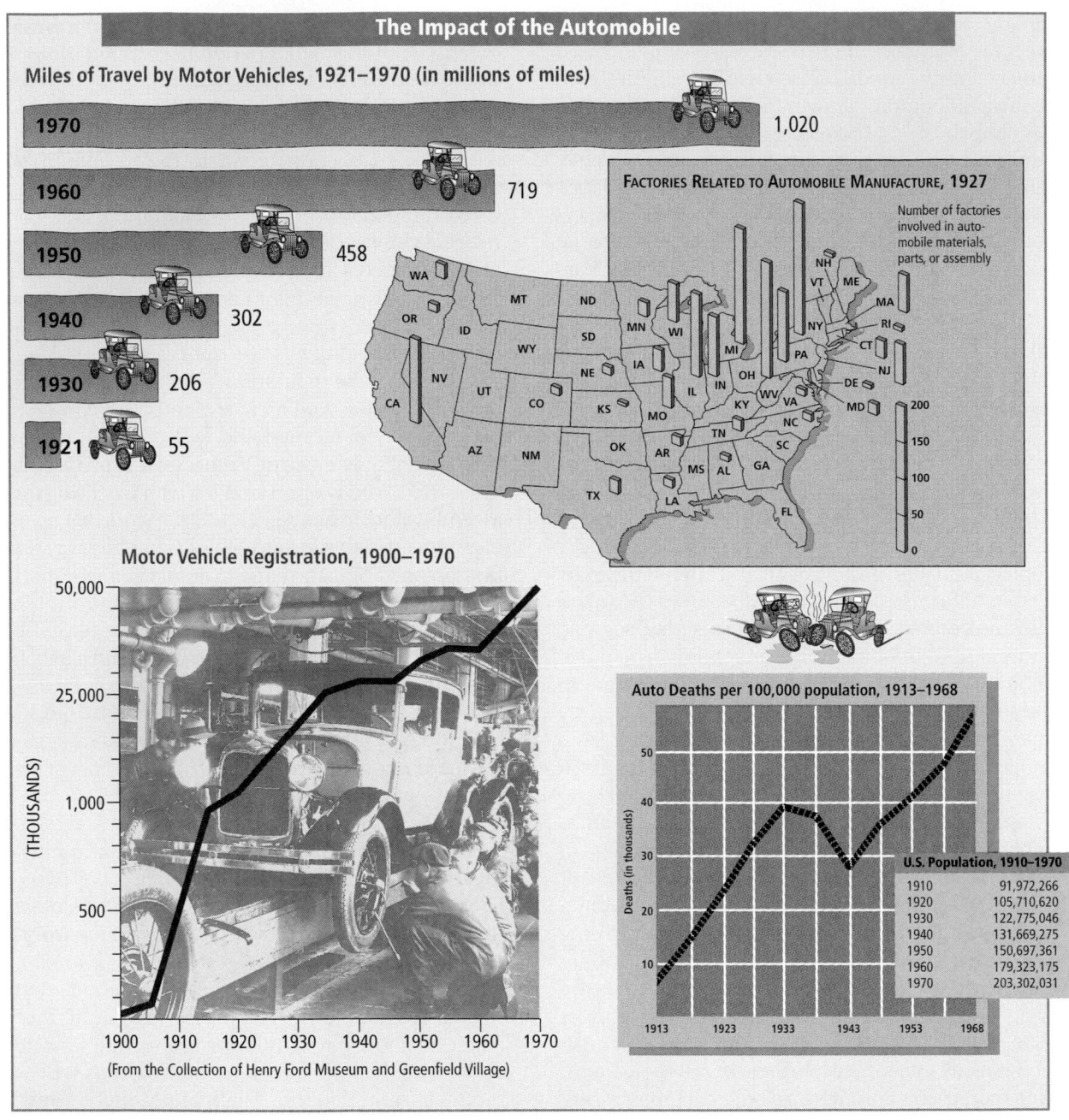

The Impact of the Automobile

Miles of Travel by Motor Vehicles, 1921–1970 (in millions of miles)

1970   1,020
1960   719
1950   458
1940   302
1930   206
1921   55

FACTORIES RELATED TO AUTOMOBILE MANUFACTURE, 1927

Number of factories involved in automobile materials, parts, or assembly

200
150
100
50
0

Motor Vehicle Registration, 1900–1970

(THOUSANDS)

50,000
25,000
1,000
500

1900 1910 1920 1930 1940 1950 1960 1970

(From the Collection of Henry Ford Museum and Greenfield Village)

Auto Deaths per 100,000 population, 1913–1968

Deaths (in thousands)

50
40
30
20
10

1913   1923   1933   1943   1953   1968

U.S. Population, 1910–1970	
1910	91,972,266
1920	105,710,620
1930	122,775,046
1940	131,669,275
1950	150,697,361
1960	179,323,175
1970	203,302,031

bail him out of difficult financial situations. Instead of borrowing money from a bank, he forced dealers to buy extra cars, trucks, and tractors. He used spies on the assembly lines and fired workers and executives at the least provocation. But he did produce a car that transformed America.

The Model T, which cost $600 in 1912, was reduced gradually in price until it sold for only $290 in 1924. The "Tin Lizzie," as it was affectionately called, was light and easily repaired. Some owners claimed all one needed was a pair of pliers and some baling wire to keep it running. If it got stuck on bad roads, as it often did, it could be lifted out by a reasonably healthy man. Replacement parts were standardized and widely available.

The Model T did not change from year to year, and it did not deviate from its one color, black. Except for adding a self-starter, offering a closed model, and making a few minor face-lift changes, Ford kept the Model T in 1927 much as he had introduced it in 1909. By that time, its popularity had declined as many people traded up to sleeker, more colorful, and, they thought, more prestigious autos put out by Ford's competitors, and wages at Ford dipped below the industry average. The Model A, introduced in 1927, was never as popular or as successful as the Model T, but the gigantic River Rouge factory, built especially to produce the new model, became the symbol of mass production in the new era.

The Exploding Metropolis

The automobile caused American cities to expand into the countryside. In the late nineteenth century, railroads and streetcars had created suburbs near the major cities, but the great expansion of suburban population occurred in the 1920s. Shaker Heights, a Cleveland suburb, was in some ways a typical development. Built on the site of a former Shaker community, the new suburb was planned and developed by two businessmen. They controlled the size and style of the homes and restricted buyers. No blacks were allowed. Curving roads led off the main auto boulevards, and landscaping and natural areas contributed to a parklike atmosphere. The suburb increased in population from 1,700 in 1919 to over 15,000 in 1929, and the price of lots multiplied by 10 during the decade.

Other suburbs grew in an equally spectacular manner. Beverly Hills, near Los Angeles, increased in population by 2,485 percent during the decade. Grosse Point Park, near Detroit, grew by 725 percent, and Elmwood Park, near Chicago, by 716 percent. The automobile also allowed industry to move to the suburbs. Employees in manufacturing establishments in the suburbs of the 11 largest cities increased from 365,000 in 1919 to 1.2 million in 1937.

Barger, Texas, "as it was in 1926 in the middle of its rise from road crossing to an oil city," here depicted by Thomas Hart Benton, one of the best known of the regionalist painters. (Memorial Art Gallery of the University of Rochester; Marion Stratton Gould Fund)

Advertising

Have you ever noticed that television commercials can often be more interesting and creative than the programs? One authority has suggested that the best way for a foreign visitor to understand the American character and popular culture is to study television commercials. Television advertising, the thesis goes, appeals to basic cultural assumptions. The nature of advertising not only reveals for historians the prejudices, fears, values, and aspirations of a people, but also makes an impact on historical development itself, influencing patterns of taste and purchasing habits. One modern critic calls advertising a "peculiarly American force that now compares with such long-standing institutions as the school and church in the magnitude of its social impact."

As long as manufacturing was local and limited, there was no need to advertise. Before the Civil War, for example, the local area could usually absorb all that was produced; therefore, a simple announcement in a local paper was sufficient to let people know that a particular product was available. But when factories began producing more than the local market could ordinarily consume, advertising came into play to create a larger demand.

Although national advertising began with the emergence of "name brands" in the late nineteenth century, it did not achieve the importance it now holds until the 1920s. In 1918, the total gross advertising revenue in magazines was $58.5 million. By 1920, it had more than doubled to $129.5 million, and by 1929, it was nearly $200 million. These figures should not be surprising in a decade that often equated advertising with religion. The biblical Moses was called the "ad-writer for the Deity," and in a best-selling book, Bruce Barton, a Madison Avenue advertiser, reinterpreted Jesus, the "man nobody knows," as a master salesman. Wrote Barton: "He would be a national advertiser today."

The designers of ads began to study psychology to determine what motives, conscious or unconscious, influenced consumers. One psychologist concluded that the appeal to the human instinct for "gaining social prestige" would sell the most goods. Another way to sell products, many learned, was to create anxiety in the mind of the consumer over body odor, bad breath, oily hair, dandruff, pimples, and other embarrassing ailments. In 1921, the Lambert Company used the term *halitosis* for bad breath in an ad for Listerine. Within six years, sales of Listerine had increased from a little over 100,000 bottles a year to more than 4 million.

The appeal to sex also sold products, advertisers soon found, as did the desire for the latest style or invention. But perhaps the most important thing advertisers marketed was youth. "We are going to sell every artificial thing there is," a cosmetic salesman wrote in 1926, "and above all it is going to be young-young-young! We make women feel young." A great portion of the ads were aimed at women. As one trade journal announced: "The proper study of mankind is man ..., but the proper study of markets is woman."

Mouthwash advertisement.

Look at the accompanying advertisements carefully. What do they tell you about American culture in the 1920s? What do they suggest about attitudes toward women? Do they reveal any special anxieties? How are they similar to and different from advertising today?

Automobile advertisement (1929). (Corbis-Bettmann)

For Clean-up King
I Nominate . . .

by LOU GEHRIG

New York Yankees' Clean-up Ace Makes
Novel Choice for All-Time Honor

I DON'T need to tell baseball fans how important the "clean-up" (number four) man is in the batting line-up. With three reliable hitters batting ahead of him, it is his wallops that bring in the runs.

In my thirteen years of big league baseball I have watched some of the most famous "clean-up" men in the history of the game. But the other day in Boston I had the pleasure of seeing the "clean-up" king that gets my vote for the "all-time" honors. Strangely enough, this "clean-up" king isn't a slugger at all. Instead of cleaning up the bases, this one's specialty is cleaning up faces.

Here's how it happened. While in Boston playing the Red Sox, I made an inspection trip through the Gillette Safety Razor factory. There I discovered that what is true of baseball is also true of Gillette Blades. In baseball, the pick of the raw material is tried out, tested, and trained for the big league teams. At the Gillette factory I found that they buy only the finest steel, and put it through gruelling tests before it is made into Gillette Blades.

For instance, like a rookie baseball player, Gillette Blade steel has to be hardened and tempered.

To do this, Gillette uses electric furnaces, each one controlled by a device which can tell in an instant if the steel passing through the furnaces requires more heat or less heat. Faster than a speedball, the signal is flashed from the box to a great battery of switches, and the heat is raised or lowered accordingly. Then to make doubly sure that there is no possibility of error, they X-ray the steel with an electro-magnetic tester to detect hidden flaws.

A good ball player has to have precision and accuracy, too . . . and that's where Gillette chalks up a winning score. Grinding machines, adjustable to 1/10,000 of an inch give Gillette Blades shaving edges so keen you can't see them, even with the most powerful microscope.

These are some of the reasons why I nominate the Gillette Blade for all-time Clean-up King. For when it comes to cleaning up on stubborn bristles—with the greatest of ease and comfort—Gillette hits a home run with the bases loaded. Yes, Sir!—if baseball could only train players as accurately and efficiently as Gillette makes razor blades, we'd all find it easy to bat 1000.

With these important facts before you, why let anyone deprive you of shaving comfort by selling you a substitute! Ask for Gillette Blades and be sure to get them.

GILLETTE SAFETY RAZOR COMPANY, BOSTON, MASS.

Razor blade advertisement.
(R. Kravette, Jericho, New York)

809

Ten Largest Cities in 1900 and 1930*			
1900		1930	
1. New York	4,023,000	1. New York	9,423,000
2. Chicago	1,768,000	2. Chicago	3,870,000
3. Philadelphia	1,458,000	3. Philadelphia	2,399,000
4. Boston	905,000	4. Detroit	1,837,000
5. Pittsburgh	622,000	5. Los Angeles	1,778,000
6. St. Louis	612,000	6. Boston	1,545,000
7. Baltimore	543,000	7. Pittsburgh	1,312,000
8. San Francisco	444,000	8. San Francisco	1,104,000
9. Cincinnati	414,000	9. St. Louis	1,094,000
10. Cleveland	402,000	10. Cleveland	1,048,000

*Figures are for the entire metropolitan areas, including suburbs.
Source: U.S. Bureau of the Census.

The biggest land boom of all occurred in Florida, where the city of Miami mushroomed from 30,000 in 1920 to 75,000 in 1925. One plot of land in West Palm Beach sold for $800,000 in 1923 and two years later was worth $4 million. A hurricane in 1926 ended the Florida land boom temporarily, but most cities and their suburbs continued to grow during the decade.

The census of 1920 indicated that for the first time, more than half the population of the United States lived in "urban areas" of more than 2,500. The census designation of an urban area was a little misleading because a town of 5,000 could still be more rural than urban. A more significant concept was the metropolitan area of at least 100,000 people. There were only 52 of these areas in 1900, but in 1930 there were 115.

The automobile transformed every city, but the most spectacular growth of all took place in two cities that the car virtually created. Detroit grew from 300,000 in 1900 to 1,837,000 in 1930, and Los Angeles expanded from 114,000 in 1900 to 1,778,000 in 1930. With sprawling subdivisions connected by a growing network of roads, Los Angeles was the city of the future.

Cities expanded horizontally during the 1920s, sprawling into the countryside, but city centers grew vertically. A building boom that peaked near the end of the decade created new skylines for most urban centers. Even cities such as Tulsa, Dallas, Kansas City, Memphis, and Syracuse built skyscrapers. By 1929, there were 377 buildings of over 20 stories in American cities. Many were started just before the stock market crash ended the building boom, and the empty offices stood as a stark reminder of the limits of expansion. The most famous skyscraper of all, the Empire State Building in New York, which towers 102 stories in the air, was finished in 1931, but not completely occupied until after World War II.

A Communications Revolution

Changing communications altered the way many Americans lived as well as the way they conducted business. The telephone was first demonstrated in 1876. By 1899, more than a million phones were in operation. During the 1920s, the number of homes with phones increased from 9 to 13 million. Still, by the end of the decade, more than half of American homes were without phones.

The radio even more than the telephone symbolized the technological and communicational changes of the 1920s. Department stores quickly began to stock radios, or crystal sets as they were called, but many Americans in the 1920s built their own receivers. The first station to begin commercial broadcasting was WWJ in Detroit in the summer of 1920. When WWJ and KDKA in Pittsburgh broadcast the election returns in 1920, they ushered in a new era in politics. The next year WJZ of Newark, New Jersey, broadcast the World Series, beginning a process that would transform baseball and eventually football and basketball as well. Five hundred stations took to the airwaves in 1922 alone, many of them sponsored by department stores, and others by newspapers and colleges. In the same year, a radio station in New York broadcast the first commercial, an indication that the airways would be used to increase the demand for the goods the factories were producing.

Much early broadcasting consisted of classical music, but soon came news analysis and coverage of presidential inaugurals and important events. Some stations produced live dramas, but it was the serials such as "Amos 'n' Andy" that more than any other programs made radio a national medium. Millions of people scattered across the country could sit in their living rooms (and after 1927, in their cars) listening to the same program. The record industry grew just as rapidly. By the end of the decade, people in all sections of the country were humming the same popular songs. Actors and announcers became celebrities. The music, voice, and sound of the radio, even more than the sound of the automobile, marked the end of silence and, to a certain extent, the end of privacy.

Even more dramatic was the phenomenon of the movies. Forty million viewers a week went to the movies in 1922, and by 1929, that had increased to over 100 million. Men, women, and children flocked to small theaters in the towns and to movie palaces in the cities, where they could dream of romance or adventure. Charlie Chaplin, Rudolph Valentino, Lillian Gish, and Greta Garbo were more famous and more important to millions of Americans than were most government officials. The motion pictures, which before the war had attracted mostly the working class, now seemed to appeal across class, regional, and generational lines.

The movies had the power to influence attitudes and ideas. In the 1920s, many parents feared that the movies would dictate ideas about sex and life. One young college woman remembered, "One day I went to see Viola Dana in *The Five Dollar Baby*. The scenes which showed her as a baby

Most farmers did not own a radio until the end of the 1930s when they finally got electricity, but for those living in the cities, the radio altered lives and brought a new magic of sound into 2 or 3 million households in the 1920s. This early radio was battery-powered and had an antenna wire (seen at left) that connected to an outside aerial antenna. Still, even with antenna and headset, the reception was probably poor. (Corbis-Bettmann)

Sports figures like Jack Dempsey, depicted here by artist George Bellows, became celebrities largely because of the radio and the newspapers. (Dempsey and Firpo, 1924/The Whitney Museum of American Art, New York)

fascinated me so that I stayed to see it over four times. I forgot home, dinner and everything. About eight o'clock mother came after me." She also admitted that the movies taught her how to smoke, and in some of the movies "there were some lovely scenes which just got me all hot 'n' bothered."

Not only movie stars became celebrities in the 1920s. Sports figures such as Babe Ruth, Bobby Jones, Jack Dempsey, and Red Grange were just as famous. The great spectator sports of the decade owed much to the increase of leisure time and to the automobile, the radio, and the mass-circulation newspaper. Thousands drove automobiles to college towns to watch football heroes perform. Millions listened for scores or read about the results the next day. One writer in 1924 called this era "the age of play." He might better have called it "the age of the spectator." The popularity of sports, like the movies and radio, was in part the product of technology.

The year 1927 seemed to mark the beginning of the new age of mechanization and progress. That was the year Henry Ford produced his fifteen millionth car and introduced the Model A. During that year, radio-telephone service was established between San Francisco and Manila. The first radio network was organized (CBS), and the first talking movie was released (*The Jazz Singer*). In 1927, the Holland Tunnel, the first underwater vehicular

roadway, connected New York and New Jersey. It was also the year that Charles Lindbergh flew from New York to Paris in his single-engine plane in 33 1/2 hours. Lindbergh was not the first to fly the Atlantic, but he was the first to fly it alone, an accomplishment that won him $25,000 in prize money and captured the world's imagination. He was young and handsome, and his feat seemed to represent not only the triumph of an individual, but also the triumph of the machine. Lindbergh never talked of his accomplishments in the first person; he always said "we," meaning his airplane as well. He was greeted by 4 million people when he returned to New York for a triumphant ticker-tape parade. Like many a movie star or sports hero, he had become an instant celebrity. When Americans cheered Lindbergh, they were reaffirming their belief in the American dream and their faith in individual initiative as well as in technology.

Hopes Raised, Promises Deferred

The 1920s was a time when all kinds of hopes seemed realizable. "Don't envy successful salesmen—be one!" one advertisement screamed. Buy a car. Build a house. Start a career. Invest in land. Invest in stocks. Make a fortune.

Charles Lindbergh standing next to his plane, "The Spirit of St. Louis." His feat of flying alone from New York to Paris in 1927 and his youthful good looks made him an instant hero. President Coolidge presented him with the Distinguished Flying Cross and called his achievement a shining example of heroic individualism combined with American genius and industry. (Library of Congress)

Not all Americans, of course, were intent on making a stock market killing or expected to win a huge fortune. Some merely wished to retain traditional values in a society that seemed to question them. Others wanted a steady job and a little respect. Still others hungered for the new appliances so alluringly described in ads and on the radio. Many discovered, however, that no matter how modest their hopes might be, they lay tantalizingly out of reach.

Clash of Values

During the 1920s, radio, movies, advertising, and mass-circulation magazines promoted a national, secular culture. But this new culture, which emphasized consumption, pleasure, upward mobility, even sex, clashed with traditional values of hard work, thrift, church, family, and home. Although it would be easy to see these cultural differences as a reflection of an urban-rural conflict, in fact, many people clinging to the old ways had

moved into the cities. Still, many Americans feared that new cultural values, scientific breakthroughs, and new ideas like bolshevism, relativism, Freudianism, and biblical criticism threatened their familiar way of life. A trial over the teaching of evolutionary ideas in high school in the little town of Dayton, Tennessee, symbolized, even as it exaggerated, the clash of the old versus the new, the traditional versus the modern, the city versus the country.

The scientific community and most educated people had long accepted the basic concepts of evolution, if not all the details of Charles Darwin's theories. But many Christians, especially those from Protestant evangelical churches, accepted the Bible as the literal truth. They believed that faith in the Gospel message was crucial to living a virtuous life on earth and, more important, going to heaven. Many of these faithful saw in the dramatic changes of the 1920s a major spiritual crisis. Resistance to the concept of evolution resulted in legislative efforts in several states to forbid its teaching. The Tennessee law enacted in 1925 became the most famous, for it made it illegal

for any teacher in any of the universities, normal and all other public schools of the state to teach any theory that denies the story of the divine creation of man as taught in the Bible and to teach instead that man has descended from a lower order of animals.

John Scopes, a young biology teacher, broke the law by teaching evolutionary theory to his class, and the state of Tennessee brought him to trial. The American Civil Liberties Union hired Clarence Darrow, perhaps the country's most famous defense lawyer, to defend Scopes; the World Christian Fundamentalist Association engaged William Jennings Bryan, former presidential candidate and secretary of state, to assist the prosecution. Bryan was old and tired (he died only a few days after the trial), but he was still an eloquent and deeply religious man. In cross-examination, Darrow reduced Bryan's statements to intellectual rubble and revealed also that Bryan was at a loss to explain much of the Bible. He could not explain how Eve was created from Adam's rib or where Cain got his wife. Nevertheless, the jury declared Scopes guilty, for he had clearly broken the law.

John Steuart Curry was one of the 1920s regionalist painters who found inspiration in the American heartland. In Baptism in Kansas, *he depicts a religious ritual that underscores the persistence of faith and the importance of religion in creating a sense of community. (The Whitney Museum of American Art, New York)*

The press from all over the country covered the trial and upheld science and academic freedom. Journalists like H. L. Mencken had a field day poking fun at Bryan and the fundamentalists. "Heave an egg out a Pullman window," Mencken wrote, "and you will hit a Fundamentalist almost anywhere in the United States today.... They are everywhere where learning is too heavy a burden for mortal minds to carry."

Religious Fundamentalism

Some observers, including Mencken, thought that the Scopes trial ended what one writer in 1926 called "the fundamentalist menace." Yet religious fundamentalism, continued to survive in a world fast becoming urban, modern, and sophisticated. Fundamentalism cut across many denominations and covered over many differences, but all funda-

mentalists believed in the literal interpretation and the infallibility of the Bible, and that Jesus Christ was the only road to salvation. They rejected secularism, liberal theology, pluralism, the social gospel, and any sense that reform on earth could lead to perfection. They had a strong and unshakable belief in what they knew was the truth and they were willing to stand up and fight for their belief.

Throughout the 1920s and the 1930s, attendance at Christian colleges, and the circulation of fundamentalist periodicals and newspapers increased dramatically, and evangelical ministers reached large audiences. One of the most popular and flamboyant of the ministers was Billy Sunday, an ex-baseball player who jumped about the stage as he pitched his brand of Christianity. For Sunday, Christianity and patriotism were synonymous. Another popular preacher was Aimee Semple McPherson, a faith healer who founded her own church, the International Church of the Four Square Gospel, in Los Angeles in 1927. Dressed as a University of Southern California football player, she ran across the stage "carrying the ball for Christ," or wielding a pitchfork, she drove the devil out of the auditorium.

Sunday and McPherson may have been flamboyant performers, but it was the radio that extended the reach of the fundamentalist preachers even more dramatically. McPherson was the first woman to hold a radio license and she had the second most popular radio show in Los Angeles in the late 1920s. In the 1930s "The Old Fashioned Revival Hour" was carried on 356 stations and reached an audience of over 20 million people, more than any other prime-time broadcast. For many, the period between the wars was an age of secular humanism, technological marvels, and modernism in all fields, but for many others, it was a time when fundamentalist religion and old-fashioned values not only survived, but also prospered.

Immigration and Migration

Immigrants and anyone else perceived as "un-American" seemed to threaten the old ways. A movement to restrict immigration had existed for decades. An act passed in 1882 prohibited the entry of criminals, paupers, and the insane, and special agreements between 1880 and 1908 restricted both Chinese and Japanese immigration. But it was the fear and intolerance of the war years and the period right after the war that resulted in major restrictive legislation.

The first strongly restrictive immigration law passed in 1917 over President Wilson's veto. It required a literacy test for the first time (an immigrant had to read a passage in one of a number of languages). The bill also prohibited the immigration of certain political radicals. The literacy test did not stop the more than one million immigrants who poured into the country in 1920 and 1921, however.

In 1921, Congress limited European immigration in any one year to 3 percent of the number of each nationality present in the country in 1910. Congress changed the quota in 1924 to 2 percent of those in the country in 1890, in order to limit immigration from southern and eastern Europe and ban all immigration from Asia. The National Origins Act of 1927 set an overall limit of 150,000

Evangelist William Ashley ("Billy") Sunday (1862–1935) was a professional baseball player before experiencing a religious conversion that led him to work with the YMCA. He conducted religious revivals all over the country, captivating listeners with his flamboyant style and converting millions. (The Granger Collection, New York)

European immigrants a year, with more than 60 percent coming from Great Britain and Germany, but fewer than 4 percent from Italy.

Ethnicity increasingly became a factor in political alignments during the 1920s. Restrictive immigration laws, sponsored by Republicans, helped attract American Jews, Italians, and Poles to the Democratic party. By 1924, the Democratic party was so evenly divided between northern urban Catholics and southern rural Protestants that the party voted to condemn the Ku Klux Klan, by a very small margin.

The immigration acts of 1921, 1924, and 1927, in sharply limiting European immigration and virtually banning Asian immigrants, cut off the streams of cheap labor that had provided muscle for an industrializing country since the early nineteenth century. At the same time, by exempting immigrants from the Western Hemisphere, the new laws opened the country to Mexican laborers who were eager to escape poverty in their own land and to work in the fields and farms of California and the Southwest.

Though they never matched the flood of eastern and southern Europeans who entered the country before World War I, Mexican immigrants soon became the country's largest first-generation immigrant group. Nearly half a million arrived in the 1920s, in contrast to only 31,000 in the first decade of the century. Mexican farm workers often lived in primitive camps, where conditions were unsanitary and health care was nonexistent. "When they have finished harvesting my crops I will kick them out on the country road," one employer announced. "My obligation is ended."

Mexicans also migrated to industrial cities such as Detroit, St. Louis, and Kansas City. Northern companies recruited them and paid their transportation. The Bethlehem Steel Corporation brought 1,000 Mexicans into its Pennsylvania plant in 1923, and U.S. Steel imported 1,500 as strikebreakers to Lorain, Ohio, about the same time. During the 1920s, El Paso, Texas, became more than half Mexican, San Antonio a little less than half. The Mexican population in California reached 368,000 in 1929, and Los Angeles was about 20 percent Mexican. Like African Americans, the Mexicans found opportunity by migrating, but they did not escape prejudice or hardship.

African Americans migrated north in great numbers from 1915 to 1920. Reduced European immigration and industrial growth caused many northern companies to recruit southern blacks. Trains stopped at the depots in small southern towns, sometimes picking up hundreds of blacks in a single day. Lured by editorials and advertisements placed by industries in northern black newspapers such as the Chicago *Defender* and driven out of the South by an agricultural depression, many African Americans eagerly headed north.

One young black man wrote to the Chicago *Defender* from Texas that he would prefer to go to Chicago or Philadelphia, but "I don't care where so long as I go where a man is a man." It was the young who tended to move. "Young folks just aren't satisfied to see so little and stay around on the farm all their lives like old folks did," one older man from

South Carolina pointed out. Most black migrants were unskilled. They found work in the huge meat-packing plants of Chicago, East St. Louis, Omaha, and Kansas City and in the shipyards and steel mills. Only 50 African Americans worked for the Ford Motor Company in 1916, but there were 2,500 working there in 1920 and 10,000 in 1926. The black population of Chicago increased from 44,000 in 1910 to 234,000 by 1930. Cleveland's black population grew eightfold between 1910 and 1930.

African Americans unquestionably improved their lives by moving north. But most were like the Parkers, their dreams only partly fulfilled. Most crowded into segregated housing and faced prejudice and hate. "Black men stay South," the Chicago *Tribune* advised, and offered to pay the transportation for any who would return. In one section of Chicago, a group of white residents, fearing the encroachment of blacks, stretched across the street a banner that read: "THEY SHALL NOT PASS."

Often the young black men moved first, and only later brought their wives and children, putting great pressure on many black families. Some young men, like John Parker, restrained their anger, but others, like Richard Wright's fictional Bigger Thomas, portrayed movingly in *Native Son* (1940), struck out violently against white society. The presence of more African Americans in the industrial cities of the North led to the development of black ghettos and increased the racial tension that occasionally flared into violence.

One of the worst race riots took place in Chicago in 1919. The riot began at a beach on a hot July day. A black youth drowned in a white swimming area. Blacks claimed he had been hit by stones, but the police refused to arrest any of the white men. A group of African Americans attacked the police, and the riot was on. It lasted four days. White youths drove through the black sections shooting blacks from car windows. Blacks returned the fire. Several dozen were killed, and hundreds were wounded. The tension between the races did not die when the riot was over.

Race riots broke out in other places as well. In the early 1920s, few cities escaped racial tension and violence. Riots exploded in Knoxville, Tennessee; Omaha, Nebraska; and Tulsa, Oklahoma. Racial conflict in Elaine, Arkansas, demonstrated that not even the rural South was immune.

The wave of violence and racism angered and disillusioned W. E. B. Du Bois, who had urged African Americans to close ranks and support the American cause during the war. In an angry editorial for *The Crisis,* he called on blacks to

> fight a sterner, longer, more unbending battle against the forces of hell in our own land. We return. We return from fighting. We return fighting. Make way for Democracy; we saved it in France, and by the Great Jehovah, we will save it in the United States of America, or know the reason why.

Marcus Garvey: Black Messiah

Du Bois was not the only militant black leader in the postwar years. A flamboyant Jamaican fed a growing sense of black pride during that time. Marcus Garvey arrived in New York at the age of 29. Largely self-taught, he was an admirer of Booker T. Washington. Although he never abandoned Washington's philosophy of self-help, he thoroughly transformed it. Washington focused on economic betterment through self-help; Garvey saw self-help as a means of political empowerment by which African peoples would reclaim their homelands from European powers.

In Jamaica, Garvey had founded the Universal Negro Improvement Association. By 1919, he had established 30 branches in the United States and the Caribbean. He also set up the newspaper *The Negro World,* the Black Cross Nurses, and a chain of grocery stores, millinery shops, and restaurants. His biggest project was the Black Star Line, a steamship company, to be owned and operated by African Americans. Advocating the return of blacks to Africa, he declared himself the "provisional president of Africa," a title he adopted from Eamon De Valera, the first "provisional president of Ireland." Garvey glorified the African past and preached that God and Jesus were black.

He won converts, mostly among lower-middle-class blacks, through the force of his oratory and the power of his personality, but especially through his message that blacks should be proud of being black. "Up you mighty race, you can accomplish what you will," Garvey thundered. Thousands of blacks cheered as his Universal

Marcus Garvey, (second from the right), shown dressed in his favorite uniform, became a hero for many black Americans. (Archive Photos)

African Legions, dressed in blue and red uniforms, marched by. They waved the red, black, and green flag and sang "Ethiopia, the Land of Our Fathers," and thousands invested their money in the Black Star Line. The line soon collapsed, however, in part because white entrepreneurs sold Garvey inferior ships and equipment. Garvey was arrested for using the mails to defraud shareholders and was sentenced to five years in prison. President Coolidge commuted the sentence. Ordered deported as an undesirable alien, Garvey left America in 1927. Despite his failures, he convinced thousands of black Americans, especially the poor and discouraged, that they could join together and accomplish something and that they should feel pride in their heritage and their future.

The Harlem Renaissance and the Lost Generation

A group of black writers, artists, and intellectuals who settled in Harlem after the war led a movement related in some ways to Garvey's black nationalism crusade. It was less flamboyant, but in the end more important. They studied anthropology, art, history, and music, and they wrote novels and poetry that explored the ambivalent role of blacks in America. Like Garvey, they expressed their pride in being black and sought their African roots and the folk tradition of blacks in America. But unlike Garvey, they had no desire to go back to Africa. They sought a way to be both black and American.

Alain Locke, the first black Rhodes scholar and a dapper professor of philosophy at Howard University, was in one sense the father of the renaissance. His collection of essays and art, *The New Negro* (1925), announced the movement to the outside world and outlined black contributions to American culture and civilization. Langston Hughes, a poet and novelist born in Missouri, went to high school in Cleveland, lived in Mexico, and traveled in Europe and Africa before settling in Harlem. He wrote bitter but laughing poems, using black vernacular to describe the pathos and the pride of African Americans. In *Weary Blues,* he adapted the rhythm and beat of black jazz and the blues to his poetry.

Jazz was an important force in Harlem in the 1920s, and many prosperous whites came from downtown to listen to Louis Armstrong, Fletcher Henderson, Duke Ellington, and other black musicians. The promise of expressing primitive emotions, the erotic atmosphere, the music, and the illegal sex, drugs, and liquor made Harlem an intriguing place for many brought up in Victorian white America.

The Jamaican Claude McKay, who came to Harlem by way of Tuskegee and Kansas, wrote about the underside of life in Harlem in *Home to Harlem* (1925), one of the most popular of the "new Negro" novels. McKay portrayed two black men— one, Jake, who has deserted the white man's army and finds a life of simple and erotic pleasure in Harlem's cabarets, the other an intellectual who is unable to make such an easy choice. "My damned white education has robbed me of much of the primitive vitality, the pure stamina, the simple unwaggering strength of the Jakes of the negro race," he laments.

This was the dilemma of many of the Harlem writers: how to be both black and intellectual. They worried that they depended on white patrons, who introduced them to writers and artists in Greenwich Village and made contacts for them at New York publishing houses. Many of the white patrons pressured the black writers to conform to the white elite idea of black authenticity. The black writers resented this intrusion, but it was their only hope to be recognized. Jean Toomer, more self-consciously avant-garde than many of the other black writers, wrote haunting poems trying to explore the difficulty of black identity, and in a novel, *Cane* (1923), he sketched maladjusted, almost grotesque characters who expressed some of the alienation that many writers felt in the 1920s.

Many African American writers felt alienated from American society. They tried living in Paris or in Greenwich Village, but most felt drawn to Harlem, which in the 1920s was rapidly becoming the center of black population in New York City. Over 117,000 white people left the neighborhood during the decade, while over 87,000 blacks moved in. Countee Cullen, the only writer in the group actually born in New York, remarked, "In spite of myself I find that I am activated by a strong sense of race consciousness." So was Zora Neale Hurston, born in Florida, who came to New York to study at Barnard College, earned an advanced degree in anthropology from Columbia University, and used her interest in folklore to write stories of robust and passionate rural blacks. Much of the work of the Harlem writers was read by very small numbers, but another generation of young black intellectuals in the 1960s still struggling with the dilemma of how to be both black and American would rediscover it.

One did not need to be black to be disillusioned with society. Many white intellectuals, writers, and artists also felt alienated from what they perceived as the materialism, conformity, and provincial prejudice that dominated American life. Many writers, including F. Scott Fitzgerald, Ernest Hemingway, E. E. Cummings, and T. S. Eliot, moved to Europe. They wanted to divorce themselves from the country they pretended to detest, but cheap rents and inexpensive food in Paris also influenced their decisions. Many of those who gathered at European cafés, drinking the wine that was illegal in the United States, wrote novels, plays, and poems about America. Like so many American intellectuals in all periods, they had a love-hate relationship with their country.

For many writers, the disillusionment began with the war itself. Hemingway eagerly volunteered to go to Europe as an ambulance driver. But when he was wounded on the Italian front, he reevaluated the purpose of the war and the meaning of all the slaughter. His novel *The Sun Also Rises* (1926) is the story of the purposeless European wanderings of a group of Americans. But it is also the story of Jake Barnes, made impotent by a war injury. His "unreasonable wound" is a symbol of the futility of life in the postwar period.

F. Scott Fitzgerald, who loved to frequent the cafés and the parties in Paris, became a celebrity during the 1920s. He was sometimes confused, even in his own mind, with the dashing heroes about whom he wrote. He epitomized some of the despair of his generation, which had "grown up to find all Gods dead, all wars fought, all faiths in man shaken." His best novel, *The Great Gatsby* (1925), was a critique of the American success myth. The book describes the elaborate parties given by a mysterious businessman, who, it turns out, has made his money illegally as a bootlegger. Gatsby hopes to win back a beautiful woman who has forsaken him for another man. But wealth won't buy happiness, and Gatsby's life ends tragically, as so many lives seemed to end in the novels written during the decade.

Paris was the place to which many American writers flocked, but it was not necessary to live in France to criticize American society. Sherwood Anderson, born in Camden, Ohio, created a fictional midwestern town in *Winesburg, Ohio* (1919), to describe the dull, narrow, warped lives that seemed to provide a metaphor for American culture. Sinclair Lewis, another midwesterner, created scathing parodies of middle-class, small-town life in *Main Street* (1920) and *Babbitt* (1922). The "hero" of the latter novel is a salesman from the town of Zenith. He is a "he-man," a "regular guy" who distrusts "red professors," foreign-born people, and anyone from New York. He lives in a world of gadgets and booster clubs and seems to be the worst product of a standardized civilization. But no one had more fun laughing at the American middle class than H. L. Mencken, who edited the *American Mercury* in Baltimore and denounced what he called the "booboisie." He labeled Woodrow Wilson a "self-bamboozled Pres-

byterian," and poked fun at Warren Harding's prose, which he said reminded him of "a string of wet sponges, . . . of stale bean soup, of college yells, of dogs barking idiotically through endless nights."

Ironically, while intellectuals despaired over American society and complained that art could not survive in a business-dominated civilization, literature flourished. The novels of Hemingway, Fitzgerald, Lewis, William Faulkner, and Gertrude Stein, the plays of Eugene O'Neill and Maxwell Anderson, the poetry of T. S. Eliot, Hart Crane, E. E. Cummings, and Marianne Moore, and the work of many black writers, such as Langston Hughes, Claude McKay, and Zora Neale Hurston, marked the 1920s as one of the most creative decades in American literature.

Women Struggle for Equality

Any mention of the role of women in the 1920s brings to mind the image of the flapper—a young woman with a short skirt, bobbed hair, and a boyish figure doing the Charleston, smoking, drinking, and being very casual about sex. F. Scott Fitzgerald's heroines in novels like *This Side of Paradise* (1920) and *The Great Gatsby* (1925) provided the role models for young people to imitate, and movie stars such as Clara Bow and Gloria Swanson, aggressively seductive on the screen, supplied even more dramatic examples of flirtatious and provocative behavior.

Without question, women acquired more sexual freedom in the 1920s. "None of the Victorian mothers had any idea how casually their daughters were accustomed to being kissed," F. Scott Fitzgerald wrote. However, it is difficult, if not impossible, to know how accustomed those daughters (and their mothers) were to kissing and enjoying other sexual activity. Contraceptives, especially the diaphragm, became more readily available during the decade, and Margaret Sanger, who had been indicted for sending birth control information through the mail in 1914, organized the first American birth control conference in 1921. Still, most states made the selling or prescribing of birth control devices illegal, and federal laws prohibited sending literature discussing birth control through the mail.

Family size declined during the decade (from 3.6 children in 1900 to 2.5 in 1930), and young people were apparently more inclined to marry for

The revolution created by electricity remained out of reach for many rural and working-class women, who continued to use the scrub board rather than the washing machine. (Culver Pictures)

spent doing housework. Standards of cleanliness rose, and women were urged to make their houses more spotless than any nineteenth-century housekeeper would have felt necessary. At the same time, magazines and newspapers bombarded women with advertising urging them to buy products to make themselves better housekeepers, yet still beautiful. It must have been frustrating for those who could not afford the magic new products or whose hands and teeth and skin failed to look youthful despite all their efforts. The ads also promoted new dress styles, shorter skirts, no corsets. The young adopted them quickly, and they also learned to swim (and to display more of their bodies on the beach), to play tennis (but only if they belonged to a tennis club), and to ride a bicycle.

More women worked outside the home. Whereas in 1890 only 17 percent of women were employed, by 1933 some 22 percent were. But their share of manufacturing jobs fell from 19 to 16 percent between 1900 and 1930. The greatest expansion of jobs was in white-collar occupations that were being feminized—secretary, bookkeeper, clerk, telephone operator. In 1930, fully 96 percent of stenographers were women. Although more married women had jobs (an increase of 25 percent during the decade), most of them held low-paying jobs, and most single women assumed that marriage would terminate their employment.

For some working women—secretaries and teachers, for example—marriage often led to dismissal. "A married woman's attitude toward men who come to the office is not the same as that of an unmarried woman," one employment agency decided. Married women are "very unstable in their work; their first claim is to home and children," concluded a businessman. Although women might not be able to work after their weddings (in one poll of college men, only one in nine said he would allow his wife to work after marriage), a job as a secretary could be good preparation for marriage. A business office was a good place to meet eligible men, but more than that, a secretary learned endurance, self-effacement, and obedience, traits that would make her a good wife. Considering these attitudes, it is not surprising that the disparity between male and female wages widened during the decade. By 1930, women earned only 57 percent of what men were paid.

love than for security. More women expected sexual satisfaction in marriage (nearly 60 percent in one poll) and felt that divorce was the best solution for an unhappy marriage. Nearly 85 percent in another poll approved of sexual intercourse as an expression of love and affection and not simply for procreation. But the polls were hardly scientific and tended to be biased toward the attitudes of the urban middle class. Despite more freedom for women, the double standard persisted. "When lovely woman stoops to folly, she can always find someone to stoop with her," one male writer announced, "but not always someone to lift her up again to the level where she belongs."

Women's lives were shaped by other innovations of the 1920s. Electricity, running water, washing machines, vacuum cleaners, and other laborsaving devices made housework easier for the middle class. Yet these developments did not touch large numbers of rural and urban working-class women. Even middle-class women discovered that new appliances did not reduce time

Women in the Labor Force, 1900–1930						
				Percentage of Women in Labor Force		
Year	Women in Labor Force	Percent of Women in Total Labor Force	Women in Labor Force as Percent of Total Women of Working Age	Single	Married	Widowed or Divorced
1900	4,997,000	18.1	20.6	66.2	15.4	18.4
1910*	7,640,000	NA	25.4	60.2	24.7	15.0
1920	8,347,000	20.4	23.7	77.0[†]	23.0	—[†]
1930	10,632,000	21.9	24.8	53.9	28.9	17.2

*Data not comparable with other censuses due to a difference in the basis of enumeration.

[†]Single includes widowed and divorced.

Source: U.S. Bureau of the Census.

The image of the flapper in the 1920s promised more freedom and equality for women than they actually achieved. The flapper was young, white, slender, and upper class (Fitzgerald fixed her ideal age at 19), and most women did not fit those categories. The flapper was frivolous and daring, not professional and competent. Although the proportion of women lawyers and bankers increased slightly during the decade, the rate of growth declined, and the number of women doctors and scientists dropped. In the 1920s, women acquired some sexual freedom and a limited amount of opportunity outside the home, but the promise of the prewar feminist movement and the hopes that accompanied the suffrage amendment remained unfulfilled.

Winning the vote for women did not assure equality. In most states, a woman's service belonged to her husband. Women could vote, but often they could not serve on juries. In some states, women could not hold office, own a business, or sign a contract without their husbands' permission. Women were usually held responsible for an illegitimate birth, and divorce laws almost always favored men. Many women leaders were disappointed in the small turnout of women in the presidential election of 1920. To educate women in

the reality of politics, they organized the National League of Women Voters to "finish the fight." A nonpartisan organization, it became an important educational organization for middle-class women, but it did little to eliminate inequality.

Alice Paul, who had led the militant National Women's Party in 1916, chained herself to the

Although the flapper look of short skirts and bobbed hair appeared in the workplace in the 1920s, for most working women of the era, employed in low-paying jobs as file clerks, typists, and telephone operators, the flapper lifestyle of freedom and equality was more illusion than reality. (Corbis-Bettmann)

White House fence once again to promote an equal rights amendment to the Constitution. The amendment got support in Wisconsin and several other states, but many women opposed it on the grounds that such an amendment would cancel the special legislation to protect women in industry that had taken so long to enact in the two decades before. Feminists disagreed in the 1920s on the proper way to promote equality and rights for women, but the political and social climate was not conducive to feminist causes.

Rural America in the 1920s

Most farmers did not share in the prosperity of the 1920s. Responding to worldwide demands and rising prices for wheat, cotton, and other products, many farmers invested in more land, tractors, and farm equipment during the war. Then prices tumbled. By 1921, the price of wheat had dropped 40 percent, corn 32 percent, and hogs 50 percent. Total farm income fell from $10 to $4 million in the postwar depression. Many farmers could not make payments on their tractors. Because the value of land fell, they often lost both mortgage and land and still owed the bank money. One Iowa farmer remembered, "We gave the land back to the mortgage holder, and then we're sued for the remainder—the deficiency judgment—which we have to pay."

The changing nature of farming was part of the problem. The use of chemical fertilizers and new hybrid seeds, some developed by government experiment stations and land-grant colleges, increased the yield per acre. By 1930, some 920,000 tractors and 900,000 trucks were in use on American farms. They not only made farming more efficient, but they also released for cash crops land formerly used to raise feed for horses and mules. Production increased at the very time that worldwide demand for American farm products declined. The United States shipped abroad in 1929 only one-third the wheat it had exported in 1919, and only one-ninth the meat.

Not all farmers suffered. During the 1920s, the farming class separated into those who were getting by barely or not at all and those who earned large profits. Large commercial operations, using mechanized equipment, produced most of the cash crops. At the same time, many small farmers found themselves unable to compete with agribusiness. Some of them, along with many farm laborers, solved the problem of declining rural profitability by leaving the farms. In 1900, fully 40 percent of the labor force worked on farms; by 1930, only 21 percent earned their living from the land.

Few farmers could afford the products of the new technology. Although many middle-class urban families were more prosperous than they had ever been, buying new cars, radios, and bathrooms, only one farm family in ten had electricity in the 1920s. The lot of the farm wife had not changed for centuries. She ran a domestic factory, did all the household chores, and helped on the farm as well.

As they had done in the nineteenth century, farmers tried to act collectively. After the failure of the People's party in 1896, they gave up on direct political action, but relied instead on influencing legislation in the state capital and in Washington. Most of their effort went into the McNary-Haugen Farm Relief Bill, which provided for government support for key agricultural products. The idea was for the government to buy wheat, cotton, and other crops at a "fair exchange value" and then market the excess on the world market at a lower price, thus isolating and protecting the American farmer from the worldwide swing in prices. The bill passed Congress in February 1927, only to be vetoed by President Coolidge. It passed again in revised form the next year, and again the president vetoed it. But farm organizations in all parts of the country learned how to cooperate and how to influence Congress. That would have important ramifications for the future.

The Workers' Share of Prosperity

Hundreds of thousands of workers improved their standard of living in the 1920s, yet inequality grew. Real wages increased 21 percent between 1923 and 1929, but corporate dividends went up by nearly two-thirds in the same period. The workers did not profit from the increased production they helped to create, and that boded ill for the future. The richest 5 percent of the population increased their share of the wealth from a quarter to a third, and the wealthiest 1 percent controlled a whopping 19 percent of all income.

Even among workers there was great disparity. Those employed on the auto assembly lines or in the new factories producing radios saw their wages go up, and many saw their hours decline. Yet the majority of American working-class families did not earn enough to move them much beyond the subsistence level. One study suggested that a family needed $2,000 to $2,400 in 1924 to maintain an "American standard of living." But in that year, 16 million families earned under $2,000. For the chambermaids in New York hotels who worked seven days a week or the itinerant Mexican migrant laborers in the Southwest, labor was so exhausting that at the end of the day, it was impossible to take advantage of new consumer products and modern life-styles, even if they had the money.

Although some workers prospered in the 1920s, organized labor fell on hard times. Labor union membership fell from about 5 million in 1921 to less than 3.5 million in 1929. Although a majority of American workers had never supported unions, unions now faced competition from employers' new policies. A number of large employers lured workers away from unions with promises that seemed to equal union benefits: profit-sharing plans, pensions, and their own company unions. The National Manufacturing Association and individual businesses carried on a vigorous campaign to restore the open shop. The leadership of the AFL became increasingly conservative during the decade and had little interest in launching movements to organize the large industries.

The more aggressive unions like the United Mine Workers, led by the flamboyant John L. Lewis, also encountered difficulties. The union's attempt to organize the mines in West Virginia had led to violent clashes between union members and imported guards. President Harding called out troops in 1921 to put down an "army organized by the strikers." The next year, Lewis called the greatest coal strike in history, and further violence erupted, especially in Williamson County, Illinois. Internal strife also weakened the union, and Lewis had to accept wage reductions in the negotiations of 1927.

Organized labor, like so many other groups, struggled desperately during the decade to take advantage of the prosperity. It won some victories, and it made some progress. But American affluence was beyond the reach of many groups during the decade. Eventually, the inequality would lead to disaster.

The Business of Politics

"Among the nations of the earth today America stands for one idea: *Business*," a popular writer announced in 1921. "Through business, properly conceived, managed and conducted, the human race is finally to be redeemed." Bruce Barton, the head of the largest advertising firm in the country, was the author of one of the most popular nonfiction books of the decade. In *The Man Nobody Knows* (1925), he depicted Christ as "the founder of modern business." He took 12 men from the bottom ranks of society and forged them into a successful organization. "All work is worship; all useful service prayer," Barton argued. If the businessman would just copy Christ, he could become a supersalesman.

Business, especially big business, prospered in the 1920s, and the image of businessmen, enhanced by their important role in World War I, rose further. The government reduced regulation, lowered taxes, and cooperated to aid business expansion at home and abroad. Business and politics, always intertwined, were especially allied during the decade. Wealthy financiers such as Andrew Mellon and Charles Dawes played important roles in formulating both domestic and foreign policy. Even more significant, a new kind of businessman was elected president in 1928. Herbert Hoover, international engineer and efficiency expert, was the very symbol of the modern techniques and practices that many people confidently expected to transform the United States and the world.

Harding and Coolidge

The Republicans, almost assured of victory in 1920 because of bitter reaction against Woodrow Wilson, might have preferred nominating their old standard-bearer, Theodore Roosevelt, but he had died the year before. Warren G. Harding, a former newspaper editor from Ohio, captured the nomination after meeting late at night with some of the party's most powerful men in a hotel room in Chicago. What Harding promised no one ever discovered, but the meeting in the "smoke-filled room" became legendary. To balance the ticket, the Republicans chose as their vice-presidential candidate Calvin Coolidge of Massachusetts, who had gained attention by his firm stand during the Boston police strike. The Democrats seemed equally unimaginative. After 44 roll calls, they finally nominated Governor James Cox of Ohio and picked Franklin D. Roosevelt, a young politician from New York, as vice-president. Roosevelt had been the assistant secretary of the navy, but otherwise had not distinguished himself.

Harding won in a landslide. His 60.4 percent of the vote was the widest margin yet recorded in a presidential election. More significant, fewer than 50 percent of the eligible voters went to the polls. The newly enfranchised women, especially in working-class neighborhoods, stayed away from the voting booths. So did large numbers of men. To many people, it did not seem to matter who was president.

Warren G. Harding (left) and Calvin Coolidge were immensely popular in the 1920s, but later historians have criticized them and rated them among the worst of American presidents. (Library of Congress)

In contrast to the reform-minded presidents Roosevelt and Wilson, Harding reflected the conservatism of the 1920s. He was a jovial man who brought many Ohio friends to Washington and placed them in positions of power. A visitor to the White House described Harding and his cohorts discussing the problems of the day, with "the air heavy with tobacco smoke, trays with bottles containing every imaginable brand of whiskey" near at hand.

At a little house a few blocks from the White House on K Street, Harry Daugherty, Harding's attorney general and longtime associate, held forth with a group of friends. Amid bootleg liquor and the atmosphere of a brothel, they did a brisk business in selling favors, taking bribes, and organizing illegal schemes. Harding, however, was not personally corrupt, and the nation's leading businessmen approved of his policies of higher tariffs and lower taxes. Nor did Harding spend all his time drinking with his cronies. He called a conference on disarmament and another to deal with the problems of unemployment, and he pardoned Eugene Debs, who had been in prison since the war. Harding once remarked that he could never be considered one of the great presidents, but he thought perhaps he might be "one of the best loved." He was probably right. When he died suddenly in August 1923, the American people genuinely mourned him.

Only after Calvin Coolidge became president did the full extent of the corruption and scandals of the Harding administration come to light. A Senate committee discovered that the secretary of the interior, Albert Fall, had illegally leased government-owned oil reserves in the Teapot Dome section of Wyoming to private business interests in return for over $300,000 in bribes. Illegal activities were also discovered in the Veterans Administration and elsewhere in government. Harding's attorney general resigned in disgrace, the secretary of the Navy barely avoided prison, two of Harding's advisers committed suicide, and the secretary of the interior was sentenced to jail.

Coolidge was dour and taciturn, but honest. No hint of scandal infected his administration or his personal life. Born in a little town in Vermont, he was sworn in as president by his father, a justice of the peace, in a ceremony conducted by the light of kerosene lamps at his ancestral home. To many, Coolidge represented old-fashioned rural values, simple religious faith, and personal integrity—a world fast disappearing in the 1920s. In reality, Coolidge was uncomfortable playing the rural yokel. He was ill at ease posing for photographers holding a pitchfork or sitting on a hay rig; he was much more comfortable around corporate executives.

Coolidge ran for reelection in 1924 with the financier Charles Dawes as his running mate. There was little question that he would win. The Democrats were so equally divided between northern urban Catholics and southern rural Protestants that it took 103 ballots before they nominated John Davis, an affable, corporate lawyer with little national following.

A group of dissidents, mostly representing the farmers and the laborers dissatisfied with both nominees, formed a new Progressive party. They adopted the name, but little else, from Theodore Roosevelt's party of 1912. Nominating Robert La Follette of Wisconsin for president, they drafted a platform calling for government ownership of railroads and ratification of the child labor amendment. La Follette attacked the "control of government and industry by private monopoly." He received nearly 5 million votes, only 3.5 million short of Davis's total. But Coolidge and prosperity won easily.

Like Harding, Coolidge was a popular president. Symbolizing his administration was his wealthy secretary of the treasury, Andrew Mellon, who set out to lower individual and corporate taxes. In 1922, Congress, with Mellon's endorsement, repealed the wartime excess profits tax. Although it raised some taxes slightly, it exempted most families from any tax at all by giving everyone a $2,500 exemption, plus $400 for each dependent. In 1926, the rate was lowered to 5 percent and the maximum surtax to 40 percent. Only families with incomes above $3,500 paid any taxes at all. In 1928, Congress reduced taxes further, removed most excise taxes, and lowered the corporate tax rate. The 200 largest corporations increased their assets during the decade from $43 to $81 billion.

"The chief business of the American people is business," Coolidge announced. "The man who builds a factory builds a temple.... The man who works there worships there." Coolidge's idea of the proper role of the federal government was to have as little as possible to do with the functioning of business and the lives of the people. Not everyone approved of his policies, or his personality. "No other president in my time slept so much," a White House usher remembered. But most Americans approved of his inactivity.

Herbert Hoover

One bright light in the lackluster Harding and Coolidge administrations was Herbert Hoover, who served as secretary of commerce under both presidents. Hoover had made a fortune as an international mining engineer before 1914 and then earned the reputation as a great humanitarian for his work managing the Belgian Relief Committee and directing the Food Administration. He was mentioned as a candidate for president in 1920, when he had the support of such progressives as Jane Addams, Louis Brandeis, and Walter Lippmann.

Hoover was a dynamo of energy and efficiency. He expanded his department to control and regulate the airlines, radio, and other new industries. By directing the Bureau of Standards to work with the trade associations and with individual businesses, Hoover managed to standardize the size of almost everything manufactured in the United States, from nuts and bolts and bottles to automobile tires, mattresses, and electric fixtures. He supported zoning codes, the eight-hour day in major industries, better nutrition for children, and the conservation of national resources. He pushed through the Pollution Act of 1924, the first attempt to control oil pollution along the American coastline.

While secretary of commerce, Hoover used the force of the federal government to regulate, stimulate, and promote, but he believed first of all in American free enterprise and local volunteer action to solve problems. In 1921, he convinced Harding of the need to do something about unemployment during the postwar recession. The president's conference on unemployment, convened in September 1921, marked the first time the national government had admitted any responsibility to the unemployed. The result of the conference (the first of many on a variety of topics that Hoover was to organize) was a flood of publicity, pamphlets, and advice from experts. Most of all, the conference urged state and local governments and businesses to cooperate on a volunteer basis to solve the problem. The primary responsibility of the federal government, Hoover believed, was to educate and promote. With all his activity and his organizing, Hoover got the reputation during the Harding and Coolidge years as an efficient and progressive administrator, and he became one of the most popular figures in government service.

Foreign Policy in the 1920s

The decade of the 1920s is often remembered as a time of isolation, when the United States rejected the League of Nations treaty and turned its back on the rest of the world. It is true that many Americans had little interest in what was going on in Paris, Moscow, or Rio de Janeiro, and it is also true that a bloc of congressmen was determined that the United States would never again enter another European war. But the United States remained involved—indeed, increased its involvement—in international affairs during the decade. Although the United States never joined the League of Nations, and a few dedicated isolationists, led by Senator William Borah, blocked membership in the World Court, the United States cooperated with many League agencies and conferences and took the lead in trying to reduce naval armaments and to solve the problems of international finance caused in part by the war.

Indeed, business, trade, and finance marked the decade as one of international expansion. With American corporate investments overseas growing sevenfold during the decade, the United States was transformed from a debtor to a creditor nation. The continued involvement of the

United States in the affairs of South and Central American countries also indicated that the country had little interest in hiding behind its national boundaries. Yet the United States took up its role of international power reluctantly and with a number of contradictory and disastrous results.

"We seek no part in directing the destiny of the world," Harding announced in his inaugural address, but even Harding discovered that international problems would not disappear. One that required immediate attention was the naval arms race. Although moderates in Japan and Great Britain wanted to restrict the production of battleships, it was the United States, encouraged by men like William Borah, that took the lead and called the first international conference to discuss disarmament.

At the Washington Conference on Naval Disarmament, which convened in November 1921, Secretary of State Charles Evans Hughes startled the delegates by proposing a ten-year "holiday" on the construction of warships and by offering to sink or scrap 845,000 tons of American ships, including 30 battleships. He urged Britain and Japan to do the same. The delegates greeted Hughes's speech with enthusiastic cheering and applause, and they set about the task of sinking more ships than the admirals of all their countries had managed to do in a century.

The conference participants ultimately agreed to fix the tonnage of capital ships at a ratio of the United States and Great Britain, 5; Japan, 3; and France and Italy, 1.67. Japan agreed only reluctantly, but when the United States promised not to fortify its Pacific island possessions, Japan yielded. Retrospectively, in the light of what happened in 1941, the Washington Naval Conference has often been criticized, but in 1921, it was appropriately hailed as the first time in history that the major nations of the world had agreed to disarm. The conference did not cause World War II; neither, as it turned out, did it prevent it. But it was a creative beginning to reducing tensions and to meeting the challenges of the modern arms race. And it was the United States that took the lead by offering to be the first to scrap its battleships.

American foreign policy in the 1920s tried to reduce the risk of international conflict, resist revolution, and make the world safe for trade and investment. Nobody in the Republican administrations even suggested that the United States should remain isolated from Latin America. American diplomats argued for an open door to trade in China, in Latin America, but the United States had always assumed a special and distinct role. Throughout the decade, American investment in agriculture, minerals, petroleum, and manufacturing increased in the countries to the south. The United States bought nearly 60 percent of Latin America's exports and sold the region nearly 50 percent of its imports. "We are seeking to establish a Pax Americana maintained not by arms but by mutual agreement and good will," Hughes maintained.

Still, the United States continued the process of intervention begun earlier. By the end of the decade, the United States controlled the financial affairs of ten Latin American nations. The Marines were withdrawn from the Dominican Republic in 1924, but that country remained a virtual protectorate of the United States until 1941. The government ordered the Marines from Nicaragua in 1925, but sent them back the next year when a liberal insurrection threatened the conservative government. But the American Marines, and the Nicaraguan troops they had trained, had a difficult time containing a guerrilla band led by Augusto Sandino, a charismatic leader and one of Latin America's greatest heroes. The Sandinistas, supported by the great majority of peasants, came out of the hills to attack the politicians and their American supporters. One American coffee planter decided in 1931 that the American intervention had been a disaster. "Today we are hated and despised," he announced. "This feeling has been created by employing American Marines to hunt down and kill Nicaraguans in their own country." In 1934, Sandino was murdered by General Anastasio Somoza, a ruthless leader supported by the United States. For more than 40 years, Somoza and his two sons ruled Nicaragua as a private fiefdom, a legacy not yet resolved in that strife-torn country.

Mexico frightened American businessmen in the mid-1920s by beginning to nationalize foreign holdings in oil and mineral rights. Fearing that further military activity would "injure American interests," businessmen and bankers urged Coolidge not to send Marines but to negotiate instead. Coolidge appointed Dwight W. Morrow of the J. P. Morgan Company as ambassador, and his conciliatory attitude led to agreements protecting American investments. Throughout the decade, the goal of U.S. policy toward Central and South America, whether in the form of negotiations or intervention, was to maintain a special sphere of influence.

The United States' policy of promoting peace, stability, and trade was not always consistent or carefully thought out, and this was especially true in its relationships with Europe. At the end of the war, European countries owed the United States over $10 billion, with Great Britain and France responsible for about three-fourths of that amount. Both countries, mired in postwar economic problems, suggested that the United States forgive the debts, arguing that they had paid for the war in lives and property destroyed. But the United States, although adjusting the interest and the payment schedule, refused to forget the debt. "They hired the money, didn't they?" Coolidge supposedly remarked.

International debt was not the same as money borrowed at the neighborhood bank; it influenced trade and investment, which the United States wanted to promote. Practically the only way European nations could repay the United States was by exporting products, but in a series of tariff acts, especially the Fordney-McCumber Tariff of 1922, Congress erected a protective barrier to trade. This act also gave the president power to lower or raise individual rates; both Harding and Coolidge used the power, in almost every case, to raise them. Finally, in 1930, the Hawley-Smoot Tariff raised rates even further, despite the protests of many economists and 35 countries. American policy of high tariffs (a counterproductive policy for a creditor nation) caused retaliation and restrictions on American trade, which American corporations were trying to increase.

The inability of the European countries to export products to the United States and to repay their loans was intertwined with the reparation agreement made with Germany. Germany's economy was in disarray after the war, with inflation raging and its industrial plant throttled by the peace treaty. By 1921, Germany was defaulting on its payments. The United States, which believed a healthy Germany important to the stability of Europe and of world trade, instituted a plan engineered by Charles Dawes whereby the German debt would be renegotiated and spread over a longer period. In the meantime, American bankers and the American government lent Germany hundreds of millions of dollars. In the end, the United States lent money to Germany so it could make payments to Britain and France so that those countries could continue their payments to the United States.

The United States had replaced Great Britain as the dominant force in international finance, but the nation in the 1920s was a reluctant and inconsistent world leader. The United States had stayed out of the League of Nations and was hesitant to get involved in multinational agreements. However, some agreements seemed proper to sign, and the most idealistic of all was the Kellogg-Briand pact to outlaw war. The French foreign minister, Aristide Briand, suggested a treaty between the United States and France in large part to commemorate long years of friendship between the two countries, but Secretary of State Frank B. Kellogg in 1928 expanded the idea to a multinational treaty to outlaw war. Fourteen nations agreed to sign the treaty, and eventually 62 nations signed, but the only power behind the treaty was moral force rather than economic or military sanctions.

The Survival of Progressivism

The decade of the 1920s was a time of reaction against reform, but progressivism did not simply die. It survived in many forms through the period that Jane Addams called a time of "political and social sag." Progressives who sought efficiency and order were perhaps happier during the 1920s than those who tried to promote social justice, but even the fight against poverty and for better housing and the various campaigns to protect children per-

sisted. In a sense, the reformers went underground, but they did not disappear or give up the fight. Child labor reformers worked through the Women's Trade Union League, the Consumers League, and other organizations to promote a child labor amendment to the Constitution after the 1919 law was declared unconstitutional in 1922.

The greatest success of the social justice movement was the 1921 Sheppard-Towner Maternity Act, one of the first pieces of federal social welfare legislation, the product of long progressive agitation. A study conducted by the Children's Bureau discovered that more than 3,000 mothers died in childbirth in 1918 and that more than 250,000 infants also died. The United States ranked eighteenth out of 20 countries in maternal mortality and eleventh in infant deaths. Josephine Baker, the pioneer physician and founder of the American Child Health Association, was not being ironic when she remarked, "It's six times safer to be a soldier in the trenches in France than to be born a baby in the United States."

The maternity bill called for a million dollars a year to assist the states in providing medical aid, consultation centers, and visiting nurses to teach expectant mothers how to care for themselves and their babies. The bill was controversial from the beginning. The American Medical Association, which had supported pure food and drug legislation and laws to protect against health quacks and to enforce standards for medical schools, attacked this bill as leading to socialism and interfering with the relationship between doctor and patient and with the "fee for service" system. Others, especially those who had opposed woman suffrage, argued that it was put forward by extreme feminists, that it was "inspired by foreign experiments in Communism and backed by radical forces in the country," that it "strikes at the heart of American Civilization," and that it would lead to socializing medicine and radicalizing the children.

Despite the opposition, the bill passed Congress and was signed by President Harding in 1921. The appropriation for the bill was only for six years, and the opposition, again raising the specter of a feminist-Socialist-Communist plot, succeeded in repealing the law in 1929. Yet the Sheppard-Towner Act, promoted and fought for by a group of progressive women, indicated that concern for social justice was not dead in the age of Harding and Coolidge.

Temperance Triumphant

For one large group of progressives, prohibition, like child labor reform and maternity benefits, was an important effort to conserve human resources. At first, they argued for local option, whereby states, counties, or cities could decide whether to make the sale of alcohol illegal. Then, after 1913, they pressed for an amendment to the Constitution. The modern prohibition movement had more success than the earlier movement in translating the reformers' zeal into the passage of laws.

By 1918, over three-fourths of the people in the country lived in dry states or counties, but it was the war that allowed the antisaloon advocates to associate prohibition with patriotism. At first, the beer manufacturers supported limited prohibition, but in the end, patriotic fervor prohibited the sale of all alcoholic beverages, including beer and wine. "We have German enemies across the water," one prohibitionist announced. "We have German enemies in this country too. And the worst of all our German enemies, the most treacherous, the most menacing are Pabst, Schlitz, Blatz and Miller."

In 1919, Congress passed the Volstead Act banning the brewing and selling of beverages containing more than 0.5 percent alcohol. The thirty-sixth state ratified the Eighteenth Amendment in June 1919, but the country had, for all practical purposes, been dry since 1917. One social worker confidently predicted that the Eighteenth Amendment would reduce poverty, nearly wipe out prostitution and crime, improve labor, and "substantially increase our national resources by setting free vast suppressed human potentialities."

The prohibition experiment probably did reduce the total consumption of alcohol in the country, especially in rural areas and urban working-class neighborhoods. Fewer arrests for drunkenness occurred, and deaths from alcoholism declined. But the legislation showed the difficulty of using law to promote moral reform. Most people who wanted to drink during the "noble experiment" found a way. Speakeasies replaced saloons, and people consumed bathtub gin, home brew, and many strange and dangerous concoctions. Bartenders invented the cocktail to disguise the poor quality of liquor, and women, at least middle- and upper-class women, began to drink in public for the first time.

Prohibition also created great bootlegging rings, which were tied to organized crime in many cities. Al Capone of Chicago was the most famous underworld figure whose power and wealth were based on the sale of illegal alcohol. His organization alone is supposed to have grossed over $60 million in 1927; ironically, most of the profit came from distributing beer. Many supporters of prohibition slowly came to favor its repeal, some because it reduced the power of the states, others because it stimulated too much illegal activity and because it did not seem to be worth the social and political costs.

The Election of 1928

On August 2, 1927, President Coolidge announced simply, "I do not choose to run for President in 1928." Hoover immediately became the logical Republican candidate. Hoover and Coolidge were not especially close. Coolidge resented what he considered Hoover's spendthrift ways. "That man has offered me unsolicited advice for six years, all of it bad," Coolidge once remarked. Though lacking an enthusiastic endorsement from the president and opposed by some Republicans who thought him too progressive, Hoover easily won the nomination. In a year when the country was buoyant with optimism and when prosperity seemed as if it would go on forever, few doubted that Hoover would be elected.

Herbert Hoover, one of the most popular politicians of the 1920s and one of the most unpopular after 1929, is seen here campaigning from the platform of his private railway car. Note the hats worn by all the men and the few women in the audience. (Corbis-Bettmann)

The Democrats nominated Alfred Smith, a Catholic Irish American from New York. With his New York accent, his opposition to prohibition, and his flamboyant style, he contrasted sharply with the more sedate Hoover. On one level, it was a bitter contest between Catholic "wets" and Protestant "drys," between the urban, ethnic Tammany politician and former governor of New York against the rural-born but sophisticated secretary of commerce. Religious prejudice, especially a persistent anti-Catholicism, played an important role in the campaign. But looked at more closely, the two candidates differed little. Both were self-made men, both were "progressives." Social justice reformers

Presidential Elections, 1920–1928				
Year	Candidate	Party	Popular Vote	Electoral Vote
1920	WARREN G. HARDING	Republican	16,152,200 (60.4%)	404
	James M. Cox	Democratic	9,147,353 (34.2%)	127
	Eugene V. Debs	Socialist	919,799 (3.4%)	0
1924	CALVIN COOLIDGE	Republican	15,725,016 (54.0%)	382
	John W. Davis	Democratic	8,385,586 (28.8%)	136
	Robert M. La Follette	Progressive	4,822,856 (16.6%)	13
1928	HERBERT C. HOOVER	Republican	21,392,190 (58.2%)	444
	Alfred E. Smith	Democratic	15,016,443 (40.9%)	87

Note: Winners' names appear in capital letters.

campaigned for each candidate. Both candidates tried to attract women voters, both were favorable to organized labor, both defended capitalism, and both had millionaires and corporate executives among their advisers.

Hoover won in a landslide, 444 electoral votes to 76 for Smith, who carried only Massachusetts and Rhode Island outside the Deep South. But the 1928 campaign revitalized the Democratic party. Smith polled nearly twice as many votes as the Democratic candidate in 1924, and for the first time the Democrats carried the 12 largest cities.

Stock Market Crash

Hoover, as it turned out, had only six months to apply his progressive and efficient methods to running the country because in the fall of 1929, the prosperity that seemed endless suddenly came to a halt. In 1928 and 1929, rampant speculation made the stock market boom. Money could be made everywhere—in real estate and business ventures, but especially in the stock market. "Everybody ought to be Rich," Al Smith's campaign manager argued in an article in the *Ladies' Home Journal* early in 1929. Just save $15 a month and

TIMELINE

1900–1930	Electricity powers the "second industrial revolution"
1917	Race riot in East Saint Louis, Illinois
1918	World War I ends
1919	Treaty of Versailles
	Strikes in Seattle, Boston, and elsewhere
	Red Scare and Palmer raids
	Race riots in Chicago and other cities
	Marcus Garvey's Universal Negro Improvement Association spreads
1920	Warren Harding elected president
	Women vote in national elections
	First commercial radio broadcast
	Sacco and Vanzetti arrested
	Sinclair Lewis, *Main Street*
1921	Immigration Quota Law
	Disarmament Conference
	First birth control conference
	Sheppard-Towner Maternity Act
1921–1922	Postwar depression
1922	Fordney-McCumber Tariff
	Sinclair Lewis, *Babbitt*
1923	Harding dies; Calvin Coolidge becomes president
	Teapot Dome scandal
1924	Coolidge reelected president
	Peak of Ku Klux Klan activity
	Immigration Quota Law
1925	Scopes trial in Dayton, Tennessee
	F. Scott Fitzgerald, *The Great Gatsby*
	Bruce Barton, *The Man Nobody Knows*
	Alain Locke, *The New Negro*
	Claude McKay, *Home to Harlem*
	5 million enameled bathroom fixtures produced
1926	Ernest Hemingway, *The Sun Also Rises*
1927	National Origins Act
	McNary-Haugen Farm Relief Bill
	Sacco and Vanzetti executed
	Lindbergh flies solo, New York to Paris
	First talking movie, *The Jazz Singer*
	Henry Ford produces 15 millionth car
1928	Herbert Hoover elected president
	Kellogg-Briand Treaty
	Stock market soars
1929	27 million registered cars in country
	10 million households own radios
	100 million people attend movies
	Stock market crash

buy good common stock with it, and that money would turn into $80,000 in 20 years (a considerable fortune in 1929). Good common stock seemed to be easy to find in 1929.

Only a small percentage of the American people invested in the stock market, for many had no way of saving even $15 a month. But a large number got into the game in the late 1920s because it seemed a safe and sure way to make money. For many, the stock market came to represent the American economy, and the economy was booming. The *New York Times* index of 25 industrial stocks reached 100 in 1924, moved up to 181 in 1925, dropped a bit in 1926, and rose again to 245 by the end of 1927.

Then the orgy started. During 1928, the market rose to 331. Many investors and speculators began to buy on margin (borrowing in order to invest). Businessmen and others began to invest money in the market that would ordinarily have gone into houses, cars, and other goods. Yet even at the peak of the boom, probably only about 1.5 million Americans owned stock.

In early September 1929, the *New York Times* index peaked at 452 and then began to drift downward. On October 23, the market lost 31 points. The next day ("Black Thursday"), it first seemed that everyone was trying to sell, but at the end of the day, the panic appeared over. It was not. By mid-November, the market had plummeted to 224, about half what it had been two months before. This represented a loss on paper of over $26 billion. Still, a month later, the chairman of the board of Bethlehem Steel could announce, "Never before has American business been as firmly entrenched for prosperity as it is today." Some businessmen even got back into the market, thinking that it had reached its low point. But it continued to go down. Tens of thousands of investors lost everything. Those who had bought on margin had to keep coming up with money to pay off their loans as the value of their holdings declined. There was panic and despair, but the legendary stories of executives jumping out of windows were grossly exaggerated.

Conclusion

A New Era of Prosperity and Problems

The stock market crash ended the decade of prosperity. The crash did not cause the depression, but the stock market debacle revealed the weakness of the economy. The fruits of economic expansion had been unevenly distributed. Not enough people could afford to buy the autos, refrigerators, and other products pouring from American factories. Prosperity had been built on a shaky foundation. When that foundation crumbled in 1929, the nation slid into a major depression.

Looking back from the vantage point of the 1930s or later, the 1920s seemed a golden era—an age of flappers, bootleg gin, constant parties, literary masterpieces, sports heroes, and easy wealth. The truth is much more complicated. More than most decades, the 1920s was a time of paradox and contradictions.

The 1920s was a time of prosperity, yet a great many people, including farmers, blacks, and other ordinary Americans, did not prosper. It was a time of modernization, but only about 10 percent of rural families had electricity. It was a time when women achieved more sexual freedom, but the feminist movement declined. It was a time of prohibition, but many Americans increased their consumption of alcohol. It was a time of reaction against reform, yet progressivism survived. It was a time when intellectuals felt disillusioned with America, yet it was one of the most creative and innovative periods for American writers. It was a time of flamboyant heroes, yet the American people elected the lackluster Harding and Coolidge as their presidents. It was a time of progress, when almost every year saw a new technological breakthrough, but it was also a decade of hate and intolerance. The complex and contradictory legacy of the 1920s continues to fascinate and to influence our time.

Recommended Reading

General References

Frederick Lewis Allen, *Only Yesterday* (1931); William E. Leuchtenburg, *The Perils of Prosperity, 1914–1932* (1970); Paul Carter, *Another Part of the Twenties* (1977).

Politics, Economics, and Foreign Policy

John D. Hicks, *Republican Ascendancy, 1921–1933* (1960); George Soule, *Prosperity Decade: From War to Depression* (1947); John Kenneth Galbraith, *The Great Crash, 1929* (1954); Andrew Sinclair, *The Available Man* (1965); Donald R. McCoy, *Calvin Coolidge* (1967); Oscar Handlin, *Al Smith and His America* (1958); Joan Hoff Wilson, *Herbert Hoover: The Forgotten Progressive* (1975) and *American Business and Foreign Policy, 1920–1933* (1971); David Burner, *The Politics of Provincialism* (1967); Lawrence Levine, *Defender of the Faith: William Jennings Bryan, The Last Decade* (1965); Warren I. Cohen, *Empire Without Tears* (1987).

Society and Culture

Robert K. Murray, *Red Scare* (1955); Frederick Hoffman, *The Twenties: American Writing in the Postwar Decade* (1955); Nathan Huggins, *Harlem Renaissance* (1971); Houston A. Baker, Jr., *Modernism and the Harlem Renaissance* (1987); Gary Wills, *Under God: Religion and American Politics* (1990); Lyle W. Dorsett, *Billy Sunday and the Redemption of Urban America* (1991); George M. Marsden, *Fundamentalism and American Culture* (1980); David M. Chalmers, *Hooded Americanism: The History of the Ku Klux Klan* (1965); John Higham, *Strangers in the Land: Patterns of American Nativism, 1860–1925* (1955); Sarah Deutsch, *No Separate Refuge* (1987); Paula Fass, *The Damned and Beautiful: American Youth in the 1920s* (1977); Robert Sklar, *Movie Made America* (1975); James J. Flink, *The Car Culture* (1975); Roland Marchand, *Advertising the American Dream* (1985); William H. Chafe, *The American Woman: Her Changing Social and Economic Roles, 1920–1970* (1972); Nancy F. Cott, *The Grounding of Modern Feminism* (1987); J. Stanley Lemons, *The Woman Citizen* (1972); Ruth Schwartz, *More Work for Mother* (1983); Margaret Marsh, *Suburban Lives* (1990); Lizabeth Cohen, *Making a New Deal: Industrial Workers in Chicago, 1919–1939* (1990); Irving Bernstein, *The Lean years: A History of the American Worker* (1960); David E. Nye, *Electrifying America: Social Meaning of a New Technology* (1991); Tom Lewis, *Empire of the Air: The Men Who Made Radio* (1991); Ellen Chesler, *Woman of Valor: Margaret Sanger and the Birth Control Movement* (1992); Ann Douglas, *Terrible Honesty: Mongrel Manhattan in the 1920s* (1995); George Chauncey, *Gay New York: Gender, Urban Culture and the Meaning of the Gay Male World* (1994).

Fiction

Ernest Hemingway's novel *The Sun Also Rises* (1926) is a classic tale of disillusionment and despair in the 1920s; F. Scott Fitzgerald gives a picture of the life of the rich in *The Great Gatsby* (1925); and Claude McKay's novel *Home to Harlem* (1928) is one of the best to come out of the Harlem Renaissance.

The Great Depression and the New Deal

Diana Morgan grew up in a small North Carolina town, the daughter of a prosperous cotton merchant. She lived the life of a "southern belle," oblivious to the country's social and political problems, but the Great Depression changed that. She came home from college for Christmas vacation during her junior year to discover that the telephone had been disconnected. Her world suddenly fell apart. Her father's business had failed, her family didn't have a cook or a cleaning woman anymore, and their house was being sold for back taxes. She was confused and embarrassed. Sometimes it was the little things that were the hardest. Friends would come from out of town, and there would be no ice because her family did not own an electric refrigerator and they could not afford to buy ice. "There were those frantic arrangements of running out to the drugstore to get Coca-Cola with crushed ice, and there'd be this embarrassing delay, and I can remember how hot my face was."

Like many Americans, Diana Morgan and her family blamed themselves for what happened during the Great Depression. Americans had been taught to believe that if they worked hard, saved their money, and lived upright and moral lives, they could succeed. Success was an individual matter for Americans. When so many failed during the Depression, they blamed themselves rather than society or larger forces for their plight. The shame and the guilt affected people at all levels of society. The businessman who lost his business, the farmer who watched his farm being sold at auction, the worker who was suddenly unemployed and felt his manhood stripped away because he could not provide for his family were all devastated by the Depression.

Diana Morgan had never intended to get a job; she expected to get married and let her husband support her. But the failure of her father's business forced her to join the growing number of women who worked outside the home in the 1930s. She finally found a position with the Civil Works Administration, a New Deal agency, where at first she had to ask humiliating questions of the people applying for assistance to make sure they were destitute. "Do you own a car?" "Does anyone in the family work?" Diana was appalled at the conditions she saw when she traveled around the county to corroborate their stories. She found dilapidated houses, a dirty, "almost paralyzed-looking mother," and a drunken father, together with malnourished children. She felt helpless that she could do nothing more than write out a food order. One day, a woman who had formerly cooked for her family came in to apply for help. Each was embarrassed to see the other in changed circumstances.

Diana had to defend the New Deal programs to many of her friends, who accused her of being sentimental and told her that the poor, especially poor blacks, did not know any better than to live in squalor. "If you give them coal, they'd put it in the bathtub," was a charge she often heard. But she knew "they didn't have bathtubs to put coal in. So how did anybody know that's what they'd do with coal if they had it?"

Diana Morgan's experience working for a New Deal agency influenced her life and her attitudes; it made her more of a social activist. Her Depression experience gave her a greater appreciation for the struggles of the country's poor and unlucky. Although she prospered in the years after the Depression, the sense of guilt and the fear that the telephone might again be cut off never left her.

The WPA (Works Progress Administration) hired artists from 1935 to 1943 to create murals for public buildings. The assumption was not only that "artists need to eat too," as Harry Hopkins announced, but also that art was an important part of culture and should be supported by the Federal government. Here Moses Soyer, a Philadelphia artist, depicts WPA artists creating a mural. (Moses Soyer, Artists on WPA, 1935/National Museum of American Art, Smithsonian Institution, Gift of Mr. and Mrs. Moses Soyer/Art Resource, New York) he Great Depression changed the lives of all Americans and separated that generation from the one that followed. An exaggerated need for security, the fear of failure, a nagging sense of guilt, and a real sense that it might happen all over again divided the Depression generation from everyone born after 1940. Like Diana Morgan, most Americans never forgot those bleak years.

This chapter explores the causes and consequences of the Great Depression. We will look at Herbert Hoover and his efforts to combat the Depression and then turn to Franklin Roosevelt, the dominant personality of the 1930s. We will examine the New Deal and Roosevelt's program to bring relief, recovery, and reform to the nation. But we will not ignore the other side of the 1930s, for the decade did not consist only of crippling unemployment and New Deal agencies. It was also a time of great strides in technology, when innovative developments in radio, movies, and the automobile affected the lives of most Americans.

The Great Depression

There had been recessions and depressions in American history, notably in the 1830s, 1870s, and 1890s, but nothing compared to the devastating economic collapse of the 1930s. The Great Depression was all the more shocking because it came after a decade of unprecedented prosperity, when most experts assumed that the United States was immune to a downturn in the business cycle. The Great Depression had an impact on all areas of American life; perhaps most important, it destroyed American confidence in the future.

The Depression Begins

Few people anticipated the stock market crash in the fall of 1929. But even after the collapse of the stock market, few expected the entire economy to go into a tailspin. General Electric stock, selling for 396 in 1929, fell to 34 in 1932; U.S. Steel declined from 261 to 21. By 1932, the median income had plunged to half what it had been in 1929. Construction spending fell to one-sixth of the 1929 level. By 1932, at least one of every four American breadwinners was out of work, and industrial production had almost ground to a halt.

Why did the nation sink deeper and deeper into depression? After all, only about 2 percent of the population owned stock of any kind. The answer is complex, but the prosperity of the 1920s, it appears in retrospect, was superficial. Farmers and coal and textile workers had suffered all through the 1920s from low prices, and the farmers were the first group in the 1930s to plunge into

depression. But other aspects of the economy also lurched out of balance. Two percent of the population received about 28 percent of the national income, but the lower 60 percent got only 24 percent. Businesses increased profits while holding down wages and the prices of raw materials. This pattern depressed consumer purchasing power. American workers, like American farmers, did not have the money to buy the goods they helped to produce. There was a relative decline in purchasing power in the late 1920s, unemployment was high in some industries, and the housing and automobile industries were already beginning to slacken before the crash.

Well-to-do Americans were speculating a significant portion of their money in the stock market. Their illusion of permanent prosperity helped fire the boom of the 1920s, just as their pessimism and lack of confidence helped exaggerate the depression in 1931 and 1932.

Other factors were also involved. The stock market crash revealed serious structural weaknesses in the financial and banking systems (7,000 banks had failed during the 1920s). The Federal Reserve Board, fearing inflation, tightened credit—exactly the opposite of the action they should have taken to fight a slowdown in purchasing. Economic relations with Europe contributed to deepening depression. High American tariffs during the 1920s had reduced trade. When American investment in Europe declined in 1928 and 1929, European economies declined. As the European financial situation worsened, the American economy spiraled downward.

The federal government might have prevented the stock market crash and the Depression by more careful regulation of business and the stock market. Central planning might have assured a more equitable distribution of income. But that kind of policy would have taken more foresight than most people had in the 1920s. It certainly would have required different people in power, and it is unlikely that the Democrats, had they been in control, would have altered the government's policies in fundamental ways.

Hoover and the Great Depression

Initial business and government reactions to the stock market crash were optimistic. "All the evidence indicates that the worst effects of the crash upon unemployment will have been passed during the next sixty days," Herbert Hoover reported. Hoover, the great planner and progressive efficiency expert, did not sit idly by and watch the country drift toward disorder. His upbeat first statements were calculated to prevent further panic.

The Agricultural Marketing Act of 1929 set up a $500 million revolving fund to help farmers organize cooperative marketing associations and to establish minimum prices. But as agricultural prices plummeted and banks foreclosed on farm mortgages, the available funds proved inadequate. The Farm Board was helpless to aid the farmer who could not meet mortgage payments because the price of grain had fallen so rapidly. Nor could it help the Arkansas woman who stood weeping in the window as her possessions, including the cows, which all had names, were sold one by one.

Hoover acted aggressively to stem the economic collapse. More than any president before him, he used the power of the federal government and the office of the president to deal with an economic crisis. Nobody called it a depression for the first year at least, for the economic problems seemed very much like earlier cyclic recessions. Hoover called conferences of businessmen and labor leaders. He met with mayors and governors and encouraged them to speed up public works projects. He created agencies and boards, such as the National Credit Corporation and the Emergency Committee for Employment, to obtain voluntary action to solve the problem. Hoover even supported a tax cut, which Congress enacted in

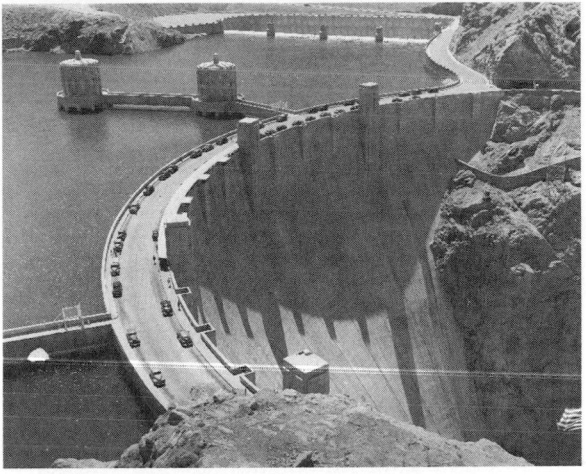

One of the New Deal's largest public works projects was actually started during the Hoover administration. Built between 1931 and 1935, the Boulder Dam (renamed the Hoover Dam) was the greatest American construction feat since the Panama Canal. Rising over 726 feet above bedrock and creating Lake Mead, the world's largest reservoir, the Hoover Dam was an engineering marvel. The project employed tens of thousands of men, but ninety-six lost their lives as they were pushed beyond endurance in 110° heat by companies trying to finish ahead of schedule. The dam provided cheap electricity to Los Angeles and parts of Arizona. And it provided water that turned the imperial valley into one of the most productive agricultural areas in the world. (Culver Pictures)

December 1929, but it did little to stimulate spending. Hoover also went on the radio in his effort to convince the American people that the fundamental structure of the economy was sound.

The Collapsing Economy

Voluntary action and psychological campaigns could not stop the Depression. The stock market, after appearing to bottom out in the winter of 1930–1931, continued its decline, responding in part to the European economic collapse that threatened international finance and trade. Of course, not everyone lost money in the market. William Danforth, founder of Ralston Purina, and Joseph Kennedy, film magnate, entrepreneur, and the father of a future president, were among those who made millions of dollars by selling short as the market went down.

More than a collapsing market afflicted the economy. Over 1,300 additional banks failed in 1930. Despite Hoover's pleas, many factories cut back on production, and some simply closed. U.S. Steel announced a 10 percent wage cut in 1931. As the auto industry laid off workers, the unemployment rate rose to over 40 percent in Detroit. More than 4 million Americans were out of work in 1930, and at least 12 million by 1932. Foreclosures and evictions created thousands of personal tragedies. There were 200,000 evictions in New York City alone in 1930. While the middle class watched in horror as their life savings and their dreams disappeared, the rich were increasingly concerned as the price of government bonds (the symbol of safety and security) dropped. They began to hoard gold and to fear revolution.

There was never any real danger of revolution. Some farmers organized to dump their milk to protest low prices, and when a neighbor's farm was sold, they gathered to hold a penny auction, bidding only a few cents for equipment and returning it to their dispossessed neighbor. But everywhere people despaired as the Depression deepened in 1931 and 1932. For unemployed blacks and for many tenant farmers, the Depression had little immediate effect because their lives were already so depressed. Most Americans (the 98 percent who did not own stock) hardly noticed the stock market crash; for them, the Depression meant the loss of a job or a bank foreclosure. For Diana Morgan, it was the discovery that the telephone had been cut off; for some farmers, it was burning corn rather than coal because the price of corn had fallen so low that it was not worth marketing.

For some in the cities, the Depression meant not having enough money to feed the children. "Have you ever heard a hungry child cry?" asked Lillian Wald of the Henry Street Settlement. "Have you seen the uncontrollable trembling of parents who have gone half starved for weeks so that the children may have food?" In Chicago, children fought with men and women over the garbage dumped by the city trucks. "We have been eating wild greens," a coal miner wrote from Harlan County, Kentucky, "such as Polk salad, violet tops, wild onions … and such weeds as cows eat." In Toledo, when municipal and private charity funds were running low, as they did in all cities, those granted assistance were given only 2.14 cents per meal per person. In another city, a social worker noticed that the children were playing a game called "Eviction." "Sometimes they play 'Relief,'" she remarked, "but 'Eviction' has more action and all of them know how to play."

Not everyone went hungry, stood in breadlines, or lost jobs during the Depression, but almost everyone was affected, and many victims tended to blame themselves. A businessman who lost his job and had to stand in a relief line remembered years later how he would bend his head low so nobody would recognize him. A 28-year-old teacher in New Orleans was released because of a cut in funds, and in desperation she took a job as a domestic servant. "If with all the advantages I've had," she remarked, "I can't make a living, I'm just no good, I guess. I've given up ever amounting to anything. It's no use."

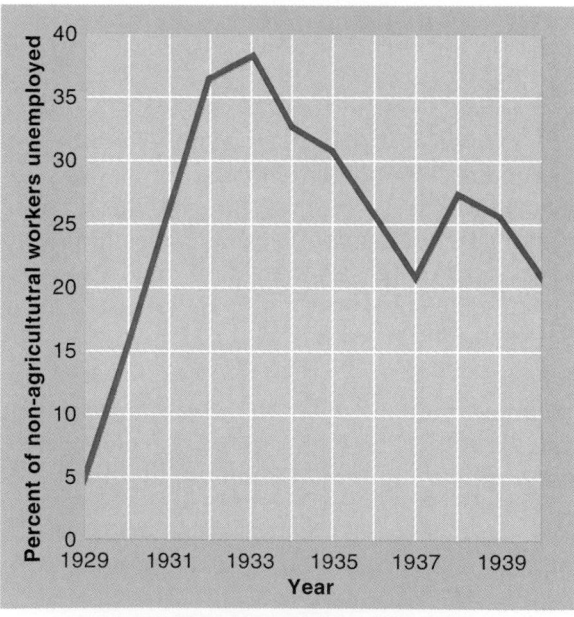

Unemployment Rate, 1929–1940

Although the unemployment rate declined during the New Deal years, the number still unemployed remained tragically high until World War II brought full employment. Source: U.S. Bureau of the Census.

The worst result of the Depression was hopelessness and despair. Those emotions are captured in this painting of an unemployment office by Isaac Soyer. (Employment Agency, 1937/Collection Whitney Museum of American Art, New York)

The Depression probably disrupted women's lives less than men's. "When hard times hit, it didn't seem to bother mother as much as it did father," one woman remembered. There were many exceptions, of course, but when men lost their jobs, their identity and sense of purpose as the family breadwinner were shattered. Some helped out with family chores, usually with bitterness and resentment. For women, however, even when money was short, there was still cooking, cleaning, and mending, and women were still in command of their households. Yet many women were forced to do extra work. They took in laundry, found room for a boarder, and made the clothes they formerly would have bought. Women also bore the psychological burden of unemployed husbands, hungry children, and unpaid bills. The Depression altered patterns of family life, and many families were forced to move in with relatives. The marriage rate, the divorce rate, and the birthrate all dropped during the decade. Many of these changes created tension that statistics cannot capture.

Hoover reacted to growing despair by urging more voluntary action. "We are going through a period," he announced in February 1931, "when character and courage are on trial, and where the very faith that is within us is under test." He insisted on maintaining the gold standard, believing it to be the only responsible currency, and a balanced budget, but so did almost everyone else. Congress was nearly unanimous in supporting those ideals, and Governor Franklin Roosevelt of New York accused Hoover of endangering the country by spending too much. Hoover increasingly blamed the Depression on international economic problems, and he was not entirely mistaken. The whole world was gripped by depression, but as it deepened, Americans began to blame Hoover for some of the disaster. The

The Election of 1932

The Republicans nominated Herbert Hoover for a second term, but in the summer of 1932, the Depression and Hoover's unpopularity opened the way for the Democrats. After a shrewd campaign, Franklin D. Roosevelt, governor of New York, emerged from the pack and won the nomination. Journalist Walter Lippmann's comment during the campaign that Roosevelt was a "pleasant man who, without any important qualifications for office, would like very much to be President" was exaggerated at the time and seemed absurd later. Roosevelt, distantly related to Theodore Roosevelt, had served as an assistant secretary of the navy during World War I and had been the Democratic vice presidential candidate in 1920. Crippled by infantile paralysis not long after, he had recovered enough to serve as governor of New York for two terms, though he was not especially well known by the general public in 1932.

Governor Roosevelt had promoted cheaper electric power, conservation, and old-age pensions. Urged on by advisers Frances Perkins and Harry Hopkins, he became the first governor to support state aid for the unemployed, "not as a matter of charity, but as a matter of social duty." But it was difficult to tell during the presidential campaign exactly what he stood for. He did announce that the government must do something for the "forgotten man at the bottom of the economic pyramid," and he struck out at the small group of men who "make huge profits from lending money and the marketing of securities." Yet he also mentioned the need for balancing the budget and maintaining the gold standard. Ambiguity was probably the best strategy in 1932, but the truth was that Roosevelt did not have a master plan to save the country. Yet he won overwhelmingly, carrying more than 57 percent of the popular vote.

During the campaign, Roosevelt had promised a "new deal for the American people." But after his

The Presidential Election of 1932

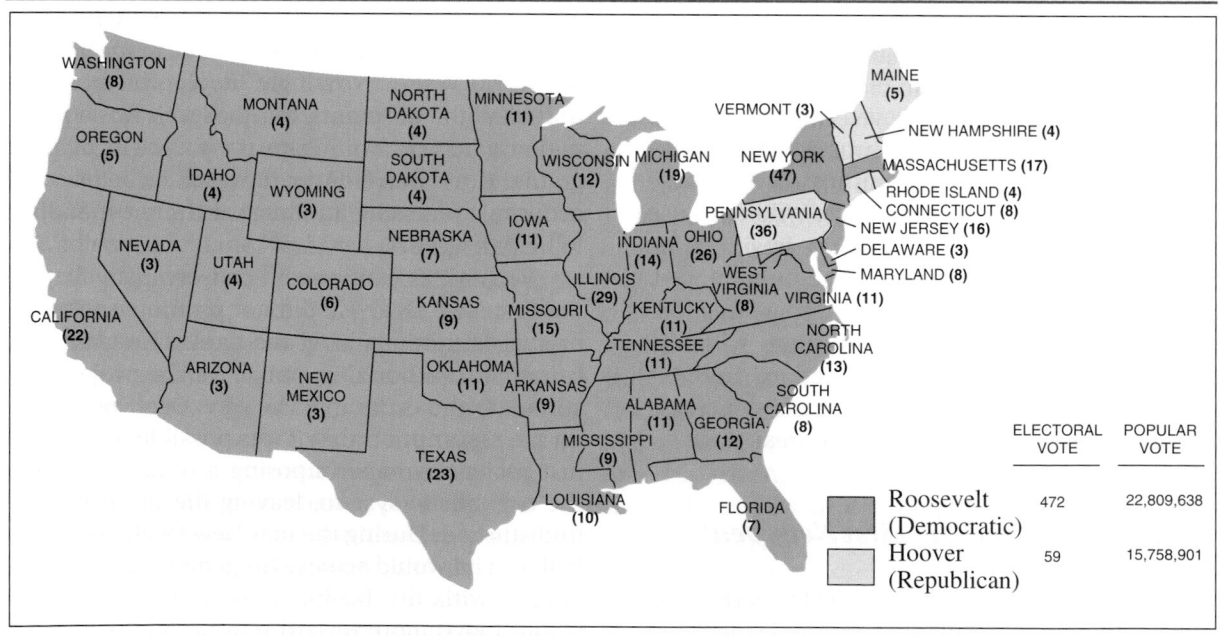

This map demonstrates the overwhelming extent of Roosevelt's landslide victory, caused largely by the economic situation.

victory, the New Deal had to wait for four months because the Constitution provided that the new president be inaugurated on March 4 (this was changed to January 20 by the Twentieth Amendment, ratified in 1933). During the long interregnum, the state of the nation deteriorated badly. The banking system seemed near collapse, and the hardship increased. Despite his bitter defeat, Hoover tried to cooperate with the president-elect and with a hostile Congress. But he could accomplish little. Everyone waited for the new president to take office and to act.

In his inaugural address, Roosevelt announced confidently, "The only thing we have to fear is fear itself." This, of course, was not true, for the country faced the worst crisis since the Civil War, but Roosevelt's confidence and his ability to communicate with ordinary Americans were obvious early in his presidency. He had clever speech writers, a sense of pace and rhythm in his speeches, and an ability, when he spoke on the radio, to convince listeners that he was speaking directly to them. He instituted a series of radio "fireside chats" to explain to the American people what he was doing to solve the nation's problems. When he said "my friends," millions believed that he meant it, and they wrote letters to him in unprecedented numbers to explain their needs.

The Cabinet and the "Brain Trust"

During the interregnum, Roosevelt surrounded himself with intelligent and innovative advisers. Some, like James A. Farley, a former New York State boxing commissioner with a genius for remembering names, and Louis Howe, Roosevelt's secretary and confidant since 1912, had helped plan his successful campaign. His cabinet was made up of a mixture of people from different backgrounds who often did not agree with one another. Harold Ickes, the secretary of the interior, was a Republican lawyer from Chicago and onetime supporter of Theodore Roosevelt. Another Republican, Henry Wallace of Iowa, a plant geneticist and agricultural statistician, became the secretary of agriculture. Frances Perkins, the first woman ever appointed to a cabinet post, became the secretary of labor. A disciple of Jane Addams and Florence Kelley, she had

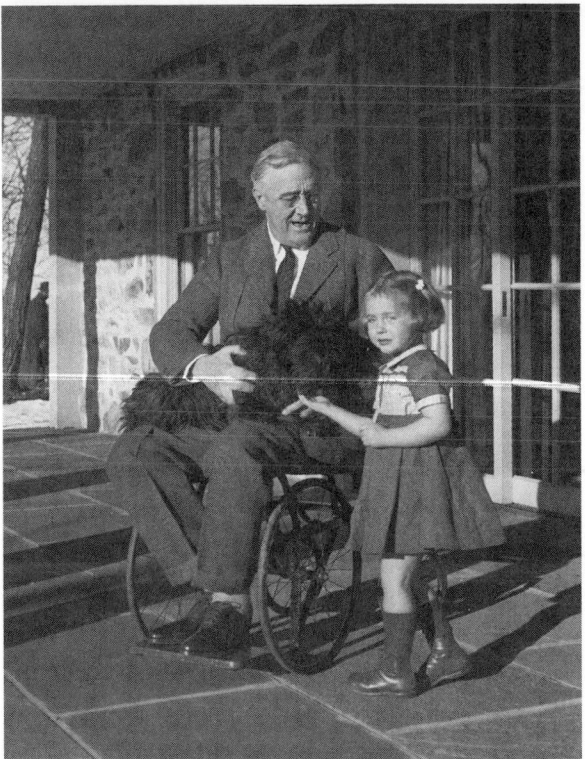

This is a rare photograph of Franklin Roosevelt in his wheelchair taken in a private moment with his dog, Fala, and a young friend. Usually FDR's advisers carefully arranged to have the president photographed only when he was seated or propped up behind a podium. Despite being paralyzed from the waist down, the president until near the end of his life gave the impression of health and vitality. (Margaret Suckley Collection, Franklin Delanor Roosevelt Library)

been a settlement resident, secretary of the New York Consumers League, and an adviser to Al Smith.

In addition to the formal cabinet, Roosevelt appointed an informal "Brain Trust," including Adolph Berle, Jr., a young expert on corporation law, and Rexford Tugwell, a Columbia University authority on agricultural economics and a committed national planner. Roosevelt also appointed Raymond Moley, another Columbia professor, who later became one of the president's severest critics, and Harry Hopkins, a nervous, energetic man who loved to bet on horse races and had left Iowa to be a social worker in New York. Hopkins's passionate concern for the poor and unemployed would play a large role in formulating New Deal policy.

Eleanor Roosevelt, the president's wife, was a controversial first lady. She wrote a newspaper column, made radio broadcasts, traveled widely, and was constantly giving speeches and listening to the concerns of women, minorities, and ordinary Americans. Attacked by critics who thought she had too much power and mocked for her protruding front teeth, her awkward ways, and her upper-class accent, she courageously took stands on issues of social justice and civil rights. She helped push the president toward social reform.

Roosevelt proved to be an adept politician. He was not well read, especially on economic matters, but he had the ability to learn from his advisers and yet not be dominated by them. He took ideas, plans, and suggestions from conflicting sources and combined them. He had a "flypaper mind," one of his advisers decided. There was no overall plan, no master strategy. An improviser and an opportunist who once likened himself to a football quarterback who called one play and if it did not work called a different one, Roosevelt was an optimist by nature. And he believed in action.

One Hundred Days

Because Roosevelt took office in the middle of a major crisis, a cooperative Congress was willing to pass almost any legislation that he put before it. Not since Woodrow Wilson's first term had a president orchestrated Congress so effectively. In three months, a bewildering number of bills were rushed through. Some of them were hastily drafted and not well thought out, and some contradicted other legislation. But many of the laws passed during Roosevelt's first 100 days would have far-reaching implications for the relationship of government to society. Roosevelt was an opportunist, but unlike Hoover, he was willing to use direct government action to solve the problems of depression and unemployment. As it turned out, none of the bills passed during the first 100 days cured the Depres-

sion, but taken together, the legislation constituted one of the most innovative periods in American political history.

The Banking Crisis

The most immediate problem Roosevelt faced was the condition of the banks. Many had closed, and American citizens, no longer trusting the financial institutions, were hoarding money and putting their assets into gold. Using a forgotten provision of a World War I law, Roosevelt immediately declared a four-day bank holiday. Three days later, an emergency session of Congress approved his action and within hours passed the Emergency Banking Relief Act. The bill gave the president broad powers over financial transactions, prohibited the hoarding of gold, and allowed for the reopening of sound banks, sometimes with loans from the Reconstruction Finance Corporation.

Within the next few years, Congress passed additional legislation that gave the federal government more regulatory power over the stock market and over the process by which corporations issued stock. It also passed the Banking Act of 1933, which strengthened the Federal Reserve System, established the Federal Deposit Insurance Corporation (FDIC), and insured individual deposits up to $5,000. Although the American Bankers Association opposed the plan as "unsound, unscientific, unjust and dangerous," banks were soon attracting depositors by advertising that they were protected by government insurance.

The Democratic platform in 1932 called for reduced government spending and an end to prohibition. Roosevelt moved quickly on both. The Economy Act, which passed Congress easily, called for a 15 percent reduction in government salaries as well as a reorganization of federal agencies in order to save money. The bill also cut veterans' pensions, over their protests. However, the Economy Act's small savings were dwarfed by other bills passed the same week, which called for increased spending. The Beer-Wine Revenue Act legalized 3.2 beer and light wines and levied a tax on both. The Twenty-first Amendment, ratified on December 5, 1933, repealed the Eighteenth Amendment and ended the prohibition experiment. The veterans and the antiliquor forces, two of the strongest lobbying groups in the nation, were both overwhelmed by a Congress that seemed ready to give the president free rein.

Congress granted Roosevelt great power to devalue the dollar and to manipulate inflation. Some members argued for the old Populist solution of free and unlimited coinage of silver, while others called for issuing billions of dollars in paper currency. Bankers and businessmen feared inflation, but farmers and debtors favored an inflationary policy as a way to raise prices and put more money in their pockets. "I have always favored sound money," Roosevelt announced, "and I do now, but it is 'too darned sound' when it takes so much of farm products to buy a dollar." He rejected the more extreme inflationary plans supported by many congressmen from the agricultural states, but he did take the country off the gold standard. No longer would paper currency be redeemable in gold. The action terrified some conservative businessmen, who argued that it would lead to "uncontrolled inflation and complete chaos." Even Roosevelt's director of the budget announced solemnly that going off the gold standard "meant the end of Western Civilization."

Devaluation did not end Western civilization, but neither did it lead to instant recovery. After experimenting with pushing the price of gold up by buying it in the open market, Roosevelt and his advisers fixed the price at $35 an ounce in January 1934 (against the old price of $20.63). This inflated the dollar by about 40 percent. Roosevelt also tried briefly to induce inflation through the purchase of silver, but soon the country settled down to a slightly inflated currency and a dollar based on both gold and silver. Some experts still believed that gold represented fiscal responsibility, even morality, and others still cried for more inflation.

Relief Measures

Roosevelt believed in economy in government and in a balanced budget, but he also wanted to help the unemployed and the homeless. One survey estimated in 1933 that 1.5 million Ameri-

cans were homeless. One man with a wife and six children from Latrobe, Pennsylvania, who was being evicted wrote, "I have 10 days to get another house, no job, no means of paying rent, can you advise me as to which would be the most humane way to dispose of myself and family, as this is about the only thing that I see left to do."

Roosevelt's answer was the Federal Emergency Relief Administration (FERA), which Congress authorized with an appropriation of $500 million in direct grants to cities and states. A few months later, Roosevelt created a Civil Works Administration (CWA) to put more than 4 million people to work on various state, municipal, and federal projects. Hopkins, who ran both agencies, had experimented with work relief programs in New York. Like most social workers, he believed it was much better to pay people to work than to give them charity. A woman with two daughters from Houston, Texas, wrote and asked, "Why don't they give us materials and let us make our children's clothes … you've no idea how children hate wearing relief clothes." An accountant working on a road project said, "I'd rather stay out here in that ditch the rest of my life than take one cent of direct relief."

The CWA was not always effective, but in just over a year, the agency built or restored a half-million miles of roads and constructed 40,000 schools and 1,000 airports. It hired 50,000 teachers to keep rural schools open and others to teach adult education courses in the cities. The CWA helped millions of people get through the bitterly cold winter of 1933–1934. It also put over a billion dollars of purchasing power into the economy. Roosevelt, who later would be accused of deficit spending, feared that the program was costing too much and might create a permanent class of relief recipients. In the spring of 1934, he ordered the CWA closed down.

The Public Works Administration (PWA), directed by Harold Ickes, in some respects overlapped the work of the CWA, but it lasted longer. Between 1933 and 1939, the PWA built hospitals, courthouses, and school buildings. It helped construct structures as diverse as the port of Brownsville, Texas, a bridge that linked Key West to the Florida mainland, and the library at the University of New Mexico. It built the aircraft

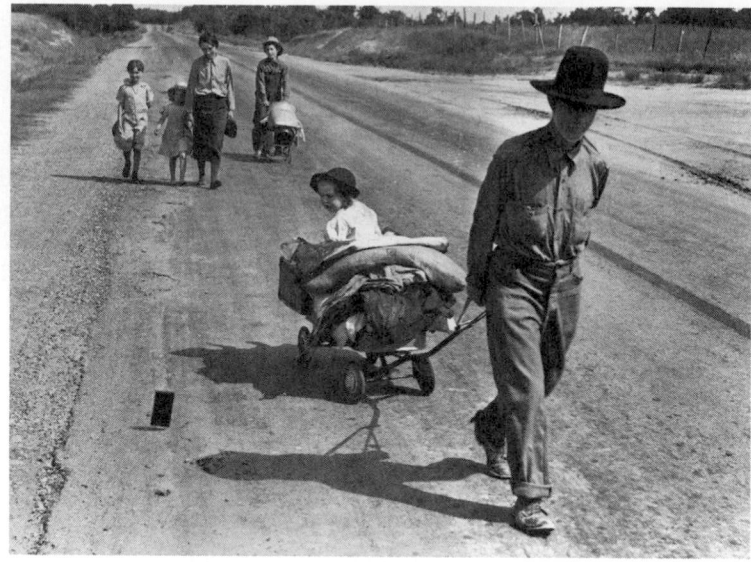

For many people, the Depression meant homeless despair. Here an Oklahoma family who have lost their farm walk with all their possessions along the highway. This compelling photograph was taken by Dorothea Lange, one of several accomplished photographers who documented the impact of the Depression for the Farm Security Administration. (Corbis-Bettmann)

carriers *Yorktown* and *Enterprise,* planes for the Army Air Corps, and low-cost housing for slum dwellers.

One purpose of the PWA was economic pump priming—the stimulation of the economy and consumer spending through the investment of government funds. Afraid that there might be scandals in the agency, Ickes spent money slowly and carefully. Thus during the first years, PWA projects, worthwhile as most of them were, did little to stimulate the economy.

Agricultural Adjustment Act

In 1933, most farmers were desperate, as mounting surpluses and falling prices drastically cut their incomes. Some in the Midwest talked of open rebellion, even of revolution. Many observers saw only hopelessness and despair in farmers who had worked hard but were still losing their farms.

Congress passed a number of bills in 1933 and 1934 to deal with the agricultural crisis. They included the Emergency Farm Mortgage Act, designed to prevent more farm foreclosures and evictions. But the New Deal's principal solution to the farm problem was the Agricultural Adjustment Act (AAA), which sought to control the overproduc-

tion of basic commodities so that farmers might regain the purchasing power they had enjoyed before World War I. To guarantee these "parity prices" (the average prices in the years 1909–1914), the production of major agricultural staples— wheat, cotton, corn, hogs, rice, tobacco, and milk—would be controlled by paying the farmers to reduce their acreage under cultivation. The AAA levied a tax at the processing stage to pay for the program.

The act aroused great disagreement among farm leaders and economists, but the controversy was nothing compared with the outcry from the public over the initial action of the AAA in the summer of 1933. To prevent a glut on the cotton and pork markets, the agency ordered 10 million acres of cotton plowed up and 6 million young pigs slaughtered. It seemed unnatural, even immoral, to kill pigs and plow up cotton when millions of people were underfed and in need of clothes. The story circulated that in the South, mules trained for many years to walk between the rows of cotton now refused to walk on the cotton plants. Some suggested that those mules were more intelligent than the government bureaucrats who had ordered the action.

The Agricultural Adjustment Act did raise the prices of some agricultural products. But it helped the larger farmers more than the small operators, and it was often disastrous for the tenant farmers and sharecroppers, whom crop reduction made expendable. Landowners often discharged tenant families when they reduced the acres under cultivation. There were provisions in the act to help marginal farmers, but little trickled down to them. Many were simply cast out on the road with a few possessions and nowhere to go. As for large farmers, they cultivated their fewer acres more intensely, so that the total crop was little reduced. In the end, the prolonged drought that hit the Southwest in 1934 did more than the AAA to limit production and raise agricultural prices. But the long-range significance of the AAA, which was later declared unconstitutional, was the establishment of the idea that the government should subsidize farmers for limiting production.

Industrial Recovery

The flurry of legislation during the first days of the Roosevelt administration contained something for almost every group. The National Industrial Recovery Act (NIRA) was designed to help business, raise prices, control production, and put people back to work. The act established the National Recovery Administration (NRA) with the power to set fair competition codes in all industries. For a time, everyone forgot about antitrust laws and talked of cooperation and planning rather than competition.

To run the NRA, Roosevelt appointed Hugh Johnson, who had helped organize the World War I draft and served on the War Industries Board. Johnson used his wartime experiences and the enthusiasm of the bond drives to rally the country around the NRA and, implicitly, around all New Deal measures. There were parades and rallies, even a postage stamp, and industries that cooperated could display a blue eagle, the symbol of the NRA. "We Do Our Part," the posters and banners proclaimed, but the results were somewhat less than the promise.

Section 7a of the NIRA, included at the insistence of organized labor, guaranteed labor's right to organize and to bargain collectively and established the National Labor Board to see that their rights were respected. But the board, usually dominated by businessmen, often interpreted the labor provisions of the contracts loosely. In addition, small businessmen complained that the NIRA was unfair to their interests. Any attempt to set prices led to controversy.

Many consumers suspected that the codes and contracts were raising prices, while others feared the return of monopoly in some industries. One woman wrote the president that she was taking down her blue eagle because she had lost her job; another wrote from Tennessee to denounce the NIRA as a joke because it helped only the chain stores. Johnson's booster campaign backfired in the end because anyone with a complaint about a New Deal agency seemed to take it out on the symbol of the blue eagle. When the Supreme Court declared the NIRA unconstitutional in 1935, few people complained. Still, the NIRA was an ambitious attempt to bring some order into a confused business situation, and the labor provisions of the act were picked up later by the National Labor Relations Act.

Civilian Conservation Corps

One of the most popular and successful of the New Deal programs, the Civilian Conservation Corps (CCC), combined work relief with the preservation of natural resources. It put young unemployed men between the ages of 18 and 25 to work on reforestation, road and park construction, flood control, and other projects. The men lived in work camps (there were over 1,500 camps in all) and earned $30 a month, $25 of which had to be sent home to their families. Some complained that the CCC camps, run by the U.S. Army, were too military, and one woman wrote from Minnesota to point out that all the best young men were at CCC camps when they ought to be home looking for real jobs and finding brides. Others complained that the CCC did nothing for unemployed young women, so a few special camps were organized for them, but only 8,000 women took part in a program that by 1941 had included 2.5 million men participants. Overall, the CCC was one of the most successful and least controversial of all the New Deal programs.

Tennessee Valley Authority

Roosevelt, like his Republican ancestor, believed in conservation. He promoted flood-control projects and added millions of acres to the country's national forests, wildlife refuges, and fish and game sanctuaries. But the most important New Deal conservation project, the Tennessee Valley Authority (TVA), owed more to Republican George Norris, a progressive senator from Nebraska, than to Roosevelt.

During World War I, the federal government had built a hydroelectric plant and two munitions factories at Muscle Shoals, on the Tennessee River in Alabama. The government tried unsuccessfully to sell these facilities to private industry, but all through the 1920s, Norris campaigned to have the federal government operate them for the benefit of the valley's residents. Twice Republican presidents vetoed bills that would have allowed federal operation, but Roosevelt endorsed Norris's idea and expanded it into a regional development plan.

Congress authorized the TVA as an independent public corporation with the power to sell electricity and fertilizer and to promote flood control and land reclamation. The TVA built nine major dams and many minor ones between 1933 and 1944, affecting parts of Virginia, North Carolina, Georgia, Alabama, Mississippi, Tennessee, and Kentucky. Some private utility companies claimed that TVA offered unfair competition to private industry, but it was an imaginative experiment in regional planning. It promoted everything from flood control to library bookmobiles. For residents of the valley, it meant cheaper electricity and changed life-styles. The TVA meant radios, electric irons, washing machines, and other appliances for the first time. The largest federal construction project ever launched, it also created jobs for many thousands who helped build the dams. But government officials and businessmen who feared that the experiment would lead to socialism always curbed the regional planning possibilities of the TVA.

The Tennessee Valley Authority

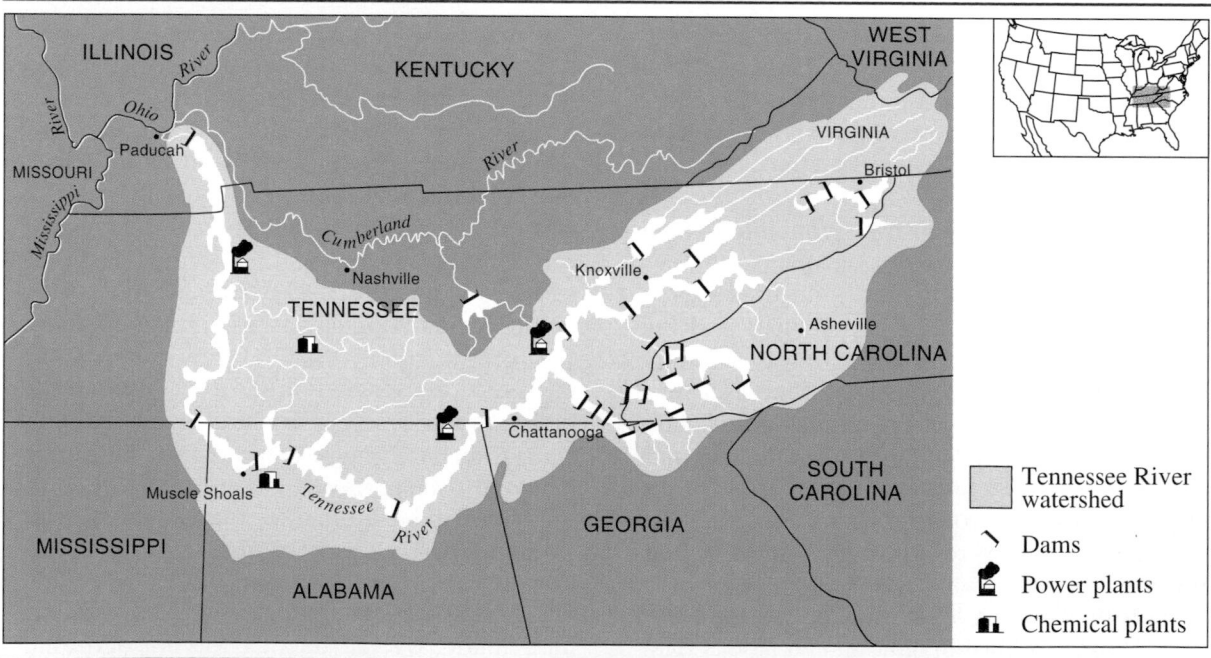

The TVA transformed the way the Tennessee valley looked; it replaced a wild river with a series of flood-control and hydroelectric dams and created a series of lakes behind the dams. It stopped short of the coordinate regional planning that some people wanted, but it was one of the most important New Deal projects.

Critics of the New Deal

The furious legislative activity during the first 100 days of the New Deal helped alleviate the pessimism and despair hanging over the country. Stock market prices rose slightly, and industrial production was up 11 percent at the end of 1933. Still, the country remained locked in depression, and nearly 12 million Americans were without jobs. Yet Roosevelt captured the imagination of ordinary Americans everywhere. Hundreds of thousands of letters poured into the White House, so many that eventually 50 people had to be hired to answer them. "I've always thought of F.D.R. as my personal friend," a man wrote from Georgia. "I feel very grateful to you for all the good you have already done for all of us," another added from Missouri. "If ever there was a saint, he is one," declared a Wisconsin woman.

But conservatives were not so sure that Roosevelt was a savior; in fact, many businessmen, after being impressed with Roosevelt's early economy measures and approving programs such as the NIRA, began to fear that the president was leading the country toward socialism. Appalled by work relief programs, regional planning such as the TVA, and the abandonment of the gold standard, many businessmen were also annoyed by the style of the president, whom they called "that man in the White House."

The conservative revolt against Roosevelt surfaced in the summer of 1934 as the congressional elections approached. A group of disgruntled politicians and businessmen formed the Liberty League. Led by Alfred E. Smith and John W. Davis, two unsuccessful Democratic presidential candidates, the league stood for states' rights, free enterprise, and the "American system of the open shop." The league supported conservative or at least anti–New Deal candidates for Congress, but it had little influence. In the election of 1934, the Democrats increased their majority from 310 to 319 in the House and from 60 to 69 in the Senate (only the second time in the twentieth century that the party in power had increased its control of Congress in the mid-term election). A few people were learning to hate Roosevelt, but it was obvious that most Americans approved of what he was doing.

Much more disturbing to Roosevelt and his advisers in 1934 and 1935 than people who thought the New Deal too radical were those on the left who maintained that the government had not done enough to help the poor. One source of criticism was the Communist party. Attracting supporters from all walks of life during a time when capitalism seemed to have failed, the Communist party increased its membership from 7,500 in 1930 to 75,000 in 1938. The Communists organized protest marches and tried to reach out to the oppressed and unemployed. While a majority who joined the party came from the working class, communism had a special appeal to writers, intellectuals, and some college students during a decade when the American dream had turned into a nightmare.

A larger number of Americans, however, were influenced by other movements promising easy solutions to poverty and unemployment. In Minnesota, Governor Floyd Olson, elected on a Farm-Labor ticket, accused capitalism of causing the Depression and startled some listeners when he thundered, "I hope the present system of government goes right to hell." In California, Upton Sinclair, the muckraking socialist and author of *The Jungle*, ran for governor on the platform "End Poverty in California." He promised to pay everyone over 60 years of age a pension of $50 a month using higher income and inheritance taxes to finance the program. He won in the primary but lost the election, and his program collapsed.

California also produced Dr. Francis E. Townsend, who claimed he had a national following of over 5 million. His supporters backed the Townsend Old Age Revolving Pension Plan, which promised $200 a month to all unemployed citizens over 60 on the condition that they spend it in the same month they received it. Economists laughed at the utopian scheme, but followers organized thousands of Townsend Pension Clubs across the country. As one Minnesota woman wrote to Eleanor Roosevelt, "The old folks who have paid taxes all their lives and built this country up will live in comfort." The plan "will banish crime, give the young a chance to work, pay off the national debt which is mounting every day."

More threatening to Roosevelt and the New Deal than Sinclair and Townsend were the protest movements led by Father Charles E. Coughlin and Senator Huey P. Long. Father Coughlin, a Roman Catholic priest from a Detroit suburb, attracted an audience of 30 to 45 million to his national radio show. At first, he supported Roosevelt's policies, but later he savagely attacked the New Deal as excessively probusiness. Mixing religious commentary with visions of a society operating without bankers and big businessmen, he roused his audience with blatantly anti-Semitic appeals. Most often the "evil" bankers he described were Jewish—the Rothschilds, Warburgs, and Kuhn-Loebs. Anti-Semitism reached a peak in the 1930s, so Jews, rather than Catholics, bore the brunt of nativist fury. Groups like the Silver Shirts and the German-American Bund lashed out against Jews. To members of these groups and others like them, Father Coughlin's attacks made sense.

Huey Long, like Coughlin, had a charisma that won support from the millions still trying to survive in a country where the continuing depression made day-to-day existence a struggle. Elected governor of Louisiana in 1928, Long promoted a "Share the Wealth" program. He taxed the oil refineries and built hospitals, schools, and thousands of miles of new highways. By 1934, he was the virtual dictator of his state, personally controlling the police and the courts. Long talked about a guaranteed $2,000 to $3,000 income for all American families (18.3 million families earned less than $1,000 per year in 1936) and promised pensions for the elderly and college educations for the young. He would pay for these programs by taxing the rich and liquidating the great fortunes. Had not an assassin's bullet cut Long down in September 1935, he might have mounted a third-party challenge to Roosevelt.

The Second New Deal

Responding in part to the discontent of the lower middle class but also to the threat of various utopian schemes, Roosevelt moved his programs in 1935 toward the goals of social reform and social justice. At the same time, he departed from attempts to cooperate with the business community. "We find our population suffering from old inequalities," Roosevelt announced in his annual message to Congress in January 1935. "In spite of our efforts and in spite of our talk, we have not weeded out the overprivileged and we have not effectively lifted up the underprivileged."

Work Relief and Social Security

The Works Progress Administration (WPA), authorized by Congress in April 1935, was the first massive attempt to deal with unemployment and its demoralizing effect on millions of Americans. The WPA employed about 3 million people a year on a variety of socially useful projects. The WPA workers, who earned wages lower than private industry paid, built bridges, airports, libraries, roads, and golf courses. Nearly 85 percent of the funds went directly into salaries and wages.

A minor but important part of the WPA funding supported writers, artists, actors, and musicians. Richard Wright, Jack Conroy, and Saul Bellow were among the 10,000 writers who were paid less than $100 a month. Experimental theater, innovative and well-written guides to all the states, murals painted in municipal and state buildings, and the Historical Records Survey were among the long-lasting results of these projects.

Only one member of a family could qualify for a WPA job, and first choice always went to the man. A woman could qualify only if she headed the household. But eventually more than 13 percent of the people who worked for the WPA were women, although their most common employment was in the sewing room, where old clothes were made over. "For unskilled men we have the shovel. For unskilled women we have only the needle," one official remarked.

The WPA was controversial from the beginning. Critics charged that the agency had hired Communists to paint murals or work on the state guides. For others, a lazy good-for-nothing leaning on a shovel symbolized the WPA. The initials WPA, some wags charged, stood for "We Pay for All" or "We Putter Around." Yet for all the criticism, the WPA did useful work; the program built nearly

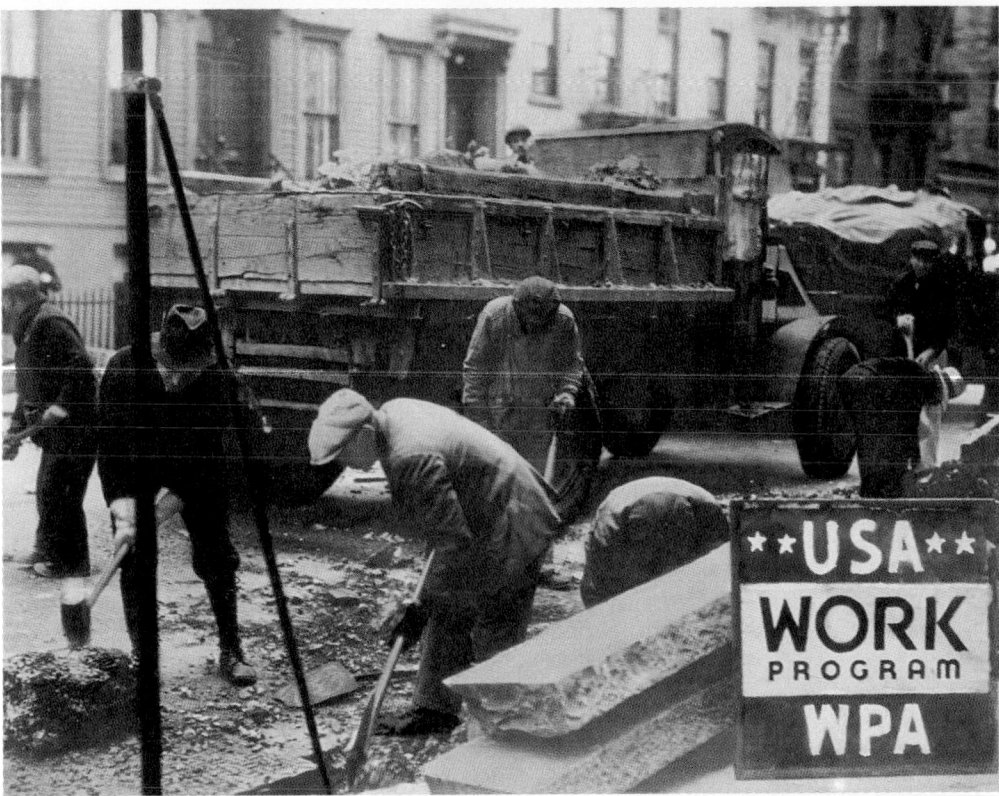

The WPA (which some wags said stood for "We Putter Around") employed many people for a great variety of jobs. This is an unusual photograph because it is in color. A few photographers who worked for government agencies were beginning to experiment with color film, but most of the photographs that survive from the 1930s are black and white. (Corbis-Bettmann)

6,000 schools, more than 2,500 hospitals, and 13,000 playgrounds. More important, it gave millions of unemployed Americans a sense that they were working and bringing in a paycheck to support their families.

The National Youth Administration (NYA) supplemented the work of the WPA and assisted young men and women between the ages of 16 and 25, many of them students. A young law student named Richard Nixon earned 35 cents an hour working for the NYA while he was at Duke University, and Lyndon Johnson began his political career as director of the Texas NYA.

By far the most enduring reform came with the passage of the Social Security Act of 1935. Since the progressive period, social workers and reformers had argued for a national system of health insurance, old-age pensions, and unemployment insur-

ance. By the 1930s, the United States remained the only major industrial country without such programs. Within the Roosevelt circle, Frances Perkins argued most strongly for social insurance, but the popularity of the Townsend Plan and other schemes to aid the elderly helped convince Roosevelt of the need to act. The number of people over 65 in the country increased from 5.7 million in 1925 to 7.8 million in 1935, and that group demanded action.

The Social Security Act of 1935 was a compromise. Congress quickly dropped a plan for federal health insurance because of opposition from the medical profession. The most important provision of the act was old-age and survivor insurance to be paid for by a tax of 1 percent on both employers and employees. The benefits initially ranged from $10 to $85 a month. The act also established a cooperative federal-state system of unemployment compensation. Other provisions authorized federal grants to the states to assist in caring for the disabled and the blind. Finally, the Social Security Act provided some aid to dependent children. This provision would eventually expand to become the largest federal welfare program.

The National Association of Manufacturers denounced social security as a program that would regiment the people and destroy individual self-reliance. In reality, it was a conservative and incomplete system. In no other country was social insurance paid for in part by a regressive tax on the workers' wages. "We put those payroll contributions there so as to give the contributors a legal, moral, and political right to collect their pensions and unemployment benefits," Roosevelt later explained. "With those taxes in there, no damn politician can ever scrap my social security program." But the law also excluded many people, including those who needed it most, such as farm laborers and domestic servants. It discriminated against married women wage earners, and it failed to protect against sickness. Yet for all its weaknesses, it was one of the most important New Deal measures. A landmark in American social legislation, it marked the beginning of the welfare state that would expand significantly after World War II.

Aiding the Farmers

The Social Security Act and the Works Progress Administration were only two signs of Roosevelt's greater concern for social reform. The flurry of legislation in 1935 and early 1936, often called the "second New Deal," also included an effort to help American farmers. Over 1.7 million farm families had incomes of under $500 annually in 1935, and 42 percent of all those who lived on farms were tenants. The Resettlement Administration (RA), motivated in part by a Jeffersonian ideal of yeoman farmers working their own land, set out to relocate tenant farmers on land purchased by the government. Lack of funds and fears that the Roosevelt administration was trying to establish Soviet-style collective farms limited the effectiveness of the RA program.

Much more important in improving the lives of farm families was the Rural Electrification Administration (REA), which was authorized in 1935 to lend money to cooperatives to generate and distribute electricity in isolated rural areas not served by private utilities. Only 10 percent of the nation's farms had electricity in 1936. When the REA's lines were finally attached, they dramatically changed the lives of millions of farm families who had been able only to dream about the radios, washing machines, and farm equipment advertised in magazines.

In the hill country west of Austin, Texas, for example, no electricity existed until the end of the 1930s. Life went on in small towns and on ranches much as it had for decades. Houses were illuminated by kerosene lamps whose wicks had to be trimmed just right or the lamp smoked or went out, but even with perfect adjustment it was difficult to read by them. There were no bathrooms, because bathrooms required running water, and running water depended on an electric pump. "Yes, we had running water," one woman remembered. "I always said we had running water because I grabbed those two buckets up and ran the two hundred yards to the house with them."

Women and children hauled water constantly—for infrequent baths, for continuous canning (because without a refrigerator, fruits and vegetables had to be put up almost immediately or they spoiled), and for washday. Washday, always Monday, meant scrubbing clothes by hand with harsh soap on a washboard; it meant boiling clothes in a large copper vat over a woodstove and stirring them with a wooden fork. It was a hot and backbreaking job, especially in summer. Then the women had to lift the hot, heavy clothes into a rinsing tub. After the clothes were thoroughly mixed with bluing (to make them white), they had to be wrung out by hand, then carried to the lines, where they were hung to dry. Tuesday was for ironing, and even in summer a wood fire was needed to heat the irons. When irons got dirty on the stove, as could easily happen, dirt got on a white shirt or blouse and it had to be washed all over again.

It was memory of life in the hill country and personal knowledge of how hard his mother and grandmother toiled that inspired a young congressman from Texas, Lyndon Johnson, to work to bring rural electrification to the area. In November 1939, the lights finally came on in the hill country, plugging the area into the twentieth century.

The Dust Bowl: An Ecological Disaster

The ultimate goal of the New Deal was to alter and stabilize agriculture through planning and by promoting efficiency. Some farmers profited from the agricultural legislation of the 1930s, but those who tried to farm on the Great Plains fell victim to years of drought and dust storms. Record heat waves and below-average rainfall in the 1930s turned an area from the Oklahoma panhandle to western Kansas into a giant dust bowl. A single storm on May 11, 1934, removed 300 million tons of topsoil and turned day into night. Between 1932 and 1939 there was an average of fifty storms a year. Cities kept their street lights on for 24 hours a day. Dust covered everything from food to bedspreads and piled up in dunes in city streets and barnyards.

Thousands died of "dust pneumonia." One woman remembered what it was like at night: "A trip for water to rinse the grit from our lips, and then back to bed with washcloths over our noses, we try to lie still, because every turn stirs the dust on the blankets."

A 1936 survey of twenty counties in the heart of the dust bowl concluded that 97.6 percent of the land suffered from erosion and more than 50 percent was seriously damaged. By the end of the decade 10,000 farm homes were abandoned to the elements, and 9 million acres of farmland was reduced to a wasteland. By the end of the decade 3.5 million people had abandoned their farms and joined a massive migration to find a better life.

Not all were forced out by the dust storms; some fell victim to large-scale agriculture, and many tenant farmers and hired hands were expendable during the Depression. In most cases they not only lost their jobs, but they also were evicted from their houses. More than 350,000 left Oklahoma during the decade and moved to California, a place

A farmer and his sons race to find shelter from a dust storm in Cimarron County, Oklahoma, in 1936. A combination of factors, including overplanting which destroyed the natural sod of the Great Plains, resulted in the devastating dust storms of the 1930s. Without sod to protect the soil from the wind, thousands of acres of the Great Plains just blew away. (Library of Congress)

that seemed to many like the promised land. But the name *Okie* came to mean any farm migrant. The plight of these wayfarers was immortalized by John Steinbeck in his novel about the Joad family, *The Grapes of Wrath* (1939). The next year John Ford made a powerful movie based on the book starring Henry Fonda as Tom Joad. Many Americans sympathized with the plight of the embattled farm family trying to escape the dust bowl and find a better life in California; others interpreted their defeat as a symbol of the failure of the American dream.

The dust bowl was a natural disaster, but it was aided and exaggerated by human actions and inactions. The semiarid plains west of the 98th meridian were not suitable for intensive agriculture. Overgrazing, too much plowing, and indiscriminate planting over a period of 60 years exposed the thin soil to the elements. When the winds came in the 1930s, much of the land simply blew away. In the end it was a matter of too little government planning and regulation and too many farmers using new technology to exploit natural resources for their own gain.

The Roosevelt administration did try to deal with the problem. The Taylor Grazing Act of 1934 restricted the use of the public range in an attempt to prevent overgrazing, and it also closed 80 million acres of grassland to further settlement. The Civilian Conservation Corps and other New Deal agencies planted trees, and the Soil Conservation Service promoted drought-resistant crops and contour plowing, but it was too little and too late. Even worse, according to some authorities, government measures applied after the disaster of 1930 encouraged farmers to return to raising wheat and other inappropriate crops, leading to more dust bowl crises in the 1950s and 1970s.

The New Deal and the West

The New Deal probably aided the West more than any other region. The CCC, AAA, drought relief measures, and various federal agencies helped the region out of proportion to the people who lived there. In fact, the top fourteen states in per capita expenditure by federal agencies during the 1930s were all in the West. Most important were the large-scale water projects. The Boulder Dam (later renamed the Hoover Dam) on the Colorado River not only provided massive amounts of hydroelectric power but, with the construction of a 259-mile aqueduct, also provided the water that caused the city of Los Angeles to boom.

The largest power project of all was the Grand Coulee Dam on the Columbia River northwest of Spokane, Washington. Employing tens of thousands of men and pouring millions of dollars into the economy, the dam, finally completed in 1941, provided cheap electricity for the Pacific Northwest and eventually irrigated over a million acres of arid land.

Despite all the federal aid to the region many Westerners, holding fast to the myth of frontier individualism, bitterly criticized the regulation and the bureaucracy that went with the grants. The cattlemen in Wyoming, Colorado, and Montana desperately needed the help of the federal government, but even as they accepted the aid they denounced Roosevelt and the New Deal.

Controlling Corporate Power and Taxing the Wealthy

In the summer of 1935, Roosevelt also moved to control the large corporations, and he even toyed with radical plans to tax the well-to-do heavily and redistribute wealth in the United States. The Public Utility Holding Company Act, passed in 1935, attempted to restrict the power of the giant utility companies, the 12 largest of which controlled more than half the country's power. The act gave various government commissions the authority to regulate and control the power companies and included a "death sentence" clause that gave each company five years to demonstrate that its services were efficient. If it could not demonstrate this, the government could dissolve the company. This was one of the most radical attempts to control corporate power in American history.

In his message to Congress in 1935, Roosevelt also pointed out that the federal revenue laws had "done little to prevent an unjust concentration of wealth and economic power." He suggested steeper income taxes for wealthy groups and a much larger inheritance tax. When Congress dropped the inheritance tax provision, however, Roosevelt did not fight to have it restored. Even the weakened bill, increasing estate and gift taxes and raising the income tax rates at the top, angered many in the business community who thought that Roosevelt had sold out to Huey Long's "Share the Wealth" scheme.

The New Deal for Labor

Like many progressive reformers, Roosevelt was more interested in improving the lot of working people by passing social legislation than by strengthening the bargaining position of organized labor. Yet he saw labor as an important balance to the power of industry, and he listened to his advisers, especially to Frances Perkins and to Senator Robert Wagner of New York, who persistently brought up the needs of organized labor.

After strikes in San Francisco, Minneapolis, and Toledo, Roosevelt supported the Wagner Act, officially called the National Labor Relations Act, which outlawed blacklisting and a number of other practices and reasserted labor's right to organize and to bargain collectively. The act also established a Labor Relations Board with the power to certify a properly elected bargaining unit. The act did not require workers to join unions, but it made the federal government a regulator, or at least a neutral force, in management-labor relations. That alone made the national Labor Relations Act one of the most important New Deal reform measures.

The Roosevelt administration's friendly attitude toward organized labor helped increase union membership from under 3 million in 1933 to 4.5 million by 1935. Many groups, however, were left out, including farm laborers, unskilled workers, and women. Only about 3 percent of working women belonged to unions, and women earned only about 60 percent of wages paid to men for equivalent work.

Still, many people resented the fact that women were employed at all. The Brotherhood of Railway and Steamship Clerks ruled that no married woman whose husband could support her was eligible for a job. One writer had a perfect solution for the unemployment problem: "Simply fire the women, who shouldn't be working anyway, and hire the men."

The American Federation of Labor (AFL) had little interest in organizing unskilled workers, but a

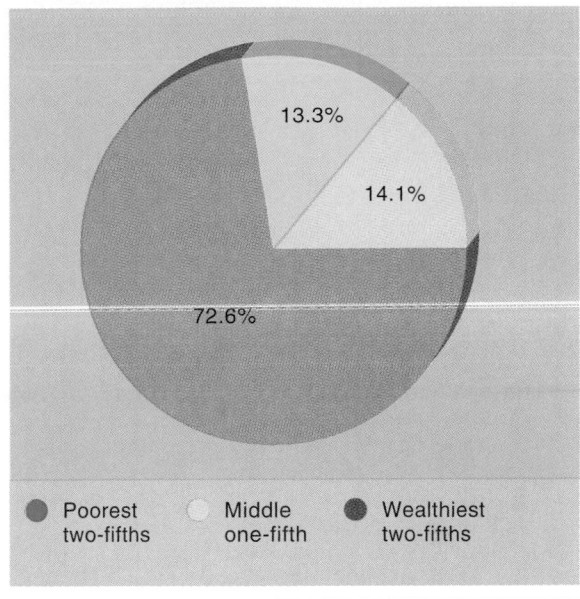

Distribution of Income, 1935–1936

- 13.3%
- 14.1%
- 72.6%

- ● Poorest two-fifths
- ○ Middle one-fifth
- ● Wealthiest two-fifths

Roosevelt and the New Deal never sought consistently to redistribute wealth in America, and a great disparity in income and assets remained. Source: U.S. Bureau of the Census.

new group of committed and militant labor leaders emerged in the 1930s to take up that task. John L. Lewis, the eloquent head of the United Mine Workers, was the most aggressive. He was joined by David Dubinsky of the International Ladies' Garment Workers and Sidney Hillman, president of the Amalgamated Clothing Workers. Both were socialists who believed in economic planning, but both had worked closely with social justice progressives. These new progressive labor leaders formed the Committee of Industrial Organization (CIO) within the AFL and set out to organize workers in the steel, auto, and rubber industries. Rather than separating workers by skill or craft as the AFL preferred, they organized everyone into an industrywide union much as the Knights of Labor had done in the 1880s. They also used new and aggressive tactics. When a foreman tried to increase production or enforce discipline, the union leaders would simply pull the switch and declare a spontaneous strike. This "brass knuckle unionism" worked especially well in the auto and rubber industries.

Frances Perkins, FDR's secretary of labor, was an important defender of organized labor within the administration. As the first woman to hold a cabinet position, she was often greeted by surprised stares as she traveled around the country. (Brown Brothers)

In 1936, the workers at three rubber plants in Akron, Ohio, went on strike without permission from the leaders. Instead of picketing outside the factory, they occupied the buildings and took them over. The "sit-down strike" became a new protest technique. After sit-down strikes against General Motors plants in Atlanta, Georgia, and Flint, Michigan, General Motors finally accepted the United Auto Workers (UAW) as their employees' bargaining agent.

The General Motors strike was the most important event in a critical period of labor upheaval. A group of workers using disorderly but largely nonviolent tactics (as would the civil rights advocates in the mid-1960s) demanded their rights under the law. They helped make labor's voice heard in the decision-making process in major industries where labor had long been denied any role. They also helped raise the status of organized labor in the eyes of many Americans.

"Labor does not seek industrial strife," Lewis announced. "It wants peace, but a peace with justice." As the sit-down tactic spread, violence often accompanied justice. Chrysler capitulated, but the Ford Motor Company used hired gunmen to dis-

courage the strikers. A bloody struggle ensued before Ford agreed to accept the UAW as the bargaining agent. Even U.S. Steel, which had been militantly antiunion, signed an agreement with the Steel Workers Organizing Committee calling for a 40-hour week and an eight-hour day. But other steel companies refused to go along. In Chicago on Memorial Day in 1937, a confrontation between the police and peaceful pickets at the Republic Steel plant resulted in ten deaths. In the "Memorial Day Massacre," as it came to be called, the police fired without provocation into a crowd of workers and their families, who had gathered near the plant in a holiday mood. All ten of the dead were shot in the back.

Despite the violence and management's use of undercover agents within unions, the CIO gained many members. William Green and the leadership of the AFL were horrified at the aggressive tactics of the new labor leaders. They expelled the CIO leaders from the AFL, only to see them form a separate Congress of Industrial Organization (the initials stayed the same). By the end of the decade, the CIO had infused the labor movement with a new spirit. Accepting unskilled workers, African Americans, and others who had never belonged to a union before, the CIO won increased pay, better working conditions, and the right to bargain collectively in most of the basic American industries.

America's Minorities in the 1930s

A half-million African Americans joined unions through the CIO during the 1930s, and many blacks were aided by various New Deal agencies. Yet the familiar pattern of discrimination, low-paying jobs, and intimidation through violence persisted. Lynchings in the South actually increased in the New Deal years, rising from 8 in 1932 to 28 in 1933 and 20 in 1935.

One particular case came to symbolize and dramatize discrimination against African Americans in the 1930s. On March 25, 1931, in Scottsboro, Alabama, two young white women accused nine black men of raping them in a railroad boxcar as they all hitched a free ride. A jury of white men found all nine blacks guilty, and the court sentenced eight to die. The United States Supreme Court ordered new trials in 1933, on the grounds that the accused rapists had not received proper legal counsel. The case garnered much publicity in the United States and abroad. The youth of the defendants, their quick trial, and the harsh sentences made the "Scottsboro boys" a popular cause for many northern liberals and especially the Communist party.

For many southerners, however, it was a matter of defending the honor of white women. As one observer remarked of one of the accusers, she "might be a fallen woman, but by God she is a white woman." However, evidence supporting the alleged rapes was never presented, and eventually one of the women recanted. Yet the case dragged on. In new trials, five of the young men were convicted and given long prison terms. Charges against the other four were dropped in 1937. Four of the remaining five were paroled in 1944, and the fifth escaped to Michigan.

African Americans did not have to be accused of rape to want to flee to the North, however, and the migration of blacks to northern cities, which had accelerated during World War I, continued during the 1930s. The collapse of cotton prices forced black farmers and farm laborers to flee north for survival. But since most were poorly educated, they soon became trapped in northern ghettos, where they were eligible for only the most menial jobs. The black unemployment rate was triple that of whites, and blacks often received less per person in welfare payments.

Black leaders attacked the Roosevelt administration for supporting or allowing segregation in government-sponsored facilities. The TVA model town of Norris, Tennessee, was off limits for blacks, and AAA policies actually drove blacks off the land in the South. The CCC segregated black and white workers, and the PWA financed segregated housing projects. Some charged that NRA stood for "Negroes Rarely Allowed." Many African Americans wrote to the president or the first lady to protest discrimination in New Deal agencies. As one woman from Georgia put it, "I can't sign my name, Mr. President, they will beat me up and run me away from here and this is my home." Blacks ought to realize, a writer in the NAACP journal *The Crisis* warned in 1935, "that the powers-that-be in the Roosevelt administration have nothing for them."

Roosevelt, dependent on the vote of the solid South and fearing that he might antagonize southern congressmen whose backing he needed, refused to support the two major civil rights bills of the era, an antilynching bill and a bill to abolish the poll tax. Yet Harold Ickes and Harry Hopkins worked to ensure that blacks were given opportunities in the CCC, the WPA, and other agencies. By 1941, black federal employees totaled 150,000, more than three times the number during the Hoover administration. Most worked in the lower ranks, but some were lawyers, architects, office managers, and engineers.

Partly responsible for the presence of more black employees was the "black cabinet," a group of more than 50 young blacks who had appointments in almost every government department and New Deal agency. The group met on Friday evenings at the home of Mary McLeod Bethune to discuss problems and plan strategy. The daughter of a sharecropper and one of 17 children, Bethune had worked her way through the Moody Bible Institute in Chicago. She had founded a black primary school in Florida and then transformed it into Bethune-Cookman College. In the 1920s, she had organized the National Council of Negro Women. In 1934, Harry Hopkins, following the advice of Eleanor Roosevelt, appointed her to the advisory committee of the National Youth Administration. Bethune had a large impact on New Deal policy and on the black cabinet. She spoke out forcefully, she picketed and protested, and she intervened shrewdly to obtain civil rights and more jobs for African Americans.

W. E. B. Du Bois, in the meantime, had become increasingly discouraged with token appointments and the reform of race relations through integration with white society. In the 1920s, he supported a series of pan-African conferences designed to unite black people from around the world. He resigned from the NAACP and from his position as editor of *The Crisis* in 1934 and devoted his time to promoting "voluntary segregation" and a "Negro Nation within a nation." Eventually, he joined the Communist party and moved to Ghana, where he died in 1963.

Although Roosevelt appointed a number of blacks to government positions, he was never particularly committed to civil rights. That was not true of Eleanor Roosevelt, who was educated in part by Mary McLeod Bethune. In 1939, when the Daughters of the American Revolution refused to allow Marian Anderson, a black concert singer, to use

their stage, Mrs. Roosevelt publicly protested and resigned her membership in the DAR. She also arranged for Anderson to sing from the steps of the Lincoln Memorial, where 75,000 people gathered to listen and to support civil rights for all black citizens.

Many Mexicans who had been actively recruited for American farms and businesses in the 1920s discovered that they were not needed in the Depression decade. Hundreds of thousands lost their jobs and drifted from the urban *barrios* to small towns and farms in the Southwest looking for work. By one estimate, there were 400,000 Mexican migrants in Texas alone. The competition for jobs increased ethnic prejudice. Signs inscribed "Only White Labor Employed" and "No Niggers, Mexicans, or Dogs Allowed" expressed the hate and fear that the Mexicans encountered everywhere.

Some New Deal agencies helped destitute Mexicans. A few worked for the CCC and the WPA, but to be employed, an applicant had to qualify for state relief, and that eliminated most migrants. The primary solution was not to provide aid for Mexicans but to ship them back to Mexico. Both federal and local authorities encouraged and sometimes coerced Mexican aliens into returning to Mexico. In Los Angeles and other cities, the police and immigration authorities rounded up

Eleanor Roosevelt meeting in 1937 with the National Youth Administration's executive director, Aubrey Williams, and its director of Negro activities, Mary McLeod Bethune. Eleanor Roosevelt was the most visible and the most active of first ladies. She was both praised and attacked for her activities. (UPI/Corbis-Bettmann)

Mexican farm workers, eagerly recruited in the 1920s, often found themselves deported back to Mexico in the 1930s. That even the migrants drove cars and trucks, though old and repaired, shocked foreign observers. In much of the rest of the world autos were still owned only by the wealthy. (Library of Congress)

aliens and held them illegally. A trainload of repatriates left Los Angeles every month during 1933, and officials deported thousands from other cities. One estimate placed the number sent back in 1932 at 200,000, including some American citizens.

Not all the Mexicans were repatriated, however, and some who remained adopted militant tactics to obtain fair treatment. Mexican strawberry pickers went on strike in El Monte, California, and 18,000 cotton pickers walked away from their jobs in the San Joaquin Valley in 1933. In Gallup, New Mexico, several thousand Mexican coal miners walked out on strike. They constructed a village of shacks and planned to wait out the strike. The miners, who were aided by writers and artists from Santa Fe and Taos, were evicted from their village by the city authorities. Federal agents arrested their leader, Jesus Pallares, and deported him to Mexico.

During the Depression, Native Americans also experienced hunger, disease, and despair, and their plight was compounded by years of exploitation. Since the Dawes Act of 1887 (described in Chapter 17), government policy had sought to make the Indian into a property-owning farmer and to limit tribal rights. Native Americans lost over 60 percent of the 138 million acres granted them in 1887. The government declared some of the land surplus and encouraged individuals to settle on 160 acres and adopt the "habits of civilized life." Few Native Americans profited from this system, but many whites did.

Just as other progressives sought the quick assimilation of immigrants, the progressive era Indian commissioners sped up the allotment process to increase Indian detribalization. But many Native Americans who remained on the reservations were not even citizens. Finally, in 1924, Congress granted citizenship to all Indians born in the United States. The original Americans became United States citizens, but that did not end their suffering.

Franklin Roosevelt brought a new spirit to Indian policy by appointing John Collier as commissioner of Indian affairs. Collier had organized the American Indian Defense Association in 1923, but he built on the work of a group of Native American leaders, sometimes called the "Red Progressives." They included Dr. Carlos Montezuma, an Apache physician; Henry Roe Cloud, a Winnebago teacher; and Gertrude Bonnin, a Sioux writer and musician. As commissioner, Collier was primarily responsible for the passage of the Indian Reorganization Act of 1934, which sought to restore the political independence of the tribes and to end the allotment policy of the Dawes Act. "Even where a tribal group is split into factions, where leadership has broken down, where Indians clamor to distribute the tribal property, even there deep forces of cohesion persist and can be evoked," Collier wrote.

The bill also sought to promote the "study of Indian civilization" and to "preserve and develop the special cultural contributions and achievements of such civilization, including Indian arts, crafts, skills and traditions." Not all Indians agreed with the new policies. Some chose to become members of the dominant culture, and the Navajos voted to reject the Reorganization Act. Some Americans charged that the act was inspired by Communism. Others argued that its principal result would be to increase government bureaucracy, while missionaries claimed that the government was promoting paganism by allowing the Indians to practice their native religions.

The paradox and contradictions of United States policy toward the Indians can be illustrated by Collier's attempt to solve the Navajo problem. Genuinely sympathetic to Native Americans, he was also a modern man who believed in soil conservation, science, and progress. The Navajo lands, like most of the West, were overgrazed, and soil erosion threatened to fill the new lake behind the Hoover Dam with silt. By supporting a policy of reducing the herds of sheep and goats on Indian land and by promoting soil conservation, Collier contributed to the change in the Navajo life-style and to the end of their self-sufficiency, something his other policies supported.

Women and the New Deal

Women made some gains during the 1930s, and more women occupied high government positions than in any previous administration. Besides Frances Perkins, the secretary of labor, there was Molly Dewson, a social worker with the Massachusetts Girls Parole Department and the National Consumers League before becoming head of the Women's Division of the Democratic Committee and then an adviser to Roosevelt. Working closely with Eleanor Roosevelt to promote women's causes, she helped achieve a number of firsts: two women appointed ambassadors, a judge on the U.S. Court of Appeals, the director of the mint, and many women in government agencies. Katharine

Lenroot, director of the Children's Bureau, and Mary Anderson, head of the Women's Bureau, selected many other women to serve in their agencies. Some of these women had collaborated as social workers and now joined government bureaus to continue the fight for social justice. But they were usually in offices where they did not threaten male prerogatives.

Despite the number of women working for the government, feminism declined in the 1930s. The older feminists died or retired, and younger women did not replace them. Despite some dramatic exceptions, the image of woman's proper role in the 1930s continued to be housewife and mother.

The Last Years of the New Deal

The New Deal was not a consistent or well-organized effort to end the Depression and restructure society. Roosevelt was a politician and a pragmatist, unconcerned about ideological or programmatic consistency. The first New Deal in 1933 and 1934 concentrated on relief and recovery, while the legislation passed in 1935 and 1936 was more involved with social reform. In many ways, the election of 1936 marked the high point of Roosevelt's power and influence. After 1937, in part because of the growing threat of war but also because of increasing opposition in Congress, the pace of social legislation slowed. Yet several measures passed in 1937 and 1938 had such far-reaching significance that some historians refer to a third New Deal. Among the new measures were bills that provided for a minimum wage and for housing reform.

The Election of 1936

The Republicans in 1936 nominated a moderate, Governor Alfred Landon of Kansas. Although he attacked the New Deal, charging that new government programs were wasteful and created a dangerous federal bureaucracy, Landon only promised to do the same thing more cheaply and efficiently. Two-thirds of the newspapers in the country

FDR's Successful Presidential Campaigns, 1932–1944				
Year	Candidate	Party	Popular Vote	Electoral Vote
1932	FRANKLIN D. ROOSEVELT	Democratic	22,809,638 (57.4%)	472
	Herbert C. Hoover	Republican	15,758,901 (39.7%)	59
	Norman Thomas	Socialist	881,951 (2.2%)	0
1936	FRANKLIN D. ROOSEVELT	Democratic	27,751,612 (60.8%)	523
	Alfred M. Landon	Republican	16,681,913 (36.5%)	8
	William Lemke	Union	891,858 (1.9%)	0
1940	FRANKLIN D. ROOSEVELT	Democratic	27,243,466 (54.8%)	449
	Wendell L. Willkie	Republican	22,304,755 (44.8%)	82
1944	FRANKLIN D. ROOSEVELT	Democratic	25,602,505 (53.5%)	432
	Thomas E. Dewey	Republican	22,006,278 (46.0%)	99

Note: Winners' names appear in capital letters.

supported him, and the *Literary Digest* predicted his victory on the basis of a "scientific" telephone poll.

Roosevelt, helped by signs that the economy was recovering and supported by a coalition of the Democratic South, organized labor, farmers, and urban voters, won easily. A majority of African Americans for the first time deserted the party of Lincoln, not because of Roosevelt's interest in civil rights for blacks but because New Deal relief programs assisted many poor blacks. A viable candidate to the left of the New Deal failed to materialize. In fact, the Socialist party candidate, Norman Thomas, polled fewer than 200,000 votes. Roosevelt won by over 10 million votes, carrying every state except Maine and Vermont. Even the traditionally Republican states of Pennsylvania, Delaware, and Connecticut, which had voted Republican in almost every election since 1856, went for Roosevelt. "To some generations much is given," Roosevelt announced in his acceptance speech; "of other generations much is expected. This generation has a rendezvous with destiny." Now he had a mandate to continue his New Deal social and economic reforms.

The Battle of the Supreme Court

"I see one-third of a nation ill-housed, ill-clad, ill-nourished," Roosevelt declared in his second inau-

gural address, and he vowed to alter that situation. But the president's first action in 1937 did not call for legislation to alleviate poverty. Instead he announced a plan to reform the Supreme Court and the judicial system. The Court had not only invalidated a number of New Deal measures—including the NIRA and the first version of the AAA—but other measures as well.

Increasingly angry at the "nine old men" who seemed to be destroying New Deal initiatives and defying Congress's will, Roosevelt determined to create a more sympathetic Court. He hoped to gain power to appoint an extra justice for each justice over 70 years of age, of whom there were six. His plan also called for modernizing the court system at all levels, but that plan got lost in the public outcry over the Court-packing scheme.

Roosevelt's plan to nullify the influence of the older and more reactionary justices foundered. Republicans accused him of being a dictator and of subverting the Constitution. Many congressmen from his own party refused to support him. Led by Vice President John H. Garner of Texas, a number of southern Democrats broke with the president and formed a coalition with conservative Republicans that lasted for more than 30 years. After months of controversy, Roosevelt withdrew the legislation and admitted defeat. He had perhaps misunderstood his mandate, and he certainly underestimated the respect, even the reverence, that most Americans felt for the Supreme Court. Even in times of economic catastrophe, Americans proved themselves fundamentally conservative toward their institutions, in stark contrast to Europeans, who experimented radically with their governments.

Ironically, though he lost the battle of the Supreme Court, Roosevelt won the war. By the spring of 1937, the Court began to reverse its position and in a 5–4 decision upheld the National Labor Relations Act. When Justice Willis Van Devanter retired, Roosevelt was able to make his first Supreme Court appointment, thus assuring at least a shaky liberal majority on the Court. But Roosevelt triumphed at great cost. His attempt to reorganize the Court dissipated energy and slowed the momentum of his legislative program. The most unpopular action he took as president, it made him vulnerable to criticism from opponents of the New Deal, and even some of his supporters were dismayed by what they regarded as an attack on the principle of separation of powers.

In late 1936 and early 1937, it appeared that the country was finally recovering from the long Depression; employment was up, and even the stock market had recovered some of its losses. But in August, the fragile prosperity collapsed. Unemployment shot back up nearly to the peak levels of 1934, industrial production fell, and the stock market plummeted. Roosevelt had probably helped cause the recession by assuming that the prosperity of 1936 was permanent. He cut federal spending and reduced outlays for relief. He had always believed in balanced budgets and limited government spending, but now, facing an embarrassing economic slump that evoked charges that the New Deal had failed, he gave in to those of his advisers who were followers of John Maynard Keynes, the British economist.

Keynes argued that to get out of a depression, the government must spend massive amounts of money on goods and services. This action would increase demand and revive production. By increasing the money spent on the WPA and other agencies, Roosevelt's administration consciously practiced deficit spending for the first time in order to stimulate the economy. It was not a well-planned or well-coordinated effort, however. The economy responded slowly but never fully recovered until wartime expenditures, beginning in 1940, eliminated unemployment and ended the Depression.

The Third New Deal

Despite increasing hostility, Congress passed a number of important bills in 1937 and 1938 that completed the New Deal reform legislation. The Bankhead-Jones Farm Tenancy Act of 1937 created the Farm Security Administration (FSA) to aid tenant farmers, sharecroppers, and farm owners who had lost their farms. The FSA, which provided loans to grain collectives, also set up camps for migratory workers. Some people saw such policies as the first step toward Communist collectives, but the FSA in fact never had enough money to make a real difference.

Congress passed a new Agricultural Adjustment Act in 1938 that tried to solve the problem of farm surpluses, which persisted even after hundreds of thousands of farmers had lost their farms. The new act replaced the processing tax, which the Supreme Court had declared unconstitutional, with direct payments from the federal treasury to farmers; added a soil conservation program; and provided for the marketing of surplus crops. Like its predecessor, the new act tried to stabilize farm prices by controlling production. But only the outbreak of World War II would end the problem of farm surplus, and then only temporarily.

In the cities, housing continued to be a problem. Progressive reformers had dreamed of providing better housing for the urban poor. They had campaigned for city ordinances and state laws and had built model tenements, but the first experiment with federal housing occurred during World War I. That brief experience encouraged a number of social reformers, who later became advisers to Roosevelt. They convinced him that federal low-cost housing should be part of New Deal reform.

The Reconstruction Finance Corporation made low-interest loans to housing projects, and the Public Works Administration constructed some apartment buildings. But not until the National Housing Act of 1937 did Roosevelt and his advisers try to develop a comprehensive housing policy for the poor. The act provided federal funds for slum clearance projects and for the con-

Key 1930s Reform Legislation		
Year	Legislation	Provisions
1932	Reconstruction Finance Corporation (RFC)	Granted emergency loans to banks, life insurance companies, and railroads (passed during Hoover administration)
1933	Civilian Conservation Corps (CCC)	Employed young men (and a few women) in reforestation, road construction, and flood control projects
1933	Agricultural Adjustment Act (AAA)	Granted farmers direct payments for reducing production of certain products; funds for payments provided by a processing tax, which was later declared unconstitutional
1933	Tennessee Valley Authority (TVA)	Created independent public corporation to construct dams and power projects and to develop the economy of a nine-state area in the Tennessee River valley
1933	National Industrial Recovery Act (NIRA)	Sought to revive business through a series of fair-competition codes; Section 7a guaranteed labor's right to organize (later declared unconstitutional)
1933	Public Works Administration (PWA)	Sought to increase employment and business activity through construction of roads, buildings, and other projects
1934	National Housing Act—created Federal Housing Administration (FHA)	Insured loans made by banks for construction of new homes and repair of old homes
1935	Emergency Relief Appropriation Act—created Works Progress Administration (WPA)	Employed over 8 million people to repair roads, build bridges, and work on other projects; also hired artists and writers
1935	Social Security Act	Established unemployment compensation and old-age and survivors' insurance paid for by a joint tax on employers and employees
1935	National Labor Relations Act (Wagner-Connery Act)	Recognized the right of employees to join labor unions and to bargain collectively; created a National Labor Relations Board to supervise elections and to prevent unfair labor practices
1935	Public Utility Holding Act	Outlawed pyramiding of gas and electric companies through the use of holding companies and restricted these companies to activity in one area; a "death sentence" clause gave companies five years to prove local, useful, and efficient operation or be dissolved
1937	National Housing Act (Wagner-Steagall Act)	Authorized low-rent public housing projects
1938	Agricultural Adjustment Act (AAA)	Continued price supports and payments to farmer to limit production, as in 1933 Act, but replaced processing tax with direct federal payment
1938	Fair Labor Standards Act	Established minimum wage of 40 cents an hour and maximum workweek of 40 hours in enterprises engaged in interstate commerce

struction of low-cost housing. By 1939, however, only 117,000 units had been built. Most of these housing projects were bleak and boxlike, and many of them soon became problems rather than solutions. Though it made the first effort, the New Deal did not meet the challenge of providing decent housing for millions of American citizens.

In the long run, New Deal housing legislation had a greater impact on middle-class housing poli-

cies and patterns. During the first 100 days of the New Deal, at Roosevelt's urging, Congress passed a bill creating the Home Owners Loan Corporation (HOLC), which over the next two years made more than $3 billion in low-interest loans and helped over a million people save their homes from foreclosure. The HOLC also had a strong impact on housing policy by introducing the first long-term fixed-rate mortgages. Formerly, all mortgages were for periods of no more than five years and were subject to frequent renegotiation.

The HOLC also introduced a uniform system of real estate appraisal that tended to undervalue urban property, especially in neighborhoods that were old, crowded, and ethnically mixed. The system gave the highest ratings to suburban developments where, according to the HOLC, there had been no "infiltration of Jews" or other undesirable groups. This was the beginning of the practice later called "redlining" that made it nearly impossible for certain prospective homeowners to obtain a mortgage in many urban areas.

The Federal Housing Administration (FHA), created in 1934 by the National Housing Act, expanded and extended many of these HOLC policies. The FHA insured mortgages, many of them for 25 or 30 years, reduced the down payment required from 30 percent to under 10 percent, and allowed over 11 million families to buy homes between 1934 and 1972. The system, however, tended to favor purchasing new suburban homes rather than repairing older urban residences. New Deal housing policies helped make the suburban home with the long FHA mortgage part of the American way of life, but the policies also contributed to the decline of many urban neighborhoods.

Just as important as housing legislation was the Fair Labor Standards Act, which Congress passed in June 1938. Roosevelt's bill proposed for all industries engaged in interstate commerce a minimum wage of 25 cents an hour, to rise in two years to 40 cents an hour, and a maximum work week of 44 hours, to be reduced to 40 hours. Congress amended the legislation and exempted many groups, including farm laborers and domestic servants. Nevertheless, when it went into effect, 750,000 workers immediately received raises, and by 1940, some 12 million had had pay increases. The law also prohibited child labor in interstate commerce, making it the first permanent federal law to prohibit youngsters under 16 from working. And without emphasizing the matter, the law made no distinction between men and women, thus diminishing, if not completely ending, the need for special legislation for women.

The New Deal had many weaknesses, but it did dramatically increase government support for the needy. In 1913, local, state, and federal government spent $21 million on public assistance. By 1932, that had risen to $218 million; by 1939, it was $4.9 billion.

The Other Side of the 1930s

The Great Depression and the New Deal so dominate the history of the 1930s that it is easy to conclude that nothing else happened, that there were only breadlines and relief agencies. But there is another side of the decade. A communications revolution changed the lives of middle-class Americans. The sale of radios and attendance at movies increased during the 1930s, and literature flourished. Americans were fascinated by technology, especially automobiles. Many people traveled during the decade; they stayed in motor courts and looked ahead to a brighter future dominated by streamlined appliances and gadgets that would mean an easier life.

Taking to the Road

"People give up everything in the world but their car," a banker in Muncie, Indiana, remarked during the Depression, and that seems to have been true all over the country. Although automobile production dropped off after 1929 and did not recover until the end of the 1930s, the number of motor vehicles registered, which declined from 26.7 million in 1930 to just over 24 million in 1933, increased to over 32 million by 1940. People who could not afford new cars drove used ones. Even the "Okies" fleeing the dust bowl of the Southwest traveled in cars. They were secondhand, run-down cars to be sure, but the fact that even many poor Americans owned cars shocked visitors from Europe, where automobiles were still only for the rich.

The American middle class traveled at an increasing rate after the low point of 1932 and 1933. In 1938, the tourist industry was the third largest in the United States, behind only steel and automobile production. Over 4 million Americans traveled every year, and four out of five went by car. Many dragged a trailer for sleeping or stopped at the growing number of tourist courts and overnight cabins. In these predecessors of the motel there were no doormen, no bellhops, no reg-

Household Appliance Production, 1922–1939

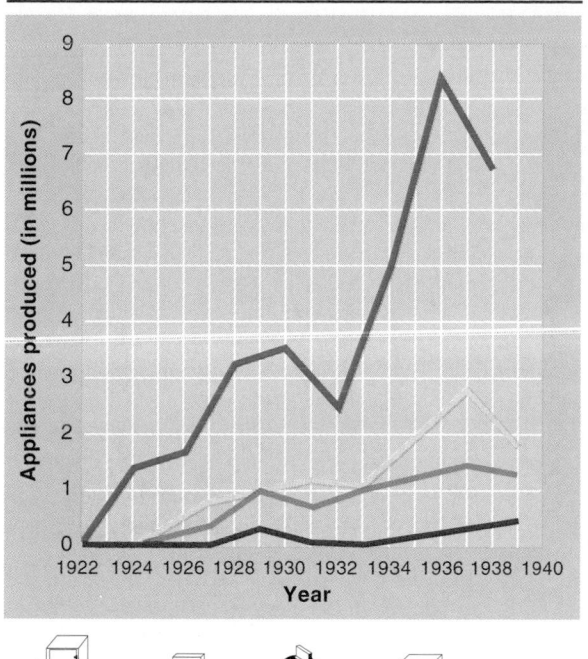

Electric appliances altered the lives of many American middle-class families during the 1930s. The replacement of the icebox with the electric refrigerator was especially dramatic. Source: U.S. Bureau of the Census.

The radio played an important role in the 1930s. Here a family crowds around a typical floor model to listen to the latest news or to a favorite program. (UPI/Corbis-Bettmann)

ister to sign. The tourist court was much more informal than the hotel, and you could park your car next to your cabin.

The Electric Home

If the 1920s was the age of the bathroom, the 1930s was the era of the modern kitchen. The sale of electrical appliances increased throughout the decade, with refrigerators leading the way. In 1930, the number of refrigerators produced exceeded the number of iceboxes for the first time. Refrigerator production continued to rise throughout the decade, reaching a peak of 2.3 million in 1937. At first, the refrigerator was boxy and looked very much like an icebox with a motor sitting on top. In 1935, however, the refrigerator, like most other appliances, became streamlined. Sears, Roebuck advertised "The New 1935 Super Six Coldspot ... Stunning in Its Streamlined Beauty." The Coldspot,

which quickly influenced the look of all other models, was designed by Raymond Loewy, one of a group of industrial designers who emphasized sweeping horizontal lines, rounded corners, and a slick modern look. They hoped modern design would stimulate an optimistic attitude and, of course, increase sales.

Replacing an icebox with an electrical refrigerator, as many middle-class families did in the 1930s, altered more than the appearance of the kitchen. It also changed habits and life-styles, especially for women. An icebox was part of a culture that included icemen, ice wagons (or ice trucks), picks, tongs, and a pan that had to be emptied continually. The refrigerator required no attention beyond occasional defrosting of the freezer compartment. Like the streamlined automobile, the sleek refrigerator became a symbol of progress and modern civilization in the 1930s. At the end of the decade, in 1939, the World's Fair in New York

The Movies

Just as some historians have used fiction to help define the cultural history of a decade, others in the twentieth century have turned to film to describe the "spirit of an age." On an elementary level, the movies help us appreciate changing styles in dress, furniture, and automobiles. We can even get some sense of how a particular time defined a beautiful woman or a handsome man, and we can learn about ethnic and racial stereotypes and assumptions about gender and class.

The decade of the 1930s is sometimes called the "golden age of the movies." Careful selection among the 500 or so feature films Hollywood produced each year during the decade—ranging from gangster and cowboy movies to Marx Brothers comedies, from historical romances to Busby Berkeley musical extravaganzas—could support a number of interpretations about the special myths and assumptions of the era. But one historian has argued that especially after 1934, "Not only did the movies amuse and entertain the nation through its most severe economic and social disorder, holding it together by their capacity to create unifying myths and dreams, but movie culture in the 1930s became a dominant culture for many Americans, providing new values and social ideals to replace shattered old traditions."

The year 1934 was a dividing line for two reasons. The motion picture industry, like all other industries, had suffered during the Depression; 1933 marked the low point in attendance, with more than a third of the theaters in the country shut down. The next year, however, attendance picked up, heralding a revival that lasted until 1946. Also in 1934, the movie industry adopted a code for which the Catholic Legion of Decency and other religious groups had lobbied. The new code prohibited the depiction of "sex perversion, interracial sex, abortion, incest, drugs and profanity." Even married couples could not be shown together in a double bed. Although a movie could depict immoral behavior, sin always had to be punished. "Evil and good should never be confused," the code announced.

Before the code, Hollywood had indeed produced graphic films, such as *The Public Enemy* (1931) and *Scarface* (1932), with a considerable amount of violence; musicals, such as *Gold Diggers of 1933,* filled with scantily clad young women; films featuring prostitutes, such as Jean Harlow in *Red Dust* (1932) and Marlene Dietrich in *Blond Venus* (1930); and other films that confronted the problems of real life. But after 1934, Hollywood concentrated on movies that created a mythical world where evil was

A scene from It Happened One Night, *1934. (The Museum of Modern Art Film Stills Archive)*

A scene from Drums Along the Mohawk, *1939. (The Museum of Modern Art Film Stills Archive)*

always punished, family moral values won out in the end, and patriotism and American democracy were never questioned. Although the code was modified from time to time, it was not abandoned until 1966, when it was replaced by a rating system.

It Happened One Night (1934) and *Drums Along the Mohawk* (1939), two films out of thousands, illustrate some of the myths the movies created and sustained. Frank Capra, one of Hollywood's masters at entertaining without disturbing, directed *It Happened One Night,* a comedy-romance. A rich girl (played by Claudette Colbert) dives from her father's yacht off the coast of Florida and takes a bus for New York. She meets a newspaper reporter (Clark Gable). They have a series of madcap adventures and fall in love. But mix-ups and misunderstandings make it appear that she will marry her old boyfriend. In the end, however, they are reunited and marry in an elaborate outdoor cere-mony. Afterward, they presumably live happily ever after. The movie is funny and entertaining and presents a varia-tion on the poor-boy-marries-rich-girl theme. Like so many movies of the time, this one suggests that life is fulfilled for a woman only if she can find the right man to marry.

Claudette Colbert also stars in *Drums Along the Mohawk,* this time with Henry Fonda. Based on a 1936 novel by Walter Edmonds, *Drums* is a sentimental story about a man who builds a house in the wilderness, marries a pretty girl, fights off the Indians, and works with the simple country folk to create a satisfying life in the very year the American colonies rebel against Great Britain. *Drums* was one of a number of films based on historical themes that Hollywood released just before World War II. *The Howards of Virginia* (1940), *Northwest Passage* (1939), and most popular of all, *Gone with the Wind* (1939) were others in the same genre. Historical themes had been popular before, but with the world on the brink of war, the story of men and women in the wilderness struggling for family and country against the Indians (stereotyped as savages) proved comforting as well as entertaining.

Can a historian use movies to describe the values and myths of a particular time, or are the complexities and exaggerations too great? Are the most popular or most critically acclaimed films more useful than others in get-ting at the "spirit of an age"? What films popular today tell us most about our time and culture? Is there too much sex and violence in movies today? Should the government control the language, themes, and values depicted in movies? Are movies as important today as they were in the 1930s in defining and influencing the country's myths and values?

The General Motors Building at the 1939 New York World's Fair. With the world hovering on the brink of war and the country still caught in the grip of depression, millions of Americans flocked to the fair to see a planned, streamlined world of the future. (Archive Photos)

glorified the theme of a streamlined future, carefully planned and based on new technology.

This reverence for technological progress contrasted with the economic despair in the 1930s, but people adapted to it selectively. For example, the electric washing machine and electric iron revolutionized washday. Yet even with labor-saving machines, most women continued to do their wash on Monday and their ironing on Tuesday. Packaged and canned goods became more widely available during the decade, and many women discovered that it was easier, and in some cases cheaper, to serve Kellogg's Corn Flakes or Nabisco Shredded Wheat than to make oatmeal, to heat Van Camp's pork and beans or Heinz spaghetti from a can than to prepare a meal, or to use commercially baked bread than to bake their own.

Ironically, despite these new conveniences, a great many middle-class families maintained their standard of living during the 1930s only because the women in the family learned to stretch and save and make do, and most wives spent as much time on housework as before. Some also took jobs outside the home to maintain their level of consumption. The number of married women who worked increased substantially during the decade.

At the same time, many rural women, like those in the hill country of Texas and other remote areas, and many wives of the unemployed simply made do. They continued to cook, clean, and sew as their ancestors had for generations.

The Age of Leisure

During the Depression, many middle-class people found themselves with time on their hands and sought out ways of spending it. The 1920s was a time of spectator sports, of football and baseball heroes, of huge crowds that turned out to see boxing matches. Those sports continued during the Depression decade, although attendance suffered. Softball and miniature golf, which were cheap forms of entertainment and did not require expensive travel, also became popular. But leisure in the 1930s actually grew to be a problem, and professionals published some 450 new books on the subject. Leisure was mechanized; millions put their nickels in a slot and listened to a record played on a jukebox. Millions more played a pinball machine, a mechanized device that had no practical use other than entertainment and could end the game with one word: "Tilt."

Double features, newsreels, cartoons, an occasional stage show, and often a gift of free dinnerware (now called "depression glass") made the movie theater a popular place even during the Depression. (Culver Pictures)

Many popular games of the period had elaborate rules and directions. Contract bridge swept the country during the decade, and Monopoly was the most popular game of all. Produced by Parker Brothers, Monopoly was a fantasy of real estate speculation in which chance, luck, and the roll of the dice determined the winner. But one still had to obey the rules: "Go Directly to Jail. Do Not Pass Go. Do Not Collect $200." During a depression brought on in part by frenzied speculation, Americans were fascinated by a game whose purpose was to obtain real estate and utility monopolies and drive one's opponents into bankruptcy.

The 1930s was also a time of fads and instant celebrities, created by radio, newsreels, and businessmen ready to turn almost anything to commercial advantage. The leading box office attraction between 1935 and 1938 was Shirley Temple, a blond and adorable child star. She inspired dolls, dishes, books, and clothes. Even stranger was the excitement created by the birth of five identical girl babies to a couple in northern Ontario in 1934. The Dionne quintuplets appeared on dozens of magazine covers and endorsed every imaginable product. Millions of people waited eagerly for the latest news about the babies, and over 3 million traveled to see their home in Canada. The crazes over Shirley Temple and the Dionne quintuplets were products of the new technology, especially radio and the movies.

Literary Reflections of the 1930s

Though much of the literature of the 1930s reflected the decade's troubled currents, reading continued to be a popular and cheap entertainment. John Steinbeck, whose later novel *The Grapes of Wrath* (1939) followed the fortunes of the Joad family, described the plight of Mexican migrant workers in *Tortilla Flat* (1935). His novels expressed his belief that there was in American life a "crime ... that goes beyond denunciation." "In the eyes of the hungry there is a growing wrath," he warned.

TIMELINE

1929   Stock market crashes

Agricultural Marketing Act

1930   Depression worsens

Hawley-Smoot Tariff

1932   Reconstruction Finance Corporation established

Federal Home Loan Bank Act

Glass-Steagall Banking Act

Federal Emergency Relief Act

Bonus march on Washington

Franklin D. Roosevelt elected president

1933   Emergency Banking Relief Act

Home Owners Loan Corporation

Twenty-first Amendment repeals Eighteenth Amendment, ending prohibition

Agricultural Adjustment Act

National Industrial Recovery Act

Civilian Conservation Corps

Tennessee Valley Authority established

Public Works Administration established

1934   Unemployment peaks

Federal Housing Administration established

Indian Reorganization Act

1935   Second New Deal begins

Works Progress Administration established

Social Security Act

Rural Electrification Act

National Labor Relations Act

Public Utility Holding Company Act

Committee for Industrial Organization (CIO) formed

1936   United Auto Workers hold sit-down strikes against General Motors

Roosevelt reelected president

Economy begins to rebound

1937   Attempt to expand the Supreme Court

Economic collapse

Farm Security Administration established

National Housing Act

1938   Fair Labor Standards Act

Agricultural Adjustment Act

1939   John Steinbeck, *The Grapes of Wrath*

Margaret Mitchell, *Gone with the Wind*

Other writers also questioned the American dream. John Dos Passos's trilogy *U.S.A.* (1930–1936) conveyed a deep pessimism about American capitalism that many other intellectuals shared. Less political were the novels of Thomas Wolfe and William Faulkner, who more sympathetically portrayed Americans caught up in the web of local life and facing the complex problems of the modern era. Faulkner's fictional Yoknapatawpha County, brought to life in *The Sound and the Fury, As I Lay Dying, Sanctuary,* and *Light in August* (1929–1932), documented the South's racial problems and its poverty as well as its stubborn pride. But the book about the South that became one of

the decade's best-sellers was far more optimistic and far less complex than Faulkner's work—Margaret Mitchell's *Gone with the Wind* (1936). Its success suggested that many Americans read to escape, not to explore their problems.

Radio's Finest Hour

The number of radio sets purchased increased steadily during the decade. In 1929, slightly more than 10 million households owned radios; by 1939, fully 27.5 million households had radio sets. The radio was not just a source of music and news but a focal point of the living room. In many homes, the top of the radio became the symbolic mantel where cherished photos were displayed. Families gathered around the radio at night to listen to and laugh at Jack Benny or Edgar Bergen and Charlie McCarthy or to try to solve a murder mystery with Mr. and Mrs. North. "The Lone Ranger," another popular program, had 20 million listeners by 1939.

During the day there were soap operas. "Between thick slices of advertising," wrote James Thurber, "spread twelve minutes of dialogue, add predicament, villainy, and female suffering in equal measure, throw in a dash of nobility, sprinkle with tears, season with organ music, cover with a rich announcer sauce and serve five times a week." After school, teenagers and younger children argued over whether to listen to "Jack Armstrong, the All-American Boy" and "Captain Midnight" or "Stella Dallas" and "The Young Widder Brown."

Most families had only one radio, but everyone could join in the contests or send for magic rings or secret decoders. In Chicago's working-class neighborhoods in 1930 there was one radio for every two or three households but often families and friends gathered to listen to the radio. The reception was sometimes poor, especially in rural areas and small towns. Voices faded in and out and disappeared during storms. But the magic of radio allowed many people to feel connected to distant places and to believe they knew the radio performers personally. Radio was also responsible for one of the most widespread episodes of mass hysteria of all time. On October 31, 1938, Orson Welles broadcast "The War of the Worlds" so realistically that thousands of listeners really believed that Martians had landed in New Jersey. If anyone needed proof, that single program demonstrated the power of the radio.

The Silver Screen

The 1930s were the golden decade of the movies. Between 60 and 90 million Americans went to the movies every week. The medium was not entirely Depression-proof, but talking films had replaced the silent variety in the late 1920s, and attendance soared. Though it fell off slightly in the early 1930s, by 1934 movie viewing was climbing again. For many families, even in the depth of the Depression, movie money was almost as important as food money.

In the cities, one could go to an elaborate movie palace and live in a fantasy world far removed from the reality of Depression America. In small towns across the country, for 25 cents (10 cents under age 12) one could go to at least four movies during the week. There was a Sunday–Monday feature film (except in communities where the churches had prevented Sunday movies), a different feature of somewhat lesser prominence on Tuesday–Wednesday, and another on Thursday–Friday. On Saturday there was a cowboy or detective movie. Sometimes a double feature played, and always there were short subjects, a cartoon, and a newsreel. On Saturday there was usually a serial that left the heroine or hero in such a dire predicament that one just had to come back the next week to see how she or he survived.

The movies were a place to take a date, to go with friends, or to go as a family. Movies could be talked about for days. Young women tried to speak like Greta Garbo or to hold a cigarette like Joan Crawford. Jean Harlow and Mae West so popularized blonde hair that sales of peroxide shot up. Young men tried to emulate Clark Gable or Cary Grant, and one young man admitted that it was "directly through the movies that I learned to kiss a girl on her ears, neck, and cheeks, as well as on the mouth."

The animated cartoons of Walt Disney, one of the true geniuses of the movie industry, were so popular that Mickey Mouse was more famous and familiar than most human celebrities. In May 1933, halfway into Roosevelt's first 100 days, Disney released *The Three Little Pigs,* whose theme song "Who's Afraid of the Big Bad Wolf?" became a national hit overnight. Some people felt it boosted the nation's morale as much as New Deal legislation. One critic suggested that the moral of the story, as retold by Disney, was that the little pig survived because he was conservative, diligent, and hardworking; others felt that it was the pig who used modern tools and planned ahead who won out.

Conclusion

The Ambivalence of the Great Depression

The New Deal, despite its great variety of legislation, did not end the Depression, nor did it solve the problem of unemployment. For many Americans looking back on the decade of the 1930s, the most vivid memory was the shame and guilt of being unemployed, the despair and fear that came from losing a business or being evicted from a home or an apartment. Parents who lived through the decade urged their children to find a secure job, to get married, and to settle down. "Every time I've encountered the Depression it has been used as a barrier and a club," one daughter of Depression parents remembered; "older people use it to explain to me that I can't understand anything: I didn't live through the Depression."

New Deal legislation did not solve the country's problems, but it did strengthen the federal government, especially the executive branch. Federal agencies like the Federal Deposit Insurance Corporation and programs like social security influenced the daily lives of most Americans, and rural electrification, the WPA, and the CCC changed the lives of millions. The New Deal also established the principle of federal responsibility for the health of the economy, initiated the concept of the welfare state, and dramatically increased government spending to help the poor. Federally subsidized housing, minimum-wage laws, and a policy for paying farmers to limit production, all aspects of these principles, had far-reaching implications.

The New Deal was as important for what it did not do as for what it did. It did not promote socialism or redistribute income or property. It promoted social justice and social reform, but it provided little for people at the bottom of American society. The New Deal did not prevent business consolidation, and, in the end, it probably strengthened corporate capitalism:

Roosevelt, with his colorful personality and his dramatic response to the nation's crisis, dominated his times in a way few presidents have done. Yet for some people who lived through the decade, neither Roosevelt nor breadlines but a new streamlined refrigerator or a Walt Disney movie symbolized the Depression decade.

Recommended Reading

General Accounts

Anthony J. Badger, *The New Deal: The Depression Years* (1989); Paul Conkin, *The New Deal* (1967); William E. Leuchtenburg, *Franklin D. Roosevelt and the New Deal* (1963); Robert S. McElvaine, *The Great Depression* (1984).

The Depression

James Agee, *Let Us Now Praise Famous Men* (1941); Lester V. Chandler, *America's Greatest Depression* (1970); Richard White, *The Roots of Dependency: Subsistence, Environment and Social Change Among the Choctaws, Pawnees, and Navajos* (1983); Joan Hoff Wilson, *Herbert Hoover: Forgotten Progressive* (1975); Donald Worster, *Dust Bowl* (1979); Studs Terkel, *Hard Times* (1970).

Roosevelt and the New Deal

Irving Bernstein, *The Turbulent Years: A History of the American Worker, 1933–1941* (1969); Alan Brinkley, *Voices of Protest: Huey Long, Father Coughlin and the Great Depression* (1982) and *The End of Reform: New Deal Liberalism in Recession and War* (1995); James MacGregor Burns, *Roosevelt: The Lion and the Fox* (1956); Dan T. Carter, *Scottsboro* (1969); Lizabeth Cohen, *Making a New Deal: Industrial Workers in Chicago, 1919–1939* (1990); Blanche Wiesen Cook, *Eleanor Roosevelt* (1992); Steve Fraser and Gary Gerstle, eds., *The Rise and Fall of the New Deal Order* (1989); Frank Freidel, *Franklin Roosevelt: A Rendezvous with Destiny* (1990); Abraham Hoffman, *Unwanted: Mexican Americans and the Great Depression* (1974); Joseph Lash, *Eleanor and Franklin* (1971); Richard Lowitt, *The New Deal and the West*

(1984); Roy Lubove, *The Struggle for Social Security* (1968); Jerre Mangione, *The Dream and the Deal* (1972); Richard Pells, *Radical Visions and American Dreams* (1973); Kenneth R. Philip, *John Collier's Crusade for Indian Reform* (1977); Leo P. Ribuffo, *The Old Christian Right: The Protestant Far Right from the Great Depression to the Cold War* (1983); Jordan A. Schwartz, *The New Dealers: Power Politics in the Age of Roosevelt* (1993); Harvard Sitkoff, *A New Deal for Blacks* (1978); Susan Ware, *Beyond Suffrage* (1981).

The Other Side of the Thirties

Andrew Bergman, *We're in the Money* (1972); Lizabeth Cohen, *Making a New Deal: Industrial Workers in Chicago, 1919–1939* (1990); Terry A. Cooney, *Balancing Acts: American Thought and Culture in the 1930s* (1995); David Gelernter, *1939: The Lost World of the Fair* (1995); Siegfreid Giedion, *Mechanization Takes Command* (1948); Jeffrey L. Meikle, *American Plastic: A Cultural History* (1995); Marjorie Rosen, *Popcorn Venus: Women, Movies and the American Dream* (1971); William Stott, *Documentary Expression in Thirties America* (1973); Warren Sussman, ed., *Culture and Commitment* (1968); Susan Ware, *Amelia Earhart and the Search for Modern Feminism* (1993).

Fiction

James Farrell describes growing up in Depression Chicago in *Studs Lonigan* (1932–1935); John Steinbeck shows Okies trying to escape the dust bowl in his novel, *The Grapes of Wrath* (1939); Richard Wright details the trials of a young black man in *Native Son* (1940).

World War II

Scott Momaday, a Kiowa Indian born at Lawton, Oklahoma, in 1934, grew up on Navajo, Apache, and Pueblo reservations. He was only 11 when World War II ended, yet the war changed his life. Shortly after the United States entered the war, Momaday's parents moved to New Mexico, where his father got a job with an oil company and his mother worked in the civilian personnel office at an Army Air Force base. Like many couples, they had struggled through the hard times of the Depression. The war meant jobs.

Reading Right to Left—FIRST ROW: Britain, Canada, Australia, New Zealand, SECOND ROW: Southern Rhodesia, Newfoundland, South Africa, THIRD ROW: India, FOURTH ROW: The Colonial Empire

Reading Left to Right—FIRST ROW: U.S.A., China, U.S.S.R., Yugoslavia, SECOND ROW: Holland, France, Poland, Czechoslovakia, THIRD ROW: Greece, Norway, Belgium

FREEDOM SHALL PREVAIL!

Momaday's best friend was Billy Don Johnson, a "reddish, robust boy of great good humor and intense loyalty." Together they played war, digging trenches and dragging themselves through imaginary minefields. They hurled grenades and fired endless rounds from their imaginary machine guns, pausing only to drink Kool-Aid from their canteens. At school, they were taught history and math and also how to hate the enemy and be proud of America. They recited the Pledge of Allegiance to the flag and sang "God Bless America," "The Star-Spangled Banner," and "Remember Pearl Harbor." Like most Americans, they believed that World War II was a good war fought against evil empires. The United States was always right, the enemy always wrong. It was an attitude that would influence Momaday and his generation for the rest of their lives.

Momaday's only difficulty was that his Native American face was often mistaken for that of an Asian. Almost every day on the playground, someone would yell, "Hi ya, Jap," and a fight was on. Billy Don always came to his friend's defense, but it was disconcerting to be taken for the enemy. His father read old Kiowa tales to Momaday, who was proud to be an Indian but prouder still to be an American. On Saturday, he and his friends would go to the local theater to cheer as they watched a Japanese Zero or a German ME-109 go down in flames. They pretended that they were P-40 pilots. "The whole field of vision shuddered with our fire: the 50-caliber tracers curved out, fixing brilliant arcs upon the span, and struck; then there was a black burst of smoke, and the target went spinning down to death."

Near the end of the war, his family moved again, as so many families did, so that his father might get a better job. This time they lived right next door to an air force base, and Momaday fell in love with the B-17 "Flying Fortress," the bomber that military strategists thought would win the war in the Pacific and in Europe. He felt a real sense of resentment and loss when the B-17 was replaced by the larger but not nearly so glamorous B-29.

Looking back on his early years, Momaday reflected on the importance of the war in his growing up. "I see now that one experiences easily the ordinary things of life," he decided, "the things which cast familiar shadows upon the sheer, transparent panels of time, and he perceives his experience in the only way he can, according to his age." Though Momaday's life during the war differed from the lives of boys old enough to join the armed forces, the war was no less real for him. Though his youth was affected by the fact that he was male, was an Indian, and lived in the Southwest, the most important influence was that he was an American growing up during the war. Ironically, his parents, made U.S. citizens by an act of Congress in 1924, like all Native Americans living in Arizona and New Mexico were denied the right to vote by state law.

The Momadays fared better than most Native Americans, who found prejudice against them undiminished and jobs, even in wartime, hard to find. Native American servicemen returning from the war discovered that they were still treated like "Indians." They were prohibited from buying liquor in many states, and those who returned to the reservations learned that they were ineligible for veterans' benefits. Still, Momaday thought of himself not so much as an Indian as an American, and that too was a product of his generation. But as he grew to maturity, he became a successful writer and spokesman for his people. In 1969, he won the Pulitzer Prize for his novel *House Made of Dawn*. He also recorded his experiences and memories in a book called *The Names* (1976). In his writing, he stresses the Indian's close identification with the land. Writing about his grandmother, he says: "The immense landscape of the continental interior lay like memory in her blood."

A World War II poster depicting the many nations united in the fight against the Axis powers. In reality there were often disagreements. Notice to the right the American sailor is marching next to Chinese and Soviet soldiers. Within a few years after victory they would be enemies. (Courtesy The American Legion) espite the fact that no American cities were bombed and the country was never invaded, World War II influenced almost every aspect of American life. The war ended the Depression. Industrial jobs were plentiful, and even though prejudice and discrimination did not disappear, blacks, Hispanics, women, and other minorities had new opportunities. Like World War I, the second war expanded cooperation between government and industry and increased the influence of government in all areas of American life. The war also ended the last remnants of American isolationism. The United States emerged from the war in 1945 as the most powerful and most prosperous nation in the world.

This chapter traces the gradual involvement of the United States in the international events during the 1930s that finally led to participation in the most devastating war the world had seen. It recounts the diplomatic and military struggles of the war and the search for a secure peace. It also seeks to explain the impact of the war on ordinary people and on American attitudes about the world, as well as its effect on patriotism and the American way of life. The war brought prosperity to some as it brought death to others. It left the American people the most affluent in the world and the United States the most powerful nation.

The Twisting Road to War

Looking back on the events between 1933 and 1941 that eventually led to American involvement in World War II, it is easy either to be critical of decisions made or actions not taken or to see everything that happened during the period as inevitable. Historical events are never inevitable, and leaders who must make decisions never have the advantage of retrospective vision; they have to deal with situations as they find them, and they never have all the facts.

Foreign Policy in the 1930s

In March 1933, Roosevelt faced not only overwhelming domestic difficulties but also international crisis. The worldwide depression had caused near financial disaster in Europe. Germany had defaulted on its reparations installments, and most European countries were unable to keep up the payments on their debts to the United States. President Hoover had agreed to a brief moratorium on war debts in 1931 and had pledged American participation in an international economic conference to be held in London in June 1933.

Roosevelt had no master plan in foreign policy, just as he had none in the domestic sphere. In the first days of his administration, he gave conflicting signals as he groped to respond to the international situation. At first, it seemed that the president would cooperate in some kind of international economic agreement on tariffs and currency. But then he undercut the American delegation in London by refusing to go along with any international agreement. Solving the American domestic economic crisis seemed more important to Roosevelt in 1933 than international economic cooperation. His actions signaled a decision to go it alone in foreign policy in the 1930s.

Roosevelt did, however, alter some of the foreign policy decisions of previous administrations. For example, he recognized the Soviet government. There were many reasons why the United States had not recognized the Soviet Union during the 1920s. The new regime had failed to accept the debts of the tsar's government, but more important, Americans feared communism and believed that recognition meant approval. In reversing this nonrecognition policy, Roosevelt hoped to gain a market for surplus American grain. Although the expected trade bonanza never materialized, the Soviet Union agreed to pay the old debts and to extend rights to American citizens living in the Soviet Union. Diplomatic recognition opened communications between the two emerging world powers.

Led by Secretary of State Cordell Hull, Roosevelt's administration also reversed the earlier policy of intervention in South America. The United States continued to support dictators, especially in Central America, because they promised to promote stability and preserve American economic interests. But Roosevelt, extending the Good Neighbor policy Hoover had initiated, completed the removal of American military forces from Haiti and Nicaragua in 1934, and, in a series of pan-American conferences, he joined in pledging that no country in the hemisphere would intervene in the "internal or external affairs" of any other. The United States still had economic and trade interests in Latin America, however, and with many of the Latin American economies in disarray because of the Depression, pressures mounted to resume the policy of military intervention.

The first test case came in Cuba, where a revolution threatened American investments of more than a billion dollars. But the United States did not send troops. Instead Roosevelt dispatched special envoys to work out a conciliatory agreement with the revolutionary government. A short time later, when a coup led by Fulgencio Batista overthrew the revolutionary government, the United States not only recognized the Batista government but also offered a large loan and agreed to abrogate the Platt Amendment (which made Cuba a virtual protectorate of the United States) in return for the rights to a naval base.

The Trade Agreements Act of 1934 gave the president power to lower tariff rates by as much as 50 percent and took the tariff away from the pressure of special-interest groups in Congress. Using this act, the Roosevelt administration negotiated a series of agreements that improved trade. By 1935, half of American cotton exports and a large proportion of other products were going to Latin America. So the Good Neighbor policy was also good business for the United States. But increased trade did not solve the economic problems for either the United States or Latin America.

Another test for Latin American policy came in 1938 when Mexico nationalized the property of a number of American oil companies. Instead of intervening, as many businessmen urged, the State Department patiently worked out an agreement that included some compensation for the companies. The American government might have acted differently, however, if the threat of war in Europe in 1938 had not created a fear that all the Western Hemisphere nations would have to cooperate to resist the growing power of Germany and Italy. At a pan-American conference held that year, the United States and most Latin American countries agreed to resist all foreign intervention in the hemisphere.

Neutrality in Europe

Around the time that Roosevelt was first elected president, Adolf Hitler came to power in Germany. Born in Austria in 1889, Hitler had served as a corporal in the German army during World War I. Like many other Germans, he was angered by the Treaty of Versailles. But he blamed Germany's defeat on the Communists and the Jews.

Hitler had a checkered life after the war. He became the leader of the National Socialist party of the German workers (*Nazi* is short for *National*), and in 1923, after leading an unsuccessful coup, he was sentenced to prison. While in jail he wrote *Mein Kampf* ("My Struggle"), a long, rambling book spelling out his theories of racial purity, his hopes for Germany, and his venomous hatred of the Jews. After his release from prison, Hitler's following grew. He had a charismatic style and a plan. On January 30, 1933, he became chancellor of Germany, and within months the Reichstag (parliament) suspended the constitution, making Hitler Führer (leader) and dictator. His Fascist regime concentrated political and economic power in a centralized state. He intended to conquer Europe and to make the German Third Reich (empire) the center of a new civilization.

In 1934, Hitler announced a program of German rearmament, violating the Versailles Treaty of 1919. Meanwhile, in Italy, a Fascist dictator, Benito Mussolini, was building a powerful military force, and in 1934, he threatened to invade the East African country of Ethiopia. These ominous rumblings in Europe frightened Americans at the very time they were reexamining American entry into the Great War and vowing that they would never again get involved in a European conflict.

Senator Gerald P. Nye of North Dakota, a conscientious and determined man who had helped expose the Teapot Dome scandal in 1924, turned to an investigation of the connection between corporate profits and American participation in World War I. His committee's public hearings revealed that many American businessmen had close relationships with the War Department. Businesses producing war materials had made huge profits. Though the committee failed to prove a conspiracy, it was easy to conclude that the United States had been tricked into going to war by the people who profited most from it.

On many college campuses, students demonstrated against war. On April 13, 1934, a day of protest around the country, students at Smith College placed white crosses on the campus as a memorial to the people killed in the Great War and those who would die in the next one. The next year, even more students went on strike for a day. Students joined organizations like Veterans of Future Wars and Future Gold Star Mothers and protested the presence of the Reserve Officer Training Corps on their campuses. One college president, who supported the peace movement, announced, "We will be called cowards … [but] I say that war must be banished from civilized society if democratic civilization and culture are to be perpetuated." Not all students supported the peace movement, but in the mid-1930s, many young people as well as adults joined peace societies such as the Fellowship of Reconciliation and the Women's International League for Peace and Freedom. They were determined never again to support a foreign war. But in Europe, Asia, and Africa, there were already rumblings of another great international conflict.

Newsreels and popular magazines such as Life *and* Look *made Hitler's image and mannerisms familiar to all Americans. (The Granger Collection, New York)*

Ethiopia and Spain

In May 1935, Italy invaded Ethiopia after rejecting the League of Nations' offer to mediate the difficulties between the two countries. Italian dive bombers and machine guns made quick work of the small and poorly equipped Ethiopian army. The Ethiopian war, remote as it seemed, frightened Congress, which passed a Neutrality Act authorizing the president to prohibit all arms shipments to nations at war and to advise all United States citizens not to travel on belligerents' ships except at their own risk. Remembering the process that led the United States into World War I, Congress was determined that it would not happen again.

Though he would have preferred a more flexible bill, Roosevelt used the authority of the Neutrality Act of 1935 to impose an arms embargo. The League of Nations condemned Italy as the aggressor in the war, and Great Britain moved its fleet to

the Mediterranean. But neither Britain nor the United States wanted to stop shipments of oil to Italy or to commit its own soldiers to the fight. The embargo on arms had little impact on Italy, but it was disastrous for the poor African nation. Italy quickly defeated Ethiopia, and by 1936, Mussolini had joined forces with Germany to form the Rome-Berlin Axis.

"We shun political commitments which might entangle us in foreign war," Roosevelt announced in 1936. "We are not isolationist except in so far as we seek to isolate ourselves completely from war." But isolation became more difficult when a civil war broke out in Spain in 1936. General Francisco Franco, supported by the Catholic church and large landowners, revolted against the republican government. Germany and Italy aided Franco, sending planes and other weapons, while the

Soviet Union came to the support of the Spanish republican Loyalists.

The war in Spain polarized the United States. Most Catholics and many anti-Communists sided with Franco. But many American radicals, even those opposed to all war a few months before, found the Loyalist cause worth fighting and dying for. Over 3,000 Americans joined the Abraham Lincoln Brigade, and hundreds were killed fighting fascism in Spain. "If this were a Spanish matter, I'd let it alone," Sam Levenger, a student at Ohio State, wrote. "But the rebellion would not last a week if it weren't for the Germans and the Italians. And if Hitler and Mussolini can send troops to Spain to attack the government elected by the people, why can't they do so in France? And after France?" Levenger was killed in Spain in 1937 at the age of 20.

Not everyone agreed that the moral issues in Spain were worth dying for. The U.S. government tried to stay neutral and to ship arms and equipment to neither side. The Neutrality Act, extended in 1936, technically did not apply to civil wars, but the State Department imposed a moral embargo. However, when an American businessman disregarded it and attempted to send 400 used airplane engines to the Loyalists, Roosevelt asked Congress to extend the arms embargo to Spain. While the United States, along with Britain and France, carefully protected its neutrality, Franco consolidated his dictatorship with the active aid of Germany and Italy. Meanwhile, Congress in 1937 passed another Neutrality Act, this time making it illegal for American citizens to travel on belligerents' ships. The act extended the embargo on arms and made even nonmilitary items available to belligerents only on a cash-and-carry basis.

In a variety of ways, the United States tried to avoid repeating the mistakes that had led it into World War I. Unfortunately, World War II, which moved closer each day, would be a different kind of war, and the lessons of the first war would be of little use.

War in Europe

Roosevelt had no carefully planned strategy to deal with the rising tide of war in Europe in the late 1930s. He was by no means an isolationist, but he wanted to keep the United States out of the European conflagration. When he announced, "I hate war," he was expressing a deep personal belief that wars solve few problems. Unlike his distant cousin Theodore Roosevelt, he did not view war as a test of one's manhood. In foreign policy, just as in domestic affairs, he responded to events, but he moved reluctantly (and with agonizing slowness, from the point of view of many of his critics) toward more and more American involvement in the war.

In March 1938, Hitler's Germany annexed Austria and then in September, as a result of the Munich Conference, occupied the Sudetenland, a part of Czechoslovakia. Within six months, Hitler's armies had overrun the rest of Czechoslovakia. Little protest came from the United States. Most Americans sympathized with the victims of Hitler's aggression, and eventually some were horrified at rumors of the murder of hundreds of thousands of Jews. But because newspapers avoided intensive coverage of the well-documented but unpleasant stories, many Americans did not learn of the Holocaust of the early 1940s until near the end of the war.

At first, almost everyone hoped that compromises could be worked out and that Europe could settle its own problems. But that notion was destroyed on August 23, 1939, by the news of a Nazi-Soviet pact. Fascism and Communism were political philosophies supposedly in deadly opposition. Many Americans had secretly hoped that Nazi Germany and Soviet Russia would fight it out, neutralizing each other. Now they had signed a non-aggression pact. A week later, Hitler's army attacked Poland, marking the official beginning of World War II. Britain and France honored their treaties and came to Poland's defense. "This nation will remain a neutral nation," Roosevelt announced, "but I cannot ask that every American remain neutral in thought as well."

Roosevelt asked for a repeal of the embargo section of the Neutrality Act and for the approval of the sale of arms on a cash-and-carry basis to France and Britain. The United States would help the countries struggling against Hitler, but not at the risk of entering the war or even at the threat of disrupting the civilian economy. Yet Roosevelt did take some secret risks. In August 1939, Albert Einstein, a Jewish refugee from Nazi Germany, and other distinguished scientists warned the president that German researchers were at work on an atomic bomb. Fearing the consequences of a powerful new weapon in Hitler's hands, Roosevelt authorized funds for a top-secret project to build an American bomb first. Only a few advisers and key members of Congress knew of the project, which was officially organized in 1941 and would ultimately change the course of human history.

The war in Poland ended quickly. With Germany attacking from the west and the Soviet Union from the east, the Poles were overwhelmed in a month. The fall of Poland in September 1939 brought a lull in the fighting. A number of Americans, including the American ambassador to Great Britain, Joseph Kennedy, who feared Communist Russia more than Fascist Germany, urged the United States to take the lead in negotiating a peace settlement that would recognize the German and Russian occupation of Poland. The British and French, however, were not interested in such a solution, and neither was Roosevelt.

Great Britain sent several divisions to aid the French against the expected German attack, but for months nothing happened. This interlude, sometimes called the "phony war," dramatically ended on April 9, 1940, when Germany attacked Norway and Denmark with a furious air and sea assault. A few weeks later, using armored vehicles supported by massive air strikes, the German *Blitzkrieg* ("lightning war") swept through Belgium, Luxembourg, and the Netherlands. A week later, the Germans stormed into France.

The famed Maginot line, a series of fortifications designed to repulse a German invasion, was useless, as German mechanized forces swept around the end of the line and attacked from the rear. The French guns, solidly fixed in concrete and pointing toward Germany, were never fired. The Maginot line, which would have been an effective defensive weapon in World War I, was ineffective in the new mechanized and mobile war of the 1940s. France surrendered in June as the British army fled back across the English Channel from Dunkirk.

How should the United States respond to the new and desperate situation in Europe? William Allen White, journalist and editor, and other concerned Americans organized the Committee to Defend America by Aiding the Allies, but others, including Charles Lindbergh, the hero of the 1920s, supported a group called America First. They argued that the United States should forget about England and concentrate on defending America. Roosevelt steered a cautious course. He approved the shipment to Britain of 50 overage American destroyers. In return, the United States received the right to establish naval and air bases on British territory from Newfoundland to Bermuda and British Guiana.

Winston Churchill, prime minister of Great Britain, asked for much more, but Roosevelt hesitated. In July 1940, the president did sign a measure authorizing $4 billion to increase the number of American naval warships. In September, Congress passed the Selective Service Act, which provided for the first peacetime draft in the history of the United States. Over a million men were to serve in the army for one year, but only in the Western Hemisphere. As the war in Europe reached a crisis in the fall of 1940, the American people were still undecided about the proper response.

The Election of 1940

Part of Roosevelt's reluctance to aid Great Britain more energetically came from his genuine desire to keep the United States out of the war, but it was also related to the presidential campaign waged during the crisis months of the summer and fall of 1940. Roosevelt broke a long tradition by seeking a third term. He marked the increasing support he was drawing from the liberal wing of the Democratic party by selecting liberal farm economist Henry Wallace of Iowa as his running mate.

The Republicans nominated Wendell Willkie of Indiana. Despite his big-business ties, Willkie approved of most New Deal legislation and supported aid to Great Britain. Energetic and attractive, Willkie was the most persuasive and exciting Republican candidate since Theodore Roosevelt, and he appealed to many people who distrusted or disliked Roosevelt. Yet in an atmosphere of international crisis, most voters chose to stay with Roosevelt. He won, 27 million to 22 million, and carried 38 of 48 states.

Lend-Lease

After the election, Roosevelt invented a scheme for sending aid to Britain without demanding payment. He called it "lend-lease." He compared the situation to lending a garden hose to a neighbor whose house was on fire. Senator Robert Taft of Ohio, however, thought the idea of lending military equipment and expecting it back was absurd. He decided it was more like lending chewing gum to a friend: "Once it had been used you did not want it back." Others were even more critical. Senator Burton K. Wheeler, an extreme isolationist, branded lend-lease "Roosevelt's triple A foreign policy" (after the Agricultural Adjustment Act) because it was designed to "plow under every fourth American boy."

The Lend-Lease Act, which Congress passed in March 1941, destroyed the fiction of neutrality. By that time, German submarines were sinking a half-million tons of shipping each month in the Atlantic. In June, Roosevelt proclaimed a national emergency and ordered the closing of German and Italian consulates in the United States. On June 22, Germany suddenly attacked the Soviet Union. It was one of Hitler's biggest blunders of the war, for now his armies had to fight on two fronts.

The surprise attack created a dilemma for the United States. Suddenly the great Communist "enemy" had become America's friend and ally. When Roosevelt extended lend-lease aid to Russia in November 1941, many Americans were shocked. But most made a quick transition from viewing the Soviet Union as an enemy to treating it like a friend.

By the autumn of 1941, the United States was virtually at war with Germany in the Atlantic. On September 11, Roosevelt issued a "shoot on sight" order for all American ships operating in the Atlantic, and on October 30, a German submarine sank an American destroyer off the coast of New-foundland. The war in the Atlantic, however, was undeclared, and many Americans opposed it. Eventually the sinking of enough American ships or another crisis would probably have provided the excuse for a formal declaration of war against Germany. It was not Germany, however, but Japan that catapulted the United States into World War II.

The Path to Pearl Harbor

Japan, controlled by ambitious military leaders, was the aggressor in the Far East as Hitler's Germany was in Europe. Intent on becoming a major world power yet desperately needing natural resources, especially oil, Japan was willing to risk war with China, the Soviet Union, and even the United States to get those resources. Japan invaded Manchuria in 1931 and launched an all-out assault on China in 1937. The Japanese leaders assumed that at some point the United States would go to war if Japan tried to take the Philippines, but the Japanese attempted to delay that moment as long as possible by diplomatic means. For its part, the United States feared the possibility of a two-front war and was willing to delay the confrontation with Japan until it had dealt with the German threat. Thus between 1938 and 1941, the United States and Japan engaged in a kind of diplomatic shadow boxing.

The United States did exert economic pressure on Japan. In July 1939, the United States gave the required six months' notice regarding cancellation of the 1911 commercial agreement between the two countries. In September 1940, the Roosevelt administration forbade the shipment of airplane fuel and scrap metal to Japan. Other items were added to the embargo until by the spring of 1941, the United States allowed only oil to be shipped to Japan, hoping that the threat of cutting off the important resource would lead to negotiations and avert a crisis. Japan did open negotiations with the United States, but there was little to discuss. Japan would not withdraw from China as the United States demanded. Indeed, Japan, taking advantage of the situation in Europe, occupied French Indochina in 1940 and 1941. In July 1941, Roosevelt froze all Japanese assets in the United States, effectively embargoing trade with Japan.

Roosevelt had an advantage in the negotiations with Japan, for the United States had broken the Japanese secret diplomatic code. But Japanese intentions were hard to decipher from the intercepted messages. The American leaders knew that Japan planned to attack, but they didn't know where. In September 1941, the Japanese decided to strike sometime after November unless the United States offered real concessions. The strike came not in the Philippines but at Pearl Harbor, the main American Pacific naval base, in Hawaii.

On the morning of December 7, 1941, Japanese airplanes launched from aircraft carriers attacked the United States fleet at Pearl Harbor. The surprise attack destroyed or disabled 19 ships (including five battleships) and 150 planes and killed 2,335 soldiers and sailors and 68 civilians. On the same day, the Japanese launched attacks on the Philippines, Guam, and the Midway Islands, as well as on the British colonies of Hong Kong and Malaya. The next day, with only one dissenting vote, Congress declared war on Japan. Jeannette Rankin, a member of Congress from Montana who had voted against the war resolution in 1917, voted no again in 1941. She recalled that in 1917, after a week of tense debate, 50 voted against going to war. "This time I stood alone."

Corporal John J. "Ted" Kohl, a 25-year-old from Springfield, Ohio, was standing guard that Sunday morning near an ammunition warehouse at Hickam Field, near Pearl Harbor. He had joined the army two years before when his marriage failed and he could not find work. A Japanese bomb hit

nearby, and Ted Kohl blew up with the warehouse. It was not until Wednesday evening, December 10, that the telegram arrived in Springfield. "The Secretary of War desires to express his deep regrets that your son Cpl. John J. Kohl was killed in action in defense of his country." Ted's younger brothers cried when they heard the news. There would be hundreds of thousands of telegrams and even more tears before the war was over.

December 7, 1941, was a day that "would live in infamy," in the words of Franklin Roosevelt. It was also a day that would have far-reaching implications for American foreign policy and for American attitudes toward the world. The surprise attack united the country as nothing else could have. Even isolationists and "America first" advocates quickly rallied behind the war effort.

After the shock and anger subsided, Americans searched for a villain. Someone must have blundered, someone must have betrayed the country to have allowed the "inferior" Japanese to have carried out such a successful and devastating attack. A myth persists to this day that the villain was Roosevelt, who, the story goes, knew of the Japanese attack but failed to warn the military commanders so that the American people might unite behind the war effort against Germany. But

An exploding American destroyer at Pearl Harbor, December 7, 1941. The attack on Pearl Harbor united the country and came to symbolize Japanese treachery and American lack of preparedness. Photographs such as this were published throughout the war to inspire Americans to work harder. (Superstock, Inc.)

Roosevelt did not know. There was no specific warning that the attack was coming against Pearl Harbor, and the American ability to read the Japanese coded messages was no help because the fleet kept radio silence.

The irony was that the Americans, partly because of racial prejudice against the Japanese, underestimated their ability. They ignored many warning signals because they did not believe that the Japanese could launch an attack on a target as far away as Hawaii. Most of the experts, including Roosevelt, expected the Japanese to attack the Philippines or perhaps Thailand. Many people blundered, but there was no conspiracy on the part of Roosevelt and his advisers to get the United States into the war.

Even more important in the long run than the way the attack on Pearl Harbor united the American people was its effect on a generation of military and political leaders. Pearl Harbor became the symbol of unpreparedness. For a generation that experienced the anger and frustration of the attack on Pearl Harbor by an unscrupulous enemy, the lesson was to be prepared and ready to stop an aggressor before it had a chance to strike at the United States. The smoldering remains of the sinking battleships at Pearl Harbor on the morning of December 7, 1941, and the history lesson learned there would influence American policy not only during World War II but also in Korea, Vietnam, and the international confrontations of the 1980s.

The Home Front

Too often wars are described in terms of presidents and generals, emperors and kings, in terms of grand strategy and elaborate campaigns. But wars affect the lives of all people—the soldiers who fight and the women and children and men who stay home. World War II especially had an impact on all aspects of society—the economy, the movies and radio, even attitudes toward women and blacks. For many people, the war represented opportunity and the end of the Depression. For others, the excitement of faraway places meant that they could never return home again. For still others, the war left lasting scars.

Mobilizing for War

Converting American industry to war production was a complex task. Many corporate executives refused to admit that an emergency existed. Shortly after Pearl Harbor, Roosevelt created the War Production Board (WPB) and appointed Donald Nelson, executive vice president of Sears, Roebuck, to mobilize the nation's resources for an all-out war effort. The WPB offered businesses cost-plus contracts, guaranteeing a fixed and generous profit. Often the government also financed new plants and equipment. Secretary of War Henry Stimson remarked, "If you … go to war … in a capitalist country, you have to let business make money out of the process or business won't work." Roosevelt seemed to agree.

The Roosevelt administration leaned over backward to gain the cooperation of businessmen, many of whom New Deal policies had alienated. The president appointed many business executives to key positions, some of whom, like Nelson, served for a dollar a year. Roosevelt also abandoned antitrust actions in all industries that were remotely war-related. The probusiness policies angered some of his supporters. "The New Dealers are a vanishing tribe," one remarked, "and the moneychangers who were driven from the temple are now quietly established in government offices."

The policy worked, however. Both industrial production and net corporate profits nearly doubled during the war. Large commercial farmers also profited. With many members of Congress supporting their demands, the farmers exacted high support prices for basic commodities. The war years accelerated the mechanization of the farm. Between 1940 and 1945, a million tractors joined those already in use. At the same time, the farm population declined by 17 percent. The consolidation of small farms into large ones and the dramatic increase in the use of fertilizer made farms more productive and farming more profitable for the large operators.

Many government agencies in addition to the War Production Board helped run the war effort efficiently. The Office of Price Administration (OPA), eventually placed under the direction of Chester Bowles, an advertising executive, set prices on thousands of items to control inflation. The OPA also rationed scarce products. Because the OPA's decisions affected what people wore and ate and whether they had gasoline, many regarded it as oppressive. The National War Labor Board (NWLB) had the authority to set wages and hours and to monitor working conditions and could, under the president's wartime emergency powers, seize industrial plants whose owners refused to cooperate.

Membership in labor unions grew rapidly during the war, from a total of 10.5 million in 1941 to 14.7 million in 1945. This increase was aided by government policy. In return for a "no-strike pledge," the NWLB allowed agreements that required workers to retain their union membership through the life of a contract. Labor leaders, however, complained about increased government regulations and argued that wage controls coupled with wartime inflation were unfair. The NWLB finally allowed a 15 percent cost-of-living increase on some contracts, but that did not apply to overtime pay, which helped drive up wages in some industries during the war by about 70 percent.

Labor leaders were often not content with the raises. In the most famous incident, John L. Lewis broke the no-strike pledge of organized labor by calling a nationwide coal strike in 1943. When Roosevelt ordered the secretary of the interior to take over the mines, Lewis called off the strike. But this bold protest did help raise miners' wages.

In addition to wage and price controls and rationing, the government tried to reduce inflation by selling war bonds and by increasing taxes. The Revenue Act of 1942 raised tax rates, broadened the tax base, increased corporate taxes to 40 percent, and raised the excess-profits tax to 90 percent. In addition, the government initiated a payroll deduction for income taxes. The war made the income tax a reality for most Americans for the first time.

Despite some unfairness and much confusion, the American economy responded to the wartime crisis and turned out the equipment and supplies that eventually won the war. American industries built 300,000 airplanes, 88,140 tanks, and 3,000 merchant ships. In 1944 alone, American factories produced 800,000 tons of synthetic rubber to replace the supply of natural rubber captured by the Japanese. Although the national debt grew from about $143 billion in 1943 to $260 billion in 1945, the government policy of taxation paid for about 40 percent of the war's cost. At the same time, full employment and the increase in two-income families, together with forced savings, helped provide capital for postwar expansion. In a limited way, the tax policy also tended to redistribute wealth, which the New Deal had failed to do. The top 5 percent income bracket, which controlled 23 percent of the disposable income in 1939, accounted for only 17 percent in 1945.

The war stimulated the growth of the federal bureaucracy and accelerated the trend, begun during World War I and extended in the 1920s and

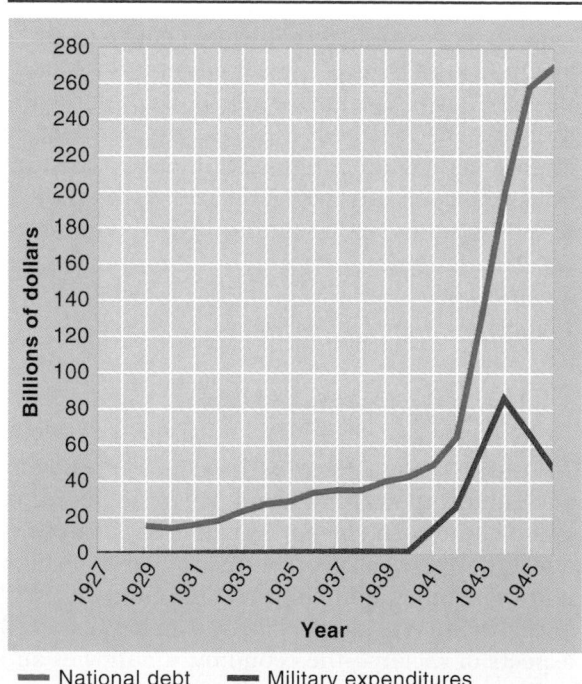

Military Expenditures and the National Debt, 1929–1945

Increased taxes, the sale of war bonds, and price controls kept inflation under relative control during the war. Still, the war industry not only stimulated the economy, but also increased the national debt. Source: U.S. Bureau of the Census.

1930s, toward the government's central role in the economy. The war also increased the cooperation between industry and government, creating what would later be called a military-industrial complex. But for most Americans, despite anger at the OPA and the income tax, the war meant the end of the Depression.

Patriotic Fervor

In European and Asian cities, the horror and destruction of war were everywhere. But in the United States, the war was remote. Thousands of American families felt the tragedy of war directly with the arrival of an official telegram telling of a son or husband killed in action. For most Americans, however, it was a foreign war, far removed from the reality of daily life.

The government tried to keep the conflict alive in the minds of Americans and to keep the country united behind the war effort. The Office of War Information, staffed by writers and advertising executives, controlled the news the American public received about the war. It promoted patriotism and presented the American war effort in the best possible light. The government also sold war bonds, not only to help pay for the war and reduce inflation but also to sell the war to the American people. As had been true during World War I, movie stars and other celebrities appeared at war bond rallies. Dorothy Lamour, one of Hollywood's glamorous actresses, took credit for selling $350 million worth of bonds. Schoolchildren purchased war stamps and faithfully pasted them in an album until they had accumulated stamps worth $18.75, enough to buy a $25 bond (redeemable ten years later). Their bonds, they were told, would purchase bullets or a part for an airplane to kill "Japs" and Germans and defend the American way of life. "For Freedom's Sake, Buy War Bonds," one poster announced. Working men and women purchased bonds through payroll deduction plans and looked forward to spending the money on consumer goods after the war. In the end, the government sold over $135 billion in war bonds. While the bond drives did help control inflation, they were most important in making millions of Americans feel that they were contributing to the war effort.

Gross National Product and Unemployment, 1940–1945

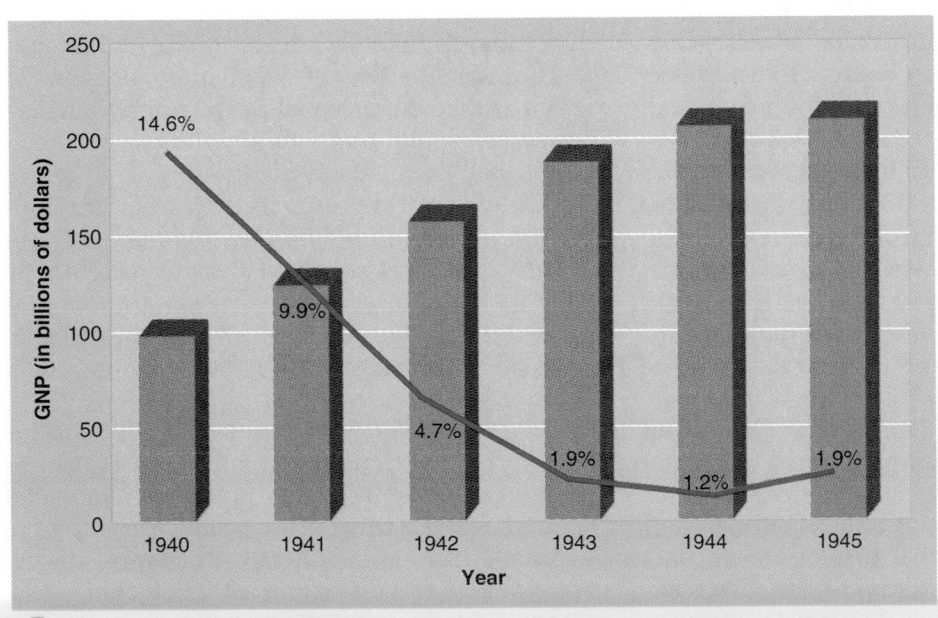

The war economy virtually wiped out unemployment and increased production to unprecedented levels. Source: U.S. Bureau of the Census.

Those too old or too young to join the armed forces served in other ways. Thousands became air raid wardens or civilian defense and Red Cross volunteers. They raised victory gardens and took part in scrap drives. Even small children could join the war effort by collecting old rubber, wastepaper, and kitchen fats. Boys dived into lakes and rivers to recover old tires and even ripped down iron fences to aid their towns and neighborhoods in meeting their scrap quota. Some items, including gasoline, sugar, butter, and meat, were rationed, but few people complained. Even horsemeat hamburgers seemed edible if they helped win the war. Newspaper and magazine advertising characterized ordinary actions as either speeding victory or impeding the war effort. "Hoarders are the same as spies," one ad announced. "Every time you decide not to buy something you help win the war."

Internment of Japanese Americans

Cooperating with the war effort fostered a sense of pride, a feeling of community. But wartime campaigns not only stimulated patriotism but also promoted hate for the enemy. The Nazis, especially Hitler and his Gestapo, had become synonymous with evil even before 1941. But at the beginning of the war, there was little animosity toward the German people. "You and I don't hate the Nazis because they are Germans. We hate the Germans because they are Nazis," announced a character in one of Helen MacInnes's novels. But before long, most Americans ceased to make distinctions. All Germans seemed evil, although the anti-German hysteria that had swept the country during World War I never developed.

The Japanese were easier to hate than the Germans. The attack on Pearl Harbor created a special animosity toward the Japanese, but the depiction of the Japanese as warlike and subhuman owed something to a long tradition of fear of the so-called yellow peril and a distrust of all Asians. The movies, magazine articles, cartoons, and posters added to the image of the Japanese soldier or pilot with a toothy grin murdering innocent women and children or shooting down helpless Americans. Two weeks after Pearl Harbor, *Time* magazine explained to Americans how they could distinguish our Asian friends the Chinese "from the Japs." "Vir-

tually all Japanese are short, Japanese are seldom fat; they often dry up with age," *Time* declared. "Most Chinese avoid horn-rimmed spectacles. Japanese walk stiffly erect, hard-heeled. Chinese, more relaxed, have an easy gait. The Chinese expression is likely to be more kindly, placid, open; the Japanese more positive, dogmatic, arrogant."

The racial stereotype of the Japanese played a role in the treatment of Japanese Americans during the war. Some prejudice was shown against German and Italian Americans, but Japanese Americans were the only group confined in concentration camps, in the greatest mass abridgment of civil liberties in American history.

At the time of Pearl Harbor, about 127,000 Japanese Americans lived in the United States, most on the West Coast. About 80,000 were *nisei* (Japanese born in the United States and holding American citizenship) and *sansei* (the sons and daughters of nisei); the rest were *issei* (aliens born in Japan who were ineligible for U.S. citizenship). The Japanese had long suffered from racial discrimination and prejudice in the United States. They were barred from intermarriage with other groups and excluded from many clubs, restaurants, and recreation facilities. Many worked as tenant farmers, fishermen, or small businessmen. Others made up a small professional class of lawyers, teachers, and doctors and a large number of land-owning farmers.

Although many retained cultural and linguistic ties to Japan, they posed no more threat to the country than did the much larger groups of Italian Americans and German Americans. But their physical characteristics made them stand out as the others did not. After Pearl Harbor, an anti-Japanese panic seized the West Coast. A Los Angeles newspaper reported that armed Japanese were in Baja, California, ready to attack. Rumors suggested that Japanese fishermen were preparing to sow mines in the harbor, blow up tunnels, and poison the water supply.

West Coast politicians and ordinary citizens urged the War Department and the president to evacuate the Japanese. The president capitulated and issued Executive Order 9066 authorizing the evacuation in February 1942. "The continued pressure of a largely unassimilated, tightly knit racial group, bound to an enemy nation by strong ties of race, culture, custom and religion, constituted a menace which had to be dealt with," General John De Witt argued, justifying the removal on military grounds. But racial fear and animosity, not military necessity, stood behind the order.

Eventually, the government built the "relocation centers" in remote, often arid, sections of the West. "The Japs live like rats, breed like rats, and act like rats. We don't want them," the governor of Idaho announced. The camps were primitive and unattractive. "When I first entered our room, I became sick to my stomach," a Japanese American woman remembered. "There were seven beds in the room and no furniture nor any partitions to separate the males and the females of the family. I just sat on the bed, staring at the bare wall."

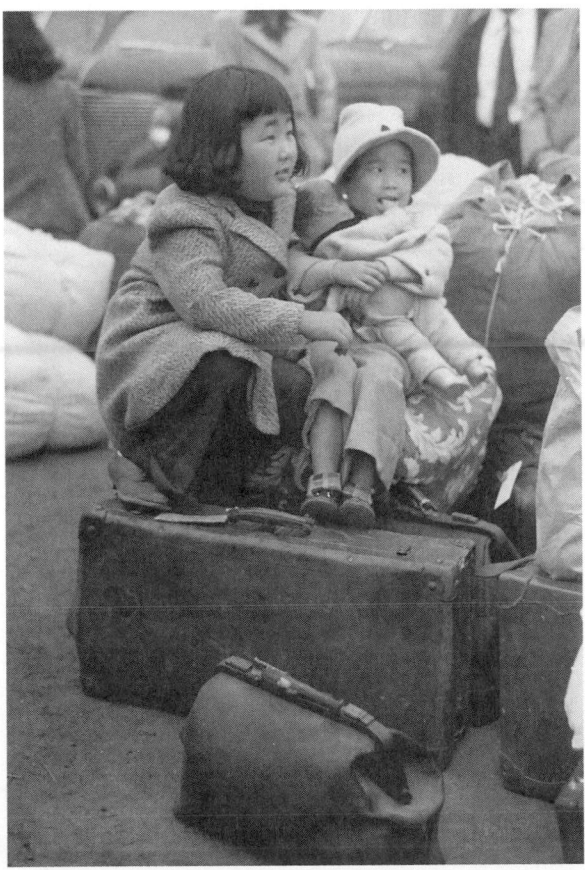

Japanese American children on their way to a "relocation center." For many Japanese Americans, but especially for the children, the nightmare of the relocation camp experience would stay with them all their lives. (Library of Congress)

The government evacuated about 110,000 Japanese. Those who were forced to leave their homes, farms, and businesses lost almost all their property and possessions. Farmers left their crops to be harvested by their American neighbors. Store owners sold out for a small percentage of what their goods were worth. No personal items or household goods could be transported. The Japanese Americans lost their worldly possessions, and something more—their pride and respect. One 6-year-old kept asking his mother to "take him back to America." He thought his relocation center was in Japan.

The evacuation of the Japanese Americans appears in retrospect to have been unjustified. Even in Hawaii, where a much larger Japanese population existed, the government attempted no evacuation, and no sabotage and little disloyalty occurred. The government allowed Japanese American men to volunteer for military service, and many served bravely in the European theater. The 442nd Infantry Combat Team, made up entirely of *nisei,* became the most decorated unit in all the military service—another indication of the loyalty and patriotism of the Japanese Americans. In 1988, Congress belatedly voted limited compensation for the Japanese Americans relocated during World War II.

African and Hispanic Americans at War

The United States in 1941, even in much of the North, remained a segregated society. African Americans could not live, eat, travel, work, or go to school with the same freedom whites enjoyed. Black Americans profited little from the revival of prosperity and the expansion of jobs early in the war. Those who joined the military were usually assigned to menial jobs as cooks or laborers and were always assigned to segregated units with whites as the high-ranking officers. The myth that black soldiers had failed to perform well in World War I persisted. "Leadership is not embedded in the negro race yet," Secretary of War Henry Stimson wrote, "and to try to make commissioned officers ... lead men into battle—colored men—is only to work a disaster to both."

Some black leaders found it especially ironic that as the country prepared to fight Hitler and his racist policies, the United States persisted in its own brand of racism. "A jim crow Army cannot fight for a free world," announced *The Crisis,* the journal of the NAACP. A. Philip Randolph decided to act rather than talk. The son of a Methodist minister, Randolph had worked with the first wave of African Americans migrating from the South to the northern cities during and just after World War I. He spent years trying "to carry the gospel of unionism to the colored world." He organized and led the Brotherhood of Sleeping Car Porters, and in 1937, he finally won grudging recognition of the union from the Pullman Company.

Respected and admired by black leaders of all political persuasions, Randolph convinced many of them in 1941 to join him in a march on Washington to demand equal rights. "Dear fellow Negro Americans," Randolph wrote, "be not dismayed in these terrible times. You possess power, great power. Our problem is to harness and hitch it up for action on the broadest, daring and most gigantic scale."

The threat of as many as 100,000 African Americans marching in protest in the nation's capital alarmed Roosevelt. At first, he sent his assistants, including his wife Eleanor, who was greatly admired in the black community, to dissuade Randolph from such drastic action. Finally, he talked to Randolph in person on June 18, 1941. Randolph and Roosevelt struck a bargain. Roosevelt refused to desegregate the armed forces, but in return for Randolph's calling off the march, the president issued Executive Order 8802, which stated that it was the policy of the United States that "there shall be no discrimination in the employment of workers in defense industries or government because of race, creed, color or national origin." He also established the Fair Employment Practices Commission (FEPC) to enforce the order.

By threatening militant action, the black leaders wrested a major concession from the president. But the executive order did not end prejudice, and the FEPC, which its chairman described as the "most hated agency in Washington," had limited success in erasing the color line. Many black soldiers were angered and humiliated throughout the war by being made to sit in the back of buses and being barred from hotels and restaurants. Years later, one former black soldier recalled being refused service in a restaurant in Salina, Kansas, while the same restaurant served German prisoners from a camp nearby. "We continued to stare," he recalled. "This was really happening. . . . The people of Salina would serve these enemy soldiers and turn away black American G.I.'s."

Many African Americans improved their economic conditions during the war by taking jobs in war industries. Continuing the migration that had begun during World War I, 750,000 southern blacks moved to northern and western cities in search of economic opportunity. Some became skilled workers and a few became professionals, but they did not escape racial prejudice. In Detroit, where a major race riot broke out in the summer of 1943, Polish Americans had protested a public housing development that promised to bring blacks into their neighborhood. In one year, more than 50,000 blacks moved into that city, already overcrowded with many others seeking wartime jobs. The new arrivals increased the pressure on housing and other facilities, and the war accentuated the tension among the various groups.

The riot broke out on a hot, steamy day at a municipal park where a series of incidents led to fights between black and white young people and then to looting in the black community. Before federal and state troops restored order, 34 had been killed (25 blacks and 9 whites) and rioters had destroyed more than $2 million worth of property. Groups of whites roamed the city attacking blacks, overturning cars, setting fires, and sometimes killing wantonly. A group of young men murdered a 58-year-old black "just for the hell of it." "We didn't know him," one of the boys admitted. "He wasn't bothering us. But other people were fighting and killing and we felt like it too." Other riots broke out in Mobile, Los Angeles, New York, and Beaumont, Texas. In all these cities, and in many others where the tension did not lead to open violence, the legacy of bitterness and hate lasted long after the war.

Mexican Americans, like most minority groups, profited during the war from the increased job opportunities provided by wartime industry, but they, too, faced racial prejudice. In California and in many parts of the Southwest, Mexicans could not use public swimming pools. Often

Even before the United States entered the war, black families like this one moved north to look for work and a better life. This massive migration would change the racial mix in northern cities. (Library of Congress)

lumped together with blacks, they were excluded from certain restaurants. Usually they were limited to menial jobs and were constantly harassed by the police, picked up for minor offenses, and jailed on the smallest excuse. In Los Angeles, the anti-Mexican prejudice flared into violence. The increased migration of Mexicans into the city and old hatreds created a volatile situation. Most of the hostility and anger focused on Mexican gang members, or *pachuchos,* especially those wearing zoot suits. The suits consisted of long, loose coats with padded shoulders, ballooned pants, pegged at the ankles, and a wide-brimmed hat. A watch chain and a ducktail haircut completed the uniform. The zoot suit had originated in the black sections of northern cities and became a national craze during the war. It was a look some teenage males adopted to call attention to themselves and shock conventional society.

The zoot-suiters especially angered soldiers and sailors who were stationed or on leave in Los Angeles. After a number of provocative incidents, violence broke out between the Mexican American youths and the servicemen in the spring of 1943. The violence reached a peak on June 7 when gangs of servicemen, often in taxicabs, combed the city, attacking all the young zoot-suiters they could find or anyone who looked Mexican. The servicemen, joined by others, beat up the Mexicans, stripped them of their offensive clothes, and then gave them haircuts. The police, both civilian and military, looked the other way, and when they did move in, they arrested the victims rather than their attackers. The local press and the chamber of commerce hotly denied that race was a factor in the riots, but *Time* magazine was probably closer to the truth when it called the riots the "ugliest brand of mob action since the coolie race riots of the 1870s."

Social Impact of the War

Modern wars have been incredibly destructive of human lives and property, but they have social results as well. The Civil War ended slavery and ensured the triumph of the industrial North for years to come; in so doing, it left a legacy of bitterness and transformed the race question from a sectional to a national problem. World War I assured the success of woman suffrage and prohibition, caused a migration of blacks to northern

Oral History

World War II influenced every family in some significant way. For those who lost sons, husbands, or fathers, the war was tragic. But for others, it meant jobs, travel, adventure, and romance. The war is still the subject of many movies and books, and thousands of people still collect World War II weapons, model airplanes, and other memorabilia. The generation that lived through the war is inclined to look back nostalgically and to recall the war as a wonderful period in their lives, unlike those who look back at the Vietnam War. In fact, almost as many Americans landed in France in June 1994 to celebrate the fiftieth anniversary of D-Day as invaded Normandy on June 6, 1944. Taking former soldiers and their families back to World War II battlegrounds has become a major tourist industry in Europe.

How did the war influence your family? The study of the family, "humanity's most fundamental and most durable institution," is as important for historians as the study of wars, elections, depressions, and social currents. One's own family, in fact, is a part of these events. By interviewing family members and writing about their lives, which is called oral history, the past is made both more vivid and more personal. Oral history goes beyond names and dates to the rich immediate texture of people's recollections of personal experiences and feelings. Investigating family members is an opportunity not only to "put your own family into history" but also to develop deeper relations and understanding. As such, it is an act requiring a high degree of respect and responsibility.

You can become an oral historian by asking members of your family about their World War II experience, recovering a partial history of both your family and the war. Talk to your father and mother, your grandparents, and other older relatives. Who in your family served in the armed forces? Who went overseas? Did anyone work in a war industry? Was there a "Rosie the Riveter" in your family? Did your family move during the war? For many people, the war meant jobs and the end of depression. Was that true for your family? Many young people met their future spouses during that war. Was that true in your family?

Can anyone in your family remember rationing, scrap drives, blackouts, victory gardens? Did anyone eat horsemeat or mix yellow food coloring with oleomargarine? Can anyone recall the big bands, the movie stars, the newsreels? Although there was widespread support for the war, and patriotism was popular, prejudice and hate still remained. In what ways did your family share in the patriotism or the prejudice? Whether in battles abroad or on the home front, how does the war as recalled by your family differ from the war as described in this chapter?

Look around your home. Are there any surviving memorabilia from the war—old photographs or uniforms, discharge papers, ration books, war stamps, souvenirs, magazines, or other things from the war years? Go to your library and look at a few issues of *Life* or *Look* for the 1940s. What do you notice about the advertisements and the news stories? How do they differ from magazine advertising and reporting today? What happened to the automotive industry and to professional baseball and college football during the war? What do you notice about women's dress styles? What do the two photographs shown here tell you about the American people in World War II?

Did the war mean tragedy or opportunity for your family? "World War II was a holy war and FDR a saint," one writer has remarked. Does your family agree? World

Collecting scrap to aid the war effort.
(Library of Congress)

War II may have been the last time the country was really united; those who lived through it have inevitably looked at recent events through the perspective of the war years. How did the "Good War," as Studs Terkel called it, influence the political and social views of members of your family old enough to remember it? How do their attitudes about World War II compare with their feelings about more recent American wars?

If the experience of World War II is too distant for the recollections of members of your family, ask them instead about either the Korean War or the Vietnam War. Similar questions are appropriate: Ask those who went abroad to describe what the war was like and how they felt about it, and ask those who stayed at home how the war affected or changed their lives.

The accompanying brief excerpt from Studs Terkel's book *"The Good War": An Oral History of World War Two* illustrates how the world transformed the family and neighborhood of young Mike Royko, now a Chicago journalist.

Alfred Eisenstadt, Soldier's Farewell, *Penn Station, New York, 1944. (Alfred Eisenstadt/LIFE Magazine ©Time Inc.)*

Remembering the Good War

I was nine years old when the war started. It was a typical Chicago working-class neighborhood. It was predominantly Slavic, Polish. There were some Irish, some Germans. When you're a kid, the borders of the world are the few blocks of two-flats, bungalows, cottages, with a lot of little stores in between. My father had a tavern. In those days they put out extras. I remember the night the newsboys came through the neighborhood. Skid-row kind of guys, hawking the papers. Germany had invaded Poland: '39. It was the middle of the night, my mother and father waking. People were going out in the streets in their bathrobes to buy the papers. In our neighborhood with a lot of Poles, it was a tremendous story.

Suddenly you had a flagpole. And a marker. Names went on the marker, guys from the neighborhood who were killed. Our neighborhood was decimated. There were only kids, older guys, and women.

Suddenly I saw something I hadn't seen before. My sister became Rosie the Riveter. She put a bandanna on her head every day and went down to this organ company that had been converted to war

work. There was my sister in slacks. It became more than work. There was a sense of mission about it. Her husband was Over There....

There was the constant idea that you had to be doing something to help. It did filter down to the neighborhood: home-front mobilization. We had a block captain....

We'd listen to the radio every night. My father would turn it on to find out what was happening. The way a kid's mind could be shaped by those dulcet voices. The world was very simple. I saw Hitler and Mussolini and Tojo: those were the villains. We were the good guys. And the Russians were the good guys too. The war was always being talked about in the bar. Everybody was a military strategist.

The big event was my brother-in-law coming home, my sister's husband. He had been a combat soldier all the way through. He had all his ribbons and medals on. He was the family hero.

Source: Mike Royko, in Studs Terkel, *"The Good War": An Oral History of World War Two*. Copyright ©1984 by Studs Terkel. Reprinted by permission of Pantheon Books, a division of Random House, Inc.

cities, and ushered in a time of intolerance. World War II also had many social results. It altered patterns of work, leisure, education, and family life; caused a massive migration of people; created jobs; and changed life-styles. It is difficult to overemphasize the impact of the war on the generation that lived through it.

Wartime Opportunities

More than 15 million American civilians moved during the war. Like the Momadays, many left home to find better jobs. In fact, for many Native Americans, wartime opportunities led to a migration from the rural areas and the reservations into the cities. Americans moved off the farms and away from the small towns, flocking to cities, where defense jobs were readily available. They moved west: California alone gained more than 2 million people during the war. But they also moved out of the South into the northern cities, while a smaller number moved from the North to the South. Late in the war, when a shortage of farm labor developed, some reversed the trend and moved back onto the farms. But a great many people moved somewhere. One observer, noticing the heavily packed cars heading west, decided that it was just like *The Grapes of Wrath,* without the poverty and the hopelessness.

The World War II migrants poured into industrial centers; 200,000 came to the Detroit area, nearly a half-million to Los Angeles, and about 100,000 to Mobile, Alabama. They put pressure on the schools, housing, and other services. Often they had to live in new Hoovervilles, trailer parks, or temporary housing. In San Pablo, California, a family of four adults and seven children lived in an 8-by-10-foot shack. In Los Angeles, Mrs. Colin Kelley, the widow of a war hero, could find no place to live until a local newspaper publicized her plight. Bill Mauldin, the war cartoonist, showed a young couple with a child buying tickets for a movie with the caption: "Matinee, heck—we want to register for a week."

Nowhere was the change more dramatic than in the West, especially in California, where the wartime boom transformed the region more dramatically than any development since the nineteenth-century economic revolution created by

the railroads and mining. The federal government spent over $70 billion in the state (one-tenth of the total for the entire country) to build army bases, shipyards, supply depots, and testing sites. In addition, private industry constructed so many facilities that the region became the center of a growing military-industrial complex. San Diego, for example, was transformed from a sleepy port and naval base into a sprawling metropolis. The population grew by 147 percent between 1941 and 1945, from 202,000 to 380,000. Vallezo, a small city near Oakland, grew from 20,000 to over 100,000 in just two years. The United States Navy's Mare Island Shipyard nearby increased its work force from 5,000 to 45,000. Vanport, just north of Portland, Oregon, was an empty mud flat in 1940; three years later it was a bustling city of more than 40,000. Almost everyone in the new town worked for the Kaiser Ship Yards.

This spectacular growth created problems. There was a housing shortage, schools were overcrowded, and hospitals and municipal services could not keep up with the demand. Crime and prostitution increased as did racial tension, though few cities reproduced the zoot-suit riots of Los Angeles. The war years were like a "perpetual American Legion convention," one San Diego official remarked.

The overcrowded conditions, the uneasiness at being away from home, the volatile mixture of people from different backgrounds living close together, and the wartime situation often created tension and sometimes open conflict. Some migrants had never lived in a city and were homesick. On one occasion in a Willow Grove, Michigan, school, the children were all instructed to sing "Michigan, My Michigan"; no one knew the words because they all came from other states. One of the most popular country songs of the period, when thousands had left their rural homes to find work in the city, was "I Wanna Go Back to West Virginia."

For the first time in years, many families had money to spend, but they had nothing to spend it on. The last new car rolled off the assembly line in February 1942. There were no washing machines, refrigerators, or radios in the stores, no gasoline and no tires to permit weekend trips. Even when people had time off, they tended to stay at home or in the neighborhood. Some of the new housing

Changing work shifts at an airplane plant in Inglewood, California, in 1942. The war suddenly meant jobs for most Americans. But it was still difficult, especially early in the war, for some groups to find employment. These workers seem to be almost entirely white and male. Two years later there probably would have been more women workers. (Library of Congress)

developments had the atmosphere of a mining camp, complete with drinking, prostitution, and barroom brawls.

The war required major adjustments in American family life. With several million men in the service and others far away working at defense jobs, the number of households headed by a woman increased dramatically. The number of marriages also rose sharply. Early in the war, a young man could be deferred if he had a dependent, and a wife qualified as a dependent. Later, many servicemen got married, often to women they barely knew, because they wanted a little excitement and perhaps someone to come home to. Reversing a decline that extended back as far as the colonial period, the birthrate also began to rise in 1940, as young couples started a family as fast as they could. Birthrates had been especially low during the Depression, so the shift marked a significant change. Some children were "good-bye babies," conceived just before the husband left to join the military or go overseas. The illegitimacy rate also went up, and from the outset of the war, the divorce rate began to climb sharply. Yet most of the wartime marriages survived, and many of the women left at

home looked ahead to a time after the war when they could settle down to a normal life.

Women Workers for Victory

Thousands of women took jobs in heavy industry that formerly would have been considered unladylike. They built tanks, airplanes, and ships, but they still earned less than men. At first, women were rarely taken on because as the war in Europe pulled American industry out of its long slump, unemployed men snapped up the newly available positions. In the face of this male labor pool, one government official remarked that we should "give the women something to do to keep their hands busy as we did in the last war, then maybe they won't bother us."

But by 1943, with many men drafted and male unemployment virtually nonexistent, the government was quick to suggest that it was women's patriotic duty to take their place on the assembly line. A government poster showed a woman worker and her uniformed husband standing in front of an American flag with the caption: "I'm proud … my husband wants me to do my part."

The government tried to convince women that if they could run a vacuum cleaner or a sewing machine or drive a car, they could operate power machinery in a factory. Advertisers in women's magazines joined the campaign by showing fashion models in work clothes. A popular song was "Rosie the Riveter," who was "making history working for victory." She also helped her marine boyfriend by "working overtime on the riveting machine."

At the end of the war, the labor force included 19.5 million women, but three-fourths of them had been working before the conflict, and some of the additional ones might have sought work in normal times. The new women war workers tended to be older, and they were more often married than single. Some worked for patriotic reasons. "Every time I test a batch of rubber, I know it's going to

"Rosie the Riveter" became perhaps the most familiar symbol of women's contribution to the war effort during World War II. Here women rivet sections of an aircraft engine compartment. The government recruited women to work in war industries, but after the war ended, it urged women to return to the traditional roles of wife and mother. (Library of Congress)

help bring my three sons home quicker," a woman worker in a rubber plant remarked. But others worked for the money or to have something useful to do. Yet in 1944, women's weekly wages averaged $31.21, compared with $54.65 for men, reflecting women's more menial tasks and their low seniority as well as outright discrimination. Still, many women enjoyed factory work. "Boy have the men been getting away with murder all these years," exclaimed a Pittsburgh housewife. "Why I worked twice as hard selling in a department store and got half the pay."

Black women faced the most difficult situation during the war, and often when they applied for work, they were told, "We have not yet installed separate toilet facilities" or "We can't put a Negro in the front office." Not until 1944 did the telephone company in New York City hire a black telephone operator. Still, some black women moved during the war from domestic jobs to higher-paying factory work. Married women with young children also found it difficult to obtain work. There were few day-care facilities and the women were often informed that they should be home with their children.

Women workers often had to endure catcalls, whistles, and more overt sexual harassment on the job. Still, most persisted, and they tried to look feminine despite the heavy work clothes. In one Boston factory, a woman was hooted at for carrying a lunch box. Only men, it seemed, carried lunch boxes; women brought their lunch in a paper bag.

Many women war workers quickly left their jobs after the war ended. Some left by choice, but dismissals ran twice as high for women as for men. The war had barely shaken the notion that a woman's place was at home. Some women who learned what an extra paycheck meant for the family's standard of living would have preferred to keep working. But most women, and an even larger percentage of men, agreed at the end of the war that women did not deserve an "equal chance with men" for jobs. War work altered individual lives and attitudes, but it did not change dramatically either sex's perception of women's proper role.

Entertaining the People

According to one survey, Americans listened to the radio an average of 4-1/2 hours a day during the war. The major networks increased their news programs from less than 4 percent to nearly 30 percent of broadcasting time. Americans heard Edward R. Murrow broadcasting from London during the German air blitz with the sound of the air raid sirens in the background. They listened to Eric Sevareid cover the battle of Burma and describe the sensation of jumping out of an airplane. Often the signal faded out and the static made listening difficult, but the live broadcasts had drama and authenticity never before possible.

Even more than the reporters, the commentators became celebrities on whom the American people depended to explain what was going on around the world. Millions listened to the clipped, authoritative voice of H. V. Kaltenborn or to Gabriel Heatter, whose trademark was "Ah, there's good news tonight." But the war also intruded on almost all other programming. Even the advertising, which took up more and more air time, reminded listeners of the war. Lucky Strike cigarettes, which changed the color of its package from green to white, presumably because there was a shortage of green pigment, made "Lucky Strike Green Has Gone to War" almost as famous as "Remember Pearl Harbor."

The serials, the standard fare of daytime radio, also adopted wartime themes. Dick Tracy tracked down spies, and Captain Midnight fought against the enemy on remote jungle islands. Superman outwitted Nazi agents, and Stella Dallas took a job in a defense plant.

Music, which took up a large proportion of radio programming, also conveyed a war theme. There were "Goodbye, Mama (I'm Off to Yokohama)" and "Praise the Lord and Pass the Ammunition," but more numerous were songs of romance and love, songs about separation and hope for a better time after the war. The danceable tunes of Glenn Miller and Tommy Dorsey became just as much a part of wartime memories as ration books and far-off battlefields.

For many Americans, the motion picture became the most important leisure activity and a part of their fantasy life during the war. Attendance at the movies averaged about 100 million viewers a week. There might not be gasoline for weekend trips or Sunday drives, but the whole family could go to the movies; and then, like Scott Momaday, they could replay them in their imaginations. Even those in the military service could watch American movies on board ship or at a remote outpost. "Pinup" photographs of Hollywood stars decorated the barracks and even tanks and planes wherever American troops were stationed.

Musical comedies, cowboy movies, and historical romances remained popular during the war, but the conflict intruded even on Hollywood. Newsreels that offered a visual synopsis of the war news, always with an upbeat message and a touch of human interest, preceded most movies. Their theme was that the Americans were winning the war, even if early in the conflict there was little evidence to that effect. Many feature films also had a wartime theme, picturing the war in the Pacific complete with grinning, vicious Japanese villains (usually played by Chinese or Korean character actors). In the beginning of these films, the Japanese were always victorious, but in the end, they always got "what they deserved."

The movies set in Europe differed somewhat from those depicting the Far Eastern war. British and Americans, sometimes spies, sometimes downed airmen, could dress up like Germans and get away with it. They outwitted the Germans at every turn, sabotaging important installations and finally escaping in a captured plane.

A number of Hollywood actors went into the service, and some even became heroes. Most, like Ronald Reagan, were employed to produce, narrate, or act in government films. The Office of War Information produced short subjects and documentaries, some of them distinguished, like John Huston's *Battle of San Pietro,* a realistic depiction of war on the Italian front. More typical were propaganda films meant to indoctrinate American soldiers into the reasons they were fighting the war. *Letter from Bataan,* a short film made in 1942, portrayed a wounded GI who wrote home asking his brother-in-law to save his razor blades because "it takes twelve thousand razor blades to make a one-thousand-pound bomb." The film ended with the announcement that the soldier had died in the hospital.

The GIs' War

GI, the abbreviation for *government issue,* became the affectionate designation for the ordinary soldier in World War II. The GIs came from every background and ethnic group. Some served reluctantly, some eagerly. A few became genuine heroes. All were turned into heroes by the press and the public, who seemed to believe that one American could easily defeat at least 20 Japanese or Germans. Ernie Pyle, one of the war correspondents who chronicled the authentic story of the ordinary GI, wrote of soldiers "just toiling from day to day in a world full of insecurity, discomfort, homesickness, and a dulled sense of danger."

Bill Mauldin, another correspondent, told the story of the ordinary soldier in a series of cartoons featuring two tired and resigned infantrymen, Willie and Joe. Joe tries to explain what the war is about, "when they run we try to ketch 'em, when we ketch 'em we try to make 'em run." In another cartoon, Willie says, "Joe, yestiddy ya saved my life an' I swore I'd pay you back. Here's my last pair of dry socks." For the soldier in the front line, the big strategies were irrelevant. The war seemed a constant mix-up; much more important were the little comforts and staying alive.

In the midst of battle, the war was no fun, but only one soldier of eight who served ever saw combat, and even for many of those the war was a great adventure (just as World War I had been). "When World War II broke out I was delighted," Mario Puzo, author of *The Godfather*, remembered. "There is no other word, terrible as it may sound. My country called. I was delivered from my mother, my family, the girl I was loving passionately but did not love. And delivered *without guilt.* Heroically my country called, ordered me to defend it." World War II catapulted young men and women out of their small towns and urban neighborhoods into exotic places where they met new people and did new things.

The war was important for Mexican Americans, who were drafted and volunteered in great numbers. A third of a million served in all branches of the military, a larger percentage than for many other ethnic groups. Although they encountered prejudice, they probably found less in the armed forces than they had at home, and many returned to civilian life with new ambitions and a new sense of self-esteem.

Many Native Americans also served. In fact, many Indians were recruited for special service in the Marine Signal Corps. One group of Navajos completely befuddled the Japanese with a code based on their native language. "Were it not for the Navajos, the Marines would never have taken Iwo Jima," one Signal Corps officer declared. But the Navajo code talkers and all other Indians who chose to return to the reservations after the war were ineligible for veterans' loans, hospitalization, and other benefits. They lived on federal land, and that, according to the law, canceled all the advantages that other veterans enjoyed after the war.

For African Americans, who served throughout the war in segregated units and faced prejudice wherever they went, the military experience also had much to teach. Fewer blacks were sent overseas (about 79,000 of 504,000 blacks in the service in 1943), and fewer were in combat outfits, so the percentage of black soldiers killed and wounded was low. Many illiterate blacks, especially from the South, learned to read and write in the service. Blacks who went overseas began to realize that not everyone viewed them as inferior. One black army officer said, "What the hell do we want to fight the Japs for anyhow? They couldn't possibly treat us any worse than these 'crackers' right here at home." Most realized the paradox of fighting for freedom when they themselves had little freedom; they hoped things would improve after the war.

Because the war lasted longer than World War I, its impact was greater. In all, over 16 million men and women served in some branch of the military service. About 322,000 were killed in the war, and more than 800,000 were wounded. The 12,000 listed as missing just disappeared. The war claimed many more lives than World War I and was the nation's costliest after the Civil War. But because of penicillin, blood plasma, sulfa drugs, and rapid battlefield evacuation, the wounded in World War II were twice as likely to survive as in World War I. Penicillin also minimized the threat of venereal disease, but all men who served saw an anti-VD film, just as their predecessors had in World War I.

Women in Uniform

Women had served in all wars as nurses and cooks and in other support capacities, and during World War II many continued in these traditional roles. A few nurses landed in France just days after the

Over 300,000 American servicemen died during the war, but the government tried to protect the American people from learning the real cost of the battles. This photograph, published in 1943, was the first to show dead American soldiers. (George Strock/LIFE Magazine ©1943 Time Inc.)

could free men for combat duty. World War II thus became the first war in which women were given regular military status. About 350,000 women joined up, most in the Women's Army Corps (WACS) and the women's branch of the Navy (WAVES), but others served in the Coast Guard and the Marines. Oveta Culp Hobby, wife of a former governor of Texas and the mother of two children, directed the Women's Army Corps.

Many recruiting posters suggested that the services needed women "for the precision work at which women are so adept" or for work in hospitals to comfort and attend to the wounded "as only women can do." Most women served in traditional female roles, doing office work, cooking, and cleaning. But others were engineers and pilots. Still, men and women were not treated equally. Women were explicitly kept out of combat situations and were often underused by male officers who found it difficult to view women in nontraditional roles.

Men were informed about contraceptives and encouraged to use them, but information about birth control was explicitly prohibited for women. Rumors charged many servicewomen with sexual promiscuity. On one occasion, the secretary of war defended the morality and the loyalty of the women in the service, but the rumors continued, spread apparently by men made uncomfortable by women's invasion of the male military domain. One cause for immediate discharge was pregnancy; yet the pregnancy rate for both married and unmarried women remained low.

Thus, despite difficulties, women played important roles during the war, and when they left the service (unlike the women who had served in other wars), they had the same rights and privileges as the male veterans. The women in the service did not permanently alter the military or the public's perception of women's proper role, but they did change a few minds, and many of the women who served had their lives changed and their horizons broadened.

A War of Diplomats and Generals

Pearl Harbor catapulted the country into war with Japan, and on December 11, 1941, Hitler declared war on the United States. Why he did so has never

Normandy invasion. Nurses served with the Army and the Marines in the Pacific. They dug their own foxholes and treated men under enemy fire. Sixty-six nurses spent the entire war in the Philippines as prisoners of the Japanese. Most nurses, however, served far behind the lines tending the sick and wounded. Army nurses who were given officer rank were forbidden to date enlisted men. "Not permitting nurses and enlisted men to be seen together is certainly not American," one soldier decided.

Though nobody objected to women's serving as nurses, not until April 1943 did women physicians win the right to join the Army and Navy Medical Corps. Some people questioned whether it was right for women to serve in other capacities, but Congress authorized full military participation for women (except for combat) because of the military emergency and the argument that women been fully explained; he was perhaps impressed by the apparent weakness of America demonstrated at Pearl Harbor. He was not required by his treaty with Japan to go to war with the United States, and without his declaration, the United States might have concentrated on the war against Japan. But Hitler forced the United States into the war against the Axis powers in both Europe and Asia.

War Aims

Why was the United States fighting the war? What did it hope to accomplish in a peace settlement once the war was over? Roosevelt and the other American leaders never really decided. In a speech before Congress in January 1941, Roosevelt had mentioned the four freedoms: freedom of speech and expression, freedom of worship, freedom from want, and freedom from fear. For many Americans, especially after Norman Rockwell expressed those freedoms in four sentimental paintings, this was what they were fighting for. Roosevelt spoke vaguely of the need to extend democracy and to establish a peacekeeping organization, but in direct contrast to Woodrow Wilson's Fourteen Points, he never spelled out in any detail the political purposes for fighting. The only American policy was to end the war as quickly as possible and to solve the political problems it created when the time came. That policy, or lack of policy, would have important ramifications.

Roosevelt and his advisers, realizing that it would be impossible to mount an all-out war against both Japan and Germany, decided to fight a holding action in the Pacific while concentrating efforts against Hitler in Europe, where the immediate danger seemed greater. But the United States was not fighting alone. It joined the Soviet Union and Great Britain in what became a difficult, but ultimately effective alliance to defeat Nazi Germany. Churchill and Roosevelt got along well, although they often disagreed on strategy and tactics. Roosevelt's relationship with Stalin was much more strained, but often he agreed with the Russian leader about the way to fight the war. Stalin, a ruthless leader who had maintained his position of power only after eliminating hundreds of thousands of opponents, distrusted both the British

and the Americans, but he needed them, just as they depended on him. Without the tremendous sacrifices of the Russian army and the Russian people in 1941 and 1942, Germany would have won the war before the vast American military and industrial might could be mobilized.

Year of Disaster, 1942

Despite the potential of the American-British-Soviet alliance, the first half of 1942 was disastrous for the Allied cause. In the Pacific, the Japanese captured the Dutch East Indies with their vast riches in rubber, oil, and other resources. They swept into Burma, took Wake Island and Guam, and invaded the Aleutian Islands of Alaska. They pushed the American garrison on the Philippines onto the Bataan peninsula and finally onto the tiny island of Corregidor, where U.S. General Jonathan Wainwright surrendered more than 11,000 men to the Japanese. American reporters tried to play down the disasters, concentrating their stories on the few American victories and on tales of American heroism against overwhelming odds. One of the soldiers on a Pacific island picked up an American broadcast one night. "The news commentators in the States had us all winning the war," he discovered, "their buoyant cheerful voices talking of victory. We were out here where we would see these victories. They were all Japanese."

In Europe, the Germans pushed deep into Russia, threatening to capture all the industrial centers and the valuable oil fields. For a time, it appeared that they would even take Moscow. In North Africa, General Erwin Rommel and his mechanized divisions, the Afrika Korps, drove the British forces almost to Cairo in Egypt and threatened the Suez Canal. In contrast to World War I, which had been a war of stalemate, the opening phase of World War II was marked by air strikes and troops supported by trucks and tanks covering many miles a day. In the Atlantic, German submarines sank British and American ships more rapidly than they could be replaced. For a few dark months in 1942, it seemed that the Berlin-Tokyo Axis would win the war before the United States got itself ready to fight.

The Allies could not agree on the proper military strategy in Europe. Churchill advocated tight-

World War II: Pacific Theater

After the surprise attack on Pearl Harbor, the Japanese extended their control in the Pacific from Burma to the Aleutian Islands and almost to Australia. But after American naval and air victories at Coral Sea and Midway in 1942, the Japanese were increasingly on the defensive.

ening the ring around Germany, using bombing raids to weaken the enemy and encouraging resistance among the occupied countries but avoiding any direct assault on the continent until success was assured. Remembering the vast loss of British lives during World War I, he was determined to avoid similar casualties in this conflict. Stalin demanded a second front, an invasion of Europe in 1942, to relieve the pressure on the Russian army, which faced 200 German divisions along a 2,000-mile front. Roosevelt agreed to an offensive in 1942. But in the end, the invasion in 1942 came not in France but in North Africa. The decision was

probably right from a military point of view, but it taught Russia to distrust Britain and the United States. The delay in opening the second front probably contributed indirectly to the Cold War after 1945.

Attacking in North Africa in November 1942, American and British troops tried to link up with a beleaguered British army. The American army, enthusiastic but inexperienced, met little resistance in the beginning, but at Kasserine Pass in Tunisia, the Germans counterattacked and destroyed a large American force, inflicting 5,000 casualties. Roosevelt, who launched the invasion

World War II: European and North African Theaters

The German war machine swept across Europe and North Africa and almost captured Cairo and Moscow, but after major defeats at Stalingrad and El Alamein in 1943, the Axis powers were in retreat. Many lives were lost on both sides before the Allied victory in 1945.

in part to give the American people a victory to relieve the dreary news from the Far East, learned that victories often came with long casualty lists.

He also learned the necessity of political compromise. To gain a cease-fire in conquered French territory in North Africa, the United States recognized Admiral Jean Darlan as head of its provisional government. Darlan persecuted the Jews, exploited the Arabs, imprisoned his opponents, and collaborated with the Nazis. He seemed diametrically opposed to the principles the Americans said they were fighting for. Did the Darlan deal mean the United States would negotiate with

Mussolini? Or with Hitler? The Darlan compromise reinforced Soviet distrust of the Americans and angered many Americans as well.

Roosevelt never compromised or made a deal with Hitler, but he did aid General Francisco Franco, the Fascist dictator in Spain, in return for safe passage of American shipping into the Mediterranean. But the United States did not aid only right-wing dictators. It also supplied arms to the left-wing resistance in France, to the Communist Tito in Yugoslavia, and to Ho Chi Minh, the anti-French resistance leader in Indochina. Roosevelt also authorized large-scale, lend-lease aid to the Soviet Union. Although liberals criticized his support of dictators, Roosevelt was willing to do almost anything to win the war. Military expediency often dictated his political decisions.

Even on one of the most sensitive issues of the war, the plight of the Jews in occupied Europe, Roosevelt's solution was to win the war as quickly as possible. By November 1942, confirmed information had reached the United States that the Nazis were systematically exterminating Jews. Yet the Roosevelt administration did nothing for more than a year, and even then it did scandalously little to rescue European Jews from the gas chambers. Only 21,000 refugees were allowed to enter the United States over a period of 3 1/2 years, just 10 percent of those who could have been admitted under immigration quotas. The U.S. War Department rejected suggestions that the Auschwitz gas chambers be bombed, and government officials turned down many rescue schemes. Widespread anti-Semitic feelings in the United States in the 1940s and the fear of massive Jewish immigration help explain the failure of the Roosevelt administration to act. The fact that the mass media, Christian leaders, and even American Jews failed to mount effective pressure on the government does not excuse the president for his shameful indifference to the systematic murder of millions of people. Roosevelt could not have prevented the Holocaust, but vigorous action on his part could have saved many thousands of lives during the war. Roosevelt was not always right, nor was he even consistent, but people who assumed he had a master strategy or a fixed ideological position misunderstood the American president.

A Strategy for Ending the War

The commanding general of the Allied armies in the North African campaign emerged as a genuine leader. Born in Texas, Dwight D. Eisenhower spent his boyhood in Abilene, Kansas. His small-town background made it easy for biographers and newspaper reporters to make him into an American hero. Eisenhower, however, had not come to hero status easily. He saw no action in World War I; he spent that war training soldiers in Texas. Even though he served as assistant to General Douglas MacArthur in the 1930s in the Philippines, he was

Only at the end of the war did the world learn of the horrors of the Nazi concentration camps and the gas chambers. (UPI/Corbis-Bettmann)

only a lieutenant colonel when World War II erupted.

General George Marshall had discovered Eisenhower's talents even before the war began. Eisenhower was quickly promoted to general and achieved a reputation as an expert planner and organizer. Gregarious and outgoing, he had a broad smile that made most people like him instantly. He was not a brilliant field commander and made many mistakes in the African campaign, but he had the ability to get diverse people working together, which was crucial where British and American units had to cooperate.

The American army moved slowly across North Africa, linked up with the British, invaded Sicily in July 1943, and finally stormed ashore in Italy in September. The Italian campaign proved long and bitter. Despite the fact that the Italians overthrew Mussolini and surrendered in September 1943, the Germans occupied the peninsula and gave ground only after bloody fighting. The whole American army seemed to be bogged down for months. One soldier described the "slushy mud that reaches almost up to your knees,... making the roads dangerously slippery." The Allies did not reach Rome until June 1944, and they never controlled all of Italy.

Despite the decision to make the war in Europe the first priority, American ships and planes halted the Japanese advance in the spring of 1942. In the Battle of Coral Sea in May 1942, American carrier-based planes inflicted heavy damage on the Japanese fleet and prevented the invasion of the southern tip of New Guinea and probably of Australia as well. It was the first naval battle in history in which no guns were fired from one surface ship against another; airplanes caused all the damage. In World War II, the aircraft carrier proved more important than the battleship. A month later, at the Battle of Midway, American planes sank four Japanese aircraft carriers and destroyed nearly 300 planes. This was the first major Japanese defeat; it restored some balance of power in the Pacific and ended the threat to Hawaii.

In 1943, the American sea and land forces leapfrogged from island to island, gradually retaking territory from the Japanese and building bases to attack the Philippines and eventually Japan itself. Progress often had terrible costs, however. In November 1943, about 5,000 marines landed on the coral beaches of the tiny island of Tarawa. Despite heavy naval bombardment and the support of hundreds of planes, the marines met heavy opposition. The four-day battle left more than 1,000 Americans dead and over 3,000 wounded. One marine general thought it was all wasted effort. He thought the island should have been bypassed. Others disagreed. No one asked the marines who stormed the beaches. Less than half of the first wave survived.

The Invasion of Europe

Operation Overlord, the code name for the largest amphibious invasion in history, the invasion Stalin had wanted in 1942, began only on June 6, 1944. It

was, according to Churchill, "the most difficult and complicated operation that has ever taken place." The initial assault along a 60-mile stretch of the Normandy coast was conducted with 175,000 men supported by 600 warships and 11,000 planes. Within a month, over a million troops and more than 170,000 vehicles had landed. Such an invasion would have been impossible during World War I.

Eisenhower, now bearing the title Supreme Commander of the Allied Expeditionary Force in Western Europe, coordinated and planned the operation. British and American forces, with some units from other countries, worked together, but Overlord was made possible by American industry, which, by the war's end, was turning out an astonishing 50 percent of all the world's goods. During the first few hours of the invasion, there seemed to be too many supplies. "Everything was confusing," one soldier remembered. It cost 2,245 killed and 1,670 wounded to secure the beachhead. "It was much lighter than anybody expected," one observer remarked. "But if you saw faces instead of numbers on the casualty list, it wasn't light at all."

For months before the invasion, American and British planes had bombed German transportation lines, industrial plants, and even cities. In all, over 1.5 million tons of bombs were dropped on Europe. The massive bombing raids helped make the invasion a success, but evidence gathered after the war suggests that the bombs did not disrupt German war production as seriously as Allied strategists believed at the time. Often a factory or a rail center would be back in operation within a matter of days, sometimes within hours, after an attack. In the end, the bombing of the cities, rather than destroying morale, may have strengthened the resolve of the German people to fight to the bitter end. And the destruction of German cities did not come cheaply. German fighters and anti-aircraft guns shot down 22 of 60 B-17s on June 23, 1943, and on August 17, the Americans lost 60 bombers.

The most destructive bombing raid of the war, carried out against Dresden on the night of February 13–14, 1945, had no strategic purpose. It was launched by the British and Americans to help demonstrate to Stalin that they were aiding the Russian offensive. Dresden, a city of 630,000, was a communications center. Three waves of planes

President Roosevelt inspects General Eisenhower's troops in Sicily before returning home from the Cairo-Tehran Conference in 1943. These were two dominant personalities of the war years. (Department of the Army)

dropped 650,000 incendiary bombs, causing a firestorm that swept over 8 square miles, destroyed everything in its path, and killed 135,000 civilians. One of the American pilots remarked, "For the first time I felt sorry for the population below."

With the dashing and eccentric General George Patton leading the charge and the more staid General Omar Bradley in command, the American army broke out of the Normandy beachhead in July 1944. Led by the tank battalions, it swept across France. American productive capacity and the ability to supply a mobile and motorized army eventually brought victory. But not all American equipment was superior. The American fighter plane, the P-40, could not compete early in the war with the German ME-109. The United States was also far behind Germany in the development of rockets, but that was not as important in the actual fighting as the inability of the United States, until the end of the war, to develop a tank that could compete in armament or firepower with the German tanks. The American army made up for the deficiency of its tanks in part by having superior artillery. Perhaps even more important, most of the American soldiers had grown up tin-

kering with cars and radios. Children of the machine age, they managed to make repairs and to keep tanks, trucks, and guns functioning under difficult circumstances. They helped give the American army the superior mobility that eventually led to the defeat of Germany.

By late 1944, the American and British armies had swept across France, while the Russians had pushed the German forces out of much of eastern Europe. The war seemed nearly over. However, just before Christmas in 1944, the Germans launched a massive counterattack along an 80-mile front, much of it held by thinly dispersed and inexperienced American troops. The Germans drove 50 miles inside the American lines before they were checked. During the Battle of the Bulge, as it was called, Eisenhower was so desperate for additional infantry that he offered to pardon any military prisoners in Europe who would take up a rifle and go into battle. Most of the prisoners, who were serving short sentences, declined the opportunity to clear their record. Eisenhower also promised any black soldiers in the service and supply outfits an opportunity to become infantrymen in the white units, though usually with a lower rank.

However, Walter Bedell Smith, his chief of staff, pointed out that this was against War Department regulations and was the "most dangerous thing I have seen in regard to race relations." Eisenhower recanted, not wishing to start a social revolution. Black soldiers who did volunteer to join the battle fought in segregated platoons commanded by white officers.

The Politics of Victory

As the American and British armies raced across France into Germany in the winter and spring of 1945, the political and diplomatic aspects of the war began to overshadow military concerns. It became a matter not only of defeating Germany but also of determining who was going to control Germany and the rest of Europe once Hitler fell. The relationship between the Soviet Union and the other Allies had been badly strained during the war; with victory in sight, the tension became even greater. Although the American press pictured Stalin as a wise and democratic leader and the Russian people as quaint and heroic, a number of high-level American diplomats and presidential advisers distrusted the Russians and looked ahead to a confrontation with Soviet communism after the war. These men urged Roosevelt to make military decisions with the postwar political situation in mind.

The main issue in the spring of 1945 concerned who would capture Berlin. The British wanted to beat the Russians to the capital city. Eisenhower, however, fearing that the Germans might barricade themselves in the Austrian Alps and hold out indefinitely, ordered the armies south rather than toward Berlin. He also wanted to avoid unnecessary American casualties, and he planned to meet the Russian army at an easily marked spot to avoid any unfortunate incidents. The British and American forces could probably not have arrived in Berlin before the Russians in any case, but Eisenhower's decision generated controversy after the war. Russian and American troops met on April 25, 1945, at the Elbe River. On May 2, the Russians took Berlin. Hitler committed suicide. The long war in Europe finally came to an end on May 8, 1945, but political problems remained.

In 1944, the United States continued to tighten the noose on Japan. American long-range B-29 bombers began sustained strikes on the Japanese mainland in June 1944, and by November they were dropping firebombs on Tokyo. In a series of naval and air engagements, especially at the Battle of Leyte Gulf, American planes destroyed most of the remaining Japanese navy. By the end of 1944, an American victory in the Pacific was all but assured. American forces recaptured the Philippines early the next year, yet the American forces had barely touched Japan itself. It might take years to conquer the Japanese on their home islands.

While the military campaigns reached a critical stage in both Europe and the Pacific, Roosevelt took time off to run for an unprecedented fourth term. To appease members of his own party, he agreed to drop Vice President Henry Wallace from the ticket because some thought him too radical and impetuous. To replace him, the Democratic convention selected a relatively unknown senator from Missouri. Harry S Truman, a World War I veteran, had been a judge in Kansas City before being elected to the Senate in 1934. His only fame came when, as chairman of the Senate Committee to Investigate the National Defense Program, he had insisted on honesty and efficiency in war contracts. He got some publicity for saving the taxpayers' dollars.

The Republicans nominated Thomas Dewey, the colorless and politically moderate governor of New York, who had a difficult time criticizing Roosevelt without appearing unpatriotic. Roosevelt seemed haggard and ill during much of the campaign, but he won the election easily. He would need all his strength to deal with the difficult political problems of ending the war and constructing a peace settlement.

The Big Three at Yalta

Roosevelt, Churchill, and Stalin, together with many of their advisers, met at Yalta in the Crimea in February 1945 to discuss the problems of the peace settlements. Most of the agreements reached at Yalta were secret, and in the atmosphere of the subsequent Cold War, many would become controversial. Roosevelt wanted the help of the Soviet Union in ending the war in the Pacific so as to avoid the needless slaughter of American men in an invasion of the Japanese mainland. In return for a promise to enter the war within three months after the war in Europe was over, the Soviet Union was granted the Kurile Islands, the southern half of Sakhalin, and railroads and port facilities in North Korea, Manchuria, and Outer Mongolia. Later that seemed like a heavy price to pay for the promise, but realistically the Soviet Union controlled most of this territory and could not have been dislodged short of going to war.

When the provisions of the secret treaties were revealed much later, many people would accuse Roosevelt of trusting the Russians too much. But Roosevelt wanted to retain a working relationship with the Soviet Union. If the peace was to be preserved, the major powers of the Grand Alliance would have to work together. Moreover, Roosevelt hoped to get the Soviet Union's agreement to cooperate with a new peace-preserving United Nations organization after the war.

The European section of the Yalta agreement proved even more controversial than its Far Eastern provisions. It was decided to partition Germany and to divide the city of Berlin. The Polish agreements were even more difficult to swallow, in part because the invasion of Poland in 1939 had precipitated the war. The Polish government in exile in London was militantly anti-Communist and looked forward to returning to Poland after the war. Stalin, however, demanded that the eastern half of Poland be given to the Soviet Union to protect its western border. Churchill and Roosevelt finally agreed to the Russian demands with the proviso that Poland be compensated with German territory on its western border. Stalin also agreed to include some members of the London-based Polish group in the new Polish government. He also promised to carry out "free and unfettered elections as soon as possible."

The Polish settlement would prove divisive after the war, and it quickly became clear that what the British and Americans wanted in eastern Europe contrasted with what the Soviet Union intended. Yet at the time it seemed imperative that Russia enter the war in the Pacific, and the reality was that in 1945 the Soviet army occupied most of eastern Europe.

The most potentially valuable accomplishment at Yalta was agreement on the need to construct a United Nations, an organization for preserving peace and fostering the postwar reconstruction of battered and underdeveloped coun-

tries. In 1942, a total of 26 Allied nations had subscribed to the Atlantic Charter, drafted by Churchill and Roosevelt, which laid down several principles for a lasting peace. Discussions among the Allied powers continued during the war, and Stalin agreed with Roosevelt and Churchill to call a conference in San Francisco in April 1945 to draft a United Nations charter.

Spirited debate occurred in San Francisco when the representatives of 50 nations gathered for this task. As finally accepted, amid optimism about a quick end to the war, the charter provided for a General Assembly in which every member nation had a seat. However, this General Assembly was designed mainly as a forum for discussing international problems. The responsibility for keeping global peace was lodged in the Security Council, composed of five permanent members (the United States, the Soviet Union, Great Britain, France, and China) and six other nations elected for two-year terms. The Security Council's responsibility was to suppress international violence by applying economic, diplomatic, or military sanctions against any nation that all permanent members agreed threatened the peace. In addition, the charter established an International Court of Justice and a number of agencies to promote "collaboration among the nations through education, science, and culture." Among these agencies were the International Monetary Fund, the World Health Organization, and the UN Educational, Scientific, and Cultural Organization (UNESCO).

The Atomic Age Begins

Two months after Yalta, on April 12, 1945, as the United Nations charter was being drafted, Roosevelt died suddenly of a massive cerebral hemorrhage. The nation was shocked. When an industrial worker in Springfield, Ohio, heard the news, he remarked that he was glad that "the old son of a bitch was gone"; another worker punched him in the face. Roosevelt, both hated and loved to the end, was replaced by Harry Truman, who was both more difficult to hate and harder to love. In the beginning, Truman seemed tentative and unsure of himself. Yet it fell to the new president to make some of the most difficult decisions of all time. The most momentous of all was the decision to drop the atomic bomb.

The Manhattan Project, first organized in 1941, was one of the best-kept secrets of the war. The task of the distinguished group of scientists whose work on the project was centered at Los Alamos, New Mexico, was to manufacture an atomic bomb before Germany did. But by the time the bomb was successfully tested in the New Mexico desert on July 16, 1945, the war in Europe had ended.

The scientists working on the bomb assumed that they were perfecting a military weapon. Yet when they saw the ghastly power of that first bomb, remembered J. Robert Oppenheimer, a leading scientist on the project, "some wept, a few cheered. Most stood silently." Some opposed the military use of the bomb. They realized its revolutionary power and worried about the future reputation of the United States if it unleashed this new force. But a presidential committee made up of scientists, military leaders, and politicians recom-

mended that it be used on a military target in Japan as soon as possible.

"The final decision of where and when to use the atomic bomb was up to me," Truman later remembered. "Let there be no doubt about it. I regarded the bomb as a military weapon and never had any doubt that it should be used." But the decision had both military and political ramifications. Even though Japan had lost most of its empire by the summer of 1945, it still had a military force of several million men and thousands of kamikaze planes that had already wreaked havoc on the American fleet. The kamikaze pilots gave up their own lives to make sure that their planes, heavily laden with bombs, crashed on an American ship. There was little defense against such fanaticism.

Even with the Russian promise to enter the war, it appeared that an amphibious landing on the Japanese mainland would be necessary to end

The incredible destruction caused by the atomic bombs dropped on Japan is recalled by this 1984 Osaka department store display. The decision to drop the atomic bomb on two Japanese cities is still controversial a half century later. (Kitamura/Gamma Liaison)

TIMELINE

1931–1932	Japan seizes Manchuria
1933	Hitler becomes German chancellor
	United States recognizes the Soviet Union
	Roosevelt extends Good Neighbor policy
1934	Germany begins rearmament
1935	Italy invades Ethiopia
	First Neutrality Act
1936	Spanish civil war begins
	Second Neutrality Act
	Roosevelt reelected
1937	Third Neutrality Act
1938	Hitler annexes Austria, occupies Sudetenland
	German persecution of Jews intensifies
1939	Nazi-Soviet Pact
	German invasion of Poland; World War II begins
1940	Roosevelt elected for a third term
	Selective Service Act
1941	FDR's "Four Freedoms" speech
	Proposed black march on Washington
	Executive order outlaws discrimination in defense industries
	Lend-Lease Act
	Germany attacks Russia
	Japanese assets in United States frozen
	Japanese attack Pearl Harbor; United States declares war on Japan
	Germany declares war on United States
1942	Internment of Japanese Americans
	Second Allied front in Africa launched
1943	Invasion of Sicily
	Italian campaign; Italy surrenders
	United Mine Workers strike
	Race riots in Detroit and other cities
1944	Normandy invasion (Operation Overlord)
	Congress passes GI Bill
	Roosevelt elected for a fourth term
1945	Yalta Conference
	Roosevelt dies; Harry Truman becomes president
	Germany surrenders
	Successful test of atomic bomb
	Hiroshima and Nagasaki bombed; Japan surrenders

the war. The monthlong battle for Iwo Jima, only 750 miles from Tokyo, had resulted in over 4,000 American dead and 15,000 wounded, and the battle for Okinawa was even more costly. An invasion of the Japanese mainland would presumably be even more expensive in human lives. The bomb, many thought, could end the war without an invasion. But some people involved in the decision wanted to retaliate for Pearl Harbor, and still others needed to justify spending over $2 billion on the project in the first place. The timing of the first bomb, however, indicates to some that the decision was intended to impress the Russians and ensure that they had little to do with the peace settlement in the Far East. One British scientist later charged that the decision to drop the bomb on Hiroshima was the "first major operation of the cold diplomatic war with Russia."

Historians still debate whether the use of the atomic bomb on Japanese cities was necessary to end the war, but for the hundreds of thousands of American troops waiting on board ships and on island bases, even in Europe, to invade the Japanese mainland there was no question about the rightness of the decision. They believed that the bombs ended the war and saved their lives. On August 6, 1945, two days before the Soviet Union had promised to enter the war against Japan, a B–29 bomber, the "Enola Gay," dropped a single atomic bomb over Hiroshima. It killed or severely wounded 160,000 civilians and destroyed 4 square miles of the city. One of the men on the plane saw the thick cloud of smoke and thought that they had missed their target. "It looked like it had landed on a forest. I didn't see any sign of the city." The Soviet Union entered the war on August 8.

When Japan refused to surrender, a second bomb was dropped on Nagasaki on August 9. The Japanese surrendered five days later. The war was finally over, but the problems of the atomic age and the postwar world were just beginning.

Conclusion

Peace, Prosperity, and International Responsibilities

The United States emerged from World War II with an enhanced reputation as the world's most powerful industrial and military nation. The demands of the war had finally ended the Great Depression and brought prosperity to most Americans. The war had also increased the power of the federal government. The payroll deduction of federal income taxes, begun during the war, symbolized the growth of a federal bureaucracy that affected the lives of all Americans. The war had also ended American isolationism and made the United States into the dominant international power. Of all the nations that fought in the war, the United States had suffered the least. No bombs were dropped on American factories, and no cities were destroyed. Although more than 300,000 Americans lost their lives, even this carnage seemed minimal when compared with the more than 20 million Russian soldiers and civilians who died or the 6 million Jews and millions of others systematically exterminated by Hitler.

Americans greeted the end of the war with joy and relief. They looked forward to the peace and prosperity for which they had fought. Yet within two years, the peace would be jeopardized by the Cold War, and the United States would be rearming its former enemies, Japan and Germany, to oppose its former friend, the Soviet Union. The irony of that situation reduced the joy of the hard-won peace and made the American people more suspicious of their government and its foreign policy.

Recommended Reading

General Accounts

A. Russell Buchanan, *The United States and World War II* (2 vols., 1964); Robert A. Divine, *Roosevelt and World War II* (1969); Gerhard Weinberg, *A World at Arms: A Global History of World War II* (1994); Gordon Wright, *The Ordeal of Total War* (1968).

Diplomatic and Military

Gar Alperovitz, *Atomic Diplomacy* (1965); Stephen E. Ambrose, *D-Day, June 6, 1944: The Climactic Battle of World War II* (1994); Richard M. Dalfiume, *Desegregation of the U.S. Armed Forces* (1975); Robert A. Divine, *The Reluctant Belligerent* (1979); John Dower, *War Without Mercy* (1986); Paul Fussell, *Wartime* (1989); Lloyd C. Gardner, *Economic Aspects of New Deal Diplomacy* (1964); Waldo Heinrichs, *Threshold*

of War (1988); Akira Iriye, *The Origins of the Secod World War in Asia and the Pacific* (1988); Walter LaFeber, *Inevitable Revolutions: The United States and Central America* (1983); Gordon W. Prange, *At Dawn We Slept* (1981); Martin J. Sherwin, *A World Destroyed* (1975); Gaddis Smith, *Diplomacy During the Second World War* (1965); Russell F. Weigley, *Eisenhower's Lieutenants: The Campaigns in France and Germany* (1981).

The War at Home

Alison Bernstein, *American Indians and World War II* (1991); John Morton Blum, *V Was for Victory* (1976); D'Ann Campbell, *Women at War with America* (1984); Roger Daniels, *Concentration Camp U.S.A.* (1971); Bill Gilbert, *They Also Served: Baseball and the Homefront* (1992); Doris

Kearns Goodwin, *No Ordinary Time: Franklin and Eleanor Roosevelt, The Home Front in World War II* (1994); Ross Gregory, *America 1941* (1988); Susan M. Hartman, *The Homefront and Beyond: Women in the 1940s* (1982); Nicholas Lemann, *The Promised Land: The Great Black Migration and How It Changed America* (1991); Richard R. Lingeman, *Don't You Know There Is a War On?* (1970); Ruth Milkman, *Gender at Work* (1987); Gerald D. Nash, *The American West Transformed: The Impact of the Second World War* (1985); Richard Polenberg, *War and Society* (1972); George H. Roseder, Jr. *The Censored War: American Visual Experience During World War Two* (1993); William Tuttle, "*Daddy's Gone to War*" (1993); Allan M. Winkler, *The Politics of Propaganda: The Office of War Information, 1942–1945* (1978); David S. Wyman, *The Abandonment of the Jews* (1984); Neil A. Wynn, *The Afro-American and the Second World War* (1976).

Fiction

In the *Dollmaker* (1954), Harriette Arnow tells the story of a young woman from Kentucky who finds herself in wartime Detroit; two powerful novels that tell the story of the battlefield experience are Norman Mailer, *The Naked and the Dead* (1948), and Irwin Shaw, *The Young Lions* (1948).

PART VI

A Resilient People, 1945–1996

COMPARATIVE CHRONOLOGIES

Political and Diplomatic	Social and Economic	Cultural and Technological

1945

Political and Diplomatic	Social and Economic	Cultural and Technological
1945 Roosevelt dies; Truman becomes president; first atomic bomb dropped on Japan; World War II ends	1945–1946 Wave of strikes	1946 Benjamin Spock, *Baby and Child Care*
1946 Employment Act	1952 United States tests first hydrogen bomb	1947 Jackie Robinson becomes first African American to play major league baseball
1947 Truman Doctrine; Taft-Hartley Act; Truman establishes Federal Loyalty Program; HUAC probes movie industry	1953 Introduction of termination policy to eliminate reservations for Native Americans	1948 Kinsey publishes first report on human sexuality; Bell Laboratories develops transistor
1948 Marshall Plan launched; Berlin Airlift; Truman reelected	1953–1954 Operation Wetback	1951 J. D. Salinger, *The Catcher in the Rye*
1949 NATO established; Truman announces Fair Deal		
1950 Alger Hiss convicted; Korean War begins; McCarran Internal Security Act		
1951 *Dennis* v. *United States*		
1952 Dwight D. Eisenhower elected president		
1953 Rosenbergs executed; Korean War ends		
1954 Army-McCarthy hearings; *Brown* v. *Board of Education*		

1955

Political and Diplomatic	Social and Economic	Cultural and Technological
1956 Eisenhower reelected; Interstate Highway Act	1955 AFL and CIO merge; Montgomery bus boycott; first McDonald's opens	1956 Elvis Presley hits No. 1 with "Heartbreak Hotel"; Allen Ginsburg, "Howl"
1957 Civil Rights Act	1957 Baby boom peaks; Little Rock school desegregation crisis	1957 First nuclear power plant opens in Shippingport, Pennsylvania
1960 John F. Kennedy elected president; Civil Rights Act	1960 Birth control pills made available; sit-ins begin; SDS founded	1957 USSR launches *Sputnik*
1961 Bay of Pigs invasion	1960s Wave of mergers in American industry	1960s Electronic calculators in office use; Jet planes used for commercial purposes
1962 Cuban missile crisis	1961 Freedom rides to the South	1961 Rachel Carson, *Silent Spring*
1963 JFK assassinated; Lyndon B. Johnson becomes president	1962 James Meredith crisis at University of Mississippi	1962 Bob Dylan gains recognition with "Blowin' in the Wind"; first American orbits the earth; Michael Harrington, *The Other America*
1964 Civil Rights Act; War on Poverty launched; LBJ reelected	1963 Birmingham demonstration; march on Washington	1963 Betty Friedan, *The Feminine Mystique*
	1964 Free speech movement at Berkeley	

1965

Political and Diplomatic	Social and Economic	Cultural and Technological
1965 Voting Rights Act; escalation in Vietnam	1965 Teach-ins begin; Malcolm X assassinated	1965 Ralph Nader, *Unsafe at Any Speed*
1968 Robert F. Kennedy assassinated; Richard M. Nixon elected president	1966 "Black Power"; NOW founded	1966 Masters and Johnson, *Human Sexual Response*
1969 Nixon Doctrine	1968 Martin Luther King, Jr., assassinated; AIM established	1969 U.S. lands man on the moon; Woodstock and Altamont rock festivals
1970 Environmental Protection Agency created	1970 Kent State and Jackson State incidents	1970s Electronics transform traditional industries
	1971–1975 Busing controversies	

Political and Diplomatic	Social and Economic	Cultural and Technological

1965 (continued)

Political and Diplomatic	Social and Economic	Cultural and Technological
1971 Pentagon Papers published; Congress passes Equal Rights Amendment	1973 Occupation of Wounded Knee; Arab oil embargo	1972 *Ms.* magazine founded; 99.8 percent of U.S. households have TV sets
1972 Nixon visits China; SALT I agreement; Watergate break-in; Nixon reelected	1974 OPEC price increases	1972–1973 Development of minicomputers; introduction of calculators for home use
1973 U.S. withdraws from Vietnam; *Roe* v. *Wade*		1973 More than 1 million photocopiers in use
1974 Nixon resigns; Gerald Ford becomes president; Runaway and Homeless Youth Act		

1975

Political and Diplomatic	Social and Economic	Cultural and Technological
1976 Jimmy Carter elected president	1977 Department of Energy created; U.S. trade deficit $26.72 billion	1976–1979 Space probes to Saturn, Pluto, Jupiter, Venus, and Mars
1977 Panama Canal treaties	1979 Three Mile Island accident	1980s Increasing sales of personal home computers
1978 Proposition 13 in California; *Bakke* decision	1980s Rise in number of deaths from AIDS	1982 Vietnam Veterans Memorial dedicated
1979–1981 Iranian hostage crisis	1981–1983 Tax cuts; deficit spending increases	
1979 SALT II agreement		
1980 Ronald Reagan elected president		
1981 Sandra Day O'Connor becomes first woman to sit on U.S. Supreme Court		
1982 Equal Rights Amendment fails		
1984 Democrats name Geraldine Ferraro as vice presidential candidate; Reagan reelected		

1985

Political and Diplomatic	Social and Economic	Cultural and Technological
1986 Tax reform bill passed	1986 Federal budget deficit hits $221 billion	1985 17 million VCRs in use; shift of film entertainment into the home
1988 Intermediate-Range Nuclear Forces Treaty; George Bush elected president	1987 Stock market crash	1986 *Challenger* space shuttle explodes
1989 Berlin Wall breached	1989 Federal bailout of savings and loan industry; one hundred thousandth case of AIDS in United States reported	1990 Fifty million computers in use in United States
1990 Immigration reform enacted	1990 National debt reaches $3.1 trillion	1993 Toni Morrison becomes first African American to win Nobel Prize for Literature
1991 Strategic Arms Reduction Treaty (START); Soviet Union dissolved; Cold War ends; Persian Gulf War	1991 Rodney King incident in Los Angeles	
1992 Bill Clinton elected president; civil war in Bosnia-Herzegovina	1992 Verdicts in Rodney King case spur protests and violence in Los Angeles	
1993 START II; Israel and PLO sign accord	1993 World Trade Center in New York City bombed; North American Free Trade Agreement (NAFTA) signed	
1994 Nelson Mandela elected president of South Africa		

1995

Political and Diplomatic	Social and Economic	Cultural and Technological
1995 Israeli Prime Minister Yitzhak Rabin assassinated	1995 Terrorist bomb kills 169 in Oklahoma City; O. J. Simpson acquitted in criminal trial	1996 TWA plane crash off Long Island
1996 Bill Clinton reelected president	1996 Budget deficit narrows to lowest level since 1981	

Postwar Growth and Social Change

ay Kroc, an ambitious salesman, headed toward San Bernardino, California, on a business trip in 1954. For more than a decade he had been selling "multimixers"—stainless steel machines that could make six milkshakes at once—to restaurants and soda shops around the United States. On this trip, he was particularly interested in checking out a hamburger stand run by Richard and Maurice McDonald, who had bought eight of his "contraptions" and could therefore make 48 shakes at the same time.

Always eager to increase sales, Kroc wanted to see the McDonalds' operation for himself. The 52-year-old son of Slavic parents had sold everything from real estate to radio time to paper cups before peddling the multimixers but had enjoyed no stunning success. Yet he was still on the alert for the key to the fortune that was part of the American dream. As he watched the lines of people at the San Bernardino McDonald's, the answer seemed at hand.

The McDonald brothers sold only standard hamburgers and french fries, but they had developed a system that was fast, efficient, and clean. It drew on the automobile traffic that moved along Route 66. And it was profitable indeed. Sensing the possibilities, Kroc proposed that the two owners open other establishments as well. When they balked, he negotiated a 99-year contract that allowed him to sell the fast-food idea and the name—and their golden arches design—wherever he could.

On April 15, 1955, Kroc opened his first McDonald's in Des Plaines, a suburb of Chicago. Three months later, he sold his first franchise in Fresno, California. Others soon followed. Kroc scouted out new locations, almost always on highway "strips," persuaded people to put up the capital, and provided them with specifications guaranteed to ensure future success. For his efforts, he received a percentage of the gross take.

From the start, Kroc insisted on standardization. Every McDonald's was the same—from the two func-tional arches supporting the glass enclosure that housed the kitchen and take-out window to the single arch near the road bearing a sign indicating how many 15-cent hamburgers had already been sold. All menus and prices were exactly the same, and Kroc demanded that everything from hamburger size to cooking time be constant. He insisted, too, that the establishments be clean. No pinball games or cigarette machines were permitted; the premium was on a good, inexpensive hamburger, quickly served, at a nice place.

McDonald's, of course, was an enormous success. In 1962, total sales exceeded $76 million. In 1964, before the company had been in operation ten years, it had sold over 400 million hamburgers and 120 million pounds of french fries. By the end of the next year, there were 710 McDonald's stands in 44 states. In 1974, only 20 years after Kroc's vision of the hamburger's future, McDonald's did $2 billion worth of business. When Kroc died in 1984, a total of 45 billion burgers had been sold at 7,500 outlets in 32 countries. Ronald McDonald, the clown who came to represent the company, became known to children around the globe after his Washington, D.C., debut in November 1963. When McDonald's began to advertise, it became the country's first restaurant to buy TV time. Musical slogans like "You deserve a break today" and "We do it all for you" became better known than some popular songs.

The post–World War II years saw tremendous suburban development, which reflected the more general economic growth and economic prosperity of the period. (Robert Bechtle, '58 Rambler/Sloan Collection, Valparaiso University Museum of Art, gift of Mrs. McCauley Conner in memory of her father Barklie McK. Henry)

*T*he success of McDonald's provides an example of the development of new trends in the United States in the post–World War II years. Kroc capitalized on the changes of the automobile age. He understood that a restaurant, not in the city but along the highways, where it could draw on heavier traffic, had a better chance of success. The drive-in design, catering to a new and ever-growing clientele, soon became common.

He understood, too, that the franchise notion provided the key to rapid growth. Not prepared to open up thousands of stands himself, he sold the idea to eager entrepreneurs who stood to make sizable profits as long as they remained a part of the larger whole. In numerous other product areas as well as the hamburger business, the franchise method helped create a nationwide web of firms.

Finally, Kroc sensed the importance of standardization and uniformity. He understood the mood of the time, the quiet conformity of Americans searching for success. The McDonald's image may have been monotonous, but that was part of its appeal. Customers always knew what they would get wherever they found the golden arches. If the atmosphere was "bland," that too was deliberate. As Kroc said, "Our theme is kind of synonymous with Sunday school, the Girl Scouts and the YMCA. McDonald's is clean and wholesome." It was a symbol of the age.

This chapter describes the structural changes in American society in the 25 years following World War II. Even as the nation became involved in the Cold War with the Soviet Union (a story we will take up in Chapter 27), Americans were preoccupied with the shifts in social and economic patterns that were taking place. This chapter examines how economic growth, spurred by technological advances, transformed the patterns of work and daily life in the United States, and provided the context for the development of the liberal state described in Chapter 28. Self-interest triumphed over idealism as most people gained a level of material comfort previously unknown. Working-class Americans shared in the gains, as the union movement pressed its claims more successfully than it had ever done in the past, and workers entered into a new equilibrium with the world of management. Life for most Americans was more comfortable than it had ever been before. For many of them, this period appeared to promise the possibility of living the American dream.

But even as the nation prospered, it experienced serious social and economic divisions. This chapter also shows the enormous gaps that existed between rich and poor, even in the best of times. It shows the continuing presence of what one critic eloquently called "the other America" and documents the considerable income disparity and persistent prejudice African Americans (like members of other minority groups) encountered in their effort to share in the postwar prosperity. The frustrations they experienced led to the reform movements described in Chapter 29 and highlighted the limits of the postwar American dream.

Economic Boom

In spite of anxieties about the Cold War, most Americans were optimistic after 1945. As servicemen returned home, their very presence caused a change in family patterns. A baby boom brought unprecedented population growth. The simultaneous and unexpected economic boom had an even greater impact. Large corporations increasingly dominated the business world, but unions grew as well, and most workers improved their lives. Technology appeared triumphant, with new products flooding the market and finding their way into most American homes. For the growing middle class, increased prosperity conveyed the sense that all was well in the United States.

The Thriving Peacetime Economy

The wartime return of prosperity after the Great Depression continued in the postwar years. Even though Americans feared another collapse, for the next several decades they enjoyed one of the most sustained periods of economic expansion the country had ever known, as the United States solidified its position as the richest nation in the world.

McDonald's provided a model for other franchisers in the 1950s and the years that followed. The golden arches, shown here in an early version, were virtually the same wherever they appeared. Initially found along highways around the country, they were later built within cities and towns as well. (Courtesy McDonald's Corporation)

The statistical evidence of economic success was impressive. The gross national product (GNP) jumped from just over $200 billion in 1945 to almost $300 billion in 1950 and by 1960 climbed above $500 billion. The growth continued in the next decade as well. In 1965 it reached $685 billion, and by 1970, it soared to $970 billion. Per capita personal income rose from $1,223 in 1945 to $2,987 in 1966 and then reached $3,945 in 1970. Almost 60 percent of all families in the country were now part of the middle class, a dramatic change from the class structure in the nineteenth and early twentieth centuries.

Personal resources fueled economic growth. During World War II, American consumers had been unable to spend all they earned because factories had concentrated on manufacturing the ships, planes, tanks, and other equipment needed for war. With accumulated savings of $140 billion at war's end, consumers were ready to buy whatever they could. Equally important was the 22 percent rise in real purchasing power between 1946 and 1960. Families now had far more discretionary income—money to satisfy wants as well as needs—than before. At the end of the Great Depression, fewer than one-quarter of all households had any discretionary income; in 1960, three of every five did.

The United States, which produced half the world's goods, was providing new products that average Americans, unlike their parents, could afford. Higher real wages allowed people across social classes to buy consumer goods, and that consumer power, in contrast to the underconsumption of the 1920s and 1930s, spurred the economy. In the words of one government official, Adolf A. Berle, Jr., Americans were caught up in a spirit of "galloping capitalism."

The automobile industry played a key part in the economic boom. Just as cars and roads transformed America in the 1920s when mass production came of age, so they contributed to the equally great transformation three decades later. Limited to the production of military vehicles during World War II, the auto industry expanded dramatically in the postwar period. Two million cars were made in 1946; four times as many were built in 1955; and the number rose to over 9 million in 1965. Customers now chose from a wide variety of engines, colors, and optional accessories. Fancy grills and tail fins distinguished each year's models.

A major economic transformation had occurred in the United States. Peaceful, prosperous, and productive, the nation had become the "affluent society," in economist John Kenneth Galbraith's phrase. Inflation, a problem in the immediate postwar period, slowed from an average of 7 percent per year in the 1940s to 2 to 3 percent per year in the 1950s. It remained stable in the 1960s, averaging 2.7 percent per year. The concentration of income remained the same—the bottom half of the population still earned less than the top tenth—but the ranks of middle-class Americans grew. Charles Lehman, a veteran from Missouri, later summed up the sentiments of many workers as the postwar era began: "I was a twenty-one-year-old lieutenant with a high school education, and my only prewar experience was as a stock boy in a grocery store. But on V-J day, I knew it was only a matter of time before I was rich—or well-off, anyway."

The Corporate Impact on American Life

After 1945, the major corporations increased their hold on the American economy. Government policy in World War II had encouraged the growth of big business and produced tremendous industrial concentration. The government suspended antitrust actions in the interest of wartime production, while government contracts spurred expansion. During the war, two-thirds of all military contracts were awarded to 100 firms, and half of all contracts went to three dozen giants. Firms such as the Ford Motor Company dominated wartime production. In 1940, some 100 companies accounted for 30 percent of all manufacturing output in the United States. Three years later, those same 100 firms controlled 70 percent of output.

Industrial concentration continued after the war. Several waves of mergers had taken place in the past, including one in the 1890s and another in the 1920s. Still another occurred in the 1950s, making oligopoly—domination of a given industry by a few firms—a feature of American capitalism. At the same time, the booming economy encouraged the development of conglomerates—firms that diversified with holdings in a variety of industries. International Telephone and Telegraph, for example, purchased Avis Rent-a-Car, Continental Baking, Sheraton Hotels, Levitt and Sons Home Builders, and Hartford Fire Insurance. That pattern, widely duplicated, protected companies against instability in one particular area. It also led to the further development of finance capitalism to help put the deals together, just as the demands of consolidation in the late nineteenth century had opened the way for bankers like J. P. Morgan (see Chapter 18).

Expansion took other forms as well. Even as the major corporations expanded, so did smaller franchise operations like McDonald's, Kentucky Fried Chicken, and Burger King. Ray Kroc, introduced at the start of this chapter, provided a widely imitated pattern.

While expanding at home, large corporations also moved increasingly into foreign markets, as they had in the 1890s. But at the same time they began to build plants overseas, where labor costs were cheaper. A General Electric plant in Massachusetts might have to pay a worker $3.40 an hour, whereas a plant in Singapore paid only 30 cents an hour for the same job. In the decade after 1957, General Electric built 61 plants abroad, and numerous other firms did the same.

Corporate planning, meanwhile, developed rapidly, as firms sought managers who could assess information, weigh marketing trends, and make rational decisions. Andrew Carnegie had pioneered such an approach in the late nineteenth century by paying meticulous attention to his costs (see Chapter 18). Now managers, trained in business schools, were even more precise in the effort to maximize profit.

Changing Work Patterns

As corporations changed, so did the world of work. In the years after World War II, the United States reversed a 150-year trend and became less a nation of goods producers and more a country of service providers. Between 1947 and 1957, the number of factory workers fell by 4 percent, while the number of clerical workers increased 23 percent and the number of salaried middle-class employees rose 61 percent. By 1956, a majority of American workers held white-collar jobs, and the percentage rose in the years that followed. These new white-collar workers, paid by salary rather than by the hour, served as corporate managers, office workers, salespeople, and teachers.

People lived comfortably, enjoying an abundance of leisure time. Experts predicted that a four-day work week loomed ahead. Indeed, the *Harvard Business Review* announced in 1959 that "boredom, which used to bother only aristocrats, has become a common curse." The American Council of Churches met to consider the question of how to deal with spare time. Housewives worried about how to get their work done if their husbands were home for extended weekends on a regular basis.

Yet white-collar employees paid a price for comfort. Work in the huge corporations became even more impersonal than before. In many firms, the bureaucratic style predominated, with white-collar employees seemingly dressing, thinking, and acting the same (as depicted in a popular novel and film of the 1950s, *The Man in the Gray Flannel Suit*). Corporations, preaching that teamwork was all-important, indoctrinated employees with the appropriate standards of conduct. RCA issued company neckties. IBM had training programs to teach employees the company line. Some large firms even set up training programs to show wives how their own behavior could help their husbands' careers. Just as product standardization became increasingly important, individual acceptance of company norms became necessary. "Personal views can cause a lot of trouble," an oil company recruiting pamphlet noted, suggesting that business favored moderate or conservative ideas that would not threaten the system. William H. Whyte, an analyst of organizational behavior, vividly described the lives of young executives whose ultimate goal was "belongingness." Social critic C. Wright Mills observed, "When white-collar people get jobs, they sell not only their time and energy but their personalities as well."

But not all Americans held white-collar jobs. Many were still blue-collar factory workers, who worked on assembly lines and made the goods others enjoyed. They too dreamed of owning a suburban home and several cars and providing more for their children than they had enjoyed while growing up. Their lives were now more comfortable than ever before, as the union movement

brought substantial gains (see the next section). They were the more fortunate members of the working class. Millions of others, perhaps totaling 40 percent of the work force, held less appealing and less well-paying positions. More and more worked as taxi drivers or farm laborers or dime-store sales clerks. For them, jobs were less stable, less secure, and less interesting. Casual employment had involved manual labor in the past; now it consisted of service work, and much of this was done by minorities, teenagers, and women gradually returning to the labor force.

The Union Movement at High Tide

The union movement had come of age during the New Deal (see Chapter 24). By the end of World War II, it had become even stronger. There were more union members—14.5 million—than ever before. Ten million belonged to the American Federation of Labor (AFL); the other 4.5 million belonged to the Congress of Industrial Organizations (CIO). Unions had taken a no-strike pledge and given their full support to the war effort. Now they looked forward to salary enhancements and a greater voice in workplace management.

The immediate postwar period was difficult. The cancellation of military orders led to layoffs of war workers and prompted fears of a postwar depression, like the one that had followed World War I. Even workers who held their jobs lost the overtime pay they had enjoyed during the war. Workers scrapped their no-strike pledge, leading to a series of strikes. In 1946 alone, 4.6 million workers went out on strike—more than ever before in the history of the United States. There were work stoppages in the automobile, coal, steel, and electrical industries, and a threatened strike by railway workers. These disruptions alienated middle-class Americans who looked for stable employment patterns and provoked the antagonism of conservative Republicans who felt that unionization had gone too far.

In the late 1940s, the situation improved. Unions adopted a less confrontational approach toward management, and a new accord emerged. Gone was the era of bitter industrial warfare. Now big business recognized the basic rights of industrial workers, and union leaders and members in

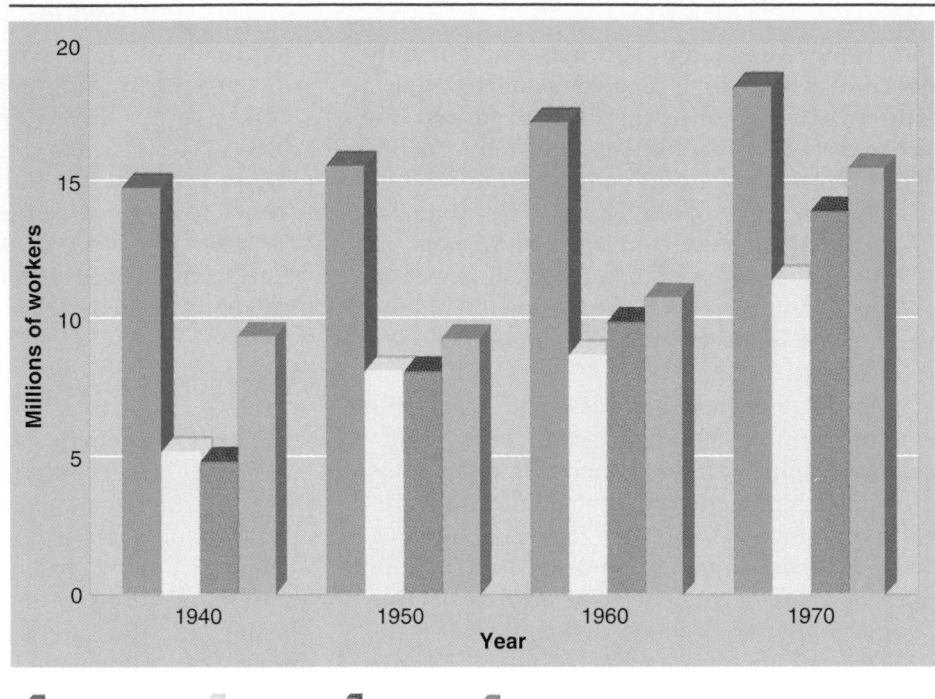

In the postwar years, the size of the work force increased considerably. In this graph, observe how all categories grew, particularly the number of clerical workers and service and sales workers in the decades after 1950. Sources: U.S. Department of Labor and *Historical Statistics of the United States.*

turn acknowledged the prerogatives of management and the need for a fair profit. In this new arrangement, an equilibrium, encouraged by Democrats as well as Republicans, governed business-labor relations. Corporations in the same industry agreed to cooperate rather than compete with one another over labor costs. This meant that once a leading firm reached agreement with the union, the other firms in that area would adopt similar terms, and the costs of the new contract would be met by a general increase in prices.

At the same time, companies made material concessions to workers that improved their daily lives. For example, they agreed to protect workers against inflation. In 1948, General Motors offered the United Automobile Workers a contract that included a cost-of-living adjustment (COLA) and a 2 percent "annual improvement factor" wage increase intended to share GM's productivity gains with workers. In 1950, GM again took the lead, this time with a five-year agreement providing pensions along with a cost-of-living adjustment and

wage increase. Five years later, automobile workers won a guaranteed annual wage. The merger of the AFL and CIO in 1955 ratified the changes that had occurred in the labor movement, as the new organization, led by building trade unionist George Meany, represented more than 90 percent of the country's now larger cohort of 17.5 million union members. By the end of the decade the COLA principle was built into most union contracts.

Union gains came at a price. With higher, more predictable incomes, workers were more willing to limit strike activity and surrender the last vestiges of autonomy in the workplace. Co-opted by the materialistic benefits big business provided, workers fell increasingly under the control of middle-level managers and watched anxiously as companies automated at home or expanded abroad, where labor was cheaper. But the agreements they had reached often precluded any response.

The union movement stalled in the 1960s. The heavy industries whose workers gravitated to the union movement stagnated. The unionized percentage of the nonfarm work force remained stable in the decade and a half following World War II but then began to fall. Unions tried to expand their base by reaching out to new groups—less skilled minority workers and white-collar, service-oriented employees—but these groups proved difficult to organize.

Agricultural Workers in Trouble

The agricultural world changed even more than the industrial world in the postwar United States. Prior to World War II, agriculture had supported one of every five Americans. In the course of one generation, mechanization and consolidation forced that figure down to one of every twenty. Altogether, some 15 million rural jobs disappeared.

New technology revolutionized farming. Improved planting and harvesting machines and better fertilizers and pesticides brought massive gains in productivity. Increasing profitability led to agricultural consolidation. In the 25 years after 1945, average farm size almost doubled. Farms specialized more in cash crops like corn or soybeans that were more profitable than hay or oats that could be used to feed animals. Demanding large-scale investment, farming became a big business. Family farms often found it difficult to compete with the technologically superior "agribusinesses" and watched their share of the market fall. In response, farmers left the land in increasing numbers.

Some of those displaced were whites from such midwestern states as Iowa and Ohio. Most of them found jobs in offices and factories that made up the urban economy of the region. In the South, the upheaval was more disruptive. Many of the uprooted agricultural workers were African Americans, who became part of the huge migration north that had been going on since World War I. In the years between 1910 and 1970, more than 6.5 million African Americans left the South; 5 million of those moved north after 1940. Most of them gravitated to cities, where they faced difficulties described later in this chapter. The agricultural life, as it had been known for decades, even centuries, was over.

Demographic and Technological Trends

The postwar economic boom was interwoven with a series of demographic changes. The population grew dramatically and continued to move west, while at the same time, millions of white Americans left the cities for the suburbs that began to grow exponentially in the postwar years. New patterns, revolving around television and other gadgets provided by the advances of technology, came to characterize the consumer culture that dominated suburban life.

Population Shifts

In post–World War II America, a growing population marked prosperity's return. During the Great Depression, the birthrate had dropped to an all-time low of 19 births per 1,000 population as hard times obliged people to delay marriage and parenthood. As the Second World War boosted the economy, the birthrate began to rise again. Some experts questioned whether the trend was a long-term one. The Census Bureau cautiously claimed that it was at least partly due to "occasional furloughs," but in fact a real shift was underway.

The birthrate soared in the postwar years as millions of Americans began families. The "baby boom" peaked in 1957, with a rate of more than 25 births per 1,000. In that year, 4.3 million babies were born, one every seven seconds. While the population growth of 19 million in the 1940s was double the rise of the decade before, that increase paled against the increase in the 1950s, which totaled 29 million.

The effects of the baby boom were visible everywhere. Monroe Park, a community of 95 house trailers for veterans and their families at the University of Wisconsin, was called the "state's most fertile five acres." In one week alone in 1947, five families had babies. Similar fertility was evident in communities throughout the United States.

The rising birthrate was the dominant factor affecting population growth, but the death rate was also declining. Miracle drugs made a difference. Federal sponsorship of medical research during World War II had spurred the development of penicillin and streptomycin, now widely available in the

Birth and Population Rates, 1900–1970

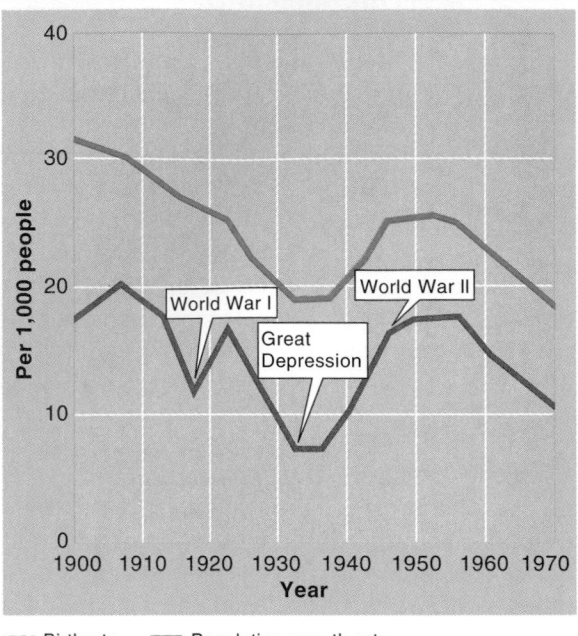

Birthrate ▬   Population growth rate ▬

Both birth and population rates increased dramatically after the difficult years of the Great Depression. Note the baby boom that began at the end of World War II and continued for the next several decades. Sources: U.S. Bureau of the Census and *Statistical Abstract of the United States.*

United States. They helped cure strep throat and other bacterial infections, intestinal ailments, and more serious illnesses such as tuberculosis. A polio vaccine introduced a decade after the war virtually eliminated that dreaded disease. Life expectancy rose: midway through the 1950s, the average was 70 years for whites and 64 for blacks, compared with 55 for whites and 45 for blacks in 1920.

The baby boom shaped family and social patterns and material needs. Many women who had taken jobs during the war now left the work force to rear their children and care for their homes. Their lives changed considerably as they substituted housework for paid work. The demand grew for diaper services and baby foods. When they entered school, the members of the baby boom generation strained the educational system. Between 1946 and 1956, enrollment in grades 1 through 8 soared from 20 million to 30 million. Since school construction had slowed during the Depression and had virtually halted during the

Second World War, classrooms were needed. Teachers, too, were in short supply.

As Americans became more populous, they also became more mobile. For many generations, working-class Americans had been the most likely to move; now geographic mobility spread to the middle class. Each year in the 1950s, over a million farmers left their farms in search of new employment. Other Americans picked up stakes and headed on as well. Some moved to look for better jobs. Others, like Bob Moses of Baltimore, simply wandered awhile after returning home from the war and then settled down. Moses, traveling in a 1937 Chevrolet with some high school friends, was going "nowhere in particular, just roaming. We'd see a kink in a river on the map, and head there." After regimented military life, it was good to be free.

The war had produced increasing movement, most of it westward. Although the scarcity of water in the West would require massive water projects to support population growth, war workers and their families streamed to western cities where shipyards, airplane factories, and other industrial plants were located. After the war, this migration pattern persisted, as the West and the Southwest continued to grow. The Sun Belt—the region stretching along the southern tier of the United States from Florida to California—attracted new arrivals. Cities like Houston, Albuquerque, Tucson, and Phoenix underwent phenomenal expansion. The population of Phoenix soared from 65,000 in 1940 to 439,000 in 1960. In the 1950s, Los Angeles pulled ahead of Philadelphia as the third-largest city in the United States. One-fifth of all the growth in the period took place in California's promised land; even baseball teams—the Brooklyn Dodgers and the New York Giants—left the East Coast for western shores. By 1963, in a dramatic illustration of the importance of the West, California passed New York as the nation's most populous state.

The migration west resulted from a number of reasons. Servicemen who had been stationed in the West liked the scenery, climate, and pace of life. Many returned with their families after the war. With funds from the Federal Housing Administration or Veterans Administration, they could afford to borrow money and buy new homes. That spending, in turn, helped fuel the region's economic growth.

Meanwhile, as noted earlier in this chapter, Cold War spending promoted economic develop-

Population Shifts, 1940–1950

POPULATION SHIFT	
■	Over 20% increase
■	5%–20% increase
■	Under 5% increase
■	Decrease

This map reveals the huge growth of population in the West and the sizable, though less extensive, increase in the Northeast and Southeast between 1940 and 1950.

ment, and much of that expansion occurred in the West. As the Korean War sparked increased military expenditures, the economy of California grew more rapidly than that of the country as a whole. Aircraft production in the state accounted for more than 40 percent of the total increase in manufacturing employment there between 1949 and 1953. In the 1950s, rocket research further stimulated the aerospace industry. In 1959, California had nearly a quarter of all prime military contracts in the nation. By 1962, the Pacific Coast as a whole held almost half of all Defense Department research and development contracts.

The West also benefited from the development of the service economy. Many western workers in postwar America were part of the growing service sector. The percentage of workers in such jobs was higher in virtually all western states than in eastern counterparts. Denver became a major regional center of the federal bureaucracy in the postwar years. From 14,000 people on the payroll in 1951, the number rose to 23,000 in 1961, and to 31,500 in 1975, when it had more such employees than any city other than Washington, DC. Albuquerque like-

wise gained numerous federal offices and became known as "little Washington." The old West of cowboys, farmers, and miners was turning into a new West of bureaucrats, lawyers, and clerks.

The New Suburbs

As the population shifted westward after World War II, another form of movement was taking place. Although the proportion of Americans defined as residents of metropolitan areas increased from 51 to 63 percent between 1940 and 1960, this disguised another shift. Millions of white Americans fled the inner city to suburban fringes, intensifying a movement that had begun before the war. Fourteen of the nation's largest cities, including New York, Boston, Chicago, Philadelphia, and Detroit, actually lost population in the 1950s. As central cities became places where poor nonwhites clustered, new urban and racial problems emerged.

For people of means, cities were places to work and then to leave at five o'clock. In Manhattan, south of the New York borough's City Hall, the

Growth of Sun Belt Cities, 1920–1980 Population (in thousands)				
	1920	1940	1960	1980
Los Angeles	879	2,916	6,039	7,478
Houston	168	529	1,418	2,905
Dallas	185	527	1,084	2,430
Atlanta	249	559	1,017	2,030
San Diego	74	289	1,033	1,862
Miami	30	268	935	1,626
Phoenix	29	186	664	1,509
New Orleans	398	552	907	1,256
San Antonio	191	338	716	1,072
Tucson	20	37	266	531

Source: U.S. Bureau of the Census.

noontime population of 1.5 million dropped to 2,000 during the night. The outlying regions, writer John Brooks argued, were

> draining downtown of its nighttime population, except for night watchmen and derelicts; it was becoming a part-time city, tidally swamped with bustling humanity every weekday morning when the cars and commuter trains arrived, and abandoned again at nightfall when the wave sucked back—left pretty much to thieves, policemen, and rats.

As the cities declined, new suburbs blossomed. If the decade after World War I had witnessed a rural-to-urban shift, the decades after World War II saw a reverse shift to the regions outside the central cities, usually accessible only by car. By the end of the 1950s, a third of all Americans resided in suburbs. That figure continued to rise in the next decade, reaching nearly 38 percent in 1970.

Americans moved to the suburbs to buy homes that could accommodate their larger families. Often rapidly constructed and overpriced, these suburban tract houses provided the appearance of comfort and space and the chance to have at least one part of the American dream, a place of one's own. Set in developments with names like Scarborough Manor, Peppermill Village, and Woodbury Knoll, they seemed protected from the growing troubles of the cities, insulated from the difficulties of the world outside.

A major figure in the suburbanization movement was William J. Levitt, a builder eager to gamble and reap the rewards of a growing demand. Levitt had recognized the advantages of mass production during World War II, when his firm constructed housing for war workers. Aware that the GI Bill made mortgage money readily available, he saw the possibilities of suburban development. But to cash in, Levitt knew he had to use new construction methods.

Shifts in Population Distribution, 1940–1970

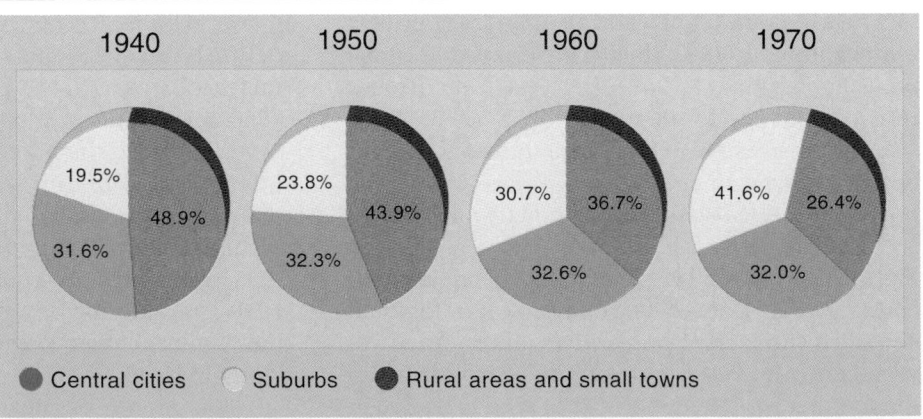

This graph shows the progressive decline in rural population, and the corresponding increase in suburban population, between 1940 and 1970. Source: U.S. Bureau of the Census.

Mass production was the key. Individually designed houses were a thing of the past, he believed. "The reason we have it so good in this country," he said, "is that we can produce lots of things at low prices through mass production." Houses were among them. Working on a careful schedule, Levitt's team brought precut and pre-assembled materials to each site, put them together, and then moved on to the next location. As on an assembly line, tasks were broken down into individual steps. Groups of workers performed but a single job, moving from one tract to another.

Levitt proved that his system worked. Construction costs at Levittown, New York, a new community of 17,000 homes built in the late 1940s, were only $10 per square foot, compared with the $12 to $15 common elsewhere. The next Levittown appeared in Bucks County, Pennsylvania, several years after the first, and another went up in Willingboro, New Jersey, at the end of the 1950s. Levitt's success provided a model for other developers.

Government-insured mortgages, especially for veterans, fueled the housing boom. So did fairly low postwar interest rates. With many American families vividly remembering the Depression and saving significant parts of their paychecks, the nation had a pool of savings large enough to keep mortgage interest rates in the affordable 5 percent range.

Suburbanization transformed the American landscape. Huge tracts of former fields, pastures, and forests were now divided into standardized squares, each bearing a house with a two-car garage and a manicured lawn. Stands of trees disappeared, for it was cheaper to cut them down than to work around them. Folksinger Malvina Reynolds described the new developments she saw:

> *Little boxes on the hillside*
> *Little boxes made of ticky tacky*
> *Little boxes on the hillside*
> *Little boxes all the same.*
> *There's a green one and a pink one*
> *And a blue one and a yellow one*
> *And they're all made out of ticky tacky*
> *And they all look just the same.*

As suburbs flourished, businesses followed their customers out of the cities. Shopping centers led the way. At the end of World War II, there were eight, but the number multiplied rapidly in the

Step-by-step mass production, with units completed in assembly-line fashion, was the key to William Levitt's approach to housing. But the suburban developments he and others created were marked by street after street of houses that all looked the same. (Lambert/Archive Photos)

1950s. In a single three-month period in 1957, 17 new centers opened; by 1960, there were 3,840 in the United States. Developers like Don M. Casto, who built the Miracle Mile near Columbus, Ohio, understood the importance of location as Americans moved out of the cities. "People have path-habits," he said, "like ants."

Shopping centers catered to the suburban clientele and transformed consumer patterns. They offered easy parking and convenient late hours; if they wished, suburb dwellers could remain entirely insulated from the cities. Their new shopping patterns, however, undermined the downtown department stores and further eroded urban health.

The Environmental Impact

Fast-food restaurants, shopping centers, and suburban housing developments all had a pronounced effect on the environment. Rapid development often took place without extensive planning and encroached on some of the nation's most attractive rural areas. Before long, virtually every American city was ringed by an ugly highway lined with the eating places, shopping malls, and auto dealerships that catered to the suburban population. Billboard advertisements filled whatever space was not yet developed.

Responding to the increasingly cluttered terrain, architect Peter Blake ruthlessly attacked the practices of the 1950s in his muckraking book *God's Own Junkyard: The Planned Deterioration of America's Landscape,* published in 1964. The largely pictorial account indicted the careless attitudes toward the environment that led to the "uglification" of a once lovely land. After describing breathtaking natural resources, Blake declared, "The only trouble is that we are about to turn this beautiful inheritance into the biggest slum on the face of the earth." Public policy and the pursuit of private profit, coupled with general citizen indifference, he charged, led to the unconscionable desecration of the American landscape:

> Our suburbs are interminable wastelands dotted with millions of monotonous little houses on monotonous little lots and crisscrossed by highways lined with billboards,

Highways surrounding cities and towns were filled with commercial establishments advertising their wares with brightly colored, but often tasteless, signs. Here hotels along such a roadway try to entice travelers to come in. (Photograph by Wallace Litwin)

jazzed-up diners, used-car lots, drive-in movies, beflagged gas stations, and garish motels. Even the relatively unspoiled countryside beyond these suburban fringes has begun to sprout more telephone poles than trees, more trailer camps than national parks.

Despite occasional accounts like Blake's, there was little real consciousness of environmental issues in the early post–World War II years. The term *environment* itself was hardly used prior to the war. Americans had been concerned with conservation earlier in the century and had first focused on efficient use and development of water and forests. Later they turned their attention to the preservation of grasslands, soils, and game.

Yet the very prosperity that created the dismal highway strips in the late 1940s and 1950s was leading more and more Americans to appreciate natural environments as treasured parts of their rising standard of living. The shorter workweek provided more free time, and many Americans now had the means for longer vacations. By 1950, most wage laborers worked a 40-hour week, and 60 percent of nonagricultural workers enjoyed paid vacations, whereas few had been able to take regular holidays in 1930. They began to explore mountains and rivers and ocean shores, and to ponder how they might be used for recreation. They also began to consider how to protect them. In 1958, Congress established the National Outdoor Recreation Review Commission, a first step toward consideration of environmental issues that became far more common in the next decade. In 1964, Congress went still further, passing a National Wilderness Preservation Act, followed by a Wild and Scenic Rivers Act and a National Trails Act in 1968. Americans also began to recognize the need for open space in their communities, to compensate for the urban overdevelopment that was often taking place.

Technology Supreme

Rapid technological change occurred in the postwar years. Some developments—the use of atomic energy, for example—flowed directly from war research. Federal support for scientific activity increased dramatically, as the pattern of wartime collaboration continued. The government established the National Institutes of Health in 1948 to coordinate medical research and the National Science Foundation in 1950 to fund basic scientific research. Meanwhile, the advent of the Cold War led to ever greater government involvement, through research and development (R & D) funding from the Atomic Energy Commission, created in 1946, and from the Department of Defense, set up in 1947. Money went to large research universities and fueled their growth. Scientists engaged in both basic and applied research, and helped develop nuclear weapons, jet planes, satellites, and consumer goods that were often the side products of military research. But not all innovations came from government funding. Others emerged from the research and development activities sponsored by big business.

Computers both reflected and assisted the process of technological development. Wartime advances resulted in large but workable calculators, followed in the postwar years by machines that contained their own internal instructions and memories. In 1946, the Electronic Numerical Integrator and Calculator, called ENIAC, was built at the University of Pennsylvania. Although it contained 18,000 electronic tubes and required tremendous amounts of electricity and special cooling procedures, the machine worked. In an advertised test, it set out to multiply 97,367 by itself 5,000 times. A reporter pushed the necessary button, and the task was completed in less than half a second.

After the development of the transistor by three scientists at Bell Laboratories in 1948, the computer became faster and more reliable, and transformed American society as surely as industrialization had changed it a century before. Computers allowed for sophisticated forms of space

The Computer

WORLDWIDE SHIPMENTS OF PCs, 1985—1995

(MILLIONS)

MILESTONES IN COMPUTER DEVELOPMENT

- Vacuum tube
- Transistor
- Intergrated Circuit
- Microprocessor (computer on a chip)
- Internet
- World Wide Web

Personal Computers in American Homes (in millions)

0.75 17.38 22.60
1984 1989 1993

Growth of World Wide Web sites in two years (6/93–6/95)

Web sites (in thousands)

6/93 6/94 6/95

Employment of Computer programmers, 1984–1994

Employment (in thousands)

1984 1988 1992 1994

The ENIAC computer, first used in 1946, was a huge machine that took up an entire room. Yet it was far slower and far less powerful than the tiny desktop computers that became popular several decades later. (Courtesy, Moore School of Engineering)

exploration. Airlines, hotels, and other businesses computerized their reservation systems. Business accounting and inventory control began to depend on computers. Computer programmers and operators were in increasing demand.

One ominous technological trend was the advent of automation. Mechanization was not new, but now it became far more widespread, threatening both skilled and unskilled workers. In 1952, the Ford Motor Company began using automatic drilling machines in an engine plant and found that 41 workers could do a job 117 had done before. The implications of falling purchasing power as machines replaced workers were serious for an economy dependent on consumer demand.

The Consumer Culture

Tiny transistors powered not only computers but also a wide variety of new appliances and gadgets designed for personal use. A transistorized miniature hearing aid, for example, could fit into the frame of a pair of eyeglasses. Stereophonic high fidelity systems, using new transistor components, provided better sound.

Television, developed in the 1930s, became a major influence on American life after World War II. In 1946, there were fewer than 17,000 TV sets, but by 1960, three-quarters of all American families

owned at least one set. In 1955, the average American family tuned in four to five hours each day. Some studies predicted that an American student, on graduating from high school, would have spent 11,000 hours in class and 15,000 hours before the "tube." Young Americans grew up to the strains of "Winky Dink and You," "The Mickey Mouse Club," and "Howdy Doody Time" in the 1950s. Older viewers attended to situation comedies like "I Love Lucy" and "Father Knows Best" and live dramas such as "Playhouse 90." They watched Elvis Presley play his guitar and sing, and they danced to the rock and roll music played on "American Bandstand." Many of the programs aimed at children depicted violence and crime. Hopalong Cassidy was one of America's defenders who became a cult hero in his time. The gunslinging cowboy provided a role model that hundreds of American manufacturing firms capitalized on by making toy guns.

Americans maintained an ardent love affair with the appliances and gadgets produced by modern technology. By the end of the 1950s, most families had at least one automobile, as well as the staple appliances they had begun to purchase before—refrigerator, washing machine, television, and vacuum cleaner. Dozens of less essential items also became popular. There were electric can openers, electric pencil sharpeners, and electric toothbrushes. There were push-button phones and aerosol bombs, and automatic transmissions to eliminate the manual shifting of car gears.

The American economy came to depend on consumption as the expansion of consumer credit made purchasing new goods and gadgets easier. Installment plans facilitated buying a new car, while credit cards encouraged the purchase of smaller items such as television sets and household appliances. Eating out became easier when meals could be charged on a card. The first of the consumer credit cards—the Diner's Club card—appeared in 1950, followed at the end of the decade by the American Express card and the BankAmericard. By 1965, American Express and Diner's Club each had more than 2 million cardholders. By the end of the decade, there were just about 50 million credit cards of all kinds in use in the United States. Consumer credit—total private indebtedness—increased from $8.4 billion in 1946 to nearly $45 billion in 1958, and reached $113.2 billion in 1968.

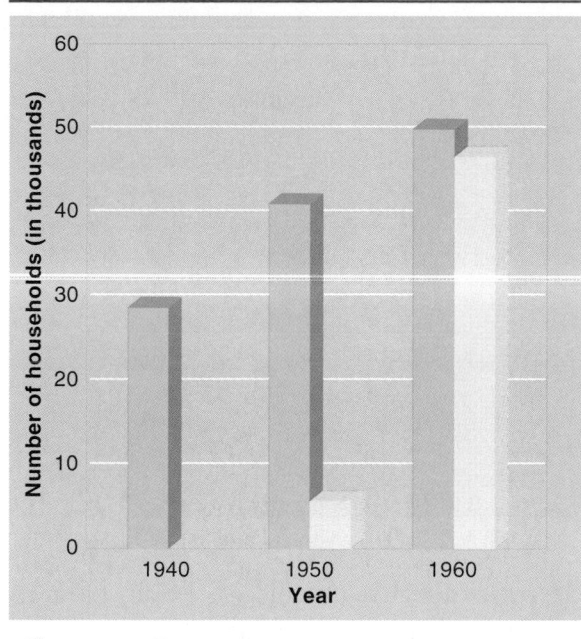

Households Owning Radios and Televisions, 1940–1960

Radio became increasingly popular in the postwar years, but observe the astronomical increase in the number of households owning television sets in the decade after 1950. Source: U.S. Bureau of the Census.

"The Mickey Mouse Club" was a popular daily feature on television in the 1950s. Millions of American children were glued to their TV sets each day after school, as they shared a common experience and absorbed the values promoted by the television networks. (Photofest)

For consumers momentarily unsure about new purchases, a revitalized advertising industry was ready to convince them to go ahead. Advertising had come of age in the 1920s, as businesses persuaded customers that buying new products brought status and satisfaction. Advertising faltered when the economy collapsed in the 1930s but began to revive during the war, as firms kept the public aware of consumer goods, even those in short supply. With the postwar boom, advertisers again began to hawk their wares, this time even more aggressively than before.

Motivational research became more sophisticated, uncovering new ways of persuading people to buy. Television played an important part in conveying the spirit of consumption to millions of Americans. Unlike radio, which could only describe new commodities, television could show products to consumers. Advertisements featuring the luxury items needed for the good life bombarded television viewers. Programs such as "The Price Is Right" stressed consumption in direct ways: Contestants won goods for quoting their correct retail price. Drawing on a talent honed in shopping centers and department stores, the show encouraged the acquisition of ever more material goods.

If the appeal often seemed overdone, advertisers had their defenders, too. Vance Packard argued in 1957 in his best-selling book *The Hidden Persuaders* that advertisers "fill an important and constructive role in our society. Advertising, for example, not only plays a vital role in promoting our economic growth but [serves] as a colorful, diverting aspect of American life, and many of the creations of admen are tasteful, honest works of artistry." That may have been true of some ads, but others were garish and conveyed a sense of material wealth run amok.

The supermarket, filled with convenience foods, was an important part of the consumer revolution. Suburban residents could drive to a supermarket and in aisle after aisle find all the goods that had been sold by a variety of smaller specialty stores in an earlier age. (George Silk/LIFE Magazine ©Time Inc.)

Americans welcomed the postwar affluence. Having weathered the poverty and unemployment of the 1930s and made sacrifices during a long war, they now intended to enjoy their newfound abundance and leisure time. Most Americans regarded all this as their due, sometimes neglecting to look beyond the immediate objects of their desire. The decade, journalist William Shannon wrote, was one of "self-satisfaction and gross materialism.... The loudest sound in the land has been the oink and grunt of private hoggishness.... It has been the age of the slob."

Consensus and Conformity

As the economy expanded, an increasing sense of sameness pervaded American society. Some believed this was the great age of conformity, when members of all social groups learned to emulate those around them rather than strike out on their own. Third- and fourth-generation ethnic Americans became much more alike. With immigration slowed to a trickle after 1924, ties to Europe weakened, and assimilation occurred. Television contributed to growing conformity by providing young and old with a common, shared, visually seductive experience. Escaping the homogenizing tenden-

cies was difficult. Sociologist David Riesman pointed out that in the classic nursery rhyme "This Little Pig Went to Market," each pig went his own way. "Today, however, all little pigs go to market; none stay home; all have roast beef, if any do; and all say 'we-we.'"

Conformity in School and Religious Life

The willingness to conform to group norms affected students at all levels. Elementary school children watched the same television shows and coveted the same toys. High school students, always concerned with group norms, dressed in similar ways and shared a common vocabulary that came from television programs and the products featured in advertising jingles. College and university students seemed most concerned with security, both during their years of study and after graduation. They joined fraternities and sororities and engaged in panty raids and other pranks but took little interest in world affairs. "I observe," Yale president A. Whitney Griswold told a graduating class in 1950, "that you share the prevailing mood of the hour, which in your case consists of bargains privately struck with fate—on fate's terms."

Americans in the postwar years discovered a shared religious sense and returned to their churches in record numbers. By the end of the

1950s, fully 95 percent of all Americans identified with some religious denomination. Church membership doubled between 1945 and 1970.

In part, church attendance reflected a desire to challenge "godless communism" at the height of the Cold War and to find some solace from the threat of annihilation in a nuclear war (see Chapter 27). Clergyman Billy James Hargis founded his Christian Crusade in 1947 and preached the close connection between religion and politics. Hargis claimed: "Patriotism and Christianity are very close to each other. It is impossible to be a true Christian and not be a true patriot." Evangelist Billy Graham, often introduced as a "man with God's message for these crisis days," was in the forefront of the anti-Communist campaign in the 1950s and 1960s. He preached to millions at his revivals, and capitalized on the media, using radio, television, and film to spread his message. "Hour of Decision" was a regular radio ministry in the 1950s, in which Graham tried to convert sinners and so save the nation. In one sermon, he declared: "Unless America at this tragic hour is willing to turn to Jesus Christ and be cleansed by the blood of Christ and know the regenerating power of the Holy Spirit, Christ will never save the nation." How could the nation be saved? "When you make your decision for Jesus Christ," Graham said, "it is America making her decision through you."

The religious resurgence had other roots as well. Ecumenical activities—worldwide efforts on the part of different Christian churches—became more common following a first World Council of Churches meeting in Amsterdam, in The Netherlands, in 1948. These helped draw attention to the place of religion in modern life. Catholicism made its traditions more accessible in the 1960s, as Pope John XXIII convened the Vatican Ecumenical Council to reform the Church. He pushed for the substitution of modern languages for Latin and for doctrinal changes that made Catholicism more accessible to the laity. Judaism, likewise, experienced important shifts in the postwar years. Second- and third-generation Jews became increasingly affluent, and between 1945 and 1965, a third of all American Jews left cities for the suburbs. There they built new synagogues, most of which adhered to the easier-to-follow patterns of Reform or Conservative, rather than Orthodox,

Evangelist Billy Graham preached a fiery message to millions of Americans in the 1950s. On the radio, on television, and in huge revivals, he urged sinners to embrace God and so save their nation from the perils of the Communist threat. (UPI/Corbis-Bettmann)

Judaism. In part, this shift reflected an effort by Jews to seek greater acceptance from mainstream American society.

The religious revival resulted to some degree as well from the power of suggestion that led Americans to do what others did. It seemed to reinforce the importance of family life. As one slogan put it, "The family that prays together stays together." The renewal of interest in religion also offered an acceptable means of escape from the anxieties of a middle-class executive's life. In the 1950s, the Full Gospel Businessmen's Fellowship not only provided religious camaraderie but also enjoyed access to the White House.

President Dwight Eisenhower reflected the national mood when he observed that "our government makes no sense unless it is founded in a deeply felt religious faith—and I don't care what it is." In 1954, Congress added the words "under God" to the pledge to the flag, and the next year voted to require the phrase "In God We Trust" on all U.S. currency. Yet the revival sometimes seemed to rest on a shallow base of religious knowledge. In one public opinion poll, 80 percent of the respondents indicated that the Bible was God's revealed word, but only 35 percent were able to name the four Gospels and over half were unable to name even one.

Back to the Kitchen

World War II had interrupted traditional patterns of behavior for both men and women. As servicemen went overseas, women left their homes to work. After 1945, there was a period of adjustment as the men returned, and many working women were told that they were no longer needed in their jobs. In the 1950s, traditional gender roles were reaffirmed and women faced tremendous pressure to conform to accepted prewar patterns, even though, paradoxically, more women entered the work force than ever before.

Men and women had different expectations in the postwar years. Most men expected to go to school and then find jobs to support their families. Viewing themselves as the primary breadwinners, they wanted their jobs waiting for them after the war. It was fine for women to have worked during the conflict, but now men wanted things the way they had been before. For women, the situation was more complex. While they wanted to resume patterns of family life that had been disrupted by the war, many had enjoyed working in the military plants and were reluctant to retreat to the home, although the government and their employers persistently encouraged them to do so.

In 1947, *Life* magazine ran a long photo essay called "The American Woman's Dilemma" that summed up the problem. The essay observed that women were caught in a conflict between the traditional expectation to stay home and the desire to have a paid job. A 1946 *Fortune* magazine poll also captured the discontent of some women. Asked whether they would prefer to be born again as men or women, 25 percent of the women interviewed said they would prefer to be men. That dissatisfaction was strongest among white, well-educated,

middle-class women, which was understandable, since family economic circumstances usually required black and lower-class white women to continue working outside the home.

By the 1950s, doubts and questions had largely receded. The baby boom increased average family size and made the decision to remain home easier. The flight to the suburbs gave women more to do, and they settled into the routines of redecorating their homes and gardens and transporting children to and from activities and schools.

In 1956, when *Life* produced a special issue on women, the message differed strikingly from that of nine years before. Profiling Marjorie Sutton, the magazine spoke of the "Busy Wife's Achievements" as "Home Manager, Mother, Hostess, and Useful Civic Worker." Married at 16, Marjorie was now involved with the PTA, Campfire Girls, and charity causes. She cooked and sewed for her family, which included four children, supported her husband by entertaining 1,500 guests a year, and worked out on the trampoline "to keep her size 12 figure."

Marjorie Sutton reflected the widespread social emphasis on marriage and home. Many women went to college to find husbands; if they succeeded, they dropped out. Almost two-thirds of the women in college left before completing a degree, compared with less than half the men. Women were expected to marry young, have children early, and encourage their husbands' careers. An article in *Esquire* magazine in 1954 called working wives a "menace."

The traditional view of women extended throughout American society. Adlai Stevenson, Democratic presidential candidate in 1952 and 1956, defined the female role in politics, telling a group of women that "the assignment for you, as wives and mothers, you can do in the living room with a baby in your lap or in the kitchen with a can opener in your hand." As in much of the nineteenth century, a woman was "to influence man and boy" in her "humble role of housewife" and mother.

Pediatrician Benjamin Spock agreed. In 1946 he published *Baby and Child Care*, the book most responsible for the child-rearing patterns of the postwar generation. In it, he advised mothers to stay at home if they wanted to raise stable and secure youngsters. Working outside the home might jeopardize their children's mental and emotional health. Subsequent editions argued much the same thing.

Popular culture highlighted the stereotype of the woman concerned only about marriage and family. Author Betty Friedan described these patterns in her explosive 1963 critique, *The Feminine Mystique.* Through an exhaustive examination of women's magazines and other publications, she provided a profile of women in the 1950s and early 1960s. They "could desire no greater destiny than to glory in their own femininity.... All they had to do was to devote their lives from earliest girlhood to finding a husband and bearing children." Their role was clear. "It was unquestioned gospel," she wrote, "that women could identify with *nothing* beyond the home—not politics, not art, not science, not events large or small, war or peace, in the United States or the world, unless it could be approached through female experience as a wife or mother or translated into domestic detail."

Movies likewise played upon on conventional images. Doris Day, charming and wholesome, was a favorite heroine. In film after film, she showed how an attractive woman who played her cards right could land her man—the assumed goal of every woman.

The family was all important in this scenario. Fewer than 10 percent of all Americans felt that an unmarried person could be happy. A popular advice book declared: "The family is the center of your living. If it isn't, you've gone far astray." A healthy family strengthened the nation in its Cold War struggle against the Communist menace. In the pattern pictured in many of the popular television programs mentioned earlier in this chapter, the family was meant to provide all satisfaction and contentment. The single-story ranch house that became so popular in this period reflected the focus on the family as the source of recreation and fun. No longer were kitchen and den private, as they had been earlier in a reflection of the notion of separate spheres. Now houses, with far more shared and open space, stressed livability and family comfort.

Film star Doris Day was enormously popular in the 1950s. She was pert and pretty, with a winning smile and a captivating charm, and she looked like the special girl next door many men dreamed of marrying. (Archive Photos)

Sexuality was a troublesome if compelling topic in the postwar years. In 1948, Alfred C. Kinsey published *Sexual Behavior in the Human Male.* Kinsey was an Indiana University zoologist who had previously studied the gall wasp. When asked to teach a course on marriage problems, he found little published material about human sexual activity and decided to collect his own. He compiled case histories of 5,300 white males, analyzed their personal backgrounds, and recorded patterns of sexual behavior.

Kinsey shocked the country with his statistics on premarital, extramarital, and otherwise illicit sexual acts. Among males who went to college, he concluded, 67 percent had engaged in sexual intercourse before marriage; 84 percent of those who went to high school but not beyond had done the same. Thirty-seven percent of the total male population had experienced some kind of overt

Clothing

Clothing can be an important source of information about the past. The clothes people wear often announce their age, sex, and class, and frequently transmit some sense of their origin, occupation, and even their politics. The vocabulary of dress includes more than garments alone: hairstyles, jewelry, and makeup all contribute to the way people choose to present themselves. Clothing can signal strong emotions; a torn, unbuttoned shirt, for example, can indicate that a person who seldom dresses that way is really upset. Bright colors can demonstrate a daring sense and a willingness to make a strong statement. By examining clothing styles in a number of different decades, we can begin to understand something of the changing patterns of people's lives.

In the 1920s, flappers and other women often dressed like children, with loose dresses usually in pastel colors ending just below the knee. Large trimmings, like huge artificial flowers, accentuated the effect. A "boyish" figure was considered most attractive. The clothes conveyed a feeling of playfulness and a willingness to embrace the freedom of the young. Men's suits in the same period were now made out of lighter materials, and looked less padded than before. As the tall, stiff collar of

an earlier age disappeared and trousers became more high-waisted, men too had a more youthful look.

The Great Depression of the 1930s brought a change in style. Flappers now looked silly, especially as millions of people were starving. Advertisements and films promoted a new maturity and sophistication, more appropriate to hard times. Men's suits became heavier and darker, as if symbolically to provide protection in a breadline. Trousers were wider, and jackets were frequently double-breasted. Overcoats became longer. Women's clothes were likewise made out of heavier fabrics and used darker colors. Skirts fell, almost to the ankles on occasion, and were covered by longer coats. Clothes indicated that there was no place for the playfulness of the decade before.

As conditions improved during and after World War II, styles changed once more. In the 1940s, young teenage girls frequently wore bobby socks, rolled down to their ankles. Working women wore overalls, but with their own adornments to maintain their femininity. Rosie the Riveter, drawn by noted artist Norman Rockwell, wore her overalls proudly as she sat with a riveting gun in her lap and an attractive scarf around her hair. In the postwar years, the Man in the Gray Flannel Suit looked serious, sober, and well-tailored, ready to go work for corporate America. His female partner wanted to look equally worldly and sophis

Frances Perkins with laborers in the 1930s. (Brown Brothers)

Harlem women in the 1920s. (Schomburg Collection, New York Public Library)

World War II women at work. (Oregon Historical Society, Portland)

A woman and child in the 1950s. (From the negative by Dorothea Lange, collection of The Oakland Museum, California)

ticated, and wore carefully tailored adult clothing, with the waist drawn in (often by a girdle) and heels as tall as three inches, when going out. The fashion industry helped define the decorative role women should play in supporting men as they advanced their business careers.

Then came the 1960s and an entirely new look. Casual clothing became a kind of uniform. The counterculture was a movement of the young, and clothing took on an increasingly youthful look. Skirts rose above the knee in 1963 and a few years later climbed to midthigh. Women began to wear pants and trouser suits. Men and women both favored jeans and informal shirts and let their hair grow longer. Men broke away from the gray suits of the preceding decade and indulged themselves in bright colors in what has been called the "peacock revolution."

Look carefully at the pictures on these pages. They show fashions from different periods and can tell us a good deal about how these people defined themselves. Examine first the photo of the three black women from the 1920s. What kinds of adornments do you notice? What impression do these women convey?

Look at the photograph of Frances Perkins, Secretary of Labor in the 1930s. What kind of dress is she wearing? How do her clothes differ from those of the women in the 1920s? In the picture, she is talking to a number of working men. What do their clothes tell you about the kind of work they might be doing?

In the picture of two drill press operators during World War II, the women are dressed to handle the heavy machinery. Are their clothes different from those of the laborers in the preceding picture? How have the women accommodated themselves to their work, while still maintaining their individuality?

Now look at the picture of a woman in the 1950s. What kind of work might she do? What kind of flexibility do these clothes give her? What do the stylistic touches convey?

Finally, examine the photogaph of the man and woman at an outdoor music festival in the 1960s. What does their clothing remind you of? Where might it come from? What impression are these people trying to create by their dress?

Countercultural dress in the 1960s. (Ken Heyman)

935

Sex goddess Marilyn Monroe—shown here in Gentlemen Prefer Blonds—*stirred the fantasies of American males in the 1950s. Despite the family orientation of suburban America, millions were captivated by her seductive appeal. (UPI/Corbis-Bettmann)*

homosexual activity. One out of every six farm boys in America, he claimed, had copulated with animals. Five years later, Kinsey published a companion volume, *Sexual Behavior in the Human Female,* that detailed many of the same sexual patterns. Although critics denounced Kinsey for his methodology and his results, both of his books sold widely, for they opened the door to a subject that had previously been considered taboo.

Interest in sexuality was reflected in the fascination with sex goddesses like Marilyn Monroe. With her blonde hair, breathy voice, and raw sexuality, she personified the forbidden side of the good life and became one of Hollywood's most

popular stars. The images of such film goddesses corresponded to male fantasies of women, visible in *Playboy* magazine, which first appeared in 1953 and soon achieved a huge readership. As for these men's wives, they were expected to manage their suburban homes and to be cheerful and willing objects of their husbands' desire.

Despite the reaffirmation of the old ideology that a woman's place was in the home, the 1950s were years of unnoticed but important change. Because the supply of single women workers was diminished by the low birthrate of the Depression years and by increased schooling and early marriage, older married women continued the pattern begun during the war and entered the labor force in larger numbers than before. In 1940, only 15 percent of American wives had jobs. By 1950, 21 percent were employed, and ten years later, the figure had risen to 30 percent. Moreover, married women now accounted for more than half of all working women, a dramatic reversal of pre–World War II patterns. Although the media hailed those women who primarily tended to their families, some magazine articles, in fact, did stress the achievements of women outside the home.

Although many working women were poor, divorced, or widowed, many others worked to acquire the desirable new products that were badges of middle-class status. They stepped into the new jobs created by economic expansion, clustering in office, sales, and service positions, occupations already defined as female. They and their employers considered their work subordinate to their primary role as wives and mothers. The conviction that women's main role was homemaking justified low wages and the denial of promotions. Comparatively few women entered professions where they would have challenged traditional notions of a woman's place. As *Life* magazine pointed out in 1956, "Household skills take her into the garment trades; neat and personable, she becomes office worker and sales lady; patient and dexterous, she does well on competitive, detailed factory work; compassionate, she becomes teacher and nurse."

African American women worked as always but often lost the jobs they had held during the war. As the percentage of women in the Detroit automobile industry, for example, dropped from 25 to 7.5 in the immediate postwar period, black women who had held some of the jobs were the first to go. Bernice McCannon, an African American employee at a Virginia military base, observed, "I have always done domestic work for families. When war came, I made the same move many domestics did. I took a higher paying job in a government cafeteria as a junior baker. If domestic work offers a good living, I see no reason why most of us will not return to our old jobs. We will have no alternative." These jobs, however, did not pay well at all. In the 1950s, the employment picture improved somewhat. African American women succeeded both in moving into white-collar positions and in increasing their income. By 1960, more than a third of all black women held clerical, sales, service, or professional jobs. The income gap between white women and black women holding similar jobs dropped from about 50 percent in 1940 to about 30 percent in 1960.

Some of these patterns that dominated in the 1950s persisted in the next decade. By the middle of the 1960s, however, the roots of what became a powerful women's movement were visible. Women challenged stereotypical patterns of behavior and patterns of dress. They demanded and seized greater control over their own lives, in a story we will take up in much greater detail in Chapter 29.

Cultural Rebels

Not all Americans fit the stereotypes of the 1950s. Some were alienated from the culture and rebelled against its values. Even as young people struggled to meet the standards and expectations of their peers, they were intrigued by Holden Caulfield, the main figure in J. D. Salinger's popular novel *The Catcher in the Rye* (1951). Holden, a sensitive student at boarding school, felt surrounded by "phonies" who threatened his individuality and independence. Holden's ill-fated effort to preserve his own integrity in the face of pressures to conform aroused readers' sympathy and struck a resonant chord.

A group of writers, often called the "beat generation," espoused unconventional values in their stories, poems, and "happenings." They challenged the apathy and conformity of the period. Stressing spontaneity and spirituality, they claimed that intuition was more important than reason, Eastern mysticism more valuable than Western faith. The "beats" went out of their way to attack the standard norms of respectability. They rejected materialism, engaged in overt sexual activity designed to shock, and helped popularize marijuana.

Their literary work reflected their approach to life. Finding conventional academic forms confining, they rejected them. Jack Kerouac typed his best-selling novel *On the Road* (1957), describing freewheeling trips across country, on a 250-foot roll of paper. Lacking conventional punctuation and paragraph structure, the book was a song of praise to the free life-style the beats espoused.

Poet Allen Ginsberg, like Kerouac a Columbia University dropout, became equally well known for his poem "Howl." Written during a wild weekend in 1955 while Ginsberg was under the influence of drugs, the poem was a scathing critique of the modern, mechanized culture and its effects. Reading the poem to a group of poets in San Francisco, Ginsberg bobbed and wove as he communicated the electric rhythm of his verse. He became a celebrity when "Howl" appeared in print in 1956. The poem developed into a cult piece, particularly after the police seized it on the grounds that it was obscene. When the work survived a court test, national acclaim followed for Ginsberg. He and the other beats furnished a model for rebellion in the 1960s, as the counterculture described in Chapter 29 became increasingly powerful.

The popularity of Salinger, Kerouac, and Ginsberg owed much to a revolution in book publishing and to the democratization of education that accompanied the program of GI educational benefits. More Americans than ever before acquired a taste for literature, and they found huge numbers of inexpensive books available because of the "paperback revolution." The paperback, introduced in 1939, dominated the book market after World War II. By 1965, readers could choose among some 25,000 titles, available in bookstores, supermarkets, drugstores, and airplane terminals, and they purchased these cheap volumes at the rate of nearly 7 million copies per week.

Allen Ginsberg was one of the most influential "beats" who went out of his way to protest what he considered the stultifying patterns of American life. His poetry (and appearance in later years) challenged more conventional norms. (Courtesy Mellon)

Jackson Pollock often stood over the canvas and flung the paint around him as he moved across the painting in progress. Here he is shown in 1951 dripping the paint on the work that became Autumn Rhythm. *(Photo by Hans Namuth/ Courtesy, Center for Creative Photography, The University of Arizona. © 1991 Hans Namuth Estate)*

The signs of cultural rebellion also appeared in popular music. Parents recoiled as their children flocked to hear a young Tennessee singer named Elvis Presley belt out rock and roll songs. Presley's sexy voice, gyrating hips, and other techniques borrowed from black singers made him the undisputed "king of rock and roll." A multimedia blitz of movies, television, and radio helped make songs like "Heartbreak Hotel," "Don't Be Cruel," and "Hound Dog" smash singles. Eighteen Presley hits sold more than a million copies in the last four years of the 1950s. His black leather jacket and ducktail haircut became standard dress for rebellious male teenagers. His music provided a pattern for rock musicians in the 1960s.

American painters, shucking off European influences that had shaped American artists for two centuries, also became a part of the cultural rebellion. Led by Jackson Pollock and the "New York school," some artists discarded the easel, laid gigantic canvases on the floor, and then used trowels, putty knives, and sticks to apply paint, glass shards, sand, and other materials in wild explosions of color. Known as abstract expressionists, these painters regarded the unconscious as the source of their artistic creations. "I am not aware of what is taking place [as I paint]," Pollock explained; "it is only after that I see what I have done." Like much of the literature of rebellion, abstract expressionism reflected the artist's alienation from a world becoming filled with nuclear threats, computerization, and materialism.

The Other America

In the years after World War II, not all Americans shared the prosperity of the growing middle class. Although most Americans were barely conscious of poverty, it clearly existed in inner cities and rural areas. African Americans, uprooted from rural roots and transplanted into urban slums, were among the hardest hit. But members of other minority groups, as well as less fortunate whites, suffered similar dislocations that more prosperous Americans often ignored.

Poverty Amid Affluence

Many people in the "affluent society" lived in poverty. Economic growth favored the upper and middle classes. Although the popular "trickle-down" theory argued that economic expansion benefited all classes, little wealth, in fact, reached the citizens at the bottom of the ladder. In 1960, according to the Federal Bureau of Labor Statistics, a yearly subsistence-level income for a family of four was $3,000 and for a family of six, $4,000. The Bureau reported that 40 million people (almost a quarter of the population) lived below those levels, with nearly the same number only marginally above the line. Two million migrant workers labored long hours for a subsistence wage. Many less mobile people were hardly better off. According to the 1960 census, 27 percent of the residential units in the United States were substandard, and even acceptable dwellings were often hopelessly overcrowded in some slums.

Michael Harrington, socialist author and critic, shocked the country with his 1962 study, *The Other America*. The poor, Harrington argued, were everywhere. He described New York City's "economic underworld," where "Puerto Ricans and Negroes, alcoholics, drifters, and disturbed people" haunted employment agencies for temporary positions as "dishwashers and day workers, the fly-by-night jobs." In the afternoon, he continued, "the jobs have all been handed out, yet the people still mill around. Some of them sit on benches in the larger offices. There is no real point to their waiting, yet they have nothing else to do."

Harrington also described the conditions faced by the rural poor living in what songwriter Woody Guthrie had called in an earlier era the "pastures of plenty." Despite the prosperity that surrounded them, the mountain folk of Appalachia, the tenant farmers of Mississippi, and the migrant farmers of Florida, Texas, and California were all caught in poverty's relentless cycle. Life for them was as harsh as the existence of the slum-dweller in the cities of the United States.

Hard Times for African Americans

African Americans were among the least prosperous citizens in the nation in the postwar period. They had long suffered from poverty. Now, however, most of them were concentrated in cities rather than on farms. In the South, agricultural workers continued to experience the transformation, mentioned earlier in this chapter, that had been underway for decades. New Deal farm legislation, the popularity of synthetic fabrics, and foreign competition robbed "King Cotton" of world markets. Mechanized cotton picking, first introduced in Mississippi in 1944, wiped out jobs in the Delta. As cotton farmers turned to less labor-intensive crops like soybeans and peanuts, they ousted their tenants, most of whom were African Americans.

The southern agricultural population declined dramatically, as millions of blacks moved to southern cities, where they found better jobs, better schooling, and freedom from landlord control. Some achieved middle-class status. Many more did not. They remained poor, with even less of a support system than they had known before.

Millions of African Americans also headed for northern cities in the years after 1940. In the 1950s, Detroit's black population increased from 16 to 29 percent, Chicago's from 14 to 23 percent. At one point in this decade, Chicago's black population rose by more than 2,200 people each week. The new arrivals congregated in urban slums, where the growth of facilities and social services failed to keep pace with population growth.

The black ghetto that had begun to develop earlier in the twentieth century became a permanent fixture in the post–World War II years. African

While the 1950s were prosperous years for some Americans, others lived in poverty in urban slums. Here a back street in a Chicago ghetto is a lonely and forbidding place. (Courtesy Peter Blake)

The experiences of African Americans in the cities often proved different from what they had expected. As author Claude Brown recalled, blacks were told that in the North, "Negroes lived in houses with bathrooms, electricity, running water, and indoor toilets. To them, this was the 'promised land' that Mammy had been singing about in the cotton fields for many years." But no one had told them "about one of the most important aspects of the promised land: it was a slum ghetto.... There were too many people full of hate and bitterness crowded into a dirty, stinky, uncared-for closet-size section of a great city."

Novelist and essayist James Baldwin likewise described slum conditions and their corrosive effect on American blacks. In his 1961 book *Nobody Knows My Name,* he wrote:

> They work in the white man's world all day and come home in the evening to this fetid block. They struggle to instill in their children some private sense of honor or dignity, which will help the child to survive. This means, of course, that they must struggle, stolidly, incessantly, to keep this sense live in them-selves, in spite of the insults, the indifference, and the cruelty they are certain to encounter in their working day. They patiently browbeat the landlord into fixing the heat, the plaster, the plumbing; this demands prodigious patience, nor is patience usually enough.... Such frustration, so long endured, is driving many strong and admirable men and women whose only crime is color to the very gates of paranoia.

Housing was one problem; employment was another. Men had more difficulty finding work than women. Unemployment often led to idleness and frustration, and sometimes resulted in public drunkenness and neighborhood brawls. The inability to secure work challenged black masculinity, which in turn, had an impact on the stability of African American family life. Despite all obstacles, the black family managed to hold together until the 1960s, with 70 percent of all units including both husband and wife. In the years that followed, this pattern changed. By 1983,

Americans attempting to move elsewhere often found the way blocked. In 1951, a black couple purchasing a home in Cicero, Illinois, was driven away when an angry crowd broke the house's win-dows, defaced the walls, and shouted vile insults. This pattern was repeated throughout the postwar years around the country—in Birmingham, Chicago, Detroit, and countless other cities. Even passage in 1968 of the Fair Housing Act barring racial discrimination in the sale, rental, or financ-ing of housing units failed to end this kind of resi-dential segregation.

50 percent of all black children under 18 lived in households headed by women, and many of these suffered from oppressive poverty from which there appeared to be no escape.

Still, the larger black community remained intact. Chicago's South Side neighborhood was a vibrant place, replacing New York's Harlem as black America's cultural capital. This section of the city included such figures as boxing champion Joe Louis, gospel singer Mahalia Jackson, and Representative William Dawson, the only African American member of Congress.

Here and elsewhere, the black church played an important role in sustaining African American life. Blacks moving into the cities retained church-going habits and commitment to religious institutions from their rural days. Older, established churches assisted newcomers in the transition to urban America, while new religious groups began to form as well, to create a sense of community for recent arrivals. The churches offered more than religious sustenance alone. Many provided day-care facilities, ran Boy Scout and Girl Scout troops, and sponsored a variety of other social services.

These activities gave them a crucial place in the civil rights movement that began to flourish in these years (see Chapter 29).

The growth of the black urban population fostered the development of businesses that catered to the African American community. Black newspapers now provided a more regional, rather than a national, focus, but magazines such as *Jet*, a pocket-size weekly with a large countrywide circulation, filled the void. Black-owned or black-operated banks and other financial institutions increased in number.

Yet most African Americans remained second-class citizens. Escape from the slums was difficult for many, impossible for most. Persistent poverty was a dismal fact of life, even as the rest of the United States enjoyed prosperous times.

Minorities on the Fringe

Other groups had similar difficulties in the postwar United States. Latino immigrants from Cuba, Puerto Rico, Mexico, and Central America, often unskilled and illiterate, followed other less

Chicanos, like these in the broccoli fields of Texas, often faced grim conditions in their effort to make a living. Many were migrant workers who took temporary jobs on American farms, then moved on when their work was done, without ever enjoying the security or stability of permanent employment. (Standard Oil (New Jersey) Co. Collection, Photographic Archives, University of Louisville, Neg. #57292)

TIMELINE

1944	4.6 million workers on strike
	ENIAC computer built
	Benjamin Spock's *Baby and Child Care*
1947	Defense budget of $13 billion
1948	GM offers UAW cost-of-living adjustment
	Transistor developed at Bell Laboratories
	Kinsey report on male sexuality
1950s	Each year a million farmers leave farms
1950	Diner's Card inaugurated
1951	J.D. Salinger's *The Catcher in the Rye*
1953	Defense budget of $47 billion
	Operation Wetback begins
1954	Congress adds "under God" to pledge to flag
1955	First McDonald's opens in Illinois
	Merger of AFL and CIO
	Congress adds "In God We Trust" to currency
1956	Interstate Highway Act
	Majority of US workers hold white-collar jobs
	Allen Ginsberg's "Howl"
1957	Baby boom peaks
	Vance Packard's *The Hidden Persuaders*
	Jack Kerouac's *On the Road*
1960	3/4 of all Americans own a TV set
1962	Michael Harrington's *The Other America*
1963	California passes NY as most populous state
	Betty Friedan's *The Feminine Mystique*
1964	Peter Blake's *God's Own Junkyard*
1970	38% of all Americans live in suburbs

fortunate Americans to the cities. In the face of persistent discrimination, these groups maintained a strong sense of group identity. The urban *barrios* where they settled preserved a sense of community and close-knit cohesive culture, even in the midst of pervasive poverty. The ties fostered in these communities provided a strong base on which a growing political consciousness could rest as it emerged in the next decade (see Chapter 29).

Chicanos, or Mexican Americans, the most numerous of the newcomers, faced peculiar difficulties and widespread discrimination. During World War II, as the country experienced a labor shortage at home, American farmers sought Mexican *braceros* (helping hands) to harvest their crops. A program to encourage the seasonal immigration of farm workers continued after the war when the government signed a Migratory Labor Agreement with Mexico. Between 1948 and 1964, some 4.5 million Mexicans were brought to the United States for temporary work. *Braceros* were expected to return to Mexico at the end of their labor contract, but often they stayed. Joining them were millions more who entered the country illegally.

Conditions were harsh for the *braceros* in the best of times. In periods of economic difficulty, troubles worsened. During a serious recession in 1953–54, the government mounted Operation Wetback to deport illegal entrants and *braceros* who had remained in the country illegally. Deportations numbered 1.1 million. As immigration officials searched out illegal workers, all Chicanos found themselves vulnerable. They bitterly protested the violations of their rights, to little effect.

Operation Wetback did not end the reliance on poor Mexican farm laborers. A coalition of southern Democrats and conservative Republicans, mostly representing farm states, extended the Migratory Labor Agreement with Mexico, for they wanted to continue to take advantage of the inordinately cheap labor. Two years after the massive deportations of 1954, a record 445,000 *braceros* crossed the border to work on American farms.

Not all Spanish-speaking Americans were Chicano. A steady stream of immigrants had been coming to New York from Puerto Rico since the

1920s. As the island's sugarcane economy became more mechanized, nearly 40 percent of the inhabitants left their homes. By the end of the 1960s, New York City had more Puerto Ricans than San Juan, the island's capital. El Barrio, in East Harlem, became the center of Puerto Rican activity, the home of *salsa* music and small *bodegas,* grocery stores that served the neighborhood. Author Guillermo Cotto-Thorner described the place in his autobiographical novel *Trópico en Manhattan* through the words of Antonio, an older resident.

> This … is our neighborhood, El Barrio…. It's said that we Latins run things here. And that's how we see ourselves. While the American take most of the money that circulates around here, we consider this part of the city to be ours…. The stores, barbershops, restaurants, butcher shops, churches, funeral parlors, greasy spoons, pool halls, everything is all Latino. Every now and then you see a business run by a Jew or an Irishman or an Italian, but you'll also see that even these people know a little Spanish.

Puerto Ricans, like many other immigrants, hoped to earn money in America and then return home. Some did; others stayed. Like countless Latinos, they failed to enjoy the promise of the American dream.

Native Americans were likewise outsiders in the postwar years. They faced the consequences of the same technological developments affecting other Americans, but often had greater difficulty coping with the changes they faced, given the persistent discrimination they had experienced over an extended period of years. As power lines reached their reservations, Indians purchased televisions, refrigerators, washing machines, and automobiles. As they partook of the consumer culture, old patterns inevitably changed. Reservation life lost its cohesiveness. Indians who gravitated to the cities often had difficulty adjusting to urban life and faced hostility from white Americans, much like that experienced by Latinos and blacks. They too began to protest in a movement that gained strength in succeeding years (see Chapter 29).

onclusion

Qualms amid Affluence

In general, the United States during the decade and a half after World War II was stable and secure. Structural adjustments caused occasional moments of friction but were seldom visible in prosperous times. Recessions occurred periodically, but the economy righted itself after short downturns. For the most part, business boomed. The standard of living for many of the nation's citizens reached new heights, especially compared with standards in other parts of the world. Millions of middle-class Americans joined the ranks of suburban property owners, enjoying the benefits of shopping centers and fast-food establishments and other material manifestations of what they considered the good life. Workers found themselves savoring the materialistic advantages of the era.

Some Americans did not share in the prosperity, but they were not visible in the affluent suburbs. Many African Americans and members of other minority groups were seriously disadvantaged, although still believed they could share in the American dream and remained confident that deeply rooted patterns of discrimination could be changed. Even when they began to mobilize, their protest was peaceful at first.

Beneath the calm surface, though, there were signs of discontent. The seeds for the protest movements of the 1960s had already been sown. Disquieting signs were likewise evident on other fronts. The divorce rate increased, as a third of all marriages in the 1950s broke apart. Americans more than doubled their use of tranquilizers between 1958 and 1959, in an effort to cope with problems in their lives. Some Americans began to criticize the materialism that seemed to undermine American efforts in the Cold War. Such criticisms in turn legitimized challenges by other groups, in the continuing struggle to make the realities of American life match the nation's ideals.

Criticisms and anxieties notwithstanding, the United States—for most whites and some people of color—continued to develop according to Ray Kroc's dreams as he first envisioned McDonald's establishments across the land. Healthy and comfortable, upper- and middle-class Americans expected prosperity and growth to continue in the years ahead.

Recommended Reading

Domestic Issues

American Social History Project, *Who Built America? Working People & the Nation's Economy, Politics, Culture, and Society* (1992); Stephen Kemp Bailey, *Congress Makes a Law* (1950); Lois W. Banner, *American Beauty* (1983); Peter Blake, *God's Own Junkyard: The Planned Deterioration of America's Landscape* (1964); David Brody, *Workers in Industrial America* (1980); Paul A. Carter, *Another Part of the Fifties* (1983); James R. Green, *The World of the Worker* (1980); David Halberstam, *The Fifties* (1993); Samuel P. Hays, *Beauty, Health, and Permanence: Environmental Politics in the United States, 1955–1985* (1987); Daniel Horowitz, ed., *American Social Classes in the 1950s: Selections from Vance Packard's The Status Seekers* (1995); Kenneth T. Jackson, *Crabgrass Frontier: The Suburbanization of the United States* (1985); William E. Leuchtenburg, *A Troubled Feast: American Society Since 1945* (1983); Alison Lurie, *The Language of Clothes* (1981); Zane L. Miller, *The Urbanization of Modern America* (1973); C. Wright Mills, *White Collar: The American Middle Classes* (1951); J. Carroll Moody and Alice Kessler-Harris, eds. *Perspectives on American Labor History: The Problems of Synthesis* (1989); Richard Polenberg, *One Nation Divisible: Class, Race, and Ethnicity in the United States Since 1938* (1980); David Riesman, *The Lonely Crowd: A Study of the Changing American Character* (1950); Juliet B. Schor, *The Overworked American: The Unexpected Decline of Leisure* (1991); Richard White, "*It's Your Misfortune and None of My Own": A History of the American West* (1991); Robert H. Zieger, *American Workers, American Unions*, 2d ed. (1994) and *The CIO, 1935–1955* (1995).

Religious Developments

David Chidester, *Patterns of Power: Religion and Politics in American Culture* (1988); Nathan Glazer, *American Judaism*, 2d ed. (1989); Philip Gleason, *Keeping the Faith: American Catholicism Past and Present* (1987); Andrew Greeley, *American Catholics Since the Council* (1985); Arthur Hertzberg, *The Jews in America: Four Centuries of Uneasy Encounter* (1989); Erling Jorstad, *Holding Fast/Pressing On: Religion in America in the 1980s* (1990); R. Laurence Moore, *Selling God: American Religion in the Marketplace of Culture* (1994); Gerald Showstack, *Suburban Communities: The Jewishness of American Reform Jews* (1988); Peter W. Williams, *Popular Religion in America: Symbolic Change and the Modernization Process in Historical Perspective* (1980); Garry Wills, *Under God: Religion and American Politics* (1990).

Women's Role in the 1950s

Beth L. Bailey, *From Front Porch to Back Seat: Courtship in Twentieth-Century America* (1988); William H. Chafe, *The American Woman: Her Changing Social, Economic, and Political Roles, 1920–1970* (1972); Stephanie Coontz, *The Way We Never Were: American Families and the Nostalgia Trap* (1992); John D'Emilio and Estelle B. Freedman, *Intimate Matters: A History of Sexuality in America* (1988); Sara Evans, *Born for Liberty: A History of Women in America* (1989); Betty Friedan, *The Feminine Mystique* (1963); Susan M. Hartmann, *The Home Front and Beyond: American Women in the 1940s* (1982); Bret Harvey: *The Fifties: A Women's Oral History* (1993); Eugenia Kaledin, *Mothers and More: American Women in the 1950s* (1984); Elaine Tyler May, *Homeward Bound: American Families in the Cold War Era* (1988);

Joanne Meyerowitz, ed., *Not June Cleaver: Women and Gender in Postwar America, 1945–1960* (1994); Susan Allen Toth, *Blooming: A Small-Town Girlhood* (1981).

African Americans

James Baldwin, *Nobody Knows My Name* (1961); Claude Brown, *Manchild in the Promised Land* (1965); John Egerton, *Speak Now Against the Day: The Generation Before the Civil Rights Movement in the South* (1994); John Hope Franklin and Alfred A. Moss, Jr., *From Slavery to Freedom: A History of African Americans*, 7th ed. (1994); Jacqueline Jones, *Labor of Love, Labor of Sorrow: Black Women, Work, and the Family from Slavery to the Present* (1985).

Chicanos

Rodolfo Acuña, *Occupied America: A History of Chicanos*, 3d ed. (1988); George J. Sánchez, *Becoming Mexican American: Ethnicity, Culture and Identity in Chicano Los Angeles, 1900–1945* (1993); Peter Skerry, *Mexican Americans: The Ambivalent Minority* (1993).

Native Americans

Frederick E. Hoxie, ed., *Indians in American History* (1988); Alvin M. Josephy, Jr., *Now That the Buffalo's Gone* (1982); David Hurst Thomas, Jay Miller, Richard White, Peter Nabokov, and Philip J. Deloria, *The Native Americans: An Illustrated History* (1993).

Novels

Jack Kerouac, *On the Road* (1957); J. D. Salinger, *The Catcher in the Rye* (1951); Sloan Wilson, *The Man in the Gray Flannel Suit* (1955).

Chills and Fever During the Cold War

al Lorwin was in Paris in November 1950 when word of the charges against him arrived. A State Department employee, on leave of absence after 16 years of government service, he was in France working on a book. Now he had to return to the United States to defend himself against the accusation that he was a member of the Communist party and thus a loyalty and security risk.

The accusation surprised Lorwin. It almost seemed like a tasteless joke. Yet it was no joke but a grim consequence of the Cold War. Suspicions of the Soviet Union escalated after 1945, and a wave of paranoia swept through the United States. The threat of communism was no laughing matter at home.

Lorwin was an unlikely candidate to be caught up in the fallout of the Cold War. He had begun to work for the government in 1935, serving in a number of New Deal agencies, then in the Labor Department and on the War Production Board before he was drafted during World War II. While in the Army, he was assigned to the Office of Strategic Services, an early intelligence agency, and he was frequently granted security clearances in the United States and abroad.

Lorwin, however, did have a left-wing past as an active Socialist in the 1930s. His social life then had revolved around Socialist party causes, particularly the unionization of southern tenant farmers and the provision of aid to the unemployed. He and his wife Madge drafted statements or stuffed envelopes to support their goals. But that activity was wholly open and legal, and Lorwin had from the start been aggressively anti-Communist in political affairs.

Suddenly, Lorwin, like others in the period, faced the nightmare of secret charges against which the burden of proof was entirely on him and the chance of clearing his name slim. Despite his spotless record, Lorwin was told that an unnamed accuser had identified him as a Communist. He was entitled to a hearing if he chose, or he could resign.

Lorwin requested a hearing, held late in 1950. Still struck by the absurdity of the situation, he refuted all accusations but made little effort to cite his own positive achievements. At the conclusion, he was informed that the government no longer doubted his loyalty but considered him a security risk, likewise grounds for dismissal from his job.

When he appealed the judgment, Lorwin was again denied access to the identity of his accuser. This time, however, he thoroughly prepared his defense. At the hearing, a total of 97 witnesses either spoke under oath on Lorwin's behalf or left sworn written depositions testifying to his good character and meritorious service.

The issues in the hearings might have been considered comic in view of Lorwin's record, had not a man's reputation been at stake. The accuser had once lived with the Lorwins in Washington, D.C. Fifteen years later, he claimed that in 1935 Lorwin had revealed that he was holding a Communist party meeting in his home and had even shown him a party card.

Lorwin proved all the charges groundless. He also showed that in 1935 the Socialist party card was red, the color the accuser reported seeing, while the Communist party card was black. In March 1952, Lorwin was finally cleared for both loyalty and security.

Though he thought he had weathered the storm, Lorwin's troubles were not yet over. His name appeared on one of the lists produced by Senator Joseph McCarthy of Wisconsin, the most aggressive anti-Communist of the era, and Lorwin was again victimized. The next year, he was indicted for making false statements to the State Department Loyalty-Security Board. The charges this time proved as specious as before. Finally, in May 1954, admitting that its special prosecutor had deliberately lied to the grand jury and had no legitimate case, the Justice Department asked for dismissal of the indictment. Lorwin was cleared at last and went on to a distinguished career as a labor historian.

The Cold War created a climate of confrontation between East and West and led to wars in Korea and Vietnam that left millions of people injured or dead. (Edward Keinholz, O'er the Ramparts We Watched Fascinated/Courtesy of L.A. Louver Gallery, Venice, CA)

*L*orwin was more fortunate than some victims of the anti-Communist crusade. People rallied around him and gave him valuable support. Despite considerable emotional cost, he survived the witch-hunt of the early 1950s, but his case still reflected vividly the ugly domestic consequences of the breakdown in relations between the Soviet Union and the United States.

The Cold War, which unfolded soon after the end of World War II and lasted for nearly fifty years, powerfully affected all aspects of American life. Rejecting for good the isolationist impulse that had governed foreign policy in the 1920s and 1930s, the United States began to play a major role in the world in the postwar years. Doubts about intervention in other lands faded as the nation acknowledged its dominant international position and resolved to do whatever was necessary to maintain it. The same sense of mission that had infused the United States in the Spanish-American War, World War I, and World War II now committed most Americans to the struggle against communism at home and abroad.

This chapter explores that continuing sense of mission and its consequences. It shows how basic beliefs about American destiny drove the United States forward in this latest struggle against forces that stood in its way. It examines the roots of the Cold War both in the idealistic aim to keep the world safe for democracy and in the pursuit of economic self-interest that had long fueled American capitalism. It records how the determination to prevent the spread of communism led American policy makers to consider vast parts of the world as pivotal to American security and to act accordingly, particularly in Korea and Vietnam. It examines the impact on economic development, particularly in the West, where the mighty defense industry flourished. And it considers the tragic consequences of the effort to promote ideological unity within the United States, where excesses threatened the principles of democracy itself.

Origins of the Cold War

The Cold War developed by degrees. It stemmed from the crumbling of colonial empires in Asia, Africa, and the Middle East in the post–World War II years. The major powers held divergent views about the shape of the changing postwar world. The United States, strong and secure, was intent on spreading its vision of freedom and free trade around the world to maintain its own economic hegemony. The Soviet Union, concerned about its own security after a devastating war, demanded politically sympathetic neighbors on its borders to preserve its own autonomy. Suppressed during World War II, these differences now brought the United States and the Soviet Union into conflict. As confrontations occurred, the two nations behaved, according to Senator J. William Fulbright, "like two big dogs, chewing on a bone."

The American Stance

The United States emerged from World War II more powerful than any nation ever before. Now it sought to use that might to achieve the kind of order that could sustain American aims. American policy makers, following in Woodrow Wilson's footsteps, hoped to spread the values of liberty, equality, and democracy that provided the underpinning of the American dream. They assumed that they could furnish the stability that postwar reconstruction required. They did not always recognize that what they considered universal truths were rooted in specific historical circumstances in their own country and might not flourish elsewhere.

At the same time, American leaders sought to create a world where economic enterprise could thrive. Recollections of the Depression decade haunted leaders. With the American economy operating at full speed as a result of the war, world markets were needed once the fighting stopped.

Government officials wanted to eliminate trade barriers—imposed by the Soviet Union and other nations—to provide outlets for industrial products and for surplus farm commodities such as wheat, cotton, and tobacco. As the largest source of goods for world markets, with exports totaling $14 billion in 1947, the United States required open channels for growth to continue. Americans assumed that their prosperity would benefit the rest of the world, even when other nations disagreed.

Soviet Aims

The Soviet Union formulated its own goals after World War II. Historically, Russia had usually been governed by a strongly centralized, sometimes even autocratic government, and that tradition—as much as Communist ideology, with its stress on class struggle and the inevitable triumph of a proletarian state—guided Soviet policy.

During the war, the Russians had played down the notion of world revolution they knew the other allies found threatening and had mobilized support for more nationalistic goals. As the struggle drew to a close, the Soviets talked little of world conquest, emphasizing socialism within the nation itself.

Rebuilding was the first priority. Devastated by the war, Soviet agriculture and industry were in shambles. But revival required internal security. At the same time, the Russians feared vulnerability along their western flank. Such anxieties had a historical basis, for in the early nineteenth century, Napoleon had reached the gates of Moscow. Twice in the twentieth century, invasions had come from the west, most recently when Hitler had attacked in 1941. Haunted by fears that the Germans would recover quickly, the Soviets demanded defensible borders and neighboring regimes sympathetic to Russian aims. They insisted on military and political stability in the regions closest to them.

Early Cold War Leadership

Both the United States and the Soviet Union had strong leadership in the early years of the Cold War. On the American side, first Harry Truman, then Dwight Eisenhower accepted the centralization of authority Franklin Roosevelt had begun, as

the executive branch became increasingly powerful in guiding foreign policy. In the Soviet Union, first Joseph Stalin, then Nikita Khrushchev provided equally forceful direction.

Harry S Truman served as president of the United States in the first postwar years. He was an unpretentious man who took a straightforward approach to public affairs. He was, however, ill prepared for the office he assumed in the final months of World War II. His three months as vice president had done little to school him in the complexity of postwar issues. Nor had Franklin Roosevelt confided in Truman. No wonder that the new president felt insecure. To a former colleague in the Senate, he groaned, "I'm not big enough for this job." Critics agreed.

Yet Truman matured rapidly. A feisty politician, he responded ably to new challenges. Impulsive and aggressive, he made a virtue out of rapid response. At his first press conference, he answered questions so quickly that reporters could not record his replies. A sign on the president's White House desk read "The Buck Stops Here," and he was willing to make quick decisions on issues, even though associates sometimes wondered if he understood all the implications. His rapid-fire decisions had important consequences for the Cold War.

Truman served virtually all of the term to which Roosevelt had been elected in 1944, then won another for himself in 1948. In 1952, war hero Dwight D. Eisenhower won the presidency for the Republican party for the first time in 20 years.

Eisenhower stood in stark contrast to his predecessor. His easy manner and warm smile made him widely popular. On occasion, in press conferences or other public gatherings, his comments came out convoluted and imprecise. Yet appearances were deceiving, for beneath his casual approach was real shrewdness. At one point, as he prepared for a session with newsmen and his aides briefed him on a delicate matter, he said, "Don't worry. . . . If that question comes up, I'll just confuse them."

Eisenhower had not taken the typical route to the presidency. After his World War II success, he served as army chief of staff, president of Columbia University, and then head of the North Atlantic Treaty Organization (NATO). Despite his lack of formal political background, he had a genuine ability to get people to compromise and to work together. Though he remained aloof from party politics, he may have entertained hopes of holding office after the war. General George Patton commented in 1943 that "Ike wants to be President so badly you can taste it," yet Eisenhower made no move in that direction until he sought the Republican nomination in 1952.

Ike's limited experience with everyday politics conditioned his sense of the presidential role. Whereas Truman was accustomed to political infighting and wanted to take charge, Eisenhower saw things differently. The presidency for him was no "bully pulpit," as it had been for Theodore Roosevelt and even FDR. "I am not one of those desk-pounding types that likes to stick out his jaw and look like he is bossing the show," he said. "You do not lead by hitting people over the head. Any damn fool can do that, but it's usually called 'assault'— not 'leadership.'" Even so, Ike knew exactly where he wanted to go and worked behind the scenes to get there.

Though the personal styles of Truman and Eisenhower differed, they both subscribed to traditional American attitudes about self-determina-tion and the superiority of American political institutions and values. Truman accepted collaboration with the Soviet Union during World War II as a marriage of necessity, but he became increasingly uncomfortable with Soviet moves as the war drew to an end. It was now time, he said, "to stand up to the Russians." Like Truman, Eisenhower believed that communism was a monolithic force struggling for world supremacy and agreed that the Kremlin in Moscow was orchestrating subversive activity around the globe. Like Truman, he saw issues in black and white terms and regarded the Soviet system as a "tyranny that has brought thousands, millions of people into slave camps and is attempting to make all mankind its chattel." Eisenhower, however, more than Truman, was willing to practice accommodation when it served his ends.

The leader of the Soviet Union at the war's end was Joseph Stalin. Possessing almost absolute

Harry Truman was a simple, unassuming man who became a strong and decisive president when he moved into the White House. Here he is shown in his office with the famous sign "The Buck Stops Here" that sat on his desk and characterized his approach to the presidency. (Harry S Truman Library)

Dwight Eisenhower provided a reassuring presence in the White House in the 1950s. His wide smile made Americans feel good about themselves and their country, and conveyed the message that everything was going to be all right. (National Park Service)

power, he had presided over ruthless purges against his opponents in the 1930s. Now he was determined to do whatever was necessary to rebuild Soviet society, if possible with Western assistance, and to keep eastern Europe within the Russian sphere of influence.

Stalin's death in March 1953 left a vacuum in Soviet political affairs. His successor, Nikita S. Khrushchev, used his position as party secretary to consolidate his power. Five years after Stalin's death, Khrushchev held the offices of both prime minister and party secretary. Known for rude behavior, Khrushchev once pounded a table at the United Nations with his shoe and did his best to bully opponents, at home and abroad.

Disillusionment with the USSR

Support in the United States for the Soviet Union quickly began to fade after the war. In September 1945, more than half (54 percent) of a national sample trusted the Russians to cooperate with the Americans in the postwar years. Two months later, the figure had dropped to 44 percent, and by February 1946, to 35 percent.

As Americans soured on Russia, they began to equate the Nazi and Soviet systems and to transfer their hatred of Nazi Germany to Communist Russia. Just as they had in the 1930s, authors, jour-

Joseph Stalin's autocratic approach to foreign and domestic affairs affronted American sensibilities. Here he stands in front of a bust of Lenin, father of the Russian Revolution. (Corbis-Bettmann)

nalists, and public officials pointed to similarities between the regimes, some of them legitimate. Both states, they contended, maintained total control over communications and could eliminate political opposition whenever they chose. Both states used terror to silence dissidents. Stalin's

Soviet leader Nikita Khrushchev was an aggressive leader who sometimes spoke out belligerently in defense of his country's interests. Here he appears at the podium at the United Nations delivering a speech. (Archive Photos)

Conflicting Aims During the Cold War	
United States	Soviet Union
Spread ideological values of liberty, equality, democracy	Spread ideological values of class struggle, triumph of the proletariat
Extend the tradition of representative government	Extend the tradition of strong centralized government
Maintain stability around the world	Support revolutionary movements around the world
Fill vacuum created by the end of imperialism with regimes sympathetic to Western ideals	Support regimes sympathetic to the Soviet Union, particularly to avoid attack on its western flank
Maintain a world free for economic enterprise by eliminating trade barriers, providing markets for American exports	Rebuild the devastated Soviet economy by creating preferential trading arrangements in the region of Soviet dominance

labor camps in Siberia were now compared to Hitler's concentration camps. After the U.S. publication in 1949 of George Orwell's frightening novel *1984, Life* magazine noted in an editorial that the ominous figure Big Brother was but a "mating" of Hitler and Stalin. Truman spoke for many Americans when he said in 1950 that "there isn't any difference between the totalitarian Russian government and the Hitler government.... They are all alike. They are ... police state governments."

The lingering sense that the nation had not been quick enough to resist totalitarian aggression in the 1930s heightened American fears. Had the United States stopped the Germans, Italians, or Japanese, it might have prevented the long, devastating war. The free world had not responded quickly enough before and was determined never to repeat the same mistake.

The Troublesome Polish Question

The first clash between East and West came, even before the war ended, over Poland. Soviet demands for a government willing to accept Russian influence clashed with American hopes for a more representative structure patterned after the Western model. The Yalta Conference of February 1945 attempted to resolve the issue of a government for the postwar state (see Chapter 25), but the agreement was loosely worded and correspondingly imprecise.

When Truman assumed office, the situation was still unresolved. Averell Harriman, the U.S. ambassador to the Soviet Union, warned that the United States faced a "barbarian invasion of Europe" unless the Soviets could be checked and Western-style democracies established. The president agreed.

Truman's unbending stance was clear in an April 1945 meeting with Soviet foreign minister Vyacheslav Molotov on the question of Poland. Concerned that the Russians were breaking the Yalta agreements, imprecise as they were, the American leader demanded a new democratic government there. Though Molotov appeared conciliatory, Truman insisted on Russian acquiescence. Truman later recalled that when Molotov protested, "I have never been talked to like that in my life," he himself retorted bluntly, "Carry out your agreements and you won't get talked to like that." Such bluntness contributed to the deterioration of Soviet-American relations.

Truman and Stalin met face to face for the first time at the Potsdam Conference in July 1945, the last of the meetings held by the Big Three—the United States, the Soviet Union, and Great Britain—during the war. There, as they considered the Russian-Polish boundary, the fate of Germany, and the American desire to obtain an unconditional surrender from Japan, the two leaders sized each other up. It was Truman's first exposure to international diplomacy at the highest level, and it left him confident of his abilities. When he learned during the meeting of the first successful atomic bomb test in New Mexico, he became even more determined to insist on his positions.

Economic Pressure on the USSR

One major source of controversy in the last stage of the Second World War was the question of U.S. aid to its allies. Responding to congressional pressure at home to limit foreign assistance as hostilities ended, Truman acted impulsively. Six days after V-E Day signaled the end of the European war in May 1945, he issued an executive order cutting off lend-lease supplies to the Allies. Though the policy affected all nations receiving aid, it hurt the Soviet Union most of all.

The United States intended to use economic pressure in other ways as well. The USSR desperately needed financial assistance to rebuild after the war and, in January 1945, had requested a $6 billion loan. Roosevelt hedged, hoping to win concessions in return. In August, four months after FDR's death, the Russians renewed their application, this time for only $1 billion. The new president dragged his heels, hoping to use the loan as a lever to gain access to markets in areas traditionally dominated by the Soviet Union. The United States first claimed to have lost the Soviet request, then in March 1946 indicated a willingness to consider the matter—but only if Russia pledged "nondiscrimination in world commerce." Stalin refused the offer and launched his own five-year plan instead.

Declaring the Cold War

As Soviet-American relations deteriorated, both sides stepped up their rhetorical attacks. Stalin spoke out first, in 1946, asserting his confidence in the triumph of the Soviet system. Capitalism and communism were on a collision course, he argued, and a series of cataclysmic disturbances would tear the capitalist world apart. Stalin's speech was a stark and ominous statement that worried the West. Supreme Court Justice William O. Douglas called it the "declaration of World War III."

The response to Stalin's speech came not from an American but from England's former prime minister, Winston Churchill, long suspicious of the Soviet state. Speaking in Fulton, Missouri, in 1946, with Truman on the platform during the address, Churchill declared that "from Stettin in the Baltic to Trieste in the Adriatic, an iron curtain has descended across the Continent." To counter the threat, he urged that a vigilant association of English-speaking peoples work to contain Soviet designs.

Containing the Soviet Union

Containment formed the basis of postwar American policy. Both Democrats and Republicans were determined to check Soviet expansion. In an increasingly contentious world, the American government formulated rigid anti-Soviet policies. The Soviet Union responded in an equally uncompromising way.

Containment Defined

George F. Kennan was primarily responsible for defining the new policy. Chargé d'affaires at the American embassy in the Soviet Union, he sent off an 8,000-word telegram to the State Department after Stalin's speech in February 1946. Kennan argued that Soviet-American hostility stemmed from the "Kremlin's neurotic view of world affairs," which in turn came from the "traditional and instinctive Russian sense of insecurity." The stiff Soviet stance was not so much a response to American actions as a reflection of the Russian leaders' own efforts to maintain their autocratic rule. Russian fanaticism would not soften, regardless of how accommodating American policy became. Therefore, it had to be opposed at every turn.

Kennan's analysis struck a resonant chord in Washington. It made his diplomatic reputation, led to his assignment to a more influential position in the State Department, and encouraged him to publish an important article, under the pseudonym "Mr. X," in the influential journal *Foreign Affairs*. "The whole Soviet governmental machine, including the mechanism of diplomacy," he wrote, "moves inexorably along the prescribed path, like a persistent toy automobile wound up and headed in a given direction, stopping only when it meets with some unanswerable force." Many Americans agreed with Kennan that Soviet pressure had to "be contained by the adroit and vigilant application of counter-force at a series of constantly shifting geographical and political points."

The concept of containment provided the philosophical justification for the hard-line stance that Americans, both in and out of government, adopted. Containment created the framework for military and economic assistance around the globe.

The First Step: The Truman Doctrine

The Truman Doctrine represented the first major application of containment policy. The new policy was devised to respond to conditions in the eastern Mediterranean, an area that Americans had never before considered vital to their national security. The Soviet Union was pressuring Turkey for joint control of the Dardanelles, the passage between the Black Sea and the Mediterranean. Meanwhile, a civil war in Greece pitted Communist elements against the ruling English-aided right-wing monarchy. Revolutionary pressures threatened to topple the government.

In February 1947, the British ambassador to the United States informed the State Department that his exhausted country could no longer give Greece and Turkey economic and military aid. Would the United States now move into the void?

Administration officials, who were willing to move forward, knew they needed bipartisan sup-

port to accomplish such a major policy shift. A conservative Congress wanted smaller budgets and lower taxes rather than massive and expensive aid programs. Senator Arthur Vandenberg of Michigan, a key Republican, warned that the top policy makers had to begin "scaring hell out of the country" if they were serious about a bold new course of containment.

Undersecretary of State Dean Acheson took the lead. Meeting with congressional leaders, he declared that "like apples in a barrel infected by one rotten one, the corruption of Greece would infect Iran and all to the east." He warned ominously that a Communist victory would "open three continents to Soviet penetration." The major powers were now "met at Armageddon," as the Soviet Union pressed forward. Only the United States had the power to resist.

Truman likewise played on the Soviet threat. On March 12, 1947, he told Congress, in a statement that came to be known as the Truman Doctrine, "I believe that it must be the policy of the United States to support free peoples who are resisting subjugation by armed minorities or by outside pressures." Unless the United States acted, the free world might not survive. "If we falter in our leadership," Truman said, "we may endanger the peace of the world—and we shall surely endanger the welfare of our own Nation." To avert that calamity, he urged Congress to appropriate $400 million for military and economic aid to Turkey and Greece.

Not everyone approved of Truman's request or of his overblown description of the situation. Autocratic regimes controlled Greece and Turkey, some observers pointed out. And where was the proof that Stalin had a hand in the Greek conflict? Others

Americans in the early postwar years were afraid that communism was a contagious disease spreading around the globe. In this picture from the spring of 1946, Time *magazine pictured the relentless spread of this infection that would need to be contained. (© 1946* TIME *Magazine. Reprinted by permission.)*

warned that the United States could not by itself stop encroachment in all parts of the world. Nonetheless, Congress passed Truman's foreign aid bill.

In its assumption that Americans could police the globe, the Truman Doctrine was a major step in the advent of the Cold War. Truman's address, observed financier Bernard Baruch, "was tantamount to a declaration of … an ideological or religious war." Journalist Walter Lippmann was more critical. He termed the new containment policy a "strategic monstrosity" that could embroil the United States in disputes around the world. In the two succeeding decades, Lippmann proved correct.

The Next Steps: The Marshall Plan, NATO, and NSC-68

The next step involved extensive economic aid for postwar recovery in Western Europe. At the war's end, most of Europe was economically and politically unstable, thereby offering opportunities to the Communist movement. In France and Italy, large Communist parties grew stronger and refused to cooperate with established governments. In such circumstances, administration officials believed, the Soviet Union might easily intervene. Decisive action was needed, for as the new secretary of state, George Marshall, declared, "The patient is sinking while the doctors deliberate."

Another motive was eagerness to bolster the European economy to provide markets for American goods. Western Europeans had been excellent customers earlier. In the aftermath of the war, they were able to purchase less at a time when the United States was producing much more.

Marshall revealed the administration's willingness to assist European recovery in June 1947. He asked all troubled European nations to draw up an aid program that the United States could support, a program "directed not against any country or doctrine but against hunger, poverty, desperation, and chaos." Soviet-bloc countries were welcome to participate, Marshall announced, aware that their involvement was unlikely since they would have to disclose economic records to join, and Communist nations maintained rigorous secrecy about their internal affairs.

The proposed program would assist the ravaged nations while advancing American economic ends. It would also underscore the nation's ideolog-

ical aims. American aid, Marshall pointed out, would permit the "emergence of political and social conditions in which free institutions can exist." The Marshall Plan and the Truman Doctrine, Truman noted, were "two halves of the same walnut."

Responding quickly to Marshall's invitation, the Western European nations worked out the details of massive requests in the summer of 1947. In the end, American officials agreed to provide $17 billion over a period of four years to 16 cooperating nations.

Not all Americans supported the Marshall Plan. Henry A. Wallace, former vice president and secretary of agriculture, who had broken with the administration, called the scheme the "Martial Plan" and argued that it was another step toward war. Some members of Congress feared spreading American resources too thin. But in early 1948, Congress committed the nation to funding European economic recovery, and the containment policy moved forward another step.

Closely related to the Marshall Plan was a concerted Western effort to rebuild Germany and to reintegrate it into a reviving Europe. At Yalta, Allied leaders had agreed on zonal occupation of Germany and on reparations Germany would pay the victors. Four zones, occupied by the Russians, Americans, British, and French, had been established for postwar administration. A year after the end of the war, however, the balance of power in Europe had shifted. With the Soviet Union threatening to dominate eastern Europe, the West moved to fill the vacuum in central Europe. In late 1946, the Americans and British merged their zones for economic purposes and began to assign administrative duties to Germans. By the middle of 1947, the process of rebuilding West German industry was under way.

Despite French fears, the United States sought to make Germany strong enough to anchor Europe. Secretary Marshall cautiously laid out the connections for Congress:

> The restoration of Europe involves the restoration of Germany. Without a revival of German production there can be no revival of Europe's economy. But we must be very careful to see that a revived Germany cannot again threaten the European community.

In mid-1948, the Soviet Union attempted to force the other nations out of Berlin, which, like

An American and British airlift in 1948 brought badly needed supplied to West Berliners isolated by a Soviet blockade of the city. By refusing to allow the Western powers to reach the city, located within the Soviet zone, the Russians hoped to drive them from Berlin, but the airlift broke the blockade. (Corbis-Bettmann)

Germany itself, was divided into zones after the war. Soviet refusal to allow the other Allies land access to West Berlin, located in the Russian zone of Germany, led to a U.S. and Royal Air Force airlift that flew supplies to the beleaguered Berliners. The fliers named it Operation Vittles, and it broke the Russian blockade.

The next major link in the containment strategy was the creation of a military alliance in Europe to complement the economic program. After the Soviets tightened their control of Hungary and Czechoslovakia, the United States in 1949 took the lead in establishing the North Atlantic Treaty Organization (NATO). Twelve nations formed the alliance, vowing that an attack against any one member would be considered an attack against all, to be met by appropriate armed force.

The Senate, long opposed to such military pacts, approved this time, and the United States established its first military treaty ties with Europe since the American Revolution. Congress went further than merely authorizing membership by voting military aid for its NATO allies. The Cold War had caused a major transformation in the American approach to foreign affairs.

In 1949, two significant events—the success of the Communists in the Chinese civil war and the Russian detonation of an atomic device—led the United States to define its aims still more specifically. Truman asked for a full-fledged review of U.S. foreign and defense policy. The National Security Council, organized in 1947 to provide policy coordination, produced a document, NSC-68, which shaped U.S. policy for the next 20 years.

Presented to the National Security Council in 1950, NSC-68 built on the Cold War rhetoric of the Truman Doctrine, describing challenges facing the United States in cataclysmic terms. "The issues that face us are momentous," the paper said, "involving the fulfillment or destruction not only of this Republic but of civilization itself." Conflict between East and West, the document assumed, was unavoidable, for amoral Soviet objectives ran totally counter to U.S. aims. Negotiation was useless, for the Soviets could never be trusted to bargain in good faith.

NSC-68 then argued that the nation could continue on its present course, with relatively limited military budgets, but would fail to achieve its objectives. If the United States hoped to meet the Russian challenge, it must increase defense spend-

Cold War Europe in 1950

This map shows the rigid demarcation between East and West during the Cold War. Although there were a number of neutral countries in Europe, the other nations found themselves in a standoff, as each side tried to contain the possible advances of the other. The small insert map in the upper-right-hand corner shows the division of Berlin that paralleled the division of Germany itself after World War II.

ing from the $13 billion set for 1950 to as much as $50 billion per year and increase the percentage of its budget allotted to defense from 5 to 20 percent. The costs were huge but necessary if the free world was to survive.

Containment in the 1950s

Containment, the keystone of American policy throughout the Truman years, was the rationale for the Truman Doctrine, the Marshall Plan, NATO, and NSC-68. Containment required the extensive use of government resources to resist the spread of communism. It also demanded detailed and up-to-date information about Communist moves. In

the 1950s, the government relied increasingly on the Central Intelligence Agency (CIA). Established by the National Security Act of 1947, which had also created the National Security Council, it sought to conduct espionage in foreign lands and to analyze what that information meant. Some of its work was aboveboard and visible; some was secret and seldom seen. During the Eisenhower administration, Allen Dulles, brother of the secretary of state, headed the agency and provided close foreign policy coordination. With the president's approval the CIA rearranged its priorities so that by 1957, 80 percent of its budget went toward covert activities. More and more, Eisenhower relied on clandestine CIA actions to undermine foreign governments, subsidize friendly newspapers in distant lands, and assist those who supported the American stance in the Cold War.

At the same time, the administration reassessed the impact of the containment policy itself, especially in light of attacks that it was too cautious to counter the threat of communism. For most of Eisenhower's two terms, John Foster Dulles was secretary of state. A devout Presbyterian who hated atheistic communism, he sought to move beyond containment. Eager to counter the "God-less terrorism" of communism, Dulles wanted to commit the nation to a holy crusade to promote democracy and to free the countries under Soviet domination. Instead of advocating containment, the United States should make it "publicly known that it wants and expects liberation to occur."

Eisenhower's own rhetoric was equally strong. In his 1953 inaugural address, he declared, "Forces of good and evil are massed and armed and opposed as rarely before in history. Freedom is pitted against slavery, lightness against dark." Yet Eisenhower was more conciliatory and realistic than Dulles and recognized the need for caution. He also understood the impossibility of changing the governments of the USSR's satellites. When, in mid-1953, East Germans mounted anti-Soviet demonstrations, in a challenge that foreshadowed the revolt against communism three and a half decades later, the United States maintained its distance and did not move in. In 1956, when Hungarian "freedom fighters" likewise took to the streets and aggressively defied Russian domination, the United States again stood back as Soviet forces smashed the rebels and maintained control of their satellite. Because Western action could have precipitated a more general conflict, Eisenhower refused to translate rhetoric into action. Throughout the 1950s, the policy of containment, largely as it had been defined earlier, remained in effect.

Containment in Asia, the Middle East, and Latin America

In a dramatic departure from its history of noninvolvement, the United States extended the policy of containment to meet challenges around the globe.

Secretary of State John Foster Dulles viewed the Cold War as a moral struggle between good and evil. Opposed to "godless communism," he often appeared as a religious crusader for measures he believed were necessary for the survival of the free world. (Corbis-Bettmann)

Colonial empires were disintegrating, and countries seeking and attaining their independence now found themselves caught in the middle of the super-power struggle. Decolonization became even more complicated as it became intertwined with the Cold War. Although the containment initiative had resulted from the effort to promote European stability, it now became worldwide. In Asia, the Middle East, and Latin America, the United States discovered the tremendous appeal of communism as a social and political system in emerging nations and found that ever greater efforts were required to advance American aims.

The Shock of the Chinese Revolution

The U.S. commitment to containment became stronger with the Communist victory in the Chinese Revolution. China, an ally during World War

II, had struggled against the Japanese, even as it fought a bitter civil war. The roots of the civil war lay deep in the Chinese past—in widespread poverty, disease, oppression by the landlord class, and national humiliation at the hands of foreign powers. Mao Zedong (Mao Tse-tung),* founder of a branch of the Communist party, gathered followers who wished to reshape China in a Communist mold. Opposing the Communists were the Nationalists, led by Jiang Jieshi (Chiang Kai-shek). By the early 1940s, Jiang Jieshi's regime was exhausted, inefficient, and corrupt. Mao's movement, meanwhile, grew stronger during the Second World War as he opposed the Japanese invaders and won the loyalty of the peasant class. Mao finally prevailed, as Jiang fled in 1949 to the island of Taiwan (Formosa) and nursed the improbable belief that he was still the rightful ruler of all China and would one day return.

The United States failed to understand the long internal conflict in China or the immense popular support Mao had garnered. As the Communist army moved toward victory, the *New York Times* termed the group a "nauseous force," a "compact little oligarchy dominated by Moscow's nominees." Mao's proclamation of the People's Republic of China on October 1, 1949, fanned fears of Russian domination, for he had already announced his regime's support for the Soviet Union against the "imperialist" United States.

Events in China caused near hysteria in America. Staunch anti-Communists argued that Truman and the United States were to blame for Jiang's defeat by failing to provide him sufficient support. Secretary of State Dean Acheson briefly considered granting diplomatic recognition to the new government but backed off after the Communists seized American property, harassed American citizens, and openly allied themselves with the Russians. Like other Americans, he viewed the Chinese as Soviet puppets.

Tension with China increased during the Korean War (1950–1953) and then again in 1954 when Mao's government began shelling National-

Mao Zedong, chairman of the Chinese Communist Party, was a powerful and popular leader who drove Jiang Jieshi from power in 1949 and established a strong hold over the People's Republic of China he created at that time. (Corbis-Bettmann)

ist positions on the offshore islands of Quemoy and Matsu. Eisenhower, now president, was committed to defending the Nationalists on Taiwan from a Communist attack, but he was unwilling to risk war over the islands. Again he showed an understanding of the need to proceed with caution.

Stalemate in the Korean War

The Korean War, on the other hand, highlighted growing U.S. intervention in Asian affairs. Concern about China and determination to contain communism led the United States into involvement in a bloody struggle in a faraway land. But American objectives were not always clear and were largely unrealized after three years of war.

The conflict in Korea stemmed from tensions lingering after World War II. Korea, long under

---

*Chinese names are rendered in their modern *pinyin* spelling. At first occurrence, the older but perhaps more familiar spelling (usually Wade-Giles) is given in parentheses.

Japanese control, hoped for independence after Japan's defeat. Instead, the Allies temporarily divided Korea along the 38th parallel when the rapid end to the Pacific struggle allowed Soviet troops to accept Japanese surrender in the north while American forces did the same in the south. The Soviet-American line, initially intended as a matter of military convenience, hardened after 1945, just as a similar division rigidified in Germany, and in time the Soviets set up a government in the north and the Americans a government in the south. Though the major powers left Korea, they continued to support the regimes they had created. Each government hoped to reunify the country on its own terms.

North Korea moved first. On June 25, 1950, North Korean forces crossed the 38th parallel to invade South Korea. Following Soviet-built tanks, the North Korean troops steadily advanced. They operated on their own initiative. Kim Il Sung, the North Korean leader, had visited Moscow earlier and spoken to Stalin about instability in South Korea. Although the Russians may have acquiesced in the idea of an attack, both the planning and the timing occurred in Korea.

North Korea's action took the United States by surprise. Earlier, the nation had seemed reluctant to defend Korea, but the Communist victory in China had changed the balance of power in Asia. Certain that Russia had masterminded the North Korean offensive and was testing the American policy of containment, Truman responded vigorously. "If this was allowed to go unchallenged," he declared, "it would mean a third world war, just as similar incidents had brought on the second world war."

Truman readied American naval and air forces and directed General Douglas MacArthur in Japan to supply South Korea. The United States also went to the United Nations Security Council. With the Soviet Union absent in protest of the UN's refusal to admit the People's Republic of China, the United States secured a unanimous resolution branding North Korea an aggressor, then another resolution calling on members of the organization to assist South Korea in repelling aggression and restoring peace.

The president first ordered American air and naval forces, then American ground forces, into battle south of the 38th parallel. Following a daring amphibious invasion that pushed the North Kore-

The Korean War

This map shows the ebb and flow of the Korean War. North Korea crossed the 38th parallel first, then the UN offensive drove the North Koreans close to the Chinese border, and finally the Chinese Communists entered the war and drove the UN forces back below the 38th parallel. The armistice signed at Panmunjom in 1953 provided a dividing line very close to the prewar line.

ans back to the former boundary line, United Nations troops crossed the 38th parallel, hoping to reunify Korea under an American-backed government. Despite Chinese signals that this movement toward their border threatened their security, the United States pressed on. In October, Chinese troops appeared briefly in battle, then disappeared. The next month, the Chinese mounted a full-fledged counterattack, which pushed the UN forces back below the dividing line again.

The resulting stalemate provoked a bitter struggle between MacArthur and his civilian commander in chief. The brilliant but arrogant general called for retaliatory air strikes against China, but Truman remained committed to conducting a limited war. MacArthur's statements, issued from the field, finally went too far. In April 1951, he argued that the American approach in Korea was wrong and asserted publicly that "there is no substitute for victory." Truman had no choice but to relieve the general for insubordination. The decision outraged many Americans. After the stunning victories of World War II, limited war was frustrating and difficult to understand.

The Korean War continued into Eisenhower's presidency. During the campaign of 1952, Ike promised to go to Korea, and three weeks after his election, he did so. When truce talks bogged down in May 1953, the new administration privately threatened the Chinese with the use of atomic weapons. Peace talks resumed, and on July 27, an armistice was signed. The Republican administration had managed to do what the preceding Democratic administration could not accomplish. After three long years, the unpopular war had ended.

American involvement carried a heavy price: over 33,000 Americans killed in action and many more wounded. But those figures paled beside the number of Korean casualties. As many as 2 million may have died in North and South Korea, and countless others were maimed.

The war also significantly changed American attitudes and institutions. This was the first war in

General Douglas MacArthur was a superb tactician but a supremely egotistical commander of UN forces in Korea. When he challenged Truman's policy, the president relieved him of his command, although, as shown in this picture, MacArthur returned home to a hero's welcome. (Wayne Miller/Magnum Photos)

The Korean War disrupted numerous families in both the north and south and led them to flee their homes. Here fleeing Korean civilians, with the belongings they could carry with them, pass U.S. soldiers as the bitter struggle dragged on. (UPI/Corbis-Bettmann)

which U.S. forces fought in integrated units. Truman, as commander in chief, had ordered the integration of the armed forces in 1948, over the opposition of many generals, and African Americans became part of all military units. Their successful performance led to acceptance of military integration.

During the Korean War, military expenditures soared from $13 billion in 1950 to about $47 billion three years later as defense spending followed the guidelines proposed in NSC-68. In the process, the United States accepted the demands of permanent mobilization. Whereas the military absorbed less than a third of the federal budget in 1950, a decade later it took half. More than a million soldiers were stationed around the world. At home, an increasingly powerful military establishment became closely tied to corporate and scientific communities and created a military-industrial complex that employed 3.5 million Americans by 1960.

The Korean War had important political effects as well. It led the United States to sign a peace treaty with Japan in September 1951 and to rely on that nation to maintain the balance of power in the Pacific. At the same time, the struggle poisoned relations with the People's Republic of China and ensured a diplomatic standoff that lasted more than 20 years.

Turbulence in the Middle East

Cold War attitudes also influenced American diplomacy in the Middle East. That part of the world had tremendous strategic importance as the supplier of oil for industrialized nations. During World War II, the major Allied powers occupied Iran, with the provision that they would leave within six months of the war's end. As of early 1946, both Great Britain and the United States had withdrawn, but the Soviet Union, which bordered on Iran, remained. Stalin claimed that earlier security agreements had not been honored and then went a step further and demanded oil concessions. A threat of vigorous American action forced the Russians to back down and depart.

The Eisenhower administration maintained its interest in Iran. In 1953, the CIA helped the local army overthrow the government of Mohammed Mossadegh, which had nationalized oil wells formerly under British control, and placed the shah of Iran securely on the Peacock Throne. After the coup, British and American companies regained command of the wells, and thereafter the United States government provided military assistance to the shah.

A far more serious situation emerged west of Iran. In 1948, the United Nations attempted to partition Palestine into an Arab state and a Jewish state. Truman officially recognized the new state of Israel 15 minutes after it was proclaimed. But recognition could not end bitter animosities between Arabs, who judged they had been robbed of their territory, and Jews, who felt they had finally regained a homeland after the horrors of the Holocaust. As Americans looked on, Arab forces from Egypt, Trans-Jordan, Syria, Lebanon, and Iraq invaded Israel, but the Israelis won the war and added territory to what they had been given by the United Nations.

While cultivating close ties with Israel, the United States also tried to maintain the friendship of oil-rich Arab states or, at the very least, to prevent them from falling into the Soviet orbit. In Egypt, the policy ran into trouble when Arab nationalist General Gamal Abdel Nasser planned a huge dam on the Nile River to produce electric power. Nasser hoped to follow a middle course by proclaiming his country's neutrality in the Cold War. Although Dulles offered U.S. financial support for the Aswan Dam project, Nasser also began discussions with the Soviet Union. Furious, the secretary of state withdrew the American offer. Left without funds for the dam, in July 1956 Nasser seized and nationalized the British-controlled Suez Canal and closed it to Israeli ships. Now Great Britain was enraged. All of Europe feared that Nasser would disrupt the flow of oil from the Middle East.

In October and November, Israeli, British, and French military forces invaded Egypt. Eisenhower, who had not been consulted, was irate. Realizing that the attack might push Nasser into Moscow's arms, the United States sponsored a UN resolution condemning the attacking nations and also cut off oil from England and France. These actions persuaded the invaders to withdraw.

It was not long before the United States again intervened in the Middle East. Concerned about the region's stability, Eisenhower declared in 1957 that "the existing vacuum in the Middle East must be filled by the United States before it is filled by Russia." A year later, in line with a congressional resolution that committed the United States to stop suspected Communist aggression, he authorized the landing of 14,000 soldiers in Lebanon to prop up a right-wing government challenged from within.

The Middle East remained a battleground in subsequent years. In 1967, Israeli forces defeated the Egyptian army in the Six Day War. Then in 1973, the Egyptians seized the initiative in the Yom Kippur War. In each case, the United States was concerned with maintaining both regional stability and uninterrupted supplies of oil and used its influence to bring fighting to an end.

Restricting Revolt in Latin America

The Cold War also affected relations in Latin America, the United States' traditional sphere of influence, and provided fresh reasons for intervention. In 1954, Dulles sniffed Communist activity in Guatemala and ordered CIA support for a coup aimed at ousting the elected government of reform-minded Colonel Jacobo Arbenz Guzmán. It trained and equipped Guatemalans to overthrown the legitimate regime, which had appropriated

The Middle East in 1949

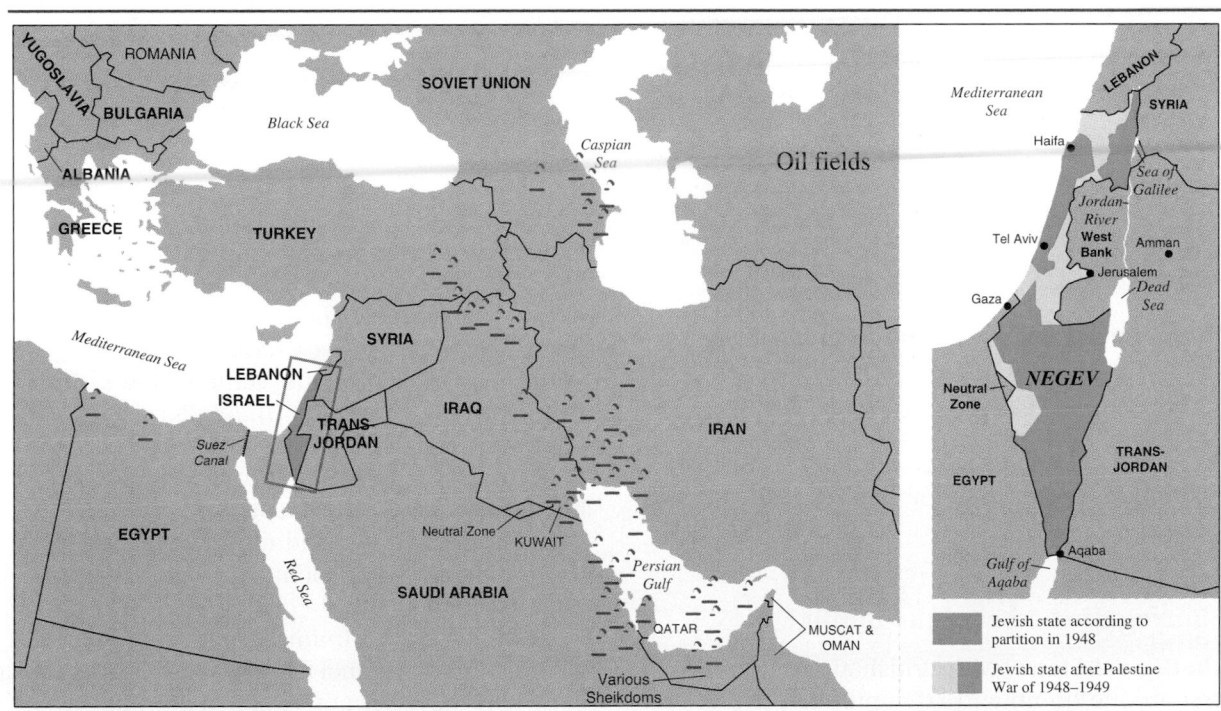

This map shows the extensive oil reserves that made the Middle East such an important region, and the shifting boundaries of Israel as a result of the war following its independence in 1948. Notice how its size increased after its victory in the first of a series of Middle Eastern conflicts.

property of the American-owned United Fruit Company. The right-wing takeover succeeded, established a military dictatorship that responded to U.S. wishes, and restored the property of the United Fruit Company. These actions demonstrated again the shortsighted American commitment to stability and private investment, whatever the internal effect or ultimate cost. The interference in Guatemala fed anti-American feeling throughout Latin America.

In 1959, when Fidel Castro overthrew the dictatorial regime of Fulgencio Batista in Cuba, the shortsightedness of American policy became even clearer. Nationalism and the thrust for social reform were powerful forces in Latin America, as in the rest of the Third World. As Milton Eisenhower, Ike's brother and adviser, pointed out: "Revolution is inevitable in Latin America. The people are angry. They are shackled to the past with bonds of ignorance, injustice, and poverty. And they no longer accept as universal or inevitable the oppressive prevailing order." But when Castro confiscated American property in Cuba, the Eisenhower administration cut off exports and severed diplomatic ties. In response, Cuba turned to the Soviet Union for support.

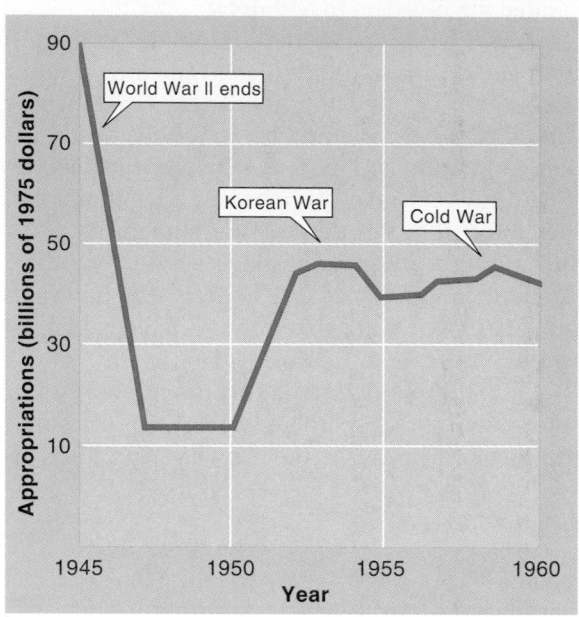

Defense Expenditures, 1945–1960

Defense spending plummeted after World War II, only to quadruple with the onset of the Korean War. After that increase, spending levels never dropped dramatically, even after the end of the war. Source: U.S. Bureau of the Census.

Atomic Weapons and the Cold War

Throughout the Cold War period, the atomic bomb was a crucial factor in world affairs. It hung over all diplomatic discussions and military initiatives. Atomic weapons were destructive enough, but when the United States and the Soviet Union both developed hydrogen bombs, an age of overkill began.

Sharing the Secret of the Bomb

The United States, with British aid, had built the first atomic bomb and attempted to conceal the project from its wartime ally, the Soviet Union. Soviet spies, however, discovered that the Americans were working on the bomb, and, even before

the war was over, the Soviets had initiated a program to create a bomb of their own.

The question of sharing the atomic secret was considered in the immediate postwar years. Just before he retired, Secretary of War Henry L. Stimson argued that the United States should cooperate with the Soviet Union. Recognizing the futility of trying to cajole the Russians while "having this weapon ostentatiously on our hip," he warned that "their suspicions and their distrust of our purposes and motives will increase." Only mutual accommodation could bring international cooperation.

For a time the administration contemplated a system of international arms control. Realizing by early 1946 that mere possession of the bomb by the United States did not make the Russians more malleable, Truman decided to offer an atomic energy plan to the United Nations. It proposed an international agency to control atomic energy. The Russians balked at a plan they argued favored the United States and negotiations collapsed.

The United States gave up on the process of sharing atomic secrets. Intent on retaining the technological advantage until the creation of a "foolproof method of control," Truman endorsed the Atomic Energy Act, passed by Congress in 1946. It established the Atomic Energy Commission to supervise all atomic energy development in the United States and, under the tightest security, to authorize all nuclear activity in the nation at large. It also opened the way to a nuclear arms race once Russia developed its own bomb.

Nuclear Proliferation

As the atomic bomb found its way into popular culture, Americans at first showed more excitement than fear. In Los Angeles, the "Atombomb Dancers" appeared at the Burbank Burlesque Theater. In 1946, the Buchanan Brothers released a record called "Atomic Power."

Anxiety lurked beneath the exuberance, though it did not surface while the United States maintained a nuclear monopoly. Then, in September 1949, reporters were called to the White House and told: "We have evidence that within recent weeks an atomic explosion occurred in the U.S.S.R." Over the Labor Day weekend, a U.S. Air Force weather reconnaissance plane on a routine mission had picked up air samples showing higher than normal radioactivity counts. Other samples confirmed the reading, and scientists soon concluded that Russia had conducted a nuclear test.

The American public was shocked. Suddenly the security of being the world's only atomic power vanished. People wondered whether the Soviet test foreshadowed a nuclear attack. Harold C. Urey, a Nobel Prize–winning scientist, summed up the feelings of many Americans: "There is only one thing worse than one nation having the atomic bomb—that's two nations having it."

In early 1950, Truman authorized the development of a new hydrogen superbomb, potentially far more devastating than the atomic bomb. Edward Teller, a physicist on the Manhattan Project, was intrigued with the novelty of the puzzle. During the war, as other scientists struggled with the problem of fission, he contemplated the possibility that fusion might release energy in even greater amounts. Now he had his chance to proceed.

By 1953, both the United States and the Soviet Union had unlocked the secret of the hydrogen bomb. As kilotons gave way to megatons, the stakes rose. The government remained quiet about MIKE, the first test of a hydrogen device in the Pacific Ocean in 1952, but rumors circulated that it had created a hole in the ocean floor 175 feet deep and a mile wide. Later, after the 1954 BRAVO test, Lewis Strauss, Atomic Energy Commission chairman, admitted that "an H-bomb can be made … large enough to take out a city," even New York. Then, in 1957, shortly after the news that the Soviets had successfully tested their first intercontinental ballistic missile (ICBM), Americans learned that the Soviets had fired the first satellite, *Sputnik,* into outer space, with a rocket that could deliver a hydrogen bomb.

The discovery of radioactive fallout added another dimension to the nuclear dilemma. Fallout became publicly known after the BRAVO blast in 1954 showered Japanese fishermen 85 miles away with radioactive dust. They became ill with radiation sickness, and several months later, one of them died. The Japanese, who had been the first to experience the effects of atomic weapons, were outraged. Other people around the world were similarly alarmed.

Authors in both the scientific and the popular press focused attention on radioactive fallout. Radiation, physicist Ralph Lapp observed, "cannot be felt and possesses all the terror of the unknown. It is something which evokes revulsion and helplessness—like a bubonic plague." Nevil Shute's best-selling 1957 novel *On the Beach,* and the film that followed, also sparked public awareness and fear. The story described a war that released so much radioactive waste that all life in the northern hemisphere disappeared, while the southern hemisphere awaited the same deadly fate. When *Consumer Reports* warned of the contamination of milk with the radioactive isotope strontium-90 in 1959, the public grew even more anxious.

The mushroom cloud resulting from an atomic blast became a familiar sight as it accompanied hundreds of nuclear tests in the postwar United States. But while the cloud was beautiful, it also filled the atmosphere with fallout that contaminated people, plants, and animals below. (Gamma Liaison)

The discovery of fallout provoked a shelter craze. Bob Russell, a Michigan sheriff, declared that "to build a new home in this day and age without including such an obvious necessity as a fallout shelter would be like leaving out the bathroom 20 years ago." *Good Housekeeping* magazine carried a full-page editorial in November 1958 that urged the construction of family shelters.

More and more companies advertised ready-made shelters to eager consumers. A firm in Miami reported numerous inquiries about shelters costing between $1,795 and $3,895, depending on capacity, and planned 900 franchises. *Life* magazine in 1955 featured an "H-Bomb Hideaway" for $3,000. By the end of 1960, the Office of Civil and Defense Mobilization estimated that a million family shelters had been built.

The Nuclear West

The bomb stimulated more than just shelter building. It sparked an enormous increase in defense spending and encouraged the development of a huge nuclear industry, particularly in the West. Contractors preferred to work in this region, which was unfriendly to union activity, arguing that labor stability would make it easier to meet government demands.

During World War II, a number of the Manhattan Project's major centers were located in the West. The plant at Hanford, Washington, was one of the most important producers of fissionable material for a bomb. The actual fabrication of the first atomic weapon occurred at Los Alamos, New Mexico. Development in this area expanded after the war. Hanford continued to produce plutonium. A facility at Rocky Flats, outside Denver, Colorado, made plutonium triggers for thermonuclear bombs. The new Sandia National Laboratory in Albuquerque, New Mexico, provided the production engineering of nuclear bombs, while the Los Alamos laboratory remained a major center of atomic activity. In 1951, the United States opened the Nevada Test Site, 65 miles north of Las Vegas, to try out nuclear weapons, and the facility had a major impact on the city. The Chamber of Commerce offered schedules of test shots, and the mushroom cloud became the logo for the Southern Nevada Telephone Directory.

Defense spending promoted other development as well. Naval commands had headquarters in Seattle, San Francisco, San Diego, and Honolulu. Radar sites, aimed at tracking incoming missiles, stretched all the way up to Alaska. The Boeing Company, located in the state of Washington, stimulated the tremendous development of Seattle, as it produced B-47 and B-52 airplanes, which became major delivery vehicles for nuclear bombs.

*Americans sought protection from fallout in shelters that civil defense authorities told them would be just like home. Here a typical family in 1955 practices in the Kiddie Kokoon, which has beds and supplies of food and water to last for several weeks. (©J. Edward Bailey/*TIME *Magazine)*

"Massive Retaliation"

As Americans grappled with the consequences of nuclear weapons, government policy came to depend increasingly on an atomic shield. The Soviet success in building its own bomb encouraged the conviction that America must beef up its atomic forces. Truman authorized the development of a nuclear arsenal but also stressed conventional forms of defense. After his election in 1952, Eisenhower found the effort fragmented and wasteful. Concerned with controlling the budget and cutting taxes, his administration decided to rely on atomic weapons rather than combat forces as the key to American defense.

Secretary of State Dulles developed the policy of "massive retaliation." The United States, he declared, was willing and ready to use nuclear weapons against Communist aggression "at places of our own choosing." The policy allowed troop cutbacks and promised to be cost-effective by giving "more bang for the buck."

Massive retaliation provided for an all-or-nothing response, leaving no middle course, no alternatives between nuclear war and retreat. Still, it reflected Dulles's willingness to threaten direct retaliation to deter Soviet challenges around the world. "The ability to get to the verge without getting into war is the necessary art," he said. "If you cannot master it you inevitably get into war." Critics called the policy "brinkmanship" and wondered what would happen if the line was crossed in the new atomic age. Eisenhower himself was horrified when he saw reports indicating what nuclear weapons could do, and with characteristic caution he did his best to ensure that the rhetoric of massive retaliation did not lead to war.

Atomic Protest

As nuclear development continued, critics demanded an end to the arms race. In 1956, Democratic presidential candidate Adlai Stevenson pointed to "the danger of poisoning the atmosphere," and demanded an end to nuclear tests. Eisenhower did not respond to Stevenson, but Dulles minimized the hazards of radiation by arguing, "From a health standpoint, there is greater danger from wearing a wrist watch with a luminous dial."

In 1957, activists organized SANE, the National Committee for a Sane Nuclear Policy. One of its most effective advertisements featured internationally known pediatrician Benjamin Spock, looking down at a little girl with a frown on his face. "Dr. Spock is worried," the caption read, and the text below amplified on his concern. "I *am* worried," he said, "not so much about the effect of past tests but

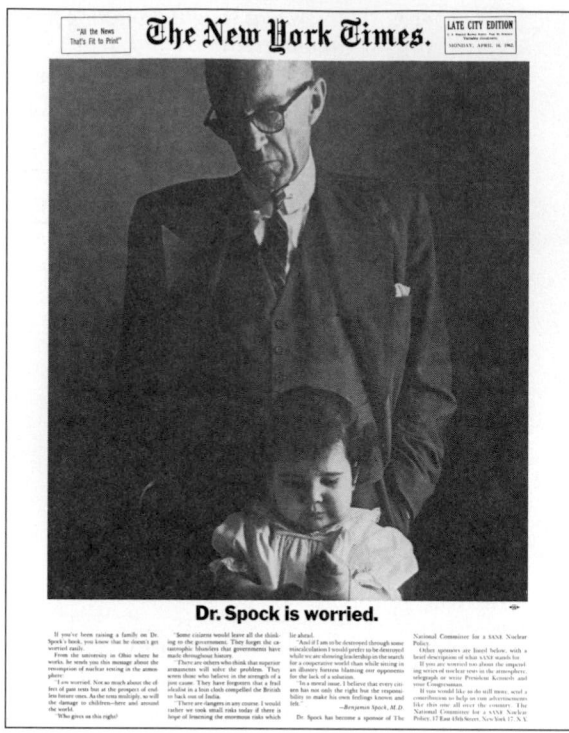

SANE tried to get the United States, and the rest of the world, to stop testing nuclear weapons and dumping huge amounts of fallout in this atmosphere. This newspaper advertisement, which appeared in 1962, was part of the larger effort to make the world a safer place. (The Peace Collection, Swarthmore College, PA)

at the prospect of endless future ones. As the tests multiply, so will the damage to children—here and around the world."

Several years later, a number of women who had worked with SANE took the protest movement a step further. As one activist later recalled, "This movement was inspired and motivated by mothers' love for children.... When they were putting their breakfasts on the table, they saw not only Wheaties and milk, but they also saw Strontium 90 and Iodine 131." To challenge continued testing, which dropped such lethal elements on all inhabitants of the globe, the protesters called on women all over the country to suspend normal activities for a day and strike for peace." An estimated 50,000 women marched in 60 communities around the nation. Their slogans included "Let the Children Grow" and "End the Arms Race—Not the Human Race."

Pressure from many groups produced a political breakthrough and sustained it for a time. The

superpowers began a voluntary moratorium on testing in the fall of 1958. It lasted until the Soviet Union resumed testing in September 1961, the United States the following March.

The Cold War at Home

The Cold War also affected domestic affairs and led to the creation of an internal loyalty program that seriously violated civil liberties. Americans had feared radical subversion before and after the Russian Revolution (see Chapters 16, 21, and 22). Now the Soviet Union appeared ever more ominous in confrontations around the world. Maps showed half the world colored red to dramatize the spread of the monolithic Communist system. As Americans began to suspect Communist infiltration at home, some determined to root out all traces of communism inside the United States.

Truman's Loyalty Program

When the Truman administration mobilized support for its containment program in the immediate postwar years, its rhetoric became increasingly shrill. Spokesmen contrasted American virtues to diabolical Russian designs. For Truman, the issue confronting the world was one of "tyranny or freedom." According to Attorney General J. Howard McGrath, there were "many Communists in America," each bearing the "germ of death for society."

When administration officials perceived an internal threat to security after the discovery of classified documents in the offices of the allegedly pro-Communist *Amerasia* magazine, Truman responded by appointing a Temporary Commission on Employee Loyalty. Republican gains in the midterm elections of 1946 led him to fear a congressional loyalty probe that could be used for partisan ends, especially since Republicans had accused the Democrats of being "soft on communism." Truman hoped to head off such an investigation by starting his own.

On the basis of the report from his temporary commission, Truman established a new Federal Employee Loyalty Program by executive decree in

1947. In the same week that he announced his containment policy, Truman ordered the FBI to check its files for evidence of subversive activity and then to bring suspects before a new Civil Service Commission Loyalty Review Board. Initially, the program included safeguards and assumed that a challenged employee was innocent until proved guilty. But as the Loyalty Review Board assumed more and more power, it systematically ignored individual rights. Employees about whom there was any doubt, regardless of proof, found themselves under attack, with little chance to fight back. Val Lorwin, met at the start of the chapter, was just one of many victims.

The Truman loyalty program examined several million employees and found grounds for dismissing only several hundred. Nonetheless, it bred the unwarranted fear of subversion, led to the assumption that absolute loyalty could be achieved, and legitimated investigatory tactics that were used irresponsibly to harm innocent individuals.

The Congressional Loyalty Program

While Truman's loyalty probe investigated government employees, Congress embarked on its own program. In the early years of the Cold War, the law became increasingly explicit about what was illegal in the United States. The Smith Act of 1940 made it a crime to advocate or teach the forcible overthrow of the U.S. government. In 1949, Eugene Dennis and ten other Communist leaders were found guilty under its terms. In 1951, in *Dennis* v. *United States,* the Supreme Court upheld the Smith Act, clearing the way for the prosecution of nearly 100 other Communists.

The McCarran Internal Security Act of 1950 further circumscribed Communist activity. It declared that it was illegal to conspire to act in a way that would "substantially contribute" to establishing a totalitarian dictatorship in America. Members of Communist organizations had to register with the attorney general and could not obtain passports or work in areas of national defense. Congress passed the measure over Truman's veto. The American Communist party, which had never been large, even in the Depression, declined still further. Membership, numbering about 80,000 in 1947, fell to 55,000 in 1950 and 25,000 in 1954.

The investigations of the House Un-American Activities Committee (HUAC) contributed to that decline. Intent on rooting out subversion, HUAC probed the motion picture industry in 1947. Protesting its scare tactics, some people summoned by the committee refused to testify under oath. They were scapegoated for their stand. The so-called Hollywood Ten, a group of writers, were cited for contempt of court and sent to federal prison. At that, Hollywood knuckled under and blacklisted anyone with even a marginally questionable past. No one on these lists could find jobs at the studios anymore.

Congress made a greater splash with the Hiss-Chambers case. Whittaker Chambers, a former Communist who had broken with the party in 1938 and had become a successful editor of *Time,* charged that Alger Hiss had been a Communist in the 1930s. Hiss was a distinguished New Dealer who had served in the Agriculture Department before becoming assistant secretary of state. Now out of the government, he was president of the Carnegie Endowment for International Peace. He denied Chambers's charge, and the matter might have died there had not freshman congressman Richard Nixon taken up the case. Nixon finally extracted from Hiss an admission that he had once known Chambers. Outside the hearing room, Hiss sued Chambers for libel, whereupon Chambers changed his story and charged that Hiss was a Soviet spy.

Hiss was indicted for perjury, for lying under oath about his former relationship with Chambers. The case made front-page news around the nation. Millions of Americans read about the case at about the same time they learned of Russia's first atomic explosion and the final victory of the Communist revolution in China. Chambers appeared unstable and changed his story several times. Yet Hiss, too, seemed contradictory in his testimony and never adequately explained how some copies of stolen State Department documents had been typed on a typewriter he had once owned. The first trial ended in a hung jury; the second trial, in January 1950, sent Hiss to prison for almost four years.

For many Americans, the Hiss case proved a Communist threat indeed existed in the United States. It "forcibly demonstrated to the American people that domestic Communism was a real and present danger to the security of the nation," Richard Nixon declared after using the case to win

Alger Hiss's conviction for perjury helped heighten American fears of communism at home. Despite damaging evidence that became public in later years, Hiss never ceased proclaiming his innocence, but he became an isolated and subdued figure, far different from the prominent government official he had once been. (Elliott Erwitt/Magnum Photos)

a Senate seat from California and then the Republican vice presidential nomination in 1952. The case also led people to question the Democratic approach to the problem. Critics attacked Dean Acheson for supporting Hiss, his friend. They likewise questioned Truman's own commitment to protect the nation from internal subversion. The dramatic Hiss case helped justify the even worse witch-hunt that followed.

The Second Red Scare

The key anti-Communist warrior in the 1950s was Joseph R. McCarthy. Coming to the Senate from Wisconsin in 1946, McCarthy had an undistin-

guished career. As he began to contemplate reelection two years hence, he seized on the Communist issue. Truman had carried Wisconsin in 1948, and McCarthy saw in the Communist question a way of mobilizing Republican support. He first gained national attention with a speech before the Wheeling, West Virginia, Women's Club in February 1950, not long after the conviction of Alger Hiss. In that address, McCarthy claimed he had in his hand a list of 205 known Communists in the State Department. When pressed for details, McCarthy said first that he would release his list only to the president, then reduced the number of names to 57.

Early reactions to McCarthy were mixed. A subcommittee of the Senate Foreign Relations Committee, after investigating, called his charge a "fraud and a hoax." Even other Republicans like Robert Taft and Richard Nixon questioned his effectiveness. As his support grew, however, Republicans realized his partisan value and egged him on. Senator John Bricker of Ohio allegedly told him, "Joe, you're a dirty s.o.b., but there are times when you've got to have an s.o.b. around, and this is one of them."

McCarthy selected assorted targets. In the elections of 1950, he attacked Millard Tydings, the Democrat from Maryland who had chaired the subcommittee that dismissed McCarthy's first accusations. A doctored photograph, showing Tydings with deposed American Communist party head Earl Browder, helped bring about Tydings's defeat. McCarthy called Dean Acheson the "Red Dean of the State Department" and slandered George C. Marshall, the architect of victory in World War II and a powerful figure in formulating Far Eastern policy, as a "man steeped in falsehood … who has recourse to the lie whenever it suits his convenience."

A demagogue throughout his career, McCarthy gained visibility through extensive press and television coverage. Playing on his tough reputation, he did not mind appearing disheveled, unshaven, and half sober. He used obscenity and vulgarity freely as he lashed out against his "vile and scurrilous" enemies.

McCarthy's tactics worked because of public alarm about the Communist threat. The Korean War revealed the aggressiveness of Communists in Asia. The arrest in 1950 of Julius and Ethel Rosenberg fed fears of subversion from within. The

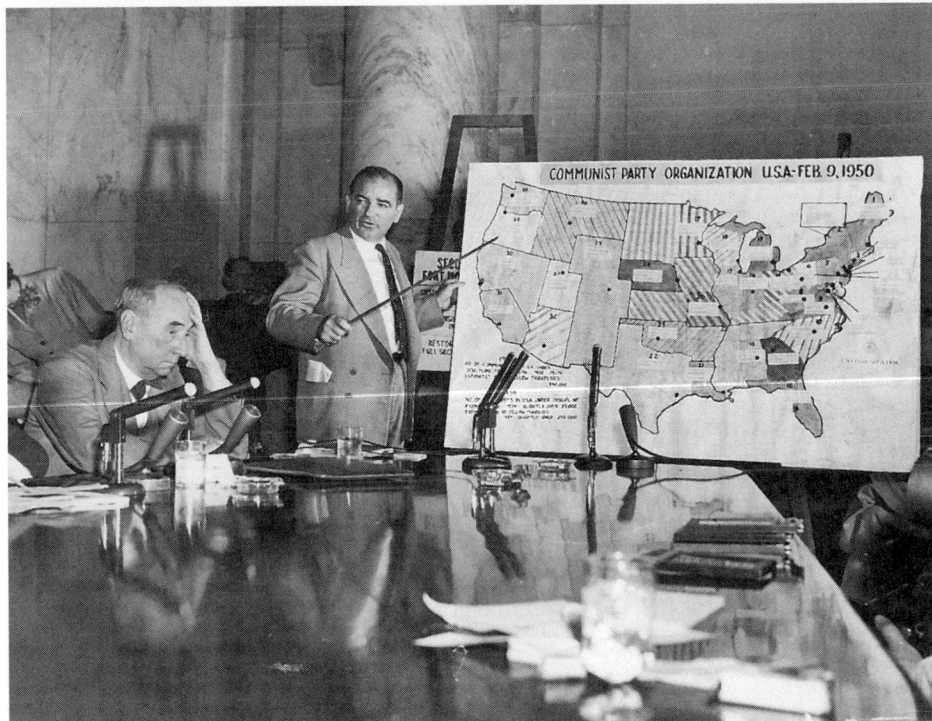

Senator Joseph McCarthy's spurious charges inflamed anti-Communist sentiment in the 1950s. Here he uses a chart of Communist party organization in the United States to suggest that the nation was at risk unless subversives were rooted out. (Corbis-Bettmann)

Rosenbergs, a seemingly ordinary American couple with two small children, were charged with stealing and transmitting atomic secrets to the Russians. To many Americans, it was inconceivable that the Soviets could have developed the bomb on their own. Treachery helped explain the Soviet explosion of an atomic device.

The next year, the Rosenbergs were found guilty of espionage. Judge Irving Kaufman expressed the rage of an insecure nation as he sentenced them to death. "Your conduct in putting into the hands of the Russians the A-bomb," he charged, "has already caused, in my opinion, the Communist aggression in Korea, . . . and who knows but that millions more of innocent people may pay the price of your treason."

When the Republicans won control of the Senate in 1952, McCarthy's power grew. He became chairman of the Government Operations Committee and head of its Permanent Investigations Subcommittee. He now had a stronger base and two dedicated assistants, Roy Cohn and G. David Schine, who helped keep attention focused on the ostensible Communist threat. The lists of

suspects, including Val Lorwin, introduced at the start of this chapter, continued to grow.

As McCarthy's anti-Communist witch-hunt continued, Eisenhower became uneasy. He disliked the senator but, recognizing his popularity, was reluctant to challenge him. At the height of his influence, polls showed that McCarthy had half the public behind him. With the country so inclined, Eisenhower voiced his disapproval quietly and privately.

With the help of Cohn and Schine, McCarthy pushed on, and finally he pushed too hard. In 1953, the army drafted Schine and then refused to allow the preferential treatment that Cohn insisted his colleague deserved. Angered, McCarthy began to investigate army security and even top-level army leaders themselves. When the army charged that McCarthy was going too far, the Senate investigated the complaint.

The Army-McCarthy hearings began in April 1954 and lasted 36 days. Televised to a fascinated nationwide audience, they demonstrated the power of TV to shape people's opinions. Americans saw McCarthy's savage tactics on screen. He came across to viewers as irresponsible and destructive, particularly in contrast to Boston lawyer Joseph Welch, who argued the army's case with quiet eloquence.

The hearings shattered McCarthy's mystical appeal. In broad daylight, before a national television audience, his ruthless tactics no longer made sense. The Senate finally summoned the courage to condemn him for his conduct. Even conservatives turned against McCarthy because he was no longer limiting his venom to Democrats and liberals. Although McCarthy remained in office, his influence disappeared. Three years later, at the age of 48, he died a broken man.

Yet for a time he had exerted a powerful hold in the United States. "To many Americans," radio commentator Fulton Lewis, Jr., said, "McCarthyism is Americanism." Seizing upon the frustrations and anxieties of the Cold War, McCarthy struck a resonant chord. As his appeal grew, he put together a following that included both lower-class ethnic groups, who responded to the charges against established elites, and conservative midwestern Republicans. But his real power base was the Senate, where, particularly after 1952, conservative Republicans saw McCarthy as a means of reasserting their own authority. Their support encouraged the vicious crusade.

The Casualties of Fear

The anti-Communist campaign promoted a pervasive sense of suspicion in American society. In the late 1940s and early 1950s, dissent no longer seemed safe. Civil servants, government workers, academics, and actors all came under attack and found that the right of due process often evaporated as the Cold War Red Scare gained ground. Seasoned China experts lost their positions in the diplomatic service, and social justice legislation faltered.

This paranoia affected American life in countless ways. In New York, subway workers were fired when they refused to answer questions about their own political actions and beliefs. In Seattle, a fire department officer who denied current membership in the Communist party but refused to speak of his past was dismissed just 40 days before he reached the 25 years of service that would have

qualified him for retirement benefits. Navajos in Arizona and New Mexico, facing starvation in the bitter winter of 1947–1948, were denied government relief because of charges that their communal way of life was communistic and therefore un-American. Racism became intertwined with the anti-Communist crusade as African American actor Paul Robeson was accused of Communist leanings for criticizing American foreign policy and denied opportunities to perform. Subsequently the State Department revoked his passport. Black author W. E. B. Du Bois, who joined the Communist party, faced even more virulent attacks and likewise lost his passport. Hispanic laborers faced deportation for membership in unions with left-wing sympathies. In 1949, the Congress of Industrial Organizations (CIO) expelled 11 unions with a total membership of more than one million for alleged domination by Communists. Val Lorwin, met at the start of this chapter, weathered the storm of malicious accusations and was finally vindicated, but others were less lucky. They were the unfortunate victims as the United States became consumed by the passions of the Cold War.

Continuing Confrontations with Communists

The Cold War continued into the 1960s and 1970s. Presidents John F. Kennedy and Lyndon B. Johnson shared the assumptions that had guided the United States in the post–World War II years. Both were aggressive cold warriors who subscribed to the policies of their predecessors. Their commitment to stopping the spread of communism kept the nation locked in the same bitter conflict that had dominated foreign policy in the 1950s and led to continuing confrontations around the globe.

John Kennedy and the Bay of Pigs Fiasco

Kennedy, who won the presidency in 1960, was an activist who wanted to take charge of the White House. At 43, he was the youngest man ever elected president, and he hoped to use his youthful vigor to make good on his campaign promise to get the country moving again. The new president was determined to stand firm in the face of Russian power. During the campaign, he had declared: "The enemy is the communist system itself—implacable, insatiable, unceasing in its drive for world domination." In his inaugural address, he eloquently described the dangers and challenges the United States faced. "In the long history of the world," he cried out, "only a few generations have been granted the role of defending freedom in its hour of maximum danger." The United States would "pay any price, bear any burden, meet any hardship, support any friend, oppose any foe, to assure the survival and success of liberty."

Kennedy perceived direct challenges from the Soviet Union almost from the beginning of his presidency. The first came at the Bay of Pigs in Cuba in the spring of 1961. Cuban-American relations had been strained since Fidel Castro's revolutionary army had seized power in 1959. A radical regime in Cuba, leaning toward the Soviet Union, could provide a model for upheaval elsewhere in Latin America and threaten the venerable Monroe Doctrine.

Just before Kennedy assumed office, the United States broke diplomatic relations with Cuba. The CIA, meanwhile, was covertly training anti-Castro exiles to storm the Cuban coast at the Bay of Pigs. The American planners assumed the invasion would lead to an uprising of the Cuban people against Castro. When Kennedy learned of the plan, he approved it.

The invasion, on April 17, 1961, was an unmitigated disaster. Cuban forces kept troops from coming ashore, and there was no popular uprising to greet the invaders. The United States stood exposed to the world, attempting to overthrow a sovereign government. It had broken agreements not to interfere in the internal affairs of hemispheric neighbors and had intervened clumsily and unsuccessfully.

Although chastened by the debacle at the Bay of Pigs, Kennedy remained determined to deal sternly with the perceived Communist threat. Following a hostile meeting with Soviet leader Nikita Khrushchev in Vienna in June 1961, where

Aerial photographs in the fall of 1962 showed the Soviet missile sites in Cuba and this evidence led President Kennedy to insist on removal of the weapons. The Cuban missile crisis threatened to engulf the world in a nuclear war. (UPI/Corbis-Bettmann)

discussion centered on the question of a permanent settlement for the divided city of Berlin, to prevent refugees from fleeing from East Germany to the West, Kennedy reacted aggressively. He asked Congress for $3 billion more in defense appropriations, more men for the armed forces, and funds for a civil defense fallout shelter program, as if to warn of the possibility of nuclear war. After the USSR erected a wall in Berlin to seal off its section, the crisis eased.

The Cuban Missile Face-off

The next year, a new crisis arose. Fidel Castro, understandably fearful of the American threat to Cuban independence after the Bay of Pigs invasion, sought and secured Soviet assistance. American aerial photographs taken in October 1962 revealed that the USSR had begun to place what Kennedy considered offensive missiles on Cuban soil, though Cuba insisted they were defensive. The missiles did not change the strategic balance significantly; the Soviets could still wreak untold

damage on American targets from bases farther away. But with Russian weapons installed just 90 miles from American shores, appearance was more important than reality. Kennedy was determined to confront the Soviet Union in Cuba and this time to win.

Kennedy went on nationwide TV to tell the American people about the missiles and to demand their removal. He declared that the United States would not shrink from the risk of nuclear war and announced a naval blockade around Cuba to prevent Soviet ships from bringing in additional missiles. He called the move a quarantine, for a blockade was an act of war.

As the Soviet ships steamed toward the blockade and the nations stood "eyeball to eyeball" at the brink, the people around the world held their breath. After several days, the tension broke, but only because Khrushchev called the Soviet ships back. Khrushchev then sent a long letter to Kennedy pledging to remove the missiles if the United States ended the blockade and promised to stay out of Cuba altogether. A second letter demanded that

Lyndon Johnson succeeded John Kennedy and sought to emphasize that he would follow in the slain president's footsteps. This photograph, sent to government posts around the world, showed the connection between the two leaders and thereby tried to highlight the continuity of the American government. (AP/Wide World Photos)

America remove its missiles from Turkey as well. The United States responded affirmatively to the first letter, ignored the second, and said nothing about its intention, already voiced, of removing its own missiles from Turkey. With that the crisis ended.

The Cuban missile crisis was the most terrifying confrontation of the Cold War. Yet the president emerged from the crisis as a hero who had stood firm. His reputation was enhanced, as was the image of his party in the coming congressional elections. As the relief of the moment began to fade, however, critics charged that what Kennedy saw as his finest hour was in fact an unnecessary crisis. One consequence of the affair was the establishment of a Soviet-American hot line to avoid similar episodes in the future. Another was the USSR's determination to increase its nuclear arsenal so that it would never again be exposed as inferior to the United States.

Confrontation and Containment under Johnson

After Kennedy's brutal assassination in 1963, Vice President Lyndon Johnson assumed the presidency. He was an extraordinarily effective legislative leader (see Chapter 28), with considerably less experience in foreign affairs. Yet he shared many of Kennedy's assumptions about the threat of communism. His understanding of the past led him to believe that aggressors had to be stopped or their actions would lead to further aggression, as had been true in World War II. Like Kennedy, Johnson believed in the domino theory, which held that if one country in a region fell, others were bound to follow. He was determined to keep the power of the United States intact and contain the Communist menace. He assumed he could treat foreign adversaries just as he treated political opponents in the United States.

In 1965, Johnson dispatched over 20,000 troops to the Dominican Republic in Central America, believing that "Castro-type elements" might win in a civil war there. In fact, the group Johnson called Communist was led by the former president, Juan Bosch, who had been overthrown by a military junta. Bosch ruefully pointed out that "this was a democra-

tic revolution smashed by the leading democracy of the world." Johnson's claims about the threat of communism and the importance of protecting American tourists seemed deceptive to critics.

The Quagmire of Vietnam

The commitment to stopping the spread of communism led to the massive U.S. involvement in Vietnam. That struggle, which tore the United States apart and wrought enormous damage in Southeast Asia, finally forced a reevaluation of the policies that had guided America foreign policy in the first decades of the Cold War.

Roots of the Conflict

The roots of the war extended far back in the past. Indochina had been under French control since the middle of the nineteenth century. During World War II, the Japanese occupied the area but allowed French collaborators to direct internal affairs. An independence movement, led by the Communist organizer and revolutionary Ho Chi Minh, sought to expel the Japanese conquerors.

In 1945, the Allied powers faced the decision of how to deal with Ho and his nationalist movement. Franklin Roosevelt, like Woodrow Wilson, believed in self-determination and wanted to end colonialism. But France was determined to regain its colony, and by the time of his death, Roosevelt had backed down.

Meanwhile, Ho Chi Minh had established the Democratic Republic of Vietnam in 1945. Although the new government enjoyed widespread support, the United States refused to extend it formal diplomatic recognition. A long, bitter struggle broke out between French and Vietnamese forces and became entangled with the larger Cold War.

Though Ho did not have close ties to the Soviet state and was committed to his independent nationalist crusade, Truman and his advisers, who saw communism as a monolithic force, assumed wrongly that Ho took orders from Moscow. Hence, in 1950, the United States formally recognized a French puppet government in Vietnam. Because

Public Opinion Polls

In recent years, historians have used a new source of evidence, the public opinion poll. People have always been concerned with what others think, and leaders have often sought to frame their behavior according to the preferences of the populace. As techniques of assessing the mind of the public have become more sophisticated, the poll has emerged as an integral part of the analysis of social and political life. Polls now measure opinion on many questions—social, cultural, intellectual, political, and diplomatic. Because of their increasing importance, it is useful to know how to use the polls in an effort to understand and recover the past.

The principle of polling is not new. In 1824 the *Harrisburg Pennsylvanian* sought to predict the winner of that year's presidential race, and in the 1880s, the *Boston Globe* sent reporters to selected precincts on election night to forecast final returns. In 1916, *Literary Digest* began conducting postcard polls to predict political results. By the 1930s, Elmo Roper and George Gallup had further developed the field of market research and public opinion polling. Notwithstanding an embarrassing mistake by *Literary Digest* in predicting a Landon victory over FDR in 1936, polling had by World War II become a scientific enterprise.

According to Gallup, a poll is not magic but "merely an instrument for gauging public opinion," especially the views of those often unheard. As Elmo Roper said, the poll is "one of the few ways through which the so-called common man can be articulate." Polling, therefore, is a valuable way to recover the attitudes, beliefs, and voices of ordinary people.

Yet certain cautions should be observed. Like all instruments of human activity, polls are imperfect and may even be dangerous. Historians using information from polls need to be aware of how large the samples were, when the interviewing was done, and how opinions might have been molded by the form of the poll itself. Questions can be poorly phrased. Some hint at the desirable answer or plant ideas in the minds of those interviewed. Polls sometimes provide ambiguous responses that can be interpreted many ways. More seriously, some critics worry that human freedom itself is threatened by the pollsters' manipulative and increasingly accurate predictive techniques.

Despite these limitations, polls have become an ever-present part of American life. In the late 1940s and early 1950s, Americans were polled frequently about topics ranging from foreign aid, the United Nations, and the occupation of Germany and Japan to labor legislation, child punishment, and whether women should wear slacks in public (39 percent of men said no, as did 49 percent of women). Such topics as the first use of nuclear arms, presidential popularity, national defense, and U.S. troop intervention in a troubled area of the world remain as pertinent today as they were then.

A number of the polls included here deal with foreign policy during the Cold War in the early 1950s. How did people respond to Soviet nuclear capability? How did they regard Russian intentions and the appropriate American response? How do you analyze the results of these polls? What do you think is the significance of rating responses by levels of education? In what ways are the questions "loaded"? How might the results of these polls influence American foreign policy? What do you think is significant about the Indochina poll? These polls show the challenge-and-response nature of the Cold War. How do you think Americans would respond today to these questions?

Polls also shed light on domestic issues. Consider the poll on professions for young men and women taken in 1950. What does it tell us about the attitudes of the pollster on appropriate careers for men and women? Why do you think both men and women had nearly identical views on this subject? How do you think people today would answer these questions? Would they be presented in the same way? Also observe the poll on women in politics. To what extent have attitudes on this issue changed in the intervening years?

Foreign Policy Polls

December 2, 1949—Atom Bomb

Now that Russia has the atom bomb, do you think another war is more likely or less likely?

More likely	45%
Less likely	28%
Will make no difference	17%
No opinion	10%

BY EDUCATION

College

More likely	36%	Will make no difference	23%
Less likely	35%	No opinion	6%

High School

More likely	44%	Will make no difference	19%
Less likely	28%	No opinion	9%

Grade School

More likely	50%	Will make no difference	12%
Less likely	26%	No opinion	12%

May 1, 1950—National Defense

Do you think United States Government spending on national defense should be increased, decreased, or remain about the same?

Increased	63%	Same	24%
Decreased	7%	No opinion	6%

September 18, 1953—Indochina

The United States is now sending war materials to help the French fight the Communists in Indochina. Would you approve or disapprove of sending United States soldiers to take part in the fighting there?

Approve	8%	Disapprove	85%
No opinion	7%		

January 11, 1950—Russia

As you hear and read about Russia these days, do you believe Russia is trying to build herself up to be the ruling power of the world—or is Russia just building up protection against being attacked in another war?

Rule the world	70%
Protect herself	18%
No opinion	12%

BY EDUCATION

College

Rule the world	73%	Protect herself	21%
No opinion	6%		

High School

Rule the world	72%	Protect herself	18%
No opinion	10%		

Grade School

Rule the world	67%	Protect herself	17%
No opinion	16%		

February 12, 1951—Atomic Warfare

If the United States gets into an all-out war with Russia, do you think we should drop atom bombs on Russia first—or do you think we should use the atom bomb only if it is used on us?

Drop A-bomb first	66%
Only if used on us	19%
No opinion	15%

The greatest difference was between men and women–72% of the men questioned favored our dropping the bomb first, compared to 61% of the women.

Source: George H. Gallup, *The Gallup Poll: Public Opinion, 1935–1971*, vol. 2 (New York: Random House, 1972). ©American Institute of Public Opinion.

Domestic Policy Polls

October 29, 1949—Women in Politics

If the party whose candidate you most often support nominated a woman for President of the United States, would you vote for her if she seemed qualified for the job?

Yes	48%	No	48%
No opinion	4%		

BY SEX

Men

Yes	45%	No	50%
No opinion	5%		

Women

Yes	51%	No	46%
No opinion	3%		

BY POLITICAL AFFILIATION

Democrats

Yes	50%	No	48%
No opinion	2%		

Republicans

Yes	46%	No	50%
No opinion	4%		

Would you vote for a woman for Vice President of the United States if she seemed qualified for the job?

Yes	53%	No	43%
No opinion	4%		

May 5, 1950—Most Important Problem

What do you think is the most important problem facing the entire country today?

War, threat of war	40%
Atomic bomb control	6%
Economic problems, living costs, inflation, taxes	15%
Strikes and labor troubles	4%
Corruption in government	3%
Unemployment	10%
Housing	3%
Communism	8%
Others	11%

July 12, 1950—Professions

Suppose a young man came to you and asked your advice about taking up a profession. Assuming that he was qualified to enter any of these professions, which one of them would you first recommend to him?

Doctor of medicine	29%	Government worker	6%
Engineer, builder	16%	Professor, teacher	5%
Business executive	8%	Banker	4%
Clergyman	8%	Dentist	4%
Lawyer	8%	Veterinarian	3%
None, don't know	9%		

July 15, 1950—Professions

Suppose a young girl came to you and asked your advice about taking up a profession. Assuming that she was qualified to enter any of these professions, which one of them would you first recommend?

CHOICE OF WOMEN

Nurse	33%	Actress	3%
Teacher	15%	Journalist	2%
Secretary	8%	Musician	2%
Social service worker	8%	Model	2%
Dietician	7%	Librarian	2%
Dressmaker	4%	Medical, dental technician	1%
Beautician	4%	Others	2%
Airline stewardess	3%	Don't know	4%

The views of men on this subject were nearly identical with those of women.

Source: George H. Gallup, *The Gallup Poll: Public Opinion, 1935–1971*, vol. 2 (New York: Random House, 1972). ©American Institute of Public Opinion.

President Truman needed France to balance Soviet strength in Europe, he was willing to provide economic aid that freed the French to use their own resources in the struggle. By 1954, the United States was paying over three-quarters of the cost of the war.

After Eisenhower took office, France's position deteriorated. Secretary of State Dulles was eager to assist the French. The chairman of the Joint Chiefs of Staff even contemplated using nuclear weapons. But Eisenhower refused to intervene directly. As a French fortress at Dien Bien Phu finally fell, an international conference in Geneva divided Vietnam along the 17th parallel, with elections promised in 1956 to unify the country and determine its political fate.

The Start of U.S. Involvement in Vietnam

The Geneva agreement created two Vietnams. Ho Chi Minh held power in the north, while in the south Premier Ngo Dinh Diem, a fierce anti-Communist, formed a separate government. Intent on taking France's place in Southeast Asia, the United States supported the Diem government

and refused to sign the Geneva pact. In the next few years, American aid increased and military advisers—675 by the time Ike left office—began to assist the South Vietnamese. The United States had taken its first steps toward direct involvement in a ruinous war halfway around the world that would escalate out of control.

John Kennedy's commitment to Cold War victory led him to expand the American role in the conflict. He had once called Vietnam the "cornerstone of the free world in Southeast Asia," and now resolved to resist the spread of communism. After the Bay of Pigs, Kennedy decided to provide more American assistance. By the end of 1963, the number of advisers had risen to more than 16,000.

Despite American backing, South Vietnamese leader Diem was rapidly losing support within his own country. Buddhist priests burned themselves alive in the capital of Saigon to dramatize his unpopularity. After receiving assurances that the United States would not object to an internal coup, South Vietnamese military leaders assassinated Diem and seized the government. Kennedy understood the importance of popular support for the South Viet-

In 1963, Buddhist priests in Vietnam burned themselves to death in Saigon to dramatize their opposition to the Diem government. Photographs in American newspapers horrified readers and created suspicion that South Vietnam was led by a corrupt and autocratic leader. (UPI/Corbis-Bettmann)

namese government if that country was to maintain its independence. But he was reluctant to withdraw and let the Vietnamese solve their own problems.

Lyndon Johnson shared the same reservations. He recognized the problems the United States faced, noting after an early briefing that he felt like a catfish that had "grabbed a big juicy worm with a right sharp hook in the middle of it." Soon after assuming the presidency, he reached a fundamen-

tal decision that guided policy for the next four years. South Vietnam was more unstable than ever after the assassination of Diem. Guerrillas, known as Viet Cong, challenged the regime, sometimes covertly, sometimes through the National Liberation Front, their political arm. Aided by Ho Chi Minh and the North Vietnamese, the insurgent Viet Cong slowly gained ground. Henry Cabot Lodge, the American ambassador to South Vietnam, told

Johnson that if he wanted to save that country, and indeed the whole region, he had to stand firm. "I am not going to lose Vietnam," Johnson replied. "I am not going to be the President who saw Southeast Asia go the way China went."

In the election campaign of 1964, Johnson posed as a man of peace. "We don't want our American boys to do the fighting for Asian boys," he declared. "We are not going to send American boys nine or ten thousand miles away from home to do what Asian boys ought to be doing for themselves." He criticized those who suggested moving in with American bombs. All the while, however, he was planning to escalate the American role.

Escalation

In August 1964, Johnson cleverly obtained congressional authorization for the war. North Vietnamese torpedo boats, he announced, had, without provocation, attacked American destroyers in the international waters of the Gulf of Tonkin, 30 miles from North Vietnam. Only later did it become clear that the American ships had violated the territorial waters of North Vietnam by assisting South Viet-

namese commando raids in offshore combat zones. With the details of the attack still unclear, Johnson used the episode to obtain from Congress a resolution giving him authority to "take all necessary measures to repel any armed attack against the forces of the United States and to prevent further aggression." It gave Johnson the leverage he sought. As he noted, it was "like grandma's nightshirt—it covered everything."

Military escalation began in earnest in February 1965, after Viet Cong forces killed 7 Americans and wounded 109 in an attack on an American base at Pleiku. Johnson responded by authorizing retaliatory bombing of North Vietnam to cut off the flow of supplies and to ease pressure on South Vietnam. He personally ratified all bombing decisions. The forces he commanded "can't even bomb an outhouse without my approval," he boasted. A few months later, the president sent American ground troops into action. This marked the crucial turning point in the Americanization of the Vietnam War. Only 25,000 American soldiers were in Vietnam at the start of 1965. By the end of the year there were 184,000. The number swelled to 385,000 in 1966, to 485,000 in 1967, and to 543,000 in 1968.

Napalm, a jellylike chemical dropped by American planes, stuck to people as it burned. In this picture, widely circulated throughout the world, a small girl whose skin was seared off by napalm tries unsuccessfully to escape the ravages of war. (AP/Wide World Photos)

American forces became direct participants in the fight to prop up a dictatorial regime in faraway South Vietnam. Although a somewhat more effective government headed by Nguyen Van Thieu and Nguyen Cao Ky was finally established, the level of violence increased. Saturation bombing of North Vietnam continued. Fragmentation bombs, killing and maiming countless civilians, and napalm, which seared off human flesh, were used extensively. Similar destruction wracked South Vietnam.

Protesting the War

Americans began to protest their involvement in the war. As escalation began, 82 percent of the public felt that American forces should stay in Vietnam until the Communist elements withdrew. Then students began to question basic Cold War assumptions, first espoused by Truman, about the need to battle communism around the globe. The first antiwar teach-in took place in March 1965 at the University of Michigan. Others soon followed. Initially, both supporters and opponents of the war appeared at the teach-ins, but soon the sessions became more like antiwar rallies than instructional affairs. Boxer Muhammad Ali legitimated draft resistance when he declared, "I ain't got no quarrel with them Viet Cong," and refused military induction. Working through Students for a Democratic Society (SDS) and other organizations, radical activists campaigned against the draft, attacked ROTC units on campus, and sought to discredit firms that produced the destructive tools of war (see Chapter 29 for a full discussion of student activism). "Make love, not war," students proclaimed.

The antiwar movement expanded. Women Strike for Peace, the most forceful women's antiwar organization, mobilized support by saying, "Stop! Don't drench the jungles of Asia with the blood of our sons. Don't force our sons to kill women and children whose only crime is to live in a country ripped by civil war." Students became even more shrill. "Hey, hey, LBJ. How many kids did you kill today?" they chanted. In 1967, some 300,000 people marched in New York City. In Washington, D.C., 100,000 tried to close down the Pentagon.

Working-class and middle-class Americans began to sour on the war at the time of the Tet offensive, in early 1968. The North Vietnamese

mounted a massive attack on provincial capitals and district towns in South Vietnam. In Saigon, they struck the American embassy, Tan Son Nhut air base, and the presidential palace. Though beaten back, they won a psychological victory. American

The Vietnam War

This map shows the major campaigns of the Vietnam War. The North Vietnamese Tet offensive of early 1968, pictured with red arrows, turned the tide against U.S. participation in the war and led to peace talks. The U.S. invasion of Cambodia in 1970, pictured with blue arrows, provoked serious opposition.

audiences watched the fighting on television, as they had for several years. In the past, they had seen images of burning huts and wounded soldiers each evening. During the Tet offensive, American TV networks showed scenes of a kind never screened before. One such clip, from NBC News, appears here in still photograph form. Viewers who watched the television clip saw the corpse drop to the ground, blood spouting from his head. As they gazed at such graphic representations of death and destruction, many Americans wondered about their nation's purposes and actions, and began to ask whether the war could be won.

When Richard Nixon assumed office in 1969, he understood the need to heal the rifts that split American society. A lonely, aloof man who had gained political prominence as one of the nation's most aggressive anti-Communists, he now promised to bring the nation together. He gave top priority to extricating the United States from Vietnam while still seeking a way to win the war. To that end, he announced the Nixon Doctrine, which asserted that the United States would aid friends and allies but would not undertake the full burden of troop defense. The policy of Vietnamization entailed removing American forces and replacing them with Vietnamese ones. At the same time, Americans launched ferocious air attacks on North Vietnam. "Let's blow the hell out of them," Nixon instructed the Joint Chiefs of Staff. Between 1968 and 1972, American troop strength dropped from 543,000 to 39,000, and the reduction won political support for Nixon at home. Yet as the transition occurred, the South Vietnamese steadily lost ground to the Viet Cong.

War protests multiplied in 1969 and 1970. In November 1969, as a massive protest demonstration took place in Washington, D.C., stories surfaced about a horrifying massacre of civilians in Vietnam the year before. My Lai, a small village in South Vietnam, was allegedly harboring 250 members of the Viet Cong. An American infantry company was helicoptered in to clear out the village. C Company had already taken heavy combat losses as it prepared to confront the enemy soldiers. Instead of troops, it found women, children, and old men. Perhaps hardened to the random destruction already wrought by the American military, perhaps concerned with the sometimes fuzzy distinction between combatants and civilians in a guerrilla war, the American forces lost control and mowed down the civilians in cold blood. Private

In this picture, General Loan, the chief of the South Vietnamese National Police, looks at a Viet Cong prisoner, lifts his gun, and calmly blows out the captive's brains. This prizewinning photograph captured the horror of the war for many Americans. (AP/Wide World Photos)

When Ohio National Guardsmen fired on a crowd of antiwar demonstrators and killed four students, even prowar Americans were shocked. This photograph shows the grief and outrage of others who survived the savage shooting of innocent bystanders. (Valley Daily News, Tarantum, Pennsylvania)

Paul Meadlo, one of the soldiers involved in the massacre, later recalled:

> We huddled them up. We made them squat down.... I poured about four clips into the group.... The mothers was hugging their children.... Well, we kept right on firing. They was waving their arms and begging.... I still dream about it. About the women and children in my sleep. Some days ... some nights, I can't even sleep.

Much as Nixon wanted to defuse opposition to the war, he was determined not to lose the struggle either. Realizing that the Vietnamese relied on supplies funneled through Cambodia, Nixon announced in mid-1970 that American and Vietnamese troops were invading that country to clear out Communist enclaves there. The United States, he said, would not stand by as a "pitiful helpless giant" when there were actions it could take to stem the Communist advance.

Nixon's invasion of Cambodia brought renewed demonstrations on college campuses, some with tragic results. At Kent State University in Ohio, the response was fierce. The day after the president announced his moves, disgruntled students gathered downtown. Worried about the crowd, the local police called in sheriff's deputies to disperse the students. The next evening, groups of students collected on the college grounds. Assembling around the ROTC building, they began throwing firecrackers and rocks at the structure, which had become a hated symbol of the war. Then they set it on fire and watched it burn to the ground.

The governor of Ohio ordered the National Guard to the university. Tension grew and finally the situation exploded. The Guardsmen watched as students gathered on campus. Though most were so far away they could not have reached the troops, the soldiers reacted by firing without provocation on the students. When the shooting stopped, four students lay dead, nine wounded. Two of the dead had been demonstrators, who were more than 250 feet away when shot. The other two were innocent bystanders, almost 400 feet from the troops.

Students around the country, as well as other Americans, were outraged by the attack. Many

Major Events of the Cold War		
Year	Event	Effect
1946	Winston Churchill's "Iron Curtain" speech	First Western "declaration" of the Cold War
	George F. Kennan's long telegram	Spoke of Soviet insecurity and the need for containment
1947	George F. Kennan's article signed "Mr. X"	Elaborated on arguments in the telegram
	Truman Doctrine	Provided economic and military aid to Greece and Turkey
	Federal Employee Loyalty Program	Sought to root out subversion in the U.S. government
	HUAC investigation of the motion picture industry	Sought to expose Communist influences in the movies
1948	Marshall Plan	Provided massive American economic aid in rebuilding postwar Europe
	Berlin airlift	Brought in supplies when USSR closed off land access to the divided city
1949	NATO	Created a military alliance to withstand a possible Soviet attack
	First Soviet atomic bomb	Ended the American nuclear monopoly
	Communist victory in China	Made Americans fear the worldwide spread of communism
1950	Conviction of Alger Hiss	Seemed to bear out Communist danger at home
	Joseph McCarthy's first charges	Launched aggressive anti-Communist campaign in the United States
	NSC-68	Called for vigilance and increased military spending to counter the Communist threat
	Outbreak of the Korean War	North Korean invasion of South Korea viewed as part of Soviet conspiracy
1953	Armistice in Korea	Brought little change after years of bitter fighting
1954	Vietnamese victory over French at Dien Bien Phu	Early triumph for nationalism in Southeast Asia
	Army-McCarthy hearings	Brought downfall of Joseph McCarthy
1961	Invasion at the Bay of Pigs	Showed U.S. efforts to check the spread of communism in the Americas
1962	Cuban Missile Crisis	Showed U.S. determination to resist Soviet intrusion in Cuba
1973	Cease-fire in Vietnam	Allowed the United States to withdraw from Vietnam
1975	North Vietnamese victory in Vietnam	Ended the war and allowed for unification of Vietnam

were equally disturbed about a similar attack at Jackson State University in Mississippi. As students there returned to their dormitories one evening, they saw police officers and National Guardsmen responding to a bonfire. A few taunted the law officers. The troops responded without warning by firing 460 rounds of automatic weapon fire into a women's dormitory. When the gunfire ceased, two people were dead, more wounded. The dead, however, were black students at a black institution, and white America paid less attention to this attack.

In 1971, the Vietnam War made major headlines once more when the *New York Times* began publishing a secret Department of Defense account of American involvement. The so-called Pentagon Papers, leaked by Daniel Ellsberg, a defense analyst, gave Americans a firsthand look at the fabrications and faulty assumptions that had guided the steady expansion of the struggle. Even though the study stopped with the Johnson years, the Nixon administration was furious and tried, without success, to halt publication of the series.

Peace and Its Consequences

Vietnam remained a political football as Nixon ran for reelection in 1972. Negotiations aimed at a settlement were under way, and just days before the election, Secretary of State Henry Kissinger announced, "Peace is at hand." When South Vietnam seemed to balk at the proposed settlement, however, the administration responded with the most intensive bombing campaign of the war. Hanoi, the capital of North Vietnam, was hit hard; then the North Vietnamese harbors were mined. Only in the new year was a cease-fire finally signed.

The conflict in Vietnam lingered on into the spring of 1975. When at last the North Vietnamese consolidated their control over the entire country, Gerald Ford, Nixon's successor as president, called for another $1 billion in aid, even as the South Vietnamese were abandoning arms and supplies in chaotic retreat. Congress refused to authorize further funding, leaving the crumbling government of South Vietnam to fend for itself. Republicans hailed Kissinger for having finally freed the United States from the Southeast Asian quagmire. Antiwar critics condemned him for remaining involved for so long. The *New Republic* wryly observed that Kissinger brought peace to Vietnam in the same way Napoleon brought peace to Europe: by losing.

The long conflict had enormous consequences for American society. In foreign policy, disillusionment with the war undermined assumptions about America's role in world affairs. In human terms, the costs were immense. In the longest war in its history, the United States lost almost 58,000 men, with far more wounded or maimed. Blacks and Chicanos suffered more than whites, since they were disproportionately represented in combat units. Many minority men saw military service as a means of advancement. In 1965, 24 percent of all soldiers killed in Vietnam were African American—a figure far higher than their percentage of the population as a whole.

Financially, the nation spent over $150 billion on the unsuccessful war. Domestic reform slowed, then stopped. Cynicism about the government increased. American society was deeply divided. Only time would heal the wounds.

Post-Vietnam Détente

If the Republicans' Vietnam policy was a questionable success, accomplishments were impressive in other areas. Nixon, the consummate Red-baiter of the past, was able to deal imaginatively and successfully with the major Communist powers. In so doing, he reversed the direction of American policy since the Second World War.

Nixon's most dramatic step was opening formal relations with the People's Republic of China. In the two decades since Mao Zedong's victory in the Chinese revolution in 1949, the United States had never recognized the Communist government on the mainland, regarding Jiang Jieshi's rump command on Taiwan as the rightful government of the Chinese people. In 1971, with an eye on the forthcoming political campaign, the administration began

Nixon shifted the course of Chinese-U.S. relations by his dramatic visit to the People's Republic. He met Chinese officials for the first time, visited the Great Wall and other sites, and then reported back enthusiastically to the American people. (Sygma)

TIMELINE

1945	Yalta Conference
	Roosevelt dies; Harry Truman becomes president
	Potsdam Conference
1946	American plan for control of atomic energy fails
	Atomic Energy Act
	Iran crisis
	Churchill's "Iron Curtain" speech
1947	Truman Doctrine
	Federal Employee Loyalty Program
	House Un-American Activities Committee (HUAC) investigates the movie industry
1948	Marshall Plan launched
	Berlin airlift
	Israel created by the United Nations
	Hiss-Chambers case
	Truman elected president
1949	Soviet Union tests atomic bomb
	North Atlantic Treaty Organization (NATO) established
	George Orwell, *1984*
	Mao Zedong's forces win Chinese civil war; Jiang Jieshi flees to Taiwan
1950	Truman authorizes development of the hydrogen bomb
	Alger Hiss convicted
	Joseph McCarthy's Wheeling (W. Va.) speech on subversion
	NSC-68
	McCarran Internal Security Act
1950–1953	Korean War
1951	Japanese-American treaty
	Dennis v. *United States*
1952	Dwight D. Eisenhower elected president
	McCarthy heads Senate Permanent Investigations Subcommittee
1953	Stalin dies; Khrushchev consolidates power
	East Germans stage anti-Soviet demonstrations
	Shah of Iran returns to power in CIA-supported coup

1954	Fall of Dien Bien Phu ends French control of Indochina
	Geneva Conference
	Guatemalan government overthrown with CIA help
	Mao's forces shell Quemoy and Matsu
	Army-McCarthy hearings
1956	Suez incident
	Hungarian "freedom fighters" suppressed
	Eisenhower reelected
1957	Russians launch *Sputnik* satellite
1958	U.S. troops sent to support Lebanese government
1959	Castro deposes Batista in Cuba
1960	John F. Kennedy elected president
1961	Bay of Pigs invasion fails
	Khrushchev and Kennedy meet in Berlin
	Berlin Wall constructed
1962	Cuban missile crisis
1963	Buddhist demonstrations in Vietnam
	President Diem assassinated in Vietnam
	Kennedy assassinated; Lyndon B. Johnson becomes president
1964	Gulf of Tonkin resolution
	Johnson reelected
1965	Vietnam conflict escalates
	Marines sent to Dominican Republic
1967–1968	Antiwar demonstrations
1968	Tet offensive in Vietnam
	Richard Nixon elected president
	My Lai incident
1969	Nixon Doctrine announced
	Moratorium against the Vietnam War
	SALT talks begin
1970	U.S. invasion of Cambodia
	Shootings at Kent State and Jackson State universities
1971	*New York Times* publishes the Pentagon Papers
1972	Nixon visits People's Republic of China and Soviet Union
	Nixon reelected
	SALT I treaty on nuclear arms
1973	Vietnam cease-fire agreement
1975	South Vietnam falls to the Communists; end of the Vietnam War

softening its rigid stance. After the Chinese invited an American table tennis team to visit the mainland, the United States eased some trading restrictions. Then Nixon announced that he intended to visit China the following year. He suspected that he could use Chinese friendship as a bargaining chip when he dealt with the Soviet Union. He acknowledged what most nations already knew: Communism was not monolithic. He believed that he could open a dialogue with the Chinese Communists without political harm, for he had long ago established his anti-Communist credentials. Finally, he recognized that the press and television coverage of a dramatic trip could boost his image.

Nixon went to China in February 1972. He met with Chinese leaders Mao Zedong and Zou Enlai (Chou En-lai), talked about international problems, exchanged toasts, and saw some of the major sights. Wherever he went, American television cameras followed, helping introduce to the American public a nation about which it knew little. Though formal relations were not yet restored, détente between the two countries had begun.

Seeking to play one Communist state against the other, Nixon also visited Russia, where he was likewise warmly welcomed. At a cordial summit meeting, the president and Soviet premier Leonid Brezhnev signed the first Strategic Arms Limitation Treaty (SALT I). In addition to this move to limit missile stockpiles, they agreed to work together in space and eased long-standing restrictions on trade. Business applauded the new approach, and most Americans approved of détente.

Nixon's policy of détente resulted in improved relations with the Soviet Union. Here he and Soviet leader Leonid Brezhnev toast one another at the signing of the Strategic Arms Limitation Treaty. (UPI/Corbis-Bettmann)

When Gerald Ford assumed office, he followed the policies begun under Nixon, even if he ceased calling the approach détente. He continued the strategic arms limitation talks that provided hope for eventual nuclear disarmament, and culminated in the even more comprehensive SALT II agreement, signed but never ratified during Jimmy Carter's presidency.

*C*onclusion

The Cold War in Perspective

The Cold War had a powerful impact on American society in the decades following World War II. Tensions grew throughout the postwar years as the United States and the Soviet Union found themselves engaged in a bitter standoff. Altogether, this struggle dominated international relations for nearly 50 years.

What caused the Cold War? Historians have long differed over the question of where responsibility should be placed. In the early years after the Second World War,

policy makers and commentators justified the American stance as a bold and courageous effort to meet the Communist threat. Later, particularly in the 1960s, as the war
in Vietnam eroded confidence in American foreign policy, revisionist historians began
to argue that American actions were misguided, insensitive to Soviet needs, and at
least partially responsible for escalating friction. As with most historical questions,
there are no easy answers, but both sides must be weighed.

The Cold War stemmed from a competition for international influence between
the two great world powers. After World War II, the U.S. goal was to exercise economic
and political leadership in the world and thus to institute capitalist economies and
democratic political institutions throughout Europe and in nations emerging from
colonial rule. But these goals put the United States on a collision course with nations,
such as the Soviet Union, that had a different vision of what the postwar world should
be like and with anticolonial movements in emerging countries around the globe.
Perceiving threats from the Soviet Union, China, and other Communist countries, the
United States clung to its deep-rooted sense of mission and embarked on an increasingly aggressive effort at containment, culminating in the ill-fated war in Vietnam.
Here, as elsewhere, policy makers followed the advice of George Kennan as they
sought to preserve and extend America's influence. The Cold War, with its profound
effects at home and abroad, was the unfortunate result.

Recommended Reading

Background and Development of the Cold War

Stephen E. Ambrose, *Rise to Globalism: American Foreign Policy Since 1938*, 3d rev. ed. (1983); Thomas H. Etzold and John Lewis Gaddis, *Containment: Documents on American Policy and Strategy, 1945–1950* (1978); John Lewis Gaddis, *The Long Peace: Inquiries into the History of the Cold War* (1987), *Strategies of Containment: A Critical Appraisal of Postwar American National Security Policy* (1982), and *The United States and the Origins of the Cold War, 1941–1947* (1972); Michael J. Hogan, *The Marshall Plan: America, Britain, and the Reconstruction of Western Europe* (1987); Walter LaFeber, *America, Russia, and the Cold War, 1945–1990*, 7th ed. (1993); Melvyn P. Leffler, *A Preponderance of Power: National Security, the Truman Administration, and the Cold War* (1992); Ralph B. Levering, *The Cold War: A Post–Cold War History* (1994); Thomas J. McCormick, *America's Half Century: United States Foreign Policy in the Cold War* (1992); Thomas G. Patterson, *Meeting the Communist Threat: Truman to Reagan* (1988) and *On Every Front: The Making of the Cold War* (1979); Daniel Yergin, *Shattered Peace: The Origins of the Cold War and the National Security State* (1977).

Foreign Policy in the Eisenhower Years

H. W. Brands, Jr., *Cold Warriors: Eisenhower's Generation and American Foreign Policy* (1988); Robert A. Divine, *Eisenhower and the Cold War* (1981) and *The Sputnik Challenge: Eisenhower's Response to the Soviet Satellite* (1993); Townsend Hoopes, *The Devil and John Foster Dulles* (1973).

The Korean War

Joseph C. Goulden, *Korea: The Untold Story of the War* (1982); Burton I. Kaufman, *The Korean War: Challenges in Crisis, Credibility, and Command* (1986); David Rees, *Korea: The Limited War* (1964).

The Nuclear Threat

Paul Boyer, *By the Bomb's Early Light: American Thought and Culture at the Dawn of the Atomic Age* (1985); McGeorge Bundy, *Danger and Survival: Choices About the Bomb in the First Fifty Years* (1988); Gregg Herken, *Counsels of War* (1985); Richard G. Hewlett and Francis Duncan, *Atomic Shield: Volume II: A History of the United States Atomic Energy Commission, 1947–1952* (1972); Richard G. Hewlett and Jack M. Holl, *Atoms for Peace and War: Eisenhower and the Atomic Energy Commission, 1953–1961* (1989); Fred Kaplan, *The Wizards of Armageddon* (1983); John Newhouse, *War and Peace in the Nuclear Age* (1989); Spencer R. Weart, *Nuclear Fear: A History of Images* (1988); Allan M. Winkler, *Life Under a Cloud: American Anxiety About the Atom* (1993); Herbert F. York, *The Advisors: Oppenheimer, Teller, and the Superbomb* (1976).

The Anti-Communist Crusade

David Caute, *The Great Fear: The Anti-Communist Purge Under Truman and Eisenhower* (1978); Richard Freeland, *The Truman Doctrine and the Origins of McCarthyism: Foreign Policy, Domestic Politics, and Internal Security, 1946–1948* (1971); Robert Griffith, *The Politics of Fear: Joseph*

R. McCarthy and the Senate (1970); David M. Oshinsky, *A Conspiracy So Immense: The World of Joe McCarthy* (1983); Ronald Radash and Joyce Milton, *The Rosenberg File: A Search for Truth* (1984); Thomas C. Reeves, *The Life and Times of Joe McCarthy: A Biography* (1982); Richard H. Rovere, *Senator Joe McCarthy* (1960); Ellen W. Schrecker, *No Ivory Tower: McCarthyism and the Universities* (1986) and *The Age of McCarthyism: A Brief History with Documents* (1994); Allen Weinstein, *Perjury: The Hiss-Chambers Case* (1978).

The War in Vietnam

Christian G. Appy, *Working-Class War: American Combat Soldiers and Vietnam* (1993); Frances FitzGerald, *Fire in the Lake: The Vietnamese and the Americans in Vietnam* (1972); David Halberstam, *The Best and the Brightest* (1972); Le Ly Hayslip, *When Heaven and Earth Changed Places* (1989); George C. Herring, *America's Longest War: The United States and Vietnam, 1950–1975* (1979) and *LBJ and Vietnam: A Dif-ferent Kind of War* (1994); Stanley Karnow, *Vietnam: A History: The First Complete Account of Vietnam at War* (1983); Jeffrey P. Kimball, ed., *To Reason Why: The Debate about the Causes of U.S. Involvement in the Vietnam War* (1990); Ron Kovic, *Born on the Fourth of July* (memoir, 1976); Guenter Lewy, *America in Vietnam* (1978); Robert S. McNamara, *In Retrospect* (1995); Al Santoli, *Everything We Had: An Oral History of the Vietnam War by Thirty-three American Soldiers Who Fought It* (1981); Neil Sheehan, *A Bright Shining Lie: John Paul Vann and America in Vietnam* (1988).

Novels

John M. Del Vecchio, *The 13th Valley* (1982); Pat Frank, *Alas, Babylon* (1959); Norman Mailer, *The Armies of the Night* (history as a novel, 1968); James A. Michener, *The Bridges at Toko-ri* (1953); Walter M. Miller, Jr., *A Canticle for Leibowitz* (1959); Tim O'Brien, *Going After Cacciato* (1978); Nevil Shute, *On the Beach* (1957); Robert Stone, *Dog Soldiers* (1974).

High Water and Ebb Tide of the Liberal State

*P*aul Cowan was an idealist in the 1960s. Like many students who came of age in these years, he believed in the possibility of social change and plunged into the struggle for liberal reform. He shared the hopes and dreams of other members of his generation, who felt that their government could make a difference in people's lives.

Cowan's commitment had developed slowly. He was a child of the 1950s, when most Americans were caught up in the consumer culture and paid little attention to the problems of people less fortunate than themselves. His grandfather had sold used cement bags in Chicago, but his father had become an executive at CBS television, and Cowan grew up in comfortable surroundings. He graduated from the Choate School (where John Kennedy had gone) in 1958, and then from Harvard University (where Kennedy had also been a student) in 1963.

When he entered college, Cowan was interested in politically conscious writers like John Dos Passos, John Steinbeck, and James Agee, and folk singers like Pete Seeger and Woody Guthrie. They offered him entrance, he later recalled, into a "nation that seemed to be filled with energy and decency," one that lurked "beneath the dull, conformist facade of the Eisenhower years." While at Harvard, he was excited by antinuclear campaigns in New England and civil rights demonstrations in the South.

After college, he made good on his commitment to civil rights by going to Mississippi to work in the Summer Freedom Project of 1964. He was inspired by the example of John Kennedy, the liberal president whose administration promised "a new kind of politics" that could make the nation, and the world, a better place. During that summer, he wrote, "it was possible to believe that by changing ourselves we could change, and redeem, our America."

The Peace Corps came next. Paul and his wife Rachel were convinced that this organization, the idea of the young president, "really was a unique government agency, permanently protected by the lingering magic of John F. Kennedy's name." They were assigned to the city of Guayaquil, in Ecuador, in South America. Their task was to serve as mediators between administrators of the city hall and residents of the slums. They wanted to try to raise the standard of living by encouraging local governments to provide basic services such as garbage disposal and clean water.

But the work proved more frustrating than they had imagined. They bristled at the restrictions imposed by the Peace Corps bureaucracy. They despaired at the inadequate resources local government officials had to accomplish their aims. They wondered if they were simply new imperialists, trying to impose their values on others who had priorities of their own. "From the day we moved into the *barrio*," Cowan later recalled, "the question we were most frequently asked by the people we were supposed to be organizing was whether we would leave them our clothes when we returned to the States."

Cowan came home disillusioned. "I saw that even the liberals I had wanted to emulate, men who seemed to be devoting their lives to fighting injustice, were unable to accept people from alien cultures on any terms but their own." He called his account of his own odyssey *The Making of an Un-American*.

The United States was comfortable and confident as the 1960s began. The basic consensus about the responsibility of the government to help those who could not help themselves eroded in the turbulent years that followed. (George Giusti, "Civilization is a method of living, an attitude of equal respect for all men," Jane Addams, 1993. From the series Great Ideas of Western Man, 1955/National Museum of American Art, Washington, DC/Art Resource, New York)

*P*aul Cowan's passage through the 1960s mirrored the passage of American society as a whole. Millions of Americans shared his views as the period began. Mostly comfortable and confident, they supported the liberal agenda advanced by the Democratic party of John Kennedy and Lyndon Johnson. They endorsed the proposition that the government had responsibility for the welfare of all its citizens and accepted the need for a more active governmental role to help those who were unable to help themselves. That commitment lay behind the legislative achievements of the "Great Society," the last wave of twentieth-century reform that built upon the gains of the Progressive era and the New Deal years before.

Then political reaction set in, as the nation was torn apart by the ravages of the Vietnam War. Liberal assumptions eroded, as conservatives argued that an activist approach was responsible for the chaos consuming the country. Republicans who assumed power at the end of the 1960s accepted the basic outlines of the welfare state but rejected many of the liberal initiatives of Democratic administrations as expensive failures. Under Richard Nixon and Gerald Ford, Republicans capitalized on disillusionment with federal policy and crafted a new consensus that kept them in the White House for most of the next decade and a half. The presidency of Democrat Jimmy Carter was unable to reverse the conservative shift. Liberals despaired as they watched the destruction of their dreams.

This chapter describes both the climax of twentieth-century liberalism and its subsequent decline. It focuses on the effort of the government, begun in the New Deal of Franklin Roosevelt, to help those caught short by the advances of industrial capitalism. It examines first the initiatives in the 1940s and 1950s and early 1960s to provide necessary assistance to the less fortunate members of American society, then the efforts in the late 1960s and 1970s to limit such aid. In pondering the possibilities of reform, this chapter outlines the various attempts to devise an effective political response to the major structural changes in the post–World War II economy outlined in Chapter 26. It explores the debates that took place and the shifts that occurred as the political system struggled to cope with the problems of wholesale economic transformation and to maintain the promise of American life.

The Origins of the Welfare State

The modern American welfare state originated in the New Deal of FDR. Roosevelt's efforts to deal with the ravages of the Great Depression and protect Americans from the problems stemming from industrial capitalism (see Chapter 24) provided the basis for subsequent reform. Harry Truman's Fair Deal built squarely on Roosevelt's New Deal, though Truman often found himself stymied by a conservative Congress. His Republican successor, Dwight Eisenhower, sought to scale down spending but made no effort to roll back the most important initiatives of the welfare state. Actions taken in the post–World War II years

provided the groundwork for the major reforms of the 1960s.

Truman's Approach

Like Roosevelt, Harry Truman believed that the federal government had the responsibility for ensuring the social welfare of all Americans. He shared his predecessor's commitment to assisting less comfortable inhabitants of the country in a systematic, rational way. Truman wanted his administration to embrace and act upon a series of carefully defined social and economic goals. Immediate problems of reconversion had to be resolved first, to be sure. He had to deal with

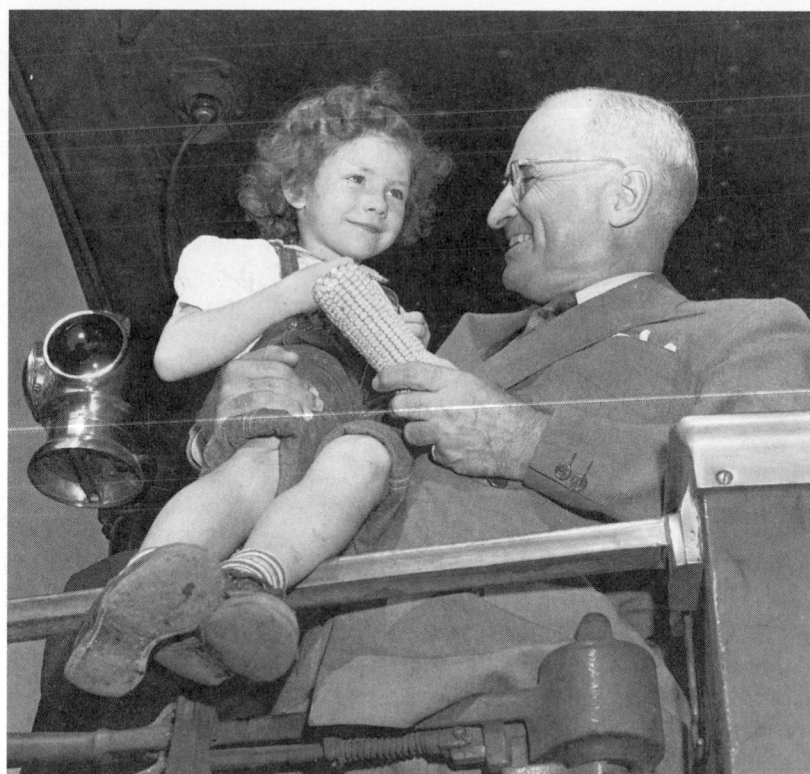

Truman was a down-to-earth politician who was most comfortable when he could appeal informally to his constituents. His direct approach, however, sometimes got him into trouble. (UPI/Corbis-Bettmann)

demands for the return of servicemen, fears of inflation, and the consequences of labor unrest. But even as he worked (not always successfully) to handle these issues, Truman outlined his vision of the welfare state.

Truman took the same feisty approach to public policy that characterized his conduct of foreign affairs (see Chapter 27). He stated his position clearly and simply, often in black and white terms. Persuaded that plain speaking was the best approach, he seldom hesitated to let others know exactly where he stood. He attacked his political enemies vigorously when they resisted his initiatives and often took his case to the American people in an effort to gain support for his goals. He was, in many ways, an old-style Democratic politician, schooled and supported by Missouri's Democratic machine, who hoped to use his authority to benefit the middle-class and working-class Americans who made up his political base.

Less than a week after the end of World War II, Truman called on Congress to pass a 21-point program that would produce stability and security in the postwar era. He wanted full-employment legislation, a higher minimum wage, greater unemployment compensation, and housing assistance. During the next ten weeks, Truman sent blueprints of further proposals to Congress, including health insurance and atomic energy legislation. But this liberal program soon ran into fierce political opposition.

The debate surrounding the Employment Act of 1946 hinted at the fate of Truman's proposals. This measure was a deliberate effort to apply the theory of English economist John Maynard Keynes to preserve economic equilibrium and prevent depression. Keynes had argued a decade earlier that massive spending was necessary to extricate a nation from depression (see Chapter 24). The money spent during World War II caused the economy to respond precisely as Keynes had predicted. Now economists wanted to institutionalize his ideas to forestall further problems. The initial bill, which enjoyed the strong support of labor, committed the government to maintaining full employment by monitoring the economy and taking remedial action in case of decline. These actions included tax cuts and spending programs to stimulate the economy and reduce unemployment.

Liberals and labor leaders hailed the measure, but business groups such as the National Association of Manufacturers condemned it. They claimed that government intervention would undermine free enterprise and move the United States one step closer to socialism. Responding to the business community, Congress cut the proposal to bits. As finally passed, the act created a Council of Economic Advisers to make recommendations to the president, who was to report annually to Congress and the nation on the state of the economy. But it stopped short of committing the government to using fiscal tools to maintain full employment when economic indicators turned downward. The act was only a modest continuation of New Deal attempts at economic planning.

Truman's Struggle with a Conservative Congress

As the midterm elections of 1946 approached, Truman and his supporters knew they were vulnerable. Many Democrats still pined for FDR, and when they questioned what Roosevelt would have done had he been alive, the standard retort was, "I wonder what Truman would do if he were alive." Truman appeared to be a petty, bungling administrator and became the butt of countless political jokes. His support dropped from 87 percent of those polled after he assumed the presidency to 32 percent in November 1946. Gleeful Republicans asked the voters, "Had enough?"

The voters answered that they had. Republicans won majorities in both houses of Congress for the first time since the 1928 elections, and gained a majority of the governorships as well. In Atlantic City, New Jersey, a Republican candidate for justice of the peace who had died a week before the election was victorious in the sweep.

After the 1946 elections, Truman faced an unsympathetic 80th Congress. Republicans and conservative Democrats, dominating both houses, planned to reverse the liberal policies of the Roo-

sevelt years. Hoping to reestablish congressional authority and cut the power of the executive branch, they insisted on less government intervention in the business world and in private life. Their goals included tax reduction and curtailment of the privileged position they felt labor had come to enjoy.

When the new Congress met, it moved to slash federal spending and reduce taxes. Robert A. Taft, one of the Republican leaders in the Senate, believed that $5 to $6 billion could be cut to bring the overall budget down to $30 billion. In 1947, Congress twice passed tax-cut measures. Both times Truman vetoed them, but in 1948, another election year, Congress overrode the veto.

Congress also struck at Democratic labor policies. Angry at the gains won by labor in the 1930s and 1940s, Republicans wanted to check unions and to circumscribe their right to engage in the kind of disruptive strikes that had occurred immediately after the war. Early in Truman's presidency, Congress had passed a bill requiring notice for strikes as well as a cooling-off period if a strike occurred. Truman had vetoed that measure. But in 1947, commanding more votes, the Republicans passed the Taft-Hartley Act, which intended to limit the power of unions by restricting the weapons they could employ. Revising the Wagner Act of 1935, the legislation spelled out unfair labor practices (such as preventing nonunion workers from working if they wished) and outlawed the closed shop whereby an employee had to join a union before getting a job. The law likewise allowed states to prohibit the union shop, which forced workers to join the union after they had been hired. It also gave the president the right to call for an 80-day cooling-off period in strikes affecting national security and required union officials to sign non-Communist oaths in order to use governmental machinery designed to protect their rights.

Understandably, union leaders and members were furious. They argued vigorously that the measure eliminated many of their hard-won rights and left labor-management relations like they had been in pre–New Deal days. Vetoing the measure, Truman claimed that it was unworkable and unfair and went on nationwide radio to seek public approval. In the process he regained some of the support he had earlier lost when he had sought to force strikers to go back to work in the immediate postwar period. Congress, however, passed the Taft-Hartley measure over the president's veto.

The Fair Deal and Its Fate

In 1948, Truman wanted a chance to consolidate a liberal program and decided to seek the presidency in his own right. He understood that some people considered him an accidental occupant of the White House. He knew that some Democrats wanted to replace him with Dwight Eisenhower or Supreme Court Justice William O. Douglas or anyone else. That effort failed, but Truman was left with what most people thought was a worthless nomination. Not only was his own popularity waning, but the Democratic party itself seemed to be falling apart.

The civil rights issue—aimed at securing rights for African Americans—split the Democrats. Truman hoped to straddle the issue, at least until after the election, to avoid alienating the South. When liberals defeated a moderate platform proposal and pressed for a stronger stand on black civil rights, angry delegates from Mississippi and Alabama stormed out of the convention. They later formed the States' Rights, or Dixiecrat, party. At their own convention, delegates from 13 states nominated Governor J. Strom Thurmond of South Carolina as their presidential candidate and affirmed their support for continued racial segregation.

Meanwhile, Henry A. Wallace, for seven years secretary of agriculture, then vice president during Roosevelt's third term and secretary of commerce after that, mounted his own challenge. Truman had fired Wallace from his cabinet for supporting a more temperate approach to the Soviet Union. Now Wallace became the presidential candidate of the Progressive party. Initially, he attracted widespread liberal interest because of his moderate position on Soviet-American affairs, his promotion of desegregation, and his promise to nationalize the railroads and major industries. But as Communists and "fellow travelers" appeared active in his organization, other support dropped off.

In that fragmented state, facing the first real third-party challenges since 1912, the Democrats

took on the Republicans, who coveted the White House after 16 years out of power. Once again the GOP nominated New York Governor Thomas E. Dewey, their unsuccessful candidate in 1944. Stiff and egocentric, Dewey was hardly a charismatic figure. Still, the polls uniformly picked the Republicans to win. Dewey saw little value in brawling with his opponent and campaigned, in the words of one commentator, "with the humorless calculation of a Certified Public Accountant in pursuit of the Holy Grail."

Truman, as the underdog, conducted a two-fisted campaign. He appealed to ordinary Americans as an unpretentious man engaged in an uphill fight. Believing that everyone was against him but the people, he addressed Americans in familiar language. He called the Republicans a "bunch of old mossbacks" out to destroy the New Deal. He attacked the "do nothing" 80th Congress, which he had called into special session in 1948 with instructions to live up to the Republican platform. Predictably, the legislators failed, providing Truman with handy ammunition. Speaking without a prepared text in his choppy, aggressive style, he warmed to crowds, and they warmed to him. "Give 'em hell, Harry," they yelled. "Pour it on." He did.

All the polls predicted a Republican victory. But the pollsters were wrong. On election day, despite the bold headline "Dewey Defeats Truman" in the *Chicago Daily Tribune*, the incumbent president scored one of the most unexpected political upsets in American history, winning 303–189 in the Electoral College. Democrats also swept both houses of Congress.

Truman won primarily because he was able to revive the major elements of the Democratic coalition that Franklin Roosevelt had constructed more than a decade before. Despite the rocky days of 1946, Truman managed to hold on to labor, farm, and black votes. Labor's support, in particular, made a major difference. Working men and women had been irritated by his response to the strikes in the immediate postwar period but had been buoyed by his veto, even though unsuccessful, of the Taft-Hartley Act. Still, union leaders at first seemed unwilling to support Truman's bid for a second term. Some hoped for a new party, or a new coalition within the Democratic party, that would better support their goals. Henry Wallace,

In one of the nation's most extraordinary political upsets, Harry Truman beat Thomas E. Dewey in 1948. Here an exuberant Truman holds a newspaper headline printed while he slept, before the vote turned his way. (Corbis-Bettmann)

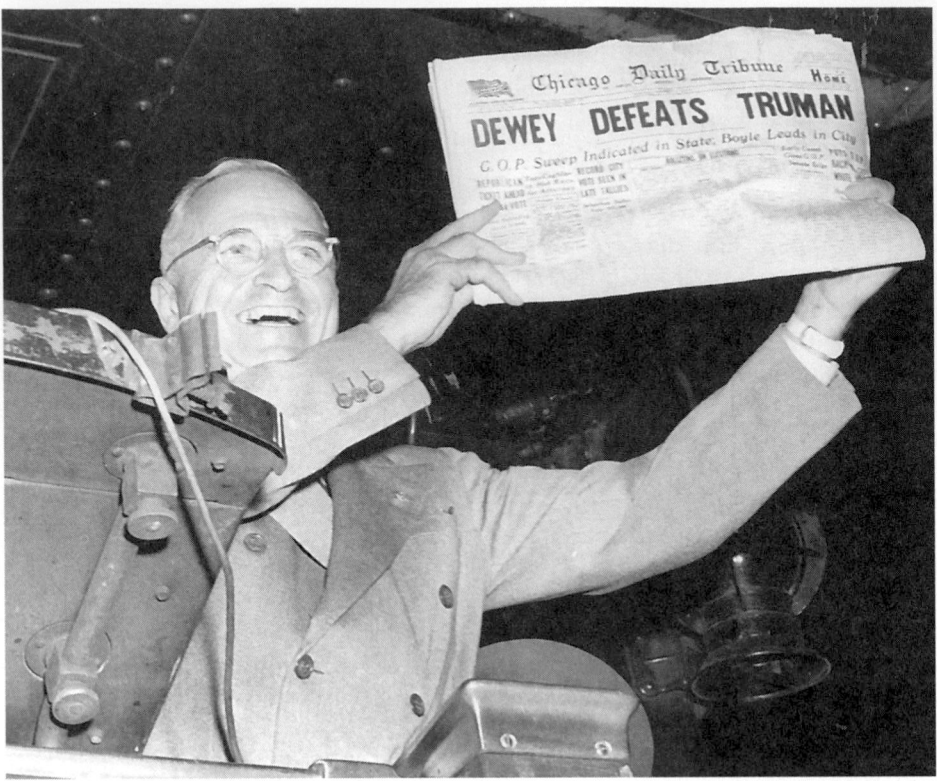

however, worried them, and they feared being tarnished with the Communist label as the Cold War unfolded. They therefore backed Truman.

The fragmentation of the Democratic party, which had threatened to hurt the president severely, helped instead. The splinter parties drew off some votes but allowed Truman to make a more aggressive, direct appeal to the center, and that ultimately accounted for his success.

With the election behind him, Truman pursued his liberal program. In his 1949 State of the Union message, he declared, "Every segment of our population and every individual has a right to expect from our Government a fair deal." Fair Deal became the name for his domestic program, which included the measures he had proposed over and over since 1945.

Some parts of Truman's Fair Deal worked; others did not. Lawmakers raised the minimum wage and expanded social security programs. A housing program brought modest gains but did not really meet housing needs. A farm program, aimed at providing income support to farmers if prices fell, never made it through Congress. Although he desegregated the military, other parts of his civil rights program failed to win congressional support (see Chapter 29). The American Medical Association undermined the effort to provide national health insurance, and Congress rejected a measure to provide federal aid to education.

The mixed record was not entirely Truman's fault. Conservative legislators were largely responsible for the president's inability to achieve his goals. They sought to sabotage his efforts whenever they could and by and large they succeeded. At the same time, critics charged correctly that Truman was often unpragmatic and shrill in his struggles with an unsympathetic Congress. They argued that he sometimes seemed to provoke the confrontations that became a hallmark of his presidency. They also claimed that he was most concerned with foreign policy as he strove to secure bipartisan support for Cold War initiatives (see Chapter 27). Committed to checking the perceived Soviet threat, he allowed his domestic program to suffer. As defense expenditures mounted, correspondingly less money was available for projects at home.

Still, Truman had kept the liberal vision alive. The Fair Deal had ratified many of the initiatives begun during the New Deal, and had led Americans to take programs like social security for granted. Truman had not achieved everything he wanted—he had not even come close—but the nation had taken another step toward endorsing liberal goals.

The Election of Eisenhower

Acceptance of the liberal state continued in the 1950s, even as the Republicans took control. By 1952, Truman's popularity had plummeted, leaving him with the support of only 23 percent of the American people, and all indicators pointed to a political shift. The Democrats nominated Adlai Stevenson, Illinois's able, articulate, and moderately liberal governor. The Republicans turned to Dwight Eisenhower, the World War II hero Americans knew as Ike.

Stevenson approached political issues in intellectual terms. "Let's talk sense to the American people," he said. "Let's tell them the truth." While liberals loved his approach, Stevenson himself anticipated the probable outcome. How, he wondered, could a man named Adlai beat a soldier called Ike?

The Republicans focused on communism, corruption, and Korea as major issues. They called the Democrats "soft on communism." They criticized assorted scandals surrounding Truman's cronies and friends. The president himself was blameless, but some of the people near him were not. The Republicans also promised to end the unpopular Korean War.

Eisenhower proved to be a highly effective campaigner. Though this was his first effort to win political office, he had a natural talent for taking his case to the American people. He spoke in simple, reassuring terms they could understand. Throughout the campaign, he struck a grandfatherly pose, unified the various wings of his party, and went on to victory at the polls. He received 55 percent of the vote and carried 41 states. The new president took office with a Republican Congress as well and had little difficulty gaining a second term four years later.

"Modern Republicanism"

Eisenhower believed firmly in limiting the presidential role. He was uncomfortable with the growth of the executive office that had been taking place for the past 20 years. Like the Republicans in Congress with whom Truman had tangled, he wanted to restore the balance between the branches of government and to reduce the authority of the national government. He recognized,

Presidential Elections, 1948–1956

Year	Candidate	Party	Popular Vote	Electoral Vote
1948	HARRY S TRUMAN	Democratic	24,105,812 (49.5%)	303
	Thomas E. Dewey	Republican	21,970,065 (45.1%)	189
	J. Strom Thurmond	States' Rights	1,169,063 (2.4%)	39
	Henry A. Wallace	Progressive	1,157,172 (2.4%)	0
1952	DWIGHT D. EISENHOWER	Republican	33,936,234 (55.1%)	442
	Adlai E. Stevenson	Democratic	27,314,992 (44.4%)	89
1956	DWIGHT D. EISENHOWER	Republican	35,590,472 (57.4%)	457
	Adlai E. Stevenson	Democratic	26,022,752 (42.0%)	73

Note: Winners' names appear in capital letters.

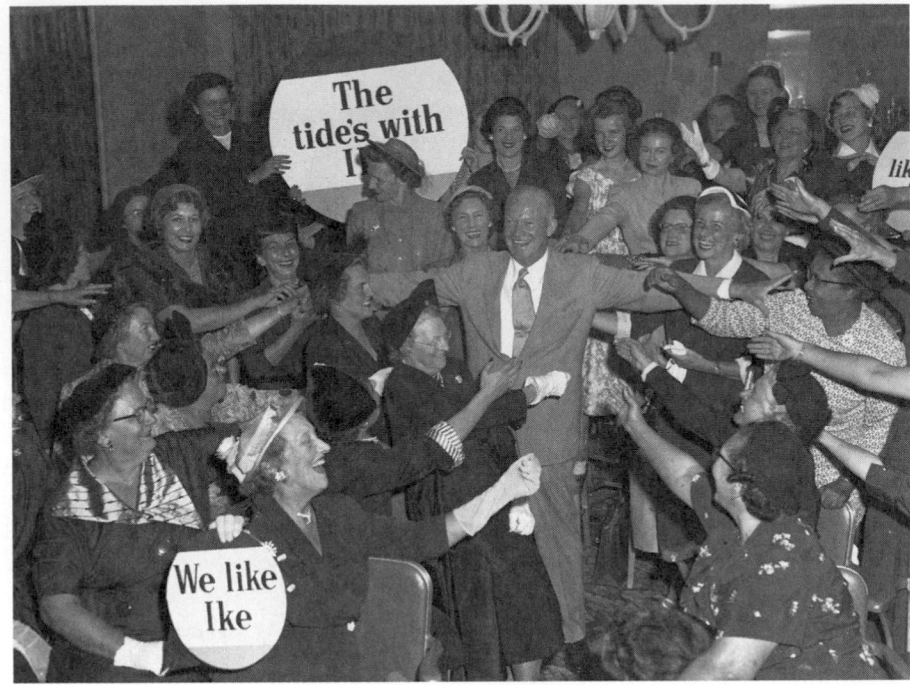

Eisenhower's indirect approach and low-key public image made him popular throughout the 1950s. His intent gaze and wide smile gave Americans a sense of confidence that the country was in good hands. Here "Ike" greets a delegation of Republican National Committee women during the 1952 presidential campaign. (UPI/Corbis-Bettmann)

however, that it was impossible to scale back federal power to the limited levels of the 1920s, and he wanted to preserve social gains that even Republicans now accepted. Eisenhower sometimes termed his approach "dynamic conservatism" or "modern Republicanism," which, he explained, meant "conservative when it comes to money, liberal when it comes to human beings." Liberals quipped that his approach meant endorsing social projects and then failing to authorize the funds.

Above all, economic concerns dominated the Eisenhower years. The president and his chief aides wanted desperately to preserve the value of the dollar, pare down levels of funding, cut taxes, and balance the budget after years of deficit spending.

To achieve those aims, the president appointed George Humphrey, a fiscal conservative, as secretary of the treasury. Humphrey placed a picture of Andrew Mellon, Calvin Coolidge's ultraconservative treasury head, in his office and declared, "We have to cut one-third out of the budget and you can't do that just by eliminating waste. This means, whenever necessary, using a meat axe." His words reflected the administration's approach to economic affairs. In times of economic stagnation,

Republican leaders were willing to risk unemployment to keep inflation under control. The business orientation became obvious when Defense Secretary Charles E. Wilson, former president of General Motors, stated his position at confirmation hearings. "What is good for our country is good for General Motors," he declared, "and vice versa."

Eisenhower fulfilled his promise to reduce government's economic role. After Republicans received financial support from oil companies during the campaign, the new Congress, with a strong endorsement from the president, passed the Submerged Lands Act in 1953. That measure transferred control of about $40 billion worth of oil lands from the federal government to the states. The *New York Times* called it "one of the greatest and surely the most unjustified give-away programs in all the history of the United States."

The administration also sought to reduce federal activity in the electric power field. Eisenhower favored private rather than public development of power. That sentiment came out clearly in a private comment about the Tennessee Valley Authority, the extensive public power and development project begun during the New Deal. "I'd like to see us sell the whole thing," Eisenhower said, "but I suppose we can't go that far." He opposed a TVA proposal for expansion to provide power to the Atomic Energy Commission and instead authorized a private group, the Dixon-Yates syndicate, to build a plant in Arkansas for that purpose. Later, when charges of scandal arose, the administration canceled the agreement, but the basic preference for private development remained.

Committed to supporting business interests, the administration sometimes saw its program backfire. As a result of its reluctance to stimulate the economy too much, the annual rate of economic growth declined from 4.3 percent between 1947 and 1952 to 2.5 percent between 1953 and 1960. The economy was still growing, but more slowly than before. The country also suffered three recessions in Eisenhower's eight years. During the slumps, tax revenues fell and the deficits that Eisenhower so wanted to avoid increased. Liberal economists argued that Keynesian tools were available to avoid such troubles, but they had to be used to bring results.

Eisenhower's understated approach led to a legislative stalemate, particularly when the Democrats regained control of Congress in 1954. Opponents of the president gibed at Ike's restrained stance and laughed about limited White House leadership. One observed that Eisenhower proved that the country did not "need" a president. Another spoke of the Eisenhower doll—you wound it up, and it did nothing for eight years.

Yet Eisenhower understood just what he was doing and had a better grasp of public policy than his critics realized. He worked quietly to create the consensus that he believed was necessary to make legislative progress and often actively pushed his favorite programs behind the scenes. He practiced what later observers called a "hidden hand" approach to the presidency, unobtrusively orchestrating support for his own ends, just as he had done as supreme commander of the Allied forces in World War II.

Even more important was his role in ratifying the welfare state. By 1960, the government had become a major factor in ordinary people's lives. It had grown enormously, employing close to 2.5 million people throughout the 1950s. Federal expenditures, which had stood at $3.1 billion in 1929, rose to $75 billion in 1953 and passed $150 million in the 1960s. The White House was now instrumen-

tal in initiating legislation and in steering bills through Congress. Individuals had come to expect old-age pensions, unemployment payments, and a minimum wage. By accepting the fundamental features of the national state the Democrats had created, Eisenhower ensured its survival. Now the debate about social policy broadened, as issues such as educational assistance, federal health care, and increased welfare benefits became part of the political agenda of the 1960s.

For all the jokes at his expense, Eisenhower remained popular with the voters. He accomplished most of the things he had wanted to do. He was one of the few presidents to leave office as highly regarded by the people as when he entered it. He was the kind of leader Americans wanted in prosperous times.

The High Water Mark of Liberalism

The commitment to a welfare state became even stronger in the 1960s. The Democrats who won office in these years wanted to broaden the role of government even further. Dismayed at the problems of poverty, unemployment, and racism, John F. Kennedy and Lyndon B. Johnson sought to manage the economy more effectively, eradicate poverty, and protect the civil rights of all Americans. Midway through the decade they came close to achieving their goals.

The Election of 1960

In the 1960 campaign, Kennedy argued that the government in general, and the president in particular, had to play an even more active role than they had in the Eisenhower years. He charged that the country had become lazy as it reveled in the prosperity of the 1950s. There were, in fact, problems that needed to be addressed.

Kennedy squared off against Richard Nixon, the Republican nominee, in the first televised presidential debates. Seventy million Americans tuned in to watch the two men in the first contest. The debates made a major difference in the campaign (see the Recovering the Past section of this chapter). Kennedy himself admitted, "It was TV more than anything else that turned the tide." From now

Television

In the last 50 years, television has played an increasingly important part in American life, providing historians with another source of evidence about American culture and society in the recent past.

Television's popularity by the 1950s was the result of decades of experimentation dating back to the nineteenth century. In the 1930s, NBC installed a television station in the new Empire State Building in New York. With green makeup and purple lipstick to provide better visual contrast, actors began to perform before live cameras in studios. At the end of the decade, "Amos 'n' Andy," a popular radio show, was telecast, and as the 1940s began, Franklin D. Roosevelt became the first president to appear on television. World War II interrupted the development of television, as Americans relied on radio to bring them news. After the war, however, the commercial development of television quickly resumed. Assembly lines that had made electronic implements of war were now converted to consumer production, and thousands of new sets appeared on the market. The opening of Congress could be seen live in 1947; baseball coverage improved that same year owing to the zoom lens; children's shows like "Howdy Doody" made their debut; and "Meet the Press," a radio interview program, made the transition to television.

Although sports programs, variety shows hosted by Ed Sullivan and Milton Berle, TV dramas, and episodic series ("I Love Lucy" and "Gunsmoke," for example) dominated TV broadcasting in the 1950s, television soon became entwined with politics and public affairs. Ameri-cans saw Senator Joseph McCarthy for themselves in the televised Army-McCarthy hearings in 1954; his malevolent behavior on camera contributed to his downfall. The 1948 presidential nominating conventions were the first to be televised, but the use of TV to enhance the public image of politicians was most thoroughly developed by the fatherly Dwight D. Eisenhower and the charismatic John F. Kennedy.

In November 1963, people throughout the United States shared the tragedy of John Kennedy's assassination, sitting stunned before their sets trying to understand the events of his fateful Texas trip. The shock and sorrow of the American people was repeated in the spring of 1968 as they watched the funerals of Martin Luther King, Jr., and Robert Kennedy. A year later, a quarter of the world's population watched as Neil Armstrong became the first man to set foot on the moon. In that same era, television played an important part in shaping impressions of the war in Vietnam. More and more Americans began to understand the nature and impact of the conflict from what they saw on TV.

This combination of visual entertainment and enlightenment made owning a television set virtually a necessity. By 1970, fully 95 percent of American households owned a TV set, a staggering increase from the 9 percent only 20 years earlier. Fewer families owned refrigerators or indoor toilets.

The implications of the impact of television on American society are of obvious interest to historians. How has television affected other communications and entertain-

The candidates squaring off in their debate. (AP/Wide World Photos)

ment industries, such as radio, newspapers, and movies? Look at the "Television Tonight" listings shown here. What does the content of TV programming tell us about the values, interests, and tastes of the American people?

Perhaps most significant, what impact has TV had on the course of historical events like presidential campaigns, human relations, and wars? The pictures you see here come from the Kennedy-Nixon debates in the presidential campaign of 1960. The first picture shows the two candidates in the studio. The second picture shows a relaxed and energetic Kennedy staring directly into the TV camera. The third picture shows a taut and tense Nixon challenging the points made by his opponent. Which candidate seems to be speaking directly to the American people? Which candidate makes the better impression? Why? Polls of radio listeners taken after the first debate showed Nixon the winner; surveys of television surveys placed Kennedy in front. How do you account for this discrepancy?

John Kennedy (above) and Richard Nixon (right). (AP/Wide World Photos)

Television Tonight

6:00—WTTV 4: Leave It to Beaver. Beaver tries to help a friend who has run away from home. Repeat.

6:30—WLTW-I 13: Cheyenne has a Laramie adventure in which Slim, Jess, and Jonesy work on a cattle drive. Repeat.

7:30—WTTV 4: The Untouchables. Eliot Ness tries to deal with a late gangster's niece who has a record of the murdered hood's career. Repeat.

7:30—WLW-I 13: Voyage to the Bottom of the Sea presents "Mutiny," in which Admiral Nelson shows signs of a mental breakdown during the search for a giant jellyfish which supposedly consumed a submarine.

7:30—WFBM-TV 6: Members of the Indianapolis Rotary Club discuss the 1965 business outlook with former U.S. Sen. Homer Capehart.

8:00—WFBM-TV 6: The Man from UNCLE is in at a new time and night. Thrush agents try to recapture one of their leaders before Napoleon Solo can deliver him to the Central Intelligence Agency. Ralph Taeger is guest star.

8:00—WISH-TV 8: I've Got a Secret welcomes the panel from To Tell the Truth: Tom Poston, Peggy Cass, Kitty Carlisle, and Orson Bean.

8:30—WLW-I 13: Basketball, I.U. vs. Iowa.

8:30—WISH-TV 8: Andy Griffith's comedy involves Goober's attempts to fill in at the sheriff's office.

9:00—WFBM-TV 6: Andy Williams is visited by composer Henry Mancini, Bobby Darin, and Vic Damone. Musical selections include "Charade," "Hello Dolly," and "Moon River."

9:00—WTTV 4: Lloyd Thaxton welcomes vocal group, Herman's Hermits.

9:30—WISH-TV 8: Many Happy Returns. Walter's plan for currying favor with the store's boss hits a snag.

10:00—WFBM-TV 6: Alfred Hitchcock presents Margaret Leighton as a spinster who goes mad when she cannot cope with the strain of rearing an orphaned niece in "Where the Woodbine Twineth."

10:00—WLW-I 13: Ben Casey gets help in diagnosing a boy's illness from an Australian veterinarian with terminal leukemia. The vet's knowledge of bats provides the key.

10:00—WISH-TV 8: "Viet Nam: How We Got In—Can We Get Out?" is the topic of CBS Reports.

Source: Indianapolis News, January 11, 1965.

on, television would play a major role in the political process and reshape its character.

Kennedy overcame seemingly insuperable odds to become the first Catholic in the White House. Yet his victory over Nixon was razor-thin. The electoral margin of 303 to 219 concealed the close popular tally, in which he triumphed by fewer than 120,000 of 68 million votes cast. If but a few thousand people had voted differently in Illinois and Texas, the election would have gone to Nixon. While Kennedy had Democratic majorities in Congress, many members of his party came from the South and were less sympathetic to liberal causes.

Kennedy had a charismatic public presence. He was able to voice his aims in eloquent yet understandable language. During the campaign, he pointed to "uncharted areas of science and space, unsolved problems of peace and war, unconquered pockets of ignorance and prejudice, unanswered questions of poverty and surplus" that Americans must confront, for "the New Frontier is here whether we seek it or not." He made the same point even more movingly in his inaugural address: "The torch has been passed to a new generation of Americans—born in this century, tempered by war, disciplined by a hard and bitter peace, proud of our ancient heritage." Many, like Paul Cowan met at the start of the chapter, were inspired by Kennedy's concluding call to action: "And so, my fellow Americans: Ask not what your country can do for you—ask what you can do for your country."

For Kennedy, strong leadership was all-important. The president, he believed, "must serve as a catalyst, an energizer." He must be able and willing to perform "in the very thick of the fight." Viewing himself as "tough-minded" and "hard-nosed," he was determined to provide firm direction and play a leading role in creating the national agenda, just as Franklin Roosevelt had done.

The Presidential Election of 1960

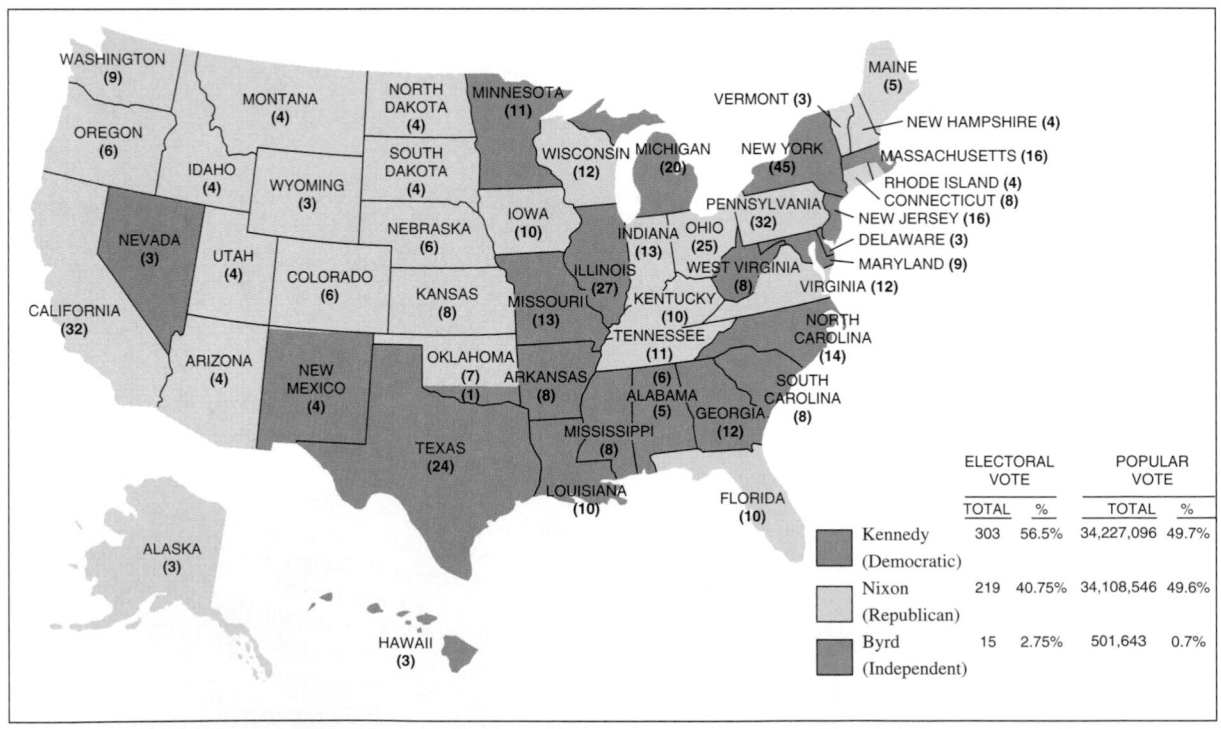

In the close election of 1960, Kennedy's strength in the industrial Northeast and the South helped him revive significant elements of the liberal Democratic coalition of the 1930s.

Energy, exuberance, and excitement filled the air. The administration seemed like the Camelot of King Arthur's day, popularized in a Broadway musical in 1960.

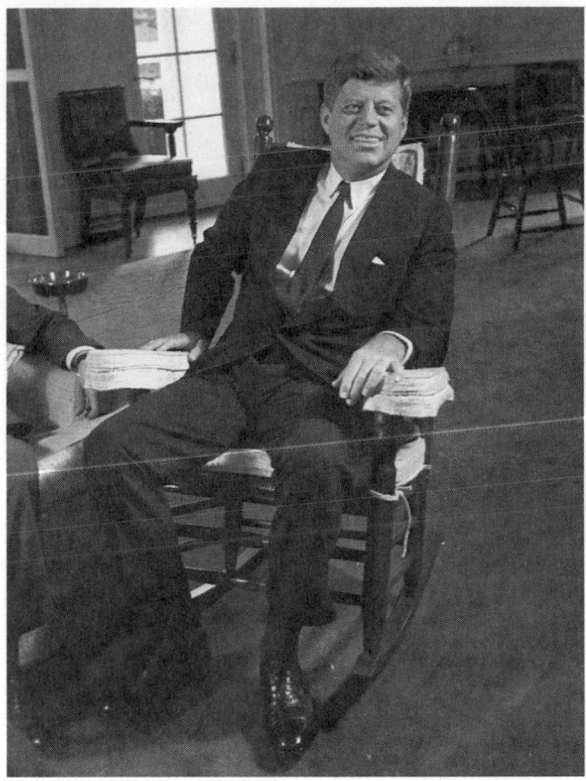

John Kennedy's energy and enthusiasm captured the imagination of Americans and people around the world, though few were aware of the physical ailments that affected him. He was fond of using this rocking chair in the White House, which he found comfortable for his ailing back. (Corbis-Bettmann)

The New Frontier

In office, Kennedy was committed to extending the welfare state. He sought to maintain an expanding economic system and to enlarge social welfare programs. As he told one of his advisers in 1962, "I want to go beyond the things that have already been accomplished. Give me facts and figures on things we still have to do." Regarding civil rights, Kennedy espoused liberal goals and social justice although his policies were limited (see Chapter 29 for a full discussion of civil rights). On the economic front, he tried to end the lingering recession by working with the business community, while controlling price inflation at the same time.

These two goals conflicted when, in the spring of 1962, the large steel companies decided on a major price increase after steel unions had accepted a modest wage package. The angry president termed the price increases unjustifiable and on television charged that the firms pursued "private power and profit" rather than the public interest. Determined to force the steel companies to their knees, Kennedy pressed for executive and congressional action. In the end, the large companies capitulated, but they disliked Kennedy's heavy-handed approach and decided that this Democratic administration, like all the others, was hostile to business. In late May, six weeks after the steel crisis, the stock market plunged in the greatest drop since the Great Crash of 1929. Kennedy received the blame. "When Eisenhower had a heart attack," Wall Street analysts joked, "the market broke." If Kennedy would have a heart attack, the market would go up."

It now seemed doubly pressing to end the recession. Earlier a proponent of a balanced budget, Kennedy began to listen to his liberal advisers who proposed a Keynesian approach to economic growth. Budget deficits had promoted prosperity during the Second World War and might work in the same way in peacetime too. By the summer of 1962, the president was convinced. In early 1963, he called

Kennedy surrounded himself with talented assistants. On his staff were 15 Rhodes scholars and several famous authors. The secretary of state was Dean Rusk, a former member of the State Department who had then served as president of the Rockefeller Foundation. The secretary of defense was Robert S. McNamara, the highly successful president of the Ford Motor Company, who had proved creative in mobilizing talented assistants—"whiz kids"—and in using computer analysis to turn the company around.

Further contributing to Kennedy's attractive image were his glamorous wife Jacqueline and the glittering social occasions the couple hosted. Nobel Prize winners, musicians, and artists attended White House dinners. The Kennedys and their friends played touch football on the White House lawn and charged off on 50-mile hikes.

Glamour and grace characterized the Kennedy White House, as artists, authors, and other celebrities were invited to official functions. Here the President and First Lady greet poet Robert Frost at a party for Nobel Prize winners. (UPI/Corbis-Bettmann)

for a $13.5 billion cut in corporate taxes over the next three years. While that cut would cause a large deficit, it would also provide capital to stimulate the economy and ultimately increase tax revenues.

Opposition mounted. Conservatives refused to accept the basic premise that deficits would stimulate economic growth and argued, in Eisenhower's words, that "no family, no business, no nation can spend itself into prosperity." Some liberals claimed that it would be better to stimulate the economy by spending for social programs rather than by cutting taxes. Why, economist John Kenneth Galbraith wondered, have "a few more dollars to spend if the air is too dirty to breathe, the water is too polluted to drink, the commuters are losing out in the struggle to get in and out of cities, the streets are filthy, and the schools are so bad that the young, perhaps wisely, stay away?" In Congress, where Democrats had thin majorities but still had to contend with conservative Southerners within the party, opponents pigeonholed the proposal in committee, and there it remained.

On other issues on the liberal agenda, Kennedy encountered similar resistance. Though he proposed legislation increasing the minimum wage and providing for federal aid for education, medical care for the elderly, housing subsidies, and urban renewal, the results were disappointing. His new minimum-wage measure passed Congress in pared-down form, but Kennedy did not have the votes in Congress to achieve most of his legislative program.

His inability to win necessary congressional support became even more evident in the struggle to aid public education. Soon after taking office, Kennedy proposed a $2.3 billion program of grants to the states over a three-year period to help build schools and raise teachers' salaries. Immediately, a series of prickly questions emerged. Was it appropriate to spend large sums of money for social goals? Would federal aid bring federal control of school policies and curriculum? Should assistance go to segregated schools? Should it go to parochial schools? The administration proved willing to allow assistance to segregated schools, thereby easing white southern minds. On the Catholic question, however, it stumbled to a halt. Kennedy at first insisted that he would not allow his religion to influence his actions and opposed aid for parochial schools. As Catholic pressure mounted and the administration realized that Catholic votes were necessary for passage, Kennedy began to reconsider. In the end, compromise proved impossible and the school aid measure died in the House Rules Committee.

Kennedy was more successful in securing funding for the exploration of space. As first Alan Shepard, then John Glenn, flew in space, Kennedy proposed that the United States commit itself to landing a man on the moon and returning him to earth before the end of the decade. Congress, caught up in the glamour of the proposal and worried about Soviet achievements in space, assented and increased funding of the National Aeronautics and Space Administration (NASA).

Kennedy also established the Peace Corps, which sent men and women overseas to assist developing countries. According to Kennedy aide Arthur M. Schlesinger, Jr., the Peace Corps was an effort "to replace protocol-minded, striped-pants officials by reform-minded missionaries of democracy who mixed with the people, spoke the native dialects, ate the food, and involved themselves in local struggles against ignorance and want." Paul Cowan, introduced at the start of this chapter, was one of thousands of volunteers who hoped that they could share their liberal dreams.

If Kennedy's successes were modest, he had at least made commitments that could be broadened in subsequent years. He had reaffirmed the importance of executive leadership in the effort to extend the boundaries of the welfare state. And he had committed himself to using modern economics to maintain fiscal stability. The nation was poised to achieve liberal goals.

Change of Command

Facing reelection in 1964, Kennedy wanted not only to win the presidency for a second term but also to increase liberal Democratic strength in Congress. In November 1963, he traveled to Texas, where he hoped to unite the state's Democratic party for the upcoming election. Dallas, one of the stops on the trip, was reputed to be hostile to the administration. Four weeks before, a conservative mob had abused Adlai Stevenson, ambassador to the United Nations. Now, on November 22, Kennedy had a chance to see the city for himself. Arriving at the airport, Henry González, a con-

The American landing on the moon in 1969 resulted from Kennedy's commitment to the space program. Here an astronaut stands next to the lunar module on the moon's surface. (NASA)

gressman accompanying the president in Texas, remarked jokingly, "Well, I'm taking my risks. I haven't got my steel vest yet." As the party entered the city in an open car, the president encountered friendly crowds. Suddenly shots rang out, and Kennedy slumped forward as bullets ripped through his head and throat. Mortally wounded, he died a short time later at a Dallas hospital. Lee Harvey Oswald, the accused assassin, was himself shot and killed a few days later by a minor underworld figure as he was being moved in the jail where he was held.

Americans were stunned when they learned of Kennedy's death. For days people stayed at home and watched endless replays of the assassination and its aftermath on television. The images of the handsome president felled by bullets, the funeral cortege, the president's young son saluting his father's casket as it rolled by on the way to final burial at Arlington National Cemetery were all imprinted on people's minds. United around the event, members of an entire generation remembered where they had been when Kennedy was

shot, just as an earlier generation recalled Pearl Harbor.

Vice President Lyndon Johnson succeeded Kennedy as president of the United States. Though less polished, Johnson was a more effective political leader than Kennedy and brought his own special skills and vision to the presidency.

Johnson was a man of elemental force. Always manipulative, he reminded people of a riverboat gambler, according to one White House aide. Though he desperately wanted to be loved, he was, former secretary of state Dean Acheson once told him, "not a very likable man." There was a streak of vulgarity that contributed to his earthy appeal but offended some of his associates. Asked once why he had not responded more sympathetically to a suggestion from Richard Nixon, he said to his friends in Congress, "Boys, I may not know much, but I know the difference between chicken shit and chicken salad."

Those qualities notwithstanding, he was successful in the passion of his life—politics. Schooled in Congress and influenced by FDR, Johnson was

John Kennedy seemed comfortable and relaxed as he rode in a motorcade through the streets of Dallas. This picture was taken just moments before bullets ended the Camelot dream. (Corbis-Bettmann)

the most able legislator of the postwar years. As Senate majority leader, he became famous for his ability to get things done. Ceaseless in his search for information, tireless in his attention to detail, he knew the strengths and weaknesses of everyone he faced. When he approached someone in the hall, one senator remarked, he was like a "great overpowering thunderstorm that consumed you as it closed in on you." He could flatter and cajole, and became famous for what came to be called the "Johnson treatment." He zeroed in, according to columnists Rowland Evans, Jr., and Robert Novak, "his face a scant millimeter from his target, his eyes widening and narrowing, his eyebrows rising and falling." He grabbed people by the lapels, made them listen, and usually got his way.

Johnson ran the Senate with tight control and established a credible record for himself and his party during the Eisenhower years. He was the Democrat most responsible for keeping liberal goals alive in a conservative time, as he tried to broaden his own appeal in his quest for the presidency. Unsuccessful in his own bid for the White House in 1960, he agreed to take the second spot under JFK and helped Kennedy win the election, then went into a state of eclipse as vice president.

He felt uncomfortable with the Kennedy crowd, useless and stifled in his new role. He told friends that he agreed with John Nance Garner, a vice president under FDR, who once observed that the vice presidency "wasn't worth a pitcher of warm spit."

Despite his own ambivalence about Kennedy, Johnson sensed the profound shock that gripped the United States after the assassination and was determined to utilize Kennedy's memory to achieve legislative success. Even more than Kennedy, he was willing to wield presidential power aggressively and to use the media to shape public opinion in pursuit of his vision of a society in which the comforts of life would be more widely shared and poverty would be eliminated once and for all.

The Great Society in Action

Lyndon Johnson had an expansive vision of the possibilities of reform. Using his considerable political skills, he succeeded in pushing through Congress the most extensive reform program in American history. "Is a new world coming?" the president asked. "We welcome it, and we will bend it to the hopes of man."

Kennedy's assassination thrust Lyndon Johnson into the presidency in an atmosphere of shocked grief and loss. Here, with Jacqueline Kennedy by his side, he takes the oath of office as he flew back from Dallas to Washington on the presidential plane. (Corbis-Bettmann)

Presidential Election of 1964				
Year	Candidate	Party	Popular Vote	Electoral Vote
1964	LYNDON B. JOHNSON	Democratic	43,126,584 (61.1%)	486
	Barry M. Goldwater	Republican	27,177,838 (38.5%)	52

Note: Winner's name appears in capital letters.

Johnson began to develop the support he needed the day he took office. In his first public address, delivered to Congress and televised nationwide, he sought to dispel the image of impostor as he embraced Kennedy's liberal program. He began, in a measured tone, with the words, "All I have, I would have given gladly not to be standing here today." He asked members of Congress to work with him, and he underscored the theme "Let us continue" throughout his speech.

As a first step, Johnson resolved to secure the measures Kennedy had been unable to extract from Congress. He took the bills to reduce taxes and ensure civil rights as his first and most pressing priorities, but he was interested too in aiding public education, providing medical care for the aged, and eliminating poverty. By the spring of 1964, the outlines of his own expansive vision were taking shape, and he had begun to use the phrase "Great Society" to describe his reform program.

Successful even before the election of 1964, his landslide victory over conservative Republican challenger Barry Goldwater of Arizona validated his approach. LBJ received 61 percent of the popular vote and an electoral tally of 486 to 52 and gained Democratic congressional majorities of 68–32 in the Senate and 295–140 in the House. Goldwater's candidacy reflected the growing power of conservatism within the Republican party and the ability of a grass-roots group to organize a successful campaign in party primaries. It also drove moderate Republicans to vote for the Democratic party this time and gave Johnson a far more impressive mandate than Kennedy had ever enjoyed.

Johnson knew how to make things happen in the world of politics. He appointed task forces that included legislators to study problems and suggest solutions, worked with them to draft bills, and maintained close contact with congressional leaders through a sophisticated liaison staff. Not since the FDR years had there been such a coordinated effort.

Civil rights reform was LBJ's first legislative priority and an integral part of the Great Society program (see Chapter 29). But other measures were equally important in extending the boundaries of government action and bolstering the welfare state.

Following Kennedy's lead, Johnson pressed for a tax cut to stimulate the economy. He accepted the Keynesian theory that deficits, properly managed, could promote prosperity. To gain conservative support, he agreed to hold down spending. On one occasion, he applied such pressure that the author of an amendment to provide a tax credit for families with children in college ended up voting against his own proposal. Soon the tax bill passed.

With the tax cut in hand, the president pressed for the poverty program that Kennedy had begun to plan. Such an effort was bold and unprecedented. In the Progressive era, at the turn of the century, some legislation had attempted to alleviate conditions associated with poverty. During the New Deal, Franklin Roosevelt had proposed programs to assist the one-third of a nation that could not help itself. Now Johnson took a step that no president had taken before; in his 1964 State of the Union message, he declared an "unconditional war on poverty in America."

The center of this utopian effort to eradicate poverty was the Economic Opportunity Act of 1964. It created an Office of Economic Opportunity (OEO) to provide education and training through programs such as the Job Corps for unskilled young people trapped in the poverty cycle. VISTA

(Volunteers in Service to America), patterned after the Peace Corps, offered assistance to the poor at home, while Head Start tried to give disadvantaged children a chance to succeed in school. Assorted community action programs gave the poor themselves a voice in improving housing, health, and education in their own neighborhoods.

Aware of the escalating costs of medical care, Johnson also proposed a medical assistance plan. Both Truman and Kennedy had supported such an initiative but had failed to win congressional approval. Johnson succeeded. To head off conservative attacks, the administration tied the Medicare measure to the social security system and limited the program to the elderly. Medicaid met the needs of those on welfare and certain other groups who could not afford private insurance. The Medicare-Medicaid program was the most important extension of federally directed social benefits since the Social Security Act of 1935. By 1976 the two programs were paying for the medical costs of 20 percent of the American people.

Johnson was similarly successful in his effort to provide aid for elementary and secondary schools. Kennedy had met defeat when Catholics had insisted on assistance to parochial schools. Johnson, a Protestant, was able to deal with the ticklish religious question without charges of favoritism. His legislation allocated education money to the states based on the number of children from low-income families. Those funds would then be distributed to assist deprived children in public as well as private schools.

In LBJ's expansive vision, the federal government would ensure that everyone shared in the promise of American life. As a result of his prodding, Congress passed a new housing act to give rent supplements to the poor and created a Cabinet Department of Housing and Urban Development. The federal government provided new forms of aid, such as legal assistance for those who could not afford to pay for it themselves. It moved further in funding higher education, including colleges and universities in its financial grants. Congress also provided artists and scholars with assistance through the National Endowments for the Arts and Humanities, created in 1965. Not since the Works Progress Administration in the New Deal had such groups been granted government aid.

Johnson's administration also provided much-needed immigration reform. It replaced the restrictive immigration policy, set in place in 1924 (which had limited immigration severely and favored northern Europeans), with a measure that vastly increased the ceiling on immigration and opened the door to immigrants from Asia and Latin America. The Immigration Act of 1965 also exempted from the quotas family members of U.S. citizens and political refugees, including at first Cuban and later Indochinese immigrants. By the late 1960s, some 350,000 immigrants were entering the United States annually; in the 1970s, the number exceeded 400,000 a year. This new stream of immigration—largely from Asia and Latin America—created a population more diverse than it had been since the early decades of the twentieth century. The consequences of this new diversity were far-ranging and affected many areas of American life, from politics, radio programming, and consumer products to street signs and public school classrooms.

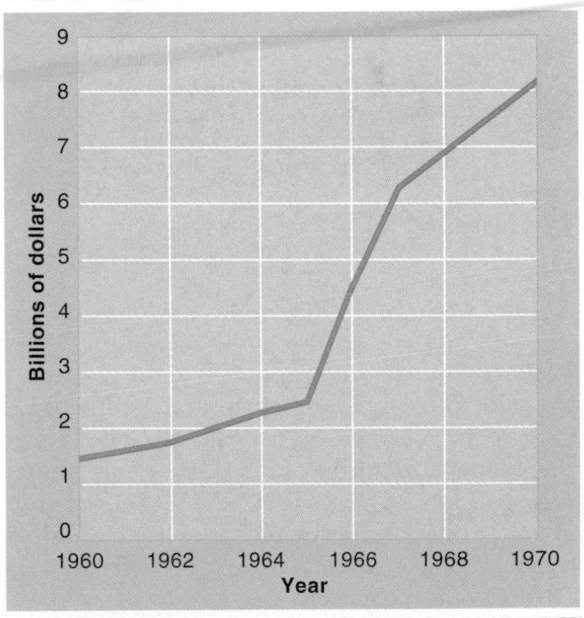

Federal Aid to Education in the 1960s

Passage of a bill to provide federal aid to education in 1965 led to rapidly increasing government support at all levels for the remainder of the decade. Source: U.S. Bureau of the Census.

Immigration from Asia and Latin America brought greater diversity to the United States. Here a Cuban refugee waits to enter the United States at the immigration processing facility at the Miami, Florida, airport in 1974 (Michael Heron/Woodfin Camp & Associates)

The Great Society also reflected the stirring of the environmental movement. In 1962, naturalist Rachel Carson alerted the public to the dangers of pesticide poisoning and environmental pollution in her book *Silent Spring* (see Chapter 29). Though the chemical industry fought Carson and argued that she left readers "unable to sort fact from fancy," a special presidential advisory committee warned against widespread pesticide use.

Johnson recognized the need to go even further. He was determined to deal with caustic fumes in the air, lethal sludge in rivers and streams, and the steady disappearance of wildlife. The National Wilderness Preservation Act of 1964 set aside 9.1 million acres of wilderness, while Lady Bird Johnson, the president's wife, led a beautification campaign to eliminate unsightly billboards and junkyards along the nation's highways, and Congress passed other measures to limit air and water pollution.

A Sympathetic Supreme Court

With the addition of four new liberal justices appointed by Kennedy and Johnson, the Supreme Court supported and promoted the liberal agenda in the 1960s. Under the leadership of Chief Justice Earl Warren, the Court followed the lead it had taken in the 1954 landmark civil rights case *Brown* v. *Board of Education* (see Chapter 29). Several decisions reaffirmed the Court's support of black rights, by moving against Jim Crow practices in other public establishments.

The Court also supported civil liberties. Where earlier judicial decisions had affirmed restrictions on members of the Communist party and radical groups, now the Court began to protect the rights of individuals with radical political views. Similarly, the Court sought to protect accused suspects from police harassment. In *Gideon* v. *Wainwright* (1963), the justices decided that poor defendants in serious cases had the right to free legal counsel. In *Escobedo* v. *Illinois* (1964), they ruled that a suspect had to be given access to an attorney during questioning. In *Miranda* v. *Arizona* (1966), they argued that offenders had to be warned that statements extracted by the police could be used against them and that they could remain silent.

Other decisions similarly broke new ground. *Baker* v. *Carr* (1962) opened the way to reapportionment of state legislative bodies, according to the standard, defined a year later in Justice William O. Douglas's words, of "one person, one vote." This crucial ruling helped break the political control of lightly populated rural districts in many state assemblies and similarly made the U.S. House of Representatives much more responsive to urban and suburban issues. Meanwhile, the Court outraged conservatives by ruling that prayer could not be required in the public schools and that obscenity laws could no longer restrict allegedly pornographic material that might have some "redeeming social value."

Major Great Society Programs

Date of Passage	Program	Effect
January 23, 1964 (ratified)	Twenty-fourth Amendment	Banned poll tax as prerequisite in federal elections
February 26, 1964	Tax Reduction Act	Lowered federal personal tax rates
July 2, 1964	Civil Rights Act	Banned discrimination in public accommodations; gave attorney general right to file suit to desegregate schools or other facilities; banned discrimination in employment on basis of race, color, religion, sex, or national origin
July 9, 1964	Urban Mass Transportation Act	Provided $375 million in financial aid to urban transit systems
August 30, 1964	Economic Opportunity Act	Authorized ten separate programs to be conducted by the Office of Economic Opportunity, including Job Corps and Vista
September 3, 1964	National Wilderness Preservation Act	Designated 9.1 million acres of land as national forest to be safeguarded permanently against commercial use and construction of permanent roads and buildings
April 11, 1965	Elementary and Secondary Education Act	Provided $1.3 billion in aid to elementary and secondary schools
July 30, 1965	Medicare	Provided medical care for the aged through the social security system
August 6, 1965	Voting Rights Act	Suspended literacy tests and other voter tests; authorized federal supervision of registration in states and districts where few voting-age residents had voted earlier
August 10, 1965	Omnibus Housing Act	Provided rent supplements to low-income families and federal aid to place low-income people in private housing
September 9, 1965	Department of Housing and Urban Development	Provided special programs concerned with housing needs, fair-housing opportunities, and the improvement and development of communities
September 29, 1965	National Endowments for the Arts and Humanities	Provided financial assistance for painters, actors, dancers, musicians, and others in the arts and humanities
October 2, 1965	Water Quality Act	Required states to establish and enforce water quality standards for all interstate waters within their boundaries
October 3, 1965	Immigration Act	Revision set new quotas
October 20, 1965	Air Quality Act	Amended earlier laws
October 20, 1965	Higher Education Act	Provided federal scholarships to undergraduates and others
September 9, 1966	National Traffic and Motor Vehicle Safety Act	Set federal safety standards
September 9, 1966	Highway Safety Act	Required states to set up federally approved safety programs
September 23, 1966	Minimum wage	Raised minimum wage from $1.25 to $1.40 per hour; extended coverage
October 15, 1966	Department of Transportation	Provided federal agencies to administer policies, in conjunction with state and local officials, regarding highway planning, development, and construction; urban mass transit; railroads; aviation; and safety of waterways, ports, highways; and oil and gas pipelines
November 3, 1966	Model Cities	Encouraged rehabilitation of slums

The Great Society Under Attack

Supported by healthy economic growth, the Great Society worked for a few years as Johnson had hoped. The tax cut proved effective. After its passage, gross national product (GNP) rose steadily: 7.1 percent in 1964, 8.1 percent in 1965, and 9.5 percent in 1966. At the same time, the budget deficit dropped. Unemployment fell, and inflation remained under control. Medical programs provided basic security for the old and the poor. Education flourished as schools were built, and salaries increased in response to the influx of federal aid.

Yet Johnson's dream of the Great Society proved illusory. Some programs, like the effort to eliminate poverty, promised too much, and the administration's rhetorical oversell led to disillusionment when problems failed to disappear. Other programs, planned in haste, were simply ill-conceived and did not work. Never were the massive sums allocated to these programs that some argued were necessary to make them successful.

Factionalism also plagued the Great Society. Lyndon Johnson had reconstituted the old Democratic coalition in his triumph in 1964, with urban Catholics and southern whites joining organized labor, the black electorate, and the middle class. But diverse interests within the coalition soon clashed. Conservative white southerners and blue-collar white northerners felt threatened by the government's support of civil rights. Local urban bosses, long the backbone of the Democratic party, objected to grass-roots participation of the urban poor, which threatened their own political control.

Criticisms of the Great Society and its liberal underpinnings came from across the political spectrum. There had never been widespread popular enthusiasm for much of the effort. Conservatives disliked the centralization of authority and the government's increased role in defining the national welfare. They also questioned involving the poor themselves in reform programs, arguing poor people lacked a broad vision of the nation's needs. Even middle-class Americans, generally supportive of liberal goals, sometimes grumbled that the government was paying too much attention to the underprivileged and thereby neglecting their own needs.

Radicals attacked the Great Society as a warmed-over version of the New Deal. The same middle-class liberal orientation remained, they claimed, with the real intent of programs to provide the working-class poor with middle-class values. "The welfare state is more machinery than substance," activist Tom Hayden declared. Furthermore, radicals charged, the assumption of Great Society programs that the American system was basically sound and that economic growth would finance benefits of the American dream for all meant that no real effort was being made to redistribute income. Only the redistribution of wealth, in their view, could transform American life.

The Vietnam War (discussed in Chapter 27) dealt the Great Society a fatal blow. LBJ wanted to maintain both the war and his treasured domestic reform programs, but his effort to pursue these goals simultaneously produced serious inflation. The economy was already booming as a result of the tax cut and the spending for reform. As military expenditures increased, the productive system of the country could not keep up with demand. When Johnson refused to raise taxes, in an effort to hide the costs of the war, inflation spiraled out of control. Congress finally got into the act and slashed Great Society programs. As hard economic choices became increasingly necessary, many decided the country could no longer afford social reform on the scale Johnson had proposed.

The Decline of Liberalism

After eight years of Democratic rule, many Americans became frustrated with the liberal approach. They questioned the liberal agenda and the ability of the government to solve social problems. The war in Vietnam had polarized the country and fragmented the Democratic Party. Critics now questioned the entire liberal agenda and argued that the government was trying to do too much. Capitalizing on the alienation sparked by the war, Republicans determined to scale down the commitment to social change. Like Dwight Eisenhower a decade and a half before, they accepted some social programs as necessary for the well-being of modern America but were still resolved to reduce spending and cut back the federal bureaucracy. Furthermore, they were determined to pay more attention to white, middle-class Americans who disliked the social disorder they perceived as one of the consequences of rapid social change and resented the government's perceived favoritism toward the poor and dispossessed.

The Election of 1968

Richard Nixon had long dreamed of the nation's highest office. He had failed in his first bid in 1960 and then two years later lost a race for governor of California. His political career seemed over, as he told the press in 1962, "You won't have Nixon to kick around any more because, gentlemen, this is my last press conference." Written off by most politicians, he staged a comeback after the Goldwater disaster of 1964, and by 1968 seemed to have a good shot at the presidency again.

In the election, Nixon faced Vice President Hubert H. Humphrey. The war in Vietnam had fractured the Democratic party and made Johnson so unpopular that he chose not to run for reelection. The turbulent Democratic convention in Chicago, where police ran amok and clubbed demonstrators, reporters, and bystanders, all on nationwide TV, undermined the Democrats' hopes of unification and worked in Nixon's favor. But he faced a serious threat from Governor George C. Wallace of Alabama, a third-party candidate, who exploited social and racial tensions in his campaign. Appealing to northern working-class voters as well as southern whites, Wallace characterized those who wanted to reform American life as "left-wing theoreticians, briefcase-totin' bureaucrats, ivory-tower guideline writers, bearded anarchists, smart-aleck editorial writers and pointy-headed professors." He hoped to ride into office on blue-collar resentment of social disorder and the liberal agenda.

Nixon addressed the same constituency who made up what he called the country's "silent majority." Capitalizing on the dismay these Americans

Roots of Selected Great Society Programs		
Progressive Period	**New Deal**	**Great Society**
Settlement house activity of Jane Addams and others	Relief efforts to ease unemployment (FERA, WPA)	Poverty programs (OEO)
Efforts to clean up slums (tenement house laws)	Housing program	Rehabilitation of slums through Model Cities program
Progressive party platform calling for federal accident, old-age, and unemployment insurance	Social security system providing unemployment compensation and old-age pensions	Medical care for the aged through social security (Medicare)
Activity to break up monopolies and regulate business	Regulation of utility companies	Regulation of highway safety and transportation
Efforts to regulate working conditions and benefits	Establishment of standards for working conditions and minimum wage	Raising of minimum wage
Efforts to increase literacy and spread education at all levels	Efforts to keep college students in school through NYA	Assistance to elementary, secondary, and higher education
Theodore Roosevelt's efforts at wilderness preservation	Conservation efforts (CCC, TVA planning)	Safeguarding of wilderness lands
Establishment of federal income tax	Tax reform to close loopholes and increase taxes for the wealthy	Tax cut to stimulate business activity
Theodore Roosevelt's overtures to Booker T. Washington	Discussion (but not passage) of antilynching legislation	Civil rights measures to ban discrimination in public accommodations and to guarantee right to vote

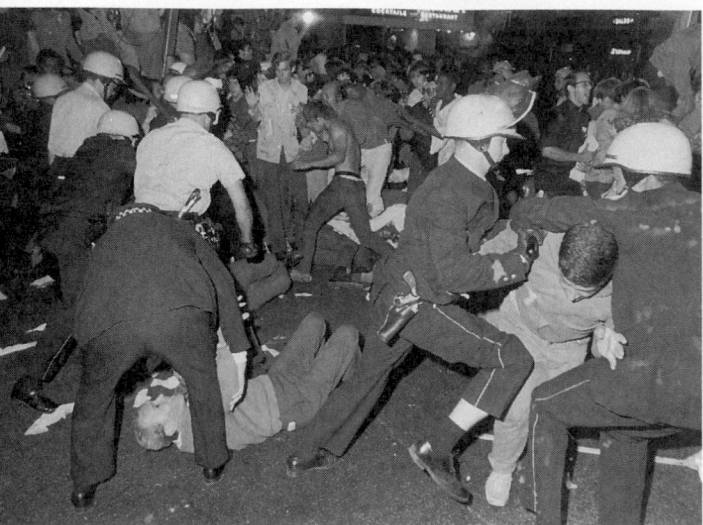

Policemen attacked demonstrators and bystanders alike at the turbulent Democratic convention of 1968. The senseless violence, pictured in graphic detail on national television, undermined the Democratic party and helped Nixon win the election. (UPI/Corbis-Bettmann)

felt over campus disruptions and inner-city riots and appealing to latent racism, he promised to preserve law and order if elected. He also called the Great Society a costly mistake, declaring that it was "time to quit pouring billions of dollars into programs that have failed." Heeding the advice of public-relations advisers, Nixon took the high ground and avoided shrill criticism himself. He gave Governor Spiro Agnew of Maryland, his vice-presidential running mate, the task of leading the attack. Agnew, much like the Nixon of old, called Hubert Humphrey "squishy soft on communism" and declared that "if you've seen one city slum, you've seen them all."

When the results were in, Nixon received 43 percent of the popular vote, not quite 1 percent more than Humphrey, with Wallace capturing the rest. It was enough to give the Republicans a majority in the electoral college and Nixon the presidency at last. Sixty-two percent of all white voters (but only 12 percent of black voters) had cast their votes for either Nixon or Wallace, suggesting the covert racial appeal had worked. Because many Americans split their tickets, the Democrats won both houses of Congress.

In and out of office, Nixon was a complex, remote man, who carefully concealed his private self. There was, one of his aides noted, "a mean side to his nature" that he sought to keep from public view. Nixon embraced political life, but never with the exuberance of Lyndon Johnson. Physically awkward and humorless, he was most comfortable alone or with a few wealthy friends. Even at work he insulated himself, preferred written contacts to personal ones, and often retreated to a small room in the executive office building to be alone.

Nixon was keenly aware of the psychology of politics in the electronic age. He believed that "in the modern presidency, concern for image must rank with concern for substance." Thus, he posed as the defender of American morality, though in private he was frequently coarse and profane. Earlier in his career he had been labeled "Tricky Dick" for his apparent willingness to do anything to advance his career. He had spent years trying to create the appearance of a "new Nixon," but to many he still appeared to be a mechanical man, always calculating his next step.

Philosophically, Nixon disagreed with the liberal faith in federal planning and wanted to decentralize social policy. But he agreed with his liberal predecessors that the presidency ought to be the engine of the political system. Faced with a Congress dominated by Democrats and their allocations of money for programs he opposed, he impounded, or refused to spend, funds Congress had authorized. Later commentators would see the Nixon years as the height of the "imperial presidency."

Nixon's cabinet appointees, sworn in with NBC "Today" cameras relaying the ceremony directly to television viewers, were white, male Republicans. For the most part, however, the president worked around his cabinet, relying on other White House staff members. In domestic affairs, Arthur Burns, a former chairman of the Council of Economic Advisers, and Daniel Patrick Moynihan, a Harvard professor of government (and a Democrat) were the most important. In foreign affairs, the talented and ambitious Henry A. Kissinger, another Harvard government professor, directed the National Security Council staff and later became secretary of state.

Still another tier of White House officials insulated the president from the outside world and carried out his commands. None had public policy experience, but all shared an intense loyalty to their leader, a quality that Nixon prized, and a keen sense of the importance of the Nixon image. Advertising executive H. R. Haldeman, a tireless Nixon campaigner, became chief of staff. Of his relationship with the president, Haldeman remarked, "I get done what he wants done and I take the heat instead of him." Working with Haldeman was lawyer John Ehrlichman. Starting as a legal counselor, he rose to the post of chief domestic adviser. Haldeman and Ehrlichman framed issues and narrowed options for Nixon. They came to be called the "Berlin Wall" for the way they guarded the president's privacy. John Mitchell was known as "El Supremo" by the staff, as the "Big Enchilada" by Ehrlichman. A tough, successful bond lawyer from Nixon's New York law office, he became a fast friend and managed the 1968 campaign. In the new administration, he became attorney general and gave the president daily advice.

The Republican Agenda

Although Nixon had come to political maturity in Republican circles, he understood that it was impossible to roll back the government's expanded role altogether. Accepting the basic contours of the welfare state, he sought to systematize and scale back its programs. Furthermore, he was determined "to reverse the flow of power and resources" away from the federal government to state and local governments, where he believed they belonged.

Despite initial reservations, Nixon proved willing to use economic tools to maintain stability. The economy was faltering when he assumed office. Inflation had risen from 2.2 percent in 1965 to 4.5 percent in 1968, largely as a result of the Vietnam War. Nixon responded by reducing government spending and pressing the Federal Reserve Board to raise interest rates. Although parts of the conservative plan worked, a mild recession occurred in 1969–1970 and inflation continued. Realizing the political dangers of pursuing this policy, Nixon shifted course, imposed wage and price controls to stop inflation, and used monetary and fiscal policies to stimulate the economy. After his reelection in 1972, however, he lifted wage and price controls, and inflation began its upward course once more.

A number of factors besides the Vietnam War contributed to the troubling spiral of rising prices. Eager to court the farm vote, the administration made a large wheat sale to Russia in 1972. The sale proved to be a major miscalculation. With insufficient wheat left for the American market, grain prices shot up. Twenty-five years of grain surpluses suddenly vanished and shortages occurred. Other agricultural setbacks like corn blight compounded the problem. Between 1971 and 1974, farm prices rose 66 percent, as agricultural inflation accompanied industrial inflation.

The most critical factor in disrupting the economy, though, was the Arab oil embargo. American economic expansion had rested on cheap energy

Speaking to the "silent majority," Nixon promised to reinstitute traditional values and restore law and order. A private man, Nixon tried to insulate himself from the public and present a carefully crafted image through the national media. (Hiroji Kubota/Magnum Photos)

Rate of Inflation, 1940–1980

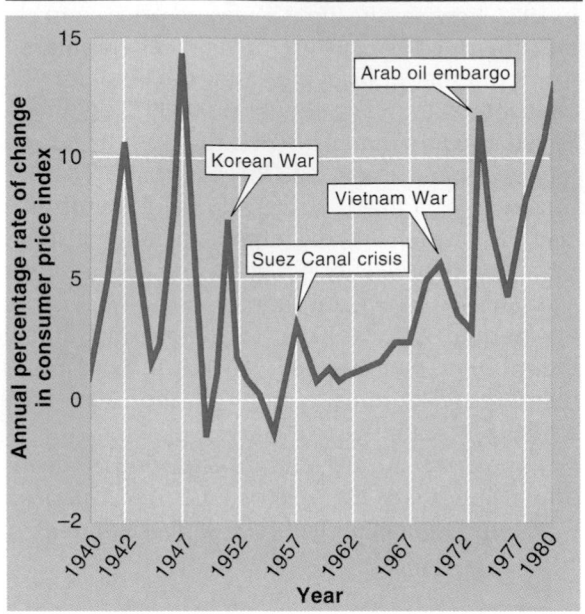

Inflation has often accompanied military spending in the postwar years. In the early 1970s, the Arab oil embargo contributed to an even higher rate. Source: U.S. Bureau of the Census.

Unemployment Rate, 1940–1980

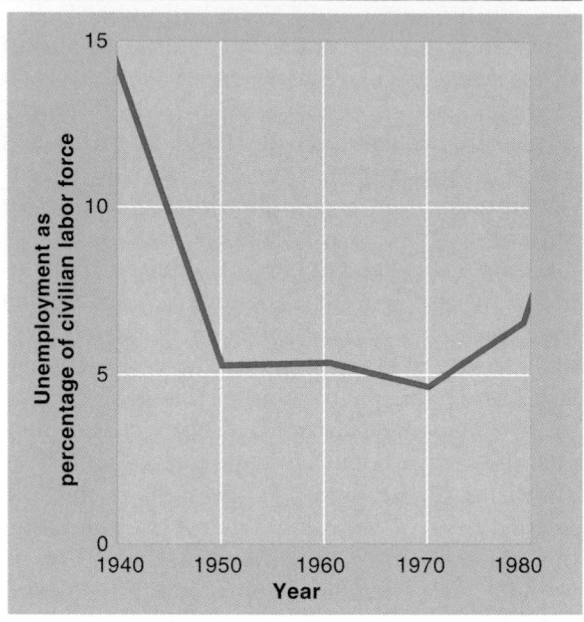

The unemployment rate, which had fallen dramatically during World War II and remained relatively constant in the 1950s and 1960s, rose at the same time inflation increased in the 1970s. Source: U.S. Bureau of Labor Statistics.

just as American patterns of life had depended on inexpensive gasoline. Although the Organization of Petroleum Exporting Countries (OPEC) had slowly raised oil prices in the early 1970s, the 1973 Arab-Israeli war led Saudi Arabia to impose an embargo on oil shipped to Israel's ally, the United States. Other OPEC nations quadrupled their prices. Dependent on imports for one-third of their energy needs, Americans faced shortages and skyrocketing prices. When the embargo ended in 1974, prices remained high.

The oil crisis affected all aspects of American economic life. Manufacturers, farmers, homeowners—all were touched by high energy prices. A loaf of bread that had cost 28 cents in the early 1970s jumped to 89 cents, and automobiles cost 72 percent more in 1978 than they had in 1973. Accustomed to filling up their cars' tanks for only a few dollars, Americans were shocked at paying 65 cents a gallon. In 1974, inflation reached 11 percent. But then as higher energy prices encouraged consumers to cut back on their purchases, the

nation entered a recession as well. Unemployment climbed to 9 percent, the highest level since the 1930s. Inflation and high unemployment were worrisome bedfellows.

As economic growth and stability eluded him, Nixon also tried to reorganize rapidly expanding and expensive welfare programs. Changes in welfare during the years of the Great Society had led the government to spend considerably more in this area. Critics claimed that welfare was inefficient and that benefits discouraged people from seeking work. Nixon faced a dilemma. He recognized the conservative tide growing in the Sun Belt regions of the country from Florida to Texas to California, where many voters wanted cutbacks in what they viewed as excessive government programs. At the same time, he wanted to create a new Republican coalition by winning over traditionally Democratic blue-collar workers with reassurances that the Republicans would not dismantle the parts of the welfare state on which they relied.

Oil Imports, 1973–1980

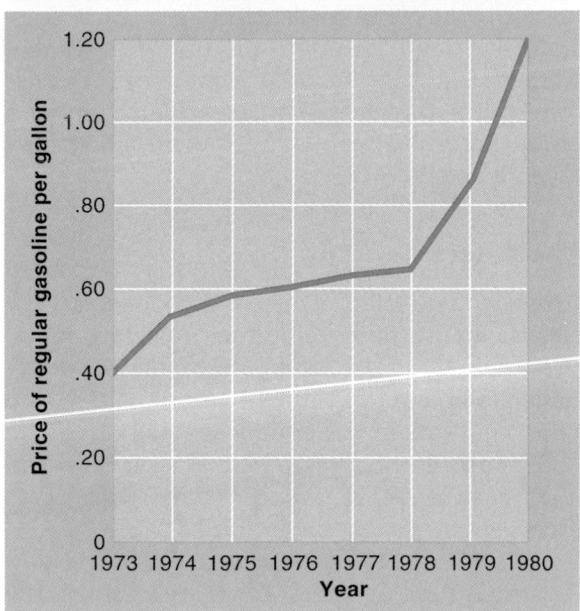

American reliance on foreign oil increased in the mid-1970s, until the United States tried to respond to price increases by reducing reliance on imports. Source: U.S. Energy Information Administration.

Gasoline Prices, 1973–1980

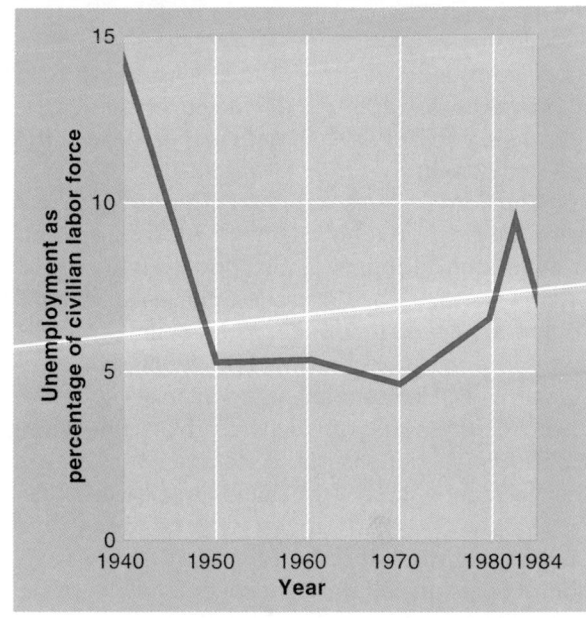

Gasoline prices rose steadily in the years following the Arab oil embargo and affected the entire American economy. Source: U.S. Energy Information Administration.

At the urging of domestic adviser Daniel Moynihan, Nixon endorsed an expensive but feasible new program. The Family Assistance Plan would have guaranteed a minimum yearly stipend of $1,600 to a family of four, with food stamps providing about $800 more. The program, aiming to cut "welfare cheaters" who took unfair advantage of the system and to encourage recipients to work, required all participants to register for job training and to accept employment when found. Proponents, who doubtless exaggerated the number of cheaters, wanted to make it more profitable to work than to subsist on the public rolls. Though promising, the program was attacked by both liberals, who felt it was too limited, and conservatives, who claimed it tried to do too much, and it died in the Senate.

As he struggled with the economy and with what many called the "welfare mess," Nixon irritated liberals still further in his effort to restore "law and order." Political protest—and rising crime rates, increased drug use, and more permissive attitudes toward sex—created a growing backlash among working-class and many middle-class Americans (see Chapter 29 for the development of youth culture). Nixon decided to use government power to silence disruption and thereby strengthen his conservative political constituency.

One part of the administration's campaign involved denouncing disruptive elements. Nixon lashed out at demonstrators—at one point he called student activists "bums." More and more, however, he relied on his vice president to play the part of hatchet man. As he had demonstrated during the 1968 campaign, Agnew had a gift for jugular attack. Opposition elements, students in particular, were "ideological eunuchs" who made up an "effete corps of impudent snobs." At the same time, Nixon and Agnew appealed for support to blue-collar youth, whom they described as patriotic supporters of the Vietnam War.

Another part of Nixon's effort to circumscribe the liberal approach involved attacking the communications industry. Although Nixon himself was well aware of the power of the media and used both television and radio effectively, he believed the media represented the opinions of the "Eastern establishment" and viewed him with hostility. After commentators responded negatively to a major address in 1969, he decided to challenge the television networks. Again Agnew spearheaded the pointed attack.

The third and strongest part of Nixon's plan was Attorney General John Mitchell's effort to demonstrate that the administration supported the values of citizens upset by domestic upheavals. Mitchell sought enhanced powers for a campaign on crime, sometimes at the expense of individuals' constitutional rights. He intended to send a message to the entire country that the new team in the White House would not tolerate certain actions, even if they were protected by the right to free speech.

Mitchell's plan included reshaping the Supreme Court, which had rendered increasingly liberal decisions on the rights of defendants in the past decade and a half. That shift, Republican leaders argued, had resulted in moral and ethical laxity. During his first term, Nixon had the opportunity to name four judges to the Court, and he nominated men who shared his views. His first choice was Warren E. Burger as chief justice to replace the liberal Earl Warren, who was retiring. Burger, a moderate, was confirmed quickly. Other appointments, however, were more partisan and reflected Nixon's aggressively conservative approach. Intent on appealing to white southerners, he first selected Clement Haynesworth of South Carolina, then G. Harold Carswell of Florida. Both men on examination showed such racial biases or limitations that the Senate refused to confirm them. Nixon then appointed Harry Blackmun, Lewis F. Powell, Jr., and William Rehnquist, all able and qualified, and all inclined to tilt the Court in a more conservative direction.

Not surprisingly, the Court gradually shifted to the right. It narrowed defendants' rights in an attempt to ease the burden of the prosecution in its cases and slowed the process of liberalization by upholding pornography laws if they reflected community standards. It supported Nixon's assault on the media by ruling that journalists did not have the right to refuse to answer questions for a grand jury, even if they had promised sources confidentiality. On other questions, however, the Court did not always act as the president had hoped. In the controversial 1973 *Roe* v. *Wade* decision, the Court legalized abortion, stating that women's rights included the right to control their own bodies. This decision was one that feminists, a group hardly supported by the president, had ardently sought.

The Watergate Affair

Faced with a solidly Democratic Congress, the Nixon administration found its legislative initiatives blocked. In this situation, Nixon was determined to end the stalemate by winning a second term and sweeping Republican majorities into both houses of Congress in 1972. His efforts to gain a decisive Republican victory at the polls led to excesses that brought his demise.

Nixon's reelection campaign was even better organized than the effort four years earlier. The president relied on fiercely loyal aides who were prepared to do anything to win. Special counsel Charles W. Colson described himself as a "flag-waving, kick-'em-in-the-nuts, anti-press, anti-liberal Nixon fanatic." He had earlier played an important part in developing an "enemies list" of prominent figures judged to be unsympathetic to the administration. White House counsel John Dean defined his task as finding a way to "use the available federal machinery to screw our political enemies." Active in carrying out commands were E. Howard Hunt, a former CIA agent and a specialist in "dirty tricks," and G. Gordon Liddy, a onetime member of the FBI, who prided himself on his willingness to do anything without flinching.

The Committee to Re-elect the President (CREEP), headed by John Mitchell, who resigned as attorney general, spared no expense in pursuit of its goal. It launched a massive fund-raising drive, aimed at collecting as much money as it could before the reporting of contributions became necessary under a new campaign-finance law. That money could be used for any purpose, including payments for the performance of dirty tricks aimed at disrupting the opposition's campaign. Other funds financed an intelligence branch within CREEP that had Liddy at its head and included Hunt.

Early in 1972, Liddy and his lieutenants proposed an elaborate scheme to wiretap the phones of various Democrats and to disrupt their nominating convention. Twice Mitchell refused to go along, arguing that the proposal was too risky and expensive. Finally he approved a modified version of the plan to tap the phones of the Democratic National Committee at its headquarters in the Watergate apartment complex in Washington, D.C. Mitchell, formerly the top justice official in the land, had authorized breaking the law.

The wiretapping attempt took place on the evening of June 16, 1972, and ended with the arrest of those involved. They carried with them money and documents that could be traced to CREEP and incriminate the reelection campaign. Top officials of the Nixon reelection team had to decide quickly what to do.

Reelection remained the most pressing priority, so Nixon's aides played the matter down and used federal resources to head off the investigation. When the FBI traced the money carried by the burglars to CREEP, the president authorized the CIA to call off the FBI on the grounds that national security was at stake. Though not involved in the planning of the break-in, the president was now party to the cover-up. In the succeeding months, he authorized payment of hush money to silence Hunt and others. Members of the administration, including Mitchell, perjured themselves in court to shield the top officials who were involved.

Nixon trounced Democrat George McGovern in the election of 1972, receiving 61 percent of the popular vote. In a clear indication of the collapse of the Democratic coalition, 70 percent of southern voters cast their ballots for Nixon. The president, however, failed to gain the congressional majorities necessary to support his programs.

When the Watergate burglars were brought to trial, they pleaded guilty and were sentenced to jail, but the case refused to die. Judge John Sirica was not satisfied that justice had been done, asserting that the evidence indicated that others had played a part. Meanwhile, two zealous reporters, Bob Woodward and Carl Bernstein of the *Washington Post,* were following a trail of leads on their own. Slowly they recognized who else was involved. On one occasion, when they reached Mitchell and asked him about a story tying him to Watergate, he turned on them in fury. "All that crap you're putting in the paper?" he said. "It's all been denied."

Mitchell's irritation notwithstanding, the unraveling of Watergate continued. The Senate Select Committee on Presidential Campaign Activities undertook an investigation, and one of the convicted burglars testified that the White House had been involved in the episode. Newspaper stories provided further leads, and the Senate hearings in turn provided new material for the press. Faced with rumors that the White House was actively involved, Nixon decided that he had to release Haldeman and Ehrlichman, his two closest aides, to save his own neck. On nationwide TV he declared that he would take the ultimate responsibility for the mistakes of others, for "there can be no whitewash at the White House."

Presidential Elections, 1968–1972				
Year	Candidate	Party	Popular Vote	Electoral Vote
1968	RICHARD M. NIXON	Republican	31,783,783 (43.4%)	301
	Hubert M. Humphrey	Democratic	31,271,839 (42.7%)	191
	George C. Wallace	American Independent	9,899,557 (13.5%)	46
1972	RICHARD M. NIXON	Republican	45,767,218 (60.7%)	520
	George S. McGovern	Democratic	28,357,668 (37.5%)	17

Note: Winners' names appear in capital letters.

In May 1973, the Senate committee began televised public hearings, reminiscent of the McCarthy hearings of the 1950s. As millions of Americans watched, the drama built. John Dean, seeking to save himself, testified that Nixon knew about the cover-up, and other staffers revealed a host of illegal activities undertaken at the White House: Money had been paid to the burglars to silence them; State Department documents had been forged to smear a previous administration; wiretaps had been used to prevent top-level leaks. The most electrifying moment was the disclosure that the president had installed a secret taping system in his office that recorded all conversations. Tapes could verify or disprove the growing rumors that Nixon had in fact been party to the cover-up all along.

In an effort to demonstrate his own honesty, Nixon agreed to appoint Harvard law professor Archibald Cox as a special prosecutor in the Department of Justice. But when Cox tried to gain access to the tapes, Nixon resisted and finally fired him. Nixon's own popularity plummeted, and even the appointment of another special prosecutor, Leon Jaworski, did not help. More and more Americans now believed that the president had played at least some part in the cover-up and should take responsibility for his acts. *Time* magazine ran an editorial headlined "The President Should Resign," and Congress considered impeachment.

The first steps, in accordance with constitutional mandate, began in the House of Representatives. The House Judiciary Committee, made up of 21 Democrats and 17 Republicans, began to debate the impeachment case in late July 1974. By sizable tallies, it voted to impeach the president on the grounds of obstruction of justice, abuse of power, and refusal to obey a congressional subpoena to turn over his tapes. A full House of Representatives vote still had to occur, and the Senate would have to preside over a trial before removal could take place. But for Nixon the handwriting was on the wall.

After a brief delay, on August 5 Nixon obeyed a Supreme Court ruling and released the tapes. Despite a suspicious 18½-minute silence, they contained the "smoking gun"—clear evidence of his complicity in the cover-up. His ultimate resignation became but a matter of time. Four days later, on August 9, 1974, the extraordinary episode came to an end, as Nixon became the first American president ever to resign.

The Watergate affair seemed disturbing and scandalous evidence that the appropriate balance of power had disappeared. As the scandal wound down, many began to question the centralization of power in the American political system and to cite the "imperial presidency" as the cause of recent abuses. Others simply lost faith in the presidency altogether. A 1974 survey showed that

DOONESBURY   **by Garry Trudeau**

Although Nixon steadfastly denied his complicity in the Watergate affair, his tape recordings of White House conversations told a different story. In this classic "Doonesbury" cartoon from September 17, 1973, Garry Trudeau notes Nixon's efforts to head off the investigation. (Universal Press Syndicate)

Gerald Ford, a genial man, sought to reestablish confidence in the government after succeeding Nixon as president. Far different from his predecessor, he served just over two years, as his bid for election to the presidency in 1976 ended in defeat. (UPI/Corbis-Bettmann)

trust in the presidency had declined by 50 percent in a two-year period. Coming on the heels of Lyndon Johnson's lying to the American people about involvement in Vietnam, the Watergate affair contributed to the cumulative disillusionment with politics in Washington and to the steady decrease in political participation. Barely half of those eligible to vote bothered to go to the polls in the presidential elections of 1976, 1980, and 1984. Even fewer cast ballots in nonpresidential contests.

Gerald Ford: Caretaker President

When Nixon resigned in disgrace midway through his second term, he was succeeded by Gerald Ford. An unpretentious middle-American Republican who believed in the traditional virtues, Ford had been appointed vice president in 1973 when Spiro Agnew resigned in disgrace for accepting bribes. After the appointment, Richard Rovere, a noted journalist, wrote in the *New Yorker:* "That he is thoroughly equipped to serve as Vice President seems unarguable; the office requires only a warm body

and occasionally a nimble tongue. However ... neither Richard Nixon nor anyone else has come forward to explain Gerald Ford's qualifications to serve as Chief Executive." The new president acknowledged his own limitations, declaring, "I am a Ford, not a Lincoln."

More important than his limitations were his views about public policy. Throughout his tenure in Congress, Ford had voted according to the Republican convictions he shared with his Michigan constituents. Over the years he had opposed federal aid to education, the poverty program, and mass transit. He had voted for civil rights measures only when weaker substitutes he had favored had gone down to defeat. Like his predecessor, he was determined to stop the liberal advances promoted by the Democrats in the 1960s.

Ford faced a daunting task. In the aftermath of the Watergate affair, Washington was in turmoil. Americans wondered whether any politician could be trusted to guide public affairs. The new president had to use his authority to restore national confidence at a time when the misuse of presidential power itself had precipitated the crisis.

Ford worked quickly to restore trust in the government. He emphasized conciliation and compromise, and he promised to cooperate both with Congress and with American citizens. The nation responded gratefully. *Time* magazine pointed to a "mood of good feeling and even exhilaration in Washington that the city had not experienced for many years."

The new feeling did not last long. The new president weakened his base of support by pardoning Richard Nixon barely a month after his resignation. Ford's decidedly conservative bent in domestic policy often threw him into confrontation with a Democratic Congress. Economic problems proved most pressing in 1974, as inflation, fueled by oil price increases, rose to 11 percent a year, unemployment stood at 5.3 percent, and GNP declined. Home construction slackened and interest rates rose, while stock prices fell. Nixon, preoccupied with the Watergate crisis, had been unable to curb rising inflation and unemployment. Not since Franklin Roosevelt took office in the depths of the Great Depression had a new president faced economic difficulties so severe.

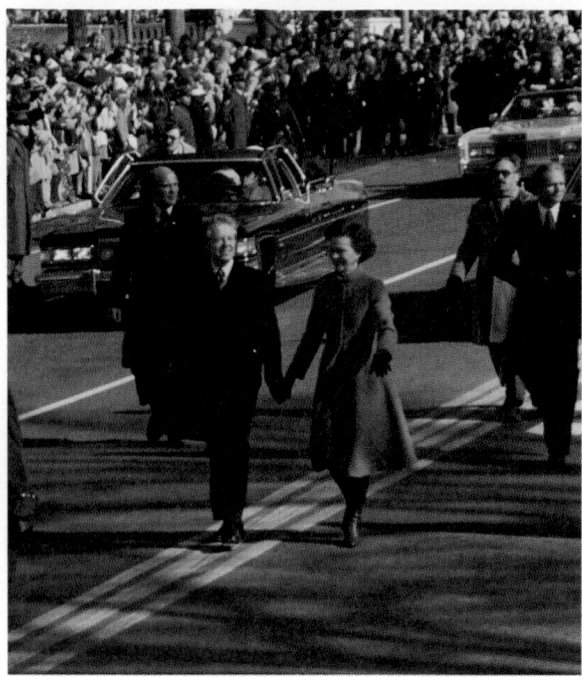

Jimmy Carter holds hands with his wife, Rosalyn, as they walk to his inauguration in early 1977. As much as possible, Carter tried to avoid actions that reminded people of the "imperial presidency" of the Nixon years. (The White House)

Like Herbert Hoover 45 years before, the conservative Ford hoped to restore confidence and persuade the public that conditions would improve with patience and goodwill. But his campaign to cajole Americans to "Whip Inflation Now" voluntarily failed dismally. At last convinced of the need for strong governmental action, the administration introduced a tight-money policy as a means of curbing inflation. It led to the most severe recession since the Depression, with unemployment peaking at 12 percent in 1975. In response, Congress pushed for an antirecession spending program. Recognizing political reality, Ford endorsed a multibillion-dollar tax cut coupled with higher unemployment benefits. The economy made a modest recovery, although inflation and unemployment remained high, and federal budget deficits soared.

Ford's dilemma was that his belief in limited presidential involvement set him against liberals who argued that strong executive leadership was necessary to make the welfare state work. When he failed to take the initiative, Congress intervened, and the two branches of government became embroiled in conflict. Ford vetoed numerous bills, including those creating a consumer protection agency and expanding programs in education, housing, and health. In response, Congress overrode a higher percentage of vetoes than at any time since the presidency of Franklin Pierce more than a century before.

The Carter Interlude

In the election of 1976, the nation's bicentennial year, Ford faced Jimmy Carter, former governor of Georgia. Carter, appealing to voters distrustful of political leadership, portrayed himself as an outsider. He stressed that he was not from Washington and that, unlike many of those mired in past scandals, he was not a lawyer. Carter's quest for the Democratic nomination benefited from reforms that increased the significance of primary elections in selecting a presidential candidate and decreased the influence of party professionals. Assisted by public relations experts, he effectively utilized the media, especially television, which

Presidential Election of 1976				
Year	Candidate	Party	Popular Vote	Electoral Vote
1976	JIMMY CARTER	Democratic	40,830,763 (50.0%)	297
	Gerald R. Ford	Republican	39,147,793 (48.0%)	240

Note: Winner's name appears in capital letters.

allowed him to bypass party machines and establish a direct electronic relationship with voters.

In the election, most elements of the old Democratic coalition came together once again, as the Democrats benefited from the fallout of the Watergate affair. Carter won a 50 to 48 percent majority of the popular vote and a 297 to 240 tally in the Electoral College. He did well with members of the working class, African Americans, and Catholics. He won most of the South, heartening to the Democrats after Nixon's gains there. Racial voting differences continued, however, as Carter attracted less than half of all white voters but an overwhelming majority of black voters.

Carter stood in stark contrast to his recent predecessors in the White House. Rooted in the rural South, he was a peanut farmer who shared the values of the region. He was also a graduate of the Naval Academy, trained as a manager and an engineer. A modest man by nature, he was not wholly comfortable with the pomp and incessant political activity in Washington. He hoped to take a more restrained approach to the presidency and thereby defuse its imperial stamp.

Initially, voters saw Carter as a reform Democrat committed to his party's liberal goals. When he had accepted the Democratic nomination, he had called for an end to race and sex discrimination. He had challenged the "political and economic elite" in America and sought a new approach to providing for the poor, old, and weak.

But Carter was hardly the old-line liberal some Democrats had hoped for. Though he called himself a populist, his political philosophy and priorities were never clear. His critics charged that he had no legislative strategy to communicate to Congress. Rather, they said with some truth, he responded to problems in a haphazard way and failed to provide firm direction. His status as an outsider, touted during the campaign, led him to ignore traditional political channels when he assumed power. He also seemed to become mired in detail, and to lose sight of larger issues. Like Herbert Hoover, he was a technocrat in the White House when liberals wanted a visionary to help them overcome hard times.

In economic affairs, Carter gave liberals some hope at first as he permitted a policy of deficit spending. When the Federal Reserve Board increased the money supply to help meet mount-

TIMELINE

1946	Employment Act
1947	Taft-Hartley Act
1948	"Dixiecrat" party formed
	Truman defeats Dewey
1949	Truman launches Fair Deal
1952	Dwight D. Eisenhower elected president
1953	Submerged Lands Act
1956	Eisenhower reelected
1960	John F. Kennedy elected president
1962	JFK confronts steel companies
1963	Kennedy assassinated; Lyndon B. Johnson becomes president
1964	Economic Opportunity Act initiates War on Poverty
	Johnson reelected president
1965	Department of Housing and Urban Development established
	Elementary and Secondary Education Act
1968	Robert F. Kennedy assassinated
	Police and protesters clash at Democratic national convention
	Richard Nixon elected president
1972	Nixon reelected
1973	Watergate hearings in Congress
	Spiro Agnew resigns as vice president
1974	OPEC price increases
	Inflation hits 11 percent
	Unemployment reaches 7.1 percent
	Nixon resigns; Gerald Ford becomes president
	Ford pardons Nixon
1975	Unemployment reaches 12 percent
1976	Jimmy Carter elected president
1977	Carter energy program

ing deficits, which reached peacetime records in these years, inflation rose to about 10 percent a year. Seeking to reduce inflation in 1979, Carter slowed down the economy by reducing spending and cut the deficit slightly. Contraction of the money supply led to greater unemployment and many small-business failures. Budget cuts fell largely on social programs and distanced Carter from reform-minded Democrats who had supported him three years before. Yet even that effort to arrest growing deficits was not enough. When the budget released in early 1980 still showed high spending levels, the financial community reacted strongly. Bond prices fell, and interest rates rose dramatically.

Similarly, Carter disappointed liberals by failing to construct an effective energy policy. OPEC had been increasing oil prices rapidly since 1973. Americans began to resent their dependence on foreign oil—over 40 percent was being imported by the end of the decade—and clamored for energy self-sufficiency. Carter responded in April 1977 with a comprehensive energy program, which he called the "moral equivalent of war." Critics seized on the acronym of that expression, MEOW, to describe the plan and had a field day attacking the president. Never an effective leader in working with the leg-

islative branch, Carter watched his proposals bog down in Congress for 26 months. Eventually, the program committed the nation to move from oil dependence to reliance on coal, possibly even on sun and wind, and established a new synthetic-fuel corporation. Nuclear power, another alternative, seemed less attractive as costs rose and accidents, like the one at Three Mile Island, occurred.

Carter further upset liberals by beginning deregulation—the removal of governmental controls in economic life. Arguing that certain restrictions established over the past century ended competition and increased consumer costs, he supported decontrol of oil and natural gas prices to spur production. He also deregulated the railroad, trucking, and airline industries.

Liberals were disappointed as the 1970s came to a close. Their hopes for a stronger commitment to a welfare state had been dashed and conservatives had the upper hand. Despite a tenuous Democratic hold on the presidency at the end of the decade, liberalism was in trouble in the United States.

 onclusion

Political Readjustment

The course of public policy shifted significantly in the post–World War II years. In the late 1940s and 1950s, American leaders took the first steps toward consolidating the welfare state that Franklin Roosevelt had begun to create in the decade before. In the 1960s, liberal Democrats went even further, as they pressed for large-scale government intervention to meet the social and economic problems that accompanied the modern industrial age. They were inspired by John Kennedy's rhetoric and saw the triumph of their approach in Lyndon Johnson's Great Society, as the nation strengthened its commitment to a capitalist welfare state. When the Democratic party became impaled on the Vietnam War and lost the presidency, the Republicans began dismantling the Great Society programs. While accepting some provisions of the modern welfare state, they objected to the aggressive liberal effort to make the government the major player in the political game and took exception to many of the programs aimed at the poor.

Most Americans, like Paul Cowan, met at the start of this chapter, embraced the message of John Kennedy and the New Frontier in the 1960s and endorsed the liberal approach. But over time, they began to question the tenets of liberalism as the economy faltered, as hard economic choices had to be made, and as the country became mired in Vietnam. Republicans challenging Democratic priorities gained the upper hand and disillusioned liberals like Cowan wondered if their approach could ever succeed.

Recommended Reading

General Works

Terry Anderson, *The Movement and the Sixties: Protest in America from Greensboro to Wounded Knee* (1995); Edward D. Berkowitz and Kim McQuaid, *Creating the Welfare State: The Political Economy of 20th Century Reform* (1992); John Morton Blum, *Years of Discord: American Politics and Society, 1961–1974* (1991); Paul Cowan, *The Making of an Un-American: A Dialogue with Experience* (1970); David Farber, *The Age of Great Dreams: America in the 1960s* (1994); James Gilbert, *Another Chance: Postwar America, 1945–1985* (1986); Todd Gitlin, *The Sixties: Years of Hope, Days of Rage* (1987); Jim F. Heath, *Decade of Disillusionment: The Kennedy-Johnson Years* (1975); Godfrey Hodgson, *America in Our Time* (1976); Allen J. Matusow, *The Unraveling of America: A History of Liberalism in the 1960s* (1984); William L. O'Neill, *Coming Apart: An Informal History of America in the 1960s* (1971); James L. Sundquist, *Politics and Policy: The Eisenhower, Kennedy, and Johnson Years* (1968).

Harry S Truman

Barton J. Bernstein and Allen J. Matusow, eds., *The Truman Administration: A Documentary History* (1966); Robert J. Donovan, *Conflict and Crisis: The Presidency of Harry S Truman, 1945–1948* (1977) and *Tumultuous Years: The Presidency of Harry S Truman, 1949–1953* (1982); Robert H. Ferrell, *Harry S. Truman and the Modern American Presidency* (1983); Alonzo L. Hamby, *Harry S. Truman and the Fair Deal* (1974); David McCullough, *Truman* (1992); Cabell Phillips, *The Truman Presidency: The History of a Triumphant Succession* (1966); Harry S Truman, *Memoirs*, 2 vols. (1955, 1956).

Dwight D. Eisenhower

Charles C. Alexander, *Holding the Line: The Eisenhower Era, 1952–1961* (1975); Craig Allen, *Eisenhower and the Mass Media: Peace, Prosperity, and Prime-Time TV* (1993); Stephen E. Ambrose, *Eisenhower: The President* (1984); Günter Bischof and Stephen E. Ambrose, eds., *Eisenhower: A Centenary Assessment* (1995); Dwight D. Eisenhower, *Mandate for Change, 1953–1956* (1963) and *Waging Peace* (1965); Fred I. Greenstein, *The Hidden-Hand Presidency: Eisenhower as Leader* (1982); Peter Lyon, *Eisenhower: Portrait of the Hero* (1974); Herbert S. Parmet, *Eisenhower and the American Crusades* (1972); Gary W. Reichard, *The Reaffirmation of Republicanism: Eisenhower and the 83rd Congress* (1975).

John F. Kennedy and the New Frontier

Henry Fairlie, *The Kennedy Promise* (1972); James N. Giglio, *The Presidency of John F. Kennedy* (1991); Nigel Hamilton, *JFK: Reckless Youth* (1992); Herbert S. Parmet, *Jack: The Struggles of John F. Kennedy* (1980) and *JFK: The Presidency of John F. Kennedy* (1983); Richard Reeves, *President Kennedy: Profile of Power* (1993); Thomas C. Reeves, *A Question of Character: A Life of John F. Kennedy* (1991); Arthur M. Schlesinger, Jr., *A Thousand Days: John F. Kennedy in the White House* (1965); Theodore C. Sorensen, *Kennedy* (1965).

Lyndon B. Johnson and the Great Society

Robert A. Caro, *The Years of Lyndon Johnson: The Path to Power* (1983) and *The Years of Lyndon Johnson: Means of Ascent* (1990); Robert Dallek, *Lone Star Rising: Lyndon Johnson and His Times* (1990); Robert A. Divine, ed., *Exploring the Johnson Years* (1981) and *The Johnson Years, Volume Two: Vietnam, the Environment, and Science* (1984); Rowland Evans, Jr., and Robert Novak, *Lyndon B. Johnson: The Exercise of Power* (1966); Julie Roy Jeffrey, *Education for the Children of the Poor* (1976); Lyndon Johnson, *The Vantage Point: Perspectives of the Presidency* (1971); Doris Kearns, *Lyndon Johnson and the American Dream* (1976); Sar A. Levitan and Robert Taggart, *The Promise of Greatness: The Social Programs of the Last Decade and Their Major Achievements* (1976); James T. Patterson, *America's Struggle Against Poverty* (1976).

Richard Nixon and Watergate

Stephen Ambrose, *Nixon: The Education of a Politician, 1913–1962* (1987); Rowland Evans, Jr., and Robert D. Novak, *Nixon in the White House* (1972); Stanley I. Kutler, *The Wars of Watergate: The Last Crisis of Richard Nixon* (1990); J. Anthony Lukas, *Nightmare: The Underside of the Nixon Years* (1976); Richard Nixon, *RN: The Memoirs of Richard Nixon* (1978); Jonathon Schell, *The Time of Illusion: An Historical and Reflective Account of the Nixon Era* (1975); Garry Wills, *Nixon Agonistes: The Crisis of the Self-made Man* (1969); Bob Woodward and Carl Bernstein, *All the President's Men* (1974) and *The Final Days* (1976).

Gerald Ford

John Robert Greene, *The Limits of Power: The Nixon and Ford Administrations* (1992); John Hersey, *The President* (1975); Richard Reeves, *A Ford, Not a Lincoln* (1975).

Jimmy Carter

Jimmy Carter, *Keeping Faith: Memories of a President* (1982); Gaddis Smith, *Morality, Reason, and Power: American Diplomacy in the Carter Years* (1985); Jules Witcover, *Marathon: The Pursuit of the Presidency, 1972–1976* (1977).

The Struggle for Social Reform

A nn Clarke—as she chooses to call herself now—always wanted to go to college. But girls from Italian families rarely did when she was growing up. Her mother, a Sicilian immigrant and widow, asked her brother for advice: "Should Antonina go to college?" "What's the point?" he replied. "She's just going to get married."

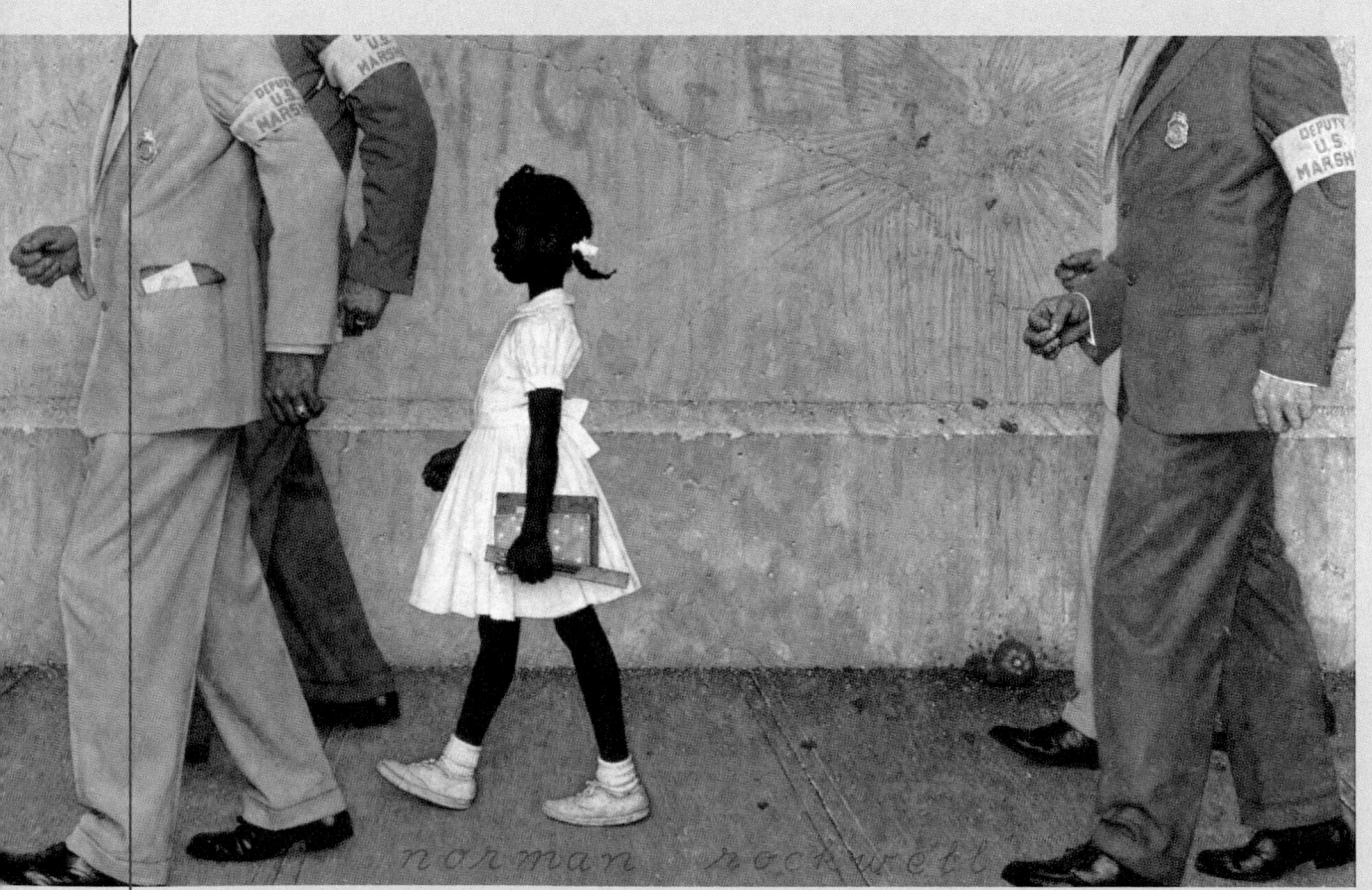

Life had not been easy for Antonina Rose Rumore. As a child in the 1920s, her Italian-speaking grandmother cared for her while her mother worked to support the family, first in the sweatshops, then as a seamstress. Even as she dreamed, Ann accommodated her culture's demands for dutiful daughters. Responsive to family needs, Ann finished the high school commercial course in three years. She struggled with ethnic prejudice as a legal secretary on Wall Street but still believed in the American dream and the Puritan work ethic. She was proud of her ability to bring money home to her family.

When World War II began, Ann wanted to join the WACS. "Better you should be a prostitute," her mother said. Ann went off to California instead, where she worked at resorts. When she left California, she vowed to return to that land of freedom and opportunity.

After the war, Ann married Gerard Clarke, a college man with an English background. Her children would grow up accepted with Anglo-Saxon names. Over the next 15 years, Ann devoted herself to her family. She was a mother above all, and that took all her time. But she still waited for her own chance. "I had this hunger to learn, this curiosity," she later recalled. By the early 1960s, her three children were all in school. Promising her husband to have dinner on the table every night at six, she enrolled at Pasadena City College. It was not easy. Family still came first. A simple problem was finding time to study. When doing dishes or cleaning house, she memorized lists of dates, historical events, and other material for school. Holiday time was difficult. Ann occasionally felt compelled to give everything up "to make Christmas." Forgetting about a whole semester's work two weeks before finals one year, she sewed nightgowns instead of writing her art history paper.

Her conflict over her studies was intensified by her position as one of the first older women to go back to college. "Sometimes I felt like I wanted to hide in the woodwork," she admitted. Often her teachers were younger than she was. It took four years to complete the two-year program. But she was not yet done. She wanted a bachelor's degree. Back she went, this time to California State College at Los Angeles.

As the years passed and the credits piled up, Ann became an honors student. Her children, now in college themselves, were proud and supportive; dinners became arguments over Faulkner and foreign policy. Even so, Ann still felt caught between her world at home and outside. Since she was at the top of her class, graduation should have been a special occasion. But she was only embarrassed when a letter from the school invited her parents to attend the final ceremonies. Ann could not bring herself to go.

With a college degree in hand, Ann returned to school for a teaching credential. Receiving her certificate at age 50, she faced the irony of social change. Once denied opportunities, Italians had assimilated into American society. Now she was just another Anglo in Los Angeles, caught in a changing immigration wave; now the city sought Hispanics and other minorities to teach in the schools. Jobs in education were scarce, and she was close to "retirement age," so she became a substitute in Mexican-American areas for the next ten years, specializing in bilingual education.

Meanwhile, Ann was troubled by the Vietnam War. "For every boy that died, one of us should lie down," she told fellow workers. She was not an activist, rather one of the millions of quieter Americans who ultimately helped bring about change. The social adjustments caused by the war affected her. Her son grew long hair and a beard and attended protest rallies. She worried that he would antagonize the ladies in Pasadena. Her daughter came home from college in boots and a leather miniskirt designed to shock. Ann accepted her children's changes as relatively superficial, confident in their fundamental values; "they were good kids," she knew. She trusted them, even as she worried about them.

Federal officials and local law enforcement authorities frequently had to assist African American children attending integrated schools in the sometimes turbulent aftermath of the *Brown* v. *Board of Education* decision of 1954. (Printed by permission of the Norman Rockwell Family Trust Copyright ©1964 The Norman Rockwell Family Trust)

*A*nn Clarke's experience paralleled that of millions of women in the post–World War II years. Caught up in traditional patterns of family life, these women began to recognize their need for something more. Like blacks, Hispanics, Native Americans, and members of other groups, American women struggled to transform the conditions of their lives and the rights they enjoyed within American society. In the process, they changed the nation itself.

This chapter describes the reform impulse that accompanied the effort to define the government's responsibility for economic and social stability described in Chapter 28. Like earlier reform efforts, particularly those during the Progressive era and the New Deal, this modern struggle sought to fulfill the promise of the American past and to provide liberty and equality in racial, gender, and social relations. The third reform cycle of the twentieth century, however, drew more from the militancy of those on the mudsills of society than from the pleas of middle-class activists. It reflected the attempt of often marginalized Americans to make the nation live up to its professed values. This chapter highlights the voices of such "outsiders" as it describes their efforts to square the ideals of American life with the realities many Americans faced. The chapter records the continuing frustrations of integrating diverse groups into American society while acknowledging their integrity and identity. And it notes the still-present tension accompanying the sharp debate over power and its distribution in the United States.

The Black Struggle for Equality

The quest for equality by African Americans played a central role in the struggle for civil rights in the postwar era. It influenced the long-standing protest movements of Native Americans and Latinos noted later in this chapter. It also provided an example for other groups, such as Asian Americans, whose experiences are detailed in the section on changes in immigration patterns in the following chapter. Stemming from an effort dating back to the Civil War and Reconstruction, the black movement had gained momentum by the mid-twentieth century. African Americans continued to press for reform through peaceful protest and political pressure. But change came slowly. Despite a number of major victories in the 1950s, rigid segregation of public accommodations remained the rule in the South. In the North, urban ghettos grew, as the influx of southern blacks continued. Crowded public housing, poor schools, and limited economic opportunities fostered serious discontent.

Mid-Twentieth Century Roots

African Americans had increased their demands for change in the 1930s and 1940s and had made significant gains during World War II (see Chapter 25). Black servicemen returning from the war vowed to reject second-class citizenship and helped mobilize a grass-roots movement to counter discrimination. In the postwar years, African struggles for independence, such as the Kenyan Mau Mau revolt against the British, inspired African American leaders who now saw the quest for black equality in a broader context. As Adam Clayton Powell, a Harlem preacher (and later congressman), warned, the black man "is ready to throw himself into the struggle to make the dream of America become flesh and blood, bread and butter, freedom and equality. He walks conscious of the fact that he is no longer alone—no longer a minority."

The racial question was dramatized in 1947 when Jackie Robinson broke the color line and began playing major-league baseball with the Brooklyn Dodgers. Sometimes teammates were hostile, sometimes opponents crashed into him with spikes flying high, but Robinson kept his frustrations to himself. A splendid first season helped ease the way, and after Robinson's trailblazing effort, other blacks, formerly confined to the old Negro leagues, started to move into the major leagues, then into professional football and basketball.

Many Americans began to respond as the nation's racial problems became entangled with

Jackie Robinson's electrifying play as the first African American in the major leagues led to acceptance of the integration of baseball. A spectacular rookie season in 1947 opened the way for other African Americans who had earlier been limited to the Negro leagues. (UPI/Corbis-Bettmann)

Cold War politics. As leader of the "free world," America appealed for support in Africa and Asia. Discrimination in the United States was an obvious drawback in the struggle to gain new friends.

A somewhat reluctant Truman supported the civil rights movement. A moderate on questions of race who believed in political, not social, equality, he responded to the growing strength of the African American vote. In 1946, he appointed a Committee on Civil Rights to investigate the problem of lynchings and other brutalities against blacks and to recommend what could be done. The committee's report, released in October 1947, showed that black Americans remained second-class citizens in every area of American life. The first report set a civil rights agenda for the next two decades.

Though Truman hedged at first, in February 1948, he sent a ten-point civil rights program to Congress—the first presidential civil rights plan since Reconstruction. When the southern wing of the Democratic party bolted later that year (see Chapter 28), he moved forward even more aggressively. First he issued an executive order barring discrimination in the federal establishment. Then he ordered equality of treatment in the military

services. Manpower needs in the Korean War led to the elimination of the last restrictions, particularly when the army found that integrated units performed well.

Elsewhere the administration pushed reforms as well. The Justice Department, not previously supportive of litigation from the National Association for the Advancement of Colored People (NAACP) on behalf of equal rights for African Americans, now entered the battle against segregation and filed briefs challenging the constitutionality of restrictions in housing, education, and interstate transportation. These actions helped build the pressure for change that influenced the Supreme Court. Congress, however, took little action.

Integrating the Schools

As the civil rights struggle gained momentum during the 1950s, the judicial system played a crucial role. The NAACP was determined to overturn the 1896 Supreme Court decision *Plessy* v. *Ferguson,* in which the Court had declared that segregation of the black and white races was constitutional if the facilities used by each were "separate but equal." The decree had been used for generations to sanction rigid segregation, primarily in the South, even though separate facilities were seldom, if ever, equal.

A direct challenge came in 1951. Oliver Brown, the father of 8-year-old Linda Brown, sued the school board of Topeka, Kansas, to allow his daughter to attend a school for white children she passed as she walked to the bus that carried her to a black school farther away. The case reached the Supreme Court, which added other school segregation cases to this one.

On May 17, 1954, the Supreme Court released its bombshell ruling in *Brown* v. *Board of Education*. For more than a decade, Supreme Court decisions had gradually expanded black civil rights. Now the Court unanimously decreed that "separate facilities are inherently unequal" and concluded that the "separate but equal" doctrine had no place in public education. A year later, the

Court turned to the question of implementation and declared that local school boards, acting with the guidance of lower courts, should move "with all deliberate speed" to desegregate their facilities.

President Dwight Eisenhower had the ultimate responsibility for executing the law. Doubting that simple changes in the law could improve race relations, he once observed, "I don't believe you can change the hearts of men with laws or decisions." Privately he thought that the *Brown* ruling was wrong, but he knew that it was his constitutional duty to see that the law was carried out. Even while urging sympathy for the South in its period of transition, he acted immediately to desegregate the Washington, D.C. schools as a model for the rest of the country. He also ordered desegregation in navy yards and veterans' hospitals.

The South resisted. In district after district, vicious scenes occurred. The crucial confrontation came in Little Rock, Arkansas, in 1957. A desegre-

National Guardsmen, under federal command, escorted African American students into Central High School in Little Rock, Arkansas, in 1957. Notice the number of students and the number of soldiers as forcible integration began. (Burt Glinn/Magnum Photos)

gation plan, to begin with the token admission of a few black students to Central High School, was ready to go into effect. Just before the school year began, Governor Orval Faubus declared on television that it would not be possible to maintain order if integration took place. National Guardsmen, posted by the governor to keep the peace and armed with bayonets, turned away nine black students as they tried to enter the school. After three weeks, a federal court ordered the troops to leave. When the black children entered the building, the white students, spurred on by their elders, belligerently opposed them, chanting such slogans as "Two, four, six, eight, we ain't gonna integrate." In the face of hostile mobs, the black children left the school.

With the lines drawn, attention focused on the moderate man in the White House, who faced a situation in which Little Rock whites were clearly defying the law. As a former military officer, Ike knew that such resistance could not be tolerated, and he finally took the one action he had earlier called unthinkable. For the first time since the end of Reconstruction, an American president called out federal troops to protect the rights of black citizens. Eisenhower ordered paratroopers to Little Rock and placed National Guardsmen under federal command. The black

children entered the school and attended classes with the military protecting their rights. Thus desegregation began.

Black Gains on Other Fronts

Meanwhile, African Americans themselves began organizing to take direct action and their efforts significantly advanced the civil rights movement. In the 1930s, some had joined the "Don't Buy Where You Can't Work" campaign begun in Chicago by itinerant street preacher Sufi Abdul Hamid. During World War II, others had marched under the slogan "We Die Together. Let's Eat Together" in the effort to integrate segregated restaurants. Now they were ready for an even more dramatic confrontation. The crucial event occurred in Montgomery, Alabama, in December 1955. Rosa Parks, a 42-year-old black seamstress who was also secretary of the Alabama NAACP, sat down in the front of a bus in a section reserved by custom for whites. Tired from a hard day's work, she refused to move when ordered to move back. The bus driver called the police at the next stop, and Parks was arrested and ordered to stand trial for violating the segregation laws. Although she had not intended to challenge the law or cause a

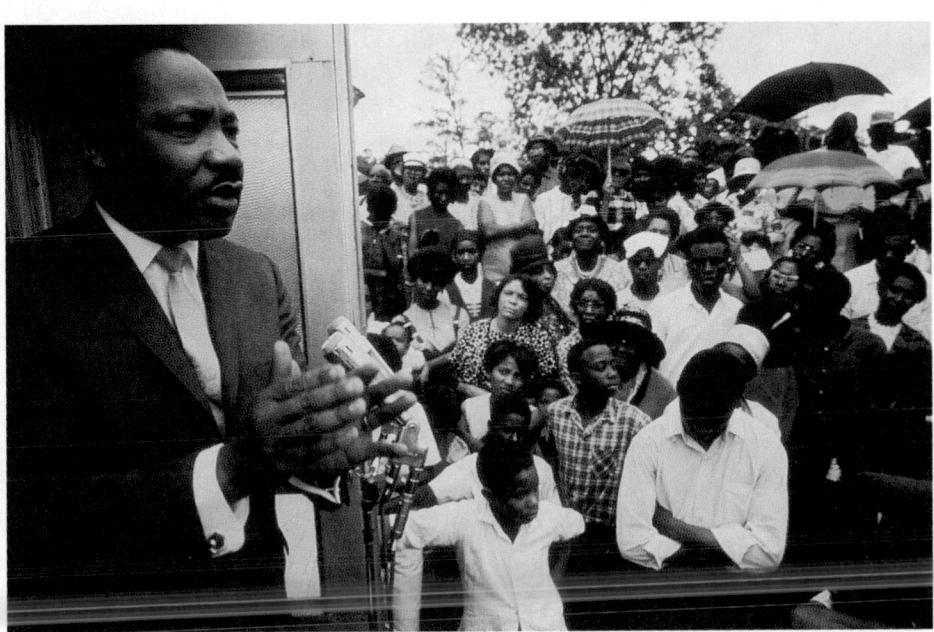

Baptist minister Martin Luther King, Jr., emerged as the black spokesman in the Montgomery, Alabama, bus boycott and soon became the most eloquent African American leader of the entire civil rights movement. Drawing on his religious background, he was able to mobilize blacks and whites alike in the struggle for equal rights. (Bob Adelman/Magnum Photos)

scene, her stance marked a new phase in the civil rights struggle. Like Rosa Parks, ordinary black men and women would challenge the racial status quo and force both white and black leaders to respond.

In Montgomery, black civil rights officials seized the issue. E. D. Nixon, state NAACP president, told Parks, "This is the case we've been looking for. We can break this situation on the bus with your case." Fifty black leaders met to discuss the case and decided to organize a massive boycott of the bus system.

Martin Luther King, Jr., the 27-year-old minister of the Baptist church where the meeting was held, soon emerged as the preeminent spokesman of the protest. King was an impressive figure and an inspiring speaker. "There comes a time when people get tired … of being kicked about by the brutal feet of oppression," he declared. It was time to be more assertive, to cease being "patient with anything less than freedom and justice."

Although King, like others, was arrested on the trumped-up charge of speeding and jailed, grassroots support bubbled up. In Montgomery, 50,000 African Americans walked or formed car pools to avoid the transit system. Their actions cut gross revenue on city buses by 65 percent. Almost a year later, the Supreme Court ruled that bus segregation, like school segregation, violated the Constitution, and the boycott ended. But the mood it fostered continued, and for many blacks peaceful protest became a way of life.

Meanwhile, a concerted effort developed to guarantee black voting rights. The provisions of the Fifteenth Amendment notwithstanding, many states had circumvented the law for decades (see Chapter 16). Some states required a poll tax or a literacy test or an examination of constitutional understanding. Blacks often found themselves excluded from the polls.

Largely because of the legislative genius of Senate majority leader Lyndon B. Johnson of Texas, a civil rights bill, the first since Reconstruction, moved toward passage. With his eye on the presidency, Johnson wanted to establish his credentials as a man who could look beyond narrow southern interests. Paring the bill down to the provisions he felt would pass, Johnson pushed the measure through.

The Civil Rights Act of 1957 created a Civil Rights Commission and empowered the Justice Department to go to court in cases where blacks were denied the right to vote. The bill was a compromise measure, yet it was the first successful effort to protect civil rights in 82 years.

Again led by Johnson, Congress passed the Civil Rights Act of 1960, which set stiffer penalties for people who interfered with the right to vote, but again stopped short of authorizing federal registrars to register blacks to vote and so, like its predecessor, was generally ineffective.

The civil rights movement made important strides during the Eisenhower years, though little of the progress resulted from the president's leadership. Rather, the efforts of blacks themselves and the rulings of the Supreme Court brought the most significant changes. The period of grass-roots civil rights activity, now launched, would continue in the 1960s.

Confrontation Continues

A spectrum of organizations, some old, some new, carried the fight forward. The NAACP, founded in 1910, remained committed to overturning the legal bases for segregation. The Congress of Racial Equality (CORE), an interracial group established in 1942, promoted change through peaceful confrontation. In 1957, after their victory in Montgomery, Martin Luther King, Jr., and others formed the Southern Christian Leadership Conference (SCLC), an organization of southern black clergy. The Student Nonviolent Coordinating Committee (SNCC, pronounced "snick") began to operate in 1960 and recruited young Americans who had not been involved in the civil rights struggle. SNCC, an offshoot of SCLC, was far more militant than the older, gradualist organizations.

Confrontations continued in the 1960s. On January 31, 1960, four black college students from the Agricultural and Technical College in Greensboro, North Carolina, sat down at a segregated Woolworth's lunch counter and deliberately violated southern segregation laws by refusing to leave. When a reporter inquired how long they had been planning the protest, the students responded, "All our lives!" The sit-ins captured media attention, and soon involved thousands of

African Americans. Those protesting often met with a brutal response. John Lewis, an African American activist who participated in a sit-in in Nashville, Tennessee, described his experience:

> A group of young white men came in and they started pulling and beating primarily the young women. They put lighted cigarettes down their backs, in their hair, and they were really beating people. In a short time police officials came in and placed all of us under arrest, and not a single member of the white group, the people that were opposing our sit-in, was arrested.

The following year, sit-ins gave rise to freedom rides, aimed at testing southern transportation facilities, recently desegregated by a Supreme Court decision. Organized initially by CORE and aided by SNCC, the program sent groups of blacks and whites together on buses heading south and stopping at terminals along the way. The riders, peaceful themselves, anticipated confrontations that would publicize their cause and generate political support. In Anniston, Alabama, CORE leader James Farmer depicted the confrontation that occurred as a mob of white men attacked a bus that was preparing to leave:

> Before the bus pulled out … members of the mob took their sharp instruments and slashed tires. The bus got to the outskirts of Anniston and the tires blew out and the bus ground to a halt. Members of the mob had boarded cars and followed the bus, and now with the disabled bus standing there, the members of the mob surrounded it, held the door closed, and a member of the mob threw a firebomb into the bus, breaking a window to do so.

In Birmingham, police made an agreement with the Ku Klux Klan to give Klansmen 15 minutes alone to beat the Freedom Riders. Although the FBI knew about the plan, the federal agency did nothing to stop it.

In North and South alike, consciousness of the need to combat racial discrimination grew. The civil rights movement became the most powerful moral campaign since the abolitionist crusade before the Civil War. Often working together

In violation of southern law, black college students refused to leave a lunch counter, launching a new campaign in the struggle. Here the students wait patiently for service, or forcible eviction, as a way of dramatizing their determination to end segregation. (Bruce Roberts/Photo Researchers)

closely, blacks and whites vowed to eliminate racial barriers.

Anne Moody, who grew up in a small town in Mississippi, personified the awakening of black consciousness. As a child, she had watched the murder of friends and acquaintances who had somehow transgressed the limits set for blacks. Overcoming the hardships of growing up poor and black in the rural South, Moody became the first member of her family to go to college, enrolling at Tougaloo College, near Jackson, Mississippi. Once there, she found her own place in the civil rights movement. She joined the NAACP and became involved in the activities of SNCC and CORE. Slowly, she noted, "I could feel myself beginning to change. For the first time I began to think something would be done about whites killing, beating, and misusing Negroes. I knew I was going to be a part of whatever happened." Participating in sit-ins where she was thrashed and jailed for her activities, she remained deeply involved in the movement.

Many whites also joined the struggle in the South. Mimi Feingold, a white student at Swarthmore College in Pennsylvania, helped picket Woolworth's in Chester, Pennsylvania, and worked to unionize Swarthmore's black dining hall workers. In 1961, after her sophomore year, she headed south to join the freedom rides sponsored by CORE. Like many others, Feingold found herself in the midst of often-violent confrontations and went to jail as an act of conscience. In Jackson, Mississippi, she spent a month behind bars.

In 1962, the civil rights movement accelerated. James Meredith, a black air force veteran and student at Jackson State College, applied to the all-white University of Mississippi, only to be rejected on racial grounds. Suing to gain admission, he carried his case to the Supreme Court, where Justice Hugo Black affirmed his claim. But then Governor Ross Barnett, an adamant racist, announced defiantly that Meredith would not be admitted, whatever the Court decision, and on one occasion personally blocked the way. A major riot followed; tear gas covered the university grounds; and by the riot's end, two men lay dead and hundreds were hurt.

An even more violent confrontation began in April 1963, in Birmingham, Alabama, where local black leaders encouraged Martin Luther King, Jr., to launch another attack on southern segregation. The city, 40 percent black, was rigidly segregated along racial and class lines. "We believed that while a campaign in Birmingham would surely be the toughest fight of our civil rights careers," King later explained, "it could, if successful, break the back of segregation all over the nation."

Though the demonstrations were nonviolent, the responses were not. City officials declared that protest marches violated city regulations against parading without a license, and, over a five-week period, they arrested 2,200 blacks, some of them schoolchildren. Police Commissioner Eugene "Bull" Connor used high-pressure fire hoses, electric cattle prods, and trained police dogs to force the protesters back. As the media recorded the

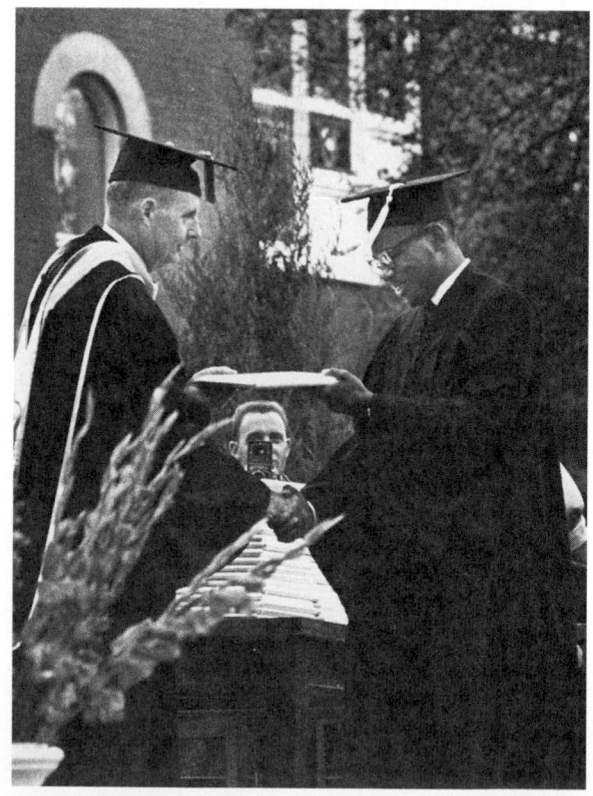

James Meredith refused to be driven from the University of Mississippi, despite the opposition of the governor and a campus riot. His perseverance paid off, as he ultimately earned his degree. (UPI/Corbis-Bettmann)

events, Americans watching television and reading newspapers were horrified. The images of violence created mass sympathy for black Americans' civil rights struggle.

Kennedy's Response

John Kennedy claimed to be sickened by the pictures from Birmingham but insisted that he could do nothing, even though he had sought and won black support in 1960. The narrowness of his electoral victory made him reluctant to press white southerners on civil rights when he needed their votes on other issues. Kennedy initially failed to propose any civil rights legislation. Nor did he fulfill a campaign promise to end housing discrimination by presidential order, despite gifts of numerous bottles of ink. Not until November 1962, after the midterm elections, did he take a modest action—an executive order ending segregation in federally financed housing.

Events finally forced Kennedy to act more boldly. In the James Meredith confrontation, the president, like his predecessor in the Little Rock crisis, had to send federal troops to restore control and to guarantee Meredith's right to attend. The administration also forced the desegregation of the University of Alabama and helped arrange a compromise providing for desegregation of Birmingham's municipal facilities, implementation of more equitable hiring practices, and formation of a biracial committee. And when white bombings aimed at eliminating black leaders in Birmingham caused thousands of blacks to abandon nonviolence and rampage through the streets, Kennedy readied federal troops to intervene.

He also spoke out more forcefully than before. In a nationally televised address, he called the

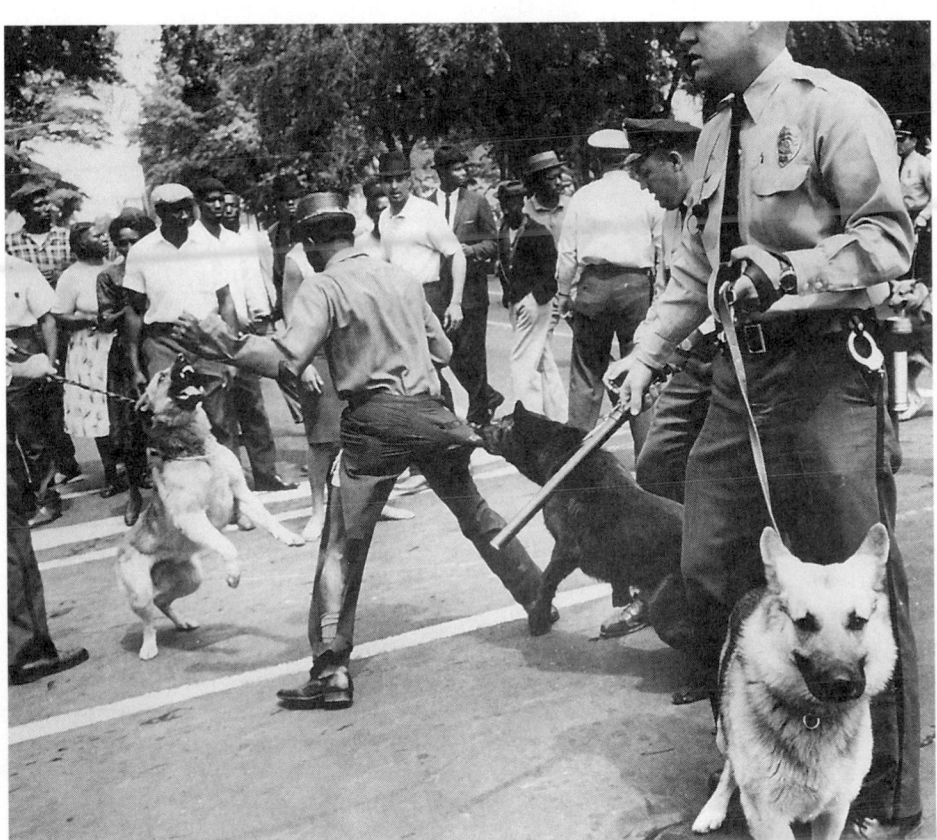

In Birmingham, city officials resisted peaceful demonstrators with brutal force. Here, city police use trained dogs to drive marchers back. Televised nationally, the police response appalled the American public. As newsman Eric Sevareid observed, "A newspaper or television picture of a snarling police dog set upon a human being is recorded on the permanent photoelectric file of every human brain." (Charles Moore/Black Star)

quest for equal rights a "moral issue" and asked, "are we to say to the world, and, much more importantly, to each other that this is a land of the free except for the Negroes ..." Just hours after the president spoke, assassins killed Medgar Evers, a black NAACP official, in his own driveway in Jackson, Mississippi.

Kennedy sent Congress a new civil rights bill, far stronger than a moderate one proposed earlier in the year. The legislation prohibited segregation in public places, banned discrimination wherever federal money was involved, and advanced the process of school integration. Polls showed that 63 percent of the nation supported his stand.

To lobby for passage of this measure, civil rights leaders, pressed from below by black activists, arranged a massive march on Washington in August 1963. More than 200,000 people gathered from across the country and demonstrated enthusiastically. Celebrities present included diplomat Ralph Bunche, writer James Baldwin, entertainers Sammy Davis, Jr., Harry Belafonte, and Lena Horne, and former baseball player Jackie Robinson. The folk music artists of the early 1960s were there as well. Joan Baez, Bob Dylan, and Peter, Paul, and Mary led the crowd in songs associated with the movement such as "Blowin' in the Wind" and "We Shall Overcome."

The high point of the day was the address by Martin Luther King, Jr., the nation's preeminent spokesman for civil rights and proponent of nonviolent protest. King proclaimed his faith in the decency of his fellow citizens and in their ability to extend the promises of the Constitution and the Declaration of Independence to every American. With all the power of a southern preacher, he implored his audience to share his faith.

"I have a dream," King declared, "that one day this nation will rise up and live out the true meaning of its creed: 'We hold these truths to be self-evident, that all men are created equal.' I have a dream that one day on the red hills of Georgia, the sons of former slaves and the sons of former slaveowners will be able to sit together at the table of brotherhood." It was a fervent appeal, and one to which the crowd responded. Each time King used the refrain "I have a dream," thousands of blacks and whites roared together. King concluded by

The 1963 march on Washington was a high point in the civil rights movement. Several hundred thousand demonstrators lined the reflecting pool leading out from the Washington Monument and heard Martin Luther King, Jr., and other black leaders eloquently plead for racial equality. (Fred Ward/Black Star)

quoting from an old hymn: "Free at last! Free at last! Thank God almighty, we are free at last!"

Despite the power of the rhetoric, not all were moved. Anne Moody, who had come up from her activist work in Mississippi to attend the event, sat on the grass by the Lincoln Memorial as the speaker's words rang out. "Martin Luther King went on and on talking about his dream," she said. "I sat there thinking that ... we never had time to sleep, much less dream." Nor was the Congress prompted to do much. Despite large Democratic majorities, strong white southern resistance to the cause of civil rights remained, and as of November 1963, Kennedy's bill was still bottled up in committee.

Legislative Success in the Johnson Years

Lyndon Johnson was more successful than Kennedy in advancing the cause of civil rights. His first priority on assuming office was civil rights reform. In 1963, Johnson revived Kennedy's sidetracked civil rights proposal. Seizing the opportunity provided by Kennedy's assassination, Johnson told Congress, "No memorial oration or eulogy could more eloquently honor President Kennedy's memory than the earliest possible passage of the civil rights bill." He pushed the bill through Congress, heading off a Senate filibuster by persuading his old colleague, minority leader Everett Dirksen of Illinois, to work for cloture—a two-thirds vote to cut off debate. In June 1964, the Senate for the first time imposed cloture to advance a civil rights measure, and passage soon followed. "No army can withstand the strength of an idea whose time has come," Dirksen explained.

The Civil Rights Act of 1964 outlawed racial discrimination in all public accommodations and authorized the Justice Department to act with greater authority in school and voting matters. In addition, an equal opportunity provision prohibited discriminatory hiring on grounds of race, gender, religion, or national origin in firms with more than 25 employees. The law was one of the great achievements of the 1960s.

Johnson realized that the Civil Rights Act of 1964 was only a starting point, since widespread discrimination still existed in American society. Despite the voting rights measures of 1957 and 1960, African Americans still found it difficult to vote in large areas of the South. Freedom Summer, sponsored by SNCC and other civil rights groups in 1964, focused attention on the problem by sending black and white students to Mississippi to work for black rights. Early in the summer, two whites, Michael Schwerner and Andrew Goodman, and one black, James Chaney, were murdered. By the end of the summer, 80 workers had been beaten, 1,000 arrests had been made, and 37 churches had been bombed.

Early in 1965, another confrontation made national headlines. Alabama police clubbed and tear-gassed demonstrators in an aborted march from Selma to the state capital at Montgomery.

President Johnson sent the National Guard to protect another march to Montgomery and then asked Congress for a voting bill that would close the loopholes of the previous two acts.

The Voting Rights Act of 1965, perhaps the most important law of the decade, singled out the South for its restrictive practices and authorized the U.S. attorney general to appoint federal examiners to register voters where local officials were obstructing the registration of blacks. In the year after passage of the act, 400,000 blacks registered to vote in the Deep South; by 1968, the number reached a million.

Black Power Challenges Liberal Reform

Despite passage of the Civil Rights Act of 1964 and the Voting Rights Act of 1965, racial discrimination remained in both North and South. Still-segregated schools, wretched housing, and inadequate job opportunities were continuing problems. As the struggle for civil rights moved north, dramatic divisions within the movement emerged.

Initially, the civil rights campaign had been integrated and nonviolent. Its acknowledged leader was Martin Luther King, Jr. But now tensions between blacks and whites flared within

Fannie Lou Hamer, pictured here, provided eloquent testimony about the discrimination that kept many Southern blacks from voting as she lobbied unsuccessfully for seating the delegates of the Mississippi Freedom Democratic party at the Democratic national convention of 1964. (AP/Wide World Photos)

organizations, and younger black leaders began to challenge King's nonviolent approach. They were tired of beatings, jailings, church bombings, and the slow pace of change when dependent on white liberal support and government action. Anne Moody, the stalwart activist in Mississippi, voiced the doubts so many blacks harbored about the possibility of real change. Discouraged after months of struggle, she boarded a bus taking civil rights workers north to testify about the abuses that still remained. As she listened to the others singing the movement's songs, she was overwhelmed by the suffering she had so often seen. "We Shall Overcome" reverberated around her, but all she could think was, "I wonder. I really wonder."

One episode that contributed to many blacks' suspicion of white liberals occurred at the Democratic national convention of 1964 in Atlantic City. SNCC, active in the Freedom Summer project in Mississippi, had founded the Freedom Democratic party as an alternative to the all-white delegation that was to represent the state. Testifying before the credentials committee, black activist Fannie Lou Hamer reported that she had been beaten, jailed, and denied the right to vote. Yet the committee's final compromise, pressed by President Johnson, who worried about losing southern support in the coming election, was that the white delegation would still be seated, with two members of the protest organization offered seats at large. That response hardly satisfied those who had risked their lives and families to try to vote in Mississippi. As civil rights leader James Forman observed, "Atlantic City was a powerful lesson, not only for the black people from Mississippi, but for all of SNCC.... No longer was there any hope ... that the federal government would change the situation in the Deep South." SNCC, once a religious, integrated organization, began to change into an all-black cadre that could mobilize poor blacks for militant action. "Liberation" replaced civil rights as a goal.

Increasingly, angry blacks argued that the nation must no longer withhold the rights pledged in its founding credo. Black author James Baldwin wrote in one of his eloquent essays that unless change came soon, the worst could be expected: "If we do not now dare everything, the fulfillment of that prophecy, recreated from the Bible in song

by a slave, is upon us: God gave Noah the rainbow sign, No more water, the fire next time!"

Even more responsible for channeling black frustration into a new set of goals and tactics was Malcolm X. Born Malcolm Little and reared in ghettos from Detroit to New York, he hustled numbers and prostitutes in the big cities. Arrested and imprisoned, he became a convert to the Nation of Islam and a disciple of black leader Elijah Muhammad. He began to preach that the white man was responsible for the black man's condition and that blacks had to help themselves.

Malcolm was impatient with the moderate civil rights movement. He grew tired of hearing "all of this non-violent, begging-the-white-man kind of dying ... all of this sitting-in, sliding-in, wading-in, eating-in, diving-in, and all the rest." Espousing black separatism and black nationalism for most of

"The day of nonviolence is over," Malcolm X proclaimed, as many African Americans listened enthusiastically. A compelling speaker, Malcolm made a powerful case for a more aggressive campaign for black rights. (UPI/Corbis-Bettmann)

	The Struggle for Equal Rights	
Year	**Event**	**Effect**
1947	Report of Truman's Committee on Civil Rights	Showed that African Americans remained second-class citizens in the United States
1948	Truman's executive order integrating the armed services	Opened the way for equal opportunity in the armed forces
1954	*Brown* v. *Board of Education* decision	Supreme Court ruled that "separate but equal" schools were unconstitutional; first step in ending school segregation
1955	Montgomery bus boycott	Black solidarity tested local petty segregation laws and customs
1957	Little Rock school integration crisis	White resistance to integration of Little Rock's Central High School resulted in Eisenhower's calling in federal troops
	Civil Rights Act	Created Civil Rights Commission and empowered Justice Department to go to court to guarantee blacks the right to vote
1960	Civil Rights Act	Plugged loopholes in Civil Rights Act of 1957
	Sit-in demonstrations	Gained support for desegregation of public facilities
1961	Freedom rides	Dramatized struggle to desegregate transportation facilities
1962	James Meredith's attempt to attend University of Mississippi	Required federal intervention to uphold blacks' right to attend public institutions
1963	Effort to desegregate Birmingham, Alabama	Brutal response of police televised, sensitizing entire nation to plight of blacks
	March on Washington	Gathered support and inspiration for the civil rights movement; scene of Rev. Martin Luther King, Jr.'s "I Have a Dream" speech
1964	Civil Rights Act	Outlawed racial discrimination in public accommodations
1965	Voting Rights Act	Allowed federal examiners to register black voters where necessary
1971	Busing decision	Supreme Court ruled that court-ordered desegregation was constitutional, even if it employed busing
1978	*Bakke* decision	Supreme Court ruled that affirmative action was constitutional but that firm racial quotas were not

his public career, he argued for black control of black communities, preached an international perspective embracing African peoples in diaspora, and appealed to blacks to fight racism "by any means necessary."

Malcolm X became the most dynamic spokesman for poor northern blacks since Marcus Garvey in the 1920s. Though he was assassinated by black antagonists in 1965, his African-centered, uncompromising perspective helped shape the struggle against racism.

One man influenced by Malcolm's message was Stokely Carmichael. Born in Trinidad, he came to the United States at the age of 11, where he grew up with an interest in political affairs and black protest. While at Howard University, he participated in pickets and demonstrations and was beaten and jailed. Frustrated with the strategy of civil disobedience as he became active in SNCC, he urged field-workers to carry weapons for self-defense. It was time for blacks to cease depending on whites, he argued, and to make SNCC into a black organization. His election as head of the student group reflected SNCC's growing radicalism.

The split in the black movement was dramatized in June 1966 when Carmichael's followers challenged those of Martin Luther King, Jr., during a march in Mississippi. King still adhered to nonviolence and interracial cooperation. Carmichael, just out of jail after arrest for his protest activities, jumped onto a flatbed truck to address the group. "This is the twenty-seventh time I have been arrested—and I ain't going to jail no more!" he shouted. "The only way we gonna stop them white men from whippin' us is to take over. We been saying freedom for six years and we ain't got nothing. What we gonna start saying now is Black Power!" Carmichael had the audience in his hand as he repeated, and the crowd shouted back, "We ... want ... Black ... Power!"

Black Power was a call for a broad-based campaign to build independent institutions in the African American community. It drew on growing demands for an end to abuse of black women. When Malcolm X heard about a vicious beating Fannie Lou Hamer had received in Winona, Mississippi, he cried, "I ask myself how in the world we can expect to be respected as *men* when we will allow something like this to be done to our women, and we do nothing about it." Black Power fostered a powerful sense of black pride. The movement included a wide variety of different figures: cultural nationalists such as Maulana Ron Karenga, an activist scholar and early authority on Black Studies; advocates of black capitalism such as Nathan Wright, Jr., chairman of 1967 and 1968 National and International Conferences on Black Power; and revolutionary nationalists such as Huey P. Newton, a proponent of aggressive liberation measures. Its most enduring legacy was political and cultural mobilization at the grass-roots level, even if it only partially realized the goals it sought.

Black Power led to demands for more drastic action. The Black Panthers, radical activists who organized first in Oakland, California, and then in other cities, formed a militant organization that vowed to eradicate not only racial discrimination but capitalism as well. H. Rap Brown, who succeeded Carmichael as head of SNCC, became known for his statement that "violence is as American as cherry pie."

Violence accompanied the more militant calls for reform and showed that racial injustice was not a southern problem but an American one. Riots erupted in Rochester, New York City, and several New Jersey cities in 1964. In 1965, in the Watts neighborhood of Los Angeles, a massive uprising lasting five days left 34 dead, more than 1,000 injured, and hundreds of structures burned to the ground. Violence broke out again in other cities in 1966 and 1967. When Martin Luther King, Jr., fell to a white assassin's bullet in April 1968, angry blacks reacted by rioting once more in cities around the country.

"Southern Strategy" and Showdown on Civil Rights

Richard Nixon, elected president in 1968, was less sympathetic to the cause of civil rights than his predecessors. In 1968, the Republicans had won only 12 percent of the black vote, leading Nixon to conclude that any effort to woo the black elec-

When busing was mandated to end de facto school segregation in the North, the order frequently prompted fierce resistance. Here police provide protection for the children being bused. (Owen Franken/Gamma Liaison)

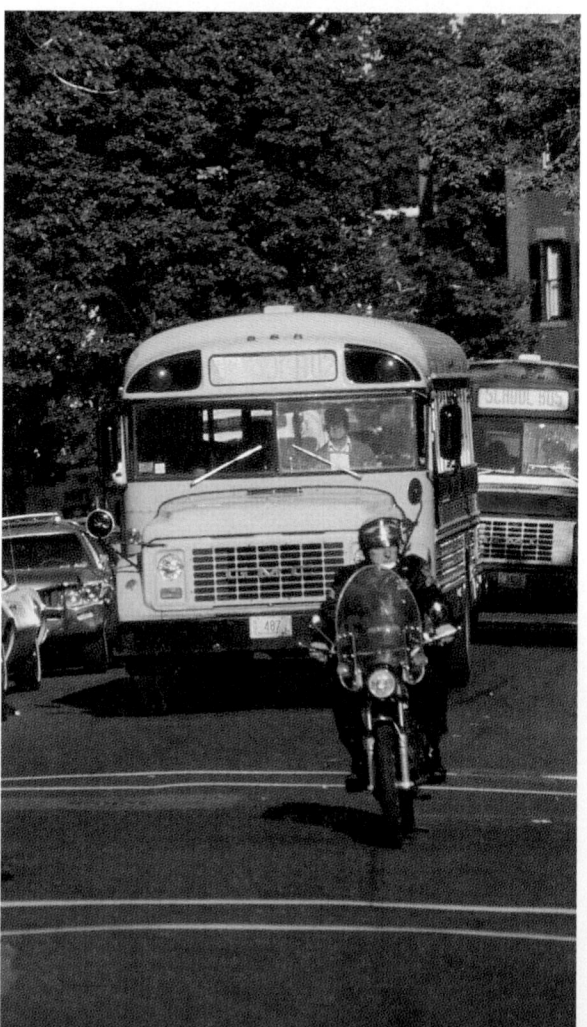

torate would endanger his attempt to obtain white southern support.

From the start, the Nixon administration sought to scale back the federal commitment to civil rights. It moved at the start to reduce appropriations for fair-housing enforcement. Then the Department of Justice tried to block an extension of the Voting Rights Act of 1965. Although Congress approved the extension, the administration's position on racial issues was clear. When South Carolina Senator Strom Thurmond and others tried to suspend federal school desegregation guidelines, the Justice Department lent support by urging a delay in meeting desegregation deadlines in 33 of Mississippi's school districts. When a unanimous Supreme Court rebuffed the effort, the president disagreed publicly with the decision.

Nixon also faced the growing controversy over busing as a means of desegregation, a highly charged issue in the 1970s. Transporting students from one area to another to attend school was nothing new. By 1970, over 18 million students, almost 40 percent of those in the United States, rode buses to school. Yet when busing became tangled with the question of integration, it inflamed passions.

In the South, before the Supreme Court endorsed integration, busing had long been used to maintain segregated schools. Some black students in Selma, Alabama, for example, traveled 50 miles by bus to an entirely black trade school in Montgomery, even though a similar school for whites stood nearby. Now, however, busing was a means of breaking down racial barriers.

The issue came to a head in North Carolina, in the Charlotte-Mecklenburg school system. A desegregation plan involving voluntary transfer was in effect, but many blacks still attended largely segregated schools. A federal judge ruled that the district was not in compliance with the latest Supreme Court decisions, and in 1971, the Supreme Court ruled that district courts had broad authority to order the desegregation of school systems—by busing, if necessary.

Earlier, Nixon had opposed such busing. Now he proposed a moratorium or even a restriction on busing and went on television to denounce it.

Although Congress did not accede to his request, southerners knew where the president stood.

As the busing mandate spread to the North, resistance spilled out of the South. In many of the nation's largest northern cities, schools were as rigidly segregated as in the South, largely because of residential patterns. This segregation was called *de facto* to differentiate it from the *de jure* or legal segregation that had existed in the South. Mississippi senator John C. Stennis, a bitter foe of busing, hoped to stir up the North by making it subject to the same standards as the South. He proposed requiring the government to enforce federal desegregation guidelines uniformly throughout the country or not use them at all. Court decisions subsequently ordered many northern cities to desegregate their schools.

The effort to integrate proved rockier in Boston than anywhere else in the North. In 1973, 85 percent of the blacks in the city attended schools that had a black majority. More than half of the African American students were in schools that were 90 percent black. In June 1974, a federal judge ordered busing to begin. The first phase, involving 17,000 pupils, was to start in the fall of that year.

For many younger students, attendance at different elementary schools went smoothly. Reassigned high school students were less fortunate. A white boycott at South Boston High cut attendance from the anticipated 1500 to fewer than 100 on the first day. Buses bringing in black students were stoned, and some children were injured. White working-class South Bostonians felt that they were being asked to carry the burden of middle-class liberals' racial views. Similar resentments triggered racial episodes elsewhere. In many cases, white families either enrolled their children in private schools or fled the city altogether.

The Republicans managed to slow down the school desegregation movement. Nixon catered successfully to his conservative constituents and demonstrated he was on their side. His successor, Gerald Ford, never came out squarely against civil rights, but his lukewarm approach to desegregation demonstrated a further weakening of the federal commitment.

The situation was less inflamed at the college level, but the same pattern held. Blacks made significant progress until the Republican administrations in the late 1960s and 1970s slowed the movement for civil rights. Integration at the postsecondary level came easier as federal affirmative-action guidelines brought more blacks into colleges and universities. In 1950, only 83,000 black students were enrolled in institutions of higher education. A decade later, more than one million were working for college degrees. Black enrollment in colleges reached 9.3 percent of the college population in 1976, then dropped back slightly to 9.1 percent in 1980, just what it had been in 1973.

As blacks struggled on the educational and occupational fronts, some whites protested that gains came at their expense and amounted to "reverse discrimination." In 1973 and 1974, for example, Allan Bakke, a white, applied to the medical school at the University of California at Davis. Twice rejected, he sued on the grounds that a racial quota reserving 16 of 100 places for minority-group applicants was a form of reverse discrimination that violated the Civil Rights Act of 1964. In 1978, the Supreme Court ordered Bakke's admission to the medical school, but in a complex ruling involving six separate opinions, the Court upheld the consideration of race in admissions policies, even while arguing that quotas could no longer be imposed.

Jimmy Carter, president when the *Bakke* decision was handed down, tried to adopt a more aggressive approach than his Republican predecessors. He brought a large number of qualified blacks into his administration. Some, like Andrew Young, his ambassador to the United Nations, were highly visible. But Carter's lack of support for increased social programs for the poor hurt the majority of black citizens and strained their loyalty to the Democratic party.

The civil rights movement underscored the democratic values on which the nation was based, but the gap between rhetoric and reality remained. In an era when industrial and farming employment shrank and rents rose at a highly inflationary rate, most black families remained poor. African American income was substantially lower than white income, as the chart on this page shows. After early optimism in the years when the movement made its greatest strides, blacks and sympathetic whites were troubled by the direction of public policy. Given a wavering national commitment to reform in the 1970s, only pressures from reform groups kept the faltering civil rights movement alive.

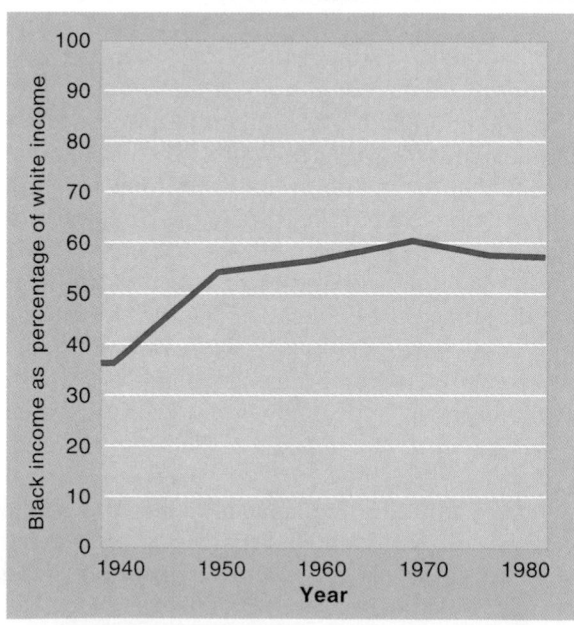

Ratio of Median Black-to-White Family Income, 1940–1980

This chart shows the substantial difference between family income for blacks and whites and reveals it has changed slowly since World War II. Source: Data from U.S. Department of Labor and *Statistical Abstract of the United States*, 1991.

Pressure from the Women's Movement

The black struggle for equality in the 1960s and 1970s was accompanied by a women's movement that grew out of the agitation for civil rights but soon developed a life of its own. This struggle, like the struggles by Hispanics and Native Americans, employed the confrontational approach and the vocabulary of the civil rights movement to create pressure for change. Using proven strategies, it sometimes proceeded even faster than the black effort.

Attacking the Feminine Mystique

Many white women joined the civil rights movement only to find that they were second-class citizens. Men, black and white, held the policy positions and relegated women to menial chores when not actually involved in demonstrations or voter drives. Many women also felt sexually exploited by male leaders. Stokely Carmichael's comment only underscored their point. "The only position for women in SNCC," he said, "is prone."

Although the civil rights movement helped spark the women's movement, broad social changes provided the preconditions. During the 1950s and 1960s, increasing numbers of married women entered the labor force (see Chapter 26). Equally important, many more young women were attending college. By 1970, women earned 41 percent of all B.A. degrees awarded, in comparison with only 25 percent in 1950. These educated young women held high hopes for themselves, even if they still earned substantially less than men.

Just as in the civil rights movement, reform legislation played a part in ending sexual discrimination. Title 7 of the 1964 Civil Rights bill, as originally drafted, prohibited discrimination on the grounds of race. During legislative debate, conservatives opposed to black civil rights seized on an amendment to include discrimination on the basis of gender, in the hope of defeating the entire bill.

Women in the Work Force, 1920–1980

This graph shows the dramatic increase in the number of women in the work force. Note particularly the rise in the number of working women 25–44 years old in the 1970s. Source: U.S. Bureau of the Census.

But the amendment passed, and then the full measure was approved, giving women a legal tool for attacking discrimination. They discovered, however, that the Equal Employment Opportunities Commission regarded women's complaints of discrimination as far less important than those of blacks.

In 1966, a group of 28 professional women, including author Betty Friedan, established the National Organization for Women (NOW) "to take action to bring American women into full participation in the mainstream of American society now." By full participation the founders meant not only fair pay and equal opportunity but a new, more egalitarian form of marriage. NOW also attacked the "false image of women ... in the media." By 1967, some 1,000 women had joined the organization, and four years later, its membership reached 15,000.

NOW was a pressure group. It sought to reform American society by promoting equal opportunity for women. To radical feminists, who had come up through the civil rights movement, NOW's agenda failed to confront adequately the problem of gender discrimination. Jo Freeman, a radical activist, observed, "Women's liberation does not mean equality with men ... [because] equality in an unjust society is meaningless." These feminists wanted to educate millions of discontented but unpoliticized women about the oppression they faced. They tried, through the technique of consciousness raising, to help women understand the extent of their oppression and to analyze their experience as a political phenomenon. They wanted to demonstrate, in their phrase, that the personal was political.

They gained the attention of the mass media at the Miss America pageant in Atlantic City, New Jersey, in September 1968. There, in the words of activist author Robin Morgan, they "announced our existence to the world." On the boardwalk, a hundred women nominated a sheep as their candidate for Miss America. They also set up a "freedom trash can," and placed in it "instruments of torture": bras, girdles, hair curlers, high heels, and copies of *Playboy* and *Cosmopolitan* magazines. In the pageant hall, they chanted "Freedom for women" and unfurled banners reading "Women's Liberation."

Awareness of racial discrimination led women to speak out against discrimination based on gender, as shown in this pointed advertisement sponsored by the National Organization for Women. (NOW Legal Defense and Education Fund)

Feminism at High Tide

In 1971, Helen Reddy expressed the energy of the women's movement in a song called "I Am Woman" that rose to the top of the charts:

> *I am woman, hear me roar*
> *In numbers too big to ignore*
> *And I know too much to go back and pretend*
> *'Cause I've heard it all before*
> *And I've been down there on the floor,*
> *No one's ever gonna keep me down again.*
> *Oh, yes, I am wise*
> *But it's wisdom born of pain.*
> *Yes, I've paid the price*
> *But look how much I gained*
> *If I have to*
> *I can do anything.*
> *I am strong,*
> *I am invincible,*
> *I am woman.*

Reddy's song reflected a new militancy and sense of self-confidence among women.

Real changes were under way. A 1970 survey of first-year college students showed that men interested in such fields as business, medicine, engineering, and law outnumbered women eight to one; by 1975, the ratio had dropped to three to one. The proportion of women beginning law school quadrupled between 1969 and 1973. Women gained access to the military academies and entered senior officer ranks, although they were still restricted from combat command ranks. According to the Census Bureau, 45 percent of mothers with preschool children held jobs outside the home in 1980. That figure was four times greater than it had been 30 years before. To be sure, many employers systematically excluded women from certain positions, and women usually held "female" jobs in the clerical, sales, and service sectors, but the progress was still unmistakable.

Legal changes brought women more benefits and opportunities. Title 9 of the Education Amendments of 1972 broadened the provisions of the Civil Rights Act of 1964. The new legislation, which barred gender bias in federally assisted educational activities and programs, made easier the admission of women to colleges and changed the nature of intercollegiate athletics by requiring schools to funds sports teams for women. By 1980, fully 30 percent of the participants in intercollegiate sports were women, compared with 15 percent before Title 9 became law.

A flurry of publications spread the principles of the women's movement. In 1972, journalist Gloria Steinem and several other women founded a new magazine, *Ms.,* which succeeded beyond their wildest dreams. By 1973, there were almost 200,000 subscribers. *The New Woman's Survival Catalogue* provided useful advice to women readers. *Our Bodies, Ourselves,* a handbook published by a women's health collective, encouraged women to understand and control their bodies; it sold 850,000 copies between 1971 and 1976.

These new books and magazines differed radically from older women's magazines like *Good Housekeeping* and *Ladies' Home Journal,* which focused on domestic interests and needs. *Ms.,* in dramatic contrast, dealt with abortion, employ-ment, discrimination, and other feminist issues, such as the Equal Rights Amendment.

Women both in and out of NOW worked for congressional passage, then ratification, of the Equal Rights Amendment (ERA) to the Constitution. Passed by Congress in 1972, with ratification seemingly assured, it stated simply, "Equality of rights under the law shall not be denied or abridged by the United States or by any State on account of sex."

More radical feminists became increasingly vocal. Legal changes were not enough, they argued. Traditional gender and family rolls would have to be discarded to end social exploitation. Socialist feminists claimed that it was not enough to strike out at male domination, for capitalist society itself was responsible for women's plight. Only through the process of revolution could women be free.

The women's movement spawned a number of publications that attempted to give women greater control over various aspects of their own lives. The book Our Bodies, Ourselves *and* Ms. *magazine were two important sources in that effort. (Ms. Magazine)*

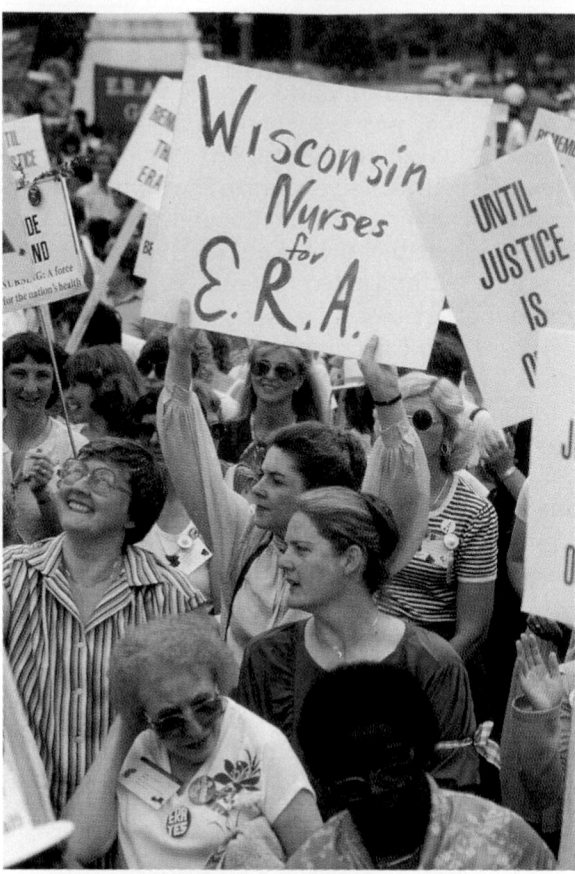

Women marched to mobilize support for ratification of the Equal Rights Amendment, but the campaign failed, as opponents aroused public fears and blocked support in a number of key states. A decade after passage, the ERA was dead. (J. L. Atlan/Sygma)

Black women frequently viewed the women's movement with ambivalence. Some became feminists; others felt that the struggle for racial equality took precedence, and they were reluctant to divert energy and attention from it. Race, more than gender, was the source of their oppression. They were also suspicious of the middle-class orientation of many white feminists. Members of NOW and similar organizations, they claimed, "suffered little more than boredom, gentle repression, and dishpan hands," and were hardly confronting the most important issues when they burned their bras and insisted on using the title Ms. rather than Mrs. or Miss.

Not all women were feminists, to be sure. Many felt the women's movement was contemptuous of women who stayed at home to perform traditional tasks. Marabel Morgan was one who still insisted that the woman had a place at home by her husband's side. The wife of a Florida attorney, she argued that "it is only when a woman surrenders her life to her husband, reveres and worships him, and is willing to serve him, that she becomes really beautiful to him." In her book *The Total Woman* (1973), she counseled others to follow the 4A approach: accept, admire, adapt, appreciate. As of 1975, some 500,000 copies of the hardcover volume had been sold.

In politics, Phyllis Schlafly headed a nationwide campaign to block ratification of the ERA. "It won't do anything to help women," she said, "and it will take away from women the rights they already have, such as the right of a wife to be supported by her husband, the right of a woman to be exempted from military combat, and the right, if you wanted it, to go to a single-sex college." The ERA, she predicted, would lead to the establishment of coed bathrooms, the elimination of alimony, and the legalization of homosexual marriage.

Schlafly and her allies had their way. Within a few years after passage of the ERA, 35 states had agreed to the measure, but then the momentum disappeared. Even with an extension in the deadline granted in 1979, the amendment could not win support of the necessary 38 states. By mid-1982, the ERA was dead.

Despite the counterattacks, the women's movement flourished in the 1960s and 1970s. In the tenth anniversary issue of *Ms.* magazine, in 1982, founding editor Gloria Steinem noted the differences a decade had made. "Now, we have words like 'sexual harassment' and 'battered women,'" she wrote. "Ten years ago, it was just called 'life.'" She also observed that "now, we are becoming the men we wanted to marry. Ten years ago, we were trained to marry a doctor, not be one."

Latino Mobilization

Latinos, like women, profited from the example of blacks in the struggle for equality. Long denied equal access to the American dream, they became more vocal and confrontational as their numbers

Changes in Female Employment, 1940–1980 (Percent of all employed women)					
	1940	1950	1960	1970	1980
Professional and technical	13.2	10.8	12.4	15.3	16.7
Managers and administrators	3.8	5.5	5.7	3.6	6.9
Sales	7.0	8.8	7.7	7.4	6.8
Clerical	21.2	26.4	30.3	34.5	35.1
Craft workers	0.9	1.1	1.6	1.8	1.8
Operatives	18.4	18.7	15.2	15.1	10.7
Laborers	0.8	0.4	0.4	1.0	1.3
Service workers	28.9	22.9	23.7	20.5	19.5
Farmworkers	5.8	5.4	4.4	0.8	1.2

Sources: Oppenheimer, *The Female Labor Force in the United States* (1976), and *Statistical Abstract of the United States, 1991.*

increased dramatically in the postwar years. In 1970, some 9 million residents of the United States declared they were of Spanish origin; in 1980, the figure was 14.6 million. But median household income remained less than three-fourths that of Anglos and inferior education and political weakness reinforced social and cultural separation. Latinos comprised Puerto Ricans in the Northeast, Cubans in Florida, Chicanos in California, and Tejanos in Texas. Chicanos took the lead in the protest struggle, though all groups developed a heightened sense of solidarity and group pride as they began to assert their own rights.

Early Efforts for Equality

The roots of the Latino struggle dated back to the World War II years. Chicanos established the American GI Forum because a Texas funeral home refused to bury a Mexican American casualty of World War II. When the group's protest led to a burial in Arlington National Cemetery, the possibilities of concerted action became clear. In the waning months of the war, a court case challenged Mexican American segregation in the schools. Gonzalo Méndez, an asparagus grower and a U.S. citizen who had lived in Orange County, Califor-

nia, for 25 years, filed suit to permit his children to attend the school reserved for Anglo Americans, which was far more attractive than the Mexican one to which they had been assigned. A federal district court upheld his claim in the spring of 1945, and two years later, the circuit court affirmed the original ruling. With the favorable decision, other communities filed similar suits and began to press for integration of their schools. Meanwhile, Mexican Americans returning from wartime service, where they had often been racially invisible, chafed under continuing discrimination at home.

A number of new organizations assisted in the struggle for equal rights. The Community Service Organization mobilized Chicanos against discrimination, as did the more radical Asociación Nacional México-Americana. And the League of United Latin American Citizens continued efforts to promote educational programs and other reforms.

Advances, however, came slowly. In the late 1940s, many Chicanos sought official classification as Caucasian, hoping that the change would lead to better treatment. But even when the designation changed, their status did not. They still faced discrimination and police brutality, particularly in the cities with the largest Chicano populations.

César Chávez organized the United Farm Workers to give migrant Mexican workers representation in their struggle for better wages and working conditions. Here he works with laborers in his tireless campaign for their support. (Bob Fitch/Black Star)

Los Angeles, with its large number of Chicanos, was the scene of numerous unsavory racial episodes. In mid-1951, on receiving a complaint about a loud record player, police officers raided a baptismal gathering at the home of Simon Fuentes. Breaking into the house without a warrant, they assaulted the members of the party. In the "Bloody Christmas" case at the end of the year, officers removed seven Mexican Americans from jail cells and beat them severely.

Protests continued, yet in the 1950s, Chicano activism was fragmented. Some Mexican Americans considered their situation hopeless. While new and aggressive challenges appeared, fully effective mobilization had to wait for another day.

César Chávez and the Politics of Confrontation

In the 1960s and 1970s, Mexican Americans became more active politically. In the election of 1960, Chicanos supported Kennedy, helping him win Texas, and began to see the benefits of such support. In 1961, Henry B. González was elected to Congress from San Antonio. Three years later, Elizo ("Kika") de la Garza of Texas won election to the House and Joseph Montoya of New Mexico went to the Senate. Chicanos were gaining a political voice.

More important than political representation, which came only slowly, was direct action. César Chávez, founder of the United Farm Workers, proved what could be done by organizing one of the most exploited and ignored groups of laboring people in the country, the migrant farm workers of the West. Chávez, who came from a family whose members were "the first ones to leave the fields if anyone shouted 'Huelga!'— which is Spanish for 'Strike!'" concentrated on migrant Mexican field hands, who worked long hours for meager pay. By 1965, his organization had recruited 1,700 people and was beginning to attract volunteer help.

Chávez first took on the grape growers of California. Calling the grape workers out on strike, the union demanded better pay and working conditions as well as recognition of the union. When the growers did not concede, Chávez launched a nationwide consumer boycott of their products. Although the Schenley Corporation and several wine companies came to terms, others held out. In 1966, the DiGiorgio Corporation agreed to permit a union election but then rigged the results. When California governor Edmund G. Brown, Sr., launched an investigation that resulted in another election, he became the first major political figure to support the long-powerless Chicano field hands. This time, the United Farm Workers won. Similar boycotts of lettuce and other products harvested by exploited labor also ended in success.

In 1975, César Chávez's long struggle for farmworkers won passage in California of a measure that required growers to bargain collectively with the elected representatives of the workers. Farmworkers had never been covered by the National Labor Relations Board. Now they had achieved the legal basis for representation that could help bring higher wages and improved working conditions. And Chávez had become a national figure.

Meanwhile, Mexican Americans pressed for reform in other areas as well. In the West and Southwest, Mexican American studies programs flourished. In 1969, at least 50 were available in California alone. They offered degrees, built library collections, and gave Chicanos access to their own past. The campuses also provided a network linking students together and mobilizing them for political action.

Beginning in 1968, Mexican American students began to protest conditions in secondary schools. They pointed to overcrowded and run-down institutions and to the 50 percent dropout rate that came from expulsion, transfer, or failure because students had never been taught to read. In March 1968, some 10,000 Chicano students walked out of five high schools in Los Angeles. Their actions inspired other walkouts in Colorado, Texas, and other parts of California and led to successful demands for Hispanic teachers, counselors, and courses and better facilities.

At the same time, new organizations emerged. Young Citizens for Community Action, founded by teenager David Sánchez and four Chicanos in East Los Angeles, began as a service club to assist the neighborhood. Later the organization adopted a paramilitary stance and evolved into a defensive patrol, now known as Young Chicanos for Community Action, which tried to protect local residents. Its members became identified as the Brown Berets and formed chapters throughout the Midwest and Southwest.

Other Hispanics followed a more political path. In Texas, José Angel Gutiérrez formed a citizens' organization which developed into the La Raza Unida political party and successfully promoted Mexican American candidates for political offices. Throughout the 1970s, it gained strength in the West and Southwest.

Among the new Chicano leaders was the charismatic Reis López Tijerina, or "El Tigre." A

Chicano leaders worked to mobilize their communities behind the campaign for equal rights. This mural in an East Los Angeles housing project helped foster a sense of Chicano pride. (Craig Aurness/Woodfin Camp & Associates)

preacher, he became interested in land-grant issues and argued that the United States government had fraudulently deprived Chicanos of village lands. He formed an organization, La Alianza Federal de Mercedes (the Federal Alliance of Land Grants), which marched on the New Mexico state capital and occupied a number of national forests. Arrested, he stood trial and eventually served time in prison, where he became a symbol of political repression.

Rodolfo "Corky" Gonzáles was another such leader. A Golden Gloves boxing champion as a youth, he later served as a district captain for the Democratic party in Denver. He helped direct Denver poverty programs until he was fired for being overly zealous in his support of the Chicano community. Eloquently he described the despair many Chicanos felt:

> I am Joaquin,
> lost in a world of confusion,
> caught up in the whirl of a gringo society,
> confused by the rules,
> scorned by attitudes,
> suppressed by manipulation
> and destroyed by modern society.

In 1966, Gonzáles founded the Crusade for Justice to advance the Chicano cause through community organization. Like Tijerina, he was arrested for his part in a demonstration but was subsequently acquitted.

Latinos made a particular point of protesting against the Vietnam War. Because the draft drew most heavily from the poorer segments of society, the Hispanic casualty rate was far higher than that of the population at large. In 1969, the Brown Berets organized the National Chicano Moratorium Committee and staged antiwar demonstrations. They argued that this was a racial war, with black and brown Americans being used against their Third World compatriots. Some of the rallies ended in confrontations with the police. News reporter Rubén Salazar, active in exposing questionable police activity, was killed in one such episode in 1970, and his death brought renewed charges of police brutality.

Aware of the growing numbers and growing demands of Latinos, the Nixon administration sought to defuse their anger and win their support. Cuban American refugees, strongly opposed to communism, shifted toward the Republican party, which they assumed was more likely eventually to intervene against Fidel Castro. Meanwhile, Nixon courted Chicanos by dangling political positions, government jobs, and promises of better programs for Mexican Americans. The effort paid off; Nixon received 31 percent of the Hispanic vote in 1972. Rather than reward his Hispanic followers, however, the president moved to cut back the poverty program, begun under Johnson, that assisted many of them.

Despite occasional gains, Hispanics from all groups faced continuing problems. Discrimination persisted in housing, education and employment. Activists had laid the groundwork for a campaign for equal rights, but the struggle had just begun.

Native American Protest

Like Latinos, Native Americans continued to suffer second-class status as the 1960s began. But, partly inspired by the confrontational tactics of other groups, they became more aggressive in their efforts to claim their rights and to improve living and working conditions. As their numbers soared—from 550,000 in 1960 to 1,480,000 in 1980—Native Americans became increasingly determined to improve their own lot.

Origins of the Struggle

Native Americans began the struggle for equality well before the 1960s. They achieved an important victory just after the end of World War II when Congress established the Indian Claims Commission. The commission was mandated to review tribal cases arguing that ancestral lands had been illegally seized and federal treaties violated. Hundreds of tribal suits against the government in federal courts were now possible. Many of them would lead to large settlements of cash—a form of reparation for past injustices—and sometimes the return of long-lost lands.

In the 1950s, federal Indian policy shifted course. As part of its effort to limit the role of the national government, the Eisenhower administration turned away from the New Deal policy of government support for tribal autonomy. In the Indian Reorganization Act of 1934, the government had stepped in to restore lands to tribal ownership and end their loss or sale to outsiders. In 1953, instead of trying to encourage Native American self-government, the administration adopted a new approach, known as the "termination" policy. The government proposed settling all outstanding claims and eliminating reservations as legitimate political entities. To encourage their assimilation into mainstream society, the government offered small subsidies to families who would leave the reservations and relocate in the cities.

The new policy victimized the Native Americans. With their lands no longer federally protected and their members deprived of treaty rights, many tribes became unwitting victims of people who wanted to seize their land. Though promising more freedom, the new policy caused great disruption as the government terminated tribes like the Klamaths in Oregon, the Menominees in Wisconsin, the Alabamas and Coushattas in Texas, and bands of Paiutes in Utah.

An unintended consequence of the policy was increased Indian activism. The National Congress of American Indians mobilized opposition to the federal program. A Seminole petition to the president in 1954 summed up a general view:

> We do not say that we are superior or inferior to the White Man and we do not say that the White Man is superior or inferior to us. We do say that we are not White Men but Indians, do not wish to become White Men but wish to remain Indians, and have an outlook on all things different from the outlook of the White Man.

Not only did the termination policy foster a sense of Indian identity, but it also sparked a dawning awareness among whites of the Indians' right to maintain their heritage. In 1958, the Eisenhower administration changed the policy of termination so that it required a tribe's consent. The policy continued to have the force of law, but implementation ceased.

Tribal Voices

In the 1960s, Native Americans began to assert themselves even more. At a conference in Chicago in 1961, several hundred Indians asked the Kennedy administration for the right to help make decisions about programs and budgets for the tribes. A group of college-educated Indians at the conference formed a National Indian Youth Council aimed at reestablishing Indian national pride. Over the next several decades, the council helped change the attitudes of tribal leaders, who were frequently called Uncle Tomahawks and "apples" (red outside, white inside) for their willingness to sacrifice their people's needs to white demands.

Native Americans learned from the examples of protest they saw around them. Watching the development of nationalism in Third World countries and, even more important, following the progress of the civil rights revolution, they too came to understand the place of interest-group politics in a diverse society. Finally, they were chastened by the excesses of the Vietnam War. They recognized a pattern of killing people of color that connected Indian-white relations to the excesses in the Philippines at the turn of the century and to atrocities in Korea and Vietnam.

Indians successfully promoted their own values and designs. Native American fashions became more common, museums and galleries displayed Indian art, and Indian jewelry found a new market. The larger culture came to appreciate important work by Native Americans. In 1968, N. Scott Momaday won the Pulitzer Prize for his book *House Made of Dawn*. Vine Deloria, Jr.'s *Custer Died for Your Sins* (1969) had even wider readership. Meanwhile popular films such as *Little Big Man* (1970) provided sympathetic portrayals of Indian history. Indian studies programs developed in colleges and universities. Organizations like the American Indian Historical Society in San Francisco protested traditional textbook treatment of Indians and demanded more honest portrayals.

Confrontational Tactics

At the same time, Native Americans became more confrontational. Like other groups, they worked through the courts when they could but also challenged authority more aggressively when necessary.

Led by a new generation of leaders, Native Americans tried to protect what was left of their tribal lands. Elders reminded young people, "Once we owned all the land." For generations, federal and state governments had steadily encroached on Native American territory. That intrusion had to cease. "Everything is tied to our homeland," D'Arcy McNickle, a Flathead anthropologist, told other Indians in 1961.

The protest spirit was apparent on the Seneca Nation's Allegany reservation in New York State. Although a 1794 treaty had established the Seneca's right to the land, the federal government had planned since 1928 to build the Kinzua Dam there as part of a flood control project. In 1956, after hearings to which the Indians were not invited and about which they were not informed, Congress appropriated funds for the project. Court appeals failed to block the scheme and the dam was eventually built. Although the government belatedly passed a $15 million reparations bill, money did not compensate for the loss of 10,000 acres of land that contained sacred sites, hunting and fishing grounds, and homes.

The Seneca did somewhat better in the 1970s. When New York State tried to condemn a section of Seneca land in order to build a superhighway to run through part of the Allegany reservation, the Indians again went to court. In 1981, the state finally agreed to an exchange: state land elsewhere in addition to a cash settlement in return for an easement through the reservation. That decision encouraged tribal efforts in Montana, Wyoming, Utah, New Mexico, and Arizona to resist similar incursions on reservation lands.

Native American leaders recognized that they could use the legal process in other areas as well and brought a wave of lawsuits charging violations of treaty rights. In 1967, in the first of many decisions upholding the Indian side, the U.S. Court of Claims ruled that the government in 1823 had forced the Seminole in Florida to cede their land for an unreasonably low price. The court directed the government to pay additional funds 144 years later. That decision was a source of some satisfaction to the Seminole population.

Native Americans also vigorously protested a new assault on their long-abused water rights. On the northern plains, large conglomerates, responding to the international oil shortage, vastly extended their coal strip-mining operations. Fierce legal struggles over possession of limited water resources resulted. Litigating tribes gained some legal ammunition when a federal court ruled in 1973, in a landmark case involving the water rights of the Paiute on the Nevada-California border, that the government must carry out its obligation as trustee to protect Indian property.

Another effort involved the reassertion of fishing rights. In various parts of the nation, the Nisqually, Puyallup, Muckleshoot, Chippewa, and other Indian tribes argued that they had treaty rights to fish where they chose, without worrying about the intrusive regulatory efforts of the states. Despite pressure from other fishermen, a series of court cases provided the tribes with some of the protection they claimed by ruling that nineteenth-century treaties allowing Indians fishing rights "in common with" whites meant that Indians could take up to 50 percent of allowable limits.

In 1968, George Mitchell and Dennis Banks, Chippewa living in Minneapolis, founded the activist American Indian Movement (AIM). AIM sought to help neglected Indians in the city. It managed to get Office of Economic Opportunity funds channeled to Indian-controlled organizations. It also established patrols to protect drunken Indians from harassment by the police. As its successes became known, chapters formed in other cities.

An incident in November 1969 dramatized Native American militancy. A landing party of 78 Indians seized Alcatraz Island in San Francisco Bay in an effort to protest symbolically the inability of the Bureau of Indian Affairs to "deal practically" with questions of Indian welfare. The Indians converted the island, with its defunct federal prison, into a cultural and educational center. As author Vine Deloria, Jr., noted, "By making Alcatraz an experimental Indian center operated and planned by Indian people, we would be given a chance to see what we could do toward developing answers to modern social problems.... It just seems to a lot of Indians that this continent was a lot better off when we were running it." In 1971 federal officials removed the Indians from Alcatraz.

Similar protests followed. In 1972, militants launched the Broken Treaties Caravan to Washington. For six days, insurgents occupied the Bureau of Indian Affairs. In 1973, AIM took over the South Dakota village of Wounded Knee, where in 1890 the U.S. 7th Cavalry had massacred the Sioux. The reservation surrounding the town was mired in poverty. Half the families were on welfare, alcoholism was widespread, and 81 percent of the student population had dropped out of school. The occupation was meant to dramatize these conditions and to draw attention to the 371 treaties AIM leaders claimed the government had broken. Federal officials responded by encircling the area and, when AIM tried to bring in supplies, killed one Indian and wounded another. The confrontation ended with a government agreement to reexamine the treaty rights of the Indians, although little of substance was subsequently done.

At the same time, Native Americans devoted increasing attention to providing education and developing legal skills. Because roughly half of the Indian population continued to live on reservations, many tribal communities founded their own colleges. In 1971, the Oglala Sioux established Oglala Lakota College on the Pine Ridge Reservation in South Dakota. The motto "Wa Wo Ici Ya" ("We can do it ourselves") revealed the college's goal. Nearby Sinte Gleska College on the Rosebud Reservation was the first to offer accredited four-year and graduate programs. The number of Indians in college increased from a few hundred in the early 1960s to tens of thousands by 1980.

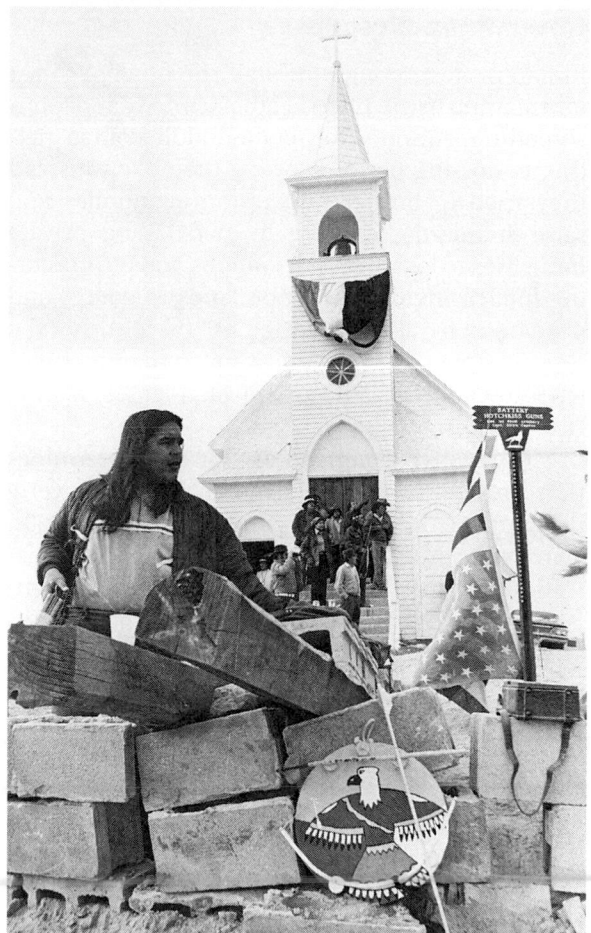

The American Indian Movement's armed occupation of Wounded Knee, South Dakota, site of a late-nineteenth-century massacre of the Sioux, resulted in bloodshed that dramatized unfair government treatment of Native Americans. (AP/Wide World Photos)

Indians themselves studied law and acted as legal advocates for their own people in the court cases they were filing. In 1968, funding from the Office of Economic Opportunity helped the University of New Mexico Law School start a Native American scholarship program. Since 1971, that program has graduated 35 to 40 Indian lawyers each year. They have worked for tribes directly and have successfully argued for tribal jurisdiction in conflicts between whites and Indians on the reservations.

Government Response

Indian protest brought results. The outcry against termination in the 1960s led the Kennedy and Johnson administrations to steer a middle course, neither endorsing nor disavowing the policy. Instead they tried to bolster reservation economies and raise standards of living by persuading private industries to locate on reservations and by promoting the leasing of reservation lands to energy and development corporations. In the 1970s, the Navajo, Northern Cheyenne, Crow, and other tribes tried to cancel or renegotiate such leases, fearing "termination by corporation."

The Native American cry for self-determination brought Indian involvement in the poverty program of the Great Society in the mid-1960s. Two agencies, the Area Redevelopment Administration (later the Economic Development Administration) and the Office of Economic Opportunity, responded to Indian pressure by allowing Indians to devise programs and budgets and administer programs themselves. Indians were similarly involved with Great Society housing, health, and education initiatives.

Finally, in 1975, Congress passed Indian Self-determination and Education Assistance Acts. Five years earlier, Richard Nixon had declared that self-determination had replaced termination as American policy. The self-determination measure was a largely rhetorical statement of that position. The education act involved subcontracting federal services to tribal groups. Though both laws were limited, they nonetheless reflected the government's decision to respond to Indian pressure and created a framework to guide federal policy in the decades ahead.

Social and Cultural Protest

As blacks, Hispanics, and Native Americans agitated, middle-class American society experienced an upheaval unlike any it had known before. Young people in particular rejected the stable patterns of affluent life their parents had forged. Some embraced radical political activity; many more adopted new standards of sexual behavior, music, and dress. In time their actions spawned still other protests as Americans tried to make the political and social world more responsive.

Student Activism

The demographic patterns of the post–World War II years lay behind youthful activism and helped explain the generation gap. Members of the baby boom generation came of age in the 1960s, and many of them, especially from the large middle class, moved on to some form of higher education. Between 1950 and 1964, the number of students in college more than doubled. By the end of the 1960s, college enrollment was more than four times what it had been in the 1940s. College served as a training ground for industry and corporate life; more important, it gave students time to experiment and grow before they had to make a living.

In college, some students joined the struggle for civil rights. Hopeful at first, they gradually became discouraged by the limitations of the government's commitment, despite the rhetoric of Kennedy and the New Frontier.

Out of that disillusionment arose the radical spirit of the New Left. Civil rights activists were among those who in 1960 organized Students for a Democratic Society (SDS). In 1962, SDS issued a manifesto, the Port Huron Statement, written largely by Tom Hayden of the University of Michigan. "We are people of this generation, bred in at least modest comfort, housed now in universities, looking uncomfortably at the world we inherit," it began. It went on to deplore the vast social and economic distances separating people from each other and to condemn the isolation and estrangement of modern life. The document called for a better system, a "democracy of individual participation."

The first blow of the growing student rebellion came at the University of California in Berkeley. There civil rights activists became involved in a confrontation that quickly became known as the free speech movement. It began in September 1964 when the university refused to allow students

In 1968, the demonstrators pictured here barricaded themselves inside Columbia University's main library to protest U.S. involvement in the Vietnam War and the school's relations with the neighboring African American community. (Archive Photos)

to distribute protest material outside the main campus gate. The students, many of whom had worked in the movement in the South, argued that their tables were off campus and therefore not subject to university restrictions on political activity. When police arrested one of the leaders, students surrounded the police car and kept it from moving all night.

The university regents brought charges against the student leaders, including Mario Savio, who was accused of biting a policeman on the thigh. When the regents refused to drop the charges, the students occupied the administration building. Savio called the university an impersonal machine: "It becomes odious, so we must put our bodies against the gears, against the wheels ... and make the machine stop until we're free." Folksinger Joan Baez sang "We Shall Overcome," the marching song of the civil rights movement. Then, as in the South, police stormed in and arrested the students in the building. A student strike, with faculty aid, mobilized wider support for the right to free speech.

The free speech movement at Berkeley was basically a plea for traditional liberal reform. Stu-

dents sought only the reaffirmation of the long-standing right to express themselves as they chose, and they aimed their attacks at the university, not at society as a whole. Later, in other institutions, the attack broadened. Students sought greater involvement in university affairs, argued for curricular reform, and demanded admission of more minority students. Their success in gaining their demands changed the shape of American higher education.

The mounting protest against the escalation of the Vietnam War fueled and refocused the youth movement. Confrontation became the new tactic of radical students, and protest became a way of life. Between January 1 and June 15, 1968, hundreds of thousands of students staged 221 major demonstrations at more than 100 educational institutions.

One of the most dramatic episodes came in April 1968 at Columbia University, where the issues of civil rights and war were tightly intertwined. A strong SDS chapter urged the university to break ties with the Institute of Defense Analysis, which specialized in military research. The Students' Afro-American Society tried to stop the building of a new gymnasium, which it claimed encroached on the Harlem community and disrupted life there. Whites occupied one building, blacks another. Finally, the president of the university called in the police. Hundreds of students were arrested; many were hurt. A student sympathy strike followed, and Columbia closed for the summer several weeks early.

The next year, in October 1969, the Weathermen, a militant fringe group of SDS, sought to show that the revolution had arrived with a frontal attack on Chicago, scene of the violent Democratic convention of 1968. The Weathermen, taking their name from a line in a Bob Dylan song—"You don't need a weatherman to know which way the wind blows"—came from all over the country. Dressed in hard hats, jackboots, work gloves, and other padding, they rampaged through the streets with clubs and pipes, chains and rocks. They ran into the police, as they had expected and hoped, and continued the attack. Some were arrested, others were shot, and the rest withdrew to regroup. For the next two days, they plotted strategy, engaged in minor skirmishes, and prepared for the final thrust. It came on the fourth day, once again pitting aggressive Weathermen against hostile police.

Why had the Weathermen launched their attack? "The status quo meant to us war, poverty, inequality, ignorance, famine and disease in most of the world," Bo Burlingham, a participant from Ohio, reflected. "To accept it was to condone and help perpetuate it. We felt like miners trapped in a terrible poisonous shaft with no light to guide us out. We resolved to destroy the tunnel even if we risked destroying ourselves in the process." The rationale of the Chicago "national action" may have been clear to the participants, but it convinced few other Americans. Citizens around the country were infuriated at what they saw.

The New Left was, briefly, a powerful force. Although activists never composed a majority, radicals attracted students and other sympathizers to their cause until the movement fragmented. But while it was healthy, the movement focused opposition to the Vietnam War and challenged inequities in American society in a more pointed way than ever before.

The Counterculture

Cultural change accompanied political upheaval. In the 1960s, many Americans, particularly young people, lost faith in the sanctity of the American system. "There was," observed Joseph Heller, the irreverent author of *Catch-22* (1961), "a general feeling that the platitudes of Americanism were horseshit." The protests exposed the emptiness of some of the old patterns, and many Americans, some politically active, some not, found new ways to assert their individuality and independence. As in the political sphere, the young led the way, often drawing on the example of the beats of the 1950s as they sought new means of self-gratification and self-expression.

Surface appearances were most visible and, to older Americans, most troubling. The "hippies" of the 1960s carried themselves in different ways. Men let their hair grow and sprouted beards; men and women both donned jeans, muslin shirts, and other simple garments. Stressing spontaneity above all else, some rejected traditional marital customs and gravitated to communal living groups. Their example, shocking to some, soon found its way into the culture at large.

Sexual norms underwent a revolution as more people separated sex from its traditional ties to family life. A generation of young women came of age with access to "the pill"—an oral contraceptive that was effortless to use and freed sexual experimentation from the threat of pregnancy. Americans of all social classes became more open to exploring, and enjoying, their sexuality. Scholarly findings supported natural inclinations. In 1966, William H. Masters and Virginia E. Johnson published *Human Sexual Response*, based on intensive laboratory observation of couples engaged in sexual activities. Describing the kinds of response that women, as well as men, could experience, they destroyed the myth of the sexually passive woman.

Nora Ephron, author and editor, summed up the sexual changes in the 1960s as she reflected on her own experiences. Initially she had "a hangover from the whole Fifties virgin thing," she recalled. "The first man I went to bed with, I was in love with and wanted to marry. The second one I was in love with, but I didn't have to marry him. With the third one, I thought I might fall in love."

The arts reflected the sexual revolution. Federal courts ruled that books like D. H. Lawrence's *Lady Chatterley's Lover,* earlier considered obscene, could not be banned. Many suppressed works, long available in Europe, now began to appear. Nudity became more common on stage and screen. In *Hair,* a rock musical, one scene featured the disrobing of performers of both sexes in the course of an erotic celebration.

Paintings reflected both the mood of dissent and the urge to innovate apparent in the larger society. "Op" artists painted sharply defined geometric figures in clear, vibrant colors, starkly different from the flowing, chaotic work of the abstract expressionists. "Pop" artists such as Andy Warhol, Roy Lichtenstein, and Jasper Johns made ironic comments on American materialism and taste with their representations of everyday objects like soup cans, comic strips, or pictures of Marilyn Monroe. Their paintings broke with formal artistic conventions. Some used spray guns and fluorescent paints to gain effect. Others even tried to make their pictures look like giant newspaper photographs.

Hallucinogenic drugs also became a part of the counterculture. One prophet of the "drug scene" was Timothy Leary, a scientific researcher experimenting with LSD at Harvard University. Fired for violating a pledge not to use undergraduates as subjects, Leary aggressively asserted that drugs were necessary to free the mind. Working through his group, the League for Spiritual Discovery, he dressed in long robes and preached his message, "Tune in, turn on, drop out."

Another apostle of life with drugs was Ken Kesey. While writing his first novel, *One Flew Over the Cuckoo's Nest,* he began participating in medical experiments at a hospital where he was introduced to LSD. With the profits from his novel, Kesey established a commune of "Merry Pranksters" near Palo Alto, California. In 1964, the group headed east in a converted school bus painted in psychedelic Day-Glo colors, wired for sound, and stocked with enough orange juice and "acid" (LSD) to sustain the Pranksters across the continent.

Drug use was no longer confined to an urban subculture of musicians, artists, and the streetwise. Soldiers brought experience with drugs back from Vietnam. Young professionals began experimenting

Andy Warhol's painting of a Campbell's soup can was one of the best-known examples of "pop" art in the 1960s. Warhol and other artists drew on advertising images, comic strips, and other elements of popular culture in their painting and sculpture. (© 1997 Andy Warhol Foundation for the Visual Arts/ARS, New York/Superstock, Inc.)

with cocaine as a stimulant. Taking a "tab" of LSD became part of the coming-of-age ritual for many middle-class college students. Marijuana became phenomenally popular in the 1960s. "Joints" of "grass" were passed around at high school, neighborhood, and college parties as readily as cans of beer had been in the previous generation.

Music became intimately connected with these cultural changes. The rock and roll of the 1950s and the gentle strains of folk music gave way to a new kind of rock that swept the country—and the world (see the Recovering the Past section of this chapter for a discussion of the music of the 1960s and The American People Gather: at Rock Music Festivals for a detailed examination of the concerts held).

The counterculture had an underside that was most visible in the Haight-Ashbury section of San Francisco, where runaway "flower children" mingled with "burned-out" drug users and radical

Popular Music

One way to recover the past is through music. Popular songs not only provide insight into attitudes and beliefs but also quickly convey the mood and feelings of an era. Through their lyrics, songwriters express the hopes and fears of a people and the emotional tone of an age. Consider, for example, the powerful message conveyed in the Democratic party adoption of "Happy Days Are Here Again" as a campaign theme during the Great Depression. The decline of pop music and the rise of rock and roll in the 1950s tells historians a great deal about the mood of that period. Similarly, the popularity of both folk music and rock in the 1960s provides another way of following social change in that turbulent decade.

The music of the 1960s moved beyond the syrupy ballads of the early 1950s and the rock and roll movement that Elvis Presley helped launch in the middle of the decade. As the United States confronted the challenges of the counterculture and the crosscurrents of political and social reform, new kinds of music began to be played.

Folk music took off at the start of the period. Building on a tradition launched by Woody Guthrie, Pete Seeger, and the Weavers, Joan Baez was one of the first to become popular. Accompanying herself on a guitar as she performed at coffee shops in Harvard Square and at the Newport Folk Festival, she soon overwhelmed audiences with her crystal-clear voice. She sang ballads, laments, and spirituals like "We Shall Overcome" and became caught up in the protest activities of the period.

Equally active was Bob Dylan, who grew up playing rock and roll in high school, then folk music in college at the University of Minnesota. Disheveled and gravelly voiced, he wrote remarkable songs like "Blowin' in the Wind" that were soon sung by other artists like Peter, Paul and Mary as well. His song "The Times They Are A-Changin' " (excerpted here) captured the inexorable force of the student protest movement best of all.

But the 1960s were marked by far more than folk music alone. In the early 1960s, an English group from Liverpool began to build a following in Great Britain. In early 1964, the Beatles released "I Want to Hold Your Hand" in the United States and appeared on the popular Ed Sullivan television show. Within weeks, Beatles songs held the first, second, third, fourth, and fifth positions on the *Billboard* singles chart, and *Meet the Beatles* became the best-selling LP record to date. With *Sergeant Pepper's Lonely Hearts Club Band* a few years later, the Beatles branched out in new musical directions and reflected the influence of the counterculture with songs like "Lucy in the Sky with Diamonds" (which some people said referred to the hallucinogenic drug LSD).

Bob Dylan. (AP/Wide World Photos)

Joan Baez. (John Launois/Black Star)

The Beatles.
(Archive Photos)

The Supremes. (Brown Brothers)

Come mothers and fathers
Throughout the land
And don't criticize
What you can't understand
Your sons and daughters
Are beyond your command
There's a battle
Outside and it's ragin'
It'll soon shake your windows
And rattle your walls ...
For the times they are a-changin'.

From "The Times They Are A-Changin'"

Mick Jagger and the Rolling Stones followed at the end of the decade. Another English group that changed the nature of American music, the Stones played a blues-based rock music that proclaimed a commitment to drugs, sex, and a decadent life of social upheaval. Jagger was an aggressive, sometimes violent showman on stage, whose androgynous style showed his contempt for conventional sexual norms. Other artists, such as Jim Morrison of the Doors and Janis Joplin, reflected the same intensity of the new rock world, and both died from drug overdoses.

Meanwhile, other groups were setting off in different directions. On the pop scene, Motown Records in Detroit popularized a new kind of black rhythm and blues. By 1960, the gospel-pop-soul fusion was gaining followers. By the late 1960s, Motown Records was one of the largest black-owned companies in America and one of the most successful independent recording ventures in the business. Stevie Wonder, the Temptations, and the Supremes were among the groups who became enormously popular. The Supremes, led by Diana Ross, epitomized the Motown sound with such hits as "Where Did Our Love Go."

What songs come to your mind when you think of the 1960s? How is the music different from that of the 1950s? What do the lyrics tell you about the period?

Look at the lyrics for "The Times They Are A-Changin'" reprinted here. What do they tell you about the social upheaval of the 1960s? What, if anything, does the song imply can be done about the changes in the air? What other songs can you think of that give you a similar handle on the decade?

1059

activists. Joan Didion, a perceptive essayist, wrote of American society in 1967: "Adolescents drifted from city to torn city, sloughing off both the past and the future as snakes shed their skins, children who were never taught and would never now learn the games that had held the society together." For all the spontaneity and exuberance, the counterculture's darker side could not be ignored.

Gay and Lesbian Rights

Closely tied to the revolution in sexual norms that affected sexual relations, marriage, and family life was a fast-growing and increasingly militant gay liberation movement. There had always been people who accepted the "gay" life-style, but American society as a whole was unsympathetic, and many homosexuals kept their preferences to themselves. The climate of the 1970s encouraged gays to "come out of the closet." A nightlong riot in 1969, in response to a police raid on the Stonewall Inn, a homosexual bar in Greenwich Village in New York, helped spark a new consciousness and a movement for gay rights. Throughout the next decade, homosexuals made important gains in ending the most blatant forms of discrimination against them. In 1973, the American Psychiatric Association ruled that homosexuality should no longer be classified as a mental illness, and that decision was overwhelmingly supported in a vote by the membership the next year. In 1975, the U.S. Civil Service Commission lifted its ban on employment of homosexuals.

In this new climate of acceptance, many gays who had hidden or suppressed their sexuality revealed their darkest secret. Women, too, became more open about their sexual preferences and demanded that they not be penalized for choosing other females as partners. A lesbian movement developed, sometimes involving women active in the more radical wing of the women's movement. But many Americans remained unsympathetic to anyone who challenged traditional sexual norms. Churches and some religious groups often lashed out against gays.

Environmental and Consumer Agitation

Although many of the social movements that arose in the 1960s were defined by race, gender, and sexual preference, one further movement united many of these reformers across such boundaries.

Emerging in the early 1960s, a powerful movement of Americans concerned with the environment began to revive issues raised in the Progressive era and to push them further. In the mid-1960s, a Gallup poll revealed that only 17 percent of the public considered air and water pollution to be one of the three major governmental problems. By 1970, that figure had risen to 53 percent.

The modern environmental movement stemmed in part from a desire in the post–World War II years for a better "quality of life." Many Americans began to recognize that clear air, unpolluted waters, and unspoiled wilderness were indispensable to a decent existence (see Chapter 26). They worried about threats to their natural surroundings, particularly after naturalist Rachel Carson published her brilliant book *Silent Spring*

The accident at the reactor on Three Mile Island helped spark opposition to nuclear power. For people around the world, the cooling towers pictured here came to represent the horrifying possibilities of a nuclear reaction out of control. (UPI/Corbis-Bettmann)

in 1962. She took aim at chemical pesticides, especially DDT, which had increased crop yields but had disastrous side effects:

> The most alarming of all man's assaults upon the environment is the contamination of air, earth, rivers, and sea with dangerous and even lethal materials. This pollution is for the most part irrecoverable; the chain of evil it initiates not only in the world that must support life but in living tissues is for the most part irreversible. In this now universal contamination of the environment, chemicals are the sinister and little-recognized partners of radiation in changing the very nature of the world—the very nature of its life.

Chemicals entered the food chain and caused a cycle of poisoning and death. Something clearly needed to be done. As Americans learned of the pollutants surrounding them, they became increasingly worried about pesticides, motor vehicle exhaust, and industrial wastes that filled the air, earth, and water. Earth Day in 1970 celebrated the world's natural resources and warned of continuing threats.

Public concern focused on a variety of targets. Americans were troubled in 1969 to learn how thermal pollution from nuclear power plants was killing fish in both eastern and western rivers. An article in *Sports Illustrated* aroused fishermen, sailors, and other recreational enthusiasts who had not been previously concerned. A massive oil spill off the coast of southern California turned white beaches black and wiped out much of the marine life in the immediate area. Concern about the deterioration of the environment increased as people learned more about substances they had once taken for granted. In 1978, the public became alarmed about the lethal effects of toxic chemicals dumped in the Love Canal neighborhood of Niagara Falls, New York. A few years later, attention focused on dioxin, one of the poisons in the Love Canal, which now surfaced in other areas in more concentrated form. Thousands of times more potent than cyanide, it was one of the most deadly substances ever made.

Equally frightening was the potential environmental damage from a nuclear accident. That possibility became more real as a result of a mishap at one of the reactors at Three Mile Island near Harrisburg, Pennsylvania, in 1979. There a faulty pressure relief valve led to a loss of coolant. Initially, plant operators refused to believe indicators showing a serious malfunction. Part of the nuclear core became uncovered, part began to disintegrate, and the surrounding steam and water became highly radioactive. An explosion releasing radioactivity into the atmosphere appeared possible, and thousands of residents of the area fled. The scenario of nuclear disaster

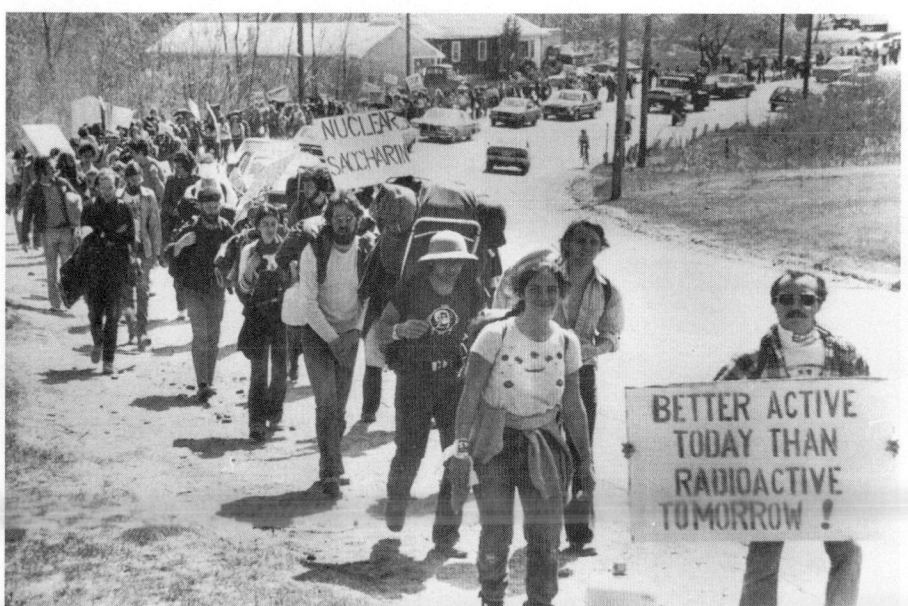

Antinuclear activists protested the proliferation of both atomic weapons and atomic power plants. Here members of the Clamshell Alliance agitate in 1977 against construction of a nuclear power plant in Seabrook, New Hampshire. (AP/Wide World Photos)

At Rock Music Festivals

The rock music festival became a popular gathering place for young Americans in the 1960s. Between 1967 and 1971, more than 3 million people attended 300 festivals around the United States. The largest of these brought together hundreds of thousands of members of the baby boom generation, who listened to the live music of rock legends, camped without inhibition in open fields with friends and strangers, and celebrated a sense of liberation from conventional society.

The festivals focused on the rock music of the era. Frenzied Americans had flocked to theaters to hear Frank Sinatra sing in the 1940s and had then become even more passionate about Elvis Presley and other rock and roll stars of the 1950s. Now they gathered outside to hear artists such as the Rolling Stones, Jimi Hendrix, Janis Joplin, The Who, Crosby, Stills, Nash, and Young, and Three Dog Night, who provided a syncopated backdrop for the countercultural life-style of dedicated followers.

For the rock festivals were about more than music alone. They reflected a powerful challenge to traditional authority. Fans, some naked, wandered about freely as the pulse of ear-splitting music pounded on. Some flaunted their sexuality in front of their friends. More enjoyed the marijuana, LSD, and other drugs, that were easily available. They hailed the sense of community they hoped represented a revolution in values.

These celebrations began with the Fairie Fantasy and Magic Mountain Music Festival at Mount Tamalpais in California in June 1967 and reached a high point with the Woodstock Festival in upstate New York in the summer of

(Jim Marshall/Gamma Liaison)

(Elliot Landy/Magnum Photos

1969. That gathering, the largest to date, brought together 400,000 young people for the better part of a week. Despite torrential rain and inadequate supplies of water and food, the festival unfolded in a spirit of affection. The police chose not to enforce the drug laws and thereby avoided confrontations. The gathering ended with Jimi Hendrix offering a psychedelic version of "The Star Spangled Banner."

The 300,000 fans at the Rolling Stones festival in Altamont, California, later in 1969 fared less well. The immensely popular English group hired a band of Hell's Angels, tough motorcyclists, to keep control. An undercurrent of violence simmered from the very start, music critic Greil Marcus observed, as "all day long people … speculated on who would be killed, on when the killing would take place. There were few doubts that the Angels would do the job." They did. They beat one oung black man to death and hurt others. Accidents claimed several more

lives, and drug-overdosed revelers found inadequate medical support.

Still the festivals continued. At Watkins Glen, in upstate New York, 600,000 people gathered for one day in July 1973. But the uninhibited mood of Woodstock was hard to maintain. Top-line rock groups demanded more and more money to play the festivals, as commercial greed replaced the naive enthusiasm of the early events. Local authorities began to pass laws regulating or even prohibiting the festivals. Middle Americans were uncomfortable with the idea of hundreds of thousands of turned-on hippies invading their towns.

Like the counterculture itself, the rock music festivals ran their course and then died out. But rock groups continued to play their songs, fans continued to turn out (sometimes in large sports arenas), and the rock music that blared out in the 1960s remains an important part of contemporary American life.

depicted in the film *The China Syndrome* (1979) seemed frighteningly real. *Mad* magazine's Alfred E. Newman posed in front of the now-famous cooling towers and said, "Yes, me worry!" The worst never occurred and the danger period passed, but the plant remained shut down, filled with radioactive debris, a monument to a form of energy that was once hailed as the wave of the future but now appeared more destructive than any ever known.

The threat of a nuclear catastrophe underscored the arguments of grass-roots environmental activists. Groups like the Clamshell Alliance in New Hampshire and the Abalone Alliance in northern California campaigned aggressively against licensing new nuclear plants at Seabrook, New Hampshire, and Diablo Canyon, California. While activist tactics did not always succeed in their immediate goals, they mobilized opinion sufficiently that no new plants were authorized after 1978.

Western environmentalists were particularly worried about excessive use of water. The American West, one critic observed, had become "the greatest hydraulic society ever built in history." With massive irrigation systems, the nation's use of water rose from 40 billion gallons a day in 1900 to 393 billion gallons by 1975, though the population had only tripled. Americans used three times as much water per capita as the world's average, and far more than other industrialized societies.

One serious source of concern was the Ogallala aquifer in the Great Plains. The drawing of enormous amounts of water in the 1950s and 1960s to make arid areas productive for farming had by the mid-1970s dramatically depleted the water stored in the aquifer. Conservation measures might delay the day of reckoning, but inevitable shortages loomed ahead.

The situation was similar in California. Naturally dry, the state's prosperity rested on massive irrigation projects. In the late 1970s, the state had 1,251 major reservoirs. Virtually every large river had at least one dam. Almost as much water was pumped from the ground, with little natural replenishment, and even less regulation. Pointing to the destruction of the nation's rivers and streams and the severe lowering of the water table in many areas, environmentalists argued that something needed to be done before it was too late. Slowly, they made themselves heard. Critic Marc Reisner later noted, "Forty years ago,

only a handful of heretics, howling at wilderness, challenged the notion that the West needed hundreds of new dams. Today they are almost vindicated."

Environmental agitation produced legislative results in the 1960s and 1970s. Lyndon Johnson, whose vision of the Great Society included an "environment that is pleasing to the senses and healthy to live in," won basic legislation to halt the depletion of the country's natural resources (see Chapter 28). In the next few years, environmentalists went further, pressuring legislative and administrative bodies to regulate polluters. During Richard Nixon's presidency, Congress passed the Clean Air Act, the Water Quality Improvement Act, and the Resource Recovery Act and mandated a new Environmental Protection Agency (EPA) to spearhead the effort to control abuses. Initially, these measures aimed at controlling the toxic by-products of the modern industrial order. In subsequent years, environmentalists broadened the effort to include occupational health and social justice issues.

One such effort developed into an extraordinarily bitter economic and ecological debate. The Endangered Species Act of 1973 prohibited the federal government from supporting any projects that might jeopardize species threatened with extinction. It ran into direct conflict with commercial imperatives in the Pacific Northwest. Loggers in the Olympic Peninsula had long exploited the land by clearcutting (cutting down all trees in a region, without leaving any standing). Environmentalists claimed that the forests they cut provided the last refuge for the spotted owl. Scientists and members of the U.S. Forest Service pushed to set aside timberland so that the owl could survive. Loggers protested that this action jeopardized their livelihood. As the issue wound its way through the courts, logging fell off drastically.

Another protest against regulation in the late 1970s and early 1980s came to be called the Sagebrush Rebellion. Critics argued that large federal landholdings in the West put that region at a disadvantage in economic competition with the East. They demanded that the national government cede the lands to states, which could sell or lease them for local gain. Conservative state legislatures in the Rocky Mountain states supported the scheme. Ranchers applauded the notion. In the end, it went nowhere, though the agitation did persuade federal authorities to endorse a less restrictive policy on grazing.

Related to the environmental movement was a consumer movement. As Americans bought fashionable clothes, house furnishings, and electrical and electronic gadgets, they began to worry about unscrupulous sellers, just as they had earlier in the twentieth century. Over the years, Congress had established a variety of regulatory efforts as it started to safeguard citizens from marketplace abuse. In the 1970s, a stronger consumer movement developed, aimed at protecting the interests of the purchasing public and making business more responsible to consumers.

TIMELINE

1947	Jackie Robinson breaks the color line in major league baseball
1950	Asociación Nacional México-Americana formed
1954	*Brown* v. *Board of Education*
1955	Montgomery, Alabama, bus boycott begins
1957	Little Rock, Arkansas, school integration crisis
	Civil Rights Act
1960	Civil Rights Act
	Birth control pill becomes available
	Sit-ins begin
	Students for a Democratic Society (SDS) founded
1961	Freedom rides
	Joseph Heller, *Catch-22*
	Ken Kesey, *One Flew Over the Cuckoo's Nest*
1962	James Meredith crisis at the University of Mississippi
	SDS's Port Huron Statement
	Rachel Carson, *Silent Spring*
1963	Birmingham demonstration
	Civil rights march on Washington
	Betty Friedan's, *The Feminine Mystique*
1964	Civil Rights Act
	Free speech movement, Berkeley
1965	Martin Luther King, Jr., leads march from Selma to Montgomery
	Voting Rights Act
	United Farm Workers grape strike
	Malcolm X assassinated
	Riot in Watts section of Los Angeles
	Ralph Nader, *Unsafe at Any Speed*
1966	Stokely Carmichael becomes head of SNCC and calls for "black power"
	Black Panthers founded
	NOW founded
	Masters and Johnson, *Human Sexual Response*
1967	Urban riots in 22 cities
1968	Martin Luther King, Jr., assassinated
	Student demonstrations at Columbia University and elsewhere
	Chicano student walkouts
	American Indian Movement (AIM) founded
1969	Woodstock and Altamont rock festivals
	Weathermen's "Days of Rage" in Chicago
	Native Americans seize Alcatraz
	La Raza Unida founded
1971–1975	School busing controversies in North and South
1972	*Ms.* magazine founded
	Congress passes Equal Rights Amendment
1973	AIM occupies Wounded Knee, South Dakota
1975	Farmworkers' grape boycott
	Indian Self-determination and Education Assistance Acts
1978	*Bakke* v. *Regents of the University of California*
1979	Accident at Three Mile Island nuclear power plant
1982	Ratification of ERA fails

Ralph Nader led the movement. He had become interested in the issue of automobile safety while studying law at Harvard and had pursued that interest as a consultant to the Department of Labor. His book *Unsafe at Any Speed: The Designed-in Dangers of the American Automobile* (1965) argued that many cars were coffins on wheels. Head-on collisions, even at low speeds, could easily kill, for cosmetic bumpers could not withstand modest shocks. He termed the Chevrolet Corvair "one of the nastiest-handling cars ever built" because of its tendency to roll over in certain situations. His efforts paved the way for the National Traffic and Motor Vehicle Safety Act of 1966, which set minimum safety standards for vehicles on public highways, provided for inspection to ensure compliance, and created a National Motor Vehicle Safety Advisory Council.

Nader's efforts attracted scores of volunteers, called "Nader's Raiders." They turned out critiques and reports and, more important, inspired consumer activists at all levels of government—city, state, and national. Consumer protection offices began to monitor a flood of complaints as ordinary citizens became more vocal in defending their rights.

Conclusion

Extending the American Dream

The 1960s and 1970s were turbulent years. Yet this third major reform era of the twentieth century accomplished a good deal for the groups fighting to expand the meaning of equality. African Americans now enjoyed greater access to the rights and privileges enjoyed by mainstream American society, despite the backlash the movement brought. Women, like Ann Clarke, introduced at the start of the chapter, returned to school in ever-increasing numbers and found jobs and sometimes independence after years of being told that their place was at home. Native Americans and Latinos mobilized too and could see the stirrings of change. Environmentalists created a new awareness of the global dangers the nation and the world faced. Slowly reformers succeeded in pressuring the government to help the national fulfill its promise and ensure the realization of the ideals of American life.

But the course of change was ragged. The reform effort reached its high-water mark during Lyndon Johnson's Great Society and in the years immediately following, then faltered with the rise of conservatism and disillusionment with liberalism (see Chapter 28). Some movements were circumscribed by the changing political climate; others simply ran out of steam. Still, the various efforts left a legacy of ferment which could help spark further change in future years.

Recommended Reading

The Civil Rights Movement

James Baldwin, *The Fire Next Time* (1962); Taylor Branch, *Parting the Waters: America in the King Years, 1954–1963* (1988); Carl M. Brauer, *John F. Kennedy and the Second Reconstruction* (1977); Clayborne Carson, *In Struggle: SNCC and the Black Awakening of the 1960s* (1981); William H. Chafe, *Civilities and Civil Rights: Greensboro, North Carolina, and the Black Struggle for Freedom* (1980); James Forman, *The Making of Black Revolutionaries* (1972); John Hope Franklin and Alfred A. Moss, Jr., *From Slavery to Freedom: A History of African Americans,* 7th ed. (1994); David J.

Garrow, *Bearing the Cross: Martin Luther King, Jr., and the Southern Christian Leadership Conference* (1986); Andrew Hacker, *Two Nations: Black and White, Separate, Hostile, Unequal* (1992); Christopher Jencks, *Rethinking Social Policy: Race, Poverty, and the Underclass* (1992); Martin Luther King, Jr., *I Have a Dream: Writings and Speeches that Changed the World* [ed. by James M. Washington] (1992); Richard Kluger, *Simple Justice: The History of* Brown v. Board of Education *and Black America's Struggle for Equality* (1975); Malcolm X (with Alex Haley), *The Autobiography of Malcolm X* (1966); August Meier and Elliott Rudwick, *CORE:*

A Study in the Civil Rights Movement, 1942–1968 (1973); Anne Moody, *Coming of Age in Mississippi* (1968); Harvard Sitkoff, *The Struggle for Black Equality, 1954–1992*, revised ed. (1993); Ronald Takaki, *A Different Mirror: A History of Multicultural America* (1993); Jules Tygiel, *Baseball's Great Experiment: Jackie Robinson and his Legacy* (1983); Stephen J. Whitfield, *A Death in the Delta: The Story of Emmett Till* (1988).

The Women's Movement

Rosalyn Baxandall and Linda Gordon, eds., *America's Working Women: A Documentary History, 1600 to the Present* (revised and updated, 1995); William H. Chafe, *The American Woman: Her Changing Social, Political, and Economic Roles, 1920–1970* (1972); Sara Evans, *Personal Politics: The Roots of Women's Liberation in the Civil Rights Movements and the New Left* (1979); Peter Gabriel Filene, *Him/Her/Self: Sex Roles in Modern America*, 2d ed. (1986); Shulamith Firestone, *The Dialectic of Sex: The Case for Feminist Revolution* (1970); Betty Friedan, *The Feminine Mystique* (with a new introduction and epilogue, 1983); Jacqueline Jones, *Labor of Love, Labor of Sorrow: Black Women, Work, and the Family from Slavery to the Present* (1985); Alice Kessler-Harris, *Out to Work: A History of Wage-earning Women in the United States* (1982); Blanche Linden-Ward, *Changing the Future: American Women in the 1960s* (1993); Sheila M. Rothman, *Woman's Proper Place: A History of Changing Ideals and Practices, 1870 to the Present* (1978); Winifred D. Wandersee, *On the Move: American Women in the 1970s* (1988).

The Movement for Latino Rights

Rodolfo Acuña, *Occupied America: A History of Chicanos*, 3d ed. (1988); Cletus Daniel, "César Chávez and the Unionization of California Farm Workers," in Melvyn Dubofsky and Warren Van Tine, eds., *Labor Leaders in America* (1987); Mario T. García, *Memories of Chicano History: The Life and Narrative of Bert Corona* (1994) and *Mexican Americans: Leadership, Ideology, and Identity, 1930–1960* (1989); Ed Ludwig and James Santibañez, eds., *The Chicanos: Mexican American Voices* (stories and essays, 1971); Beatrice Rodriguez Owsley, *The Hispanic-American Entrepreneur: An Oral History of the American Dream* (1992); Delia Poey and Virgil Suarez, eds., *Iguana Dreams: New Latino Fiction* (1992); Edward Rivera, *Family Installments: Memories of Growing Up Hispanic* (1982); Peter Skerry, *Mexican Americans: The Ambivalent Minority* (1993).

The Native American Struggle

Dee Brown, *Bury My Heart at Wounded Knee: An Indian History of the American West* (1971); Stephen Cornell, *The Return of the Native: American Indian Political Resurgence* (1988); Vine Deloria, Jr., *Custer Died for Your Sins: An Indian Manifesto* (1969); Frederick E. Hoxie, ed., *Indians in American History* (1988); Alvin M. Josephy, Jr., *Now That the Buffalo's Gone* (1982); D'Arcy McNickle, *Native American Tribalism: Indian Survivals and Renewals* (1973); David Hurst Thomas, Jay Miller, Richard White, Peter Nabokov,

Philip J. Deloria, *The Native Americans: An Illustrated History* (1993).

Social and Cultural Protest

Terry Anderson, *The Movement and the Sixties: Protest in America from Greensboro to Wounded Knee* (1995); Beth L. Bailey, *From Front Porch to Back Seat: Courtship in Twentieth Century America* (1988); David Chalmers, *And the Crooked Places Made Straight: The Struggle for Social Change in the 1960s* (1991); John D'Emilio and Estelle B. Freedman, *Intimate Matters: A History of Sexuality in America* (1988); Morris Dickstein, *Gates of Eden: American Culture in the 1960s* (1977); Joan Didion, *Slouching Towards Bethlehem* (1968); Barbara Epstein, *Political Protest and Cultural Revolution: Nonviolent Direct Action in the 1970s and 1980s* (1991); David Farber, *The Age of Great Dreams: America in the 1960s* (1994); Todd Gitlin, *The Sixties: Years of Hope, Days of Rage* (1987); James Miller, *"Democracy Is in the Streets": From Port Huron to the Siege of Chicago* (1987); Steven Mintz and Susan Kellogg, *Domestic Revolutions: A Social History of American Family Life* (1988); William L. O'Neill, *Coming Apart: An Informal History of America in the 1960s* (1971); Charles A. Reich, *The Greening of America* (1978); W. J. Rorabaugh, *Berkeley at War: The 1960s* (1989); Theodore Roszak, *The Making of a Counter Culture* (1969); Hunter S. Thompson, *Fear and Loathing in Las Vegas* (1971); Milton Viorst, *Fire in the Streets: America in the 1960s* (1979); Tom Wolfe, *The Electric Kool-Aid Acid Test* (1968).

The Environmental Movement

Rachel Carson, *Silent Spring* (1962); William Dietrich, *The Final Forest: The Battle for the Last Great Trees of the Pacific Northwest* (1992); Barbara Epstein, *Political Protest and Cultural Revolution: Nonviolent Direct Action in the 1970s and 1980s* (1991); Robert Gottlieb, *Forcing the Spring: The Transformation of the American Environmental Movement* (1993); Samuel P. Hays, *Beauty, Health, and Permanence: Environmental Politics in the United States, 1955–1985* (1987); Patricia Nelson Limerick, *The Legacy of Conquest: The Unbroken Past of the American West* (1987); John Opie, *The Law of the Land: Two Hundred Years of American Farmland Policy* (1987); Marc Reisner, *Cadillac Desert: The American West and Its Disappearing Water*, revised and updated ed. (1993); Kirkpatrick Sale, *The Green Revolution: The American Environmental Movement, 1962–1992* (1993); Richard White, *"It's Your Misfortune and None of My Own": A History of the American West* (1991); Charles F. Wilkinson, *Crossing the Next Meridian: Land, Water, and the Future of the West* (1992); Donald Worster, *Rivers of Empire: Water, Aridity and the Growth of the American West* (1985).

Novels

Sara Davidson, *Loose Change* (1977); Richard Fariña, *Been Down So Long It Looks Like Up to Me* (1966); Marilyn French, *The Women's Room* (1977); N. Scott Momaday, *House Made of Dawn* (1968); Alix Kates Shulman, *Memoirs of an Ex-Prom Queen* (1972).

The Revival of Conservatism

raig Miller lived comfortably in the early 1990s. As a sheet-metal worker for TWA, he earned a healthy $15.65 an hour. He, his wife, and their four children rented a pleasant house in a suburban section of Overland Park, Kansas. They were saving money to buy their own home.

Then in the summer of 1992, Miller lost his job. The airline industry was financially troubled, and TWA began to lay off blue-collar workers. Miller looked for a comparable position with another company but found nothing. Manufacturing jobs were drying up throughout the United States, as American firms moved tens of thousands of jobs abroad, where labor costs were cheaper. Other jobs were lost to advances in technology, which rendered old production methods obsolete.

Miller had no alternative but to piece together a living as best he could. He found a job at McDonald's, taking orders for Quarter Pounders and Big Macs. He drove a school bus every morning and afternoon. He also started a small business of his own, changing furnace filters. With the income from his various jobs and his wife's part-time position at Toys "R" Us, the family now earned $18,000 a year, less than half of what Miller made as a sheet-metal worker.

The decline in their standard of living was hard to accept. Miller and his wife had worked hard and prospered modestly, but suddenly any security they had known was gone. Before the layoff, they had moved comfortably in a middle-class world of backyard barbecues and church picnics. Now they struggled to make ends meet. They could have qualified for food stamps to supplement their income but refused to apply. Those were only for the really poor, they believed. "We're middle-class people," Miller said. "It's just that we have a lower-class income."

Gone was the pride Miller had once felt in his work. He had enjoyed fixing dents in the fuselages of jets. When other children boasted about what their parents did, his son Peter said, "My daddy can fix planes so they can fly high in the sky." That was the same feeling Miller had about his own father, also a blue-collar laborer, who had worked hard in a factory all his life, bought a two-story house for his family, and earned enough to provide vacations out West in the summer. Now all Miller could do was to take out his old tools, stroke them with his hands, and put them away again.

Miller still worked hard, only now he spent his time in nearly skill-less jobs. At McDonald's, he forced himself to be polite to rude teenagers who frequented the establishment. "I still have some pride, you know," he said. "But what am I going to do? I think the needs of my children are a little more important than my ego."

But those needs were hard to meet. In mid-1994, the family fell $3,000 behind in medical bills. Miller bought one newspaper a week, to get the food coupons. If a child left a light burning, Miller's wife asked, "Have you got stock in the electric company? Well, neither do I." The dream of their own home disappeared.

After two years of struggle, neither Miller nor his wife expected conditions to improve for members of the working class. "For people like us," she said, "I'm afraid the good times are gone for good."

American society became more and more aware of its multicultural past and present in the 1980s and 1990s. Different groups competed with each other for positions in the marketplace and other public spaces as the gap between rich and poor grew greater in these years. (Billy Morrow Jackson, Station, 1981–82, Courtesy of the Artist) he Miller family's struggle unfolded against the backdrop of a conservative era that was marked by extravagance and a widening gap between rich and poor. Middle-class incomes, like the Millers', shrank, and it became increasingly difficult for many Americans to make ends meet. In this situation, members of minority groups had the most trouble finding jobs, just as they had in past decades. Then a deep recession in the early 1990s eroded the security of the middle and upper-middle classes as well. The national debt continued to climb and the stock market tumbled as investors, for a while at least, questioned the stability of the economy.

Within that economic framework, the nation struggled with questions about the government's responsibility for those who could not help themselves. The relentless shift toward a service economy left millions of people like the Millers either jobless or in positions far less attractive than before. Yet even as the nation's underclass and homeless population grew, the welfare system came under renewed attack from conservatives who argued that the government was trying to do too much. As discontent mounted, they managed to cut back on payments to millions of Americans who had relied on federal assistance in the past.

At the same time, cataclysmic events shook Communist governments in the USSR and Eastern Europe, ending nearly a half century of Cold War and requiring the United States to redefine its international role. This led to substantial debate, as conservative Republicans were often unwilling to play an activist, and potentially expensive, role abroad.

This chapter describes the enormous changes that occurred in the 1980s and 1990s. It highlights the economic and technological shifts that affected the daily lives of millions of Americans. It then notes the social, political, and diplomatic adjustments that affected the lives of millions of Americans in these years.

The Conservative Transformation

In the 1980s, the Republican party reestablished itself as the dominant force in national politics. The Republican ascendancy that had begun in the Nixon era was now largely complete. The liberal agenda that had governed national affairs ever since the New Deal of Franklin Roosevelt gave way to a new Republican coalition determined to scale back the social welfare state and prevent what its proponents perceived as the erosion of the nation's moral values. Firmly in control of the presidency, sometimes in control of the Senate and later the whole Congress, the Republican party directed the new national agenda.

The New Politics

Conservatism gained new respect in the 1980s. It attracted countless new adherents after the turbulence of the 1960s and the backlash of the Vietnam War. New advertising and fund-raising techniques capitalized on national disaffection with liberal solutions to continuing social problems and made the conservative movement an almost unstoppable national force.

Conservatives seized on Thomas Jefferson's maxim "That government is best which governs least." They argued that the United States in the 1980s had entered an era of limits, as international competition made resources scarcer than before. The dramatic economic growth of the 1960s and 1970s, they believed, left a legacy of rising inflation, falling productivity, enormous waste, and out-of-control entitlements. The liberal solution of "throwing money at social problems" no longer worked, argued conservatives. They therefore sought to downsize government, reduce the tax burden, and cut back the regulations they claimed hampered business competition. In the process, they would restore the focus on individual initiative and private enterprise that they believed had made the nation strong.

The conservative philosophy had tremendous appeal. It promised profitability to those who worked hard and showed initiative in the economic arena. It attracted middle-class Americans who were troubled that they were being forgotten in the commitment to assist minorities and the poor. And it offered hope for the revival of basic social and religious values that many citizens worried had been eaten away by rising divorce rates, legalized abortion, homosexuality, and media preoccupation with violence and sex.

The new conservative coalition covered a broad spectrum. Some followers embraced the economic doctrines of the University of Chicago's Milton Friedman, who promoted the free play of market forces and a sharp restriction of governmental activism in regulating the economy. Other supporters embraced the social and political conservatism of North Carolina Senator Jesse Helms, a tireless foe of any forms of expression he deemed pornographic and a fervent campaigner for a more limited federal role. Many others flocked to the Republican fold because of their conviction that civil rights activists and "bleeding heart liberals" practiced "reverse racism" with their programs of affirmative action, job quotas, and school busing to promote equal opportunity.

The conservative coalition also drew deeply from religious fundamentalists who advocated a far more literal interpretation of Scriptures. Millions, ranging from devout Catholics to orthodox Jews to evangelical Protestants, demanded a return to stricter standards of morality. Muslims, relying on the Koran, took an equally fundamentalist approach. All groups worried about sexual permissiveness and gay rights. They were disturbed at the increase of women working outside the home, a practice they believed eroded family life. They were bothered by a sizable increase in crime. They were likewise troubled by the increase in drug use. Marijuana was not simply a youthful fad but an institution for a broad segment of society. Cocaine use was increasingly common. In short, fundamentalists objected to what they viewed as the liberalizing tendencies of American life and sought to refashion society by reaffirming the morality dictated by the Bible. They wanted to return religion to a central place in American life.

Many of these activists belonged to the so-called Moral Majority. The Reverend Jerry Falwell of Virginia and other television evangelists who focused the concerns of religious fundamentalism attracted large followings in the 1980s. Emulating Father Charles E. Coughlin, the radio priest of the

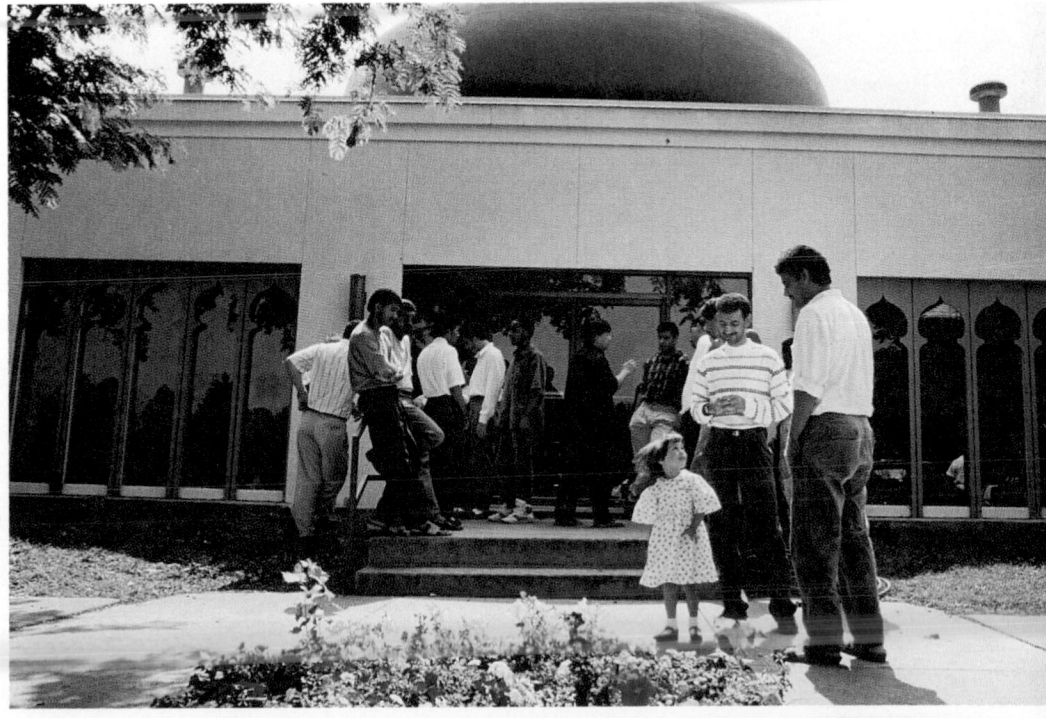

Islam became increasingly popular in the United States in the 1980s and 1990s. This mosque, located in Cedar Rapids, Iowa, is just one of numerous mosques around the country used for worship by American Muslims. (AP/Wide World Photos)

1930s, they appealed to audiences who knew them only on the airwaves. Using electronic means to preach fiery sermons to enormous audiences, they focused their television congregations on specific political ends. They also used their fund-raising ability to support candidates sympathetic to their cause. Moral Majority money began to fund politicians who demanded reinstituting school prayer, ending legalized abortion, and defeating the Equal Rights Amendment. Later a group calling itself the Christian Coalition became even more powerful in supporting—and electing—candidates who met its litmus test on conservative values.

Conservatives from all camps capitalized on changing political techniques more successfully than their liberal opponents. They understood the importance of television in providing instant access to the American public. Politicians became increasingly adept at using brief "sound bites," often lasting no more than 15 or 30 seconds, to state their views. They also relied on new electronic systems, such as e-mail, internet, and fax, to mobilize their followers.

Similarly, conservatives, even more than liberals, seized on negative advertising in political campaigns. Mudslinging has always been a part of the American political tradition, but now carefully crafted television ads concentrated not so much on conveying a positive image of a candidate's platform but on subtly attacking an opponent's character in order to create fundamental doubt in a voter's mind. That effort was visible in both presidential and congressional campaigns.

Conservatives led the way in refining their appeal to voters. Polls, sometimes taken daily, showed which part of a candidate's image needed polishing most or where one's opponent was most vulnerable. "Spin doctors" moved into action after a candidate made a public statement to put the best possible gloss on what had been said. Small wonder that Americans became increasingly cynical about politics and stayed away from the voting booth in record numbers as the twentieth century drew to a close.

Conservatives also were most successful in raising unprecedented sums of money for their campaigns. Richard Viguerie, the New Right mastermind, understood how to tap the huge conservative constituency for political ends. A young Houston activist who later moved to Washington, he developed direct-mail appeals that assisted conservative candidates around the country.

Conservatives understood as well the need to provide an intellectual grounding for their positions. Conservative scholars worked in think tanks and other research organizations, such as the Hoover Institution at Stanford University or the American Enterprise Institute in Washington, D.C., that gave conservatism a solid institutional base. Their books, articles, and reports helped elect Ronald Reagan and other conservative politicians.

Conservative Leadership

More than any other Republican, Ronald Reagan was responsible for the success of the conservative cause. An actor turned politician, he had been a radio broadcaster in his native Midwest, then gravitated to California, where he began a movie career. His success affected his political inclinations, and he changed his affiliation from Democrat to Republican. His visibility and ability to articulate corporate values as a public spokesman for General Electric attracted the attention of conservatives who recognized his political potential and helped him win election as governor of Cali-

The Reverend Jerry Falwell, founder of the Moral Majority, called for a crusade to revive moral values in the United States. His constituency was an important part of the new conservative movement. (UPI/Corbis-Bettmann)

fornia in 1966. He failed in his first bid for the presidency in 1976 but consolidated his strength over the next four years. By 1980, he had the firm support of the growing right, which applauded his promise to reduce the size of the federal government but bolster military might.

Running against incumbent Jimmy Carter in 1980, Reagan scored a landslide victory, gaining a popular vote of 51 to 41 percent and a 489 to 49 Electoral College advantage. He also led the Republican party to control of the Senate for the first time since 1955. In 1984, he was reelected by an even larger margin. He received 59 percent of the popular vote and swamped Democratic candidate Walter Mondale in the Electoral College 525 to 13, losing only Minnesota, Mondale's home state, and the District of Columbia. The Democrats, however, netted two additional seats in the Senate and maintained superiority in the House of Representatives.

Reagan had a pleasing manner and a special skill as a media communicator. Relying on lessons learned in his acting days, he used television as Franklin D. Roosevelt had used radio in the 1930s. He was a gifted storyteller, who loved using anecdotes or one-liners to make his point. In 1980, for example, he quibbled playfully with

Richard Viguerie pioneered direct-mail, fund-raising techniques that raised huge amounts of money for conservative political campaigns. Viguerie's large lists of donors helped candidates around the country as the conservative movement gained momentum. (AP/Wide World Photos)

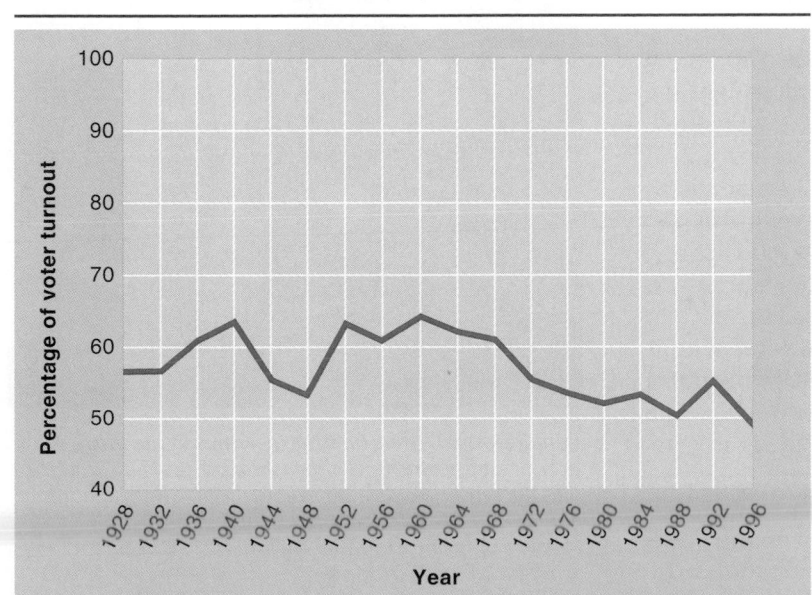

Voter Turnout, 1928–1996

Voter turnout was far lower in the twentieth century than it had been in the nineteenth century. The fact that barely 50 percent of the electorate voted in the last decade reflects a pervasive sense of disillusionment with the political process. Source: Data from *Historical Statistics of the United States* and *Statistical Abstract of the United States.*

Carter over definitions of economic doldrums. "I'm talking in human terms and he is hiding behind a dictionary," Reagan said. "If he wants a definition, I'll give him one. A recession is when your neighbor loses his job. A depression is when you lose yours. A recovery is when Jimmy Carter loses his."

Reagan enjoyed enormous popularity. People talked about a "Teflon" presidency, making a comparison with nonstick frying pans, for even serious criticisms failed to stick and disagreements over policy never diminished his personal approval ratings. When he left the White House, an overwhelming 68 percent of the American public approved of his performance over the past eight years.

But Reagan had a number of liabilities that surfaced over time. As the oldest president the nation had ever had, his attention often drifted, and he occasionally fell asleep during meetings. In press conferences, he was frequently unsure about what was being asked. Uninterested in governing, he delegated a great deal of authority, even if that left him unclear about policy decisions.

Worst of all, he suffered from charges of "sleaze" in his administration. In a period of several months during his last year in office, one former aide was convicted of lying under oath to conceal episodes of influence peddling. Another was convicted of illegally lobbying former government colleagues. His attorney general escaped indictment but nonetheless resigned after severe criticism for improprieties.

In 1988, Republican George Bush, who served eight years as Reagan's vice president, sought the presidency. Though he came from New England, he had prospered in the oil industry in Texas, then served in Congress, as top envoy to China, and as head of the CIA. Termed a preppy wimp by the press, he became a pit bull who ran a mudslinging campaign against his Democratic opponent, Michael Dukakis, governor of Massachusetts. On election day, Bush claimed a 54 to 46 percent popular vote victory and carried 40 states, giving him a 426–112 electoral vote win. But he did not have the kind of mandate Reagan had enjoyed eight years earlier, and Democrats controlled both houses of Congress.

Bush quickly put his own imprint on the presidency. Despite his upper-crust background, he was an unpretentious man, who made a point of trying to appear down-to-earth. He also maintained his own network of friends and political contacts through handwritten notes, telephone calls, and personal visits. More than a year and a half into his term, he was still on his political honeymoon, with a personal approval rating of 67 percent. Support grew even stronger as he presided over the Persian Gulf War in 1991. Then, as the economy faltered and the results of the war seemed suspect, approval levels began to drop.

Though the Democrats won the presidency in 1992, the Republicans won control of both houses of Congress in the midterm elections of 1994. Legislative leaders were now responsible for promoting the Republican cause. Robert Dole of Kansas became the Majority Leader of the Senate. Newt Gingrich, a brash, aggressive, and outspoken congressman from Georgia, was elected new Speaker of the House of Representatives, and became the most visible advocate of the conservative Republican agenda.

Ronald Reagan drew on his experience in the movies to project an appealing, if old-fashioned, image. Though he was the nation's oldest president, he gave the appearance of vitality. Here he is pictured with his wife Nancy, who was one of his most influential advisers. (Diana Walker/Gamma Liaison)

Republican Policies at Home

Republicans in the 1980s aimed to reverse the stagnation of the Carter years and to provide new opportunities for business to prosper. To that end Reagan proposed and implemented an economic recovery program that rested on the theory of supply-side economics. According to this much-criticized theory, reduction of taxes would encourage business expansion, which in turn would lead to a larger supply of goods to help stimulate the system as a whole. Even George Bush, during his brief run for the Republican nomination in 1980, was critical, charging that Reagan was promoting "voodoo economics." Despite these criticisms, Republicans followed the president's lead and endorsed "Reaganomics" with its promise of a revitalized economy.

One early initiative involved tax reductions. The bill finally passed provided for a 5 percent cut in the tax rate that went into effect on October 1, 1981, followed by 10 percent cuts in 1982 and 1983. Although all taxpayers enjoyed tax relief, the rich gained far more than middle- and lower-income Americans. Poverty-level Americans did not bene-

fit at all. Tax cuts and enormous defense expenditures increased the budget deficit. From $74 billion in 1980, it rose to $208 billion in 1983, and then jumped to $290 billion in 1992. Such massive deficits drove the gross federal debt—the total national indebtedness—upward from $909 billion in 1980 to $4.4 trillion in 1992. When Reagan assumed office, the per capita national debt was $4,035; ten years later, in 1990, it was about $12,400.

Faced with the need to raise more money and to rectify the increasingly skewed tax code, in 1986 Congress passed and Reagan signed the most sweeping tax reform revision since the federal income tax began in 1913. It lowered rates, simplified brackets, and closed loopholes to expand the tax base. Though it ended up neither increasing nor decreasing the government's tax take, the measure was an important step toward treating low-income Americans more equitably. Still, most of the benefits went to the richest 5 percent of Americans, whose tax rate dropped from 50 to 38 percent.

At the same time, Reagan embarked on a major program of deregulation. In a campaign more comprehensive than President Carter's, he

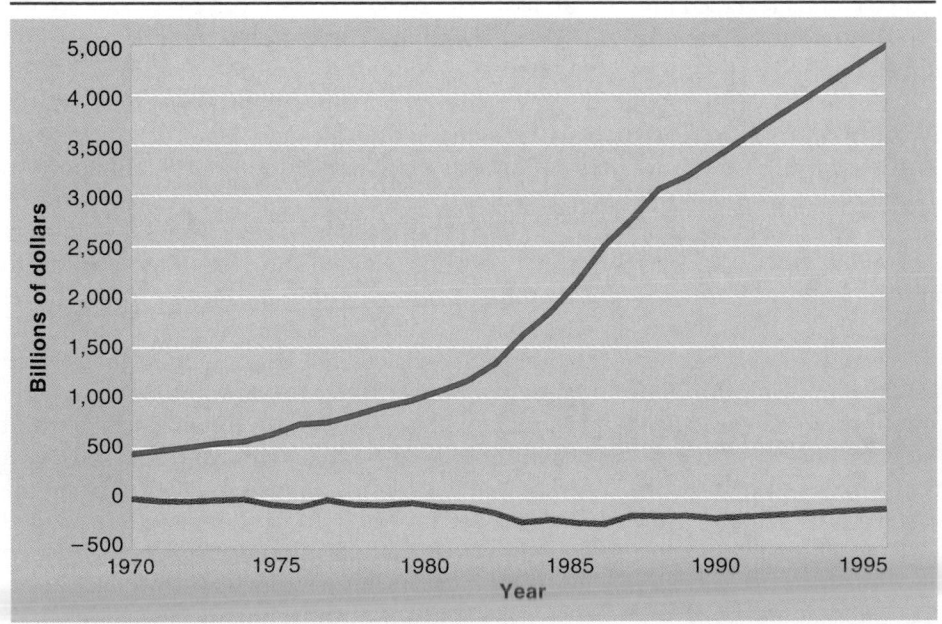

Federal Budget Deficits and the National Debt, 1970–1995

In the 1970s and 1980s, the yearly federal deficit grew steadily larger, and the gross federal debt skyrocketed, topping $3 trillion in 1990. Despite cuts in the deficit in the 1990s, the gross federal debt continued to climb, moving closer to $5 trillion. Source: Data from *Statistical Abstract of the United States.*

— Total yearly deficit   — Gross federal debt

focused on agencies of the 1970s such as the Environmental Protection Agency, the Consumer Product Safety Commission, and the Occupational Safety and Health Administration. The Republican administration argued that regulations pertaining to the consumer, the workplace, and the environment were inefficient, paternalistic, and excessively expensive. They impeded business growth and needed to be eliminated.

Meanwhile, Reagan challenged the consensus fostered by the New Deal that the national government should monitor the economy and assist the least fortunate citizens. He had played by the rules of the system and had won fame and fortune. Others could do the same. He charged that government intruded into too many aspects of American life and declared it was time to eliminate "waste, fraud, and abuse" by cutting unnecessary programs.

Reagan needed to make cuts in social programs, both because of sizable tax cuts and because of enormous military expenditures. Committed to a massive arms buildup, over a five-year period, the administration sought an unprecedented military budget of $1.5 trillion. By 1985, with a budget of $300 billion, the United States was spending half a million dollars a minute on defense and four times as much as at the height of the Vietnam War.

The huge cuts in social programs reversed the approach of liberals over the past 50 years. Republicans in the 1970s had begun to question the social policy goals of Lyndon Johnson's Great Society (see Chapter 28). Now, in the 1980s, they attacked those liberal aims head-on. They eliminated public service jobs, mandated under the Comprehensive Employment and Training Act, and reduced other aid to the cities, where the poor congregated. They cut back unemployment compensation and required Medicare patients to pay more for treatment. They lowered welfare benefits and reduced food stamp allocations. They slashed the Legal Services Corporation, which provided legal services for those too poor to afford lawyers' fees. They replaced grants for college students with loans. Spending on human resources fell by $101 billion between 1980 and 1982. The process continued even after Reagan left office. Between 1981 and 1992, U.S. spending, after adjustment for inflation, fell 82 percent for subsidized housing, 63 percent for job training and employment services,

and 40 percent for community services. Middle-class Americans, benefiting from the tax cuts, were not hurt by the slashes in social programs. But for millions of the nation's poorest citizens, the administration's approach caused real suffering.

As a political conservative distrustful of central government, Reagan wanted to place more power in the hands of state and local governments and to reduce the involvement of the federal government in people's lives. His "New Federalism" attempted to shift responsibilities from the federal to the state level. By eliminating federal funding and instead making grants to the states, which could spend the money as they saw fit, he hoped to fortify local initiative. Critics charged, with some justification, that the proposal was merely a backhanded way of moving programs from one place to another, while eliminating federal funding. When a prolonged recession began in 1990, the administration's policy contributed to the near-bankruptcy of a number of states and municipalities, which now bore responsibility for programs formerly funded in Washington.

Reagan took a conservative approach to social issues as well. Accepting the support of the New Right, he strongly endorsed conservative social goals. To avoid compromising his economic program, however, he provided only symbolic support at first. He spoke out for public prayer in the schools without expending political capital in Congress to support the issue. In the same way, he showed his opposition to abortion by making sure that the first nongovernmental group to receive an audience at the White House was an antiabortion March for Life contingent.

George Bush followed directly in his predecessor's footsteps. Having forsworn his objection to "voodoo economics" as soon as he received the vice presidential nomination, Bush faithfully adhered to Reagan's general economic policy, even after he became president. In the 1988 campaign, he admonished voters to "read my lips" and promised "no new taxes." Though he backed down from that pledge in a bipartisan effort to bring the budget deficit under control, he later renounced his own agreement to modest tax increases when he went back on the campaign trail in 1992.

Like Reagan, Bush wanted deep cuts in social programs. Tireless in his criticism of the Democratic majorities in the Senate and House of Representa-

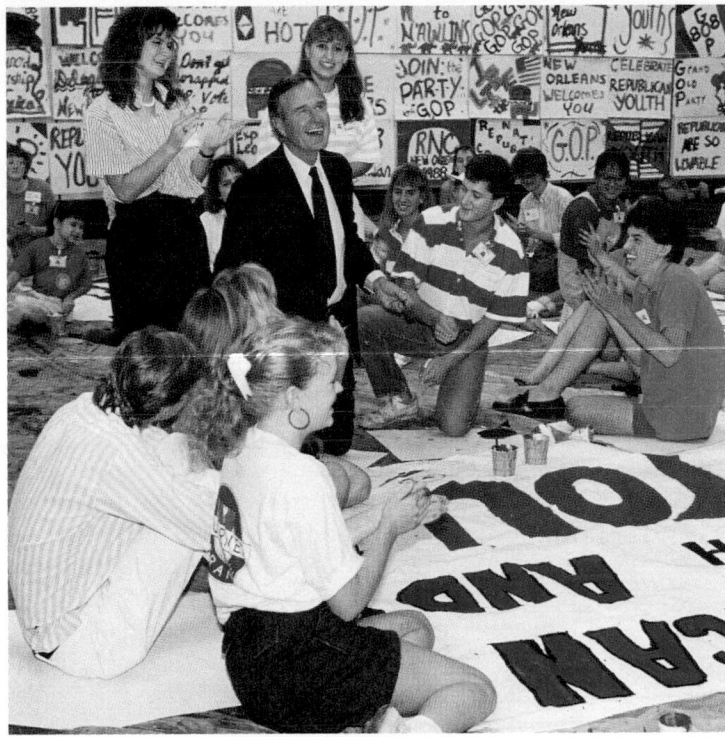

Although he trailed Democrat Michael Dukakis by 17 percentage points four months before the 1988 presidential election, George Bush rapidly overtook his opponent through effective campaigning. Bush won 85 percent of the voters who had supported Reagan in 1984. (UPI/Corbis-Bettmann)

tives, he vetoed measure after measure to assist those caught in the ravages of a troubling recession that sent unemployment rates up to 8 percent and left one of every four urban children living in poverty.

Bush was more outspoken than Reagan in his support of conservative social goals. At the start of the 1980s, conservatives had questioned Bush's commitment to their social agenda, and, indeed, Bush had been sympathetic to a woman's right to choice in the abortion issue. As president, however, he firmly opposed abortion, and his Supreme Court appointments, like Reagan's, guaranteed that the effort to roll back or overturn *Roe* v. *Wade* would continue.

The Republican philosophy under Reagan and Bush dramatically reversed the nation's domestic agenda. Liberalism in the 1960s had reached a high-water mark in a time of steady growth, when hard choices about where to spend money had been less necessary. As limits began to loom, decisions about social programs became more difficult, and millions of Americans came to believe that most of the Great Society programs had failed to conquer poverty and in fact had created lifelong welfare dependency. Conservatism offered a more attractive answer, particularly to those Americans in the middle and upper classes who were already comfortable.

But the transformation was accompanied by a number of serious problems that emerged in the early 1990s. Bush faced a crisis in the long-mismanaged savings and loan industry. The Republican deregulation policy had allowed owners of savings and loan institutions to operate without previous restrictions. Many, paying themselves lavish salaries, made unwise high-risk investments that proved profitable for a while but then produced tremendous losses. To protect depositors whose assets had been lost by these questionable lending practices, Congress approved a $166 billion rescue plan (that soon reached more than $250 billion) committing taxpayers to bail out the industry.

Republican policy also widened the gap between rich and poor. Tax breaks for the wealthy, deregulation initiatives, high interest rates for investors, permissiveness toward mergers, and an enormous growth in the salaries of business executives all contributed to the disparity. So did more lenient antitrust enforcement and a general sympathy for speculative finance.

The Wealthiest Americans

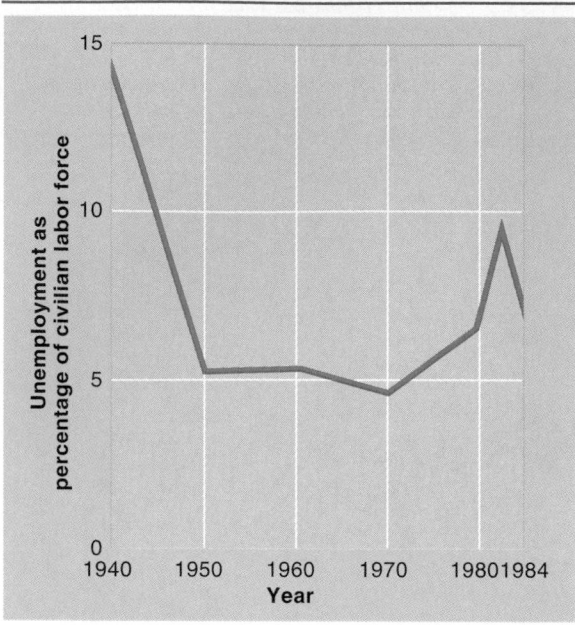

During the 1980s, the percentage of national wealth held by the richest 1 percent of Americans reached the highest level since the 1930s. Source: *New York Times,* August 16, 1992.

The results were clear. "The 1980s," analyst Kevin Phillips observed, "were the triumph of upper America—an ostentatious celebration of wealth, the political ascendancy of the rich and a glorification of capitalism, free markets and finance." The concentration of capital increased, and the sums involved took what Phillips termed a "megaleap" forward. Now there was an extraordinary amassing of wealth at the top levels, among the dekamillionaires, centmillionaires, half-billionaires, and billionaires. "Garden-variety millionaires," Phillips noted, "had become so common that there were about 1.5 million of them by 1989." According to one study, the share of national wealth of the richest 1 percent of the nation rose from about 18 percent in 1976 to 36 percent in 1989. The net worth of the *Forbes* magazine 400 richest Americans nearly tripled between 1981 and 1989.

Meanwhile, less fortunate Americans were hurting more than they had since the Great Depression of the 1930s. Financial expert Felix Rohatyn decried the "huge transfer of wealth from lower-skilled, middle-class American workers to

owners of capital assets and a new technological aristocracy." Millions of people, ranging from foreclosed farmers to laid-off industrial workers, were struggling to make ends meet.

Liberal Interlude

In 1992, the Democratic Party mounted an aggressive challenge to Republican rule. After a fierce primary campaign, Governor Bill Clinton of Arkansas triumphed over a crowded field of candidates. Overcoming allegations of marital instability, marijuana use, and draft evasion, he argued that it was time for a new generation to take command. Forty-six years old, he had reached maturity in the 1960s and stood in stark contrast to George Bush, now running for reelection, who had come of age during World War II. The third candidate in what became a three-way race was H. Ross Perot, a billionaire businessman from Texas who had made a fortune in the computer data-processing field and declared that he alone could provide the leadership the nation needed.

This campaign, more than any in the past, was fought on television. In addition to three televised presidential debates, the candidates appeared on talk shows and interview programs. Perot energized his campaign with appearances on "Larry King Live." Bill Clinton used a post–Super Bowl appearance on "60 Minutes" to answer charges questioning his character and later played his saxophone on the "Arsenio Hall Show" and appeared on MTV. This reliance on the electronic marketplace reoriented American campaign politics.

On election day, Clinton won 43 percent of the popular vote to 38 percent for Bush and 19 percent for Perot. The electoral vote margin was even larger: 357 for Clinton, 168 for Bush, 0 for Perot. The Democrats retained control of both houses of Congress, with more women and minority members than ever before.

The president-elect quickly demonstrated his intention of shifting the nation's course after 12 years of Republican rule. His Cabinet nominations included four women, four African Americans, and two Latinos. He held a televised "economic summit" to explore national options and demonstrated a keen grasp of the details of policy. In his inaugural address, Clinton declared that "a new season of American renewal has begun."

Bill Clinton was an exuberant campaigner who used his musical talent to attract support as he ran for president in 1992. Here he plays his saxophone on nationwide television on "The Arsenio Hall Show" in Los Angeles. (AP/Wide World Photos)

Clinton soon found his hands full at home. Although the economy finally began to improve, the public gave the president little credit for the upturn. He gained Senate ratification of the North American Free Trade Agreement (NAFTA)—aimed at promoting free trade between Canada, Mexico, and the United States—in November 1993 after a bitter battle. He secured passage of a crime bill banning manufacture, sale, or possession of 19 different assault weapons (though not of a much larger number of semiautomatic guns). But he failed to win approval of his major legislative initiative: health care reform. "This health-care system of ours is badly broken," he said in September 1993, "and it's time to fix it." Particularly troublesome were escalating costs and the lack of

Presidential Elections, 1980–1996				
Year	Candidate	Party	Popular Vote	Electoral Vote
1980	RONALD REAGAN	Republican	43,899,248 (50.8%)	489
	Jimmy Carter	Democratic	36,481,435 (41.0%)	49
	John B. Anderson	Independent	5,719,437 (6.6%)	0
1984	RONALD REAGAN	Republican	53,428,357 (58.7%)	525
	Walter F. Mondale	Democratic	36,930,923 (40.6%)	13
1988	GEORGE BUSH	Republican	47,946,422 (53.9%)	426
	Michael Dukakis	Democratic	41,016,429 (46.1%)	112
1992	BILL CLINTON	Democratic	43,728,275 (43.2%)	357
	George Bush	Republican	38,167,416 (37.7%)	168
	H. Ross Perot	Independent	19,237,245 (19.0%)	0
1996	BILL CLINTON	Democratic	47,401,185 (49.2%)	379
	Robert Dole	Republican	39,197,469 (40.7%)	159
	H. Ross Perot	Reform	8,085,294 (8.4%)	0

Note: Winners' names appear in capital letters.

universal medical care, which left 35 million Americans with no medical insurance. Clinton's complicated proposal for a system of health alliances in each state provoked intense opposition from the health care and insurance industries and from politicians with plans of their own. In the end he was unable to persuade Congress either to accept his approach or adopt a workable alternative.

Conservative Resurgence

Voters demonstrated their dissatisfaction in the midterm elections of 1994. Republicans swept control of both the Senate and the House for the first time in over 40 years. In the House, they made the largest gains since 1946, winning over 50 races against Democratic incumbents. Some of the strongest and most senior Representatives, including Speaker Thomas Foley, lost their seats. At the state level, Republicans picked up 12 governorships and took control in seven of the eight largest states.

The election marked the end of the commitment to the welfare state. The 104th Congress moved aggressively to make good on its promises—outlined during the campaign in the Republicans' "Contract with America"—to scale back the role of the federal government, eliminate troublesome regulations, reduce taxes, and balance the budget. Newt Gingrich, as the new Speaker of the House of Representatives, pushed through changes in the House rules that provided him with far greater power in appointing committee members and moving legislation along. Under his leadership, Congress launched a frontal attack on the budget, proposing massive cuts in virtually all social services. It demanded the elimination of three Cabinet departments and insisted on gutting the National Endowment for the Humanities, the National Endowment for the Arts, and the Public Broadcasting System. When, at the end of 1995 the President and the Speaker tangled with one another on the size of the cuts and refused to compromise on a budget, the government shut down and 800,000 federal employees found themselves temporarily "furloughed."

While the House of Representatives passed many of the measures proposed in the "Contract with America," only a few of them became law. The Senate balked at some; the president vetoed others. As the election of 1996 approached, Newt Gingrich found himself out of favor as millions of

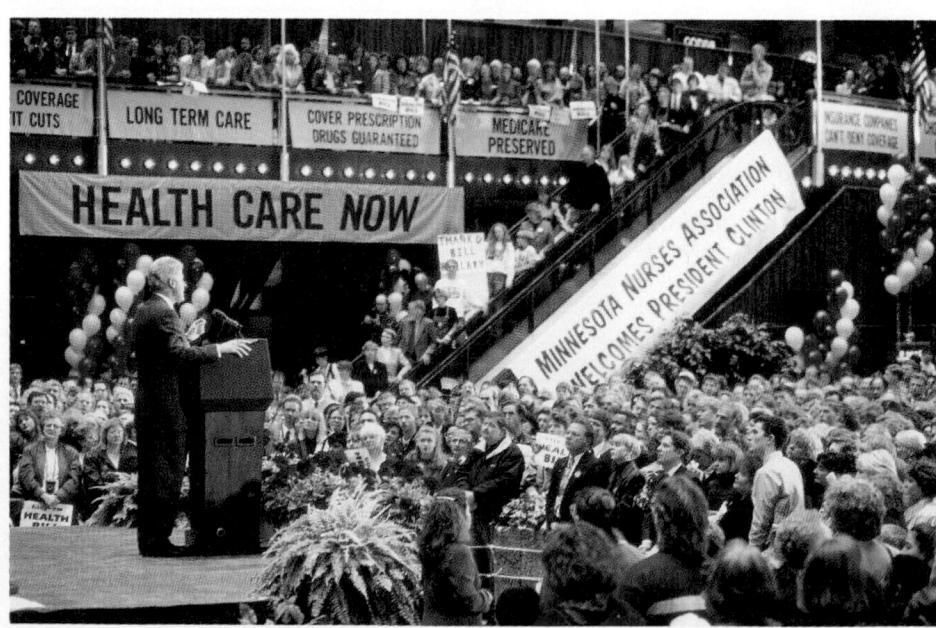

Bill Clinton enjoyed leaving Washington and addressing crowds in an effort to gain support for his programs. Here he speaks about his health care reform proposal to a noontime rally in Minneapolis. (David Rae Morris/Impact Visuals)

Americans began to realize that they would suffer from the cuts more aggressive Republicans sought.

A Second Term for Clinton

As Bill Clinton sought a second term in 1996, the Republicans nominated Senate Minority Leader Robert Dole as their presidential candidate. The 73-year-old Dole ran a lackluster campaign. His pledge to push through a sweeping 15 percent tax reduction failed to excite voter interest. Even supporters wondered how he would balance the budget at the same time. Stung by Democratic congressional defeats two years before, Clinton reshaped his own image and announced that the "era of big government is over." He coopted Republican issues, pledging to balance the budget himself and enraging liberal supporters by signing a welfare reform bill that slashed benefits and removed millions of people from the rolls. At the same time, he posed as the protector of Medicare and other programs that were threatened by proposed Republican cuts.

Clinton's strategy worked. On election day, he won a resounding victory over Dole. He received 49 percent of the popular vote to 41 percent for Dole and 8 percent for Ross Perot, who ran again, though this time less successfully than four years before. In the electoral tally, Clinton received 379 votes to 159 for Dole. Yet the Republicans kept control of Congress. In the House of Representatives, they lost a number of seats but retained a majority. In the Senate, they added two seats to what they had won in 1994. Around the country, voters seemed willing to support Clinton, but not to give him the blanket mandate he sought. In California, voters voiced their opposition to affirmative action when they approved Proposition 209 prohibiting preferential treatment based on gender or race.

An End to Social Reform

The Republican attack on the welfare state included an effort to limit the commitment to social reform. Enough had been done already, conservatives argued, and gains for less fortunate Americans came at the expense of the middle class. It was time to end federal "intrusion" in this area.

Slowdown in the Struggle for Civil Rights

Republican policies slowed the civil rights movement. Ronald Reagan opposed busing to achieve racial balance, and his attorney general worked to dismantle affirmative action programs. Initially reluctant to support extension of the enormously successful Voting Rights Act of 1965, Reagan relented only under severe criticism from Republicans as well as Democrats. He directed the Internal Revenue Service to cease banning tax exemptions for private schools that discriminated against blacks, only to see that move overturned by the Supreme Court in 1983. He also launched an assault on the Civil Rights Commission and hampered its effectiveness by appointing members who did not support its main goals.

The courts similarly weakened the commitment to equal rights. As a result of Reagan's and Bush's judicial appointments, federal courts stopped pushing for school integration, and in some cases actively encouraged the pattern of separation. The Supreme Court's *Freeman* v. *Pitts* decision in 1992 granted a suburban Atlanta school board relief from a desegregation order on the grounds that it was not possible to counteract massive demographic shifts. Then in 1995, the Court let stand a lower court ruling prohibiting colleges and universities from awarding special scholarships to African Americans or other minorities.

That last decision was part of a larger backlash against the policy of affirmative action. Energized by their political victories in 1994, conservatives launched a powerful attack on the policy of giving preferential treatment to groups that had suffered discrimination in the past. Arguing that government leaders had never intended affirmative action to be a permanent policy, they pushed ballot initiatives and pressured public agencies to bring the practice to an end.

Despite significant progress in the electoral arena—where African Americans won mayoral elections in major cities, captured the governor's office in Virginia, and helped the Reverend Jesse Jackson mount two impressive presidential campaigns in 1984 and 1988—black-white relations remained tense. As Joseph Lattimore, an African American from Chicago, observed, "As far as integrating with you—we have sang 'We Shall Overcome,' we have prayed at the courthouse steps, we have made all these gestures, and the door is not open." Sylvia Matthews, from the same city, noted, "Today it seems more acceptable to be racist. Just in the kinds of things you hear people say." African American historian John Hope Franklin, looking back in 1995 at the eight decades of his life, said, "Just about the time you sit down or sit back and say, 'Oh, yes, we're really moving,' you get slapped back down."

Obstacles to Women's Rights

Women had a similar experience in the 1980s and 1990s. They too made significant electoral gains. In 1981, President Ronald Reagan appointed Sandra Day O'Connor as the first woman Supreme Court justice, and in 1984, Geraldine Ferraro, a Democratic member of Congress, became the first woman vice presidential candidate for a major party.

Yet women still faced serious problems that were compounded by conservative social policies. Access to new positions did not change their concentration in lower-paying jobs. In 1985, most women still served as secretaries, cashiers, bookkeepers, registered nurses, and waitresses—the same jobs most frequently held ten years before. Even when women moved into positions traditionally held by men, their progress often stopped at the lower and middle levels. Interruptions of work—to bear children or assume family responsibilities—impeded advancement. A "glass ceiling" seemed to prevent them from moving up.

Wage differentials between women and men continued to exist. In 1985, full-time working women still earned only 63.6 cents for every dollar earned by men. Their concentration in the so-called pink-collar positions—traditional women's jobs—made further improvement difficult. Comparable-worth cases—arguing that women should receive equal pay for different jobs of similar value—met with conservative resistance.

Conservative activists also waged a dedicated campaign against the right to legal abortion. Despite the 1973 Supreme Court decision legalizing abortion, the issue remained very much alive. The number of abortions increased dramatically in the decade after the decision. In response, "pro-life" forces mobilized. Opponents lobbied to cut off federal funds that allowed the poor to obtain the abortions the better-off could pay for themselves; they insisted that abortions should be performed in hospitals and not in less expensive clinics; and they worked to reverse the original decision itself.

Though the Supreme Court underscored its judgment in 1983, the pro-life movement was not deterred. In 1989, a solidifying conservative major-

Jesse Jackson demonstrated that an African American could attract a substantial level of support as he ran for president in 1984 and 1988. Here he is shown on the campaign trail in Chicago in 1988. (Marc Pokempner/ Impact Visuals)

ity on the Court ruled in *Webster* v. *Reproductive Health Services* that while women's right to abortion remained intact, state legislatures could impose limitations if they chose. With that judgment, a major legislative debate over the issue began, and numerous states began to mandate restrictions.

In 1992, in *Planned Parenthood* v. *Casey,* the Supreme Court reaffirmed what it termed the essence of the right to abortion, while permitting further state restrictions. It declared that a 24-hour waiting period for women seeking abortions was acceptable and required teenage girls to secure the permission of a parent (or a judge) before ending a pregnancy. The ruling clearly gave states greater latitude in the overall restrictive effort and made an abortion harder to obtain, particularly for poor women and young women.

In response to a conservative backlash, the larger women's liberation movement became more inclusive, and more sensitive to issues of race. Black women still had their own concerns, but now found more common ground. While black women in the early 1990s still earned less, on a weekly basis, than white men and white women, that situation began to improve. The dramatic confrontation between Supreme Court nominee Clarence Thomas and lawyer Anita Hill during confirmation hearings in 1991 dramatized both racial questions and the issue of sexual harassment. In the aftermath, Americans in Congress, in the business community, and in the larger workplace all became more aware of inappropriate behavior that could no longer be tolerated.

The Limited Commitment to Latino Rights

Latinos from all groups likewise faced continuing problems in the 1980s and 1990s as the commitment to reform eroded. Spanish-speaking students often found it difficult to move through the educational system. In 1987, fully 40 percent of all Latino high school students did not graduate. Only 31 percent of the Latino seniors were enrolled in college-preparatory courses. Latino students frequently received little help from guidance counselors. Anel Albarran, a Mexican immigrant who arrived in East Los Angeles when she was 11, applied to UCLA when a special high school teacher encouraged her and made sure that she

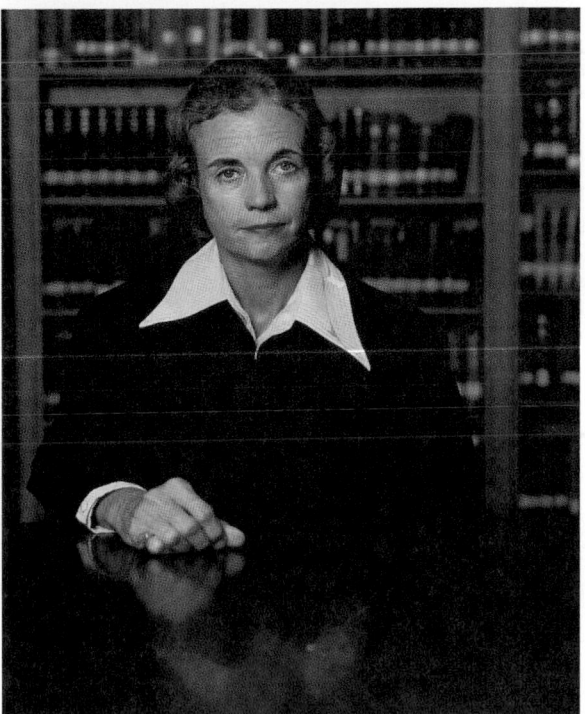

Sandra Day O'Connor became the first woman justice to sit on the United States Supreme Court. Her pre-Court career was similar to that of many other women, as she was denied numerous jobs when she emerged from law school. A decade later, Ruth Bader Ginsburg joined O'Connor on the nation's highest Court. (Tom Zimberoff/Sygma)

received help in choosing the necessary courses. By contrast, her regular counselor asked her two months before graduation whether she had considered college: "All he had wanted to do during high school was give me my classes and get me out of the room."

College itself was another problem. Of those Latinos who went to college, 56 percent attended community colleges. Graduation often proved difficult; fewer than 7 percent completed a course of study. When forced to take courses that had little connection to their background and less relevance to their lives, many students became frustrated and dropped out.

Like other groups, Latinos slowly extended their political gains. Henry Cisneros became mayor of San Antonio and Colorado state legislator Federico Peña was elected mayor of Denver. In New Mexico, Governor Toney Anaya called himself

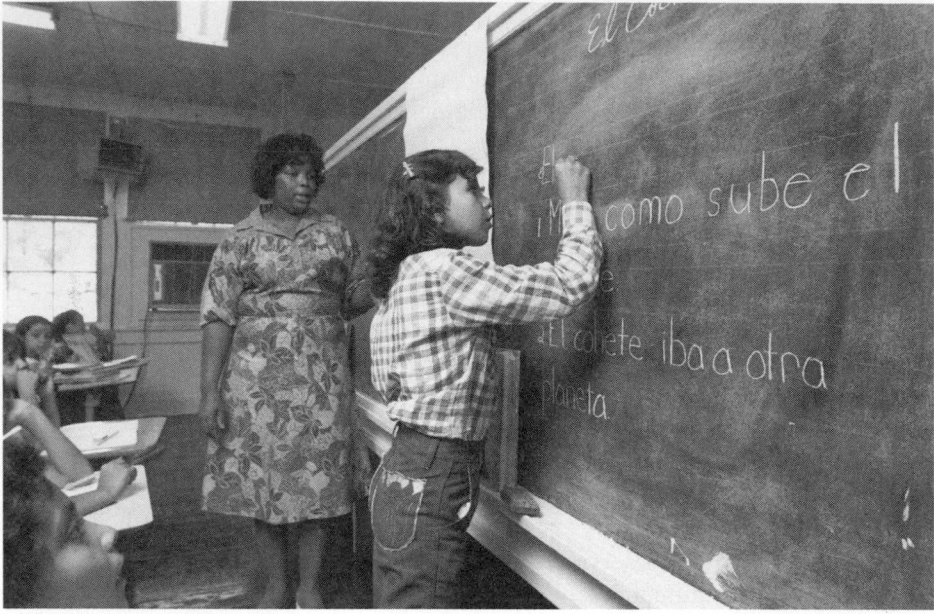

the nation's highest elected Hispanic. The number of Latinos holding elective offices nationwide increased 3.5 percent between 1986 and 1987, and the number of Latina women in such offices increased 20 percent in that time. Lauro Cavazos became U.S. Secretary of Education in 1988, while Henry Cisneros became Secretary of Housing and Urban Development and Federico Peña Secretary of Transportation in 1993.

Latino workers, however, continued to have a hard time in the employment market. As the nation's overall unemployment rate dropped in the mid-1990s, the rate for the 12 million Latino workers barely budged and worsened in relation to the rate for African Americans. Many found themselves suffering from outmoded skills and weaker educational backgrounds. They also experienced greater scrutiny than in the past. "They ask you for your Social Security card, your alien card," according to Efrain Castillo, a 43-year-old truck driver who had come to the United States from Mexico in the early 1970s. Discrimination seemed increasingly prevalent.

Continuing Problems for Native Americans

Native Americans likewise experienced the waning commitment to reform. Gains achieved came as a result of their own efforts. Some tribal communities developed business skills, although traditional Indian attitudes hardly fostered the capitalist perspective. As Dale Old Horn, an MIT graduate and department head at Little Big Horn College in Crow Agency, Montana, explained:

> The Crow Indian child is taught that he is part of a harmonious circle of kin relations, clans and nature. The white child is taught that he is the center of the circle. The Crow believe in sharing wealth, and whites believe in accumulating wealth.

Even so, a number of Indian groups adopted at least some of the capitalist ethos. "Now we're beginning to realize that, if we want to be self-sufficient, we're going to have to become entrepreneurs ourselves," observed Iola Hayden, the Comanche executive director of Oklahomans for Indian Opportunity. The Choctaw in Mississippi were among the most successful. Before they began a drive toward self-sufficiency in 1979, their unemployment rate was 50 percent. By the middle of the 1980s, Choctaws owned all or part of three businesses on the reservation, employed 1,000 people, generated $30 million in work annually, and cut the unemployment rate in half. The Pequots in Connecticut built a casino in the Ledyard woods in the southeastern part of the state. By 1995, it had become the most profitable casino in

Native Americans became more politically active in the 1990s. In the election of 1992, Ben Nighthorse Campbell was elected to the Senate from his home state of Colorado. (AP/Wide World Photos)

growth. The Department of the Interior opened forest lands, wilderness areas, and coastal waters to economic development, with no concern for preserving the natural environment. George Bush initially proved more sympathetic to environmental causes and delighted environmentalists by signing new clean air legislation. Later, as the economy faltered, he was less willing to support environmental action that he claimed might slow economic growth. In 1992, he accommodated business by easing clean air restrictions. That same year, at a United Nations–sponsored Earth Summit in Rio de Janeiro, Brazil, with 100 other heads of state, Bush stood alone in his refusal to sign a biological diversity treaty framed to conserve plant and animal species.

Bill Clinton seemed to promise a new approach for the 1990s. His vice president was Al Gore, a dedicated environmentalist. His Secretary of the Interior was Bruce Babbitt, who had gained environmental support during his tenure as governor of Arizona. The Clinton administration tried to take the middle ground in the still-continuing spotted owl controversy, by protecting substantial stretches of forest but permitting more logging than had been done in recent years. But Clinton too discovered that the issues were hardly subject to easy resolution in a conservative age.

the nation, grossing more than $800 million the year before.

Despite those efforts, the 1990 census revealed that Indians remained the nation's poorest group. As Ben Nighthorse Campbell, Republican Senator from Colorado, noted in 1995, average Indian household income fell by 5 percent in the 1980s, while it rose for all other ethnic and racial groups. Average annual income for Native Americans on reservations was less than $5,000. There was still much to be done.

Pressures on the Environmental Movement

Environmentalists too were discouraged by the direction of public policy in the 1980s and 1990s. Activists now found that they faced fierce opposition. Ronald Reagan systematically restrained the EPA in his avowed effort to promote economic

The Postindustrial Economy

Republicans sought to reorganize the government against the backdrop of an economy that grew more volatile in the 1980s and 1990s. As patterns of employment changed in an increasingly mechanized workplace, millions of workers struggled to survive the shocks they faced. Under Republican supply-side economics, the business cycle began to follow a pattern of moving from recession to boom and back to recession again. When Reagan took office in 1980, the economy was reeling under the impact of declining productivity, galloping inflation, oil shortages, and high unemployment. Reagan's policies brought improvement in the early 1980s, particularly for middle- and upper-income individuals. But even renewed growth and higher employment rates could not help those of lesser means, as stiff competition from abroad led to continuing trouble in balancing budgets. The recession that gripped the country from 1990 to 1992 only underscored the need for renewed productivity, full employment, and equitable distribution of wealth.

The Changing Nature of Work

Automation and other technological advances had a powerful impact on the American workplace and brought about a shift in the occupational structure of the working class. Because of such advances, the *New York Times* reported in 1990 in an article on the industrial Midwest, "Some factories look as if they have been hit by a kind of economic neutron bomb, which left assembly lines running at full speed but eliminated most of the people who worked on them." Formerly profitable jobs disappeared. One pulp mill worker voiced gloom about the future: "I think the country has a problem. The managers want everything run by computers. But if no one has a job, no one will know how to do anything anymore. Who will pay the taxes? What kind of society will it be when people have lost their knowledge and depend on computers for everything?"

In human terms, the introduction of the computer had other consequences as well. Now workers sat for hours before their screens. Some described the feeling of "floating in space" as they worked, or of being "lost behind the screen." Others worried about radiation from the monitor or muscular fatigue from sitting at a keyboard all day. Still others complained that they could no longer touch their work.

Yet even as the nature of work changed, people seemed to be working more. In past decades leisure time had seemed to expand. By the late 1950s, people spoke of the four-day workweek which seemed to "loom on the immediate horizon." In the last 20 years, however, the amount of time Americans worked has steadily risen. In the mid–1990s, American employees worked 320 hours more each year than their counterparts in Germany or France.

In the process, they experienced more stress, as they attempted to juggle the pressures between employment and family life. Problems were particularly severe for women, still trying to cope with the pressures of a double load, as they main-

tained responsibility for the home even when working outside. Marriages came under significant strain. One 26-year-old legal secretary in California spoke for many as she summed up her frustration. Her husband, she noted, "does no cooking, no washing, no anything else. How do I feel? Furious. If our marriage ends, it will be on this issue."

The Shift to a Service Economy

The scarcity of good jobs stemmed in part from the restructuring of the economy that occurred in the 1980s. In a trend underway for more than half a century, the United States continued the shift from an industrial base, where most workers actually produced things, to a service base, where most provided expertise or service to others in the work force. By the mid-1980s, three-fourths of the 113 million employees in the country worked in the service sector—as fast-food workers, clerks, computer programmers, doctors, lawyers, bankers, teachers, and public employees.

That shift, in turn, had its roots in the decline of the country's industrial sector. The United States had been the world's industrial leader since the late nineteenth century. By the 1970s, however, the United States began to lose that position. After 1973, productivity slowed in virtually all American industries, in a pattern that continued in the 1980s and 1990s. Economic growth in the early 1970s averaged 2.3 percent annually in contrast to its average of 3.2 percent in the 1950s. In the early 1980s, during the worst recession since the 1930s, economic growth virtually ceased.

The causes of this decline in productivity were complex. The most important factor was a widespread and systematic failure on the part of the United States to invest sufficiently in its basic productive capacity. During the Reagan years, investment of capital in real plants and equipment within the United States gave way to speculation, mergers, and spending abroad. Gross private domestic investment in national industries rose modestly during the boom years, though most companies became caught up in an acquisition mania that consumed even more resources. At the end of the 1980s, domestic investment was down—5.7 percent in 1990 and 9.5 percent in 1991.

The oil crisis and rising oil prices (see Chapter 28) also contributed to the industrial decline. Finally, the war in Vietnam diverted federal funds from support for research and development.

While American industry became less productive, other industrial nations moved forward. German and Japanese industries, rebuilt after World War II with U.S. aid and aggressively modernized thereafter, reached new heights of efficiency. As a result, the United States began to lose its share of the world market for industrial goods. In 1946, the country had provided 60 percent of the world's iron and steel. In 1978, it provided a mere 16 percent. So efficient and cost-effective were foreign steel producers that the United States found itself importing a fifth of its iron and steel. By 1980, Japanese car manufacturers had also captured nearly a quarter of the American automobile market, and they continued to hold that substantial share in 1990. The auto industry, which had been a mainstay of economic growth for much of the twentieth century, suffered plant shutdowns and massive layoffs. In 1991, its worst year ever, Ford lost a staggering $2.3 billion.

Workers in Transition

In the 1980s and 1990s, American labor struggled to hold on to the gains realized by the post–World War II generation of blue-collar workers. The largest problems involved adjusting to the nation's changing economic needs. The shift to a service economy, while providing new jobs, was problematic for many American workers. Millions of men and women, like Craig Miller, met at the start of the chapter, who had lost positions as a result of plant closings and permanent economic contractions, now found themselves in low-paying jobs with few opportunities for advancement. Entry-level posts were seldom located in the central cities, where most of the poor lived. Even when new jobs were created in the cities, minority residents often lacked the skills to acquire or hold them.

Meanwhile, the trade union movement faltered as the economy moved from an industrial to a service base. Unions had been most successful in organizing the nation's industrial workers in the years since the 1930s, and the United States emerged from World War II with unions strong. In the years that followed, the percentage of workers belonging to unions dropped. As the chart shows, it was just over 25 percent in 1980, barely over 16 percent a decade later. As the total number of wage and salary workers rose substantially between 1983 and 1993, the overall number of union members dropped from 17.7 to 16.6 million.

The pattern was visible in the example of U.S. Steel. It had once relied on a unionized work force of 200,000 employees. In the early 1980s, it reconstituted itself as USX Corporation and shut many of its steel mills, while branching out into the more profitable oil business. The union—the United Steelworkers of America—lost half of its members in the process.

Union membership declined for a number of reasons. The shift from blue-collar to white-collar work contributed to the contraction. The increase in the numbers of women and young people in the work force (groups that have historically been difficult to organize) was another factor, as was the more forceful opposition to unions by managers

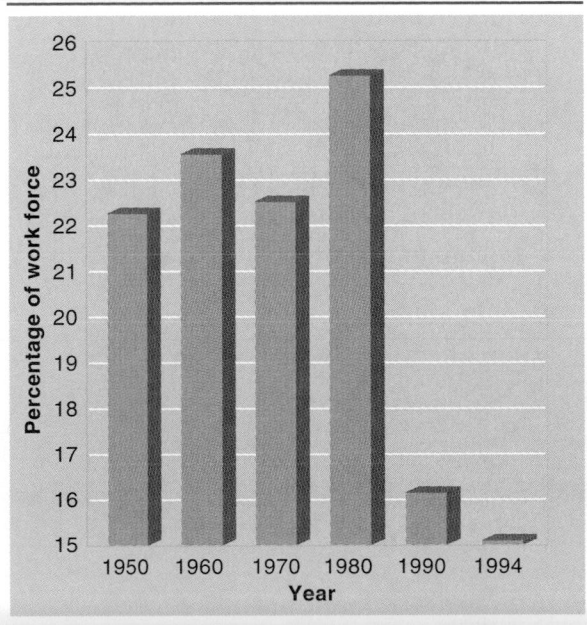

Union Membership, 1950–1994

The percentage of workers belonging to unions dropped dramatically after 1980 and continued to fall in the 1990s. Source: U.S. Bureau of Labor Statistics.

applying the provisions of the Taft-Hartley Act of 1947, which restricted the tactics labor leaders could use. Union organizing efforts fell off significantly. One study showed a drop in spending to organize from $1.03 per nonunion member in 1953 to $0.71 in 1974. At the same time, managerial opposition to unions increased. A 1994 report presented to the Secretaries of Labor and Commerce found that "There is a dismal side to American labor relations in which the rights of some individual workers are violated by some employers who resist the right to organize." Such unfair labor practices, the report noted, were on the rise.

Union vulnerability was visible early in Ronald Reagan's first term, when the Professional Air Traffic Controllers Organization (PATCO) went out on strike. Charging that the strike violated the law, the president fired the strikers, decertified the union, and ordered the training of new air controllers at a cost of $1.3 billion. The message was clear: Government employees could not challenge the public interest.

Antiunion sentiments reverberated throughout the nongovernment sector as well, as was evident in a 1983 strike by Arizona miners. The management of Phelps Dodge, one of the world's largest copper producers, was beset by falling prices and company losses. It decided to end the cost-of-living allowance that enabled workers, many of them Mexican Americans, to earn $12 an hour. When negotiations failed, workers struck, only to find that the company, working with antiunion experts at the University of Pennsylvania's Wharton School of Business, had hired permanent replacement workers. The company president later acknowledged, "I had decided to break the union."

Work Stoppages, 1960–1993	
Year	Number of Stoppages
1960	222
1970	381
1980	187
1990	44
1993	35

Even strikers who kept their jobs seldom fared well. In Groton, Connecticut, an affiliate of the United Auto Workers (UAW) called a strike of ship workers in 1983. After 15 months, workers accepted a "very bad" contract, leaving 43 percent of the strikers unemployed. As union leaders admitted, "No one will attempt ... to defend the package." But it was all they could get. In 1984, the same union ended a strike at General Motors by trading a pledge that GM would guarantee up to 70 percent of the production workers' lifetime jobs for a smaller wage increase than the union sought and a modification of the cost-of-living allowance that had been a part of UAW contracts since 1948. In 1988, General Electric workers in the Midwest accepted a pay cut to save their jobs and keep GE from relying on foreign labor.

Farmers also had to adjust as the larger work force was reconstituted. Continuing a trend that began in the early twentieth century, the number of farms and farmers declined steadily. When Franklin Roosevelt took office in 1933, some 6.7 million farms covered the American landscape. Fifty years later, there were only 2.4 million. In 1980, farm residents made up 2.7 percent of the total population; by 1989, that figure had fallen to 1.9 percent. As family farms disappeared, farming income became more concentrated in the hands of the largest operators. In 1983, the largest 1 percent of the nation's farmers produced 30 percent of all farm products; the top 12 percent generated 90 percent of all farm income. The top 1 percent of the growers in the United States had average annual incomes of $572,000, but the small and medium-size farmers who were being forced off the land frequently had incomes below the official government poverty line.

The extraordinary productivity of the most successful American farmers derived in part from the use of chemical fertilizers, irrigation, pesticides, and scientific agricultural management. Equally important were the government's price support programs, initiated during the New Deal to shield struggling farmers from unstable prices and continued thereafter.

Yet that very productivity caused unexpected setbacks in the 1980s. In the 1970s, as food shortages developed in many countries, the United States became the "breadbasket of the world."

Farmers increased their output to meet multibillion-bushel grain orders from India, China, Russia, and other countries and profited handsomely from high grain prices caused by global shortages. Often farmers borrowed heavily to increase production, sometimes at interest rates reaching 18 percent. Then, the fourfold increase in oil prices beginning in 1973 drove up the cost of running the modern mechanized farm. When a worldwide economic slump began in 1980, overseas demand for American farm products declined sharply and farm prices fell. Farmers who had borrowed money at high interest rates, when corn sold at $3 to $4 per bushel, now found themselves trying to meet payments on these loans with corn that brought only $2 per bushel.

Thousands of farmers, caught in the cycle of overproduction, heavy indebtedness, and falling prices, watched helplessly as banks and federal agencies foreclosed on their mortgages and drove them out of business. Dale Christensen, an Iowa corn grower, faced foreclosure in 1983 when the Farmers Home Administration called in his over-

due payments on debts totaling $300,000. "I am 58 years old," he said. "My whole life has gone into this farm." He was one of many struggling farmers, who, in spite of government crop support programs that cost more in 1982 than all welfare programs for the poor, could not make ends meet.

Conditions were little changed at the end of the decade. Family farms continued to disappear amid predictions that the trend would continue to the turn of the century. A drought in the Southeast in 1986 led to burned and stunted fields. An even worse drought in 1988 stretched across most of the Midwest. Devastating crops and forcing up prices, it demonstrated how vulnerable farmers remained. Then in 1993, a massive flood wrought even further damage on the region. As the Mississippi and other rivers overflowed their banks, many farmers lost their crops and other belongings. Some lost everything.

The Roller Coaster Economy

The economy shifted several times during the 1980s and 1990s. The Reagan years began with a recession that lasted for several years. An economic boom between 1983 and 1990 gave way to a punishing recession as the new decade began. It appeared that the United States had embarked on another cycle of boom and bust as unsettling as that which had prevailed in the early years of the twentieth century.

The recession of 1980–1982 began during Jimmy Carter's administration when the Federal Reserve Board tried to deal with mounting deficits by increasing the money supply. To counter the resulting inflation and cool down the economy, Carter cut programs but succeeded only in bringing on a recession, with substantial unemployment in the work force. Under Carter, the unemployment rate had hovered between 5.6 and 7.8 percent. During Reagan's first year, the job situation deteriorated further, and by the end of 1982, the unemployment rate had climbed to 10.8 percent, with joblessness among African Americans exceeding 20 percent. Nearly a third of the nation's industrial capacity lay idle, and 12 million Americans were out of work.

Inflation continued to be a problem and accompanied widespread unemployment. The

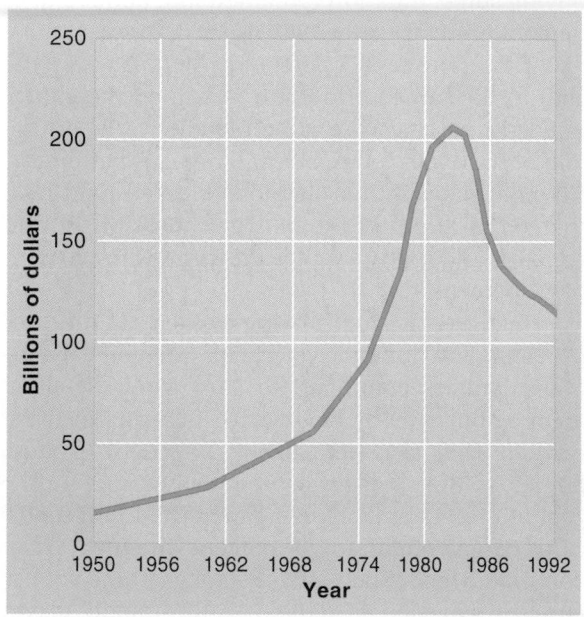

Farm Indebtedness, 1950–1992

Farm indebtedness was a continuing problem in the postwar years. Even modest improvement in the early 1980s did not change the overall picture. Source: U.S. Department of Agriculture.

inflation rate, which reached 12.4 percent a year under Carter in 1980, fell after Reagan assumed office, to 8.9 percent in his first year and to about 5 percent during the remainder of his first term. But even the lower rate eroded the purchasing power of people already in difficulty.

The recession of 1980–1982 afflicted every region of the country. Business failures proliferated in every city and state, as large and small businesses closed their doors and fired their employees. In 1982, business bankruptcies rose 50 percent from the previous year. In one week in June 1982, a total of 548 businesses failed, close to the 1932 weekly record of 612.

No area was immune from the recession. Louisville, Kentucky, had considered itself safe from the threats other areas faced. In 1982, the Brown & Williamson Tobacco Corporation, manufacturer of Kool, Raleigh, and Viceroy cigarettes, closed down its Louisville branch. Then Joseph E. Seagram & Sons shut its bottling plant. General Electric released almost 10,000 of its 23,000 workers, and International Harvester closed a plant employing 6,500 people.

Detroit was one of the hardest-hit areas in the United States. An industrial city revolving around automobile manufacturing, it suffered both from Japanese competition and from the high interest rates that made car sales plummet. The Detroit unemployment rate rose to more than 19 percent. The entire city suffered from the decline. The $357 million Renaissance Center, which included a large hotel surrounded by four modern office buildings, had been expected to revitalize downtown Detroit when it opened in 1977. Instead its owners defaulted on a huge mortgage.

Even the Sun Belt—the vast southern region stretching from coast to coast—showed the effects of the recession. It had enjoyed economic growth fostered by the availability of cheap, nonunion labor, tax advantages that state governments offered corporations willing to locate plants there, and a favorable climate. Now it too began to suffer economic problems, and large areas began to stagnate. Overexpansion in the oil industry led to a collapse in prices that disrupted the economy in Texas, Oklahoma, Louisiana, and other oil-producing regions. Worldwide gluts of some minerals, copper for example, added to unemployment else-

where in the Southwest. Since many parts of the rural South had never prospered, a gloomy economic picture spread from the Gulf states almost to California. In Jefferson County, Mississippi, 67 percent of the population lived below the poverty line. The unemployment rate in California in mid–1982 reached the national average of 9.5 percent, while in Texas it was 7 percent, higher than it had been for ten years.

While not all Americans suffered, most felt the recession in some way. Everyone had a jobless friend or relative. Nobody could avoid the numerous "For Sale" signs on the lawns of houses around the country where residents, unable to meet their mortgage payments, had moved out, their faith in the American dream of home ownership now gone.

Economic conditions improved in late 1983 and early 1984, particularly for Americans in the middle and upper income ranges. The federal tax cut Reagan pushed through encouraged consumer spending, and huge defense expenditures had a stimulating effect. The Republican effort to reduce restrictions and cut waste sparked business confidence. A voluntary Japanese quota on car exports assisted the ailing automobile industry. The stock market climbed as it reflected the optimistic buying spree. Inflation remained low, about 3 to 4 percent annually from 1982 to 1988. Interest rates likewise fell from 16.5 percent in 1982 to 10.5 percent in the same period and remained thereafter under 11 percent. The unemployment rate at the end of the 1980s fell to below 6 percent nationally (though many of the new jobs created paid less than $13,000 per year). Between the start of the recovery and 1988, real GNP grew at an annual rate of 4.2 percent.

But the economic upswing masked a number of problems. Millions of Americans remained poor. Many families continued to earn a middle-class income, but only by having two full-time income earners. They also went deeply into debt. To buy homes, young people accepted vastly higher mortgage interest rates than their parents had. Stiff credit card debts, often at 20 percent interest, were common. Under such circumstances, some young families struggled to remain in the middle class. Blue-collar workers, like Craig Miller, introduced at the start of this chapter, had to accept lower standards of living. Single mothers were hit hardest of all.

The huge and growing budget deficits reflected the fundamental economic instability. Those deficits provoked doubts that resulted in the stock market crash of 1987. Six weeks of falling prices ended with a 22.6 percent drop on Monday, October 19, almost double the plunge of "Black Tuesday," October 29, 1929. The deficits, negative trade balances, and exposures of Wall Street fraud all combined to puncture the bubble. The stock market revived, but the crash foreshadowed further problems.

Those problems surfaced in the early 1990s, as the country experienced another recession. The combination of extravagant military spending, the uncontrolled growth of entitlements—programs such as Medicare and Medicaid which provided benefits for millions of Americans on the basis of need—and the tax cut sent budget deficits skyward. As bond traders in the 1980s speculated recklessly and pocketed huge profits, the basic productive structure of the country continued to decline. The huge increase in the national debt eroded business confidence, and this time the effects were felt not simply in the stock market but in the economy as a whole.

American firms suffered a serious decline as corporate profits fell from $327 billion in 1989 to $315.5 billion in 1991. In an effort to cope with declining profits and decreased consumer demand, companies scaled back dramatically. In late 1991, General Motors announced that it would close 21 plants, lay off 9,000 white-collar employees the next year, and eliminate more than 70,000 jobs in the next several years. Hundreds of other companies did the same thing, trimming corporate fat but also cutting thousands of jobs.

The unemployment rate rose once again. In mid-1991, it reached 7 percent, the highest level in nearly five years. About 8.7 million Americans were without jobs, up 2 million in the year since the recession began. Near the end of 1991, first-time claims for unemployment insurance increased by 79,000, more than double the number forecast. In the New York City metropolitan area, more than 400,000 jobs were lost between 1989 and 1991. In Manhattan alone, job losses eliminated virtually all of the private sector growth of the 1980s. In a chilling indication of the city's economic woes, over a million New Yorkers, one out of every seven,

were on the welfare rolls in July 1992. Most of the welfare newcomers were unskilled workers who were unable to find jobs during the recession. Meanwhile, for those working, real incomes, after adjustment for inflation, began to fall. The upshot, the *New York Times* reported, was that "most Americans are entering the 1990s worse off than they were in the early 1970s."

Around the nation, state governments found it impossible to balance their budgets without resorting to massive spending cuts. Reagan's efforts to move programs from the federal to the state level worked as long as funding lasted, but as national support dropped and state tax revenues declined, states found themselves in a budgetary gridlock. Most had constitutional prohibitions against running deficits, and so they had to slash spending for social services and education, even after yearly budgets had been approved.

After a number of false starts, the economy began to recover in mid-1992. The unemployment rate dropped from 7.4 percent that year to 5.6 percent in mid-1995. The productivity index maintained a steady rise. And a concerted effort brought the federal deficit down from its high of $290 billion in 1992 to under $200 billion in 1995.

Demographic and Regional Change

As the American people dealt with the swings of the economy, demographic patterns changed in significant ways. According to the 1990 census, the population of the United States increased from 228 million to approximately 250 million between 1980 and 1990. The rise of 9.6 percent in the 1980s, down from 11.5 percent in the 1970s, was one of the lowest rates of growth in American history. At the same time, the complexion of the country changed. As a result of increased immigration and minority birthrates significantly higher than the rate for whites, an all-time high of 25 percent of the population in 1992 was black, Hispanic, Asian, or Native American. The population shifted as well. Suburban growth continued, leaving ever larger minority populations in the cities. Meanwhile, in the West a pattern of urban and regional development underway since World

War II continued and provided a model for the rest of the country.

Urban and Suburban Shifts

American cities increasingly filled with members of the nation's minorities. White families continued to leave for the steadily growing suburbs, which by 1990 contained almost half the population, more than ever before. In 15 of the nation's 28 largest cities—New York, Chicago, and Houston among them—minorities made up at least half the population. Minority representation varied by urban region. In Detroit, Washington, New Orleans, and Chicago, blacks were the largest minority; in Phoenix, El Paso, San Antonio, and Los Angeles, Hispanics held that position; in San Francisco, Asians outnumbered other groups.

The cities grew steadily poorer. In Houston, for example, although increasing numbers of blacks, Hispanics, and Asians lived in the suburbs, most of the poorest minority families concentrated in the city itself. As had been the case since World War II, commuters from the suburbs took the better-paying jobs, while people living in the cities held lower-paying positions. Mario Perez, a 27-year-old Hispanic immigrant, noted in 1991 that the increase in the number of Spanish-speaking immigrants in the nine years since he arrived in Houston made it easier to find a job but harder to secure well-paying work. Perez himself worked seven days a week sweeping streets downtown and tending plants for $5.50 an hour.

Western Development

At the same time, the population was moving west. In 1900, the region consisting of the Mountain and Pacific states contained about 5 percent of the nation's population. By 1990 that figure stood at 21 percent. The population of the nation as a whole rose by less than 10 percent in the 1980s, but the population of the West increased by 22 percent.

That population was becoming much more urbanized. In the 50 years following 1940, the six largest metropolitan areas in the West grew by 380 percent; the six largest in the East expanded by only 64 percent. While the West remained the nation's emptiest region, it was nonetheless the most urbanized. By 1990, 80 percent of all Westerners lived in metropolitan areas (compared to 76 percent of the people in the rest of the United States). Writer Wallace Stegner observed, the West "*is* urban; it's an oasis civilization."

With its urban development, the West became a pacesetter for the rest of the country. If the New England village had been a representative symbol of the 18th century, and the midwestern town a similar symbol of the 19th century, now in the late twentieth century the western metropolis was singled out for special symbolic attention. The Stanford Industrial Park, established in California in 1951, focused on research-oriented manufacturing and became a model for other high-tech centers. Western cities were often unbounded, open-ended, sprawling in all directions. They seemed capable of expanding indefinitely. Horizontal, low-slung homes made western neighborhoods look very different from those in the Northeast. Tourism became a dynamic industry, with the West in the forefront. The motel, a western invention, made automobile travel easier. Western cities were among the most popular tourist destinations, catering to visitors from both the Pacific Basin and the rest of the world.

California was the nation's fastest growing state, with the population increasing in the 1980s by nearly 26 percent. Responding to a question about California's impact on the rest of the country, Wallace Stegner said, "We *are* the national culture, at its most energetic end."

Within the state, Los Angeles became the most dynamic example of American vitality and creativity. The motion picture industry exerted a worldwide impact. The city became a capital of consumption. Novelist Thomas Pynchon caught the energy of Los Angeles in his 1990 novel *Vineland*. In the following passage, he described the city as seen at night from the freeway. There were:

> screaming black motorcades that could have carried any of several office seekers, cruisers heading for treed and more gently roaring boulevards, huge double and triple trailer rigs that loved to find Volkswagens laboring up

Population Shifts, 1980–1990

WASHINGTON (17.8%)

MONTANA (1.6%)

NORTH DAKOTA (–2.7%)

MINNESOTA (7.3%)

MAINE (9.2%)

VERMONT (10.0%)

NEW HAMPSHIRE (20.5%)

OREGON (7.9%)

IDAHO (6.7%)

WYOMING (–3.4%)

SOUTH DAKOTA (0.8%)

WISCONSIN (4.0%)

MICHIGAN (0.4%)

NEW YORK (2.5%)

MASSACHUSETTS (4.9%)

RHODE ISLAND (5.9%)

CONNECTICUT (5.8%)

NEW JERSEY (5.0%)

NEVADA (50.1%)

UTAH (17.9%)

COLORADO (14.0%)

NEBRASKA (0.5%)

IOWA (–4.7%)

INDIANA (1.0%)

OHIO (0.5%)

PENNSYLVANIA (0.1%)

DELAWARE (12.1%)

MARYLAND (13.4%)

CALIFORNIA (25.7%)

KANSAS (4.8%)

MISSOURI (4.1%)

ILLINOIS (0%)

KENTUCKY (0.7%)

WEST VIRGINIA (–8.0%)

VIRGINIA (15.7%)

ARIZONA (34.8%)

NEW MEXICO (16.3%)

OKLAHOMA (4.0%)

ARKANSAS (2.8%)

TENNESSEE (6.2%)

NORTH CAROLINA (12.7%)

ALABAMA (3.8%)

GEORGIA (18.6%)

SOUTH CAROLINA (11.7%)

TEXAS (19.4%)

MISSISSIPPI (2.1%)

LOUISIANA (0.3%)

FLORIDA (32.7%)

ALASKA (36.9%)

HAWAII (14.9%)

POPULATION SHIFT

Over 20% increase

10%–20% increase

Under 10% increase

Decrease

This map shows the population shifts between 1980 and 1990. Note the substantial increases in western regions of the country and the much smaller increases along the Atlantic seaboard.

grades and go sashaying around them gracefully and at gnat's-ass tolerances, plus flirters, deserters, wimps and pimps, speeding like bullets, grinning like chimps, above the heads of the TV watchers, lovers under the overpasses, movies at the mall letting out, bright gas-station oases in the pure fluorescent spill, . . . the adobe air, the smell of distant fireworks, the spilled, the broken world.

The New Pilgrims

The second great wave of immigrants in the twentieth century brought about another demographic shift. The number of immigrants has risen dramatically in the past 30 years. In the 1970s, the number averaged 450,000 a year, far higher than in the decade before. In the 1980s, it averaged 730,000. In 1990, as the chart here shows, more people arrived than in any single year in this century. Altogether, a fifth of the pop-

ulation growth in the 1980s stemmed from immigration.

The influx was spurred by the Immigration Act of 1965 (see Chapter 28). Part of Lyndon Johnson's Great Society program, this act authorized the acceptance of immigrants impartially from all parts of the world. The result in the 1980s, as in the 1970s, was far greater numbers of Asians and Latin Americans. In this latter decade, 37 percent came from Asia, and 47 percent came from Mexico, the Caribbean, and Latin America. Always a nation of immigrants, the United States was once again receiving new, and very different, ethnic infusions.

As has long been true, the desire for jobs fostered immigration. But foreign crises also fueled the influx. After 1975, the United States accepted more than a half million Vietnamese refugees, uprooted by the war that had finally come to an end. In 1980, more than 160,000 arrived. That same year, the nation admitted 125,000 Cubans and

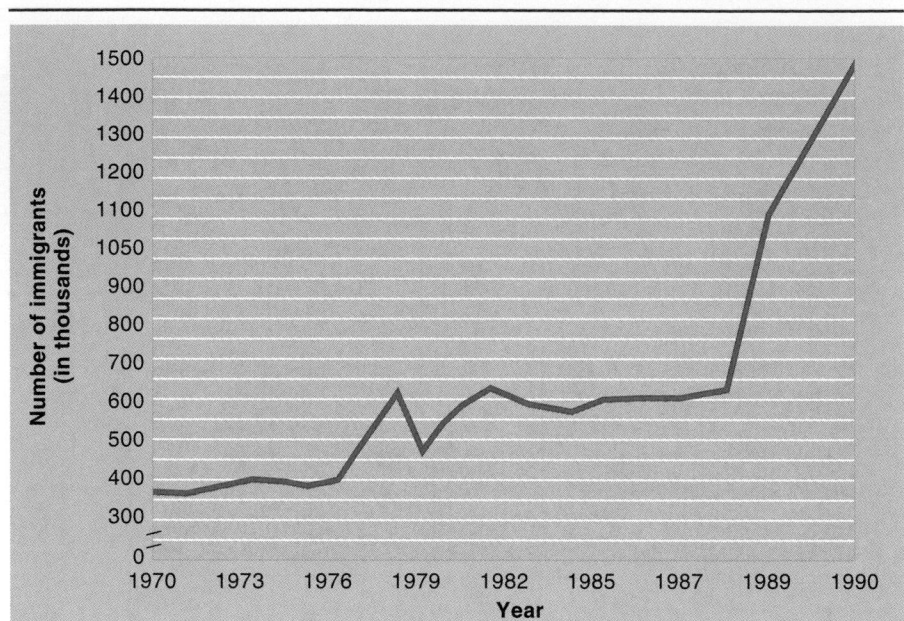

Immigration, 1970–1990

This chart shows the significant rise in immigration after 1970, as the tightly restricted quotas in force from the 1920s to 1965 were liberalized. Note the most rapid rise in the 1980s, as Asians and Latin Americans have come in ever larger numbers. Source: Data from *Statistical Abstract of the United States.*

Haitians to southern Florida, as they fled persecution in their own lands.

Millions more arrived illegally. As the populations of Latin American nations soared and as economic conditions deteriorated, more and more people looked to the United States for relief. In the mid-1970s, Leonard Chapman, commissioner of the Immigration and Naturalization Service, estimated that there might be 12 million foreigners in the nation illegally. While official estimates were lower, Attorney General William French Smith declared in 1983, "Simply put, we've lost control of our own borders."

Several legislative measures sought to rationalize the immigration process. In 1986, Congress passed the Immigration Reform and Control Act, aimed at curbing illegal immigration while offering amnesty to aliens who had lived in the United States since 1982. As the mid-1988 deadline approached, 50,000 per week applied to stay. The Immigration Act of 1990 revised the level and preference system for admission of immigrants to the United States and refined administrative procedures for naturalization. Raising immigration quotas by 40 percent per year, the act cut back on restrictions based on ideology or sexual orienta-

tion that had been used to deny entry in the past. It also set aside a substantial number of visas for large investors and provided for swift deportation of aliens who committed crimes. "This act recognizes the fundamental importance and historic contributions of immigrants to our country," President Bush said in signing the measure.

The more than 10 million immigrants who arrived between 1976 and 1990 belonged to two very different economic classes. In the 1970s and early 1980s, as the chart here shows, about 25 percent were professionals, and more than 40 percent were white-collar employees. Many of these immigrants brought skills, funds, and family support networks that could assist in business ventures in America. At the same time, the United States absorbed a large group of less skilled workers. In this decade and a half, about 46 percent of all employed immigrants were laborers, service sector workers, and semiskilled employees. The flow of this group increased in the 1980s and 1990s.

This new wave of immigration changed the complexion of the United States, just as it had in decades past. Once again, as had been the case before 1924, the nation was a refuge for people from very different parts of the world. The Sun Belt in particular, from Florida to California, felt the impact of the new Asians and Hispanics. In Los Angeles, Samoans, Taiwanese, Koreans, Vietnamese, Filipinos, and Cambodians competed for jobs and apartments with Mexicans, African Americans, and Anglos, just as newcomers from different countries had contended with one another in New York City a century before. Throughout the country, in Miami, in Houston, in Brooklyn, the languages heard in the schools and on the streets changed.

These groups left a new imprint on the United States. As African Americans and Hispanics became major figures in the urban equation, the number of Asians in the country doubled in the 1980s, and they made up nearly half of all immigrants by the end of the decade. Immigrants from India, the Philippines, China, and Korea often brought skills and professional expertise. Southeast Asian refugees were frequently less well off when they arrived. Many of these unskilled immigrants provided the labor for the rapidly expanding West Coast electronics industry. The Asian immigrants, following a pattern established decades before, sought better and better opportunities for their children, and in California they became the largest group of entering students at a number of college campuses.

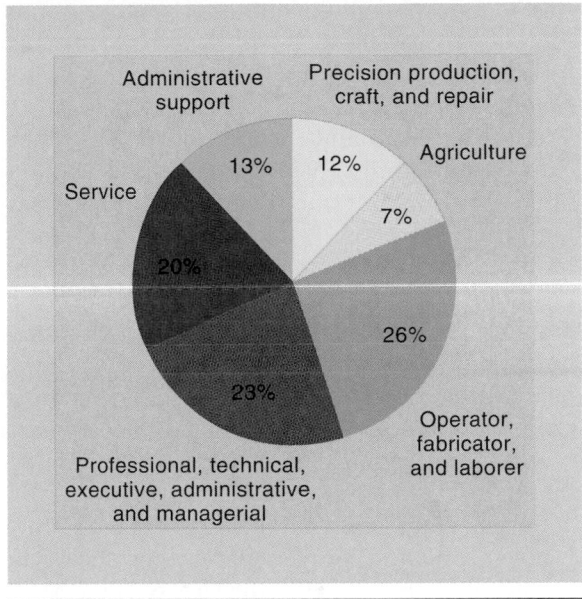

Immigration by Occupational Group, 1976–1990

This graph shows the large fraction of immigrants in the past two decades who have been white-collar and professional workers. Source: *1990 Statistical Yearbook of the Immigration and Naturalization Service.*

Cuban "boat people," classified as refugees from Fidel Castro's Communist regime, were permitted to register for resident status. They were among the many immigrants from Asia and Latin America who were permitted to enter the United States in the 1970s and 1980s. (Reuters/Bettmann)

Sometimes the media highlighted the successes of Asian immigrants, particularly in contrast to the problems encountered by other groups. In 1986, *U.S. News & World Report* noted Asian American advances in a cover story, while *Newsweek* ran a lead article on "Asian Americans: A 'Model Minority,'" and *Fortune* called them "America's Super Minority." Asian Americans were proud of the exposure but pointed out that many members of the working class still struggled for a foothold. In the Chinatowns of San Francisco and Los Angeles, 40 to 50 percent of the workers were employed in the ill-paid service sector or garment industry; in New York's Chinatown the figure was close to 70 percent. Chinese immigrant women, in particular, often had little choice but to work as seamstresses, just as women from other nationalities had earlier in the century.

Each group, each family, had its own story. Nguyen Ninh and Nguyen Viet, two brothers who remained in Vietnam after the victory of the North Vietnamese in 1975, were among the many who finally fled their war-torn country by boat. The boat sank, but they were rescued, only to be shuttled to Kuwait, then Greece, and finally to the United States, where another brother had arrived a few years before. Though they spoke no English,

they immediately began to look for work. One became a carpenter's helper; the other, an attendant at a valet parking firm. With the money they earned, they helped other members of their family emigrate. Slowly they learned English, obtained better jobs, and saved enough money to purchase a home.

Professionals often had a hard time. Frequently, training in their country of birth had little bearing in the United States. One Vietnamese physician who resettled in Oklahoma noted, "When I come here, I am told that I must be a beginner again and serve like an apprentice for two years. I have no choice, so I will do it, but I have been wronged to be asked to do this."

In the 1970s and 1980s, America's efforts to help immigrants coincided with still-intact social assistance programs of the liberal welfare state. Affirmative action programs, in particular, provided aid for both legal and illegal arrivals. Bilingual classrooms became more common, and multiculturalism, stressing the different values that made up a larger American identity, became a dominant theme in many schools.

Yet those efforts brought increasing resistance from Americans already here, particularly as the structure of the economy changed and good jobs

Asian workers often found themselves trapped in low-paying jobs with little hope of advancement. Here women work at sewing machines in a cluttered factory in Queens, New York in 1993, in conditions similar to those earlier in the 20th century. (Donna Binder/ Impact Visuals)

Immigration: Volume and Sources, 1945–1990

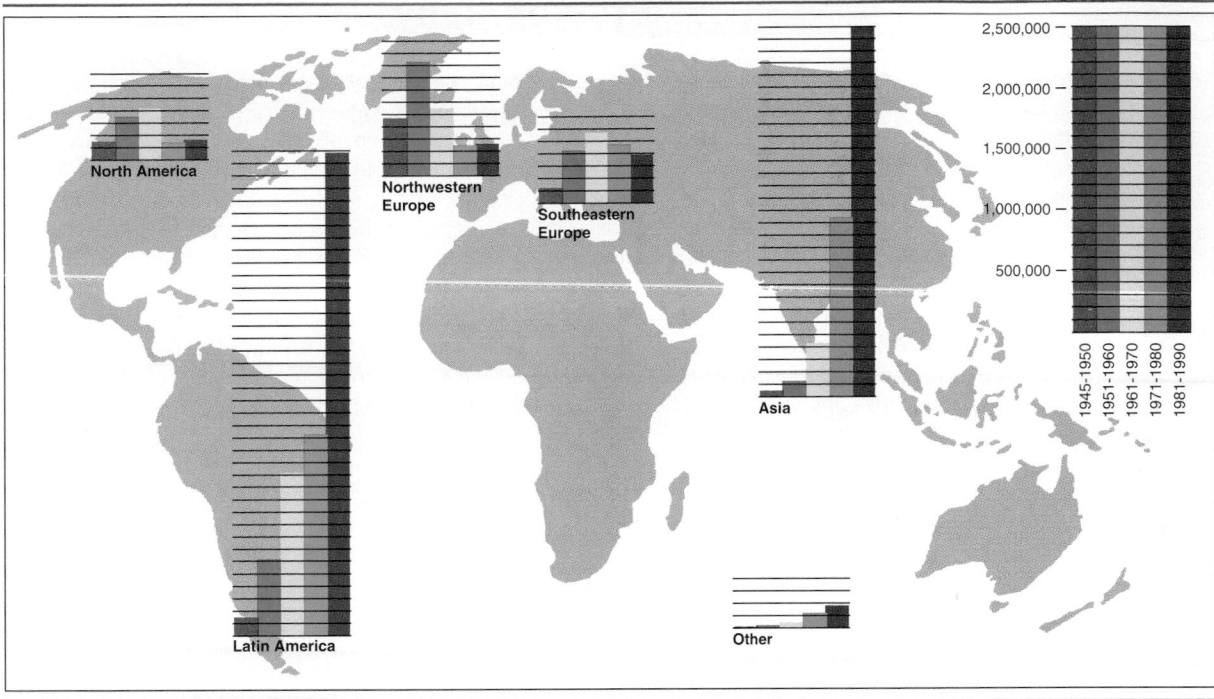

This map shows the shifting patterns of American immigration in the postwar years. In particular, note the large increase in Asian and Latin American immigration in the past several decades.

became more scarce. That opposition, which echoed anti-immigrant feeling of the past, included strenuous efforts to restrict illegal immigration and a move to lower annual quotas for new arrivals. Resistance came to a head in California, in the midterm elections of 1994. Proposition 187 required teachers and clinic doctors to deny assistance to illegal aliens and to report them to police. While its constitutionality is still being weighed by the courts, it provided a model for other states to follow, and caught the attention of national legislators as the Republicans took control.

Growing Up

In the mid-1970s, the birthrate began to rise slowly after a decade and a half of decline. The baby boom, which had created a population explosion in the years after World War II, peaked in 1960 with a rate of 24 births per 1,000 people. In 1981, the rate stood at 16, then rose to nearly 17 in 1990, as demographers viewed the new increase in births as part of a long-term trend.

But children less frequently lived in traditional homes. The Labor Department estimated that by the late 1970s only 7 percent of the nation's families matched the stereotypical pattern of the breadwinner father, the homemaker mother, and two children. Divorce shattered the mold. In 1980, the courts granted nearly 1.2 million divorces, the highest total in the nation's history. In 1990, the figure of 1.175 million was almost as high. For each 1,000 marriages there were 480 divorces, down slightly from 490 in 1980, but significantly higher than 328 per 1,000 in 1970 and 258 per 1,000 in 1960. The social stigma once attached to divorce disappeared; Reagan was the first divorced person to be elected president. "Nonfamily households" became increasingly common. Between 1980 and 1990, such households, which might be led by either a man or a woman, increased from 26 to 29 percent of the total number, while the percentage

Autobiography

As we reach our own time, the historical past most worth recovering, perhaps, is our own. Our own story is as valid a part of the story of American history as the tale of Revolutionary War soldiers, frontier women, reform politicians, and immigrant grandparents. In this increasingly computerized and depersonalized age, the person we need to recover and know is ourself, a self that has been formed, at least in part, by the entire American experience we have been studying.

Autobiography is the form of writing in which people tell their own life's history. Although written autobiographies are at least as old as the literature of the early Christians, for example, *The Confessions of St. Augustine*, the word *autobiography* dates from the late eighteenth century, around the time of the French and American revolutions. That is no accident. These momentous events represented the triumph of individual liberty and the sovereignty of the self. *The Autobiography of Benjamin Franklin*, written between 1771 and his death in 1790, and excerpted here, is a classic celebration of the American success story. Franklin's work set the standard for one autobiographical form, the memoir of one's public achievements and success. The other brief autobiographical memoir, from the reminiscences of Elizabeth Cady Stanton, also reflects the tone and range of this tradition.

AUTOBIOGRAPHICAL MEMOIRS

Benjamin Franklin

DEAR SON,

I have ever had a pleasure in obtaining any little anecdotes of my ancestors. You may remember the enquiries I made among the remains of my relations when you were with me in England and the journey I undertook for that purpose. Imagining it may be equally agreeable to you to know the circumstances of my life—many of which you are yet unacquainted with—and expecting a week's uninterrupted leisure in my present country retirement, I sit down to write them for you. Besides, there are some other inducements that excite me to this undertaking. From the poverty and obscurity in which I was born and in which I passed my earliest years, I have raised myself to a state of affluence and some degree of celebrity in the world. As constant good fortune has accompanied me even to an advanced period of life, my posterity will perhaps be desirous of learning the means, which I employed, and which, thanks to Providence, so well succeeded with me. They may also deem them fit to be imitated, should any of them find themselves in similar circumstances.

Source: *The Autobiography of Benjamin Franklin* (1771).

Elizabeth Cady Stanton

Elizabeth Cady Stanton

It was 'mid such exhilarating scenes that Miss Anthony and I wrote addresses for temperance, anti-slavery, educational and woman's rights conventions. Here we forged resolutions, protests, appeals, petitions, agricultural reports, and constitutional arguments; for we made it a matter of conscience to accept every invitation to speak on every question, in order to maintain woman's right to do so. To this end we took turns on the domestic watchtowers, directing amusements, settling disputes, protecting the weak against the strong, and trying to secure equal rights to all in the home as well as the nation.

It is often said, by those who know Miss Anthony best, that she has been my good angel, always pushing and goading me to work, and that but for her pertinacity I should never have accomplished the little I have. On the other hand it has been said that I forged the thunderbolts and she fired them. Perhaps all this is, in a measure, true. With the cares of a large family I might, in time, like too many women, have become wholly absorbed in a narrow family selfishness, had not my friend been continually exploring new fields for missionary labors. Her description of a body of men on any platform, complacently deciding questions in which women had an equal interest, without an equal voice, readily aroused me to a determination to throw a firebrand into the midst of their assembly.

Source: Elizabeth Cady Stanton, *Eighty Years and More: Reminiscences, 1815–1897* (1898).

CONFESSIONAL AUTOBIOGRAPHIES

Black Elk

And so it was all over.

I did not know then how much was ended. When I look back now from this high hill of my old age, I can still see the butchered women and children lying heaped and scattered all along the crooked gulch as plain as when I saw them with eyes still young. And I can see that something else died there in the bloody mud, and was buried in the blizzard. A people's dream died there. It was a beautiful dream.

And I, to whom so great a vision was given in my youth,—you see me now a pitiful old man who has done nothing, for the nation's hoop is broken and scattered. There is no center any longer, and the sacred tree is dead.

Source: *Black Elk Speaks*, as told through John G. Neihardt (1932).

Malcolm X

I want to say before I go on that I have never previously told anyone my sordid past in detail. I haven't done it now to sound as though I might be proud of how bad, how evil, I was.

But people are always speculating—why am I as I am? To understand that of any person, his whole life, from birth, must be reviewed. All of our experiences fuse into our personality. Everything that ever happened to us is an ingredient.

Today, when everything that I do has an urgency, I would not spend one hour in the preparation of a book which has the ambition to perhaps titillate some readers. But I am spending many hours because the full story is the best many hours because the full story is the best way that I know to have it seen, and understood, that I had sunk to the very bottom of the American white man's society when—soon now, in prison—I found Allah and the religion of Islam and it completely transformed my life.

Source: *The Autobiography of Malcolm X*, with the assistance of Alex Haley (1964).

Not all autobiographies are written late in life to celebrate one's accomplishments. The confessional autobiography, unlike most memoirs, explores the author's interior life, acknowledging flaws and failures as well as successes; it may be written at any age. The purpose of this type of autobiography is not just to reconstruct one's past to preserve it for posterity, but to find from one's past an identity in order to know better how to live one's future. The story of religious confessions and conversions is an obvious example. This form also includes secular self-examinations such as those by Maxine Hong Kingston in *The Woman Warrior* (1976), Piri Thomas in *Down These Mean Streets* (1967), or Maya Angelou in a series of five autobiographical sketches beginning with *I Know Why the Caged Bird Sings* (1969). The other two excerpts presented here are among the finest examples of confessional autobiography and suggest its variety.

These examples hardly convey the full range of the autobiographical form or how available to all people is the opportunity to tell the story of one's life. In 1909, William Dean Howells called autobiography the "most democratic province in the republic of letters." A recent critic agrees, pointing out:

To this genre have been drawn public and private figures: poets, philosophers, prizefighters; actresses, artists, political activists; statesmen and penitentiary prisoners; financiers and football players; Quakers and Black Muslims; immigrants and Indians. The range of personality, experience, and profession reflected in the forms of American autobiography is as varied as American life itself.

Your story, too, is a legitimate part of American history. But writing an autobiography, while open to all, is deceptively difficult. Like historians, autobiographers face problems of sources, selection, interpretation, and style. As in the writing of any history, the account of one's past must be objective, not only in the verifiable accuracy of details but also in the honest selection of representative events to be described. Moreover, as in fiction as well as history, the autobiographer must provide a structured form, an organizing principle, literary merit, and thematic coherence to the story. Many other challenges face the would-be autobiographer, such as finding a balance between one's public life and the private self and handling problems of memory, ego (should one, for example, use the first or third person?), and death.

To get an idea of the difficulties of writing an autobiography, try writing your own. Limit yourself to 1,000 words. Good luck.

The growing disparity in wealth, and the neglect of the urban poor and resurgent racism noted earlier in this chapter, became horrifyingly visible in the terrible rioting that swept through Los Angeles in the spring of 1992. The year before, Americans had watched a videotaped savage beating of black motorist Rodney King by white police officers, the most dramatic of a long string of incidents involving police brutality. When a California jury, which contained no African Americans, acquitted the policemen, many people throughout the country became convinced that people of color could not obtain equal justice under the law. In Los Angeles thousands reacted with uncontrolled fury. As widespread arson and looting swept through many neighborhoods, the police proved unable to control the mayhem. Much of it was led by gang members but involved as well hundreds of ordinary citizens who acted irresponsibly yet with a sense that the social contract had been broken by politicians and the rich who were unresponsive to their plight. Several days later, after the riot had run its course, 51 people (most of them black and Hispanic) lay dead, 2,000 were injured, and $1 billion in damage had been done to the city. It was the worst riot in decades, more deadly even than the Watts riot 27 years before. Political candidates from both parties scurried around trying to define an urban policy, as the upheaval served notice that racial injustice, social inequality, and poverty could no longer be ignored.

The United States in a Changed World

In the 1980s and 1990s, the United States emerged triumphant in the Cold War that had dominated world politics since the end of World War II. In one of the most momentous developments in modern world history, communism collapsed in Eastern Europe and in the Soviet Union, and the various republics in the Soviet orbit embraced both capitalism and democracy. Other regions—the Middle East and Africa—experienced equally breathtaking change.

In the midst of this international tumult, the United States had to examine its own assump-

tions about its role in the world. What kind of leadership would the United States exert as the one remaining superpower on the globe? How involved would it become in peacekeeping missions in troubled lands? What kind of assistance would it extend to developing nations once the competition with the Soviet Union that had fueled foreign aid was over? These questions, asked in different forms over the course of past centuries, helped shape foreign policy in transitional times.

Triumph in the Cold War

The Cold War was very much alive when Reagan assumed power in 1981. In foreign affairs, the new president asserted U.S. interests far more aggressively than had President Carter. Like most of his contemporaries, Reagan believed in large defense budgets and a militant approach toward the Soviet Union. He wanted to cripple the Russians militarily and economically by forcing them to spend more than they could afford.

Viewing the Soviet Union as an "evil empire" in his first term, Reagan promoted an increased atomic arsenal by arguing that a nuclear war could be fought and won. The administration abandoned Senate ratification of SALT II, the arms reduction plan negotiated under Carter, although it observed the pact's restrictions. Then Reagan proposed the enormously expensive and bitterly criticized Strategic Defense Initiative, popularly known as "Star Wars" after a 1977 movie, to intercept Soviet missiles by means of a shield in outer space.

In his second term, however, Reagan softened his belligerent stance. Mikhail Gorbachev, the new Soviet leader, watching his own economy collapse under the pressure of the superheated arms race, realized the need for greater accommodation with the West. He understood that the only way the Soviet Union could survive was through arms negotiations with the United States that would help reduce his overextended budget. He therefore proposed a policy of *perestroika* (restructuring the economy) and *glasnost* (political openness to encourage personal initiative). His overtures opened the way to better relations with the United States.

Mikhail Gorbachev was the Soviet leader who initiated the process that helped ease tensions with the United States and ultimately ended the Cold War. Gorbachev's policies provided for major readjustments in Soviet society, but those eventually tore the Soviet Union apart. (AP/Wide World Photos)

Concerned with his own place in history, Reagan met with Gorbachev, and the two heads of state developed a close working relationship. Summit meetings led to an Intermediate-Range Nuclear Forces Treaty in 1987 that provided for withdrawal and destruction of 2,500 Soviet and American nuclear missiles in Europe.

George Bush maintained Reagan's comfortable relationship with Gorbachev. At several summit meetings in 1989 and 1990, the two leaders signed agreements reducing the number of long-range nuclear weapons to a maximum of 1,600 rockets and 6,000 warheads, ending manufacture of chemical weapons, and easing trade restrictions between the two nations. The Strategic Arms Reduction Treaty (START) signed in 1991 dramatically decreased the stockpiles of long-range weapons.

Hailed around the world for his part in easing tensions, Gorbachev encountered trouble at

home. In mid-1991, he faced a conservative coup, led by those who opposed *glasnost* and *perestroika* and wanted to slow the process of change. He survived this right-wing challenge, but he could not resist those who wanted to go even further to establish democracy and capitalism. The forces he had unleashed within the Soviet Union finally tore the USSR apart.

Boris Yeltsin, president of Russia, the strongest and most populous of the Soviet republics, emerged as the dominant leader, but even he could not contain the forces of disintegration. Independence movements in the tiny Baltic republics began the dismantling of the Soviet Union, and other republics likewise went their own way. The once-powerful superpower was now a collection of separate states. Although the republics coalesced loosely in a Commonwealth of Independent States, led by Russia, they retained their autonomy—and independent leadership—in domestic and foreign affairs.

Early in 1992, Bush and Yeltsin proclaimed a new era of "friendship and partnership" and formally declared an end to the Cold War. After half a

Boris Yeltsin, president of Russia, the largest of the republics in what had been the Soviet Union, became the most influential leader after Gorbachev's fall. But Yeltsin's efforts at economic reform met with serious opposition and left him vulnerable as well. (Corbis-Bettmann)

century of conflict, the United States had won. Yeltsin abandoned the notion of nuclear parity—maintaining an arsenal similar to that of the United States—and agreed to cut back conventional Russian forces to complement nuclear cuts. The United States then extended aid to the former Soviet republics which needed help in reorganizing their economies as free enterprise systems. Relations became strained in 1994, when Russia sought to prevent further fragmentation and moved aggressively to squelch a rebellion in the republic of Chechnya. The brutal nature of Yeltsin's response led allies to question both his democratic values and his ability to govern, yet they continued to support him for lack of a better alternative.

Meanwhile, Communist regimes throughout Europe collapsed. In a series of remarkable developments that occurred at the same time and intertwined with the turbulence in the Soviet Union, many of the Communist satellites broke loose, rejected communism, and proclaimed a new commitment to democracy.

The most dramatic chapter in this story unfolded in Germany in November 1989. Responding to Gorbachev's softening stance toward the West, East Germany's Communist party boss announced unexpectedly that citizens of his country would be free to leave East Germany. Within hours, thousands of people gathered on both sides of the 28-mile Berlin Wall—the symbol of the Cold War that divided Berlin into east and west sectors. As the border guards stepped aside, East Germans flooded into West Berlin amidst dancing, shouting, and fireworks. All through the night noisy celebrators reveled in what one observer called the "greatest street party in the history of the world."

Within days, sledgehammer-wielding Germans pulverized the Berlin Wall, and soon the Communist government itself came tumbling down. By October 1990, less than a year after the free movement of East Germans across their borders began, the two Germanys were reunited.

The fall of the Berlin Wall reverberated all over Eastern Europe. Everywhere it brought in its wake the pell-mell overthrow of Communist regimes. In Poland, the 10-year-old Solidarity movement led by Lech Walesa triumphed in its long struggle against Soviet domination and found itself in power, with Walesa as president. Governing, however, sometimes proved more difficult than leading the revolt. The nation faced enormous economic problems, and Americans had to decide just how much help they could afford to give.

In Czechoslovakia, two decades after Soviet tanks had rolled into the streets of Prague to suppress a policy of liberalization, the forces of freedom were victorious. A month after the Berlin Wall dismantlement, playwright Vaclav Havel was elected president of Czechoslovakia. Like Walesa, he sought and received aid from the United States. But not even economic assistance could keep the nation intact, as turbulence led to the creation of separate and independent Czech and Slovak republics. The same forces that culminated in the independence of

The destruction of the Berlin Wall in November 1989 was a symbolic blow to the entire Cold War structure that had grown up in Europe in the postwar years. The fall of the Wall touched off joyous celebrations. (R. Bossu/Sygma)

Czechoslovakia brought new regimes in Bulgaria, Hungary, Romania, and Albania.

Former Yugoslavia proved to be the extreme case of resurgent ethnic hostility in the face of collapsing central authority. The Balkan region had long been a powder keg—a spark there had set off World War I—and only dictatorship had held the diverse republics together. When two of these states declared their independence in 1991, the fragile nation fell apart. The decision of the Muslim and Croatian majority in Bosnia to secede from Serbian-dominated Yugoslavia led Bosnian Serbs, backed by the Serbian republic, to embark upon a brutal siege of the city of Sarajevo and an even more ruthless "ethnic cleansing" campaign to liquidate opponents in newly independent Bosnia and Herzegovina. In the mid-1990s, ethnic and religious violence worsened. Brutal killing escalated out of control; rape became commonplace; and civilians suffered most from the uncurbed violence. As the region became increasingly volatile, the United States remained out of the conflict, while the United Nations proved unable to bring about peace. In mid-1995, a NATO bombing campaign forced the Bosnian Serbs into negotiations, and a peace conference held in Dayton, Ohio, led to the commitment of American troops, along with soldiers from other countries, but even that effort failed to end hostilities.

Steps Toward Peace in the Middle East

Americans were equally involved with events in the Middle East. Here too they were concerned with preserving stability as the Cold War drew to an end. During President Bush's first term, the United States went to war in the region. When Saddam Hussein, ruler of Iraq, invaded neighboring Kuwait in August 1990 and annexed the territory, the United States reacted strongly. Saddam seemed intent on unifying Arab nations, thereby threatening Israel and dominating the region's production of oil on which the United States relied.

Working through the United Nations, as Truman had done in Korea, the United States persuaded the Security Council to vote unanimously

to condemn the attack and endorse an embargo on trade with Iraq. In mid-January 1991, a 28-nation coalition struck at Iraq in Operation Desert Storm with a multinational army of nearly half a million troops.

The coalition forces, with their sophisticated missiles, airplanes, and tanks, overwhelmed the Iraqis. Americans were initially enthusiastic about their victory. Then the mood of euphoria in the United States soured as Saddam used his remaining military power against minorities in Iraq. Bush's unwillingness to become bogged down in an Iraqi civil war and his eagerness to return U.S. troops home left the conflict unfinished. A year after his defeat, Saddam was as strong as he had been before.

Meanwhile, the United States was involved in a larger, and ultimately more important, effort to bring peace to the Middle East. In the early 1990s, Secretary of State James Baker finally secured agreement from the major parties in the region to speak to one another face-to-face. Though intense squabbling continued, the discussions themselves

A multinational coalition freed Kuwait after Iraqi leader Saddam Hussein—whose image appears on the signs at the anti-American demonstration in Baghdad—annexed the oil-rich land in 1990. The Persian Gulf War gave George Bush a quick victory, but the long-range results of U.S. involvement were more questionable. (Chris Morris/Black Star)

were a step forward. A victory in the Israeli parliamentary elections in mid-1992 for Yitzhak Rabin, a soldier who recognized the need for peace and was ready to compromise, offered further hope for the talks.

During his first year in office, Clinton played the part of peacemaker, just as Jimmy Carter had done 15 years before. On September 13, 1993, in a dramatic ceremony on the White House lawn, Palestine Liberation Organization leader Yasir Arafat and Israeli prime minister Rabin took the first public step toward ending years of conflict as they shook hands and signed a peace agreement that led to Palestinian self-rule in the Gaza strip. In 1995, Israel and the PLO signed a further agreement and the Israelis handed over control of the West Bank of the Jordan River to the Palestinians. A treaty between Jordan and Israel brought peace on still another border. While extremists tried to destroy the peace process by continued violence, and assassinated Rabin in a move deplored worldwide, the effort to heal old animosities continued.

Turbulence in Latin America

The United States intervened frequently in Latin American affairs, just as it had in the past, in an effort to stabilize this volatile region. Viewing Central America as a Cold War battlefield early in his presidency, Reagan openly opposed left-wing guerrillas in El Salvador who fought to overthrow a repressive right-wing regime. He was fearful that still another nation might follow the Marxist examples of Cuba and Nicaragua. The United States increased its assistance to the antirevolutionary Salvadoran government, heedless of a similar course followed years before in Vietnam. Efforts to destroy the radical forces failed, despite the expenditure of about $1 million a day. Then in

President Bill Clinton helped orchestrate this famous handshake between Israeli Prime Minister Yitzhak Rabin and Palestine Liberation Organization Chairman Yasir Arafat in 1993. Though the two men had long been adversaries, they now began to work together to settle the bitter conflicts in the Middle East. (AP/Wide World Photos)

1989, a far-right faction won Salvadoran elections and polarized the country. As fighting continued, U.S. officials despaired of finding a solution.

Nicaragua became an even bloodier battleground in the effort to promote stability. In 1979, revolutionaries calling themselves Sandinistas (after César Sandino, who fought in the 1920s against U.S. occupation troops) overthrew the repressive Somoza family, which had ruled for three decades. President Carter initially extended aid to the Sandinistas and recognized the new regime, then cut off support to show his disapproval of their curbs on civil liberties and their alleged efforts to assist rebels in El Salvador. The Republicans adopted a far stronger position. Their 1980 platform pledged to replace the Sandinistas with a "free and independent" government. Once in office, Reagan circumvented congressional opposition to his efforts to defeat the revolutionary reformers and signed a National Security directive in November 1981 authorizing the CIA to arm and train counterrevolutionaries known as *contras*.

The *contras* began to attack from bases outside the country and Nicaragua became enmeshed in a bitter civil war. When the war went badly for the *contras*, the CIA assumed the military initiative and mined Nicaraguan harbors, violating international law. Upon discovering these secret missions, Congress cut off military aid to the *contras*. Peaceful elections in early 1990 finally drove the Sandinistas out and brought the fighting to an end. Though the economy remained in desperate straits, the new regime seemed to offer the best hope of healing the wounds of the bloody conflict.

Middle Eastern and Central American concerns became entangled in the Iran-*contra* affair. In 1987, Congress learned that the National Security Council had launched an effort to free American hostages in the Middle East by selling arms to Iran and then using the funds to aid the *contras*, in direct violation of both the law and congressional will. The trial of Oliver North, the National Security Council official responsible for the policy, focused on his distortions and falsifications before congressional committees and on his destruction of official documents that could have substantiated charges of wrongdoing by top officials. Convicted in 1989, North received a light sentence requiring no time in prison from a judge who recognized that North was not acting entirely on his own.

Reagan was more successful in maintaining stability on the tiny Caribbean island of Grenada. The president ordered marines there in October 1983, after a military coup installed a government sympathetic to Fidel Castro's Cuba. Concerned about the construction of a large airfield on the island, 2,000 marines invaded the island, rescued a number of American medical students, and claimed triumph. Though the United Nations condemned the incursion, Americans still cheered what the administration called its "rescue mission."

George Bush took credit for a similar incursion in Panama, ostensibly to protect American lives. Invoking memories of past imperialism, the United States invaded Panama, it said, to protect the Panama Canal, defend American citizens following a number of attacks, and stop drug traffic. The campaign resulted in the capture of military

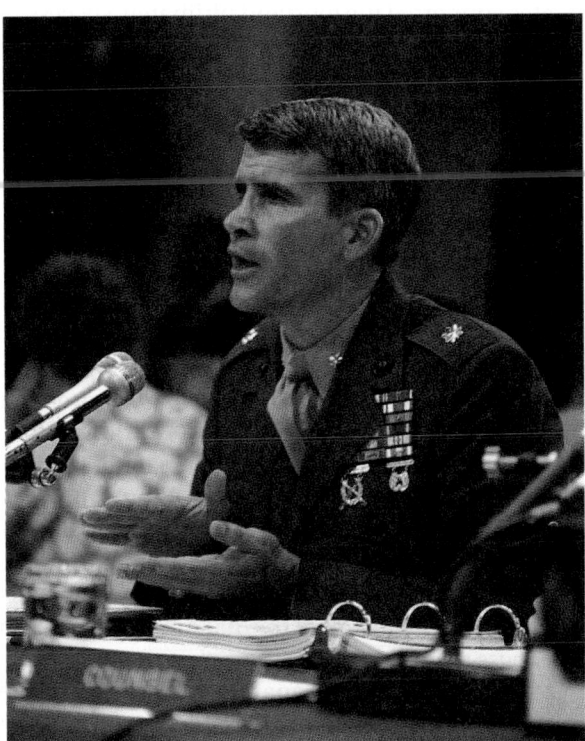

Oliver North, shown here testifying before a congressional committee, flouted the law in the Iran-contra affair. Convicted for his cavalier distortions and fabrications, North was not the only one involved in the illegal government program. (Fred Ward/Black Star)

For abolishing the free system of English laws in a neighboring province, establishing therein an arbitrary government, and enlarging its boundaries, so as to render it at once an example and fit instrument for introducing the same absolute rule into these colonies;

For taking away our charters abolishing our most valuable laws, and altering fundamentally the forms of our governments;

For suspending our own legislatures, and declaring themselves invested with power to legislate for us in all cases whatsoever.

He has abdicated government here, by declaring us out of his protection and waging war against us.

He has plundered our seas, ravaged our coasts, burned our towns, and destroyed the lives of our people.

He is at this time transporting large armies of foreign mercenaries to complete the works of death, desolation, and tyranny already begun with circumstances of cruelty and perfidy scarcely paralleled in the most barbarous ages, and totally unworthy the head of a civilized nation.

He has constrained our fellow-citizens, taken captive on the high seas, to bear arms against their country, to become the executioners of their friends and brethren, or to fall themselves by their hands.

He has excited domestic insurrection among us, and has endeavored to bring on the inhabitants of our frontiers the merciless Indian savages, whose known rule of warfare is an undistinguished destruction of all ages, sexes, and conditions.

In every stage of these oppressions we have petitioned for redress in the most humble terms; our repeated petitions have been answered only by repeated injury. A prince, whose character is thus marked by every act which may define a tyrant, is unfit to be the ruler of a free people.

Nor have we been wanting in our attentions to our British brethren. We have warned them, from time to time, of attempts by their legislature to extend an unwarrantable jurisdiction over us. We have reminded them of the circumstances of our emigration and settlement here. We have appealed to their native justice and magnanimity; and we have conjured them, by the ties of our common kindred, to disavow these usurpations, which would inevitably interrupt our connections and correspondence. They, too, have been deaf to the voice of justice and of consanguinity. We must, therefore, acquiesce in the necessity which denounces our separation, and hold them, as we hold the rest of mankind, enemies in war, in peace friends.

We, therefore, the representatives of the United States of America, in General Congress assembled, appealing to the Supreme Judge of the world for the rectitude of our intentions, do, in the name and by the authority of the good people of these colonies, solemnly publish and declare, that these United Colonies are, and of right, ought to be, FREE AND INDEPENDENT STATES; that they are absolved from all allegiance to the British crown, and that all political connection between them and the state of Great Britain is, and ought to be, totally dissolved; and that, as free and independent states, they have full power to levy war, conclude peace, contract alliances, establish commerce, and do all other acts and things which independent states may of right do. And for the support of this declaration, with a firm reliance on the protection of Devine Providence, we mutually pledge to each other our lives, our fortunes, and our sacred honor.

JOHN HANCOCK

BUTTON GWENNETT
LYMAN HALL
GEO. WALTON
WM. HOOPER
JOSEPH HEWES
JOHN PENN
EDWARD RUTLEDGE
THOS. HEYWARD, JUNR.
THOMAS LYNCH, JUNR.
ARTHUR MIDDLETON
SAMUEL CHASE
WM. PACA
THOS. STONE
CHARLES CARROLL OF CARROLLTON
GEORGE WYTHE
RICHARD HENRY LEE
TH. JEFFERSON
BENJA. HARRISON

THS. NELSON, JR.
FRANCIS LIGHTFOOT LEE
CARTER BRAXTON
ROBT. MORRIS
BENJAMIN RUSH
BENJA. FRANKLIN
JOHN MORTON
GEO. CLYMER
JAS. SMITH
GEO. TAYLOR
JAMES WILSON
GEO. ROSS
CAESAR RODNEY
GEO. READ
THO. MiKEAN
WM. FLOYD
PHIL. LIVINGSTON
FRANS. LEWIS
LEWIS MORRIS

RICHD. STOCKTON
JNO. WITHERSPOON
FRAS. HOPKINSON
JOHN HART
ABRA. CLARK
JOSIAH BARTLETT
WM. WHIPPLE
SAML. ADAMS
JOHN ADAMS
ROBT. TREAT PAINE
ELBRIDGE GERRY
STEP. HOPKINS
WILLIAM ELLERY
ROGER SHERMAN
SAMiEL. HUNTINGTON
WM. WILLIAMS
OLIVER WOLCOTT
MATHEW THORNTON

The Constitution of the United States of America

PREAMBLE

We the People of the United States, in Order to form a more perfect Union, establish Justice, insure domestic Tranquility, provide for the common defence, promote the general Welfare, and secure the Blessings of Liberty to ourselves and our Posterity, do ordain and establish this Constitution for the United States of America.

ARTICLE I.

Section 1   All legislative Powers herein granted shall be vested in a Congress of the United States, which shall consist of a Senate and House of Representatives.

Section 2   The House of Representatives shall be composed of Members chosen every second Year by the People of the several States, and the Electors in each State shall have the Qualifications requisite for Electors of the most numerous Branch of the State Legislature.

No Person shall be a Representative who shall not have attained to the Age of twenty five Years, and been seven Years a Citizen of the United States, and who shall not, when elected, be an Inhabitant of that State in which he shall be chosen.

Representatives and direct Taxes shall be apportioned among the several States which may be included within this Union, according to their respective Numbers, *which shall be determined by adding to the whole Number of free Persons, including those bound to Service for a Term of Years, and excluding Indians not taxed, three fifths of all other Persons.* * The actual Enumeration shall be made within three Years after the first Meeting of the Congress of the United States, and within every subsequent Term of ten Years, in such Manner as they shall by Law direct. The Number of Representatives shall not exceed one for every thirty Thousand, but each State shall have at Least one Representative; *and until such enumeration shall be made, the State of New Hampshire shall be entitled to chuse three, Massachusetts eight, Rhode-Island and Providence Plantations one, Connecticut five, New-York six, New Jersey four, Pennsylvania eight, Delaware one, Maryland six, Virginia ten, North Carolina five, South Carolina five, and Georgia three.*

When vacancies happen in the Representation from any State, the Executive Authority thereof shall issue Writs of Election to fill such Vacancies.

The House of Representatives shall chuse their Speaker and other Officers; and shall have the sole Power of Impeachment.

Section 3   The Senate of the United States shall be composed of two Senators from each State, chosen by the Legislature thereof, for six Years; and each Senator shall have one Vote.

Immediately after they shall be assembled in Consequence of the first Election, they shall be divided as equally as may be into three Classes. The Seats of the Senators of the first Class shall be vacated at the Expiration of the second Year, of the second Class at the Expiration of the fourth Year, and of the third Class at the Expiration of the sixth Year, so that one third may be chosen every second Year; and if Vacancies happen by Resignation, or otherwise, during the Recess of the Legislature of any State, the Executive thereof may make temporary Appointments until the next Meeting of the Legislature, which shall then fill such Vacancies.

No Person shall be a Senator who shall not have attained to the Age of thirty Years, and been nine Years a Citizen of the United States, and who shall not, when elected, be an Inhabitant of that State for which he shall be chosen.

The Vice President of the United States shall be President of the Senate, but shall have no Vote, unless they be equally divided.

The Senate shall choose their other Officers, and also a President *pro tempore,* in the Absence of the Vice President, or when he shall exercise the Office of President of the United States.

The Senate shall have the sole Power to try all Impeachments. When sitting for that Purpose, they shall be on Oath or Affirmation. When the President of the United States is tried the Chief Justice shall preside: And no Person shall be convicted without the Concurrence of two thirds of the Members present.

Judgment in Cases of Impeachment shall not extend further than to removal from Office, and disqualification to hold and enjoy any Office of honor, Trust or Profit under the United States: but the Party convicted shall nevertheless be liable and subject to Indictment, Trial, Judgment and Punishment, according to Law.

Section 4   The Times, Places and Manner of holding Elections for Senators and Representatives, shall be prescribed in each State by the Legislature thereof; but the Congress may at any time by Law make or alter such Regulations, except as to the Places of chusing Senators.

The Congress shall assemble at least once in every Year, and such Meeting *shall be on the first Monday in December, unless they shall by Law appoint a different Day.* *

Section 5   Each House shall be the Judge of the Elections, Returns and Qualifications of its own Members, and a Majority of each shall constitute a Quorum to do Business; but a smaller Number may adjourn from day to day, and may be authorized to compel the Attendance of absent Members, in such Manner, and under such Penalties as each House may provide.

Each House may determine the Rules of its Proceedings, punish its Members for disorderly Behaviour, and, with the Concurrence of two thirds, expel a Member.

Each House shall keep a Journal of its Proceedings, and from time to time publish the same, excepting such Parts as may in their Judgment require Secrecy; and the Yeas and Nays of the Members of either House on any question shall, at the Desire of one fifth of those Present, be entered on the Journal.

Neither House, during the Session of Congress, shall, without the Consent of the other, adjourn for more than three days, nor to any other Place than that in which the two Houses shall be sitting.

Section 6   The Senators and Representatives shall receive a Compensation for their Services, to be ascertained by Law, and paid out of the Treasury of the United States. They shall in all Cases, except Treason, Felony and Breach of the Peace, be privileged from Arrest during their Attendance at the Session of their respective Houses, and in going to and returning from the same; and for any Speech or Debate in either House, they shall not be questioned in any other Place.

No Senator or Representative shall, during the Time for which he was elected, be appointed to any civil Office under the Authority of the United States, which shall have been created, or the Emoluments whereof shall have been encreased during such time; and no Person holding any Office under the United States, shall be a Member of either House during his Continuance in Office.

Section 7   All Bills for raising Revenue shall originate in the House of Representatives; but the Senate may propose or concur with Amendments as on other Bills.

Every Bill which shall have passed the House of Representatives and the Senate, shall, before it become a Law, be presented to the President of the United States; If he approve he shall sign it, but if not he shall return it, with his Objections to that House in which it shall have originated, who shall enter the Objections at large on their Journal, and proceed to reconsider it. If after such Reconsideration two thirds of that House shall agree to pass the Bill, it shall be sent, together with the Objections, to the other House, by which it shall likewise be reconsidered, and if approved by two thirds of that House, it shall become a Law. But in all such Cases the Votes of both Houses shall be determined by yeas and Nays, and the Names of the Persons voting for and against the Bill shall be entered on the Journal of each House respectively. If any Bill shall not be returned by the President within ten Days (Sundays excepted) after it shall have been presented to him, the Same shall be a Law, in like Manner as if he had signed it, unless the Congress by their Adjournment prevent its Return, in which Case it shall not be a Law.

Every Order, Resolution, or Vote to which the Concurrence of the Senate and House of Representatives may be necessary (except on a question of Adjournment) shall be presented to the President of the United States; and before the Same shall take Effect, shall be approved by him, or being disapproved by him, shall be repassed by two thirds of the Senate and House of Representatives, according to the Rules and Limitations prescribed in the Case of a Bill.

Section 8   The Congress shall have Power:

To lay and collect Taxes, Duties, Imposts and Excises, to pay the Debts and provide for the common Defence and general Welfare of the United States; but all Duties, Imposts and Excises shall be uniform throughout the United States;

To borrow Money on the credit of the United States;

To regulate Commerce with foreign Nations, and among the several States, and with the Indian Tribes;

To establish an uniform Rule of Naturalization, and uniform Laws on the subject of Bankruptcies throughout the United States;

To coin Money, regulate the Value thereof, and of foreign Coin, and fix the Standard of Weights and Measures;

To provide for the Punishment of counterfeiting the Securities and current Coin of the United States;

To establish Post Offices and post Roads;

To promote the Progress of Science and useful Arts, by securing for limited Times to Authors and Inventors the exclusive Right to their respective Writings and Discoveries;

To constitute Tribunals inferior to the supreme Court;

To define and punish Piracies and Felonies committed on the high Seas, and Offences against the Law of Nations;

To declare War, grant Letters of Marque and Reprisal, and make Rules concerning Captures on Land and Water;

To raise and support Armies, but no Appropriation of Money to that Use shall be for a longer Term than two Years;

To provide and maintain a Navy;

To make Rules for the Government and Regulation of the land and naval Forces;

To provide for calling forth the Militia to execute the Laws of the Union, suppress Insurrections and repel Invasions;

To provide for organizing, arming, and disciplining, the Militia, and for governing such Part of them as may be employed in the Service of the United States, reserving to the States respectively, the Appointment of the Officers, and the Authority of training the Militia according to the discipline prescribed by Congress;

To exercise exclusive Legislation in all Cases whatsoever, over such District (not exceeding ten Miles square) as may, by Cession of particular States, and the Acceptance of Congress, become the Seat of the Government of the United States, and to exercise like Authority over all Places purchased by the Consent of the Legislature of the State in which the Same shall be, for the Erection of Forts, Magazines, Arsenals, dock-Yards, and other needful Buildings;—And

To make all Laws which shall be necessary and proper for carrying into Execution the foregoing Powers, and all other Powers vested by this Constitution in the Government of the United States, or in any Department or Officer thereof.

Section 9 *The Migration or Importation of such Persons as any of the States now existing shall think proper to admit, shall not be prohibited by the Congress prior to the Year one thousand eight hundred and eight, but a Tax or duty may be imposed on such Importation, not exceeding ten dollars for each Person.*

The Privilege of the Writ of Habeas Corpus shall not be suspended, unless when in Cases of Rebellion or Invasion the public Safety may require it.

No Bill of Attainder or ex post facto Law shall be passed.

No Capitation, or other direct, Tax shall be laid, unless in Proportion to the Census or Enumeration herein before directed to be taken.

No Tax or Duty shall be laid on Articles exported from any State.

No Preference shall be given by any Regulation of Commerce or Revenue to the Ports of one State over those of another: nor shall Vessels bound to, or from, one State, be obliged to enter, clear, or pay Duties in another.

No Money shall be drawn from the Treasury, but in Consequence of Appropriations made by Law; and a regular Statement and Account of the Receipts and Expenditures of all public Money shall be published from time to time.

No Title of Nobility shall be granted by the United States: And no Person holding any Office of Profit or Trust under them, shall, without the Consent of the Congress, accept of any present, Emolument, Office, or Title, of any kind whatever, from any King, Prince, or foreign State.

Section 10 No State shall enter into any Treaty, Alliance, or Confederation; grant Letters of Marque and Reprisal; coin Money; emit Bills of Credit; make any Thing but gold and silver Coin a Tender in Payment of Debts; pass any Bill of Attainder, ex post facto Law, or Law impairing the Obligation of Contracts, or grant any Title of Nobility.

No State shall, without the Consent of the Congress, lay any Imposts or Duties on Imports or Exports, except what may be absolutely necessary for executing it's inspection Laws: and the net Produce of all Duties and Imposts, laid by any State on Imports or Exports, shall be for the Use of the Treasury of the United States; and all such Laws shall be subject to the Revision and Controul of the Congress.

No State shall, without the Consent of Congress, lay any Duty of Tonnage, keep Troops, or Ships of War in time of Peace, enter into any Agreement or Compact with another State, or with a foreign Power, or engage in War, unless actually invaded, or in such imminent Danger as will not admit of delay.

ARTICLE II.

Section 1 The executive Power shall be vested in a President of the United States of America. He shall hold his Office during the Term of four Years, and, together with the Vice President, chosen for the same Term, be elected, as follows

Each State shall appoint, in such Manner as the Legislature thereof may direct, a Number of Electors, equal to the whole Number of Senators and Representatives to which the State may be entitled in the Congress: but no Senator or Representative, or Person holding an Office of Trust or Profit under the United States, shall be appointed an Elector.

The Electors shall meet in their respective States, and vote by Ballot for two Persons, of whom one at least shall not be an Inhabitant of the same State with themselves. And they shall make a List of all the Persons voted for, and of the Number of Votes for each; which List they shall sign and certify, and transmit sealed to the Seat of Government of the United States, directed to the President of the Senate. The President of the Senate shall, in the Presence of the Senate and House of Representatives, open all the Certificates, and the Votes shall then be counted. The Person having the greatest Number of Votes shall be the President, if such Number be a Majority of the whole Number of Electors appointed; and if there be more than one who have such Majority, and have an equal Number of Votes, then the House of Representatives shall immediately chuse by Ballot one of them for President; and if no Person have a Majority, then from the five highest on the List the said House shall in like Manner chuse the President. But in chusing the President, the Votes shall be taken by States, the Representation from each State having one Vote; A quorum for this Purpose shall consist of a Member or Members from two thirds of the States, and a Majority of all the States shall be necessary to a Choice. In every Case, after the Choice of the President, the Person having the greatest Number of Votes of the Electors shall be the Vice President. But if there should remain two or more who have equal Votes, the Senate shall chuse from them by Ballot the Vice President. The Congress may determine the Time of chusing the Electors, and the Day on which they shall give their Votes; which Day shall be the same throughout the United States.

No Person except a natural born Citizen, *or a Citizen of the United States, at the time of the Adoption of this Constitution,* shall be eligible to the Office of President; neither shall any Person be eligible to that Office who shall not have attained to the Age of thirty five Years, and been fourteen Years a Resident within the United States.

In Case of the Removal of the President from Office, or of his Death, Resignation, or Inability to discharge the Powers and Duties of the said Office, the Same shall devolve on the Vice President, and the Congress may by Law provide for the Case of Removal, Death, Resignation or Inability, both of the President and Vice President declaring what Officer shall then act as President, and such Officer shall act accordingly, until the Disability be removed, or a President shall be elected.

The President shall, at stated Times, receive for his Services, a Compensation, which shall neither be encreased nor diminished during the Period for which he shall have been elected, and he shall not receive within that Period any other Emolument from the United States, or any of them.

Before he enter on the Execution of his Office, he shall take the following Oath or Affirmation: "I do solemnly swear (or affirm) that I will faithfully execute the Office of President of the United States, and will to the best of my Ability, preserve, protect and defend the Constitution of the United States."

Section 2   The President shall be Commander in Chief of the Army and Navy of the United States, and of the Militia of the several States, when called into the actual Service of the United States; he may require the Opinion, in writing, of the principal Officer in each of the executive Departments, upon any Subject relating to the Duties of their respective Offices, and he shall have Power to grant Reprieves and Pardons for Offences against the United States, except in Cases of Impeachment.

He shall have Power, by and with the Advice and Consent of the Senate, to make Treaties, provided two thirds of the Senators present concur; and he shall nominate, and by and with the Advice and Consent of the Senate, shall appoint Ambassadors, other public Ministers and Consuls, Judges of the supreme Court, and all other Officers of the United States, whose Appointments are not herein otherwise provided for, and which shall be established by Law: but the Congress may by Law vest the Appointment of such inferior Officers, as they think proper, in the President alone, in the Courts of Law, or in the Heads of Departments.

The President shall have Power to fill up all Vacancies that may happen during the Recess of the Senate, by granting Commissions which shall expire at the End of their next Session.

Section 3   He shall from time to time give to the Congress Information of the State of the Union, and recommend to their Consideration such Measures as he shall judge necessary and expedient; he may, on extraordinary Occasions, convene both Houses, or either of them, and in Case of Disagreement between them, with Respect to the Time of Adjournment, he may adjourn them to such Time as he shall think proper; he shall receive Ambassadors and other public Ministers; he shall take Care that the Laws be faithfully executed, and shall Commission all the Officers of the United States.

Section 4   The President, Vice President and all civil Officers of the United States, shall be removed from Office on Impeachment for, and Conviction of, Treason, Bribery, or other high Crimes and Misdemeanors.

ARTICLE III.

Section 1   The judicial Power of the United States, shall be vested in one supreme Court, and in such inferior Courts as the Congress may from time to time ordain and establish. The Judges, both of the supreme and inferior Courts, shall hold their Offices during good Behaviour, and shall, at stated Times, receive for their Services, a Compensation which shall not be diminished during their Continuance in Office.

Section 2   The judicial Power shall extend to all Cases, in Law and Equity, arising under this Constitution, the Laws of the United States, and Treaties made, or which shall be made, under their Authority;—to all Cases affecting Ambassadors, other public Ministers and Consuls;— to all Cases of admiralty and maritime Jurisdiction;—to Controversies to which the United States shall be a Party;—to Controversies between two or more States;—*between a State and Citizens of another State;*—between Citizens of different States;—between Citizens of the same State claiming Lands under Grants of different States, and between a State, or the Citizens thereof, and foreign States, Citizens or Subjects.

In all Cases affecting Ambassadors, other public Ministers and Consuls, and those in which a State shall be Party, the supreme Court shall have original Jurisdiction. In all the other Cases before mentioned, the supreme Court shall have appellate Jurisdiction, both as to Law and Fact, with such Exceptions, and under such Regulations as the Congress shall make.

The Trial of all Crimes, except in Cases of Impeachment, shall be by Jury; and such Trial shall be held in the State where the said Crimes shall have been committed; but when not committed within any State, the Trial shall be at such Place or Places as the Congress may by Law have directed.

Section 3 Treason against the United States, shall consist only in levying War against them, or in adhering to their Enemies, giving them Aid and Comfort. No Person shall be convicted of Treason unless on the Testimony of two Witnesses to the same overt Act, or on Confession in open Court.

The Congress shall have Power to declare the Punishment of Treason, but no Attainder of Treason shall work Corruption of Blood, or Forfeiture except during the Life of the Person attainted.

ARTICLE IV

Section 1 Full Faith and Credit shall be given in each State to the public Acts, Records, and judicial Proceedings of every other State. And the Congress may by general Laws prescribe the Manner in which such Acts, Records and Proceedings shall be proved, and the Effect thereof.

Section 2 The Citizens of each State shall be entitled to all Privileges and Immunities of Citizens in the several States.

A Person charged in any State with Treason, Felony, or other Crime, who shall flee from Justice, and be found in another State, shall on Demand of the executive Authority of the State from which he fled, be delivered up, to be removed to the State having Jurisdiction of the Crime.

No Person held to Service or Labour in one State, under the Laws thereof, escaping into another, shall, in Consequence of any Law or Regulation therein, be discharged from such Service or Labour, but shall be delivered up on Claim of the Party to whom such Service or Labour may be due. *

Section 3 New States may be admitted by the Congress into this Union; but no new State shall be formed or erected within the Jurisdiction of any other State; nor any State be formed by the Junction of two or more States, or Parts of States, without the Consent of the Legislatures of the States concerned as well as of the Congress.

The Congress shall have Power to dispose of and make all needful Rules and Regulations respecting the Territory or other Property belonging to the United States; and nothing in this Constitution shall be so construed as to Prejudice any Claims of the United States, or of any particular State.

Section 4 The United States shall guarantee to every State in this Union a Republican Form of Government, and shall protect each of them against Invasion; and on Application of the Legislature, or of the Executive (when the Legislature cannot be convened) against domestic Violence.

ARTICLE V

The Congress, whenever two thirds of both Houses shall deem it necessary, shall propose Amendments to this Constitution, or, on the Application of the Legislatures of two thirds of the several States, shall call a Convention for proposing Amendments, which, in either Case, shall be valid to all Intents and Purposes, as Part of this Constitution, when ratified by the Legislatures of three fourths of the several States, or by Conventions in three fourths thereof, as the one or the other Mode of Ratification may be proposed by the Congress; Provided *that no Amendment which may be made prior to the Year One thousand eight hundred and eight shall in any Manner affect the first and fourth Clauses in the Ninth Section of the first Article; and* that no State, without its Consent, shall be deprived of its equal Suffrage in the Senate.

ARTICLE VI

All Debts contracted and Engagements entered into, before the Adoption of this Constitution, shall be as valid against the United States under this Constitution, as under the Confederation.

This Constitution, and the Laws of the United States which shall be made in Pursuance thereof; and all Treaties made or which shall be made, under the Authority of the United States, shall be the supreme Law of the Land; and the Judges in every State shall be bound thereby, any Thing in the Constitution or Laws of any State to the Contrary notwithstanding.

The Senators and Representatives before mentioned, and the Members of the several State Legislatures, and all executive and judicial Officers, both of the United States and of the several States, shall be bound by Oath or Affirmation, to support this Constitution; but no religious Test shall ever be required as a Qualification to any Office or public Trust under the United States.

ARTICLE VII

The Ratification of the Conventions of nine States, shall be sufficient for the Establishment of this Constitution between the States so ratifying the Same.

Done in Convention by the Unanimous Consent of the States present the Seventeenth Day of September in the Year of our Lord one thousand seven hundred and Eighty seven and of the Independence of the United States of America the Twelfth* IN WITNESS whereof We have hereunto subscribed our Names,

GEORGE WASHINGTON,
President and Deputy from Virginia

North Carolina
WILLIAM BLOUNT
RICHARD DOBBS SPRAIGHT
HU WILLIAMSON

Pennsylvania
BENJAMIN FRANKLIN
THOMAS MIFFLIN
ROVERT MORRIS
GEORGE CLYMER
THOMAS FITZSIMONS
JARED INGERSOLL
JAMES WILSON
GOUVERNEUR MORRIS

Delaware
GEORGE READ
GUNNING BEDFORD, JR.
JOHN DICKINSON
RICHARD BASSETT
JACOB BROOM

South Carolina
J. RUTLEDGE
CHARLES C. PINCKNEY
PIERCE BUTLER

Virginia
JOHN BLAIR
JAMES MADISON, JR.

New Jersey
WILLIAM LIVINGSTON
DAVID BREARLEY
WILLIAM PATERSON
JONATHAN DAYTON

Maryland
JAMES MCHENRY
DANIEL OF ST. THOMAS
JENIFER
DANIEL CARROLL

Massachusetts
NATHANIEL GORHAM
RUFUS KING

Connecticut
WILLIAM S. JOHNSON
ROGER SHERMAN

New York
ALEXANDER HAMILTON

New Hampshire
JOHN LANGDON
NICHOLAS GILMAN

Georgia
WILLIAM FEW
ABRAHAM BALDWIN

AMENDMENTS TO THE CONSTITUTION*

*The first ten amendments (the Bill of Rights) were adopted in 1791.

Amendment I
Congress shall make no law respecting an establishment of religion, or prohibiting the free exercise thereof; or abridging the freedom of speech, or of the press; or the right of the people peaceably to assemble, and to petition the Government for a redress of grievances.

Amendment II
A well regulated Militia, being necessary to the security of a free State, the right of the people to keep and bear Arms, shall not be infringed.

Amendment III
No Soldier shall, in time of peace be quartered in any house, without the consent of the Owner, nor in time of war, but in a manner to be prescribed by law.

Amendment IV
The right of the people to be secure in their persons, houses, papers, and effects, against unreasonable searches and seizures, shall not be violated, and no Warrants shall issue, but upon probable cause, supported by Oath or affirmation, and particularly describing the place to be searched, and the persons or things to be seized.

Amendment V
No person shall be held to answer for a capital, or otherwise infamous crime, unless on a presentment or indictment of a Grand Jury, except in cases arising in the land or naval forces, or in the Militia, when in actual service in time of War or public danger; nor shall any person be subject for the same offence to be twice put in jeopardy of life or limb; nor shall be compelled in any criminal case to be a witness against himself, nor be deprived of life, liberty, or property, without due process of law; nor shall private property be taken for public use, without just compensation.

Amendment VI
In all criminal prosecutions, the accused shall enjoy the right to a speedy and public trial, by an impartial jury of the State and district wherein the crime shall have been committed, which district shall have been previously ascertained by law, and to be informed of the nature and cause of the accusation; to be confronted with the witnesses against him; to have compulsory process for obtaining witnesses in his favor, and to have the Assistance of Counsel for his defence.

Amendment VII
In Suits at common law, where the value in controversy shall exceed twenty dollars, the right of trial by jury shall be preserved, and no fact tried by a jury, shall be otherwise re-examined in any Court of the United States, than according to the rules of the common law.

Amendment VIII
Excessive bail shall not be required, nor excessive fines imposed, nor cruel and unusual punishments inflicted.

Amendment IX
The enumeration in the Constitution, of certain rights, shall not be construed to deny or disparage others retained by the people.

Amendment X*
The powers not delegated to the United States by the Constitution, nor prohibited by it to the States, are reserved to the States respectively, or to the people.

Amendment XI [Adopted 1798]
The Judicial power of the United States shall not be construed to extend to any suit in law or equity, commenced or prosecuted against one of the United States by Citi-

zens of another State, or by Citizens or Subjects of any Foreign State.

Amendment XII [Adopted 1804]

The Electors shall meet in their respective states, and vote by ballot for President and Vice-President, one of whom, at least, shall not be an inhabitant of the same state with themselves; they shall name in their ballots the person voted for as President, and in distinct ballots the person voted for as Vice-President, and they shall make distinct lists of all persons voted for as President, and of all persons voted for as Vice-President, and of the number of votes for each, which list they shall sign and certify, and transmit sealed to the seat of the government of the United States, directed to the President of the Senate;—The President of the Senate shall, in the presence of the Senate and House of Representatives, open all the certificates and the votes shall then be counted;—The person having the greatest number of votes for President, shall be the President, if such number be a majority of the whole number of Electors appointed; and if no person have such majority, then from the persons having the highest numbers not exceeding three on the list of those voted for as President, the House of Representatives shall choose immediately, by ballot, the President. But in choosing the President, the votes shall be taken by states, the representation from each state having one vote; a quorum for this purpose shall consist of a member or members from two thirds of the states, and a majority of all the states shall be necessary to a choice. And if the House of Representatives shall not choose a President whenever the right of choice shall devolve upon them, before *the fourth day of March* next following, then the Vice-President shall act as President, as in the case of the death or other constitutional disability of the President.

The person having the greatest number of votes as Vice-President, shall be the Vice-President, if such number be a majority of the whole number of Electors appointed, and if no person have a majority, then from the two highest numbers on the list, the Senate shall choose the Vice-President; a quorum for the purpose shall consist of two thirds of the whole number of Senators, and a majority of the whole number shall be necessary to a choice. But no person constitutionally ineligible to the office of President shall be eligible to that of Vice-President of the United States.

Amendment XIII [Adopted 1865]

Section 1   Neither slavery nor involuntary servitude, except as a punishment for crime whereof the party shall have been duly convicted, shall exist within the United States, or any place subject to their jurisdiction.

Section 2   Congress shall have power to enforce this article by appropriate legislation.

Amendment XIV [Adopted 1868]

Section 1   All persons born or naturalized in the United States, and subject to the jurisdiction thereof, are citizens of the United States and of the State wherein they reside. No State shall make or enforce any law which shall abridge the privileges or immunities of citizens of the United States; nor shall any State deprive any person of life, liberty, or property, without due process of law; nor deny to any person within its jurisdiction the equal protection of the laws.

Section 2   Representatives shall be apportioned among the several States according to their respective numbers, counting the whole number of persons in each State, excluding Indians not taxed. But when the right to vote at any election for the choice of electors for President and Vice-President of the United States, Representatives in Congress, the Executive and Judicial officers of a State, or the members of the Legislature thereof, is denied to any of the male inhabitants of such State, being twenty-one years of age, and citizens of the United States, or in any way abridged, except for participation in rebellion, or other crime, the basis of representation therein shall be reduced in the proportion which the number of such male citizens shall bear to the whole number of male citizens twenty-one years of age in such State.

Section 3   No person shall be a Senator or Representative in Congress, or elector of President and Vice-President, or hold any office, civil or military, under the United States, or under any State, who, having previously taken an oath, as a member of Congress, or as an officer of the United States, or as a member of any State legislature, or as an executive or judicial officer of any State, to support the Constitution of the United States, shall have engaged in insurrection or rebellion against the same, or given aid or comfort to the enemies thereof. But Congress may by a vote of two thirds of each House, remove such disability.

Section 4   The validity of the public debt of the United States, authorized by law, including debts incurred for payment of pensions and bounties for services in suppressing insurrection or rebellion, shall not be questioned. But neither the United States nor any State shall assume or pay any debt or obligation incurred in aid of insurrection or rebellion against the United States, or any claim for the loss or emancipation of any slave; but all such debts, obligations and claims shall be held illegal and void.

Section 5   The Congress shall have power to enforce, by appropriate legislation, the provisions of this article.

Amendment XV [Adopted 1870]

Section 1   The right of citizens of the United States to vote shall not be denied or abridged by the United States or by any State on account of race, color, or previous condition of servitude

Section 2 The Congress shall have power to enforce this article by appropriate legislation.

Amendment XVI [Adopted 1913]
The Congress shall have power to lay and collect taxes on incomes, from whatever source derived, without apportionment among the several States, and without regard to any census or enumeration.

Amendment XVII [Adopted 1913]
The Senate of the United States shall be composed of two Senators from each State, elected by the people thereof, for six years; and each Senator shall have one vote. The electors in each State shall have the qualifications requisite for electors of the most numerous branch of the State legislatures.

When vacancies happen in the representation of any State in the Senate, the executive authority of such State shall issue writs of election to fill such vacancies: *Provided,* That the legislature of any State may empower the executive thereof to make temporary appointments until the people fill the vacancies by election as the legislature may direct.

This amendment shall not be so construed as to affect the election or term of any Senator chosen before it becomes valid as part of the Constitution.

Amendment XVIII [Adopted 1919; Repealed 1933]

Section 1 After one year from the ratification of this article the manufacture, sale, or transportation of intoxicating liquors within, the importation thereof into, or the exportation thereof from the United States and all territory subject to the jurisdiction thereof for beverage purposes is hereby prohibited.*

Section 2 The Congress and the several States shall have concurrent power to enforce this article by appropriate legislation.

Section 3 This article shall be inoperative unless it shall have been ratified as an amendment to the Constitution by the legislatures of the several States, as provided in the Constitution, within seven years from the date of the submission hereof to the States by the Congress.

Amendment XIX [Adopted 1920]

Section 1 The right of citizens of the United States to vote shall not be denied or abridged by the United States or by any State on account of sex.

Section 2 Congress shall have power to enforce this article by appropriate legislation.

Amendment XX [Adopted 1933]

Section 1 The terms of the President and Vice-President shall end at noon on the 20th day of January, and the terms of Senators and Representatives at noon on the third day of January, of the years in which such terms would have ended if this article had not been ratified; and the terms of their successors shall then begin.

Section 2 The Congress shall assemble at least once in every year, and such meeting shall begin at noon on the third day of January, unless they shall by law appoint a different day.

Section 3 If, at the time fixed for the beginning of the term of the President, the President elect shall have died, the Vice-President elect shall become President. If a President shall not have been chosen before the time fixed for the beginning of his term, or if the President elect shall have failed to qualify, then the Vice-President elect shall act as President until a President shall have qualified; and the Congress may by law provide for the case wherein neither a President elect nor a Vice-President elect shall have qualified, declaring who shall then act as President, or the manner in which one who is to act shall be selected, and such person shall act accordingly until a President or Vice-President shall have qualified.

Section 4 The Congress may by law provide for the case of the death of any of the persons from whom the House of Representatives may choose a President whenever the right of choice shall have devolved upon them, and for the case of the death of any of the persons from whom the Senate may choose a Vice-President whenever the right of choice shall have devolved upon them.

Section 5 Sections 1 and 2 shall take effect on the 15th day of October following the ratification of this article.

Section 6 This article shall be inoperative unless it shall have been ratified as an amendment to the Constitution by the legislatures of three fourths of the several States within seven years from the date of its submission.

Amendment XXI [Adopted 1933]

Section 1 The eighteenth article of amendment to the Constitution of the United States is hereby repealed.

Section 2 The transportation or importation into any State, Territory, or possession of the United States for delivery or use therein of intoxicating liquors, in violation of the laws thereof, is hereby prohibited.

Section 3 This article shall be inoperative unless it shall have been ratified as an amendment to the Constitution by conventions in the several States, as provided in the Constitution, within seven years from the date of the submission hereof to the States by the Congress.

Amendment XXII [Adopted 1951]

Section 1 No person shall be elected to the office of the President more than twice, and no person who has held the office of President, or acted as President, for more than two years of a term to which some other person was elected President shall be elected to the office of the President more than once. But this Article shall not apply to any person holding the office of President when this Article was proposed by the Congress, and shall not prevent any person who may be holding the office of President, or acting as President, during the term within which this Article becomes operative from holding the office of President or acting as President during the remainder of such term.

Section 2   This article shall be inoperative unless it shall have been ratified as an amendment to the Constitution by the legislatures of three fourths of the several States within seven years from the date of its submission to the States by the Congress.

Amendment XXIII [Adopted 1961]

Section 1   The District constituting the seat of Government of the United States shall appoint in such manner as the Congress may direct:

A number of electors of President and Vice-President equal to the whole number of Senators and Representatives in Congress to which the District would be entitled if it were a State, but in no event more than the least populous State; they shall be in addition to those appointed by the States, but they shall be considered, for the purposes of the election of President and Vice-President, to be electors appointed by a State; and they shall meet in the District and perform such duties as provided by the twelfth article of amendment.

Section 2   The Congress shall have power to enforce this article by appropriate legislation.

Amendment XXIV [Adopted 1944]

Section 1   The right of citizens of the United States to vote in any primary or other election for President or Vice-President, for electors for President or Vice-President, or for Senator or Representative in Congress, shall not be denied or abridged by the United States or any State by reason of failure to pay any poll tax or other tax.

Section 2   The Congress shall have power to enforce this article by appropriate legislation.

Amendment XXV [Adopted 1967]

Section 1   In case of the removal of the President from office or his death or resignation, the Vice-President shall become President.

Section 2   Whenever there is a vacancy in the office of the Vice-President, the President shall nominate a Vice-President who shall take the office upon confirmation by a majority vote of both houses of Congress.

Section 3   Whenever the President transmits to the President pro tempore of the Senate and the Speaker of the House of Representatives his written declaration that he is unable to discharge the powers and duties of his office, and until he transmits to them a written declaration to the contrary, such powers and duties shall be discharged by the Vice-President as Acting President.

Section 4   Whenever the Vice-President and a majority of either the principal officers of the executive departments, or of such other body as Congress may by law provide, transmit to the President pro tempore of the Senate and the Speaker of the House of Representatives their written declaration that the President is unable to discharge the powers and duties of his office, the Vice-President shall immediately assume the powers and duties of the office as Acting President.

Thereafter, when the President transmits to the President pro tempore of the Senate and the Speaker of the House of Representatives his written declaration that no inability exists, he shall resume the powers and duties of his office unless the Vice-President and a majority of either the principal officers of the executive department, or of such other body as Congress may by law provide, transmit within four days to the President pro tempore of the Senate and the Speaker of the House of Representatives their written declaration that the President is unable to discharge the powers and duties of his office. Thereupon Congress shall decide the issue, assembling within 48 hours for that purpose if not in session. If the Congress, within 21 days after receipt of the latter written declaration, or, if Congress is not in session, within 21 days after Congress is required to assemble, determines by two-thirds vote of both houses that the President is unable to discharge the powers and duties of his office, the Vice-President shall continue to discharge the same as Acting President; otherwise, the President shall resume the powers and duties of his office.

Amendment XXVI [Adopted 1971]

Section 1   The right of citizens of the United States, who are eighteen years of age or older, to vote shall not be denied or abridged by the United States or any state on account of age.

Section 2   The Congress shall have power to enforce this article by appropriate legislation.

Amendment XXVII [Adopted 1992]

No law, varying the compensation for the services of Senators and Representatives, shall take effect until an election of Representatives have intervened.

Presidential Elections

Year	Candidates	Parties	Popular Vote	Electoral Vote	Voter Participation
1789	GEORGE WASHINGTON		*	69	
	John Adams			34	
	Others			35	
1792	GEORGE WASHINGTON		*	132	
	John Adams			77	
	George Clinton			50	
	Others			5	
1796	JOHN ADAMS	Federalist	*	71	
	Thomas Jefferson	Democratic-Republican		68	
	Thomas Pinckney	Federalist		59	
	Aaron Burr	Dem.-Rep.		30	
	Others			48	
1800	THOMAS JEFFERSON	Dem.-Rep.	*	73	
	Aaron Burr	Dem.-Rep.		73	
	C. C. Pinckney	Federalist		64	
	John Jay	Federalist		1	
1804	THOMAS JEFFERSON	Dem.-Rep.	*	122	
	C. C. Pinckney	Federalist		14	
1808	JAMES MADISON	Dem.-Rep.	*	122	
	C. C. Pinckney	Federalist		47	
	George Clinton	Dem.-Rep.		6	
1812	JAMES MADISON	Dem.-Rep.	*	128	
	De Witt Clinton	Federalist		89	
1816	JAMES MONROE	Dem.-Rep.	*	183	
	Rufus King	Federalist		34	
1820	JAMES MONROE	Dem.-Rep.	*	231	
	John Quincy Adams	Dem.-Rep.		1	
1824	JOHN Q. Adams	Dem.-Rep.	108,740 (10.5%)	84	26.9%
	Andrew Jackson	Dem.-Rep.	153,544 (43.1%)	99	
	William H. Crawford	Dem.-Rep.	46,618 (13.1%)	41	
	Henry Clay	Dem.-Rep.	47,136 (13.2%)	37	
1828	ANDREW JACKSON	Democratic	647,286 (56.0%)	178	57.6%
	John Quincy Adams	National Republican	508,064 (44.0%)	83	
1832	ANDREW JACKSON	Democratic	687,502 (55.0%)	219	55.4%
	Henry Clay	National Republican	530,189 (42.4%)	49	
	John Floyd	Independent		11	
	William Wirt	Anti-Mason	33,108 (2.6%)	7	
1836	MARTIN VAN BUREN	Democratic	765,483 (50.9%)	170	57.8%
	W. H. Harrison	Whig		73	
	Hugh L. White	Whig	739,795 (49.1%)	26	
	Daniel Webster	Whig		14	
	W. P. Magnum	Independent		11	
1840	WILLIAM H. HARRISON	Whig	1,274,624 (53.1%)	234	80.2%
	Martin Van Buren	Democratic	1,127,781 (46.9%)	60	
	J. G. Birney	Liberty	7069	—	
1844	JAMES K. POLK	Democratic	1,338,464 (49.6%)	170	78.9%
	Henry Clay	Whig	1,300,097 (48.1%)	105	
	J. G. Birney	Liberty	62,300 (2.3%)	—	
1848	ZACHARY TAYLOR	Whig	1,360,967 (47.4%)	163	72.7%
	Lewis Cass	Democratic	1,222,342 (42.5%)	127	
	Martin Van Buren	Free-Soil	291,263 (10.1%)	—	

Year	Candidates	Parties	Popular Vote	Electoral Vote	Voter Participation
1852	FRANKLIN PIERCE	Democratic	1,601,117 (50.9%)	254	69.6%
	Winfield Scott	Whig	1,385,453 (44.1%)	42	
	John P. Hale	Free-Soil	155,825 (5.0%)	—	
1856	JAMES BUCHANAN	Democratic	1,832,955 (45.3%)	174	78.9%
	John C. Fremont	Republican	1,339,932 (33.1%)	114	
	Millard Fillmore	American	871,731 (21.6%)	8	
1860	ABRAHAM LINCOLN	Republican	1,865,593 (39.8%)	180	81.2%
	Stephen A. Douglas	Democratic	1,382,713 (29.5%)	12	
	John C. Breckinridge	Democratic	848,356 (18.1%)	72	
	John Bell	Union	592,906 (12.6%)	39	
1864	ABRAHAM LINCOLN	Republican	2,213,655 (55.0%)	212	73.8%
	George B. McClellan	Democratic	1,805,237 (45.0%)	21	
1868	ULYSSES S. GRANT	Republican	3,012,833 (52.7%)	214	78.1%
	Horatio Seymour	Democratic	2,703,249 (47.3%)	80	
1872	ULYSSES S. GRANT	Republican	3,597,132 (55.6%)	286	71.3%
	Horace Greeley	Democratic; Liberal Republican	2,834,125 (43.9%)	66	
1876	RUTHERFORD B. HAYES	Republican	4,036,298 (48.0%)	185	81.8%
	Samuel J. Tilden	Democratic	4,300,590 (51.0%)	184	
1880	JAMES A. GARFIELD	Republican	4,454,416 (48.5%)	214	79.4%
	Winfield S. Hancock	Democratic	4,444,952 (48.1%)	155	
1884	GROVER CLEVELAND	Democratic	4,874,986 (48.5%)	219	77.5%
	James G. Blaine	Republican	4,851,981 (48.2%)	182	
1888	BENJAMIN HARRISON	Republican	5,439,853 (47.9%)	233	79.3%
	Grover Cleveland	Democratic	5,540,309 (48.6%)	168	
1892	GROVER CLEVELAND	Democratic	5,556,918 (46.1%)	277	74.7%
	Benjamin Harrison	Republican	5,176,108 (43.0%)	145	
	James B. Weaver	People's	1,041,028 (8.5%)	22	
1896	WILLIAM McKINLEY	Republican	7,104,779 (51.1%)	271	79.3%
	William J. Bryan	democratic People's	6,502,925 (47.7%)	176	
1900	WILLIAM McKINLEY	Republican	7,207,923 (51.7%)	292	73.2%
	William J. Bryan	Dem.-Populist	6,358,133 (45.5%)	155	
1904	THEODORE ROOSEVELT	Republican	7,623,486 (57.9%)	336	65.2%
	Alton B. Parker	Democratic	5,077,911 (37.6%)	140	
	Eugene V. Debs	Socialist	402,283 (3.0%)	—	
1908	WILLIAM H. TAFT	Republican	7,678,908 (51.6%)	321	65.4%
	William J. Bryan	democratic	6,409,104 (43.1%)	162	
	Eugene V. Debs	Socialist	420,793 (2.8%)	—	
1912	WOODROW WILSON	Democratic	6,293,454 (41.9%)	435	58.8%
	Theodore Roosevelt	Progressive	4,119,538 (27.4%)	88	
	William H. Taft	Republican	3,484,980 (23.2%)	8	
	Eugene V. Debs	Socialist	900,672 (6.0%)	—	
1916	WOODROW WILSON	Democratic	9,129,606 (49.4%)	277	61.6%
	Charles E. Hughes	Republican	8,538,221 (46.2%)	254	
	A. L. Benson	Socialist	585,113 (3.2%)	—	
1920	WARREN G. HARDING	Republican	16,152,200 (60.4%)	404	49.2%
	James M. Cox	Democratic	9,147,353 (34.2%)	127	
	Eugene V. Debs	Socialist	919,799 (3.4%)	—	
1924	CALVIN COOLIDGE	Republican	15,725,016 (54.0%)	382	48.9%
	John W. Davis	Democratic	8,386,503 (28.8%)	136	
	Robert M. La Follette	Progressive	4,822,856 (16.6%)	13	

Year	Candidates	Parties	Popular Vote	Electoral Vote	Voter Participation
1928	HERBERT HOOVER	Republican	21,391,381 (58.2%)	444	56.9%
	Alfred E. Smith	Democratic	15,016,443 (40.9%)	87	
	Normal Thomas	Socialist	267,835 (0.7%)	—	
1932	FRANKLIN D. ROOSEVELT	Democratic	22,821,857 (57.4%)	472	56.9%
	Herbert Hoover	republican	15,761,841 (39.7%)	59	
	Norman Thomas	Socialist	881,951 (2.2%)	—	
1936	FRANKLIN D. ROOSEVELT	Democratic	27,751,597 (60.8%)	523	61.0%
	Alfred M. Landon	Republican	16,679,583 (36.5%)	8	
	William Lemke	Union	882,479 (1.9%)	—	
1940	FRANKLIN D. ROOSEVELT	Democratic	27,244,160 (54.8%)	449	62.5%
	Wendell L. Willkie	Republican	22,305,198 (44.8%)	82	
1944	FRANKLIN D. ROOSEVELT	Democrat	25,602,504 (53.5%)	432	55.9%
	Thomas E. Dewey	Republican	22,006,285 (46.0%)	99	
1948	HARRY S TRUMAN	Democratic	24,105,695 (49.5%)	304	53.0%
	Thomas E. Dewey	Republican	21,969,170 (45.1%)	189	
	J. Strom Thurmond	State-Rights Democratic	1,169,021 (2.4%)	38	
	Henry A. Wallace	Progressive	1,156,103 (2.4%)	—	
1952	DWIGHT D. EISENHOWER	Republican	33,936,252 (55.1%)	442	63.3%
	Adlai E. Stevenson	Democratic	27,314,992 (44.4%)	89	
1956	DWIGHT D. EISENHOWER	Republican	35,575,420 (57.6%)	457	60.5%
	Adlai E. Stevenson	Democratic	26,033,066 (42.1%)	73	
	Other	—	—	1	
1960	JOHN F. KENNEDY	Democratic	34,227,096 (49.9%)	303	62.8%
	Richard M. Nixon	Republican	34,108,546 (49.6%)	219	
	Other	—	—	15	
1964	LYNDON B. JOHNSON	Democratic	43,126,506 (61.1%)	486	61.7%
	Barry M. Goldwater	Republican	27,176,799 (38.5%)	52	
1968	RICHARD M. NIXON	Republican	31,770,237 (43.4%)	301	60.6%
	Hurbert H. Humphrey	Democratic	31,270,633 (42.7%)	191	
	George Wallace	American Indep.	9,906,141 (13.5%)	46	
1972	RICHARD M. NIXON	Republican	47,169,911 (60.7%)	520	55.2%
	George S. McGovern	Democratic	29,170,383 (37.5%)	17	
	Other	—	—	1	
1976	JIMMY CARTER	Democratic	40,828,587 (50.0%)	297	53.5%
	Gerald R. Ford	Republican	39,147,613 (47.9%)	241	
	Other	—	1,575,459 92.1%)	—	
1980	RONALD REAGAN	Republican	43,901,812 (50.7%)	489	52.6%
	Jimmy Carter	Democratic	35,483,820 (41.0%)	49	
	John B. Anderson	Independent	5,719,722 (6.6%)	—	
	Ed Clark	Libertarian	921,188 (1.1%)	—	
1984	RONALD REAGAN	Republican	54,455,075 (59.0%)	525	53.3%
	Walter Mondale	Democratic	37,577,185 (41.0%)	13	
1988	GEORGE H. W. BUSH	Republican	48,886,000 (45.6%)	426	57.4%
	Michael S. Dukakis	Democratic	41,809,000 (45.6%)	111	
1992	WILLIAM J. CLINTON	Democratic	43,728,375 (43%)	370	55.0%
	George H. W. Bush	Republican	38,167,416 (38%)	168	
	Ross Perot	—	19,237,247 (19%)	—	
1996	WILLIAM J. CLINTON	Democratic	45,590,703 (50%)	379	48.8%
	Robert Dole	Republican	37,816,307 (41%)	159	
	Ross Perot	Independent	7,866,284 (9%)	—	

NAME	SERVICE	APPOINTED BY...	NAME	SERVICE	APPOINTED BY...
John Jay*	1789–1795	Washington	Joseph McKenna	1898–1925	McKinley
James Wilson	1789–1798	Washington	Oliver W. Holmes	1902–1932	T. Roosevelt
John Blair	1789–1796	Washington	William R. Day	1903–1922	T. Roosevelt
John Rutledge	1790–1791	Washington	William H. Moody	1906–1910	T. Roosevelt
William Cushing	1790–1810	Washington	Horace H. Lurton	1910–1914	Taft
James Iredell	1790–1799	Washington	Charles E. Hughes	1910–1916	Taft
Thomas Johnson	1791–1793	Washington	Willis Van Devanter	1910–1937	Taft
William Paterson	1793–1806	Washington	Joseph R. Lamar	1911–1916	Taft
John Rutledge†	1795	Washington	**Edward D. White**	1910–1921	Taft
Samuel Chase	1796–1811	Washington	Mahlon Pitney	1912–1922	Taft
Oliver Ellsworth	1796–1799	Washington	James C. McReynolds	1914–1941	Wilson
Bushrod Washington	1798–1829	J. Adams	Louis D. Brandeis	1916–1939	Wilson
Alfred Moore	1799–1804	J. Adams	John H. Clarke	1916–1922	Wilson
John Marshall	1801–1835	J. Adams	**William H. Taft**	1921–1930	Harding
William Johnson	1804–1834	Jefferson	George Sutherland	1922–1938	Harding
Henry B. Livingston	1806–1823	Jefferson	Pierce Butler	1923–1939	Harding
Thomas Todd	1807–1826	Jefferson	Edward T. Sanford	1923–1930	Harding
Gabriel Duval	1811–1836	Madison	Harlan F. Stone	1925–1941	Coolidge
Joseph Story	1811–1845	Madison	**Charles E.Hughes**	1930–1941	Hoover
Smith Thompson	1823–1843	Monroe	Owen J. Roberts	1930–1945	Hoover
Robert Trimble	1826–1828	J. Q. Adams	Benjamin N. Cardozo	1932–1938	Hoover
John McLean	1829–1861	Jackson	Hugo L. Black	1937–1971	F. Roosevelt
Henry Baldwin	1830–1844	Jackson	Stanley F. Reed	1938–1957	F. Roosevelt
James M. Wayne	1835–1867	Jackson	Felix Frankfurter	1939–1962	F. Roosevelt
Rager B. Taney	1836–1864	Jackson	William O. Douglas	1939–1975	F. Roosevelt
Philip P. Barbour	1836–1841	Jackson	Frank Murphy	1940–1949	F. Roosevelt
John Catron	1837–1865	Van Buren	**Harlan F. Stone**	1941–1946	F. Roosevelt
John McKinley	1837–1852	Van Buren	James F. Byrnes	1941–1942	F. Roosevelt
Peter V. Daniel	1841–1860	Van Buren	Robert H. Jackson	1941–1954	F. Roosevelt
Samuel Nelson	1845–1872	Tyler	Wiley B. Rutledge	1943–1949	F. Roosevelt
Levi Woodbury	1845–1851	Polk	Harold H. Burton	1945–1958	Truman
Robert C. Grier	1846–1870	Polk	**Frederick M. Vinson**	1946–1953	Truman
Benjamin R. Curtis	1851–1857	Fillmore	Tom C. Clark	1949–1967	Truman
John A. Campbell	1853–1861	Pierce	Sherman Minton	1949–1956	Truman
Nathan Clifford	1858–1881	Buchanan	**Earl Warren**	1953–1969	Eisenhower
Noah H. Swayne	1862–1881	Lincoln	John Marshall Harlan	1955–1971	Eisenhower
Samuel F. Miller	1862–1890	Lincoln	William J. Brennan, Jr.	1956–1990	Eisenhower
David Davis	1862–1877	Lincoln	Charles E.Whittaker	1957–1962	Eisenhower
Stephen J. Field	1863–1897	Lincoln	Potter Stewart	1958–1981	Eisenhower
Salmon P. Chase	1864–1873	Lincoln	Byron R.White	1962–1993	Kennedy
William Strong	1870–1880	Grant	Arthur J. Goldberg	1962–1965	Kennedy
Joseph P. Bradley	1870–1892	Grant	Abe Fortas	1965–1969	Johnson
Ward Hunt	1873–1882	Grant	Thurgood Marshall	1967–1991	Johnson
Morrison R. Waite	1874–1888	Grant	**Warren E. Burger**	1969–1986	Nixon
John M. Harlan	1877–1911	Hayes	Harry A. Blackmun	1970– 1994	Nixon
William B. Woods	1880–1887	Hayes	Lewis F. Powell, Jr.	1972–1988	Nixon
Stanley Matthews	1881–1889	Garfield	William H. Rehnquist	1972–1986	Nixon
Horace Gray	1882–1902	Arthur	John Paul Stevens	1975–	Ford
Samuel Blatchford	1882–1893	Arthur	Sandra Day O'Connor	1981–	Reagan
Lucious Q. C. Lamar	1888–1893	Cleveland	**William H. Rehnquist**	1986–	Reagan
Melville W.Fuller	1888–1910	Cleveland	Antonin Scalia	1986–	Reagan
David J. Brewer	1889–1910	B. Harrison	Anthony M. Kennedy	1988–	Reagan
Henry B. Brown	1890–1906	B. Harrison	David H. Souter	1990–	Bush
George Shiras	1892–1903	B. Harrison	ClarenceThomas	1991–	Bush
Howell E. Jackson	1893–1895	B. Harrison	Ruth Bader Ginsburg	1993–	Clinton
Edward D. White	1894–1910	Cleveland	Stephen Breyer	1994–	Clinton
Rufus W. Peckham	1896–1909	Cleveland			

***Chief Justices appear in bold type.**
†Acting Chief Justice; Senate refused to confirm appointment.

States of the United States

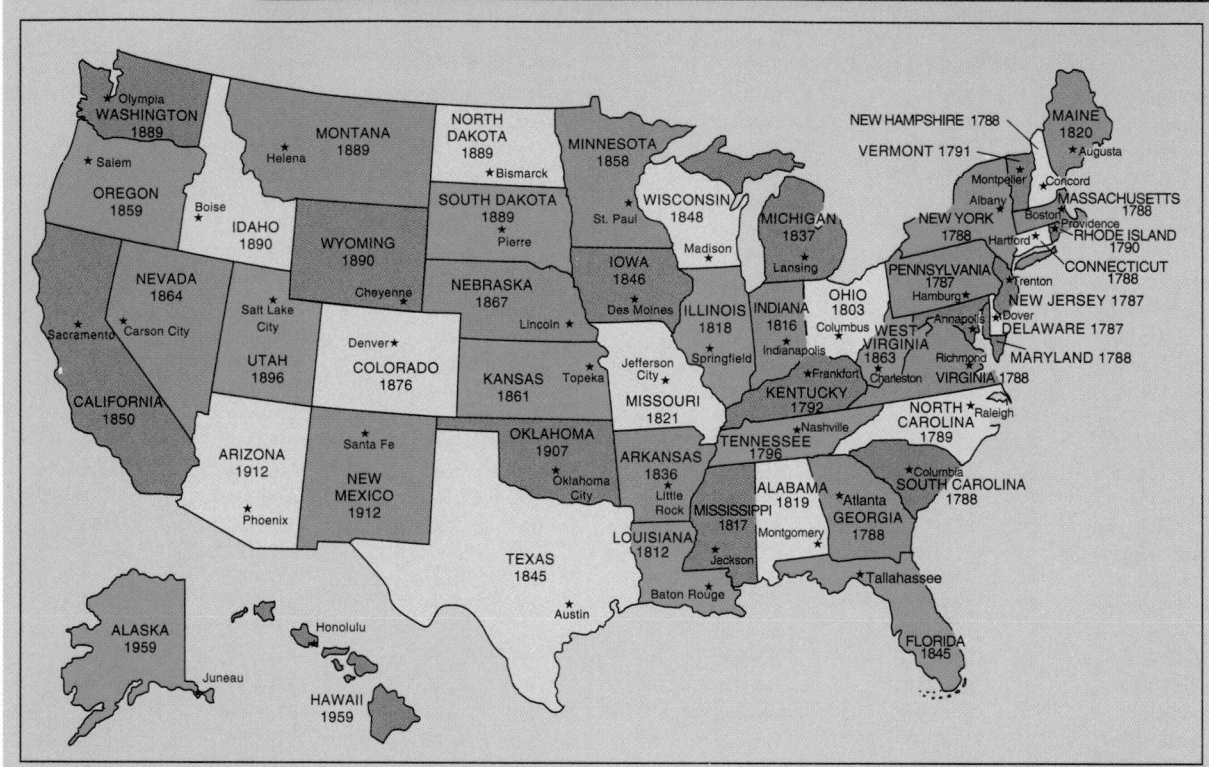

STATE	DATE OF ADMISSION	STATE	DATE OF ADMISSION
Delaware	December 7, 1787	Michigan	January 16, 1837
Pennsylvania	December 12, 1787	Florida	March 3, 1845
New Jersey	December 18, 1787	Texas	December 29, 1845
Georgia	January 2, 1788	Iowa	December 28, 1846
Connecticut	January 9, 1788	Wisconsin	May 29, 1848
Massachusetts	February 6, 1788	California	September 9, 1850
Maryland	April 28, 1788	Minnesota	May 11, 1858
South Carolina	May 23, 1788	Oregon	February 14, 1859
New Hampshire	June 21, 1788	Kansas	January 29, 1861
Virginia	June 25, 1788	West Virginia	June 19, 1863
New York	July 26, 1788	Nevada	October 31, 1864
North Carolina	November 21, 1789	Nebraska	March 1, 1867
Rhode Island	May 29, 1790	Colorado	August 1, 1876
Vermont	March 4, 1791	North Dakota	November 2, 1889
Kentucky	June 1, 1792	South Dakota	November 2, 1889
Tennessee	June 1, 1796	Montana	November 8, 1889
Ohio	March 1, 1803	Washington	November 11, 1889
Louisiana	April 30, 1812	Idaho	July 3, 1890
Indiana	December 11, 1816	Wyoming	July 10, 1890
Mississippi	December 10, 1817	Utah	January 4, 1896
Illinois	December 3, 1818	Oklahoma	November 16, 1907
Alabama	December 14, 1819	New Mexico	January 6, 1912
Maine	March 15, 1820	Arizona	February 14, 1912
Missouri	August 10, 1821	Alaska	January 3, 1959
Arkansas	June 15, 1836	Hawaii	August 21, 1959

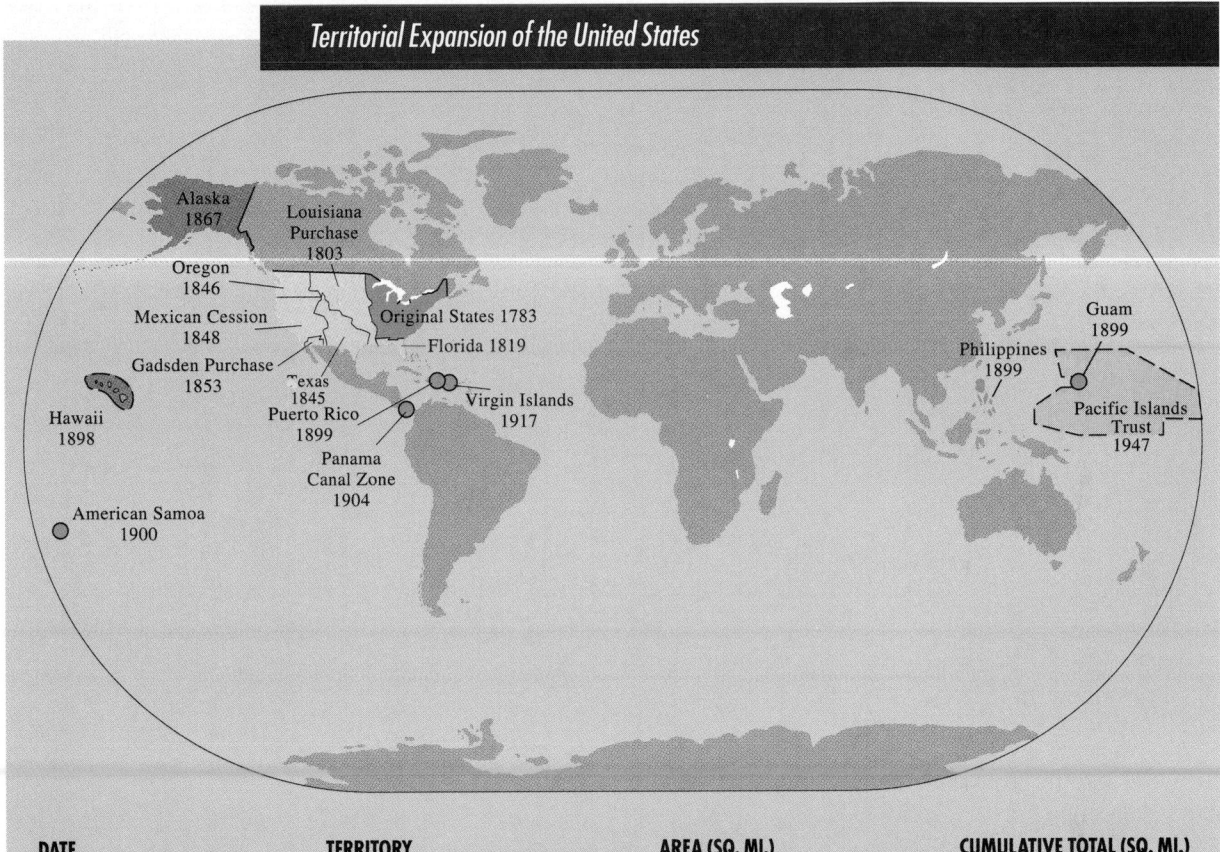

Territorial Expansion of the United States

DATE	TERRITORY	AREA (SQ. MI.)	CUMULATIVE TOTAL (SQ. MI.)
1793	Original states	888,685	888,685
1803	Louisiana Purchase	827,192	1,715,877
1819	Florida	72,003	1,787,880
1845	Texas	390,143	2,178,023
1846	Oregon	285,580	2,463,603
1848	Mexican Cession	529,017	2,992,620
1853	Gadsden Purchase	29,640	3,022,260
1867	Alaska	589,757	3,612,017
1898	Hawaii	6,450	3,618,467
1899	Philippines	115,600	3,734,067
1899	Puerto Rico	3,435	3,737,502
1899	Guam	212	3,737,714
1900	American Samoa	76	3,737,790
1904	Panama Canal Zone	553	3,738,343
1917	Virgin Islands	133	3,738,476
1947	Pacific Islands Trust	8,489	3,746,965
	All others	46	3,747,011

Population of the United States

YEAR	NUMBER OF STATES	POPULATION	% INCREASE	POPULATION PER SQUARE MILE
1790	13	3,929,214		4.5
1800	16	5,308,483	35.1	6.1
1810	17	7,239,881	36.4	4.3
1820	23	9,638,453	33.1	5.5
1830	24	12,866,020	33.5	7.4
1840	26	17,069,453	32.7	9.8
1850	31	23,191,876	35.9	7.9
1860	33	31,443,321	35.6	10.6
1870	37	39,818,449	26.6	13.4
1880	38	50,155,783	26.0	16.9
1890	44	62,947,714	25.5	21.2
1900	45	75,994,575	20.7	25.6
1910	46	91,972,266	21.0	31.0
1920	48	105,710,620	14.9	35.6
1930	48	122,775,046	16.1	41.2
1940	48	131,669,275	7.2	44.2
1950	48	150,697,361	14.5	50.7
1960	50	179,323,175	19.0	50.6
1970	50	203,235,298	13.3	57.5
1980	50	226,545,805	11.5	64.1
1990	50	248,709,873	9.8	70.3

Source: U.S. Bureau of the Census estimates.

Index

The World

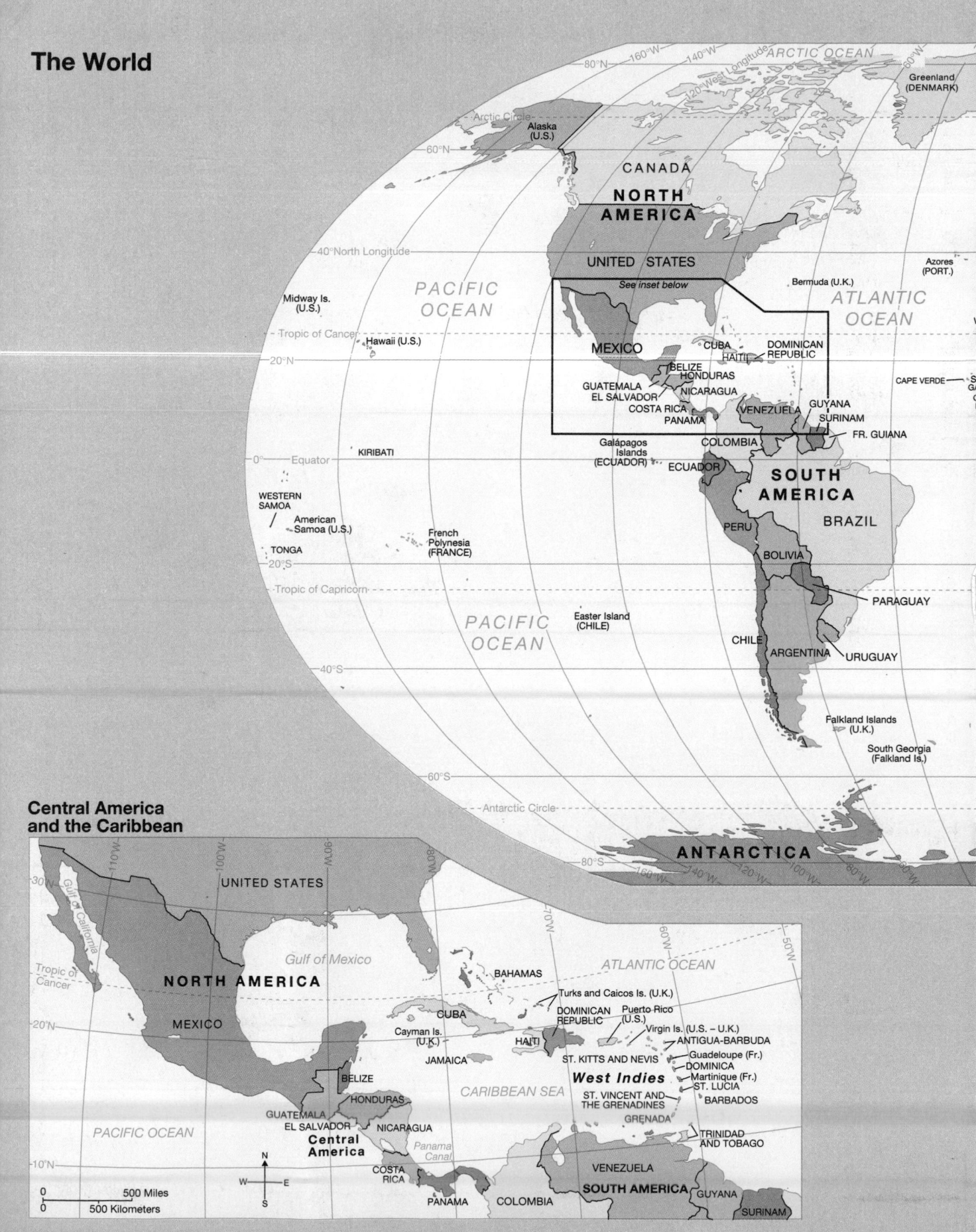

ARCTIC OCEAN

Greenland
(DENMARK)

80°N

160°W

140°W

120°West Longitude

90°W

Alaska
(U.S.)

60°N

Arctic Circle

CANADA

NORTH
AMERICA

40°North Longitude

UNITED STATES

Azores
(PORT.)

Bermuda (U.K.)

See inset below

ATLANTIC
OCEAN

Midway Is.
(U.S.)

PACIFIC
OCEAN

Tropic of Cancer

Hawaii (U.S.)

20°N

MEXICO

CUBA

HAITI

DOMINICAN
REPUBLIC

CAPE VERDE

S.
GA

BELIZE
HONDURAS

GUATEMALA
EL SALVADOR

NICARAGUA

COSTA RICA
PANAMA

VENEZUELA

GUYANA

SURINAM

FR. GUIANA

Galápagos
Islands
(ECUADOR)

COLOMBIA

KIRIBATI

0°   Equator

ECUADOR

SOUTH
AMERICA

WESTERN
SAMOA

American
Samoa (U.S.)

French
Polynesia
(FRANCE)

PERU

BRAZIL

TONGA

20°S

BOLIVIA

Tropic of Capricorn

PACIFIC
OCEAN

Easter Island
(CHILE)

PARAGUAY

CHILE

ARGENTINA

URUGUAY

40°S

Falkland Islands
(U.K.)

South Georgia
(Falkland Is.)

60°S

Antarctic Circle

80°S

ANTARCTICA

160°W

140°W

120°W

100°W

80°

Central America
and the Caribbean

30°

120°W

110°W

100°W

90°W

80°W

UNITED STATES

70°W

60°W

50°W

Gulf of California

Tropic of
Cancer

Gulf of Mexico

BAHAMAS

ATLANTIC OCEAN

NORTH AMERICA

20°N

MEXICO

CUBA

DOMINICAN
REPUBLIC

Turks and Caicos Is. (U.K.)

Puerto Rico
(U.S.)

Virgin Is. (U.S. – U.K.)

ANTIGUA-BARBUDA

Cayman Is.
(U.K.)

HAITI

Guadeloupe (Fr.)

JAMAICA

ST. KITTS AND NEVIS

West Indies

DOMINICA

Martinique (Fr.)

ST. LUCIA

CARIBBEAN SEA

ST. VINCENT AND
THE GRENADINES

BARBADOS

BELIZE

GRENADA

GUATEMALA

HONDURAS

PACIFIC OCEAN

EL SALVADOR

NICARAGUA

Central
America

TRINIDAD
AND TOBAGO

10°N

COSTA
RICA

PANAMA

Panama
Canal

COLOMBIA

VENEZUELA

SOUTH AMERICA

GUYANA

SURINAM

N
W   E
S

0   500 Miles

0   500 Kilometers